MOVIE STILL IDENTIFICATION SUPPLEMENT

By
Ed and Susan Poole

2018 Edition

A Must Reference Tool For Anyone
Who Handles Movie Studio Production, Short,
Portrait, Studio and Television Stills

A Publication by
LearnAboutMoviePosters.com
of the
Learn About Network, L.L.C.

Movie Still Identification Supplement

2018 Edition

Published by:
Ed and Susan Poole
Gretna, LA
edp@LearnAboutMoviePosters.com

ISBN: 978-0-9965015-5-2

LIMIT OF LIABILITY/DISCLAIMER OF WARRANTY

ADDITIONAL COPIES:

Additional copies of this publication are
available through the authors.

Ed Poole
(504) 298-5267
Email: edp@LearnAboutMoviePosters.com

or online at www.MovieStillID.com or www.LearnAboutMoviePosters.com

From the Authors

The declaration that over 90% of all silent films made in the U.S., plus 50% of all U.S. films produced before 1951 (when they created safety film) are already lost forever makes the preservation of the film accessories as the remaining historical documents of this social media even more imperative.

But what good is it to preserve these historical movie stills when you can't identify them.

This has been our guiding principle since we were first made aware of their importance at the 2007 Cinevent. That quest has led to this final printed supplement which contains 28,255 production codes. These additional codes bring the 2011, 2013 and 2015 editions of the *Movie Still Identification Book* to over 58,000 codes.

But, the quest does not end here. It just changes to a different format and continues. The books have become too large to continue printing.

However, we have now created the first Production Code Data Base which will allow us to continue to document and grow. It is going online with the entire 58,000+ codes in the member area of LAMP (LearnAboutMoviePosters.com) as we release this supplement. This also allows us to immediately add and update the database without having to wait for the next edition to be released.

We have only been able to accomplish this monumental feat through the support of our wonderful sponsors and members. We limited the advertisements in this book to just our regular sponsors to honor them. So when you see an advertisement, please remember that these wonderful sponsors care enough about the research, documentation and preservation of film accessories to sponsor us, which in turn allows us to present you this supplement. We have a list of these wonderful sponsors at the end of this book.

But there have also been numerous people along the way that have also helped that we want to thank but unfortunately they are far too many to mention. Our final wish...

May all your production codes – be identified!

Ed and Susan

How to Use This Book

If you are reading this, you must already have one of the editions of our *Movie Still Identification Books*. This supplement contains 28,255 codes and updates our 2011, 2013 and 2015 editions to over 58,000 for each. Since these editions were slightly different in their layout, we wanted to step through the breakdown of this supplement to make it easier for you to use it.

Our focus is upon stills that were created either during the production of the film OR re-marked during distribution of the film. In other words, those that had a control code on them. We do NOT cover pre-production, promotional, publicity, paparazzi, photographer, celebrity, autographed or homemade stills as these do not have production or distribution markings.

Besides covering just production codes as was the focus of the 2011 edition, we expanded into portrait codes, serial codes, series codes, tv codes, and studio codes.

To help you identify such a wide variety of codes AND present it in a simplified fashion, we also had to use our own type of codes. **Please read this section carefully** -- it explains how we present each column to help with your identification as no explanations are presented in the remainder of the book.

If the code **starts** with a LETTER, it will be in the LETTER section. If it **starts** with a NUMBER, use the NUMBER section. Many codes are alpha-numeric but that does not matter. Simply look at what the code starts with.

You will see the same 5 columns in each volume:

1. Code; **2.** Title/Name; **3.** Director/Type; **4.** Studio/Distributor; **5.** Year

1. Code: Whether it is a production code, portrait code, series code, serial code or studio code, all codes are together.

> In the LETTERS section, following the initial letter, we used the general rule of numbers before letters, so A400 would come BEFORE AA.

> In the NUMBERS section, all will start with a number. We DO HAVE some codes starting with the number "0" and they precede "1." Codes are in numeric order. When a letter is used in the middle of the code, they will be in alphabetic order and then any numbers afterwards starting over in numeric order.

Also, because the majority of the codes listed are taken directly from the stills, numerous oddities occur. IMPORTANT: When checking multiple stills from the same title, we noticed that the codes were NOT consistent and written in a variety of ways. For example, a code such as MC42 could be found on the stills as M C42; MC-42; or MC4/2. We tried to place them in the most common form that we found. BUT, for this reason, **ONLY IN THIS COLUMN**, we have ignored ALL **spaces and dashes**. The codes are presented in order as if they were not there.

2. Title/Name - This column has the film title, personality name or studio name (plus a LOT more information). This is the most complex column with the majority of OUR codes to try to help you with that identification, so PLEASE read this section carefully.

ALL TITLES, NAMES AND STUDIOS ARE IN ALL CAPITAL LETTERS

If the code was identified as a "Working Title," we placed an asterisk **(*)** behind it. If we also had the release title, we placed the working title BEHIND the release title and in parenthesis.

For non-US titles that we identified, we place a code for the country of origin. Here are the country codes that are used in the edition:

(ARG) – ARGENTINA	(GR) – GREECE	(POL) – POLAND
(AUS) – AUSTRALIA	(HK) – HONG KONG	(RUS) – RUSSIA
(BRA) – BRAZIL	(IND) – INDIA	(SP) – SPAIN
(CAN) – CANADA	(IS) – ISRAEL	(SWE) – SWEDEN
(CZ) – CZECH REPUBLIC	(IT) – ITALY	(SWIT) – SWITZERLAND
(DEN) – DENMARK	(JAP) – JAPAN	(UK) –UNITED KINGDOM
(FR) – FRANCE	(MEX) – MEXICO	(YUGO) – YUGOSLAVIA
(GER) - GERMANY	(NETH) - NETHERLANDS	Combos divided with (/)

If there was a time difference between the original release title and distribution, we placed the year behind the title of origin.

For rereleases, we put them behind the title and in () parenthesis when room allowed and the year behind it.

instructions, variations and additional info are written in small letters.

The standards are: **(t)** for toon or animation; **(sh)** for shorts; **(tv)** for tv movies; **(serial)**; and **(series)** are as stated.

Other instructions include: an (aka) was used if it was a portrait code for an alias used (Not used on film titles); (changed to...) was used when the studio made changes in the code.

When we found mistakes in the coding or pieces mis-marked, we marked it as **(mistake)** and put the correct code if we had it.

If it was a portrait code for multiple people, we placed an (*) behind the names.

If there was a distribution oddity, we placed it in **[ ]** brackets.

3. Director/Type - The primary director is listed in all caps by last name only. If multiple directors were used, we place both divided by a comma when possible. When it is a portrait, series, serial or studio code, they are shown in small letters.

4. Studio/Distributor - The major distributor is listed (NOT the production company) for production codes. For major studios, they are the same so no problem.

For smaller, independent distributors and import/export distributor, check the date and title columns for more information.

For portrait, series, serials, tv or studio codes, we tried to list the major distributor when available.

5. Year - Year of release is shown for production codes. When it is a reissue, the year is shown as "R" plus a 2 digit reissue year.

If the film was in import, also look to the title line for original country, title and release year.

Some series and portrait codes have ranges shown by decade.

We have also included some lined pages behind each section to give you a place when you make new code discoveries.

We truly hope this will help in your identification of production stills, studio portraits and costumes. If you find any that we have not documented and want to share – we gladly accept all production code additions as we continue trying to fill in all the codes. You can email them to ed at edp@LearnAboutMoviePosters.com

Ed and Susan

DO YOU want to buy vintage movie paper?

There is NO auctioneer of vintage movie paper who auctions more items than eMoviePoster.com, and we auction every type of movie paper, 3,000 different items each week. Go to our website to start bidding!

CODE	TITLE/NAME	DIRECTOR/TYPE	STUDIO/DISTRIBUTOR	YEAR
A	ACCUSED	KAPLAN	PARAMOUNT	1988
A	AGENT 8 3/4 (UK: HOT ENOUGH FOR JUNE 1964)	THOMAS	CONSOLIDATED	1965
A	AIRHEADS	LEHMANN	20th CENTURY FOX	1994
A	AIRPLANE	ZUCKER	20th CENTURY FOX	1980
A	ALADDIN (IT: SUPERFANTAGENIO)	CORBUCCI	CANNON	1986
A	ALAMO	WAYNE	UNITED ARTISTS	1960
A	ALICE	ALLEN	ORION	1990
A	ALICE WHITE	portrait		
A	ALIEN	SCOTT	20TH CENTURY FOX	1979
A	ALIEN 3	FINCHER	20th CENTURY FOX	1992
A	ALIENS	CAMERON	20th CENTURY FOX	1986
A	ALIMONY	HORNE	FILM BOOKING OFF	1924
A	ALLIGATOR	TEAGUE	WARNER BROS	1980
A	ANNA	LATTUADA	LUX FILM	1951
A	APARAJITO (IND 1957)	RAY	EDWARD HARRISON	1959
A	ASHANTI	FLEISCHER	WARNER BROS	1979
A	ASSASSINATION	HUNT	CANNON	1986
A	ASSAULT	RADEMAKERS	CANNON	1986
A	ASSIGNMENT REDHEAD (UK: UNDERCOVER GIRL)	SEARLE	UNITED ARTISTS	1958
A	DEATH OF AN ANGEL (UK)	SAUNDERS	HAMMER-EXCLUSIVE	1952
A	FRENZY (UK: LATIN QUARTER)	SEWELL	FOUR CONTINENTS	1945
A	GEISHA GIRL	BREAKSTON	REALART	1952
A	HER SECRET	MILLAIS	IDEAL PICTURES	1933
A	I'LL STICK TO YOU (UK)	HISCOTT	BRITISH LION	1933
A-1	CATCH AS CATCH CAN (sh)	NEILAN	MGM	1931
A-1	LUKE RIDES ROUGHSHOD (sh)	ROACH	PATHE EXCHANGE	1916
A-1	ONE NIGHT OF LOVE	SCHERTZINGER	COLUMBIA	1934
A-1	OUR GANG (sh)	MCGOWAN	PATHE EXCHANGE	1922
A2	AIRPLANE II: THE SEQUEL	FINKLEMAN	PARAMOUNT	1982
A-2	BROADWAY BILL	CAPRA	COLUMBIA	1934
A-2	FIRE FIGHTERS (sh)	MCGOWAN	PATHE EXCHANGE	1922
A-2	LUKE, CRYSTAL GAZER (sh)	ROACH	PATHE EXCHANGE	1916
A-2	PAJAMA PARTY (sh)	ROACH	MGM	1931
A-3	LUKE'S LOST LAMB (sh)	ROACH	PATHE EXCHANGE	1916
A-3	WAR MAMAS (sh)	NEILAN	MGM	1931
A-3	YOUNG SHERLOCKS (sh)	MCGOWAN	PATHE EXCHANGE	1922
A3D	AMITYVILLE 3-D	FLEISHER	ORION	1983
A-4	LUKE DOES THE MIDWAY (sh)	ROACH	PATHE EXCHANGE	1916
A-4	ON THE LOOSE (sh)	ROACH	MGM	1931
A-4	ONE TERRIBLE DAY (sh)	MCGOWAN	PATHE EXCHANGE	1922
A-4	THAT'S GRATITUDE	CRAVEN	COLUMBIA	1934
A-5	A QUIET STREET (sh)	MCGOWAN	PATHE EXCHANGE	1922
A-5	JEALOUSY	NEILL	COLUMBIA	1934
A-5	LUKE AND THE BANGTAILS (sh)	ROACH	PATHE EXCHANGE	1916
A-5	SEAL SKINS (sh)	LIGHTFOOT	MGM	1932
A-6	CHAMPAGNE FOR BREAKFAST	BROWN	COLUMBIA	1935
A-6	LUKE JOINS THE NAVY (sh)	ROACH	PATHE EXCHANGE	1916
A-6	RED NOSES (sh)	HORNE	MGM	1932
A-6	SATURDAY MORNING (sh)	MCGOWAN	PATHE EXCHANGE	1922
A-7	BIG SHOW (sh)	MCGOWAN	PATHE EXCHANGE	1923
A-7	LUKE AND THE MERMAIDS (sh)	ROACH	PATHE EXCHANGE	1916
A-7	STRICTLY UNRELIABLE (sh)	MARSHALL	MGM	1932
A-8	COBBLER (sh)	MCNAMARA	PATHE EXCHANGE	1923
A-8	LUKE'S SPEEDY CLUB LIFE (sh)	ROACH	PATHE EXCHANGE	1916
A-8	OLD BULL (sh)	MARSHALL	MGM	1932
A-8	WHITE LIES	BULGAKOV	COLUMBIA	1934
A-9	CHAMPEEN (sh)	MCGOWAN	PATHE EXCHANGE	1923
A-9	LUKE THE CHAUFFEUR (sh)	ROACH	PATHE EXCHANGE	1916
A-9	SHOW BUSINESS (sh)	WHITE	MGM	1932
A-9	WHOLE TOWN'S TALKING	FORD	COLUMBIA	1935
A-10	ALUM AND EVE (sh)	MARSHALL	MGM	1932
A-10	BOYS TO BOARD (sh)	MCNAMARA	PATHE EXCHANGE	1923
A-10	LUKE'S PREPAREDNESS PREPARATIONS (sh)	ROACH	PATHE EXCHANGE	1916
A-10	MILLS OF THE GODS	NEILL	COLUMBIA	1935
A10	REBECCA OF SUNNYBROOK FARM	NEILAN	ARTCRAFT	1917

A-11	BEST MAN WINS	KENTON	COLUMBIA	1935
A-11	LUKE THE GLADIATOR (sh)	ROACH	PATHE EXCHANGE	1916
A-11	PLEASANT JOURNEY (sh)	MCGOWAN	PATHE EXCHANGE	1923
A-11	SOILERS (sh)	MARSHALL	MGM	1932
A-12	CARNIVAL	LANG	COLUMBIA	1935
A-12	GIANTS VS. YANKS (sh)	MCGOWAN	PATHE EXCHANGE	1923
A-12	LUKE, PATIENT PROVIDER (sh)	ROACH	PATHE EXCHANGE	1916
A-12	SNEAK EASILY (sh)	MEINS	MGM	1932
A-13	ASLEEP IN THE FLEET (sh)	MEINS	MGM	1933
A-13	BACK STAGE (sh)	MCGOWAN	PATHE EXCHANGE	1923
A-14	DOGS OF WAR (sh)	MCGOWAN	PATHE EXCHANGE	1923
A-14	LUKE'S NEWSIE KNOCKOUT (sh)	ROACH	PATHE EXCHANGE	1916
A-14	MAIDS A LA MODE (sh)	MEINS	MGM	1933
A-15	BARGAIN OF THE CENTURY (sh)	CHASE	MGM	1933
A-15	LODGE NIGHT (sh)	MCGOWAN	PATHE EXCHANGE	1923
A-15	LUKE'S MOVIE MUDDLE - LUKE'S MODEL MOVIE (sh)	ROACH	PATHE EXCHANGE	1916
A-16	FAST COMPANY (sh)	MCGOWAN	PATHE EXCHANGE	1924
A-16	LUKE'S RANK IMPERSONATOR (sh)	ROACH	PATHE EXCHANGE	1916
A-16	ONE TRACK MINDS (sh)	MEINS	MGM	1933
A-17	BEAUTY AND THE BUS (sh)	MEINS	MGM	1933
A-17	LUKE'S FIREWORKS FIZZLE (sh)	ROACH	PATHE EXCHANGE	1916
A-17	STAGE FRIGHT (sh)	MCGOWAN	PATHE EXCHANGE	1923
A-18	BACK TO NATURE (sh)	MEINS	MGM	1933
A-18	JULY DAYS (sh)	MCGOWAN	PATHE EXCHANGE	1923
A-18	LUKE LOCATES THE LOOT (sh)	ROACH	PATHE EXCHANGE	1916
A-19	AIR FRIGHT (sh)	MEINS	MGM	1933
A-19	LUKE'S SHATTERED SLEEP (sh)	ROACH	PATHE EXCHANGE	1916
A-19	SUNDAY CALM (sh)	MCGOWAN	PATHE EXCHANGE	1923
A-20	BABES IN THE GOODS (sh)	MEINS	MGM	1934
A-20	LUKE'S LOST LIBERTY (sh)	ROACH	PATHE EXCHANGE	1917
A-20	NO NOISE (sh)	MCGOWAN	PATHE EXCHANGE	1923
A-21	DERBY DAY (sh)	MCGOWAN	PATHE EXCHANGE	1923
A-21	LUKE'S BUSY DAY (sh)	ROACH	PATHE EXCHANGE	1917
A-21	SOUP AND FISH (sh)	MEINS	MGM	1934
A-22	LUKE'S TROLLEY TROUBLES (sh)	ROACH	PATHE EXCHANGE	1917
A-22	MAID IN HOLLYWOOD (sh)	MEINS	MGM	1934
A-22	TIRE TROUBLE (sh)	MCGOWAN	PATHE EXCHANGE	1924
A-23	BIG BUSINESS (sh)	MCGOWAN	PATHE EXCHANGE	1924
A-23	I'LL BE SUING YOU (sh)	MEINS	MGM	1934
A-23	LONESOME LUKE, LAWYER (sh)	ROACH	PATHE EXCHANGE	1917
A-24	BUCCANEERS (sh)	MCGOWAN, GOLDAINE	PATHE EXCHANGE	1924
A-24	LUKE WINS YE LADYE FAIRE (sh)	ROACH	PATHE EXCHANGE	1917
A-24	THREE CHUMPS AHEAD (sh)	MEINS	MGM	1934
A-25	DONE IN OIL (sh)	MEINS	MGM	1934
A-25	LONESOME LUKE'S LIVELY LIFE (sh)	ROACH	PATHE EXCHANGE	1917
A-25	SEEIN' THINGS (sh)	MCGOWAN	PATHE EXCHANGE	1924
A-26	COMMENCEMENT DAY (sh)	MCGOWAN, GOLDAINE	PATHE EXCHANGE	1924
A-26	LONESOME LUKE, MECHANIC (sh)	ROACH	PATHE EXCHANGE	1917
A-26	ONE HORSE FARMERS (sh)	MEINS	MGM	1934
A-27	FIGHTING TEXAN	ABBOTT	AMBASSADOR	1937
A-27	IT'S A BEAR (sh)	MCGOWAN	PATHE EXCHANGE	1924
A-27	LONESOME LUKE'S HONEYMOON (sh)	ROACH	PATHE EXCHANGE	1917
A-27	OPENED BY MISTAKE (sh)	PARROTT	MGM	1934
A-28	BUM VOYAGE (sh)	GRINDE	MGM	1934
A-28	CRADLE ROBBERS (sh)	MCGOWAN	PATHE EXCHANGE	1924
A-28	LONESOME LUKE, PLUMBER (sh)	ROACH	PATHE EXCHANGE	1917
A-29	JUBLIO, JR. (sh)	MCGOWAN	PATHE EXCHANGE	1924
A-29	STOP! LUKE! LISTEN! (sh)	ROACH	PATHE EXCHANGE	1917
A-29	TREASURE BLUES (sh)	PARROTT	MGM	1935
A-30	HIGH SOCIETY (sh)	MCGOWAN	PATHE EXCHANGE	1924
A-30	LONESOME LUKE'S WILD WOMEN (sh)	ROACH	PATHE EXCHANGE	1917
A-30	TIN MAN (sh)	PARROTT	MGM	1935
A-31	LONESOME LUKE ON TIN CAN ALLEY (sh)	ROACH	PATHE EXCHANGE	1917
A-31	MISSES STOOGE (sh)	PARROTT	MGM	1935
A-31	SUN DOWN LIMITED (sh)	MCGOWAN	PATHE EXCHANGE	1924
A-32	EVERY MAN FOR HIMSELF (sh)	MCGOWAN	PATHE EXCHANGE	1924

A-32	LONESOME LUKE LOSES PATIENTS (sh)	ROACH	PATHE EXCHANGE	1917
A-32	SING, SISTER, SING (sh)	PARROTT	MGM	1935
A-33	LONESOME LUKE IN LOVE, LAUGHS AND LATHER (sh)	ROACH	PATHE EXCHANGE	1917
A-33	MYSTERIOUS MYSTERY! (sh)	MCGOWAN	PATHE EXCHANGE	1924
A-33	SLIGHTLY STATIC (sh)	TERHUNE	MGM	1935
A-34	BIG TOWN (sh)	MCGOWAN	PATHE EXCHANGE	1925
A-34	LONESOME LUKE, MESSENGER (sh)	ROACH	PATHE EXCHANGE	1917
A-34	TWIN TRIPLETS (sh)	TERHUNE	MGM	1935
A-35	CIRCUS FEVER (sh)	MCGOWAN	PATHE EXCHANGE	1925
A-35	HOT MONEY (sh)	HORNE	MGM	1935
A-35	LONESOME LUKE IN FROM LONDON TO LARAMIE (sh)	ROACH	PATHE EXCHANGE	1917
A-36	DOG DAYS (sh)	MCGOWAN	PATHE EXCHANGE	1925
A-36	LONESOME LUKE IN BIRDS OF A FEATHER (sh)	ROACH	PATHE EXCHANGE	1917
A-36	TOP FLAT (sh)	JEVNE, TERHUNE	MGM	1935
A-37	ALL AMERICAN TOOTHACHE (sh)	MEINS	MGM	1936
A-37	LOVE BUG (sh)	MCGOWAN	PATHE EXCHANGE	1925
A-37	TRUMPS (sh)	ROACH	PATHE EXCHANGE	1917
A-38	ASK GRANDMA (sh)	MCGOWAN	PATHE EXCHANGE	1925
A-38	LONESOME LUKE IN WE NEVER SLEEP (sh)	ROACH	PATHE EXCHANGE	1917
A-38	PAN HANDLERS (sh)	TERHUNE	MGM	1936
A-39	AT SEA ASHORE (sh)	TERHUNE	MGM	1936
A-39	SHOOTIN' INJUNS (sh)	MCGOWAN	PATHE EXCHANGE	1925
A-40	AGAINST THE LAW	HILLYER	COLUMBIA	1934
A-40	HILL TILLIES (sh)	MEINS	MGM	1936
A-40	OFFICIAL OFFICERS (sh)	MCGOWAN	PATHE EXCHANGE	1925
A-41	MARY, QUEEN OF TOTS (sh)	MCGOWAN	PATHE EXCHANGE	1925
A-41	MEN OF THE NIGHT	HILLYER	COLUMBIA	1934
A-42	BEHIND THE EVIDENCE	HILLYER	COLUMBIA	1935
A-42	BOYS WILL BE JOYS (sh)	MCGOWAN	PATHE EXCHANGE	1925
A-43	BETTER MOVIES (sh)	MCGOWAN	PATHE EXCHANGE	1925
A-46	SWELL HEAD	STOLOFF	COLUMBIA	1935
A-47	TOGETHER WE LIVE	MACK	COLUMBIA	1935
A50	CAR OF DREAMS (UK)	CUTTS, MELFORD	GAUMONT BRITISH	1935
A-50	PRESCOTT KID	SELMAN	COLUMBIA	1934
A-50	UNDER THE TOP	CRISP	PARAMOUNT	1919
A-51	WESTERNER	SELMAN	COLUMBIA	1934
A-52	SQUARE SHOOTER	SELMAN	COLUMBIA	1935
A53	FIRST A GIRL (UK)	SAVILLE	GAUMONT BRIT. AMER.	1935
A-53	LAW BEYOND THE RANGE	BEEBE	COLUMBIA	1935
A-54	REVENGE RIDER	SELMAN	COLUMBIA	1935
A-55	FIGHTING SHADOWS	SELMAN	COLUMBIA	1935
A-56	RIDING WILD	SELMAN	COLUMBIA	1935
A-57	JUSTICE OF THE RANGE	SELMAN	COLUMBIA	1935
A57	RHODES (UK: RHODES OF AFRICA)	VIERTEL	GAUMONT BRIT. AMER.	1936
A59	SECRET AGENT (UK)	HITCHCOCK	GAUMONT BRIT. AMER.	1936
A60	IT'S LOVE AGAIN (UK)	SAVILLE	GAUMONT BRIT. AMER.	1936
A61	DOOMED CARGO (UK: SEVEN SINNERS)	DE COURVILLE	GAUMONT BRIT. AMER.	1936
A62	EVERYTHING IS THUNDER (UK)	ROSMER	GAUMONT BRITISH	1936
A-63	WAY OF A MAN WITH A MAID	CRISP	PARAMOUNT	1918
A64	SILENT BARRIERS (UK)	ROSMER	GAUMONT BRITISH	1937
A65	STRANGERS ON HONEYMOON (UK)	DE COURVILLE	GAUMONT BRIT. AMER.	1936
A67	DON'T CHANGE YOUR HUSBAND	DEMILLE	PARAMOUNT	1918
A67	MAN OF AFFAIRS (UK: HIS LORDSHIP)	MASON	GAUMONT BRIT. AMER.	1936
A68	HEAD OVER HEELS IN LOVE (UK: HEAD OVER HEELS)	HALE	GAUMONT BRIT. AMER.	1937
A-69	YOU'RE IN THE ARMY NOW	WALSH	GAUMONT BRITISH	1937
A70	KING SOLOMON'S MINES (UK)	STEVENSON	GAUMONT BRIT. AMER.	1937
A72	NON-STOP NEW YORK (UK: LISBON CLIPPER MYSTERY)	STEVENSON	GAUMONT BRIT. AMER.	1937
A73	GANGWAY (UK)	HALE	GAUMONT BRIT. AMER.	1937
A74	GIRL WAS YOUNG (UK: YOUNG AND INNOCENT)	HITCHCOCK	GAUMONT BRIT. AMER.	1937
A75	SAILING ALONG (UK)	HALE	GAUMONT BRIT. AMER.	1938
A83	WHITE HEATHER	TOURNEUR	PARAMOUNT	1919
A-90	ONE WAY OUT (sh)	HILLYER	COLUMBIA	1934
A-91	HIDDEN EVIDENCE	HILLYER	COLUMBIA	1934
A-92	SIMPLE SOLUTION (sh)	LEDERMAN	COLUMBIA	1934
A-93	BY PERSONS UNKNOWN (sh)	LEDERMAN	COLUMBIA	1934
A-94	PROFESSOR GIVES A LESSON	HILLYER	COLUMBIA	1934

A99	HIS HOUSE IN ORDER	FORD	PARAMOUNT	1920
A100	DESERT FLOWER, THE	CUMMINGS	FIRST NATIONAL	1925
A102	MY LADY'S GARTER	TOURNEUR	PARAMOUNT	1920
A-103	RADIO DOUGH	BOASBERG	COLUMBIA	1934
A-105	TEN BABY FINGERS (sh)	WHITE	COLUMBIA	1934
A-106	SCHOOL FOR ROMANCE (LESSONS IN LOVE*) (sh)	GOTTLER	COLUMBIA	1934
A-107	ELMER STEPS OUT (PLAYFUL HUSBANDS*) (sh)	WHITE	COLUMBIA	1934
A-108	LOVE DETECTIVES (sh)	GOTTLER	COLUMBIA	1934
A-109	WHEN DO WE EAT? (SHOWMANSHIP*) (sh)	GOULDING	COLUMBIA	1934
A-110	STABLE MATES (sh)	WHITE	COLUMBIA	1934
A-111	FISHING FOR TROUBLE (HOLY MACKERAL*) (sh)	WHITE	COLUMBIA	1934
A111	THAT LADY (UK)	YOUNG	20TH CENTURY FOX	1955
A-112	WOMAN HATERS (sh)	GOTTLER	COLUMBIA	1934
A-113	SUSIE'S AFFAIRS (sh)	GOTTLER	COLUMBIA	1934
A-114	GET ALONG LITTLE HUBBY (sh)	MCCAREY	COLUMBIA	1934
A-115	PLUMBING FOR GOLD (sh)	LAMONT	COLUMBIA	1934
A-116	PUNCH DRUNKS (sh)	BRESLOW	COLUMBIA	1934
A-117	TRIPPING THRU THE TROPICS (sh)	GOTTLER	COLUMBIA	1934
A-118	BACK TO THE SOIL (PAYDIRT*) (sh)	WHITE	COLUMBIA	1934
A-119	HOLLYWOOD HERE WE COME (sh)	GOTTLER	COLUMBIA	1934
A125	BLACK ROSE, THE (UK)	HATHAWAY	20TH CENTURY FOX	1950
A-150	COUNSEL ON DE FENCE (sh)	RIPLEY	COLUMBIA	1934
A-151	IT'S THE CATS (sh)	RAY	COLUMBIA	1934
A-152	MEN IN BLACK (sh)	MCCAREY	COLUMBIA	1934
A-153	PERFECTLY MISMATED (SCRAMBLE WIVES*) (sh)	HORNE	COLUMBIA	1934
A-154	SHIVERS (sh)	RIPLEY	COLUMBIA	1934
A-155	IN THE DOG HOUSE (sh)	RIPLEY	COLUMBIA	1934
A-158	ONE TOO MANY (sh)	MCGOWAN	COLUMBIA	1934
A311	NO HIGHWAY IN THE SKY (UK: NO HIGHWAY)	KOSTER	20TH CENTURY FOX	1951
A-315	MY SON, THE HERO	ULMER	PRODUCERS RELEASING	1943
A334	I'LL NEVER FORGET YOU (UK: HOUSE IN THE SQUARE)	BAKER	20TH CENTURY FOX	1951
A478	ANNA AND THE KING OF SIAM	CROMWELL	20th CENTURY FOX	1946
A-500	ALICE	ALLEN	ORION	1990
AA	ANNE AUBREY	portrait		1950s
AA	ARABIAN ADVENTURE	CONNOR	ASSOCIATED FILM	1979
AA	AUTHOR! AUTHOR!	HILLER	20TH CENTURY FOX	1982
AA	SPRING AND PORT WINE (UK)	HAMMOND	ALLIED ARTISTS	1970
AA	WHATEVER HAPPENED TO AUNT ALICE	KATZIN	CINERAMA	1969
AA1	BLOOD OF THE VAMPIRE (UK)	CASS	UNIVERSAL	1958
AAA	ALMOST AN ANGEL	CORNELL	PARAMOUNT	1990
AAR	ALONE AGAINST ROME (IT: SOLO CONTRO ROMA 1962)	RICCI	MEDALLION	1963
AAV	ATOM AGE VAMPIRE (IT: SEDDOK, L'EREDE DI SATANA)	MAJANO	TOPAZ	1960
AAW	RUN FOR YOUR WIFE (IT: UNA MOGLIE AMERICANA 1965)	POLIDORO	MONOGRAM	1966
AB	ABDUCTORS	MCLAGLAN	LIPPERT	1957
AB	ADVENTURE IN BLACKMAIL (UK: BREACH OF PROMISE)	HUTH, PERTWEE	ENGLISH	1942
AB	AIRBORNE	BOWMAN	WARNER BROS	1993
AB	ALAMO BAY	MALLE	TRI STAR	1985
AB	ALF'S BUTTON AFLOAT (UK)	VARNEL	GFD	1938
AB	ARRIVEDERCI, BABY! (UK: DROP DEAD DARLING)	HUGHES	PARAMOUNT	1966
AB	BULLDOG SEES IT THROUGH (UK)	HUTH	PATHE	1940
AB	MAGIC BOW (UK)	KNOWLES	UNIVERSAL	1946
ABBB	ADVENTURES IN BABYSITTING	COLUMBUS	BUENA VISTA	1987
ABL	BUG'S LIFE	LASSETER	BUENA VISTA	1998
ABL8	WINSLOW BOY (UK)	ASQUITH	EAGLE-LION	1948
AC	ACE VENTURA: PET DETECTIVE	SHADYAC	WARNER BROS	1994
AC	ADVENTURES OF ROBINSON CRUSOE (MEX: ROBINSON CRUSOE)	BUNUEL	UNITED ARTISTS	1954
AC	ALAN CURTIS	portrait	UNIVERSAL	1940s
AC	ALLEY CATS, THE	METZGAR	AUDUBON FILMS	1966
AC	AMAZING MR. CALLAGHAN (FR: TOI JOUER CALLAGHAN 1955)	ROZIER	ATLANTIS FILMS	1960
AC	AMERICAN CYBORG	DAVIDSON	CANNON	1993
AC	ANTARTIC CROSSING	LOWE	SCHOENFELD FILMS	1959
AC	APACHE CHIEF	MCDONALD	LIPPERT	1949
AC	CIVIL ACTION, A	ZAILLIAN	BUENA VISTA	1998
AC-105	UNNAMED DIPPY DOO DADS (sh)		PATHE EXCHANGE	1923
AC-113	KNOCKOUT (sh)	POWERS	PATHE EXCHANGE	1923
AC-124	BAR-FLY (sh)	POWERS	PATHE EXCHANGE	1924

AC-128	MAN PAYS (sh)	POWERS	PATHE EXCHANGE	1924
ACK	ALIEN	SCOTT	20th CENTURY FOX	1979
ACK	MAN UPSTAIRS	DEL RUTH	WARNER BROS	1926
A COL-1	ONE NIGHT OF LOVE	SCHERTZINGER	COLUMBIA	1934
A COL-2	BROADWAY BILL	CAPRA	COLUMBIA	1934
A COL-3	GIRL FRIEND	BUZZELL	COLUMBIA	1935
A COL-4	THAT'S GRATITUDE	CRAVEN	COLUMBIA	1934
A COL-5	JEALOUSY	NEILL	COLUMBIA	1934
A COL-6	CHAMPAGNE FOR BREAKFAST	BROWN	COLUMBIA	1935
A COL-7	EIGHT BELLS	NEILL	COLUMBIA	1935
A COL-8	WHITE LIES	BULGAKOV	COLUMBIA	1934
A COL-10	MILLS OF THE GODS	NEILL	COLUMBIA	1935
A COL-11	BEST MAN WINS	KENTON	COLUMBIA	1935
A COL-12	CARNIVAL	LANG	COLUMBIA	1935
A COL-14	LET'S LIVE TONIGHT	SCHERTZINGER	COLUMBIA	1935
A COL-15	DEATH FLIES EAST	ROSEN	COLUMBIA	1935
A COL-16	UNWELCOME STRANGER	ROSEN	COLUMBIA	1935
A COL 17	PARTY WIRE	KENTON	COLUMBIA	1935
A COL-19	AIR HAWKS	ROGELL	COLUMBIA	1935
A COL-20	AWAKENING OF JIM BURKE	HILLYER	COLUMBIA	1935
A COL-22	UNKNOWN WOMAN	ROGELL	COLUMBIA	1935
A COL-23	AFTER THE DANCE	BULGAKOV	COLUMBIA	1935
A COL-24	FEATHER IN HER HAT	SANTELL	COLUMBIA	1935
A COL-25	BLACK ROOM	NEILL	COLUMBIA	1935
A COL-26	SHE MARRIED HER BOSS	LA CAVA	COLUMBIA	1935
A COL-29	PUBLIC MENACE	KENTON	COLUMBIA	1935
A COL-40	AGAINST THE LAW	HILLYER	COLUMBIA	1934
A COL-41	MEN OF THE NIGHT	HILLYER	COLUMBIA	1934
A COL-42	BEHIND THE EVIDENCE	HILLYER	COLUMBIA	1935
A COL-43	IN SPITE OF DANGER	HILLYER	COLUMBIA	1935
A COL-44	MEN OF THE HOUR	HILLYER	COLUMBIA	1935
A COL-46	SWELL HEAD	STOLOFF	COLUMBIA	1935
A COL-47	TOGETHER WE LIVE	MACK	COLUMBIA	1935
A COL-48	SUPERSPEED	HILLYER	COLUMBIA	1935
A COL-50	PRESCOTT KID	SELMAN	COLUMBIA	1934
A COL-51	WESTERNER	SELMAN	COLUMBIA	1934
A COL-52	SQUARE SHOOTER	SELMAN	COLUMBIA	1935
A COL-53	LAW BEYOND THE RANGE	BEEBE	COLUMBIA	1935
A COL-54	REVENGE RIDER	SELMAN	COLUMBIA	1935
A COL-55	FIGHTING SHADOWS	SELMAN	COLUMBIA	1935
A COL-56	RIDING WILD	SELMAN	COLUMBIA	1935
A COL-57	JUSTICE OF THE RANGE	SELMAN	COLUMBIA	1935
ACP	ANYONE CAN PLAY (IT/FR: DOLCE SIGNORE)	ZAMPA	PARAMOUNT	1968
ACT	GUNS OF DARKNESS (UK)	ASQUITH	WARNER BROS.	1962
ACT-1	GREEN GROW THE RUSHES (UK)	TWIST	BRITISH LION	1951
ACT-5	KITCHEN (UK)	HILL	KINGSLEY INT'L	1961
ACT-6	HER THREE BACHELORS (UK: ALF'S BABY)	ROGERS	ADELPHI	1953
ACT-9	BLUE PARROT (UK)	HARLOW	MONARCH	1953
ACT-11	BURNT EVIDENCE (UK)	BIRT	MONARCH	1954
ACT-22	DON'T PANIC CHAPS (UK)	POLLOCK	COLUMBIA	1959
AD	AFTER DARK (UK)	PARKER	FOX	1932
AD	AMERICAN DREAMER	ROSENTHAL	WARNER BROS	1984
AD	ARLENE DAHL	portrait	RKO, UNIV	
AD	ASHES AND DIAMONDS (POL: POPOL I DIAMENT)	WAJDA	JANUS	1958
AD	AWFUL DR. ORLOF, THE (SP: GRITOS EN LA NOCHE 1962)	FRANCO	SIGMA III CORP	1964
AD	DIAMONDS	GOLAN	AVCO EMBASSY	1975
AD	ON ANY SUNDAY	BROWN	CINEMA 5	1971
AD	SLEUTH	MANKIEWICZ	20th CENTURY FOX	1972
AD-372	STATE POLICE	RAWLINS	UNIVERSAL	1938
AD/ART	SLEUTH	MANKIEWICZ	20th CENTURY-FOX	1972
ADM	DAVID MANNERS	portrait	FN/WARNER BROS	
ADS	DIFFERENT STORY, A	AARON	AVCO EMBASSY	1978
AE	ACE ELI AND RODGER OF THE SKIES	SAMPSON (ERMAN)	20th CENTURY FOX	1973
AE	ANGEL EYES	MANDOKI	WARNER BROS	2001
AE	AVALANCHE EXPRESS	ROBSON	COLUMBIA	1979
AE-6	HONOR BOUND	GREEN	FOX FILM	1928

AF	ADDAMS FAMILY	SONNENFELD	PARAMOUNT	1991
AF	ANIMAL FARM (t) (UK)	BATCHELOR, HALAS	LOUIS DE ROCHEMONT	1954
AF	AVENGING FORCE	FIRSTENBERG	CANNON	1986
AF1	UNSTOPPABLE MAN (UK)	BISHOP	SUTTON	1961
AF-368	SKABENGA (KILLER LUST) (doc)	MICHAEL	ALLIED ARTISTS	1955
AFD	APRIL FOOLS DAY	WALTON	PARAMOUNT	1986
AFF	FRIEND OF THE FAMILY (FR: L'AMI DE LA FAMILLE)	PINOTEAU	INT'L CLASSICS	1957
AFI	KING IN NEW YORK	CHAPLIN	ARCHWAY	1957
AFS	AT FIRST SIGHT	WINKLER	MGM	1999
AG	AMAZING GRACE AND CHUCK (SILENT VOICE*)	NEWELL	TRI STAR	1987
AG	AMERICAN GIGOLO	SCHRADER	PARAMOUNT	1980
AG	ANY GIVEN SUNDAY	STONE	WARNER BROS.	1999
AGP	CAESAR AND CLEOPATRA (UK)	PASCAL	UNITED ARTISTS	1945
AH	ACE HIGH (IT)	COLIZZI	PARAMOUNT	1968
AH	AFTER HOURS	SCORSESE	WARNER BROS	1985
AH	AIRHEADS	LEHMANN	20th CENTURY FOX	1994
AH	ALEXANDRA HAY (ALSO A. HAY)	portrait	COLUMBIA	
AH	ALMOST A HONEYMOON (UK)	LEE	PATHE	1938
AH	ANNABELLE HAYES	portrait	RKO	
AH	ASSASSIN FOR HIRE (UK)	MCCARTHY	HORNE & DIETZ	1951
AH	LIFE OF ADOLF HITLER (GER: DAS LEBEN ADOLF HITLER) (doc)	ROTHA	BRITISH LION	1962
AH	STORY OF ADELE H (FR: L'HISTOIRE D'ADELE H)	TRUFFANT	NEW WORLD	1976
AHW	AMERICAN HOT WAX	MUTRUX	PARAMOUNT	1978
AHW	AMONG HUMAN WOLVES (UK: SECRET JOURNEY)	BAXTER	FILM ALLIANCE	1939
AI	A.I. ARTIFICIAL INTELLIGENCE	SPIELBERG	WARNER BROS	2001
AIBB	ANGIE	COOLIDGE	BUENA VISTA	1994
AIN	AUTUMN IN NEW YORK	CHEN	MGM	2000
AIT	ANGEL IN A TAXI	LEONVIOLA	MAGNA PICTURES	1963
AIT	GYPSY MELODY (UK)	GREVILLE	WARDOUR	1936
AJ	ALL THAT JAZZ	FOSSE	20TH CEN + COLUMBIA	1979
AJ	AND JUSTICE FOR ALL	JEWISON	COLUMBIA	1979
AJ	EYES OF ANNIE JONES (UK)	LE BORG	20TH CENTURY FOX	1964
AK	ALICE KELLEY	portrait	UNIV	
AK	ANDREA KING	portrait	WARNER BROS	1940s, 50s
AK	ANNA KARENINA	ROSE	WARNER BROS	1997
AK	ARTHUR KENNEDY	portrait	RKO, UNIV	
AK04	LION HAS WINGS (UK)	BRUNEL,HURST,POWELL	UNITED ARTISTS	1939
AKO-AW	THIEF OF BAGDAD (UK)	BERGER, POWELL,	UNITED ARTISTS	1940
AL	ABE LYMAN (& HIS ORCHESTRA)	portrait	MCA	
AL	ADDICTED TO LOVE	DUNNE	WARNER BROS	1997
AL	AGNES LAURENT	portrait	UNITED ARTISTS	
AL	ALAN LADD	portrait	RKO, WARNER BROS	
AL	ALLAN LANE	portrait	REP	
AL	ANITA LOUISE	portrait	TIFFANY, UNIV	
AL	AUDRA LINDLEY	portrait	WARNER BROS	
ALA	ALIEN FROM L.A.	PYUN	CANNON	1988
ALA	ME TRAES DE UN ALA	SOLARES	FILMEX	1953
ALBB	ALIVE	MARSHALL	BUENA VISTA	1993
ALC	ALL THE LOVING COUPLES	BING	U-M FILM	1969
ALF	ALFIE (UK)	GILBERT	PARAMOUNT	1966
ALL	WINDY CITY	BERNSTEIN	WARNER BROS	1984
ALN	ABOUT LAST NIGHT	ZWICK	TRI STAR	1986
ALVIN	ALVIN PURPLE (AUST -tv)	various	FAY FILMS	1976
AM	ADELE MARA	portrait	REP	
AM	ALINE MACMAHON	portrait	WARNER BROS	1930s-50s
AM	ANN MILLER		RKO	
AM	ANNA MAGNANI	portrait		
AM	ARSENAL STADIUM MYSTERY (UK)	DICKINSON	GFD	1939
AM	ATOMIC MAN (UK: TIMESLIP)	HUGHES	ALLIED ARTISTS	1955
AMC	AMARCORD	FELLINI	NEW WORLD	1974
AML	ALIKI (UK: ALIKI MY LOVE)	MATE	LIONEX	1963
AN	AFFAIR OF THE NECKLACE	SHYER	WARNER BROS	2001
AN	ALL NEAT IN BLACK STOCKINGS (UK)	MORAHAN	NATIONAL GENERAL	1969
AN	AMERICAN NINJA	FIRSTENBERG	CANNON	1985
AN	ANASTASIA (t)	BLUTH	20th CENTURY FOX	1997
AN	ANNA NEAGLE	portrait	RKO	

AN	LITTLE DARK ANGELS	RODRIGUEZ	DISTRIBUIDORA RODRIGU	1954
AN2	AMERICAN NINJA 2	FIRSTENBERG	CANNON	1987
AN3	AMERICAN NINJA 3	SUNDSTROM	CANNON	1989
AN4	AMERICAN NINJA 4	SUNDSTROM	CANNON	1990
AN5	AMERICAN NINJA 5 (video)	BRALVER	CANNON	1993
ANBS	ALL NEAT IN BLACK STOCKINGS (UK)	MORAHAN	NATIONAL GENERAL	1969
ANCW	ANY NUMBER CAN WIN	VERNEUIL	MGM	1963
ANJ	THERE AIN'T NO JUSTICE (UK)	TENNYSON	ABFD	1939
ANV	ANNIVERSARY (UK)	BAKER	20TH CENTURY FOX	1968
AO	OUTLAND	HYAMS	WARNER BROS	1981
AOG-192	MILLIONAIRESS (UK)	ASQUITH	20TH CENTURY FOX	1960
AOT	IT'S ALL OVER TOWN (UK)	HICKOX	BRITISH LION	1963
AP	AMOROUS MR. PRAWN (UK: AMOROUS PRAWN)	KIMMINS	MEDALLION	1962
AP	ANATOMY OF A PSYCHO	PETROFF	UNITED OF CALIFORNIA	1961
AP	ASK A POLICEMAN (UK)	VARNEL	MGM	1939
A-P	MACOMBER AFFAIR (aka GREAT WHITE HUNTER 1953)	Z. KORDA	UNITED ARTISTS	1947
AP-1	SHAKE HANDS WITH MURDER	HERMAN	PRODUCERS RELEASING	1944
AP-314	BEHIND PRISON WALLS	SEKELY	PRODUCERS RELEASING	1943
APA	ALMOST PERFECT AFFAIR	RITCHIE	PARAMOUNT	1979
APBB	ARACHNOPHOBIA	MARSHALL	BUENA VISTA	1990
APBB	FLUBBER	MAYFIELD	BUENA VISTA	1997
AP-F	ROLLING HOME	BERKE	SCREEN GUILD	1946
APM	PERFECT MURDER, A	DAVIS	WARNER BROS	1998
AQ	ALLAN QUATERMAIN AND THE LOST CITY OF GOLD	NELSON	CANNON	1986
AR	ARNOLD	FENADY	CINERAMA RELEASING	1973
AR	ARTHUR 2: ON THE ROCKS	YORKIN	WARNER BROS	1988
AR	MILLION DOLLAR MANHUNT (UK: ASSIGNMENT REDHEAD)	ROGERS	TUDOR	1956
ARBB	ARMAGEDDON	BAY	BUENA VISTA	1998
ARG	3 GODFATHERS	FORD	MGM	1948
ARG	ARGYLE SECRETS, THE	ENDFIELD	FILM CLASSICS	1948
ARGO-1	SON OF ROBIN HOOD (UK)	SHERMAN	20TH CENTURY FOX	1958
ARM	ALL THE RIGHT MOVES	CHAPMAN	20TH CENTURY FOX	1983
ARMS	INTO THE ARMS OF STRANGERS (doc)	HARRIS	WARNER BROS	2000
ARR	ADVENTURES OF REX AND RINTY (serial)	BEEBE, EASON	MASCOT	1935
AR-R	BADMAN'S TERRITORY	WHELAN	RKO	1946
ART	ARTICLE 99	DEUTCH	ORION PICTURES	1992
ARW	AFTER THE RAIN, WHERE?		BRANDON FILMS	
AS	AIR STRIKE	ROTH	LIPPERT	1955
AS	ALONG CAME SALLY (UK: AUNT SALLY)	WHELAN	GAUMONT BRIT. AMER.	1934
AS	ANITA STEWART	portrait	MGM	
AS	ANN SAVAGE	portrait	UNIVERSAL	
AS	ANOTHER SKY (UK)	LAMBERT		1954
AS	ASSASSINS	DONNER	WARNER BROS	1995
AS	GRIP OF THE STRANGLER (UK: HAUNTED STRANGLER)	DAY	AMALGAMATED	1957
AS	SIMON BIRCH	JOHNSON	BUENA VISTA	1998
ASS	AND NOW THE SCREAMING STARTS (UK)	BAKER	CINERAMA RELEASING	1973
AT	ACCIDENTAL TOURIST	KASDAN	WARNER BROS	1988
AT	ACTION OF THE TIGER (UK)	YOUNG	MGM	1957
AT	ANALYZE THIS	RAMIS	WARNER BROS	1999
AT	ARIZONA THOROUGHBRED			
AT	ASKING FOR TROUBLE (UK)	MITCHELL	ANGLO-AMERICAN	1942
AT	ASSASSINATION	LOSEY	CINERAMA RELEASING	1972
AT	ATTILA	FRANCISCI	EMBASSY	1958
AT	GENTLEMAN FROM ARIZONA (ARIZONA THOROUGHBRED)	HALEY	ASTOR	1939
ATBB	ATLANTIS THE LOST EMPIRE	WISE	BUENA VISTA	2001
ATG	ALEX THE GREAT	MURPHY	FILM BOOKING (FBO)	1928
ATG	ALFRED THE GREAT (UK)	DONNER	MGM	1969
ATW	ALL THESE WOMEN (SWE)	BERGMAN	JANUS	1964
ATX	AVONNE TAYLOR	portrait	MGM	
AUBB	AIR UP THERE	GLASER	BUENA VISTA	1994
AV	ALIDA VALLI	portrait	RKO	1950
AV	AVENGERS	CHECHIK	WARNER BROS	1998
AV	AVIATOR	MILLER	MGM/UA	1985
AV1	EIGHT O'CLOCK WALK (UK)	COMFORT	AAP	1954
AW	ALICE IN WONDERLAND (UK)	BOWER	SOUVAINE SELECTIVE	1949
AW	ALICE IN WONDERLAND (x)	TOWNSEND		1976

AW	ANDY WILLIAMS	portrait	UNIV	
AW	APACHE WARRIOR	WILLIAMS	20TH CENTURY FOX	1957
AWC	ALL I WANT FOR CHRISTMAS	LIEBERMAN	PARAMOUNT	1991
AWN	ACE VENTURA: WHEN NATURE CALLS	OEDEKERK	WARNER BROS	1995
AWW	ANGELS' WILD WOMEN	ADAMSON	INDEPENDENT INTL	1972
AXR	ANN RUTHERFORD	portrait	MGM	
AXS	ANN SOTHERN	portrait	MGM	
AYW	ALL THE YOUNG WIVES	DIEHL	UNITED FILM	1973
B	ALIAS BULLDOG DRUMMOND (UK: BULLDOG JACK)	FORDE	GAUMONT BRIT. AMER.	1935
B	ANY WHICH WAY YOU CAN	VAN HORN	WARNER BROS	1980
B	BACKFIRE (FR: ECHAPPEMENT LIBRE)	BECKER	ROYAL	1962
B	BARBARELLA	VADIM	PARAMOUNT	1968
B	BARTLEBY (UK)	FRIEDMAN	MARON	1970
B	BEAR (FR: L'OURS 1960)	SECHAN	EMBASSY	1963
B	BEAST WITH A MILLION EYES	KRAMARSKY	AMERICAN RELEASING	1955
B	BEDAZZLED (UK)	DONEN	20TH CENTURY FOX	1967
B	BEDELIA (UK)	COMFORT	EAGLE-LION	1946
B	BELLE DE JOUR (FR) (BELLE OF THE DAY)	BUNUEL	ALLIED ARTISTS	1968
B	BIG	MARSHALL	20TH CENTURY FOX	1988
B	BILLY JACK (on some US int'l - see BJ)	LAUGHLIN	WARNER BROS	1971
B	BIRD	EASTWOOD	WARNER BROS	1988
B	BIRDY	PARKER	TRI-STAR PICTURES	1985
B	BLAZING SADDLES	BROOKS	WARNER BROS	1974
B	BLOWN AWAY	HOPKINS	MGM	1994
B	BODY HEAT	KASDAN	WARNER BROS	1981
B	BODY OF EVIDENCE	EDEL	MGM	1992
B	BOPHA!	FREEMAN	PARAMOUNT	1993
B	BOUNTY	DONALDSON	ORION	1984
B	BOY AND THE BRIDGE (UK)	MCCLORY	COLUMBIA	1959
B	BOY WHO COULD FLY	CASTLE	LORIMAR	1986
B	BRAIN (GER: TOTER SEINEN MORDER 1962) (VENGEANCE)	FRANCIS	GOVERNOR	1964
B	BRAIN, THE (FR/IT: LE CERVEAU)	OURY	PARAMOUNT	1969
B	BRAVEHEART	GIBSON	20TH CENTURY FOX	1995
B	BREAKAWAY (UK)	CASS	AAP	1955
B	BREAKOUT (UK: DANGER WITHIN)	CHAFFEY	CONTINENTAL	1959
B	BREATHLESS	GODARD	FILMS AROUND WORLD	1960
B	BUSHBABY (UK)	TRENT	MGM	1969
B	BUSHWHACKED	BEEMAN	20th CENTURY FOX	1995
B	BUTLEY	PINTER	AMERICAN FILM	1975
B	BUTTERFLY	NEVE	AUDUBON	1970
B	CADDYSHACK	RAMIS	ORION	1980
B	CANCEL MY RESERVATION	BOGART	WARNER BROS	1972
B	EXORCIST	FRIEDKIN	WARNER BROS	1973
B	FIREFOX	EASTWOOD	WARNER BROS	1982
B	FRIENDLY ENEMIES	MELFORD	PRODUCERS DIST (PDC)	1925
B	GOING IN STYLE	BREST	WARNER BROS	1979
B	HIGH ROAD TO CHINA	HUTTON	WARNER BROS	1983
B	IN-LAWS, THE	HILLER	WARNER BROS	1979
B	INSIDE OUT	DUFFELL	WARNER BROS	1975
B	JUST TELL ME WHAT YOU WANT	LUMET	WARNER BROS	1979
B	LEPKE	GOLAN	WARNER BROS	1975
B	MAN WITH THE BALLOONS (FR: L'UOMO DEI CINQU PALLONI)	FERRERI	CIGMA III CORP	1968
B	O LUCKY MAN	ANDERSON	WARNER BROS	1973
B	ONE TRICK PONY	YOUNG	WARNER BROS	1980
B	OUR TIME	HYAMS	WARNER BROS	1974
B	PERMISSION TO KILL (EXECUTIONER)	FRANKEL	AVCO EMBASSY	1975
B	PRETTY BUT WICKED	DE CARVALHO	TIMES FILM CORP	1965
B	SATANIC RITES OF DRACULA	GIBSON	WARNER BROS	1973
B	TERMINAL MAN, THE	HODGES	WARNER BROS	1974
B	WHEN TIME RAN OUT	GOLDSTONE	WARNER BROS	1980
B-090	SO FINE	BERGMAN	WARNER BROS	1981
B1	BATTLE OF THE SEXES (UK)	CRICHTON	CONTINENTAL	1960
B1	RAGGED HEIRESS	BEAUMONT	FOX FILM	1922
B-1	365 DAYS (sh)	CHASE	PATHE EXCHANGE	1922
B-1	CARETAKER'S DAUGHTER (sh)	MCCAREY	PATHE EXCHANGE	1925
B-1	GO GET 'EM HUTCH (sh)	SEITZ	PATHE EXCHANGE	1922

B-1	MICKEY	JONES	W. H. PRODUCTIONS	1918
B-1	MOVIE DAZE (sh)	MEINS	MGM	1934
B-1	SCHEMER SKINNY'S SCHEMES (sh)		PATHE EXCHANGE	1917
B2	BASKETBALL FIX	FEIST	REALART	1951
B-2	BEFORE THE PUBLIC (sh)	CHASE	PATHE EXCHANGE	1923
B-2	CROOK'S TOUR (sh)	MCGOWAN	MGM	1933
B2	ENTERTAINER (UK)	RICHARDSON	CONTINENTAL	1960
B-2	SKINNY'S LOVE TRIANGLE (sh)		PATHE EXCHANGE	1917
B-2	SPIDER AND THE ROSE	MCDERMOTT	PRINCIPAL PICTURES	1923
B-2	UNEASY THREE (sh)	CHASE	PATHE EXCHANGE	1925
B-3	HIS WOODEN WEDDING (sh)	MCCAREY	PATHE EXCHANGE	1925
B-3	NEWLY RICH (sh)	CHASE	PATHE EXCHANGE	1922
B-3	SCHEEMER SKINNY'S SCHEMES (sh)		PATHE EXCHANGE	1917
B-3	TWIN SCREWS (sh)	PARROTT	MGM	1933
B-4	CHARLEY MY BOY (sh)	MCCAREY	PATHE EXCHANGE	1926
B-4	DRAMA'S DREADFUL DEAL (sh)		PATHE EXCHANGE	1917
B-4	GREEN CAT (sh)	CHASE	PATHE EXCHANGE	1922
B-4	KATHLEEN MAVOURNEEN	BRABIN	FOX FILM	1919
B-4	MIXED NUTS (sh)	PARROTT	MGM	1934
B4	SKYWATCH (UK: LIGHT UP THE SKY)	GILBERT	CONTINENTAL	1960
B-5	BALLAD OF A SOLDIER (RUS: BALLADA O SOLDATE 1959)	CHUKHRAY	UNION FILM	1960
B5	BOY WHO STOLE A MILLION (UK)	CRICHTON	PARAMOUNT	1960
B-5	BROKEN SABER	MCEVEETY	SENTINEL	1965
B-5	MAMA BEHAVE (sh)	CHASE	PATHE EXCHANGE	1926
B-5	NEXT WEEKEND (sh)	DUNN	MGM	1934
B-5	SKINNY GETS A GOAT (sh)	ROACH	PATHE EXCHANGE	1917
B-5	WHERE AM I? (sh)	CHASE	PATHE EXCHANGE	1923
B-6	CARETAKER'S DAUGHTER (sh)	FRENCH	MGM	1934
B-6	DOG SHY (sh)	MCCAREY	PATHE EXCHANGE	1926
B-6	OLD SEA DOG (sh)	CHASE	PATHE EXCHANGE	1922
B-6	SKINNY'S FALSE ALARM (sh)	ROACH	PATHE EXCHANGE	1917
B-7	DIG UP (sh)	HUTCHINSON	PATHE EXCHANGE	1923
B-7	MRS. BARNACLE BILL (sh)	FRENCH	MGM	1934
B-7	MUM'S THE WORD (sh)	McCAREY	PATHE EXCHANGE	1926
B-7	SKINNY'S SHIP-WRECKED SAND-WITCH (sh)	ROACH	PATHE EXCHANGE	1917
B-8	HOOK, LINE AND SINKER (sh)	CHASE	PATHE EXCHANGE	1922
B-8	LONG FLIV THE KING (sh)	MCCAREY	PATHE EXCHANGE	1926
B-8	SKINNY ROUTS A ROBBER (sh)		PATHE EXCHANGE	1917
B-8	SPEAKING OF RELATIONS (sh)	YATES	MGM	1934
B-9	BOARDER BUSTERS (sh)		PATHE EXCHANGE	1917
B-9	CALIFORNIA OR BUST (sh)	HUTCHINSON	PATHE EXCHANGE	1923
B9	LINDA (UK)	SHARP	BRYANSTON	1960
B-9	MIGHTY LIKE A MOOSE (sh)	MCCAREY	PATHE EXCHANGE	1926
B10	DOUBLE BUNK (UK)	PENNINGTON-RICHARDS	SHOWCORPORATION	1961
B-10	CRAZY LIKE A FOX (sh)	MCCAREY	PATHE EXCHANGE	1926
B-10	ETERNAL STRUGGLE	BARKER	METRO	1923
B-10	TOUGH WINTER (sh)	CHASE	PATHE EXCHANGE	1923
B-11	BROMO AND JULIET (sh)	MCCAREY	PATHE EXCHANGE	1926
B-11	IT'S A GIFT (sh)	FAY	PATHE EXCHANGE	1923
B11	SPARE THE ROD (UK)	NORMAN	BRYANSTON	1961
B-12	SOLD AT AUCTION (sh)	CHASE	PATHE EXCHANGE	1923
B-12	TELL 'EM NOTHING (sh)	MCCAREY	PATHE EXCHANGE	1926
B-13	BE YOUR AGE (sh)	CHASE	PATHE EXCHANGE	1926
B13	BROKEN BARRIERS	BARKER	METRO-GOLDWYN	1924
B-13	CALLING OF DAN MATHEWS	ROSEN	COLUMBIA	1935
B-13	WALKOUT, THE (sh)	JESKE	PATHE EXCHANGE	1923
B-13	WHY WORRY? (sh)	TAYLOR, NEWMEYER	PATHE EXCHANGE	1923
B-14	MANY SCRAPY RETURNS (sh)	PARROTT	PATHE EXCHANGE	1927
B-14	MYSTERY MAN (sh)	FAY	PATHE EXCHANGE	1923
B-15	JACK FROST (sh)	CHASE	PATHE EXCHANGE	1923
B-15	THERE AIN'T NO SANTA CLAUS (sh)	PARROTT	PATHE EXCHANGE	1926
B-16	ARE BRUNETTES SAFE? (sh)	PARROTT	PATHE EXCHANGE	1927
B-16	COURTSHIP OF MILES SANDWICH (sh)	CHASE	PATHE EXCHANGE	1923
B16	GIRL ON APPROVAL (UK)	FREND	CONTINENTAL	1961
B-17	ONE MAMA MAN (sh)	PARROTT	PATHE EXCHANGE	1927
B17	STRONGROOM (UK)	SEWELL	UNION	1962

B-18	FORGOTTEN SWEETIES (sh)	PARROTT	PATHE EXCHANGE	1927
B18	QUARE FELLOW, THE (UK)	DREIFUSS	ASTOR	1962
B-19	BIGGER AND BETTER BLONDS (sh)	PARROTT	PATHE EXCHANGE	1927
B-19	MINE WITH THE IRON DOOR	HOWARD	COLUMBIA	1936
B-20	FLUTTERING HEARTS (sh)	PARROTT	PATHE EXCHANGE	1927
B20	LONELINESS OF THE LONG DISTANCE RUNNER (UK)	RICHARDSON	CONTINENTAL	1962
B-21	WHAT WOMEN DID FOR ME (sh)	PARROTT	PATHE EXCHANGE	1927
B-21-P	LOST HORIZON	CAPRA	COLUMBIA	1937
B22	DON'T TALK TO STRANGE MEN (UK)	JACKSON	BRYANSTON	1962
B-22	NOW I'LL TELL ONE (sh)	PARROTT	PATHE EXCHANGE	1927
B-23	ASSISTANT WIVES (sh)	PARROTT	PATHE EXCHANGE	1927
B25	LUNCH HOUR (UK)	HILL	BRYANSTON	1961
B26	CALCULATED RISK (UK)	HARRISON	BRYANSTON	1963
B-27	MEET NERO WOLFE	BIBERMAN	COLUMBIA	1936
B28	MODEL MURDER CASE (UK: GIRL IN THE HEADLINES)	TRUMAN	CINEMA V	1963
B29	LADIES WHO DO (UK)	PENNINGTON-RICHARDS	CONTINENTAL	1963
B-35	LAWLESS RIDERS	BENNET	COLUMBIA	1935
B-70	WESTERN FRONTIER	HERMAN	COLUMBIA	1935
B-74	CATTLE THIEF	BENNET	COLUMBIA	1936
B-75	HEROES OF THE RANGE	BENNET	COLUMBIA	1936
B-76	AVENGING WATERS	BENNET	COLUMBIA	1936
B-77	FUGITIVE SHERIFF	BENNET	COLUMBIA	1936
B-80	GALLANT DEFENDER	SELMAN	COLUMBIA	1935
B-82	STAMPEDE	BEEBE	COLUMBIA	1936
B-83	SECRET PATROL	SELMAN	COLUMBIA	1936
B-84	TUGBOAT PRINCESS	SELMAN	COLUMBIA	1936
B-85	LUCKY FUGITIVES (CAN: STOP, LOOK AND LOVE)	GRINDE	COLUMBIA	1936
B113	HIS PEST FRIEND (sh)	GOODWINS	RKO	1938
B121	BERTH QUAKES (sh)	YARBROUGH	RKO	1938
B129	JITTERS (sh)	GOODWINS	RKO	1938
B131	HERE COME THE JETS	FOWLER JR.	20th CENTURY FOX	1959
B132	RETURN OF THE FLY	BERNDS	20th CENTURY FOX	1959
B133	MIRACLE OF THE HILLS, THE	LANDRES	20th CENTURY FOX	1959
B134	ALLIGATOR PEOPLE	DEL RUTH	20th CENTURY FOX	1959
B135	OREGON TRAIL	FOWLER JR.	20th CENTURY FOX	1959
B148	STAGE FRIGHT (sh)	GOODWINS	RKO	1938
B152	MAJOR DIFFICULTIES (sh)	BROCK	RKO	1938
B176	CRIME RAVE (sh)	YARBROUGH	RKO	1939
B184	MOVING VANITIES (sh)	BROCK	RKO	1939
B187	RING MADNESS (sh)	D'ARCY	RKO	1939
B212	MYRNA LOY	portrait		
B215	WRONG ROOM (sh)	BROCK	RKO	1939
B225	ROLAND YOUNG	portrait		
B225	TRUTH ACHES (sh)	ROBERTS	RKO	1939
B228	SCRAPPILY MARRIED (sh)	RIPLEY	RKO	1939
B262	BESTED BY A BEARD (sh)	ROBERTS	RKO	1940
B268	HE ASKED FOR IT (sh)	D'ARCY	RKO	1940
B278	WHEN WIFE'S AWAY		RKO	1940
B286	TATTLE TALEVISION (sh)	D'ARCY	RKO	1940
B291	FIRED MAN (sh)	ROBERTS	RKO	1941
B302	PANIC IN THE PARLOR (sh)	ROBERTS	RKO	1941
B304	POLO PHONY (sh)	D'ARCY	RKO	1941
B331	MAN-I-CURED (sh)	D'ARCY	RKO	1941
B336	WHO'S A DUMMY? (sh)	D'ARCY	RKO	1941
B344	HOME WORK (sh)	D'ARCY	RKO	1942
B360	WEDDED BLITZ (sh)	EDWARDS	RKO	1942
B361	FRAMING FATHER (sh)	ROBERTS	RKO	1942
B370	HOLD 'EM JAIL (shy)	FRENCH	RKO	1942
B375	MAIL TROUBLE (sh)	FRENCH	RKO	1942
B381	TWO FOR THE MONEY (sh)	FRENCH	RKO	1942
B387	DEAR! DEER! (sh)	HOLMES	RKO	1942
B391	PRETTY DOLLY (sh)	HOLMES	RKO	1942
B399	DOUBLE UP (sh)	HOLMES	RKO	1943
B406	GEM JAMS (sh)	HILLYER	RKO	1943
B411	RADIO RUNAROUND (sh)	HILLYER	RKO	1943
B422	CUTIE ON DUTY (sh)	HOLMES	RKO	1943

B425	WEDTIME STORIES (sh)	HOLMES	RKO	1943
B427	SEEING NELLIE HOME (sh)	HOLMES	RKO	1943
B439	SAY UNCLE (sh)	HOLMES	RKO	1943
B442	POPPA KNOWS WORST (sh)	HOLMES	RKO	1943
B459	GIRLS! GIRLS! GIRLS! (sh)	D'ARCY	RKO	1944
B462	TRIPLE TROUBLE (sh)	D'ARCY	RKO	1944
B478	HE FORGOT TO REMEMBER (sh)	YATES	RKO	1944
B479	LUISE RAINER	portrait	MGM	
B489	BIRTHDAY BLUES (sh)	YATES	RKO	1945
B492	LET'S GO STEPPING (sh)	YATES	RKO	1945
B499	IT SHOULDN'T HAPPEN TO A DOG (sh)	YATES	RKO	1945
B510	DOUBLE HONEYMOON (sh)	YATES	RKO	1945
B513	BEWARE OF REDHEADS (sh)	YATES	RKO	1945
B-519	OUTLAW	HUGHES	UNITED ARTISTS	1946
B530	BUDDY EBSEN	portrait		
B531	BUDDY EBSEN	portrait		
B531	MAID TROUBLE (sh)	EDWARDS	RKO	1945
B534	OH! PROFESSOR BEHAVE (sh)	YATES	RKO	1946
B543	TWIN HUSBANDS (sh)	YATES	RKO	1946
B547	I'LL TAKE MILK (sh)	YATES	RKO	1946
B549	MARIE DRESSLER	portrait		
B552	FOLLOW THAT BLONDE (sh)	YATES	RKO	1946
B-557	NIGHT FREIGHT	YARBROUGH	ALLIED ARTISTS	1955
B559	DOROTHY SEBASTIAN	portrait		
B578	BORROWED BLONDE (sh)	YATES	RKO	1947
B585	HIRED HUSBAND (sh)	YATES	RKO	1947
B586	IN ROOM 303 (sh)	YATES	RKO	1947
B599	BLONDES AWAY (sh)	YATES	RKO	1947
B618	SPOOK SPEAKS (sh)	YATES	RKO	1947
B619	BET YOUR LIFE (sh)	YATES	RKO	1948
B620	LIONEL BARRYMORE	portrait		
B625	DON'T FOOL YOUR WIFE (sh)	YATES	RKO	1948
B626	SECRETARY TROUBLE (sh)	YATES	RKO	1948
B646	BACHELOR BLUES (sh)	GOODWINS	RKO	1948
B647	UNINVITED BLONDE (sh)	YATES	RKO	1948
B648	BACKSTAGE FOLLIES (sh)	YATES	RKO	1948
B649	ELEANOR POWELL	portrait		
B650	ELEANOR POWELL	portrait		
B652	ELEANOR POWELL	portrait	MGM	
B656	FATHER'S DAY (sh)		RKO	1948
B657	CACTUS CUT-UP (sh)	ROBERTS	RKO	1949
B658	ELEANOR POWELL	portrait		
B664	OIL'S WELL THAT ENDS WELL (sh)	YATES	RKO	1949
B665	I CAN'T REMEMBER (sh)	YATES	RKO	1949
B676	SWEET CHEAT (sh)	YATES	RKO	1949
B679	SHOCKING AFFAIR (sh)	YATES	RKO	1949
B693	HIGH AND DIZZY (sh)	YATES	RKO	1950
B705	ROBERT TAYLOR	portrait		
B710	ROBERT TAYLOR	portrait		
B714	ROBERT TAYLOR	portrait		
B721	TEXAS TOUGH GUY (sh)	YATES	RKO	1950
B726	SPOOKY WOOKY (sh)	YATES	RKO	1950
B729	CHINA TOWN CHUMPS (sh)	YATES	RKO	1951
B756	LORD EPPING RETURNS (sh)	GOODWINS	RKO	1951
B1124	TED HEALY	portrait		
B1284	JAMES STEWART	portrait		
B1294	JAMES STEWART	portrait		
B1333	GRETA GARBO	portrait	MGM	
B1335	ERNESTINE SCHUMANN-HEINK	portrait		
B1337	GRETA GARBO	portrait	MGM	
B1361	GRETA GARBO	portrait	MGM	
B1397	ROBERT YOUNG	portrait		
B1583	CLARK GABLE	portrait		
B1913	EDMUND LOWE	portrait		
B1942	JEANETTE MACDONALD	portrait		
B1969	GRETA GARBO	portrait	MGM	

B1971	GRETA GARBO	portrait	MGM	
B2006	LILIAN BOND	portrait		
B2113	MYRNA LOY	portrait		
B2115	MYRNA LOY	portrait		
B2125	MYRNA LOY	portrait		
B2163	CHARLES BOYER	portrait		
B2189	LILIAN BOND	portrait	MGM	
B2198	MAUREEN O'SULLIVAN	portrait		
B2201	MAUREEN O'SULLIVAN	portrait		
B2203	MAUREEN O'SULLIVAN	portrait		
B2224	MAUREEN O'SULLIVAN	portrait		
B2254	CLARK GABLE	portrait		
B2259	CLARK GABLE	portrait		
B2276	ELEANOR POWELL	portrait	MGM	
B2442	FREDDIE BARTHOLOMEW	portrait		
B2517	LYNNE CARVER	portrait	MGM	
B2555	CLARK GABLE	portrait		
B2559	MYRNA LOY	portrait		
B2561	MYRNA LOY	portrait		
B2656	BERT LAHR	portrait		
B2741	GRETA GARBO	portrait	MGM	
B2754	GRETA GARBO	portrait	MGM	
B2838	MAUREEN O'SULLIVAN	portrait		
B2933	NELSON EDDY	portrait		
B3023	MYRNA LOY	portrait		
B3082	CLARK GABLE	portrait		
B3103	JOHN BARRYMORE	portrait		
B3208	GRETA GARBO	portrait	MGM	
B3223	GRETA GARBO	portrait	MGM	
B3234	GRETA GARBO	portrait	MGM	
B3255	GRETA GARBO	portrait	MGM	
B3290	KAREN MORLEY	portrait		
B3297	GRETA GARBO	portrait	MGM	
B3319	GRETA GARBO	portrait	MGM	
B3479	FRANK MORGAN	portrait		
B3543	ROBERT MONTGOMERY	portrait		
B3547	ROBERT MONTGOMERY	portrait		
B3575	MYRNA LOY	portrait		
B3584	GRETA GARBO	portrait	MGM	
B3593	GRETA GARBO	portrait	MGM	
B3608	ROBERT YOUNG	portrait		
B3617	ROBERT YOUNG	portrait		
B3618	ROBERT YOUNG	portrait		
B3620	ROBERT YOUNG	portrait		
B3674	LENORE BUSHMAN	portrait		
B3694	KAREN MORLEY	portrait		
B3830	HEDY LAMARR	portrait		
B3891	FAY HOLDEN	portrait		
B3960	LYNNE CARVER	portrait		
B4016	MARION DAVIES	portrait	MGM	
B4058	HEDY LAMARR	portrait		
B4073	RICHARD THORPE	portrait		
B4078	SARA HADEN	portrait		
B4120	REGINALD OWEN	portrait		
B4181	MARIE DRESSLER	portrait		
B4189	MARIE DRESSLER	portrait		
B4207	FAY HOLDEN	portrait		
B4209	GREER GARSON	portrait		
B4213	GREER GARSON	portrait		
B4343	POLLY MORAN	portrait		
B4344	POLLY MORAN	portrait		
B4351	POLLY MORAN	portrait		
B4359	LIONEL BARRYMORE	portrait		
B4378	VEREE TEASDALE	portrait		
B4527	MAUREEN O'SULLIVAN	portrait		
B4533	MAUREEN O'SULLIVAN	portrait		

B4608	CLARK GABLE	portrait		
B4609	CLARK GABLE	portrait		
B4631	GREER GARSON	portrait		
B4637	GREER GARSON	portrait		
B4686	GREER GARSON	portrait		
B4713	GREER GARSON	portrait		
B4760	GRETA GARBO	portrait	MGM	
B4765	GRETA GARBO	portrait	MGM	
B4811	ILONA MASSEY	portrait		
B4954	HEDY LAMARR	portrait		
B4973	GRETA GARBO	portrait	MGM	
B4986	GRETA GARBO	portrait	MGM	
B4988	GRETA GARBO	portrait	MGM	
B5063	WALTER HUSTON	portrait		
B5071	ROBERT MONTGOMERY	portrait		
B5158	JEANETTE MACDONALD	portrait		
B5208	MARGARET SULLAVAN	portrait	MGM	
B5211	MARGARET SULLAVAN	portrait	MGM	
B5258	SHIRLEY TEMPLE	portrait		
B5291	LANA TURNER	portrait		
B5343	FAY HOLDEN	portrait	MGM	
B5460	MARGARET SULLAVAN	portrait	MGM	
B5463	MARGARET SULLAVAN	portrait	MGM	
B5464	MARGARET SULLAVAN	portrait	MGM	
B5465	MARGARET SULLAVAN	portrait	MGM	
B5473	MARGARET SULLAVAN	portrait		
B5497	GRETA GARBO	portrait	MGM	
B5517	ELEANOR POWELL	portrait		
B5519	ELEANOR POWELL	portrait		
B5523	ANN SOTHERN	portrait		
B5539	ELEANOR POWELL	portrait		
B5542	ELEANOR POWELL	portrait		
B5552	JEANETTE MACDONALD	portrait		
B5566	KATHARINE HEPBURN	portrait	MGM	
B5614	BASIL RATHBONE	portrait		
B5617	VIRGINIA WEIDLER	portrait		
B5651	SUSAN PETERS	portrait		
B5722	MARJORIE MAIN	portrait		
B5723	MARJORIE MAIN	portrait		
B5724	MARJORIE MAIN	portrait		
B5876	NELSON EDDY	portrait		
B5882	MAUREEN O'SULLIVAN	portrait		
B5900	BARBARA STANWYCK/ROBERT TAYLOR	portrait	MGM	
B5917	KATHRYN GRAYSON	portrait		
B6260	LEWIS STONE	portrait		
B6558	MYRNA LOY	portrait		
B6710	LIONEL BARRYMORE	portrait		
B6835	CLARK GABLE	portrait		
B7108	FRANK MORGAN	portrait		
B7230	LUPE VELEZ	portrait		
B7291	LEWIS STONE	portrait		
B7343	FLORINE MCKINNEY	portrait		
B7472	POLLY MORAN	portrait		
B7482	POLLY MORAN	portrait		
B7923	GRETA GARBO	portrait	MGM	
B7970	JIMMY DURANTE	portrait	MGM	
B7991	JIMMY DURANTE	portrait	MGM	
B8021	OTTO KRUGER	portrait		
B8227	LEWIS STONE	portrait		
B8230	LEWIS STONE	portrait		
B8284	MURIEL EVANS	portrait		
B8477	MAURICE CHEVALIER	portrait	MGM	
B8677	GWEN LEE	portrait		
B8836	FRANK MORGAN	portrait		
B8837	FRANK MORGAN	portrait		
B8846	FRANK MORGAN	portrait		

B8942	CLARK GABLE	portrait		
B9015	LUPE VELEZ	portrait		
B9069	MYRNA LOY	portrait		
B9630	ANITA PAGE	portrait		
B9678	POLLY MORAN	portrait		
B9800	ROSALIND RUSSELL	portrait	MGM	
B9843	BASIL RATHBONE	portrait		
B9896	JACKIE COOPER	portrait		
B9946	JEANETTE MACDONALD	portrait		
B9953	JEANETTE MACDONALD	portrait		
B9963	JEANETTE MACDONALD	portrait		
B10036	LIONEL BARRYMORE	portrait		
B10847	ROBERT MONTGOMERY	portrait		
B10902	GWEN LEE	portrait		
B11075	GRETA GARBO	portrait	MGM	
B11084	GRETA GARBO	portrait	MGM	
B&D	BEAR AND THE DOLL	DEVILLE	PARAMOUNT	1971
B&R	BATMAN AND ROBIN	SCHUMACHER	WARNER BROS	1997
B&S	BLOOD AND SAND	NIBLO	PARAMOUNT	R-ONLY
B&S	BODY AND SOUL	BOWERS	CANNON	1981
B&T-105	BILL AND TED'S EXCELLENT ADVENTURE	HEREK	ORION	1989
BA	BARON OF ARIZONA	FULLER	LIPPERT	1950
BA	BATTLE OF ALGIERS (ITALY: BATTAGLIA DI ALGERI)	PONTECORVO	ALLIED ARTISTS	1968
BA	BERMUDA AFFAIR (UK)	SUTHERLAND	COLUMBIA	1956
BA	BEULAH BONDI	portrait		
BA	BLOOD ARROW	WARREN	20th CENTURY FOX	1958
BA	BORN AGAIN	RAPPER	AVCO EMBASSY	1978
BA	BREAKING AWAY	YATES	20th CENTURY FOX	1979
BA	BROKEN ARROW	WOO	20th CENTURY FOX	1996
BA	BRUCE ALMIGHTY	SHADYAC	BUENA VISTA	2003
BA	EVERY WHICH WAY BUT LOOSE	FARGO	WARNER BROS	1978
BA	SHADOW OF FEAR (UK)	MORRIS	BUTCHER'S	1963
BA	TIGER WALKS, A	TOKAR	BUENA VISTA	1964
BA1	GREEN SCARF (UK)	O'FERRALL	AAP	1954
BA-1	NAKED EARTH, THE (UK)	SHERMAN	20th CENTURY FOX	1958
BAB	BEAUTY AND THE BARGE (UK)	EDWARDS	WARDOUR	1937
B-AE	8 1/2	FELLINI	EMBASSY	1963
BAL	BALCONY	STRICK	CONTINENTAL	1963
BAP	PRIVATE POTTER (UK)	WREDE	MGM	1962
BAR	BARBARIANS	DEODATO	CANNON	1987
BARKER1	WHEN THE DOOR OPENED	BARKER	FOX FILM	1925
BAT	BATMAN	BURTON	WARNER BROS	1989
BAT 21	BAT 21	MARKLE	TRI STAR	1988
BAU	BUSINESS AS USUAL	AN-BARRETT	CANNON	1988
BAY	BAY BOY, THE	PETRIE	ORION	1988
BB	ADV OF BUCKAROO BANZAI	RICHTER	20th CENTURY FOX	1984
BB	AND THE SAME TO YOU (UK)	POLLOCK	MONARCH	1960
BB	BABY AND THE BATTLESHIP (UK)	LEWIS	DCA	1956
BB	BACK-ROOM BOY (UK)	MASON	GFD	1942
BB	BALLAD IN BLUE (BLUES FOR LOVERS)	HENREID	20th CENTURY FOX	1964
BB	BALTIMORE BULLET	MILLER	AVCO EMBASSY	1980
BB	BIG BLOCKADE (UK)	FREND	UNITED ARTISTS	1942
BB	BIG BLUFF, THE	WILDER	UNITED ARTISTS	1955
BB	BIG BREAK	STRICK	MADISON	1953
BB	BIGGEST BUNDLE OF THEM ALL	ANNAKIN	MGM	1968
BB	BILLY & BOBBY MAUCH	portrait	WARNER BROS	
BB	BLACK BEAUTY	HILL	PARAMOUNT	1971
BB	BLACK BIRD, THE	GILER	COLUMBIA	1975
BB	BLISS OF MRS. BLOSSOM (UK)	MCGRATH	PARAMOUNT	1968
BB	BLOOD BEAST FROM OUTER SPACE	GILLING	WORLD ENTERTAIN.	1965
BB	BOY IN BLUE	JARROTT	20th CENTURY FOX	1985
BB	BRADY BUNCH MOVIE	THOMAS	PARAMOUNT	1995
BB	BROKEN BLOSSOMS (UK)	BRAHM	TWICKENHAM (UK)	1936
BB	BRONCO BULLFROG (UK)	PLATTS-MILLS	NEW YORKER	1969
BB	BUTCHER BOY	JORDAN	GEFFEN	1998
BB	HIPPODROME	RABENALT	CONTINENTAL DIST.	1961

BB	HIS MAJESTY BUNKER BEAN	BEAUMONG	WARNER BROS	1925
BB	WILLIAM BOYD	portrait	PARAMOUNT	
BB1	BRIDGE OF SAN LUIS REY	LEE	UNITED ARTISTS	1944
BB1	KID FOR TWO FARTHINGS (UK)	REED	LOPERT	1955
BB2	RICHARD THE 3RD (UK)	OLIVIER	LOPPERT	1955
BB-210	TOO MANY WOMEN	RAY	PRODUCERS RELEASING	1942
BB-212	HOUSE OF ERRORS	RAY	PRODUCERS RELEASING	1942
BBB	BEAUTY AND THE BEAST	WISE	BUENA VISTA	1991
BBBB	BIG BUSINESS	ABRAHAMS	BUENA VISTA	1988
BBBB	BUBBLE BOY	HAYES	BUENA VISTA	2001
BBE	BATTLE BENEATH THE EARTH (UK)	TULLY	MGM	1967
BBG	BANG BANG GANG	GUYLDER	EDEN DISTRIBUTING	1970
BBG	BELL-BOTTOM GEORGE (UK)	VARNEL	COLUMBIA	1944
BBH	BEAVIS & BUTTHEAD DO AMERICA	JUDGE	GEFFEN	1996
BBL	BYE BYE LOVE	WEISMAN	20th CENTURY FOX	1995
BBS	GREEN SLIME, THE	FUKASAKU	MGM	1969
BBT	BLACK BELLY OF THE TARANTULA	CAVARA	MGM	1971
BBW	BIG BAD WOLF (GER: WOLF UND SIEBEN JUNGEN GEISSLEIN)	PODEHL	CHILDHOOD PROD	1966
BC	BED CAREER (r: SWINGIN' MODELS)	VON ANUTROFF	HEMISPHERE	1973
BC	BLACK CAT	HOFFMAN	FALCON INTL	1966
BC	BLIND CORNER/US: MAN IN THE DARK (UK)	COMFORT	UNIVERSAL	1965
BC	BREAK IN THE CIRCLE (UK)	GUEST	20TH CENTURY FOX	1955
BC	BUSH CHRISTMAS (UK)	SMART	UNIVERSAL	1947
BC	BUSTER COLLIER	portrait		
BC	BUSTER CRABBE	portrait	UNIV	
BC-86	LAW AND ORDER	NEWFIELD	PRODUCERS RELEASING	1942
BC-97	WILD HORSE RUSTLERS	NEWFIELD	TIFFANY	1943
BC-110	NABONGA	NEWFIELD	PRODUCERS RELEASING	1944
BC-111	DEVIL RIDERS (mistake? BC-107)	NEWFIELD	PRODUCERS RELEASING	1943
BCBB	BAD COMPANY	SCHUMACHER	BUENA VISTA	2002
BCBB	BLANK CHECK	WAINWRIGHT	BUENA VISTA	1994
BCBB	BREAKFAST OF CHAMPIONS	RUDOLPH	BUENA VISTA	1999
BCC	BOYS OF COMPANY C	FURIE	COLUMBIA	1978
B-COL-2	MUSIC GOES ROUND	SCHERTZINGER	COLUMBIA	1936
B-COL-3	CRIME AND PUNISHMENT	STERNBERG	COLUMBIA	1935
B-COL-4	GRAND EXIT	KENTON	COLUMBIA	1935
B-COL-5	ESCAPE FROM DEVIL'S ISLAND	ROGELL	COLUMBIA	1935
B-COL-6	ONE WAY TICKET	BIBERMAN	COLUMBIA	1935
B-COL-7	LONE WOLF RETURNS	NEILL	COLUMBIA	1935
B-COL-8	IF YOU COULD ONLY COOK	SEITER	COLUMBIA	1935
B-COL-9	HELL-SHIP MORGAN	LEDERMAN	COLUMBIA	1936
B-COL-10	YOU MAY BE NEXT	ROGELL	COLUMBIA	1936
B-COL-11	KING STEPS OUT	VON STERNBERG	COLUMBIA	1936
B-COL-12	LADY OF SECRETS	GERING	COLUMBIA	1936
B-COL-13	CALLING OF DAN MATHEWS	ROSEN	COLUMBIA	1935
B-COL-14	DEVIL'S SQUADRON	KENTON	COLUMBIA	1936
B-COL-15	DON'T GAMBLE WITH LOVE	MURPHY	COLUMBIA	1936
B-COL-16	PRIDE OF THE MARINES	LEDERMAN	COLUMBIA	1936
B-COL-17	END OF THE TRAIL	KENTON	COLUMBIA	1936
B-COL-18	ROAMING LADY	ROGELL	COLUMBIA	1936
B-COL-19	MINE WITH THE IRON DOOR	HOWARD	COLUMBIA	1936
B-COL-20	AND SO THEY WERE MARRIED	NUGENT	COLUMBIA	1936
B-COL-22	TRAPPED BY TELEVISION	LORD	COLUMBIA	1936
B-COL-23	BLACKMAILER	WILES	COLUMBIA	1936
B-COL-25	COUNTERFEIT	KENTON	COLUMBIA	1936
B-COL-27	MEET NERO WOLFE	BIBERMAN	COLUMBIA	1936
B-COL-27	MR. DEEDS GOES TO TOWN	CAPRA	COLUMBIA	1936
B-COL-29	THEODORA GOES WILD	BOLESLAWSKI	COLUMBIA	1936
B-COL-32	TWO FISTED GENTLEMAN	WILES	COLUMBIA	1936
B-COL-33	THEY MET IN A TAXI	GREEN	COLUMBIA	1936
B-COL-35	LAWLESS RIDERS	BENNET	COLUMBIA	1935
B-COL-35	WHEN YOU'RE IN LOVE	RISKIN	COLUMBIA	1937
B-COL-60	GUARD THAT GIRL	HILLYER	COLUMBIA	1935
B-COL-61	CASE OF THE MISSING MAN	LEDERMAN	COLUMBIA	1935
B-COL-62	TOO TOUGH TO KILL	LEDERMAN	COLUMBIA	1935
B-COL-63	DANGEROUS INTRIGUE	SELMAN	COLUMBIA	1936

B-COL-64	PANIC ON THE AIR	LEDERMAN	COLUMBIA	1936
B-COL-65	FINAL HOUR	LEDERMAN	COLUMBIA	1936
B-COL-66	SHAKEDOWN	SELMAN	COLUMBIA	1936
B-COL-67	ALIBI FOR MURDER	LEDERMAN	COLUMBIA	1936
B-COL-68	KILLER AT LARGE	SELMAN	COLUMBIA	1936
B-COL-70	WESTERN FRONTIER	HERMAN	COLUMBIA	1935
B-COL-74	CATTLE THIEF	BENNET	COLUMBIA	1936
B-COL-75	HEROES OF THE RANGE	BENNET	COLUMBIA	1936
B-COL-76	AVENGING WATERS	BENNET	COLUMBIA	1936
B-COL-77	FUGITIVE SHERIFF	BENNET	COLUMBIA	1936
B-COL-80	GALLANT DEFENDER	SELMAN	COLUMBIA	1935
B-COL-81	MYSTERIOUS AVENGER	SELMAN	COLUMBIA	1936
B-COL-82	STAMPEDE	BEEBE	COLUMBIA	1936
B-COL-83	SECRET PATROL	SELMAN	COLUMBIA	1936
B-COL-84	TUGBOAT PRINCESS	SELMAN	COLUMBIA	1936
B-COL-85	LUCKY FUGITIVES - CAN: STOP, LOOK AND LOVE)	GRINDE	COLUMBIA	1936
B-COL-157	HIS OLD FLAME (sh)	HORNE	COLUMBIA	1935
B-COL-159	HORSE COLLARS (sh)	BRUCKMAN	COLUMBIA	1935
B-COL-160	RESTLESS KNIGHTS (sh)	LAMONT	COLUMBIA	1935
B-COL-161	I'M A FATHER (sh)	HORNE	COLUMBIA	1935
B-COL-162	HIS BRIDAL SWEET (sh)	GOULDING	COLUMBIA	1935
B-COL-163	POP GOES THE EASEL (sh)	LORD	COLUMBIA	1935
B-COL-165	UNCIVIL WARRIORS (sh)	LORD	COLUMBIA	1935
B-COL-166	LEATHER NECKER (sh)	RIPLEY	COLUMBIA	1935
B-COL-167	GUM SHOES (sh)	LORD	COLUMBIA	1935
B-COL-168	PARDON MY SCOTCH (sh) (changed)	LORD	COLUMBIA	1935
B-COL-169	TRAMP TRAMP TRAMP (sh)	LAMONT	COLUMBIA	1935
B-COL-171	ALIMONY ACHES (sh)	LAMONT	COLUMBIA	1935
B-COL-172	STAGE FRIGHTS (sh)	RAY	COLUMBIA	1935
B-COL-173	DO YOUR STUFF (sh)	PARROTT	COLUMBIA	1935
B-COL-174	CAPTAIN HITS THE CEILING (sh)	LAMONT	COLUMBIA	1935
B-COL-175	GOBS OF TROUBLE (sh)	LORD	COLUMBIA	1935
B-COL-200	OH, MY NERVES! (sh)	LORD	COLUMBIA	1935
B-COL-202	IT ALWAYS HAPPENS (sh)	LORD	COLUMBIA	1935
B-COL-203	HIS MARRIAGE MIX-UP (sh)	WHITE	COLUMBIA	1935
B-COL-204	STAR GAZING (sh)	RUBIN	COLUMBIA	1935
B-COL-205	YOO HOO HOLLYWOOD (sh)	RUBIN	COLUMBIA	1935
B-COL-206	PARDON MY SCOTCH (sh)	LORD	COLUMBIA	1935
B-COL-207	HOI POLLOI (sh)	LORD	COLUMBIA	1935
B-COL-208	HONEYMOON BRIDGE (sh)	LORD	COLUMBIA	1935
B-COL-209	HOT PAPRIKA (sh)	WHITE	COLUMBIA	1935
B-COL-210	THREE LITTLE BEERS (sh)	LORD	COLUMBIA	1935
B-COL-211	I DON'T REMEMBER (sh)	WHITE	COLUMBIA	1935
B-COL-213	MOVIE MANIACS (sh)	LORD	COLUMBIA	1936
B COL-217	DISORDER IN THE COURT (sh)	WHITE	COLUMBIA	1936
B-COL-219	CHAMP'S A CHUMP (sh)	WHITE	COLUMBIA	1936
B-COL-220	MISTER SMARTY (sh)	WHITE	COLUMBIA	1936
B-COL-221	SLIPPERY SILKS (changed to 252)	WHITE	COLUMBIA	1936
B-COL-222	CAUGHT IN THE ACT	LORD	COLUMBIA	1936
B-COL-223	PAIN IN THE PULLMAN (sh)	WHITE	COLUMBIA	1936
B-COL-224	FALSE ALARMS (sh) (changed to 250)	LORD	COLUMBIA	1936
B-COL-225	HALF SHOT SHOOTERS (sh)	WHITE	COLUMBIA	1936
B-COL-226	WHOOPS, I'M AN INDIAN! (sh) (changed to 251)	WHITE	COLUMBIA	1936
B-COL-250	FALSE ALARMS (sh)	LORD	COLUMBIA	1936
B-COL-251	WHOOPS, I'M AN INDIAN! (sh)	WHITE	COLUMBIA	1936
B-COL-252	SLIPPERY SILKS	WHITE	COLUMBIA	1936
B-COL-253	AM I HAVING FUN! (sh)	WHITE	COLUMBIA	1936
B-COL-254	AY TANK AY GO (sh)	LORD	COLUMBIA	1936
B-COL-255	OH, DUCHESS! (sh)	LAMONT	COLUMBIA	1936
B-COL-256	LOVE COMES TO MOONEYVILLE (sh)	WHITE	COLUMBIA	1936
B-COL-257	FIBBING FIBBERS (sh)	WHITE	COLUMBIA	1936
BCP	BIRD WITH THE CRYSTAL PLUMAGE (IT)	ARGENTO	UNIVERSAL MARION	1970
BCT	ELIZABETH THREATT	portrait	RKO	
BD	BACK FROM THE DEAD	WARREN	20th CENTURY FOX	1957
BD	BAD DREAMS	FLEMING	20th CENTURY FOX	1988
BD	BELLA DONNA (UK)	MILTON	OLYMPIC	1934

BD	BEST DEFENSE	HUYCK	PARAMOUNT	1984
BD	BLACK DUKE	MERCANTI	PRODUCERS RELEASING	1964
BD	BLIND DATE	EDWARDS	TRI STAR	1987
BD	BLONDES FOR DANGER (UK)	RAYMOND	BRITISH LION	1938
BD	BOBBY DEERFIELD	POLLACK	COLUMBIA	1972
BD	BROADWAY DANNY ROSE	ALLEN	ORION	1984
BD	BROWN DERBY	HINES	FIRST NATIONAL	1926
BDB	BILLION DOLLAR BRAIN (UK)	RUSSELL	UNITED ARTISTS	1967
BDC	BLOOD OF DRACULA'S CASTLE	ADAMSON	CROWN INT'L	1969
BDH	BIG DOLL HOUSE	HILL	NEW WORLD	1971
BDMS	BIG DEAL ON MADONNA STREET (IT: I SOLITI IGNOTI)	MONICELLI	UMPO	1958
BDO	BABY'S DAY OUT	JOHNSON	20th CENTURY FOX	1994
BDR	BORDER RANGERS	BERKE	LIPPERT	1950
BDR	BROADWAY DANNY ROSE	ALLEN	ORION	1984
BE	WILD BILL ELLIOTT	portrait	REP	
BEA	BLESS 'EM ALL (UK)	HILL	ADELPHI	1949
BEAU 1	ONE INCREASING PURPOSE	BEAUMONT	FOX FILM	1927
BEAU-7	SECRET STUDIO	BEAUMONT	FOX FILM	1927
BEAUDINE-2453	BATTLING BELL BOY	BEAUDINE	UNIVERSAL	1917
BEBB	BEACHES	MARSHALL	BUENA VISTA	1988
B-E-COL 4	LAW COMES TO TEXAS	LEVERING	COLUMBIA	1939
BEL	BELLISSIMA (IT)	VISCONTI	IFE	1952
BF	BARFLY	SCHROEDER	CANNON	1987
BF	BARTON FINK	COEN BROS	20th CENTURY FOX	1991
BF	BATMAN FOREVER	SCHUMACHER	WARNER BROS	1995
BF	BELATED FLOWERS	ROOM	ARTKINO	1970
BF	BEYOND FEAR (FR: AU DELA DE LA PEUR 1975)	ANDREI	PRISM	1985
BF	BIG FOOT	SLATZER	UNIVERSAL	1971
BF	BLOOD FEAST	LEWIS	BOX OFFICE SPECT.	1963
BF	BLOOD FIEND (UK: THEATRE OF DEATH)	GALLU	HEMISPHERE	1967
BF	BOAT IS FULL, THE (GER: DAS BOOT IST VOLL)	IMHOOF	QUARTET FILMS	1981
BF	BOYFRIEND (UK)	RUSSELL	MGM	1971
BF1	TRUTH ABOUT WOMEN (UK)	BOX	CONTINENTAL	1957
BF3	MAN IN THE ROAD (UK)	COMFORT	REPUBLIC	1956
BF3	ROCK AROUND THE WORLD (UK: TOMMY STEELE STORY)	BRYANT	AIP	1957
BF/3	ROCK AROUND THE WORLD (UK: TOMMY STEELE STORY)	BRYANT	AIP	1957
BF4	TOO YOUNG TO LOVE (UK)	BOX	GO	1960
BF5	MAILBAG ROBBERY (UK: FLYING SCOT)	BENNETT	TUDOR	1957
BF-507	HOUSE OF INTRIGUE (IT: LONDRA CHIAMA POLO NORD 1956)	COLETTI	MONOGRAM	1959
BFL1	CARRY ON SERGEANT (UK)	THOMAS	GOVERNOR	1958
BFM	BRIDES OF FU MANCHU (UK)	SHARP	SEVEN ARTS	1966
BFM6	ON APPROVAL (UK)	BROOK	ENGLISH	1944
BFW	WATERLOO ROAD (UK)	GILLIAT	EAGLE-LION	1945
BG	BAD GIRLS	KAPLAN	20th CENTURY FOX	1994
BG	BADGER'S GREEN (UK)	BRUNEL	PARAMOUNT BRITISH	1934
BG	BADMAN'S GOLD	TANSEY	EAGLE-LION	1951
BG	BLACK GLOVE (UK: FACE THE MUSIC)	FISHER	LIPPERT	1954
BG	BODYGUARD	JACKSON	WARNER BROS	1992
BG	BONITA GRANVILLE	portrait	MGM, RKO, UNIV, WB	1930s-40s
BG	BOUND FOR GLORY	ASHBY	UNITED ARTISTS	1976
BG	BREAKING GLASS	GIBSON	PARAMOUNT	1980
BG	PRIDE OF THE BLUE GRASS	MCGANN	WARNER BROS	1939
BG1	RETURN OF THE SCARLET PIMPERNEL (UK)	SCHWARZ	UNITED ARTISTS	1937
BGD	BELLS GO DOWN (UK)	DEARDEN	UNITED ARTISTS	1943
BH	BAND OF THE HAND	GLASER	TRI STAR	1986
BH	BEAST FROM HAUNTED CAVE	HELLMAN	FILM GROUP	1959
BH	BENITA HUME	portrait	MGM	1930s
BH	BEVERLY HILLBILLIES	SPHEERIS	20th CENTURY FOX	1993
BH	BODY HEAT	KASDAN	WARNER BROS	1981
BH	HORROR MANIACS (UK: GREED OF WILLIAM HART)	MITCHELL	JH HOFFBERG	1948
BH	THREE ON A WEEKEND (UK: BANK HOLIDAY)	REED	GAUMONT BRIT. AMER.	1938
BHC	BEVERLY HILLS COP	BREST	PARAMOUNT	1984
BHC3	BEVERLY HILLS COP III	LANDIS	PARAMOUNT	1994
BI	BAD INFLUENCE	HANSON	TRIUMPH RELEASING	1990
BI	BEAR ISLAND	SHARP	UNITED ARTISTS	1980
BIB	BLUES FOR LOVERS (BALLAD IN BLUE)	HENREID	20th CENTURY FOX	1965

BIY	BABY ITS YOU	SAYLES	PARAMOUNT	1983
BJ	BENJAMIN	DEVILLE	PARAMOUNT	1968
BJ	BETTY JAYNES	portrait	MGM	
BJ	BIG JIM MCLAIN	LUDWIG	WARNER BROS	1952
BJ	BLIND JUSTICE (UK)	VORHAUS	OLYMPIC	1934
BJ-1	BEATNIKS, THE	FREES	BARJUL INT'L	1959
BJ-1	ROCKY RHODES (1934)	RABOCH	REALART	R48
BJ-2	WHEN A MAN SEES RED	JAMES	UNIVERSAL	1934
BJ3	CREMSON TRAIL - ®	RAVOCH	REALART	1935
BJ-4	STONE OF SILVER CREEK	GRINDE	UNIVERSAL	1935
BJ-14	LEFT HANDED LAW	SELANDER	UNIVERSAL	1937
BJ-COL-1	HOLLYWOOD ROUNDUP	SCOTT	COLUMBIA	1937
BJ-COL-2	HEADING EAST	SCOTT	COLUMBIA	1937
BJ-COL-4	STRANGER FROM ARIZONA	CLIFTON	COLUMBIA	1938
BJ-COL-5	LAW OF THE TEXAN	CLIFTON	COLUMBIA	1938
BJ-COL-6	CALIFORNIA FRONTIER	CLIFTON	COLUMBIA	1938
BK	8 1/2	FELLINI	EMBASSY	1963
BK	AFTER HOURS (see AH)	SCORSESE	WARNER BROS	1985
BK	BARBARA KNUDSON	portrait	UNIV	
BK	BEBE'S KIDS (t)	SMITH	PARAMOUNT	1992
BK	BEETLEJUICE	BURTON	WARNER BROS	1988
BK	BILL KENNEDY	portrait	WARNER BROS	
BK	BIRD	EASTWOOD	WARNER BROS	1988
BK	BLADERUNNER	SCOTT	WARNER BROS	1982
BK	BODY HEAT	KASDAN	WARNER BROS	1981
BK	BRETT KING	portrait	RKO	
BK	BRUBAKER	ROSENBERG	20th CENTURY FOX	1980
BK	BURGLER	WILSON	WARNER BROS	1987
BK	CLEAN AND SOBER	CARON	WARNER BROS	1988
BK	COBRA	COSMATOS	WARNER BROS	1986
BK	COLOR PURPLE, THE	SPIELBERG	WARNER BROS	1985
BK	CROSSING DELANCEY	SILVER	WARNER BROS	1988
BK	CUJO	TEAGUE	WARNER BROS	1983
BK	DEAD POOL	VAN HORN	WARNER BROS	1988
BK	DEAL OF THE CENTURY	FRIEDKIN	WARNER BROS	1983
BK	DEATHTRAP	LUMET	WARNER BROS	1982
BK	ELENI	YATES	WARNER BROS	1985
BK	EMPIRE OF THE SUN	SPIELBERG	WARNER BROS	1987
BK	EVERYBODY'S ALL AMERICAN	HACKFORD	WARNER BROS	1988
BK	EXCALIBUR	BOORMAN	WARNER BROS	1981
BK	EYES OF A STRANGER	WIEDERHORN	WARNER BROS	1981
BK	FUNNY FARM	HILL	WARNER BROS	1988
BK	GREAT SANTINI	CARLINO	WARNER BROS	1979
BK	GREMLINS	DANTE	WARNER BROS	1984
BK	HONKYTONK MAN	EASTWOOD	WARNER BROS	1982
BK	HOT TO TROT	DINNER	WARNER BROS	1983
BK	I SHOT BILLY THE KID	BERKE	LIPPERT	1950
BK	IRRECONCILABLE DIFFERENCES	SHYER	WARNER BROS	1984
BK	KILLING FIELDS	JOFFE	WARNER BROS	1984
BK	LOCAL HERO	FORSYTH	WARNER BROS	1983
BK	LOST BOYS	SCHUMACHER	WARNER BROS	1987
BK	LOVESICK	BRICKMAN	WARNER BROS	1983
BK	MAN WITH TWO BRAINS, THE	REINER	WARNER BROS	1983
BK	MIKE'S MURDER	BRIDGES	WARNER BROS	1983
BK	MISHIMA: LIFE IN FOUR CHAPTERS	SCHRADER	WARNER BROS	1985
BK	MISSION	JOFFE	WARNER BROS	1986
BK	MOVING	METTER	WARNER BROS	1988
BK	NEVER SAY NEVER AGAIN	KERSHNER	WARNER BROS	1983
BK	NEVERENDING STORY	PETERSEN	WARNER BROS	1984
BK	ONCE UPON A TIME IN AMERICA	LEONE	WARNER BROS	1984
BK	POLICE ACADEMY 3: BACK IN TRAINING	PARIS	WARNER BROS	1986
BK	PURPLE HEARTS	FURIE	WARNER BROS	1984
BK	RATBOY	LOCKE	WARNER BROS	1986
BK	REVOLUTION	HUDSON	WARNER BROS	1985
BK	RIGHT STUFF, THE	KAUFMAN	WARNER BROS	1983
BK	RISKY BUSINESS	BRICKMAN	WARNER BROS	1983

BK	ROUND MIDNIGHT	TAVERNIER	WARNER BROS	1986
BK	RUNNING ON EMPTY	LUMET	WARNER BROS	1988
BK	STAR 80	FOSSE	WARNER BROS	1984
BK	STEALING HOME	KAMPMANN	WARNER BROS	1988
BK	SUDDEN IMPACT	EASTWOOD	WARNER BROS	1983
BK	SURRENDER	BELSON	WARNER BROS	1987
BK	SWING SHIFT	DEMME	WARNER BROS	1984
BK	TARGET	PENN	WARNER BROS	1985
BK	TWICE UPON A TIME (UK)	KORTY	WARNER BROS	1982
BK	TWILIGHT ZONE - THE MOVIE	SPIELBERG	WARNER BROS	1983
BK	UNDER THE RAINBOW	RASH	ORION	1981
BK	WHO'S THAT GIRL	FOLEY	WARNER BROS	1987
BK	WINDY CITY	BERNSTEIN	WARNER BROS	1984
BK	WITCHES OF EASTWICK	MILLER	WARNER BROS	1987
BK	WORLD ACCORDING TO GARP	HILL	WARNER BROS	1982
BK 4	DEVIL'S ISLAND	FRANCE	WARNER BORS	1939
BL	BABY LOVE (UK)	REID	AVCO EMBASSY	1968
BL	BEA LILLIE	portrait	UNIV	
BL	BEN LYON	portrait	FN	
BL	BILLY LIAR (UK)	SCHLESINGER	CONTINENTAL	1963
BL	BLOODLINE	YOUNG	PARAMOUNT	1979
BL	BLUE LAGOON	KLEISER	COLUMBIA	1980
BL	BOMBS OVER LONDON (UK: MIDNIGHT MENACE)	HILL	FILM ALLIANCE	1937
BL	BRINK OF LIFE (SWE: NARA LIVET)	BERGMAN	AJAY	1958
BL	BURT LANCASTER	portrait	UNIV, WARNER BROS	
BL	LOVE AT STAKE	MOFFITT	TRI STAR	1987
BL	MAN IN THE DARK	COMFORT	UNIVERSAL	1965
BL	WILLIAM LUNDIGAN	portrait	UNITED ARTISTS	
BL-1	BONNIE PRINCE CHARLIE (UK)	KIMMINS, KORDA	SNADER	1948
BL-2	MAN ABOUT THE HOUSE (UK)	ARLISS	20TH CENTURY FOX	1947
BL-7	NIGHT BEAT (UK)	HUTH	BRITISH LION	1947
BL-8	WINSLOW BOY (UK)	ASQUITH	EAGLE-LION	1948
BL-9	HOUR OF GLORY (UK: SMALL BACK ROOM)	POWELL, PRESSBURGER	SNADER	1949
BL-10	WOMEN OF DOLWYN (UK: LAST DAYS OF DOLWYN)	WILLIAMS	LOPERT	1949
BL-12	WILD HEART (UK: GONE TO EARTH)	POWELL, PRESSBURGER	RKO	1950
BL-14	SEVEN DAYS TO NOON (UK)	BOULTING, BOULTING	MAYER-KINGLSEY	1950
BL-15	HAPPIEST DAYS OF YOUR LIFE (UK)	LAUNDER	BRITISH LION	1950
BL-16	WOODEN HORSE (UK)	LEE	SNADER	1950
BL-17	WONDER BOY (UK: WONDER KID)	HARTL	SNADER	1951
BL-18	CRY, THE BELOVED COUNTRY (UK)	KORDA	LOPERT	1951
BL-19	TALES OF HOFFMANN (UK)	POWELL, PRESSBURGER	LOPERT	1951
BL-20	OUTCAST OF THE ISLANDS (UK)	REED	LOPERT	1951
BL-21	BIKINI BABY (UK: LADY GODIVA RIDES AGAIN)	LAUNDER	CARROLL	1951
BL-22	BREAKING THE SOUND BARRIER (UK)	LEAN	UNITED ARTISTS	1952
BL-23	MR. DENNING DRIVES NORTH (UK)	KIMMINS	CARROLL	1951
BL-24	MURDER ON MONDAY (UK: HOME AT SEVEN)	RICHARDSON	MAYER-KINGLSEY	1952
BL-25	HOLLY AND THE IVY (UK)	O'FERRALL	PACEMAKER	1952
BL-26	PASSIONATE SENTRY (UK: WHO GOES THERE!)	KIMMINS	FINE ARTS	1952
BL-27	TWICE UPON A TIME (UK)	PRESSBURGER	BRITISH LION	1953
BL-28	RINGER (UK)	HAMILTON	BRITISH LION	1952
BL-30	FOLLY TO BE WISE (UK)	LAUNDER	FINE ARTS	1953
BL-31	HEART OF THE MATTER (UK)	O'FERRALL	AAP	1953
BL-32	CAPTAIN'S PARADISE (UK)	KIMMINS	LLOPERT	1953
BL-35	THREE CASES OF MURDER (UK)	EADY, O'FERRALL, TOYE	AAP	1955
BL-35A	THREE CASES OF MURDER: YOU KILLED ELIZABETH (UK)	EADY	AAP	1955
BL-35B	THREE CASES OF MURDER: THE PICTURE (UK)	TOYE	AAP	1955
BL-35C	THREE CASES OF MURDER: LORD MOUNTDRAGO (UK)	O'FERRALL	AAP	1955
BL36	BELLES OF ST. TRINIANS (UK)	LAUNDER	ASSOC. ARTISTS	1955
BL-38	MARRIAGE A LA MODE (UK: CONSTANT HUSBAND)	GILLIAT	STRATFORD	1955
BL-97	WILD HORSE RUSTLERS (mistake? See BC-97)	NEWFIELD	TIFFANY	1943
BLBB	BELOVED	DEMME	BUENA VISTA	1998
BLBC	WINSLOW BOY (UK - 1948)	ASQUITH	EAGLE LION	1950
BLD	BREAD, LOVE AND DREAMS (IT: PANE, AMORE E FANTASIA)	COMENCINI	IFE	1953
BLL-6	BEYOND LONDON LIGHTS	TERRISS	FILM BOOKING (FBO)	1928
BLM	BARBARA LAMARR	portrait	METRO	
BLT	BLACK BELT JONES	CLOUSE	WARNER BROS	1974

BLY-38	FAMILY UPSTAIRS	BLYSTONE	FOX FILM	1926
BLY-40	ANKLES PREFERRED	BLYSTONE	FOX FILM	1927
BLY 42	PAJAMAS	BLYSTONE	FOX FILM	1927
BM	BABY MAKER	BRIDGES	NATIONAL GENERAL	1970
BM	BAD MEDICINE	MILLER	20th CENTURY FOX	1985
BM	BARRY MACKAY	portrait	GAUMONT BRITISH	
BM	BEVERLY MICHAELS	portrait	UNIV	
BM	BLACK LIKE ME	LERNER	CONTINENTAL DIST.	1964
BM	BLUE MONKEY	FRUET	FRIES	1987
BM	BREAKER MORANT	BERESFORD	NEW WORLD QUARTET	1980
BM	BRIDE OF THE MONSTER	WOOD	FILMAKERS REL.	1956
BM	BUGSY MALONE	PARKER	PARAMOUNT	1976
BM	EXTREME ADVENTURES OF SUPER DAVE	MACDONALD	MGM	1999
BM	GIANT OF MARATHON	TOURNEUR	MGM	1959
BM	PATTERN FOR PLUNDER	AINSWORTH	HERTS-LION INT'L	1964
BM	SUPER MAN CHU	HSIUNG	CAPITAL PRODUCTIONS	1973
BM	VAGABOND VIOLINIST (UK: BROKEN MELODY)	VORHAUS	OLYMPIC	1934
BMBB	BICENTENNIAL MAN	COLUMBUS	BUENA VISTA	1999
BMBB	BRIDE IS MUCH TOO BEAUTIFUL (FR: HER BRIDAL NIGHT 1956)	GASPARD-HUIT	ELLIS FILMS	1958
BMIA3	BRADDOCK: MISSING IN ACTION 3	RICHARDS	CANNON	1987
BN	BEAUTIES OF THE NIGHT (FR: LES BELLES DE NUIT 1952)	CLAIR	LOPERT	1954
BN	BEK NELSON		COL	
BN	BIG MONEY (UK)	CARSTAIRS	LOPERT	1958
BN	BOSS NIGGER	ARNOLD	DIMENSION	1975
BN	THAT SPLENDID NOVEMBER (IT)	BOLOGNINI	UNITED ARTISTS	1969
BNB-III	BAD NEWS BEARS GO TO JAPAN	BERRY	PARAMOUNT	1978
BNO	BOYS NIGHT OUT (SEXY)	GORDON	MGM	1962
BO	BLACK ORPHEUS (BRA: ORFEU NEGRO)	CAMUS	LOPERT	1959
BO	BLACKOUT (UK)	BAKER	EROS	1950
BO	BLACKOUT (UK: MURDER BY PROXY)	FISHER	LIPPERT	1954
BO	BLOW OUT	DE PALMA	FILMWAYS	1981
BO	BORSALINO	DERAY	PARAMOUNT	1970
BOB	BRAIN OF BLOOD	ADAMSON	HEMISPHERE	1972
BOB	BRIDES OF BLOOD	ROMERO	HEMISPHERE	1968
BOB	GREYFRIARS BOBBY	CHAFFEY	RANK INTL	1961
BOR-11	RIVER	BORZAGE	FOX FILM	1929
BORDERLINE	BORDERLINE	SEITER	UNIVERSAL-INT'L	1950
BOSD	BLOOD ORGY OF THE SHE DEVILS	MIKELS	GEMINI	1972
BOV	BONFIRE OF THE VANITIES	DE PALMA	WARNER BROS	1990
BP	BATTLE FOR THE PLANET OF THE APES	THOMPSON	20th CENTURY FOX	1973
BP	BEES IN PARADISE (UK)	GUEST	GFD	1944
BP	BIRTHDAY PARTY (UK)	FRIEDKIN	CONTINENTAL	1968
BP	BLACK PIT OF DR. M	MENDEZ	UNITED PRODUCERS	1961
BP	BOAT PEOPLE	HUI	SPECTRAFILM	1983
BP	BODY PARTS	DICKERSON	PARAMOUNT	1991
BP	BRIDAL PATH (UK)	LAUNDER	KINGSLEY-UNION	1959
BP	BRIDE OF PENNACOOK (sh)		TIFFANY	1927
BP	BROKEDOWN PALACE	KAPLAN	20th CENTURY FOX	1999
BP1	MY SISTER AND I (UK)	HUTH	GFD	1948
BP1	NAKED EARTH (UK)	SHERMAN	20TH CENTURY FOX	1958
BP1	REACH FOR GLORY (UK)	LEACOCK	ROYAL	1962
BP2	COUNT FIVE AND DIE (UK)	VICAS	20TH CENTURY FOX	1957
BP2	LOOK BEFORE YOU LOVE (UK)	HUTH	GFD	1948
BP3	PRESCRIPTION FOR MURDER (UK: RX FOR MURDER)	TWIST	20TH CENTURY FOX	1958
BP7	BOBBIKINS (UK)	DAY	20TH CENTURY FOX	1959
BPP	SANDOKAN THE GREAT (IT 1963)	LENZI	MGM	1965
BPT	BOBBIKINS (UK)	DAY	20th CENTURY FOX	1959
BQ	BANDIT QUEEN	BERKE	LIPPERT	1950
BQ	MURDER ON APPROVAL (UK: BARBADOS QUEST)	KNOWLES	RKO	1956
BR	BANANA RIDGE (UK)	MYCROFT	PATHE	1942
BR	BARBARA RUSH	portrait	UNIV	
BR	BATMAN RETURNS	BURTON	WARNER BROS	1992
BR	BEFORE THE RAIN	MANCHEVSKI	GRAMERCY	1994
BR	BIG RISK (FR: CLASSE TOUS RISQUES 1960)	SAUDET	UNITED ARTISTS	1963
BR	BLACK RAIN	SCOTT	PARAMOUNT	1989
BR	BREATHLESS	MCBRIDE	ORION	1983

BR	BRIDGE TO THE SUN	PERIER	MGM	1961
BR	BRIGHTON ROCK (UK)	BOULTING	MAYER-KINGSLEY	1947
BR	CHARLES 'BUDDY' ROGERS	portrait	RKO	
BR	GIVE MY REGARDS TO BROAD ST	WEBB	20th CENTURY FOX	1984
BR	OLD BONES OF THE RIVER (UK)	VARNEL	GFD	1938
BR	ROCCO AND HIS BROTHERS (IT: ROCCO E I SUOI FRATELLI)	VISCONTI	ASTOR	1961
BR-1	MARSHALL OF HELDORADO	CARR	LIPPERT	1950
BR-2	WEST OF THE BRAZOS	CARR	LIPPERT	1950
BR-4	HOSTILE COUNTRY	CARR	LIPPERT	1950
BR-6	CROOKED RIVER	CARR	LIPPERT	1950
BS	BALLAD OF A SOLDIER (USSR)	CHUKHRAJ	KINGSLEY INT'L	1961
BS	BEAT STREET	LATHAN	ORION	1984
BS	BEAUTIFUL SWINDLERS (FR: BELLES ESCROQUERIES MONDE)	CHABROL	LUX	1964
BS	BEST SELLER	FLYNN	ORION	1987
BS	BEVERLY SIMMONS	portrait		
BS	BIG SHOW	CLARK	20TH CENTURY FOX	1961
BS	BLAZING STEWARDESSES	ADAMSON	INDEPENDENT INTL	1975
BS	BLOOD AND STEEL (TANK COMMANDOS)	KAOWALSKI	20th CENTURY FOX	1959
BS	BLOOD ON SATAN'S CLAW (UK)	HAGGARD	CANNON	1971
BS	BLOODSPORT	ARNOLD	CANNON	1987
BS	BLUE STEEL	BIGELOW	MGM	1990
BS	BOMB IN THE HIGH STREET (UK)	BEZENCENET, BISHOP	HEMISPHERE	1961
BS	BOND STREET (UK)	PARRY	STRATFORD	1948
BS	BOYS ON THE SIDE	ROSSEN	WARNER BROS	1995
BS	BUDDY SYSTEM, THE	JORDAN	20th CENTURY FOX	1984
BS	BURNING SECRET	BIRKIN	VESTRON	1988
BS	TANK COMMANDOS	TOPPER	AIP	1959
BSB-1	GEORGE TAKES THE AIR (UK: IT'S IN THE AIR)	KIMMINS	SELECT ATTRACTIONS	1938
BSH	BARBER OF STAMFORD HILL (UK)	WREDE	BRITISH LION	1962
BSI	SILVER STALLION	FINNEY	MONOGRAM	1941
BSL	BITTER SWEET LOVE	MILLER	AVCO EMBASSY	1976
B-SL	BOCCACCIO '70 (IT)	DE SICA, FELLINI	EMBASSY	1962
BSN	BODY SAID NO! (UK)	GUEST	EROS	1950
BSR	BED SITTING ROOM (UK)	LESTER	LOPERT	1969
BSR	BLACK STALLION RETURNS	DALVA	UNITED ARTISTS	1983
BSW	BLACK SHEEP OF WHITEHALL (UK)	DEARDEN, HAY	UNITED ARTISTS	1942
BT	BAIT	FUQUA	WARNER BROS	2000
BT	BAND OF THIEVES (UK)	BEZENCENET	RANK	1962
BT	BEHIND THE GREAT WALL (IT) doc	LIZZANI	CONTINENTAL	1959
BT	BITTER RICE (Riso Amaro)	DE SANTIS	LUX	1950
BT	BLACK 13 (UK)	HUGHES	20TH CENTURY FOX	1953
BT	BLACK TIDE (UK: STORMY CROSSING)	PENNINGTON-RICHARDS	ASTOR	1958
BT	BLACK TORMENT (UK)	HARTFORD-DAVIS	GOVERNOR	1964
BT	BLACK TURIN (IT: TORINO NERA)	LIZZANI	CFM	1972
BT	BONJOUR TRISTESSE (FR)	PREMINGER	COLUMBIA	1958
BT	BRONX TALE, A	DE NIRO	SAVOY	1993
BT	LAND BEYOND THE LAW	EASON	WARNER BROS	1937
BT	THAT NIGHT	NEWLAND	UNIVERSAL	1957
BT2	BILL & TED'S BOGUS JOURNEY	HEWITT	ORION	1991
BTB	BIGGER THAN BARNUMS	INCE	FILM BOOKING (FBO)	1926
BTL	BEYOND THE LIMIT	MACKENZIE	PARAMOUNT	1983
BTS	BACK TO SCHOOL	METTER	ORION	1986
BTVS	BUFFY THE VAMPIRE SLAYER	KUZUI	20th CENTURY FOX	1992
BU	BLOW-UP (UK)	ANTONIONI	PREMIER	1966
BU	BOB'S YOUR UNCLE (UK)	MITCHELL	BUTCHER'S	1942
BV	BEAVER VALLEY	ALGAR	RKO	1950
BV	BED OF VIOLENCE	SARNO	CHELEE FILMS	1967
BV	BROWNING VERSION	FIGGIS	PARAMOUNT	1994
BV1	WRONG ARM OF THE LAW (UK)	OWEN	CONTINENTAL	1963
BW	BACK TO THE WALL (FR: LE DOS AU MUR)	MOLINARO	ELLIS	1958
BW	BAND WAGGON (UK)	VARNEL	GFD	1940
BW	BLACK WHIP	WARREN	20th CENTURY FOX	1956
BW	BLACK WIDOW	RAFELSON	20th CENTURY FOX	1987
BW	BOSS' WIFE	STEINBERG	TRI STAR	1986
BW	BULWORTH	BEATTY	20th CENTURY FOX	1998
BW	BUTCHER'S WIFE	HUGHES	PARAMOUNT	1991

BWB	BRAZEN WOMEN OF BALZAC	ZACHER	GLOBE PICTURES	1969
BWBB	BETSY'S WEDDING	ALDA	BUENA VISTA	1990
BWS	BUGS BUNNY'S WILD WORLD OF SPORTS (t)	FORD, LENNON	WARNER BROS	1989
BX	BOGUS	JEWISON	WARNER BROS	1996
BX	GRAND ESCAPADE (UK)	BAXTER	BRITISH LION	1946
BYF	BEAST OF YUCCA FLATS, THE	FRANCIS	CINEMA ASSOCIATES	1962
BYN	BEAST OF THE YELLOW NIGHT	ROMERO	NEW WORLD	1971
C	CALL NORTHSIDE 777	HATHAWAY	20th CENTURY FOX	1948
C	CAMILLE 2000	METZGER	AUDUBON	1969
C	CAR 54, WHERE ARE YOU?	FISHMAN	ORION	1994
C	CARAVAN (UK)	CRABTREE	EAGLE LION	1946
C	CENTURION, THE	COSTA	PRODUCERS INT'L	1962
C	CHOCOLAT	DENIS	ORION	1989
C	CINDERELLA (IT: LA CENERENTOLA 1949)	CERCHIO	TIMES FILM CORP.	1953
C	CIRCLE (UK: VICIOUS CIRCLE)	THOMAS	KASSLER	1957
C	CLASS	CARLINO	ORION	1983
C	COMMANDO	LESTER	20th CENTURY FOX	1985
C	CONFIDENTIAL	CAHN	MASCOT	1935
C	CONGO	MARSHALL	PARAMOUNT	1995
C	CONTRABAND SPAIN (UK)	HUNTINGTON	STRATFORD	1955
C	COUNTRY	PEARCE	BUENA VISTA	1984
C	COUSINS	SCHUMACHER (sh)	PARAMOUNT	1988
C	CRACKSMAN (UK)	SCOTT	PATHE	1963
C	CRASH!	BAND	GROUP 1	1976
C	CURE, THE	CHAPLIN	MUTUAL	1917
C	HEAT WAVE (CODE*) (UK)	ELVEY	GAUMONT BRITISH	1935
C	HOW TO MURDER A RICH UNCLE (UK)	PATRICK	COLUMBIA	1957
C	INTERNAL AFFAIRS	FIGGIS	PARAMOUNT	1990
C	INTERRUPTED JOURNEY (UK)	BIRT	LOPERT	1949
C	MOULIN ROUGE	LANFIELD	UNITED ARTISTS	1934
C	NO WAY BACK (UK)	OSIECKI	EROS	1949
C	TRUE COLORS	ROSS	PARAMOUNT	1991
C	UNDERCOVER AGENT (UK: COUNTERSPY)	SEWELL	LIPPERT	1953
C	WALK IN THE CLOUDS	ARAU	20th CENTURY FOX	1995
C-1	AMERICAN MADNESS	CAPRA	COLUMBIA	1932
C-1	COUNSEL FOR CRIME	BRAHM	COLUMBIA	1937
C-1	COURT MARTIAL	SEITZ	COLUMBIA	1928
C-1	FALSE ALARM	O'CONNOR	COLUMBIA	1926
C-1	FLIGHT	CAPRA	COLUMBIA	1929
C-1	HE FORGOT TO REMEMBER (sh)	POWERS, BUCKINGHAM	PATHE EXCHANGE	1926
C-1	JUNE MADNESS (sh)	PEMBROKE	PATHE EXCHANGE	1920
C-1	LADY FOR A DAY	CAPRA	COLUMBIA	1933
C-1	LIGHTER THAT FAILED (sh)	PARROTT	MGM	1927
C-1	PANIC IS ON (sh)	PARROTT	MGM	1931
C-1	RAIN OR SHINE	CAPRA	COLUMBIA	1930
C-1	SCARLET LADY	CROSLAND	COLUMBIA	1928
C-1	SHE COULDN'T TAKE IT	GARNETT	COLUMBIA	1935
C-1	THUNDER IN THE CITY	GERING	COLUMBIA	1937
C-1	UNNAMED ROLIN PROJECT (sh)	WHITING	PATHE EXCHANGE	1915
C-2	ALIAS THE LONE WOLF	GRIFFITH	COLUMBIA	1927
C-2	BROADWAY SCANDALS	ARCHAINBAUD	COLUMBIA	1929
C-2	COURT MARTIAL	SEITZ	COLUMBIA	1928
C-2	LONE WOLF RETURNS	INCE	COLUMBIA	1926
C-2	MAN'S CASTLE	BORZAGE	COLUMBIA	1933
C-2	MURDER IN GREENWICH VILLAGE	ROGELL	COLUMBIA	1937
C-2	MUSIC GOES ROUND	SCHERTZINGER	COLUMBIA	1936
C-2	NIGHT CLUB LADY	CUMMINGS	COLUMBIA	1932
C-2	SANDMAN (sh)	NEWMEYER	PATHE EXCHANGE	1920
C-2	SCARLET LADY	CROSLAND	COLUMBIA	1928
C-2	SHOULD SAILORS MARRY? (sh)	ROBBINS	PATHE EXCHANGE	1925
C-2	SKIP THE MALOO! (sh)	PARROTT	MGM	1931
C-2	STING OF STINGS (sh)	PARROTT	MGM	1927
C-2	UNNAMED ROLIN PROJECT (sh)	WHITING	PATHE EXCHANGE	1915
C-3	ALIAS ALADDIN (sh)	ROACH	PATHE EXCHANGE	1920
C-3	ALIAS THE LONE WOLF	GRIFFITH	COLUMBIA	1927
C-3	BITTER TEA OF GENERAL YEN	CAPRA	COLUMBIA	1933

C-3	BROTHERS	LANG	COLUMBIA	1930
C-3	CRIME AND PUNISHMENT	STERNBERG	COLUMBIA	1935
C-3	GIRL FRIEND	BUZZELL	COLUMBIA	1935
C-3	MOONLIGHT AND NOSES (sh)	LAUREL, JONES	PATHE EXCHANGE	1925
C-3	RUNAWAY GIRLS	SANDRICH	COLUMBIA	1928
C-3	SALLY IN OUR ALLEY	LANG	COLUMBIA	1927
C-3	SONG OF LOVE	KENTON	COLUMBIA	1929
C-3	TIMBER WAR	NEWFIELD	AMBASSADOR	1936
C-3	UNNAMED ROLIN PROJECT (sh)	WHITING	PATHE EXCHANGE	1915
C-3	WAY OF ALL PANTS (sh)	JONES, MCCAREY	MGM	1927
C-3	WHAT A BOZO (sh)	PARROTT	MGM	1931
C-3	WHEN THE WIFE'S AWAY	STRAYER	COLUMBIA	1926
C-4	BELLE OF BROADWAY	HOYT	COLUMBIA	1926
C-4	BY WHOSE HAND?	LANG	COLUMBIA	1927
C-4	GRAND EXIT	KENTON	COLUMBIA	1935
C-4	HASTY MARRIAGE (sh)	PRATT	MGM	1931
C-4	LADY IS WILLING	MILLER	COLUMBIA	1934
C-4	LIFE BEGINS WITH LOVE	MCCAREY	COLUMBIA	1937
C-4	MAMMA'S BOY (sh)	DORAN	PATHE EXCHANGE	1920
C-4	OLD DRACULA	DONNER	COLUMBIA	1975
C4	PORT AFRIQUE (UK)	MATE	COLUMBIA	1956
C-4	STREET OF ILLUSION	KENTON	COLUMBIA	1928
C-4	THAT'S GRATITUDE	CRAVEN	COLUMBIA	1934
C-4	TOL'ABLE DAVID	BLYSTONE	COLUMBIA	1930
C-4	UNNAMED ROLIN PROJECT (sh)	WHITING	PATHE EXCHANGE	1915
C-4	US (sh)		MGM	1927
C-4	WANDERING PAPAS (sh)	LAUREL	PATHE EXCHANGE	1926
C-5	ESCAPE FROM DEVIL'S ISLAND	ROGELL	COLUMBIA	1935
C-5	FOG	ROGELL	COLUMBIA	1933
C-5	JEALOUSY	NEILL	COLUMBIA	1934
C-5	MEXICALI ROSE	KENTON	COLUMBIA	1929
C-5	NEVER THE DAMES SHALL MEET (sh)	PARROTT	MGM	1927
C-5	POWDER MANKEYS (sh)	WHITING	PATHE EXCHANGE	1915
C-5	QUEEN'S UP! (sh)	NEWMEYER	PATHE EXCHANGE	1920
C-5	SINNER'S PARADE	ADOLFI	COLUMBIA	1928
C-5	STARVATION BLUES (sh)	WALLACE	PATHE EXCHANGE	1925
C-5	SWEET ROSIE O'GRADY	STRAYER	COLUMBIA	1926
C-5	TABASCO KID (sh)	HORNE	MGM	1932
C-6	ALL FOR NOTHING (sh)	PARROTT	MGM	1928
C-6	COLLEGE HERO	LANG	COLUMBIA	1927
C-6	FASHION MADNESS (mistake)	GASNIER	COLUMBIA	1928
C-6	MAN HATERS (sh)	BARROWS	PATHE EXCHANGE	1922
C-6	MURDER ON THE ROOF	SEITZ	COLUMBIA	1930
C-6	NICKLE NURSER (sh)	DOANE	MGM	1932
C-6	OBEY THE LAW	RABOCH	COLUMBIA	1926
C-6	ONE WAY TICKET	BIBERMAN	COLUMBIA	1935
C-6	SHE MARRIED AN ARTIST	GERING	COLUMBIA	1937
C-6	SUBMARINE	CAPRA	COLUMBIA	1928
C-6	WHAT'S THE WORLD COMING TO? (sh)	JONES, WALLACE	PATHE EXCHANGE	1926
C-7	BETTER WAY	INCE	COLUMBIA	1926
C-7	DRIFTWOOD	CABANNE	COLUMBIA	1928
C-7	EIGHT BELLS	NEILL	COLUMBIA	1935
C-7	GREEK MEETS GREEK (sh)	BARROWS	PATHE EXCHANGE	1920
C-7	IN WALKED CHARLEY (sh)	DOANE	MGM	1932
C-7	LONE WOLF RETURNS	NEILL	COLUMBIA	1935
C-7	MADONNA OF THE STREETS	ROBERTSON	COLUMBIA	1930
C-7	MELODY MAN	NEILL	COLUMBIA	1930
C-7	MOVIE NIGHT (sh)	FOSTER	MGM	1929
C-7	SCARED STIFF (sh)	HORNE	PATHE EXCHANGE	1926
C-7	TIGRESS	SEITZ	COLUMBIA	1927
C-8	AIR HOSTESS	ROGELL	COLUMBIA	1932
C-8	FAMILY GROUP (sh)	GUIOL, MCCAREY	MGM	1928
C-8	FIRST IN WAR (sh)	DOANE	MGM	1932
C-8	IF YOU COULD ONLY COOK	SEITER	COLUMBIA	1935
C-8	NO GREATER GLORY	BORZAGE	COLUMBIA	1934
C-8	PERSONALITY	HEERMAN	COLUMBIA	1930

C-8		REMEMBER	SELMAN	COLUMBIA	1926
C-8		SLEEPY HEAD (sh)	BARROWS	PATHE EXCHANGE	1920
C-8		STAGE KISSES	KELLEY	COLUMBIA	1927
C-8		STOOL PIGEON	HOFFMAN	COLUMBIA	1928
C-8		WIFE TAMERS (sh)	HORNE	PATHE EXCHANGE	1926
C-9		ACHING YOUTH (sh)	GUIOL	MGM	1928
C-9		BURGLARS BOLD (sh)	BARROWS	PATHE EXCHANGE	1921
C-9		GALLOPING GHOSTS (sh)	PARROTT	PATHE EXCHANGE	1928
C-9		HELL-SHIP MORGAN	LEDERMAN	COLUMBIA	1936
C-9		LITTLE MISS ROUGHNECK	SCOTTO	COLUMBIA	1938
C-9		MERRY WIDOWER (sh)	WALLACE	PATHE EXCHANGE	1926
C-9		OPENING NIGHT	GRIFFITH	COLUMBIA	1927
C-9		POWER OF THE PRESS	CAPRA	COLUMBIA	1928
C-9		SO THIS IS AFRICA	CLINE	COLUMBIA	1933
C-9		STOLEN PLEASURE	ROSEN	COLUMBIA	1927
C-9		VENGEANCE	MAYO	COLUMBIA	1930
C-9		WHOLE TOWN'S TALKING	FORD	COLUMBIA	1935
C-9		YOUNG IRONSIDES (sh)	PARROTT	MGM	1932
C-10		DECEPTION	SEILER	COLUMBIA	1932
C-10		GIRL GRIEF (sh)	PARROTT	MGM	1932
C-10		GUILTY?	SEITZ	COLUMBIA	1930
C-10		LIMOUSINE LOVE (sh)	GUIOL	MGM	1928
C-10		MILLS OF THE GODS	NEILL	COLUMBIA	1934
C-10		NO TIME TO MARRY	LACHMAN	COLUMBIA	1938
C-10		PINNING IT ON (sh)	BARROWS	PATHE EXCHANGE	1921
C-10		SHOULD HUSBANDS PAY? (sh)	JONES, LAUREL	PATHE EXCHANGE	1926
C-10		WANDERING GIRLS	INCE	COLUMBIA	1927
C-10		WARNING	SEITZ	COLUMBIA	1927
C-10		YOU MAY BE NEXT	ROGELL	COLUMBIA	1936
C-11		AS THE DEVIL COMMANDS	NEILL	COLUMBIA	1933
C-11		BACHELOR'S BABY	STRAYER	COLUMBIA	1927
C-11		BEST MAN WINS	KENTON	COLUMBIA	1935
C-11		FASHION MADNESS	GASNIER	COLUMBIA	1928
C-11		FIGHT PEST (sh)	GUIOL, MCCAREY	MGM	1928
C-11		IT'S ALL YOURS	NUGENT	COLUMBIA	1937
C-11		KING STEPS OUT	VON STERNBERG	COLUMBIA	1936
C-11		NOW WE'LL TELL ONE (sh)	PARROTT	MGM	1932
C-11		OH, PROMISE ME (sh)	BARROWS	PATHE EXCHANGE	1921
C-12		CARNIVAL	LANG	COLUMBIA	1935
C-12		IMAGINE MY EMBARRASSMENT (sh)	YATES, MCCAREY	MGM	1928
C-12		LADY OF SECRETS	GERING	COLUMBIA	1936
C-12		MR. BRIDE (sh)	PARROTT	MGM	1932
C-12		PENITENTIARY	BRAHM	COLUMBIA	1938
C-12		PRINCE PISTACHIO (sh)	BARROWS	PATHE EXCHANGE	1921
C-12		ROYAL ROMANCE	KENTON	COLUMBIA	1930
C-12		SIREN	HASKIN	COLUMBIA	1928
C-12		SOCIAL REGISTER	NEILAN	COLUMBIA	1934
C-12		WRECK	CRAFT	COLUMBIA	1927
C-13		BELOW THE SEA	ROGELL	COLUMBIA	1933
C-13		CALL OF THE WEST	RAY	COLUMBIA	1930
C-13		CALLING OF DAN MATHEWS	ROSEN	COLUMBIA	1935
C-13		FALLEN ARCHES (sh)	MEINS	MGM	1933
C-13		I'LL LOVE YOU ALWAYS	BULGAKOV	COLUMBIA	1935
C-13		IS EVERYBODY HAPPY? (sh)	YATES	MGM	1928
C-13		LOVER COME BACK	KENTON	COLUMBIA	1931
C-13		PAINT AND POWDER (sh)	ROACH	PATHE EXCHANGE	1921
C-13		PRICE OF HONOR	GRIFFITH	COLUMBIA	1927
C-13		RESTLESS YOUTH	CABANNE	COLUMBIA	1928
C-13		TOGETHER WE LIVE	MACK	COLUMBIA	1935
C-14		BIG TIMER	BUZZELL	COLUMBIA	1932
C-14		BIRDS OF PREY	CRAFT	COLUMBIA	1927
C-14		BOOSTER (sh)	YATES	MGM	1928
C-14		DEVIL'S SQUADRON	KENTON	COLUMBIA	1936
C-14		HURRY WEST (sh)	BARROWS	PATHE EXCHANGE	1921
C-14		LET'S LIVE TONIGHT	SCHERTZINGER	COLUMBIA	1935
C-14		LONE WOLF IN PARIS	ROGELL	COLUMBIA	1938

C-14	NATURE IN THE WRONG (sh)	CHASE	MGM	1933
C-14	PRINCE OF DIAMONDS	BROWN	COLUMBIA	1930
C-14	WHEN STRANGERS MARRY	BADGER	COLUMBIA	1933
C-14	WIFE'S RELATIONS	MARSHALL	COLUMBIA	1928
C-15	ALL PARTS (sh)	YATES	MGM	1928
C-15	ARIZONA	SEITZ	COLUMBIA	1931
C-15	AROUND THE CORNER	GLENNON	COLUMBIA	1930
C-15	BRIEF MOMENT	BURTON	COLUMBIA	1933
C-15	DEATH FLIES EAST	ROSEN	COLUMBIA	1935
C-15	DON'T GAMBLE WITH LOVE	MURPHY	COLUMBIA	1936
C-15	HIS SILENT RACKET (sh)		MGM	1933
C-15	LADY RAFFLES	NEILL	COLUMBIA	1928
C-15	PLEASURE BEFORE BUSINESS	STRAYER	COLUMBIA	1927
C-15	RUNNING WILD (sh)	BARROWS	PATHE EXCHANGE	1921
C-15	SIDESHOW	KENTON	COLUMBIA	1928
C-15	THERE'S ALWAYS A WOMAN	HALL	COLUMBIA	1938
C-16	ARABIAN TIGHTS (sh)	ROACH	MGM	1933
C-16	CHASING HUSBANDS (sh)	PARROTT	MGM	1928
C-16	HOBGOBLINS (sh)	GORDON	PATHE EXCHANGE	1921
C-16	OBJECT: ALIMONY	DUNLAP	COLUMBIA	1928
C-16	PAROLE GIRL	CLINE	COLUMBIA	1933
C-16	POOR GIRLS	CRAFT	COLUMBIA	1927
C-16	PRIDE OF THE MARINES	LEDERMAN	COLUMBIA	1936
C-16	SO THIS IS LOVE	CAPRA	COLUMBIA	1928
C-16	SOLDIERS AND WOMEN	SLOMAN	COLUMBIA	1930
C-16	UNWELCOME STRANGER	ROSEN	COLUMBIA	1935
C-16	YOU CAN'T TAKE IT WITH YOU	CAPRA	COLUMBIA	1938
C-17	CIRCUS QUEEN MURDER	NEILL	COLUMBIA	1933
C-17	END OF THE TRAIL	KENTON	COLUMBIA	1936
C-17	FATHER		COLUMBIA	1928
C-17	HOLIDAY	CUKOR	COLUMBIA	1938
C-17	LOVE LESSON (sh)	BARROWS	PATHE EXCHANGE	1921
C-17	PARTY WIRE	KENTON	COLUMBIA	1935
C-17	PAYING THE PRICE	SELMAN	COLUMBIA	1927
C-17	RUBY LIPS (sh)	PARROTT	MGM	1929
C-17	SHERMAN SAID IT (sh)	CHASE	MGM	1933
C-17	TEMPTATION	HOPPER	COLUMBIA	1930
C-17	WOMAN'S WAY	MORTIMER	COLUMBIA	1928
C-18	COCKTAIL HOUR	SCHERTZINGER	COLUMBIA	1933
C-18	LOVE ME FOREVER	SCHERTZINGER	COLUMBIA	1935
C-18	MIDSUMMER MUSH (sh)	CHASE	MGM	1933
C-18	NON SKID KID (sh)	GORDON	PATHE EXCHANGE	1922
C-18	OFF TO BUFFALO (sh)	HORNE	MGM	1929
C-18	ROAMING LADY	ROGELL	COLUMBIA	1936
C-18	SISTERS	FLOOD	COLUMBIA	1930
C-18	SPORTING AGE	KENTON	COLUMBIA	1928
C-18	TRIAL MARRIAGE	KENTON	COLUMBIA	1929
C-19	AIR HAWKS	ROGELL	COLUMBIA	1935
C-19	BEHIND CLOSED DOORS	NEILL	COLUMBIA	1929
C-19	CITY STREETS (CITY SHADOWS*)	ROGELL	COLUMBIA	1938
C-19	HELL'S ISLAND	SLOMAN	COLUMBIA	1930
C-19	LOUD SOUP (sh)	FOSTER	MGM	1929
C-19	LUNCHEON AT TWELVE (sh)	CHASE	MGM	1933
C-19	MATINEE IDOL	CAPRA	COLUMBIA	1928
C-19	MINE WITH THE IRON DOOR	HOWARD	COLUMBIA	1936
C-19	ROMANTIC AGE	FLOREY	COLUMBIA	1927
C-19	STRAIGHT CROOK (sh)		PATHE EXCHANGE	1921
C-19	WOMAN I STOLE	CUMMINGS	COLUMBIA	1933
C-20	AND SO THEY WERE MARRIED	NUGENT	COLUMBIA	1936
C-20	ANN CARVER'S PROFESSION	BUZZELL	COLUMBIA	1933
C-20	AWAKENING OF JIM BURKE	HILLYER	COLUMBIA	1935
C-20	CHINK (sh)		PATHE EXCHANGE	1921
C-20	CRACKED ICEMAN (sh)	DUNN	MGM	1934
C-20	DESERT BRIDE	CAPRA	COLUMBIA	1928
C-20	GIRL'S SCHOOL	BRAHM	COLUMBIA	1938
C-20	LADIES MUST PLAY	CANNON	COLUMBIA	1930

C-20	QUITTER	HENABERY	COLUMBIA	1929
C-20	RICH MEN'S SONS	GRAVES	COLUMBIA	1927
C-20	THIN TWINS (sh)	HORNE	MGM	1929
C-21	BIG SQUAWK (sh)	DOANE	MGM	1929
C-21	BROADWAY DADDIES	WINDEMERE	COLUMBIA	1928
C-21	CLOWN	CRAFT	COLUMBIA	1927
C-21	DONOVAN AFFAIR	CAPRA	COLUMBIA	1929
C-21	FOUR PARTS (sh)	CHASE, DUNN	MGM	1934
C-21	I AM THE LAW	HALL	COLUMBIA	1938
C-21	LATE HOURS (sh)	BARROWS	PATHE EXCHANGE	1921
C-21	SQUEALER	BROWN	COLUMBIA	1930
C-21	WHAT PRICE INNOCENCE?	MACK	COLUMBIA	1933
C-22	AFTER THE STORM	SEITZ	COLUMBIA	1928
C-22	CATCH 22	NICHOLS	PARAMOUNT	1970
C-22	ETERNAL WOMAN	MCCARTHY	COLUMBIA	1929
C-22	I'LL TAKE VANILLA (sh)	DUNN	MGM	1934
C-22	KID SISTER	GRAVES	COLUMBIA	1927
C-22	LAST OF THE LONE WOLF	BOLESLAWSKI	COLUMBIA	1930
C-22	LEAPING LOVE (sh)	DOANE	MGM	1929
C-22	STOP KIDDING (sh)	KERR, BARROWS	PATHE EXCHANGE	1921
C-22	TRAPPED BY TELEVISION	LORD	COLUMBIA	1936
C-22	UNKNOWN WOMAN	ROGELL	COLUMBIA	1935
C-22	WRECKER	ROGELL	COLUMBIA	1933
C-23	AFTER THE DANCE	BULGAKOV	COLUMBIA	1935
C-23	ANOTHER WILD IDEA (sh)	CHASE, DUNN	MGM	1934
C-23	BLACKMAILER	WILES	COLUMBIA	1936
C-23	FOR LADIES ONLY	LEHRMAN, PEMBROKE	COLUMBIA	1927
C-23	FOR THE LOVE O' LIL	TINLING	COLUMBIA	1930
C-23	GOLF WIDOWS	KENTON	COLUMBIA	1928
C-23	GOOD MORNING JUDGE (sh)	ROACH	PATHE EXCHANGE	1922
C-23	LADY OBJECTS	KENTON	COLUMBIA	1938
C-23	MY WOMAN	SCHERTZINGER	COLUMBIA	1933
C-23	SNAPPY SNEEZER (sh)	DOANE	MGM	1929
C-24	BACHELOR GIRL	THORPE	COLUMBIA	1929
C-24	CRAZY FEET (sh)	DOANE (sh)	MGM	1929
C-24	FEATHER IN HER HAT	SANTELL	COLUMBIA	1935
C-24	FLIGHT TO FAME	COLEMAN	COLUMBIA	1938
C-24	FURY OF THE JUNGLE	NEILL	COLUMBIA	1933
C-24	IT HAPPENED ONE DAY (sh)	DUNN	MGM	1934
C-24	LATE LAMENTED (sh)	EDDY	PATHE EXCHANGE	1922
C-24	MODERN MOTHERS	ROSEN	COLUMBIA	1928
C-24	SWEETHEARTS ON PARADE	NEILAN	COLUMBIA	1930
C-24	SWELL HEAD	GRAVES	COLUMBIA	1927
C-25	BLACK ROOM	NEILL	COLUMBIA	1935
C-25	COUNTERFEIT	KENTON	COLUMBIA	1936
C-25	I'LL TAKE ROMANCE	GRIFFITH	COLUMBIA	1937
C-25	NAME THE WOMAN	KENTON	COLUMBIA	1928
C-25	ON THEIR WAY (sh)	BARROWS	PATHE EXCHANGE	1921
C-25	SOMETHING SIMPLE (sh)	CHASE, WEEMS	MGM	1934
C-25	STEPPING OUT (sh)	DOANE	MGM	1929
C-26	GREAT GOBS! (sh)	DOANE	MGM	1929
C-26	MASTER OF MEN	HILLYER	COLUMBIA	1933
C-26	RANSOM	SEITZ	COLUMBIA	1928
C-26	SHE MARRIED HER BOSS	LA CAVA	COLUMBIA	1935
C-26	SWEET BY AND BY (sh)	KERR	PATHE EXCHANGE	1921
C-26	YOU SAID A HATFUL! (sh)	CHASE	MGM	1934
C-27	AWFUL TRUTH	MCCAREY	COLUMBIA	1937
C-27	FATE'S FATHEAD (sh)	CHASE	MGM	1934
C-27	MANY HAPPY RETURNS (sh)	KERR	PATHE EXCHANGE	1922
C-27	MR. DEEDS GOES TO TOWN	CAPRA	COLUMBIA	1936
C-27	REAL MCCOY (sh)	DOANE	MGM	1930
C-27	WAY OF THE STRONG	CAPRA	COLUMBIA	1928
C-28	ALL TEED UP (sh)	KENNEDY	MGM	1930
C-28	ATLANTIC ADVENTURE	ROGELL	COLUMBIA	1935
C-28	BEWARE OF BLONDES	SEITZ	COLUMBIA	1928
C-28	BUSY BEES (sh)	KERR	PATHE EXCHANGE	1922

C-28		CHASES OF PIMPLE STREET (sh)	CHASE	MGM	1934
C-28		THERE'S THAT WOMAN AGAIN	HALL	COLUMBIA	1939
C-28		WAY OF THE STRONG (mistake)	CAPRA	COLUMBIA	1928
C-29		HIGH TIDE (sh)	BARROWS	PATHE EXCHANGE	1922
C-29		LITTLE ADVENTURESS	LEDERMAN	COLUMBIA	1938
C-29		OKAY TOOTS! (sh)	CHASE, TERHUNE	MGM	1935
C-29		PUBLIC MENACE	KENTON	COLUMBIA	1935
C-29		SAY IT WITH SABLES	CAPRA	COLUMBIA	1928
C-29		THEODORA GOES WILD	BOLESLAWSKI	COLUMBIA	1936
C-29		WHISPERING WHOOPEE (sh)	HORNE	MGM	1930
C-30		ACQUITTED	STRAYER	COLUMBIA	1929
C-30		ADVENTURE IN MANHATTAN	LUDWIG	COLUMBIA	1936
C-30		BETWEEN MEALS (sh)	GREY	PATHE EXCHANGE	1926
C-30		BLONDIE	STRAYER	COLUMBIA	1938
C-30		BROADWAY SCANDALS (mistake)	ARCHAINBAUD	COLUMBIA	1929
C-30		FAITH, HOPE AND CHARITY (sh)	BLAKE	COLUMBIA	1930
C-30		FIFTY MILLION HUSBANDS (sh)	HORNE, KENNEDY	MGM	1930
C-30		POKER AT EIGHT (sh)	CHASE	MGM	1935
C-30		VIRGIN LIPS	CLIFTON	COLUMBIA	1928
C-31		BROADWAY HOOFER	ARCHAINBAUD	COLUMBIA	1929
C-31		DON'T BUTT IN (ROUSTABOUT) (sh)	GREY	PATHE EXCHANGE	1926
C-31		FAST WORK (sh)	HORNE	MGM	1930
C-31		NEVER STRIKE YOUR MOTHER (sh)	BLAKE	COLUMBIA	1930
C-31		SMASHING THE SPY RING	CABANNE	COLUMBIA	1939
C-31		SOUTHERN EXPOSURE (sh)	CHASE	MGM	1935
C-32		FOUR STAR BOARDER (sh)	CHASE	MGM	1935
C-32		GIRL SHOCK (sh)	HORNE	MGM	1930
C-32		HOT AND BOTHERED (sh)	BLAKE	COLUMBIA	1930
C-32		LADY AND THE MOB	STOLOFF	COLUMBIA	1938
C-32		TRY, TRY AGAIN (sh)	GREY	PATHE EXCHANGE	1922
C-32		TWO FISTED GENTLEMAN	WILES	COLUMBIA	1936
C-33		DOLLAR DIZZY (sh)	HORNE	MGM	1930
C-33		LONE WOLF SPY HUNT	GODFREY	COLUMBIA	1939
C-33		NURSE TO YOU! (sh)	CHASE, MOFFITT	MGM	1935
C-33		PRODIGAL DAUGHTER (sh)	BUZZELL	COLUMBIA	1930
C-33		SOFT PEDAL (sh)	GREY	PATHE EXCHANGE	1926
C-33		THEY MET IN A TAXI	GREEN	COLUMBIA	1936
C-34		CAME THE PAWN (sh)	BUZZELL	COLUMBIA	1930
C-34		LOOSER THAN LOOSE (sh)	HORNE	MGM	1930
C-34		MAN WHO LIVED TWICE	LACHMAN	COLUMBIA	1936
C-34		MANHATTAN MONKEY BUSINESS (sh)	CHASE, LAW	MGM	1935
C-35		HARD BOILED YEGGS (sh)	BUZZELL	COLUMBIA	1930
C-35		HIGH C'S (sh)	HORNE	MGM	1930
C-35		LAWLESS RIDERS	BENNET	COLUMBIA	1935
C-35		PAY THE CASHIER (sh)	GREY	PATHE EXCHANGE	1926
C-35		PUBLIC GHOST #1 (sh)	CHASE, LAW	MGM	1935
C-35		WHEN YOU'RE IN LOVE	RISKIN	COLUMBIA	1937
C-36		CRYSTAL GAZER	BUZZELL	COLUMBIA	1930
C-36		LIFE HESITATES AT 40 (sh)	CHASE, LAW	MGM	1936
C-36		ONLY ANGELS HAVE WINGS	HAWKS	COLUMBIA	1939
C-36		SLEUTH (sh)	GREY	PATHE EXCHANGE	1922
C-36		THUNDERING TENORS (sh)	HORNE	MGM	1930
C-37		COAST GUARD	LUDWIG	COLUMBIA	1939
C-37		COUNT TAKES THE COUNT (sh)	LAW	MGM	1936
C-37		LONE STAR STRANGER (sh)	BUZZELL	COLUMBIA	1931
C-37		ONLY SON (sh)	GREY	PATHE EXCHANGE	1926
C-37		PIP FROM PITTSBURGH (sh)	PARROTT	MGM	1931
C-38		HIRED AND FIRED (sh)	GREY	PATHE EXCHANGE	1926
C-38		ROMANCE OF THE REDWOODS	VIDOR	COLUMBIA	1939
C-38		ROUGH SEAS (sh)	PARROTT	MGM	1931
C-38		VAMP TILL READY (sh)	CHASE, LAW	MGM	1936
C-38		WINE, WOMAN BUT NO SONG (sh)		COLUMBIA	1931
C-39		BLONDIE MEETS THE BOSS	STRAYER	COLUMBIA	1939
C-39		CHECK AND RUBBER CHECK (sh)	BUZZELL	COLUMBIA	1931
C-39		NEIGHBORHOOD HOUSE (sh)	CHASE, LAW	MGM	1936
C-39		ONE OF THE SMITHS (sh)	PARROTT	MGM	1931

C-39	RICH MAN, POOR MAN (sh)	CHASE	PATHE EXCHANGE	1922
C-40	GOLDEN BOY	MAMOULIAN	COLUMBIA	1939
C-40	KINGS OR BETTER (sh)	BUZZELL	COLUMBIA	1931
C-40	ON THE WRONG TREK (sh)	CHASE, LAW	MGM	1936
C-40	THRILL HUNTER	SEITZ	COLUMBIA	1933
C-41	ARE PARENTS PICKLES? (sh)	PRATT	PATHE EXCHANGE	1925
C-41	BLIND ALLEY	VIDOR	COLUMBIA	1939
C-41	FIGHTING CODE	HILLYER	COLUMBIA	1933
C-42	BEHIND THE EVIDENCE	HILLYER	COLUMBIA	1935
C-42	CHRIS-CROSSED (sh)	BUZZELL	COLUMBIA	1931
C-42	GOOD GIRLS GO TO PARIS	HALL	COLUMBIA	1939
C-42	WINNER TAKE ALL (sh)	SANTELL	PATHE EXCHANGE	1923
C-43	FRIDAY THE 13TH (sh)	DAVIS	PATHE EXCHANGE	1922
C-43	IN SPITE OF DANGER	HILLYER	COLUMBIA	1935
C-43	MR. SMITH GOES TO WASHINGTON	CAPRA	COLUMBIA	1939
C-43	RED MEN TELL NO TALES (sh)	BUZZELL	COLUMBIA	1931
C-44	MEN OF THE HOUR	HILLYER	COLUMBIA	1935
C-44	TRUTH JUGGLER (sh)	DAVIS	PATHE EXCHANGE	1922
C-44	WOLF IN CHEAP CLOTHING (sh)	BUZZELL	COLUMBIA	1932
C-45	BED OF ROSES (sh)	HOWE	PATHE EXCHANGE	1922
C-45	BLONDE PRESSURE (sh)	BUZZELL	COLUMBIA	1931
C-45	BLONDIE TAKES A VACATION	STRAYER	COLUMBIA	1939
C-46	BRIDE-TO-BE (sh)	DAVIS	PATHE EXCHANGE	1922
C-46	FIVE LITTLE PEPPERS AND HOW THEY GREW	BARTON	COLUMBIA	1939
C-46	SHE SERVED HIM RIGHT (sh)	BUZZELL	COLUMBIA	1931
C-46	SWELL HEAD	STOLOFF	COLUMBIA	1935
C-47	SOLDIER OF MISFORTUNE (sh)	BUZZELL	COLUMBIA	1931
C-47	TAKE THE NEXT CAR (sh)	HOWE	PATHE EXCHANGE	1922
C-47	THOSE HIGH GRAY WALLS	VIDOR	COLUMBIA	1939
C-47	TOGETHER WE LIVE	MACK	COLUMBIA	1935
C-48	CALL OF THE MOTH (sh)		COLUMBIA	1932
C-48	SUPERSPEED	HILLYER	COLUMBIA	1935
C-48	TOUCH ALL THE BASES (sh)	DAVIS	PATHE EXCHANGE	1922
C-49	BEWARE SPOOKS	SEDGWICK	COLUMBIA	1939
C-49	LOVE, HONOR AND HE PAYS (sh)	BUZZELL	COLUMBIA	1932
C-49	ROUGH ON ROMEO (sh)	DAVIS	PATHE EXCHANGE	1922
C-50	AFRICA SPEAKS	HOEFLER, FULLER	COLUMBIA	1930
C-50	SPEED DEMON	LEDERMAN	COLUMBIA	1932
C-50	WET WEATHER (sh)	HOWE	PATHE EXCHANGE	1922
C-51	BLONDIE BRINGS UP BABY	STRAYER	COLUMBIA	1939
C-51	OUT ON BAIL (sh)	DAVIS	PATHE EXCHANGE	1922
C-51	STATE TROOPER	LEDERMAN	COLUMBIA	1933
C-52	ARIZONA	RUGGLES	COLUMBIA	1940
C-52	OBEY THE LAW	STOLOFF	COLUMBIA	1933
C-52	SHOOT STRAIGHT (sh)	HOWE	PATHE EXCHANGE	1923
C-53	LANDLUBBER (sh)	DAVIS	PATHE EXCHANGE	1922
C-53	SCANDAL SHEET	GRINDE	COLUMBIA	1939
C-53	SOLDIERS OF THE STORM	LEDERMAN	COLUMBIA	1933
C-54	AMAZING MR. WILLIAMS	HALL	COLUMBIA	1939
C-54	SOAK THE SHEIK (sh)	HOWE	PATHE EXCHANGE	1922
C-55	BONE DRY (sh)	CHASE, DAVIS	PATHE EXCHANGE	1922
C-55	CAFE HOSTESS	SALKOW	COLUMBIA	1940
C-55	NIGHT OF TERROR	STOLOFF	COLUMBIA	1933
C-56	KING OF THE WILD HORSES	HALEY	COLUMBIA	1933
C-56	LOOSE TIGHT WAD (sh)	HOWE	PATHE EXCHANGE	1923
C-56	MY SON IS GUILTY	BARTON	COLUMBIA	1939
C-57	MILITARY ACADEMY	LEDERMAN	COLUMBIA	1940
C-57	SHINE 'EM UP (sh)	DAVIS	PATHE EXCHANGE	1922
C-58	FACE THE CAMERA (sh)	HOWE	PATHE EXCHANGE	1922
C-58	FIVE LITTLE PEPPERS AT HOME	BARTON	COLUMBIA	1940
C-59	GOLF BUG (sh)	DAVIS	PATHE EXCHANGE	1922
C-60	CORNERED	EASON	COLUMBIA	1932
C-60	GUARD THAT GIRL	HILLYER	COLUMBIA	1935
C-60	LONE RIDER	KING	COLUMBIA	1930
C-60	UPPERCUT (sh)	HOWE	PATHE EXCHANGE	1922
C-61	CASE OF THE MISSING MAN	LEDERMAN	COLUMBIA	1935

C-61	SHADOW RANCH	KING	COLUMBIA	1930
C-61	WHISTLING LIONS (sh)	PARROTT	PATHE EXCHANGE	1925
C-62	MEN WITHOUT LAW	KING	COLUMBIA	1930
C-62	SHIVER AND SHAKE (sh)	HOWE	PATHE EXCHANGE	1922
C-62	TOO TOUGH TO KILL	LEDERMAN	COLUMBIA	1935
C-63	BLONDIE ON A BUDGET	STRAYER	COLUMBIA	1940
C-63	DANGEROUS INTRIGUE	SELMAN	COLUMBIA	1936
C-63	DAWN TRAIL	CABANNE	COLUMBIA	1930
C-63	END OF THE TRAIL	LEDERMAN	COLUMBIA	1933
C-63	HARVEST HANDS (sh)	DAVIS	PATHE EXCHANGE	1922
C-64	FLIVVER (sh)	HOWE	PATHE EXCHANGE	1922
C-64	MAN OF ACTION	MELFORD	COLUMBIA	1933
C-64	PANIC ON THE AIR	LEDERMAN	COLUMBIA	1936
C-65	DOCTOR TAKES A WIFE	HALL	COLUMBIA	1940
C-65	FINAL HOUR	LEDERMAN	COLUMBIA	1936
C-65	I'LL TAKE VANILLA (sh)	DAVIS	PATHE EXCHANGE	1922
C-65	SILENT MEN	LEDERMAN	COLUMBIA	1933
C66	CHE!	FLEISHER	20th CENTURY-FOX	1969
C-66	SHAKEDOWN	SELMAN	COLUMBIA	1936
C-66	WASHED ASHORE (sh)	HOWE	PATHE EXCHANGE	1922
C-66	WHIRLWIND	LEDERMAN	COLUMBIA	1933
C-67	ALIBI FOR MURDER	LEDERMAN	COLUMBIA	1936
C-67	FAIR WEEK (sh)	DAVIS	PATHE EXCHANGE	1922
C-67	RUSTY RIDES ALONE	LEDERMAN	COLUMBIA	1933
C-68	BLAZE AWAY (sh)	HOWE	PATHE EXCHANGE	1922
C-68	KILLER AT LARGE	SELMAN	COLUMBIA	1936
C-69	FIRE THE FIREMAN (sh)	HOWE	PATHE EXCHANGE	1922
C-70	JUNGLE FIGHTERS (UK: LONG AND THE SHORT AND THE TALL)	NORMAN	CONTINENTAL	1961
C-70	POLICE CAR 17	HILLYER	COLUMBIA	1933
C-70	WESTERN FRONTIER	HERMAN	COLUMBIA	1935
C-70	WHITE BLACKSMITH (sh)	JESKE	PATHE EXCHANGE	1922
C-71	HOLD THE PRESS	ROSEN	COLUMBIA	1933
C-71	WATCH YOUR WIFE (sh)	HOWE	PATHE EXCHANGE	1923
C-72	PASTE AND PAPER (sh)	JESKE	PATHE EXCHANGE	1923
C-73	SPEED THE SWEDE (sh)	HOWE	PATHE EXCHANGE	1923
C-74	CATTLE THIEF	BENNET	COLUMBIA	1936
C-74	MR. HYPPO (sh)	JESKE	PATHE EXCHANGE	1923
C-75	DON'T SAY DIE (sh)	JESKE	PATHE EXCHANGE	1923
C-75	HEROES OF THE RANGE	BENNET	COLUMBIA	1936
C-76	AVENGING WATERS	BENNET	COLUMBIA	1936
C-76	ONCE OVER (sh)	JESKE	PATHE EXCHANGE	1923
C-77	FUGITIVE SHERIFF	BENNET	COLUMBIA	1936
C-77	JAILED AND BAILED (sh)	HOWE	PATHE EXCHANGE	1923
C-78	TIGHT SHOES (sh)	JESKE	PATHE EXCHANGE	1923
C-79	DO YOUR STUFF (sh)	HOWE	PATHE EXCHANGE	1923
C-80	BEFORE MIDNIGHT	HILLYER	COLUMBIA	1933
C-80	BOWLED OVER (sh)	JESKE	PATHE EXCHANGE	1923
C-80	HE STAYED FOR BREAKFAST	HALL	COLUMBIA	1940
C-81	GET YOUR MAN (sh)	JESKE	PATHE EXCHANGE	1923
C-81	MICKEY'S CHRISTMAS CAROL	MATTINSON	BUENA VISTA	1983
C-82	ANGELS OVER BROADWAY	GARMES	COLUMBIA	1940
C-82	CRIME OF HELEN STANLEY	LEDERMAN	COLUMBIA	1934
C-82	FOR SAFE KEEPING (sh)	JESKE	PATHE EXCHANGE	1923
C-82	STAMPEDE	BEEBE	COLUMBIA	1936
C-83	GIRL IN DANGER	LEDERMAN	COLUMBIA	1934
C-83	SECRET PATROL	SELMAN	COLUMBIA	1936
C-83	SMILE WINS (sh)	JESKE	PATHE EXCHANGE	1923
C-84	BEFORE I HANG	GRINDE	COLUMBIA	1940
C-84	DON'T FLIRT (sh)	POWERS	PATHE EXCHANGE	1923
C-84	TUGBOAT PRINCESS	SELMAN	COLUMBIA	1936
C-85	GOOD RIDDANCE (sh)	JESKE	PATHE EXCHANGE	1923
C-85	LUCKY FUGITIVES - (CAN: STOP, LOOK AND LOVE)	GRINDE	COLUMBIA	1936
C-86	UNDER TWO JAGS (sh)	JESKE	PATHE EXCHANGE	1923
C-87	SUNNY SPAIN (sh)	HOWE	PATHE EXCHANGE	1923
C-88	SECRET PEOPLE	DICKINSON	LIPPERT	1952
C-88	WATCH DOG (sh)	POWERS	PATHE EXCHANGE	1923

C-89	NOON WHISTLE (sh)	JESKE	PATHE EXCHANGE	1923
C-90	FOR ART'S SAKE (sh)	CHASE	PATHE EXCHANGE	1923
C-90	LAND NOBODY KNOWS		COLUMBIA	1931
C-90	ONE WAY OUT (sh)	HILLYER	COLUMBIA	1934
C-90	TIME OUT FOR RHYTHM (sh)	SALKOW	COLUMBIA	1941
C-91	HIDDEN EVIDENCE	HILLYER	COLUMBIA	1934
C-91	WHITE WINGS (sh)	JESKE	PATHE EXCHANGE	1923
C-92	PICK AND SHOVEL (sh)	JESKE	PATHE EXCHANGE	1923
C-92	SIMPLE SOLUTION (sh)	LEDERMAN	COLUMBIA	1934
C-93	FRESH EGGS (sh)	HOWE	PATHE EXCHANGE	1923
C-94	BE HONEST (sh)	POWERS	PATHE EXCHANGE	1923
C-94	PROFESSOR GIVES A LESSON	HILLYER	COLUMBIA	1934
C-94	SUNDOWN RIDER	HILLYER	COLUMBIA	1933
C-95	KILL OR CURE (sh)	PEMBROKE	PATHE EXCHANGE	1923
C-95	TREASON	SEITZ	COLUMBIA	1933
C-96	CALIFORNIA TRAIL	HILLYER	COLUMBIA	1933
C-96	FINGER PRINTS (sh)	CEDER	PATHE EXCHANGE	1923
C-96	PENNY SERENADE	STEVENS	COLUMBIA	1941
C-97	COLLARS AND CUFFS (sh)	JESKE	PATHE EXCHANGE	1923
C-97	UNKNOWN VALLEY	HILLYER	COLUMBIA	1933
C-98	BLIND GODDESS, THE (UK 1948)	FRENCH	UNIVERSAL	1949
C-98	LIVE WIRES (sh)	HOWE	PATHE EXCHANGE	1923
C-98	THIRD MAN, THE	REED	BRITISH LION	1949
C-99	GAS AND AIR (sh)	PEMBROKE	PATHE EXCHANGE	1923
C-100	HOT DAZE (sh)	MOORE	COLUMBIA	1933
C-100	POST NO BILLS (sh)	CEDER	PATHE EXCHANGE	1923
C-101	FOR GUESTS ONLY (sh)	HOWE	PATHE EXCHANGE	1923
C-102	ORANGES AND LEMONS (sh)	JESKE	PATHE EXCHANGE	1923
C-102	ROAMIN' THRU THE ROSES	GOTTLER	COLUMBIA	1933
C-103	TAKE THE AIR (sh)	CEDER	PATHE EXCHANGE	1923
C-104	DUKE OF THE NAVY	BEAUDINE	PRODUCERS RELEASING	1942
C-104	SHORT ORDERS	PEMBROKE	PATHE EXCHANGE	1923
C-105	ED CODIGO PENAL	ROSEN, VILLARREAL	COLUMBIA	1931
C-105	UNNAMED DIPPY DOO DADS (sh)		PATHE EXCHANGE	1923
C-106	SAVE THE SHIP (sh)	JESKE, ROACH	PATHE EXCHANGE	1923
C-107	UNCOVERED WAGON (sh)	HOWE	PATHE EXCHANGE	1923
C-108	BATTLE OF GREED	HIGGIN	CRESCENT PICT	1937
C-108	CARNE DE CABARET	CABANNE	COLUMBIA	1931
C-109	NO PETS (sh)	HOWE	PATHE EXCHANGE	1923
C-109	WHEN DO WE EAT? (SHOWMANSHIP*) (sh)	GOULDING	COLUMBIA	1934
C-110	STABLE MATES (sh)	WHITE	COLUMBIA	1934
C-110	STEPPING OUT (sh)	POWERS	PATHE EXCHANGE	1923
C-112	SCORCHING SANDS (sh)	WILLIAMSON, ROACH	PATHE EXCHANGE	1923
C-113	KNOCKOUT (sh)	POWERS	PATHE EXCHANGE	1923
C-114	EL PASADO ACUSA	SELMAN, VILLARREAL	COLUMBIA	1931
C-114	I WAS A PRISONER ON DEVIL'S ISLAND	LANDERS	COLUMBIA	1941
C-114	JOIN THE CIRCUS (sh)	JESKE	PATHE EXCHANGE	1923
C-115	PLUMBING FOR GOLD (sh)	LAMONT	COLUMBIA	1934
C-115	TWO IN A TAXI	FLOREY	COLUMBIA	1941
C-115	WHOLE TRUTH (sh)	CEDER	PATHE EXCHANGE	1923
C-116	GO WEST (sh)	POWERS	PATHE EXCHANGE	1923
C-116	OUR WIFE	STAHL	COLUMBIA	1941
C-116	PUNCH DRUNKS (sh)	BRESLOW	COLUMBIA	1934
C-117	HERE COMES MR. JORDAN	HALL	COLUMBIA	1941
C-117	LOVEY-DOVEY (sh)	POWERS	PATHE EXCHANGE	1923
C-117	TRIPPING THRU THE TROPICS (sh)	GOTTLER	COLUMBIA	1934
C-118	DEAR OLD PAL (sh)		PATHE EXCHANGE	1923
C-118	YOU'LL NEVER GET RICH	LANFIELD	COLUMBIA	1941
C-119	FROZEN HEARTS (sh)	HOWE	PATHE EXCHANGE	1923
C-119	HOLLYWOOD HERE WE COME (sh)	GOTTLER	COLUMBIA	1934
C-119	MYSTERY SHIP	LANDERS	COLUMBIA	1941
C-120	GET BUSY (sh)	HAYES	PATHE EXCHANGE	1924
C-120	TWO LATINS FROM MANHATTAN	BARTON	COLUMBIA	1941
C-121	OLD WAR HORSE (sh)	JESKE	PATHE EXCHANGE	1926
C-122	AT FIRST SIGHT (sh)	ROACH	PATHE EXCHANGE	1924
C-122	COUNTER-ESPIONAGE	DMYTRYK	COLUMBIA	1942

C-123	IT'S A JOY - (IT'S A BOY) (sh)	JESKE	PATHE EXCHANGE	1923
C-124	BAR-FLY (sh)	POWERS	PATHE EXCHANGE	1924
C-124	THREE GIRLS ABOUT TOWN	JASON	COLUMBIA	1941
C-125	FULLY INSURED (sh)	JESKE	PATHE EXCHANGE	1923
C-125	GO WEST YOUNG LADY	STRAYER	COLUMBIA	1941
C-126	FRIEND HUSBAND (WHY MARRY?) (sh)	HOWE	PATHE EXCHANGE	1924
C-126	HARMON OF MICHIGAN	BARTON	COLUMBIA	1941
C-127	BIG IDEA (sh)	JESKE	PATHE EXCHANGE	1924
C-127	STORK PAYS OFF	LANDERS	COLUMBIA	1941
C-128	MAN PAYS (sh)	POWERS	PATHE EXCHANGE	1924
C-128	SECRETS OF THE LONE WOLF	DMYTRYK	COLUMBIA	1941
C-129	HARD KNOCKS (sh)	PARROTT	PATHE EXCHANGE	1924
C-129	LADY IS WILLING	LEISEN	COLUMBIA	1942
C-129	PERFECT LADY (sh)	PARROTT	PATHE EXCHANGE	1924
C-130	JUST A MINUTE (sh)	PARROTT	PATHE EXCHANGE	1924
C-130	SING FOR YOUR SUPPER	BARTON	COLUMBIA	1941
C-131	ONE OF THE FAMILY (sh)	PEMBROKE	PATHE EXCHANGE	1924
C-132	HARVARD, HERE I COME	LANDERS	COLUMBIA	1941
C-132	LOVE'S REWARD (sh)	POWERS	PATHE EXCHANGE	1924
C-133	CONFESSIONS OF BOSTON BLACKIE	DMYTRYK	COLUMBIA	1941
C-133	POWDER AND SMOKE (sh)	PARROTT	PATHE EXCHANGE	1924
C-134	BLONDIE GOES TO COLLEGE	STRAYER	COLUMBIA	1942
C-134	LOVE'S DETOUR (sh)	PARROTT	PATHE EXCHANGE	1924
C-135	HONOLULU LU	BARTON	COLUMBIA	1941
C-135	OUR LITTLE NELL (sh)	POWERS	PATHE EXCHANGE	1924
C-136	CADETS ON PARADE	LANDERS	COLUMBIA	1942
C-136	HARD KNOCKS (sh)	PARROTT	PATHE EXCHANGE	1924
C-137	NORTH OF 50-50 (sh)	POWERS	PATHE EXCHANGE	1924
C-137	SHUT MY BIG MOUTH	BARTON	COLUMBIA	1942
C-138	DON'T FORGET (sh)	PARROTT	PATHE EXCHANGE	1924
C-138	TWO YANKS IN TRINIDAD	RATOFF	COLUMBIA	1942
C-139	MAN WHO RETURNED TO LIFE	LANDERS	COLUMBIA	1942
C-140	CANAL ZONE	LANDERS	COLUMBIA	1942
C-141	TRAMP TRAMP TRAMP	BARTON	COLUMBIA	1942
C-144	ALIAS BOSTON BLACKIE	LANDERS	COLUMBIA	1942
C-146	TALK OF THE TOWN	STEVENS	COLUMBIA	1942
C-147	NOT A LADIES MAN	LANDERS	COLUMBIA	1942
C-148	HELLO ANAPOLIS	BARTON	COLUMBIA	1942
C-150	COUNSEL ON DE FENCE (sh)	RIPLEY	COLUMBIA	1934
C-150	THEY ALL KISSED THE BRIDE	HALL	COLUMBIA	1942
C-152	MEN IN BLACK (sh)	MCCAREY	COLUMBIA	1934
C-152	SWEETHEART OF THE FLEET	BARTON	COLUMBIA	1942
C-153	SUBMARINE RAIDER	LANDERS	COLUMBIA	1942
C-154	SHIVERS (sh)	RIPLEY	COLUMBIA	1934
C-154	YOU WERE NEVER LOVELIER	SEITER	COLUMBIA	1942
C-155	ATLANTIC CONVOY	LANDERS	COLUMBIA	1942
C-155	IN THE DOG HOUSE (sh)	RIPLEY	COLUMBIA	1934
C-156	FLIGHT LIEUTENANT	SALKOW	COLUMBIA	1942
C-156	THREE LITTLE PIGSKINS (sh)	MCCAREY	COLUMBIA	1934
C-157	ONE DANGEROUS NIGHT	GORDON	COLUMBIA	1943
C-158	BLONDIE FOR VICTORY	STRAYER	COLUMBIA	1942
C-159	MAN'S WORLD	BARTON	COLUMBIA	1942
C-160	SABOTAGE SQUAD	LANDERS	COLUMBIA	1942
C-161	I'M A FATHER (sh)	HORNE	COLUMBIA	1935
C-161	MY SISTER EILEEN	HALL	COLUMBIA	1942
C-162	HIS BRIDAL SWEET (sh)	GOULDING	COLUMBIA	1935
C-162	LUCKY LEGS	BARTON	COLUMBIA	1942
C-162	STORK BITES MAN	ENDFIELD	UNITED ARTISTS	1947
C-163	DESPERADOES	VIDOR	COLUMBIA	1943
C-163	POP GOES THE EASEL (sh)	LORD	COLUMBIA	1935
C-164	OLD SAWBONES (sh)	LORD	COLUMBIA	1935
C-164	STAND BY ALL NETWORKS	LANDERS	COLUMBIA	1942
C-165	SPIRIT OF STANFORD	BARTON	COLUMBIA	1942
C-165	UNCIVIL WARRIORS (sh)	LORD	COLUMBIA	1935
C-166	DESTROYER	SEITER	COLUMBIA	1943
C-166	LEATHER NECKER (sh)	RIPLEY	COLUMBIA	1935

C-167	GUM SHOES (sh)	LORD	COLUMBIA	1935
C-167	LET'S HAVE FUN	BARTON	COLUMBIA	1943
C-168	DARING YOUNG MAN	STRAYER	COLUMBIA	1942
C-168	PARDON MY SCOTCH (sh) CHANGED	LORD	COLUMBIA	1935
C-169	BOSTON BLACKIE GOES HOLLYWOOD	GORDON	COLUMBIA	1942
C-169	TRAMP TRAMP TRAMP (sh)	LAMONT	COLUMBIA	1935
C-170	SMITH OF MINNESOTA	LANDERS	COLUMBIA	1942
C-171	ALIMONY ACHES (sh)	LAMONT	COLUMBIA	1935
C-171	BOOGIE MAN WILL GET YOU	LANDERS	COLUMBIA	1942
C-172	STAGE FRIGHTS (sh)	RAY	COLUMBIA	1935
C-172	UNDERGROUND AGENT	GORDON	COLUMBIA	1942
C-173	DO YOUR STUFF (sh)	PARROTT	COLUMBIA	1935
C-173	NIGHT TO REMEMBER	WALLACE	COLUMBIA	1943
C-174	CAPTAIN HITS THE CEILING (sh)	LAMONT	COLUMBIA	1935
C-174	LAUGH YOUR BLUES AWAY	BARTON	COLUMBIA	1942
C-175	GOBS OF TROUBLE (sh)	LORD	COLUMBIA	1935
C-175	JUNIOR ARMY	LANDERS	COLUMBIA	1942
C-176	MORE THE MERRIER	STEVENS	COLUMBIA	1943
C-177	POWER OF THE PRESS	LANDERS	COLUMBIA	1943
C-178	WHAT'S BUZZIN COUSIN?	BARTON	COLUMBIA	1943
C-179	REVELIE WITH BEVERLY	BARTON	COLUMBIA	1943
C-180	MURDER IN TIMES SQUARE	LANDERS	COLUMBIA	1943
C-181	SAHARA	KORDA	COLUMBIA	1943
C-182	APPOINTMENT IN BERLIN	GREEN	COLUMBIA	1943
C-183	AFTER MIDNIGHT WITH BOSTON BLACKIE	LANDERS	COLUMBIA	1943
C-184	FIRST COMES COURAGE	ARZNER	COLUMBIA	1943
C-185	SHE HAS WHAT IT TAKES	BARTON	COLUMBIA	1943
C-186	IT'S A GREAT LIFE	STRAYER	COLUMBIA	1943
C-187	BOY FROM STALINGRAD	SALKOW	COLUMBIA	1943
C-188	REDHEAD FROM MANHATTAN	LANDERS	COLUMBIA	1943
C-189	ONCE UPON A TIME	HALL	COLUMBIA	1944
C-190	TWO SENORITAS FROM CHICAGO	WOODRUFF	COLUMBIA	1943
C-192	GOOD LUCK MR. YATES	ENRIGHT	COLUMBIA	1943
C-193	DOUGHBOYS IN IRELAND	LANDERS	COLUMBIA	1943
C-194	COVER GIRL	VIDOR	COLUMBIA	1944
C-195	MY KINGDOM FOR A COOK	WALLACE	COLUMBIA	1943
C-196	HOMBRES EN MI VIDA	SELMAN	COLUMBIA	1932
C-197	PASSPORT TO SUEZ	DE TOTH	COLUMBIA	1943
C-198	DANGEROUS BLONDES	JASON	COLUMBIA	1943
C-199	THERE'S SOMETHING ABOUT A SOLDIER	GREEN	COLUMBIA	1943
C-200	EXTORTION	HILLYER	COLUMBIA	1938
C-200	OH, MY NERVES! (sh)	LORD	COLUMBIA	1935
C-201	UNRELATED RELATIONS (sh)	LORD	COLUMBIA	1936
C-202	IT ALWAYS HAPPENS (sh)	LORD	COLUMBIA	1935
C-203	HIS MARRIAGE MIX-UP (sh)	WHITE	COLUMBIA	1935
C-203	MAIN EVENT	DARE	COLUMBIA	1938
C-204	PAID TO DANCE (HARD TO HOLD)	COLEMAN	COLUMBIA	1937
C-204	STAR GAZING (sh)	RUBIN	COLUMBIA	1935
C-205	ALL AMERICAN SWEETHEART	HILLYER	COLUMBIA	1937
C-205	YOO HOO HOLLYWOOD (sh)	RUBIN	COLUMBIA	1935
C-206	PARDON MY SCOTCH (sh)	LORD	COLUMBIA	1935
C-206	SHADOW	COLEMAN	COLUMBIA	1937
C-207	HOI POLLOI (sh)	LORD	COLUMBIA	1935
C-207	SQUADRON OF HONOR	COLEMAN	COLUMBIA	1938
C-208	HONEYMOON BRIDGE (sh)	LORD	COLUMBIA	1935
C-208	WOMEN IN PRISON	HILLYER	COLUMBIA	1938
C-209	HOT PAPRIKA (sh)	WHITE	COLUMBIA	1935
C-209	WHO KILLED GAIL PRESTON?	BARSHA	COLUMBIA	1938
C-210	THREE LITTLE BEERS (sh)	LORD	COLUMBIA	1935
C-210	WHEN G-MEN STEP IN	COLEMAN	COLUMBIA	1938
C-211	HIGHWAY PATROL	COLEMAN	COLUMBIA	1938
C-211	I DON'T REMEMBER (sh)	WHITE	COLUMBIA	1935
C-212	HOMICIDE BUREAU	COLEMAN	COLUMBIA	1939
C-212	PEPPERY SALT (sh)	LORD	COLUMBIA	1936
C-213	JUVENILE COURT	LEDERMAN	COLUMBIA	1938
C-213	MOVIE MANIACS (sh)	LORD	COLUMBIA	1936

C-214	ADVENTURE IN SAHARA	LEDERMAN	COLUMBIA	1938
C-214	JUST SPEEDING (sh)	LORD	COLUMBIA	1936
C-215	NORTH OF SHANGHAI	LEDERMAN	COLUMBIA	1939
C-215	SHARE THE WEALTH (sh)	LORD	COLUMBIA	1936
C-216	MIDNIGHT BLUNDERS (sh)	LORD	COLUMBIA	1936
C-216	MY SON IS A CRIMINAL	COLEMAN	COLUMBIA	1939
C-217	DISORDER IN THE COURT (sh)	WHITE	COLUMBIA	1936
C-217	FIRST OFFENDERS	MCDONALD	COLUMBIA	1939
C-218	ANTS IN THE PANTRY (sh)	WHITE	COLUMBIA	1936
C-218	OUTSIDE THESE WALLS	MCCAREY	COLUMBIA	1939
C-219	CHAMP'S A CHUMP (sh)	WHITE	COLUMBIA	1936
C-219	MISSING DAUGHTERS	COLEMAN	COLUMBIA	1939
C-220	MISTER SMARTY (sh)	WHITE	COLUMBIA	1936
C-220	PARENTS ON TRIAL	NELSON	COLUMBIA	1939
C-221	SLIPPERY SILKS - CHANGE TO 252	WHITE	COLUMBIA	1936
C-221	WOMAN IS THE JUDGE	GRINDE	COLUMBIA	1939
C-222	BEHIND PRISON GATES	BARTON	COLUMBIA	1939
C-222	CAUGHT IN THE ACT	LORD	COLUMBIA	1936
C-223	MAN THEY COULD NOT HANG	GRINDE	COLUMBIA	1939
C-223	PAIN IN THE PULLMAN (sh)	WHITE	COLUMBIA	1936
C-224	FALSE ALARMS (sh) (changed to 250)	LORD	COLUMBIA	1936
C-224	KONGA, THE WILD STALLION	NELSON	COLUMBIA	1940
C-225	HALF SHOT SHOOTERS (sh)	WHITE	COLUMBIA	1936
C-226	WHOOPS, I'M AN INDIAN! (sh) (changed to 251)	WHITE	COLUMBIA	1936
C-250	FALSE ALARMS (sh)	LORD	COLUMBIA	1936
C-251	WHOOPS, I'M AN INDIAN! (sh)	WHITE	COLUMBIA	1936
C-252	SLIPPERY SILKS	WHITE	COLUMBIA	1936
C-253	AM I HAVING FUN! (sh)	WHITE	COLUMBIA	1936
C-254	AY TANK AY GO (sh)	LORD	COLUMBIA	1936
C-255	OH, DUCHESS! (sh)	LAMONT	COLUMBIA	1936
C-256	LOVE COMES TO MOONEYVILLE (sh)	WHITE	COLUMBIA	1936
C-257	FIBBING FIBBERS (sh)	WHITE	COLUMBIA	1936
C-258	FREE RENT (sh)	LORD	COLUMBIA	1936
C-259	GRIPS, GRUNTS AND GROANS (sh)	WHITE	COLUMBIA	1937
C-260	SAILOR MAID (sh)	LAMONT	COLUMBIA	1937
C-261	KNEE ACTION (sh)	LAMONT	COLUMBIA	1937
C-262	SUPER SNOOPER (sh)	WHITE	COLUMBIA	1937
C-263	DIZZY DOCTORS (sh)	LORD	COLUMBIA	1937
C-264	BURY THE HATCHET (sh)	LORD	COLUMBIA	1937
C-265	STUCK IN THE STICKS (sh)	WHITE	COLUMBIA	1937
C-266	3 DUMB CLUCKS (sh)	LORD	COLUMBIA	1937
C-267	NEW NEWS (sh)	LAMONT	COLUMBIA	1937
C-268	BACK TO THE WOODS (sh)	WHITE	COLUMBIA	1937
C-269	GRAND HOOTER (sh)	WHITE	COLUMBIA	1937
C-270	LODGE NIGHT (sh)	WHITE	COLUMBIA	1937
C-271	FROM BAD TO WORSE (sh)	LORD	COLUMBIA	1937
C-272	MY LITTLE FELLER (sh)	LAMONT	COLUMBIA	1937
C-273	WRONG MISS WRIGHT (sh)	LAMONT	COLUMBIA	1937
C-274	GOOFS AND SADDLES (sh)	LORD	COLUMBIA	1937
C-275	CALLING ALL DOCTORS (sh)	LAMONT	COLUMBIA	1937
C-280	COMMUNITY SING - #3	series	COLUMBIA	1937
C-281	COMMUNITY SING - #4	series	COLUMBIA	1937
C-282	COMMUNITY SING - #5	series	COLUMBIA	1937
C-283	COMMUNITY SING - SERIES 2 #1	series	COLUMBIA	1937
C-284	COMMUNITY SING - SERIES 2 #2	series	COLUMBIA	1937
C-300	OUTLAWS OF THE PRAIRIE	NELSON	COLUMBIA	1937
C-301	CATTLE RAIDERS	NELSON	COLUMBIA	1938
C-302	OLD WYOMING TRAIL	BLANGSTED	COLUMBIA	1937
C-303	CALL OF THE ROCKIES	JAMES	COLUMBIA	1938
C-304	LAW OF THE PLAINS	NELSON	COLUMBIA	1938
C-305	WEST OF CHEYENNE	NELSON	COLUMBIA	1938
C-306	SOUTH OF ARIZONA	NELSON	COLUMBIA	1938
C-307	WEST OF SANTA FE	NELSON	COLUMBIA	1938
C-308	COLORADO TRAIL	NELSON	COLUMBIA	1938
C-309	RIO GRANDE	NELSON	COLUMBIA	1938
C-310	THUNDERING WEST	NELSON	COLUMBIA	1939

C-311	TEXAS STAMPEDE	NELSON	COLUMBIA	1939
C-312	NORTH OF THE YUKON	NELSON	COLUMBIA	1939
C-313	SPOILERS OF THE RANGE	COLEMAN	COLUMBIA	1939
C-314	WESTERN CARAVANS	NELSON	COLUMBIA	1939
C-315	MAN FROM SUNDOWN	NELSON	COLUMBIA	1939
C-316	OUTPOST OF THE MOUNTIES	COLEMAN	COLUMBIA	1939
C-317	STRANGER FROM TEXAS	NELSON	COLUMBIA	1939
C-318	RIDERS OF BLACK RIVER	DEMING	COLUMBIA	1939
C-319	TAMING OF THE WEST	DEMING	COLUMBIA	1939
C-320	MAN FROM TUMBLEWEEDS	LEWIS	COLUMBIA	1940
C-321	TWO FISTED RANGERS	LEWIS	COLUMBIA	1939
C-322	BULLETS FOR RUSTLERS	NELSON	COLUMBIA	1940
C-323	PIONEERS OF THE FRONTIER	NELSON	COLUMBIA	1940
C-324	BLAZING SIX SHOOTERS	LEWIS	COLUMBIA	1940
C-325	THUNDERING FRONTIER	LEDERMAN	COLUMBIA	1940
C-326	TEXAS STAGECOACH	LEWIS	COLUMBIA	1940
C-327	PINTO KID	HILLYER	COLUMBIA	1941
C-328	WEST OF ABILENE	CEDER	COLUMBIA	1940
C-329	RETURN OF WILD BILL	LEWIS	COLUMBIA	1940
C-330	DURANGO KID	HILLYER	COLUMBIA	1940
C-331	PRAIRIE SCHOONERS	NELSON	COLUMBIA	1940
C-332	OUTLAWS OF THE PANHANDLE	NELSON	COLUMBIA	1941
C-334	BEYOND THE SACRAMENTO	HILLYER	COLUMBIA	1940
C-335	ACROSS THE SIERRAS	LEDERMAN	COLUMBIA	1941
C-337	WILDCAT OF TUCSON	HILLYER	COLUMBIA	1940
C-338	NORTH FROM THE LONE STAR	HILLYER	COLUMBIA	1941
C-339	RETURN OF DANIEL BOONE	HILLYER	COLUMBIA	1941
C-340	HANDS ACROSS THE ROCKIES	HILLYER	COLUMBIA	1941
C-341	SON OF DAVY CROCKETT	HILLYER	COLUMBIA	1941
C-342	MEDICO OF PAINTED SPRINGS	HILLYER	COLUMBIA	1941
C-343	KING OF DODGE CITY	HILLYER	COLUMBIA	1941
C-344	THUNDER OVER THE PRAIRIE	HILLYER	COLUMBIA	1941
C-345	ROARING FRONTIERS	HILLYER	COLUMBIA	1941
C-346	PRAIRIE STRANGER	HILLYER	COLUMBIA	1941
C-347	LONE STAR VIGILANTES	FOX	COLUMBIA	1942
C-348	ROYAL MOUNTED PATROL	HILLYER	COLUMBIA	1941
C-349	BULLETS FOR BANDITS	FOX	COLUMBIA	1942
C-350	RIDERS OF THE BADLANDS	BRETHERTON	COLUMBIA	1941
C-351	NORTH OF THE ROCKIES	HILLYER	COLUMBIA	1942
C-352	DEVIL'S TRAIL	HILLYER	COLUMBIA	1942
C-353	WEST OF TOMBSTONE	BRETHERTON	COLUMBIA	1942
C-354	LAWLESS PLAINSMEN	BERKE	COLUMBIA	1942
C-355	DOWN RIO GRANDE WAY	BERKE	COLUMBIA	1942
C-356	PRAIRIE GUNSMOKE	HILLYER	COLUMBIA	1942
C-357	OVERLAND TO DEADWOOD	BERKE	COLUMBIA	1942
C-358	BADMEN OF THE HILLS	BERKE	COLUMBIA	1942
C-359	RIDERS OF THE NORTHLAND	BERKE	COLUMBIA	1942
C-360	VENGEANCE OF THE WEST	HILLYER	COLUMBIA	1942
C-362	RIDING THROUGH NEVADA	BERKE	COLUMBIA	1942
C-363	PARDON MY GUN	BERKE	COLUMBIA	1942
C-364	TORNADO IN THE SADDLE	BERKE	COLUMBIA	1942
C-365	LONE PRAIRIE	BERKE	COLUMBIA	1942
C-366	FIGHTING BUCKAROO	BERKE	COLUMBIA	1943
C-367	LAW OF THE NORTHWEST	BERKE	COLUMBIA	1943
C-368	SILVER CITY RAIDERS	BERKE	COLUMBIA	1943
C-369	RIDERS OF THE NORTHWEST MOUNTED	BERKE	COLUMBIA	1943
C-370	HAIL TO THE RANGERS	BERKE	COLUMBIA	1943
C-371	ROBIN HOOD OF THE RANGE	BERKE	COLUMBIA	1943
C-372	SADDLES AND THE SAGEBRUSH	BERKE	COLUMBIA	1943
C-373	VIGILANTES RIDE	BERKE	COLUMBIA	1943
C-374	WYOMING HURRICANE	BERKE	COLUMBIA	1944
C-375	LAST HORSEMAN	BERKE	COLUMBIA	1944
C-376	RIDING WEST	BERKE	COLUMBIA	1944
C-377	FRONTIER FURY	BERKE	COLUMBIA	1943
C-400	CASH AND CARRY (sh)	LORD	COLUMBIA	1937
C-401	PLAYING THE PONIES (sh)	LAMONT	COLUMBIA	1937

C-402	SITTER DOWNERS (sh)	LORD	COLUMBIA	1937
C-403	JUMP, CHUMP, JUMP! (sh)	LORD	COLUMBIA	1938
C-404	WEE WEE MONSIER (sh)	LORD	COLUMBIA	1938
C-405	DOGGONE MIXUP (sh)	LAMONT	COLUMBIA	1938
C-406	BIG SQUIRT (sh)	LORD	COLUMBIA	1937
C-407	GRACIE AT THE BAT (sh)	LORD	COLUMBIA	1937
C-408	OH, WHAT A KNIGHT! (sh)	CHASE	COLUMBIA	1937
C-409	CALLING ALL CURTAINS (sh)	LORD	COLUMBIA	1937
C-410	FIDDLING AROUND (sh)	LAMONT	COLUMBIA	1938
C-411	HE DONE HIS DUTY (sh)	LAMONT	COLUMBIA	1937
C-412	MIND NEEDER (sh)	LORD	COLUMBIA	1938
C-413	MANY SAPPY RETURNS (sh)	LORD	COLUMBIA	1938
C-414	MAN BITES LOVEBUG (sh)	LORD	COLUMBIA	1937
C-415	TIME OUT FOR TROUBLE (sh)	LORD	COLUMBIA	1938
C-416	TERMITES OF 1938 (sh)	LORD	COLUMBIA	1938
C-417	OLD RAID MULE (sh)	CHASE	COLUMBIA	1938
C-418	NIGHTSHIRT BANDIT (sh)	WHITE	COLUMBIA	1938
C-419	THREE LITTLE SEW AND SEWS (sh)	LORD	COLUMBIA	1939
C-420	TASSELS IN THE AIR (sh)	CHASE	COLUMBIA	1938
C-421	ANKLES AWAY (sh)	CHASE	COLUMBIA	1938
C-422	HEALTHY, WEALTHY AND DUMB (sh)	LORD	COLUMBIA	1938
C-423	VIOLENT IS THE WORD FOR CURLY (sh)	CHASE	COLUMBIA	1938
C-424	SOUL OF A HEEL (sh)	LORD	COLUMBIA	1938
C-425	HALF-WAY TO HOLLYWOOD (sh)	CHASE	COLUMBIA	1938
C-426	THREE MISSING LINKS (sh)	WHITE	COLUMBIA	1938
C-427	MUTTS TO YOU (sh)	CHASE	COLUMBIA	1938
C-428	SUE MY LAWYER (sh)	WHITE	COLUMBIA	1938
C-429	NAG IN THE BAG (sh)	CHASE	COLUMBIA	1938
C-430	SAVED BY THE BELLE (sh)	CHASE	COLUMBIA	1939
C-431	PIE A LA MAID (sh)	LORD	COLUMBIA	1938
C-432	NOT GUILTY ENOUGH (sh)	LORD	COLUMBIA	1938
C-433	MUTINY ON THE BODY (sh)	CHASE	COLUMBIA	1939
C-434	SWING YOU SWINGERS (sh)	WHITE	COLUMBIA	1939
C-435	SAP TAKES A WRAP (sh)	LORD	COLUMBIA	1939
C-436	HOME ON THE RAGE (sh)	LORD	COLUMBIA	1938
C-437	CHUMP TAKES A BUMP (sh)	LORD	COLUMBIA	1939
C-438	YES WE HAVE NO BONANZA (sh)	LORD	COLUMBIA	1939
C-439	FLAT FOOT STOOGES (sh)	CHASE	COLUMBIA	1938
C-440	BOOM GOES THE GROOM (sh)	CHASE	COLUMBIA	1939
C-441	STAR IS SHORN (sh)	LORD	COLUMBIA	1939
C-442	TROUBLE FINDS ANDY CLYDE (sh)	WHITE	COLUMBIA	1939
C-443	WE WANT OUR MUMMY (sh)	LORD	COLUMBIA	1939
C-444	DUCKING THEY DID GO (sh)	LORD	COLUMBIA	1939
C-445	CALLING ALL CURS (sh)	WHITE	COLUMBIA	1939
C-446	RATTLING ROMEO (sh)	LORD	COLUMBIA	1939
C-448	NOW IT CAN BE SOLD (sh)	LORD	COLUMBIA	1939
C-449	OILY TO BED, OILY TO RISE (sh)	WHITE	COLUMBIA	1939
C-450	SKINNY THE MOOCHER (sh)	LORD	COLUMBIA	1939
C-451	THREE SAPPY PEOPLE (sh)	WHITE	COLUMBIA	1939
C-452	TEACHER'S PEST (sh)	KRAMER, ULLMAN	COLUMBIA	1939
C-453	STATIC IN THE ATTIC (sh)	CHASE	COLUMBIA	1939
C-454	PEST FROM THE WEST (sh)	LORD	COLUMBIA	1939
C-455	COOKOO CAVALIERS (sh)	WHITE	COLUMBIA	1940
C-456	MOOCHING THROUGH GEORGIA (sh)	WHITE	COLUMBIA	1939
C-457	GLOVE SLINGERS (sh)	WHITE	COLUMBIA	1939
C-458	HOW HIGH IS UP? (sh)	LORD	COLUMBIA	1940
C-459	MONEY SQUAWKS (sh)	WHITE	COLUMBIA	1940
C-460	ALL AMERICAN BLONDES (sh)	LORD	COLUMBIA	1939
C-461	ROCKIN' THRU THE ROCKIES (sh)	WHITE	COLUMBIA	1940
C-462	PLUMBING WE WILL GO (sh)	LORD	COLUMBIA	1940
C-463	ANDY CLYDE GETS SPRING CHICKEN (sh)	WHITE	COLUMBIA	1939
C-464	AWFUL GOOF (sh)	LORD	COLUMBIA	1939
C-465	NUTTY BUT NICE (sh)	WHITE	COLUMBIA	1940
C-466	MR. CLYDE GOES TO BROADWAY (sh)	LORD	COLUMBIA	1940
C-467	HECKLER (sh)	LORD	COLUMBIA	1940
C-468	FROM NURSE TO WORSE (sh)	WHITE	COLUMBIA	1940

C-469	HIS BRIDAL FRIGHT (sh)	LORD	COLUMBIA	1940
C-470	NOTHING BUT PLEASURE (sh)	WHITE	COLUMBIA	1940
C-471	YOU'RE NEXT (sh)	LORD	COLUMBIA	1940
C-472	YOU NAZTY SPY (sh)	WHITE	COLUMBIA	1940
C-473	SOUTH OF THE BOUDOIR (sh)	LORD	COLUMBIA	1940
C-474	NO CENSUS, NO FEELING (sh)	LORD	COLUMBIA	1940
C-475	PARDON MY BERTH MARKS (sh)	WHITE	COLUMBIA	1940
C-476	BOOBS IN THE WOODS (sh)	LORD	COLUMBIA	1940
C-477	TAMING OF THE SNOOD (sh)	WHITE	COLUMBIA	1940
C-478	FIREMAN, SAVE MY CHOO CHOO (sh)	LORD	COLUMBIA	1940
C-479	PLEASED TO MITT YOU (sh)	WHITE	COLUMBIA	1940
C-480	COLD TURKEY (sh)	LORD	COLUMBIA	1940
C-481	SPOOK SPEAKS (sh)	WHITE	COLUMBIA	1940
C-482	IN THE SWEET PIE AND PIE (sh)	WHITE	COLUMBIA	1941
C-483	BLONDES AND BLUNDERS (sh)	LORD	COLUMBIA	1940
C-484	SO LONG MR. CHUMPS (sh)	WHITE	COLUMBIA	1941
C-485	DUTIFUL BUT DUMB (sh)	LORD	COLUMBIA	1941
C-486	BOOBS IN ARMS (sh)	WHITE	COLUMBIA	1940
C-487	ALL THE WORLD'S A STOOGE (sh)	LORD	COLUMBIA	1941
C-488	ACHE IN EVERY STAKE (sh)	LORD	COLUMBIA	1941
C-489	WATCHMAN TAKES A WIFE (sh)	LORD	COLUMBIA	1941
C-490	BUNDLE OF BLISS (sh)	WHITE	COLUMBIA	1940
C-491	HIS EX MARKS THE SPOT (sh)	WHITE	COLUMBIA	1940
C-493	SO YOU WON'T SQUAWK (sh)	LORD	COLUMBIA	1941
C-494	RING AND THE BELLE (sh)	LORD	COLUMBIA	1941
C-495	FRESH AS A FRESHMAN (sh)	WHITE	COLUMBIA	1941
C-496	BLITZ KISS (sh)	LORD	COLUMBIA	1941
C-497	YUMPIN' YIMMINY!	WHITE	COLUMBIA	1941
C-498	YANKEE DOODLE ANDY (sh)	WHITE	COLUMBIA	1941
C-499	READY, WILLING BUT UNABLE (sh)	LORD	COLUMBIA	1941
C-500	I'LL NEVER HEIL AGAIN (sh)	WHITE	COLUMBIA	1941
C-501	LOVE AT FIRST FRIGHT (sh)	LORD	COLUMBIA	1941
C-502	THREE BLONDE MICE (sh)	WHITE	COLUMBIA	1942
C-503	FRENCH FRIED PATOOTIE (sh)	WHITE	COLUMBIA	1941
C-504	WHAT MAKES LIZZY DIZZY (sh)	WHITE	COLUMBIA	1942
C-505	BLACK EYES AND BLUES (sh)	WHITE	COLUMBIA	1941
C-506	HALF SHOT AT SUNRISE (sh)	LORD	COLUMBIA	1941
C-507	EVEN AS I.O.U. (sh)	LORD	COLUMBIA	1942
C-508	GENERAL NUISANCEE (sh)	WHITE	COLUMBIA	1941
C-509	HOST TO A GHOST (sh)	LORD	COLUMBIA	1941
C-510	LOCO BOY MAKES GOOD (sh)	WHITE	COLUMBIA	1942
C-511	SOME MORE OF SOMOA (sh)	LORD	COLUMBIA	1941
C-512	MITT ME TONIGHT (sh)	WHITE	COLUMBIA	1941
C-513	CACTUS MAKES PERFECT	LORD	COLUMBIA	1942
C-514	ALL WORK AND NO PAY (sh)	LORD	COLUMBIA	1942
C-515	PHONY CRONIES (sh)	EDWARDS	COLUMBIA	1942
C-516	LOVEABLE TROUBLE (sh)	LORD	COLUMBIA	1941
C-517	SAPPY BIRTHDAY (sh)	EDWARDS	COLUMBIA	1942
C-518	KINK OF THE CAMPUS (sh)	LORD	COLUMBIA	1941
C-519	WHAT'S THE MATADOR? (sh)	WHITE	COLUMBIA	1942
C-520	GLOVE BIRDS (sh)	WHITE	COLUMBIA	1942
C-521	SWEET SPIRITS OF NIGHTER (sh)	LORD	COLUMBIA	1941
C-522	BACK FROM THE FRONT (sh)	WHITE	COLUMBIA	1943
C-523	GROOM AND BORED (sh)	LORD	COLUMBIA	1942
C-524	HOW SPRY I AM (sh)	WHITE	COLUMBIA	1942
C-525	GLOVE AFFAIR (sh)	WHITE	COLUMBIA	1941
C-525	STUDY IN SOCKS (sh)	LORD	COLUMBIA	1942
C-526	SHE'S OIL MINE (sh)	WHITE	COLUMBIA	1941
C-527	MATRI-PHONY (sh)	EDWARDS	COLUMBIA	1942
C-528	OLAF LAUGHS LAST (sh)	WHITE	COLUMBIA	1942
C-529	DIZZY DETECTIVES (sh)	WHITE	COLUMBIA	1943
C-530	KISS AND WAKE UP (sh)	WHITE	COLUMBIA	1942
C-531	QUACK SERVICE (sh)	EDWARDS	COLUMBIA	1943
C-532	THREE SMART SAPS (sh)	WHITE	COLUMBIA	1942
C-533	THEY STOOGE TO CONGA (sh)	LORD	COLUMBIA	1943
C-534	TIREMAN, SPARE MY TIRES (sh)	WHITE	COLUMBIA	1942

C-535	HAM AND YEGGS (sh)	WHITE	COLUMBIA	1942
C-536	CARRY HARRY (sh)	EDWARDS	COLUMBIA	1942
C-537	BLITZ ON THE FRITZ (sh)	WHITE	COLUMBIA	1943
C-538	WOLF IN THIEF'S CLOTHING (sh)	WHITE	COLUMBIA	1943
C-539	SOCK-A-BYE BABY (sh)	WHITE	COLUMBIA	1942
C-540	SAPPY PAPPY (sh)	EDWARDS	COLUMBIA	1942
C-541	HIS WEDDING SCARE (sh)	LORD	COLUMBIA	1943
C-543	PIANO MOONER (sh)	EDWARDS	COLUMBIA	1942
C-544	GREAT GLOVER (sh)	WHITE	COLUMBIA	1942
C-545	HIS GIRL'S WORST FRIEND (sh)	WHITE	COLUMBIA	1943
C-546	FARMER FOR A DAY (sh)	WHITE	COLUMBIA	1943
C-547	MAID MADE MAD (sh)	LORD	COLUMBIA	1943
C-548	SOCKS APPEAL (sh)	EDWARDS	COLUMBIA	1943
C-549	SPOOK LOUDER (sh)	LORD	COLUMBIA	1943
C-550	I SPIED FOR YOU (sh)	WHITE	COLUMBIA	1943
C-551	THREE LITTLE TWERPS (sh)	EDWARDS	COLUMBIA	1943
C-552	BLONDE AND GROOM (sh)	EDWARDS	COLUMBIA	1943
C-553	COLLEGE BELLES (sh)	EDWARDS	COLUMBIA	1942
C-554	HERE COMES MR. ZERK (sh)	EDWARDS	COLUMBIA	1943
C-555	DIZY PILOTS (sh)	WHITE	COLUMBIA	1943
C-556	TWO SAPLINGS (sh)	EDWARDS	COLUMBIA	1943
C-558	WHAT A SOLDIER (sh) (not released)		COLUMBIA	1943
C-559	SHOT IN THE ESCAPE (sh)	WHITE	COLUMBIA	1943
C-561	HE WAS ONLY FEUDIN' (sh)	EDWARDS	COLUMBIA	1943
C-562	ROOKIE'S COOKIE (sh)	WHITE	COLUMBIA	1943
C-563	BOOBS IN THE NIGHT (sh)	LORD	COLUMBIA	1943
C-564	NO DOUGH BOYS (sh)	WHITE	COLUMBIA	1944
C-565	HUGH HERBERT (sh)		COLUMBIA	
C-566	PITCHIN' IN THE KITCHEN (sh)	WHITE	COLUMBIA	1943
C-568	HIGHER THAN A KITE (sh)	LORD	COLUMBIA	1943
C-569	PHONEY EXPRESS (sh)	LORD	COLUMBIA	1943
C-570	I CAN HARDLY WAIT (sh)	WHITE	COLUMBIA	1943
C-571	YOKE'S ON ME (sh)	WHITE	COLUMBIA	1944
C-572	TO HEIR IS HUMAN (sh)	GODSOE	COLUMBIA	1944
C-573	GARDEN OF EATIN' (sh)	EDWARDS	COLUMBIA	1943
C-574	WHO'S HUGH (sh)	EDWARDS	COLUMBIA	1943
C-575	GEM OF A JAM (sh)	LORD	COLUMBIA	1943
C-595	STOOGES (sh)		COLUMBIA	
C-600	COMMUNITY SING - SERIES 2 #3	series	COLUMBIA	1937
C-602	COMMUNITY SING - SERIES 2 #4	series	COLUMBIA	1937
C-610	COMMUNITY SING - SERIES 2 #8	series	COLUMBIA	1938
C-611	COMMUNITY SING - SERIES 2 #9	series	COLUMBIA	1938
C-614	THE LITTLE HUT	ROBSON	MGM	1957
C-615	COMMUNITY SING - SERIES 2 #10	series	COLUMBIA	1938
C-620	COMMUNITY SING - SERIES 2 #11	series	COLUMBIA	1938
C-621	COMMUNITY SING - SERIES 2 #12	series	COLUMBIA	1938
C-622	COMMUNITY SING - SERIES 3 #1	series	COLUMBIA	1938
C-623	COMMUNITY SING - SERIES 3 #2	series	COLUMBIA	1938
C-624	COMMUNITY SING - SERIES 3 #3	series	COLUMBIA	1938
C-625	COMMUNITY SING - SERIES 3 #6	series	COLUMBIA	1938
C-631	COMMUNITY SING - SERIES 3 #4	series	COLUMBIA	1939
C-632	COMMUNITY SING - SERIES 3 #5	series	COLUMBIA	1939
C-635	COMMUNITY SING - SERIES 3 #7	series	COLUMBIA	1939
C-636	COMMUNITY SING - SERIES 3 #10	series	COLUMBIA	1939
C-637	COMMUNITY SING - SERIES 3 #8	series	COLUMBIA	1939
C-638	COMMUNITY SING - SERIES 4 #2	series	COLUMBIA	1939
C-639	COMMUNITY SING - SERIES 3 #9	series	COLUMBIA	1939
C-640	COMMUNITY SING - SERIES 4 #1	series	COLUMBIA	1939
C-646	FOOLS WHO MADE HISTORY-ELIAS HOWE	series	COLUMBIA	1939
C-647	FOOLS WHO MADE HISTORY-CHARLES GOODYEAR	series	COLUMBIA	1939
C-655	COMMUNITY SING - SERIES 4 #3	series	COLUMBIA	1939
C-656	COMMUNITY SING - SERIES 4 #4	series	COLUMBIA	1939
C-683	JUNIOR QUIZ PARADE		COLUMBIA	
C-697	MR. SMUG (sh)	CASTLE	COLUMBIA	1943
C-729	CITY WITHOUT MEN	SALKOW	COLUMBIA	1943
C-735	HEAT'S ON	RATOFF	COLUMBIA	1943

C-762	CRIME DR.'S STRANGEST CASE	FORDE	COLUMBIA	1943
C-770	SECRET COMMAND	SUTHERLAND	COLUMBIA	1944
C-773	ADDRESS UNKNOWN	MENZIES	COLUMBIA	1944
C-787	WHISTLER	CASTLE	COLUMBIA	1944
C-788	TEXAS	MARSHALL	COLUMBIA	1941
C-789	SHADOWS IN THE NIGHT	FORDE	COLUMBIA	1944
C-791	EVER SINCE VENUS	DREIFUSS	COLUMBIA	1944
C-803	MARK OF THE WHISTLER	CASTLE	COLUMBIA	1944
C-808	BRENDA STARR – REPORTER (serial)	FOX	COLUMBIA	1945
C-811	RIDERS OF THE WHISTLING PINES	ENGLISH	COLUMBIA	1949
C-812	CRIME DR.'S COURAGE	SHERMAN	COLUMBIA	1945
C-813	POWER OF THE WHISTLER	LANDERS	COLUMBIA	1945
C-814	KISS AND TELL	WALLACE	COLUMBIA	1945
C-818	MONSTER AND THE APE	BRETHERTON	COLUMBIA	1945
C-822	OVER 21	VIDOR	COLUMBIA	1945
C-830	ADVENTURES OF RUSTY	BURNFORD	COLUMBIA	1945
C-834	SNAFU	MOSS	COLUMBIA	1945
C-835	JUNGLE RAIDERS - (serial)	SELANDER	COLUMBIA	1945
C-838	CRIME DR.'S WARNING	CASTLE	COLUMBIA	1945
C-841	PERILOUS HOLIDAY	GRIFFITH	COLUMBIA	1946
C-844	WHO'S GUILTY?	BRETHERTON, GRISSELL	COLUMBIA	1945
C-850	JOHNNY O'CLOCK	ROSSEN	COLUMBIA	1947
C-851	MR. DISTRICT ATTORNEY	SINCLAIR	COLUMBIA	1947
C-855	HOP HARRIGAN	ABRAHAMS	COLUMBIA	1946
C-856	TO THE ENDS OF THE EARTH	STEVENSON	COLUMBIA	1948
C-862	CHICK CARTER DETECTIVE	ABRAHAMS	COLUMBIA	1946
C-863	RETURN OF MONTE CRISTO	LEVIN	COLUMBIA	1946
C-868	SON OF THE GUARDSMAN	ABRAHAMS	COLUMBIA	1946
C-869	LAST OF THE REDMEN	SHERMAN	COLUMBIA	1947
C-873	BETTY CO-ED	DREIFUSS	COLUMBIA	1946
C-876	CORPSE CAME C.O.D.	LEVIN	COLUMBIA	1947
C-878	JACK ARMSTRONG	FOX	COLUMBIA	1947
C-879	GUNFIGHTERS	WAGGNER	COLUMBIA	1947
C-882	VIGILANTE - (serial)	FOX	COLUMBIA	1947
C-883	RELENTLESS	SHERMAN	COLUMBIA	1948
C-884	LITTLE MISS BROADWAY	DREIFUSS	COLUMBIA	1947
C-885	HER HUSBANDS AFFAIRS	SIMON	COLUMBIA	1947
C-886	SEA HOUND	EASON, WRIGHT	COLUMBIA	1947
C-887	PRINCE OF THIEVES	BRETHERTON	COLUMBIA	1948
C-888	I LOVE TROUBLE	SIMON	COLUMBIA	1948
C-889	MUSIC IN MY HEART	SANTLEY	COLUMBIA	1940
C-889	STRAWBERRY ROAN	ENGLISH	COLUMBIA	1948
C-890	SWEET GENEVIEVE	DREIFUSS	COLUMBIA	1947
C-891	TWO BLONDES AND A REDHEAD	DREIFUSS	COLUMBIA	1947
C-892	LAST ROUNDUP	ENGLISH	COLUMBIA	1947
C-893	BIG SOMBRERO	MCDONALD	COLUMBIA	1949
C-895	TEX GRANGER (serial)	ABRAHAMS	COLUMBIA	1948
C-896	SIGN OF THE RAM	STURGES	COLUMBIA	1948
C-897	BLACK ARROW	DOUGLAS	COLUMBIA	1948
C-899	BRICK BRADFORD (serial)	BENNET, CARR	COLUMBIA	1947
C-900	GREAT ADV OF WILD BILL HICKOK (serial)	NELSON, WRIGHT	COLUMBIA	1938
C-900	MARY LOU	DREIFUSS	COLUMBIA	1948
C-901	SPIDER'S WEB (SERIAL)	HORNE, TAYLOR	COLUMBIA	1938
C-902	ALL THE KING'S MEN	ROSSEN	COLUMBIA	1950
C-902	FLYING G-MEN (serial)	HORNE, TAYLOR	COLUMBIA	1939
C-903	MANDRAKE THE MAGICIAN (serial)	DEMING, NELSON	COLUMBIA	1939
C-904	OVERLAND WITH KIT CARSON	DEMING, NELSON	COLUMBIA	1939
C-905	LOADED PISTOLS	ENGLISH	COLUMBIA	1948
C-908	GLAMOUR GIRL	DREIFUSS	COLUMBIA	1948
C-908	HOWARDS OF VIRGINIA	LLOYD	COLUMBIA	1940
C-909	MANHATTAN ANGEL	DREIFUSS	COLUMBIA	1949
C-910	SUPERMAN (serial)	BENNET, CARR	COLUMBIA	1948
C-911	ADVENTURE IN WASHINGTON	GREEN	COLUMBIA	1941
C-912	I SURRENDER DEAR	DREIFUSS	COLUMBIA	1948
C-913	FULLER BRUSH MAN	SIMON	COLUMBIA	1948
C-914	RACING LUCK	BERKE	COLUMBIA	1948

C-915	LOVES OF CARMEN	VIDOR	COLUMBIA	1948
C-916	SHE KNEW ALL THE ANSWERS	WALLACE	COLUMBIA	1941
C-918	MUTINEERS	YARBROUGH	COLUMBIA	1949
C-919	LULU BELLE	FENTON	COLUMBIA	1948
C-920	UNDERCOVER MAN	LEWIS	COLUMBIA	1949
C-921	SONS OF NEW MEXICO	ENGLISH	COLUMBIA	1949
C-923	ANNA LUCASTA	RAPPER	COLUMBIA	1949
C-924	COWBOY AND THE INDIANS	ENGLISH	COLUMBIA	1949
C-926	CONGO BILL	BENNET, CARR	COLUMBIA	1948
C-927	UNTAMED BREED	LAMONT	COLUMBIA	1948
C-928	LADIES OF THE CHORUS	KARLSON	COLUMBIA	1948
C-931	ADAM HAD FOUR SONS	RATOFF	COLUMBIA	1941
C-931	KNOCK ON ANY DOOR	RAY	COLUMBIA	1949
C-932	TOKYO JOE	HEISLER	COLUMBIA	1949
C-933	TRIPLE THREAT	YARBROUGH	COLUMBIA	1948
C-934	SONG OF INDIA	ROGELL	COLUMBIA	1949
C-935	JUNGLE JIM	BERKE	COLUMBIA	1948
C-937	BRUCE GENTRY	BENNET, CARR	COLUMBIA	1949
C-939	WE WERE STRANGERS	HUSTON	COLUMBIA	1949
C-942	LOST TRIBE	BERKE	COLUMBIA	1949
C-944	ADVENTURES OF BATMAN AND ROBIN	BENNET	COLUMBIA	1949
C-945	DOOLINS OF OKLAHOMA	DOUGLAS	COLUMBIA	1949
C-946	JOLSON SINGS AGAIN	LEVIN	COLUMBIA	1949
C-947	RIM OF THE CANYON	ENGLISH	COLUMBIA	1949
C-949	LADIES IN RETIREMENT	VIDOR	COLUMBIA	1941
C-950	STATE PENITENTIARY	LANDERS	COLUMBIA	1950
C-951	BARBARY PIRATE	LANDERS	COLUMBIA	1949
C-952	COW TOWN	ENGLISH	COLUMBIA	1950
C-953	ADVENTURES OF SIR GALAHAD	BENNET	COLUMBIA	1949
C-953	MEN IN HER LIFE	RATOFF	COLUMBIA	1941
C-954	CAPTIVE GIRL	BERKE	COLUMBIA	1950
C-955	MARK OF THE GORILLA	BERKE	COLUMBIA	1950
C-956	ATOM MAN VS. SUPERMAN	BENNET	COLUMBIA	1950
C-957	CODY OF THE PONY EXPRESS	BENNET	COLUMBIA	1950
C-958	CHINATOWN AT MIDNIGHT	FRIEDMAN	COLUMBIA	1949
C-962	TYRANT OF THE SEA	LANDERS	COLUMBIA	1950
C-964	ADVENTURES OF MARTIN EDEN	SALKOW	COLUMBIA	1942
C-964	RECKLESS MOMENT	OPHULS	COLUMBIA	1949
C-965	TRAVELING SALESWOMAN	REISNER	COLUMBIA	1950
C-966	AND BABY MAKES THREE	LEVIN	COLUMBIA	1949
C-967	BLAZING SUN	ENGLISH	COLUMBIA	1950
C-968	NEVADAN	DOUGLAS	COLUMBIA	1950
C-970	IN A LONELY PLACE	RAY	COLUMBIA	1950
C-971	RIDERS IN THE SKY	ENGLISH	COLUMBIA	1949
C-975	BRAVE BULLS	ROSSON	COLUMBIA	1951
C-976	MULE TRAIN	ENGLISH	COLUMBIA	1950
C-977	BEYOND THE PURPLE HILLS	ENGLISH	COLUMBIA	1950
C-981	INDIAN TERRITORY	ENGLISH	COLUMBIA	1950
C-982	SOMETHING TO SHOUT ABOUT	RATOFF	COLUMBIA	1943
C-986	LAST OF THE BUCCANEERS	LANDERS	COLUMBIA	1950
C-988	GENE AUTRY AND THE MOUNTIES	ENGLISH	COLUMBIA	1951
C-989	REVENUE AGENT	LANDERS	COLUMBIA	1950
C-990	PIRATES OF THE HIGH SEAS	BENNET, CARR	COLUMBIA	1950
C-991	SIROCCO	BERNHARDT	COLUMBIA	1951
C-992	HURRICANE ISLAND	LANDERS	COLUMBIA	1951
C-993	CHAIN GANG	LANDERS	COLUMBIA	1950
C-994	PYGMY ISLAND	BERKE	COLUMBIA	1950
C-995	FURY OF THE CONGO	BERKE	COLUMBIA	1951
C-996	COMMANDOES STRIKE AT DAWN	FARROW	COLUMBIA	1942
C-998	SATURDAY'S HERO	MILLER	COLUMBIA	1951
C-999	FAMILY SECRET	LEVIN	COLUMBIA	1951
C-1001	FOOTLIGHT GLAMOUR	STRAYER	COLUMBIA	1943
C-1002	IS EVERYBODY HAPPY?	BARTON	COLUMBIA	1943
C-1004	WHAT A WOMAN	CUMMINGS	COLUMBIA	1943
C-1005	NINE GIRLS	JASON	COLUMBIA	1944
C-1006	NONE SHALL ESCAPE	DE TOTH	COLUMBIA	1944

C-1007	VAMPIRE IN BROOKLYN	CRAVEN	PARAMOUNT	1985
C-1009	RACKET MAN	LEDERMAN	COLUMBIA	1944
C-1010	RETURN OF THE VAMPIRE	LANDERS	COLUMBIA	1944
C-1011	SONG TO REMEMBER	VIDOR	COLUMBIA	1945
C-1012	CHANCE OF A LIFETIME	CASTLE	COLUMBIA	1943
C-1014	MR. WINKLE GOES TO WAR	GREEN	COLUMBIA	1944
C-1015	KLONDIKE KATE	CASTLE	COLUMBIA	1943
C-1016	SWING OUT OF THE BLUES	ST. CLAIR	COLUMBIA	1943
C-1017	BEAUTIFUL BUT BROKE	BARTON	COLUMBIA	1944
C-1019	GHOST THAT WALKS ALONE	LANDERS	COLUMBIA	1944
C-1021	GIRL IN THE CASE	BERKE	COLUMBIA	1944
C-1022	TONIGHT AND EVERY NIGHT	SAVILLE	COLUMBIA	1945
C-1023	SAILOR'S HOLIDAY	BERKE	COLUMBIA	1944
C-1024	TOGETHER AGAIN	VIDOR	COLUMBIA	1944
C-1025	TWO MAN SUBMARINE	LANDERS	COLUMBIA	1944
C-1026	CAROLINA BLUES	JASON	COLUMBIA	1944
C-1027	STARS ON PARADE	LANDERS	COLUMBIA	1944
C-1028	BLACK PARACHUTE	LANDERS	COLUMBIA	1944
C-1029	SHE'S A SOLDIER TOO	CASTLE	COLUMBIA	1944
C-1030	JOLSON STORY (some marked 1130)	GREEN	COLUMBIA	1946
C-1031	COUNTER-ATTACK	KORDA	COLUMBIA	1945
C-1032	THEY LIVE IN FEAR	BERNE	COLUMBIA	1944
C-1033	U-BOAT PRISONER	LANDERS	COLUMBIA	1944
C-1035	LOUISIANA HAYRIDE	BARTON	COLUMBIA	1944
C-1036	IMPATIENT YEARS	CUMMINGS	COLUMBIA	1944
C-1037	CRY OF THE WEREWOLF	LEVIN	COLUMBIA	1944
C-1038	UNWRITTEN CODE	ROTSTEN	COLUMBIA	1944
C-1039	EVE KNEW HER APPLES	JASON	COLUMBIA	1945
C-1040	KANSAS CITY KITTY	LORD	COLUMBIA	1944
C-1042	MEET MISS BOBBY SOCKS	TRYON	COLUMBIA	1944
C-1043	STRANGE AFFAIR	GREEN	COLUMBIA	1944
C-1044	SOUL OF A MONSTER	JASON	COLUMBIA	1944
C-1045	ONE MYSTERIOUS NIGHT	BOETTICHER	COLUMBIA	1944
C-1046	SERGEANT MIKE	LEVIN	COLUMBIA	1944
C-1047	MISSING JUROR	BOETTICHER	COLUMBIA	1944
C-1048	ESCAPE IN THE FOG	BOETTICHER	COLUMBIA	1945
C-1049	SHE'S A SWEETHEART	LORD	COLUMBIA	1944
C-1050	TARS AND SPARS	GREEN	COLUMBIA	1946
C-1051	EADIE WAS A LADY	DREIFUSS	COLUMBIA	1945
C-1052	DANCING IN MANHATTAN	LEVIN	COLUMBIA	1944
C-1054	THOUSAND AND ONE NIGHTS	GREEN	COLUMBIA	1945
C-1055	TAHITI NIGHTS	JASON	COLUMBIA	1944
C-1056	LEAVE IT TO BLONDIE	BERLIN	COLUMBIA	1945
C-1057	LET'S GO STEADY	LORD	COLUMBIA	1945
C-1058	I LOVE A MYSTERY	LEVIN	COLUMBIA	1945
C-1059	YOUTH ON TRIAL	BOETTICHER	COLUMBIA	1945
C-1060	SHE WOULDN'T SAY YES	HALL	COLUMBIA	1945
C-1061	MEET ME ON BROADWAY	JASON	COLUMBIA	1946
C-1062	GUY, A GAL AND A PAL	BOETTICHER	COLUMBIA	1945
C-1063	ROUGH TOUGH AND READY	LORD	COLUMBIA	1945
C-1064	FIGHTING GUARDSMAN	LEVIN	COLUMBIA	1946
C-1066	TEN CENTS A DANCE	JASON	COLUMBIA	1945
C-1069	BOSTON BLACKIE HOOKED ON SUSPICION	DREIFUSS	COLUMBIA	1945
C-1070	BLONDE FROM BROOKLYN	LORD	COLUMBIA	1945
C-1071	GAY SENORITA	DREIFUSS	COLUMBIA	1945
C-1072	BOSTON BLACKIE'S RENDEZVOUS	DREIFUSS	COLUMBIA	1945
C-1074	BANDIT OF SHERWOOD FOREST	LEVIN, SHERMAN	COLUMBIA	1946
C-1075	I LOVE A BANDLEADER	LORD	COLUMBIA	1945
C-1076	VOICE OF THE WHISTLER	CASTLE	COLUMBIA	1945
C-1078	GIRL OF THE LIMBERLOST	FERRER	COLUMBIA	1945
C-1079	RENEGADES	SHERMAN	COLUMBIA	1946
C-1080	ONE WAY TO LOVE	ENRIGHT	COLUMBIA	1946
C-1081	HIT THE HAY	LORD	COLUMBIA	1945
C-1082	MY NAME IS JULIA ROSS	LEWIS	COLUMBIA	1945
C-1083	OUT OF THE DEPTHS	LEDERMAN	COLUMBIA	1945
C-1084	LIFE WITH BLONDIE	BERLIN	COLUMBIA	1945

C-1086	PRISON SHIP	DREIFUSS	COLUMBIA	1945
C-1087	GILDA	VIDOR	COLUMBIA	1946
C-1088	BLONDIE'S LUCKY DAY	BERLIN	COLUMBIA	1946
C-1089	CLOSE CALL FOR BOSTON BLACKIE	LANDERS	COLUMBIA	1946
C-1090	SO DARK THE NIGHT	LEWIS	COLUMBIA	1946
C-1091	NOTORIOUS LONE WOLF	LEDERMAN	COLUMBIA	1946
C-1092	GENTLEMEN MISBEHAVES	SHERMAN	COLUMBIA	1946
C-1093	JUST BEFORE DAWN	CASTLE	COLUMBIA	1946
C-1094	WALLS CAME TUMBLING DOWN	MENDES	COLUMBIA	1946
C-1095	DEVIL'S MASK	LEVIN	COLUMBIA	1946
C-1096	DANGEROUS BUSINESS	LEDERMAN	COLUMBIA	1946
C-1097	TALK ABOUT A LADY	SHERMAN	COLUMBIA	1946
C-1098	MYSTERIOUS INTRUDER	CASTLE	COLUMBIA	1946
C-1099	NIGHT EDITOR	LEVIN	COLUMBIA	1946
C-1100	DOWN TO EARTH	HALL	COLUMBIA	1947
C-1101	PHANTOM THIEF	LEDERMAN	COLUMBIA	1946
C-1102	MAN WHO DARED	STURGES	COLUMBIA	1946
C-1103	GALLANT JOURNEY	WELLMAN	COLUMBIA	1946
C-1104	THRILL OF BRAZIL	SIMON	COLUMBIA	1946
C-1105	RETURN OF RUSTY	CASTLE	COLUMBIA	1946
C-1106	UNKNOWN	LEVIN	COLUMBIA	1946
C-1107	BLONDIE KNOWS BEST	BERLIN	COLUMBIA	1946
C-1108	SING WHILE YOU DANCE	LEDERMAN	COLUMBIA	1946
C-1109	PERSONALITY KID	SHERMAN	COLUMBIA	1946
C-1110	CRIME DR.'S MANHUNT	CASTLE	COLUMBIA	1946
C-1111	DEAD RECKONING	CROMWELL	COLUMBIA	1947
C-1112	IT'S GREAT TO BE YOUNG	LORD	COLUMBIA	1946
C-1113	FRAMED	WALLACE	COLUMBIA	1947
C-1114	SECRET OF THE WHISTLER	SHERMAN	COLUMBIA	1946
C-1115	GUILT OF JANET AMES	LEVIN	COLUMBIA	1947
C-1116	SHADOWED	STURGES	COLUMBIA	1946
C-1117	SWORDSMAN	LEWIS	COLUMBIA	1948
C-1118	SINGING IN THE CORN	LORD	COLUMBIA	1946
C-1119	BLONDIE'S BIG MOMENT	BERLIN	COLUMBIA	1947
C-1120	BOSTON BLACKIE AND THE LAW	LEDERMAN	COLUMBIA	1946
C-1121	RETURN OF OCTOBER	LEWIS	COLUMBIA	1948
C-1122	LONE WOLF IN MEXICO	LEDERMAN	COLUMBIA	1947
C-1123	ALIAS MR. TWILIGHT	STURGES	COLUMBIA	1946
C-1124	BLIND SPOT	GORDON	COLUMBIA	1947
C-1125	MILLIE'S DAUGHTER	SALKOW	COLUMBIA	1947
C-1126	LADY FROM SHANGHAI		COLUMBIA	1947
C-1127	CIGARETTE GIRL	VON FRITSCH	COLUMBIA	1947
C-1128	THIRTEENTH HOUR	CLEMENS	COLUMBIA	1947
C-1129	KING OF THE WILD HORSES	ARCHAINBAUD	COLUMBIA	1947
C-1130	BLONDIE'S HOLIDAY	BERLIN	COLUMBIA	1947
C-1130	JOLSON STORY (some marked 1030)	GREEN	COLUMBIA	1946
C-1131	MILLERSON CASE	ARCHAINBAUD	COLUMBIA	1947
C-1132	BULLDOG DRUMMOND AT BAY	SALKOW	COLUMBIA	1947
C-1133	FOR THE LOVE OF RUSTY	STURGES	COLUMBIA	1947
C-1135	MAN FROM COLORADO	LEVIN	COLUMBIA	1948
C-1136	BLONDIE IN THE DOUGH	BERLIN	COLUMBIA	1947
C-1137	SPORT OF KINGS	GORDON	COLUMBIA	1947
C-1138	IT HAD TO BE YOU	HARTMAN, MATE	COLUMBIA	1947
C-1139	KEEPER OF THE BEES	STURGES	COLUMBIA	1947
C-1140	SON OF RUSTY	LANDERS	COLUMBIA	1947
C-1141	KEY WITNESS	LEDERMAN	COLUMBIA	1947
C-1142	BULLDOG DRUMMOND STRIKES AGAIN	MCDONALD	COLUMBIA	1947
C-1143	MATING OF MILLIE	LEVIN	COLUMBIA	1948
C-1144	WHEN A GIRL'S BEAUTIFUL	MCDONALD	COLUMBIA	1947
C-1145	SLIGHTLY FRENCH	SIRK	COLUMBIA	1949
C-1146	LONE WOLF IN LONDON	GOODWINS	COLUMBIA	1947
C-1148	CRIME DR.'S GAMBLE	CASTLE	COLUMBIA	1947
C-1149	DEVIL SHIP	LANDERS	COLUMBIA	1947
C-1152	ADVENTURES IN SILVERADO	KARLSON	COLUMBIA	1948
C-1153	WRECK OF THE HESPERUS	HOFFMAN	COLUMBIA	1948
C-1154	PORT SAID	LE BORG	COLUMBIA	1948

C-1155	BLONDIE'S REWARD	BERLIN	COLUMBIA	1948
C-1156	BLONDIE'S ANNIVERSARY	BERLIN	COLUMBIA	1947
C-1157	WOMAN FROM TANGIER	DANIELS	COLUMBIA	1948
C-1159	RETURN OF THE WHISTLER	LEDERMAN	COLUMBIA	1948
C-1160	GALLANT BLADE	LEVIN	COLUMBIA	1948
C-1161	MY DOG RUSTY	LANDERS	COLUMBIA	1948
C-1162	BEST MAN WINS	STURGES	COLUMBIA	1948
C-1163	TRAPPED BY BOSTON BLACKIE	FRIEDMAN	COLUMBIA	1948
C-1164	THUNDERHOOF	KARLSON	COLUMBIA	1948
C-1165	LEATHER GLOVES	ASHER, QUINIE	COLUMBIA	1948
C-1166	RUSTY LEADS THE WAY	JASON	COLUMBIA	1948
C-1167	WALKING HILLS	STURGES	COLUMBIA	1949
C-1168	DARK PAST	MATE	COLUMBIA	1948
C-1169	BLACK EAGLE	GORDON	COLUMBIA	1948
C-1170	GENTLEMEN FROM NOWHERE	CASTLE	COLUMBIA	1948
C-1171	RUSTY SAVES A LIFE	FRIEDMAN	COLUMBIA	1949
C-1172	BLONDIE'S SECRET	BERNDS	COLUMBIA	1948
C-1173	BOSTON BLACKIE'S CHINESE VENTURE	FRIEDMAN	COLUMBIA	1949
C-1174	SHOCKPROOF	SIRK	COLUMBIA	1949
C-1175	MR. SOFT TOUCH	DOUGLAS, LEVIN	COLUMBIA	1949
C-1176	HOLIDAY IN HAVANA	YARBROUGH	COLUMBIA	1949
C-1177	LAW OF THE BARBARY COAST	LANDERS	COLUMBIA	1949
C-1178	LONE WOLF AND HIS LADY	HOFFMAN	COLUMBIA	1949
C-1179	CRIME DR.'S DIARY	FRIEDMAN	COLUMBIA	1949
C-1180	BLONDIE'S BIG DEAL	BERNDS	COLUMBIA	1949
C-1181	AIR HOSTESS	LANDERS	COLUMBIA	1949
C-1182	MAKE BELIEVE BALLROOM	SANTLEY	COLUMBIA	1949
C-1183	LUST FOR GOLD	SIMON	COLUMBIA	1949
C-1185	BLONDIE HITS THE JACKPOT	BERNDS	COLUMBIA	1949
C-1186	DEVIL'S HENCHMEN	FRIEDMAN	COLUMBIA	1949
C-1187	JOHNNY ALLEGRO	TETZLAFF	COLUMBIA	1949
C-1188	SECRET OF ST. IVES	ROSEN	COLUMBIA	1949
C-1189	KAZAN	JASON	COLUMBIA	1949
C-1190	RUSTY'S BIRTHDAY	FRIEDMAN	COLUMBIA	1949
C-1191	MISS GRANT TAKES RICHMOND	BACON	COLUMBIA	1949
C-1192	TELL IT TO THE JUDGE	FOSTER	COLUMBIA	1949
C-1193	PALOMINO	NAZARRO	COLUMBIA	1950
C-1194	PRISON WARDEN	FRIEDMAN	COLUMBIA	1949
C-1195	BLONDIE'S HERO	BERNDS	COLUMBIA	1950
C-1196	GOOD HUMOR MAN	BACON	COLUMBIA	1950
C-1197	BORN YESTERDAY	CUKOR	COLUMBIA	1950
C-1198	CARGO TO CAPETOWN	MCEVOY	COLUMBIA	1950
C-1199	MARY RYAN, DETECTIVE	BERLIN	COLUMBIA	1949
C-1200	GIRL'S SCHOOL	BRAHM	COLUMBIA	1938
C-1201	ROGUES OF SHERWOOD FOREST	DOUGLAS	COLUMBIA	1950
C-1202	WOMAN OF DISTINCTION	BUZZELL	COLUMBIA	1950
C-1204	FATHER IS A BACHELOR	BERLIN, FOSTER	COLUMBIA	1950
C-1205	BODYHOLD	FRIEDMAN	COLUMBIA	1949
C-1206	FORTUNES OF CAPTAIN BLOOD	DOUGLAS	COLUMBIA	1950
C-1207	PETTY GIRL	LEVIN	COLUMBIA	1950
C-1208	BEWARE OF BLONDIE	BERNDS	COLUMBIA	1950
C-1209	KILL THE UMPIRE	BACON	COLUMBIA	1950
C-1210	MILITARY ACADEMY	LEDERMAN	COLUMBIA	1940
C-1211	FULLER BRUSH GIRL	BACON	COLUMBIA	1950
C-1212	FRIGHTENED CITY	MCEVOY	COLUMBIA	1950
C-1213	BEAUTY ON PARADE	LANDERS	COLUMBIA	1950
C-1214	NO SAD SONGS FOR ME	MATE	COLUMBIA	1950
C-1215	CUSTOMS AGENT	FREIDMAN	COLUMBIA	1950
C-1218	WHEN YOU'RE SMILING	SANTLEY	COLUMBIA	1950
C-1219	CONVICTED	LEVIN	COLUMBIA	1950
C-1220	ROOKIE FIREMAN	FRIEDMAN	COLUMBIA	1950
C-1221	DAVID HARDING – COUNTER SPY	NAZARRO	COLUMBIA	1950
C-1222	BETWEEN MIDNIGHT AND DAWN	DOUGLAS	COLUMBIA	1950
C-1223	HE'S A COCKEYED WONDER	GODFREY	COLUMBIA	1950
C-1224	HARRIET CRAIG	SHERMAN	COLUMBIA	1950
C-1225	ON THE ISLE OF SOMOA	BERKE	COLUMBIA	1950

C-1226	TWO OF A KIND	LEVIN	COLUMBIA	1951
C-1228	STAGE TO TUCSON	MURPHY	COLUMBIA	1950
C-1230	EMERGENCY WEDDING	BUZZELL	COLUMBIA	1950
C-1231	AL JENNINGS OF OKLAHOMA	NAZARRO	COLUMBIA	1951
C-1232	FLYING MISSING	LEVIN	COLUMBIA	1950
C-1233	MASK OF THE AVENGER	KARLSON	COLUMBIA	1951
C-1234	COUNTERSPY MEETS SCOTLAND YARD	FRIEDMAN	COLUMBIA	1950
C-1235	HER FIRST ROMANCE	FRIEDMAN	COLUMBIA	1951
C-1237	TOUGHER THEY COME	NAZARRO	COLUMBIA	1950
C-1238	FLAME OF STAMBOUL	NAZARRO	COLUMBIA	1951
C-1239	LADY AND THE BANDIT	MURPHY	COLUMBIA	1951
C-1240	GASOLINE ALLEY	BERNDS	COLUMBIA	1951
C-1241	BAREFOOT MAILMAN	MCEVOY	COLUMBIA	1951
C-1242	SUNNY SIDE OF THE STREET	QUINE	COLUMBIA	1951
C-1243	NEVER TRUST A GAMBLER	MURPHY	COLUMBIA	1951
C-1244	SMUGGLERS GOLD	BERKE	COLUMBIA	1951
C-1245	MOB	PARRISH	COLUMBIA	1951
C-1246	CRIMINAL LAWYER	FRIEDMAN	COLUMBIA	1951
C-1248	PAULA	MATE	COLUMBIA	1952
C-1249	MY TRUE STORY	ROONEY	COLUMBIA	1951
C-1250	CHINA CORSAIR	NAZARRO	COLUMBIA	1951
C-1251	BIG GUSHER	LANDERS	COLUMBIA	1951
C-1252	SON OF DR. JEKYL	FRIEDMAN	COLUMBIA	1951
C-1253	ASSIGNMENT-PARIS	PARRISH	COLUMBIA	1952
C-1254	CHAIN OF CIRCUMSTANCES	JASON	COLUMBIA	1951
C-1255	CORKY OF GASOLINE ALLEY	BERNDS	COLUMBIA	1951
C-1256	SOUND OFF	QUINE	COLUMBIA	1952
C-1257	CAPT. PIRATE	MURPHY	COLUMBIA	1952
C-1258	MARRYING KIND	CUKOR	COLUMBIA	1952
C-1259	OKINAWA	JASON	COLUMBIA	1952
C-1260	MONTANA TERRITORY	NAZARRO	COLUMBIA	1952
C-1261	HAREM GIRL	BERNDS	COLUMBIA	1952
C-1263	LAST OF THE COMMANCHES	DE TOTH	COLUMBIA	1953
C-1264	RAINBOW 'ROUND MY SHOULDER	QUINE	COLUMBIA	1952
C-1265	TARGET HONG KONG	SEARS	COLUMBIA	1953
C-1266	ALL ASHORE	QUINE	COLUMBIA	1953
C-1267	AMBUSH AT TOMAHAWK GAP	SEARS	COLUMBIA	1953
C-1268	LET'S DO IT AGAIN	HALL	COLUMBIA	1953
C-1269	MISSION OVER KOREA	SEARS	COLUMBIA	1953
C-1270	LAST POSSE	WERKER	COLUMBIA	1953
C-1271	FROM HERE TO ETERNITY	ZINNEMANN	COLUMBIA	1953
C-1272	CRUISIN' DOWN THE RIVER	QUINE	COLUMBIA	1953
C-1273	EL ALAMEIN (GER: THAT WAS OUR ROMMEL)	WIGANKO	COLUMBIA	1953
C-1274	CHINA VENTURE	SIEGEL	COLUMBIA	1953
C-1276	BIG HEAT	LANG	COLUMBIA	1953
C-1278	GUN FURY	WALSH	COLUMBIA	1953
C-1280	MAN IN THE DARK	LANDERS	COLUMBIA	1953
C-1281	HUMAN DESIRE	LANG	COLUMBIA	1954
C-1283	NEBRASKAN	SEARS	COLUMBIA	1953
C-1284	BAD FOR EACH OTHER	RAPPER	COLUMBIA	1953
C-1285	IT SHOULD HAPPEN TO YOU	CUKOR	COLUMBIA	1954
C-1287	THREE FOR THE SHOW	POTTER	COLUMBIA	1955
C-1288	MASSACRE CANYON	SEARS	COLUMBIA	1954
C-1289	DRIVE A CROOKED MILE	QUINE	COLUMBIA	1954
C-1290	THEY RODE WEST	KARLSON	COLUMBIA	1954
C-1291	PUSHOVER	QUINE	COLUMBIA	1954
C-1292	OUTLAW STALLION	SEARS	COLUMBIA	1954
C-1293	THREE HOUSE TO FILL	WERKER	COLUMBIA	1954
C-1295	BLACK DAKOTAS	NAZARRO	COLUMBIA	1954
C-1296	VIOLENT MEN	MATE	COLUMBIA	1955
C-1298	PHFFT	ROBSON	COLUMBIA	1954
C-1299	WYOMING RENEGADES	SEARS	COLUMBIA	1954
C-1300	TIGHT SPOT	KARLSON	COLUMBIA	1955
C-1301	MY SISTER EILEEN	QUINE	COLUMBIA	1955
C-1302	CELL 2455-DEATH ROW	SEARS	COLUMBIA	1955
C-1303	THREE STRIPES IN THE SUN	MURPHY	COLUMBIA	1955

C-1305	BRING YOUR SMILE ALONG	EDWARDS	COLUMBIA	1955
C-1306	LAST FRONTIER	MANN	COLUMBIA	1955
C-1307	APACHE AMBUSH	SEARS	COLUMBIA	1955
C-1308	QUEEN BEE	MACDOUGALL	COLUMBIA	1955
C-1309	PICNIC	LOGAN	COLUMBIA	1955
C-1310	JUBAL	DAVES	COLUMBIA	1956
C-1311	EDDIE DUCHIN STORY	SIDNEY	COLUMBIA	1956
C-1313	FURY AT GUNSIGHT PASS	SEARS	COLUMBIA	1956
C-1314	YOU CAN'T RUN AWAY FROM IT	POWELL	COLUMBIA	1956
C-1315	HARDER THEY FALL	ROBSON	COLUMBIA	1956
C-1316	SECRET OF TREASURE MOUNTAIN	FRIEDMAN	COLUMBIA	1956
C-1318	SOLID GOLD CADILLAC	QUINE	COLUMBIA	1956
C-1319	OVER-EXPOSED	SEILER	COLUMBIA	1956
C-1320	HE LAUGHED LAST	EDWARDS	COLUMBIA	1956
C-1322	FULL OF LIFE	QUINE	COLUMBIA	1956
C-1323	SHADOW ON THE WINDOW	ASHER	COLUMBIA	1957
C-1329	GUNMAN'S WALK	KARLSON	COLUMBIA	1958
C-1332	GUNMEN FROM LAREDO	MACDONALD	COLUMBIA	1959
C-1334	GIDGET	WENDKOS	COLUMBIA	1959
C-1400	PIRATE	MINNELLI	MGM	1948
C-1401	HUCKSTERS	CONWAY	MGM	1947
C-1402	SONG OF THE THIN MAN	BUZZELL	MGM	1947
C-1403	CASS TIMBERLANE	SIDNEY	MGM	1948
C-1404	GOOD NEWS	WALTERS	MGM	1947
C-1405	ALIAS A GENTLEMAN	BEAUMONT	MGM	1948
C-1406	KISSING BANDIT	BENEDEK	MGM	1949
C-1407	IF WINTER COMES	SAVILLE	MGM	1948
C-1408	KILLER MCCOY	ROWLAND	MGM	1948
C-1409	HIGH WALL	BERNHARDT	MGM	1948
C-1410	BRIDGE GOES WILD	TAUROG	MGM	1948
C-1411	ON AN ISLAND WITH YOU	THORPE	MGM	1948
C-1412	LUXURY LINER	WHORF	MGM	1948
C-1413	HOMECOMING	LEROY	MGM	1948
C-1414	STATE OF THE UNION	CAPRA	MGM	1948
C-1415	HILLS OF HOME	WILCOX	MGM	1948
C-1416	B.F.'S DAUGHTER	LEONARD	MGM	1948
C-1417	BIG CITY	TAUROG	MGM	1948
C-1418	EASTER PARADE	WALTERS	MGM	1948
C-1419	DATE WITH JUDY	THORPE	MGM	1948
C-1420	THREE MUSKETEERS	SIDNEY	MGM	1948
C-1421	SECRET LAND	NARRATED DOCUMENTARY	MGM	1948
C-1422	JULIA MISBEHAVES	CONWAY	MGM	1948
C-1423	SOUTHERN YANKEE	SEDGWICK	MGM	1948
C-1424	STRATTON STORY	WOOD	MGM	1949
C-1425	COMMAND DECISION	WOOD	MGM	1948
C-1426	SUN COMES UP	THORPE	MGM	1949
C-1427	WORDS AND MUSIC	TAUROG	MGM	1949
C-1428	ACT OF VIOLENCE	ZINNEMANN	MGM	1949
C-1429	NEPTUNE'S DAUGHTER	BUZZELL	MGM	1949
C-1430	LITTLE WOMEN	LEROY	MGM	1949
C-1431	BRIBE	LEONARD	MGM	1949
C-1432	TAKE ME OUT TO THE BALL GAME	BERKELEY	MGM	1949
C-1433	BARKLEYS OF BROADWAY	WALTERS	MGM	1949
C-1435	SECRET GARDEN	WILCOX	MGM	1949
C-1436	BIG JACK	THORPE	MGM	1949
C-1437	GREAT SINNER	SIODMAK	MGM	1949
C-1438	THAT FORSYTE WOMAN	BENNETT	MGM	1950
C-1439	RED DANUBE	SIDNEY	MGM	1950
C-1440	IN THE GOOD OLD SUMMERTIME	LEONARD	MGM	1949
C-1441	MADAME BOVARY	MINNELLI	MGM	1949
C-1442	CHALLENGE TO LASSIE	THORPE	MGM	1950
C-1443	THAT MIDNIGHT KISS	TAUROG	MGM	1949
C-1444	ANY NUMBER CAN PLAY	LEROY	MGM	1949
C-1445	EDWARD, MY SON (UK)	CUKOR	MGM	1949
C-1446	CONSPIRATOR (UK)	SAVILLE	MGM	1950
C-1447	SCENE OF THE CRIME	ROWLAND	MGM	1949

C-1448	BORDER INCIDENT	MANN	MGM	1949
C-1449	MALAYA	THORPE	MGM	1950
C-1450	ANNIE GET YOUR GUN	SIDNEY	MGM	1950
C-1451	INTRUDER IN THE DUST	BROWN	MGM	1949
C-1452	BATTLEGROUND	WELLMAN	MGM	1949
C-1453	ON THE TOWN	DONEN, KELLY	MGM	1949
C-1454	SIDE STREET	MANN	MGM	1950
C-1455	SHADOW ON THE WALL	JACKSON	MGM	1950
C-1456	DOCTOR AND THE GIRL	BERNHARDT	MGM	1949
C-1457	ADAM'S RIB	CUKOR	MGM	1950
C-1458	TENSION	BERRY	MGM	1950
C-1459	STARS IN MY CROWN	TOURNEUR	MGM	1950
C-1460	AMBUSH	WOOD	MGM	1950
C-1461	NANCY GOES TO RIO	LEONARD	MGM	1950
C-1462	PLEASE BELIEVE ME	TAUROG	MGM	1950
C-1463	KEY TO THE CITY	SIDNEY	MGM	1950
C-1464	EAST SIDE, WEST SIDE	LEROY	MGM	1949
C-1466	BLACK HAND	THORPE	MGM	1950
C-1467	KING SOLOMON'S MINES	BENNETT	MGM	1950
C-1468	DEVIL'S DOORWAY	MANN	MGM	1950
C-1469	OUTRIDERS	ROWLAND	MGM	1950
C-1470	BIG HANGOVER	KRASNA	MGM	1950
C-1471	YELLOW CAB MAN	DONOHUE	MGM	1950
C-1472	MINIVER STORY	POTTER	MGM	1950
C-1473	HAPPY YEARS	WELLMAN	MGM	1950
C-1474	REFORMER AND THE REDHEAD	FRANK, PANAMA	MGM	1950
C-1475	DUCHESS OF IDAHO	LEONARD	MGM	1950
C-1476	KIM	SAVILLE	MGM	1951
C-1477	SUMMER STOCK	WALTERS	MGM	1950
C-1478	LADY WITHOUT A PASSPORT	LEWIS	MGM	1950
C-1479	ASPHAULT JUNGLE	HUSTON	MGM	1950
C-1480	SKIPPER SURPRISED HIS WIFE	NUGENT	MGM	1950
C-1481	MYSTERY STREET	STURGES	MGM	1950
C-1482	THREE LITTLE WORDS	THORPE	MGM	1950
C-1483	TOAST OF NEW ORLEANS	TAUROG	MGM	1950
C-1484	FATHER OF THE BRIDE	MINNELLI	MGM	1950
C-1485	LIFE OF HER OWN	CUKOR	MGM	1950
C-1486	CRISIS	BROOKS	MGM	1950
C-1487	RIGHT CROSS	STURGES	MGM	1950
C-1488	NEXT VOICE YOU HEAR	WELLMAN	MGM	1950
C-1489	PAGAN LOVE SONG	ALTON	MGM	1950
C-1490	DIAL 1119	MAYER	MGM	1950
C-1491	TWO WEEKS WITH LOVE (TENDER HOURS*)	ROWLAND	MGM	1950
C-1492	TO PLEASE A LADY	BROWN	MGM	1950
C-1494	CAUSE FOR ALARM	GARNETT	MGM	1951
C-1495	GROUNDS FOR MARRIAGE	LEONARD	MGM	1951
C-1496	VENGEANCE VALLEY	THORPE	MGM	1951
C-1497	WATCH THE BIRDIE	DONOHUE	MGM	1951
C-1498	IT'S A BIG COUNTRY - INTERRUPTIONS	series	MGM	1952
C-1499	IT'S A BIG COUNTRY - CENSUS TAKER	series	MGM	1952
C-1500	IT'S A BIG COUNTRY - FOUR EYES	series	MGM	1952
C-1501	IT'S A BIG COUNTRY - ROSIKA	series	MGM	1952
C-1502	ROYAL WEDDING	DONEN	MGM	1951
C-1503	MRS. O'MALLEY AND MR. MALONE	TAUROG	MGM	1951
C-1504	PAINTED HILLS	KRESS	MGM	1951
C-1505	IT'S A BIG COUNTRY - LOAD	series	MGM	1952
C-1506	MAGNIFICENT YANKEE	STURGES	MGM	1950
C-1507	AMERICAN IN PARIS	MINNELLI	MGM	1951
C-1508	ACROSS THE WIDE MISSOURI	WELLMAN	MGM	1951
C-1509	THREE GUYS NAMED MIKE	WALTERS	MGM	1951
C-1510	SHOWBOAT	SIDNEY	MGM	1951
C-1511	MR. IMPERIUM	HARTMAN	MGM	1951
C-1512	RED BADGE OF COURAGE	HUSTON	MGM	1951
C-1513	CALLING BULLDOG DRUMMOND	SAVILLE	MGM	1951
C-1514	GREAT CARUSO	THORPE	MGM	1951
C-1515	IT'S A BIG COUNTRY - TEXAS	series	MGM	1951

C-1516	GO FOR BROKE	PIROSH	MGM	1951
C-1517	SOLDIERS THREE	GARNETT	MGM	1951
C-1518	EXCUSE MY DUST	ROWLAND	MGM	1951
C-1519	FATHER'S LITTLE DIVIDEND	MINNELLI	MGM	1951
C-1520	SHOW BOAT	SIDNEY	MGM	1951
C-1521	KIND LADY	STURGES	MGM	1951
C-1522	RICH, YOUNG AND PRETTY	TAUROG	MGM	1951
C-1523	NIGHT INTO MORNING	MARKEL	MGM	1951
C-1524	LOVE IS BETTER THAN EVER	DONEN	MGM	1952
C-1525	IT'S A BIG COUNTRY - LETTER FROM KOREA	series	MGM	1952
C-1526	NO QUESTIONS ASKED	KRESS	MGM	1951
C-1527	TALL TARGET	MANN	MGM	1951
C-1528	STRIP	KARDOS	MGM	1951
C-1529	UNKNOWN MAN	THORPE	MGM	1951
C-1530	STRICTLY DISHONORABLE	FRANK, PANAMA	MGM	1951
C-1531	LAW AND THE LADY	KNOPF	MGM	1951
C-1532	TEXAS CARNIVAL	WALTERS	MGM	1951
C-1533	SCARAMOUCHE	SIDNEY	MGM	1952
C-1534	PEOPLE AGAINST O'HARA	STURGES	MGM	1951
C-1535	WILD NORTH	MARTON	MGM	1952
C-1536	WESTWARD THE WOMEN	WELLMAN	MGM	1951
C-1537	ANGELS IN THE OUTFIELD	BROWN	MGM	1951
C-1538	SHADOW IN THE SKY	WILCOX	MGM	1952
C-1539	BANNERLINE	WEIS	MGM	1951
C-1540	LIGHT TOUCH	BROOKS	MGM	1952
C-1541	TOO YOUNG TO KISS	LEONARD	MGM	1951
C-1542	CALLAWAY WENT THATAWAY	FRANK, PANAMA	MGM	1952
C-1544	MAN WITH A CLOAK	MARKLE	MGM	1951
C-1545	BELLE OF NEW YORK	WALTERS	MGM	1952
C-1546	SINGIN' IN THE RAIN	DONEN, KELLY	MGM	1952
C-1547	LONE STAR	SHERMAN	MGM	1952
C-1548	WHEN IN ROME	BROWN	MGM	1952
C-1549	IVANHOE (UK)	THORPE	MGM	1952
C-1550	JUST THIS ONCE	WEIS	MGM	1952
C-1551	SELLOUT	MAYER	MGM	1952
C-1552	PLYMOUTH ADVENTURE	BROWN	MGM	1952
C-1553	BECAUSE YOU'RE MINE	HALL	MGM	1952
C-1554	TALK ABOUT A STRANGER	BRADLEY	MGM	1952
C-1555	LOVELY TO LOOK AT	LEROY	MGM	1952
C-1557	MERRY WIDOW	BERNHARDT	MGM	1952
C-1558	INVITATION	REINHARDT	MGM	1952
C-1559	YOUNG MAN WITH IDEAS	LEISEN	MGM	1952
C-1560	HOUR OF 13	FRENCH	MGM	1952
C-1561	GIRL IN WHITE	STURGES	MGM	1952
C-1564	GLORY ALLEY	WALSH	MGM	1952
C-1565	CARBINE WILLIAMS	THORPE	MGM	1952
C-1566	PAT AND MIKE	CUKOR	MGM	1952
C-1567	MILLION DOLLAR MERMAID	LEROY	MGM	1952
C-1568	WASHINGTON STORY	PIROSH	MGM	1952
C-1569	DEVIL MAKES THREE	MARTON	MGM	1952
C-1570	HOLIDAY FOR SINNERS	MAYER	MGM	1952
C-1572	STORY OF THREE LOVES - MADEMOISELLE	MINNELLI, REINHARDT	MGM	1953
C-1573	FEARLESS FAGAN	DONEN	MGM	1952
C-1574	ABOVE AND BEYOND	FRANK, PANAMA	MGM	1953
C-1575	LILI	WALTERS	MGM	1953
C-1576	EVERYTHING I HAVE IS YOURS	LEONARD	MGM	1952
C-1577	STORY OF THREE LOVES (mistake 1571)	MINNELLI, REINHARDT	MGM	1953
C-1578	MY MAN AND I	WELLMAN	MGM	1952
C-1579	PRISONER OF ZENDA	THORPE	MGM	1952
C-1580	YOU FOR ME	WEIS	MGM	1952
C-1581	BAD AND THE BEAUTIFUL	MINNELLI	MGM	1952
C-1582	TERROR ON A TRAIN (TIME BOMB)	TETZLAFF	MGM	1953
C-1583	SKY FULL OF MOON	FOSTER	MGM	1952
C-1584	I LOVE MELVIN	WEIS	MGM	1953
C-1585	ROGUE'S MARCH	DAVIS	MGM	1953
C-1586	NAKED SPUR	MANN	MGM	1953

C-1587	APACHE WAR SMOKE	KRESS	MGM	1952
C-1588	SOMBRERO	FOSTER	MGM	1953
C-1589	SMALL TOWN GIRL	WELLMAN	MGM	1953
C-1590	DESPERATE SEARCH	LEWIS	MGM	1953
C-1591	SCANDAL AT SCOURIE	NEGULESCO	MGM	1953
C-1592	CONFIDENTIALLY CONNIE	BUZZELL	MGM	1953
C-1593	NEVER LET ME GO	DAVES	MGM	1953
C-1594	JEOPARDY	STURGES	MGM	1953
C-1595	BATTLE CIRCUS	BROOKS	MGM	1953
C-1596	STUDENT PRINCE	THORPE	MGM	1954
C-1597	RIDE, VAQUERO	FARROW	MGM	1953
C-1598	GIRL WHO HAD EVERYTHING	THORPE	MGM	1953
C-1600	BRIGHT ROAD	MAYER	MGM	1953
C-1601	STORY OF THREE LOVES	MINNELLI, REINHARDT	MGM	1953
C-1602	DANGEROUS WHEN WET	WALTERS	MGM	1953
C-1603	CRY OF THE HUNTED	LEWIS	MGM	1953
C-1604	YOUNG BESS	SIDNEY	MGM	1953
C-1605	INVITATION TO THE DANCE	KELLY	MGM	1956
C-1606	HOAXTERS	HOFFMAN	MGM	1953
C-1607	DREAM WIFE	SHELDON	MGM	1953
C-1608	GIVE A GIRL A BREAK	DONEN	MGM	1954
C-1609	CODE TWO	WILCOX	MGM	1953
C-1610	BAND WAGON	MINNELLI	MGM	1953
C-1611	CLOWN	LEONARD	MGM	1953
C-1612	REMAINS TO BE SEEN	WEIS	MGM	1953
C-1613	FAST COMPANY	STURGES	MGM	1953
C-1614	ALL THE BROTHERS WERE VALIANT	THORPE	MGM	1953
C-1616	MOGAMBO	FORD	MGM	1953
C-1617	ACTRESS	CUKOR	MGM	1953
C-1618	LATIN LOVERS	LEROY	MGM	1953
C-1619	SLIGHT CASE OF LARCENY	WEIS	MGM	1953
C-1620	GREAT DIAMOND ROBBERY	LEONARD	MGM	1954
C-1621	EASY TO LOVE	WALTERS	MGM	1954
C-1622	SAADIA	LEWIN	MGM	1954
C-1623	TAKE THE HIGH GROUND	BROOKS	MGM	1953
C-1624	AFFAIRS OF DOBIE GILLIS	WEIS	MGM	1953
C-1625	BIG LEAGUER	ALDRICH	MGM	1953
C-1626	ARENA	FLEISCHER	MGM	1953
C-1627	ESCAPE FROM FORT BRAVO	STURGES	MGM	1953
C-1628	RHAPSODY	VIDOR	MGM	1954
C-1629	KISS ME KATE	SIDNEY	MGM	1953
C-1630	HALF A HERO	WEIS	MGM	1953
C-1631	TORCH SONG	WALTERS	MGM	1953
C-1632	LONG, LONG TRAILER	MINNELLI	MGM	1954
C-1633	CREST OF THE WAVE	BOULTING, BOULTING	MGM	1954
C-1634	KNIGHTS OF THE ROUND TABLE	THORPE	MGM	1953
C-1635	FLAME AND THE FLESH	BROOKS	MGM	1954
C-1636	TENNESSEE CHAMP	WILCOX	MGM	1954
C-1637	ROSE MARIE	LEROY	MGM	1954
C-1638	GYPSY COLT	MARTON	MGM	1954
C-1639	HER TWELVE MEN	LEONARD	MGM	1954
C-1640	EXECUTIVE SUITE	WISE	MGM	1954
C-1641	MEN OF THE FIGHTING LADY	MARTON	MGM	1954
C-1642	VALLEY OF THE KINGS	PIROSH	MGM	1954
C-1644	BAD DAY AT BLACK ROCK	STURGES	MGM	1955
C-1645	BRIGADOON	MINNELLI	MGM	1954
C1646	BETRAYED	REINHARDT	MGM	1954
C-1647	BEAU BRUMMEL (UK)	BERNHARDT	MGM	1954
C-1648	PRISONER OF WAR	MARTON	MGM	1954
C-1649	LAST TIME I SAW PARIS	BROOKS	MGM	1954
C-1650	ATHENA	THORPE	MGM	1954
C-1651	GREEN FIRE	MARTON	MGM	1955
C-1652	JUPITER'S DARLING	SIDNEY	MGM	1955
C-1653	ROGUE COP	ROWLAND	MGM	1954
C-1654	DEEP IN MY HEART	DONEN	MGM	1954
C-1655	GLASS SLIPPER	WALTERS	MGM	1955

C-1656	MANY RIVERS TO CROSS	ROWLAND	MGM	1955
C-1657	INVITATION TO THE DANCE	KELLY	MGM	1957
C-1658	PRODIGAL	THORPE	MGM	1955
C-1659	HIT THE DECK	ROWLAND	MGM	1955
C-1660	MOONFLEET	LANG	MGM	1955
C-1661	INTERRUPTED MELODY	BERNHARDT	MGM	1955
C-1662	BEDEVILLED	LEISEN	MGM	1955
C1663	IT'S ALWAYS FAIR WEATHER	DONEN, KELLY	MGM	1955
C-1664	MARAUDERS	MAYER	MGM	1955
C-1665	SCARLET COAT	STURGES	MGM	1955
C-1666	BLACKBOARD JUNGLE	BROOKS	MGM	1955
C-1667	COBWEB	MINNELLI	MGM	1955
C-1668	LOVE ME OR LEAVE ME	VIDOR	MGM	1955
C-1669	KING'S THIEF	LEONARD	MGM	1955
C-1670	IT'S A DOG'S LIFE	HOFFMAN	MGM	1955
C-1671	FORBIDDEN PLANET	WILCOX	MGM	1956
C-1672	BHOWANI JUNCTION	CUKOR	MGM	1956
C-1673	TRIBUTE TO A BADMAN	WISE	MGM	1956
C-1674	QUENTIN DURWARD (UK)	THORPE	MGM	1955
C-1675	DIANE	MILLER	MGM	1956
C-1676	KISMET	MINNELLI	MGM	1955
C-1677	TRIAL	ROBSON	MGM	1955
C-1678	LAST HUNT	BROOKS	MGM	1956
C-1679	I'LL CRY TOMORROW	MANN	MGM	1955
C-1680	MEET ME IN LAS VEGAS	ROWLAND	MGM	1956
C-1681	TENDER TRAP	WALTERS	MGM	1955
C-1682	LUST FOR LIFE	MINNELLI	MGM	1956
C-1683	GABY	BERNHARDT	MGM	1956
C-1684	SWAN	VIDOR	MGM	1956
C-1685	RANSOM	SEGAL	MGM	1956
C-1686	RACK	LAVEN	MGM	1956
C-1686	RACK	LAVEN	MGM	1956
C-1687	CATERED AFFAIR	BROOKS	MGM	1956
C-1688	OPPOSITE SEX	MILLER	MGM	1956
C-1689	FASTEST GUN ALIVE	ROUSE	MGM	1956
C-1690	HIGH SOCIETY	WALTERS	MGM	1956
C-1691	SOMEBODY UP THERE LIKES ME	WISE	MGM	1956
C-1692	RAINTREE COUNTY	DMYTRYK	MGM	1957
C-1693	TEAHOUSE OF THE AUGUST MOON	MANN	MGM	1956
C-1694	TEA AND SYMPATHY	MINNELLI	MGM	1956
C-1697	POWER AND THE PRIZE	KOSTER	MGM	1956
C-1698	BARRETTS OF WIMPOLE STREET	FRANKLIN	MGM	1957
C-1699	GREAT AMERICAN PASTIME	HOFFMAN	MGM	1956
C-1700	SOMETHING OF VALUE	BROOKS	MGM	1957
C-1701	WINGS OF EAGLES	FORD	MGM	1957
C-1702	VINTAGE	HAYDEN	MGM	1957
C-1703	HOT SUMMER NIGHT	FRIEDKIN	MGM	1957
C-1704	SLANDER	ROWLAND	MGM	1957
C-1705	TEN THOUSAND BEDROOMS	THORPE	MGM	1957
C-1706	DESIGNING WOMAN	MINNELLI	MGM	1957
C-1707	LES GIRLS	CUKOR	MGM	1957
C-1708	THIS COULD BE THE NIGHT	WISE	MGM	1957
C-1709	SILK STOCKINGS	MAMOULIAN	MGM	1957
C-1710	SEVENTH SIN	NEAME	MGM	1957
C-1711	GUN GLORY	ROWLAND	MGM	1957
C-1712	UNTIL THEY SAIL	WISE	MGM	1957
C-1713	MAN ON FIRE	MACDOUGALL	MGM	1957
C-1714	HOUSE OF NUMBERS	ROUSE	MGM	1957
C-1715	DON'T GO NEAR THE WATER	WALTERS	MGM	1957
C-1716	TIP ON A DEAD JOCKEY	THORPE	MGM	1957
C-1717	I ACCUSE!	FERRER	MGM	1958
C-1718	MERRY ANDREW	KIDD	MGM	1958
C-1719	JAILHOUSE ROCK	THORPE	MGM	1957
C-1720	BROTHERS KARAMAZOV	BROOKS	MGM	1958
C-1721	SADDLE THE WIND	PARRISH	MGM	1958
C-1722	HIRED GUN aka HOSTILE GUN	NAZARRO	MGM	1957

C-1723	GIGI	MINNELLI	MGM	1958
C-1724	BEN-HUR	WYLER	MGM	1959
C-1725	HIGH COST OF LOVING	FERRER	MGM	1958
C-1726	SHEEPMAN	MARSHALL	MGM	1958
C-1727	HANDLE WITH CARE	FRIEDKIN	MGM	1958
C-1728	LAW AND JAKE WADE	STURGES	MGM	1958
C-1729	TUNNEL OF LOVE	KELLY	MGM	1958
C-1730	RELUCTANT DEBUTANTE	MINNELLI	MGM	1958
C-1731	IMITATION GENERAL	MARSHALL	MGM	1958
C-1732	BADLANDERS	DAVES	MGM	1958
C-1733	HIGH SCHOOL CONFIDENTIAL	ARNOLD	MGM	1958
C-1734	GREEN MANSIONS	FERRER	MGM	1958
C-1735	CAT ON A HOT TIN ROOF	BROOKS	MGM	1958
C-1736	PARTY GIRL	RAY	MGM	1958
C-1737	WORLD, FLESH AND THE DEVIL	MACDOUGALL	MGM	1958
C-1739	ANDY HARDY COMES HOME	KOCH	MGM	1958
C-1740	WATUSI	NEUMANN	MGM	1959
C-1741	SOME CAME RUNNING	MINNELLI	MGM	1958
C-1742	COUNT YOUR BLESSINGS	NEGULESCO	MGM	1959
C-1743	NORTH BY NORTHWEST	HITCHCOCK	MGM	1959
C-1744	NIGHT OF THE QUARTER MOON	HAAS	MGM	1959
C-1746	BEAT GENERATION	HAAS	MGM	1959
C-1747	ASK ANY GIRL	WALTERS	MGM	1959
C-1748	NEVER SO FEW	STURGES	MGM	1959
C-1749	BIG OPERATOR	HAAS	MGM	1959
C-1750	WRECK OF THE MARY DEARE	ANDERSON	MGM	1959
C-1751	IT STARTED WITH A KISS	MARSHALL	MGM	1959
C-1752	TARZAN THE APE MAN	NEWMAN	MGM	1959
C-1753	GIRLS TOWN	HAAS	MGM	1960
C-1754	HOME FROM THE HILL	MINNELLI	MGM	1960
C-1755	TIME MACHINE	PAL	MGM	1960
C-1756	PLEASE DON'T EAT THE DAISIES	WALTERS	MGM	1960
C-1757	SUBTERRANEANS	MACDOUGALL	MGM	1960
C-1758	GAZEBO	MARSHALL	MGM	1959
C-1759	KEY WITNESS	KARLSON	MGM	1960
C-1760	BELLS ARE RINGING	MINNELLI	MGM	1960
C-1761	ADVENTURES OF HUCKLEBERRY FINN	CURTIZ	MGM	1960
C-1762	PLATINUM HIGH SCHOOL	HAAS	MGM	1960
C-1763	CIMARRON	MANN	MGM	1960
C-1764	ALL THE FINE YOUNG CANNIBALS	ANDERSON	MGM	1960
C-1765	BUTTERFIELD 8	MANN	MGM	1960
C-1766	GO NAKED IN THE WORLD	MACDOUGALL	MGM	1961
C-1767	ATLANTIS, THE LOST CONTINENT	PAL	MGM	1961
C-1768	WHERE THE BOYS ARE	LEVIN	MGM	1960
C-1769	MUTINY ON THE BOUNTY	MILESTONE	MGM	1962
C-1770	TWO LOVES	WALTERS	MGM	1961
C-1771	FOUR HORSEMEN OF THE APOCALYPSE	MINNELLI	MGM	1962
C-1772	ADVENTURES OF TARTU (UK)	BUCQUET	MGM	1943
C-1773	ADA	MANN	MGM	1961
C-1774	HONEYMOON MACHINE	THORPE	MGM	1961
C-1775	THUNDER OF DRUMS	NEWMAN	MGM	1961
C-1776	HOW THE WEST WAS WON	FORD, HATHAWAY	MGM	1963
C-1783	BACHELOR IN PARADISE	ARNOLD	MGM	1961
C-1784	SWEET BIRD OF YOUTH	BROOKS	MGM	1962
C-1785	WONDERFUL WORLD BROTHERS GRIMM (t)	LEVIN, PAL	MGM	1962
C-1792	HORIZONTAL LIEUTENANT	THORPE	MGM	1962
C-1793	RIDE THE HIGH COUNTRY	PECKINPAH	MGM	1962
C-1794	TWO WEEKS IN ANOTHER TOWN	MINNELLI	MGM	1962
C-1795	BOYS' NIGHT OUT	GORDON	MGM	1962
C-1796	BILLY ROSES' JUMBO	WALTERS	MGM	1962
C-1797	PERIOD OF ADJUSTMENT	HILL	MGM	1962
C-1798	HOOK	SEATON	MGM	1963
C-1801	COURTSHIP OF EDDIE'S FATHER	MINNELLI	MGM	1963
C-1802	IT HAPPENED AT THE WORLD'S FAIR	TAUROG	MGM	1963
C-1803	DRUMS OF AFRICA	CLARK	MGM	1963
C-1804	TICKLISH AFFAIR	SIDNEY	MGM	1963

C-1805	WHEELER DEALERS	HILLER	MGM	1963
C-1806	TWILIGHT OF HONOR	SAGAL	MGM	1963
C-1807	SUNDAY IN NEW YORK	TEWKSBURY	MGM	1964
C-1808	PRIZE	ROBSON	MGM	1963
C-1809	GLOBAL AFFAIR	ARNOLD	MGM	1964
C-1810	ADVANCE TO THE REAR	MARSHALL	MGM	1964
C-1812	VIVA LAS VEGAS	SIDNEY	MGM	1964
C-1813	MAIL ORDER BRIDE	KENNEDY	MGM	1964
C-1814	HOOTENANNY HOOT	NELSON	MGM	1963
C-1815	UNSINKABLE MOLLY BROWN	WALTERS	MGM	1963
C-1816	HONEYMOON HOTEL	LEVIN	MGM	1964
C-1817	LOOKING FOR LOVE	WEIS	MGM	1964
C-1818	SIGNPOST TO MURDER	ENGLUND	MGM	1964
C-1819	KISSIN' COUSINS	NELSON	MGM	1964
C-1820	AMERICANIZATION OF EMILY	HILLER	MGM	1964
C-1823	OUTRAGE	RITT	MGM	1964
C-1824	QUICK, BEFORE IT MELTS	MANN	MGM	1965
C-1825	ROUNDERS	KENNEDY	MGM	1965
C-1826	36 HOURS	SEATON	MGM	1965
C-1827	BARBARA KENT	portrait	MGM	
C-1827	RED BUTTONS	portrait	MGM	
C-1828	JOY IN THE MORNING	SEGAL	MGM	1965
C-1829	GIRL HAPPY	SAGAL	MGM	1965
C-1830	GET YOURSELF A COLLEGE GIRL	MILLER	MGM	1964
C-1831	SANDPIPER	MINNELLI	MGM	1965
C-1832	ONCE A THIEF	NELSON	MGM	1965
C-1833	CINCINNATI KID	JEWISON	MGM	1965
C-1834	MONEY TRAP	KENNEDY	MGM	1966
C-1835	7 WOMEN	FORD	MGM	1966
C-1836	MISTER BUDDWING	MANN	MGM	1966
C-1837	PATCH OF BLUE	GREEN	MGM	1965
C-1838	HARUM SCARUM	NELSON	MGM	1965
C-1839	MADE IN PARIS	SAGAL	MGM	1966
C-1840	ICE STATION ZEBRA	STURGES	MGM	1968
C-1841	WHEN THE BOYS MEET THE GIRLS	GANZER	MGM	1965
C-1842	GLASS BOTTOM BOAT	TASHLIN	MGM	1966
C-1843	SINGING NUN	KOSTER	MGM	1966
C-1844	HOLD ON!	LUBIN	MGM	1966
C-1845	SPINOUT	TAUROG	MGM	1966
C-1846	DOCTOR, YOU'VE GOT TO BE KIDDING	TEWKSBURY	MGM	1967
C-1847	VENETIAN AFFAIR	THORPE	MGM	1967
C-1848	PENELOPE	HILLER	MGM	1967
C-1849	DON'T MAKE WAVES	MACKENDRICK	MGM	1967
C-1850	DOUBLE TROUBLE	TAUROG	MGM	1967
C-1851	FASTEST GUITAR ALIVE	MOORE	MGM	1967
C-1852	LAST CHALLENGE	THORPE	MGM	1967
C-1854	GUNS FOR SAN SEBASTIAN	VERNEUIL	MGM	1968
C-1855	EXTRAORDINARY SEAMAN	FRANKENHEIMER	MGM	1969
C-1856	POWER, THE	HASKIN	MGM	1968
C-1857	SOL MADRID	HUTTON	MGM	1968
C-1858	PHANTOM TOLLBOOTH (t)	JONES, LEVITOW	MGM	1970
C-1859	LEGEND OF LYLAH CLARE	ALDRICH	MGM	1968
C-1860	SPEEDWAY	TAUROG	MGM	1968
C-1861	WHERE WERE YOU WHEN LIGHTS WENT OUT	AVERBACK	MGM	1968
C-1862	DAY OF THE EVIL GUN	THORPE	MGM	1968
C-1863	IMPOSSIBLE YEARS	GORDON	MGM	1969
C-1864	STAY AWAY, JOE	TEWKSBURY	MGM	1968
C-1866	TIME TO SING	DREIFUSS	MGM	1968
C-1867	SPLIT	FLEMYNG	MGM	1968
C-1868	LIVE A LITTLE, LOVE A LITTLE	TAUROG	MGM	1968
C-1869	HEAVEN WITH A GUN	KATZIN	MGM	1969
C-1870	YOUNG RUNAWAYS	DREIFUSS	MGM	1968
C-1871	GYPSY MOTHS	FRANKENHEIMER	MGM	1969
C-1872	MARLOWE	BOGART	MGM	1969
C-1873	ZABRISKIE POINT	ANTONIONI	MGM	1970
C-1875	TROUBLE WITH GIRLS	TEWKSBURY	MGM	1969

C-1876	MALTESE BIPPY	PANAMA	MGM	1969
C-1878	MAGIC GARDEN STANLEY SWEETHEART	HORN	MGM	1970
C-1879	BAMBOLE (IT)	BOLOGNINI, COLOGINI	COLUMBIA	1965
C-1880	ZIGZAG	COLLA	MGM	1970
C-1881	STRAWBERRY STATEMENT	HAGMANN	MGM	1970
C-1884	DIRTY DINGUS MAGEE	KENNEDY	MGM	1970
C-1885	TRAVELING EXECUTIONER	SMIGHT	MGM	1970
C-1886	HOUSE OF DARK SHADOWS	CURTIS	MGM	1970
C-1887	ALEX IN WONDERLAND	MAZURSKY	MGM	1970
C-1888	BREWSTER MCCLOUD	ALTMAN	MGM	1971
C-1889	ELVIS- THAT'S THE WAY IT IS	SANDERS	MGM	1970
C-1890	PRETTY MAIDS ALL IN A ROW	VADIM	MGM	1971
C-1891	CORKY	HORN	MGM	1973
C-1892	BELIEVE IN ME	HAGMANN	MGM	1971
C-1893	FORTUNE AND MEN'S EYES	HART	MGM	1971
C-1894	WILD ROVERS	EDWARDS	MGM	1971
C-1895	SHAFT	PARKS	MGM	1971
C-1896	NIGHT OF DARK SHADOWS	CURTIS	MGM	1971
C-1897	GANG THAT COULDN'T SHOOT STRAIGHT	GOLDSTONE	MGM	1971
C-1898	GOING HOME	LEONARD	MGM	1971
C-1899	EVERY LITTLE CROOK AND NANNY	HOWARD	MGM	1972
C-1902	GUNS A POPPIN' (sh)	WHITE	COLUMBIA	1957
C-1905	TRICKY CHICKS (sh)	WHITE	COLUMBIA	1957
C-1908	PIES AND GUYS (sh)	WHITE	COLUMBIA	1958
C-1911	OIL'S WELL THAT ENDS WELL (sh)	WHITE	COLUMBIA	1958
C-3002	CYCLONE PRAIRIE RANGERS	KLINE	COLUMBIA	1944
C-3003	COWBOY IN THE CLOUDS	KLINE	COLUMBIA	1943
C-3004	SUNDOWN VALLEY	KLINE	COLUMBIA	1944
C-3005	COWBOY CANTEEN	LANDERS	COLUMBIA	1944
C-3006	SADDLE LEATHER LAW	KLINE	COLUMBIA	1944
C-3007	SAGEBRUSH HEROES	KLINE	COLUMBIA	1945
C-3008	ROUGH RIDING JUSTICE	ABRAHAMS	COLUMBIA	1945
C-3009	SWING IN THE SADDLE	LANDERS	COLUMBIA	1944
C-3010	RETURN OF THE DURANGO KID	ABRAHAMS	COLUMBIA	1945
C-3011	BOTH BARRELS BLAZING	ABRAHAMS	COLUMBIA	1945
C-3012	RUSTLERS OF THE BADLANDS	ABRAHAMS	COLUMBIA	1945
C-3013	FRONTIER GUNLAW	ABRAHAMS	COLUMBIA	1946
C-3014	SING ME A SONG OF TEXAS	KEAYS	COLUMBIA	1945
C-3015	BLAZING THE WESTERN TRAIL	KEAYS	COLUMBIA	1945
C-3016	LAWLESS EMPIRE	KEAYS	COLUMBIA	1945
C-3017	ROCKIN' IN THE ROCKIES	KEAYS	COLUMBIA	1945
C-3018	RHYTHM ROUNDUP	KEAYS	COLUMBIA	1945
C-3019	OUTLAWS OF THE ROCKIES	NAZARRO	COLUMBIA	1945
C-3020	TEXAS PANHANDLE	NAZARRO	COLUMBIA	1945
C-3021	SONG OF THE PRAIRIE	NAZARRO	COLUMBIA	1945
C-3022	DESERT HORSEMAN	NAZARRO	COLUMBIA	1946
C-3023	GUNNING FOR VENGEANCE	NAZARRO	COLUMBIA	1946
C-3024	ROARING RANGERS	NAZARRO	COLUMBIA	1946
C-3025	THROW A SADDLE ON A STAR	NAZARRO	COLUMBIA	1946
C-3026	HEADING WEST	NAZARRO	COLUMBIA	1946
C-3027	GALLOPING THUNDER	NAZARRO	COLUMBIA	1946
C-3028	TWO-FISTED STRANGER	NAZARRO	COLUMBIA	1946
C-3029	THAT TEXAS JAMBOREE	NAZARRO	COLUMBIA	1946
C-3030	TERROR TRAIL	NAZARRO	COLUMBIA	1946
C-3031	LANDRUSH	KEAYS	COLUMBIA	1946
C-3032	COWBOY BLUES	NAZARRO	COLUMBIA	1946
C-3033	SINGING ON THE TRAIL	NAZARRO	COLUMBIA	1946
C-3034	FIGHTING FRONTIERSMAN	ABRAHAMS	COLUMBIA	1946
C-3035	SOUTH OF THE CHISHOLM TRAIL	ABRAHAMS	COLUMBIA	1947
C-3036	LONE STAR MOONLIGHT	NAZARRO	COLUMBIA	1946
C-3037	OVER THE SANTA FE TRAIL	NAZARRO	COLUMBIA	1947
C-3038	WEST OF DODGE CITY	NAZARRO	COLUMBIA	1947
C-3039	LONE HAND TEXAS	NAZARRO	COLUMBIA	1947
C-3040	LAW OF THE CANYON	NAZARRO	COLUMBIA	1947
C-3041	PRAIRIE RAIDERS	ABRAHAMS	COLUMBIA	1947
C-3042	STRANGER FROM PONCA CITY	ABRAHAMS	COLUMBIA	1947

C-3043	RIDERS OF THE LONE STAR	ABRAHAMS	COLUMBIA	1947
C-3044	SWING THE WESTERN WAY	ABRAHAMS	COLUMBIA	1947
C-3045	SMOKEY RIVER SERENADE	ABRAHAMS	COLUMBIA	1947
C-3046	SIX GUN LAW	NAZARRO	COLUMBIA	1948
C-3047	BUCKAROO FROM POWDER RIVER	NAZARRO	COLUMBIA	1947
C-3048	PHANTOM VALLEY	NAZARRO	COLUMBIA	1948
C-3049	LAST DAYS OF BOOTHILL	NAZARRO	COLUMBIA	1947
C-3050	ROSE OF SANTA ROSA	NAZARRO	COLUMBIA	1947
C-3051	WHIRLWIND RAIDERS	KEAYS	COLUMBIA	1948
C-3052	WEST OF SONORA	NAZARRO	COLUMBIA	1948
C-3053	SONG OF IDAHO	NAZARRO	COLUMBIA	1948
C-3054	BLAZING ACROSS THE PECOS	NAZARRO	COLUMBIA	1948
C-3055	TRAIL TO LAREDO	NAZARRO	COLUMBIA	1948
C-3056	ARKANSAS SWING	NAZARRO	COLUMBIA	1948
C-3057	SINGIN' SPURS	NAZARRO	COLUMBIA	1948
C-3058	EL DORADO PASS	NAZARRO	COLUMBIA	1948
C-3059	QUICK ON THE TRIGGER	NAZARRO	COLUMBIA	1948
C-3060	CHALLENGE OF THE RANGE	NAZARRO	COLUMBIA	1949
C-3061	SMOKY MOUNTAIN MELODY	NAZARRO	COLUMBIA	1948
C-3062	SOUTH OF DEATH VALLEY	NAZARRO	COLUMBIA	1949
C-3063	DESERT VIGILANTE	SEARS	COLUMBIA	1949
C-3064	LARAMIE	NAZARRO	COLUMBIA	1949
C-3065	HOME IN SAN ANTONE	NAZARRO	COLUMBIA	1949
C-3066	BLAZING TRAIL	NAZARRO	COLUMBIA	1949
C-3067	HORSEMEN OF THE SIERRAS	SEARS	COLUMBIA	1949
C-3068	BANDITS OF EL DORADO	NAZARRO	COLUMBIA	1949
C-3069	RENEGADES OF THE SAGE	NAZARRO	COLUMBIA	1949
C-3070	HOEDOWN	NAZARRO	COLUMBIA	1950
C-3071	FEUDIN' RHYTHM	BERNDS	COLUMBIA	1949
C-3072	OUTCAST OF BLACK MESA	NAZARRO	COLUMBIA	1950
C-3073	FRONTIER OUTPOST	NAZARRO	COLUMBIA	1950
C-3074	TRAIL OF THE RUSTLERS	NAZARRO	COLUMBIA	1950
C-3075	TEXAS DYNAMO	NAZARRO	COLUMBIA	1950
C-3076	STREETS OF GHOST TOWN	NAZARRO	COLUMBIA	1950
C-3078	RAIDERS OF TOMAHAWK CREEK	SEARS	COLUMBIA	1950
C-3079	LIGHTNING GUNS	SEARS	COLUMBIA	1950
C-3080	PRAIRIE ROUNDUP	SEARS	COLUMBIA	1951
C-3081	RIDIN' THE OUTLAW TRAIL	SEARS	COLUMBIA	1951
C-3082	FORT SAVAGE RAIDERS	NAZARRO	COLUMBIA	1951
C-3083	SNAKE RIVER DESPERADOES	SEARS	COLUMBIA	1951
C-3084	BONANZA TOWN	SEARS	COLUMBIA	1951
C-3085	CYCLONE FURY	NAZARRO	COLUMBIA	1951
C-3086	KID FROM AMARILLO	NAZARRO	COLUMBIA	1951
C-3087	KID FROM AMARILLO	NAZARRO	COLUMBIA	1951
C-3087	PECOS RIVER	SEARS	COLUMBIA	1951
C-3088	SMOKY CANYON	SEARS	COLUMBIA	1952
C-3089	HAWK OF WILD RIVER	SEARS	COLUMBIA	1952
C-3090	LARAMIE MOUNTAINS	NAZARRO	COLUMBIA	1952
C-3091	ROUGH TOUGH WEST	NAZARRO	COLUMBIA	1952
C-3092	JUNCTION CITY	NAZARRO	COLUMBIA	1952
C-3093	KID FROM BROKEN GUN	SEARS	COLUMBIA	1952
C-3400	CORONER CREEK	ENRIGHT	COLUMBIA	1948
C-4001	BUSY BUDDIES (sh)	LORD	COLUMBIA	1944
C-4002	WEDDED BLISS (sh)	EDWARDS	COLUMBIA	1944
C-4003	BACHELOR DAZE (sh)	WHITE	COLUMBIA	1943
C-4004	YOU DEAR BOY (sh)	WHITE	COLUMBIA	1943
C-4005	DOCTOR, FEEL MY PULSE (sh)	WHITE	COLUMBIA	1944
C-4006	BOOBY DUPES (sh)	LORD	COLUMBIA	1945
C-4007	HIS TALE IS TOLD (sh)	EDWARDS	COLUMBIA	1944
C-4008	YOU WERE NEVER UGLIER (sh)	WHITE	COLUMBIA	1944
C-4009	GOLD IS WHERE YOU LOSE IT (sh)	WHITE	COLUMBIA	1944
C-4010	CRASH GOES THE HAS (sh)	WHITE	COLUMBIA	1944
C-4011	CRAZY LIKE A FOX (sh)	WHITE	COLUMBIA	1944
C-4012	HIS HOTEL SWEET (sh)	EDWARDS	COLUMBIA	1944
C-4013	IDLE ROOMERS (sh)	LORD	COLUMBIA	1943
C-4014	OH, BABY (sh)	WHITE	COLUMBIA	1944

C-4015	OFF AGAIN, ON AGAIN (sh)	WHITE	COLUMBIA	1945
C-4016	OPEN SEASON FOR SAPS (sh)	WHITE	COLUMBIA	1944
C-4017	DEFECTIVE DETECTIVES (sh)	EDWARDS	COLUMBIA	1944
C-4018	PICK A PECK OF PLUMBERS (sh)	WHITE	COLUMBIA	1944
C-4019	MOPEY DOPE (sh)	LORD	COLUMBIA	1944
C-4020	GENTS WITHOUT CENTS (sh)	WHITE	COLUMBIA	1944
C-4021	HEATHER AND YON (sh)	EDWARDS	COLUMBIA	1944
C-4022	THREE PESTS IN A MESS (sh)	LORD	COLUMBIA	1945
C-4023	WOO WOO (I SHOULD WORRY*)	WHITE	COLUMBIA	1945
C-4024	TWO LOCAL YOKELS (sh)	WHITE	COLUMBIA	1945
C-4025	KNIGHT AND A BLONDE (sh)	EDWARDS	COLUMBIA	1944
C-4025	WOO WOO (I SHOULD WORRY*)	WHITE	COLUMBIA	1945
C-4026	SHE SNOOPS TO CONQUER (sh)	WHITE	COLUMBIA	1944
C-4027	STRIFE OF THE PARTY (sh)	EDWARDS	COLUMBIA	1944
C-4028	DANCE DUNCE, DANCE (sh)	WHITE	COLUMBIA	1945
C-4029	SNOOPER SERVICE (sh)	EDWARDS	COLUMBIA	1945
C-4030	IDIOTS DELUXE (sh)	WHITE	COLUMBIA	1945
C-4031	JURY GOES ROUND AND ROUND (sh)	WHITE	COLUMBIA	1945
C-4032	HISS AND YELL (sh)	WHITE	COLUMBIA	1946
C-4033	IF A BODY MEETS A BODY (sh)	WHITE	COLUMBIA	1945
C-4035	PISTOL PACKIN' NITWITS (sh)	EDWARDS	COLUMBIA	1945
C-4036	WIFE DECOY (sh)	EDWARDS	COLUMBIA	1945
C-4037	SPOOK TO ME (sh)	EDWARDS	COLUMBIA	1945
C-4038	HIT WITH A MISS (sh)	WHITE	COLUMBIA	1945
C-4039	MAYOR'S HUSBAND (sh)	EDWARDS	COLUMBIA	1945
C-4040	MINER AFFAIR (sh)	WHITE	COLUMBIA	1945
C-4041	BLONDE STAYED ON (sh)	EDWARDS	COLUMBIA	1946
C-4042	CALLING ALL FIBBERS (sh)	WHITE	COLUMBIA	1945
C-4043	BIRD IN THE HEAD (sh)	BERNDS	COLUMBIA	1946
C-4044	MICRO-PHONIES (sh)	BERNDS	COLUMBIA	1945
C-4045	BEER BARREL POLECATS (sh)	WHITE	COLUMBIA	1946
C-4046	THREE TROUBLEDOERS (sh)	BERNDS	COLUMBIA	1946
C-4047	WHEN THE WIFE'S AWAY (sh)	BERNDS	COLUMBIA	1946
C-4048	JIGGERS, MY WIFE (sh)	WHITE	COLUMBIA	1946
C-4048	WHERE THE PEST BEGINS	EDWARDS	COLUMBIA	1945
C-4049	YOU CAN'T FOOL A FOOL (sh)	WHITE	COLUMBIA	1946
C-4050	UNCIVIL WAR BIRDS (sh)	WHITE	COLUMBIA	1946
C-4051	HIGH BLOOD PLEASURE (sh)	WHITE	COLUMBIA	1945
C-4052	SOCIETY MUGS (sh)	BERNDS	COLUMBIA	1946
C-4053	THREE LOAN WOLVES (sh)	WHITE	COLUMBIA	1946
C-4054	MR. NOISY (sh)	BERNDS	COLUMBIA	1946
C-4055	GET ALONG LITTLE ZOMBIE (sh)	BERNDS	COLUMBIA	1946
C-4056	HALF-WITS HOLIDAY (sh)	WHITE	COLUMBIA	1947
C-4057	RHYTHM AND WEEP (sh)	WHITE	COLUMBIA	1946
C-4058	MONKEY BUSINESSMEN (sh)	BERNDS	COLUMBIA	1946
C-4059	ANDY PLAYS HOOKEY (sh)	BERNDS	COLUMBIA	1946
C-4060	HEADIN' FOR A WEDDIN' (sh)	WHITE	COLUMBIA	1946
C-4061	SCOOPER DOOPER (sh)	BERNDS	COLUMBIA	1947
C-4062	AIN'T LOVE CUCKOO (sh)	WHITE	COLUMBIA	1946
C-4063	G. I. WANNA HOME (sh)	WHITE	COLUMBIA	1946
C-4064	BRIDE AND GLOOM (sh)	BERNDS	COLUMBIA	1947
C-4065	MR. WRIGHT GOES WRONG (sh)	WHITE	COLUMBIA	1946
C-4066	HOT WATER (sh)	BERNDS	COLUMBIA	1946
C-4067	THREE LITTLE PIRATES (sh)	BERNDS	COLUMBIA	1946
C-4068	PARDON MY TERROR (sh)	BERNDS	COLUMBIA	1946
C-4069	SUNK IN THE SINK (sh)	WHITE	COLUMBIA	1949
C-4070	FIDDLERS THREE (sh)	WHITE	COLUMBIA	1948
C-4071	FRIGHT NIGHT	BERNDS	COLUMBIA	1947
C-4072	SHOULD HUSBANDS MARRY? (sh)	LORD	COLUMBIA	1947
C-4073	CRABBIN' IN THE CABIN (sh)	WHITE	COLUMBIA	1948
C-4074	HONEYMOON BLUES (sh)	BERNDS	COLUMBIA	1946
C-4075	HOT HEIR (sh)	BERNDS	COLUMBIA	1947
C-4076	HECTIC HONEYMOON (sh)	BERNDS	COLUMBIA	1947
C-4077	OUT WEST (sh)	BERNDS	COLUMBIA	1947
C-4078	SO'S YOUR ANTENNA (sh)	WHITE	COLUMBIA	1946
C-4079	TWO JILLS AND A JACK (sh)	WHITE	COLUMBIA	1947

C-4080	SLAPPILY MARRIED (sh)	BERNDS	COLUMBIA	1946
C-4081	MEET MR. MISCHIEF (sh)	BERNDS	COLUMBIA	1947
C-4082	SQUAREHEADS OF THE ROUND TABLE (sh)	BERNDS	COLUMBIA	1948
C-4083	RENO-VATED (sh)	WHITE	COLUMBIA	1946
C-4084	NERVOUS SHAKEDOWN (sh)	LORD	COLUMBIA	1947
C-4085	MORON THAN OFF (sh)	WHITE	COLUMBIA	1946
C-4086	GOOD BAD EGG (sh)	WHITE	COLUMBIA	1947
C-4087	HOLD THAT LION (sh)	WHITE	COLUMBIA	1947
C-4088	SING A SONG OF SIX PANTS (sh)	WHITE	COLUMBIA	1947
C-4089	ROLLING DOWN TO RENO (sh)	WHITE	COLUMBIA	1947
C-4091	I'M A MONKEY'S UNCLE (sh)	WHITE	COLUMBIA	1948
C-4093	PARDON MY CLUTCH (sh)	BERNDS	COLUMBIA	1948
C-4094	HOT SCOTS (sh)	BERNDS	COLUMBIA	1948
C-4095	BRIDELESS GROOM (sh)	BERNDS	COLUMBIA	1947
C-4096	WIFE TO SPARE (sh)	BERNDS	COLUMBIA	1947
C-4097	CUPID GOES NUTS (sh)	WHITE	COLUMBIA	1947
C-4098	TRAINING FOR TROUBLE (sh)	WHITE	COLUMBIA	1947
C-4099	WEDDING BELLE (sh)	BERNDS	COLUMBIA	1947
C-4100	TALL, DARK AND GRUESOME (sh)	LORD	COLUMBIA	1948
C-4101	WAITING IN THE LURCH (sh)	BERNDS	COLUMBIA	1949
C-4102	STOOGES (sh)		COLUMBIA	
C-4103	SHIVERING SHERLOCKS (sh)	LORD	COLUMBIA	1948
C-4104	ALL GUMMED UP (sh)	WHITE	COLUMBIA	1947
C-4105	MUMMY'S DUMMIES (sh)	BERNDS	COLUMBIA	1948
C-4106	WEDLOCK DEADLOCK (sh)	BERNDS	COLUMBIA	1947
C-4107	THREE HAMS ON RYE (sh)	WHITE	COLUMBIA	1950
C-4108	GHOST TALKS (sh)	WHITE	COLUMBIA	1949
C-4109	RADIO ROMEO (sh)	BERNDS	COLUMBIA	1947
C-4110	MAN OR MOUSE (sh)	WHITE	COLUMBIA	1948
C-4111	CRIME ON THEIR HANDS (sh)	BERNDS	COLUMBIA	1948
C-4112	WHO DONE IT? (sh)	BERNDS	COLUMBIA	1949
C-4113	EIGHT BALL ANDY (sh)	BERNDS	COLUMBIA	1948
C-4114	FUELIN' AROUND (sh)	BERNDS	COLUMBIA	1949
C-4115	HUGS AND MUGS (sh)	WHITE	COLUMBIA	1950
C-4116	HOKUS POKUS (sh)	WHITE	COLUMBIA	1949
C-4117	FLAT FEAT (sh)	BERNDS	COLUMBIA	1948
C-4118	GO CHASE YOURSELF (sh)	WHITE	COLUMBIA	1948
C-4119	MALICE IN THE PALACE (sh)	WHITE	COLUMBIA	1949
C-4120	JITTER BUGHOUSE (sh)	WHITE	COLUMBIA	1948
C-4121	PARDON MY LAMBCHOP (sh)	WHITE	COLUMBIA	1948
C-4122	SILLY BILLY (sh)	WHITE	COLUMBIA	1948
C-4123	HE'S IN AGAIN (sh)	BERNDS	COLUMBIA	1949
C-4124	TWO NUTS IN A RUT (sh)	BERNDS	COLUMBIA	1948
C-4125	BILLIE GETS HER MAN (sh)	BERNDS	COLUMBIA	1948
C-4126	SHEEPISH WOLF (sh)	BERNDS	COLUMBIA	1948
C-4127	PARLOR, BEDROOM AND WRATH (sh)	WHITE	COLUMBIA	1948
C-4128	PINCH IN TIME (sh)	LORD	COLUMBIA	1948
C-4129	LOVE AT FIRST BITE (sh)	WHITE	COLUMBIA	1950
C-4130	MICROSPOOK (sh)	BERNDS	COLUMBIA	1949
C-4131	DOPEY DICKS (sh)	BERNDS	COLUMBIA	1950
C-4132	RADIO RIOT (sh)	BERNDS	COLUMBIA	1949
C-4133	TRAPPED BY A BLOND (sh)	LORD	COLUMBIA	1949
C-4134	FLUNG BY A FLING (sh)	BERNDS	COLUMBIA	1949
C-4135	CLUNKED IN THE CLINK (sh)	WHITE	COLUMBIA	1949
C-4136	MISS IN A MESS (sh)	WHITE	COLUMBIA	1949
C-4137	DUNKED IN THE DEEP (sh)	WHITE	COLUMBIA	1949
C-4138	DIZZY YARDBIRD (sh)	WHITE	COLUMBIA	1950
C-4139	SLAPHAPPY SLEUTHS (sh)	WHITE	COLUMBIA	1950
C-4140	VAGABOND LOAFERS (sh)	BERNDS	COLUMBIA	1949
C-4141	SELF MADE MAIDS (sh)	WHITE	COLUMBIA	1950
C-4142	PUNCHY COWPUNCHERS (sh)	BERNDS	COLUMBIA	1950
C-4143	STUDIO STOOPS (sh)	BERNDS	COLUMBIA	1950
C-4144	HOLD THAT MONKEY (sh)	WHITE	COLUMBIA	1950
C-4145	HIS BAITING BEAUTY (sh)	BERNDS	COLUMBIA	1950
C-4146	SUPER WOLF (sh)	LORD	COLUMBIA	1949
C-4147	LET DOWN YOUR AERIAL (sh)	BERNDS	COLUMBIA	1949

C-4148	ONE SHIVERY NIGHT (sh)	LORD	COLUMBIA	1950
C-4149	WHA' HAPPEN? (sh)	WHITE	COLUMBIA	1949
C-4150	NURSIE BEHAVE (sh)	WHITE	COLUMBIA	1950
C-4151	FRENCH FRIED FROLIC (sh)	WHITE	COLUMBIA	1949
C-4152	HOUSE ABOUT IT (sh)	WHITE	COLUMBIA	1950
C-4153	MARINATED MARINER (sh)	WHITE	COLUMBIA	1950
C-4154	SNITCH IN TIME (sh)	BERNDS	COLUMBIA	1950
C-4155	BABY SITTERS JITTERS (sh)	WHITE	COLUMBIA	1951
C-4156	THREE ARABIAN NUTS (sh)	BERNDS	COLUMBIA	1951
C-4157	SCRAMBLED BRAINS (sh)	WHITE	COLUMBIA	1951
C-4158	DON'T THROW THAT KNIFE (sh)	WHITE	COLUMBIA	1951
C-4159	MALICE IN THE PALACE (sh) (see 4119)	WHITE	COLUMBIA	1949
C-4159	MISSED FORTUNE (sh)	WHITE	COLUMBIA	1952
C-4160	BLUNDERFUL TIME (sh)	WHITE	COLUMBIA	1949
C-4161	MERRY MAVERICKS (sh)	BERNDS	COLUMBIA	1951
C-4162	TOOTH WILL OUT (sh)	BERNDS	COLUMBIA	1951
C-4163	PEST MAN WINS (sh)	WHITE	COLUMBIA	1951
C-4164	WINE, WOMEN AND BONG (sh)	WHITE	COLUMBIA	1951
C-4165	TWO ROAMING CHAMPS (sh)	BERNDS	COLUMBIA	1950
C-4166	HE FLEW THE SHREW (sh)	WHITE	COLUMBIA	1951
C-4167	FUN ON THE RUN (sh)	WHITE	COLUMBIA	1951
C-4168	SLIP AND A MISS (sh)	MCCOLLUM	COLUMBIA	1950
C-4169	WOO WOO BLUES (sh)	QUINE	COLUMBIA	1951
C-4170	BLONDE ATOM BOMB (sh)	WHITE	COLUMBIA	1951
C-4171	PLEASURE TREASURE (sh)	WHITE	COLUMBIA	1951
C-4172	INNOCENTLY GUILTY (sh)	WHITE	COLUMBIA	1950
C-4173	AWFUL SLEUTH (sh)	QUINE	COLUMBIA	1951
C-4174	FOY MEETS GIRL (sh)	ULLMAN	COLUMBIA	1950
C-4175	WEDDING YELLS (sh)	WHITE	COLUMBIA	1951
C-4176	HAPPY GO WACKY (sh)	WHITE	COLUMBIA	1952
C-4177	SHE TOOK A POWDER (sh)	WHITE	COLUMBIA	1951
C-4178	CORNY CASANOVAS (sh)	WHITE	COLUMBIA	1952
C-4179	HULA-LA-LA (sh)	MCCOLLUM	COLUMBIA	1951
C-4180	LISTEN, JUDGE (sh)	BERNDS	COLUMBIA	1952
C-4181	HE COOKED HIS GOOSE (sh)	WHITE	COLUMBIA	1952
C-4182	UP IN DAISY'S PENTHOUSE (sh)	WHITE	COLUMBIA	1953
C-4183	GENTS IN A JAM (sh)	BERNDS	COLUMBIA	1952
C-4184	TROUBLE IN-LAWS (sh)	MCCOLLUM	COLUMBIA	1951
C-4185	CHAMPS STEP OUT (sh)	BERNDS	COLUMBIA	1951
C-4186	ROOTIN' TOOTIN' TENDERFEET (sh)	WHITE	COLUMBIA	1952
C-4187	GINK AT THE SINK (sh)	WHITE	COLUMBIA	1952
C-4188	HEEBIE GEE-GEES (sh)	BERNDS	COLUMBIA	1952
C-4189	FOOL AND HIS HONEY (sh)	WHITE	COLUMBIA	1952
C-4190	BLISSFUL BLUNDER (sh)	WHITE	COLUMBIA	1952
C-4191	HOOKED AND ROOKED (sh)	WHITE	COLUMBIA	1952
C-4192	FRAIDY CAT (sh)	WHITE	COLUMBIA	1951
C-4193	AIM, FIRE, SCOOT (sh)	WHITE	COLUMBIA	1952
C-4194	CUCKOO ON A CHOO CHOO (sh)	WHITE	COLUMBIA	1952
C-4195	CAUGHT ON THE BOUNCE (sh)	WHITE	COLUMBIA	1952
C-4196	BOOTY AND THE BEAST (sh)	WHITE	COLUMBIA	1953
C-4197	LOOSE LOOT (sh)	WHITE	COLUMBIA	1953
C-4198	STROP, LOOK AND LISTEN (sh)	WHITE	COLUMBIA	1952
C-4199	TRICKY DICKS (sh)	WHITE	COLUMBIA	1953
C-4200	THREE DARK HORSES (sh)	WHITE	COLUMBIA	1952
C-4201	BUBBLE TROUBLE (sh)	WHITE	COLUMBIA	1953
C-4201	RIP, SEW AND STITCH (sh)	WHITE	COLUMBIA	1953
C-4203	GOOF ON THE ROOF (sh)	WHITE	COLUMBIA	1953
C-4204	HE POPPED HIS PISTOL (sh)	WHITE	COLUMBIA	1953
C-4205	SPIES AND GUYS (sh)	WHITE	COLUMBIA	1953
C-4206	LOVE'S A POPPIN' (sh)	WHITE	COLUMBIA	1953
C-4207	OH, SAY CAN YOU SUE (sh)	WHITE	COLUMBIA	1953
C-4207	TWO JILLS AND A JACK (sh) (see 4079)	WHITE	COLUMBIA	1947
C-4208	INCOME TAX SAPPY (sh)	WHITE	COLUMBIA	1954
C-4209	MUSTY MUSKATEERS (sh)	WHITE	COLUMBIA	1954
C-4210	SPOOKS (sh)	WHITE	COLUMBIA	1953
C-4211	PALS AND GALS (sh)	WHITE	COLUMBIA	1954

C-4212	PARDON MY BACKFIRE (sh)	WHITE	COLUMBIA	1953
C-4213	A-HUNTING THEY DID GO	WHITE	COLUMBIA	1948
C-4214	DOGGIE IN THE BEDROOM (sh)	WHITE	COLUMBIA	1954
C-4215	DOWN THE HATCH (sh)	WHITE	COLUMBIA	1953
C-4216	SHOT IN THE FRONTIER (sh)	WHITE	COLUMBIA	1954
C-4217	KNUTZY KNIGHTS (sh)	WHITE	COLUMBIA	1954
C-4218	SCOTCHED IN SCOTLAND (sh)	WHITE	COLUMBIA	1954
C-4219	TOOTING TOOTERS (sh)	WHITE	COLUMBIA	1954
C-4220	MINER AFFAIR	WHITE	COLUMBIA	1945
C-4220	TWO APRIL FOOLS (sh)	WHITE	COLUMBIA	1954
C-4221	KIDS WILL BE KIDS (sh)	WHITE	COLUMBIA	1954
C-4222	BLUNDER BOYS (sh)	WHITE	COLUMBIA	1955
C-4223	FLING IN THE RING	WHITE	COLUMBIA	1955
C-4224	GYPPED IN THE PENTHOUSE (sh)	WHITE	COLUMBIA	1955
C-4225	OF CASH AND HASH (sh)	WHITE	COLUMBIA	1955
C-4226	FIRE CHASER (sh)	WHITE	COLUMBIA	1954
C-4227	CREEPS (sh)	WHITE	COLUMBIA	1956
C-4227	G. I. DOOD IT (sh)	WHITE	COLUMBIA	1955
C-4228	BEDLAM IN PARADISE (sh)	WHITE	COLUMBIA	1955
C-4228	HEAVENLY DAZE (sh)	WHITE	COLUMBIA	1948
C-4229	STONE AGE ROMEOS (sh)	WHITE	COLUMBIA	1955
C-4230	HIS PEST FRIEND (sh)	WHITE	COLUMBIA	1955
C-4231	NOBODY'S HOME (sh)	WHITE	COLUMBIA	1955
C-4232	WHAM-BAM-SLAM! (sh)	WHITE	COLUMBIA	1955
C-4233	HOT ICE (sh)	WHITE	COLUMBIA	1955
C-4234	ONE SPOOKY NIGHT (sh)	WHITE	COLUMBIA	1955
C-4235	SCRATCH SCRATCH SCRATCH	WHITE	COLUMBIA	1955
C-4236	HUSBANDS BEWARE (sh)	WHITE	COLUMBIA	1956
C-4238	FLAGPOLE JITTERS (sh)	WHITE	COLUMBIA	1956
C-4239	FOR CRIMIN' OUT LOUD (sh)	WHITE	COLUMBIA	1956
C-4240	HOOK A CROOK (sh)	WHITE	COLUMBIA	1955
C-4241	HE TOOK A POWDER (sh)	WHITE	COLUMBIA	1955
C-4242	ARMY DAZE (sh)	WHITE	COLUMBIA	1956
C-4243	COME ON SEVEN (sh)	WHITE	COLUMBIA	1956
C-4244	RUMPUS IN THE HAREM (sh)	WHITE	COLUMBIA	1956
C-4245	HOT STUFF (sh)	WHITE	COLUMBIA	1956
C-4246	SCHEMING SCHEMERS (sh)	WHITE	COLUMBIA	1956
C-4247	COMMOTION ON THE OCEAN (sh)	WHITE	COLUMBIA	1956
C-4248	ANDY GOES WILD (sh)	WHITE	COLUMBIA	1956
C-4249	PARDON MY NIGHTSHIRT (sh)	WHITE	COLUMBIA	1956
C-4250	MUSCLE UP A LITTLE CLOSER (sh)	WHITE	COLUMBIA	1957
C-4251	HOOFS AND GOOFS (sh)	WHITE	COLUMBIA	1957
C-4252	MERRY MIXUP (sh)	WHITE	COLUMBIA	1957
C-4253	SPACE SHIP SAPPY (sh)	WHITE	COLUMBIA	1957
C5011	JOURNEY, THE	LITVAK	MGM	1959
C5016	ANGRY HILLS (UK)	ALDRICH	MGM	1959
C5019	HOUSE OF SEVEN HAWKS	THORPE	MGM	1959
C5021	DOCTOR'S DILEMMA (UK)	ASQUITH	MGM	1958
C5025	LAST VOYAGE, THE	STONE	MGM	1960
C5026	LIBEL (UK)	ASQUITH	MGM	1959
C5031	DAY THEY ROBBED THE BANK OF ENGLAND (UK)	GUILLERMIN	MGM	1960
C5032	ANGEL WORE RED	JOHNSON	MGM	1960
C5033	VILLAGE OF THE DAMNED	RILLA	MGM	1960
C5035	KING OF KINGS	RAY	MGM	1961
C5036	GREEN HELMET (UK)	FORLONG	MGM	1961
C5036	RED HELMET (UK)	FORLONG	MGM	1961
C5037	RING OF FIRE	STONE	MGM	1961
C5038	INVASION QUARTET (UK)	LEWIS	MGM	1961
C5042	FOLLOW THE BOYS	THORPE	MGM	1963
C5046	COLOSSUS OF RHODES (IT: IL COLOSSO DI RODI)	LEONI	MGM	1961
C5047	SECRET PARTNER	DEARDEN	MGM	1961
C5060	PASSWORD IS COURAGE (UK)	STONE	MGM	1963
C5061	VERY PRIVATE AFFAIR, A (FR: VIE PRIVEE 1962)	MALLE	MGM	1962
C5062	LIGHT IN THE PIAZZA	GREEN	MGM	1962
C5074	CAPTAIN SINDBAD	HASKIN	MGM	1963
C5075	TARZAN GOES TO INDIA	GUILLERMIN	MGM	1962

C5076	DAY AND THE HOUR, THE (FR: LE JOUR ET L'HEURE 1963)	CLEMENT	MGM	1964
C5096	YOUNG AND THE BRAVE	LYON	MGM	1963
C5097	CATTLE KING	GARNETT	MGM	1963
C5102	TARZAN'S THREE CHALLENGES (UK)	DAY	MGM	1963
C5118	FLIPPERS NEW ADVENTURE	BENSON	MGM	1964
C5307	DIME WITH A HALO	SAGAL	MGM	1963
C5309	B.I.P.S	ASQUITH	MGM	1963
C5314	AROUND THE WORLD UNDER THE SEA	MARTON	MGM	1966
C6052	SCORPIO LETTERS	THORPE	MGM	1967
C6055	WELCOME TO HARD TIMES	KENNEDY	MGM	1967
C6056	HONDO AND THE APACHES	KATZIN	MGM	1967
C-8007	LORNA DOONE	KARLSON	COLUMBIA	1951
C-8008	ROAR OF THE IRON HORSE	BENNET, CARR	COLUMBIA	1951
C-8009	TEXANS NEVER CRY	MCDONALD	COLUMBIA	1951
C-8010	VALLEY OF FIRE	ENGLISH	COLUMBIA	1951
C-8011	MAGIC CARPET	LANDERS	COLUMBIA	1951
C-8011	MYSTERIOUS ISLAND (serial)	BENNET	COLUMBIA	1951
C-8014	TEXAS RANGERS	LEDERMAN	COLUMBIA	1951
C-8015	BRIGAND	KARLSON	COLUMBIA	1952
C-8016	SILVER CANYON	ENGLISH	COLUMBIA	1951
C-8017	SCANDAL SHEET	KARLSON	COLUMBIA	1952
C-8026	WHIRLWIND	ENGLISH	COLUMBIA	1951
C-8029	INDIAN UPRISING	NAZARRO	COLUMBIA	1952
C-8030	CALIFORNIA CONQUEST	LANDERS	COLUMBIA	1952
C-8031	YANK IN KOREA	LANDERS	COLUMBIA	1951
C-8032	HILLS OF UTAH	ENGLISH	COLUMBIA	1951
C-8033	HARLEM GLOBETROTTERS	BROWN, JASON	COLUMBIA	1951
C-8035	MAN IN THE SADDLE	DE TOTH	COLUMBIA	1951
C-8036	PURPLE HEART DIARY	QUINE	COLUMBIA	1951
C-8037	JUNGLE JIM IN THE FORBIDDEN LAND	LANDERS	COLUMBIA	1952
C-8038	JUNGLE MAN-HUNT	LANDERS	COLUMBIA	1951
C-8039	KING OF THE CONGO (serial)	BENNET, GRISSELL	COLUMBIA	1952
C-8040	CAPTAIN VIDEO (serial)	BENNET, GRISSELL	COLUMBIA	1951
C-8041	BOOTS MALONE	DIETERLE	COLUMBIA	1952
C-8042	TEN TALL MEN	GOLDBECK	COLUMBIA	1951
C-8043	FIRST TIME	TASHLIN	COLUMBIA	1952
C-8044	BRAVE WARRIOR	BENNET	COLUMBIA	1952
C-8045	OLD WEST	ARCHAINBAUD	COLUMBIA	1952
C-8047	MEMBER OF THE WEDDING	ZINNEMANN	COLUMBIA	1952
C-8049	GOLDEN HAWK	SALKOW	COLUMBIA	1952
C-8053	PRINCE OF PIRATES	SALKOW	COLUMBIA	1953
C-8054	MY SIX CONVICTS	FREGONESE	COLUMBIA	1952
C-8055	BLACKHAWK	BENNET	COLUMBIA	1952
C-8056	DEATH OF A SALESMAN	BENEDEK	COLUMBIA	1951
C-8057	FOUR POSTER	REIS	COLUMBIA	1952
C-8061	CRIPPLE CREEK	NAZARRO	COLUMBIA	1952
C-8062	SNIPER	DMYTRYK	COLUMBIA	1952
C-8063	NIGHT STAGE TO GALVESTON	ARCHAINBAUD	COLUMBIA	1952
C-8064	5000 FINGERS OF DR. T	ROWLAND	COLUMBIA	1953
C-8066	AFFAIR IN TRINIDAD	SHERMAN	COLUMBIA	1952
C-8067	BLUE CANADIAN ROCKIES	ARCHAINBAUD	COLUMBIA	1952
C-8068	PRISONERS OF THE CASBAH	BARE	COLUMBIA	1953
C-8071	HAPPY TIME	FLEISCHER	COLUMBIA	1952
C-8072	APACHE COUNTRY	ARCHAINBAUD	COLUMBIA	1952
C-8074	MEMBER OF THE WEDDING	ZINNEMANN	COLUMBIA	1952
C-8078	EIGHT IRON MEN	DMYTRYK	COLUMBIA	1952
C-8079	BARBED WIRE	ARCHAINBAUD	COLUMBIA	1952
C-8082	CAINE MUTINY	DMYTRYK	COLUMBIA	1954
C-8085	YANK IN INDO-CHINA	GRISSELL	COLUMBIA	1952
C-8087	SERPENT OF THE NILE	CASTLE	COLUMBIA	1953
C-8088	LAST TRAIN FROM BOMBAY	SEARS	COLUMBIA	1952
C-8089	SAVAGE MUTINY	BENNET	COLUMBIA	1953
C-8090	VOODOO TIGER	BENNET	COLUMBIA	1952
C-8091	JUGGLER	DMYTRYK	COLUMBIA	1953
C-8092	JACK MCCALL – DESPERADO	SALKOW	COLUMBIA	1953
C-8093	PIRATES OF TRIPOLI	FEIST	COLUMBIA	1955

C-8094	WAGON TEAM	ARCHAINBAUD	COLUMBIA	1952
C-8095	LOST PLANET	BENNET	COLUMBIA	1953
C-8100	SON OF GERONIMO (serial)	BENNET	COLUMBIA	1952
C-8103	PATHFINDER	SALKOW	COLUMBIA	1952
C-8109	SLAVES OF BABYLON	CASTLE	COLUMBIA	1953
C-8115	SKY COMMANDS	SEARS	COLUMBIA	1953
C-8116	HANGMAN'S KNOT	HUGGINS	COLUMBIA	1952
C-8117	SALOME	DIETERLE	COLUMBIA	1953
C-8118	ON TOP OF OLD SMOKY	ARCHAINBAUD	COLUMBIA	1953
C-8120	FLAME OF CALCUTTA	FRIEDMAN	COLUMBIA	1953
C-8121	STRANGE FASCINATION	HAAS	COLUMBIA	1952
C-8122	SIREN OF BAGDAD	QUINE	COLUMBIA	1953
C-8125	WINNING OF THE WEST, THE	ARCHAINBAUD	COLUMBIA	1953
C-8127	IRON GLOVE	CASTLE	COLUMBIA	1954
C-8128	GOLDTOWN GHOST RIDERS	ARCHAINBAUD	COLUMBIA	1953
C-8130	CONQUEST OF COCHISE	CASTLE	COLUMBIA	1953
C-8132	CHARGE OF THE LANCERS	CASTLE	COLUMBIA	1954
C-8140	ONE GIRL'S CONFESSION	HAAS	COLUMBIA	1953
C-8146	PACK TRAIN	ARCHAINBAUD	COLUMBIA	1953
C-8149	GREAT ADV OF CAPTAIN KIDD (serial)	ABRAHAMS, GOULD	COLUMBIA	1953
C-8150	KILLER APE	BENNET	COLUMBIA	1953
C-8151	SAGINAW TRAIL	ARCHAINBAUD	COLUMBIA	1953
C-8157	49TH MAN	SEARS	COLUMBIA	1953
C-8170	MISS SADIE THOMPSON	BERNHARDT	COLUMBIA	1953
C-8173	FORT TI	CASTLE	COLUMBIA	1953
C-8178	STRANGER WORE A GUN	DE TOTH	COLUMBIA	1953
C-8188	LAST OF THE PONY RIDERS	ARCHAINBAUD	COLUMBIA	1953
C-8191	JESSE JAMES VS DALTSON	CASTLE	COLUMBIA	1954
C-8193	DRUMS OF TAHITI	CASTLE	COLUMBIA	1954
C-8194	GUNFIGHTERS OF THE NORTHWEST	BENNET, GOULD	COLUMBIA	1954
C-8197	SARACEN BLADE	CASTLE	COLUMBIA	1954
C-8204	JUNGLE MAN-EATERS	SHOLEM	COLUMBIA	1954
C-8205	RIDING WITH BUFFALO BILL (serial)	BENNET	COLUMBIA	1954
C-8206	LAW VS. BILLY THE KID	CASTLE	COLUMBIA	1954
C-8211	TEENAGE CRIME WAVE	SEARS	COLUMBIA	1955
C-8214	BATTLE OF ROGUE RIVER	CASTLE	COLUMBIA	1954
C-8247	MIAMI STORY	SEARS	COLUMBIA	1954
C-8249	CHICAGO SYNDICATE	SEARS	COLUMBIA	1955
C-8250	SEMINOLE UPRISING	BELLAMY	COLUMBIA	1955
C-8252	MASTERSON OF KANSAS	CASTLE	COLUMBIA	1954
C-8253	MAD MAGICIAN	BRAHM	COLUMBIA	1954
C-8257	ADVENTURES OF CAPTAIN AFRICA (serial)	BENNET	COLUMBIA	1955
C-8260	IT CAME FROM BENEATH THE SEA	GORDON	COLUMBIA	1955
C-8262	CANNIBAL ATTACK	SHOLEM	COLUMBIA	1954
C-8263	DEVIL GODDESS	BENNET	COLUMBIA	1955
C-8264	BAMBOO PRISON	SEILER	COLUMBIA	1954
C-8265	JUNGLE MOON-MEN	GOULD	COLUMBIA	1955
C-8271	MAN FROM LARAMIE	MANN	COLUMBIA	1955
C-8273	TEN WANTED MEN	HUMBERSTONE	COLUMBIA	1955
C-8274	WOMEN'S PRISON	SEILER	COLUMBIA	1955
C-8281	NEW ORLEANS UNCENSORED	CASTLE	COLUMBIA	1955
C-8284	GUN THAT WON THE WEST	CASTLE	COLUMBIA	1955
C-8285	CREATURE WITH THE ATOM BRAIN	CAHN	COLUMBIA	1955
C-8286	DUEL ON THE MISSISSIPPI	CASTLE	COLUMBIA	1955
C-8289	BATTLE STATIONS	SEILER	COLUMBIA	1956
C-8289	BROTHERS RICO	KARLSON	COLUMBIA	1957
C-8294	LONG GREY LINE	FORD	COLUMBIA	1955
C-8301	FIVE AGAINST THE HOUSE	KARLSON	COLUMBIA	1955
C-8305	NIGHT HOLDS TERROR	STONE	COLUMBIA	1955
C-8306	LAWLESS STREET	LEWIS	COLUMBIA	1955
C-8307	EARTH VS. THE FLYING SAUCERS	SEARS	COLUMBIA	1956
C-8308	COUNT THREE AND PRAY	SHERMAN	COLUMBIA	1955
C-8310	HOUSTON STORY	CASTLE	COLUMBIA	1956
C-8311	BLACKJACK KETCHUM-DESPERADO	BELLAMY	COLUMBIA	1956
C-8313	INSIDE DETROIT	SEARS	COLUMBIA	1956
C-8319	FLYING FONTAINES	SHERMAN	COLUMBIA	1959

C-8321	CROOKED WEB	JURAN	COLUMBIA	1955
C-8322	AUTUMN LEAVES	ALDRICH	COLUMBIA	1956
C-8323	BELL BOOK AND CANDLE	QUINE	COLUMBIA	1958
C-8330	NIGHTFALL	TOURNEUR	COLUMBIA	1957
C-8333	STORM CENTER	TARADASH	COLUMBIA	1956
C-8335	HOT BLOOD	RAY	COLUMBIA	1956
C-8336	BLAZING THE OVERLAND TRAIL (serial)	BENNET	COLUMBIA	1956
C-8342	GUNS OF FORT PETTICOAT	MARSHALL	COLUMBIA	1957
C-8344	SEVENTH CALVARY	LEWIS	COLUMBIA	1956
C-8346	REPRISAL	SHERMAN	COLUMBIA	1956
C-8352	ROCK AROUND THE CLOCK	SEARS	COLUMBIA	1956
C-8354	RUMBLE ON THE DOCKS	SEARS	COLUMBIA	1956
C-8355	MIAMI EXPOSE	SEARS	COLUMBIA	1956
C-8359	GIANT CLAW	SEARS	COLUMBIA	1957
C-8359	WHITE SQUAW	NAZARRO	COLUMBIA	1956
C-8363	CHA-CHA-CHA BOOM	SEARS	COLUMBIA	1956
C-8365	20 MILLION MILES TO EARTH	JURAN	COLUMBIA	1957
C-8366	NIGHT THE WORLD EXPLODED	SEARS	COLUMBIA	1957
C-8368	CHA CHA CHA BOOM	SEARS	COLUMBIA	1956
C-8372	LINEUP	SIEGEL	COLUMBIA	1958
C-8373	MAN WHO TURNED TO STONE	KARDOS	COLUMBIA	1957
C-8375	BRIDGE ON THE RIVER KWAI	LEAN	COLUMBIA	1957
C-8376	HELLCATS OF THE NAVY	JURAN	COLUMBIA	1957
C-8379	TALL T	BOATTICHER	COLUMBIA	1957
C-8381	UTAH BLAINE	SEARS	COLUMBIA	1957
C-8383	DON'T KNOCK THE ROCK	SEARS	COLUMBIA	1956
C-8394	RETURN TO WARBOW	NAZARRO	COLUMBIA	1958
C-8395	GARMENT JUNGLE	SHERMAN	COLUMBIA	1957
C-8396	NO TIME TO BE YOUNG	RICH	COLUMBIA	1957
C-8397	3:10 TO YUMA	DAVES	COLUMBIA	1957
C-8398	ESCAPE FROM SAN QUENTIN	SEARS	COLUMBIA	1957
C-8400	SEVENTH VOYAGE OF SINBAD	JURAN	COLUMBIA	1958
C-8403	JEANNE EAGELS	SIDNEY	COLUMBIA	1957
C-8406	CRASH LANDING	SEARS	COLUMBIA	1958
C-8407	PAL JOEY	SIDNEY	COLUMBIA	1957
C-8414	HARD MAN	SHERMAN	COLUMBIA	1957
C-8417	THIS ANGRY AGE	CLEMENT	COLUMBIA	1958
C-8420	DECISION AT SUNDOWN	BOETTICHER	COLUMBIA	1957
C-8422	LIFE BEGINS AT 17	DREIFUSS	COLUMBIA	1958
C-8423	OPERATION MADBALL	QUINE	COLUMBIA	1957
C-8426	BATTLE OF THE CORAL SEA	WENDKOS	COLUMBIA	1959
C-8427	TARAWA BEACHHEAD	WENDKOS	COLUMBIA	1958
C-8428	CASE AGAINST BROOKLYN	WENDKOS	COLUMBIA	1958
C-8431	SCREAMING MIMI	OSWALD	COLUMBIA	1958
C-8449	TRUE STORY OF LYNN STUART	SEILER	COLUMBIA	1958
C-8453	COWBOY	DAVES	COLUMBIA	1958
C-8461	LAST BLITZKRIEG	DREIFUSS	COLUMBIA	1959
C-8462	1001 ARABIAN NIGHTS (t)	KINNEY	COLUMBIA	1959
C-8464	13 WEST STREET	LEACOCK	COLUMBIA	1962
C-8465	GODDESS	CROMWELL	COLUMBIA	1958
C-8468	JUKE BOX RHYTHM	DREIFUSS	COLUMBIA	1959
C-8470	FORBIDDEN ISLAND	GRIFFITH	COLUMBIA	1959
C-8472	APACHE TERRITORY	NAZARRO	COLUMBIA	1958
C-8475	ME AND THE COLONEL	GLENVILLE	COLUMBIA	1958
C-8476	PEPE	SIDNEY	COLUMBIA	1960
C-8484	13 WEST STREET	LEACOCK	COLUMBIA	1962
C-8485	LAST HURRAH	FORD	COLUMBIA	1958
C-8495	GOOD DAY FOR A HANGING	JURAN	COLUMBIA	1959
C-8496	IT HAPPENED TO JANE	QUINE	COLUMBIA	1959
C-8498	GENE KRUPA STORY	WEIS	COLUMBIA	1959
C-8500	CHASE		COLUMBIA	1958
C-8501	GUNS OF NAVARONE (UK)	THOMPSON	COLUMBIA	1961
C-8502	SONG WITHOUT END	VIDOR	COLUMBIA	1960
C-8503	THEY CAME TO CORDURA	ROSSEN	COLUMBIA	1959
C-8504	MOUNTAIN ROAD	MANN	COLUMBIA	1960
C-8506	RIDE LONESOME	BOETTICHER	COLUMBIA	1959

C-8507	SENIOR PROM	RICH	COLUMBIA	1958
C-8508	LET NO MAN WRITE MY EPITAPH	LEACOCK	COLUMBIA	1960
C-8511	I AIM AT THE STARS	THOMPSON	COLUMBIA	1960
C-8512	SURPRISE PACKAGE	DONEN	COLUMBIA	1960
C-8513	HEY BOY HEY GIRL	RICH	COLUMBIA	1959
C-8514	MAN ON A STRING	DE TOTH	COLUMBIA	1960
C-8515	MYSTERIOUS ISLAND	ENDFIELD	COLUMBIA	1962
C-8516	FACE OF A FUGITIVE	WENDKOS	COLUMBIA	1959
C-8518	WHO WAS THAT LADY?	SIDNEY	COLUMBIA	1960
C-8519	CRIMSON KIMONO	FULLER	COLUMBIA	1959
C-8520	LAST ANGRY MAN	MANN	COLUMBIA	1959
C-8525	DEVIL AT 4 O'CLOCK	LEROY	COLUMBIA	1961
C-8535	30 FOOT BRIDE OF CANDY ROCK	MILLER	COLUMBIA	1959
C-8536	MIDDLE OF THE NIGHT	MANN	COLUMBIA	1959
C-8539	STRANGERS WHEN WE MEET	QUINE	COLUMBIA	1960
C-8542	3 WORLDS OF GULLIVER (t)	SHERMAN	COLUMBIA	1960
C-8543	NOTORIOUS LANDLADY	QUINE	COLUMBIA	1962
C-8546	EDGE OF ETERNITY	SIEGEL	COLUMBIA	1959
C-8550	LEGEND OF TOM DOOLEY	POST	COLUMBIA	1959
C-8556	HAVE ROCKET WILL TRAVEL	RICH	COLUMBIA	1959
C-8557	COMANCHE STATION	BOETTICHER	COLUMBIA	1960
C-8559	TINGLER	CASTLE	COLUMBIA	1959
C-8566	CRY FOR HAPPY	MARSHALL	COLUMBIA	1961
C-8569	BECAUSE THEY'RE YOUNG	WENDKOS	COLUMBIA	1960
C-8570	RAISIN IN THE SUN	PETRIE	COLUMBIA	1961
C-8572	ENEMY GENERAL	SHERMAN	COLUMBIA	1960
C-8573	ALL THE YOUNG MEN	BARTLETT	COLUMBIA	1960
C-8581	GIDGET GOES HAWAIIAN	WENDKOS	COLUMBIA	1961
C-8583	THIRTEEN GHOSTS	CASTLE	COLUMBIA	1960
C-8588	DIAMOND HEAD	GREEN	COLUMBIA	1963
C-8591	STOP, LOOK AND LAUGH	APPELL, BRANDT	COLUMBIA	1960
C-8594	HOMICIDAL	CASTLE	COLUMBIA	1961
C-8596	INTERNS	SWIFT	COLUMBIA	1962
C-8602	SAIL A CROOKED SHIP	BRECHER	COLUMBIA	1961
C-8603	FIVE FINGER EXERCISE	MANN	COLUMBIA	1962
C-8610	MR. SARDONICUS	CASTLE	COLUMBIA	1961
C-8617	THREE STOOGES MEET HERCULES	BERNDS	COLUMBIA	1962
C-8624	EVERYTHING'S DUCKY	TAYLOR	COLUMBIA	1961
C-8625	BYE BYE BIRDIE	SIDNEY	COLUMBIA	1963
C-8626	EXPERIMENT IN TERROR	EDWARDS	COLUMBIA	1962
C-8629	WALK ON THE WILD SIDE	DYMTRYK	COLUMBIA	1962
C-8633	MAN FROM THE DINER'S CLUB	TASHLIN	COLUMBIA	1963
C-8650	13 FRIGHTENED GIRLS	CASTLE	COLUMBIA	1963
C-8652	WILD WESTERNERS	RUDOLPH	COLUMBIA	1962
C-8657	DON'T KNOCK THE TWIST	RUDOLPH	COLUMBIA	1962
C-8666	THREE STOOGES IN ORBIT	BERNDS	COLUMBIA	1962
C-8689	KING RAT	FORBES	COLUMBIA	1965
C-8691	STRAIGHT-JACKET	CASTLE	COLUMBIA	1964
C-8699	GOOD NEIGHBOR SAM	SWIFT	COLUMBIA	1964
C-8701	CAT BALLOU	SILVERSTEIN	COLUMBIA	1965
C-8705	3 STOOGES GO AROUND THE WORLD IN A DAZE	MAURER	COLUMBIA	1963
C-8709	BABY THE RAIN MUST FALL	MULLIGAN	COLUMBIA	1965
C-8712	PROFESSIONALS	BROOKS	COLUMBIA	1966
C-8715	MAJOR DUNDEE	PECKINPAH	COLUMBIA	1965
C-8719	COLLECTOR	WYLER	COLUMBIA	1965
C-8720	HEY THERE IT'S YOGI BEAR (t)	HANNA, BARBERA	COLUMBIA	1964
C-8722	LIFE BEGINS AT 17	DREIFUSS	COLUMBIA	1958
C-8724	QUICK GUN	SALKOW	COLUMBIA	1964
C-8731	OUTLAWS IS COMING	MAURER	COLUMBIA	1965
C-8732	RIDE THE WILD SURF	TAYLOR	COLUMBIA	1964
C-8741	SILENCERS	KARLSON	COLUMBIA	1966
C-8744	ALVAREZ KELLY	DMYTRYK	COLUMBIA	1966
C-8755	WALK DON'T RUN	WALTERS	COLUMBIA	1966
C-8761	ARIZONA RAIDERS	WITNEY	COLUMBIA	1965
C-8774	WINTER A GO-GO	BENEDICT	COLUMBIA	1965
C-8802	RIDE BEYOND VENGEANCE	MCEVEETY	COLUMBIA	1966

C-8817	THREE ON A COUCH	LEWIS	COLUMBIA	1966
C-8818	BIRDS DO IT	MARTON	COLUMBIA	1966
C-8826	RAGE	GAZCON	COLUMBIA	1966
C#	CORONADO PRODUCTIONS AT COLUMBIA		COL	
CA	AFRICA: TEXAS STYLE (UK)	MARTON	PARAMOUNT	1967
CA	CARRINGTON	HAMPTON	GRAMERCY	1995
CA	CHANCES ARE	ARDOLINO	TRI STAR	1989
CA	CHARLEY'S AUNT (UK: CHARLEY'S BIG HEARTED AUNT)	FORDE	GFD	1940
CA	CITY OF ANGELS	SILBERLING	WARNER BROS	1998
CA	CLASS ACT	MILLER	WARNER BROS	1992
CA	CLASS ACTION	APTED	20th CENTURY FOX	1991
CA	CONQUEST OF THE AIR (UK)	ESWAY, KORDA	UNITED ARTISTS	1936
CA	CROOKS ANONYMOUS (UK)	ANNAKIN	JANUS	1962
CA	QUESTION OF ADULTERY (UK)	CHAFFEY	EROS	1958
CA-84	DON'T FLIRT (sh)	POWERS	PATHE EXCHANGE	1923
CA-88	WATCH DOG (sh)	POWERS	PATHE EXCHANGE	1923
C-AA	GOODBYE GEMINI/ASK AGAMEMNON* (UK)	GIBSON	CINERAMA	1970
CAA	QUESTION OF ADULTERY (UK)	CHAFFEY	EROS	1958
CAC	CAMELS ARE COMING (UK)	WHELAN	GAUMONT BRITISH	1934
CAI	CAIRO	RILLA	MGM	1963
CAL	CHANCE OF A LIFETIME (UK)	MILES	BALLANTINE	1950
CAL	CRIMINAL AT LARGE (UK: FRIGHTENED LADY)	HUNTER	HELBER	1932
CAP	CAPRICORN ONE	HYAMS	WARNER BROS	1977
CAT	CAT, THE	KADISON	EMBASSY	1966
CB	CALLED BACK (UK)	DENHAM, HARRIS	RKO	1933
CB	CANADIAN BACON	MOORE	GRAMERCY	1995
CB	CHINESE DEN (UK: CHINESE BUNGALOW)	KING	FILM ALLIANCE	1940
CB	CLARA BOW	portrait		
CB	COLONEL BLOOD (UK)	LIPSCOMB	MGM	1934
CB	COMPANY BUSINESS	MEYER	MGM	1991
CB	CONJUGAL BED	FERRERI	EMBASSY	1963
CB	COOL BREEZE	POLLACK	MGM	1972
CB	CORRIDORS OF BLOOD (UK)	DAY	MGM	1958
CB	COUNTRY BOY	CAIN	HOWCO	1966
CB	CRIMEBUSTERS (IT: I DUE SUPERPIEDI QUASI PIATTI 1977)	BARBONI	UNITED ARTISTS	1979
CB	CRIMSON BLADE (UK: SCARLET BLADE)	GILLING	COLUMBIA	1963
CB	KILLING OF A CHINESE BOOKIE	CASAVETTES	FACES	1976
CBBB	CABIN BOY	RESNICK	BUENA VISTA	1994
CBC	CHEER BOYS CHEER (UK)	FORDE	ABFD	1939
CBR	CANNONBALL RUN	NEEDHAM	20th CENTURY FOX	1981
CBS	THEY CAME FROM BEYOND SPACE (UK)	FRANCIS	EMBASSY	1967
CC	BOAT FROM SHANGHAI (UK: CHIN CHIN CHINAMAN)	NEWALL	FIRST DIVISION	1931
CC	C. C. AND COMPANY	ROBBIE	AVCO EMBASSY	1970
CC	CALVALRY COMMAND	DE LEON	EAGLE FILMS	1958
CC	CARAVAN OF COURAGE: EWOK ADVENTURE	KORTY	20th CENTURY FOX	1984
CC	CARBON COPY	SCHULTZ	AVCO EMBASSY	1981
CC	CAROLYN CHERIE (DEAR CAROLINE)	PATELLIERE	ARTHUR DAVIS REL.	1968
CC	CHARLIE CHAN AND THE CURSE OF THE DRAGON QUEEN	DONNNER	AMERICAN CINEMA	1981
CC	CHICKEN CHRONICLES	SIMON	AVCO EMBASSY	1977
CC	CHU CHU AND THE PHILLY FLASH	RICH	20th CENTURY FOX	1981
CC	CINDY CAROL AKA CAROL SYDES		COL	
CC	CLAIRE CARLETON	portrait	RKO	
CC	COAST TO COAST	SARGENT	PARAMOUNT	1980
CC	COCKEYED CAVALIERS	SANDRICH	RKO	1934
CC	COCOON	HOWARD	20th CENTURY FOX	1985
CC	COPYCAT	AMIEL	WARNER BROS	1995
CC	COTTON CLUB	COPPOLA	ORION	1984
CC	CRITICAL CONDITION	APTED	PARAMOUNT	1986
CC	HAVING A WILD WEEKEND (UK: CATCH US IF YOU CAN)	BOORMAN	WARNER BROS	1965
CC	SOPHIE'S PLACE (UK: CROOKS AND CORONETS)	O'CONNELLY	WARNER BROS.	1969
CC-129	HARD KNOCKS (sh)	PARROTT	PATHE EXCHANGE	1924
CC-131	ONE OF THE FAMILY (sh)	PEMBROKE	PATHE EXCHANGE	1924
CC-394	COTTON CLUB	COPPOLA	ORION	1984
CCBB	COLD CREEK MANOR	FIGGIS	BUENA VISTA	2003
CCC	CULPEPPER CATTLE CO	RICHARDSON	20th CENTURY FOX	1972
CCF	CURE, THE	CHAPLIN	MUTUAL	1917

CC-K	CASSANDRA CROSSING	COSMATOS	AVCO EMBASSY	1976
C-COL-1	CRAIG'S WIFE	ARZNER	COLUMBIA	1936
C-COL-1	THUNDER IN THE CITY	GERING	COLUMBIA	1937
C-COL-3	COME CLOSER FOLKS	LEDERMAN	COLUMBIA	1936
C-COL-4	DEVIL'S PLAYGROUND	KENTON	COLUMBIA	1937
C-COL-7	MORE THAN A SECRETARY	GREEN	COLUMBIA	1936
C-COL-8	WOMEN OF GLAMOUR	WILES	COLUMBIA	1937
C-COL-9	I PROMISE TO PAY	LEDERMAN	COLUMBIA	1937
C-COL-10	WOMAN IN DISTRESS	SHORES	COLUMBIA	1937
C-COL-11	IT'S ALL YOURS	NUGENT	COLUMBIA	1937
C-COL-14	LET'S GET MARRIED	GREEN	COLUMBIA	1937
C-COL-15	RACKETEERS IN EXILE	KENTON	COLUMBIA	1937
C-COL-17	VENUS MAKES TROUBLE	WILES	COLUMBIA	1937
C-COL-19	LEAGUE OF FRIGHTENED MEN	GREEN	COLUMBIA	1937
C-COL-21	LOST HORIZON	CAPRA	COLUMBIA	1937
C-COL-22	IT HAPPENED IN HOLLYWOOD	LACHMAN	COLUMBIA	1937
C-COL-24	IT CAN'T LAST FOREVER	MACFADDEN	COLUMBIA	1937
C-COL-26	LADY FROM NOWHERE	WILES	COLUMBIA	1936
C-COL-30	ADVENTURE IN MANHATTAN	LUDWIG	COLUMBIA	1936
C-COL-31	DEVIL IS DRIVING	LACHMAN	COLUMBIA	1937
C-COL-34	MAN WHO LIVED TWICE	LACHMAN	COLUMBIA	1936
C-COL-60	LEGION OF TERROR	COLEMAN	COLUMBIA	1936
C-COL-61	COUNTERFEIT LADY	LEDERMAN	COLUMBIA	1936
C-COL-62	FIND THE WITNESS	SELMAN	COLUMBIA	1937
C-COL-63	PAROLE RACKET	COLEMAN	COLUMBIA	1937
C-COL-64	SPEED TO SPARE	HILLYER	COLUMBIA	1937
C-COL-65	MOTOR MADNESS	LEDERMAN	COLUMBIA	1937
C-COL-66	CRIMINALS OF THE AIR	COLEMAN	COLUMBIA	1937
C-COL-68	FRAMEUP	LEDERMAN	COLUMBIA	1937
C-COL-70	DANGEROUS ADVENTURE	LEDERMAN	COLUMBIA	1937
C-COL-71	FIGHT TO THE FINISH	COLEMAN	COLUMBIA	1937
C-COL-80	CODE OF THE RANGE	COLEMAN	COLUMBIA	1936
C-COL-81	COWBOY STAR	SELMAN	COLUMBIA	1936
C-COL-82	DODGE CITY TRAIL	COLEMAN	COLUMBIA	1936
C-COL-83	WESTBOUND MAIL	BLANGSTED	COLUMBIA	1937
C-COL-84	TRAPPED	BARSHA	COLUMBIA	1937
C-COL-86	TWO GUN LAW	BARSHA	COLUMBIA	1937
C-COL-87	TWO FISTED SHERIFF	BARSHA	COLUMBIA	1937
C-COL-88	ONE MAN JUSTICE	BARSHA	COLUMBIA	1937
C-COL-201	UNRELATED RELATIONS (sh)	LORD	COLUMBIA	1936
C-COL-212	PEPPERY SALT (sh)	LORD	COLUMBIA	1936
C-COL-214	JUST SPEEDING (sh)	LORD	COLUMBIA	1936
C-COL-215	SHARE THE WEALTH (sh)	LORD	COLUMBIA	1936
C-COL-216	MIDNIGHT BLUNDERS (sh)	LORD	COLUMBIA	1936
C-COL-218	ANTS IN THE PANTRY (sh)	WHITE	COLUMBIA	1936
C-COL-259	GRIPS, GRUNTS AND GROANS (sh)	WHITE	COLUMBIA	1937
C-COL-260	SAILOR MAID (sh)	LAMONT	COLUMBIA	1937
C-COL-261	KNEE ACTION (sh)	LAMONT	COLUMBIA	1937
C-COL-262	SUPER SNOOPER (sh)	WHITE	COLUMBIA	1937
C-COL-263	DIZZY DOCTORS (sh)	LORD	COLUMBIA	1937
C-COL-264	BURY THE HATCHET (sh)	LORD	COLUMBIA	1937
C-COL-265	STUCK IN THE STICKS (sh)	WHITE	COLUMBIA	1937
C-COL-266	3 DUMB CLUCKS (sh)	LORD	COLUMBIA	1937
C-COL-267	NEW NEWS (sh)	LAMONT	COLUMBIA	1937
C-COL-268	BACK TO THE WOODS (sh)	WHITE	COLUMBIA	1937
C-COL-269	GRAND HOOTER (sh)	WHITE	COLUMBIA	1937
C-COL-270	LODGE NIGHT (sh)	WHITE	COLUMBIA	1937
C-COL-271	FROM BAD TO WORSE (sh)	LORD	COLUMBIA	1937
C-COL-273	WRONG MISS WRIGHT (sh)	LAMONT	COLUMBIA	1937
C-COL-274	GOOFS AND SADDLES (sh)	LORD	COLUMBIA	1937
C-COL-275	CALLING ALL DOCTORS (sh)	LAMONT	COLUMBIA	1937
C-COL-280	COMMUNITY SING - #3	series	COLUMBIA	1937
C-COL-281	COMMUNITY SING - #4	series	COLUMBIA	1937
C-COL-282	COMMUNITY SING - #5	series	COLUMBIA	1937
C-COL-400	CASH AND CARRY (sh)	LORD	COLUMBIA	1937
C-COL-401	PLAYING THE PONIES (sh)	LAMONT	COLUMBIA	1937

C-COL-402	SITTER DOWNERS (sh)	LORD	COLUMBIA	1937
C-COL-406	BIG SQUIRT (sh)	LORD	COLUMBIA	1937
C-COL-407	GRACIE AT THE BAT (sh)	LORD	COLUMBIA	1937
C-COL-408	OH, WHAT A KNIGHT! (sh)	CHASE	COLUMBIA	1937
C-COL-411	HE DONE HIS DUTY (sh)	LAMONT	COLUMBIA	1937
C-COL-414	MAN BITES LOVEBUG (sh)	LORD	COLUMBIA	1937
CCS	KATHY'S LOVE AFFAIR (UK: COURTNEYS OF CURZON STREET)	WILCOX	SNADER	1947
CD	CAROL DOUGLAS		COL	
CD	CATS AND DOGS	GUTERMAN	WARNER BROS	2001
CD	CHALLENGE OF THE DRAGON	WEI	CANNON	1974
CD	CHARLES DRAKE	portrait	WARNER BROS	
CD	CHARMING DECEIVER (UK)	BANKS	MAJESTIC	1933
CD	CIRCLE OF DECEPTION	LEE	20th CENTURY-FOX	1960
CD	COLLEGE DAYS	THORPE	TIFFANY PRODUCTIONS	1926
CD	CONSTANCE DOWLING	portrait	RKO	
CD	COUNTESS DRACULA	SASDY	20th CENTURY FOX	1971
CD	CROCODILE DUNDEE	FAIMAN	PARAMOUNT	1986
CD	CROCODILE DUNDEE IN LOS ANGELES	WINCER	PARAMOUNT	2001
CD	ON A CLEAR DAY YOU CAN SEE FOREVER	MINNELLI	PARAMOUNT	1970
CD1901	HORSING AROUND (sh)	WHITE	COLUMBIA	1957
CD8307	EARTH VS FLYING SAUCIERS	SEARS	COLUMBIA	1956
CDG	COUP DE GRACE (GER: DER FANGSCHUB 1976)	SCHLONDORFF	CINEMA 5	1978
CDL	CASE OF DOCTOR LAURENT, THE (FR)	LE CHANOIS	TRANS-LUX	1957
CDLA	CROCODILE DUNDEE IN LOS ANGELES	WINCER	PARAMOUNT	2001
C-DLB	DIRTY LITTLE BILLY	DRAGOTI	COLUMBIA	1972
CDS	CAST A DARK SHADOW (UK 1955)	GILBERT	DCA	1957
CDVB	COUNT DRACULA AND HIS VAMPIRE BRIDE	GIBSON	WARNER BROS	1973
CE	CAT'S EYE	TEAGUE	MGM	1985
CE	CRAWLING EYE (UK: TROLLENBERG TERROR)	LAWRENCE	DCA	1958
CE	CROWNING EXPERIENCE, THE	ANDERSON	MORAL RE-ARMAMENT	1960
CE-1	BOOLOO	ELLIOTT	PARAMOUNT	1938
CEF-2137	CASE OF THE MISSING SCENE (UK)	CHAFFEY	GFD	1951
CF	CALL OF THE FOREST	LINK SR.	LIPPERT	1949
CF	CAPTAIN PHANTOM (IT: CAPTAIN FANTASMA 1953)	ZEGLIO	R. C. I. P.	1960
CF	CARTHAGE IN FLAMES (IT: CARTAGINE IN FLAMME)	GALLONE	COLUMBIA	1961
CF1	QUIET WEDDING (UK)	ASQUITH	UNIVERSAL	1941
CFBL	CREATURE FROM BLACK LAKE	HOUCK JR	HOWCO INT'L	1976
CFF-11	SKID KIDS (UK)	CHAFFEY	ASSO. BRITISH-PATHE	1953
CFF-APE	CLUE OF THE MISSING APE (UK)	HILL	ASSO. BRITISH-PATHE	1953
CFF-CF	CIRCUS FRIENDS (UK)	THOMAS	CONTINENTAL	1956
CFF-DOG	DOG AND THE DIAMONDS (UK)	THOMAS	ASSO. BRITISH-PATHE	1953
CFF-HD	HEIGHTS OF DANGER (UK)	BRADFORD	ASSO. BRITISH-PATHE	1953
CF-III	LA CAGE AUX FOLLES III	LAUTNER	TRI STAR	1985
CFF-JOHN	JOHN OF THE FAIR (UK)	MCCARTHY	ASSOCIATED BRITISH	1954
CFF-PLAN	STOLEN PLANS (UK)	HILL	CONTINENTAL	1952
CFF S3	MURDER AT SITE 3 (UK)	SEARLE	EXCLUSIVE	1959
CFF-SA1	STOLEN AIRLINER (UK)	SHARP	BRITISH LION	1955
CFF-WISH	ONE WISH TOO MANY (UK)	DURST	STERLING	1956
CFMC	CASTLE OF FU MANCHU (UK)	FRANCO	INT'L CINEMA	1969
CFP-168	DOCTOR'S DILEMMA (UK)	ASQUITH	MGM	1958
CFT	COUNTERFEITERS OF PARIS (FR: LE CAVE SE REBIFFE 1961)	GRANGIER	MGM	1963
CG	CABINET OF CALIGARI	KAY	20th CENTURY FOX	1962
CG	CALENDAR GIRLS	COLE	BUENA VISTA	2003
CG	COLLEEN GRAY	portrait	UNIVERSAL	
CG	CONTEST GIRL (UK: BEAUTY JUNGLE)	GUEST	CONTINENTAL	1964
CGA	CHINA GATE	FULLER	20th CENTURY FOX	1957
CG-BB	CALENDAR GIRLS	COLE	BUENA VISTA	2003
CGNH	CAREER GIRLS ON A NAKED HOLIDAY	SUPPLEE		1960
CH	CHAIN OF FOOLS	LOWENHEILM	WARNER BROS	2000
CH	CHARLY	NELSON	CINERAMA RELEASING	1968
CH	CHEAPER TO KEEP HER	ANNAKIN	AMERICAN CINEMA	1980
CH	CLARA'S HEART	MULLIGAN	WARNER BROS	1988
CH	CONEHEADS	BARRON	PARAMOUNT	1993
CH	FIRE WITH FIRE	GIBBINS	PARAMOUNT	1986
CH	UNDERGROUND GUERRILLAS (UK: UNDERCOVER)	NOLBANDOV	COLUMBIA	1943
CH-37	CHEAPER TO KEEP HER	ANNAKIN	AMERICAN CINEMA	1980

CHC	CHAMPAGNE CHARLIE (UK)	CAVALCANTI	BELL	1944
CI	CUTTHROAT ISLAND	HARLIN	CAROLCO	1995
CIA	CHLOE IN THE AFTERNOON (FR: L'AMOUR L'APRES-MIDI)	ROHMER	COLUMBIA	1972
C-INT	CAVEMAN	GOTTLIEB	UNITED ARTISTS	1981
CIS	CACTUS IN THE SNOW	ZWEIBACH	GENENI FILM	1971
CJ	CLAUDE JADE	portrait	UNIV	
CJ	CLAUDE JARMAN JR.	portrait		
CJ	CONCRETE JUNGLE (UK: CRIMINAL)	LOSEY	FANFARE	1960
CK	CARNAL KNOWLEDGE	NICHOLS	AVCO EMBASSY	1971
CK	CECIL KELLAWAY	portrait	SELZNICK	
CK	CHARLES KEMPER	portrait		
CK	CHARLES KULLMAN/KULLMANN	portrait	UNIV	
CK	CHEAP KISSES	INCE	FBO	1924
CK	COVER GIRL KILLER (UK)	BISHOP	FANFARE	1960
CL	BOMBSIGHT STOLEN (UK: COTTAGE TO LET)	ASQUITH	GFD	1941
CL	CAROLE LANDIS	portrait	RKO	
CL	CAROLE LOMBARD	portrait	RKO	1930s-40s
CL	CHARLES LANG	portrait	RKO	
CL	CHARLES LAUGHTON	portrait	RKO	
CL	CHELSEA LIFE (UK)	MORGAN	PARAMOUNT BRITISH	1933
CL	CINDERELLA LIBERTY	RYDELL	20th CENTURY FOX	1973
CL	CIRCLE OF LOVE	VADIM	CONTINENTAL	1965
CL	CLASS	CARLINO	ORION	1983
CL	CLOSET LAND	BHARADWAJ	UNIVERSAL	1990
CL	CLUE	LYNN	PARAMOUNT	1985
CL	CULLEN LANDIS	portrait	METRO	
CL	HE FOUND A STAR (UK)	CARSTAIRS	GFD	1941
CL	LOS CUERVOS ESTAN DE LUTO (MEX.)	VILLAR	PEL MEX	1965
CLEO	CLEOPATRA	MANKIEWICZ	20TH CENTURY FOX	1963
CLK	CLAIRE'S KNEE (FRANCE: GENOU DE CLAIRE)	ROHMER	COLUMBIA	1971
CM	84 CHARLIE MOPIC	DUNCAN	NEW CENTURY VISTA	1989
CM	CALL ME GENIUS (UK: REBEL)	DAY	CONTINENTAL	1961
CM	CAMPUS MAN	CASDEN	PARAMOUNT	1987
CM	CAPTAIN MILKSHAKE	CRAWFORD	TWI NATIONAL	1970
CM	CHARLIE MURRAY	portrait		
CM	CHRISTINE MARTEL	portrait	UNIV	
CM	COMEDY MAN (UK)	RAKOFF	BRITISH LION	1964
CM	CORRIDOR OF MIRRORS (UK)	YOUNG	UNIVERSAL	1948
CM	COSMIC MONSTER (UK: STRANGE WORLD OF PLANET X)	GUNN	DCA	1958
CM	DESPERATE MEN (UK: CAT AND MOUSE)	ROTHA	EROS	1958
CMB	COUNTRY MUSIC ON BROADWAY	DUNCAN	MARATHON PICT.	1964
CMBB	COLOR OF MONEY	SCORSESE	BUENA VISTA	1986
C.Mc	CATHERINE MCLEOD (ALSO CM)		REPUBLIC	1940s-1950s
C-MPS	SECRETS	BORZAGE	UNITED ARTISTS	1933
CMX	CHESTER MORRIS	portrait	MGM	
CN	CAPONE	CARVER	20th CENTURY FOX	1975
CN	CAPTAIN NEMO AND THE UNDERWATER CITY (UK)	HILL	MGM-UK	1969
CN	COSA NOSTRA - AN ARCH ENEMY OF THE FBI (tv)	MEDFORD	WARNER BROS	1967
CN	ONE NIGHT STAND	FIGGIS	NEW LINE CINEMA	1997
CN-21	HOME ALONE 3	GOSNELL	20th CENTURY FOX	1997
CN23	FREQUENCY	HOBLIT	NEW LINE CINEMA	2000
CN35	15 MINUTES	HERZFELD	NEW LINE CINEMA	2001
CNT	CAT O'NINE TAILS	ARGENTO	NATIONAL GEN. PIC.	1971
CNT	CHANCE OF A LIFETIME (UK)	LYNN, WILCOX	WOOLF & FREEDMAN	1931
CO	BLOOD AND STEEL	KOWALSKI	20th CENTURY FOX	1959
CO	CIRCLE OF DECEPTION (UK)	LEE	20TH CENTURY FOX	1960
CO	CONVICT 99 (UK)	VARNEL	GFD	1938
CO	COOKIE	SEIDELMAN	WARNER BROS	1989
CO	COP-OUT (UK: STRANGER IN THE HOUSE)	ROUVE	CINERAMA	1967
CO	COUNSEL'S OPINION (UK)	DWAN	PARAMOUNT BRITISH	1933
CO-40	BLOOD AND STEEL	KOWALSKI	20th CENTURY FOX	1959
COC	CARRY ON CABBY (UK)	THOMAS	GOVERNOR	1963
COC	CARRY ON CONSTABLE (UK)	THOMAS	GOVERNOR	1960
COD	CASH ON DELIVERY (UK: TO DOROTHY A SON)	BOX	RKO	1956
COF	CITY ON FIRE	RAKOFF	AVCO EMBASSY	1979
COG	COME ON GEORGE! (UK)	KIMMINS	ABFD	1939

COL-1	AMERICAN MADNESS	CAPRA	COLUMBIA	1932
COL-1	BLOOD SHIP	SEITZ	COLUMBIA	1927
COL-1	COUNSEL FOR CRIME	BRAHM	COLUMBIA	1937
COL-1	COURT MARTIAL	SEITZ	COLUMBIA	1928
COL-1	FALSE ALARM	O'CONNOR	COLUMBIA	1926
COL-1	FLIGHT	CAPRA	COLUMBIA	1929
COL1	GET CRACKING (UK)	VARNEL	COLUMBIA BRITISH	1943
COL-1	LADY FOR A DAY	CAPRA	COLUMBIA	1933
COL-1	PAGAN LADY	DILLON	COLUMBIA	1931
COL-1	RAIN OR SHINE	CAPRA	COLUMBIA	1930
COL-1	UNKNOWN RANGER	BENNET	COLUMBIA	1936
COL-2	ALIAS THE LONE WOLF	GRIFFITH	COLUMBIA	1927
COL-2	BROADWAY SCANDALS	ARCHAINBAUD	COLUMBIA	1929
COL-2	DIRIGIBLE	CAPRA	COLUMBIA	1931
COL-2	LONE WOLF RETURNS	INCE	COLUMBIA	1926
COL-2	MAN'S CASTLE	BORZAGE	COLUMBIA	1933
COL-2	MURDER IN GREENWICH VILLAGE	ROGELL	COLUMBIA	1937
COL-2	NIGHT CLUB LADY	CUMMINGS	COLUMBIA	1932
COL-2	SALLY IN OUR ALLEY	LANG	COLUMBIA	1927
COL-2	SCARLET LADY	CROSLAND	COLUMBIA	1928
COL-2	SHANGHAIED LOVE	SEITZ	COLUMBIA	1931
COL-3	ABOVE THE CLOUDS	NEILL	COLUMBIA	1934
COL-3	BITTER TEA OF GENERAL YEN	CAPRA	COLUMBIA	1933
COL-3	BROTHERS	LANG	COLUMBIA	1930
COL-3	FORBIDDEN	CAPRA	COLUMBIA	1932
COL-3	OVERLAND EXPRESS (BUCK JONES)	EVERSON	COLUMBIA	1938
COL-3	RIO GRANDE RANGER (BOB ALLEN series)	BENNET	COLUMBIA	1936
COL-3	RUNAWAY GIRLS	SANDRICH	COLUMBIA	1928
COL-3	SALLY IN OUR ALLEY	LANG	COLUMBIA	1927
COL-3	SONG OF LOVE	KENTON	COLUMBIA	1929
COL-3	WHEN THE WIFE'S AWAY	STRAYER	COLUMBIA	1926
COL-4	BELLE OF BROADWAY	HOYT	COLUMBIA	1926
COL-4	BY WHOSE HAND?	LANG	COLUMBIA	1927
COL-4	LADY IS WILLING	MILLER	COLUMBIA	1934
COL-4	LAW OF THE RANGER (BOB ALLEN series)	BENNET	COLUMBIA	1937
COL-4	LIFE BEGINS WITH LOVE	MCCAREY	COLUMBIA	1937
COL-4	PLATINUM BLONDE	CAPRA	COLUMBIA	1931
COL-4	STREET OF ILLUSION	KENTON	COLUMBIA	1928
COL-4	THAT'S GRATITUDE	CRAVEN	COLUMBIA	1934
COL-4	TOL'ABLE DAVID	BLYSTONE	COLUMBIA	1930
COL-4	WALL STREET	NEILL	COLUMBIA	1929
COL-4	WASHINGTON MERRY-GO-ROUND	CRUZE	COLUMBIA	1932
COL-5	CRIMINAL CODE	HAWKS	COLUMBIA	1931
COL-5	FOG	ROGELL	COLUMBIA	1933
COL-5	GUILTY GENERATION	LEE	COLUMBIA	1931
COL-5	ISLE OF FORGOTTEN WOMEN	SEITZ	COLUMBIA	1927
COL-5	JEALOUSY	NEILL	COLUMBIA	1934
COL-5	MEXICALI ROSE	KENTON	COLUMBIA	1929
COL-5	RECKLESS RANGER	BENNET	COLUMBIA	1937
COL-5	SINNER'S PARADE	ADOLFI	COLUMBIA	1928
COL-5	SOS PERILS OF THE SEA	HOGAN	COLUMBIA	1925
COL-5	SWEET ROSIE O'GRADY	STRAYER	COLUMBIA	1926
COL-5	THAT'S MY BOY	NEILL	COLUMBIA	1932
COL-6	COLLEGE HERO	LANG	COLUMBIA	1927
COL-6	LION AND THE LAMB	SEITZ	COLUMBIA	1931
COL-6	MAN AGAINST WOMAN	CUMMINGS	COLUMBIA	1932
COL-6	MEN IN HER LIFE	BEAUDINE	COLUMBIA	1931
COL-6	MURDER ON THE ROOF	SEITZ	COLUMBIA	1930
COL-6	OBEY THE LAW	RABOCH	COLUMBIA	1926
COL-6	RANGERS STEP IN	BENNET	COLUMBIA	1937
COL-6	SHADOWS OF SING SING	ROSEN	COLUMBIA	1934
COL-6	SHE MARRIED AN ARTIST	GERING	COLUMBIA	1937
COL-6	SUBMARINE	CAPRA	COLUMBIA	1928
COL-7	BETTER WAY	INCE	COLUMBIA	1926
COL-7	DECEIVER	KING	COLUMBIA	1931
COL-7	DRIFTWOOD	CABANNE	COLUMBIA	1928

COL-7	LET'S FALL IN LOVE	BURTON	COLUMBIA	1934
COL-7	MADONNA OF THE STREETS	ROBERTSON	COLUMBIA	1930
COL-7	MELODY MAN	NEILL	COLUMBIA	1930
COL-7	NO MORE ORCHIDS	LANG	COLUMBIA	1932
COL-7	TIGRESS	SEITZ	COLUMBIA	1927
COL-8	AIR HOSTESS	ROGELL	COLUMBIA	1932
COL-8	NO GREATER GLORY	BORZAGE	COLUMBIA	1934
COL-8	PERSONALITY	HEERMAN	COLUMBIA	1930
COL-8	REMEMBER	SELMAN	COLUMBIA	1926
COL-8	STAGE KISSES	KELLEY	COLUMBIA	1927
COL-8	STOOL PIGEON	HOFFMAN	COLUMBIA	1928
COL-8	TEN CENTS A DANCE	BARRYMORE	COLUMBIA	1931
COL-8	THREE WISE GIRLS	BEAUDINE	COLUMBIA	1932
COL-9	LAST PARADE	KENTON	COLUMBIA	1931
COL-9	LITTLE MISS ROUGHNECK	SCOTTO	COLUMBIA	1938
COL-9	MAKER OF MEN	SEDGWICK	COLUMBIA	1931
COL-9	ONCE TO EVERY WOMAN	HILLYER	COLUMBIA	1934
COL-9	OPENING NIGHT	GRIFFITH	COLUMBIA	1927
COL-9	POWER OF THE PRESS	CAPRA	COLUMBIA	1928
COL-9	SO THIS IS AFRICA	CLINE	COLUMBIA	1933
COL-9	STOLEN PLEASURE	ROSEN	COLUMBIA	1927
COL-9	VENGEANCE	MAYO	COLUMBIA	1930
COL-9	WHOLE TOWN'S TALKING	FORD	COLUMBIA	1935
COL-10	DECEPTION	SEILER	COLUMBIA	1932
COL-10	DISCONTENTED HUSBANDS	LESAINT	COLUMBIA	1924
COL-10	GUILTY?	SEITZ	COLUMBIA	1930
COL-10	MENACE	NEILL	COLUMBIA	1932
COL-10	MILLS OF THE GODS	NEILL	COLUMBIA	1935
COL-10	NINTH GUEST	NEILL	COLUMBIA	1934
COL-10	NO TIME TO MARRY	LACHMAN	COLUMBIA	1938
COL-10	NOTHING TO WEAR	KENTON	COLUMBIA	1928
COL-10	SUBWAY EXPRESS	NEWMEYER	COLUMBIA	1931
COL-10	WANDERING GIRLS	INCE	COLUMBIA	1927
COL-10	WARNING	SEITZ	COLUMBIA	1927
COL-11	APACHE	ROSEN	COLUMBIA	1928
COL-11	AS THE DEVIL COMMANDS	NEILL	COLUMBIA	1933
COL-11	BACHELOR'S BABY	STRAYER	COLUMBIA	1927
COL-11	BEHIND THE MASK	DILLON	COLUMBIA	1932
COL-11	BEST MAN WINS	KENTON	COLUMBIA	1935
COL-11	CHILD OF MANHATTAN	BUZZELL	COLUMBIA	1933
COL-11	FASHION MADNESS	GASNIER	COLUMBIA	1928
COL-11	FLOOD	TINLING	COLUMBIA	1931
COL-11	IT HAPPENED ONE NIGHT	CAPRA	COLUMBIA	1934
COL-11	IT'S ALL YOURS	NUGENT	COLUMBIA	1937
COL-11	LADIES OF LEISURE	CAPRA	COLUMBIA	1930
COL-11	PAL O'MINE	LESAINT	COLUMBIA	1924
COL-12	CARNIVAL	LANG	COLUMBIA	1935
COL-12	FINAL EDITION	HIGGIN	COLUMBIA	1932
COL-12	LONE WOLF'S DAUGHTER	ROGELL	COLUMBIA	1929
COL-12	MIRACLE WOMAN	CAPRA	COLUMBIA	1931
COL-12	PENITENTIARY	BRAHM	COLUMBIA	1938
COL-12	ROYAL ROMANCE	KENTON	COLUMBIA	1930
COL-12	SIREN	HASKIN	COLUMBIA	1928
COL-12	SOCIAL REGISTER	NEILAN	COLUMBIA	1934
COL-12	WRECK	CRAFT	COLUMBIA	1927
COL-13	BELOW THE SEA	ROGELL	COLUMBIA	1933
COL-13	CALL OF THE WEST	RAY	COLUMBIA	1930
COL-13	LINEUP	HIGGIN	COLUMBIA	1934
COL-13	LOVER COME BACK	KENTON	COLUMBIA	1931
COL-13	PRICE OF HONOR	GRIFFITH	COLUMBIA	1927
COL-13	RESTLESS YOUTH	CABANNE	COLUMBIA	1928
COL-13	SHOPWORN	GRINDE	COLUMBIA	1932
COL-13	THAT CERTAIN THING	CAPRA	COLUMBIA	1928
COL-13	TOGETHER WE LIVE	MACK	COLUMBIA	1935
COL-14	BIG TIMER	BUZZELL	COLUMBIA	1932
COL-14	BIRDS OF PREY	CRAFT	COLUMBIA	1927

COL-14	GOOD BAD GIRL	NEILL	COLUMBIA	1931
COL-14	SISTERS UNDER THE SKIN	BURTON	COLUMBIA	1934
COL-14	WHEN STRANGERS MARRY	BADGER	COLUMBIA	1933
COL-14	WIFE'S RELATIONS	MARSHALL	COLUMBIA	1928
COL-14	YOUNGER GENERATION	CAPRA	COLUMBIA	1929
COL-15	ARIZONA	SEITZ	COLUMBIA	1931
COL-15	AROUND THE CORNER	GLENNON	COLUMBIA	1930
COL-15	BRIEF MOMENT	BURTON	COLUMBIA	1933
COL-15	LADY RAFFLES	NEILL	COLUMBIA	1928
COL-15	LOVE AFFAIR	FREELAND	COLUMBIA	1932
COL-15	MOST PRECIOUS THING IN LIFE	HILLYER	COLUMBIA	1934
COL-15	PLEASURE BEFORE BUSINESS	STRAYER	COLUMBIA	1927
COL-15	SIDESHOW	KENTON	COLUMBIA	1928
COL-15	THERE'S ALWAYS A WOMAN	HALL	COLUMBIA	1938
COL-16	ATTORNEY FOR THE DEFENSE	CUMMINGS	COLUMBIA	1932
COL-16	CAPTAIN HATES THE SEA	MILESTONE	COLUMBIA	1934
COL-16	FIFTY FATHOMS DEEP	NEILL	COLUMBIA	1931
COL-16	OBJECT: ALIMONY	DUNLAP	COLUMBIA	1928
COL-16	PAROLE GIRL	CLINE	COLUMBIA	1933
COL-16	POOR GIRLS	CRAFT	COLUMBIA	1927
COL-16	SO THIS IS LOVE	CAPRA	COLUMBIA	1928
COL-16	SOLDIERS AND WOMEN	SLOMAN	COLUMBIA	1930
COL-16	YOU CAN'T TAKE IT WITH YOU	CAPRA	COLUMBIA	1938
COL-17	CIRCUS QUEEN MURDER	NEILL	COLUMBIA	1933
COL-17	DANGEROUS AFFAIR	SEDGWICK	COLUMBIA	1931
COL-17	FATHER		COLUMBIA	1928
COL-17	HOLIDAY	CUKOR	COLUMBIA	1938
COL-17	PAYING THE PRICE	SELMAN	COLUMBIA	1927
COL-17	TEMPTATION	HOPPER	COLUMBIA	1930
COL-17	TWENTIETH CENTURY	HAWKS	COLUMBIA	1934
COL-17	WOMAN'S WAY	MORTIMER	COLUMBIA	1928
COL-18	COCKTAIL HOUR	SCHERTZINGER	COLUMBIA	1933
COL-18	HOLLYWOOD SPEAKS	BUZZELL	COLUMBIA	1932
COL-18	SISTERS	FLOOD	COLUMBIA	1930
COL-18	SPORTING AGE	KENTON	COLUMBIA	1928
COL-18	TRIAL MARRIAGE	KENTON	COLUMBIA	1929
COL-18	WHIRLPOOL	NEILL	COLUMBIA	1934
COL-19	BEHIND CLOSED DOORS	NEILL	COLUMBIA	1929
COL-19	BY WHOSE HAND?	STOLOFF	COLUMBIA	1932
COL-19	CHARLEY'S AUNT	CHRISTIE	COLUMBIA	1931
COL-19	CITY STREETS (CITY SHADOWS*)	ROGELL	COLUMBIA	1938
COL-19	HELL'S ISLAND	SLOMAN	COLUMBIA	1930
COL-19	MATINEE IDOL	CAPRA	COLUMBIA	1928
COL-19	ROMANTIC AGE	FLOREY	COLUMBIA	1927
COL-19	WHOM THE GODS DESTROY	LANG	COLUMBIA	1934
COL-19	WOMAN I STOLE	CUMMINGS	COLUMBIA	1933
COL-20	ANN CARVER'S PROFESSION	BUZZELL	COLUMBIA	1933
COL-20	DESERT BRIDE	CAPRA	COLUMBIA	1928
COL-20	GIRL'S SCHOOL	BRAHM	COLUMBIA	1938
COL-20	LADIES MUST PLAY	CANNON	COLUMBIA	1930
COL-20	MEET THE WIFE	PEARCE	COLUMBIA	1931
COL-20	PARTY'S OVER	LANG	COLUMBIA	1934
COL-20	QUITTER	HENABERY	COLUMBIA	1929
COL-20	RICH MEN'S SONS	GRAVES	COLUMBIA	1927
COL-20	WAR CORRESPONDENT	SLOANE	COLUMBIA	1932
COL-21	BROADWAY DADDIES	WINDEMERE	COLUMBIA	1928
COL-21	CLOWN	CRAFT	COLUMBIA	1927
COL-21	DONOVAN AFFAIR	CAPRA	COLUMBIA	1929
COL-21	HELLCAT	ROGELL	COLUMBIA	1934
COL-21	I AM THE LAW	HALL	COLUMBIA	1938
COL-21	SQUEALER	BROWN	COLUMBIA	1930
COL-22	AFTER THE STORM	SEITZ	COLUMBIA	1928
COL-22	BLACK MOON	NEILL	COLUMBIA	1934
COL-22	ETERNAL WOMAN	MCCARTHY	COLUMBIA	1929
COL-22	KID SISTER	GRAVES	COLUMBIA	1927
COL-22	LAST MAN	HIGGIN	COLUMBIA	1932

COL-22	LAST OF THE LONE WOLF	BOLESLAWSKI	COLUMBIA	1930
COL-22	WRECKER	ROGELL	COLUMBIA	1933
COL-23	BLIND DATE	NEILL	COLUMBIA	1934
COL-23	FATHER AND SON	KENTON	COLUMBIA	1929
COL-23	FOR LADIES ONLY	LEHRMAN, PEMBROKE	COLUMBIA	1927
COL-23	FOR THE LOVE O' LIL	TINLING	COLUMBIA	1930
COL-23	GOLF WIDOWS	KENTON	COLUMBIA	1928
COL-23	LADY OBJECTS	KENTON	COLUMBIA	1938
COL-23	MY WOMAN	SCHERTZINGER	COLUMBIA	1933
COL-23	NIGHT MAYOR	STOLOFF	COLUMBIA	1932
COL-24	BACHELOR GIRL	THORPE	COLUMBIA	1929
COL-24	DEFENSE RESTS	HILLYER	COLUMBIA	1934
COL-24	FLIGHT TO FAME	COLEMAN	COLUMBIA	1938
COL-24	FURY OF THE JUNGLE	NEILL	COLUMBIA	1933
COL-24	MODERN MOTHERS	ROSEN	COLUMBIA	1928
COL-24	SWEETHEARTS ON PARADE	NEILAN	COLUMBIA	1930
COL-24	SWELL HEAD	GRAVES	COLUMBIA	1927
COL-24	THIS SPORTING AGE	BENNISON, ERICKSON	COLUMBIA	1932
COL-25	I'LL TAKE ROMANCE	GRIFFITH	COLUMBIA	1937
COL-25	NAME THE WOMAN	KENTON	COLUMBIA	1928
COL-25	NAME THE WOMAN	ROGELL	COLUMBIA	1934
COL-25	VANITY STREET	GRINDE	COLUMBIA	1932
COL-26	FALL OF EVE	STRAYER	COLUMBIA	1929
COL-26	MASTER OF MEN	HILLYER	COLUMBIA	1933
COL-26	RANSOM	SEITZ	COLUMBIA	1928
COL-26	VIRTUE	BUZZELL	COLUMBIA	1932
COL-27	AWFUL TRUTH	MCCAREY	COLUMBIA	1937
COL-27	COLLEGE COQUETTE	ARCHAINBAUD	COLUMBIA	1929
COL-27	FUGITIVE LADY	ROGELL	COLUMBIA	1934
COL-27	WAY OF THE STRONG	CAPRA	COLUMBIA	1928
COL-28	BEWARE OF BLONDES	SEITZ	COLUMBIA	1928
COL-28	LADY BY CHOICE	BURTON	COLUMBIA	1934
COL-28	LIGHT FINGERS	HENABERY	COLUMBIA	1929
COL-28	THERE'S THAT WOMAN AGAIN	HALL	COLUMBIA	1939
COL-29	HURRICANE	INCE	COLUMBIA	1929
COL-29	I'LL FIX IT	NEILL	COLUMBIA	1934
COL-29	LITTLE ADVENTURESS	LEDERMAN	COLUMBIA	1938
COL-29	SAY IT WITH SABLES	CAPRA	COLUMBIA	1928
COL-30	ACQUITTED	STRAYER	COLUMBIA	1929
COL-30	AMONG THE MISSING	ROGELL	COLUMBIA	1934
COL-30	BLONDIE	STRAYER	COLUMBIA	1938
COL-30	FAITH, HOPE AND CHARITY (sh)	BLAKE	COLUMBIA	1930
COL-31	BROADWAY HOOFER	ARCHAINBAUD	COLUMBIA	1929
COL-31	NEVER STRIKE YOUR MOTHER (sh)	BLAKE	COLUMBIA	1930
COL-31	SMASHING THE SPY RING	CABANNE	COLUMBIA	1939
COL-32	HOT AND BOTHERED (sh)	BLAKE	COLUMBIA	1930
COL-32	LADY AND THE MOB	STOLOFF	COLUMBIA	1939
COL-33	LONE WOLF SPY HUNT	GODFREY	COLUMBIA	1939
COL-33	PRODIGAL DAUGHTER (sh)	BUZZELL	COLUMBIA	1930
COL-34	CAME THE PAWN (sh)	BUZZELL	COLUMBIA	1930
COL-35	HARD BOILED YEGGS (sh)	BUZZELL	COLUMBIA	1930
COL-36	CRYSTAL GAZER	BUZZELL	COLUMBIA	1930
COL-36	ONLY ANGELS HAVE WINGS	HAWKS	COLUMBIA	1939
COL-37	COAST GUARD	LUDWIG	COLUMBIA	1939
COL-37	LONE STAR STRANGER (sh)	BUZZELL	COLUMBIA	1931
COL-38	ROMANCE OF THE REDWOODS	VIDOR	COLUMBIA	1939
COL-38	WINE, WOMAN BUT NO SONG (sh)		COLUMBIA	1931
COL-39	BLONDIE MEETS THE BOSS	STRAYER	COLUMBIA	1939
COL-39	CHECK AND RUBBER CHECK (sh)	BUZZELL	COLUMBIA	1931
COL-40	GOLDEN BOY	MAMOULIAN	COLUMBIA	1939
COL-40	KINGS OR BETTER (sh)	BUZZELL	COLUMBIA	1931
COL-40	THRILL HUNTER	SEITZ	COLUMBIA	1933
COL-41	BLIND ALLEY	VIDOR	COLUMBIA	1939
COL-41	FIGHTING CODE	HILLYER	COLUMBIA	1933
COL-41	LAST OF THE MOE HEE GINS (sh)	BUZZELL	COLUMBIA	1931
COL-41	MEN OF THE NIGHT	HILLYER	COLUMBIA	1934

COL-42	BEHIND THE EVIDENCE	HILLYER	COLUMBIA	1935
COL-42	CHRIS-CROSSED (sh)	BUZZELL	COLUMBIA	1931
COL-42	FIGHTING RANGER	SEITZ	COLUMBIA	1934
COL-42	GOOD GIRLS GO TO PARIS	HALL	COLUMBIA	1939
COL-43	MAN TRAILER	HILLYER	COLUMBIA	1934
COL-43	MR. SMITH GOES TO WASHINGTON	CAPRA	COLUMBIA	1939
COL-43	RED MEN TELL NO TALES (sh)	BUZZELL	COLUMBIA	1931
COL-44	WOLF IN CHEAP CLOTHING (sh)	BUZZELL	COLUMBIA	1932
COL-45	BLONDE PRESSURE (sh)	BUZZELL	COLUMBIA	1931
COL-45	BLONDIE TAKES A VACATION	STRAYER	COLUMBIA	1939
COL-46	FIVE LITTLE PEPPERS AND HOW THEY GREW	BARTON	COLUMBIA	1939
COL-46	SHE SERVED HIM RIGHT (sh)	BUZZELL	COLUMBIA	1931
COL-47	SOLDIER OF MISFORTUNE (sh)	BUZZELL	COLUMBIA	1931
COL-47	THOSE HIGH GRAY WALLS	VIDOR	COLUMBIA	1939
COL-48	CALL OF THE MOTH (sh)		COLUMBIA	1932
COL-49	BEWARE SPOOKS	SEDGWICK	COLUMBIA	1939
COL-49	LOVE, HONOR AND HE PAYS (sh)	BUZZELL	COLUMBIA	1932
COL-50	AFRICA SPEAKS	HOEFLER, FULLER	COLUMBIA	1930
COL-50	SPEED DEMON	LEDERMAN	COLUMBIA	1932
COL-51	BLONDIE BRINGS UP BABY	STRAYER	COLUMBIA	1939
COL-51	STATE TROOPER	LEDERMAN	COLUMBIA	1933
COL-52	ARIZONA	RUGGLES	COLUMBIA	1940
COL-52	OBEY THE LAW	STOLOFF	COLUMBIA	1933
COL-53	SCANDAL SHEET	GRINDE	COLUMBIA	1939
COL-53	SOLDIERS OF THE STORM	LEDERMAN	COLUMBIA	1933
COL-54	AMAZING MR. WILLIAMS	HALL	COLUMBIA	1939
COL-54	DANGEROUS CROSSROADS	HILLYER	COLUMBIA	1933
COL-55	CAFÉ HOSTESS	SALKOW	COLUMBIA	1940
COL-55	NIGHT OF TERROR	STOLOFF	COLUMBIA	1933
COL-56	KING OF THE WILD HORSES	HALEY	COLUMBIA	1933
COL-56	MY SON IS GUILTY	BARTON	COLUMBIA	1939
COL-57	MILITARY ACADEMY	LEDERMAN	COLUMBIA	1940
COL-58	FIVE LITTLE PEPPERS AT HOME	BARTON	COLUMBIA	1940
COL-60	CORNERED	EASON	COLUMBIA	1932
COL-60	LONE RIDER	KING	COLUMBIA	1930
COL-61	SHADOW RANCH	KING	COLUMBIA	1930
COL-61	WESTERN CODE	MCCARTHY	COLUMBIA	1932
COL-62	FIGHTING FOR JUSTICE	BROWER	COLUMBIA	1932
COL-62	MEN WITHOUT LAW	KING	COLUMBIA	1930
COL-63	DAWN TRAIL	CABANNE	COLUMBIA	1930
COL-63	END OF THE TRAIL	LEDERMAN	COLUMBIA	1933
COL-64	DESERT VENGEANCE	KING	COLUMBIA	1931
COL-64	MAN OF ACTION	MELFORD	COLUMBIA	1933
COL-65	AVENGER	NEILL	COLUMBIA	1931
COL-65	SILENT MEN	LEDERMAN	COLUMBIA	1933
COL-66	TEXAS RANGER	LEDERMAN	COLUMBIA	1931
COL-66	WHIRLWIND	LEDERMAN	COLUMBIA	1933
COL-67	FIGHTING SHERIFF	KING	COLUMBIA	1931
COL-67	RUSTY RIDES ALONE	LEDERMAN	COLUMBIA	1933
COL-70	BRANDED	LEDERMAN	COLUMBIA	1931
COL-70	POLICE CAR 17	HILLYER	COLUMBIA	1933
COL-71	BORDER LAW	KING	COLUMBIA	1931
COL-71	HOLD THE PRESS	ROSEN	COLUMBIA	1933
COL-72	RANGE FEUD	LEDERMAN	COLUMBIA	1931
COL-72	STRAIGHTAWAY	BROWER	COLUMBIA	1934
COL-73	DEADLINE	HILLYER	COLUMBIA	1931
COL-73	SPEED WINGS	BROWER	COLUMBIA	1934
COL-74	RIDIN' FOR JUSTICE	LEDERMAN	COLUMBIA	1932
COL-74	VOICE IN THE NIGHT	COLEMAN	COLUMBIA	1934
COL-75	HELLBENT FOR LOVE	LEDERMAN	COLUMBIA	1934
COL-75	ONE MAN LAW	HILLYER	COLUMBIA	1932
COL-76	HIGH SPEED	LEDERMAN	COLUMBIA	1932
COL-76	MAN'S GAME	LEDERMAN	COLUMBIA	1934
COL-77	BEYOND THE LAW	LEDERMAN	COLUMBIA	1934
COL-77	SOUTH OF THE RIO GRANDE	HILLYER	COLUMBIA	1932
COL-80	BEFORE MIDNIGHT	HILLYER	COLUMBIA	1933

COL-80	LIGHTNING FLYER	NIGH	COLUMBIA	1931
COL-80	SHOTGUN PASS	MCGOWAN	COLUMBIA	1932
COL-81	ONE IS GUILTY	HILLYER	COLUMBIA	1934
COL-81	ONE WAY TRAIL	TAYLOR	COLUMBIA	1931
COL-81	SKY RAIDERS	BEEBE, TAYLOR	COLUMBIA	1931
COL-82	CRIME OF HELEN STANLEY	LEDERMAN	COLUMBIA	1934
COL-82	FIGHTING MARSHALL	LEDERMAN	COLUMBIA	1931
COL-83	FIGHTING FOOL	HILLYER	COLUMBIA	1932
COL-83	GIRL IN DANGER	LEDERMAN	COLUMBIA	1934
COL-84	TEXAS CYCLONE	LEDERMAN	COLUMBIA	1932
COL-85	DARING DANGER	LEDERMAN	COLUMBIA	1932
COL-86	RIDING TORNADO	LEDERMAN	COLUMBIA	1932
COL-87	TWO FISTED LAW	LEDERMAN	COLUMBIA	1932
COL-90	HELLO TROUBLE	HILLYER	COLUMBIA	1932
COL-90	LAND NOBODY KNOWS	(DOCU)	COLUMBIA	1931
COL-90	TIME OUT FOR RHYTHM (STOOGE SHORT)	SALKOW	COLUMBIA	1941
COL-91	MCKENNA OF THE MOUNTIES	LEDERMAN	COLUMBIA	1932
COL-92	WHITE EAGLE	HILLYER	COLUMBIA	1932
COL-93	FORBIDDEN TRAIL	HILLYER	COLUMBIA	1932
COL-94	SUNDOWN RACER		COLUMBIA	1933
COL-95	TREASON	SEITZ	COLUMBIA	1933
COL-96	CALIFORNIA TRAIL	HILLYER	COLUMBIA	1933
COL-97	UNKNOWN VALLEY	HILLYER	COLUMBIA	1933
COL-100	HOT DAZE (sh)	MOORE	COLUMBIA	1933
COL-101	UMPA	CONRAD, GOTTLER	COLUMBIA	1933
COL-102	ROAMIN' THRU THE ROSES	GOTTLER	COLUMBIA	1933
COL-104	HOLD YOUR TEMPER	WHITE	COLUMBIA	1933
COL-105	ED CODIGO PENAL	ROSEN, VILLARREAL	COLUMBIA	1931
COL-108	CARNE DE CABARET	CABANNE	COLUMBIA	1931
COL-114	EL PASADO ACUSA	SELMAN, VILLARREAL	COLUMBIA	1931
COL-114	I WAS A PRISONER ON DEVIL'S ISLAND	LANDERS	COLUMBIA	1941
COL-115	TWO IN A TAXI	FLOREY	COLUMBIA	1941
COL-116	OUR WIFE	STAHL	COLUMBIA	1941
COL-117	HERE COMES MR. JORDAN	HALL	COLUMBIA	1941
COL-118	YOU'LL NEVER GET RICH	LANFIELD	COLUMBIA	1941
COL-119	MYSTERY SHIP	LANDERS	COLUMBIA	1941
COL-120	TWO LATINS FROM MANHATTAN	BARTON	COLUMBIA	1941
COL-122	COUNTER-ESPIONAGE	DMYTRYK	COLUMBIA	1942
COL-124	THREE GIRLS ABOUT TOWN	JASON	COLUMBIA	1941
COL-125	GO WEST YOUNG LADY	STRAYER	COLUMBIA	1941
COL-126	HARMON OF MICHIGAN	BARTON	COLUMBIA	1941
COL-127	STORK PAYS OFF	LANDERS	COLUMBIA	1941
COL-128	SECRETS OF THE LONE WOLF	DMYTRYK	COLUMBIA	1941
COL-129	LADY IS WILLING	LEISEN	COLUMBIA	1942
COL-130	SING FOR YOUR SUPPER	BARTON	COLUMBIA	1941
COL-132	HARVARD HERE I COME	LANDERS	COLUMBIA	1941
COL-133	CONFESSIONS OF BOSTON BLACKIE	DMYTRYK	COLUMBIA	1941
COL-134	BLONDIE GOES TO COLLEGE	STRAYER	COLUMBIA	1942
COL-135	HONOLULU LU	BARTON	COLUMBIA	1941
COL-136	CADETS ON PARADE	LANDERS	COLUMBIA	1942
COL-137	SHUT MY BIG MOUTH	BARTON	COLUMBIA	1942
COL-138	TWO YANKS IN TRINIDAD	RATOFF	COLUMBIA	1942
COL-139	MAN WHO RETURNED TO LIFE	LANDERS	COLUMBIA	1942
COL-140	CANAL ZONE	LANDERS	COLUMBIA	1942
COL-141	TRAMP TRAMP TRAMP	BARTON	COLUMBIA	1942
COL-144	ALIAS BOSTON BLACKIE	LANDERS	COLUMBIA	1942
COL-146	TALK OF THE TOWN	STEVENS	COLUMBIA	1942
COL-147	NOT A LADIES MAN	LANDERS	COLUMBIA	1942
COL-148	HELLO ANAPOLIS	BARTON	COLUMBIA	1942
COL-149	MEET THE STEWARTS	GREEN	COLUMBIA	1942
COL-150	THEY ALL KISSED THE BRIDE	HALL	COLUMBIA	1942
COL-151	PARACHUTE NURSE	BARTON	COLUMBIA	1942
COL-152	SWEETHEART OF THE FLEET	BARTON	COLUMBIA	1942
COL-153	SUBMARINE RAIDER	LANDERS	COLUMBIA	1942
COL-154	YOU WERE NEVER LOVELIER	SEITER	COLUMBIA	1942
COL-155	ATLANTIC CONVOY	LANDERS	COLUMBIA	1942

COL-156	FLIGHT LIEUTENANT	SALKOW	COLUMBIA	1942
COL-156	THREE LITTLE PIGSKINS (STOOGES SHORT)	MCCAREY	COLUMBIA	1934
COL-157	ONE DANGEROUS NIGHT	GORDON	COLUMBIA	1943
COL-158	BLONDIE FOR VICTORY	STRAYER	COLUMBIA	1942
COL-159	MAN'S WORLD	BARTON	COLUMBIA	1942
COL-160	SABOTAGE SQUAD	LANDERS	COLUMBIA	1942
COL-161	MY SISTER EILEEN	HALL	COLUMBIA	1942
COL-162	LUCKY LEGS	BARTON	COLUMBIA	1942
COL-163	DESPERADOES	VIDOR	COLUMBIA	1943
COL-164	STAND BY ALL NETWORKS	LANDERS	COLUMBIA	1942
COL-165	SPIRIT OF STANFORD	BARTON	COLUMBIA	1942
COL-166	DESTROYER	SEITER	COLUMBIA	1943
COL-167	LET'S HAVE FUN	BARTON	COLUMBIA	1943
COL-168	DARING YOUNG MAN	STRAYER	COLUMBIA	1942
COL-169	BOSTON BLACKIE GOES HOLLYWOOD	GORDON	COLUMBIA	1942
COL-170	SMITH OF MINNESOTA	LANDERS	COLUMBIA	1942
COL-171	BOOGIE MAN WILL GET YOU	LANDERS	COLUMBIA	1942
COL-172	UNDERGROUND AGENT	GORDON	COLUMBIA	1942
COL-173	NIGHT TO REMEMBER	WALLACE	COLUMBIA	1943
COL-174	LAUGH YOUR BLUES AWAY	BARTON	COLUMBIA	1942
COL-175	JUNIOR ARMY	LANDERS	COLUMBIA	1942
COL-176	MORE THE MERRIER	STEVENS	COLUMBIA	1943
COL-177	POWER OF THE PRESS	LANDERS	COLUMBIA	1943
COL-178	WHAT'S BUZZIN COUSIN?	BARTON	COLUMBIA	1943
COL-179	REVELIE WITH BEVERLY	BARTON	COLUMBIA	1943
COL-180	MURDER IN TIMES SQUARE	LANDERS	COLUMBIA	1943
COL-181	SAHARA	KORDA	COLUMBIA	1943
COL-182	APPOINTMENT IN BERLIN	GREEN	COLUMBIA	1943
COL-183	AFTER MIDNIGHT WITH BOSTON BLACKIE	LANDERS	COLUMBIA	1943
COL-184	FIRST COMES COURAGE	ARZNER	COLUMBIA	1943
COL-185	SHE HAS WHAT IT TAKES	BARTON	COLUMBIA	1943
COL-186	IT'S A GREAT LIFE (BLONDIE)	STRAYER	COLUMBIA	1943
COL-187	BOY FROM STALINGRAD	SALKOW	COLUMBIA	1943
COL-188	REDHEAD FROM MANHATTAN	LANDERS	COLUMBIA	1943
COL-189	ONCE UPON A TIME	HALL	COLUMBIA	1944
COL-190	TWO SENORITAS FROM CHICAGO	WOODRUFF	COLUMBIA	1943
COL-192	GOOD LUCK MR. YATES	ENRIGHT	COLUMBIA	1943
COL-193	DOUGHBOYS IN IRELAND	LANDERS	COLUMBIA	1943
COL-194	COVER GIRL	VIDOR	COLUMBIA	1944
COL-195	MY KINGDOM FOR A COOK	WALLACE	COLUMBIA	1943
COL-196	HOMBRES EN MI VIDA	SELMAN	COLUMBIA	1932
COL-197	PASSPORT TO SUEZ	DE TOTH	COLUMBIA	1943
COL-198	DANGEROUS BLONDES	JASON	COLUMBIA	1943
COL-199	THERE'S SOMETHING ABOUT A SOLDIER	GREEN	COLUMBIA	1943
COL-200	EXTORTION	HILLYER	COLUMBIA	1938
COL-203	MAIN EVENT	DARE	COLUMBIA	1938
COL-204	PAID TO DANCE (HARD TO HOLD)	COLEMAN	COLUMBIA	1937
COL-205	ALL AMERICAN SWEETHEART	HILLYER	COLUMBIA	1937
COL-206	SHADOW		COLUMBIA	
COL-207	SQUADRON OF HONOR	COLEMAN	COLUMBIA	1938
COL-208	WOMEN IN PRISON	HILLYER	COLUMBIA	1938
COL-209	WHO KILLED GAIL PRESTON?	BARSHA	COLUMBIA	1938
COL-210	WHEN G-MEN STEP IN	COLEMAN	COLUMBIA	1938
COL-211	HIGHWAY PATROL	COLEMAN	COLUMBIA	1938
COL-212	HOMICIDE BUREAU	COLEMAN	COLUMBIA	1939
COL-213	JUVENILE COURT	LEDERMAN	COLUMBIA	1938
COL-213	MOVIE MANIACS	LORD	COLUMBIA	1936
COL-214	ADVENTURE IN SAHARA	LEDERMAN	COLUMBIA	1938
COL-215	NORTH OF SHANGHAI	LEDERMAN	COLUMBIA	1939
COL-216	MY SON IS A CRIMINAL	COLEMAN	COLUMBIA	1939
COL-217	DISORDER IN COURT (sh)	WHITE	COLUMBIA	1936
COL-217	FIRST OFFENDERS	MCDONALD	COLUMBIA	1939
COL-218	OUTSIDE THESE WALLS	MCCAREY	COLUMBIA	1939
COL-219	MISSING DAUGHTERS	COLEMAN	COLUMBIA	1939
COL-220	PARENTS ON TRIAL	NELSON	COLUMBIA	1939
COL-221	WOMAN IS THE JUDGE	GRINDE	COLUMBIA	1939

COL-222	BEHIND PRISON GATES	BARTON	COLUMBIA	1939
COL-223	MAN THEY COULD NOT HANG	GRINDE	COLUMBIA	1939
COL-224	KONGA, THE WILD STALLION	NELSON	COLUMBIA	1940
COL-300	OUTLAWS OF THE PRAIRIE	NELSON	COLUMBIA	1937
COL-301	CATTLE RAIDERS	NELSON	COLUMBIA	1938
COL-302	OLD WYOMING TRAIL	BLANGSTED	COLUMBIA	1937
COL-303	CALL OF THE ROCKIES	JAMES	COLUMBIA	1938
COL-304	LAW OF THE PLAINS	NELSON	COLUMBIA	1938
COL-305	WEST OF CHEYENNE	NELSON	COLUMBIA	1938
COL-306	SOUTH OF ARIZONA	NELSON	COLUMBIA	1938
COL-307	WEST OF SANTA FE	NELSON	COLUMBIA	1938
COL-308	COLORADO TRAIL	NELSON	COLUMBIA	1938
COL-309	RIO GRANDE	NELSON	COLUMBIA	1938
COL-310	THUNDERING WEST	NELSON	COLUMBIA	1939
COL-311	TEXAS STAMPEDE	NELSON	COLUMBIA	1939
COL-312	NORTH OF THE YUKON	NELSON	COLUMBIA	1939
COL-313	SPOILERS OF THE RANGE	COLEMAN	COLUMBIA	1939
COL-314	WESTERN CARAVANS	NELSON	COLUMBIA	1939
COL-315	MAN FROM SUNDOWN	NELSON	COLUMBIA	1939
COL-316	OUTPOST OF THE MOUNTIES	COLEMAN	COLUMBIA	1939
COL-317	STRANGER FROM TEXAS	NELSON	COLUMBIA	1939
COL-318	RIDERS OF BLACK RIVER	DEMING	COLUMBIA	1939
COL-319	TAMING OF THE WEST	DEMING	COLUMBIA	1939
COL-320	MAN FROM TUMBLEWEEDS	LEWIS	COLUMBIA	1940
COL-321	TWO FISTED RANGERS	LEWIS	COLUMBIA	1939
COL-322	BULLETS FOR RUSTLERS	NELSON	COLUMBIA	1940
COL-323	PIONEERS OF THE FRONTIER	NELSON	COLUMBIA	1940
COL-324	BLAZING SIX SHOOTERS	LEWIS	COLUMBIA	1940
COL-325	THUNDERING FRONTIER	LEDERMAN	COLUMBIA	1940
COL-326	TEXAS STAGECOACH	LEWIS	COLUMBIA	1940
COL-327	PINTO KID	HILLYER	COLUMBIA	1941
COL-328	WEST OF ABILENE	CEDER	COLUMBIA	1940
COL-329	RETURN OF WILD BILL	LEWIS	COLUMBIA	1940
COL-330	DURANGO KID	HILLYER	COLUMBIA	1940
COL-331	PRAIRIE SCHOONERS	NELSON	COLUMBIA	1940
COL-332	OUTLAWS OF THE PANHANDLE	NELSON	COLUMBIA	1941
COL-334	BEYOND THE SACRAMENTO	HILLYER	COLUMBIA	1940
COL-335	ACROSS THE SIERRAS	LEDERMAN	COLUMBIA	1941
COL-337	WILDCAT OF TUCSON	HILLYER	COLUMBIA	1940
COL-338	NORTH FROM THE LONE STAR	HILLYER	COLUMBIA	1941
COL-339	RETURN OF DANIEL BOONE	HILLYER	COLUMBIA	1941
COL-340	HANDS ACROSS THE ROCKIES	HILLYER	COLUMBIA	1941
COL-341	SON OF DAVY CROCKETT	HILLYER	COLUMBIA	1941
COL-342	MEDICO OF PAINTED SPRINGS	HILLYER	COLUMBIA	1941
COL-343	KING OF DODGE CITY	HILLYER	COLUMBIA	1941
COL-344	THUNDER OVER THE PRAIRIE	HILLYER	COLUMBIA	1941
COL-345	ROARING FRONTIERS	HILLYER	COLUMBIA	1941
COL-346	PRAIRIE STRANGER	HILLYER	COLUMBIA	1941
COL-347	LONE STAR VIGILANTES	FOX	COLUMBIA	1942
COL-348	ROYAL MOUNTED PATROL	HILLYER	COLUMBIA	1941
COL-349	BULLETS FOR BANDITS	FOX	COLUMBIA	1942
COL-350	RIDERS OF THE BADLANDS	BRETHERTON	COLUMBIA	1941
COL-351	NORTH OF THE ROCKIES	HILLYER	COLUMBIA	1942
COL-352	DEVIL'S TRAIL	HILLYER	COLUMBIA	1942
COL-353	WEST OF TOMBSTONE	BRETHERTON	COLUMBIA	1942
COL-354	LAWLESS PLAINSMEN	BERKE	COLUMBIA	1942
COL-355	DOWN RIO GRANDE WAY	BERKE	COLUMBIA	1942
COL-356	PRAIRIE GUNSMOKE	HILLYER	COLUMBIA	1942
COL-357	OVERLAND TO DEADWOOD	BERKE	COLUMBIA	1942
COL-359	RIDERS OF THE NORTHLAND	BERKE	COLUMBIA	1942
COL-360	VENGEANCE OF THE WEST		COLUMBIA	1942
COL-362	RIDING THROUGH NEVADA	BERKE	COLUMBIA	1942
COL-363	PARDON MY GUN	BERKE	COLUMBIA	1942
COL-364	TORNADO IN THE SADDLE	BERKE	COLUMBIA	1942
COL-365	LONE PRAIRIE	BERKE	COLUMBIA	1942
COL-366	FIGHTING BUCKAROO	BERKE	COLUMBIA	1943

COL-367	LAW OF THE NORTHWEST	BERKE	COLUMBIA	1943
COL-368	SILVER CITY RAIDERS	BERKE	COLUMBIA	1943
COL-369	RIDERS OF THE NORTHWEST MOUNTED	BERKE	COLUMBIA	1943
COL-370	HAIL TO THE RANGERS	BERKE	COLUMBIA	1943
COL-371	ROBIN HOOD OF THE RANGE	BERKE	COLUMBIA	1943
COL-372	SADDLES AND THE SAGEBRUSH	BERKE	COLUMBIA	1943
COL-373	VIGILANTES RIDE	BERKE	COLUMBIA	1943
COL-374	WYOMING HURRICANE	BERKE	COLUMBIA	1944
COL-375	LAST HORSEMAN	BERKE	COLUMBIA	1944
COL-376	RIDING WEST	BERKE	COLUMBIA	1944
COL-377	FRONTIER FURY	BERKE	COLUMBIA	1943
COL-400	CASH AND CARRY	LORD	COLUMBIA	1937
COL-401	PLAY THE PONIES	LAMONT	COLUMBIA	1937
COL-404	WEE WEE MONSIER	LORD	COLUMBIA	1938
COL-407	GRACIE AT THE BAT	LORD	COLUMBIA	1937
COL-409	COLLINS-KENNEDY		COLUMBIA	
COL-413	CHARLEY CHASE (sh)		COLUMBIA	
COL-416	TERMITES OF 1938	LORD	COLUMBIA	1938
COL-427	MUTTS TO YOU	CHASE	COLUMBIA	1938
COL-429	SMITH AND DALE		COLUMBIA	
COL-430	SAVED BY THE BELLE	CHASE	COLUMBIA	1939
COL-431	CHARLEY CHASE		COLUMBIA	
COL-433	SMITH AND DALE		COLUMBIA	
COL-434	ANDY CLYDE (sh)		COLUMBIA	
COL-436	ANDY CLYDE (sh)		COLUMBIA	
COL-437	CHARLEY CHASE (sh)		COLUMBIA	
COL-438	YES WE HAVE NO BONANZA	LORD	COLUMBIA	1939
COL-439	FLAT FOOT STOOGES	CHASE	COLUMBIA	1938
COL-440	ANDY CLYDE (sh)		COLUMBIA	
COL-441	DANNY WEBB		COLUMBIA	
COL-442	ANDY CLYDE (sh)		COLUMBIA	
COL-443	WE WANT OUR MUMMY	LORD	COLUMBIA	1939
COL-444	A DUCKING THEY DID GO	LORD	COLUMBIA	1939
COL-445	CALLING ALL CURS	WHITE	COLUMBIA	1939
COL-446	RATTLING ROMEO	LORD	COLUMBIA	1939
COL-448	NOW IT CAN BE SOLD	LORD	COLUMBIA	1939
COL-449	OILY TO BED	WHITE	COLUMBIA	1939
COL-450	CHARLEY CHASE (sh)		COLUMBIA	
COL-452	TEACHER'S PEST	KRAMER, ULLMAN	COLUMBIA	1939
COL-453	STATIC IN THE ATTIC	CHASE	COLUMBIA	1939
COL-454	PEST FROM THE WEST	LORD	COLUMBIA	1939
COL-458	HOW HIGH IS UP?	LORD	COLUMBIA	1940
COL-459	ANDY CLYDE (sh)		COLUMBIA	
COL-460	ALL AMERICAN BLONDES	LORD	COLUMBIA	1939
COL-462	STOOGES (sh)		COLUMBIA	
COL-463	ANDY CLYDE GETS SPRING CHICKEN	WHITE	COLUMBIA	1939
COL-464	CHARLEY CHASE		COLUMBIA	
COL-466	ANDY CLYDE		COLUMBIA	
COL-467	HECKLER	LORD	COLUMBIA	1940
COL-468	FROM NURSE TO WORSE	WHITE	COLUMBIA	1940
COL-469	CHARLEY CHASE (sh)		COLUMBIA	
COL-473	SOUTH OF THE BOUDOIR	LORD	COLUMBIA	1940
COL-476	ANDY CLYDE (sh)		COLUMBIA	
COL-482	IN THE SWEET PIE AND PIE	WHITE	COLUMBIA	1941
COL-483	BLONDES AND BLUNDERS	LORD	COLUMBIA	1940
COL-484	SO LONG MR. CHUMPS	WHITE	COLUMBIA	1941
COL-487	STOOGES (sh)		COLUMBIA	
COL-488	AN ACHE IN EVERY STAKE	LORD	COLUMBIA	1941
COL-489	ANDY CLYDE (sh)		COLUMBIA	
COL-494	ANDY CLYDE (sh)		COLUMBIA	
COL-496	EL BRENDEL (sh)		COLUMBIA	
COL-497	EL BRENDEL (sh)		COLUMBIA	
COL-498	YANKEE DOODLE ANDY	WHITE	COLUMBIA	1941
COL-499	EL BRENDEL (sh)		COLUMBIA	
COL-500	I'LL NEVER HEIL AGAIN	WHITE	COLUMBIA	1941
COL-501	LOVE AT FIRST FRIGHT	LORD	COLUMBIA	1941

COL-502	ALAN MOWBRAY (sh)		COLUMBIA	
COL-503	FRENCH FRIED PATOOTIE	WHITE	COLUMBIA	1941
COL-505	ROSCOE KARNS		COLUMBIA	
COL-506	HALF SHOT AT SUNRISE	LORD	COLUMBIA	1941
COL-507	EVEN AS I.O.U.	LORD	COLUMBIA	1942
COL-508	GENERAL NUISANCE	WHITE	COLUMBIA	1941
COL-509	ANDY CLYDE(sh)		COLUMBIA	
COL-510	LOCO BOY MAKES GOOD	WHITE	COLUMBIA	1942
COL-511	STOOGES (sh)		COLUMBIA	
COL-512	MITT ME TONIGHT – GLOVESLINGERS	WHITE	COLUMBIA	1941
COL-515	PHONY CRONIES	EDWARDS	COLUMBIA	1942
COL-519	WHAT'S THE MATADOR?	WHITE	COLUMBIA	1942
COL-520	GLOVE SLINGERS		COLUMBIA	
COL-521	SWEET SPIRITS OF NIGHTER	LORD	COLUMBIA	1941
COL-522	BACK FROM THE FRONT	WHITE	COLUMBIA	1943
COL-523	GROOM AND BORED	LORD	COLUMBIA	1942
COL-525	GLOVE AFFAIR – GLOVESLINGERS	WHITE	COLUMBIA	1941
COL-528	OLAF LAUGHS LAST	WHITE	COLUMBIA	1942
COL-529	DIZZY DETECTIVES	WHITE	COLUMBIA	1943
COL-532	3 SMART SAPS	WHITE	COLUMBIA	1942
COL-533	THEY STOOGE TO CONGA	LORD	COLUMBIA	1943
COL-536	CARRY HARRY (HARRY LANGDON)	EDWARDS	COLUMBIA	1942
COL-541	EL BRENDEL		COLUMBIA	
COL-541	HIS WEDDING SCARE (sh)	LORD	COLUMBIA	1943
COL-549	SPOOK LOUDER	LORD	COLUMBIA	1943
COL-550	I SPIED FOR YOU	WHITE	COLUMBIA	1943
COL-551	3 LITTLE TWERPS	EDWARDS	COLUMBIA	1943
COL-553	CHESTER CONKLIN		COLUMBIA	
COL-555	DIZZY PILOTS	WHITE	COLUMBIA	1943
COL-562	A ROOKIE'S COOKIE	WHITE	COLUMBIA	1943
COL-563	BOOBS IN THE NIGHT	LORD	COLUMBIA	1943
COL-564	NO DOUGH BOYS	WHITE	COLUMBIA	1944
COL-565	HUGH HERBERT (sh)	portrait	COLUMBIA	
COL-568	HIGHER THAN A KITE	LORD	COLUMBIA	1943
COL-569	PHONEY EXPRESS	LORD	COLUMBIA	1943
COL-570	I CAN HARDLY WAIT	WHITE	COLUMBIA	1943
COL-571	YOKE'S ON ME	WHITE	COLUMBIA	1944
COL-572	TO HEIR IS HUMAN – BARRY LANGDON	GODSOE	COLUMBIA	1944
COL-573	GARDEN OF EATIN	EDWARDS	COLUMBIA	1943
COL-574	WHO'S HUGH	EDWARDS	COLUMBIA	1943
COL-575	GEM OF A JAM	LORD	COLUMBIA	1943
COL-595	STOOGES (sh)		COLUMBIA	
COL-600	COMMUNITY SING – GENE MORGAN		COLUMBIA	
COL-611	COMMUNITY SING – GENE MORGAN		COLUMBIA	
COL-631	COMMUNITY SING		COLUMBIA	
COL-632	COMMUNITY SING		COLUMBIA	
COL-646	FOOLS WHO MADE HISTORY		COLUMBIA	1939
COL-647	FOOLS WHO MADE HISTORY - WALLY WALES		COLUMBIA	1939
COL-655	COMMUNITY SING – GENE MORGAN		COLUMBIA	
COL-729	CITY WITHOUT MEN	SALKOW	COLUMBIA	1943
COL-735	HEAT'S ON	RATOFF	COLUMBIA	1943
COL-762	CRIME DR.'S STRANGEST CASE	FORDE	COLUMBIA	1943
COL-770	SECRET COMMAND	SUTHERLAND	COLUMBIA	1944
COL-773	ADDRESS UNKNOWN	MENZIES	COLUMBIA	1944
COL-787	WHISTLER	CASTLE	COLUMBIA	1944
COL-788	TEXAS	MARSHALL	COLUMBIA	1941
COL-789	SHADOWS IN THE NIGHT	FORDE	COLUMBIA	1944
COL-791	EVER SINCE VENUE	DREIFUSS	COLUMBIA	1944
COL-803	MARK OF THE WHISTLER	CASTLE	COLUMBIA	1944
COL-808	BRENDA STARR – REPORTER SERIAL	FOX	COLUMBIA	1945
COL-811	RIDERS OF THE WHISTLING PINES	ENGLISH	COLUMBIA	1949
COL-812	CRIME DR.'S COURAGE	SHERMAN	COLUMBIA	1945
COL-813	POWER OF THE WHISTLER	LANDERS	COLUMBIA	1945
COL-814	KISS AND TELL	WALLACE	COLUMBIA	1945
COL-818	MONSTER AND THE APE	BRETHERTON	COLUMBIA	1945
COL-822	OVER 21	VIDOR	COLUMBIA	1945

COL-830	ADVENTURES OF RUSTY	BURNFORD	COLUMBIA	1945
COL-834	SNAFU	MOSS	COLUMBIA	1945
COL-835	JUNGLE RAIDERS (serial)	SELANDER	COLUMBIA	1945
COL-838	CRIME DR.'S WARNING	CASTLE	COLUMBIA	1945
COL-841	PERILOUS HOLIDAY	GRIFFITH	COLUMBIA	1946
COL-844	WHO'S GUILTY?	BRETHERTON, GRISSELL	COLUMBIA	1945
COL-850	JOHNNY O'CLOCK	ROSSEN	COLUMBIA	1947
COL-851	MR. DISTRICT ATTORNEY	SINCLAIR	COLUMBIA	1947
COL-855	HOP HARRIGAN	ABRAHAMS	COLUMBIA	1946
COL-856	TO THE ENDS OF THE EARTH	STEVENSON	COLUMBIA	1948
COL-862	CHICK CARTER DETECTIVE	ABRAHAMS	COLUMBIA	1946
COL-863	RETURN OF MONTE CRISTO	LEVIN	COLUMBIA	1946
COL-868	SON OF THE GUARDSMAN	ABRAHAMS	COLUMBIA	1946
COL-869	LAST OF THE REDMEN	SHERMAN	COLUMBIA	1947
COL-873	BETTY CO-ED	DREIFUSS	COLUMBIA	1946
COL-878	JACK ARMSTRONG	FOX	COLUMBIA	1947
COL-879	GUNFIGHTERS	WAGGNER	COLUMBIA	1947
COL-882	VIGILANTE - SERIAL	FOX	COLUMBIA	1947
COL-883	RELENTLESS	SHERMAN	COLUMBIA	1948
COL-884	LITTLE MISS BROADWAY	DREIFUSS	COLUMBIA	1947
COL-885	HER HUSBANDS AFFAIRS	SIMON	COLUMBIA	1947
COL-886	SEA HOUND	EASON, WRIGHT	COLUMBIA	1947
COL-887	PRINCE OF THIEVES	BRETHERTON	COLUMBIA	1948
COL-888	I LOVE TROUBLE	SIMON	COLUMBIA	1948
COL-889	MUSIC IN MY HEART	SANTLEY	COLUMBIA	1940
COL-889	STRAWBERRY ROAN	ENGLISH	COLUMBIA	1948
COL-890	SWEET GENEVIEVE	DREIFUSS	COLUMBIA	1947
COL-891	TWO BLONDES AND A REDHEAD	DREIFUSS	COLUMBIA	1947
COL-892	LAST ROUNDUP	ENGLISH	COLUMBIA	1947
COL-893	BIG SOMBRERO	MCDONALD	COLUMBIA	1949
COL-895	TEX GRANGER - SERIAL	ABRAHAMS	COLUMBIA	1948
COL-896	SIGN OF THE RAM	STURGES	COLUMBIA	1948
COL-897	BLACK ARROW	DOUGLAS	COLUMBIA	1948
COL-899	BRICK BRADFORD - SERIAL	BENNET, CARR	COLUMBIA	1947
COL-900	GREAT ADV OF WILD BILL HICKOK (serial)	NELSON, WRIGHT	COLUMBIA	1938
COL-900	MARY LOU	DREIFUSS	COLUMBIA	1948
COL-901	SPIDER'S WEB (serial)	HORNE, TAYLOR	COLUMBIA	1938
COL-902	ALL THE KING'S MEN	ROSSEN	COLUMBIA	1950
COL-902	FLYING G-MEN - SERIAL	HORNE, TAYLOR	COLUMBIA	1939
COL-903	MANDRAKE THE MAGICIAN - (serial)	DEMING, NELSON	COLUMBIA	1939
COL-904	OVERLAND WITH KIT CARSON	DEMING, NELSON	COLUMBIA	1939
COL-905	LOADED PISTOLS	ENGLISH	COLUMBIA	1948
COL-908	GLAMOUR GIRL	DREIFUSS	COLUMBIA	1948
COL-909	MANHATTAN ANGEL	DREIFUSS	COLUMBIA	1949
COL-910	SUPERMAN - SERIAL	BENNET, CARR	COLUMBIA	1948
COL-911	ADVENTURE IN WASHINGTON	GREEN	COLUMBIA	1941
COL-912	I SURRENDER DEAR	DREIFUSS	COLUMBIA	1948
COL-913	FULLER BRUSH MAN	SIMON	COLUMBIA	1948
COL-914	RACING LUCK	BERKE	COLUMBIA	1948
COL-915	LOVES OF CARMEN	VIDOR	COLUMBIA	1948
COL-916	SHE KNEW ALL THE ANSWERS	WALLACE	COLUMBIA	1941
COL-918	MUTINEERS	YARBROUGH	COLUMBIA	1949
COL-919	LULU BELLE	FENTON	COLUMBIA	1948
COL-920	UNDERCOVER MAN	LEWIS	COLUMBIA	1949
COL-921	SONS OF NEW MEXICO	ENGLISH	COLUMBIA	1949
COL-923	ANNA LUCASTA	RAPPER	COLUMBIA	1949
COL-924	COWBOY AND THE INDIANS	ENGLISH	COLUMBIA	1949
COL-926	CONGO BILL	BENNET, CARR	COLUMBIA	1948
COL-927	UNTAMED BREED	LAMONT	COLUMBIA	1948
COL-928	LADIES OF THE CHORUS	KARLSON	COLUMBIA	1948
COL-931	ADAM HAD FOUR SONS	RATOFF	COLUMBIA	1941
COL-931	KNOCK ON ANY DOOR	RAY	COLUMBIA	1949
COL-932	TOKYO JOE	HEISLER	COLUMBIA	1949
COL-933	TRIPLE THREAT	YARBROUGH	COLUMBIA	1948
COL-934	SONG OF INDIA	ROGELL	COLUMBIA	1949
COL-935	JUNGLE JIM	BERKE	COLUMBIA	1948

COL-937	BRUCE GENTRY	BENNET, CARR	COLUMBIA	1949
COL-939	WE WERE STRANGERS	HUSTON	COLUMBIA	1949
COL-942	LOST TRIBE	BERKE	COLUMBIA	1949
COL-944	ADVENTURES OF BATMAN AND ROBIN	BENNET	COLUMBIA	1949
COL-945	DOOLINS OF OKLAHOMA	DOUGLAS	COLUMBIA	1949
COL-946	.JOLSON SINGS AGAIN	LEVIN	COLUMBIA	1949
COL-947	RIM OF THE CANYON	ENGLISH	COLUMBIA	1949
COL-949	LADIES IN RETIREMENT	VIDOR	COLUMBIA	1941
COL-950	STATE PENITENTIARY	LANDERS	COLUMBIA	1950
COL-951	BARBARY PIRATE	LANDERS	COLUMBIA	1949
COL-952	COW TOWN	ENGLISH	COLUMBIA	1950
COL-953	ADVENTURES OF SIR GALAHAD	BENNET	COLUMBIA	1949
COL-953	MEN IN HER LIFE	RATOFF	COLUMBIA	1941
COL-954	CAPTIVE GIRL	BERKE	COLUMBIA	1950
COL-955	MARK OF THE GORILLA	BERKE	COLUMBIA	1950
COL-956	ATOM MAN VS. SUPERMAN	BENNET	COLUMBIA	1950
COL-957	CODY OF THE PONY EXPRESS	BENNET	COLUMBIA	1950
COL-958	CHINATOWN AT MIDNIGHT	FRIEDMAN	COLUMBIA	1949
COL-962	TYRANT OF THE SEA	LANDERS	COLUMBIA	1950
COL-964	ADVENTURES OF MARTIN EDEN	SALKOW	COLUMBIA	1942
COL-964	RECKLESS MOMENT	OPHULS	COLUMBIA	1949
COL-965	TRAVELING SALESWOMAN	REISNER	COLUMBIA	1950
COL-966	AND BABY MAKES THREE	LEVIN	COLUMBIA	1949
COL-967	BLAZING SUN	ENGLISH	COLUMBIA	1950
COL-968	NEVADAN	DOUGLAS	COLUMBIA	1950
COL-970	IN A LONELY PLACE	RAY	COLUMBIA	1950
COL-971	RIDERS IN THE SKY	ENGLISH	COLUMBIA	1949
COL-975	BRAVE BULLS	ROSSON	COLUMBIA	1951
COL-977	BEYOND THE PURPLE HILLS	ENGLISH	COLUMBIA	1950
COL-981	INDIAN TERRITORY	ENGLISH	COLUMBIA	1950
COL-982	SOMETHING TO SHOUT ABOUT	RATOFF	COLUMBIA	1943
COL-986	LAST OF THE BUCCANEERS	LANDERS	COLUMBIA	1950
COL-988	GENE AUTRY AND THE MOUNTIES	ENGLISH	COLUMBIA	1951
COL-989	REVENUE AGENT	LANDERS	COLUMBIA	1950
COL-990	PIRATES OF THE HIGH SEAS	BENNET, CARR	COLUMBIA	1950
COL-991	SIROCCO	BERNHARDT	COLUMBIA	1951
COL-992	HURRICANE ISLAND	LANDERS	COLUMBIA	1951
COL-993	CHAIN GANG	LANDERS	COLUMBIA	1950
COL-994	PYGMY ISLAND	BERKE	COLUMBIA	1950
COL-995	FURY OF THE CONGO	BERKE	COLUMBIA	1951
COL-996	COMMANDOES STRIKE AT DAWN	FARROW	COLUMBIA	1942
COL-998	SATURDAY'S HERO	MILLER	COLUMBIA	1951
COL-999	FAMILY SECRET	LEVIN	COLUMBIA	1951
COL-1001	FOOTLIGHT GLAMOUR	STRAYER	COLUMBIA	1943
COL-1002	IS EVERYBODY HAPPY?	BARTON	COLUMBIA	1943
COL-1004	WHAT A WOMAN	CUMMINGS	COLUMBIA	1943
COL-1005	NINE GIRLS	JASON	COLUMBIA	1944
COL-1006	NONE SHALL ESCAPE	DE TOTH	COLUMBIA	1944
COL-1009	RACKET MAN	LEDERMAN	COLUMBIA	1944
COL-1010	RETURN OF THE VAMPIRE	LANDERS	COLUMBIA	1944
COL-1011	SONG TO REMEMBER	VIDOR	COLUMBIA	1945
COL-1012	CHANCE OF A LIFETIME	CASTLE	COLUMBIA	1943
COL-1014	MR. WINKLE GOES TO WAR	GREEN	COLUMBIA	1944
COL-1015	KLONDIKE KATE	CASTLE	COLUMBIA	1943
COL-1016	SWING OUT OF THE BLUES	ST. CLAIR	COLUMBIA	1943
COL-1017	BEAUTIFUL BUT BROKE	BARTON	COLUMBIA	1944
COL-1019	GHOST THAT WALKS ALONE	LANDERS	COLUMBIA	1944
COL-1021	GIRL IN THE CASE	BERKE	COLUMBIA	1944
COL-1022	TONIGHT AND EVERY NIGHT	SAVILLE	COLUMBIA	1945
COL-1023	SAILOR'S HOLIDAY	BERKE	COLUMBIA	1944
COL-1024	TOGETHER AGAIN	VIDOR	COLUMBIA	1944
COL-1025	TWO MAN SUBMARINE	LANDERS	COLUMBIA	1944
COL-1026	CAROLINA BLUES	JASON	COLUMBIA	1944
COL-1027	STARS ON PARADE	LANDERS	COLUMBIA	1944
COL-1028	BLACK PARACHUTE	LANDERS	COLUMBIA	1944
COL-1029	SHE'S A SOLDIER TOO	CASTLE	COLUMBIA	1944

COL-1030	JOLSON STORY (SOME MARKED 1130)	GREEN	COLUMBIA	1946
COL-1031	COUNTER-ATTACK	KORDA	COLUMBIA	1945
COL-1032	THEY LIVE IN FEAR	BERNE	COLUMBIA	1944
COL-1033	U-BOAT PRISONER	LANDERS	COLUMBIA	1944
COL-1035	LOUISIANA HAYRIDE	BARTON	COLUMBIA	1944
COL-1036	IMPATIENT YEARS	CUMMINGS	COLUMBIA	1944
COL-1037	CRY OF THE WEREWOLF	LEVIN	COLUMBIA	1944
COL-1038	UNWRITTEN CODE	ROTSTEN	COLUMBIA	1944
COL-1039	EVE KNEW HER APPLES	JASON	COLUMBIA	1945
COL-1040	KANSAS CITY KITTY	LORD	COLUMBIA	1944
COL-1042	MEET MISS BOBBY SOCKS	TRYON	COLUMBIA	1944
COL-1043	STRANGE AFFAIR	GREEN	COLUMBIA	1944
COL-1044	SOUL OF A MONSTER	JASON	COLUMBIA	1944
COL-1045	ONE MYSTERIOUS NIGHT	BOETTICHER	COLUMBIA	1944
COL-1046	SERGEANT MIKE	LEVIN	COLUMBIA	1944
COL-1047	MISSING JUROR	BOETTICHER	COLUMBIA	1944
COL-1048	ESCAPE IN THE FOG	BOETTICHER	COLUMBIA	1945
COL-1049	SHE'S A SWEETHEART	LORD	COLUMBIA	1944
COL-1050	TARS AND SPARS	GREEN	COLUMBIA	1946
COL-1051	EADIE WAS A LADY	DREIFUSS	COLUMBIA	1945
COL-1052	DANCING IN MANHATTAN	LEVIN	COLUMBIA	1944
COL-1054	THOUSAND AND ONE NIGHTS	GREEN	COLUMBIA	1945
COL-1055	TAHITI NIGHTS	JASON	COLUMBIA	1944
COL-1056	LEAVE IT TO BLONDIE	BERLIN	COLUMBIA	1945
COL-1057	LET'S GO STEADY	LORD	COLUMBIA	1945
COL-1058	I LOVE A MYSTERY	LEVIN	COLUMBIA	1945
COL-1059	YOUTH ON TRIAL	BOETTICHER	COLUMBIA	1945
COL-1060	SHE WOULDN'T SAY YES	HALL	COLUMBIA	1945
COL-1061	MEET ME ON BROADWAY	JASON	COLUMBIA	1946
COL-1062	GUY, A GAL AND A PAL	BOETTICHER	COLUMBIA	1945
COL-1063	ROUGH TOUGH AND READY	LORD	COLUMBIA	1945
COL-1064	FIGHTING GUARDSMAN	LEVIN	COLUMBIA	1946
COL-1066	TEN CENTS A DANCE	JASON	COLUMBIA	1945
COL-1069	BOSTON BLACKIE HOOKED ON SUSPICION	DREIFUSS	COLUMBIA	1945
COL-1070	BLONDE FROM BROOKLYN	LORD	COLUMBIA	1945
COL-1071	GAY SENORITA	DREIFUSS	COLUMBIA	1945
COL-1072	BOSTON BLACKIE'S RENDEZVOUS	DREIFUSS	COLUMBIA	1945
COL-1074	BANDIT OF SHERWOOD FOREST	LEVIN, SHERMAN	COLUMBIA	1946
COL-1075	I LOVE A BANDLEADER	LORD	COLUMBIA	1945
COL-1076	VOICE OF THE WHISTLER	CASTLE	COLUMBIA	1945
COL-1078	GIRL OF THE LIMBERLOST	FERRER	COLUMBIA	1945
COL-1079	RENEGADES	SHERMAN	COLUMBIA	1946
COL-1080	ONE WAY TO LOVE	ENRIGHT	COLUMBIA	1946
COL-1081	HIT THE HAY	LORD	COLUMBIA	1945
COL-1082	MY NAME IS JULIA ROSS	LEWIS	COLUMBIA	1945
COL-1083	OUT OF THE DEPTHS	LEDERMAN	COLUMBIA	1945
COL-1084	LIFE WITH BLONDIE	BERLIN	COLUMBIA	1945
COL-1086	PRISON SHIP	DREIFUSS	COLUMBIA	1945
COL-1087	GILDA	VIDOR	COLUMBIA	1946
COL-1088	BLONDIE'S LUCKY DAY	BERLIN	COLUMBIA	1946
COL-1089	CLOSE CALL FOR BOSTON BLACKIE	LANDERS	COLUMBIA	1946
COL-1090	SO DARK THE NIGHT	LEWIS	COLUMBIA	1946
COL-1091	NOTORIOUS LONE WOLF	LEDERMAN	COLUMBIA	1946
COL-1092	GENTLEMEN MISBEHAVES	SHERMAN	COLUMBIA	1946
COL-1093	JUST BEFORE DAWN	CASTLE	COLUMBIA	1946
COL-1094	WALLS CAME TUMBLING DOWN	MENDES	COLUMBIA	1946
COL-1095	DEVIL'S MASK	LEVIN	COLUMBIA	1946
COL-1096	DANGEROUS BUSINESS	LEDERMAN	COLUMBIA	1946
COL-1097	TALK ABOUT A LADY	SHERMAN	COLUMBIA	1946
COL-1098	MYSTERIOUS INTRUDER	CASTLE	COLUMBIA	1946
COL-1099	NIGHT EDITOR	LEVIN	COLUMBIA	1946
COL-1100	DOWN TO EARTH	HALL	COLUMBIA	1947
COL-1101	PHANTOM THIEF	LEDERMAN	COLUMBIA	1946
COL-1102	MAN WHO DARED	STURGES	COLUMBIA	1946
COL-1103	GALLANT JOURNEY	WELLMAN	COLUMBIA	1946
COL-1104	THRILL OF BRAZIL	SIMON	COLUMBIA	1946

COL-1105	RETURN OF RUSTY	CASTLE	COLUMBIA	1946
COL-1106	UNKNOWN, THE	LEVIN	COLUMBIA	1946
COL-1107	BLONDIE KNOWS BEST	BERLIN	COLUMBIA	1946
COL-1108	SING WHILE YOU DANCE	LEDERMAN	COLUMBIA	1946
COL-1109	PERSONALITY KID	SHERMAN	COLUMBIA	1946
COL-1110	CRIME DR.'S MANHUNT	CASTLE	COLUMBIA	1946
COL-1111	DEAD RECKONING	CROMWELL	COLUMBIA	1947
COL-1112	IT'S GREAT TO BE YOUNG	LORD	COLUMBIA	1946
COL-1113	FRAMED	WALLACE	COLUMBIA	1947
COL-1114	SECRET OF THE WHISTLER	SHERMAN	COLUMBIA	1946
COL-1115	GUILT OF JANET AMES	LEVIN	COLUMBIA	1947
COL-1116	SHADOWED	STURGES	COLUMBIA	1946
COL-1117	SWORDSMAN	LEWIS	COLUMBIA	1948
COL-1118	SINGING IN THE CORN	LORD	COLUMBIA	1946
COL-1119	BLONDIE'S BIG MOMENT	BERLIN	COLUMBIA	1947
COL-1120	BOSTON BLACKIE AND THE LAW	LEDERMAN	COLUMBIA	1946
COL-1121	RETURN OF OCTOBER	LEWIS	COLUMBIA	1948
COL-1122	LONE WOLF IN MEXICO	LEDERMAN	COLUMBIA	1947
COL-1123	ALIAS MR. TWILIGHT	STURGES	COLUMBIA	1946
COL-1124	BLIND SPOT	GORDON	COLUMBIA	1947
COL-1125	MILLIE'S DAUGHTER	SALKOW	COLUMBIA	1947
COL-1126	LADY FROM SHANGHAI		COLUMBIA	1947
COL-1128	THIRTEENTH HOUR	CLEMENS	COLUMBIA	1947
COL-1129	KING OF THE WILD HORSES	ARCHAINBAUD	COLUMBIA	1947
COL-1130	BLONDIE'S HOLIDAY	BERLIN	COLUMBIA	1947
COL-1130	JOLSON STORY	GREEN	COLUMBIA	1946
COL-1131	MILLERSON CASE	ARCHAINBAUD	COLUMBIA	1947
COL-1132	BULLDOG DRUMMOND AT BAY	SALKOW	COLUMBIA	1947
COL-1133	FOR THE LOVE OF RUSTY	STURGES	COLUMBIA	1947
COL-1135	MAN FROM COLORADO	LEVIN	COLUMBIA	1948
COL-1136	BLONDIE IN THE DOUGH	BERLIN	COLUMBIA	1947
COL-1137	SPORT OF KINGS	GORDON	COLUMBIA	1947
COL-1138	IT HAD TO BE YOU	HARTMAN, MATE	COLUMBIA	1947
COL-1139	KEEPER OF THE BEES	STURGES	COLUMBIA	1947
COL-1140	SON OF RUSTY	LANDERS	COLUMBIA	1947
COL-1141	KEY WITNESS	LEDERMAN	COLUMBIA	1947
COL-1143	MATING OF MILLIE	LEVIN	COLUMBIA	1948
COL-1144	WHEN A GIRL'S BEAUTIFUL	MCDONALD	COLUMBIA	1947
COL-1145	SLIGHTLY FRENCH	SIRK	COLUMBIA	1949
COL-1146	LONE WOLF IN LONDON	GOODWINS	COLUMBIA	1947
COL-1148	CRIME DR.'S GAMBLE	CASTLE	COLUMBIA	1947
COL-1149	DEVIL SHIP	LANDERS	COLUMBIA	1947
COL-1152	ADVENTURES IN SILVERADO	KARLSON	COLUMBIA	1948
COL-1153	WRECK OF THE HESPERUS	HOFFMAN	COLUMBIA	1948
COL-1154	PORT SAID	LE BORG	COLUMBIA	1948
COL-1155	BLONDIE'S REWARD	BERLIN	COLUMBIA	1948
COL-1156	BLONDIE'S ANNIVERSARY	BERLIN	COLUMBIA	1947
COL-1157	WOMAN FROM TANGIER	DANIELS	COLUMBIA	1948
COL-1159	RETURN OF THE WHISTLER	LEDERMAN	COLUMBIA	1948
COL-1160	GALLANT BLADE	LEVIN	COLUMBIA	1948
COL-1161	MY DOG RUSTY	LANDERS	COLUMBIA	1948
COL-1162	BEST MAN WINS	STURGES	COLUMBIA	1948
COL-1163	TRAPPED BY BOSTON BLACKIE	FRIEDMAN	COLUMBIA	1948
COL-1164	THUNDERHOOF	KARLSON	COLUMBIA	1948
COL-1165	LEATHER GLOVES	ASHER, QUINIE	COLUMBIA	1948
COL-1166	RUSTY LEADS THE WAY	JASON	COLUMBIA	1948
COL-1167	WALKING HILLS	STURGES	COLUMBIA	1949
COL-1168	DARK PAST	MATE	COLUMBIA	1948
COL-1169	BLACK EAGLE	GORDON	COLUMBIA	1948
COL-1170	GENTLEMEN FROM NOWHERE	CASTLE	COLUMBIA	1948
COL-1171	RUSTY SAVES A LIFE	FRIEDMAN	COLUMBIA	1949
COL-1172	BLONDIE'S SECRET	BERNDS	COLUMBIA	1948
COL-1173	BOSTON BLACKIE'S CHINESE VENTURE	FRIEDMAN	COLUMBIA	1949
COL-1174	SHOCKPROOF	SIRK	COLUMBIA	1949
COL-1175	MR. SOFT TOUCH	DOUGLAS, LEVIN	COLUMBIA	1949
COL-1176	HOLIDAY IN HAVANA	YARBROUGH	COLUMBIA	1949

COL-1177	LAW OF THE BARBARY COAST	LANDERS	COLUMBIA	1949
COL-1178	LONE WOLF AND HIS LADY	HOFFMAN	COLUMBIA	1949
COL-1179	CRIME DR.'S DIARY	FRIEDMAN	COLUMBIA	1949
COL-1180	BLONDIE'S BIG DEAL	BERNDS	COLUMBIA	1949
COL-1181	AIR HOSTESS	LANDERS	COLUMBIA	1949
COL-1182	MAKE BELIEVE BALLROOM	SANTLEY	COLUMBIA	1949
COL-1183	LUST FOR GOLD	SIMON	COLUMBIA	1949
COL-1185	BLONDIE HITS THE JACKPOT	BERNDS	COLUMBIA	1949
COL-1186	DEVIL'S HENCHMEN	FRIEDMAN	COLUMBIA	1949
COL-1187	JOHNNY ALLEGRO	TETZLAFF	COLUMBIA	1949
COL-1188	SECRET OF ST. IVES	ROSEN	COLUMBIA	1949
COL-1189	KAZAN	JASON	COLUMBIA	1949
COL-1190	RUSTY'S BIRTHDAY	FRIEDMAN	COLUMBIA	1949
COL-1191	MISS GRANT TAKES RICHMOND	BACON	COLUMBIA	1949
COL-1192	TELL IT TO THE JUDGE	FOSTER	COLUMBIA	1949
COL-1193	PALOMINO	NAZARRO	COLUMBIA	1950
COL-1194	PRISON WARDEN	FRIEDMAN	COLUMBIA	1949
COL-1195	BLONDIE'S HERO	BERNDS	COLUMBIA	1950
COL-1196	GOOD HUMOR MAN	BACON	COLUMBIA	1950
COL-1197	BORN YESTERDAY	CUKOR	COLUMBIA	1950
COL-1198	CARGO TO CAPETOWN	MCEVOY	COLUMBIA	1950
COL-1199	MARY RYAN, DETECTIVE	BERLIN	COLUMBIA	1949
COL-1200	GIRL'S SCHOOL	BRAHM	COLUMBIA	1938
COL-1201	ROGUES OF SHERWOOD FOREST	DOUGLAS	COLUMBIA	1950
COL-1202	WOMAN OF DISTINCTION	BUZZELL	COLUMBIA	1950
COL-1204	FATHER IS A BACHELOR	BERLIN, FOSTER	COLUMBIA	1950
COL-1205	BODYHOLD	FRIEDMAN	COLUMBIA	1949
COL-1206	FORTUNES OF CAPTAIN BLOOD	DOUGLAS	COLUMBIA	1950
COL-1207	PETTY GIRL	LEVIN	COLUMBIA	1950
COL-1208	BEWARE OF BLONDIE	BERNDS	COLUMBIA	1950
COL-1209	KILL THE UMPIRE	BACON	COLUMBIA	1950
COL-1210	MILITARY ACADEMY	LEDERMAN	COLUMBIA	1940
COL-1211	FULLER BRUSH GIRL	BACON	COLUMBIA	1950
COL-1213	BEAUTY ON PARADE	LANDERS	COLUMBIA	1950
COL-1214	NO SAD SONGS FOR ME	MATE	COLUMBIA	1950
COL-1215	CUSTOMS AGENT	FRIEDMAN	COLUMBIA	1950
COL-1218	WHEN YOU'RE SMILING	SANTLEY	COLUMBIA	1950
COL-1219	CONVICTED	LEVIN	COLUMBIA	1950
COL-1220	ROOKIE FIREMAN	FRIEDMAN	COLUMBIA	1950
COL-1221	DAVID HARDING – COUNTER SPY	NAZARRO	COLUMBIA	1950
COL-1222	BETWEEN MIDNIGHT AND DAWN	DOUGLAS	COLUMBIA	1950
COL-1223	HE'S A COCKEYED WONDER	GODFREY	COLUMBIA	1950
COL-1224	HARRIET CRAIG	SHERMAN	COLUMBIA	1950
COL-1225	ON THE ISLE OF SOMOA	BERKE	COLUMBIA	1950
COL-1226	TWO OF A KIND	LEVIN	COLUMBIA	1951
COL-1228	STAGE TO TUCSON	MURPHY	COLUMBIA	1950
COL-1230	EMERGENCY WEDDING	BUZZELL	COLUMBIA	1950
COL-1231	AL JENNINGS OF OKLAHOMA	NAZARRO	COLUMBIA	1951
COL-1232	FLYING MISSING	LEVIN	COLUMBIA	1950
COL-1233	MASK OF THE AVENGER	KARLSON	COLUMBIA	1951
COL-1234	COUNTERSPY MEETS SCOTLAND YARD	FRIEDMAN	COLUMBIA	1950
COL-1235	HER FIRST ROMANCE	FRIEDMAN	COLUMBIA	1951
COL-1237	TOUGHER THEY COME	NAZARRO	COLUMBIA	1950
COL-1238	FLAME OF STAMBOUL	NAZARRO	COLUMBIA	1951
COL-1239	LADY AND THE BANDIT	MURPHY	COLUMBIA	1951
COL-1240	GASOLINE ALLEY	BERNDS	COLUMBIA	1951
COL-1241	BAREFOOT MAILMAN	MCEVOY	COLUMBIA	1951
COL-1242	SUNNY SIDE OF THE STREET	QUINE	COLUMBIA	1951
COL-1243	NEVER TRUST A GAMBLER	MURPHY	COLUMBIA	1951
COL-1244	SMUGGLERS GOLD	BERKE	COLUMBIA	1951
COL-1245	MOB	PARRISH	COLUMBIA	1951
COL-1246	CRIMINAL LAWYER	FRIEDMAN	COLUMBIA	1951
COL-1248	PAULA	MATE	COLUMBIA	1952
COL-1249	MY TRUE STORY	ROONEY	COLUMBIA	1951
COL-1250	CHINA CORSAIR	NAZARRO	COLUMBIA	1951
COL-1251	BIG GUSHER	LANDERS	COLUMBIA	1951

COL-1252	SON OF DR. JEKYL	FRIEDMAN	COLUMBIA	1951
COL-1253	ASSIGNMENT-PARIS	PARRISH	COLUMBIA	1952
COL-1254	CHAIN OF CIRCUMSTANCES	JASON	COLUMBIA	1951
COL-1255	CORKY OF GASOLINE ALLEY	BERNDS	COLUMBIA	1951
COL-1257	CAPT. PIRATE	MURPHY	COLUMBIA	1952
COL-1258	MARRYING KIND	CUKOR	COLUMBIA	1952
COL-1259	OKINAWA	JASON	COLUMBIA	1952
COL-1260	MONTANA TERRITORY	NAZARRO	COLUMBIA	1952
COL-1261	HAREM GIRL	BERNDS	COLUMBIA	1952
COL-1263	LAST OF THE COMMANCHES	DE TOTH	COLUMBIA	1953
COL-1264	RAINBOW 'ROUND MY SHOULDER	QUINE	COLUMBIA	1952
COL-1265	TARGET HONG KONG	SEARS	COLUMBIA	1953
COL-1268	LET'S DO IT AGAIN	HALL	COLUMBIA	1953
COL-1269	MISSION OVER KOREA	SEARS	COLUMBIA	1953
COL-1270	LAST POSSE	WERKER	COLUMBIA	1953
COL-1271	FROM HERE TO ETERNITY	ZINNEMANN	COLUMBIA	1953
COL-1272	CRUISIN' DOWN THE RIVER	QUINE	COLUMBIA	1953
COL-1273	EL ALAMEIN (GER: THAT WAS OUR ROMMEL)	WIGANKO	COLUMBIA	1953
COL-1278	GUN FURY	WALSH	COLUMBIA	1953
COL-1280	MAN IN THE DARK	LANDERS	COLUMBIA	1953
COL-1281	HUMAN DESIRE	LANG	COLUMBIA	1954
COL-1283	NEBRASKAN	SEARS	COLUMBIA	1953
COL-1287	THREE FOR THE SHOW	POTTER	COLUMBIA	1955
COL-1288	MASSACRE CANYON	SEARS	COLUMBIA	1954
COL-1289	DRIVE A CROOKED MILE	QUINE	COLUMBIA	1954
COL-1290	THEY RODE WEST	KARLSON	COLUMBIA	1954
COL-1291	PUSHOVER	QUINE	COLUMBIA	1954
COL-1292	OUTLAW STALLION	SEARS	COLUMBIA	1954
COL-1293	THREE HOUSE TO FILL	WERKER	COLUMBIA	1954
COL-1295	BLACK DAKOTAS	NAZARRO	COLUMBIA	1954
COL-1298	PHFFT	ROBSON	COLUMBIA	1954
COL-1299	WYOMING RENEGADES	SEARS	COLUMBIA	1954
COL-1300	TIGHT SPOT	KARLSON	COLUMBIA	1955
COL-1301	MY SISTER EILEEN	QUINE	COLUMBIA	1955
COL-1302	CELL 2455-DEATH ROW	SEARS	COLUMBIA	1955
COL-1303	THREE STRIPES IN THE SUN	MURPHY	COLUMBIA	1955
COL-1305	BRING YOUR SMILE ALONG	EDWARDS	COLUMBIA	1955
COL-1306	LAST FRONTIER	MANN	COLUMBIA	1955
COL-1307	APACHE AMBUSH	SEARS	COLUMBIA	1955
COL-1308	QUEEN BEE	MACDOUGALL	COLUMBIA	1955
COL-1309	PICNIC	LOGAN	COLUMBIA	1955
COL-1310	JUBAL	DAVES	COLUMBIA	1956
COL-1311	EDDIE DUCHIN STORY	SIDNEY	COLUMBIA	1956
COL-1313	FURY AT GUNSIGHT PASS	SEARS	COLUMBIA	1956
COL-1314	YOU CAN'T RUN AWAY FROM IT	POWELL	COLUMBIA	1956
COL-1315	HARDER THEY FALL	ROBSON	COLUMBIA	1956
COL-1316	SECRET OF TREASURE MOUNTAIN	FRIEDMAN	COLUMBIA	1956
COL-1318	SOLID GOLD CADILLAC	QUINE	COLUMBIA	1956
COL-1319	OVER-EXPOSED	SEILER	COLUMBIA	1956
COL-1320	HE LAUGHED LAST	EDWARDS	COLUMBIA	1956
COL-1322	FULL OF LIFE	QUINE	COLUMBIA	1956
COL-1323	SHADOW ON THE WINDOW	ASHER	COLUMBIA	1957
COL-1329	GUNMAN'S WALK	KARLSON	COLUMBIA	1958
COL-1332	GUNMEN FROM LAREDO	MACDONALD	COLUMBIA	1959
COL-1334	GIDGET	WENDKOS	COLUMBIA	1959
COL-1879	BAMBOLE (IT)	BOLOGNINI, COLOGINI	COLUMBIA	1965
COL-3001	COWBOY FROM LONESOME RIVER	KLINE	COLUMBIA	1944
COL-3002	CYCLONE PRAIRIE RANGERS	KLINE	COLUMBIA	1944
COL-3004	SUNDOWN VALLEY	KLINE	COLUMBIA	1944
COL-3005	COWBOY CANTEEN	LANDERS	COLUMBIA	1944
COL-3006	SADDLE LEATHER LAW	KLINE	COLUMBIA	1944
COL-3007	SAGEBRUSH HEROES	KLINE	COLUMBIA	1945
COL-3008	ROUGH RIDING JUSTICE	ABRAHAMS	COLUMBIA	1945
COL-3009	SWING IN THE SADDLE	LANDERS	COLUMBIA	1944
COL-3010	RETURN OF THE DURANGO KID	ABRAHAMS	COLUMBIA	1945
COL-3011	BOTH BARRELS BLAZING	ABRAHAMS	COLUMBIA	1945

COL-3012	RUSTLERS OF THE BADLANDS	ABRAHAMS	COLUMBIA	1945
COL-3013	FRONTIER GUNLAW	ABRAHAMS	COLUMBIA	1946
COL-3014	SING ME A SONG OF TEXAS	KEAYS	COLUMBIA	1945
COL-3015	BLAZING THE WESTERN TRAIL	KEAYS	COLUMBIA	1945
COL-3016	LAWLESS EMPIRE	KEAYS	COLUMBIA	1945
COL-3017	ROCKIN' IN THE ROCKIES	KEAYS	COLUMBIA	1945
COL-3018	RHYTHM ROUNDUP	KEAYS	COLUMBIA	1945
COL-3019	OUTLAWS OF THE ROCKIES	NAZARRO	COLUMBIA	1945
COL-3020	TEXAS PANHANDLE	NAZARRO	COLUMBIA	1945
COL-3021	SONG OF THE PRAIRIE	NAZARRO	COLUMBIA	1945
COL-3022	DESERT HORSEMAN	NAZARRO	COLUMBIA	1946
COL-3023	GUNNING FOR VENGEANCE	NAZARRO	COLUMBIA	1946
COL-3024	ROARING RANGERS	NAZARRO	COLUMBIA	1946
COL-3025	THROW A SADDLE ON A STAR	NAZARRO	COLUMBIA	1946
COL-3026	HEADING WEST	NAZARRO	COLUMBIA	1946
COL-3027	GALLOPING THUNDER	NAZARRO	COLUMBIA	1946
COL-3028	TWO-FISTED STRANGER	NAZARRO	COLUMBIA	1946
COL-3029	THAT TEXAS JAMBOREE	NAZARRO	COLUMBIA	1946
COL-3030	TERROR TRAIL	NAZARRO	COLUMBIA	1946
COL-3031	LANDRUSH	KEAYS	COLUMBIA	1946
COL-3032	COWBOY BLUES	NAZARRO	COLUMBIA	1946
COL-3033	SINGING ON THE TRAIL	NAZARRO	COLUMBIA	1946
COL-3034	FIGHTING FRONTIERSMAN	ABRAHAMS	COLUMBIA	1946
COL-3035	SOUTH OF THE CHISHOLM TRAIL	ABRAHAMS	COLUMBIA	1947
COL-3036	LONE STAR MOONLIGHT	NAZARRO	COLUMBIA	1946
COL-3037	OVER THE SANTA FE TRAIL	NAZARRO	COLUMBIA	1947
COL-3038	WEST OF DODGE CITY	NAZARRO	COLUMBIA	1947
COL-3039	LONE HAND TEXAS	NAZARRO	COLUMBIA	1947
COL-3040	LAW OF THE CANYON	NAZARRO	COLUMBIA	1947
COL-3041	PRAIRIE RAIDERS	ABRAHAMS	COLUMBIA	1947
COL-3042	STRANGER FROM PONCA CITY	ABRAHAMS	COLUMBIA	1947
COL-3043	RIDERS OF THE LONE STAR	ABRAHAMS	COLUMBIA	1947
COL-3044	SWING THE WESTERN WAY	ABRAHAMS	COLUMBIA	1947
COL-3045	SMOKEY RIVER SERENADE	ABRAHAMS	COLUMBIA	1947
COL-3046	SIX GUN LAW	NAZARRO	COLUMBIA	1948
COL-3047	BUCKAROO FROM POWDER RIVER	NAZARRO	COLUMBIA	1947
COL-3048	PHANTOM VALLEY	NAZARRO	COLUMBIA	1948
COL-3049	LAST DAYS OF BOOTHILL	NAZARRO	COLUMBIA	1947
COL-3050	ROSE OF SANTA FE	NAZARRO	COLUMBIA	1947
COL-3051	WHIRLWIND RAIDERS	KEAYS	COLUMBIA	1948
COL-3052	WEST OF SONORA	NAZARRO	COLUMBIA	1948
COL-3053	SONG OF IDAHO	NAZARRO	COLUMBIA	1948
COL-3054	BLAZING ACROSS THE PECOS	NAZARRO	COLUMBIA	1948
COL-3055	TRAIL TO LAREDO	NAZARRO	COLUMBIA	1948
COL-3056	ARKANSAS SWING	NAZARRO	COLUMBIA	1948
COL-3057	SINGIN' SPURS	NAZARRO	COLUMBIA	1948
COL-3058	EL DORADO PASS	NAZARRO	COLUMBIA	1948
COL-3059	QUICK ON THE TRIGGER	NAZARRO	COLUMBIA	1948
COL-3060	CHALLENGE OF THE RANGE	NAZARRO	COLUMBIA	1949
COL-3061	SMOKY MOUNTAIN MELODY	NAZARRO	COLUMBIA	1948
COL-3062	SOUTH OF DEATH VALLEY	NAZARRO	COLUMBIA	1949
COL-3063	DESERT VIGILANTE	SEARS	COLUMBIA	1949
COL-3064	LARAMIE	NAZARRO	COLUMBIA	1949
COL-3065	HOME IN SAN ANTONE	NAZARRO	COLUMBIA	1949
COL-3066	BLAZING TRAIL	NAZARRO	COLUMBIA	1949
COL-3067	HORSEMEN OF THE SIERRAS	SEARS	COLUMBIA	1949
COL-3068	BANDITS OF EL DORADO	NAZARRO	COLUMBIA	1949
COL-3069	RENEGADES OF THE SAGE	NAZARRO	COLUMBIA	1949
COL-3070	HOEDOWN	NAZARRO	COLUMBIA	1950
COL-3071	FEUDIN' RHYTHM	BERNDS	COLUMBIA	1949
COL-3072	OUTCAST OF BLACK MESA	NAZARRO	COLUMBIA	1950
COL-3073	FRONTIER OUTPOST	NAZARRO	COLUMBIA	1950
COL-3074	TRAIL OF THE RUSTLERS	NAZARRO	COLUMBIA	1950
COL-3075	TEXAS DYNAMO	NAZARRO	COLUMBIA	1950
COL-3076	STREETS OF GHOST TOWN	NAZARRO	COLUMBIA	1950
COL-3078	RAIDERS OF TOMAHAWK CREEK	SEARS	COLUMBIA	1950

COL-3079	LIGHTNING GUNS	SEARS	COLUMBIA	1950
COL-3080	PRAIRIE ROUNDUP	SEARS	COLUMBIA	1951
COL-3081	RIDIN' THE OUTLAW TRAIL	SEARS	COLUMBIA	1951
COL-3082	FORT SAVAGE RAIDERS	NAZARRO	COLUMBIA	1951
COL-3083	SNAKE RIVER DESPERADOES	SEARS	COLUMBIA	1951
COL-3084	BONANZA TOWN	SEARS	COLUMBIA	1951
COL-3085	CYCLONE FURY	NAZARRO	COLUMBIA	1951
COL-3086	KID FROM AMARILLO	NAZARRO	COLUMBIA	1951
COL-3088	SMOKY CANYON	SEARS	COLUMBIA	1952
COL-3089	HAWK OF WILD RIVER	SEARS	COLUMBIA	1952
COL-3090	LARAMIE MOUNTAINS	NAZARRO	COLUMBIA	1952
COL-3091	ROUGH TOUGH WEST	NAZARRO	COLUMBIA	1952
COL-3092	JUNCTION CITY	NAZARRO	COLUMBIA	1952
COL-3093	KID FROM BROKEN GUN	SEARS	COLUMBIA	1952
COL-3400	CORONER CREEK	ENRIGHT	COLUMBIA	1948
COL-4001	BUSY BUDDIES	LORD	COLUMBIA	1944
COL-4002	WEDDED BLISS	EDWARDS	COLUMBIA	1944
COL-4003	BACHELOR DAZE	WHITE	COLUMBIA	1944
COL-4004	YOU DEAR BOY – VERA VAGUE	WHITE	COLUMBIA	1943
COL-4005	DR. FEEL MY PULSE – VERA VAGUE	WHITE	COLUMBIA	1944
COL-4006	BOOBY DUPES GES	LORD	COLUMBIA	1945
COL-4007	HIS TALE IS TOLD – ANDY CLYDE	EDWARDS	COLUMBIA	1944
COL-4008	YOU WERE NEVER UGLIER – ANDY CLYDE	WHITE	COLUMBIA	1944
COL-4010	CRASH GOES THE HASH – STOOGES	WHITE	COLUMBIA	1944
COL-4011	CRAZY LIKE A FOX – BILLY GILBERT	WHITE	COLUMBIA	1944
COL-4013	IDLE ROOMERS – STOOGES	LORD	COLUMBIA	1943
COL-4014	OH BABY – HUGH HERBERT	WHITE	COLUMBIA	1944
COL-4015	OFF AGAIN ON AGAIN – SHEMP HOWARD	WHITE	COLUMBIA	1945
COL-4016	OPEN SEASON FOR SAPS – SHEMP HOWARD	WHITE	COLUMBIA	1944
COL-4017	DEFECTIVE DETECTIVES – EL BRENDEL	EDWARDS	COLUMBIA	1944
COL-4018	PICK A PECK OF PLUMBERS – EL BRENDEL	WHITE	COLUMBIA	1944
COL-4019	MOPEY DOPE – HARRY LANGDON	LORD	COLUMBIA	1944
COL-4020	GENTS WITHOUT CENTS – STOOGES	WHITE	COLUMBIA	1944
COL-4021	HEATHER AND YOU – ANDY CLYDE	EDWARDS	COLUMBIA	1944
COL-4022	THREE PEST IN A MESS – STOOGES	LORD	COLUMBIA	1945
COL-4023	WOO WOO (I SHOULD WORRY*)	WHITE	COLUMBIA	1945
COL-4025	WOO WOO (I SHOULD WORRY*)	WHITE	COLUMBIA	1945
COL-4026	SHE SNOOPS TO CONQUER – VERA VAGUE	WHITE	COLUMBIA	1944
COL-4027	STRIFE OF THE PARTY – VERA VAGUE	EDWARDS	COLUMBIA	1944
COL-4028	DANCE DUNCE DANCE – EDDIE FOY JR.	WHITE	COLUMBIA	1945
COL-4030	IDIOTS DELUXE – STOOGES	WHITE	COLUMBIA	1945
COL-4031	JURY GOES 'ROUND AND 'ROUND	WHITE	COLUMBIA	1945
COL-4032	HISS AND YELL – VERA VAGUE	WHITE	COLUMBIA	1946
COL-4033	IF A BODY MEETS A BODY - STOOGES	WHITE	COLUMBIA	1945
COL-4037	SPOOK TO ME – ANDY CLYDE	EDWARDS	COLUMBIA	1945
COL-4038	A HIT WITH A MISS – SHEMP HOWARD	EDWARDS, WHITE	COLUMBIA	1945
COL-4039	MAYOR'S HUSBAND – HUGH HERBERT	EDWARDS	COLUMBIA	1945
COL-4040	ANDY CLYDE SHORT		COLUMBIA	
COL-4041	ANDY CLYDE SHORT		COLUMBIA	
COL-4042	CALLING ALL FIBBERS – VERA VAGUE	WHITE	COLUMBIA	1945
COL-4043	BIRD IN THE HEAD – STOOGES	BERNDS	COLUMBIA	1946
COL-4045	BEER BARREL POLECATS – STOOGES	WHITE	COLUMBIA	1946
COL-4047	WHEN THE WIFE'S AWAY – HUGH HERBERT	BERNDS	COLUMBIA	1946
COL-4048	WHERE THE PEST BEGINS – SHEMP HOWARD	EDWARDS	COLUMBIA	1945
COL-4049	ANDY CLYDE SHORT		COLUMBIA	
COL-4051	HIGH BLOOD PLEASURE – LANE-SHILLING	WHITE	COLUMBIA	1945
COL-4052	SOCIETY MUGS – SHEMP HOWARD	BERNDS	COLUMBIA	1946
COL-4052	SOCIETY MUGS (sh)	BERNDS	COLUMBIA	1946
COL-4053	THREE LOAN WOLVES – STOOGES	WHITE	COLUMBIA	1946
COL-4055	GET ALONG LITTLE ZOMBIE – HUGH HERBERT	BERNDS	COLUMBIA	1946
COL-4056	HALF WITS HOLIDAY – STOOGES	WHITE	COLUMBIA	1947
COL-4057	RHYTHM AND WEEP – STOOGES	WHITE	COLUMBIA	1946
COL-4058	MONKEY BUSINESSMEN – STOOGES	BERNDS	COLUMBIA	1946
COL-4059	ANDY CLYDE SHORT		COLUMBIA	
COL-4060	VERA VAGUE SHORT		COLUMBIA	
COL-4061	STERLING HOLLOWAY SHORT		COLUMBIA	

COL-4062	AIN'T LOVE CUCKOO – RICHARD LANE	WHITE	COLUMBIA	1946
COL-4063	G. I. WANNA HOME – STOOGES	WHITE	COLUMBIA	1946
COL-4064	BRIDE AND GLOOM – SHEMP HOWARD	BERNDS	COLUMBIA	1947
COL-4065	MR. WRIGHT GOES WRONG – S. HOLLOWAY	WHITE	COLUMBIA	1946
COL-4067	3 LITTLE PIRATES – STOOGES	BERNDS	COLUMBIA	1946
COL-4069	ANDY CLYDE SHORT		COLUMBIA	
COL-4070	FIDDLERS THREE – STOOGES	WHITE	COLUMBIA	1948
COL-4071	FRIGHT NIGHT – STOOGES	BERNDS	COLUMBIA	1947
COL-4072	CENSORSHIP – H. HERBERT		COLUMBIA	
COL-4074	HONEYMOON BLUES – HUGH HERBERT	BERNDS	COLUMBIA	1946
COL-4075	HOT HEIR – HUGH HERBERT	BERNDS	COLUMBIA	1947
COL-4076	HECTIC HONEYMOON – STERLING HOLLOWAY	BERNDS	COLUMBIA	1947
COL-4077	OUT WEST – STOOGES	BERNDS	COLUMBIA	1947
COL-4078	SO'S YOUR ANTENNA – HARRY VON ZELL	WHITE	COLUMBIA	1946
COL-4079	TWO JILLS AND JACK – ANDY CLYDE	WHITE	COLUMBIA	1947
COL-4080	JOE DERITA		COLUMBIA	
COL-4081	MEET MR. MISCHIEF – HARRY VON ZELL	BERNDS	COLUMBIA	1947
COL-4082	SQUAREHEADS OF ROUND THE TABLE – STOOGES	BERNDS	COLUMBIA	1948
COL-4083	RENO-VATED – VERA VAGUE	WHITE	COLUMBIA	1946
COL-4084	NERVOUS SHAKEDOWN – HUGH HERBERT	LORD	COLUMBIA	1947
COL-4085	MORON THAN OFF – STERLING HOLLOWAY	WHITE	COLUMBIA	1946
COL-4086	GOOD BAD EGG – JOE DERITA	WHITE	COLUMBIA	1947
COL-4087	HOLD THAT LION – STOOGES	WHITE	COLUMBIA	1947
COL-4088	SING A SONG OF SIX PANTS – STOOGES	WHITE	COLUMBIA	1947
COL-4091	I'M A MONKEY'S UNCLE – STOOGES	WHITE	COLUMBIA	1948
COL-4093	PARDON MY CLUTCH – STOOGES	BERNDS	COLUMBIA	1948
COL-4094	HOT SCOTS – STOOGES	BERNDS	COLUMBIA	1948
COL-4095	BRIDELESS GROOM – STOOGES	BERNDS	COLUMBIA	1947
COL-4096	WIFE TO SPARE – ANDY CLYDE	BERNDS	COLUMBIA	1947
COL-4097	CUPID GOES NUTS – FRITZ FELD	WHITE	COLUMBIA	1947
COL-4098	TRAINING FOR TROUBLE – RICHARD LANE	WHITE	COLUMBIA	1947
COL-4099	RICHARD LANE SHORT		COLUMBIA	
COL-4101	WAITING IN THE LURCH – JOE BESSER	BERNDS	COLUMBIA	1949
COL-4102	STOOGES (SHORT)		COLUMBIA	
COL-4103	SHIVERING SHERLOCKS – STOOGES	LORD	COLUMBIA	1948
COL-4104	ALL GUMMED UP – STOOGES	WHITE	COLUMBIA	1947
COL-4107	THREE HAMS ON RYE – STOOGES	WHITE	COLUMBIA	1950
COL-4108	STOOGES (SHORT)		COLUMBIA	
COL-4111	CRIME ON THEIR HANDS – STOOGES	BERNDS	COLUMBIA	1948
COL-4112	WHO DONE IT? – STOOGES	BERNDS	COLUMBIA	1949
COL-4114	FUELIN' AROUND – STOOGES	BERNDS	COLUMBIA	1949
COL-4116	HOKUS POKUS – STOOGES	WHITE	COLUMBIA	1949
COL-4117	STERLING HOLLOWAY SHORT		COLUMBIA	
COL-4118	GO CHASE YOURSELF	WHITE	COLUMBIA	1948
COL-4119	STOOGES (SHORT)		COLUMBIA	
COL-4120	JOE DERITA SHORT		COLUMBIA	
COL-4121	PARDON MY LAMBCHOP	WHITE	COLUMBIA	1948
COL-4123	HE'S IN AGAIN – RICHARD LANE	BERNDS	COLUMBIA	1949
COL-4124	RICHARD LAND SHORT		COLUMBIA	
COL-4126	SHEEPISH WOLF	BERNDS	COLUMBIA	1948
COL-4128	PINCH IN TIME – HUGH HERBERT	LORD	COLUMBIA	1948
COL-4129	STOOGES (SHORT)		COLUMBIA	
COL-4132	RADIO RIOT – HARRY VON ZELL	BERNDS	COLUMBIA	1949
COL-4133	HUGH HERBERT SHORT		COLUMBIA	
COL-4134	RICHARD LANE SHORT		COLUMBIA	
COL-4135	VERA VAGUE SHORT		COLUMBIA	
COL-4136	MISS IN A MESS	WHITE	COLUMBIA	1949
COL-4140	VAGABOND LOAFERS – STOOGES		COLUMBIA	1949
COL-4159	MALICE IN THE PALACE – STOOGES	WHITE	COLUMBIA	1949
COL-4178	CORNY CASANOVAS – STOOGES	WHITE	COLUMBIA	1952
COL-4179	HULA-LA-LA – STOOGES	MCCOLLUM	COLUMBIA	1951
COL-4180	LISTEN JUDGE – STOOGES	BERNDS	COLUMBIA	1952
COL-4181	HE COOKED HIS GOOSE – STOOGES	WHITE	COLUMBIA	1952
COL-4182	UP IN DAISY'S PENTHOUSE - STOOGES	WHITE	COLUMBIA	1953
COL-4183	GENTS IN A JAM – STOOGES	BERNDS	COLUMBIA	1952
COL-4184	HUGH HERBERT SHORT		COLUMBIA	

COL-4187	HUGH HERBERT SHORT		COLUMBIA	
COL-4188	EDDIE QUILLIAN SHORT		COLUMBIA	
COL-4189	EDDIE QUILLIAN SHORT		COLUMBIA	
COL-4190	ANDY CLYDE SHORT		COLUMBIA	
COL-4191	ANDY CLYDE SHORT		COLUMBIA	
COL-4192	FRAIDY CAT – JOE BESSER AND HAWTHORNE	WHITE	COLUMBIA	1951
COL-4193	JOE BESSER AND HAWTHORN SHORT		COLUMBIA	
COL-4194	CUCKOOS ON A CHOO CHOO – STOOGES	WHITE	COLUMBIA	1952
COL-4195	JOE BESSER SHORT		COLUMBIA	
COL-4196	STOOGES (sh)		COLUMBIA	
COL-4197	LOOSE LOOT – STOOGES	WHITE	COLUMBIA	1953
COL-4198	EDDIE QUILLAN SHORT		COLUMBIA	
COL-4198	STROP, LOOK AND LISTEN (sh)	WHITE	COLUMBIA	1952
COL-4199	TRICKY DICKS – STOOGES	WHITE	COLUMBIA	1953
COL-4200	THREE DARK HORSES – STOOGES	WHITE	COLUMBIA	1952
COL-4201	BUBBLE TROUBLE – STOOGES	WHITE	COLUMBIA	1953
COL-4203	GOOF ON THE ROOF – STOOGES	WHITE	COLUMBIA	1953
COL-4204	EDDIE QUILLAN SHORT		COLUMBIA	
COL-4205	JOE BESSER SHORT		COLUMBIA	
COL-4206	ANDY CLYDE GETS SPRING CHICKEN	WHITE	COLUMBIA	1939
COL-4208	INCOME TAX SAPPY – STOOGES	WHITE	COLUMBIA	1954
COL-4209	MUSTY MUSKATEERS – STOOGES	WHITE	COLUMBIA	1954
COL-4210	SPOOKS – STOOGES	WHITE	COLUMBIA	1953
COL-4211	PALS AND GALS – STOOGES	WHITE	COLUMBIA	1954
COL-4212	PARDON MY BACKFIRE – STOOGES	WHITE	COLUMBIA	1953
COL-4213	A-HUNTING THEY DID GO – EDDIE QUILLAN	WHITE	COLUMBIA	1948
COL-4214	DOGGIE IN THE BEDROOM – EDDIE QUILLAN	WHITE	COLUMBIA	1954
COL-4216	SHOT IN THE FRONTIER – STOOGES	WHITE	COLUMBIA	1954
COL-4217	KNUTZ KNIGHTS – STOOGES	WHITE	COLUMBIA	1954
COL-4218	SCOTCHED IN SCOTLAND – STOOGES	WHITE	COLUMBIA	1954
COL-4219	ANDY CLYDE SHORT		COLUMBIA	
COL-4220	A MINER AFFAIR – ANDY CLYDE	WHITE	COLUMBIA	1945
COL-4223	FLING IN THE RING – STOOGES	WHITE	COLUMBIA	1955
COL-4224	STOOGES (sh)		COLUMBIA	
COL-4225	OF CASH AND HASH – STOOGES	WHITE	COLUMBIA	1955
COL-4227	CREEPS – STOOGES	WHITE	COLUMBIA	1956
COL-4228	HEAVENLY DAZE – STOOGES	WHITE	COLUMBIA	1948
COL-4229	STONE AGE ROMEOS – STOOGES	WHITE	COLUMBIA	1955
COL-4244	RUMPUS IN THE HAREM - STOOGES	WHITE	COLUMBIA	1956
COL-4245	HOT STUFF – STOOGES	WHITE	COLUMBIA	1956
COL-4246	SCHEMEING SCHEMERS – STOOGES	WHITE	COLUMBIA	1956
COL-4247	COMMOTION ON THE OCEAN - STOOGES	WHITE	COLUMBIA	1956
COL-4251	HOOFS AND GOOFS – STOOGES	WHITE	COLUMBIA	1957
COL-4252	MERRY MIXUP – STOOGES	WHITE	COLUMBIA	1957
COL-4253	SPACE SHIP SAPPY – STOOGES	WHITE	COLUMBIA	1957
COL-8007	LORNA DOONE	KARLSON	COLUMBIA	1951
COL-8008	ROAR OF THE IRON HORSE	BENNET, CARR	COLUMBIA	1951
COL-8009	TEXANS NEVER CRY	MCDONALD	COLUMBIA	1951
COL-8010	VALLEY OF FIRE		COLUMBIA	1951
COL-8011	MAGIC CARPET	LANDERS	COLUMBIA	1951
COL-8011	MYSTERIOUS ISLAND (serial)	BENNET	COLUMBIA	1951
COL-8014	TEXAS RANGERS	LEDERMAN	COLUMBIA	1951
COL-8015	BRIGAND	KARLSON	COLUMBIA	1952
COL-8016	SILVER CANYON	ENGLISH	COLUMBIA	1951
COL-8017	SCANDAL SHEET	KARLSON	COLUMBIA	1952
COL-8026	WHIRLWIND	ENGLISH	COLUMBIA	1951
COL-8029	INDIAN UPRISING	NAZARRO	COLUMBIA	1952
COL-8030	CALIFORNIA CONQUEST	LANDERS	COLUMBIA	1952
COL-8031	YANK IN KOREA	LANDERS	COLUMBIA	1951
COL-8032	HILLS OF UTAH	ENGLISH	COLUMBIA	1951
COL-8033	HARLEM GLOBETROTTERS	BROWN, JASON	COLUMBIA	1951
COL-8035	MAN IN THE SADDLE	DE TOTH	COLUMBIA	1951
COL-8036	PURPLE HEART DIARY	QUINE	COLUMBIA	1951
COL-8037	JUNGLE JIM IN THE FORBIDDEN LAND	LANDERS	COLUMBIA	1952
COL-8038	JUNGLE MAN-HUNT	LANDERS	COLUMBIA	1951
COL-8039	KING OF THE CONGO SERIAL	BENNET, GRISSELL	COLUMBIA	1952

COL-8040	CAPTAIN VIDEO (serial)	BENNET, GRISSELL	COLUMBIA	1951
COL-8041	BOOTS MALONE	DIETERLE	COLUMBIA	1952
COL-8042	TEN TALL MEN	GOLDBECK	COLUMBIA	1951
COL-8043	FIRST TIME	TASHLIN	COLUMBIA	1952
COL-8044	BRAVE WARRIOR	BENNET	COLUMBIA	1952
COL-8045	OLD WEST	ARCHAINBAUD	COLUMBIA	1952
COL-8047	MEMBER OF THE WEDDING	ZINNEMANN	COLUMBIA	1952
COL-8049	GOLDEN HAWK	SALKOW	COLUMBIA	1952
COL-8053	PRINCE OF PIRATES	SALKOW	COLUMBIA	1953
COL-8054	MY SIX CONVICTS	FREGONESE	COLUMBIA	1952
COL-8055	BLACKHAWK		COLUMBIA	1952
COL-8056	DEATH OF A SALESMAN	BENEDEK	COLUMBIA	1951
COL-8057	FOUR POSTER	REIS	COLUMBIA	1952
COL-8061	CRIPPLE CREEK	NAZARRO	COLUMBIA	1952
COL-8062	SNIPER	DMYTRYK	COLUMBIA	1952
COL-8063	NIGHT STAGE TO GALVESTON	ARCHAINBAUD	COLUMBIA	1952
COL-8066	AFFAIR IN TRINIDAD	SHERMAN	COLUMBIA	1952
COL-8067	BLUE CANADIAN ROCKIES	ARCHAINBAUD	COLUMBIA	1952
COL-8068	PRISONERS OF THE CASBAH	BARE	COLUMBIA	1953
COL-8071	HAPPY TIME	FLEISCHER	COLUMBIA	1952
COL-8072	APACHE COUNTRY	ARCHAINBAUD	COLUMBIA	1952
COL-8074	MEMBER OF THE WEDDING	ZINNEMANN	COLUMBIA	1952
COL-8078	EIGHT IRON MEN	DMYTRYK	COLUMBIA	1952
COL-8079	BARBED WIRE	ARCHAINBAUD	COLUMBIA	1952
COL-8082	CAINE MUTINY	DMYTRYK	COLUMBIA	1954
COL-8087	SERPENT OF THE NILE	CASTLE	COLUMBIA	1953
COL-8088	LAST TRAIN FROM BOMBAY	SEARS	COLUMBIA	1952
COL-8089	SAVAGE MUTINY	BENNET	COLUMBIA	1953
COL-8090	VOODOO TIGER	BENNET	COLUMBIA	1952
COL-8091	JUGGLER	DMYTRYK	COLUMBIA	1953
COL-8092	JACK MCCALL – DESPERADO	SALKOW	COLUMBIA	1953
COL-8093	PIRATES OF TRIPOLI	FEIST	COLUMBIA	1955
COL-8095	LOST PLANET	BENNET	COLUMBIA	1953
COL-8100	SON OF GERONIMO (serial)	BENNET	COLUMBIA	1952
COL-8103	PATHFINDER	SALKOW	COLUMBIA	1952
COL-8109	SLAVES OF BABYLON	CASTLE	COLUMBIA	1953
COL-8115	SKY COMMANDS	SEARS	COLUMBIA	1953
COL-8116	HANGMAN'S KNOT	HUGGINS	COLUMBIA	1952
COL-8117	SALOME	DIETERLE	COLUMBIA	1953
COL-8118	ON TOP OF OLD SMOKY	ARCHAINBAUD	COLUMBIA	1953
COL-8120	FLAME OF CALCUTTA	FRIEDMAN	COLUMBIA	1953
COL-8121	STRANGE FASCINATION	HAAS	COLUMBIA	1952
COL-8122	SIREN OF BAGDAD	QUINE	COLUMBIA	1953
COL-8125	WINNING OF THE WEST, THE	ARCHAINBAUD	COLUMBIA	1953
COL-8127	IRON GLOVE	CASTLE	COLUMBIA	1954
COL-8128	GOLDTOWN GHOST RIDERS	ARCHAINBAUD	COLUMBIA	1953
COL-8130	CONQUEST OF COCHISE	CASTLE	COLUMBIA	1953
COL-8132	CHARGE OF THE LANCERS	CASTLE	COLUMBIA	1954
COL-8140	ONE GIRL'S CONFESSION	HAAS	COLUMBIA	1953
COL-8146	PACK TRAIN	ARCHAINBAUD	COLUMBIA	1953
COL-8149	GREAT ADV OF CAPTAIN KIDD (serial)	ABRAHAMS, GOULD	COLUMBIA	1953
COL-8150	KILLER APE	BENNET	COLUMBIA	1953
COL-8151	SAGINAW TRAIL	ARCHAINBAUD	COLUMBIA	1953
COL-8170	MISS SADIE THOMPSON	BERNHARDT	COLUMBIA	1953
COL-8173	FORT TI	CASTLE	COLUMBIA	1953
COL-8178	STRANGER WORE A GUN	DE TOTH	COLUMBIA	1953
COL-8188	LAST OF THE PONY RIDERS	ARCHAINBAUD	COLUMBIA	1953
COL-8191	JESSE JAMES VS DALTSON	CASTLE	COLUMBIA	1954
COL-8193	DRUMS OF TAHITI	CASTLE	COLUMBIA	1954
COL-8194	GUNFIGHTERS OF THE NORTHWEST	BENNET, GOULD	COLUMBIA	1954
COL-8197	SARACEN BLADE	CASTLE	COLUMBIA	1954
COL-8204	JUNGLE MAN-EATERS	SHOLEM	COLUMBIA	1954
COL-8205	RIDING WITH BUFFALO BILL (serial)	BENNET	COLUMBIA	1954
COL-8206	LAW VS. BILLY THE KID	CASTLE	COLUMBIA	1954
COL-8211	TEENAGE CRIME WAVE	SEARS	COLUMBIA	1955
COL-8214	BATTLE OF ROGUE RIVER	CASTLE	COLUMBIA	1954

COL-8247	MIAMI STORY	SEARS	COLUMBIA	1954
COL-8249	CHICAGO SYNDICATE	SEARS	COLUMBIA	1955
COL-8250	SEMINOLE UPRISING	BELLAMY	COLUMBIA	1955
COL-8252	MASTERSON OF KANSAS	CASTLE	COLUMBIA	1954
COL-8253	MAD MAGICIAN	BRAHM	COLUMBIA	1954
COL-8257	ADVENTURES OF CAPTAIN AFRICA (serial)	BENNET	COLUMBIA	1955
COL-8260	IT CAME FROM BENEATH THE SEA	GORDON	COLUMBIA	1955
COL-8262	CANNIBAL ATTACK	SHOLEM	COLUMBIA	1954
COL-8263	DEVIL GODDESS	BENNET	COLUMBIA	1955
COL-8264	BAMBOO PRISON	SEILER	COLUMBIA	1954
COL-8265	JUNGLE MOON-MEN	GOULD	COLUMBIA	1955
COL-8271	MAN FROM LARAMIE	MANN	COLUMBIA	1955
COL-8273	TEN WANTED MEN	HUMBERSTONE	COLUMBIA	1955
COL-8274	WOMEN'S PRISON	SEILER	COLUMBIA	1955
COL-8281	NEW ORLEANS UNCENSORED	CASTLE	COLUMBIA	1955
COL-8284	GUN THAT WON THE WEST	CASTLE	COLUMBIA	1955
COL-8285	CREATURE WITH THE ATOM BRAIN	CAHN	COLUMBIA	1955
COL-8286	DUEL ON THE MISSISSIPPI	CASTLE	COLUMBIA	1955
COL-8289	BATTLE STATIONS	SEILER	COLUMBIA	1956
COL-8289	BROTHERS RICO	KARLSON	COLUMBIA	1957
COL-8294	LONG GREY LINE	FORD	COLUMBIA	1955
COL-8301	FIVE AGAINST THE HOUSE	KARLSON	COLUMBIA	1955
COL-8305	NIGHT HOLDS TERROR	STONE	COLUMBIA	1955
COL-8306	LAWLESS STREET	LEWIS	COLUMBIA	1955
COL-8307	EARTH VS. THE FLYING SAUCERS	SEARS	COLUMBIA	1956
COL-8308	COUNT THREE AND PRAY	SHERMAN	COLUMBIA	1955
COL-8310	HOUSTON STORY	CASTLE	COLUMBIA	1956
COL-8311	BLACKJACK KETCHUM-DESPERADO	BELLAMY	COLUMBIA	1956
COL-8313	INSIDE DETROIT	SEARS	COLUMBIA	1956
COL-8321	CROOKED WEB	JURAN	COLUMBIA	1955
COL-8322	AUTUMN LEAVES	ALDRICH	COLUMBIA	1956
COL-8323	BELL BOOK AND CANDLE	QUINE	COLUMBIA	1958
COL-8330	NIGHTFALL	TOURNEUR	COLUMBIA	1957
COL-8333	STORM CENTER	TARADASH	COLUMBIA	1956
COL-8335	HOT BLOOD	RAY	COLUMBIA	1956
COL-8336	BLAZING THE OVERLAND TRAIL (serial)	BENNET	COLUMBIA	1956
COL-8342	GUNS OF FORT PETTICOAT	MARSHALL	COLUMBIA	1957
COL-8344	SEVENTH CALVARY	LEWIS	COLUMBIA	1956
COL-8346	REPRISAL	SHERMAN	COLUMBIA	1956
COL-8352	ROCK AROUND THE CLOCK	SEARS	COLUMBIA	1956
COL-8354	RUMBLE ON THE DOCKS	SEARS	COLUMBIA	1956
COL-8355	MIAMI EXPOSE	SEARS	COLUMBIA	1956
COL-8359	WHITE SQUAW	NAZARRO	COLUMBIA	1956
COL-8366	NIGHT THE WORLD EXPLODED	SEARS	COLUMBIA	1957
COL-8368	CHA CHA CHA BOOM	SEARS	COLUMBIA	1956
COL-8372	LINEUP	SIEGEL	COLUMBIA	1958
COL-8373	MAN WHO TURNED TO STONE	KARDOS	COLUMBIA	1957
COL-8376	HELLCATS OF THE NAVY	JURAN	COLUMBIA	1957
COL-8379	TALL T	BOATTICHER	COLUMBIA	1957
COL-8381	UTAH BLAINE	SEARS	COLUMBIA	1957
COL-8383	DON'T KNOCK THE ROCK	SEARS	COLUMBIA	1956
COL-8394	RETURN TO WARBOW	NAZARRO	COLUMBIA	1958
COL-8395	GARMENT JUNGLE	SHERMAN	COLUMBIA	1957
COL-8396	NO TIME TO BE YOUNG	RICH	COLUMBIA	1957
COL-8398	ESCAPE FROM SAN QUENTIN	SEARS	COLUMBIA	1957
COL-8400	SEVENTH VOYAGE OF SINBAD	JURAN	COLUMBIA	1958
COL-8403	JEANNE EAGELS	SIDNEY	COLUMBIA	1957
COL-8406	CRASH LANDING	SEARS	COLUMBIA	1958
COL-8407	PAL JOEY	SIDNEY	COLUMBIA	1957
COL-8414	HARD MAN	SHERMAN	COLUMBIA	1957
COL-8417	THIS ANGRY AGE	CLEMENT	COLUMBIA	1958
COL-8420	DECISION AT SUNDOWN	BOETTICHER	COLUMBIA	1957
COL-8422	LIFE BEGINS AT 17	DREIFUSS	COLUMBIA	1958
COL-8423	OPERATION MADBALL	QUINE	COLUMBIA	1957
COL-8427	TARAWA BEACHHEAD	WENDKOS	COLUMBIA	1958
COL-8428	CASE AGAINST BROOKLYN	WENDKOS	COLUMBIA	1958

COL-8431	SCREAMING MIMI	OSWALD	COLUMBIA	1958
COL-8449	TRUE STORY OF LYNN STUART	SEILER	COLUMBIA	1958
COL-8453	COWBOY	DAVES	COLUMBIA	1958
COL-8461	LAST BLITZKRIEG	DREIFUSS	COLUMBIA	1959
COL-8465	GODDESS	CROMWELL	COLUMBIA	1958
COL-8468	JUKE BOX RHYTHM	DREIFUSS	COLUMBIA	1959
COL-8470	FORBIDDEN ISLAND	GRIFFITH	COLUMBIA	1959
COL-8472	APACHE TERRITORY	NAZARRO	COLUMBIA	1958
COL-8475	ME AND THE COLONEL	GLENVILLE	COLUMBIA	1958
COL-8476	PEPE	SIDNEY	COLUMBIA	1960
COL-8485	LAST HURRAH	FORD	COLUMBIA	1958
COL-8495	GOOD DAY FOR A HANGING	JURAN	COLUMBIA	1959
COL-8496	IT HAPPENED TO JANE	QUINE	COLUMBIA	1959
COL-8498	GENE KRUPA STORY	WEIS	COLUMBIA	1959
COL-8500	CHASE		COLUMBIA	1958
COL-8501	GUNS OF NAVARONE (UK)	THOMPSON	COLUMBIA	1961
COL-8502	SONG WITHOUT END	VIDOR	COLUMBIA	1960
COL-8503	THEY CAME TO CORDURA	ROSSEN	COLUMBIA	1959
COL-8504	MOUNTAIN ROAD	MANN	COLUMBIA	1960
COL-8506	RIDE LONESOME	BOETTICHER	COLUMBIA	1959
COL-8507	SENIOR PROM	RICH	COLUMBIA	1958
COL-8508	LET NO MAN WRITE MY EPITAPH	LEACOCK	COLUMBIA	1960
COL-8511	I AIM AT THE STARS	THOMPSON	COLUMBIA	1960
COL-8512	SURPRISE PACKAGE	DONEN	COLUMBIA	1960
COL-8513	HEY BOY HEY GIRL	RICH	COLUMBIA	1959
COL-8514	MAN ON A STRING	DE TOTH	COLUMBIA	1960
COL-8515	MYSTERIOUS ISLAND	ENDFIELD	COLUMBIA	1962
COL-8516	FACE OF A FUGITIVE	WENDKOS	COLUMBIA	1959
COL-8519	CRIMSON KIMONO	FULLER	COLUMBIA	1959
COL-8520	LAST ANGRY MAN	MANN	COLUMBIA	1959
COL-8525	DEVIL AT 4 O'CLOCK	LEROY	COLUMBIA	1961
COL-8536	MIDDLE OF THE NIGHT	MANN	COLUMBIA	1959
COL-8539	STRANGERS WHEN WE MEET	QUINE	COLUMBIA	1960
COL-8543	NOTORIOUS LANDLADY	QUINE	COLUMBIA	1962
COL-8546	EDGE OF ETERNITY	SIEGEL	COLUMBIA	1959
COL-8550	LEGEND OF TOM DOOLEY	POST	COLUMBIA	1959
COL-8556	HAVE ROCKET WILL TRAVEL	RICH	COLUMBIA	1959
COL-8557	COMANCHE STATION	BOETTICHER	COLUMBIA	1960
COL-8566	CRY FOR HAPPY	MARSHALL	COLUMBIA	1961
COL-8569	BECAUSE THEY'RE YOUNG	WENDKOS	COLUMBIA	1960
COL-8570	RAISIN IN THE SUN	PETRIE	COLUMBIA	1961
COL-8572	ENEMY GENERAL	SHERMAN	COLUMBIA	1960
COL-8573	ALL THE YOUNG MEN	BARTLETT	COLUMBIA	1960
COL-8581	GIDGET GOES HAWAIIAN	WENDKOS	COLUMBIA	1961
COL-8583	THIRTEEN GHOSTS	CASTLE	COLUMBIA	1960
COL-8588	DIAMOND HEAD	GREEN	COLUMBIA	1963
COL-8591	STOP, LOOK AND LAUGH	APPELL, BRANDT	COLUMBIA	1960
COL-8594	HOMICIDAL	CASTLE	COLUMBIA	1961
COL-8596	INTERNS	SWIFT	COLUMBIA	1962
COL-8603	FIVE FINGER EXERCISE	MANN	COLUMBIA	1962
COL-8610	MR. SARDONICUS	CASTLE	COLUMBIA	1961
COL-8617	THREE STOOGES MEET HERCULES	BERNDS	COLUMBIA	1962
COL-8625	BYE BYE BIRDIE	SIDNEY	COLUMBIA	1963
COL-8626	EXPERIMENT IN TERROR	EDWARDS	COLUMBIA	1962
COL-8629	WALK ON THE WILD SIDE	DYMTRYK	COLUMBIA	1962
COL-8633	MAN FROM THE DINER'S CLUB	TASHLIN	COLUMBIA	1963
COL-8652	WILD WESTERNERS	RUDOLPH	COLUMBIA	1962
COL-8657	DON'T KNOCK THE TWIST	RUDOLPH	COLUMBIA	1962
COL-8666	THREE STOOGES IN ORBIT	BERNDS	COLUMBIA	1962
COL-8689	KING RAT	FORBES	COLUMBIA	1965
COL-8691	STRAIGHT-JACKET	CASTLE	COLUMBIA	1964
COL-8699	GOOD NEIGHBOR SAM	SWIFT	COLUMBIA	1964
COL-8701	CAT BALLOU	SILVERSTEIN	COLUMBIA	1965
COL-8709	BABY THE RAIN MUST FALL	MULLIGAN	COLUMBIA	1965
COL-8712	PROFESSIONALS	BROOKS	COLUMBIA	1966
COL-8715	MAJOR DUNDEE	PECKINPAH	COLUMBIA	1965

COL-8719	COLLECTOR	WYLER	COLUMBIA	1965
COL-8720	HEY THERE IT'S YOGI BEAR (t)	HANNA, BARBERA	COLUMBIA	1964
COL-8722	LIFE BEGINS AT 17	DREIFUSS	COLUMBIA	1958
COL-8724	QUICK GUN	SALKOW	COLUMBIA	1964
COL-8731	OUTLAWS IS COMING	MAURER	COLUMBIA	1965
COL-8732	RIDE THE WILD SURF	TAYLOR	COLUMBIA	1964
COL-8741	SILENCERS	KARLSON	COLUMBIA	1966
COL-8744	ALVAREZ KELLY	DMYTRYK	COLUMBIA	1966
COL-8755	WALK DON'T RUN	WALTERS	COLUMBIA	1966
COL-8761	ARIZONA RAIDERS	WITNEY	COLUMBIA	1965
COL-8802	RIDE BEYOND VENGEANCE	MCEVEETY	COLUMBIA	1966
COL-8817	THREE ON A COUCH	LEWIS	COLUMBIA	1966
COL-8818	BIRDS DO IT	MARTON	COLUMBIA	1966
COL-8826	RAGE	GAZCON	COLUMBIA	1966
COL-999	FAMILY SECRET	LEVIN	COLUMBIA	1951
COL-FOR-4	ALIBI (FR: L'ALIBI)	CHENAL	COLUMBIA	1937
COL-FR	VOICE IN THE NIGHT (UK: FREEDOM RADIO)	ASQUITH	COLUMBIA	1941
COL-IN	INVADERS (UK: 49TH PARALLEL)	POWELL, PRESSBURGER	COLUMBIA	1942
COL-MC	BELOVED VAGABOND (UK)	BERNHARDT	COLUMBIA	1936
COL-S-5	WHITE EAGLE (serial)	HILLYER	COLUMBIA	1932
COMP	HAMBURGER HILL	IRVIN	RKO	1987
COMP	ODE TO BILLY JOE	BAER	WARNER BROS	1976
CON	CARRY ON NURSE (UK)	THOMAS	GOVERNOR	1959
CON	CONFESSION (FR: L'AVEU)	COSTA-GAVRAS	WARNER BROS	1970
CON	CONFORMIST (IT)	BERTOLUCCI	PARAMOUNT	1971
COP	COMING-OUT PARTY (UK: VERY IMPORTANT PERSON)	ANNAKIN	UNION	1961
COS	CARRY ON SPYING (UK)	THOMAS	GOVERNOR	1964
COS	CARRY ON SARGEANT (UK: 1958)	THOMAS	GOVERNOR	1959
C.O.S-12	VALLEY OF VANISHING MEN (serial)	BENNET	COLUMBIA	1942
COT	CHILDREN ON TRIAL	LEE	ENGLISH	1946
CP	AMBUSH AT CIMMARON PASS	COPELAN	20th CENTURY FOX	1958
CP	CENTRAL PARK	ADOLFI	WARNER BROS	1932
CP	CLAY PIGEON	SLATE, STERN	MGM	1971
CP	COMPROMISING POSITIONS	PERRY	PARAMOUNT	1985
CP	COUNTERFEIT PLAN (UK)	TULLY	WARNER BROS.	1957
CP	CRAZY PEOPLE	BILL	PARAMOUNT	1990
CP	FLAT FOOT STOOGES (sh)	CHASE	COLUMBIA	1938
CP	HEADLINE (UK)	HARLOW	EALING	1943
CP CORP-FOR-10	ABUSED CONFIDENCE	DECOIN	COLUMBIA (BERCHOLZ)	1938
CP CORP-D-COL 62	MAN WITH NINE LIVES (1940)	GRINDE	COLUMBIA	R47
CP CORP-D-COL 100	FACE BEHIND THE MASK	FLOREY	COLUMBIA	R55
CP CORP-D-COL 102	DEVIL COMMANDS	DMYTRYK	COLUMBIA	R55
CP CORP-D-COL 223	MAN THEY COULD NOT KILL (MAN COULD NOT HANG 1939)	GRINDE	COLUMBIA	R47
CP-1	MAIN STREET TO BROADWAY	GARNETT	MGM	1953
CP-3	ALIAS THE LONE WOLF	GRIFFITH	COLUMBIA	1927
CP-149	MEET THE STEWARTS	GREEN	COLUMBIA	1942
CP-151	PARACHUTE NURSE	BARTON	COLUMBIA	1942
CP-1776	1776	HUNT	COLUMBIA	1972
CP-AT	ANDERSON TAPES, THE	LUMET	COLUMBIA	1971
CP-BB	BIRDS DO IT, BEES DO IT	NOXON, ROSTEN	COLUMBIA	1974
CP-BD	BIRDS DO IT, BEES DO IT	NOXON, ROSTEN	COLUMBIA	1974
CP-BG	BLACK GUNN	HARTFORD-DAVIS	COLUMBIA	1973
CP-BS	BRIAN'S SONG	KULIK	COLUMBIA	1971
CP-BU	BURGLARS	VERNEUIL	COLUMBIA	1971
CPC 129	LADY IF WILLING	LEISEN	COLUMBIA	1942
CPC GS	GREENGAGE SUMMER (UK)	GILBERT	COLUMBIA	1961
CPC MMS	MIND OF MR. SOAMES	COOKE	COLUMBIA	1970
CPC MR	MAD ROOM, THE	GIRARD	COLUMBIA	1968
CPC MS	MODEL SHOP	DEMY	COLUMBIA	1969
CPC-1	COUNSEL FOR CRIME	BRAHM	COLUMBIA	1937
CPC-2	MURDER IN GREENWICH VILLAGE	ROGELL	COLUMBIA	1937
CPC-2WH	HAPPENING	SILVERSTEIN	COLUMBIA	1967
CPC-4	LIFE BEGINS WITH LOVE	MCCAREY	COLUMBIA	1937
CPC-4	THAT'S GRATITUDE	CRAVEN	COLUMBIA	1934
CPC-5	JEALOUSY	NEILL	COLUMBIA	1934
CPC-6	SHE MARRIED AN ARTIST	GERING	COLUMBIA	1937

CPC-8	WHITE LIES	BULGAKOV	COLUMBIA	1934
CPC-9	LITTLE MISS ROUGHNECK	SCOTTO	COLUMBIA	1938
CPC-9	WHOLE TOWN'S TALKING	FORD	COLUMBIA	1935
CPC-10	MILLS OF THE GODS	NEILL	COLUMBIA	1935
CPC-10	NO TIME TO MARRY	LACHMAN	COLUMBIA	1938
CPC-11	BEST MAN WINS	KENTON	COLUMBIA	1935
CPC-11	IT'S ALL YOURS	NUGENT	COLUMBIA	1937
CPC-12	CARNIVAL	LANG	COLUMBIA	1935
CPC-12	PENITENTIARY	BRAHM	COLUMBIA	1938
CPC-13	TOGETHER WE LIVE	MACK	COLUMBIA	1935
CPC-15	THERE'S ALWAYS A WOMAN	HALL	COLUMBIA	1938
CPC-16	YOU CAN'T TAKE IT WITH YOU	CAPRA	COLUMBIA	1938
CPC-17	HOLIDAY	CUKOR	COLUMBIA	1938
CPC-19	CITY STREETS (CITY SHADOWS*)	ROGELL	COLUMBIA	1938
CPC-20	GIRL'S SCHOOL	BRAHM	COLUMBIA	1938
CPC-21	I AM THE LAW	HALL	COLUMBIA	1938
CPC-23	LADY OBJECTS	KENTON	COLUMBIA	1938
CPC-24	FLIGHT TO FAME	COLEMAN	COLUMBIA	1938
CPC-25	I'LL TAKE ROMANCE	GRIFFITH	COLUMBIA	1937
CPC-27	AWFUL TRUTH	MCCAREY	COLUMBIA	1937
CPC-28	THERE'S THAT WOMAN AGAIN	HALL	COLUMBIA	1939
CPC-29	LITTLE ADVENTURESS	LEDERMAN	COLUMBIA	1938
CPC-30	BLONDIE	STRAYER	COLUMBIA	1938
CPC-31	SMASHING THE SPY RING	CABANNE	COLUMBIA	1939
CPC-32	LADY AND THE MOB	STOLOFF	COLUMBIA	1939
CPC-33	LONE WOLF SPY HUNT	GODFREY	COLUMBIA	1939
CPC-36	ONLY ANGELS HAVE WINGS	HAWKS	COLUMBIA	1939
CPC-37	COAST GUARD	LUDWIG	COLUMBIA	1939
CPC-38	ROMANCE OF THE REDWOODS	VIDOR	COLUMBIA	1939
CPC-39	BLONDIE MEETS THE BOSS	STRAYER	COLUMBIA	1939
CPC-40	GOLDEN BOY	MAMOULIAN	COLUMBIA	1939
CPC-41	BLIND ALLEY	VIDOR	COLUMBIA	1939
CPC-41	MEN OF THE NIGHT	HILLYER	COLUMBIA	1934
CPC-42	BEHIND THE EVIDENCE	HILLYER	COLUMBIA	1935
CPC-42	GOOD GIRLS GO TO PARIS	HALL	COLUMBIA	1939
CPC-43	MR. SMITH GOES TO WASHINGTON	CAPRA	COLUMBIA	1939
CPC-45	BLONDIE TAKES A VACATION	STRAYER	COLUMBIA	1939
CPC-46	FIVE LITTLE PEPPERS AND HOW THEY GREW	BARTON	COLUMBIA	1939
CPC-47	THOSE HIGH GRAY WALLS	VIDOR	COLUMBIA	1939
CPC-49	BEWARE SPOOKS	SEDGWICK	COLUMBIA	1939
CPC-51	BLONDIE BRINGS UP BABY	STRAYER	COLUMBIA	1939
CPC-52	ARIZONA	RUGGLES	COLUMBIA	1940
CPC-53	SCANDAL SHEET	GRINDE	COLUMBIA	1939
CPC-54	AMAZING MR. WILLIAMS	HALL	COLUMBIA	1939
CPC-55	CAFE HOSTESS	SALKOW	COLUMBIA	1940
CPC-56	MY SON IS GUILTY	BARTON	COLUMBIA	1939
CPC-57	MILITARY ACADEMY	LEDERMAN	COLUMBIA	1940
CPC-58	FIVE LITTLE PEPPERS AT HOME	BARTON	COLUMBIA	1940
CPC-83	BRIEF SEASON	CASTELLANI	COLUMBIA	1969
CPC-90	TIME OUT FOR RHYTHM (sh)	SALKOW	COLUMBIA	1941
CPC-115	TWO IN A TAXI	FLOREY	COLUMBIA	1941
CPC-116	OUR WIFE	STAHL	COLUMBIA	1941
CPC-117	HERE COMES MR. JORDAN	HALL	COLUMBIA	1941
CPC-118	YOU'LL NEVER GET RICH	LANFIELD	COLUMBIA	1941
CPC-119	MYSTERY SHIP	LANDERS	COLUMBIA	1941
CPC-120	TWO LATINS FROM MANHATTAN	BARTON	COLUMBIA	1941
CPC-122	COUNTER-ESPIONAGE	DMYTRYK	COLUMBIA	1942
CPC-124	THREE GIRLS ABOUT TOWN	JASON	COLUMBIA	1941
CPC-125	GO WEST YOUNG LADY	STRAYER	COLUMBIA	1941
CPC-126	HARMON OF MICHIGAN	BARTON	COLUMBIA	1941
CPC-127	STORK PAYS OFF	LANDERS	COLUMBIA	1941
CPC-128	SECRETS OF THE LONE WOLF	DMYTRYK	COLUMBIA	1941
CPC-129	LADY IS WILLING	LEISEN	COLUMBIA	1942
CPC-130	SING FOR YOUR SUPPER	BARTON	COLUMBIA	1941
CPC-132	HARVARD HERE I COME	LANDERS	COLUMBIA	1941
CPC-133	CONFESSIONS OF BOSTON BLACKIE	DMYTRYK	COLUMBIA	1941

CPC-134	BLONDIE GOES TO COLLEGE	STRAYER	COLUMBIA	1942
CPC-135	HONOLULU LU	BARTON	COLUMBIA	1941
CPC-136	CADETS ON PARADE	LANDERS	COLUMBIA	1942
CPC-137	SHUT MY BIG MOUTH	BARTON	COLUMBIA	1942
CPC-138	TWO YANKS IN TRINIDAD	RATOFF	COLUMBIA	1942
CPC-139	MAN WHO RETURNED TO LIFE	LANDERS	COLUMBIA	1942
CPC-140	CANAL ZONE	LANDERS	COLUMBIA	1942
CPC-141	TRAMP TRAMP TRAMP	BARTON	COLUMBIA	1942
CPC-144	ALIAS BOSTON BLACKIE	LANDERS	COLUMBIA	1942
CPC-146	TALK OF THE TOWN	STEVENS	COLUMBIA	1942
CPC-147	NOT A LADIES MAN	LANDERS	COLUMBIA	1942
CPC-148	HELLO ANAPOLIS	BARTON	COLUMBIA	1942
CPC-149	MEET THE STEWARTS	GREEN	COLUMBIA	1942
CPC-150	THEY ALL KISSED THE BRIDE	HALL	COLUMBIA	1942
CPC-151	PARACHUTE NURSE	BARTON	COLUMBIA	1942
CPC-152	SWEETHEART OF THE FLEET	BARTON	COLUMBIA	1942
CPC-153	SUBMARINE RAIDER	LANDERS	COLUMBIA	1942
CPC-154	YOU WERE NEVER LOVELIER	SEITER	COLUMBIA	1942
CPC-155	ATLANTIC CONVOY	LANDERS	COLUMBIA	1942
CPC-156	FLIGHT LIEUTENANT	SALKOW	COLUMBIA	1942
CPC-156	THREE LITTLE PIGSKINS (sh)	MCCAREY	COLUMBIA	1934
CPC-157	ONE DANGEROUS NIGHT	GORDON	COLUMBIA	1943
CPC-158	BLONDIE FOR VICTORY	STRAYER	COLUMBIA	1942
CPC-159	MAN'S WORLD	BARTON	COLUMBIA	1942
CPC-160	SABOTAGE SQUAD	LANDERS	COLUMBIA	1942
CPC-161	MY SISTER EILEEN	HALL	COLUMBIA	1942
CPC-162	LUCKY LEGS	BARTON	COLUMBIA	1942
CPC-163	DESPERADOES	VIDOR	COLUMBIA	1943
CPC-164	STAND BY ALL NETWORKS	LANDERS	COLUMBIA	1942
CPC-165	SPIRIT OF STANFORD	BARTON	COLUMBIA	1942
CPC-166	DESTROYER	SEITER	COLUMBIA	1943
CPC-167	LET'S HAVE FUN	BARTON	COLUMBIA	1943
CPC-168	DARING YOUNG MAN	STRAYER	COLUMBIA	1942
CPC-169	BOSTON BLACKIE GOES HOLLYWOOD	GORDON	COLUMBIA	1942
CPC-170	SMITH OF MINNESOTA	LANDERS	COLUMBIA	1942
CPC-171	BOOGIE MAN WILL GET YOU	LANDERS	COLUMBIA	1942
CPC-172	UNDERGROUND AGENT	GORDON	COLUMBIA	1942
CPC-173	NIGHT TO REMEMBER	WALLACE	COLUMBIA	1943
CPC-174	LAUGH YOUR BLUES AWAY	BARTON	COLUMBIA	1942
CPC-175	JUNIOR ARMY	LANDERS	COLUMBIA	1942
CPC-176	MORE THE MERRIER	STEVENS	COLUMBIA	1943
CPC-177	POWER OF THE PRESS	LANDERS	COLUMBIA	1943
CPC-178	WHAT'S BUZZIN COUSIN?	BARTON	COLUMBIA	1943
CPC-179	REVELIE WITH BEVERLY	BARTON	COLUMBIA	1943
CPC-180	MURDER IN TIMES SQUARE	LANDERS	COLUMBIA	1943
CPC-181	SAHARA	KORDA	COLUMBIA	1943
CPC-182	APPOINTMENT IN BERLIN	GREEN	COLUMBIA	1943
CPC-183	AFTER MIDNIGHT WITH BOSTON BLACKIE	LANDERS	COLUMBIA	1943
CPC-184	FIRST COMES COURAGE	ARZNER	COLUMBIA	1943
CPC-185	SHE HAS WHAT IT TAKES	BARTON	COLUMBIA	1943
CPC-186	IT'S A GREAT LIFE (BLONDIE)	STRAYER	COLUMBIA	1943
CPC-187	BOY FROM STALINGRAD	SALKOW	COLUMBIA	1943
CPC-188	REDHEAD FROM MANHATTAN	LANDERS	COLUMBIA	1943
CPC-189	ONCE UPON A TIME	HALL	COLUMBIA	1944
CPC-190	TWO SENORITAS FROM CHICAGO	WOODRUFF	COLUMBIA	1943
CPC-192	GOOD LUCK MR. YATES	ENRIGHT	COLUMBIA	1943
CPC-193	DOUGHBOYS IN IRELAND	LANDERS	COLUMBIA	1943
CPC-194	COVER GIRL	VIDOR	COLUMBIA	1944
CPC-195	MY KINGDOM FOR A COOK	WALLACE	COLUMBIA	1943
CPC-197	PASSPORT TO SUEZ	DE TOTH	COLUMBIA	1943
CPC-198	DANGEROUS BLONDES	JASON	COLUMBIA	1943
CPC-199	THERE'S SOMETHING ABOUT A SOLDIER	GREEN	COLUMBIA	1943
CPC-200	EXTORTION	HILLYER	COLUMBIA	1938
CPC-203	MAIN EVENT	DARE	COLUMBIA	1938
CPC-204	PAID TO DANCE (HARD TO HOLD)	COLEMAN	COLUMBIA	1937
CPC-205	ALL AMERICAN SWEETHEART	HILLYER	COLUMBIA	1937

CPC-206	SHADOW		COLUMBIA	
CPC-207	SQUADRON OF HONOR	COLEMAN	COLUMBIA	1938
CPC-208	WOMEN IN PRISON	HILLYER	COLUMBIA	1938
CPC-209	WHO KILLED GAIL PRESTON?	BARSHA	COLUMBIA	1938
CPC-210	WHEN G-MEN STEP IN	COLEMAN	COLUMBIA	1938
CPC-211	HIGHWAY PATROL	COLEMAN	COLUMBIA	1938
CPC-212	HOMICIDE BUREAU	COLEMAN	COLUMBIA	1939
CPC-213	JUVENILE COURT	LEDERMAN	COLUMBIA	1938
CPC-213	MOVIE MANIACS (sh)	LORD	COLUMBIA	1936
CPC-214	ADVENTURE IN SAHARA	LEDERMAN	COLUMBIA	1938
CPC-215	NORTH OF SHANGHAI	LEDERMAN	COLUMBIA	1939
CPC-216	MY SON IS A CRIMINAL	COLEMAN	COLUMBIA	1939
CPC-217	DISORDER IN COURT (sh)	WHITE	COLUMBIA	1936
CPC-217	FIRST OFFENDERS	MCDONALD	COLUMBIA	1939
CPC-218	OUTSIDE THESE WALLS	MCCAREY	COLUMBIA	1939
CPC-219	MISSING DAUGHTERS	COLEMAN	COLUMBIA	1939
CPC-220	PARENTS ON TRIAL	NELSON	COLUMBIA	1939
CPC-221	WOMAN IS THE JUDGE	GRINDE	COLUMBIA	1939
CPC-222	BEHIND PRISON GATES	BARTON	COLUMBIA	1939
CPC-223	MAN THEY COULD NOT HANG	GRINDE	COLUMBIA	1939
CPC-224	KONGA, THE WILD STALLION	NELSON	COLUMBIA	1940
CPC-300	OUTLAWS OF THE PRAIRIE	NELSON	COLUMBIA	1937
CPC-301	CATTLE RAIDERS	NELSON	COLUMBIA	1938
CPC-302	OLD WYOMING TRAIL	BLANGSTED	COLUMBIA	1937
CPC-303	CALL OF THE ROCKIES	JAMES	COLUMBIA	1938
CPC-304	LAW OF THE PLAINS	NELSON	COLUMBIA	1938
CPC-305	WEST OF CHEYENNE	NELSON	COLUMBIA	1938
CPC-306	SOUTH OF ARIZONA	NELSON	COLUMBIA	1938
CPC-307	WEST OF SANTA FE	NELSON	COLUMBIA	1938
CPC-308	COLORADO TRAIL	NELSON	COLUMBIA	1938
CPC-309	RIO GRANDE	NELSON	COLUMBIA	1938
CPC-310	THUNDERING WEST	NELSON	COLUMBIA	1939
CPC-311	TEXAS STAMPEDE	NELSON	COLUMBIA	1939
CPC-312	NORTH OF THE YUKON	NELSON	COLUMBIA	1939
CPC-313	SPOILERS OF THE RANGE	COLEMAN	COLUMBIA	1939
CPC-314	WESTERN CARAVANS	NELSON	COLUMBIA	1939
CPC-315	MAN FROM SUNDOWN	NELSON	COLUMBIA	1939
CPC-316	OUTPOST OF THE MOUNTIES	COLEMAN	COLUMBIA	1939
CPC-317	STRANGER FROM TEXAS	NELSON	COLUMBIA	1939
CPC-318	RIDERS OF BLACK RIVER	DEMING	COLUMBIA	1939
CPC-319	TAMING OF THE WEST	DEMING	COLUMBIA	1939
CPC-320	MAN FROM TUMBLEWEEDS	LEWIS	COLUMBIA	1940
CPC-321	TWO FISTED RANGERS	LEWIS	COLUMBIA	1939
CPC-322	BULLETS FOR RUSTLERS	NELSON	COLUMBIA	1940
CPC-323	PIONEERS OF THE FRONTIER	NELSON	COLUMBIA	1940
CPC-324	BLAZING SIX SHOOTERS	LEWIS	COLUMBIA	1940
CPC-325	THUNDERING FRONTIER	LEDERMAN	COLUMBIA	1940
CPC-326	TEXAS STAGECOACH	LEWIS	COLUMBIA	1940
CPC-327	PINTO KID	HILLYER	COLUMBIA	1941
CPC-328	WEST OF ABILENE	CEDER	COLUMBIA	1940
CPC-329	RETURN OF WILD BILL	LEWIS	COLUMBIA	1940
CPC-330	DURANGO KID	HILLYER	COLUMBIA	1940
CPC-331	PRAIRIE SCHOONERS	NELSON	COLUMBIA	1940
CPC-332	OUTLAWS OF THE PANHANDLE	NELSON	COLUMBIA	1941
CPC-334	BEYOND THE SACRAMENTO	HILLYER	COLUMBIA	1940
CPC-335	ACROSS THE SIERRAS	LEDERMAN	COLUMBIA	1941
CPC-337	WILDCAT OF TUCSON	HILLYER	COLUMBIA	1940
CPC-338	NORTH FROM THE LONE STAR	HILLYER	COLUMBIA	1941
CPC-339	RETURN OF DANIEL BOONE	HILLYER	COLUMBIA	1941
CPC-340	HANDS ACROSS THE ROCKIES	HILLYER	COLUMBIA	1941
CPC-341	SON OF DAVY CROCKETT	HILLYER	COLUMBIA	1941
CPC-342	MEDICO OF PAINTED SPRINGS	HILLYER	COLUMBIA	1941
CPC-343	KING OF DODGE CITY	HILLYER	COLUMBIA	1941
CPC-344	THUNDER OVER THE PRAIRIE	HILLYER	COLUMBIA	1941
CPC-345	ROARING FRONTIERS	HILLYER	COLUMBIA	1941
CPC-346	PRAIRIE STRANGER	HILLYER	COLUMBIA	1941

CPC-347	LONE STAR VIGILANTES	FOX	COLUMBIA	1942
CPC-348	ROYAL MOUNTED PATROL	HILLYER	COLUMBIA	1941
CPC-349	BULLETS FOR BANDITS	FOX	COLUMBIA	1942
CPC-350	RIDERS OF THE BADLANDS	BRETHERTON	COLUMBIA	1941
CPC-351	NORTH OF THE ROCKIES	HILLYER	COLUMBIA	1942
CPC-352	DEVIL'S TRAIL	HILLYER	COLUMBIA	1942
CPC-353	WEST OF TOMBSTONE	BRETHERTON	COLUMBIA	1942
CPC-354	LAWLESS PLAINSMEN	BERKE	COLUMBIA	1942
CPC-355	DOWN RIO GRANDE WAY	BERKE	COLUMBIA	1942
CPC-356	PRAIRIE GUNSMOKE	HILLYER	COLUMBIA	1942
CPC-357	OVERLAND TO DEADWOOD	BERKE	COLUMBIA	1942
CPC-358	BADMEN OF THE HILLS	BERKE	COLUMBIA	1942
CPC-359	RIDERS OF THE NORTHLAND	BERKE	COLUMBIA	1942
CPC-360	VENGEANCE OF THE WEST		COLUMBIA	1942
CPC-362	RIDING THROUGH NEVADA	BERKE	COLUMBIA	1942
CPC-363	PARDON MY GUN	BERKE	COLUMBIA	1942
CPC-364	TORNADO IN THE SADDLE	BERKE	COLUMBIA	1942
CPC-365	LONE PRAIRIE	BERKE	COLUMBIA	1942
CPC-366	FIGHTING BUCKAROO	BERKE	COLUMBIA	1943
CPC-367	LAW OF THE NORTHWEST	BERKE	COLUMBIA	1943
CPC-368	SILVER CITY RAIDERS	BERKE	COLUMBIA	1943
CPC-369	RIDERS OF THE NORTHWEST MOUNTED	BERKE	COLUMBIA	1943
CPC-370	HAIL TO THE RANGERS	BERKE	COLUMBIA	1943
CPC-371	ROBIN HOOD OF THE RANGE	BERKE	COLUMBIA	1943
CPC-372	SADDLES AND THE SAGEBRUSH	BERKE	COLUMBIA	1943
CPC-373	VIGILANTES RIDE	BERKE	COLUMBIA	1943
CPC-374	WYOMING HURRICANE	BERKE	COLUMBIA	1944
CPC-375	LAST HORSEMAN	BERKE	COLUMBIA	1944
CPC-376	RIDING WEST	BERKE	COLUMBIA	1944
CPC-377	FRONTIER FURY	BERKE	COLUMBIA	1943
CPC-400	CASH AND CARRY – STOOGES	LORD	COLUMBIA	1937
CPC-401	PLAY THE PONIES – STOOGES	LAMONT	COLUMBIA	1937
CPC-404	WEE WEE MONSIER – STOOGES	LORD	COLUMBIA	1938
CPC-407	GRACIE AT THE BAT	LORD	COLUMBIA	1937
CPC-409	COLLINS-KENNEDY		COLUMBIA	
CPC-413	CHARLEY CHASE		COLUMBIA	
CPC-416	TERMITES OF 1938	LORD	COLUMBIA	1938
CPC-427	MUTTS TO YOU – STOOGES	CHASE	COLUMBIA	1938
CPC-429	SMITH AND DALE		COLUMBIA	
CPC-430	SAVED BY THE BELLE – STOOGES	CHASE	COLUMBIA	1939
CPC-431	CHARLEY CHASE		COLUMBIA	
CPC-433	SMITH AND DALE		COLUMBIA	
CPC-434	ANDY CLYDE		COLUMBIA	
CPC-436	ANDY CLYDE – SHEMP HOWARD		COLUMBIA	
CPC-437	CHARLEY CHASE		COLUMBIA	
CPC-438	YES WE HAVE NO BONANZA – STOOGES	LORD	COLUMBIA	1939
CPC-439	FLAT FOOT STOOGES – STOOGES	CHASE	COLUMBIA	1938
CPC-440	ANDY CLYDE		COLUMBIA	
CPC-441	DANNY WEBB		COLUMBIA	
CPC-442	ANDY CLYDE		COLUMBIA	
CPC-443	WE WANT OUR MUMMY – STOOGES	LORD	COLUMBIA	1939
CPC-444	A DUCKING THEY DID GO – STOOGES	LORD	COLUMBIA	1939
CPC-445	CALLING ALL CURS – STOOGES	WHITE	COLUMBIA	1939
CPC-446	RATTLING ROMEO – CHARLEY CHASE	LORD	COLUMBIA	1939
CPC-448	NOW IT CAN BE SOLD – CHARLEY CHASE	LORD	COLUMBIA	1939
CPC-449	OILY TO BED – STOOGES	WHITE	COLUMBIA	1939
CPC-450	CHARLEY CHASE		COLUMBIA	
CPC-452	TEACHER'S PEST CHARLEY CHASE	KRAMER, ULLMAN	COLUMBIA	1939
CPC-453	STATIC IN THE ATTIC	CHASE	COLUMBIA	1939
CPC-454	PEST FROM THE WEST – BUSTER KEATON	LORD	COLUMBIA	1939
CPC-458	HOW HIGH IS UP? – STOOGES	LORD	COLUMBIA	1940
CPC-459	ANDY CLYDE – SHEMP HOWARD		COLUMBIA	
CPC-460	ALL AMERICAN BLONDES – ANDY CLYDE	LORD	COLUMBIA	1939
CPC-462	STOOGES (sh)		COLUMBIA	
CPC-463	ANDY CLYDE GETS SPRING CHICKEN	WHITE	COLUMBIA	1939
CPC-464	CHARLEY CHASE (sh)		COLUMBIA	

CPC-466	ANDY CLYDE (sh)		COLUMBIA	
CPC-467	HECKLER	LORD	COLUMBIA	1940
CPC-468	FROM NURSE TO WORSE	WHITE	COLUMBIA	1940
CPC-469	CHARLEY CHASE (sh)		COLUMBIA	
CPC-473	SOUTH OF THE BOUDOIR	LORD	COLUMBIA	1940
CPC-476	ANDY CLYDE – SHEMP HOWARD		COLUMBIA	
CPC-482	IN THE SWEET PIE AND PIE – STOOGES	WHITE	COLUMBIA	1941
CPC-483	BLONDES AND BLUNDERS – W. CATLETT	LORD	COLUMBIA	1940
CPC-484	SO LONG MR. CHUMPS – STOOGES	WHITE	COLUMBIA	1941
CPC-487	STOOGES (sh)		COLUMBIA	
CPC-488	AN ACHE IN EVERY STAKE – STOOGES	LORD	COLUMBIA	1941
CPC-489	ANDY CLYDE (sh)		COLUMBIA	
CPC-494	ANDY CLYDE (sh)		COLUMBIA	
CPC-496	EL BRENDEL (sh)		COLUMBIA	
CPC-497	EL BRENDEL (sh)		COLUMBIA	
CPC-498	YANKEE DOODLE ANDY – ANDY CLYDE	WHITE	COLUMBIA	1941
CPC-499	EL BRENDEL		COLUMBIA	
CPC-500	I'LL NEVER HEIL AGAIN – STOOGES	WHITE	COLUMBIA	1941
CPC-501	LOVE AT FIRST FRIGHT – EL BRENDEL	LORD	COLUMBIA	1941
CPC-502	ALAN MOWBRAY SHORT		COLUMBIA	
CPC-503	FRENCH FRIED PATOOTIE	WHITE	COLUMBIA	1941
CPC-505	ROSCOE KARNS		COLUMBIA	
CPC-506	HALF SHOT AT SUNRISE – ROSCOE KARNS	LORD	COLUMBIA	1941
CPC-507	EVEN AS I.O.U. – STOOGES	LORD	COLUMBIA	1942
CPC-508	GENERAL NUISANCE – BUSTER KEATON	WHITE	COLUMBIA	1941
CPC-509	ANDY CLYDE (sh)		COLUMBIA	
CPC-510	LOCO BOY MAKES GOOD – STOOGES	WHITE	COLUMBIA	1942
CPC-511	STOOGES (sh)		COLUMBIA	
CPC-512	MITT ME TONIGHT – GLOVESLINGERS	WHITE	COLUMBIA	1941
CPC-515	PHONY CRONIES – EL BRENDEL	EDWARDS	COLUMBIA	1942
CPC-519	WHAT'S THE MATADOR? – STOOGES	WHITE	COLUMBIA	1942
CPC-520	GLOVE SLINGERS		COLUMBIA	
CPC-521	SWEET SPIRITS OF NIGHTER – EL BRENDEL	LORD	COLUMBIA	1941
CPC-522	BACK FROM THE FRONT	WHITE	COLUMBIA	1943
CPC-523	GROOM AND BORED	LORD	COLUMBIA	1942
CPC-525	GLOVE AFFAIR – GLOVESLINGERS	WHITE	COLUMBIA	1941
CPC-528	OLAF LAUGHS LAST – EL BRENDEL	WHITE	COLUMBIA	1942
CPC-529	DIZZY DETECTIVES – STOOGES	WHITE	COLUMBIA	1943
CPC-532	3 SMART SAPS – STOOGES	WHITE	COLUMBIA	1942
CPC-533	THEY STOOGE TO CONGA – STOOGES	LORD	COLUMBIA	1943
CPC-536	CARRY HARRY (HARRY LANGDON)	EDWARDS	COLUMBIA	1942
CPC-541	EL BRENDEL		COLUMBIA	
CPC-549	SPOOK LOUDER – STOOGES	LORD	COLUMBIA	1943
CPC-550	I SPIED FOR YOU – EL BRENDEL	WHITE	COLUMBIA	1943
CPC-551	3 LITTLE TWERPS – STOOGES	EDWARDS	COLUMBIA	1943
CPC-553	CHESTER CONKLIN		COLUMBIA	
CPC-555	DIZZY PILOTS – STOOGES	WHITE	COLUMBIA	1943
CPC-562	A ROOKIE'S COOKIE	WHITE	COLUMBIA	1943
CPC-563	BOOBS IN THE NIGHT – EL BRENDEL	LORD	COLUMBIA	1943
CPC-564	NO DOUGH BOYS - STOOGES	WHITE	COLUMBIA	1944
CPC-565	HUGH HERBERT		COLUMBIA	
CPC-568	HIGHER THAN A KITE – STOOGES	LORD	COLUMBIA	1943
CPC-569	PHONEY EXPRESS – STOOGES	LORD	COLUMBIA	1943
CPC-570	I CAN HARDLY WAIT – STOOGES	WHITE	COLUMBIA	1943
CPC-571	YOKE'S ON ME – STOOGES	WHITE	COLUMBIA	1944
CPC-572	TO HEIR IS HUMAN – BARRY LANGDON	GODSOE	COLUMBIA	1944
CPC-573	GARDEN OF EATIN	EDWARDS	COLUMBIA	1943
CPC-574	WHO'S HUGH	EDWARDS	COLUMBIA	1943
CPC-575	GEM OF A JAM	LORD	COLUMBIA	1943
CPC-595	STOOGES (sh)		COLUMBIA	
CPC-600	COMMUNITY SING – GENE MORGAN		COLUMBIA	
CPC-611	COMMUNITY SING – GENE MORGAN		COLUMBIA	
CPC-631	COMMUNITY SING		COLUMBIA	
CPC-632	COMMUNITY SING		COLUMBIA	
CPC-646	FOOLS WHO MADE HISTORY		COLUMBIA	1939
CPC-647	FOOLS WHO MADE HISTORY - WALLY WALES		COLUMBIA	1939

CPC-655	COMMUNITY SING – GENE MORGN		COLUMBIA	
CPC-683	JUNIOR QUIZ PARADE		COLUMBIA	
CPC-729	CITY WITHOUT MEN	SALKOW	COLUMBIA	1943
CPC-735	HEAT'S ON	RATOFF	COLUMBIA	1943
CPC-749	SHORT		COLUMBIA	
CPC-762	CRIME DR.'S STRANGEST CASE	FORDE	COLUMBIA	1943
CPC-770	SECRET COMMAND	SUTHERLAND	COLUMBIA	1944
CPC-773	ADDRESS UNKNOWN	MENZIES	COLUMBIA	1944
CPC-787	WHISTLER	CASTLE	COLUMBIA	1944
CPC-788	TEXAS	MARSHALL	COLUMBIA	1941
CPC-789	SHADOWS IN THE NIGHT	FORDE	COLUMBIA	1944
CPC-791	EVER SINCE VENUE	DREIFUSS	COLUMBIA	1944
CPC-803	MARK OF THE WHISTLER	CASTLE	COLUMBIA	1944
CPC-808	BRENDA STARR – REPORTER SERIAL	FOX	COLUMBIA	1945
CPC-811	RIDERS OF THE WHISTLING PINES	ENGLISH	COLUMBIA	1949
CPC-812	CRIME DR.'S COURAGE	SHERMAN	COLUMBIA	1945
CPC-813	POWER OF THE WHISTLER	LANDERS	COLUMBIA	1945
CPC-814	KISS AND TELL	WALLACE	COLUMBIA	1945
CPC-818	MONSTER AND THE APE	BRETHERTON	COLUMBIA	1945
CPC-822	OVER 21	VIDOR	COLUMBIA	1945
CPC-830	ADVENTURES OF RUSTY	BURNFORD	COLUMBIA	1945
CPC-834	SNAFU	MOSS	COLUMBIA	1945
CPC-835	JUNGLE RAIDERS (serial)	SELANDER	COLUMBIA	1945
CPC-838	CRIME DR.'S WARNING	CASTLE	COLUMBIA	1945
CPC-841	PERILOUS HOLIDAY	GRIFFITH	COLUMBIA	1946
CPC-844	WHO'S GUILTY?	BRETHERTON, GRISSELL	COLUMBIA	1945
CPC-850	JOHNNY O'CLOCK	ROSSEN	COLUMBIA	1947
CPC-851	MR. DISTRICT ATTORNEY	SINCLAIR	COLUMBIA	1947
CPC-855	HOP HARRIGAN	ABRAHAMS	COLUMBIA	1946
CPC-856	TO THE ENDS OF THE EARTH	STEVENSON	COLUMBIA	1948
CPC-862	CHICK CARTER DETECTIVE	ABRAHAMS	COLUMBIA	1946
CPC-863	RETURN OF MONTE CRISTO	LEVIN	COLUMBIA	1946
CPC-868	SON OF THE GUARDSMAN	ABRAHAMS	COLUMBIA	1946
CPC-869	LAST OF THE REDMEN	SHERMAN	COLUMBIA	1947
CPC-873	BETTY CO-ED	DREIFUSS	COLUMBIA	1946
CPC-876	CORPSE CAME C.O.D.	LEVIN	COLUMBIA	1947
CPC-878	JACK ARMSTRONG	FOX	COLUMBIA	1947
CPC-879	GUNFIGHTERS	WAGGNER	COLUMBIA	1947
CPC-882	VIGILANTE (serial)	FOX	COLUMBIA	1947
CPC-883	RELENTLESS	SHERMAN	COLUMBIA	1948
CPC-884	LITTLE MISS BROADWAY	DREIFUSS	COLUMBIA	1947
CPC-885	HER HUSBANDS AFFAIRS	SIMON	COLUMBIA	1947
CPC-886	SEA HOUND	EASON, WRIGHT	COLUMBIA	1947
CPC-887	PRINCE OF THIEVES	BRETHERTON	COLUMBIA	1948
CPC-888	I LOVE TROUBLE	SIMON	COLUMBIA	1948
CPC-889	MUSIC IN MY HEART	SANTLEY	COLUMBIA	1940
CPC-889	STRAWBERRY ROAN	ENGLISH	COLUMBIA	1948
CPC-890	SWEET GENEVIEVE	DREIFUSS	COLUMBIA	1947
CPC-891	TWO BLONDES AND A REDHEAD	DREIFUSS	COLUMBIA	1947
CPC-892	LAST ROUNDUP	ENGLISH	COLUMBIA	1947
CPC-893	BIG SOMBRERO	MCDONALD	COLUMBIA	1949
CPC-895	TEX GRANGER (serial)	ABRAHAMS	COLUMBIA	1948
CPC-896	SIGN OF THE RAM	STURGES	COLUMBIA	1948
CPC-897	BLACK ARROW	DOUGLAS	COLUMBIA	1948
CPC-899	BRICK BRADFORD (serial)	BENNET, CARR	COLUMBIA	1947
CPC-900	GREAT ADV OF WILD BILL HICKOK (serial)	NELSON, WRIGHT	COLUMBIA	1938
CPC-900	MARY LOU	DREIFUSS	COLUMBIA	1948
CPC-901	SPIDER'S WEB (serial)	HORNE, TAYLOR	COLUMBIA	1938
CPC-902	ALL THE KING'S MEN	ROSSEN	COLUMBIA	1950
CPC-902	FLYING G-MEN - SERIAL	HORNE, TAYLOR	COLUMBIA	1939
CPC-903	MANDRAKE THE MAGICIAN (serial)	DEMING, NELSON	COLUMBIA	1939
CPC-904	OVERLAND WITH KIT CARSON	DEMING, NELSON	COLUMBIA	1939
CPC-905	LOADED PISTOLS	ENGLISH	COLUMBIA	1948
CPC-908	GLAMOUR GIRL	DREIFUSS	COLUMBIA	1948
CPC-909	MANHATTAN ANGEL	DREIFUSS	COLUMBIA	1949
CPC-910	SUPERMAN - SERIAL	BENNET, CARR	COLUMBIA	1948

CPC-911	ADVENTURE IN WASHINGTON	GREEN	COLUMBIA	1941
CPC-912	I SURRENDER DEAR	DREIFUSS	COLUMBIA	1948
CPC-913	FULLER BRUSH MAN	SIMON	COLUMBIA	1948
CPC-914	RACING LUCK	BERKE	COLUMBIA	1948
CPC-915	LOVES OF CARMEN	VIDOR	COLUMBIA	1948
CPC-916	SHE KNEW ALL THE ANSWERS	WALLACE	COLUMBIA	1941
CPC-918	MUTINEERS	YARBROUGH	COLUMBIA	1949
CPC-919	LULU BELLE	FENTON	COLUMBIA	1948
CPC-920	UNDERCOVER MAN	LEWIS	COLUMBIA	1949
CPC-921	SONS OF NEW MEXICO	ENGLISH	COLUMBIA	1949
CPC-923	ANNA LUCASTA	RAPPER	COLUMBIA	1949
CPC-924	COWBOY AND THE INDIANS	ENGLISH	COLUMBIA	1949
CPC-926	CONGO BILL	BENNET, CARR	COLUMBIA	1948
CPC-927	UNTAMED BREED	LAMONT	COLUMBIA	1948
CPC-928	LADIES OF THE CHORUS	KARLSON	COLUMBIA	1948
CPC-931	ADAM HAD FOUR SONS	RATOFF	COLUMBIA	1941
CPC-931	KNOCK ON ANY DOOR	RAY	COLUMBIA	1949
CPC-932	TOKYO JOE	HEISLER	COLUMBIA	1949
CPC-933	TRIPLE THREAT	YARBROUGH	COLUMBIA	1948
CPC-934	SONG OF INDIA	ROGELL	COLUMBIA	1949
CPC-935	JUNGLE JIM	BERKE	COLUMBIA	1948
CPC-937	BRUCE GENTRY	BENNET, CARR	COLUMBIA	1949
CPC-939	WE WERE STRANGERS	HUSTON	COLUMBIA	1949
CPC-942	LOST TRIBE	BERKE	COLUMBIA	1949
CPC-944	ADVENTURES OF BATMAN AND ROBIN	BENNET	COLUMBIA	1949
CPC-945	DOOLINS OF OKLAHOMA	DOUGLAS	COLUMBIA	1949
CPC-946	JOLSON SINGS AGAIN	LEVIN	COLUMBIA	1949
CPC-947	RIM OF THE CANYON	ENGLISH	COLUMBIA	1949
CPC-949	LADIES IN RETIREMENT	VIDOR	COLUMBIA	1941
CPC-950	STATE PENITENTIARY	LANDERS	COLUMBIA	1950
CPC-951	BARBARY PIRATE	LANDERS	COLUMBIA	1949
CPC-952	COW TOWN	ENGLISH	COLUMBIA	1950
CPC-953	ADVENTURES OF SIR GALAHAD	BENNET	COLUMBIA	1949
CPC-953	MEN IN HER LIFE	RATOFF	COLUMBIA	1941
CPC-954	CAPTIVE GIRL	BERKE	COLUMBIA	1950
CPC-955	MARK OF THE GORILLA	BERKE	COLUMBIA	1950
CPC-956	ATOM MAN VS. SUPERMAN	BENNET	COLUMBIA	1950
CPC-957	CODY OF THE PONY EXPRESS	BENNET	COLUMBIA	1950
CPC-958	CHINATOWN AT MIDNIGHT	FRIEDMAN	COLUMBIA	1949
CPC-962	TYRANT OF THE SEA	LANDERS	COLUMBIA	1950
CPC-964	ADVENTURES OF MARTIN EDEN	SALKOW	COLUMBIA	1942
CPC-964	RECKLESS MOMENT	OPHULS	COLUMBIA	1949
CPC-965	TRAVELING SALESWOMAN	REISNER	COLUMBIA	1950
CPC-966	AND BABY MAKES THREE	LEVIN	COLUMBIA	1949
CPC-967	BLAZING SUN	ENGLISH	COLUMBIA	1950
CPC-968	NEVADAN	DOUGLAS	COLUMBIA	1950
CPC-970	IN A LONELY PLACE	RAY	COLUMBIA	1950
CPC-971	RIDERS IN THE SKY	ENGLISH	COLUMBIA	1949
CPC-975	BRAVE BULLS	ROSSON	COLUMBIA	1951
CPC-976	MULE TRAIN	ENGLISH	COLUMBIA	1950
CPC-977	BEYOND THE PURPLE HILLS	ENGLISH	COLUMBIA	1950
CPC-981	INDIAN TERRITORY	ENGLISH	COLUMBIA	1950
CPC-982	SOMETHING TO SHOUT ABOUT	RATOFF	COLUMBIA	1943
CPC-986	LAST OF THE BUCCANEERS	LANDERS	COLUMBIA	1950
CPC-988	GENE AUTRY AND THE MOUNTIES	ENGLISH	COLUMBIA	1951
CPC-989	REVENUE AGENT	LANDERS	COLUMBIA	1950
CPC-990	PIRATES OF THE HIGH SEAS	BENNET, CARR	COLUMBIA	1950
CPC-991	SIROCCO	BERNHARDT	COLUMBIA	1951
CPC-992	HURRICANE ISLAND	LANDERS	COLUMBIA	1951
CPC-993	CHAIN GANG	LANDERS	COLUMBIA	1950
CPC-994	PYGMY ISLAND	BERKE	COLUMBIA	1950
CPC-995	FURY OF THE CONGO	BERKE	COLUMBIA	1951
CPC-996	COMMANDOES STRIKE AT DAWN	FARROW	COLUMBIA	1942
CPC-998	SATURDAY'S HERO	MILLER	COLUMBIA	1951
CPC-999	FAMILY SECRET	LEVIN	COLUMBIA	1951
CPC-1001	FOOTLIGHT GLAMOUR	STRAYER	COLUMBIA	1943

CPC-1002	IS EVERYBODY HAPPY?	BARTON	COLUMBIA	1943
CPC-1004	WHAT A WOMAN	CUMMINGS	COLUMBIA	1943
CPC-1005	NINE GIRLS	JASON	COLUMBIA	1944
CPC-1006	NONE SHALL ESCAPE	DE TOTH	COLUMBIA	1944
CPC-1009	RACKET MAN	LEDERMAN	COLUMBIA	1944
CPC-1010	RETURN OF THE VAMPIRE	LANDERS	COLUMBIA	1944
CPC-1011	SONG TO REMEMBER	VIDOR	COLUMBIA	1945
CPC-1012	CHANCE OF A LIFETIME	CASTLE	COLUMBIA	1943
CPC-1014	MR. WINKLE GOES TO WAR	GREEN	COLUMBIA	1944
CPC-1015	KLONDIKE KATE	CASTLE	COLUMBIA	1943
CPC-1016	SWING OUT OF THE BLUES	ST. CLAIR	COLUMBIA	1943
CPC-1017	BEAUTIFUL BUT BROKE	BARTON	COLUMBIA	1944
CPC-1019	GHOST THAT WALKS ALONE	LANDERS	COLUMBIA	1944
CPC-1021	GIRL IN THE CASE	BERKE	COLUMBIA	1944
CPC-1022	TONIGHT AND EVERY NIGHT	SAVILLE	COLUMBIA	1945
CPC-1023	SAILOR'S HOLIDAY	BERKE	COLUMBIA	1944
CPC-1024	TOGETHER AGAIN	VIDOR	COLUMBIA	1944
CPC-1025	TWO MAN SUBMARINE	LANDERS	COLUMBIA	1944
CPC-1026	CAROLINA BLUES	JASON	COLUMBIA	1944
CPC-1027	STARS ON PARADE	LANDERS	COLUMBIA	1944
CPC-1028	BLACK PARACHUTE	LANDERS	COLUMBIA	1944
CPC-1029	SHE'S A SOLDIER TOO	CASTLE	COLUMBIA	1944
CPC-1030	JOLSON STORY (some marked 1130)	GREEN	COLUMBIA	1946
CPC-1031	COUNTER-ATTACK	KORDA	COLUMBIA	1945
CPC-1032	THEY LIVE IN FEAR	BERNE	COLUMBIA	1944
CPC-1033	U-BOAT PRISONER	LANDERS	COLUMBIA	1944
CPC-1035	LOUISIANA HAYRIDE	BARTON	COLUMBIA	1944
CPC-1036	IMPATIENT YEARS	CUMMINGS	COLUMBIA	1944
CPC-1037	CRY OF THE WEREWOLF	LEVIN	COLUMBIA	1944
CPC-1038	UNWRITTEN CODE	ROTSTEN	COLUMBIA	1944
CPC-1039	EVE KNEW HER APPLES	JASON	COLUMBIA	1945
CPC-1040	KANSAS CITY KITTY	LORD	COLUMBIA	1944
CPC-1042	MEET MISS BOBBY SOCKS	TRYON	COLUMBIA	1944
CPC-1043	STRANGE AFFAIR	GREEN	COLUMBIA	1944
CPC-1044	SOUL OF A MONSTER	JASON	COLUMBIA	1944
CPC-1045	ONE MYSTERIOUS NIGHT	BOETTICHER	COLUMBIA	1944
CPC-1046	SERGEANT MIKE	LEVIN	COLUMBIA	1944
CPC-1047	MISSING JUROR	BOETTICHER	COLUMBIA	1944
CPC-1048	ESCAPE IN THE FOG	BOETTICHER	COLUMBIA	1945
CPC-1049	SHE'S A SWEETHEART	LORD	COLUMBIA	1944
CPC-1050	TARS AND SPARS	GREEN	COLUMBIA	1946
CPC-1051	EADIE WAS A LADY	DREIFUSS	COLUMBIA	1945
CPC-1052	DANCING IN MANHATTAN	LEVIN	COLUMBIA	1944
CPC-1054	THOUSAND AND ONE NIGHTS	GREEN	COLUMBIA	1945
CPC-1055	TAHITI NIGHTS	JASON	COLUMBIA	1944
CPC-1056	LEAVE IT TO BLONDIE	BERLIN	COLUMBIA	1945
CPC-1057	LET'S GO STEADY	LORD	COLUMBIA	1945
CPC-1058	I LOVE A MYSTERY	LEVIN	COLUMBIA	1945
CPC-1059	YOUTH ON TRIAL	BOETTICHER	COLUMBIA	1945
CPC-1060	SHE WOULDN'T SAY YES	HALL	COLUMBIA	1945
CPC-1061	MEET ME ON BROADWAY	JASON	COLUMBIA	1946
CPC-1062	GUY, A GAL AND A PAL	BOETTICHER	COLUMBIA	1945
CPC-1063	ROUGH TOUGH AND READY	LORD	COLUMBIA	1945
CPC-1064	FIGHTING GUARDSMAN	LEVIN	COLUMBIA	1946
CPC-1066	TEN CENTS A DANCE	JASON	COLUMBIA	1945
CPC-1069	BOSTON BLACKIE HOOKED ON SUSPICION	DREIFUSS	COLUMBIA	1945
CPC-1070	BLONDE FROM BROOKLYN	LORD	COLUMBIA	1945
CPC-1071	GAY SENORITA	DREIFUSS	COLUMBIA	1945
CPC-1072	BOSTON BLACKIE'S RENDEZVOUS	DREIFUSS	COLUMBIA	1945
CPC-1074	BANDIT OF SHERWOOD FOREST	LEVIN, SHERMAN	COLUMBIA	1946
CPC-1075	I LOVE A BANDLEADER	LORD	COLUMBIA	1945
CPC-1076	VOICE OF THE WHISTLER	CASTLE	COLUMBIA	1945
CPC-1078	GIRL OF THE LIMBERLOST	FERRER	COLUMBIA	1945
CPC-1079	RENEGADES	SHERMAN	COLUMBIA	1946
CPC-1080	ONE WAY TO LOVE	ENRIGHT	COLUMBIA	1946
CPC-1081	HIT THE HAY	LORD	COLUMBIA	1945

CPC-1082	MY NAME IS JULIA ROSS	LEWIS	COLUMBIA	1945
CPC-1083	OUT OF THE DEPTHS	LEDERMAN	COLUMBIA	1945
CPC-1084	LIFE WITH BLONDIE	BERLIN	COLUMBIA	1945
CPC-1086	PRISON SHIP	DREIFUSS	COLUMBIA	1945
CPC-1087	GILDA	VIDOR	COLUMBIA	1946
CPC-1088	BLONDIE'S LUCKY DAY	BERLIN	COLUMBIA	1946
CPC-1089	CLOSE CALL FOR BOSTON BLACKIE	LANDERS	COLUMBIA	1946
CPC-1090	SO DARK THE NIGHT	LEWIS	COLUMBIA	1946
CPC-1091	NOTORIOUS LONE WOLF	LEDERMAN	COLUMBIA	1946
CPC-1092	GENTLEMEN MISBEHAVES	SHERMAN	COLUMBIA	1946
CPC-1093	JUST BEFORE DAWN	CASTLE	COLUMBIA	1946
CPC-1094	WALLS CAME TUMBLING DOWN	MENDES	COLUMBIA	1946
CPC-1095	DEVIL'S MASK	LEVIN	COLUMBIA	1946
CPC-1096	DANGEROUS BUSINESS	LEDERMAN	COLUMBIA	1946
CPC-1097	TALK ABOUT A LADY	SHERMAN	COLUMBIA	1946
CPC-1098	MYSTERIOUS INTRUDER	CASTLE	COLUMBIA	1946
CPC-1099	NIGHT EDITOR	LEVIN	COLUMBIA	1946
CPC-1100	DOWN TO EARTH	HALL	COLUMBIA	1947
CPC-1101	PHANTOM THIEF	LEDERMAN	COLUMBIA	1946
CPC-1102	MAN WHO DARED	STURGES	COLUMBIA	1946
CPC-1103	GALLANT JOURNEY	WELLMAN	COLUMBIA	1946
CPC-1104	THRILL OF BRAZIL	SIMON	COLUMBIA	1946
CPC-1105	RETURN OF RUSTY	CASTLE	COLUMBIA	1946
CPC-1106	UNKNOWN, THE	LEVIN	COLUMBIA	1946
CPC-1107	BLONDIE KNOWS BEST	BERLIN	COLUMBIA	1946
CPC-1108	SING WHILE YOU DANCE	LEDERMAN	COLUMBIA	1946
CPC-1109	PERSONALITY KID	SHERMAN	COLUMBIA	1946
CPC-1110	CRIME DR.'S MANHUNT	CASTLE	COLUMBIA	1946
CPC-1111	DEAD RECKONING	CROMWELL	COLUMBIA	1947
CPC-1112	IT'S GREAT TO BE YOUNG	LORD	COLUMBIA	1946
CPC-1113	FRAMED	WALLACE	COLUMBIA	1947
CPC-1114	SECRET OF THE WHISTLER	SHERMAN	COLUMBIA	1946
CPC-1115	GUILT OF JANET AMES	LEVIN	COLUMBIA	1947
CPC-1116	SHADOWED	STURGES	COLUMBIA	1946
CPC-1117	SWORDSMAN	LEWIS	COLUMBIA	1948
CPC-1118	SINGING IN THE CORN	LORD	COLUMBIA	1946
CPC-1119	BLONDIE'S BIG MOMENT	BERLIN	COLUMBIA	1947
CPC-1120	BOSTON BLACKIE AND THE LAW	LEDERMAN	COLUMBIA	1946
CPC-1121	RETURN OF OCTOBER	LEWIS	COLUMBIA	1948
CPC-1122	LONE WOLF IN MEXICO	LEDERMAN	COLUMBIA	1947
CPC-1123	ALIAS MR. TWILIGHT	STURGES	COLUMBIA	1946
CPC-1124	BLIND SPOT	GORDON	COLUMBIA	1947
CPC-1125	MILLIE'S DAUGHTER	SALKOW	COLUMBIA	1947
CPC-1126	LADY FROM SHANGHAI		COLUMBIA	1947
CPC-1127	CIGARETTE GIRL	VON FRITSCH	COLUMBIA	1947
CPC-1128	THIRTEENTH HOUR	CLEMENS	COLUMBIA	1947
CPC-1129	KING OF THE WILD HORSES	ARCHAINBAUD	COLUMBIA	1947
CPC-1130	BLONDIE'S HOLIDAY	BERLIN	COLUMBIA	1947
CPC-1130	JOLSON STORY	GREEN	COLUMBIA	1946
CPC-1131	MILLERSON CASE	ARCHAINBAUD	COLUMBIA	1947
CPC-1132	BULLDOG DRUMMOND AT BAY	SALKOW	COLUMBIA	1947
CPC-1133	FOR THE LOVE OF RUSTY	STURGES	COLUMBIA	1947
CPC-1135	MAN FROM COLORADO	LEVIN	COLUMBIA	1948
CPC-1136	BLONDIE IN THE DOUGH	BERLIN	COLUMBIA	1947
CPC-1137	SPORT OF KINGS	GORDON	COLUMBIA	1947
CPC-1138	IT HAD TO BE YOU	HARTMAN, MATE	COLUMBIA	1947
CPC-1139	KEEPER OF THE BEES	STURGES	COLUMBIA	1947
CPC-1140	SON OF RUSTY	LANDERS	COLUMBIA	1947
CPC-1141	KEY WITNESS	LEDERMAN	COLUMBIA	1947
CPC-1142	BULLDOG DRUMMOND STRIKES AGAIN	MCDONALD	COLUMBIA	1947
CPC-1143	MATING OF MILLIE	LEVIN	COLUMBIA	1948
CPC-1144	WHEN A GIRL'S BEAUTIFUL	MCDONALD	COLUMBIA	1947
CPC-1145	SLIGHTLY FRENCH	SIRK	COLUMBIA	1949
CPC-1146	LONE WOLF IN LONDON	GOODWINS	COLUMBIA	1947
CPC-1148	CRIME DR.'S GAMBLE	CASTLE	COLUMBIA	1947
CPC-1149	DEVIL SHIP	LANDERS	COLUMBIA	1947

CPC-1152	ADVENTURES IN SILVERADO	KARLSON	COLUMBIA	1948
CPC-1153	WRECK OF THE HESPERUS	HOFFMAN	COLUMBIA	1948
CPC-1154	PORT SAID	LE BORG	COLUMBIA	1948
CPC-1155	BLONDIE'S REWARD	BERLIN	COLUMBIA	1948
CPC-1156	BLONDIE'S ANNIVERSARY	BERLIN	COLUMBIA	1947
CPC-1157	WOMAN FROM TANGIER	DANIELS	COLUMBIA	1948
CPC-1159	RETURN OF THE WHISTLER	LEDERMAN	COLUMBIA	1948
CPC-1160	GALLANT BLADE	LEVIN	COLUMBIA	1948
CPC-1161	MY DOG RUSTY	LANDERS	COLUMBIA	1948
CPC-1162	BEST MAN WINS	STURGES	COLUMBIA	1948
CPC-1163	TRAPPED BY BOSTON BLACKIE	FRIEDMAN	COLUMBIA	1948
CPC-1164	THUNDERHOOF	KARLSON	COLUMBIA	1948
CPC-1165	LEATHER GLOVES	ASHER, QUINIE	COLUMBIA	1948
CPC-1166	RUSTY LEADS THE WAY	JASON	COLUMBIA	1948
CPC-1167	WALKING HILLS	STURGES	COLUMBIA	1949
CPC-1168	DARK PAST	MATE	COLUMBIA	1948
CPC-1169	BLACK EAGLE	GORDON	COLUMBIA	1948
CPC-1170	GENTLEMEN FROM NOWHERE	CASTLE	COLUMBIA	1948
CPC-1171	RUSTY SAVES A LIFE	FRIEDMAN	COLUMBIA	1949
CPC-1172	BLONDIE'S SECRET	BERNDS	COLUMBIA	1948
CPC-1173	BOSTON BLACKIE'S CHINESE VENTURE	FRIEDMAN	COLUMBIA	1949
CPC-1174	SHOCKPROOF	SIRK	COLUMBIA	1949
CPC-1175	MR. SOFT TOUCH	DOUGLAS, LEVIN	COLUMBIA	1949
CPC-1176	HOLIDAY IN HAVANA	YARBROUGH	COLUMBIA	1949
CPC-1177	LAW OF THE BARBARY COAST	LANDERS	COLUMBIA	1949
CPC-1178	LONE WOLF AND HIS LADY	HOFFMAN	COLUMBIA	1949
CPC-1179	CRIME DR.'S DIARY	FRIEDMAN	COLUMBIA	1949
CPC-1180	BLONDIE'S BIG DEAL	BERNDS	COLUMBIA	1949
CPC-1181	AIR HOSTESS	LANDERS	COLUMBIA	1949
CPC-1182	MAKE BELIEVE BALLROOM	SANTLEY	COLUMBIA	1949
CPC-1183	LUST FOR GOLD	SIMON	COLUMBIA	1949
CPC-1185	BLONDIE HITS THE JACKPOT	BERNDS	COLUMBIA	1949
CPC-1186	DEVIL'S HENCHMEN	FRIEDMAN	COLUMBIA	1949
CPC-1187	JOHNNY ALLEGRO	TETZLAFF	COLUMBIA	1949
CPC-1188	SECRET OF ST. IVES	ROSEN	COLUMBIA	1949
CPC-1189	KAZAN	JASON	COLUMBIA	1949
CPC-1190	RUSTY'S BIRTHDAY	FRIEDMAN	COLUMBIA	1949
CPC-1191	MISS GRANT TAKES RICHMOND	BACON	COLUMBIA	1949
CPC-1192	TELL IT TO THE JUDGE	FOSTER	COLUMBIA	1949
CPC-1193	PALOMINO	NAZARRO	COLUMBIA	1950
CPC-1194	PRISON WARDEN	FRIEDMAN	COLUMBIA	1949
CPC-1195	BLONDIE'S HERO	BERNDS	COLUMBIA	1950
CPC-1196	GOOD HUMOR MAN	BACON	COLUMBIA	1950
CPC-1197	BORN YESTERDAY	CUKOR	COLUMBIA	1950
CPC-1198	CARGO TO CAPETOWN	MCEVOY	COLUMBIA	1950
CPC-1199	MARY RYAN, DETECTIVE	BERLIN	COLUMBIA	1949
CPC-1200	GIRL'S SCHOOL	BRAHM	COLUMBIA	1938
CPC-1201	ROGUES OF SHERWOOD FOREST	DOUGLAS	COLUMBIA	1950
CPC-1202	WOMAN OF DISTINCTION	BUZZELL	COLUMBIA	1950
CPC-1204	FATHER IS A BACHELOR	BERLIN, FOSTER	COLUMBIA	1950
CPC-1205	BODYHOLD	FRIEDMAN	COLUMBIA	1949
CPC-1206	FORTUNES OF CAPTAIN BLOOD	DOUGLAS	COLUMBIA	1950
CPC-1207	PETTY GIRL	LEVIN	COLUMBIA	1950
CPC-1208	BEWARE OF BLONDIE	BERNDS	COLUMBIA	1950
CPC-1209	KILL THE UMPIRE	BACON	COLUMBIA	1950
CPC-1210	MILITARY ACADEMY	LEDERMAN	COLUMBIA	1940
CPC-1211	FULLER BRUSH GIRL	BACON	COLUMBIA	1950
CPC-1213	BEAUTY ON PARADE	LANDERS	COLUMBIA	1950
CPC-1214	NO SAD SONGS FOR ME	MATE	COLUMBIA	1950
CPC-1215	CUSTOMS AGENT	FREIDMAN	COLUMBIA	1950
CPC-1218	WHEN YOU'RE SMILING	SANTLEY	COLUMBIA	1950
CPC-1219	CONVICTED	LEVIN	COLUMBIA	1950
CPC-1220	ROOKIE FIREMAN	FRIEDMAN	COLUMBIA	1950
CPC-1221	DAVID HARDING – COUNTER SPY	NAZARRO	COLUMBIA	1950
CPC-1222	BETWEEN MIDNIGHT AND DAWN	DOUGLAS	COLUMBIA	1950
CPC-1223	HE'S A COCKEYED WONDER	GODFREY	COLUMBIA	1950

CPC-1224	HARRIET CRAIG	SHERMAN	COLUMBIA	1950
CPC-1225	ON THE ISLE OF SOMOA	BERKE	COLUMBIA	1950
CPC-1226	TWO OF A KIND	LEVIN	COLUMBIA	1951
CPC-1228	STAGE TO TUCSON	MURPHY	COLUMBIA	1950
CPC-1230	EMERGENCY WEDDING	BUZZELL	COLUMBIA	1950
CPC-1231	AL JENNINGS OF OKLAHOMA	NAZARRO	COLUMBIA	1951
CPC-1232	FLYING MISSING	LEVIN	COLUMBIA	1950
CPC-1233	MASK OF THE AVENGER	KARLSON	COLUMBIA	1951
CPC-1234	COUNTERSPY MEETS SCOTLAND YARD	FRIEDMAN	COLUMBIA	1950
CPC-1235	HER FIRST ROMANCE	FRIEDMAN	COLUMBIA	1951
CPC-1237	TOUGHER THEY COME	NAZARRO	COLUMBIA	1950
CPC-1238	FLAME OF STAMBOUL	NAZARRO	COLUMBIA	1951
CPC-1239	LADY AND THE BANDIT	MURPHY	COLUMBIA	1951
CPC-1240	GASOLINE ALLEY	BERNDS	COLUMBIA	1951
CPC-1241	BAREFOOT MAILMAN	MCEVOY	COLUMBIA	1951
CPC-1242	SUNNY SIDE OF THE STREET	QUINE	COLUMBIA	1951
CPC-1243	NEVER TRUST A GAMBLER	MURPHY	COLUMBIA	1951
CPC-1244	SMUGGLERS GOLD	BERKE	COLUMBIA	1951
CPC-1245	MOB	PARRISH	COLUMBIA	1951
CPC-1246	CRIMINAL LAWYER	FRIEDMAN	COLUMBIA	1951
CPC-1248	PAULA	MATE	COLUMBIA	1952
CPC-1249	MY TRUE STORY	ROONEY	COLUMBIA	1951
CPC-1250	CHINA CORSAIR	NAZARRO	COLUMBIA	1951
CPC-1251	BIG GUSHER	LANDERS	COLUMBIA	1951
CPC-1252	SON OF DR. JEKYL	FRIEDMAN	COLUMBIA	1951
CPC-1253	ASSIGNMENT-PARIS	PARRISH	COLUMBIA	1952
CPC-1254	CHAIN OF CIRCUMSTANCES	JASON	COLUMBIA	1951
CPC-1255	CORKY OF GASOLINE ALLEY	BERNDS	COLUMBIA	1951
CPC-1256	SOUND OFF	QUINE	COLUMBIA	1952
CPC-1257	CAPT. PIRATE	MURPHY	COLUMBIA	1952
CPC-1258	MARRYING KIND	CUKOR	COLUMBIA	1952
CPC-1259	OKINAWA	JASON	COLUMBIA	1952
CPC-1260	MONTANA TERRITORY	NAZARRO	COLUMBIA	1952
CPC-1261	HAREM GIRL	BERNDS	COLUMBIA	1952
CPC-1263	LAST OF THE COMMANCHES	DE TOTH	COLUMBIA	1953
CPC-1264	RAINBOW 'ROUND MY SHOULDER	QUINE	COLUMBIA	1952
CPC-1265	TARGET HONG KONG	SEARS	COLUMBIA	1953
CPC-1266	ALL ASHORE	QUINE	COLUMBIA	1953
CPC-1267	AMBUSH AT TOMAHAWK GAP	SEARS	COLUMBIA	1953
CPC-1268	LET'S DO IT AGAIN	HALL	COLUMBIA	1953
CPC-1269	MISSION OVER KOREA	SEARS	COLUMBIA	1953
CPC-1270	LAST POSSE	WERKER	COLUMBIA	1953
CPC-1271	FROM HERE TO ETERNITY	ZINNEMANN	COLUMBIA	1953
CPC-1272	CRUISIN' DOWN THE RIVER	QUINE	COLUMBIA	1953
CPC-1273	EL ALAMEIN (GER: THAT WAS OUR ROMMEL)	WIGANKO	COLUMBIA	1953
CPC-1274	CHINA VENTURE	SIEGEL	COLUMBIA	1953
CPC-1276	BIG HEAT	LANG	COLUMBIA	1953
CPC-1278	GUN FURY	WALSH	COLUMBIA	1953
CPC-1280	MAN IN THE DARK	LANDERS	COLUMBIA	1953
CPC-1281	HUMAN DESIRE	LANG	COLUMBIA	1954
CPC-1283	NEBRASKAN	SEARS	COLUMBIA	1953
CPC-1284	BAD FOR EACH OTHER	RAPPER	COLUMBIA	1953
CPC-1285	IT SHOULD HAPPEN TO YOU	CUKOR	COLUMBIA	1954
CPC-1287	THREE FOR THE SHOW	POTTER	COLUMBIA	1955
CPC-1288	MASSACRE CANYON	SEARS	COLUMBIA	1954
CPC-1289	DRIVE A CROOKED MILE	QUINE	COLUMBIA	1954
CPC-1290	THEY RODE WEST	KARLSON	COLUMBIA	1954
CPC-1291	PUSHOVER	QUINE	COLUMBIA	1954
CPC-1292	OUTLAW STALLION	SEARS	COLUMBIA	1954
CPC-1293	THREE HOUSE TO FILL	WERKER	COLUMBIA	1954
CPC-1295	BLACK DAKOTAS	NAZARRO	COLUMBIA	1954
CPC-1298	PHFFT	ROBSON	COLUMBIA	1954
CPC-1299	WYOMING RENEGADES	SEARS	COLUMBIA	1954
CPC-1300	TIGHT SPOT	KARLSON	COLUMBIA	1955
CPC-1301	MY SISTER EILEEN	QUINE	COLUMBIA	1955
CPC-1302	CELL 2455-DEATH ROW	SEARS	COLUMBIA	1955

CPC-1303	THREE STRIPES IN THE SUN	MURPHY	COLUMBIA	1955
CPC-1305	BRING YOUR SMILE ALONG	EDWARDS	COLUMBIA	1955
CPC-1306	LAST FRONTIER	MANN	COLUMBIA	1955
CPC-1307	APACHE AMBUSH	SEARS	COLUMBIA	1955
CPC-1308	QUEEN BEE	MACDOUGALL	COLUMBIA	1955
CPC-1309	PICNIC	LOGAN	COLUMBIA	1955
CPC-1310	JUBAL	DAVES	COLUMBIA	1956
CPC-1311	EDDIE DUCHIN STORY	SIDNEY	COLUMBIA	1956
CPC-1313	FURY AT GUNSIGHT PASS	SEARS	COLUMBIA	1956
CPC-1314	YOU CAN'T RUN AWAY FROM IT	POWELL	COLUMBIA	1956
CPC-1315	HARDER THEY FALL	ROBSON	COLUMBIA	1956
CPC-1316	SECRET OF TREASURE MOUNTAIN	FRIEDMAN	COLUMBIA	1956
CPC-1318	SOLID GOLD CADILLAC	QUINE	COLUMBIA	1956
CPC-1319	OVER-EXPOSED	SEILER	COLUMBIA	1956
CPC-1320	HE LAUGHED LAST	EDWARDS	COLUMBIA	1956
CPC-1879	BAMBOLE (IT)	BOLOGNINI, COLOGINI	COLUMBIA	1965
CPC-1902	GUNS A POPPIN' (sh)	WHITE	COLUMBIA	1957
CPC-1903	FIFI BLOWS HER TOP (sh)	WHITE	COLUMBIA	1958
CPC-1904	RUSTY ROMEOS (sh)	WHITE	COLUMBIA	1957
CPC-1905	TRICKY CHICKS (sh)	WHITE	COLUMBIA	1957
CPC-1906	FLYING SAUCER DAFFY (sh)	WHITE	COLUMBIA	1958
CPC-1907	QUIZ WHIZZ (sh)	WHITE	COLUMBIA	1958
CPC-1908	PIES AND GUYS (sh)	WHITE	COLUMBIA	1958
CPC-1909	OUTER SPACE JITTERS (sh)	WHITE	COLUMBIA	1957
CPC-1910	SWEET AND HOT (sh)	WHITE	COLUMBIA	1958
CPC-1911	OIL'S WELL THAT ENDS WELL (sh)	WHITE	COLUMBIA	1958
CPC-1912	SAPPY BULLFIGHTERS (sh)	WHITE	COLUMBIA	1959
CPC-1913	TRIPLE CROSSED (sh)	WHITE	COLUMBIA	1959
CPC-3001	COWBOY FROM LONESOME RIVER	KLINE	COLUMBIA	1944
CPC-3002	CYCLONE PRAIRIE RANGERS	KLINE	COLUMBIA	1944
CPC-3003	COWBOY IN THE CLOUDS	KLINE	COLUMBIA	1943
CPC-3004	SUNDOWN VALLEY	KLINE	COLUMBIA	1944
CPC-3005	COWBOY CANTEEN	LANDERS	COLUMBIA	1944
CPC-3006	SADDLE LEATHER LAW	KLINE	COLUMBIA	1944
CPC-3007	SAGEBRUSH HEROES	KLINE	COLUMBIA	1945
CPC-3008	ROUGH RIDING JUSTICE	ABRAHAMS	COLUMBIA	1945
CPC-3009	SWING IN THE SADDLE	LANDERS	COLUMBIA	1944
CPC-3010	RETURN OF THE DURANGO KID	ABRAHAMS	COLUMBIA	1945
CPC-3011	BOTH BARRELS BLAZING	ABRAHAMS	COLUMBIA	1945
CPC-3012	RUSTLERS OF THE BADLANDS	ABRAHAMS	COLUMBIA	1945
CPC-3013	FRONTIER GUNLAW	ABRAHAMS	COLUMBIA	1946
CPC-3014	SING ME A SONG OF TEXAS	KEAYS	COLUMBIA	1945
CPC-3015	BLAZING THE WESTERN TRAIL	KEAYS	COLUMBIA	1945
CPC-3016	LAWLESS EMPIRE	KEAYS	COLUMBIA	1945
CPC-3017	ROCKIN' IN THE ROCKIES	KEAYS	COLUMBIA	1945
CPC-3018	RHYTHM ROUNDUP	KEAYS	COLUMBIA	1945
CPC-3019	OUTLAWS OF THE ROCKIES	NAZARRO	COLUMBIA	1945
CPC-3020	TEXAS PANHANDLE	NAZARRO	COLUMBIA	1945
CPC-3021	SONG OF THE PRAIRIE	NAZARRO	COLUMBIA	1945
CPC-3022	DESERT HORSEMAN	NAZARRO	COLUMBIA	1946
CPC-3023	GUNNING FOR VENGEANCE	NAZARRO	COLUMBIA	1946
CPC-3024	ROARING RANGERS	NAZARRO	COLUMBIA	1946
CPC-3025	THROW A SADDLE ON A STAR	NAZARRO	COLUMBIA	1946
CPC-3026	HEADING WEST	NAZARRO	COLUMBIA	1946
CPC-3027	GALLOPING THUNDER	NAZARRO	COLUMBIA	1946
CPC-3028	TWO-FISTED STRANGER	NAZARRO	COLUMBIA	1946
CPC-3029	THAT TEXAS JAMBOREE	NAZARRO	COLUMBIA	1946
CPC-3030	TERROR TRAIL	NAZARRO	COLUMBIA	1946
CPC-3031	LANDRUSH	KEAYS	COLUMBIA	1946
CPC-3032	COWBOY BLUES	NAZARRO	COLUMBIA	1946
CPC-3033	SINGING ON THE TRAIL	NAZARRO	COLUMBIA	1946
CPC-3034	FIGHTING FRONTIERSMAN	ABRAHAMS	COLUMBIA	1946
CPC-3035	SOUTH OF THE CHISHOLM TRAIL	ABRAHAMS	COLUMBIA	1947
CPC-3036	LONE STAR MOONLIGHT	NAZARRO	COLUMBIA	1946
CPC-3037	OVER THE SANTA FE TRAIL	NAZARRO	COLUMBIA	1947
CPC-3038	WEST OF DODGE CITY	NAZARRO	COLUMBIA	1947

CPC-3039	LONE HAND TEXAS	NAZARRO	COLUMBIA	1947
CPC-3040	LAW OF THE CANYON	NAZARRO	COLUMBIA	1947
CPC-3041	PRAIRIE RAIDERS	ABRAHAMS	COLUMBIA	1947
CPC-3042	STRANGER FROM PONCA CITY	ABRAHAMS	COLUMBIA	1947
CPC-3043	RIDERS OF THE LONE STAR	ABRAHAMS	COLUMBIA	1947
CPC-3044	SWING THE WESTERN WAY	ABRAHAMS	COLUMBIA	1947
CPC-3045	SMOKEY RIVER SERENADE	ABRAHAMS	COLUMBIA	1947
CPC-3046	SIX GUN LAW	NAZARRO	COLUMBIA	1948
CPC-3047	BUCKAROO FROM POWDER RIVER	NAZARRO	COLUMBIA	1947
CPC-3048	PHANTOM VALLEY	NAZARRO	COLUMBIA	1948
CPC-3049	LAST DAYS OF BOOTHILL	NAZARRO	COLUMBIA	1947
CPC-3050	ROSE OF SANTA FE	NAZARRO	COLUMBIA	1947
CPC-3051	WHIRLWIND RAIDERS	KEAYS	COLUMBIA	1948
CPC-3052	WEST OF SONORA	NAZARRO	COLUMBIA	1948
CPC-3053	SONG OF IDAHO	NAZARRO	COLUMBIA	1948
CPC-3054	BLAZING ACROSS THE PECOS	NAZARRO	COLUMBIA	1948
CPC-3055	TRAIL TO LAREDO	NAZARRO	COLUMBIA	1948
CPC-3056	ARKANSAS SWING	NAZARRO	COLUMBIA	1948
CPC-3057	SINGIN' SPURS	NAZARRO	COLUMBIA	1948
CPC-3058	EL DORADO PASS	NAZARRO	COLUMBIA	1948
CPC-3059	QUICK ON THE TRIGGER	NAZARRO	COLUMBIA	1948
CPC-3060	CHALLENGE OF THE RANGE	NAZARRO	COLUMBIA	1949
CPC-3061	SMOKY MOUNTAIN MELODY	NAZARRO	COLUMBIA	1948
CPC-3062	SOUTH OF DEATH VALLEY	NAZARRO	COLUMBIA	1949
CPC-3063	DESERT VIGILANTE	SEARS	COLUMBIA	1949
CPC-3064	LARAMIE	NAZARRO	COLUMBIA	1949
CPC-3065	HOME IN SAN ANTONE	NAZARRO	COLUMBIA	1949
CPC-3066	BLAZING TRAIL	NAZARRO	COLUMBIA	1949
CPC-3067	HORSEMEN OF THE SIERRAS	SEARS	COLUMBIA	1949
CPC-3068	BANDITS OF EL DORADO	NAZARRO	COLUMBIA	1949
CPC-3069	RENEGADES OF THE SAGE	NAZARRO	COLUMBIA	1949
CPC-3070	HOEDOWN	NAZARRO	COLUMBIA	1950
CPC-3071	FEUDIN' RHYTHM	BERNDS	COLUMBIA	1949
CPC-3072	OUTCAST OF BLACK MESA	NAZARRO	COLUMBIA	1950
CPC-3073	FRONTIER OUTPOST	NAZARRO	COLUMBIA	1950
CPC-3074	TRAIL OF THE RUSTLERS	NAZARRO	COLUMBIA	1950
CPC-3075	TEXAS DYNAMO	NAZARRO	COLUMBIA	1950
CPC-3076	STREETS OF GHOST TOWN	NAZARRO	COLUMBIA	1950
CPC-3077	ACROSS THE BADLANDS	SEARS	COLUMBIA	1950
CPC-3078	RAIDERS OF TOMAHAWK CREEK	SEARS	COLUMBIA	1950
CPC-3079	LIGHTNING GUNS	SEARS	COLUMBIA	1950
CPC-3080	PRAIRIE ROUNDUP	SEARS	COLUMBIA	1951
CPC-3081	RIDIN' THE OUTLAW TRAIL	SEARS	COLUMBIA	1951
CPC-3082	FORT SAVAGE RAIDERS	NAZARRO	COLUMBIA	1951
CPC-3083	SNAKE RIVER DESPERADOES	SEARS	COLUMBIA	1951
CPC-3084	BONANZA TOWN	SEARS	COLUMBIA	1951
CPC-3085	CYCLONE FURY	NAZARRO	COLUMBIA	1951
CPC-3086	KID FROM AMARILLO	NAZARRO	COLUMBIA	1951
CPC-3087	KID FROM AMARILLO	NAZARRO	COLUMBIA	1951
CPC-3088	SMOKY CANYON	SEARS	COLUMBIA	1952
CPC-3089	HAWK OF WILD RIVER	SEARS	COLUMBIA	1952
CPC-3090	LARAMIE MOUNTAINS	NAZARRO	COLUMBIA	1952
CPC-3091	ROUGH TOUGH WEST	NAZARRO	COLUMBIA	1952
CPC-3092	JUNCTION CITY	NAZARRO	COLUMBIA	1952
CPC-3093	KID FROM BROKEN GUN	SEARS	COLUMBIA	1952
CPC-3400	CORONER CREEK	ENRIGHT	COLUMBIA	1948
CPC-4001	BUSY BUDDIES – STOOGES	LORD	COLUMBIA	1944
CPC-4002	WEDDED BLISS	EDWARDS	COLUMBIA	1944
CPC-4003	BACHELOR DAZE	WHITE	COLUMBIA	1944
CPC-4004	YOU DEAR BOY – VERA VAGUE	WHITE	COLUMBIA	1943
CPC-4005	DR. FEEL MY PULSE – VERA VAGUE	WHITE	COLUMBIA	1944
CPC-4006	BOOBY DUPES – 3 STOOGES	LORD	COLUMBIA	1945
CPC-4007	HIS TALE IS TOLD – ANDY CLYDE	EDWARDS	COLUMBIA	1944
CPC-4008	YOU WERE NEVER UGLIER – ANDY CLYDE	WHITE	COLUMBIA	1944
CPC-4010	CRASH GOES THE HASH – STOOGES	WHITE	COLUMBIA	1944
CPC-4011	CRAZY LIKE A FOX – BILLY GILBERT	WHITE	COLUMBIA	1944

CPC-4013	IDLE ROOMERS – STOOGES	LORD	COLUMBIA	1943
CPC-4014	OH BABY – HUGH HERBERT	WHITE	COLUMBIA	1944
CPC-4015	OFF AGAIN ON AGAIN – SHEMP HOWARD	WHITE	COLUMBIA	1945
CPC-4016	OPEN SEASON FOR SAPS – SHEMP HOWARD	WHITE	COLUMBIA	1944
CPC-4017	DEFECTIVE DETECTIVES – EL BRENDEL	EDWARDS	COLUMBIA	1944
CPC-4018	PICK A PECK OF PLUMBERS – EL BRENDEL	WHITE	COLUMBIA	1944
CPC-4019	MOPEY DOPE – HARRY LANGDON	LORD	COLUMBIA	1944
CPC-4020	GENTS WITHOUT CENTS – STOOGES	WHITE	COLUMBIA	1944
CPC-4021	HEATHER AND YOU – ANDY CLYDE	EDWARDS	COLUMBIA	1944
CPC-4022	THREE PEST IN A MESS – STOOGES	LORD	COLUMBIA	1945
CPC-4023	WOO WOO (I SHOULD WORRY*)	WHITE	COLUMBIA	1945
CPC-4025	WOO WOO (I SHOULD WORRY*)	WHITE	COLUMBIA	1945
CPC-4026	SHE SNOOPS TO CONQUER – VERA VAGUE	WHITE	COLUMBIA	1944
CPC-4027	STRIFE OF THE PARTY – VERA VAGUE	EDWARDS	COLUMBIA	1944
CPC-4028	DANCE DUNCE DANCE – EDDIE FOY JR.	WHITE	COLUMBIA	1945
CPC-4030	IDIOTS DELUXE – STOOGES	WHITE	COLUMBIA	1945
CPC-4031	JURY GOES 'ROUND AND 'ROUND –VAGUE	WHITE	COLUMBIA	1945
CPC-4032	HISS AND YELL – VERA VAGUE	WHITE	COLUMBIA	1946
CPC-4033	IF A BODY MEETS A BODY - STOOGES	WHITE	COLUMBIA	1945
CPC-4037	SPOOK TO ME – ANDY CLYDE	EDWARDS	COLUMBIA	1945
CPC-4038	A HIT WITH A MISS – SHEMP HOWARD	EDWARDS, WHITE	COLUMBIA	1945
CPC-4039	MAYOR'S HUSBAND – HUGH HERBERT	EDWARDS	COLUMBIA	1945
CPC-4040	ANDY CLYDE SHORT		COLUMBIA	
CPC-4041	ANDY CLYDE SHORT		COLUMBIA	
CPC-4042	CALLING ALL FIBBERS – VERA VAGUE	WHITE	COLUMBIA	1945
CPC-4043	BIRD IN THE HEAD – STOOGES	BERNDS	COLUMBIA	1946
CPC-4045	BEER BARREL POLECATS – STOOGES	WHITE	COLUMBIA	1946
CPC-4047	WHEN THE WIFE'S AWAY – HUGH HERBERT	BERNDS	COLUMBIA	1946
CPC-4048	WHERE THE PEST BEGINS – SHEMP HOWARD	EDWARDS	COLUMBIA	1945
CPC-4049	ANDY CLYDE SHORT		COLUMBIA	
CPC-4051	HIGH BLOOD PLEASURE – LANE-SHILLING	WHITE	COLUMBIA	1945
CPC-4052	SOCIETY MUGS – SHEMP HOWARD	BERNDS	COLUMBIA	1946
CPC-4053	THREE LOAN WOLVES – STOOGES	WHITE	COLUMBIA	1946
CPC-4055	GET ALONG LITTLE ZOMBIE – HUGH HERBERT	BERNDS	COLUMBIA	1946
CPC-4056	HALF WITS HOLIDAY – STOOGES	WHITE	COLUMBIA	1947
CPC-4057	RHYTHM AND WEEP – STOOGES	WHITE	COLUMBIA	1946
CPC-4058	MONKEY BUSINESSMEN – STOOGES	BERNDS	COLUMBIA	1946
CPC-4059	ANDY CLYDE SHORT		COLUMBIA	
CPC-4060	VERA VAGUE SHORT		COLUMBIA	
CPC-4061	STERLING HOLLOWAY SHORT		COLUMBIA	
CPC-4062	AIN'T LOVE CUCKOO – RICHARD LANE	WHITE	COLUMBIA	1946
CPC-4063	G. I. WANNA HOME – STOOGES	WHITE	COLUMBIA	1946
CPC-4064	BRIDE AND GLOOM – SHEMP HOWARD	BERNDS	COLUMBIA	1947
CPC-4065	MR. WRIGHT GOES WRONG – S. HOLLOWAY	WHITE	COLUMBIA	1946
CPC-4067	3 LITTLE PIRATES – STOOGES	BERNDS	COLUMBIA	1946
CPC-4069	ANDY CLYDE SHORT		COLUMBIA	
CPC-4070	FIDDLERS THREE – STOOGES	WHITE	COLUMBIA	1948
CPC-4071	FRIGHT NIGHT – STOOGES	BERNDS	COLUMBIA	1947
CPC-4072	CENSORSHIP – H. HERBERT		COLUMBIA	
CPC-4074	HONEYMOON BLUES – HUGH HERBERT	BERNDS	COLUMBIA	1946
CPC-4075	HOT HEIR – HUGH HERBERT	BERNDS	COLUMBIA	1947
CPC-4076	HECTIC HONEYMOON – STERLING HOLLOWAY	BERNDS	COLUMBIA	1947
CPC-4077	OUT WEST – STOOGES	BERNDS	COLUMBIA	1947
CPC-4078	SO'S YOUR ANTENNA – HARRY VON ZELL	WHITE	COLUMBIA	1946
CPC-4079	TWO JILLS AND JACK – ANDY CLYDE	WHITE	COLUMBIA	1947
CPC-4080	JOE DERITA		COLUMBIA	
CPC-4081	MEET MR. MISCHIEF – HARRY VON ZELL	BERNDS	COLUMBIA	1947
CPC-4082	SQUAREHEADS OF ROUND THE TABLE – STOOGES	BERNDS	COLUMBIA	1948
CPC-4083	RENO-VATED – VERA VAGUE	WHITE	COLUMBIA	1946
CPC-4084	NERVOUS SHAKEDOWN – HUGH HERBERT	LORD	COLUMBIA	1947
CPC-4085	MORON THAN OFF – STERLING HOLLOWAY	WHITE	COLUMBIA	1946
CPC-4086	GOOD BAD EGG – JOE DERITA	WHITE	COLUMBIA	1947
CPC-4087	HOLD THAT LION – STOOGES	WHITE	COLUMBIA	1947
CPC-4088	SING A SONG OF SIX PANTS – STOOGES	WHITE	COLUMBIA	1947
CPC-4091	I'M A MONKEY'S UNCLE – STOOGES	WHITE	COLUMBIA	1948
CPC-4093	PARDON MY CLUTCH – STOOGES	BERNDS	COLUMBIA	1948

CPC-4094	HOT SCOTS – STOOGES	BERNDS	COLUMBIA	1948
CPC-4095	BRIDELESS GROOM – STOOGES	BERNDS	COLUMBIA	1947
CPC-4096	WIFE TO SPARE – ANDY CLYDE	BERNDS	COLUMBIA	1947
CPC-4097	CUPID GOES NUTS – FRITZ FELD	WHITE	COLUMBIA	1947
CPC-4098	TRAINING FOR TROUBLE – RICHARD LANE	WHITE	COLUMBIA	1947
CPC-4099	RICHARD LANE SHORT		COLUMBIA	
CPC-4101	WAITING IN THE LURCH – JOE BESSER	BERNDS	COLUMBIA	1949
CPC-4102	STOOGES (SHORT)		COLUMBIA	
CPC-4103	SHIVERING SHERLOCKS – STOOGES	LORD	COLUMBIA	1948
CPC-4104	ALL GUMMED UP – STOOGES	WHITE	COLUMBIA	1947
CPC-4107	THREE HAMS ON RYE – STOOGES	WHITE	COLUMBIA	1950
CPC-4108	STOOGES (SHORT)		COLUMBIA	
CPC-4111	CRIME ON THEIR HANDS – STOOGES	BERNDS	COLUMBIA	1948
CPC-4112	WHO DONE IT? – STOOGES	BERNDS	COLUMBIA	1949
CPC-4114	FUELIN' AROUND – STOOGES	BERNDS	COLUMBIA	1949
CPC-4116	HOKUS POKUS – STOOGES	WHITE	COLUMBIA	1949
CPC-4117	STERLING HOLLOWAY SHORT		COLUMBIA	
CPC-4118	GO CHASE YOURSELF	WHITE	COLUMBIA	1948
CPC-4119	STOOGES (SHORT)		COLUMBIA	
CPC-4120	JOE DERITA SHORT		COLUMBIA	
CPC-4121	PARDON MY LAMBCHOP	WHITE	COLUMBIA	1948
CPC-4123	HE'S IN AGAIN – RICHARD LANE	BERNDS	COLUMBIA	1949
CPC-4124	RICHARD LAND SHORT		COLUMBIA	
CPC-4126	SHEEPISH WOLF	BERNDS	COLUMBIA	1948
CPC-4128	PINCH IN TIME – HUGH HERBERT	LORD	COLUMBIA	1948
CPC-4129	STOOGES (SHORT)		COLUMBIA	
CPC-4132	RADIO RIOT – HARRY VON ZELL	BERNDS	COLUMBIA	1949
CPC-4133	HUGH HERBERT SHORT		COLUMBIA	
CPC-4134	RICHARD LANE SHORT		COLUMBIA	
CPC-4135	VERA VAGUE SHORT		COLUMBIA	
CPC-4136	MISS IN A MESS	WHITE	COLUMBIA	1949
CPC-4140	VAGABOND LOAFERS – STOOGES		COLUMBIA	1949
CPC-4159	MALICE IN THE PALACE – STOOGES	WHITE	COLUMBIA	1949
CPC-4178	CORNY CASANOVAS – STOOGES	WHITE	COLUMBIA	1952
CPC-4179	HULA-LA-LA – STOOGES	MCCOLLUM	COLUMBIA	1951
CPC-4180	LISTEN JUDGE – STOOGES	BERNDS	COLUMBIA	1952
CPC-4181	HE COOKED HIS GOOSE – STOOGES	WHITE	COLUMBIA	1952
CPC-4182	UP IN DAISY'S PENTHOUSE – STOOGES	WHITE	COLUMBIA	1953
CPC-4183	GENTS IN A JAM – STOOGES	BERNDS	COLUMBIA	1952
CPC-4184	HUGH HERBERT SHORT		COLUMBIA	
CPC-4187	HUGH HERBERT SHORT		COLUMBIA	
CPC-4188	EDDIE QUILLAN SHORT		COLUMBIA	
CPC-4189	EDDIE QUILLAN SHORT		COLUMBIA	
CPC-4190	ANDY CLYDE SHORT		COLUMBIA	
CPC-4191	ANDY CLYDE SHORT		COLUMBIA	
CPC-4192	FRAIDY CAT – JOE BESSER AND HAWTHORNE	WHITE	COLUMBIA	1951
CPC-4193	JOE BESSER AND HAWTHORN SHORT		COLUMBIA	
CPC-4194	CUCKOOS ON A CHOO CHOO – STOOGES	WHITE	COLUMBIA	1952
CPC-4195	JOE BESSER (sh)		COLUMBIA	
CPC-4196	STOOGES (sh)		COLUMBIA	
CPC-4197	LOOSE LOOT – STOOGES	WHITE	COLUMBIA	1953
CPC-4198	EDDIE QUILLAN SHORT		COLUMBIA	
CPC-4199	TRICKY DICKS – STOOGES	WHITE	COLUMBIA	1953
CPC-4200	THREE DARK HORSES – STOOGES	WHITE	COLUMBIA	1952
CPC-4201	BUBBLE TROUBLE – STOOGES	WHITE	COLUMBIA	1953
CPC-4203	GOOF ON THE ROOF – STOOGES	WHITE	COLUMBIA	1953
CPC-4204	EDDIE QUILLAN SHORT		COLUMBIA	
CPC-4205	JOE BESSER SHORT		COLUMBIA	
CPC-4206	ANDY CLYDE GETS SPRING CHICKEN	WHITE	COLUMBIA	1939
CPC-4208	INCOME TAX SAPPY – STOOGES	WHITE	COLUMBIA	1954
CPC-4209	MUSTY MUSKATEERS – STOOGES	WHITE	COLUMBIA	1954
CPC-4210	SPOOKS – STOOGES	WHITE	COLUMBIA	1953
CPC-4211	PALS AND GALS – STOOGES	WHITE	COLUMBIA	1954
CPC-4212	PARDON MY BACKFIRE – STOOGES	WHITE	COLUMBIA	1953
CPC-4213	A-HUNTING THEY DID GO – EDDIE QUILLAN	WHITE	COLUMBIA	1948
CPC-4214	DOGGIE IN THE BEDROOM – EDDIE QUILLAN	WHITE	COLUMBIA	1954

CPC-4216	SHOT IN THE FRONTIER – STOOGES	WHITE	COLUMBIA	1954
CPC-4217	KNUTZ KNIGHTS – STOOGES	WHITE	COLUMBIA	1954
CPC-4218	SCOTCHED IN SCOTLAND – STOOGES	WHITE	COLUMBIA	1954
CPC-4219	ANDY CLYDE SHORT		COLUMBIA	
CPC-4220	A MINER AFFAIR – ANDY CLYDE	WHITE	COLUMBIA	1945
CPC-4223	FLING IN THE RING – STOOGES	WHITE	COLUMBIA	1955
CPC-4224	STOOGES (SHORT)		COLUMBIA	
CPC-4227	CREEPS – STOOGES	WHITE	COLUMBIA	1956
CPC-4228	HEAVENLY DAZE – STOOGES	WHITE	COLUMBIA	1948
CPC-4229	STONE AGE ROMEOS – STOOGES	WHITE	COLUMBIA	1955
CPC-4244	RUMPUS IN THE HAREM - STOOGES	WHITE	COLUMBIA	1956
CPC-4245	HOT STUFF – STOOGES	WHITE	COLUMBIA	1956
CPC-4246	SCHEMEING SCHEMERS – STOOGES	WHITE	COLUMBIA	1956
CPC-4247	COMMOTION ON THE OCEAN - STOOGES	WHITE	COLUMBIA	1956
CPC-4250	MUSCLE UP A LITTLE CLOSER (sh)	WHITE	COLUMBIA	1957
CPC-4251	HOOFS AND GOOFS – STOOGES	WHITE	COLUMBIA	1957
CPC-4252	MERRY MIXUP – STOOGES	WHITE	COLUMBIA	1957
CPC-4253	SPACE SHIP SAPPY – STOOGES	WHITE	COLUMBIA	1957
CPC-8007	LORNA DOONE	KARLSON	COLUMBIA	1951
CPC-8008	ROAR OF THE IRON HORSE	BENNET, CARR	COLUMBIA	1951
CPC-8009	TEXANS NEVER CRY	MCDONALD	COLUMBIA	1951
CPC-8010	VALLEY OF FIRE		COLUMBIA	1951
CPC-8011	MAGIC CARPET	LANDERS	COLUMBIA	1951
CPC-8011	MYSTERIOUS ISLAND (serial)	BENNET	COLUMBIA	1951
CPC-8014	TEXAS RANGERS	LEDERMAN	COLUMBIA	1951
CPC-8015	BRIGAND	KARLSON	COLUMBIA	1952
CPC-8016	SILVER CANYON	ENGLISH	COLUMBIA	1951
CPC-8017	SCANDAL SHEET	KARLSON	COLUMBIA	1952
CPC-8026	WHIRLWIND	ENGLISH	COLUMBIA	1951
CPC-8029	INDIAN UPRISING	NAZARRO	COLUMBIA	1952
CPC-8030	CALIFORNIA CONQUEST	LANDERS	COLUMBIA	1952
CPC-8031	YANK IN KOREA	LANDERS	COLUMBIA	1951
CPC-8032	HILLS OF UTAH	ENGLISH	COLUMBIA	1951
CPC-8033	HARLEM GLOBETROTTERS	BROWN, JASON	COLUMBIA	1951
CPC-8035	MAN IN THE SADDLE	DE TOTH	COLUMBIA	1951
CPC-8036	PURPLE HEART DIARY	QUINE	COLUMBIA	1951
CPC-8037	JUNGLE JIM IN THE FORBIDDEN LAND	LANDERS	COLUMBIA	1952
CPC-8038	JUNGLE MAN-HUNT	LANDERS	COLUMBIA	1951
CPC-8039	KING OF THE CONGO (serial)	BENNET, GRISSELL	COLUMBIA	1952
CPC-8040	CAPTAIN VIDEO (serial)	BENNET, GRISSELL	COLUMBIA	1951
CPC-8041	BOOTS MALONE	DIETERLE	COLUMBIA	1952
CPC-8042	TEN TALL MEN	GOLDBECK	COLUMBIA	1951
CPC-8043	FIRST TIME	TASHLIN	COLUMBIA	1952
CPC-8044	BRAVE WARRIOR	BENNET	COLUMBIA	1952
CPC-8045	OLD WEST	ARCHAINBAUD	COLUMBIA	1952
CPC-8047	MEMBER OF THE WEDDING	ZINNEMANN	COLUMBIA	1952
CPC-8049	GOLDEN HAWK	SALKOW	COLUMBIA	1952
CPC-8053	PRINCE OF PIRATES	SALKOW	COLUMBIA	1953
CPC-8054	MY SIX CONVICTS	FREGONESE	COLUMBIA	1952
CPC-8055	BLACKHAWK		COLUMBIA	1952
CPC-8056	DEATH OF A SALESMAN	BENEDEK	COLUMBIA	1951
CPC-8057	FOUR POSTER	REIS	COLUMBIA	1952
CPC-8061	CRIPPLE CREEK	NAZARRO	COLUMBIA	1952
CPC-8062	SNIPER	DMYTRYK	COLUMBIA	1952
CPC-8063	NIGHT STAGE TO GALVESTON	ARCHAINBAUD	COLUMBIA	1952
CPC-8066	AFFAIR IN TRINIDAD	SHERMAN	COLUMBIA	1952
CPC-8067	BLUE CANADIAN ROCKIES	ARCHAINBAUD	COLUMBIA	1952
CPC-8068	PRISONERS OF THE CASBAH	BARE	COLUMBIA	1953
CPC-8071	HAPPY TIME	FLEISCHER	COLUMBIA	1952
CPC-8072	APACHE COUNTRY	ARCHAINBAUD	COLUMBIA	1952
CPC-8074	MEMBER OF THE WEDDING	ZINNEMANN	COLUMBIA	1952
CPC-8078	EIGHT IRON MEN	DMYTRYK	COLUMBIA	1952
CPC-8079	BARBED WIRE	ARCHAINBAUD	COLUMBIA	1952
CPC-8082	CAINE MUTINY	DMYTRYK	COLUMBIA	1954
CPC-8085	YANK IN INDO-CHINA	GRISSELL	COLUMBIA	1952
CPC-8087	SERPENT OF THE NILE	CASTLE	COLUMBIA	1953

CPC-8088	LAST TRAIN FROM BOMBAY	SEARS	COLUMBIA	1952
CPC-8089	SAVAGE MUTINY	BENNET	COLUMBIA	1953
CPC-8090	VOODOO TIGER	BENNET	COLUMBIA	1952
CPC-8091	JUGGLER	DMYTRYK	COLUMBIA	1953
CPC-8092	JACK MCCALL – DESPERADO	SALKOW	COLUMBIA	1953
CPC-8093	PIRATES OF TRIPOLI	FEIST	COLUMBIA	1955
CPC-8094	WAGON TEAM	ARCHAINBAUD	COLUMBIA	1952
CPC-8095	LOST PLANET	BENNET	COLUMBIA	1953
CPC-8100	SON OF GERONIMO (serial)	BENNET	COLUMBIA	1952
CPC-8103	PATHFINDER	SALKOW	COLUMBIA	1952
CPC-8109	SLAVES OF BABYLON	CASTLE	COLUMBIA	1953
CPC-8115	SKY COMMANDS	SEARS	COLUMBIA	1953
CPC-8116	HANGMAN'S KNOT	HUGGINS	COLUMBIA	1952
CPC-8117	SALOME	DIETERLE	COLUMBIA	1953
CPC-8118	ON TOP OF OLD SMOKY	ARCHAINBAUD	COLUMBIA	1953
CPC-8120	FLAME OF CALCUTTA	FRIEDMAN	COLUMBIA	1953
CPC-8121	STRANGE FASCINATION	HAAS	COLUMBIA	1952
CPC-8122	SIREN OF BAGDAD	QUINE	COLUMBIA	1953
CPC-8125	WINNING OF THE WEST, THE	ARCHAINBAUD	COLUMBIA	1953
CPC-8127	IRON GLOVE	CASTLE	COLUMBIA	1954
CPC-8128	GOLDTOWN GHOST RIDERS	ARCHAINBAUD	COLUMBIA	1953
CPC-8130	CONQUEST OF COCHISE	CASTLE	COLUMBIA	1953
CPC-8132	CHARGE OF THE LANCERS	CASTLE	COLUMBIA	1954
CPC-8140	ONE GIRL'S CONFESSION	HAAS	COLUMBIA	1953
CPC-8146	PACK TRAIN	ARCHAINBAUD	COLUMBIA	1953
CPC-8149	GREAT ADV OF CAPTAIN KIDD (serial)	ABRAHAMS, GOULD	COLUMBIA	1953
CPC-8150	KILLER APE	BENNET	COLUMBIA	1953
CPC-8151	SAGINAW TRAIL	ARCHAINBAUD	COLUMBIA	1953
CPC-8170	MISS SADIE THOMPSON	BERNHARDT	COLUMBIA	1953
CPC-8173	FORT TI	CASTLE	COLUMBIA	1953
CPC-8178	STRANGER WORE A GUN	DE TOTH	COLUMBIA	1953
CPC-8188	LAST OF THE PONY RIDERS	ARCHAINBAUD	COLUMBIA	1953
CPC-8191	JESSE JAMES VS DALTSON	CASTLE	COLUMBIA	1954
CPC-8193	DRUMS OF TAHITI	CASTLE	COLUMBIA	1954
CPC-8194	GUNFIGHTERS OF THE NORTHWEST	BENNET, GOULD	COLUMBIA	1954
CPC-8197	SARACEN BLADE	CASTLE	COLUMBIA	1954
CPC-8204	JUNGLE MAN-EATERS	SHOLEM	COLUMBIA	1954
CPC-8205	RIDING WITH BUFFALO BILL (serial)	BENNET	COLUMBIA	1954
CPC-8206	LAW VS. BILLY THE KID	CASTLE	COLUMBIA	1954
CPC-8211	TEENAGE CRIME WAVE	SEARS	COLUMBIA	1955
CPC-8214	BATTLE OF ROGUE RIVER	CASTLE	COLUMBIA	1954
CPC-8247	MIAMI STORY	SEARS	COLUMBIA	1954
CPC-8249	CHICAGO SYNDICATE	SEARS	COLUMBIA	1955
CPC-8250	SEMINOLE UPRISING	BELLAMY	COLUMBIA	1955
CPC-8252	MASTERSON OF KANSAS	CASTLE	COLUMBIA	1954
CPC-8253	MAD MAGICIAN	BRAHM	COLUMBIA	1954
CPC-8257	ADVENTURES OF CAPTAIN AFRICA (serial)	BENNET	COLUMBIA	1955
CPC-8260	IT CAME FROM BENEATH THE SEA	GORDON	COLUMBIA	1955
CPC-8262	CANNIBAL ATTACK	SHOLEM	COLUMBIA	1954
CPC-8263	DEVIL GODDESS	BENNET	COLUMBIA	1955
CPC-8264	BAMBOO PRISON	SEILER	COLUMBIA	1954
CPC-8265	JUNGLE MOON-MEN	GOULD	COLUMBIA	1955
CPC-8271	MAN FROM LARAMIE	MANN	COLUMBIA	1955
CPC-8273	TEN WANTED MEN	HUMBERSTONE	COLUMBIA	1955
CPC-8274	WOMEN'S PRISON	SEILER	COLUMBIA	1955
CPC-8281	NEW ORLEANS UNCENSORED	CASTLE	COLUMBIA	1955
CPC-8284	GUN THAT WON THE WEST	CASTLE	COLUMBIA	1955
CPC-8285	CREATURE WITH THE ATOM BRAIN	CAHN	COLUMBIA	1955
CPC-8286	DUEL ON THE MISSISSIPPI	CASTLE	COLUMBIA	1955
CPC-8289	BATTLE STATIONS	SEILER	COLUMBIA	1956
CPC-8294	LONG GREY LINE	FORD	COLUMBIA	1955
CPC-8301	FIVE AGAINST THE HOUSE	KARLSON	COLUMBIA	1955
CPC-8305	NIGHT HOLDS TERROR	STONE	COLUMBIA	1955
CPC-8306	LAWLESS STREET	LEWIS	COLUMBIA	1955
CPC-8307	EARTH VS. THE FLYING SAUCERS	SEARS	COLUMBIA	1956
CPC-8308	COUNT THREE AND PRAY	SHERMAN	COLUMBIA	1955

CPC-8310	HOUSTON STORY	CASTLE	COLUMBIA	1956
CPC-8311	BLACKJACK KETCHUM-DESPERADO	BELLAMY	COLUMBIA	1956
CPC-8313	INSIDE DETROIT	SEARS	COLUMBIA	1956
CPC-8319	FLYING FONTAINES	SHERMAN	COLUMBIA	1959
CPC-8321	CROOKED WEB	JURAN	COLUMBIA	1955
CPC-8322	AUTUMN LEAVES	ALDRICH	COLUMBIA	1956
CPC-8333	STORM CENTER	TARADASH	COLUMBIA	1956
CPC-8335	HOT BLOOD	RAY	COLUMBIA	1956
CPC-8336	BLAZING THE OVERLAND TRAIL (serial)	BENNET	COLUMBIA	1956
CPC-8344	SEVENTH CALVARY	LEWIS	COLUMBIA	1956
CPC-8346	REPRISAL	SHERMAN	COLUMBIA	1956
CPC-8352	ROCK AROUND THE CLOCK	SEARS	COLUMBIA	1956
CPC-8355	MIAMI EXPOSE	SEARS	COLUMBIA	1956
CPC-8357	27TH DAY	ASHER	COLUMBIA	1957
CPC-8359	WHITE SQUAW	NAZARRO	COLUMBIA	1956
CPC-8368	CHA-CHA-CHA BOOM	SEARS	COLUMBIA	1956
CPC-8383	DON'T KNOCK THE ROCK	SEARS	COLUMBIA	1957
CPC-8385	YOUNG DON'T CRY	WERKER	COLUMBIA	1957
CPC-8389	TIJUANA STORY, THE	KARDOS	COLUMBIA	1957
CPC-8400	SEVENTH VOYAGE OF SINBAD	JURAN	COLUMBIA	1958
CPC-8422	LIFE BEGINS AT 17	DREIFUSS	COLUMBIA	1958
CPC-8426	BATTLE OF THE CORAL SEA	WENDKOS	COLUMBIA	1959
CPC-8429	GOING STEADY	SEARS	COLUMBIA	1958
CPC-8450	BUCHANAN RIDES ALONE	BOETTICHER	COLUMBIA	1958
CPC-8462	1001 ARABIAN NIGHTS (t)	KINNEY	COLUMBIA	1959
CPC-8484	13 WEST STREET	LEACOCK	COLUMBIA	1962
CPC-8515	MYSTERIOUS ISLAND (UK)	ENDFIELD	COLUMBIA	1962
CPC-8518	WHO WAS THAT LADY?	SIDNEY	COLUMBIA	1960
CPC-8533	WACKIEST SHIP IN THE ARMY	MURPHY	COLUMIA	1960
CPC-8559	TINGLER	CASTLE	COLUMBIA	1959
CPC-8596	INTERNS, THE	SWIFT	COLUMBIA	1962
CPC-8622	VALLEY OF THE DRAGONS	BERNDS	COLUMBIA	1961
CPC-8649	TWIST AROUND THE CLOCK	RUDOLPH	COLUMBIA	1961
CPC-8688	SHIP OF FOOLS	KRAMER	COLUMBIA	1965
CPC-8719	COLLECTOR (UK)	WYLER	COLUMBIA	1965
CPC-AK	ASSIGNMENT K (UK)	GUEST	COLUMBIA	1968
CPC-AR	SEVERED HEAD (UK)	CLEMENT	COLUMBIA	1970
CPC-B	BERSERK (UK)	O'CONNELLY	COLUMBIA	1967
CPC-BC	BUTTERCUP CHAIN (UK)	MILLER	COLUMBIA	1970
CPC-BWC	BEFORE WINTER COMES (UK)	THOMPSON	COLUMBIA	1969
CPC-CF	CACTUS FLOWER	SAKS	COLUMBIA	1969
CPC-CK	CASTLE KEEP	POLLACK	COLUMBIA	1969
CPC-COM	COMIC	REINER	COLUMIA	1969
CPC-CP	IN COLD BLOOD	BROOKS	COLUMBIA	1967
CPC-CR	CASINO ROYALE	FELDMAN	COLUMBIA	1967
CPC-CROM	CROMWELL (UK)	HUGHES	COLUMBIA	1970
CPC-D	DUFFY (UK)	PARRISH	COLUMBIA	1968
CPC-DA	DANDY IN ASPIC (UK)	MANN	COLUMBIA	1968
CPC-DA	DEADLY AFFAIR	LUMET	COLUMBIA	1966
CPC-DAS	DIVORCE AMERICAN STYLE	YORKIN	COLUMBIA	1967
CPC-DBR	DON'T RAISE THE BRIDGE, LOWER THE RIVER (UK)	PARIS	COLUMBIA	1968
CPC-DF	DOCTOR FAUSTUS (UK)	BURTON, COGHILL	COLUMBIA	1967
CPC-EL	ENTER LAUGHING	REINER	COLUMBIA	1967
CPC-ER	EASY RIDER	HOPPER	COLUMBIA	1969
CPC-EX	EXECUTIONER (UK)	WANAMAKER	COLUMBIA	1970
CPC-FF	FRAGMENT OF FEAR (UK)	SARAFIAN	COLUMBIA	1970
CPC-GD	GUESS WHO'S COMING FOR DINNER	KRAMER	COLUMBIA	1967
CPC-GIO	GAME IS OVER	VADIM	COLUMBIA	1966
CPC-GS	GETTING STRAIGHT	RUSH	COLUMBIA	1970
CPC-H	HAMLET (UK)	RICHARDSON	COLUMBIA	1969
CPC-H	HAMMERHEAD (UK)	MILLER	COLUMBIA	1968
CPC-HLS	HOOK, LINE AND SINKER	MARSHALL	COLUMBIA	1969
CPC-HUS	HUSBANDS	CASSAVETES	COLUMBIA	1970
CPC-I	INTERLUDE	BILLINGTON	COLUMBIA	1968
CP-CIC	BROTHERHOOD OF SATAN	MCEVEETY	COLUMBIA	1970
CPC-IC	INVESTIGATION OF A CITIZEN	PETRI	COLUMBIA	1971

CPC-INS	I NEVER SANG FOR MY FATHER	CATES	COLUMBIA	1970
CPC-KL	KING LEAR (UK)	BROOK	COLUMBIA	1971
CPC-LBJ	LIBERATION OF LB JONES	WYLER	COLUMBIA	1970
CPC-LGW	LOOKING GLASS WAR (UK)	PIERSON	COLUMBIA	1969
CP-CLK	CLAIRE'S KNEE (FR: LE GENOU DE CLAIRE 1970)	ROHMER	COLUMBIA	1971
CPC-M	MAROONED	STURGES	COLUMBIA	1969
CPC-MC	MACHINE GUN MCCAIN	MONTALDO	COLUMBIA	1969
CPC-MDM	MOST DANGEROUS MAN ALIVE	DWAN	COLUMBIA	1961
CPC-MFAS	MAN FOR ALL SEASONS (UK)	ZINNEMANN	COLUMBIA	1967
CPC-MG	MCKENNA'S GOLD	STEVENSON	COLUMBIA	1969
CPC-NOG	NIGHT OF THE GENERALS (UK)	LITVAK	COLUMBIA	1967
CPC-O	OLIVER! (UK)	REED	COLUMBIA	1968
CPC-O	OTLEY (UK)	CLEMENT	COLUMBIA	1969
CPC-OM	ONCE MORE, WITH FEELING! (UK)	DONEN	COLUMBIA	1960
CPCP	COTTONPICKIN' CHICKENPICKERS	JACKSON	SOUTHEASTERN PICT.	1967
CPC-POH	PURSUIT OF HAPPINESS	MULLIGAN	COLUMBIA	1971
CPC-R	RECKONING (UK)	GOLD	COLUMBIA	1970
CP-CS	CALIFORNIA SPLIT	ALTMAN	COLUMBIA	1974
CP-CS	CHOSEN SURVIVORS	ROLEY	COLUMBIA	1974
CPC-SS	SOUTHERN STAR (UK)	HAYERS	COLUMBIA	1969
CPC-SS	SWIMMER	PERRY	COLUMBIA	1968
CPC-T	RING-A-DING RHYTHM! (UK: IT'S TRAD, DAD!)	LESTER	COLUMBIA	1962
CPC-TC	30 IS A DANGEROUS AGE, CYNTHIA (UK)	MCGRATH	COLUMBIA	1968
CPC-TG	TORTURE GARDEN (UK)	FRANCIS	COLUMBIA	1967
CPC-TGU	TAKE A GIRL LIKE YOU	MILLER	COLUMBIA	1970
CPC-TSWL	TO SIR, WITH LOVE (UK)	CLAVELL	COLUMBIA	1967
CPC-TYM	THANK YOU ALL VERY MUCH (UK: TOUCH OF LOVE)	HUSSEIN	COLUMBIA	1969
CPC-VS	VIRGIN SOLDIERS (UK)	DEXTER	COLUMBIA	1969
CPC-WB	WRONG BOX (UK)	FORBES	COLUMBIA	1966
CPC-WC	RUN WILD, RUN FREE (UK)	SARAFIAN	COLUMBIA	1969
CPC-YA	YOUNG AMERICANS	GRASSHOFF	COLUMBIA	1967
CPC-YCW	YOU CAN'T WIN 'EM ALL (UK)	COLLINSON	COLUMBIA	1970
CPD	CLEAR AND PRESENT DANGER	NOYCE	PARAMOUNT	1994
CP-DOL	DOLLARS ($)	BROOKS	COLUMBIA	1971
CP-DW	DEATH WISH	WINNER	COLUMBIA	1974
CP-DW	DOCTOR'S WIVES	SCHAEFER	COLUMBIA	1971
CP-FC	FAT CITY	HUSTON	COLUMBIA	1972
CP-FOC	FORTY CARATS	KATSELAS	COLUMBIA	1973
CP-FP	FOR PETE'S SAKE	YATES	COLUMBIA	1974
CP-GB	GO-BETWEEN (UK)	LOSEY	COLUMBIA	1971
CP-HBWJ	HAPPY BIRTHDAY WANDA JANE	ROBSON	COLUMBIA	1971
CP-HLS	HOOK, LINE AND SINKER	MARSHALL	COLUMBIA	1969
CP-HO	HORSEMAN, THE	FRANKENHEIMER	COLUMBIA	1971
CP-IM	IMAGES	ALTMAN	COLUMBIA	1972
CP-L4	LAST REBEL	MCCOY	COLUMBIA	1971
CP-LD	LAST DETAIL	ASHBY	COLUMBIA	1973
CP-LF	LIVING FREE	COUFFER	COLUMBIA	1972
CP-LGR	LET THE GOOD TIMES ROLL	ABEL; GAVIN	COLUMBIA	1973
CP-LM	LOVE MACHINE	HALEY, JR.	COLUMBIA	1971
CP-LPS	LAST PICTURE SHOW	BOGDANOVICH	COLUMBIA	1971
CP-NC	NEW CENTURIONS	FLEISCHER	COLUMBIA	1972
CP-OC	OKLAHOMA CRUDE	KRAMER	COLUMBIA	1974
CP-OF	ODESSA FILE	NEAME	COLUMBIA	1974
CP-OP	OWL & THE PUSSYCAT	ROSS	COLUMBIA	1970
CP-PJ	POPE JOAN	ANDERSON	COLUMBIA	1972
CP-SH	SHAMUS	KULIK	COLUMBIA	1972
CP-SK	STONE KILLER	WINNER	COLUMBIA	1973
CP-SOUV	SUMMER WISHES, WINTER DREAMS	CATES	COLUMBIA	1973
CP-SUBC	STAND UP AND BE COUNTED	COOPER	COLUMBIA	197S
CP-TFM	TO FIND A MAN	KULIK	COLUMBIA	1972
CP-TGS	THERE'S A GIRL IN MY SOUP (UK)	BOULTING	COLUMBIA	1970
CP-V	OLD DRACULA	DONNER	COLUMGIA	1974
CP-VP	VALACCI PAPERS	CROMWELL	UNITED ARTISTS	1944
CP-WID	LOVE AND PAIN AND THE WHOLE DAMN THING	PAKULA	COLUMBIA	1973
CP-YW	YOUNG WINSTON	ATTENBOROUGH	COLUMBIA	1972
CR	CHAIN REACTION	DAVIS	20th CENTURY FOX	1996

CR	CLAUDE RAINS	portrait	UNIV	
CR	CRAZE	FRANCIS	WARNER BROS	1974
CR	CRIMSON ROMANCE	HOWARD	MASCOT	1934
CR	CROOKED ROAD (UK)	CHAFFEY	GALA	1965
CR	CUBAN REBEL GIRLS	MAHON	JOSEPH BRENNER ASSO	1959
CR	CYCLONE RANGER	HILLER	SPECTRUM	1935
CR	HEARTBREAK RIDGE (FR: CREVECOEUR)	DUPONT	TUDOR	1955
CR	MASTER OF BANKDAM/CROWTHERS OF BANKDAM* (UK)	FORDE	EAGLE-LION	1947
CR	SANDERS OF THE RIVER/CONGO RAID* (UK)	KORDA	UNITED ARTISTS	1935
CRBB	COOL RUNNINGS	TURTELTAUB	BUENA VISTA	1993
CRISP	DONALD CRISP	portrait	WARNER BROS.	
CRS	CURSE OF THE PINK PANTHER	EDWARDS	UNITED ARTISTS	1983
CS	BATTLE OF THE SEXES (UK)	CRICHTON	CONTINENTAL	1960
CS	CHANGE OF SEASONS	LANG	20th CENTURY FOX	1980
CS	CLEAN SLATE	JACKSON	MGM	1994
CS	COAST OF SKELETONS (UK)	LYNN	SEVEN ARTS	1965
CS	CODE OF SILENCE	DAVIS	ORION	1985
CS	COLDITZ STORY (UK)	HAMILTON	DCA	1955
CS	CONFESSIONS OF A NAZI SPY	LITVAK	WARNER BROS	1939
CS	CONNIE STEVENS	portrait		
CS	COPPER SKIES	WARREN	20th CENTURY FOX	1957
CS	CROOKED SKY (UK)	CASS	TUDOR	1957
CS	CRUEL SEA (UK)	FREND	UNIVERSAL	1953
CS	CRY FROM THE STREETS (UK)	GILBERT	TUDOR	1958
CS	CUL-DE-SAC (UK)	POLANSKI	COMPTON	1966
CS	CURLY SUE	HUGHES	WARNER BROS	1991
CSTP	COME SEE THE PARADISE	PARKER	20th CENTURY FOX	1990
CT	CANTERBURY TALE (UK)	POWELL, PRESSBURGER	EAGLE-LION	1944
CT	CAROL THURSTON	portrait	RKO	
CT	CHRISTMAS TREE (UK)	CLARK	CHILDRENS FILM FOUN.	1966
CT	CLAIRE TREVOR	portrait	RKO, REPUB. UNIV.	
CT	COMMON TOUCH (UK)	BAXTER	ANGLO-AMERICAN	1941
CT	CONSPIRACY THEORY	DONNER	WARNER BROS	1997
CT	CROOK'S TOUR (UK)	BAXTER	ANGLO-AMERICAN	1941
CT	CRY TERROR!	STONE	MGM	1957
CT	GUEST (UK: CARETAKER)	DONNER	JANUS	1963
CT	HURLYBURLY	MICHAELS	FINELINE	1998
CT	IT ALL CAME TRUE	SEILER	WARNER BROS.	1940
CT	TINTAN CONTRA EL HOMBRE LOBO (MEX)	SOLARES	PELMEX	1964
CT-3	STUDIO GIRL	GIBLYN	SELECT	1918
CT-6	GOOD NIGHT, PAUL	EDWARDS	SELECT	1918
CT-10	MRS. LEFFINGWELL'S BOOTS	EDWARDS	SELECT	1918
CT-14	PRIMITIVE LOVER	FRANKLIN	ASSOCIATED FIRST NAT.	1922
CT-15	EAST IS WEST	FRANKLIN	ASSOCIATED FIRST NAT.	1922
CT-17	DANGEROUS MAID	HEERMAN	ASSOCIATED FIRST NAT.	1923
CT-3543A	THIN LINE BETWEEN LOVE AND HATE	LAWRENCE	NEW LINE CINEMA	1996
CTBB	COCKTAIL	DONALDSON	BUENA VISTA	1988
CTBB	CONFESSIONS OF A TEENAGE DRAMA QUEEN	SUGERMAN	BUENA VISTA	2004
CTC	CONSTANTINE AND THE CROSS	DE FELICE	EMBASSY	1961
CTS	CHASING THE SUN	LA VARRE	WARNER BROS	1956
CTW	CODE OF THE WEST	BERKE	RKO	1947
CU	GERT AND DAISY CLEAN UP (UK)	ROGERS	BUTCHER'S	1942
CUF	COURAGE UNDER FIRE	ZWICK	20th CENTURY FOX	1996
CUM-2	RUSTLING FOR CUPID	CUMMINGS	FOX FILM	1926
CUM-3	MIDNIGHT KISS	CUMMINGS	FOX FILM	1926
CURWOOD-2	GOLD HUNTERS	HURST	DAVIS DISTRIBUTING	1925
CUUN	FOUR A.M.	CONSULMAN	FOX FILM	1928
CV	CODE 7, VICTIM 5 (UK: VICTIM 5)	LYNN	COLUMBIA	1964
CW	CAROLE WELLS	portrait	UNIV	
CW	CAVALIER OF THE WEST	MCCARTHY	ARTCLASS	1931
CW	CIRCUS WORLD	HATHAWAY	PARAMOUNT	1965
CW	CLINT WALKER	portrait	WARNER BROS	
CW	COLD WIND IN AUGUST	SINGER	TROY FILMS	1960
CW	COOL WORLD	BAKSHI	PARAMOUNT	1992
CW	CUSTER OF THE WEST (UK)	SIODMAK	CINERAMA	1967
CW	IN SEARCH OF THE CASTAWAYS	STEVENSON	BUENA VISTA	1962

CW-ART	CHILD IS WAITING	CASSAVETES	UNITED ARTISTS	1963
CWH	COUNTRY WESTERN HOEDOWN	KING		1967
CX	COVER GIRL KILLER	BISHOP	FANFARE	1960
CXM	CONCHITA MONTENEGRO	portrait	MGM	
CY	COMIN AT YA! (IT)	BALDI	FILMWAYS	1981
CY	CYBORG	PYUN	CANNON	1989
D	D.A.R.Y.L.	WINCER	COLUMBIA	1986
D	DANGEROUS WOMAN	GYLLENHAAL	GRAMERCY	1993
D	DAREDEVIL	STRINGER	TRANS INT'L	1972
D	DECEIVER	PATE	MGM	1998
D	DEEP, THE	YATES	COLUMBIA	1977
D	DEFILERS, THE	FROST	SONNEY AMUSEMENT	1965
D	DEMOBBED (UK)	BLAKELEY	BUTCHER'S	1946
D	DESPAIR	FASSBINDER	RAINER WERNER FASS.	1978
D	DESPERADOS ARE IN TOWN	NEWMANN	20th CENTURY FOX	1956
D	DESTRUCTORS, THE	LYON	FEATURE FILM CORP	1967
D	DIABOLIQUE	CHECHIK	WARNER BROS	1996
D	DIGGSTOWN	RITCHIE	MGM	1992
D	DINGAKA	UYS	EMBASSY	1965
D	DISCLOSURE	LEVINSON	WARNER BROS	1994
D	DIVE! (GOING UNDER)	TRAVIS	WARNER BROS	1990
D	DREAMER	NOSSECK	20th CENTURY FOX	1979
D	DREAMING (UK)	BAXTER	EALING	1944
D	DREAMS	KUROSAWA	WARNER BROS	1990
D	DREAMS (SWE: KVINNODROM)	BERGMAN	JANUS	1955
D	DRIVER, THE	HILL	20th CENTURY FOX	1978
D	DUDES	SPHEERIS	NEW CENTURY/VISTA.	1987
D	DUNSTON CHECKS IN	KWAPIS	20th CENTURY FOX	1995
D	DUTCH	FAIMAN	20th CENTURY FOX	1991
D	DUTCHMAN (UK)	HARVEY	CONTINENTAL	1967
D	GOING UNDER (DIVE!*)	TRAVIS	WARNER BROS	1990
D	HEAVEN KNOWS, MR ALLISON	HUSTON	20th CENTURY FOX	1957
D	MAGNIFICENT MATADOR	BOETTICHER	20th CENTURY FOX	1955
D	TREACHERY ON THE HIGH SEAS (UK)	REINERT	FILM ALLIANCE	1936
D&B	DEAD AND BURIED	SHERMAN	AVCO EMBASSY	1981
D&S	DRACULA AND SON	MOLINARO	QUNITED ARTISTSRTET	1979
D-1	FOR ART'S SAKE (sh)	CHASE	PATHE EXCHANGE	1923
D1	KILL ME TOMORROW (UK)	FISHER	TUDOR	1957
D-1	TROLLEY TROUBLES (sh)	GOULDING	PATHE EXCHANGE	1921
D-1	UNNAMED ROLIN PROJECT (sh)	WHITING	PATHE EXCHANGE	1915
D-1	WHAT EVERY ICEMAN KNOWS (sh)	YATES, MCCAREY	MGM	1927
D-2	CALL OF THE CUCKOOS (sh)	BRUCKMAN	MGM	1927
D-2	ROUGH SEAS (sh)	GOULDING	PATHE EXCHANGE	1921
D-2	UNNAMED ROLIN PROJECT (sh)	WHITING	PATHE EXCHANGE	1915
D-2	WHITE WINGS (sh)	JESKE	PATHE EXCHANGE	1923
D-3	DODGE YOUR DEBTS (sh)	KENTON	PATHE EXCHANGE	1921
D-3	LOVE 'EM AND FEED 'EM (sh)	BRUCKMAN	MGM	1927
D-3	PICK AND SHOVEL (sh)	JESKE	PATHE EXCHANGE	1923
D-3	UNNAMED ROLIN PROJECT (sh)	WHITING	PATHE EXCHANGE	1915
D-4	FIGHTING FATHERS (sh)	GUIOL	MGM	1927
D-4	FRESH EGGS (sh)	HOWE	PATHE EXCHANGE	1923
D-4	THAT'S GRATITUDE	CRAVEN	COLUMBIA	1934
D-4	ZERO HERO (sh)	KENTON	PATHE EXCHANGE	1921
D-5	JEALOUSY	NEILL	COLUMBIA	1934
D-5	KILL OR CURE (sh)	PEMBROKE	PATHE EXCHANGE	1923
D-5	LUCKY NUMBER (sh)	KENTON	PATHE EXCHANGE	1921
D-5	TELL IT TO THE JUDGE (sh)	MCCAREY, YATES	MGM	1928
D-6	FINGER PRINTS (sh)	CEDER	PATHE EXCHANGE	1923
D-6	PASS THE GRAVY (sh)	GUIOL, MCCAREY	MGM	1928
D-7	COLLARS AND CUFFS (sh)	JESKE	PATHE EXCHANGE	1923
D-7	DUMB DADDIES (sh)	YATES	MGM	1928
D-8	CAME THE DAWN (sh)	HEATH, MCCAREY	MGM	1928
D-8	LIVE WIRES (sh)	HOWE	PATHE EXCHANGE	1923
D-8	WHITE LIES	BULGAKOV	COLUMBIA	1934
D-9	BLOW BY BLOW (sh)	MCCAREY	MGM	1928
D-9	GAS AND AIR (sh)	PEMBROKE	PATHE EXCHANGE	1923

D9	PROUD VALLEY (UK)	TENNYSON	SUPREME	1940
D-9	WHOLE TOWN'S TALKING	FORD	COLUMBIA	1935
D-9	WOULD YOU FORGIVE?	DUNLAP	FOX FILM	1920
D-10	MILLES OF GODS	NEILL	COLUMBIA	1935
D-10	SHOULD WOMEN DRIVE? (sh)	MCCAREY	MGM	1928
D-11	BEST MAN WINS	KENTON	COLUMBIA	1935
D-11	FOR GUESTS ONLY (sh)	HOWE	PATHE EXCHANGE	1923
D-11	IT'S ALL YOURS	NUGENT	COLUMBIA	1937
D-12	CARNIVAL	LANG	COLUMBIA	1935
D-12	ORANGES AND LEMONS (sh)	JESKE	PATHE EXCHANGE	1923
D13	BOY FRIEND, THE	GUIOL	MGM	1928
D-13	TAKE THE AIR (sh)	CEDER	PATHE EXCHANGE	1923
D-13	TOGETHER WE LIVE	MACK	COLUMBIA	1935
D-14	SHORT ORDERS (sh)	PEMBROKE	PATHE EXCHANGE	1923
D-15	SAVE THE SHIP (sh)	JESKE, ROACH	PATHE EXCHANGE	1923
D-16	UNCOVERED WAGON (sh)	HOWE	PATHE EXCHANGE	1923
D-17	MAN ABOUT TOWN (sh)	JESKE	PATHE EXCHANGE	1923
D-18	NO PETS (sh)	HOWE	PATHE EXCHANGE	1923
D-19	SCORCHING SANDS (sh)	WILLIAMSON, ROACH	PATHE EXCHANGE	1923
D-20	KNOCKOUT (sh)	POWERS	PATHE EXCHANGE	1923
D-21	JOIN THE CIRCUS (sh)	JESKE	PATHE EXCHANGE	1923
D-22	WHOLE TRUTH (sh)	CEDER	PATHE EXCHANGE	1923
D-23	GO WEST (sh)	POWERS	PATHE EXCHANGE	1923
D-24	DEAR OLD PAL (sh)		PATHE EXCHANGE	1923
D-25	LOVEY-DOVEY (sh)	POWERS	PATHE EXCHANGE	1923
D-26	GET BUSY (sh)	HAYES	PATHE EXCHANGE	1924
D-27	AWFUL TRUTH	MCCAREY	COLUMBIA	1937
D-27	OLD WAR HORSE (sh)	JESKE	PATHE EXCHANGE	1926
D-28	AT FIRST SIGHT (sh)	ROACH	PATHE EXCHANGE	1924
D-29	IT'S A JOY (IT'S A BOY) (sh)	JESKE	PATHE EXCHANGE	1923
D-30	BAR-FLY (sh)	POWERS	PATHE EXCHANGE	1924
D-31	FULLY INSURED (sh)	JESKE	PATHE EXCHANGE	1923
D-32	FRIEND HUSBAND (WHY MARRY?) (sh)	HOWE	PATHE EXCHANGE	1924
D-33	BIG IDEA (sh)	JESKE	PATHE EXCHANGE	1924
D-34	MAN PAYS (sh)	POWERS	PATHE EXCHANGE	1924
D-35	PERFECT LADY (sh)	PARROTT	PATHE EXCHANGE	1924
D-36	POWDER AND SMOKE (sh)	PARROTT	PATHE EXCHANGE	1924
D-37	ONE OF THE FAMILY (sh)	PEMBROKE	PATHE EXCHANGE	1924
D-38	LOVE'S REWARD (sh)	POWERS	PATHE EXCHANGE	1924
D-39	JUST A MINUTE (sh)	PARROTT	PATHE EXCHANGE	1924
D-40	LOVE'S DETOUR (sh)	PARROTT	PATHE EXCHANGE	1924
D-41	MEN OF THE NIGHT	HILLYER	COLUMBIA	1934
D-41	OUR LITTLE NELL (sh)	POWERS	PATHE EXCHANGE	1924
D-42	BEHIND OF THE EVIDENCE	HILLYER	COLUMBIA	1935
D-42	HARD KNOCKS (sh)	PARROTT	PATHE EXCHANGE	1924
D-43	NORTH OF 50-50 (sh)	POWERS	PATHE EXCHANGE	1924
D-44	DON'T FORGET (sh)	PARROTT	PATHE EXCHANGE	1924
D-45	FRAIDY CAT (sh)	PARROTT	PATHE EXCHANGE	1924
D-46	UP AND AT 'EM (sh)	POWERS	PATHE EXCHANGE	1924
D-47	PUBLICITY PAYS (sh)	MCCAREY	PATHE EXCHANGE	1924
D-48	POSITION WANTED (sh)	CEDER	PATHE EXCHANGE	1924
D-49	BIG KICK (sh)	GUIOL, ROACH	PATHE EXCHANGE	1925
D-50	ONE AT A TIME (sh)	CEDER	PATHE EXCHANGE	1924
D-51	BOUNCER (sh)	CEDER, GUIOL	PATHE EXCHANGE	1925
D-52	APRIL FOOL (sh)	CEDER	PATHE EXCHANGE	1924
D-53	SOLID IVORY (sh)	CEDER	PATHE EXCHANGE	1925
D-54	STOLEN GOODS (sh)	MCCAREY	PATHE EXCHANGE	1924
D-55	BEFORE TAKING (sh)	CEDER	PATHE EXCHANGE	1924
D-56	YOUNG OLDFIELD (sh)	MCCAREY	PATHE EXCHANGE	1924
D-57	FAST BLACK (sh)	GARNETT	PATHE EXCHANGE	1924
D-58	JEFFRIES JR. (sh)	MCCAREY	PATHE EXCHANGE	1924
D-59	RIDER OF THE KITCHEN RANGE (sh)	GARNETT, JESKE	PATHE EXCHANGE	1925
D-60	WHY HUSBANDS GO MAD (sh)	MCCAREY	PATHE EXCHANGE	1924
D-61	ALL WOOL (sh)	GARNETT	PATHE EXCHANGE	1925
D-62	SEEING NELLIE HOME (sh)	MCCAREY	PATHE EXCHANGE	1924
D-63	GRIEF OF BAGDAD (SHEIKS IN BAGDAD) (sh)	LEDERMAN	PATHE EXCHANGE	1925

D-64	TEN MINUTE EGG (sh)	MCCAREY	PATHE EXCHANGE	1924
D-65	ACCIDENTAL ACCIDENTS (sh)	MCCAREY	PATHE EXCHANGE	1924
D-66	BIG RED RIDING HOOD (sh)	MCCAREY	PATHE EXCHANGE	1925
D-67	WHY MEN WORK (sh)	MCCAREY	PATHE EXCHANGE	1924
D-68	SWEET DADDY (sh)	MCCAREY	PATHE EXCHANGE	1924
D-69	OUTDOOR PAJAMAS (sh)	MCCAREY	PATHE EXCHANGE	1924
D-70	SITTIN' PRETTY (sh)	MCCAREY	PATHE EXCHANGE	1924
D-71	TOO MANY MAMMAS (sh)	MCCAREY	PATHE EXCHANGE	1924
D-72	BUNGALOW BOOBS (sh)	MCCAREY	PATHE EXCHANGE	1924
D-73	ALL WET (sh)	MCCAREY	PATHE EXCHANGE	1924
D-74	POOR FISH (sh)	MCCAREY	PATHE EXCHANGE	1924
D-75	ROYAL RAZZ (sh)	MCCAREY	PATHE EXCHANGE	1924
D-76	RAT'S KNUCKLES (sh)	MCCAREY	PATHE EXCHANGE	1925
D-77	HELLO BABY (sh)	MCCAREY	PATHE EXCHANGE	1925
D-78	FIGHTING FLUID (sh)	MCCAREY	PATHE EXCHANGE	1925
D-79	FAMILY ENTRANCE (sh)	MCCAREY	PATHE EXCHANGE	1925
D-80	SHOULD HUSBANDS BE WATCHED? (sh)	MCCAREY	PATHE EXCHANGE	1925
D-81	PLAIN AND FANCY GIRLS (sh)	MCCAREY	PATHE EXCHANGE	1925
D-82	IS MARRIAGE THE BUNK? (sh)	MCCAREY	PATHE EXCHANGE	1925
D-83	HOLD EVERYTHING (sh)	GUIOL, MCCAREY	PATHE EXCHANGE	1925
D-84	ARE HUSBANDS HUMAN? (sh)	BARROWS	PATHE EXCHANGE	1925
D-85	SURE MIKE (sh)	GUIOL	PATHE EXCHANGE	1925
D-86	TOL'ABLE ROMEO (sh)	ROBBINS	PATHE EXCHANGE	1925
D-87	IN THE GREASE (sh)	HOWE	PATHE EXCHANGE	1925
D-88	CHASING THE CHASER (sh)	LAUREL	PATHE EXCHANGE	1925
D-89	UNFRIENDLY ENEMIES (sh)	LAUREL	PATHE EXCHANGE	1925
D-90	YES, YES NANETTE (sh)	HENNECKE, LAUREL	PATHE EXCHANGE	1925
D-118	YOU'LL NEVER GET RICH	LANFIELD	COLUMBIA	1941
D-156	3 LITTLE PIGSKINS (STOOGES)	MCCAREY	COLUMBIA	1934
D-196	JAM SESSION	BARTON	COLUMBIA	1944
D-206	SHADOW		COLUMBIA	
D-213	MOVIE MANIACS - STOOGES	LORD	COLUMBIA	1936
D-217	DISORDER IN COURT (sh)	WHITE	COLUMBIA	1936
D-339	RETURN OF DANIEL BOONE	HILLYER	COLUMBIA	1941
D-401	PLAY THE PONIES – STOOGES	LAMONT	COLUMBIA	1937
D-401	PLAYING THE PONIES (sh)	LAMONT	COLUMBIA	1937
D-402	SITTER DOWNERS (sh)	LORD	COLUMBIA	1937
D-409	COLLINS-KENNEDY		COLUMBIA	
D-413	CHARLEY CHASE		COLUMBIA	
D-419	THREE LITTLE SEW AND SEWS (sh)	LORD	COLUMBIA	1939
D-420	TASSELS IN THE AIR (sh)	CHASE	COLUMBIA	1938
D-422	HEALTHY, WEALTHY AND DUMB (sh)	LORD	COLUMBIA	1938
D-423	VIOLENT IS THE WORD FOR CURLY (sh)	CHASE	COLUMBIA	1938
D-426	THREE MISSING LINKS (sh)	WHITE	COLUMBIA	1938
D-429	SMITH AND DALE		COLUMBIA	
D-431	CHARLEY CHASE		COLUMBIA	
D-433	SMITH AND DALE		COLUMBIA	
D-434	ANDY CLYDE		COLUMBIA	
D-436	ANDY CLYDE – SHEMP HOWARD		COLUMBIA	
D-437	CHARLEY CHASE		COLUMBIA	
D-440	ANDY CLYDE		COLUMBIA	
D-441	DANNY WEBB		COLUMBIA	
D-442	ANDY CLYDE		COLUMBIA	
D-444	DUCKING THEY DID GO - STOOGES (sh)	LORD	COLUMBIA	1939
D-450	CHARLEY CHASE		COLUMBIA	
D-451	THREE SAPPY PEOPLE (sh)	WHITE	COLUMBIA	1939
D-452	TEACHER'S PEST CHARLEY CHASE (sh)	KRAMER, ULLMAN	COLUMBIA	1939
D-459	ANDY CLYDE - SHEMP HOWARD		COLUMBIA	
D-460	ALL AMERICAN BLONDES - ANDY CLYDE (sh)	LORD	COLUMBIA	1939
D-461	ROCKIN' THRU THE ROCKIES (sh)	WHITE	COLUMBIA	1940
D-462	PLUMBING WE WILL GO (sh)	LORD	COLUMBIA	1940
D-462	STOOGES (SHORT)		COLUMBIA	
D-463	ANDY CLYDE GETS SPRING CHICKEN (sh)	WHITE	COLUMBIA	1939
D-464	CHARLEY CHASE		COLUMBIA	
D-465	NUTTY BUT NICE (sh)	WHITE	COLUMBIA	1940
D-466	ANDY CLYDE		COLUMBIA	

D-469	CHARLEY CHASE		COLUMBIA	
D-471	YOU NAZTY SPY! (sh)	WHITE	COLUMBIA	1940
D-474	NO CENSUS, NO FEELING (sh)	LORD	COLUMBIA	1940
D-476	ANDY CLYDE - SHEMP HOWARD		COLUMBIA	
D-485	DUTIFUL BUT DUMB (sh)	LORD	COLUMBIA	1941
D-486	BOOBS IN ARMS (sh)	WHITE	COLUMBIA	1940
D-487	ALL THE WORLD'S A STOOGE (sh)	LORD	COLUMBIA	1941
D-487	STOOGES (SHORT)		COLUMBIA	
D-488	ACHE IN EVERY STAKE - STOOGES (sh)	LORD	COLUMBIA	1941
D-489	ANDY CLYDE		COLUMBIA	
D492	GIANT BEHEMOTH (UK: BEHEMOTH THE SEA MONSTER)	HICKOX, LOURIE	ALLIED ARTISTS	1959
D-494	ANDY CLYDE		COLUMBIA	
D-496	EL BRENDEL		COLUMBIA	
D-497	EL BRENDEL		COLUMBIA	
D-499	EL BRENDEL		COLUMBIA	
D-502	ALAN MOWBRAY SHORT		COLUMBIA	
D-505	ROSCOE KARNS		COLUMBIA	
D-509	ANDY CLYDE		COLUMBIA	
D-511	SOME MORE OF SAMOA (sh)	LORD	COLUMBIA	1941
D-519	WHAT'S THE MATADOR? – STOOGES	WHITE	COLUMBIA	1942
D-527	MATRI-PHONY (sh)	H EDWARDS	COLUMBIA	1942
D-531	QUACK SERVICE (sh)	EDWARDS	COLUMBIA	1943
D-532	3 SMART SAPS – STOOGES	WHITE	COLUMBIA	1942
D-537	BLITZ ON THE FRITZ (sh)	WHITE	COLUMBIA	1943
D-538	WOLF IN THIEF'S CLOTHING (sh)	WHITE	COLUMBIA	1943
D-539	SOCK-A-BYE BABY (sh)	WHITE	COLUMBIA	1942
D-541	EL BRENDEL		COLUMBIA	
D-541	HIS WEDDING SCARE (sh)	LORD	COLUMBIA	1943
D-545	HIS GIRL'S WORST FRIEND (sh)	WHITE	COLUMBIA	1943
D-546	FARMER FOR A DAY (sh)	WHITE	COLUMBIA	1943
D-547	MAID MADE MAD (sh)	LORD	COLUMBIA	1943
D-548	SOCKS APPEAL (sh)	EDWARDS	COLUMBIA	1943
D-551	3 LITTLE TWERPS – STOOGES	EDWARDS	COLUMBIA	1943
D-552	BLONDE AND GROOM (sh)	EDWARDS	COLUMBIA	1943
D-553	CHESTER CONKLIN		COLUMBIA	
D-554	HERE COMES MR. ZERK (sh)	EDWARDS	COLUMBIA	1943
D-556	TWO SAPLINGS (sh)	EDWARDS	COLUMBIA	1943
D-558	WHAT A SOLDIER (sh) not released		COLUMBIA	1943
D-559	SHOT IN THE ESCAPE (sh)	WHITE	COLUMBIA	1943
D-561	HE WAS ONLY FEUDIN' (sh)	EDWARDS	COLUMBIA	1943
D-562	ROOKIE'S COOKIE (sh)	WHITE	COLUMBIA	1943
D-565	HUGH HERBERT (sh)		COLUMBIA	
D-566	PITCHIN' IN THE KITCHEN (sh)	WHITE	COLUMBIA	1943
D-595	STOOGES (SHORT)		COLUMBIA	
D-600	COMMUNITY SING - GENE MORGAN		COLUMBIA	
D-611	COMMUNITY SING - GENE MORGAN		COLUMBIA	
D-631	COMMUNITY SING		COLUMBIA	
D-632	COMMUNITY SING		COLUMBIA	
D-655	COMMUNITY SING - GENE MORGAN		COLUMBIA	
D-697	MR. SMUG (sh)		COLUMBIA	1943
D-769	THE PHANTOM	EASON, WRIGHT	COLUMBIA	1943
D-805	BLACK ARROW	LANDERS	COLUMBIA	1944
D831	MAVERICK (tv)		AMERICAN BROAD.	1950s
D-911	RIDERS OF THE WHISTLING PINES	ENGLISH	COLUMBIA	1949
D-934	TRIPLE THREAT (mistake? 933)	YARBROUGH	COLUMBIA	1948
D-996	SANTA FE	PICHEL	COLUMBIA	1951
D-1106	UNKNOWN	LEVIN	COLUMBIA	1946
D-1007	HEY, ROOKIE	BARTON	COLUMBIA	1944
D-1210	MILITARY ACADEMY WITH THAT 10TH AVENUE GANG	LEDERMAN	COLUMBIA	1950
D-1212	FRIGHTENED CITY (KILLER THAT STALKED NEW YORK)	MCEVOY	COLUMBIA	1950
D-1257	CAPTAIN PIRATE (CAPTAIN BLOOD, FUGITIVE)	MURPHY	COLUMBIA	1952
D-3067	HORSEMEN OF THE SIERRAS	SEARS	COLUMBIA	1949
D-3087	KID FROM AMARILLO (error on some - should be 3086)	NAZARRO	COLUMBIA	1951
D-3087	PECOS RIVER	SEARS	COLUMBIA	1951
D-4005	DOCTOR, FEEL MY PULSE (sh)	WHITE	COLUMBIA	1944
D-4005	DR. FEEL MY PULSE – VERA VAGUE	WHITE	COLUMBIA	1944

D-4009	GOLD IS WHERE YOU LOSE IT (sh)	WHITE	COLUMBIA	1944
D-4011	CRAZY LIKE A FOX – BILLY GILBERT	WHITE	COLUMBIA	1944
D-4012	HIS HOTEL SWEET (sh)	EDWARDS	COLUMBIA	1944
D-4014	OH BABY – HUGH HERBERT	WHITE	COLUMBIA	1944
D-4024	TWO LOCAL YOKELS (sh)	WHITE	COLUMBIA	1945
D-4025	KNIGHT AND A BLONDE (sh)	EDWARDS	COLUMBIA	1944
D-4029	SNOOPER SERVICE (sh)	EDWARDS	COLUMBIA	1945
D-4035	PISTOL PACKIN' NITWITS (sh)	EDWARDS	COLUMBIA	1945
D-4036	WIFE DECOY (sh)	EDWARDS	COLUMBIA	1945
D-4038	A HIT WITH A MISS – SHEMP HOWARD	EDWARDS, WHITE	COLUMBIA	1945
D-4039	MAYOR'S HUSBAND – HUGH HERBERT	EDWARDS	COLUMBIA	1945
D-4040	ANDY CLYDE SHORT		COLUMBIA	
D-4040	MINER AFFAIR (sh)	WHITE	COLUMBIA	1945
D-4041	ANDY CLYDE SHORT		COLUMBIA	
D-4041	BLONDE STAYED ON (sh)	EDWARDS	COLUMBIA	1946
D-4044	MICRO-PHONIES (sh)	BERNDS	COLUMBIA	1945
D-4046	THREE TROUBLEDOERS (sh)	BERNDS	COLUMBIA	1946
D-4047	WHEN THE WIFE'S AWAY – HUGH HERBERT	BERNDS	COLUMBIA	1946
D-4048	JIGGERS, MY WIFE (sh)	WHITE	COLUMBIA	1946
D-4049	ANDY CLYDE SHORT		COLUMBIA	
D-4049	YOU CAN'T FOOL A FOOL (sh)	WHITE	COLUMBIA	1946
D-4050	UNCIVIL WAR BIRDS (sh)	WHITE	COLUMBIA	1946
D-4054	MR. NOISY (sh)	BERNDS	COLUMBIA	1946
D-4055	GET ALONG LITTLE ZOMBIE (sh)	BERNDS	COLUMBIA	1946
D-4059	ANDY PLAYS HOOKEY (sh)	BERNDS	COLUMBIA	1946
D-4060	HEADIN' FOR A WEDDIN' (sh)	WHITE	COLUMBIA	1946
D-4060	VERA VAGUE SHORT		COLUMBIA	
D-4061	SCOOPER DOOPER (sh)	BERNDS	COLUMBIA	1947
D-4061	STERLING HOLLOWAY SHORT		COLUMBIA	
D-4066	HOT WATER (sh)	BERNDS	COLUMBIA	1946
D-4067	THREE LITTLE PIRATES – STOOGES	BERNDS	COLUMBIA	1946
D-4068	PARDON MY TERROR (sh)	BERNDS	COLUMBIA	1946
D-4069	ANDY CLYDE SHORT		COLUMBIA	
D-4069	SUNK IN THE SINK (sh)	WHITE	COLUMBIA	1949
D-4072	CENSORSHIP – H. HERBERT		COLUMBIA	
D-4072	SHOULD HUSBANDS MARRY? (sh)	LORD	COLUMBIA	1947
D-4073	CRABBIN' IN THE CABIN (sh)	WHITE	COLUMBIA	1948
D-4078	SO'S YOUR ANTENNA – HARRY VON ZELL	WHITE	COLUMBIA	1946
D-4079	TWO JILLS AND JACK – ANDY CLYDE	WHITE	COLUMBIA	1947
D-4080	JOE DERITA		COLUMBIA	
D-4080	SLAPPILY MARRIED (sh)	BERNDS	COLUMBIA	1946
D-4089	ROLLING DOWN TO RENO (sh)	WHITE	COLUMBIA	1947
D-4091	I'M A MONKEY'S UNCLE – STOOGES	WHITE	COLUMBIA	1948
D-4099	RICHARD LANE SHORT		COLUMBIA	
D-4099	WEDDING BELLE (sh)	BERNDS	COLUMBIA	1947
D-4100	TALL, DARK AND GRUESOME (sh)	LORD	COLUMBIA	1948
D-4102	STOOGES (SHORT)		COLUMBIA	
D-4105	MUMMY'S DUMMIES (sh)	BERNDS	COLUMBIA	1948
D-4106	WEDLOCK DEADLOCK (sh)	BERNDS	COLUMBIA	1947
D-4108	GHOST TALKS (sh)	WHITE	COLUMBIA	1949
D-4108	STOOGES (SHORT)		COLUMBIA	
D-4109	RADIO ROMEO (sh)	BERNDS	COLUMBIA	1947
D-4110	MAN OR MOUSE (sh)	WHITE	COLUMBIA	1948
D-4113	EIGHT BALL ANDY (sh)	BERNDS	COLUMBIA	1948
D-4115	HUGS AND MUGS (sh)	WHITE	COLUMBIA	1950
D-4117	FLAT FEAT (sh)	BERNDS	COLUMBIA	1948
D-4117	STERLING HOLLOWAY SHORT		COLUMBIA	
D-4119	STOOGES (SHORT)		COLUMBIA	
D-4120	JITTER BUGHOUSE (sh)	WHITE	COLUMBIA	1948
D-4120	JOE DERITA SHORT		COLUMBIA	
D-4122	SILLY BILLY (sh)	WHITE	COLUMBIA	1948
D-4123	HE'S IN AGAIN - RICHARD LANE	BERNDS	COLUMBIA	1949
D-4124	TWO NUTS IN A RUT (sh)	BERNDS	COLUMBIA	1948
D-4125	BILLIE GETS HER MAN (sh)	BERNDS	COLUMBIA	1948
D-4127	PARLOR, BEDROOM AND WRATH (sh)	WHITE	COLUMBIA	1948
D-4129	LOVE AT FIRST BITE (sh)	WHITE	COLUMBIA	1950

D-4129	STOOGES (SHORT)		COLUMBIA	
D-4130	MICROSPOOK (sh)	BERNDS	COLUMBIA	1949
D-4131	DOPEY DICKS (sh)	BERNDS	COLUMBIA	1950
D-4133	HUGH HERBERT SHORT		COLUMBIA	
D-4133	TRAPPED BY A BLOND (sh)	LORD	COLUMBIA	1949
D-4134	FLUNG BY A FLING (sh)	BERNDS	COLUMBIA	1949
D-4135	CLUNKED IN THE CLINK (sh)	WHITE	COLUMBIA	1949
D-4135	VERA VAGUE SHORT		COLUMBIA	
D-4137	DUNKED IN THE DEEP (sh)	WHITE	COLUMBIA	1949
D-4138	DIZZY YARDBIRD (sh)	WHITE	COLUMBIA	1950
D-4139	SLAPHAPPY SLEUTHS (sh)	WHITE	COLUMBIA	1950
D-4141	SELF MADE MAIDS (sh)	WHITE	COLUMBIA	1950
D-4142	PUNCHY COWPUNCHERS (sh)	BERNDS	COLUMBIA	1950
D-4143	STUDIO STOOPS (sh)	BERNDS	COLUMBIA	1950
D-4144	HOLD THAT MONKEY (sh)	WHITE	COLUMBIA	1950
D-4145	HIS BAITING BEAUTY (sh)	BERNDS	COLUMBIA	1950
D-4146	SUPER WOLF (sh)	LORD	COLUMBIA	1949
D-4147	LET DOWN YOUR AERIAL (sh)	BERNDS	COLUMBIA	1949
D-4148	ONE SHIVERY NIGHT (sh)	LORD	COLUMBIA	1950
D-4149	WHA' HAPPEN? (sh)	WHITE	COLUMBIA	1949
D-4150	NURSIE BEHAVE (sh)	WHITE	COLUMBIA	1950
D-4151	FRENCH FRIED FROLIC (sh)	WHITE	COLUMBIA	1949
D-4152	HOUSE ABOUT IT (sh)	WHITE	COLUMBIA	1950
D-4153	MARINATED MARINER (sh)	WHITE	COLUMBIA	1950
D-4154	SNITCH IN TIME (sh)	BERNDS	COLUMBIA	1950
D-4155	BABY SITTERS JITTERS (sh)	WHITE	COLUMBIA	1951
D-4156	THREE ARABIAN NUTS (sh)	BERNDS	COLUMBIA	1951
D-4157	SCRAMBLED BRAINS (sh)	WHITE	COLUMBIA	1951
D-4158	DON'T THROW THAT KNIFE (sh)	WHITE	COLUMBIA	1951
D-4159	MALICE IN THE PALACE (sh) (see 4119)	WHITE	COLUMBIA	1949
D-4159	MISSED FORTUNE (sh)	WHITE	COLUMBIA	1952
D-4160	BLUNDERFUL TIME (sh)	WHITE	COLUMBIA	1949
D-4161	MERRY MAVERICKS (sh)	BERNDS	COLUMBIA	1951
D-4162	TOOTH WILL OUT (sh)	BERNDS	COLUMBIA	1951
D-4163	PEST MAN WINS (sh)	WHITE	COLUMBIA	1951
D-4164	WINE, WOMEN AND BONG (sh)	WHITE	COLUMBIA	1951
D-4165	TWO ROAMING CHAMPS (sh)	BERNDS	COLUMBIA	1950
D-4166	HE FLEW THE SHREW (sh)	WHITE	COLUMBIA	1951
D-4167	FUN ON THE RUN (sh)	WHITE	COLUMBIA	1951
D-4168	SLIP AND A MISS (sh)	MCCOLLUM	COLUMBIA	1950
D-4169	WOO WOO BLUES (sh)	QUINE	COLUMBIA	1951
D-4170	BLONDE ATOM BOMB (sh)	WHITE	COLUMBIA	1951
D-4171	PLEASURE TREASURE (sh)	WHITE	COLUMBIA	1951
D-4172	INNOCENTLY GUILTY (sh)	WHITE	COLUMBIA	1950
D-4173	AWFUL SLEUTH (sh)	QUINE	COLUMBIA	1951
D-4174	FOY MEETS GIRL (sh)	ULLMAN	COLUMBIA	1950
D-4175	WEDDING YELLS (sh)	WHITE	COLUMBIA	1951
D-4176	HAPPY GO WACKY (sh)	WHITE	COLUMBIA	1952
D-4177	SHE TOOK A POWDER (sh)	WHITE	COLUMBIA	1951
D-4180	LISTEN JUDGE – STOOGES	BERNDS	COLUMBIA	1952
D-4184	HUGH HERBERT SHORT		COLUMBIA	
D-4184	TROUBLE IN-LAWS (sh)	MCCOLLUM	COLUMBIA	1951
D-4185	CHAMPS STEP OUT (sh)	BERNDS	COLUMBIA	1951
D-4186	ROOTIN' TOOTIN' TENDERFEET (sh)	WHITE	COLUMBIA	1952
D-4187	GINK AT THE SINK (sh)	WHITE	COLUMBIA	1952
D-4187	HUGH HERBERT SHORT		COLUMBIA	
D-4188	EDDIE QUILLIAN SHORT		COLUMBIA	
D-4188	HEEBIE GEE-GEES (sh)	BERNDS	COLUMBIA	1952
D-4189	EDDIE QUILLIAN SHORT		COLUMBIA	
D-4189	FOOL AND HIS HONEY (sh)	WHITE	COLUMBIA	1952
D-4190	ANDY CLYDE SHORT		COLUMBIA	
D-4190	BLISSFUL BLUNDER (sh)	WHITE	COLUMBIA	1952
D-4191	ANDY CLYDE SHORT		COLUMBIA	
D-4191	HOOKED AND ROOKED (sh)	WHITE	COLUMBIA	1952
D-4193	AIM, FIRE, SCOOT (sh)	WHITE	COLUMBIA	1952
D-4193	JOE BESSER AND HAWTHORN (sh)		COLUMBIA	

D-4194	CUCKOOS ON A CHOO CHOO – STOOGES	WHITE	COLUMBIA	1952
D-4195	CAUGHT ON THE BOUNCE (sh)	WHITE	COLUMBIA	1952
D-4195	JOE BESSER SHORT		COLUMBIA	
D-4196	STOOGES (SHORT)		COLUMBIA	
D-4198	EDDIE QUILLAN SHORT		COLUMBIA	
D-4198	STROP, LOOK AND LISTEN (sh)	WHITE	COLUMBIA	1952
D-4201	RIP, SEW AND STITCH (sh) (2- 4201'S - Error? 4202)	WHITE	COLUMBIA	1953
D-4204	EDDIE QUILLAN SHORT		COLUMBIA	
D-4204	HE POPPED HIS PISTOL (sh)	WHITE	COLUMBIA	1953
D-4205	JOE BESSER SHORT		COLUMBIA	
D-4205	SPIES AND GUYS (sh)	WHITE	COLUMBIA	1953
D-4206	ANDY CLYDE GETS SPRING CHICKEN	WHITE	COLUMBIA	1939
D-4206	LOVE'S A POPPIN' (sh)	WHITE	COLUMBIA	1953
D-4207	OH, SAY CAN YOU SUE (sh)	WHITE	COLUMBIA	1953
D-4207	TWO JILLS AND A JACK (sh) (see 4079)	WHITE	COLUMBIA	1947
D-4215	DOWN THE HATCH (sh)	WHITE	COLUMBIA	1953
D-4219	ANDY CLYDE SHORT		COLUMBIA	
D-4219	TOOTING TOOTERS (sh)	WHITE	COLUMBIA	1954
D-4220	A MINER AFFAIR – ANDY CLYDE	WHITE	COLUMBIA	1945
D-4220	TWO APRIL FOOLS (sh)	WHITE	COLUMBIA	1954
D-4221	KIDS WILL BE KIDS (sh)	WHITE	COLUMBIA	1954
D-4222	BLUNDER BOYS (sh)	WHITE	COLUMBIA	1955
D-4224	GYPPED IN THE PENTHOUSE (sh)	WHITE	COLUMBIA	1955
D-4224	STOOGES (SHORT)		COLUMBIA	
D-4225	OF CASH AND HASH – STOOGES	WHITE	COLUMBIA	1955
D-4226	FIRE CHASER (sh)	WHITE	COLUMBIA	1954
D-4227	G. I. DOOD IT (sh)	WHITE	COLUMBIA	1955
D-4228	BEDLAM IN PARADISE (sh)	WHITE	COLUMBIA	1955
D-4230	HIS PEST FRIEND (sh)	WHITE	COLUMBIA	1955
D-4231	NOBODY'S HOME (sh)	WHITE	COLUMBIA	1955
D-4232	WHAM-BAM-SLAM! (sh)	WHITE	COLUMBIA	1955
D-4233	HOT ICE (sh)	WHITE	COLUMBIA	1955
D-4234	ONE SPOOKY NIGHT (sh)	WHITE	COLUMBIA	1955
D-4235	SCRATCH SCRATCH SCRATCH	WHITE	COLUMBIA	1955
D-4236	HUSBANDS BEWARE (sh)	WHITE	COLUMBIA	1956
D-4238	FLAGPOLE JITTERS (sh)	WHITE	COLUMBIA	1956
D-4239	FOR CRIMIN' OUT LOUD (sh)	WHITE	COLUMBIA	1956
D-4240	HOOK A CROOK (sh)	WHITE	COLUMBIA	1955
D-4241	HE TOOK A POWDER (sh)	WHITE	COLUMBIA	1955
D-4242	ARMY DAZE (sh)	WHITE	COLUMBIA	1956
D-4243	COME ON SEVEN (sh)	WHITE	COLUMBIA	1956
D-4246	SCHEMING SCHEMERS - STOOGES (sh)	WHITE	COLUMBIA	1956
D-4248	ANDY GOES WILD (sh)	WHITE	COLUMBIA	1956
D-4249	PARDON MY NIGHTSHIRT (sh)	WHITE	COLUMBIA	1956
D-4251	HOOFS AND GOOFS - STOOGES	WHITE	COLUMBIA	1957
D-4252	MERRY MIXUP - STOOGES	WHITE	COLUMBIA	1957
D-4253	SPACE SHIP SAPPY - STOOGES	WHITE	COLUMBIA	1957
D-8013	WHEN THE REDSKINS RODE	LANDERS	COLUMBIA	1951
D-8025	THIEF OF DAMASCUS	JASON	COLUMBIA	1952
D-8172	VALLEY OF HEADHUNTERS	BERKE	COLUMBIA	1953
D-8191	JESSE JAMES VS DALTONS	CASTLE	COLUMBIA	1954
D-8257	ADVENTURES OF CAPTAIN AFRICA (serial)	BENNET	COLUMBIA	1955
D-8299	BATTLE STATIONS	SEILER	COLUMBIA	1956
D-8316	URANIUM BOOM	CASTLE	COLUMBIA	1956
D-8357	27TH DAY	ASHER	COLUMBIA	1957
D-8359	GIANT CLAW	SEARS	COLUMBIA	1957
D-8385	YOUNG DON'T CRY	WERKER	COLUMBIA	1957
D-8389	TIJUANA STORY, THE	KARDOS	COLUMBIA	1957
D-8429	GOING STEADY	SEARS	COLUMBIA	1958
D-8450	BUCHANAN RIDES ALONE	BOETTICHER	COLUMBIA	1958
D-8479	GIDEON OF SCOTLAND YARD (UK: GIDEON'S DAY)	FORD	COLUMBIA	1958
D-8518	WHO WAS THAT LADY?	SIDNEY	COLUMBIA	1960
D-8559	TINGLER	CASTLE	COLUMBIA	1959
DA	CASE OF DIAMOND ANNIE (serial - Stryker of Yard)	various	HOLLYWOOD TELEVISION	1962
DA	DAMNATION ALLEY	SMIGHT	20th CENTURY FOX	1977
DA	DEAD AGAIN	BRANAGH	PARAMOUNT	1991

DA	DEATH OF AN ANGEL	POPESCU	20th CENTURY FOX	1985
DA	DEVIL'S ADVOCATE	HACKFORD	WARNER BROS	1997
DA	DOROTHY ARNOLD	portrait		
DA	DUAL ALIBI (UK)	TRAVERS	PATHE	1947
DA	HOUSE OF DARK SHADOWS	CURTIS	MGM	1970
DA-C	101 DALMATIANS (t)	GERONIMI	BUENA VISTA	R69
DAF	DECLINE AND FALL OF A BIRD WATCHER (UK)	KRISH	20th CENTURY FOX	1968
DAH	DADDY'S GONE A-HUNTING	ROBSON	NATIONAL GENERAL	1969
DAK	DAKTARI (tv series)		MGM	1966
DAR	DARBY O'GILL AND THE LITTLE PEOPLE	STEVENSON	BUENA VISTA	1959
DAY	DAYDREAMER	BASS	EMBASSY	1966
DB	ADVENTURES OF DUSTY BATES (UK: DUSTY BATES)	CATLING	GFD	1947
DB	DANCE BAND (UK)	VARNEL	FIRST DIVISION	1935
DB	DANNY BOY (UK)	MITCHELL	BUTCHER'S	1941
DB	DEADLY BEES (UK)	FRANCIS	PARAMOUNT	1966
DB	DEVIL RIDES OUT (UK: DEVIL'S BRIDE)	FISHER	20TH CENTURY FOX	1968
DB	DOUBLE BUNK (UK)	PENNINGTON-RICHARDS	SHOWCORPORATION	1961
DB	SWEENEY TODD, THE DEMON BARBER OF FLEET STREET (UK)	KING	SELECT ATTRACTIONS	1936
DB	TRIAL AND ERROR (UK: DOCK BRIEF)	HILL	MGM	1962
D-B	BAIT	HAAS	COLUMBIA	1954
DBH	DEATH AT A BROADCAST (UK: DEATH AT BROADCASTING HOUSE)	DENHAM	FILM ALLIANCE	1934
DBK	DAYBREAK (UK)	BENNETT	UNIVERSAL	1948
DBK	WHY BOTHER TO KNOCK (UK: DON'T BOTHER TO KNOCK)	FRANKEL	SEVEN ARTS	1961
DBP80	ROLLING DOWN THE GREAT DIVIDE	NEWFIELD	PRODUCERS RELEASING	1942
DBS	DEEP BLUE SEA	HARLIN	WARNER BROS	1999
DC	DANGEROUSLY CLOSE	PYUN	CANNON	1986
DC	DAVY CROCKETT, INDIAN SCOUT	LANDERS	UNITED ARTISTS	1950
DC	DEAD ON COURSE (UK: WINGS OF DANGER)	FISHER	LIPPERT	1952
DC	DESPERATE CHARACTERS	GILROY	PARAMOUNT	1971
DC	DON CHICAGO (UK)	ROGERS	ANGLO-AMERICAN	1945
DC	HIGH POWERED RIFLE	DEXTER	20th CENTURY FOX	1960
DC	LITTLE WORLD OF DON CAMILLO, THE (IT: DON CAMILLO 1952)	DUVIVIER	IFE RELEASING	1967
DC	THREE DAYS OF THE CONDOR	POLLACK	PARAMOUNT	1975
DC	WINDJAMMER; VOYAGE OF THE CHRISTIAN RADICH (doc)	DE ROCHEMONT III	NATIONAL THEATERS	1958
DC-19	WINDJAMMER; VOYAGE OF THE CHRISTIAN RADICH (doc)	DE ROCHEMONT III	NATIONAL THEATERS	1958
DC-5094	THREE DAYS OF THE CONDOR	POLLACK	PARAMOUNT	1975
DCA	THREE DAYS OF THE CONDOR	POLLACK	PARAMOUNT	1975
DCD	BLAME THE WOMAN (UK: DIAMOND CUT DIAMOND)	ELVEY, NIBLO	PRINCIPAL	1932
D-COL-8	START CHEERING	ROGELL	COLUMBIA	1938
D-COL-9	LITTLE MISS ROUGHNECK	SCOTTO	COLUMBIA	1938
D-COL-10	NO TIME TO MARRY	LACHMAN	COLUMBIA	1938
D-COL-12	VALLEY OF VANISHING MEN (serial)	BENNET	COLUMBIA	1942
D-COL-14	LONE WOLF IN PARIS	ROGELL	COLUMBIA	1938
D-COL-15	THERE'S ALWAYS A WOMAN	HALL	COLUMBIA	1938
D-COL-16	YOU CAN'T TAKE IT WITH YOU	CAPRA	COLUMBIA	1938
D-COL-17	HOLIDAY	CUKOR	COLUMBIA	1938
D-COL-19	CITY SHADOWS* (CITY STREETS)	ROGELL	COLUMBIA	1938
D-COL-19	CITY STREETS (CITY SHADOWS*)	ROGELL	COLUMBIA	1938
D-COL-21	I AM THE LAW	HALL	COLUMBIA	1938
D-COL-23	LADY OBJECTS	KENTON	COLUMBIA	1938
D-COL-24	FLIGHT TO FAME	COLEMAN	COLUMBIA	1938
D-COL-27	AWFUL TRUTH	MCCAREY	COLUMBIA	1937
D-COL-28	THERE'S THAT WOMAN AGAIN	HALL	COLUMBIA	1939
D-COL-29	LITTLE ADVENTURESS	LEDERMAN	COLUMBIA	1938
D-COL-30	BLONDIE	STRAYER	COLUMBIA	1938
D-COL-31	SMASHING THE SPY RING	CABANNE	COLUMBIA	1939
D-COL-32	LADY AND THE MOB	STOLOFF	COLUMBIA	1938
D-COL-35	LET US LIVE	BRAHM	COLUMBIA	1939
D-COL-37	COAST GUARD	LUDWIG	COLUMBIA	1939
D-COL-38	ROMANCE OF THE REDWOODS	VIDOR	COLUMBIA	1939
D-COL-39	BLONDIE MEETS THE BOSS	STRAYER	COLUMBIA	1939
D-COL-41	BLIND ALLEY	VIDOR	COLUMBIA	1939
D-COL-42	GOOD GIRLS GO TO PARIS	HALL	COLUMBIA	1939
D-COL-43	MR. SMITH GOES TO WASHINGTON	CAPRA	COLUMBIA	1939
D-COL-45	BLONDIE TAKES A VACATION	STRAYER	COLUMBIA	1939
D-COL-46	FIVE LITTLE PEPPERS AND HOW THEY GREW	BARTON	COLUMBIA	1939

D-COL-47	THOSE HIGH GRAY WALLS	VIDOR	COLUMBIA	1939
D-COL-49	BEWARE SPOOKS	SEDGWICK	COLUMBIA	1939
D-COL-51	BLONDIE BRINGS UP BABY	STRAYER	COLUMBIA	1939
D-COL-52	ARIZONA	RUGGLES	COLUMBIA	1940
D-COL-53	SCANDAL SHEET	GRINDE	COLUMBIA	1939
D-COL-54	AMAZING MR. WILLIAMS	HALL	COLUMBIA	1939
D-COL-55	CAFE HOSTESS	SALKOW	COLUMBIA	1940
D-COL-56	MY SON IS GUILTY	BARTON	COLUMBIA	1939
D-COL-57	MILITARY ACADEMY	LEDERMAN	COLUMBIA	1940
D-COL-58	FIVE LITTLE PEPPERS AT HOME	BARTON	COLUMBIA	1940
D-COL-59	LONE WOLF MEETS A LADY	SALKOW	COLUMBIA	1940
D-COL-60	CONVICTED WOMAN	GRINDE	COLUMBIA	1940
D-COL-61	TOO MANY HUSBANDS	RUGGLES	COLUMBIA	1940
D-COL-62	MAN WITH NINE LIVES (1940)	GRINDE	COLUMBIA	R47
D-COL-63	BLONDIE ON A BUDGET	STRAYER	COLUMBIA	1940
D-COL-66	FIVE LITTLE PEPPERS IN TROUBLE	BARTON	COLUMBIA	1940
D-COL-68	SO YOU WON'T TALK	SEDGWICK	COLUMBIA	1940
D-COL-72	BABIES FOR SALE	BARTON	COLUMBIA	1940
D-COL-73	TILLIE THE TOILER	SALKOW	COLUMBIA	1941
D-COL-74	BLONDE FROM SINGAPORE	DMYTRYK	COLUMBIA	1941
D-COL-75	BLONDIE HAS SERVANT TROUBLE	STRAYER	COLUMBIA	1940
D-COL-76	GIRLS OF THE ROAD	GRINDE	COLUMBIA	1940
D-COL-77	HER FIRST BEAU	REED	COLUMBIA	1941
D-COL-79	THIS THING CALLED LOVE	HALL	COLUMBIA	1940
D-COL-80	HE STAYED FOR BREAKFAST	HALL	COLUMBIA	1940
D-COL-81	THEY DARE NOT LIVE	WHALE	COLUMBIA	1941
D-COL-82	ANGELS OVER BROADWAY	GARMES	COLUMBIA	1940
D-COL-83	THE SECRET SEVEN	MOORE	COLUMBIA	1940
D-COL-84	BEFORE I HANG	GRINDE	COLUMBIA	1940
D-COL-86	GLAMOUR FOR SALE	LEDERMAN	COLUMBIA	1940
D-COL-87	BLONDIE PLAYS CUPID	STRAYER	COLUMBIA	1940
D-COL-88	GIRLS UNDER 21	NOSSECK	COLUMBIA	1940
D-COL-90	TIME OUT FOR RHYTHM (sh)	SALKOW	COLUMBIA	1941
D-COL-91	ESCAPE TO GLORY	BRAHM	COLUMBIA	1940
D-COL-95	BLONDIE GOES LATIN	STRAYER	COLUMBIA	1941
D-COL-100	FACE BEHIND THE MASK	FLOREY	COLUMBIA	1941
D-COL-102	DEVIL COMMANDS	DMYTRYK	COLUMBIA	R55
D-COL-106	BEDTIME STORY	HALL	COLUMBIA	1941
D-COL-107	BIG BOSS	BARTON	COLUMBIA	1941
D-COL-108	NAVAL ACADEMY	KENTON	COLUMBIA	1941
D-COL-109	SWEETHEART OF THE CAMPUS	DMYTRYK	COLUMBIA	1941
D-COL-111	BLONDIE IN SOCIETY	STRAYER	COLUMBIA	1941
D-COL-112	YOU BELONG TO ME	RUGGLES	COLUMBIA	1941
D-COL-113	RICHEST MAN IN TOWN	BARTON	COLUMBIA	1941
D-COL-114	I WAS A PRISONER ON DEVIL'S ISLAND	LANDERS	COLUMBIA	1941
D-COL-115	TWO IN A TAXI	FLOREY	COLUMBIA	1941
D-COL-116	OUR WIFE	STAHL	COLUMBIA	1941
D-COL-117	HERE COMES MR. JORDAN	HALL	COLUMBIA	1941
D-COL-118	YOU'LL NEVER GET RICH	LANFIELD	COLUMBIA	1941
D-COL-119	MYSTERY SHIP	LANDERS	COLUMBIA	1941
D-COL-120	TWO LATINS FROM MANHATTAN	BARTON	COLUMBIA	1941
D-COL-122	COUNTER-ESPIONAGE	DMYTRYK	COLUMBIA	1942
D-COL-124	THREE GIRLS ABOUT TOWN	JASON	COLUMBIA	1941
D-COL-125	GO WEST YOUNG LADY	STRAYER	COLUMBIA	1941
D-COL-126	HARMON OF MICHIGAN	BARTON	COLUMBIA	1941
D-COL-127	STORK PAYS OFF	LANDERS	COLUMBIA	1941
D-COL-128	SECRETS OF THE LONE WOLF	DMYTRYK	COLUMBIA	1941
D-COL-130	SING FOR YOUR SUPPER	BARTON	COLUMBIA	1941
D-COL-132	HARVARD, HERE I COME	LANDERS	COLUMBIA	1941
D-COL-133	CONFESSIONS OF BOSTON BLACKIE	DMYTRYK	COLUMBIA	1941
D-COL-134	BLONDIE GOES TO COLLEGE	STRAYER	COLUMBIA	1942
D-COL-135	HONOLULU LU	BARTON	COLUMBIA	1941
D-COL-136	CADETS ON PARADE	LANDERS	COLUMBIA	1942
D-COL-137	SHUT MY BIG MOUTH	BARTON	COLUMBIA	1942
D-COL-138	TWO YANKS IN TRINIDAD	RATOFF	COLUMBIA	1942
D-COL-139	MAN WHO RETURNED TO LIFE	LANDERS	COLUMBIA	1942

D-COL-140	CANAL ZONE	LANDERS	COLUMBIA	1942
D-COL-141	TRAMP TRAMP TRAMP	BARTON	COLUMBIA	1942
D-COL-142	BLONDIE'S BLESSED EVENT	STRAYER	COLUMBIA	1942
D-COL-144	ALIAS BOSTON BLACKIE	LANDERS	COLUMBIA	1942
D-COL-145	WIFE TAKES A FLYER (YANK IN DUTCH)	WALLACE	COLUMBIA	1942
D-COL-146	TALK OF THE TOWN	STEVENS	COLUMBIA	1942
D-COL-147	NOT A LADIES MAN	LANDERS	COLUMBIA	1942
D-COL-148	HELLO ANAPOLIS	BARTON	COLUMBIA	1942
D-COL-149	MEET THE STEWARTS	GREEN	COLUMBIA	1942
D-COL-150	THEY ALL KISSED THE BRIDE	HALL	COLUMBIA	1942
D-COL-151	PARACHUTE NURSE	BARTON	COLUMBIA	1942
D-COL-152	SWEETHEART OF THE FLEET	BARTON	COLUMBIA	1942
D-COL-153	SUBMARINE RAIDER	LANDERS	COLUMBIA	1942
D-COL-154	YOU WERE NEVER LOVELIER	SEITER	COLUMBIA	1942
D-COL-155	ATLANTIC CONVOY	LANDERS	COLUMBIA	1942
D-COL-156	FLIGHT LIEUTENANT	SALKOW	COLUMBIA	1942
D-COL-158	BLONDIE FOR VICTORY	STRAYER	COLUMBIA	1942
D-COL-159	MAN'S WORLD	BARTON	COLUMBIA	1942
D-COL-160	SABOTAGE SQUAD	LANDERS	COLUMBIA	1942
D-COL-161	MY SISTER EILEEN	HALL	COLUMBIA	1942
D-COL-162	LUCKY LEGS	BARTON	COLUMBIA	1942
D-COL-165	SPIRIT OF STANFORD	BARTON	COLUMBIA	1942
D-COL-168	DARING YOUNG MAN	STRAYER	COLUMBIA	1942
D-COL-169	BOSTON BLACKIE GOES HOLLYWOOD	GORDON	COLUMBIA	1942
D-COL-170	SMITH OF MINNESOTA	LANDERS	COLUMBIA	1942
D-COL-171	BOOGIE MAN WILL GET YOU	LANDERS	COLUMBIA	1942
D-COL-172	UNDERGROUND AGENT	GORDON	COLUMBIA	1942
D-COL-174	LAUGH YOUR BLUES AWAY	BARTON	COLUMBIA	1942
D-COL-175	JUNIOR ARMY	LANDERS	COLUMBIA	1942
D-COL-177	POWER OF THE PRESS	LANDERS	COLUMBIA	1943
D-COL-203	MAIN EVENT	DARE	COLUMBIA	1938
D-COL-206	SHADOW	COLEMAN	COLUMBIA	1937
D-COL-207	SQUADRON OF HONOR	COLEMAN	COLUMBIA	1938
D-COL-208	WOMEN IN PRISON	HILLYER	COLUMBIA	1938
D-COL-209	WHO KILLED GAIL PRESTON?	BARSHA	COLUMBIA	1938
D-COL-210	WHEN G-MEN STEP IN	COLEMAN	COLUMBIA	1938
D-COL-211	HIGHWAY PATROL	COLEMAN	COLUMBIA	1938
D-COL-212	HOMICIDE BUREAU	COLEMAN	COLUMBIA	1939
D-COL-213	JUVENILE COURT	LEDERMAN	COLUMBIA	1938
D-COL-214	ADVENTURE IN SAHARA	LEDERMAN	COLUMBIA	1938
D-COL-215	NORTH OF SHANGHAI	LEDERMAN	COLUMBIA	1939
D-COL-216	MY SON IS A CRIMINAL	COLEMAN	COLUMBIA	1939
D-COL-217	FIRST OFFENDERS	MCDONALD	COLUMBIA	1939
D-COL-218	OUTSIDE THESE WALLS	MCCAREY	COLUMBIA	1939
D-COL-219	MISSING DAUGHTERS	COLEMAN	COLUMBIA	1939
D-COL-220	PARENTS ON TRIAL	NELSON	COLUMBIA	1939
D-COL-221	WOMAN IS THE JUDGE	GRINDE	COLUMBIA	1939
D-COL-222	BEHIND PRISON GATES	BARTON	COLUMBIA	1939
D-COL-223	MAN THEY COULD NOT KILL (1939)	GRINDE	COLUMBIA	R47
D-COL-224	KONGA, THE WILD STALLION	NELSON	COLUMBIA	1940
D-COL-283	COMMUNITY SING - SERIES 2 #1	series	COLUMBIA	1937
D-COL-284	COMMUNITY SING - SERIES 2 #2	series	COLUMBIA	1937
D-COL-301	CATTLE RAIDERS	NELSON	COLUMBIA	1938
D-COL-303	CALL OF THE ROCKIES	JAMES	COLUMBIA	1938
D-COL-304	LAW OF THE PLAINS	NELSON	COLUMBIA	1938
D-COL-305	WEST OF CHEYENNE	NELSON	COLUMBIA	1938
D-COL-306	SOUTH OF ARIZONA	NELSON	COLUMBIA	1938
D-COL-307	WEST OF SANTA FE	NELSON	COLUMBIA	1938
D-COL-308	COLORADO TRAIL	NELSON	COLUMBIA	1938
D-COL-309	RIO GRANDE	NELSON	COLUMBIA	1938
D-COL-310	THUNDERING WEST	NELSON	COLUMBIA	1939
D-COL-311	TEXAS STAMPEDE	NELSON	COLUMBIA	1939
D-COL-312	NORTH OF THE YUKON	NELSON	COLUMBIA	1939
D-COL-313	SPOILERS OF THE RANGE	COLEMAN	COLUMBIA	1939
D-COL-314	WESTERN CARAVANS	NELSON	COLUMBIA	1939
D-COL-315	MAN FROM SUNDOWN	NELSON	COLUMBIA	1939

D-COL-316	OUTPOST OF THE MOUNTIES	COLEMAN	COLUMBIA	1939
D-COL-317	STRANGER FROM TEXAS	NELSON	COLUMBIA	1939
D-COL-318	RIDERS OF BLACK RIVER	DEMING	COLUMBIA	1939
D-COL-319	TAMING OF THE WEST	DEMING	COLUMBIA	1939
D-COL-320	MAN FROM TUMBLEWEEDS	LEWIS	COLUMBIA	1940
D-COL-321	TWO FISTED RANGERS	LEWIS	COLUMBIA	1939
D-COL-322	BULLETS FOR RUSTLERS	NELSON	COLUMBIA	1940
D-COL-323	PIONEERS OF THE FRONTIER	NELSON	COLUMBIA	1940
D-COL-325	THUNDERING FRONTIER	LEDERMAN	COLUMBIA	1940
D-COL-326	TEXAS STAGECOACH	LEWIS	COLUMBIA	1940
D-COL-327	PINTO KID	HILLYER	COLUMBIA	1941
D-COL-328	WEST OF ABILENE	CEDER	COLUMBIA	1940
D-COL-329	RETURN OF WILD BILL	LEWIS	COLUMBIA	1940
D-COL-330	DURANGO KID	HILLYER	COLUMBIA	1940
D-COL-331	PRAIRIE SCHOONERS	NELSON	COLUMBIA	1940
D-COL-332	OUTLAWS OF THE PANHANDLE	NELSON	COLUMBIA	1941
D-COL-334	BEYOND THE SACRAMENTO	HILLYER	COLUMBIA	1941
D-COL-335	ACROSS THE SIERRAS	LEDERMAN	COLUMBIA	1941
D-COL-337	WILDCAT OF TUCSON	HILLYER	COLUMBIA	1940
D-COL-338	NORTH FROM THE LONE STAR	HILLYER	COLUMBIA	1941
D-COL-339	RETURN OF DANIEL BOONE	HILLYER	COLUMBIA	1941
D-COL-340	HANDS ACROSS THE ROCKIES	HILLYER	COLUMBIA	1941
D-COL-341	SON OF DAVY CROCKETT	HILLYER	COLUMBIA	1941
D-COL-342	MEDICO OF PAINTED SPRINGS	HILLYER	COLUMBIA	1941
D-COL-343	KING OF DODGE CITY	HILLYER	COLUMBIA	1941
D-COL-344	THUNDER OVER THE PRAIRIE	HILLYER	COLUMBIA	1941
D-COL-345	ROARING FRONTIERS	HILLYER	COLUMBIA	1941
D-COL-346	PRAIRIE STRANGER	HILLYER	COLUMBIA	1941
D-COL-347	LONE STAR VIGILANTES	FOX	COLUMBIA	1942
D-COL-348	ROYAL MOUNTED PATROL	HILLYER	COLUMBIA	1941
D-COL-349	BULLETS FOR BANDITS	FOX	COLUMBIA	1942
D-COL-350	RIDERS OF THE BADLANDS	BRETHERTON	COLUMBIA	1941
D-COL-351	NORTH OF THE ROCKIES	HILLYER	COLUMBIA	1942
D-COL-353	WEST OF TOMBSTONE	BRETHERTON	COLUMBIA	1942
D-COL-354	LAWLESS PLAINSMEN	BERKE	COLUMBIA	1942
D-COL-355	DOWN RIO GRANDE WAY	BERKE	COLUMBIA	1942
D-COL-356	PRAIRIE GUNSMOKE	HILLYER	COLUMBIA	1942
D-COL-357	OVERLAND TO DEADWOOD	BERKE	COLUMBIA	1942
D-COL-358	BADMEN OF THE HILLS	BERKE	COLUMBIA	1942
D-COL-359	RIDERS OF THE NORTHLAND	BERKE	COLUMBIA	1942
D-COL-360	VENGEANCE OF THE WEST	HILLYER	COLUMBIA	1942
D-COL-362	RIDING THROUGH NEVADA	BERKE	COLUMBIA	1942
D-COL-363	PARDON MY GUN	BERKE	COLUMBIA	1942
D-COL-364	TORNADO IN THE SADDLE	BERKE	COLUMBIA	1942
D-COL-365	LONE PRAIRIE	BERKE	COLUMBIA	1942
D-COL-403	JUMP, CHUMP, JUMP! (sh)	LORD	COLUMBIA	1938
D-COL-404	WEE WEE MONSIER (sh)	LORD	COLUMBIA	1938
D-COL-405	DOGGONE MIXUP (sh)	LAMONT	COLUMBIA	1938
D-COL-409	CALLING ALL CURTAINS (sh)	LORD	COLUMBIA	1937
D-COL-410	FIDDLING AROUND (sh)	LAMONT	COLUMBIA	1938
D-COL-412	MIND NEEDER (sh)	LORD	COLUMBIA	1938
D-COL-413	MANY SAPPY RETURNS (sh)	LORD	COLUMBIA	1938
D-COL-415	TIME OUT FOR TROUBLE (sh)	LORD	COLUMBIA	1938
D-COL-416	TERMITES OF 1938 (sh)	LORD	COLUMBIA	1938
D-COL-417	OLD RAID MULE (sh)	CHASE	COLUMBIA	1938
D-COL-418	NIGHTSHIRT BANDIT (sh)	WHITE	COLUMBIA	1938
D-COL-419	THREE LITTLE SEW AND SEWS (sh)	LORD	COLUMBIA	1939
D-COL-420	TASSELS IN THE AIR (sh)	CHASE	COLUMBIA	1938
D-COL-421	ANKLES AWAY (sh)	CHASE	COLUMBIA	1938
D-COL-422	HEALTHY, WEALTHY AND DUMB (sh)	LORD	COLUMBIA	1938
D-COL-423	VIOLENT IS THE WORD FOR CURLY (sh)	CHASE	COLUMBIA	1938
D-COL-424	SOUL OF A HEEL (sh)	LORD	COLUMBIA	1938
D-COL-425	HALF-WAY TO HOLLYWOOD (sh)	CHASE	COLUMBIA	1938
D-COL-426	THREE MISSING LINKS (sh)	WHITE	COLUMBIA	1938
D-COL-427	MUTTS TO YOU (sh)	CHASE	COLUMBIA	1938
D-COL-428	SUE MY LAWYER (sh)	WHITE	COLUMBIA	1938

D-COL-429	NAG IN THE BAG (sh)	CHASE	COLUMBIA	1938
D-COL-430	SAVED BY THE BELLE (sh)	CHASE	COLUMBIA	1939
D-COL-431	PIE A LA MAID (sh)	LORD	COLUMBIA	1938
D-COL-432	NOT GUILTY ENOUGH (sh)	LORD	COLUMBIA	1938
D-COL-433	MUTINY ON THE BODY (sh)	CHASE	COLUMBIA	1939
D-COL-434	SWING YOU SWINGERS (sh)	WHITE	COLUMBIA	1939
D-COL-435	SAP TAKES A WRAP (sh)	LORD	COLUMBIA	1939
D-COL-436	HOME ON THE RAGE (sh)	LORD	COLUMBIA	1938
D-COL-437	CHUMP TAKES A BUMP (sh)	LORD	COLUMBIA	1939
D-COL-438	YES WE HAVE NO BONANZA (sh)	LORD	COLUMBIA	1939
D-COL-439	FLAT FOOT STOOGES (sh)	CHASE	COLUMBIA	1938
D-COL-440	BOOM GOES THE GROOM (sh)	CHASE	COLUMBIA	1939
D-COL-441	STAR IS SHORN (sh)	LORD	COLUMBIA	1939
D-COL-442	TROUBLE FINDS ANDY CLYDE (sh)	WHITE	COLUMBIA	1939
D-COL-443	WE WANT OUR MUMMY (sh)	LORD	COLUMBIA	1939
D-COL-444	DUCKING THEY DID GO (sh)	LORD	COLUMBIA	1939
D-COL-445	CALLING ALL CURS (sh)	WHITE	COLUMBIA	1939
D-COL-446	RATTLING ROMEO (sh)	LORD	COLUMBIA	1939
D-COL-448	NOW IT CAN BE SOLD (sh)	LORD	COLUMBIA	1939
D-COL-449	OILY TO BED, OILY TO RISE (sh)	WHITE	COLUMBIA	1939
D-COL-450	SKINNY THE MOOCHER (sh)	LORD	COLUMBIA	1939
D-COL-451	THREE SAPPY PEOPLE (sh)	WHITE	COLUMBIA	1939
D-COL-452	TEACHER'S PEST (sh)	KRAMER, ULLMAN	COLUMBIA	1939
D-COL-453	STATIC IN THE ATTIC (sh)	CHASE	COLUMBIA	1939
D-COL-454	PEST FROM THE WEST (sh)	LORD	COLUMBIA	1939
D-COL-455	COOKOO CAVALIERS (sh)	WHITE	COLUMBIA	1940
D-COL-456	MOOCHING THROUGH GEORGIA (sh)	WHITE	COLUMBIA	1939
D-COL-458	HOW HIGH IS UP? (sh)	LORD	COLUMBIA	1940
D-COL-459	MONEY SQUAWKS (sh)	WHITE	COLUMBIA	1940
D-COL-460	ALL AMERICAN BLONDES (sh)	LORD	COLUMBIA	1939
D-COL-461	ROCKIN' THRU THE ROCKIES (sh)	WHITE	COLUMBIA	1940
D-COL-462	PLUMBING WE WILL GO (sh)	LORD	COLUMBIA	1940
D-COL-463	ANDY CLYDE GETS SPRING CHICKEN (sh)	WHITE	COLUMBIA	1939
D-COL-464	AWFUL GOOF (sh)	LORD	COLUMBIA	1939
D-COL-465	NUTTY BUT NICE (sh)	WHITE	COLUMBIA	1940
D-COL-466	MR. CLYDE GOES TO BROADWAY (sh)	LORD	COLUMBIA	1940
D-COL-467	HECKLER (sh)	LORD	COLUMBIA	1940
D-COL-468	FROM NURSE TO WORSE (sh)	WHITE	COLUMBIA	1940
D-COL-469	HIS BRIDAL FRIGHT (sh)	LORD	COLUMBIA	1940
D-COL-470	NOTHING BUT PLEASURE (sh)	WHITE	COLUMBIA	1940
D-COL-471	YOU'RE NEXT (sh)	LORD	COLUMBIA	1940
D-COL-472	YOU NAZTY SPY (sh)	WHITE	COLUMBIA	1940
D-COL-473	SOUTH OF THE BOUDOIR (sh)	LORD	COLUMBIA	1940
D-COL-474	NO CENSUS, NO FEELING (sh)	LORD	COLUMBIA	1940
D-COL-475	PARDON MY BERTH MARKS (sh)	WHITE	COLUMBIA	1940
D-COL-476	BOOBS IN THE WOODS (sh)	LORD	COLUMBIA	1940
D-COL-477	TAMING OF THE SNOOD (sh)	WHITE	COLUMBIA	1940
D-COL-478	FIREMAN, SAVE MY CHOO CHOO (sh)	LORD	COLUMBIA	1940
D-COL-479	PLEASED TO MITT YOU (sh)	WHITE	COLUMBIA	1940
D-COL-480	COLD TURKEY (sh)	LORD	COLUMBIA	1940
D-COL-481	SPOOK SPEAKS (sh)	WHITE	COLUMBIA	1940
D-COL-482	IN THE SWEET PIE AND PIE (sh)	WHITE	COLUMBIA	1941
D-COL-483	BLONDES AND BLUNDERS (sh)	LORD	COLUMBIA	1940
D-COL-484	SO LONG MR. CHUMPS (sh)	WHITE	COLUMBIA	1941
D-COL-485	DUTIFUL BUT DUMB (sh)	LORD	COLUMBIA	1941
D-COL-486	BOOBS IN ARMS (sh)	WHITE	COLUMBIA	1940
D-COL-487	ALL THE WORLD'S A STOOGE (sh)	LORD	COLUMBIA	1941
D-COL-488	ACHE IN EVERY STAKE (sh)	LORD	COLUMBIA	1941
D-COL-489	WATCHMAN TAKES A WIFE (sh)	LORD	COLUMBIA	1941
D-COL-490	BUNDLE OF BLISS (sh)	WHITE	COLUMBIA	1940
D-COL-491	HIS EX MARKS THE SPOT (sh)	WHITE	COLUMBIA	1940
D-COL-493	SO YOU WON'T SQUAWK (sh)	LORD	COLUMBIA	1941
D-COL-494	RING AND THE BELLE (sh)	LORD	COLUMBIA	1941
D-COL-495	FRESH AS A FRESHMAN (sh)	WHITE	COLUMBIA	1941
D-COL-496	BLITZ KISS (sh)	LORD	COLUMBIA	1941
D-COL-497	YUMPIN' YIMMINY!	WHITE	COLUMBIA	1941

D-COL-498	YANKEE DOODLE ANDY (sh)	WHITE	COLUMBIA	1941
D-COL-499	READY, WILLING BUT UNABLE (sh)	LORD	COLUMBIA	1941
D-COL-500	I'LL NEVER HEIL AGAIN (sh)	WHITE	COLUMBIA	1941
D-COL-501	LOVE AT FIRST FRIGHT (sh)	LORD	COLUMBIA	1941
D-COL-502	THREE BLONDE MICE (sh)	WHITE	COLUMBIA	1942
D-COL-503	FRENCH FRIED PATOOTIE (sh)	WHITE	COLUMBIA	1941
D-COL-504	WHAT MAKES LIZZY DIZZY (sh)	WHITE	COLUMBIA	1942
D-COL-505	BLACK EYES AND BLUES (sh)	WHITE	COLUMBIA	1941
D-COL-506	HALF SHOT AT SUNRISE (sh)	LORD	COLUMBIA	1941
D-COL-507	EVEN AS I.O.U. (sh)	LORD	COLUMBIA	1942
D-COL-508	GENERAL NUISANCEE (sh)	WHITE	COLUMBIA	1941
D-COL-509	HOST TO A GHOST (sh)	LORD	COLUMBIA	1941
D-COL-510	LOCO BOY MAKES GOOD (sh)	WHITE	COLUMBIA	1942
D-COL-511	SOME MORE OF SOMOA (sh)	LORD	COLUMBIA	1941
D-COL-512	MITT ME TONIGHT (sh)	WHITE	COLUMBIA	1941
D-COL-513	CACTUS MAKES PERFECT	LORD	COLUMBIA	1942
D-COL-514	ALL WORK AND NO PAY (sh)	LORD	COLUMBIA	1942
D-COL-515	PHONY CRONIES (sh)	EDWARDS	COLUMBIA	1942
D-COL-516	LOVEABLE TROUBLE (sh)	LORD	COLUMBIA	1941
D-COL-517	SAPPY BIRTHDAY (sh)	EDWARDS	COLUMBIA	1942
D-COL-518	KINK OF THE CAMPUS (sh)	LORD	COLUMBIA	1941
D-COL-519	WHAT'S THE MATADOR? (sh)	WHITE	COLUMBIA	1942
D-COL-520	GLOVE BIRDS (sh)	WHITE	COLUMBIA	1942
D-COL-521	SWEET SPIRITS OF NIGHTER (sh)	LORD	COLUMBIA	1941
D-COL-523	GROOM AND BORED (sh)	LORD	COLUMBIA	1942
D-COL-524	HOW SPRY I AM (sh)	WHITE	COLUMBIA	1942
D-COL-525	GLOVE AFFAIR (sh)	WHITE	COLUMBIA	1941
D-COL-525	STUDY IN SOCKS (sh)	LORD	COLUMBIA	1942
D-COL-526	SHE'S OIL MINE (sh)	WHITE	COLUMBIA	1941
D-COL-527	MATRI-PHONY (sh)	EDWARDS	COLUMBIA	1942
D-COL-528	OLAF LAUGHS LAST (sh)	WHITE	COLUMBIA	1942
D-COL-530	KISS AND WAKE UP (sh)	WHITE	COLUMBIA	1942
D-COL-532	THREE SMART SAPS (sh)	WHITE	COLUMBIA	1942
D-COL-534	TIREMAN, SPARE MY TIRES (sh)	WHITE	COLUMBIA	1942
D-COL-535	HAM AND YEGGS (sh)	WHITE	COLUMBIA	1942
D-COL-536	CARRY HARRY (sh)	EDWARDS	COLUMBIA	1942
D-COL-539	SOCK-A-BYE BABY (sh)	WHITE	COLUMBIA	1942
D-COL-540	SAPPY PAPPY (sh)	EDWARDS	COLUMBIA	1942
D-COL-543	PIANO MOONER (sh)	EDWARDS	COLUMBIA	1942
D-COL-544	GREAT GLOVER (sh)	WHITE	COLUMBIA	1942
D-COL-553	COLLEGE BELLES (sh)	EDWARDS	COLUMBIA	1942
D-COL-600	COMMUNITY SING - SERIES 2 #3	series	COLUMBIA	1937
D-COL-602	COMMUNITY SING - SERIES 2 #4	series	COLUMBIA	1937
D-COL-610	COMMUNITY SING - SERIES 2 #8	series	COLUMBIA	1938
D-COL-611	COMMUNITY SING - SERIES 2 #9	series	COLUMBIA	1938
D-COL-615	COMMUNITY SING - SERIES 2 #10	series	COLUMBIA	1938
D-COL-620	COMMUNITY SING - SERIES 2 #11	series	COLUMBIA	1938
D-COL-621	COMMUNITY SING - SERIES 2 #12	series	COLUMBIA	1938
D-COL-622	COMMUNITY SING - SERIES 3 #1	series	COLUMBIA	1938
D-COL-623	COMMUNITY SING - SERIES 3 #2	series	COLUMBIA	1938
D-COL-624	COMMUNITY SING - SERIES 3 #3	series	COLUMBIA	1938
D-COL-625	COMMUNITY SING - SERIES 3 #6	series	COLUMBIA	1938
D-COL-631	COMMUNITY SING - SERIES 3 #4	series	COLUMBIA	1939
D-COL-632	COMMUNITY SING - SERIES 3 #5	series	COLUMBIA	1939
D-COL-635	COMMUNITY SING - SERIES 3 #7	series	COLUMBIA	1939
D-COL-636	COMMUNITY SING - SERIES 3 #10	series	COLUMBIA	1939
D-COL-637	COMMUNITY SING - SERIES 3 #8	series	COLUMBIA	1939
D-COL-638	COMMUNITY SING - SERIES 4 #2	series	COLUMBIA	1939
D-COL-639	COMMUNITY SING - SERIES 3 #9	series	COLUMBIA	1939
D-COL-640	COMMUNITY SING - SERIES 4 #1	series	COLUMBIA	1939
D-COL-646	FOOLS WHO MADE HISTORY-ELIAS HOWE	LEMAN	COLUMBIA	1939
D-COL-647	FOOLS WHO MADE HISTORY-CHARLES GOODYEAR		COLUMBIA	1939
D-COL-655	COMMUNITY SING - SERIES 4 #3	series	COLUMBIA	1939
D-COL-656	COMMUNITY SING - SERIES 4 #4	series	COLUMBIA	1939
D-COL-788	TEXAS	MARSHALL	COLUMBIA	1941
D-COL-902	FLYING G-MEN - SERIAL	HORNE, TAYLOR	COLUMBIA	1939

D-COL-903	MANDRAKE THE MAGICIAN - SERIAL	DEMING, NELSON	COLUMBIA	1939
D-COL-908	HOWARDS OF VIRGINIA	LLOYD	COLUMBIA	1940
D-COL-911	ADVENTURE IN WASHINGTON	GREEN	COLUMBIA	1941
D-COL-916	SHE KNEW ALL THE ANSWERS	WALLACE	COLUMBIA	1941
D-COL-931	ADAM HAD FOUR SONS	RATOFF	COLUMBIA	1941
D-COL-953	MEN IN HER LIFE	RATOFF	COLUMBIA	1941
D-COL-964	ADVENTURES OF MARTIN EDEN	SALKOW	COLUMBIA	1942
D-COL-982	SOMETHING TO SHOUT ABOUT	RATOFF	COLUMBIA	1943
D-COL-996	COMMANDOES STRIKE AT DAWN	FARROW	COLUMBIA	1942
D-COL-1210	MILITARY ACADEMY	LEDERMAN	COLUMBIA	1940
DD	DANCE OF DEATH (UK)	GILES	PARAMOUNT	1968
DD	DANGER: DIABOLIK	BAVA	PARAMOUNT	1968
DD	DAUGHTERS OF DARKNESS (FR)	KUMEL	MARON FILMS	1971
DD	DAWN OF THE DEAD	ROMERO	UNITED FILM	1978
DD	DENNIS DAY	portrait	RKO	
DD	DESIRE IN THE DUST	CLAXTON	20th CENTURY FOX	1960
DD	DEVIL DOLL (UK)	SHONTEFF	ASSOCIATED	1964
DD	DEVIL'S DAFFODIL (UK)	RATHONYI	GOLDSTONE	1961
DD	DEVILS OF DARKNESS (UK)	COMFORT	20TH CENTURY FOX	1965
DD	DIANA DORS	portrait	UNIVERSAL	
DD	DIRTY DISHES (FR: LA JUMENT VAPER)	BUNUEL	MCNEIL	1978
DD	DIRTY DOZEN	ALDRICH	MGM	1967
DD	DOCTOR AND THE DEVILS, THE	FRANCIS	20th CENTURY FOX	1985
DD	DON DOUGLAS	portrait	RKO	
DD	DREAM A LITTLE DREAM	ROCCO	VESTRON	1989
DD	TO THE DEVIL A DAUGHTER (UK)	SYKES	CINE ARTISTES	1976
DD	WE DIVE AT DAWN (UK)	ASQUITH	GFD	1943
DD1	DEVIL'S DAFFODIL (UK)	RATHONYI	GOLDSTONE	1961
DE	DEVIL'S EYE (SWE: DJAVULENS OGA)	BERGMAN	JANUS	1960
DE	HIDEOUT IN THE ALPS (UK: DUSTY ERMINE)	VORHAUS	GRAND	1937
DE	PRICE OF FOLLY (UK: DOUBLE ERROR*)	SUMMERS	PATHE	1937
DE	RICHARD EGAN	portrait	RKO	
DEBB	DECEIVED	HARRIS	BUENA VISTA	1991
DEBB	DINOSAUR	LEIGHTON	BUENA VISTA	2000
DEBB	DUECE BIGALOW: MALE GIGOLO	MITCHELL	BUENA VISTA	1999
DEGRASSE 2161	PIPER'S PRICE	DE GRASSE	UNIVERSAL	1917
DEL	DELIRIOUS	MANKIEWICZ	MGM	1991
DER	SAFECRACKER (UK)	MILLAND	MGM	1958
DF	CASTLE OF FU MANCHU	FRANCO	INT'L CINEMA	1969
DF	DELTA FORCE	GOLAN	CANNON	1986
DF	DOG OF FLANDERS	CLARK	20th CENTURY FOX	1959
DF	FOR FREEDOM (UK)	ELVEY, KNIGHT	GFD	1940
D-FB	DETECTIVE (UK: FATHER BROWN)	HAMER	COLUMBIA	1954
DFII	DELTA FORCE 2	NORRIS	CANNON	1990
DFM	DESIGN FOR MURDER (UK: TRUNK CRIME)	BOULTING	WORLD	1939
DFO	DUET FOR ONE	KONCHALOVSKI	CANNON	1986
DG	DALTON GANG	BEEBE	LIPPERT	1949
DG	DARING GAME	BENEDEK	PARAMOUNT	1967
DGL	DRACULA'S GREAT LOVE	AGUIRRE	INT'L AMUSEMENT	1974
DH	DEAN HARENS	portrait	UNIV	
DH	DEATH HUNT	HUNT	20th CENTURY FOX	1981
DH	DESERT HELL	WARREN	20th CENTURY FOX	1958
DH	DESPERATE HOURS	CIMINO	MGM	1990
DH	DEVIL HORSE	JACKMAN	PATHE	1926
DH	DIE HARD WITH A VENGEANCE	MCTIERNAN	20th CENTURY FOX	1995
DH	DOSS HOUSE (UK)	BAXTER	MGM	1933
DH2	DIE HARD 2	HARLIN	20th CENTURY FOX	1990
DI	DAMSEL IN DISTRESS	STEVENS	RKO	1937
DI	KILL ME TOMORROW	FISHER	TUDOR PICTURES	1957
DIL-8	HUMANITY	DILLION	FOX FILM	1933
DIN	DINGAKA	UYS	EMBASSY	1965
DIS	DIVORCE ITALIAN STYLE	GERMI	EMBASSY	1962
DJ	DAVID JANSSEN	portrait	UNIV	
DJ	DEAR JOHN (SWE: KARE JOHN)	LINDGREN	SIGMA III	1964
DJ	FUN WITH DICK AND JANE	KOTCHEFF	COLUMBIA	1977
DJ	GET ON WITH IT! (UK: DENTIST ON THE JOB)	PENNINGTON-RICHARDS	GOVERNOR	1961

DJ	NETWORK	LUMET	MGM/UNITED ARTISTS	1976
DJD	DOCTER DOLITTLE	FLEISCHER	20th CENTURY FOX	1967
DK	DAUN KENNEDY	portrait	UNIV	
DK	DRESSED TO KILL	DE PALMA	FILMWAYS PICTURES	1980
DL	DAVID LOEW	portrait	RKO	
DL	DIANA LEWIS	portrait	WARNER BROS	
DL	DIOS LOS CRIA (MEX)	SOLARES	PELICULAS MEX	1953
DL	DOCTOR IN LOVE (UK)	THOMAS	GOVERNOR	1960
DL	DONNA LEE	portrait	RKO	
DL	DOROTHY LOVETT	portrait	RKO	
DL	DREAM LOVER	KAZAN	GRAMERCY	1994
DM	DEMOLITION MAN	BRAMBILLA	WARNER BROS	1993
DM	DENNIS THE MENACE	CASTLE	WARNER BROS	1993
DM	DEPUTY MARSHALL	BERKE	LIPPERT	1949
DM	DICKIE MOORE	portrait	RKO	
DM	DOROTHY MORRIS	portrait	UNIV	
DM	DOUBLE MURDER (IT)	STENO	WARNER BROS	1978
DM	DOUGLASS MONTGOMERY	portrait	UNIV	
DM	SUICIDE SQUADRON (UK: DANGEROUS MOONLIGHT)	HURST	REPUBLIC	1942
DM3-26	CHICAGO	URSON	PATHE	1927
DM4-2	COP, THE	CRISP	PATHE EXCHANGE	1928
DMC	DRIVE ME CRAZY	SCHULTZ	20th CENTURY FOX	1999
DMCL	DIRTY MARY CRAZY LARRY	HOUGH	20th CENTURY FOX	1974
DME	DIVORCE MADE EASY	BURNS	PARAMOUNT	1929
DMW	DEAD MAN WALKING	ROBBINS	GRAMERCY	1995
DN	DEAD OF NIGHT (UK)	CAVALCANTI	JANUS	R60
DN	NIGHT OF PASSION (UK: DURING ONE NIGHT)	FURIE	ASTOR	1960
DN1	SOUTH AMERICAN GEORGE (UK)	VARNEL	COLUMBIA	1941
DO	DEAD ONE	MAHON	MARDI GRAS	1960
DO	DEAR OCTOPUS (UK)	FRENCH	ENGLISH	1943
DOA	DAY OF ANGER	VALERII	NATIONAL GENERAL PICTU	1969
DOC	DOC	PERRY	UNITED ARTISTS	1971
DOG	SHAGGY DOG	BARTON	BUENA VISTA	1959
DOG-Prod	SHAGGY DOG	BARTON	BUENA VISTA	1959
DOM	DIARY OF A MAD OLD MAN	RADEMAKERS	CANNON	1987
DOT	DAYS OF THUNDER	SCOTT	PARAMOUNT	1990
D-OX	OPERATION X (UK: MY DAUGHTER JOY)	RATOFF	COLUMBIA	1950
DP	DAMON AND PYTHIAS (IT: IL TIRANNO DI SIRACUSA)	BERNHARDT	MGM	1962
DP	DEVIL'S HARBOR (UK: DEVIL'S POINT)	TULLY	20th CENTURY FOX	1954
DP	DICK POWELL	portrait	RKO	
DP	DOWN PERISCOPE	WARD	20th CENTURY FOX	1996
DP	OPERATION MURDER (UK)	MORRIS	ASSO. BRITISH-PATHE	1957
DP-1	GILBERT HARDING SPEAKING OF MURDER (UK)	DICKSON	PARAMOUNT BRITISH	1954
DP3	TALE OF THREE WOMEN (UK)	CONNELL, DICKSON	PARAMOUNT BRITISH	1954
DP123E	INNOCENT MEETING (UK)	GRAYSON	UNITED ARTISTS	1959
DP158E	WEB OF SUSPICION (UK)	VARNEL	PARAMOUNT BRITISH	1959
DPBB	DEAD PRESIDENTS	HUGHES BROS	BUENA VISTA	1995
DPBS	DEAD PIGEON ON BEETHOVEN ST.	FULLER	EMERSON	1974
DPC	DRAGON OF PENDRAGON CASTLE (UK)	BAXTER	GFD	1950
DPD	DRACULA: PRINCE OF DARKNESS (UK)	FISHER	20TH CENTURY FOX	1966
DP-R	DEVIL'S HARBOR (UK: DEVIL'S POINT)	TULLY	20th CENTURY FOX	1954
DPX1	DORIS KENYON	portrait	DE LUXE PICTURES	
DQ	DEVIL BY THE TAIL (FR)	DE BROCA	LOPERT	1969
DQ	DON QUIXOTE	NUREYEV	CONTINENTAL	1973
DR	DEATH RACE 2000	BARTEL	NEW WORLD	1975
DR	DER ROSENKAVALIER (UK)	CZINNER	SCHOENFELD	1962
DR	DEVIL'S RAIN	FUEST	BRYANSTON DIST.	1975
DR	DINNER AT THE RITZ (UK)	SCHUSTER	20TH CENTURY FOX	1937
DR	DOG OF THE REGIMENT	LEDERMAN	WARNER BROS	1927
DR	DONNA REED	portrait	UNIV	
DR	DRIVEN	HARLIN	WARNER BROS	2001
DR	DUNCAN RENALDO	portrait	MGM	
DR	FUGITIVE LADY (UK)	SALKOW	REPUBLIC	1950
DS	DANGER STREET	INCE	FBO	1928
DS	DARK OF THE SUN (UK: MERCENARIES)	CARDIFF	MGM	1968
DS	DARK SECRET (UK)	ROGERS	BUTCHER'S	1949

DS	DEATH SHIP	RAKOFF	AVCO EMBASSY	1980
DS	DEMON SEED	CAMMELL	UNITED ARTISTS	1977
DS	DOCTOR SYN (UK)	NEILL	GAUMONT BRIT. AMER.	1937
DS	DOLL SQUAD	MIKELS	GENENI FILM	1973
DS	DON SIEGEL	portrait	UNIV	
DS	DRAGONSLAYER	ROBBINS	PARAMOUNT	1981
DS	DREAMSCAPE	RUBEN	20th CENTURY FOX	1984
DS	DRIVER'S SEAT	GRIFFI	AVCO EMBASSY	1974
DS	TEUFEL IN SEIDE (GER: 1956)	HANSEN	CASINO FILM	1962
DS	WHO'LL STOP THE RAIN (DOG SOLDIERS)	REISZ	UNITED ARTISTS	1978
DS6	DEEP STAR SIX	CUNNINGHAM	TRI STAR	1989
DS-B	WHO'LL STOP THE RAIN (DOG SOLDIERS)	REISZ	UNITED ARTISTS	1978
DSD	DETECTIVE SCHOOL DROP OUTS	OTTONI	CANNON	1986
DSE	DAY THE SKY EXPLODED (IT/FR: LA MORTE VIENE DALLO SPAZIO)	HEUSCH	EXCELSIOR	1961
DSG	DAUGHTER OF THE SUN GOD	HARTFORD	HERTS-LION INT'L	1963
DSM	DEATH SMILES ON A MURDERER	D'AMATO	AVCO EMBASSY	1974
DSS	DESPERATELY SEEKING SUSAN	SEIDELMAN	ORION	1985
DT	BLOOD ON SATAN'S CLAW/DEVIL'S TOUCH* (UK)	HAGGARD	CANNON	1971
DT	DEADLY TRACKERS	SHEAR	WARNER BROS	1973
DT	DISTANT THUNDER	ROSENTHAL	PARAMOUNT	1988
DT	DISTANT TRUMPET (UK)	FISHER	AREX	1952
DT	DOCTOR IN TROUBLE (UK)	THOMAS	HEMISPHERE	1970
DT	DON TERRY	portrait	UNIV	
DT	DON'T TELL MOM THE BABYSITTERS DEAD	HEREK	WARNER BROS	1991
DT	DOROTHY TREE	portrait	UNIV	
DT	DOWNTOWN	BENJAMIN	20th CENTURY FOX	1990
DT	DR. TERROR'S HOUSE OF HORRORS (UK)	FRANCIS	PARAMOUNT	1965
DT	DUMMY TALKS (UK)	MITCHELL	ANGLO-AMERICAN	1943
DT2	DEEP THROAT PART 2	SARNO	DAMIANO	1974
DTBB	DOUBLE TAKE	GALLO	TOUCHSTONE	2001
DTC	RACING LUCK	RAYMAKER	ASSOCIATED EXHIBITOR	1924
DTG	ALL MINE TO GIVE	REISNER	RKO	1957
DTOPE	DOIN' TIME ON PLANET EARTH	MATTHAU	CANNON	1987
DUBB	DUETS	PALTROW	BUENA VISTA	2000
DUN-22	GOOD AS GOLD	DUNLAP	FOX	1927
DUR-8	STRANGE IDOLS	DURNING	FOX FILM	1922
DV	DAVE	REITMAN	WARNER BROS	1993
DVSF	DRACULA VS. FRANKENSTEIN	ADAMSON	INDEPENDENT INTL	1972
DW	DANCES WITH WOLVES	COSTNER	ORION	1990
DW	DESPERATE WOMEN (tv movie)	BELLAMY	NBC	1978
DW	DEVIL IS A WOMAN (IT: IL SORRISOGRANDE TENTATORE 1973)	DAMIANI	20th CENTURY FOX	1975
DW	DOOMWATCH	SASDY	AVCO EMBASSY	1974
DW	DOWN TWISTED	PYUN	CANNON	1986
DW	DRY WHITE SEASON	PALCY	MGM	1989
DW3	DEATH WISH 3	WINNER	CANNON	1985
DW4	DEATH WISH 4	THOMPSON	CANNON	1987
DWII-85	DEATH WISH II	WINNER	FILMWAYS	1982
DWM	APPOINTMENT WITH MURDER	BERNHARD	FILM CLASSICS	1948
DWR	DEATH WARRANT	SARAFIAN	MGM	1990
DWV	THIRD MAN (UK)	REED	SELZNICK RELEASING	1949
DY	DYING YOUNG	SCHUMACHER	20th CENTURY FOX	1991
DYC	MY LOVER MY SON/DON'T YOU CRY* (UK)	NEWLAND	MGM	1970
DZ	DANGER ZONE	BERKE	LIPPERT	1951
DZ	DOCTOR ZHIVAGO (UK)	LEAN	MGM	1965
DZ	DROP ZONE	BADHAM	PARAMOUNT	1994
E	EMIL AND THE DETECTIVES (UK)	ROSMER	OLYMPIC	1935
E	ENTITY, THE	FURIE	20th CENTURY FOX	1981
E	ERNESTO	SAMPERI	INT'L SPECTRAFILM	1983
E	ESCAPADE (UK)	LEACOCK	DCA	1955
E	EVERYDAY	BRITTON	AMERICAN	1976
E	EVILSPEAK	WESTON	WARNER BROS	1981
E	EXORCIST 3	BLATTY	20th CENTURY FOX	1990
E	EYEWITNESS	YATES	20th CENTURY FOX	1981
E	FACE OF EVE/US: EVE (UK)	LYNN, SUMMERS	COMMONWEALTH	1968
E	HAPPY GO LOVELY (UK)	HUMBERSTONE	RKO	1951
E	PLAYBOY (UK: KICKING THE MOON AROUND)	FORDE	GFD	1938

E-1	HOSS AND HOSS (sh)	(UNFINISHED)	PATHE EXCHANGE	1924
E-1	PICKANINNY (sh)	KERR, PARROTT	PATHE EXCHANGE	1921
E-1	YOU BRING THE DUCKS (sh)	YATES	MGM	1934
E-2	HOT HEELS (sh)	JESKE	PATHE EXCHANGE	1924
E-2	NOSED OUT (sh)	YATES	MGM	1934
E-3	BALLAD OF PADUCAH JAIL (sh)	GRINDE	MGM	1934
E-3	SKY PLUMBER (sh)	DAVISS	PATHE EXCHANGE	1924
E-4	LUCKY BEGINNERS (sh)	DOUGLAS, ROACH	MGM	1935
E-4	UNFINISHED ARTHUR STONE (sh)		PATHE EXCHANGE	1924
E-5	INFERNAL TRIANGLE (sh)	DOUGLAS	MGM	1935
E-5	SHOULD LANDLORDS LIVE? (sh)	BARROWS, DAVIS	PATHE EXCHANGE	1924
E-6	JUST A GOOD GUY (sh)	DEL RUTH	PATHE EXCHANGE	1924
E-6	UNFINISHED ROACH (sh)		PATHE EXCHANGE	1924
E-7	JUST A GOOD GUY (sh)	DEL RUTH	PATHE EXCHANGE	1924
E-8	TAME MEN AND WILD WOMEN (sh)	DE SANO	PATHE EXCHANGE	1925
E-9	COMMAND PERFORMANCE	LANG	TIFFANY	1931
E-9	HARD WORKING LOAFERS (sh)		PATHE EXCHANGE	1925
E-10	CHANGE THE NEEDLE (sh)	ROACH	PATHE EXCHANGE	1925
E-10	HELL BOUND	LANG	TIFFANY	1931
E-11	UNNAMED ARTHUR STONE (sh)		PATHE EXCHANGE	1925
E-12	SHERLOCK SLEUTH (sh)	CEDER	PATHE EXCHANGE	1925
E-12	WOMEN GO ON FOREVER	LANG	TIFFANY	1931
E-13	HARD -BOILED (sh)	MCCAREY	PATHE EXCHANGE	1925
E-14	BAD BOY (sh)	MCCAREY	PATHE EXCHANGE	1925
E-15	LOOKING FOR SALLY (sh)	MCCAREY	PATHE EXCHANGE	1925
E-16	WHAT PRICE GOOFY? (sh)	MCCAREY	PATHE EXCHANGE	1925
E-17	ISN'T LIFE TERRIBLE? (sh)	MCCAREY	PATHE EXCHANGE	1925
E-18	INNOCENT HUSBANDS (sh)	MCCAREY	PATHE EXCHANGE	1925
E-19	NO FATHER TO GUIDE HIM (sh)	MCCAREY	PATHE EXCHANGE	1925
E-45	MURDER! (UK)	HITCHCOCK	BIP	1930
E48-1	MAN ON THE RUN (UK)	HUNTINGTON	STRATFORD	1949
E49-1	LANDFALL (UK)	ANNAKIN	STRATFORD	1949
E49-2	DANCING YEARS (UK)	FRENCH	STRATFORD	1950
E49-3	STAGE FRIGHT (UK)	HITCHCOCK	WARNER BROS.	1950
E49-4	PORTRAIT OF CLARE (UK)	COMFORT	STRATFORD	1950
E49-6	GUILT IS MY SHADOW (UK)	KELLINO	STRATFORD	1950
E49-7	HER PANELLED DOOR (UK: WOMAN WITH NO NAME)	VAJDA	SOUVAINE	1950
E50-4	LAUGHTER IN PARADISE (UK)	ZAMPI	STRATFORD	1951
E50-6	YOUNG WIVES' TALE (UK)	CASS	STRATFORD	1951
E51-2	WOMAN'S ANGLE (UK)	ARLISS	STRATFORD	1952
E51-3	SO LITTLE TIME (UK)	BENNETT	MACDONALD	1952
E51-4	ANGELS ONE FIVE (UK)	O'FERRALL	STRATFORD	1952
E51-6	AFFAIR IN MONTE CARLO (UK: 24 HOURS OF A WOMAN'S LIFE)	SAVILLE	ALLIED ARTISTS	1952
E51-7	CASTLE IN THE AIR (UK)	CASS	STRATFORD	1952
E52-1	FATHER'S DOING FINE (UK)	CASS	STRATFORD	1952
E52-5	UNCLE WILLIE'S BICYCLE SHOP (UK: ISN'T LIFE WONDERFUL!)	FRENCH	STRATFORD	1954
E52-7	VALLEY OF SONG (UK)	GUNN	STRATFORD	1953
E52-8	WILL ANY GENTLEMAN...? (UK)	ANDERSON	STRATFORD	1953
E-53	DUEL IN THE JUNGLE	MARSHALL	WARNER BROS	1954
E53-1	HOUSE OF THE ARROW (UK)	ANDERSON	STRATFORD	1953
E53-2	GOOD BEGINNING (UK)	GUNN	STRATFORD	1953
E53-4	YOUNG AND WILLING (UK: WEAK AND THE WICKED)	THOMPSON	ALLIED ARTISTS	1954
E-53-6	DUEL IN THE JUNGLE (UK)	MARSHALL	WARNER BROS	1954
E53-7	TONIGHT'S THE NIGHT (UK: HAPPILY EVER AFTER)	ZAMPI	ALLIED ARTISTS	1954
E54-1	DAM BUSTERS (UK)	ANDERSON	WARNER BROS.	1955
E54-2	COCKTAILS IN THE KITCHEN (UK: FOR BETTER, FOR WORSE)	THOMPSON	STRATFORD	1954
E-54-4	MOBY DICK	HUSTON	UNITED ARTISTS	1954
E54-5	WARRIORS/US: DARK AVENGER (UK)	LEVIN	ALLIED ARTISTS	1955
E55-1	OH... ROSALINDA!! (UK)	POWELL, PRESSBURGER	ASSO. BRITISH-PATHE	1955
E55-3	NOW AND FOREVER (UK)	ZAMPI	STRATFORD	1956
E-55-6	1984 (UK)	ANDERSON	COLUMBIA	1956
E55-7	IT'S GREAT TO BE YOUNG! (UK)	FRANKEL	FINE ARTS	1956
E55-8	IT'S NEVER TOO LATE (UK)	MCCARTHY	STRATFORD	1956
E55-10	TONS OF TROUBLE (UK)	HISCOTT	RENOWN	1956
E56-1	MY WIFE'S FAMILY (UK)	GUNN	ASSO. BRITISH-PATHE	1956
E56-3	GOOD COMPANIONS (UK)	THOMPSON	STRATFORD	1957

E56-12	NO TIME FOR TEARS (UK)	FRANKEL	ASSO. BRITISH-PATHE	1957
E57-1	ACCUSED/US: MARK OF THE HAWK (UK)	AUDLEY	UNIVERSAL	1957
E-57-3	WOMAN IN A DRESSING GOWN (UK)	THOMPSON	WARNER BROS	1957
E57-6	YOUNG AND THE GUILTY (UK)	COTES	NTA	1958
E57-8	CHASE A CROOKED SHADOW (UK)	ANDERSON	WARNER BROS.	1958
E57-9	MOONRAKER (UK)	MACDONALD	ASSO. BRITISH-PATHE	1958
E57-15	DESERT ATTACK (UK: ICE COLD IN ALEX)	THOMPSON	20TH CENTURY FOX	1958
E57-18	INDISCREET (UK 1957)	DONEN	WARNER BROS	1969
E57-19	WONDERFUL THINGS! (UK)	WILCOX	ASSO. BRITISH-PATHE	1958
E58-5	NO TREES IN THE STREET (UK)	THOMPSON	SEVEN ARTS	1959
E58-10	LADY IS A SQUARE (UK)	WILCOX	ASSO. BRITISH-PATHE	1959
E58-12	ALIVE AND KICKING (UK)	FRANKEL	SEVEN ARTS	1959
E58-16	LOOK BACK IN ANGER (UK)	RICHARDSON	WARNER BROS.	1959
E58-19	OPERATION BULLSHINE (UK)	GUNN	ASSO. BRITISH-PATHE	1959
E59-3	SCHOOL FOR SCOUNDRELS (UK)	HAMER	CONTINENTAL	1960
E59-7	TOMMY THE TOREADOR (UK)	CARSTAIRS	WARNER-PATHE	1959
E59-10	FOLLOW THAT HORSE! (UK)	BROMLY	WARNER BROS.	1960
E59-11	BOTTOMS UP (UK)	ZAMPI	WARNER BROS/7ARTS	1960
E59-12	HELL IS A CITY (UK)	GUEST	COLUMBIA	1960
E60-1	SANDS OF THE DESERT (UK)	CARSTAIRS	WARNER-PATHE	1960
E60-6	JUNGLE FIGHTERS (UK: LONG AND THE SHORT AND THE TALL)	NORMAN	CONTINENTAL	1961
E60-8	CALL ME GENIUS (UK: REBEL)	DAY	CONTINENTAL	1961
E-60-10	CHASE A CROOKED SHADOW (UK)	ANDERSON	WARNER BROS.	1958
E61-3	GO TO BLAZES (UK)	TRUMAN	WARNER-PATHE	1962
E61-4	PETTICOAT PIRATES (UK)	MACDONALD	WARNER-PATHE	1961
E61-6	WONDERFUL TO BE YOUNG! (UK: YOUNG ONES)	FURIE	PARAMOUNT	1961
E61-8	OPERATION SNATCH (UK)	DAY	CONTINENTAL	1962
E61-10	POT CARRIERS (UK)	SCOTT	WARNER-PATHE	1962
E61-11	GUNS OF DARKNESS (UK)	ASQUITH	WARNER BROS.	1962
E62-4	PUNCH AND JUDY MAN (UK)	SUMMERS	WARNER-PATHE	1963
E62-5	WE JOINED THE NAVY (UK)	TOYE	WARNER-PATHE	1962
E62-6	SUMMER HOLIDAY (UK)	YATES	AIP	1963
E63-1	WEST 11 (UK)	WINNER	WARNER-PATHE	1963
E63-3	WORLD TEN TIMES OVER (UK)	RILLA	GOLDSTONE	1963
E63-4	CROOKS IN CLOISTERS (UK)	SUMMERS	WARNER-PATHE	1964
E63-7	FRENCH DRESSING (UK)	RUSSELL	WARNER-PATHE	1964
E63-11	BARGEE (UK)	WOOD	WARNER-PATHE	1964
E64-4	RATTLE OF A SIMPLE MAN (UK)	BOX	CONTINENTAL	1964
E66-5	MISTER TEN PER CENT (UK)	SCOTT	WARNER-PATHE	1967
E67-4	VENGEANCE OF SHE (UK)	OWEN	20TH CENTURY FOX	1968
E67-5	LAST CONTINENT (UK)	CARRERAS	20TH CENTURY FOX	1968
E67-6	DEVIL RIDES OUT (UK: DEVIL'S BRIDE)	FISHER	20TH CENTURY FOX	1968
E3345	GRACE KELLY	portrait	MGM	
E3348	GRACE KELLY	portrait	MGM	
E3349	GRACE KELLY	portrait		
EA	CRY IN THE DARK (EVIL ANGELS)	SCHEPISI	WARNER BROS	1988
EA	EXECUTIVE ACTION	MILLER	NATIONAL GENERAL PICTU	1973
EA1	DECISION AGAINST TIME (UK: MAN IN THE SKY)	CRICHTON	MGM	1957
EAGLE	EAGLE VS DRAGON (DOCUMENTARY FEATURETTE)	THOMA		1944
EB	EARLY BIRD	HINES	EAST COAST	1925
EB	EDDIE BRACKEN	portrait	RKO	
EB	EDNA BEST	portrait	RKO	
EB	EXCESS BAGGAGE (UK)	DAVIS	RKO	1933
EB	EXPRESSO BONGO (UK)	GUEST	CONTINENTAL	1959
EBB	ENDURANCE	WOODHEAD	BUENA VISTA	1999
EC	ECCO (IT: 1963)	PROIA	AIP	1965
EC	EDUARDO CIANNELLI	portrait	RKO	
EC	EL CONDOR	GUILLERMANN	MGM	1970
EC	ELLEN CORBY	portrait	RKO	
EC	JANET SHAW aka ELLEN CLANCY	portrait	UNIVERSAL	
ECS	ELIZA COMES TO STAY (UK)	H EDWARDS	TWICKENHAM	1936
ED	EVE OF DESTRUCTION	GIBBINS	ORION	1991
ED	EVERYBODY DANCE (UK)	REISNER	GAUMONT BRIT. AMER.	1936
ED	EVERYBODY'S DANCIN'	JASON	LIPPERT	1950
ED	EXECUTIVE DECISION	BAIRD	WARNER BROS	1996
ED	TREASURE OF THE JAMAICA REEF/EVIL IN THE DEEP	STONE		1975

ED1	GIVE US THIS DAY (UK)	DMYTRYK	EAGLE LION	1949
ED101	WHILE I LIVE (UK)	HARLOW	20TH CENTURY FOX	1947
EE	EUROPA EUROPA	HOLLAND	ORION	1990
EF	EMERALD FOREST	BOORMAN	EMBASSY	1985
EF	JEANNIE (UK)	FRENCH	ENGLISH	1941
EF-144	NOWHERE TO GO (UK)	HOLT	MGM	1958
EFE	EYE FOR AN EYE	MOORE	EMBASSY	1966
EG	EL GOLFO (MEX)	ESCRIVA	MERCURIO FILMS	1969
EG	END OF THE GAME (GER: DER RICHTER UND SEIN HENKER 1975)	SCHELL	20TH CENTURY FOX	1978
EG	EVERY TIME WE SAY GOODBYE	MIZRAHI	TRI STAR	1986
EG	HAPPY GO LOVELY (UK)	HUMBERSTONE	RKO	1951
EH	ELEANOR HOLM	portrait	WARNER BROS	
EH	EVERY HOME SHOULD HAVE ONE (UK)	CLARK	QUARTET	1970
EIC	EAGLE IN A CAGE	COOK	NATIONAL GENERAL PICTU	1972
EIE	DISK-O-TEK HOLIDAY (UK: JUST FOR YOU)	HICKOX, SCARZA	ALLIED ARTISTS	1966
EIR	EVERYTHING IS RHYTHM (UK)	GOULDING	ASTOR	1936
EJ	ELSIE JANIS FILMS	portrait		
EJBB	ERNEST GOES TO JAIL	CHERRY	BUENA VISTA	1990
EK	ELKAY PRODUCTIONS	L'ESTRANGE-KAHN (LK)	studio	
EK	ESTHER AND THE KING	BAVA (sh)	20th CENTURY FOX	1960
EK	EVEL KNIEVEL	CHOMSKY	FANFARE	1971
EK	EVELYN KEYES		COL	
EK1	BUZZY RIDES THE RANGE	KAHN	ELKAY PROD	1940
EK2	BUZZY AND THE PHANTOM PINTO	KAHN	ELKAY PROD	1941
EL	EASY LIFE (IT: IL SORPASSO)	RISI	EMBASSY	1962
EL	EDMUND LOWE	portrait	PATHE	
EL	ELMO LINCOLN	portrait		
EL	ELSA LANCHESTER	portrait	RKO	
EL	END OF THE LINE (UK)	SAUNDERS	EROS	1957
EL1-1	CAVALCADE OF STUFF NO. 1		GRAND NATIONAL	1938
EL1-2	CAVALCADE OF STUFF NO. 2		GRAND NATIONAL	1938
EL-606	REPEAT PERFORMANCE	WEAKER	EAGLE LION	1947
ELE	ELECTRA (GR: ILEKTRA)	KAKOGIANNIS	LOPPERT	1963
EM	8 MILLION WAYS TO DIE	ASHBY	TRI STAR	1986
EM	EASY MONEY	SIGNORELLI	ORION PICTURES	1983
EM	EDWARD MONTAGNE	portrait	UNIV	
EM	ELEPHANT MAN	LYNCH	PARAMOUNT	1980
EM	ELVIRA MADIGAN	WIDERBERG	CINEMA V	1967
EM	ENEMY MINE	PETERSEN	20th CENTURY FOX	1985
EM	EVE MILLER	portrait	WARNER BROS	
EM-16	EMMANUELLE II (FR)	GIACOBETTI	PARAMOUNT	1975
EMC	EASY MONEY	SIGNORELLI	ORION PICTURES	1983
EMD	EAT MY DUST	GRIFFITH	NEW WORLD PICTURES	1976
EMERALD-2	NOT WANTED	CLIFTON	FILM CLASSICS	1949
EMO	EDNA MAY OLIVER	portrait	RKO	
EMS	ENTERTAINING MR. SLOANE (UK)	HICKOX	CONTINENTAL	1970
EN	DESERT MICE (UK)	RELPH	RANK	1959
EN	ENEMY OF THE STATE	SCOTT	BUENA VISTA	1998
ENBB	EMPEROR'S NEW GROOVE, THE (t)	DINDAL	BUENA VISTA	2000
ENY	ESCAPE FROM NEW YORK	CARPENTER	AVCO EMBASSY	1981
EOK	EAST OF KILIMANJARO (UK)	BELGARD, CAPOLINO	PARADE	1957
EOL	EAGLES OVER LONDON	CASTELLARI	MGM	1970
EOR	END OF THE ROAD	AVAKIAN	ALLIED ARTISTS	1970
EP	EAT THE PEACH (UK)	ORMROD	SKOURAS	1986
EP	ELVIS PRESLEY	portrait		
EP	EMPEROR OF THE NORTH POLE	1973	20th CENTURY FOX	1973
EP	EXTREME PREJUDICE	HILL	TRI STAR	1987
EP	FIGHTING PIMPERNEL (UK: ELUSIVE PIMPERNEL)	POWELL, PRESSBURGER	CARROLL	1950
EP	NAKED HEART (UK: MARIA CHAPDELAINE)	ALLEGRET	AAP	1950
EP 101	GUN GIRLS	DERTANO	ASTOR	1957
EQ-COL-1	ELLERY QUEEN, MASTER DETECTIVE	NEUMANN	COLUMBIA	1940
EQ-COL-3	ELLERY QUEEN AND THE PERFECT CRIME	HOGAN	COLUMBIA	1941
EQ-COL-4	ELLERY QUEEN AND THE MURDERRING	HOGAN	COLUMBIA	1941
EQ-COL-5	A CLOSE CALL FOR ELLERY QUEEN	HOGAN	COLUMBIA	1942
EQ-COL-6	A DESPERATE CHANCE FOR ELLERY QUEEN	HOGAN	COLUMBIA	1942
EQ-COL-7	ENEMY AGENTS MEET ELERY QUEEN	HOGAN	COLUMBIA	1942

ER	END OF THE ROAD (UK)	RILLA	DCA	1957
ER	ESCAPE FROM RED ROCK	BERNDS	20th CENTURY FOX	1957
ERB	LOVE, THE MAGICIAN (SP: EL AMOR BRUJO	SAURA	ORION	1986
ES	ESCAPE FROM NEW YORK	CARPENTER	AVCO EMBASSY	1981
ES	EYES OF A STRANGER	WEIDERHORN	WARNER BROS	1981
ESB	EMPIRE STRIKES BACK	KERSHNER	20th CENTURY FOX	1980
ET	ELIZABETH TAYLOR	portrait	UNIVERSAL	early 40s
ETMD	EVIL THAT MEN DO	THOMPSON	TRI STAR	1984
ETWSG	EVERY TIME WE SAY GOODBYE	MIZRAHI	COLUMBIA	1986
EU	GREATEST LOVE (IT: EUROPA '51)	ROSSELLINI	IFE	1952
EV	EASY VIRTUE (UK)	HITCHCOCK	SONO ART	1928
EV	END OF VIOLENCE, THE	WENDERS	MGM	1997
EVD	EAGLE VS DRAGON (documentary featurette)	THOMA		1944
EVS	ERICH VON STROHEIM	portrait		
EW	COWBOY	WILLIAMS	LIPPERT	1954
EW	EDGE OF THE WORLD (UK)	POWELL	PAX	1937
EW	EVERYBODY WINS	REISZ	ORION	1990
EW	LIFE IN EMERGENCY WARD 10 (UK)	DAY	EROS	1959
EW	SUDDEN TERROR	HOUGH	ITC ENTERTAINMENT	1970
EX	EXPLORERS	DANTE	PARAMOUNT	1985
EX1	JEANNIE (UK)	FRENCH	ENGLISH	1941
EX2	TALK ABOUT JACQUELINE (UK)	FRENCH, STEIN	MGM	1942
EXL-1	MEET ME AT DAWN (UK)	CRESWELL, FREELAND	20TH CENTURY FOX	1947
EXT	EXTERMINATOR	GLICKENHAUS	EMBASSY	1980
EXT2	EXTERMINATOR 2	BUNTZMAN	CANNON	1984
EYE	EYE FOR AN EYE, AN	CARTER	AVCO EMBASSY	1981
F	BAREFOOT BATTALION	TALLAS	20TH CENTURY FOX	1956
F	FAME	PARKER	UNITED ARTISTS	1980
F	FANTASIA	ALGAR	BUENA VISTA	R56
F	FAR FROM HOME	BORSOS	20th CENTURY FOX	1995
F	FAR FROM MADDING CROWD	SCHLESINGER	MGM	1968
F	FARGO	COEN BROS	GRAMERCY	1996
F	FARMER, THE	VERLATSKY	COLUMBIA	1977
F	FAST BREAK	SMIGHT	COLUMBIA	1979
F	FATAL INSTINCT	REINER	MGM	1993
F	FATHOM (UK)	MARTINSON	20TH CENTURY FOX	1967
F	FAVORITE, THE	SMIGHT	20TH CENTURY FOX	1989
F	FEARLESS	WEIR	WARNER BROS	1993
F	FIEND WITHOUT A FACE (UK)	CRABTREE	MGM	1958
F	FIRE DOWN BELOW (UK)	PARRISH	COLUMBIA	1957
F	FIRST A GIRL (UK)	SAVILLE	GAUMONT BRIT. AMER.	1935
F	FLED	HOOKS	MGM	1996
F	FLY II	WALAS	20th CENTURY FOX	1989
F	FLY, THE	CRONENBERG	20TH CENTURY FOX	1986
F	FOOTLOOSE	ROSSELLINI	PARAMOUNT	1984
F	FOR THE FARMER	DERLATSKY	COLUMBIA	1977
F	FOUR FOR THE MORGUE	SLEDGE	MPA FEATURE FILMS	1962
F	FRIEDA (UK)	DEARDEN	UNIVERSAL	1947
F	FRUSTRATION (SWED: SKEPP TILL INDIA LAND 1947)	BERGMAN	FILM CLASSICS	1949
F	FUN AT ST. FANNY'S (UK)	ELVEY	BRITISH LION	1956
F	I DIDN'T DO IT (UK)	VARNEL	COLUMBIA	1945
F	SON OF FLUBBER	STEVENSON	BUENA VISTA	R70
F	STUDY IN TERROR (UK)	HILL	COLUMBIA	1965
F007	TRUDY MARSHALL	portrait	FOX	
F-1	PARDON US	PARROTT	MGM	1931
F-1	ROUGHING IT (sh)	JACKMAN	PATHE EXCHANGE	1923
F-2	LET'S BUILD (sh)	PEMBROKE	PATHE EXCHANGE	1923
F-2	PACK UP YOUR TROUBLES (sh)	MARSHALL, MCCAREY	MGM	1932
F-3	DEVIL'S BROTHER	ROACH, ROGERS	MGM	1933
F-3	HEAVY SEAS (sh)	GUIOL, HOWE	PATHE EXCHANGE	1923
F3	ROCK AROUND THE WORLD (UK: TOMMY STEELE STORY)	BRYANT	AIP	1957
F-4	GREAT OUTDOORS (sh)	GUIOL	PATHE EXCHANGE	1923
F-4	SONS OF THE DESERT	SEITER	MGM	1933
F-5	BABES IN TOYLAND (MARCH OF THE WOODEN SOLDIERS)	MEINS, ROGERS	MGM	1934
F-5	DARKEST HOUR (sh)	HOWE	PATHE EXCHANGE	1923
F-6	POLITICAL PULL (sh)	CLEMENTS	PATHE EXCHANGE	1924

F6	STOWAWAY	SEITER	20th CENTURY FOX	1933
F-6	VAGABOND LADY	TAYLOR	MGM	1935
F-7	BONNIE SCOTLAND	HORNE	MGM	1935
F-7	HELP ONE ANOTHER (sh)	GUIOL	PATHE EXCHANGE	1924
F-8	BOHEMIAN GIRL	HORNE, ROGERS	MGM	1936
F-8	HUNTERS BOLD (sh)		PATHE EXCHANGE	1924
F-9	HIT THE HIGH SPOTS (sh)	GUIOL	PATHE EXCHANGE	1924
F-9	MR. CINDERELLA		MGM	1936
F10	BACHELOR IN PARIS (UK: SONG OF PARIS)	GUILLERMIN	LIPPERT	1952
F-10	BOTTLE BABIES (sh)	HOWE, PEMBROKE	PATHE EXCHANGE	1924
F-10	KELLY THE SECOND	MEINS	MGM	1936
F10	OLD MOTHER RILEY MEETS THE VAMPIRE/VAMPIRE OVER LONDON	GILLING	BLUE CHIP	1952
F-11	OUR RELATIONS	LACHMAN	MGM	1936
F-11	SUFFERING SHAKESPEARE (sh)	CEDER	PATHE EXCHANGE	1924
F-12	GENERAL SPANKY	DOUGLAS, NEWMEYER	MGM	1936
F-12	RADIO MAD (sh)	HOWE	PATHE EXCHANGE	1924
F-12	WITHOUT COMPROMISE	FLYNN	FOX FILM	1922
F-13	HARD-BOILED TENDERFOOT (sh)	HOWE	PATHE EXCHANGE	1924
F-13	UNRELEASED ROACH (sh)		MGM	1936
F-14	SOUTH O' THE NORTH POLE	HOWE	PATHE EXCHANGE	1924
F-14	WAY OUT WEST (sh)	HORNE	MGM	1937
F-15	LOST DOG (sh)	HOWE	PATHE EXCHANGE	1924
F-15	PICK A STAR	SEDGWICK	MGM	1937
F-16	HOT STUFF (sh)	HOWE	PATHE EXCHANGE	1924
F-16	NOBODY'S BABY	MEINS	MGM	1937
F-17	TOPPER (sh)	MCLEOD	MGM	1937
F-18	DEAF, DUMB AND DAFFY (sh)	HOWE	PATHE EXCHANGE	1924
F-18	UPSPECIFIEC TITLE	ROACH	MGM	1937
F-19	LAUGH THAT OFF (sh)	HOWE	PATHE EXCHANGE	1925
F-19	MERRILY WE LIVE	MCLEOD	MGM	1938
F-20	FOX HUNT (sh)	HOWE	PATHE EXCHANGE	1925
F-20	SWISS MISS	BLYSTONE	MGM	1938
F-21	EXCUSE MY GLOVE (sh)	HOWE	PATHE EXCHANGE	1925
F-21	THERE GOES MY HEART	MCLEOD	UNITED ARTISTS	1938
F-22	BLACK HAND BLUES (BLACK HANDS) (sh)	HOWE	PATHE EXCHANGE	1925
F-22	BLOCK-HEADS	BLYSTONE	MGM	1938
F22	JAMES DUNN	portrait	FOX	1930s
F-22	MARRIED ALIVE	FLYNN	FOX FILM	1927
F-23	ROYAL FOUR-FLUSH (sh)	HOWE	PATHE EXCHANGE	1925
F-23	ZENOBIA	DOUGLAS	UNITED ARTISTS	1939
F-24	TOPPER TAKES A TRIP	MCLEOD	UNITED ARTISTS	1939
F-24	WILD PAPA (sh)	BARROWS, HOWE	PATHE EXCHANGE	1925
F-25	CAPTAIN FURY	ROACH	UNITED ARTISTS	1939
F-25	DON KEY (sh)	GUIOL, HORNE	PATHE EXCHANGE	1926
F-26	CHUMP AT OXFORD	GOULDING	UNITED ARTISTS	1940
F-27	HOUSEKEEPER'S DAUGHTER	ROACH	UNITED ARTISTS	1939
F-28	OF MICE AND MEN	MILESTONE	UNITED ARTISTS	1940
F-29	SAPS AT SEA	DOUGLAS	UNITED ARTISTS	1940
F-30	ONE MILLION B.C.	ROACH, ROACH,JR.	UNITED ARTISTS	1940
F-31	TURNABOUT	ROACH	UNITED ARTISTS	1940
F-32	CAPTAIN CAUTION	WALLACE	UNITED ARTISTS	1940
F-33	ROAD SHOW	ROACH	UNITED ARTISTS	1941
F-34	BROADWAY LIMITED	DOUGLAS	UNITED ARTISTS	1941
F-35	TOPPER RETURNS	DEL RUTH	UNITED ARTISTS	1941
F-36	NIAGARA FALLS	DOUGLAS	UNITED ARTISTS	1941
F-37	TANKS A MILLION	GUIOL	UNITED ARTISTS	1941
F-38	ALL AMERICAN CO-ED	PRINZ	UNITED ARTISTS	1941
F-39	MISS POLLY	GUIOL	UNITED ARTISTS	1941
F-40	FIESTA	PRINZ	UNITED ARTISTS	1941
F40	SIG RUMANN	portrait	FOX	
F-41	HAY FOOT	GUIOL	UNITED ARTISTS	1941
F-42	DUDES ARE PRETTY PEOPLE	ROACH, JR.	UNITED ARTISTS	1942
F-43	BROOKLYN ORCHID	NEUMANN	UNITED ARTISTS	1942
F-44	ABOUT FACE	NEUMANN	UNITED ARTISTS	1942
F-45	FLYING WITH MUSIC	ARCHAINBAUD	UNITED ARTISTS	1942
F-46	DEVIL WITH HITLER	DOUGLAS	UNITED ARTISTS	1942

F46	RUTH PETERSON	portrait	FOX	
F-47	MCGUERINS FROM BROOKLYN	NEUMANN	UNITED ARTISTS	1942
F-48	CALABOOSE	ROACH, JR.	UNITED ARTISTS	1943
F-49	FALL IN	NEWMANN	UNITED ARTISTS	1943
F-50	NAZTY NUISANCE	TRYON	UNITED ARTISTS	1943
F-51	TAXI, MISTER?	NEUMANN	UNITED ARTISTS	1943
F-52	PRAIRIE CHICKENS	ROACH, JR.	UNITED ARTISTS	1943
F-53	YANKS AHOY	NEUMANN	UNITED ARTISTS	1943
F-54	CURLEY: HAL ROACH COMEDY CANRINVAL	CARR, FOSTER	UNITED ARTISTS	1947
F-55	HERE COMES TROUBLE: LAFFTIME	GUIOL	UNITED ARTISTS	1948
F-56	FABULOUS JOE: HAL ROACH COMEDY CANRINVAL	CARR, FOSTER	UNITED ARTISTS	1947
F-57	WHO KILLED DOC ROBBIN?: LAFFTIME	CARR	UNITED ARTISTS	1948
F81/2	8 1/2	FELLINI	EMBASSY	1963
F-101	NAKED KISS (mistake-see F-102)	FULLER	ALLIED ARTISTS	1964
F122	ROSINA LAWRENCE	portrait	FOX	
F139	GIRL LIKE THAT, A	HENDERSON	PARAMOUNT	1917
F-182	FRIENDS	GILBERT	PARAMOUNT	1971
F190	MARGARET IRVING	portrait	FOX	
F190	THANKS A MILLION	DEL RUTH	20th CENTURY FOX	1935
F207	SIMONE SIMON	portrait	FOX	1930S
F241	SARA HADEN	portrait	FOX	
F253	LYNNE BERKELEY	portrait	FOX	
F254	LUCILLE MILLER	portrait	FOX	
F278	JAYNE REGAN	portrait	FOX	
F309	FRANCES DRAKE	portrait	FOX	
F322	MARGARET SKOURAS	portrait	FOX	
F376	PETER LORRE	portrait	FOX	
F400	FRANCIS LESLIE	portrait	FOX	1937
F402	RUTH TERRY	portrait	FOX	
F409	ETHEL MERMAN	portrait	FOX	
F423	OSA MASSEN	portrait	FOX	
F480	ROBERT SHAW	portrait	FOX	
F492	KANE RICHMOND	portrait	FOX	
F522	JOHN PAYNE	portrait	FOX	
F540	SHEILA RYAN	portrait	FOX	
F564	ROBERT CORNELL	portrait	FOX	
F573	RITA HAYWORTH / RITA CANSINO	portrait	FOX	
F581	JANIS CARTER	portrait	FOX	
F585	VICTOR MATURE	portrait	FOX	
F587	HELENE REYNOLDS	portrait	FOX	
F605	VIVIAN BLAINE	portrait	FOX	
F674	MADELEINE LEBEAU	portrait	FOX	
F678	CEDRIC HARDWICKE	portrait	FOX	
F719	BRENDA MARSHALL	portrait	FOX	
F723	JOHN HARVEY	portrait	FOX	
F728	DAVE WILLOCK	portrait	FOX	
F771	RONALD GRAHAM	portrait	FOX	
F776	GLENN LANGAN	portrait	FOX	
F783	STANLEY PRAGER	portrait	FOX	
F805	WILLIAM MARSHALL	portrait	FOX	
F921	KURT KREUGER	portrait	FOX	
FA	ARSON INC.	BERKE	LIPPERT	1949
FA	FAREWELL TO ARMS	VIDOR	20th CENTURY FOX	1958
FA	FRANCIS OF ASSISI	CURTIZ	20th CENTURY FOX	1961
FA	FROZEN ALIVE (UK)	KNOWLES	FEATURE FILM CORP OF AN	1964
FA	FINAL ANALYSIS	JOANOU	WARNER BROS	1992
FAF	FORTY ACRE FEUD	ORMOND	CRADDOCK FILMS	1966
FA-K	FORT APACHE THE BRONX	PETRIE	20th CENTURY FOX	1980
FAL	FUNNY ABOUT LOVE	NIMOY	PARAMOUNT	1990
FB	BAD BLONDE (UK: FLANAGAN BOY)	LE BORG	LIPPERT	1953
FB	DETECTIVE (UK: FATHER BROWN)	HAMER	COLUMBIA	1954
FB	FEMALE BUNCH	ADAMSON	GILBRETH	1971
FB	FERRIS BUELLER'S DAY OFF	HUGHES	PARAMOUNT	1986
FB	FIGHTING BACK	LUPONE	PARAMOUNT	1987
FB	FIRE DOWN BELOW	ALCALA	WARNER BROS	1997
FB	FIREBRAND	DEXTER	20th CENTURY FOX	1962

FB	FLASHBACK	AMURRI	PARAMOUNT	1990
FB	FLESH & BLOOD (UK)	KIMMINS	SNADER	1951
FB	FLESH AND BONE	KLOVES	PARAMOUNT	1993
FB	FUNERAL IN BERLIN (UK)	HAMILTON	PARAMOUNT	1966
FB	HIS FIGHTING BLOOD	ENGLISH	AMBASSADOR	1935
FBB	FABULOUS BAKER BOYS	KLOVES	20th CENTURY FOX	1989
FBG	FIVE BLOODY GRAVES	ADAMSON	INDEPENDENT INTL	1970
FBI	FBI GIRL	BERKE	LIPPERT	1951
FBT	FRANKENSTEIN'S BLOODY TERROR	EGUILEZ	INDEPENDENT INTL	1971
FBX	FREDDIE BARTHOLOMEW	portrait	MGM	
FC	FIGHT CLUB	FINCHER	20th CENTURY FOX	1999
FC	FINAL CONFLICT	BAKER	20th CENTURY FOX	1981
FC	FRITZ THE CAT	BAKSHI	CINEMATION IND	1972
FC	RULES OF ENGAGEMENT	FRIEDKIN	PARAMOUNT	2000
FCMC	CATHERINE MCLEOD	portrait		
FCW	FRANKENSTEIN CREATED WOMAN (UK)	FISHER	20TH CENTURY FOX	1967
FCWT	FINAL CHAPTER WALKING TALL	STARRETT	AIP	1977
FD	FALLING DOWN	SCHUMACHER	WARNER BROS	1993
FD	FAMILY DAIRY (FAMILY PORTRAIT) (IT:CRONACA FAMILIARE 1962)	ZURLINI	MGM	1963
FD	FATAL DESIRE (IT)	GALLONE	ULTRA PICTURES	1963
FD	FATHER'S DAY	REITMAN	WARNER BROS	1997
FD	FLOATING DUTCHMAN (UK)	SEWELL	ALLIED ARTISTS	1952
FD	FLOOD (TV)	BELLAMY	WARNER BROS	1976
FD	FOUR DESPERATE MEN (UK: SIEGE OF PINCHGUT)	WATT	CONTINENTAL	1959
FD	FOUR DEUCES	BUSHNELL	AVCO EMBASSY	1974
FD	FRANKENSTEIN MUST BE DESTROYED (UK)	FISHER	WARNER BROS	1969
FD	FROZEN DEAD (UK)	LEDER	WARNER BROS.	1966
FDS	FIRST DEADLY SIN	HUTTON	FILMWAYS	1980
FE	HOTEL BERLIN	GODFREY	WARNER BROS	1945
FF	ADVENTURES OF FORD FAIRLANE	HARLIN	20th CENTURY FOX	1990
FF	ALONG CAME A SPIDER	TAMAHON	PARAMOUNT	2001
FF	FANFAN THE TULIP (FR)	JAQUE	LOPERT	1953
FF	FAST AND THE FURIOUS, THE	IRELAND	AMERICAN RELEASING	1954
FF	FELICIA FARR		COL	
FF	FEMALE FIENDS (UK: STRANGE AWAKENING)	TULLY	CINEMA ASSOCIATES	1958
FF	FLAMING FRONTIER	NEWFIELD	20TH CENTURY FOX	1958
FF	FLORENCE FAIR	portrait	WARNER BROS	
FF	FLYING FOOL (UK)	SUMMERS	WARDOUR	1931
FF	FOR FREEDOM (UK)	ELVEY, KNIGHT	GFD	1940
FF	FORBIDDEN FRUIT (FR: LE FRUIT DEFENDU)	VERNEUIL	FILMS AROUND WORLD	1952
FF	FORCE: FIVE	CLOUSE	UNITED ARTISTS	1981
FF	FRANCES FARMER	portrait	WARNER BROS	
FF202	MATTER OF WHO (UK)	CHAFFEY	MGM	1961
FF-508	FOR COUNTRY LIFE		20th CENTURY FOX	1940
FF-508	FORD FAIRLANE	HARLIN	20th CENTURY FOX	1990
FFA	LADY TAKES A CHANCE (r: COWBOY AND THE GIRL)	SEITER	RKO	1943
FFC	FALSTAFF'S FUR COAT (UK: TV FEATURETTE)		PARAMOUNT	1954
FFL	FIGHT FOR LIFE	LORENTZ	COLUMBIA	1940
FFPI	STOWAWAY GIRL (UK: MANUELA)	HAMILTON	PARAMOUNT	1957
FG	FAIR GAME	SIPES	WARNER BROS	1995
FG	FARLEY GRANGER	portrait	RKO	
FG	FERNGULLY	KROYER	20th CENTURY FOX	1992
FG	FLASH OF GREEN, A	NUNEZ	INT'L SPECTRAFILM	1985
FG	FLOWING GOLD	GREEN	WARNER BROS	1940
FG	FORREST GUMP	ZEMECKIS	PARAMOUNT	1994
FG	FRONTIER GUN	LANDRES	20TH CENTURY FOX	1958
FG	MAGIC BOX (UK)	BOULTING	MAYER-KINGLSEY	1951
FG	WINGED DEVILS (IT: FORZA G)	TESSARI	UNITED ARTISTS	1972
FG-A	WINGED DEVILS (IT: FORZA G)	TESSARI	UNITED ARTISTS	1972
FH	FANNY HILL (1964)	MEYER	FAMOUS PLAYERS	R65
FH	FIELD OF HONOR (FR: CHAMP D'HONNEUR)	DENIS	ORION	1987
FH	FIVE HEARTBEATS	TOWNSEND	20th CENTURY FOX	1991
FHL	48 HOURS TO LIVE (UK)	BOURNE	ARCHWAY	1959
FI	FIRE AND ICE	BAKSHI	20th CENTURY FOX	1983
FI	FLIGHT OF THE INTRUDER	MILIUS	PARAMOUNT	1991
FIL	TROUBLE AHEAD (UK: FALLING IN LOVE)	BANKS	TIMES	1934

FIRE	FIRE (tv)	BELLAMY	WARNER BROS	1977
FIW	FLESH IS WEAK (UK)	CHAFFEY	DCA	1957
FJ	FEMALE JUNGLE	VESOTA	AMERICAN RELEASING	1956
FJ	FRANKIE AND JOHNNY	MARSHALL	PARAMOUNT	1991
FJBB	FEAST OF JULY	MENAUL	BUENA VISTA	1995
FJM	FOUR JUST MEN (UK: SECRET FOUR)	FORDE	MONOGRAM	1939
FJM	KANSAS CITY CONFIDENTIAL (UK: SECRET FOUR)	KARLSON	MONOGRAM	1952
FK	FOR KEEPS	AVILDSEN	TRI STAR	1988
FK	FRED KOHLER	portrait		
FK	FRENCH KISS	KASDAN	20th CENTURY FOX	1995
FL	FINGERPRINTS DON'T LIE	NEWFIELD	LIPPERT	1951
FL	FLAREUP	NEILSON	MGM	1970
FL	FOOTLOOSE	ROSS	PARAMOUNT	1984
FL	FOREVER, LULU	KOLLEK	TRI STAR	1987
FL	FRANCES LANGFORD	portrait	RKO	
FL	FRENCH LEAVE (UK)	LEE	PATHE	1937
FL	FRIGHTENED LADY (UK: CASE OF THE FRIGHTENED LADY)	KING	HOFFBERG ZIEHM	1940
FL	FROZEN LIMITS (UK)	VARNEL	GFD	1939
FL	LOVES OF A DICTATOR (UK: DICTATOR)	SAVILLE	GAUMONT BRITISH	1935
FL2	REBOUND (UK: VIOLENT MOMENT)	HAYERS	SCHOENFELD	1959
FL2	STRANGE AFFECTION (UK: SCAMP)	RILLA	JOSEPH BRENNER	1957
FLK	FRONT LINE KIDS (UK)	ROGERS	BUTCHER'S	1942
FLOC-4	SPIN A DARK WEB (UK: SOHO INCIDENT)	SEWELL	COLUMBIA	1956
FM	FACING THE MUSIC (UK)	ROGERS	BUTCHER'S	1941
FM	FACTS OF MURDER	GERMI	SEVEN ARTS	1965
FM	FAR FROM THE MADDENING CROWD (UK)	SCHLESINGER	MGM	1968
FM	FICTION MAKERS (UK)	BAKER		1967
FM	FIFTH MUSKETEER	ANNAKIN	COLUMBIA	1979
FM	FIGHTING MARINES (serial)	EASON, KANE	REPUBLIC	1935
FM	FIGHTING MUSKETEERS (FR: LES TROIS MOUSQUETAIRES 1961)	BORDERIE	COLORAMA	1963
FM	FILLMORE	HEFFRON	20th CENTURY FOX	1972
FM	FORBIDDEN MUSIC (UK: LAND WITHOUT MUSIC)	FORDE	WORLD	1936
FM	FRANCINE LARRIMORE	portrait	MGM	
FM	FRANK MAYO	portrait	RKO	
FM	FRANK MORGAN	portrait	MGM	
FM	FRANKIE MASTERS (& ORCHESTRA)	portrait	MCA	
FM	FRED MACMURRAY	portrait	RKO	
FM	FREDRIC MARCH	portrait	UNIV	
FM	FURY AT SMUGGLER'S BAY (UK)	GILLING	EMBASSY	1961
FM7	LIFE LESS ORDINARY, A	BOYLE	20th CENTURY FOX	1997
FM/E	FIRST MEN ON THE MOON (UK)	JURAN	COLUMBIA	1964
FME	FORTUNE AND MEN'S EYES	HART	MGM	1971
FMJ	FULL METAL JACKET	KUBRICK	WARNER BROS	1987
FMLB	FAT MAN AND LITTLE BOY	JOFFE	PARAMOUNT	1989
FMO	FIRST MONDAY IN OCTOBER	NEAME	PARAMOUNT	1981
FMO	FOR MEN ONLY (TALL LIE)	HENREID	LIPPERT	1952
FMY	FIVE MILLION YEARS TO EARTH (UK: QUATERMASS AND THE PIT)	BAKER	20th CENTURY FOX	1967
FN	FRIENDS AND NEIGHBOURS (UK)	PARRY	SCHOENFELD	1959
FN	MENACE IN THE NIGHT (UK: FACE IN THE NIGHT)	COMFORT	UNITED ARTISTS	1957
FN8	FEARLESS LOVER	DUNLAP, MACRAE	COLUMBIA	1925
FNBB	FLIGHT OF THE NAVIGATOR	KLEISER	BUENA VISTA	1986
FNX-6	ANITA LOOS	portrait		
FNX-36	POLA NEGRI	portrait		
FO	FATHER O'FLYNN (UK)	NOY, TENNYSON	JH HOFFBERG	1935
FOG	FOG	CARPENTER	AVCO EMBASSY	1980
FOR-10	ABUSED CONFIDENCE	DECOIN	COLUMBIA (BERCHOLZ)	1938
FOTB2	FATHER OF THE BRIDE 2	SHYER	BUENA VISTA	1995
FOTC	NIGHT CALLER	VERNEUIL	COLUMBIA	1975
FOX1	FOXHOLE IN CAIRO (UK)	MOXEY	PARAMOUNT	1960
FP	FABIOLA (IT)	BLASETTI	UNITED ARTISTS	1951
FP	FIRST POWER	RESNIKOFF	ORION	1990
FP	FLASHPOINT	TANNEN	TRI STAR	1984
FP	FOUL PLAY	HIGGINS	PARAMOUNT	1978
FP	FRANKLIN PANGBORN	portrait	RKO	
FP	FRENCH POSTCARDS	HUYCK	PARAMOUNT	1979
FP1	MAN WITHOUT A BODY (UK)	SAUNDERS, WILDER	BUDD ROGERS	1957

FP2	KILL HER GENTLY (UK)	SAUNDERS	COLUMBIA	1957
FP5	MURDER REPORTED (UK)	SAUNDERS	COLUMBIA	1958
FPP	FANTASTIC PLASTIC MACHINE	BLUM, BLUM	CROWN INT'L	1969
FR	FACE IN THE RAIN	KERSHNER	EMBASSY	1963
FR	FALSE RAPTURE (UK: BLACK EYES)	BRENON	FILM ALLIANCE	1939
FR	FORBIDDEN RELATIONS (HUN: VISSZAESOK)	KEZDI-KOVACS	SPECTRAFILM	1983
FR	QUIET GUN	CLAXTON	20th CENTURY FOX	1957
FR	TORMENT/FRENZY (SWE: HETS)	SJOBERG	LOPERT	1944
FRO	FOUR RODE OUT	PEYSER	SAGITTARIUS	1970
FS	FALCON AND THE SNOWMAN	SCHLESINGER	ORION	1985
FS	FIGHTING STOCK (UK)	WALLS	GAUMONT BRITISH	1935
FS5	FIRE SALE	ARKIN	20th CENTURY FOX	1977
FS	FIRESTORM	SEMLER	20th CENTURY FOX	1998
FS	FOURTH SEX (FR: QUATRIEME SEXE)	GIMENO, METZGER	AUDUBON	1962
FS	FRED STONE	portrait	RKO	
FS	LUCKY NUMBER (UK)	ASQUITH	IDEAL	1932
FS	MAKE MINE A DOUBLE (UK: NIGHT WE DROPPED A CLANGER)	CONYERS	ELLIS	1961
FSP	MAXIE	AARON	ORION	1985
FST	FOUR SIDED TRIANGLE (UK)	FISHER	ASTOR	1953
FT	FACE OF TERROR (SP: 1962)	FERRY	AIP	1967
FT	FEMALE TROUBLE	WATERS	NEW LINE CINEMA	1974
FT	FIGHTING TROOPER	TAYLOR	AMBASSADOR	1934
FT	FOR THE FIRST TIME	MATE	MGM	1959
FT	FORBIDDEN TERRITORY (UK)	ROSEN	JH HOFFBERG	1934
FT	FORCE 10 FROM NAVARONE	HAMILTON	COLUMBIA	1978
FT	FRANKIE THOMAS	portrait	WARNER BROS	
FT5	KNIGHTS FOR A DAY (UK) FULL TILT*	GINEVER, LEE	PATHE	1937
FT	WHILE NERO FIDDLED (UK: FIDDLERS THREE)	WATT	BELL	1944
FTB	FOR THE BOYS	RYDELL	20th CENTURY FOX	1991
FTP	FOR THOSE IN PERIL (UK)	CRICHTON	EALING	1944
FTT	FRIDAY THE THIRTEENTH (UK)	SAVILLE	GAUMONT BRIT. AMER.	1933
FTY	RETURN TO YESTERDAY (UK)	STEVENSON	JH HOFFBERG	1940
FUGB	THREE FUGITIVES	VEBER	WARNER BROS	1989
FV	FOR VALOUR (UK)	WALLS	GFD	1937
FW	FACE AT THE WINDOW (UK)	HISCOTT	RKO	1932
FW	FANGS OF THE WILD (FOLLOW THE HUNTER)	CLAXTON	LIPPERT	1954
FW	FARMER'S WIFE (UK)	ARLISS, LEE	PATHE	1941
FW	FIREWALKER	THOMPSON	CANNON	1986
FW	I COULD NEVER HAVE SEX WITH ANY MAN ... FOR MY HUSBAND	MCCARTY	CINEMA 5	1973
FW3	FREE WILLY 3	PILLSBURY	WARNER BROS	1997
FWD	FRENCH WITHOUT DRESSING	LEVERSUCH	SAME LAKE ENT.	1965
FX40	MAE BUSCH	portrait	FOX	
FX76	LOLA LANE	portrait	FOX	
FX95	HUGH SINCLAIR	portrait	FOX	
FX102	KENNETH MACKENNA	portrait	FOX	
FX106	EL BRENDEL	portrait	FOX	
FY	FOREVER YOUNG	MINER	WARNER BROS	1992
G	BORN FOR GLORY (UK: BROWN ON RESOLUTION)	FORDE	MONOGRAM	1935
G	FOUR DIMENSIONS OF GRETA (UK)	WALKER	DIMENSION	1972
G	GALLIPOLI	WEIR	PARAMOUNT	1981
G	GAMMERA THE INVINCIBLE	HOWARD, YUASA	WORLD ENTERTAIN.	1966
G	GANG WAR (UK)	MARSHALL	UNITED ARTISTS	1962
G	GATE	TAKACS	NEW CENTURY	1986
G	GIGOLETTE	LAMONT	RKO	1935
G	GLADIATORS	WATKINS	NEW LINE CINEMA	1971
G	GODZILLA, KING OF THE MONSTERS	MORSE-HONDA	TRANSWORLD	1956
G	GUENDALINA (IT/FR 1957)	LATTUADA	LOPERT	1958
G	GUILTY? (UK)	GREVILLE	GRAND NATIONAL	1956
G	ROMOLA	KING	METRO GOLDWYN	1924
G-1	BIG EARS (sh)	MCGOWAN	MGM	1931
G-1	REGULAR PAL (sh)	ROACH	PATHE EXCHANGE	1920
G-1	YALE VS. HARVARD (sh)	MCGOWAN	MGM	1927
G2	GREMLINS 2	DANTE	WARNER BROS	1990
G-2	MERELY A MAID (sh)	ROACH	PATHE EXCHANGE	1920
G-2	OLD WALLOP (sh)	MCGOWAN	MGM	1927
G-2	SAILOR PAPA (sh)	GUIOL, WILDE	PATHE EXCHANGE	1925

G-2	SHIVER MY TIMBERS (sh)	MCGOWAN	MGM	1931
G-3	DOGS IS DOGS (sh)	MCGOWAN	MGM	1931
G-3	HEEBEE JEEBEES (sh)	MCGOWAN, MCGOWAN	MGM	1927
G-3	HELLO UNCLE (sh)	ROACH	PATHE EXCHANGE	1920
G-3	MEET THE MISSUS (sh)	CLEMENTS, GUIOL	PATHE EXCHANGE	1924
G3-2	BRANDY FOR THE PARSON (UK)	ELDRIDGE	MAYER-KINGLSEY	1952
G3-5	BRAVE DON'T CRY (UK)	LEACOCK	MAYER-KINGLSEY	1952
G3-7	ORACLE/US: HORSE'S MOUTH (UK)	PENNINGTON-RICHARDS	MAYER-KINGLSEY	1953
G3-8	SCOTCH ON THE ROCKS (UK: LAXDALE HALL)	ELDRIDGE	KINGSLEY INT'L	1953
G3-11	EDGE OF DIVORCE (UK: BACKGROUND)	BIRT	KINGSLEY INT'L	1953
G3-12	ANGEL WHO PAWNED HER HARP (UK)	BROMLY	AAP	1954
G3-13	DEVIL ON HORSEBACK (UK)	FRANKEL	BRITISH LION	1954
G3-14	CONFLICT OF WINGS (UK)	ELDRIDGE	AAP	1954
G3-15	END OF THE ROAD (UK)	RILLA	DCA	1957
G3-16	ORDERS ARE ORDERS (UK)	PALTENGHI	DCA	1954
G3-17	MAKE ME AN OFFER (UK)	FRANKEL	DOMINANT	1954
G3-18	NAVY HEROES (UK: BLUE PETER)	RILLA	DCDS	1955
G3-19	LOVE MATCH (UK)	PALTENGHI	BRITISH LION	1955
G-4	DOG HEAVEN (sh)	MCGOWAN	MGM	1927
G-4	READIN' AND WRITIN' (sh)	MCGOWAN	MGM	1932
G-4	START THE SHOW (sh)	ROACH	PATHE EXCHANGE	1920
G-4	WAGES OF TIN (sh)	CLEMENTS	PATHE EXCHANGE	1925
G-5	FREE EATS (sh)	MCCAREY	MGM	1932
G-5	SPOOK SPOOFING (sh)	MCGOWAN	MGM	1928
G-5	TELL IT TO A POLICEMAN (sh)	GUIOL	PATHE EXCHANGE	1925
G-6	HOLD MY BABY - WHOSE BABY ARE YOU? (sh)	HOWE	PATHE EXCHANGE	1925
G-6	RAINY DAYS (sh)	MCGOWAN, OELZE	MGM	1928
G-6	SPANKY (sh)	MCGOWAN	MGM	1932
G-7	CHOO CHOO (sh)	MCGOWAN	MGM	1932
G-7	EDISON, MARCONI & CO. (sh)	MCGOWAN	MGM	1928
G-7	HAUNTED HONEYMOON (sh)	GUIOL, WILDE	PATHE EXCHANGE	1925
G-8	BARNUM & RINGLING INC. (sh)	MCGOWAN	MGM	1928
G-8	POOCH (sh)	MCGOWAN	MGM	1932
G-8	THUNDERING LANDLORDS (sh)	HORNE	PATHE EXCHANGE	1925
G-9	DADDY GOES A' GRUNTING (sh)	HORNE	PATHE EXCHANGE	1925
G-9	FAIR AND MUDDY (sh)	OELZE	MGM	1928
G-9	HOOK AND LADDER (sh)	MCGOWAN	MGM	1932
G-10	CRAZY HOUSE (sh)	MCGOWAN	MGM	1928
G-10	FREE WHEELING (sh)	MCGOWAN	MGM	1932
G-10	MADAME SANS JANE (sh)	HORNE	PATHE EXCHANGE	1925
G-11	BIRTHDAY BLUES (sh)	MCGOWAN	MGM	1932
G-11	CUCKOO LOVE (sh)	GUIOL	PATHE EXCHANGE	1925
G-11	GROWING PAINS (sh)	MCGOWAN	MGM	1928
G-12	A LAD AN' A LAMP (sh)	MCGOWAN	MGM	1932
G-12	OL' GRAY HOSS (sh)	MCGOWAN	MGM	1928
G-12	PAPA, BE GOOD! (sh)	GUIOL	PATHE EXCHANGE	1925
G-13	FISH HOOKY (sh)	MCGOWAN	MGM	1933
G-13	SCHOOL BEGINS (sh)	MCGOWAN	MGM	1928
G-14	FORGOTTEN BABIES (sh)	MCGOWAN	MGM	1933
G-14	SPANKING AGE (sh)	MCGOWAN	MGM	1928
G-15	ELECTION DAY (sh)	MCGOWAN	MGM	1929
G-15	KID FROM BORNEO (sh)	MCGOWAN	MGM	1933
G15	SHARI ROBINSON	portrait	FOX	
G-16	MUSH AND MILK (sh)	MCGOWAN	MGM	1933
G-16	NOISY NOISES (sh)	MCGOWAN	MGM	1929
G-17	BEDTIME WORRIES (sh)	MCGOWAN	MGM	1933
G-17	HOLY TERROR (sh)	MCGOWAN	MGM	1929
G17	TYRONE POWER & LINDA CHRISTIAN	portrait	FOX	
G-18	WIGGLE YOUR EARS (sh)	MCGOWAN	MGM	1929
G-18	WILD POSES (sh)	MCGOWAN	MGM	1933
G-19	FAST FREIGHT (sh)	MACK	MGM	1929
G-19	HI' NEIGHBOR! (sh)	MEINS	MGM	1934
G-20	FOR PETE'S SAKE! (sh)	MEINS	MGM	1934
G-20	LITTLE MOTHER (sh)	MCGOWAN	MGM	1929
G-21	CAT, DOG & CO. (sh)	MCGOWAN	MGM	1929
G-21	FIRST ROUNDUP (sh)	MEINS	MGM	1934

G-22		HONKY DONKEY (sh)	MEINS	MGM	1934
G-22		SATURDAY'S LESSON (sh)	MCGOWAN	MGM	1929
G-23		MIKE FRIGHT (sh)	MEINS	MGM	1934
G-23		SMALL TALK (sh)	MCGOWAN	MGM	1929
G-24		RAILROADIN' (sh)	MCGOWAN	MGM	1929
G-24		WASHEE IRONEE (sh)	PARROTT	MGM	1934
G-25		BOXING GLOVES (sh)	MCGOWAN	MGM	1929
G-25		MAMA'S LITTLE PIRATE (sh)	MEINS	MGM	1935
G25		MICHELINE PRESLE	portrait	FOX	
G-26		LAZY DAYS (sh)	MCGOWAN	MGM	1929
G-26		SHRIMPS FOR A DAY (sh)	MEINS	MGM	1935
G26		THELMA RITTER	portrait	FOX	
G-27		ANNIVERSARY TROUBLE (sh)	MEINS	MGM	1935
G-27		BOUNCING BABIES (sh)	MCGOWAN	MGM	1929
G-28		BEGINNER'S LUCK (sh)	MEINS	MGM	1935
G28		JOYCE MACKENZIE	portrait	FOX	
G-28		MOAN & GROAN INC. (sh)	MCGOWAN	MGM	1929
G-29		SHIVERING SHAKESPEARE (sh)	MCGOWAN	MGM	1930
G-29		TEACHER'S BEAU (sh)	MEINS	MGM	1935
G-30		FIRST SEVEN YEARS (sh)	MCGOWAN	MGM	1930
G-30		SPRUCIN' UP (sh)	MEINS	MGM	1935
G-31		LUCKY CORNER (sh)	MEINS	MGM	1936
G-31		WHEN THE WIND BLOWS (sh)	HORNE	MGM	1930
G-32		BEAR SHOOTERS (sh)	MCGOWAN	MGM	1930
G-32		LITTLE PAPA (sh)	MEINS	MGM	1935
G-33		LITTLE SINNER (sh)	MEINS	MGM	1935
G-33		TOUGH WINTER (sh)	MCGOWAN	MGM	1930
G-34		OUR GANG FOLLIES OF 1936 (sh)	MEINS	MGM	1935
G-34		PUPS IS PUPS (sh)	MCGOWAN	MGM	1930
G-35		PINCH SINGER (sh)	NEWMEYER	MGM	1936
G-35		TEACHER'S PET (sh)	MCGOWAN	MGM	1930
G-36		DIVOT DIGGERS (sh)	MCGOWAN	MGM	1936
G-36		SCHOOL'S OUT (sh)	MCGOWAN	MGM	1930
G-37		HELPING GRANDMA (sh)	MCGOWAN	MGM	1931
G-37		SECOND CHILDHOOD (sh)	MEINS	MGM	1936
G-38		ARBOR DAY (sh)	NEWMEYER	MGM	1936
G-38		LOVE BUSINESS (sh)	MCGOWAN	MGM	1931
G-39		LITTLE DADDY (sh)	MCGOWAN	MGM	1931
G-39		OUR GANG FOLLIES OF 1938 (sh)	DOUGLAS	MGM	1937
G-40		BARGAIN DAY (sh)	MCGOWAN	MGM	1931
G-41		FLY MY KITE (sh)	MCGOWAN	MGM	1931
G-42		FLAME OF LOVE (UK: ROAD TO DISHONOUR)	EICHBERG, SUMMERS	BRITISH INT'L	1930
G63		ANN SHERIDAN	portrait	FOX	
G79		HERBIE GOES BANANAS	MCEVEETY	BUENA VISTA	1980
G79		LOUIS JOURDAN	portrait		
G80		NEVER CRY WOLF	BALLARD	BUENA VISTA	1983
G115		MICHAEL RENNIE	portrait	FOX	
G126		GORILLA AT LARGE	JONES	20th CENTURY FOX	1954
G145		SCOTT BRADY	portrait	FOX	
G147		MARISA PAVAN	portrait	FOX	
G167		LAUREN BACALL	portrait	FOX	
G168		VIRGINIA LEITH	portrait	FOX	
G169		MAGGIE MCNAMARA	portrait	FOX	
G183		RALLY 'ROUND THE FLAG, BOYS	MCCAREY	20th CENTURY FOX	1958
G214		BARBARA RUSH	portrait	FOX	
G216		DON MURRAY	portrait	FOX	
G217		GORDON MACRAE	portrait	FOX	
G255		DAVID HEDISON	portrait	FOX	
G262		TONY RANDAL	portrait		
G294		ROBERT MITCHUM	portrait	FOX	
G334		FABIAN	portrait	FOX	
G337		DEAN STOCKWELL	portrait	FOX	
G344		ANN DEL GUERCIO	portrait	FOX	
G428		RAQUEL WELCH	portrait	FOX	
G460		HAMPTON FANCHER	portrait	FOX	
G468		ELAINE DEVRY	portrait	FOX	

GA	GOING APE!	KRONSBERG	PARAMOUNT	1981
GABY	GABY	MANDOKI	TRI STAR	1987
GAC	GOLDEN AGE OF COMEDY	YOUNGSON	DCA	1958
GAC	GREAT ARMORED CAR SWINDLE (UK: BREAKING POINT)	COMFORT	FALCON	1964
GAC	LAUREL & HARDY'S LAUGHING 20'S	YOUNGSON	MGM	1965
GAS	GIRLS AT SEA (UK)	GUNN	SEVEN ARTS	1958
GB	GABY	MANDOKI	TRI STAR	1987
GB	GANGBUSTERS	KARN	VISUAL DRAMA	1954
GB	GENTLE GIANT	NEILSON	PARAMOUNT	1967
GB	GRETA BALDWIN	portrait	PARAMOUNT`	
GB	TOMORROW AT TEN (UK)	COMFORT	GOVERNOR	1965
GB	WILD HEART (UK: GONE TO EARTH)	POWELL, PRESSBURGER	RKO	1952
GBBB	GUN IN BETTY LOU'S HANDBAG	MOYLE	BUENA VISTA	1992
GBF	GREAT BALLS OF FIRE	MCBRIDE	ORION	1989
GC	GARDEN OF THE FINZI-CONTINIS	DE SICA	MGM-EMI	1970
GC	GET CARTER (UK)	HODGES	MGM	1971
GC	GHOST CAMERA (UK)	VORHAUS	OLYMPIC	1933
GC	GINGER CROWLEY	portrait	WARNER BROS.	
GC	GIRL OF THE CANAL (UK: PAINTED BOATS)	CRICHTON	AFE	1945
GC	GLASS CAGE, THE	SANTEAN	FUTURAMIC RELEASING	1963
GC	GOLDEN CHILD	RITCHIE	PARAMOUNT	1986
GC	GRAND CANYON	LANDRES	LIPPERT	1949
GC	GRAND CANYON	KASDAN	20th CENTURY FOX	1991
GC	LUCK OF GINGER COFFEY, THE (CAN)	KERSHNER	CONTINENTAL DIST.	1964
GCBB	GREEN CARD	WEIR	BUENA VISTA	1990
GCG	GUNFIGHTERS OF CASA GRANDE	ROWLAND	MGM	1964
GCS	GIRL CAN'T STOP, THE	SOLOMON	U. S. FILMS	1966
GD	DARING DESPERADOES (GAY DESPERADO 1936)	MAMOULIAN	FAVORITE FILM	R47
GD	GALLOPING DYNAMITE	FRASER	AMBASSADOR	1937
GD	GAY DOG (UK)	ELVEY	EROS	1954
GD	GHOST DIVER	WHITE	20th CENTURY FOX	1957
GD	IT'S IN THE BAG (UK)	MASON	BUTCHER'S	1944
GD-3027	GALLOPING THUNDER	NAZARRO	COLUMBIA	1946
GE	GREEN EYES	THORPE	CHESTERFIELD	1934
GE3	CHILD IN THE HOUSE (UK)	ENDFIELD	EROS	1956
GEF	WAR IS OVER (FR: GUERRE EST FINIE)	RESNEIS	BRANDON FILMS	1966
GEN	GENERATION	SCHAEFER	AVCO EMBASSY	1959
GERT	GERTRUDE MICHAEL	portrait	WARNER BROS	
GF	GIRL FRIENDS	WEILL	WARNER BROS	1978
GF	GIRL IN THE FLAT (UK)	DAVIS	PARAMOUNT BRITISH	1934
GF	GOLDEN FISH, THE (sh) (FR: HISTOIRE D'UN POISSON ROUGE)	SECHAN	COLUMBIA	1959
GF	GOODFELLAS	SCORSESE	WARNER BROS	1990
GF	POSSESSORS (FR: LES GRANDES FAMILIES 1958)	PATELLIERE	LOPERT	1959
GF1	WEE GEORDIE (UK: GEORDIE)	LAUNDER	TIMES	1955
GF II	GODFATHER II	COPPOLA	PARAMOUNT	1974
GFM	GIGANTIS THE FIRE MONSTER	ODA	WARNER BROS	1959
GFT	GRIMMS FAIRY TALES	THIEL	CINEMATION IND.	1971
GG	FLIGHT TO NOWHERE	ROWLAND	SCREEN GUILD	1946
GG	GENTLE GIANT	NEILSON	PARAMOUNT	1967
GG	GIRL AND THE GENERAL, THE (IT: LA RAGAZZA E IL GENERALE)	CAMPANILE	MGM	1967
GG	GIRL GANGS	BROOKS		1952
GG	GOOD GUYS WEAR BLACK	POST	ACTION ONE FILM	1977
GG	GORDON GEBERT	portrait	RKO	
GG	GRISSOM GANG	ALDRED	ABC PICTURES	1971
GG	GYPSY GIRL (UK: SKY WEST AND CROOKED)	MILLS	CONTINENTAL	1965
GG	MILLIONAIRE FOR CHRISTY	MARSHALL	20th CENTURY FOX	1951
GG	SCARED TO DEATH	CABANNE	SCREEN GUILD	1947
GG-8	MY DOG SHEP	BEEBE	SCREEN GUILD	1946
GGE	GIRL-GETTERS (UK: SYSTEM)	WINNER	AIP	1964
GGP	GAMES GUYS PLAY (GOODNIGHT JACKIE)	LONDON	GENERAL FILM	1975
GGP	GIRL FROM GAY PAREE	GOLDSTONE, GREGOR	TIFFANY	1927
GH	GHIDRAH THE THREE HEADED MONSTER	HONDA	CONTINENTAL	1965
GH	GIRL HUNTERS (UK)	ROWLAND	COLORAMA	1963
GH	GUNG HO	HOWARD	PARAMOUNT	1986
GH-19	LONE RIDER IN CHEYENNE	NEWFIELD	PRODUCERS RELEASING	1942
GH-70	LONE RIDER IN FRONTIER FURY	NEWFIELD	PRODUCERS RELEASING	1941

GH-124	GRASSHOPPER	PARIS	NAT'L GENERAL	1970
GHL-108	IMPORTANT WITNESS	NEWFIELD	CAPITOL (states rights)	1933
GHW	GREAT MR. HANDEL (UK)	WALKER	MIDFILM	1942
GHW3	HARD STEEL (UK)	WALKER	GFD	1942
GI	WHITE HUNTRESS (UK: GOLDEN IVORY)	BREAKSTON	AIP	1954
GIBB	G. I. JANE	SCOTT	BUENA VISTA	1997
GIJ	G. I. JANE	LE BORG	LIPPERT	1951
GIM	GINGER IN THE MORNING	WILES	PRODUCERS DIST.	1973
GIR	GIRL AND THE RIVER, THE (FR: L'EAU VIVE 1958)	VILLIERS	CONTINENTAL	1960
GIS	DANCERS	ROSS	CANNON	1987
GIS	GHOST, ITALIAN STYLE (IT: QUESTI FANTASTI 1967)	CASTELLANI	MGM	1969
GIS	GREED IN THE SUN (FR: CENT MILLE DOLLARS AU SOLEIL)	VERNEUIL	MGM	1964
GJBB	GEORGE OF THE JUNGLE	WEISMAN	BUENA VISTA	1997
GK	CHARLES KORVIN aka GEORGE KORVIN	portrait	UNIV	
GK	FORBIDDEN (UK)	KING	BRITISH LION	1949
GK	GEORGE KENNEDY	portrait	UNIV	
GK	GEORGIA KING aka ANDREA KING	portrait	WARNER BROS	
GK	ROMANCE AND RICHES (UK: AMAZING QUEST OF ERNEST BLISS)	ZEISLER	GRAND NATIONAL	1936
GK1	SHOWTIME (UK: GAIETY GIRLS)	KING, SAGAN	ENGLISH	1946
GL	ATTACK OF THE GIANT LEECHES	KOWALSKI	AIP	1959
GL	FRONTIER GAMBLER	NEWFIELD	ASSOCIATED FILM RELEASI	1956
GL	GASLIGHT (UK)	DICKINSON	COMMERCIAL	1940
GL	GENE LOCKHART	portrait	WARNER BROS	
GL	GIRL MUST LIVE (UK)	REED	UNIVERSAL	1939
GL	GWEN LEE	portrait	MGM	
GL 6503	BEACH BLANKET BINGO	ASHER	AIP	1965
GLS	FIENDISH GHOULS, THE (UK: FLESH AND THE FIENDS 1960)	GILLING	PACEMAKER PICTURES	1965
GM	GABLES MYSTERY (UK)	HUGHES	MGM	1938
GM	GALLOPING MAJOR (UK)	CORNELIUS	SOUVAINE SELECTIVE	1951
GM	GAR MOORE	portrait	UNIVERSAL	
GM	GET MEAN	SCHNEIDER	CINEMATION IND.	1975
GM	GLASS MOUNTAIN (UK)	CASS	EAGLE-LION	1949
GM	GLIMMER MAN	GRAY	WARNER BROS	1996
GM	GOLDEN MADONNA (UK)	CARPENTIERI, VAJDA	STRATFORD	1949
GM	GOLDFINGER (UK)	HAMILTON	UNITED ARTISTS	1964
GM	GOOD MAN IN AFRICA, A	BERESFORD	GRAMERCY	1994
GM	GOOD MORNING, BOYS (UK)	VARNEL	GAUMONT BRITISH	1937
GM	GORILLAS IN THE MIST	APTED	WARNER BROS	1988
GM	GREEN MAN (UK)	DAY	DCA	1956
GM	GREEN MILE	DARABONT	WARNER BROS.	1999
GM	GUY MADISON	portrait	RKO, SELZNICK	
GM	GHOST IN THE MACHINE	TALALAY	20th CENTURY FOX	1993
GM2	IT'S A WONDERFUL WORLD (UK)	GUEST	JOSEPH BRENNER	1956
GMC	GOODBYE MR. CHIPS	ROSS	MGM	1969
GMH	GRACE OF MY HEART	ANDERS	GRAMERCY	1996
GML	GIRL MOST LIKELY	LEISEN	RKO	1958
GMX	GERTRUDE MICHAEL	portrait	MGM	
GN	GIRL IN THE NEWS (UK)	REED	20TH CENTURY FOX	1940
GN	STRICTLY BUSINESS	HOOKS	WARNER BROS	1991
GND	GIRLS NEXT DOOR	HONG	COLUMBIA	1978
GO	GIRLS OF THE NIGHT	CLOCHE	CONTINENTAL	1959
GO	GORGO (UK)	LOURIE	MGM	1961
GO1	TO HELL WITH HITLER (UK: LET GEORGE DO IT!)	VARNEL	FILM ALLIANCE	1940
GOM	GRUMPY OLD MEN	PETRIE	WARNER BROS	1993
GON	GOLD OF NAPLES (IT: L'ORO DI NAPOLI)	DE SICA	DCA	1954
GP	GEORGE PEPPARD	portrait	PARAMOUNT`	
GP	GERALDINE PAGE	portrait	PARAMOUNT`	
GP	GOD IS MY PARTNER	CLAXTON	20th CENTURY FOX	1957
GP	GORKY PARK	APTED	ORION	1983
GP	GREGORY PECK	portrait	RKO, UNIV	
GP	MY KID OF A FATHER (FR: MON GOSSE DE PERE)	DE LIMUR	CAPITOL	1930
GP	OLGA SAN JUAN	portrait	PARAMOUNT	1947
GP	PIER 23	BERKE	LIPPERT	1951
GP-7	GHOST PATROL	NEWFIELD	PURITAN	1936
GP/CP	OUTSIDER (UK: GUINEA PIG)	BOULTING	BALLANTINE	1948
GR	GENERAL DELLA ROVERE (IT: IL GENERALE DELLA ROVERE)	ROSSELLINI	CONTINENTAL	1959

GR	GEORGE RAFT	portrait	UNIV	
GR	GILBERT ROLAND	portrait	MGM, RKO	
GR	GOLD RUSH	CHAPLIN	UNITED ARTISTS	1925
GR	GOLDFINGER (UK)	HAMILTON	UNITED ARTISTS	1964
GR	YOUNG GIRLS OF ROCHEFORT	DEMY	WARNER BROS - 7 ARTS	1968
GRA	GRADUATE, THE	NICHOLS	AVCO EMBASSY	1968
GRB	SEPTEMBER STORM	HASKIN	20th CENTURY FOX	1960
GRI	GRISBI (FR: TOUCHEZ PAS AU GRISBI)	BECKER	UMPO	1954
GRIB	HEART OF PARIS	ALLEGRET	TRI-NATIONAL	1973
GRM	GRUMPIER OLD MEN	DEUTCH	WARNER BROS	1995
GS	GANG (UK: GANG SHOW)	GOULDING	SYNDICATE	1938
GS	GANGSTER STORY	MATTHAU	RCIP	1960
GS	GARDENS OF STONE	COPPOLA	TRI STAR	1987
GS	GEORGE SANDERS	portrait	RKO	
GS	GEORGE SEATON	portrait	PARAMOUNT`	
GS	GET SHORTY	SONNENFELD	MGM	1995
GS	GLADIATORS 7	LAZAGA	MGM	1962
GS	GOOD SON	RUBEN	20th CENTURY FOX	1993
GS	GRAVEYARD SHIFT	SINGLETON	PARAMOUNT	1990
GS	GREAT SANTINI, THE	CARLINO	ORION	1979
GS	GREAT SWINDLE (IT: HISTORIA DE UNA TRAICION 1971)	CONDE	WORLD INT'L	1975
GS	GUILTY BY SUSPICION	WINKLER	WARNER BROS	1991
GS	GUMSHOE	FREARS	COLUMBIA	1971
GS	THEIR GENTLE SEX	CASARIL	ALLIED ARTISTS	1974
GS	THERE'S A GIRL IN MY SOUP (UK)	BOULTING	COLUMBIA	1970
GS	THIRD TIME LUCKY (UK)	PARRY	PENTAGON	1949
GS-7	TEN DAYS TO TULARA	SHERMAN	UNITED ARTISTS	1958
GSI	GIANT SPIDER INVASION	REBANE	GROUP 1	1975
GSM	GREAT SIOUX MASSACRE	SALKOW	COLUMBIA	1965
GSO	GOOSE STEPS OUT (UK)	DEARDEN, HAY	ABFD	1942
GSP	GAMES SCHOOLGIRLS PLAY (GER)	NACHMANN	SUNSET INT'L	1974
GT	FOR THE LOVE OF MIKE	SHERMAN	20th CENTURY FOX	1960
GT	GARBO TALKS	LUMET	UNITED ARTISTS	1984
GT	GHOST TRAIN (UK)	FORDE	GAUMONT BRIT. AMER.	1931
GTC	GLEAMING THE CUBE	CLIFFORD	20th CENTURY FOX	1989
GTS-F	GO TELL THE SPARTANS	POST	AVCO EMBASSY	1978
GUM	GIVE US THE MOON (UK)	GUEST	GFD	1944
GV	GLENN VERNON	portrait	RKO	
GVS	GREENWICH VILLAGE STORY	O'CONNELL	SHAWN INT'L	1963
GW	GONE WITH THE WEST	GIRARD		1974
GW	GORDON'S WAR	DAVIS	20th CENTURY FOX	1973
GW	GREAT WALTZ	STONE	MGM	1972
GW	GREAT WAR		LOPERT	1959
GW	GUY WILLIAMS	portrait	UNIVERSAL	1950s
GW1	BEHIND THE MASK (UK)	HURST	SHOWCORPORATION	1958
GW-200	CRASHING THRU	TAYLOR	MONOGRAM	1949
GW-200	HAUNTED TRAILS	HILLYER	MONOGRAM	1949
GW-202	HAUNTED TRAILS	HILLYER	MONOGRAM	1949
GW-205	FENCE RIDERS	FOX	MONOGRAM	1950
GWCQ	GIRL WHO COULDN'T QUITE (UK)	LEE	CLASSIC	1950
GWH	GREAT WHITE HYPE	HUDLIN	20th CENTURY FOX	1996
GWP	GIRL WITH THE PISTOL	MONICELLI	PARAMOUNT	1968
GWWLST	GUESS WHAT WE DID IN SCHOOL TODAY?	AVILDSEN	CANNON	1969
GWWLST	GUESS WHAT WE LEARNED IN SCHOOL TODAY?	AVILDSEN	CANNON	1970
GXS	GLORIA SWANSON	portrait	MGM	
GY	QUEEN OF DESTINY (UK: SIXTY GLORIOUS YEARS)	WILCOX	RKO	1938
H	11 HARROW HOUSE	AVAKIAN	20th CENTURY FOX	1974
H	HAMLET	RICHARDSON	COLUMBIA	1969
H	HAMLET	ZEFFIRELLI	WARNER BROS	1990
H	HAMLET (UK)	OLIVIER	UNIVERSAL	1949
H	HAMLET (UK)	RICHARDSON	COLUMBIA	1969
H	HARDBALL	ROBBINS	PARAMOUNT	2001
H	HARDLY WORKING	LEWIS	20th CENTURY FOX	1981
H	HARLOW	SEGAL	MAGNA DIST	1955
H	HEADLINE (UK)	HARLOW	EALING	1943
H	HEARTLAND	PEARCE	LEVITT-PICKMAN	1979

H	HEAT	MORRISSEY	LEVITT-PICKMAN	1972
H	HEAT	RICHARDS	NEW CENTURY/ VISTA	1986
H	HERCULES	COZZI	CANNON	1983
H	HERCULES (IT: LE FATICHE DI ERCOLE 1958)	FRANCISCI	WARNER BROS	1959
H	HERO AND THE TERROR	TANNEN	CANNON	1988
H	HIGH FLIGHT	GILLING	COLUMBIA	1957
H	HIGH INFIDELITY	MONICELLI	MAGNA	1965
H	HISTORY OF THE WORLD, PART 1	BROOKS	20th CENTURY FOX	1981
H	HITCHER	HARMON	TRI STAR	1986
H	HOFFA	DEVITO	20th CENTURY FOX	1992
H	HONEYMOON (UK: LUNA DE MIEL)	POWELL, PRESSBURGER	CONTINENTAL	1959
H	HOW TO BE A FLAYER	MARTIN	GRAMERCY	1997
H	HUMANOIDS FROM THE DEEP (MONSTER)	PEETERS	UNITED ARTISTS	1980
H	HUMONGOUS	LYNCH	EMBASSY	1982
H	HURRICANE	TROELL	PARAMOUNT	1979
H	HYSTERIA (UK)	FRANCIS	MGM	1965
H	IS YOUR HONEYMOON REALLY NECESSARY? (UK)	ELVEY	AAP	1953
H	MAYOR'S DILEMMA (FR: LES OTAGES)	BERNARD	FILM ALLIANCE	1939
H	MR. HOBO (UK - GUV'NOR)	ROSMER	GAUMONT BRITISH	1935
H	OLD FAITHFUL (UK: HANSOM*)	ROGERS	RKO	1935
H	TO HAVE AND TO HOLD (UK)	GRAYSON	EXCLUSIVE	1951
H-1	ALL AT SEA (sh)	CHASE, GOULDING	PATHE EXCHANGE	1919
H-1	FLAMING FLAPPERS (sh)	GUIOL	PATHE EXCHANGE	1925
H1	LAW AND DISORDER (UK)	CRICHTON	CONTINENTAL	1958
H-2	BLACK PANTHER	ORMOND	HOWCO	1956
H-2	LONG PANTS (sh)	GUIOL	PATHE EXCHANGE	1926
H-2	START SOMETHING (sh)	GOULDING	PATHE EXCHANGE	1919
H-3	45 MINUTES FROM HOLLYWOOD (sh)	GUIOL	PATHE EXCHANGE	1926
H-3	CALL FOR MR. CAVEMAN (sh)	CHASE	PATHE EXCHANGE	1919
H-4	GIVING THE BRIDE AWAY (sh)	CHASE, ROACH	PATHE EXCHANGE	1919
H-4	HUG BUG (sh)	GUIOL	PATHE EXCHANGE	1926
H-5	ORDER IN THE COURT (sh)	CHASE	PATHE EXCHANGE	1919
H-5	UKULELE SHEIKS (sh)	GUIOL	PATHE EXCHANGE	1926
H-6	IT'S A HARD LIFE (sh)	ROACH	PATHE EXCHANGE	1919
H-6	SAY IT WITH BABIES (sh)	GUIOL	PATHE EXCHANGE	1926
H-7	COW'S KIMONO (sh)	GUIOL, PARROTT	PATHE EXCHANGE	1926
H-7	HOW DRY I AM (sh)	ROACH	PATHE EXCHANGE	1919
H-7	KENTUCKY RIFLE	HITTLEMAN	HOWCO	1955
H-8	ALONG CAME AUNTIE (sh)	GUIOL, WALLACE	PATHE EXCHANGE	1926
H-8	UNFINISHED ROACH (sh)		PATHE EXCHANGE	1919
H-9	GETTING HIS GOAT (sh)	CHASE	PATHE EXCHANGE	1920
H9	PUBLIC LIFE OF HENRY THE NINTH (UK)	MAINWARING	MGM	1935
H-9	TWO TIME MAMA (sh)	GUIOL	PATHE EXCHANGE	1927
H-10	ONE HOUR MARRIED (sh)	STRONG, YATES	PATHE EXCHANGE	1927
H-10	TEENAGE THUNDER	HELMICK	HOWCO	1957
H-10	TOUGH LUCK (sh)	CHASE	PATHE EXCHANGE	1919
H-11	CARNIVAL ROCK	CORMAN	HOWCO	1957
H-11	LOOKING FOR TROUBLE (sh)	ROACH	PATHE EXCHANGE	1919
H-11	NICKEL HOPPER (sh)	JONES, YATES	PATHE EXCHANGE	1926
H-12	ANYTHING ONCE! (sh)	JONES, YATES	PATHE EXCHANGE	1927
H-12	BRAIN FROM PLANET AROUS	JURAN (HERTZ)	HOWCO	1957
H-12	FLOOR BELOW (sh)	CHASE, GOULDING	PATHE EXCHANGE	1919
H-13	RED HOT HOTTENTOTS (sh)	CHASE	PATHE EXCHANGE	1920
H-14	WHY GO HOME? (sh)	CHASE	PATHE EXCHANGE	1920
H-15	LOST, LONELY AND VICIOUS	MYERS	HOWCO	1958
H-15	SHOULD MEN WALK HOME? (sh)	MCCAREY	PATHE EXCHANGE	1927
H-15	SLIPPERY SLICKERS (sh)	CHASE	PATHE EXCHANGE	1920
H-16	DIPPY DENTIST (sh)	GOULDING	PATHE EXCHANGE	1920
H-16	JEWISH PRUDENCE (sh)	MCCAREY	PATHE EXCHANGE	1927
H-17	ALL LIT UP (sh)	NEWMEYER	PATHE EXCHANGE	1920
H-17	EVE'S LOVE LETTERS (sh)	MCCAREY	PATHE EXCHANGE	1927
H-18	DON'T TELL EVERYTHING (sh)	MCCAREY	PATHE EXCHANGE	1927
H-18	NIGHT OF LOVE (CONCERT OF INTRIGUE) (IT: TRADITA 1954)	BONNARD	HOWCO	1959
H-18	WALTZ ME AROUND (sh)	CHASE	PATHE EXCHANGE	1920
H-19	RAISE THE RENT (sh)	NEWMEYER	PATHE EXCHANGE	1920
H-19	SHOULD SECOND HUSBANDS COME FIRST? (sh)	MCCAREY	PATHE EXCHANGE	1927

H-20		FIND THE GIRL (sh)	CHASE	PATHE EXCHANGE	1920
H-21		FLAT BROKE (sh)	CHASE	PATHE EXCHANGE	1920
H-22		FRESH PAINT (sh)	CHASE, GOULDING	PATHE EXCHANGE	1920
H-23		CUT THE CARDS (sh)	CHASE	PATHE EXCHANGE	1920
H-24		CRACKED WEDDING BELLS (sh)	LA ROSE	PATHE EXCHANGE	1920
H-25		DINNER HOUR (sh)	CHASE	PATHE EXCHANGE	1920
H-26		SPEED TO SPARE (sh)	CHASE	PATHE EXCHANGE	1920
H-27		SHOOT ON SIGHT (sh)	CHASE	PATHE EXCHANGE	1920
H-28		DON'T WEAKEN (sh)	GOULDING	PATHE EXCHANGE	1920
H-29		DRINK HEARTY (sh)	GOULDING	PATHE EXCHANGE	1920
H-30		TROTTING THROUGH TURKEY (sh)	CHASE	PATHE EXCHANGE	1920
H-31		ALL DRESSED UP (sh)	CHASE	PATHE EXCHANGE	1920
H-32		GRAB THE GHOST (sh)	GOULDING	PATHE EXCHANGE	1920
H-33		YOU'RE PINCHED (sh)	ROACH	PATHE EXCHANGE	1920
H-34		ALL IN A DAY (sh)	CHASE	PATHE EXCHANGE	1920
H-35		ANY OLD PORT (sh)	GOULDING	PATHE EXCHANGE	1920
H-36		DON'T ROCK THE BOAT (sh)	CHASE	PATHE EXCHANGE	1920
H-37		HOME STRETCH (sh)	CHASE	PATHE EXCHANGE	1920
H-38		CALL A TAXI (sh)	CHASE	PATHE EXCHANGE	1920
H-39		LIVE AND LEARN (sh)	CHASE	PATHE EXCHANGE	1920
H-40		RUN 'EM RAGGED (sh)	GOULDING	PATHE EXCHANGE	1920
H-41		LONDON BOBBY (sh)	CHASE	PATHE EXCHANGE	1920
H-42		MONEY TO BURN (sh)	NEWMEYER	PATHE EXCHANGE	1920
H-43		ROCK A BYE BABY (sh)	CHASE	PATHE EXCHANGE	1920
H-44		GO AS YOU PLEASE (sh)	GOULDING	PATHE EXCHANGE	1920
H-45		DOING TIME (sh)	GOULDING	PATHE EXCHANGE	1920
H-46		FELLOW CITIZENS (sh)	GOULDING	PATHE EXCHANGE	1920
H-47		WHEN THE WIND BLOWS (sh)	CHASE	PATHE EXCHANGE	1920
H-48		INSULTING THE SULTAN (sh)	GOULDING	PATHE EXCHANGE	1920
H-49		DEAR DEPARTED (sh)	CHASE	PATHE EXCHANGE	1920
H-50		CASH CUSTOMERS (sh)	GOULDING	PATHE EXCHANGE	1920
H-51		PARK YOUR CAR (sh)	GOULDING	PATHE EXCHANGE	1920
H-52		OPEN ANOTHER BOTTLE (sh)	GOULDING	PATHE EXCHANGE	1921
H-53		MORNING AFTER (sh)	GOULDING	PATHE EXCHANGE	1921
H-54		WHIRL OF THE WEST (sh)	BARROWS	PATHE EXCHANGE	1921
H-55		HIS BEST GIRL (sh)	CHASE	PATHE EXCHANGE	1921
H-56		MAKE IT SNAPPY (sh)		PATHE EXCHANGE	1921
H-57		FELLOW ROMANS (sh)	ROACH	PATHE EXCHANGE	1921
H-58		RUSH ORDERS (sh)	CHASE	PATHE EXCHANGE	1921
H-59		BUBBLING OVER (sh)	ROACH	PATHE EXCHANGE	1921
H-60		NO CHILDREN (sh)	GOULDING	PATHE EXCHANGE	1921
H-61		BIG GAME (sh)	GOULDING	PATHE EXCHANGE	1921
H-62		KILLJOYS (BLUE SUNDAY) (sh)	CHASE	PATHE EXCHANGE	1921
H-63		OWN YOUR OWN HOME (sh)	ROACH	PATHE EXCHANGE	1921
H-64		WHERE'S THE FIRE (sh)	ROACH	PATHE EXCHANGE	1921
H-65		HIGH ROLLERS (sh)	GOULDING	PATHE EXCHANGE	1921
H-66		YOU'RE NEXT (sh)	CHASE	PATHE EXCHANGE	1921
H-67		SAVE YOUR MONEY (sh)	ROACH	PATHE EXCHANGE	1921
H-68		BIKE BUG (sh)	ROACH	PATHE EXCHANGE	1921
H-69		NAME THE DAY (sh)	ROACH	PATHE EXCHANGE	1921
H-70		AT THE RING SIDE (sh)	CHASE	PATHE EXCHANGE	1921
H-71		NO STOP-OVER (sh)	ROACH	PATHE EXCHANGE	1921
H-72		LATE LODGERS (sh)	CHASE	PATHE EXCHANGE	1921
H-73		WHAT A WHOPPER (sh)	CHASE	PATHE EXCHANGE	1921
H-74		TEACHING THE TEACHER (sh)	ROACH	PATHE EXCHANGE	1921
H-75		SPOT CASH (sh)	CHASE	PATHE EXCHANGE	1921
H-77		GONE TO THE COUNTRY (sh)	CHASE	PATHE EXCHANGE	1921
H-78		LAW AND ORDER (sh)	CHASE	PATHE EXCHANGE	1921
H-79		FIFTEEN MINUTES (sh)	CHASE	PATHE EXCHANGE	1921
H-80		ON LOCATION (sh)	CHASE	PATHE EXCHANGE	1921
H-81		HOCUS POCUS (sh)	CHASE	PATHE EXCHANGE	1921
H-82		PENNY-IN-THE-SLOT (sh)	CHASE	PATHE EXCHANGE	1921
H-83		JOY RIDER (sh)	ROACH	PATHE EXCHANGE	1921
H-84		HUSTLER (sh)	CHASE	PATHE EXCHANGE	1921
H-85		SINK OR SWIM (sh)	CHASE	PATHE EXCHANGE	1921
H-86		SHAKE 'EM UP (sh)	CHASE	PATHE EXCHANGE	1921

H-87	STONE AGE (sh)	CHASE	PATHE EXCHANGE	1922
H-88	CORNER POCKET (sh)	CHASE	PATHE EXCHANGE	1921
H-90	CALL THE WITNESS (sh)	CHASE	PATHE EXCHANGE	1922
H-91	BLOW 'EM UP (sh)	CHASE	PATHE EXCHANGE	1922
H-92	YEARS TO COME (sh)	CHASE	PATHE EXCHANGE	1922
H-93	STAGE STRUCK (sh)	WATSON	PATHE EXCHANGE	1922
H-94	SOME BABY (sh)	CEDER	PATHE EXCHANGE	1922
H-95	DOWN AND OUT (sh)	CEDER	PATHE EXCHANGE	1922
H-96	PARDON ME (sh)	CEDER	PATHE EXCHANGE	1922
H-97	BOW WOWS (sh)	CEDER	PATHE EXCHANGE	1922
H-98	HOT OFF THE PRESS (sh)	CEDER, CHASE	PATHE EXCHANGE	1922
H-99	ANVIL CHORUS (sh)	CEDER	PATHE EXCHANGE	1922
H-100	JUMP YOUR JOB (sh)	CEDER	PATHE EXCHANGE	1922
H-101	KILL THE NERVE (sh)	CEDER	PATHE EXCHANGE	1922
H-102	FULL O' PEP (sh)	CHASE	PATHE EXCHANGE	1922
H-103	DO YOUR DUTY (sh)	CEDER	PATHE EXCHANGE	1926
H-104	DAYS OF OLD (DAYS OF GOLD) (sh)	CHASE	PATHE EXCHANGE	1922
H-105	LIGHT SHOWERS (sh)	CHASE	PATHE EXCHANGE	1922
H-106	DO ME A FAVOR (sh)	CHASE	PATHE EXCHANGE	1922
H-107	PUNCH THE CLOCK (sh)	BEAUDINE	PATHE EXCHANGE	1922
H-108	IN THE MOVIES (sh)	CHASE	PATHE EXCHANGE	1922
H-109	HALE AND HEARTY (sh)	SANTELL	PATHE EXCHANGE	1922
H-110	STRICTLY MODERN (sh)	BEAUDINE	PATHE EXCHANGE	1922
H-111	DUMB BELL (sh)	CHASE	PATHE EXCHANGE	1922
H-5140	HUSTLE	ALDRICH	PARAMOUNT	1975
H7195	JOAN CRAWFORD	portrait	MGM	
H7197	JOAN CRAWFORD	portrait	MGM	
H7200	JOAN CRAWFORD	portrait	MGM	
HA	HIDDEN AGENDA	LOACH	HEMSDALE	1990
HA	HOME ALONE	COLUMBUS	20th CENTURY FOX	1990
HA	HOME ALONE 3	GOSNELL	20th CENTURY FOX	1997
HA	HOME AND AWAY (UK)	SEWELL	EROS	1956
HA	HOT ANGEL	PARKER	PARAMOUNT	1958
HA	TO HAVE AND TO HOLD (UK)	WISE	ANGLO-AMALGAMATED	1963
HA2	HOME ALONE 2	COLUMBUS	20th CENTURY FOX	1992
HB	HARRY BLACK AND THE TIGER (UK: HARRY BLACK)	FREGONESE	20TH CENTURY FOX	1958
HB	HEART BEAT	BYRUM	ORION	1979
HB	HILLARY BROOKE	portrait	RKO	
HB	HOUSE THAT DRIPPED BLOOD (UK)	DUFFEL	CINERAMA	1970
HB	OF HUMAN BONDAGE (UK)	HUGHES	COLUMBIA	1964
HB MPI	HARRY BLACK AND THE TIGER	FREGONESE	20th CENTURY FOX	1958
HBD	HELL'S BLOODY DEVILS	ADAMSON	INDEPENDENT INTL	1970
HBHB	HONEY BABY HONEY BABY	SCHULZ	KELLY-JORDAN ENT.	1974
HBM	HORROR OF THE BLOOD MONSTERS	ADAMSON	INDEPENDENT INTL	1970
HBT	HOLD BACK TOMORROW	HAAS	UNIVERSAL	1955
HC	DANGEROUS CARGO (UK)	HARLOW	MONARCH	1954
HC	DANGEROUS CARGO (UK: HELL'S CARGO)	HUTH	FILM ALLIANCE	1939
HC	HELL IS A CITY (UK)	GUEST	COLUMBIA	1960
HC	HELLCATS	SLATZER	CROWN INT'L	1968
HC	HIGH COMMAND (UK)	DICKINSON	GRAND NATIONAL	1937
HC	HOLCROFT COVENANT, THE	FRANKENHEIMER	UNIVERSAL	1985
HC	HOW I GOT INTO COLLEGE	HOLLAND	20th CENTURY FOX	1989
HC	HUE AND CRY (UK)	CRICHTON	FINE ARTS	1947
HC	PAGAN HELLCAT (MAEVA)	BONSIGNORI	TIMES FILM	1962
HC-1	BELLS OF SAN FERNANDO	MORSE	SCREEN GUILD	1947
HCS	HAY COUNTRY SWINGERS (SABINA) (GER 1971)	BRUMMER	HEMISPHERE PICTURES	1974
HCS	HERE COMES THE SUN (UK)	BAXTER	GFD	1946
HCT	CHOSEN (IT/UK)	De MARTINO	WARNER BROS	1978
HCT	TOMCAT (UK: MINI WEEKEND)	ROBIN	JOSEPH BRENNER	1968
HD	HILLS OF DONEGAL (UK)	ARGYLE	BUTCHER'S	1947
HD	HOUSE OF DARKNESS (UK)	MITCHELL	REALART	1948
HDG	HOTDOG THE MOVIE	MARKLE	MGM	1983
HDK	OH HEAVENLY DOG	CAMP	20th CENTURY FOX	1980
HE	HEAVEN AND EARTH	STONE	WARNER BROS	1993
HE	HOWARD'S END	IVORY	SONY PICTURES	1992
HEA	MORE THAN A MIRACLE	ROSI	MGM	1967

HEMI	THUNDERSTORM (UK)	GUILLERMIN	ALLIED ARTISTS	1956
HERC	HERCULES (t)	CLEMENTS	BUENA VISTA	1997
HF	HELLFIRE CLUB (UK)	BAKER, BERMAN	EMBASSY	1961
HF	HENRY FONDA	portrait	UNIV	
HF	HOME FRIES	PARISOT	WARNER BROS	1998
HF	HORROR OF FRANKENSTEIN (UK)	SANGSTER	CONTINENTAL	1971
HF	HOT FRUSTRATION	COMBRET	AUDUBON FILMS	1967
HF	SCREAM OF FEAR (UK: TASTE OF FEAR)	HOLT	COLUMBIA	1961
HFA	HER FIRST AFFAIRE (UK)	DWAN	STERLING	1932
HFH	TAMING OF DOROTHY (UK: HER FAVOURITE HUSBAND)	SOLDATI	EAGLE LION	1950
HFRO	HUNT FOR RED OCTOBER	MCTIERNAN	PARAMOUNT	1990
HG	GATE OF HELL	KINUGASA	HARRISON (JAP)	1954
HG	HACKERS	SOFTLEY	UNITED ARTISTS	1995
HG	HELLGATE	WARREN	LIPPERT	1952
HG	MAIL TRAIN (UK: INSPECTOR HORNLEIGH GOES TO IT)	FORDE	20TH CENTURY FOX	1941
HH	HALFWAY HOUSE (UK)	DEARDEN	AFE	1944
HH	HAPPY HOOKER	SGARRO	CANNON	1975
HH	HATE FOR HATE (IT: ODIO PER ODIO)	PAOLELLA	MGM	1967
HH	HAUNTED HONEYMOON	WILDER	ORION	1986
HH	HIPS HIPS HOORAY	SANDRICH	RKO	1934
HH	HIS AND HERS (UK)	HURST	FAVORITE	1961
HH	HONEYMOON HOTEL (UK: UNDER NEW MANAGEMENT)	BLAKELEY	BUTCHER'S	1946
HH	HORROR HOTEL	HOOPER	MARS	R1980
HH	HUSBAND HUNTERS	ADOLFI	TIFFANY	1927
HH	LEGEND OF HELL HOUSE	HOUGH	20th CENTURY FOX	1973
HH2	HAPPY HOOKER GOES TO WASHINGTON	LEVEY	CANNON	1977
HH-53	HIPS HIPS HOORAY	SANDRICH	RKO	1934
HH-101	OUTLAW	HUGHES	RKO	1943
HHGW	HAPPY HOOKER GOES TO WASHINGTON	LEVEY	CANNON	1977
HHH	HUNDRED HOUR HUNT (UK: EMERGENCY CALL)	GILBERT	ABNER J. GRESHLER	1952
HHU	HEAVEN HELP US	DINNER	TRI STAR	1985
HIB	HAPPY IS THE BRIDE (UK)	BOULTING	KASSLER	1958
HJ	HIGHJACKED	NEWFIELD	LIPPERT	1950
HK	HARDY KRUGER	portrait	PARAMOUNT`	
HK	HEAVENLY KID	MEDOWAY	ORION	1984
HK	HELL IN KOREA (UK: HILL IN KOREA)	AMYES	DCA	1956
HK	HENRY KING	portrait	ROBERTSON-COLE	
HKYA	HE KNOWS YOU'RE ALONE	MASTROIANNI	UNITED ARTISTS	1980
HL	BEST HOUSE IN LONDON (UK)	SAVILLE	MGM	1969
HL	HARBOR LIGHTS	DEXTER	20th CENTURY FOX	1963
HL	HARMONY LANE	SANTLEY	MASCOT	1935
HL	HARRY LANGDON	portrait		
HL	HARRY LEWIS	portrait	WARNER BROS	
HL	HEAT WAVE (UK: HOUSE ACROSS THE LAKE)	HUGHES	LIPPERT	1954
HL	MAN OF AFFAIRS (UK: HIS LORDSHIP)	MASON	GAUMONT BRIT. AMER.	1936
HLM	HEDY LAMARR	portrait	RKO	
HM	HEART OF THE MATTER (UK)	O'FERRALL	AAP	1953
HM	HELEN MACK	portrait	RKO	
HM	HELEN MORGAN	portrait	WARNER BROS	
HM	HORSE'S MOUTH (UK)	NEAME	UNITED ARTISTS	1958
HM	HOT MILLIONS (UK)	TILL	MGM	1968
HMBB	HAUNTED MANSION	MINKOFF	BUENA VISTA	2003
HMBB	HOLY MAN	HEREK	BUENA VISTA	1998
HMG	HOT MONEY GIRL (UK: TREASURE OF SAN TERESA)	RAKOFF	UNITED PROD. REL.	1959
HN	HARLEM NIGHTS	MURPHY	PARAMOUNT	1989
HN	HILDEGARDE NEFF/HILDEGARD KNEF	portrait		
HNE	HEAR NO EVIL	GREENWALD	20th CENTURY FOX	1993
HO	HANDS OF ORLAC (UK)	GREVILLE	CONTINENTAL	1960
HO	HEAD OFFICE	FINKLEMAN	TRI STAR	1986
HO	HENRY O'NEILL	portrait	WARNER BROS	
HO	HOOSIERS	ANSPAUGH	ORION	1986
HO	HOPSCOTCH	NEAME	AVCO EMBASSY	1980
HO	HORSEMAN, THE	FRANKENHEIMER	COLUMBIA	1971
HOBB	HOLES	DAVIS	BUENA VISTA	2003
HOD	HAND OF DEATH	NELSON	20th CENTURY FOX	1962
HOD	HOUR OF DECISION (UK)	PENNINGTON-RICHARDS	ASTOR	1957

HOG	HEART OF GLASS (GER: HERZ AUS GLAS)	HERZOG	NEW YORKER FILMS	1976
HOG	HOG WILD	COURTLAND	AVCO EMBASSY	1974
HOH	HEAD OVER HEELS (CHILLEY SCENES OF WINTER)	SILVER	UNITED ARTISTS	1979
HOND	HUNCHBACK OF NOTRE DAME	TROUSDALE, WISE	BUENA VISTA	1996
HOR	HORROR OF IT ALL (UK)	FISHER	20th CENTURY FOX	1964
HP	HALF PINT, THE	JOURDAN	MILLER CONSOLIDATED	1959
HP	HARRY POTTER AND THE PHILOSOPHER'S STONE	COLUMBUS	WARNER BROS	2001
HP	HIGHWAY PICKUP	MARQUAND	TIMES REL	1963
HP	HUDSUCKER PROXY	COEN BROS	WARNER BROS	1994
HP	IT'S HOT IN PARADISE	BOTTGER	PACEMAKER	1962
HP-2	U-BOAT 29 (UK: SPY IN BLACK)	POWELL	COLUMBIA	1939
HP-3	MINE OWN EXECUTIONER (UK)	KIMMINS	20TH CENTURY FOX	1947
HPM5	THEY MET IN THE DARK (UK)	LAMAC	ENGLISH	1943
HQ2	TIME WITHOUT PITY (UK)	LOSEY	ASTOR	1957
HR	CONFESSION	MAY	WARNER BROS	1937
HR	HIGH ROLLING IN A HOT CORVETTE (HIGH ROLLING)	AUZINS	MARTIN FILMS	1978
HR	HOTEL RESERVE (UK)	COMFORT, GREENBAUM	RKO	1944
HR A-1	CATCH AS CATCH CAN (sh)	NEILAN	MGM	1931
HR A-1	LUKE RIDES ROUGHSHOD (sh)	ROACH	PATHE EXCHANGE	1916
HR A-1	OUR GANG (sh)	MCGOWAN	PATHE EXCHANGE	1922
HR A-2	FIRE FIGHTERS (sh)	MCGOWAN	PATHE EXCHANGE	1922
HR A-2	LUKE, CRYSTAL GAZER (sh)	ROACH	PATHE EXCHANGE	1916
HR A-2	PAJAMA PARTY (sh)	ROACH	MGM	1931
HR A-3	LUKE'S LOST LAMB (sh)	ROACH	PATHE EXCHANGE	1916
HR A-3	WAR MAMAS (sh)	NEILAN	MGM	1931
HR A-3	YOUNG SHERLOCKS (sh)	MCGOWAN	PATHE EXCHANGE	1922
HR A-4	LUKE DOES THE MIDWAY (sh)	ROACH	PATHE EXCHANGE	1916
HR A-4	ON THE LOOSE (sh)	ROACH	MGM	1931
HR A-4	ONE TERRIBLE DAY (sh)	MCGOWAN	PATHE EXCHANGE	1922
HR A-5	A QUIET STREET (sh)	MCGOWAN	PATHE EXCHANGE	1922
HR A-5	LUKE AND THE BANGTAILS (sh)	ROACH	PATHE EXCHANGE	1916
HR A-5	SEAL SKINS (sh)	LIGHTFOOT	MGM	1932
HR A-6	LUKE JOINS THE NAVY (sh)	ROACH	PATHE EXCHANGE	1916
HR A-6	RED NOSES (sh)	HORNE	MGM	1932
HR A-6	SATURDAY MORNING (sh)	MCGOWAN	PATHE EXCHANGE	1922
HR A-7	BIG SHOW (sh)	MCGOWAN	PATHE EXCHANGE	1923
HR A-7	LUKE AND THE MERMAIDS (sh)	ROACH	PATHE EXCHANGE	1916
HR A-7	STRICTLY UNRELIABLE (sh)	MARSHALL	MGM	1932
HR A-8	COBBLER (sh)	MCNAMARA	PATHE EXCHANGE	1923
HR A-8	LUKE'S SPEEDY CLUB LIFE (sh)	ROACH	PATHE EXCHANGE	1916
HR A-8	OLD BULL (sh)	MARSHALL	MGM	1932
HR A-9	CHAMPEEN (sh)	MCGOWAN	PATHE EXCHANGE	1923
HR A-9	LUKE THE CHAUFFEUR (sh)	ROACH	PATHE EXCHANGE	1916
HR A-9	SHOW BUSINESS (sh)	WHITE	MGM	1932
HR A-10	ALUM AND EVE (sh)	MARSHALL	MGM	1932
HR A-10	BOYS TO BOARD (sh)	MCNAMARA	PATHE EXCHANGE	1923
HR A-10	LUKE'S PREPAREDNESS PREPARATIONS (sh)	ROACH	PATHE EXCHANGE	1916
HR A-11	LUKE THE GLADIATOR (sh)	ROACH	PATHE EXCHANGE	1916
HR A-11	PLEASANT JOURNEY (sh)	MCGOWAN	PATHE EXCHANGE	1923
HR A-11	SOILERS (sh)	MARSHALL	MGM	1932
HR A-12	GIANTS VS. YANKS (sh)	MCGOWAN	PATHE EXCHANGE	1923
HR A-12	LUKE, PATIENT PROVIDER (sh)	ROACH	PATHE EXCHANGE	1916
HR A-12	SNEAK EASILY (sh)	MEINS	MGM	1932
HR A-13	ASLEEP IN THE FLEET (sh)	MEINS	MGM	1933
HR A-13	BACK STAGE (sh)	MCGOWAN	PATHE EXCHANGE	1923
HR A-14	DOGS OF WAR (sh)	MCGOWAN	PATHE EXCHANGE	1923
HR A-14	LUKE'S NEWSIE KNOCKOUT (sh)	ROACH	PATHE EXCHANGE	1916
HR A-14	MAIDS A LA MODE (sh)	MEINS	MGM	1933
HR A-15	BARGAIN OF THE CENTURY (sh)	CHASE	MGM	1933
HR A-15	LODGE NIGHT (sh)	MCGOWAN	PATHE EXCHANGE	1923
HR A-15	LUKE'S MOVIE MUDDLE (LUKE'S MODEL MOVIE) (sh)	ROACH	PATHE EXCHANGE	1916
HR A-16	FAST COMPANY (sh)	MCGOWAN	PATHE EXCHANGE	1924
HR A-16	LUKE'S RANK IMPERSONATOR (sh)	ROACH	PATHE EXCHANGE	1916
HR A-16	ONE TRACK MINDS (sh)	MEINS	MGM	1933
HR A-17	BEAUTY AND THE BUS (sh)	MEINS	MGM	1933
HR A-17	LUKE'S FIREWORKS FIZZLE (sh)	ROACH	PATHE EXCHANGE	1916

HR A-17	STAGE FRIGHT (sh)	MCGOWAN	PATHE EXCHANGE	1923
HR A-18	BACK TO NATURE (sh)	MEINS	MGM	1933
HR A-18	JULY DAYS (sh)	MCGOWAN	PATHE EXCHANGE	1923
HR A-18	LUKE LOCATES THE LOOT (sh)	ROACH	PATHE EXCHANGE	1916
HR A-19	AIR FRIGHT (sh)	MEINS	MGM	1933
HR A-19	LUKE'S SHATTERED SLEEP (sh)	ROACH	PATHE EXCHANGE	1916
HR A-19	SUNDAY CALM (sh)	MCGOWAN	PATHE EXCHANGE	1923
HR A-20	LUKE'S LOST LIBERTY (sh)	ROACH	PATHE EXCHANGE	1917
HR A-20	NO NOISE (sh)	MCGOWAN	PATHE EXCHANGE	1923
HR A-21	DERBY DAY (sh)	MCGOWAN	PATHE EXCHANGE	1923
HR A-21	LUKE'S BUSY DAY (sh)	ROACH	PATHE EXCHANGE	1917
HR A-21	SOUP AND FISH (sh)	MEINS	MGM	1934
HR A-22	LUKE'S TROLLEY TROUBLES (sh)	ROACH	PATHE EXCHANGE	1917
HR A-22	MAID IN HOLLYWOOD (sh)	MEINS	MGM	1934
HR A-22	TIRE TROUBLE (sh)	MCGOWAN	PATHE EXCHANGE	1924
HR A-23	BIG BUSINESS (sh)	MCGOWAN	PATHE EXCHANGE	1924
HR A-23	I'LL BE SUING YOU (sh)	MEINS	MGM	1934
HR A-23	LONESOME LUKE, LAWYER (sh)	ROACH	PATHE EXCHANGE	1917
HR A-24	BUCCANEERS (sh)	MCGOWAN, GOLDAINE	PATHE EXCHANGE	1924
HR A-24	LUKE WINS YE LADYE FAIRE (sh)	ROACH	PATHE EXCHANGE	1917
HR A-24	THREE CHUMPS AHEAD (sh)	MEINS	MGM	1934
HR A-25	DONE IN OIL (sh)	MEINS	MGM	1934
HR A-25	LONESOME LUKE'S LIVELY LIFE (sh)	ROACH	PATHE EXCHANGE	1917
HR A-25	SEEIN' THINGS (sh)	MCGOWAN	PATHE EXCHANGE	1924
HR A-26	COMMENCEMENT DAY (sh)	MCGOWAN, GOLDAINE	PATHE EXCHANGE	1924
HR A-26	LONESOME LUKE, MECHANIC (sh)	ROACH	PATHE EXCHANGE	1917
HR A-26	ONE HORSE FARMERS (sh)	MEINS	MGM	1934
HR A-27	IT'S A BEAR (sh)	MCGOWAN	PATHE EXCHANGE	1924
HR A-27	LONESOME LUKE'S HONEYMOON (sh)	ROACH	PATHE EXCHANGE	1917
HR A-27	OPENED BY MISTAKE (sh)	PARROTT	MGM	1934
HR A-28	BUM VOYAGE (sh)	GRINDE	MGM	1934
HR A-28	CRADLE ROBBERS (sh)	MCGOWAN	PATHE EXCHANGE	1924
HR A-28	LONESOME LUKE, PLUMBER (sh)	ROACH	PATHE EXCHANGE	1917
HR A-29	JUBLIO, JR. (sh)	MCGOWAN	PATHE EXCHANGE	1924
HR A-29	STOP! LUKE! LISTEN! (sh)	ROACH	PATHE EXCHANGE	1917
HR A-29	TREASURE BLUES (sh)	PARROTT	MGM	1935
HR A-30	HIGH SOCIETY (sh)	MCGOWAN	PATHE EXCHANGE	1924
HR A-30	LONESOME LUKE'S WILD WOMEN (sh)	ROACH	PATHE EXCHANGE	1917
HR A-30	TIN MAN (sh)	PARROTT	MGM	1935
HR A-31	LONESOME LUKE ON TIN CAN ALLEY (sh)	ROACH	PATHE EXCHANGE	1917
HR A-31	MISSES STOOGE (sh)	PARROTT	MGM	1935
HR A-31	SUN DOWN LIMITED (sh)	MCGOWAN	PATHE EXCHANGE	1924
HR A-32	EVERY MAN FOR HIMSELF (sh)	MCGOWAN	PATHE EXCHANGE	1924
HR A-32	LONESOME LUKE LOSES PATIENTS (sh)	ROACH	PATHE EXCHANGE	1917
HR A-32	SING, SISTER, SING (sh)	PARROTT	MGM	1935
HR A-33	LONESOME LUKE IN LOVE, LAUGHS AND LATHER (sh)	ROACH	PATHE EXCHANGE	1917
HR A-33	MYSTERIOUS MYSTERY! (sh)	MCGOWAN	PATHE EXCHANGE	1924
HR A-33	SLIGHTLY STATIC (sh)	TERHUNE	MGM	1935
HR A-34	BIG TOWN (sh)	MCGOWAN	PATHE EXCHANGE	1925
HR A-34	LONESOME LUKE, MESSENGER (sh)	ROACH	PATHE EXCHANGE	1917
HR A-34	TWIN TRIPLETS (sh)	TERHUNE	MGM	1935
HR A-35	CIRCUS FEVER (sh)	MCGOWAN	PATHE EXCHANGE	1925
HR A-35	HOT MONEY (sh)	HORNE	MGM	1935
HR A-35	LONESOME LUKE IN FROM LONDON TO LARAMIE (sh)	ROACH	PATHE EXCHANGE	1917
HR A-36	DOG DAYS (sh)	MCGOWAN	PATHE EXCHANGE	1925
HR A-36	LONESOME LUKE IN BIRDS OF A FEATHER (sh)	ROACH	PATHE EXCHANGE	1917
HR A-36	TOP FLAT (sh)	JEVNE, TERHUNE	MGM	1935
HR A-37	ALL AMERICAN TOOTHACHE (sh)	MEINS	MGM	1936
HR A-37	LOVE BUG (sh)	MCGOWAN	PATHE EXCHANGE	1925
HR A-37	TRUMPS (sh)	ROACH	PATHE EXCHANGE	1917
HR A-38	ASK GRANDMA (sh)	MCGOWAN	PATHE EXCHANGE	1925
HR A-38	LONESOME LUKE IN WE NEVER SLEEP (sh)	ROACH	PATHE EXCHANGE	1917
HR A-38	PAN HANDLERS (sh)	TERHUNE	MGM	1936
HR A-39	AT SEA ASHORE (sh)	TERHUNE	MGM	1936
HR A-39	SHOOTIN' INJUNS (sh)	MCGOWAN	PATHE EXCHANGE	1925
HR A-40	HILL TILLIES (sh)	MEINS	MGM	1936

HR A-40	OFFICIAL OFFICERS (sh)	MCGOWAN	PATHE EXCHANGE	1925
HR A-41	MARY, QUEEN OF TOTS (sh)	MCGOWAN	PATHE EXCHANGE	1925
HR A-42	BOYS WILL BE JOYS (sh)	MCGOWAN	PATHE EXCHANGE	1925
HR A-43	BETTER MOVIES (sh)	MCGOWAN	PATHE EXCHANGE	1925
HR AC-105	UNNAMED DIPPY DOO DADS (sh)		PATHE EXCHANGE	1923
HR AC-113	KNOCKOUT (sh)	POWERS	PATHE EXCHANGE	1923
HR AC-124	BAR-FLY (sh)	POWERS	PATHE EXCHANGE	1924
HR AC-128	MAN PAYS (sh)	POWERS	PATHE EXCHANGE	1924
HR B-1	365 DAYS (sh)	CHASE	PATHE EXCHANGE	1922
HR B-1	CARETAKER'S DAUGHTER (sh)	MCCAREY	PATHE EXCHANGE	1925
HR B-1	GO GET 'EM HUTCH (sh)	SEITZ	PATHE EXCHANGE	1922
HR B-1	MOVIE DAZE (sh)	MEINS	MGM	1934
HR B-1	SCHEMER SKINNY'S SCHEMES (sh)		PATHE EXCHANGE	1917
HR B-2	BEFORE THE PUBLIC (sh)	CHASE	PATHE EXCHANGE	1923
HR B-2	CROOK'S TOUR (sh)	MCGOWAN	MGM	1933
HR B-2	SKINNY'S LOVE TRIANGLE (sh)		PATHE EXCHANGE	1917
HR B-2	UNEASY THREE (sh)	CHASE	PATHE EXCHANGE	1925
HR B-3	HIS WOODEN WEDDING (sh)	MCCAREY	PATHE EXCHANGE	1925
HR B-3	NEWLY RICH (sh)	CHASE	PATHE EXCHANGE	1922
HR B-3	SCHEMER SKINNY'S SCHEMES (sh)		PATHE EXCHANGE	1917
HR B-3	TWIN SCREWS (sh)	PARROTT	MGM	1933
HR B-4	CHARLEY MY BOY (sh)	MCCAREY	PATHE EXCHANGE	1926
HR B-4	DRAMA'S DREADFUL DEAL (sh)		PATHE EXCHANGE	1917
HR B-4	GREEN CAT (sh)	CHASE	PATHE EXCHANGE	1922
HR B-4	MIXED NUTS (sh)	PARROTT	MGM	1934
HR B-5	MAMA BEHAVE (sh)	CHASE	PATHE EXCHANGE	1926
HR B-5	NEXT WEEKEND (sh)	DUNN	MGM	1934
HR B-5	SKINNY GETS A GOAT (sh)	ROACH	PATHE EXCHANGE	1917
HR B-5	WHERE AM I? (sh)	CHASE	PATHE EXCHANGE	1923
HR B-6	CARETAKER'S DAUGHTER (sh)	FRENCH	MGM	1934
HR B-6	DOG SHY (sh)	MCCAREY	PATHE EXCHANGE	1926
HR B-6	OLD SEA DOG (sh)	CHASE	PATHE EXCHANGE	1922
HR B-6	SKINNY'S FALSE ALARM (sh)	ROACH	PATHE EXCHANGE	1917
HR B-7	DIG UP (sh)	HUTCHINSON	PATHE EXCHANGE	1923
HR B-7	MRS. BARNACLE BILL (sh)	FRENCH	MGM	1934
HR B-7	MUM'S THE WORD (sh)	MCCAREY	PATHE EXCHANGE	1926
HR B-7	SKINNY'S SHIP-WRECKED SAND-WITCH (sh)	ROACH	PATHE EXCHANGE	1917
HR B-8	HOOK, LINE AND SINKER (sh)	CHASE	PATHE EXCHANGE	1922
HR B-8	LONG FLIV THE KING (sh)	MCCAREY	PATHE EXCHANGE	1926
HR B-8	SKINNY ROUTS A ROBBER (sh)		PATHE EXCHANGE	1917
HR B-9	BOARDER BUSTERS (sh)		PATHE EXCHANGE	1917
HR B-9	CALIFORNIA OR BUST (sh)	HUTCHINSON	PATHE EXCHANGE	1923
HR B-9	MIGHTY LIKE A MOOSE (sh)	MCCAREY	PATHE EXCHANGE	1926
HR B-10	CRAZY LIKE A FOX (sh)	MCCAREY	PATHE EXCHANGE	1926
HR B-10	TOUGH WINTER (sh)	CHASE	PATHE EXCHANGE	1923
HR B-11	BROMO AND JULIET (sh)	MCCAREY	PATHE EXCHANGE	1926
HR B-11	IT'S A GIFT (sh)	FAY	PATHE EXCHANGE	1923
HR B-12	SOLD AT AUCTION (sh)	CHASE	PATHE EXCHANGE	1923
HR B-12	TELL 'EM NOTHING (sh)	MCCAREY	PATHE EXCHANGE	1926
HR B-13	BE YOUR AGE (sh)	CHASE	PATHE EXCHANGE	1926
HR B-13	WALKOUT (sh)	JESKE	PATHE EXCHANGE	1923
HR B-13	WHY WORRY? (sh)	TAYLOR, NEWMEYER	PATHE EXCHANGE	1923
HR B-14	MANY SCRAPY RETURNS (sh)	PARROTT	PATHE EXCHANGE	1927
HR B-14	MYSTERY MAN (sh)	FAY	PATHE EXCHANGE	1923
HR B-15	JACK FROST (sh)	CHASE	PATHE EXCHANGE	1923
HR B-15	THERE AIN'T NO SANTA CLAUS (sh)	PARROTT	PATHE EXCHANGE	1926
HR B-16	ARE BRUNETTES SAFE? (sh)	PARROTT	PATHE EXCHANGE	1927
HR B-16	COURTSHIP OF MILES SANDWICH (sh)	CHASE	PATHE EXCHANGE	1923
HR B-17	ONE MAMA MAN (sh)	PARROTT	PATHE EXCHANGE	1927
HR B-18	FORGOTTEN SWEETIES (sh)	PARROTT	PATHE EXCHANGE	1927
HR B-19	BIGGER AND BETTER BLONDS (sh)	PARROTT	PATHE EXCHANGE	1927
HR B-20	FLUTTERING HEARTS (sh)	PARROTT	PATHE EXCHANGE	1927
HR B-21	WHAT WOMEN DID FOR ME (sh)	PARROTT	PATHE EXCHANGE	1927
HR B-22	NOW I'LL TELL ONE (sh)	PARROTT	PATHE EXCHANGE	1927
HR B-23	ASSISTANT WIVES (sh)	PARROTT	PATHE EXCHANGE	1927
HR C-1	HE FORGOT TO REMEMBER (sh)	POWERS, BUCKINGHAM	PATHE EXCHANGE	1926

HR C-1	JUNE MADNESS (sh)	PEMBROKE	PATHE EXCHANGE	1920
HR C-1	LIGHTER THAT FAILED (sh)	PARROTT	MGM	1927
HR C-1	PANIC IS ON (sh)	PARROTT	MGM	1931
HR C-1	UNNAMED ROLIN PROJECT (sh)	WHITING	PATHE EXCHANGE	1915
HR C-2	SANDMAN (sh)	NEWMEYER	PATHE EXCHANGE	1920
HR C-2	SHOULD SAILORS MARRY? (sh)	ROBBINS	PATHE EXCHANGE	1925
HR C-2	SKIP THE MALOO! (sh)	PARROTT	MGM	1931
HR C-2	STING OF STINGS (sh)	PARROTT	MGM	1927
HR C-2	UNNAMED ROLIN PROJECT (sh)	WHITING	PATHE EXCHANGE	1915
HR C-3	ALIAS ALADDIN (sh)	ROACH	PATHE EXCHANGE	1920
HR C-3	MOONLIGHT AND NOSES (sh)	LAUREL, JONES	PATHE EXCHANGE	1925
HR C-3	UNNAMED ROLIN PROJECT (sh)	WHITING	PATHE EXCHANGE	1915
HR C-3	WAY OF ALL PANTS (sh)	JONES, MCCAREY	MGM	1927
HR C-3	WHAT A BOZO (sh)	PARROTT	MGM	1931
HR C-4	HASTY MARRIAGE (sh)	PRATT	MGM	1931
HR C-4	MAMMA'S BOY (sh)	DORAN	PATHE EXCHANGE	1920
HR C-4	UNNAMED ROLIN PROJECT (sh)	WHITING	PATHE EXCHANGE	1915
HR C-4	US (sh)		MGM	1927
HR C-4	WANDERING PAPAS (sh)	LAUREL	PATHE EXCHANGE	1926
HR C-5	NEVER THE DAMES SHALL MEET (sh)	PARROTT	MGM	1927
HR C-5	POWDER MANKEYS (sh)	WHITING	PATHE EXCHANGE	1915
HR C-5	QUEEN'S UP! (sh)	NEWMEYER	PATHE EXCHANGE	1920
HR C-5	STARVATION BLUES (sh)	WALLACE	PATHE EXCHANGE	1925
HR C-5	TABASCO KID (sh)	HORNE	MGM	1932
HR C-6	ALL FOR NOTHING (sh)	PARROTT	MGM	1928
HR C-6	MAN HATERS (sh)	BARROWS	PATHE EXCHANGE	1922
HR C-6	NICKLE NURSER (sh)	DOANE	MGM	1932
HR C-6	WHAT'S THE WORLD COMING TO? (sh)	JONES, WALLACE	PATHE EXCHANGE	1926
HR C-7	GREEK MEETS GREEK (sh)	BARROWS	PATHE EXCHANGE	1920
HR C-7	IN WALKED CHARLEY (sh)	DOANE	MGM	1932
HR C-7	MOVIE NIGHT (sh)	FOSTER	MGM	1929
HR C-7	SCARED STIFF (sh)	HORNE	PATHE EXCHANGE	1926
HR C-8	FAMILY GROUP (sh)	GUIOL, MCCAREY	MGM	1928
HR C-8	FIRST IN WAR (sh)	DOANE	MGM	1932
HR C-8	SLEEPY HEAD (sh)	BARROWS	PATHE EXCHANGE	1920
HR C-8	WIFE TAMERS (sh)	HORNE	PATHE EXCHANGE	1926
HR C-9	ACHING YOUTH (sh)	GUIOL	MGM	1928
HR C-9	BURGLARS BOLD (sh)	BARROWS	PATHE EXCHANGE	1921
HR C-9	GALLOPING GHOSTS (sh)	PARROTT	PATHE EXCHANGE	1928
HR C-9	MERRY WIDOWER (sh)	WALLACE	PATHE EXCHANGE	1926
HR C-9	YOUNG IRONSIDES (sh)	PARROTT	MGM	1932
HR C-10	GIRL GRIEF (sh)	PARROTT	MGM	1932
HR C-10	LIMOUSINE LOVE (sh)	GUIOL	MGM	1928
HR C-10	PINNING IT ON (sh)	BARROWS	PATHE EXCHANGE	1921
HR C-10	SHOULD HUSBANDS PAY? (sh)	JONES, LAUREL	PATHE EXCHANGE	1926
HR C-11	FIGHT PEST (sh)	GUIOL, MCCAREY	MGM	1928
HR C-11	NOW WE'LL TELL ONE (sh)	PARROTT	MGM	1932
HR C-11	OH, PROMISE ME (sh)	BARROWS	PATHE EXCHANGE	1921
HR C-12	IMAGINE MY EMBARRASSMENT (sh)	YATES, MCCAREY	MGM	1928
HR C-12	MR. BRIDE (sh)	PARROTT	MGM	1932
HR C-12	PRINCE PISTACHIO (sh)	BARROWS	PATHE EXCHANGE	1921
HR C-13	FALLEN ARCHES (sh)	MEINS	MGM	1933
HR C-13	IS EVERYBODY HAPPY? (sh)	YATES	MGM	1928
HR C-13	PAINT AND POWDER (sh)	ROACH	PATHE EXCHANGE	1921
HR C-14	BOOSTER (sh)	YATES	MGM	1928
HR C-14	HURRY WEST (sh)	BARROWS	PATHE EXCHANGE	1921
HR C-14	NATURE IN THE WRONG (sh)	CHASE	MGM	1933
HR C-15	ALL PARTS (sh)	YATES	MGM	1928
HR C-15	HIS SILENT RACKET (sh)		MGM	1933
HR C-15	RUNNING WILD (sh)	BARROWS	PATHE EXCHANGE	1921
HR C-16	ARABIAN TIGHTS (sh)	ROACH	MGM	1933
HR C-16	CHASING HUSBANDS (sh)	PARROTT	MGM	1928
HR C-16	HOBGOBLINS (sh)	GORDON	PATHE EXCHANGE	1921
HR C-17	LOVE LESSON (sh)	BARROWS	PATHE EXCHANGE	1921
HR C-17	RUBY LIPS (sh)	PARROTT	MGM	1929
HR C-17	SHERMAN SAID IT (sh)	CHASE	MGM	1933

HR C-18	MIDSUMMER MUSH (sh)	CHASE	MGM	1933
HR C-18	NON SKID KID (sh)	GORDON	PATHE EXCHANGE	1922
HR C-18	OFF TO BUFFALO (sh)	HORNE	MGM	1929
HR C-19	LOUD SOUP (sh)	FOSTER	MGM	1929
HR C-19	LUNCHEON AT TWELVE (sh)	CHASE	MGM	1933
HR C-19	STRAIGHT CROOK (sh)	ROACH	PATHE EXCHANGE	1921
HR C-20	CHINK (sh)	BARROWS	PATHE EXCHANGE	1921
HR C-20	CRACKED ICEMAN (sh)	DUNN	MGM	1934
HR C-20	THIN TWINS (sh)	HORNE	MGM	1929
HR C-21	BIG SQUAWK (sh)	DOANE	MGM	1929
HR C-21	FOUR PARTS (sh)	CHASE, DUNN	MGM	1934
HR C-21	LATE HOURS (sh)	BARROWS	PATHE EXCHANGE	1921
HR C-22	I'LL TAKE VANILLA (sh)	DUNN	MGM	1934
HR C-22	LEAPING LOVE (sh)	DOANE	MGM	1929
HR C-22	STOP KIDDING (sh)	KERR, BARROWS	PATHE EXCHANGE	1921
HR C-23	ANOTHER WILD IDEA (sh)	CHASE, DUNN	MGM	1934
HR C-23	GOOD MORNING JUDGE (sh)	ROACH	PATHE EXCHANGE	1922
HR C-23	SNAPPY SNEEZER (sh)	DOANE	MGM	1929
HR C-24	CRAZY FEET (sh)	DOANE	MGM	1929
HR C-24	IT HAPPENED ONE DAY (sh)	DUNN	MGM	1934
HR C-24	LATE LAMENTED (sh)	EDDY	PATHE EXCHANGE	1922
HR C-25	ON THEIR WAY (sh)	BARROWS	PATHE EXCHANGE	1921
HR C-25	SOMETHING SIMPLE (sh)	CHASE, WEEMS	MGM	1934
HR C-25	STEPPING OUT (sh)	DOANE	MGM	1929
HR C-26	GREAT GOBS! (sh)	DOANE	MGM	1929
HR C-26	SWEET BY AND BY (sh)	KERR	PATHE EXCHANGE	1921
HR C-26	YOU SAID A HATFUL! (sh)	CHASE	MGM	1934
HR C-27	FATE'S FATHEAD (sh)	CHASE	MGM	1934
HR C-27	MANY HAPPY RETURNS (sh)	KERR	PATHE EXCHANGE	1922
HR C-27	REAL MCCOY (sh)	DOANE	MGM	1930
HR C-28	ALL TEED UP (sh)	KENNEDY	MGM	1930
HR C-28	BUSY BEES (sh)	KERR	PATHE EXCHANGE	1922
HR C-28	CHASES OF PIMPLE STREET (sh)	CHASE	MGM	1934
HR C-29	HIGH TIDE (sh)	BARROWS	PATHE EXCHANGE	1922
HR C-29	OKAY TOOTS! (sh)	CHASE, TERHUNE	MGM	1935
HR C-29	WHISPERING WHOOPEE (sh)	HORNE	MGM	1930
HR C-30	BETWEEN MEALS (sh)	GREY	PATHE EXCHANGE	1926
HR C-30	FIFTY MILLION HUSBANDS (sh)	HORNE, KENNEDY	MGM	1930
HR C-30	POKER AT EIGHT (sh)	CHASE	MGM	1935
HR C-31	DON'T BUTT IN (ROUSTABOUT) (sh)	GREY	PATHE EXCHANGE	1926
HR C-31	FAST WORK (sh)	HORNE	MGM	1930
HR C-32	FOUR STAR BOARDER (sh)	CHASE	MGM	1935
HR C-32	GIRL SHOCK (sh)	HORNE	MGM	1930
HR C-32	TRY, TRY AGAIN (sh)	GREY	PATHE EXCHANGE	1922
HR C-33	DOLLAR DIZZY (sh)	HORNE	MGM	1930
HR C-33	NURSE TO YOU! (sh)	CHASE, MOFFITT	MGM	1935
HR C-33	SOFT PEDAL (sh)	GREY	PATHE EXCHANGE	1926
HR C-34	LOOSER THAN LOOSE (sh)	HORNE	MGM	1930
HR C-34	MANHATTAN MONKEY BUSINESS (sh)	CHASE, LAW	MGM	1935
HR C-35	HIGH C'S (sh)	HORNE	MGM	1930
HR C-35	PAY THE CASHIER (sh)	GREY	PATHE EXCHANGE	1926
HR C-35	PUBLIC GHOST #1 (sh)	CHASE, LAW	MGM	1935
HR C-36	LIFE HESITATES AT 40 (sh)	CHASE, LAW	MGM	1936
HR C-36	SLEUTH (sh)	GREY	PATHE EXCHANGE	1922
HR C-36	THUNDERING TENORS (sh)	HORNE	MGM	1931
HR C-37	COUNT TAKES THE COUNT (sh)	LAW	MGM	1936
HR C-37	ONLY SON (sh)	GREY	PATHE EXCHANGE	1926
HR C-37	PIP FROM PITTSBURGH (sh)	PARROTT	MGM	1931
HR C-38	HIRED AND FIRED (sh)	GREY	PATHE EXCHANGE	1926
HR C-38	ROUGH SEAS (sh)	PARROTT	MGM	1931
HR C-38	VAMP TILL READY (sh)	CHASE, LAW	MGM	1936
HR C-39	NEIGHBORHOOD HOUSE (sh)	CHASE, LAW	MGM	1936
HR C-39	ONE OF THE SMITHS (sh)	PARROTT	MGM	1931
HR C-39	RICH MAN, POOR MAN (sh)	CHASE	PATHE EXCHANGE	1922
HR C-40	ON THE WRONG TREK (sh)	CHASE, LAW	MGM	1936
HR C-41	ARE PARENTS PICKLES? (sh)	PRATT	PATHE EXCHANGE	1925

HR C-42	WINNER TAKE ALL (sh)	SANTELL	PATHE EXCHANGE	1923
HR C-43	FRIDAY THE 13TH (sh)	DAVIS	PATHE EXCHANGE	1922
HR C-44	TRUTH JUGGLER (sh)	DAVIS	PATHE EXCHANGE	1922
HR C-45	BED OF ROSES (sh)	HOWE	PATHE EXCHANGE	1922
HR C-46	BRIDE-TO-BE (sh)	DAVIS	PATHE EXCHANGE	1922
HR C-47	TAKE THE NEXT CAR (sh)	HOWE	PATHE EXCHANGE	1922
HR C-48	TOUCH ALL THE BASES (sh)	DAVIS	PATHE EXCHANGE	1922
HR C-49	ROUGH ON ROMEO (sh)	DAVIS	PATHE EXCHANGE	1922
HR C-50	WET WEATHER (sh)	HOWE	PATHE EXCHANGE	1922
HR C-51	OUT ON BAIL (sh)	DAVIS	PATHE EXCHANGE	1922
HR C-52	SHOOT STRAIGHT (sh)	HOWE	PATHE EXCHANGE	1923
HR C-53	LANDLUBBER (sh)	DAVIS	PATHE EXCHANGE	1922
HR C-54	SOAK THE SHEIK (sh)	HOWE	PATHE EXCHANGE	1922
HR C-55	BONE DRY (sh)	CHASE, DAVIS	PATHE EXCHANGE	1922
HR C-56	LOOSE TIGHT WAD (sh)	HOWE	PATHE EXCHANGE	1923
HR C-57	SHINE 'EM UP (sh)	DAVIS	PATHE EXCHANGE	1922
HR C-58	FACE THE CAMERA (sh)	HOWE	PATHE EXCHANGE	1922
HR C-59	GOLF BUG (sh)	DAVIS	PATHE EXCHANGE	1922
HR C-60	UPPERCUT (sh)	HOWE	PATHE EXCHANGE	1922
HR C-61	WHISTLING LIONS (sh)	PARROTT	PATHE EXCHANGE	1925
HR C-62	SHIVER AND SHAKE (sh)	HOWE	PATHE EXCHANGE	1922
HR C-63	HARVEST HANDS (sh)	DAVIS	PATHE EXCHANGE	1922
HR C-64	FLIVVER (sh)	HOWE	PATHE EXCHANGE	1922
HR C-65	I'LL TAKE VANILLA (sh)	DAVIS	PATHE EXCHANGE	1922
HR C-66	WASHED ASHORE (sh)	HOWE	PATHE EXCHANGE	1922
HR C-67	FAIR WEEK (sh)	DAVIS	PATHE EXCHANGE	1922
HR C-68	BLAZE AWAY (sh)	HOWE	PATHE EXCHANGE	1922
HR C-69	FIRE THE FIREMAN (sh)	HOWE	PATHE EXCHANGE	1922
HR C-70	WHITE BLACKSMITH (sh)	JESKE	PATHE EXCHANGE	1922
HR C-71	WATCH YOUR WIFE (sh)	HOWE	PATHE EXCHANGE	1923
HR C-72	PASTE AND PAPER (sh)	JESKE	PATHE EXCHANGE	1923
HR C-73	SPEED THE SWEDE (sh)	HOWE	PATHE EXCHANGE	1923
HR C-74	MR. HYPPO (sh)	JESKE	PATHE EXCHANGE	1923
HR C-75	DON'T SAY DIE (sh)	JESKE	PATHE EXCHANGE	1923
HR C-76	ONCE OVER (sh)	JESKE	PATHE EXCHANGE	1923
HR C-77	JAILED AND BAILED (sh)	HOWE	PATHE EXCHANGE	1923
HR C-78	TIGHT SHOES (sh)	JESKE	PATHE EXCHANGE	1923
HR C-79	DO YOUR STUFF (sh)	HOWE	PATHE EXCHANGE	1923
HR C-80	BOWLED OVER (sh)	JESKE	PATHE EXCHANGE	1923
HR C-81	GET YOUR MAN (sh)	JESKE	PATHE EXCHANGE	1923
HR C-82	FOR SAFE KEEPING (sh)	JESKE	PATHE EXCHANGE	1923
HR C-83	SMILE WINS (sh)	JESKE	PATHE EXCHANGE	1923
HR C-84	DON'T FLIRT (sh)	POWERS	PATHE EXCHANGE	1923
HR C-85	GOOD RIDDANCE (sh)	JESKE	PATHE EXCHANGE	1923
HR C-86	UNDER TWO JAGS (sh)	JESKE	PATHE EXCHANGE	1923
HR C-87	SUNNY SPAIN (sh)	HOWE	PATHE EXCHANGE	1923
HR C-88	WATCH DOG (sh)	POWERS	PATHE EXCHANGE	1923
HR C-89	NOON WHISTLE (sh)	JESKE	PATHE EXCHANGE	1923
HR C-90	FOR ART'S SAKE (sh)	CHASE	PATHE EXCHANGE	1923
HR C-91	WHITE WINGS (sh)	JESKE	PATHE EXCHANGE	1923
HR C-92	PICK AND SHOVEL (sh)	JESKE	PATHE EXCHANGE	1923
HR C-93	FRESH EGGS (sh)	HOWE	PATHE EXCHANGE	1923
HR C-94	BE HONEST (sh)	POWERS	PATHE EXCHANGE	1923
HR C-95	KILL OR CURE (sh)	PEMBROKE	PATHE EXCHANGE	1923
HR C-96	FINGER PRINTS (sh)	CEDER	PATHE EXCHANGE	1923
HR C-97	COLLARS AND CUFFS (sh)	JESKE	PATHE EXCHANGE	1923
HR C-98	LIVE WIRES (sh)	HOWE	PATHE EXCHANGE	1923
HR C-99	GAS AND AIR (sh)	PEMBROKE	PATHE EXCHANGE	1923
HR C-100	POST NO BILLS (sh)	CEDER	PATHE EXCHANGE	1923
HR C-101	FOR GUESTS ONLY (sh)	HOWE	PATHE EXCHANGE	1923
HR C-102	ORANGES AND LEMONS (sh)	JESKE	PATHE EXCHANGE	1923
HR C-103	TAKE THE AIR (sh)	CEDER	PATHE EXCHANGE	1923
HR C-104	SHORT ORDERS (sh)	PEMBROKE	PATHE EXCHANGE	1923
HR C-105	UNNAMED DIPPY DOO DADS (sh)		PATHE EXCHANGE	1923
HR C-106	SAVE THE SHIP (sh)	JESKE, ROACH	PATHE EXCHANGE	1923
HR C-107	UNCOVERED WAGON (sh)	HOWE	PATHE EXCHANGE	1923

HR C-109	NO PETS (sh)	HOWE	PATHE EXCHANGE	1923
HR C-110	STEPPING OUT (sh)	POWERS	PATHE EXCHANGE	1923
HR C-112	SCORCHING SANDS (sh)	WILLIAMSON, ROACH	PATHE EXCHANGE	1923
HR C-113	KNOCKOUT (sh)	POWERS	PATHE EXCHANGE	1923
HR C-114	JOIN THE CIRCUS (sh)	JESKE	PATHE EXCHANGE	1923
HR C-115	WHOLE TRUTH (sh)	CEDER	PATHE EXCHANGE	1923
HR C-116	GO WEST (sh)	POWERS	PATHE EXCHANGE	1923
HR C-117	LOVEY-DOVEY (sh)	POWERS	PATHE EXCHANGE	1923
HR C-118	DEAR OLD PAL (sh)		PATHE EXCHANGE	1923
HR C-119	FROZEN HEARTS (sh)	HOWE	PATHE EXCHANGE	1923
HR C-120	GET BUSY (sh)	HAYES	PATHE EXCHANGE	1924
HR C-121	OLD WAR HORSE (sh)	JESKE	PATHE EXCHANGE	1926
HR C-122	AT FIRST SIGHT (sh)	ROACH	PATHE EXCHANGE	1924
HR C-123	IT'S A JOY (IT'S A BOY) (sh)	JESKE	PATHE EXCHANGE	1923
HR C-124	BAR-FLY (sh)	POWERS	PATHE EXCHANGE	1924
HR C-125	FULLY INSURED (sh)	JESKE	PATHE EXCHANGE	1923
HR C-126	FRIEND HUSBAND (WHY MARRY?) (sh)	HOWE	PATHE EXCHANGE	1924
HR C-127	BIG IDEA (sh)	JESKE	PATHE EXCHANGE	1924
HR C-128	MAN PAYS (sh)	POWERS	PATHE EXCHANGE	1924
HR C-129	HARD KNOCKS (sh)	PARROTT	PATHE EXCHANGE	1924
HR C-129	PERFECT LADY (sh)	PARROTT	PATHE EXCHANGE	1924
HR C-130	JUST A MINUTE (sh)	PARROTT	PATHE EXCHANGE	1924
HR C-131	ONE OF THE FAMILY (sh)	PEMBROKE	PATHE EXCHANGE	1924
HR C-132	LOVE'S REWARD (sh)	POWERS	PATHE EXCHANGE	1924
HR C-133	POWDER AND SMOKE (sh)	PARROTT	PATHE EXCHANGE	1924
HR C-134	LOVE'S DETOUR (sh)	PARROTT	PATHE EXCHANGE	1924
HR C-135	OUR LITTLE NELL (sh)	POWERS	PATHE EXCHANGE	1924
HR C-136	HARD KNOCKS (sh)	PARROTT	PATHE EXCHANGE	1924
HR C-137	NORTH OF 50-50 (sh)	POWERS	PATHE EXCHANGE	1924
HR C-138	DON'T FORGET (sh)	PARROTT	PATHE EXCHANGE	1924
HR CA-84	DON'T FLIRT (sh)	POWERS	PATHE EXCHANGE	1923
HR CA-88	WATCH DOG (sh)	POWERS	PATHE EXCHANGE	1923
HR CC-129	HARD KNOCKS (sh)	PARROTT	PATHE EXCHANGE	1924
HR CC-131	ONE OF THE FAMILY (sh)	PEMBROKE	PATHE EXCHANGE	1924
HR D-1	FOR ART'S SAKE (sh)	CHASE	PATHE EXCHANGE	1923
HR D-1	TROLLEY TROUBLES (sh)	GOULDING	PATHE EXCHANGE	1921
HR D-1	UNNAMED ROLIN PROJECT (sh)	WHITING	PATHE EXCHANGE	1915
HR D-1	WHAT EVERY ICEMAN KNOWS (sh)	YATES, MCCAREY	MGM	1927
HR D-2	CALL OF THE CUCKOOS (sh)	BRUCKMAN	MGM	1927
HR D-2	ROUGH SEAS (sh)	GOULDING	PATHE EXCHANGE	1921
HR D-2	UNNAMED ROLIN PROJECT (sh)	WHITING	PATHE EXCHANGE	1915
HR D-2	WHITE WINGS (sh)	JESKE	PATHE EXCHANGE	1923
HR D-3	DODGE YOUR DEBTS (sh)	KENTON	PATHE EXCHANGE	1921
HR D-3	LOVE 'EM AND FEED 'EM (sh)	BRUCKMAN	MGM	1927
HR D-3	PICK AND SHOVEL (sh)	JESKE	PATHE EXCHANGE	1923
HR D-3	UNNAMED ROLIN PROJECT (sh)	WHITING	PATHE EXCHANGE	1915
HR D-4	FIGHTING FATHERS (sh)	GUIOL	MGM	1927
HR D-4	FRESH EGGS (sh)	HOWE	PATHE EXCHANGE	1923
HR D-4	ZERO HERO (sh)	KENTON	PATHE EXCHANGE	1921
HR D-5	KILL OR CURE (sh)	PEMBROKE	PATHE EXCHANGE	1923
HR D-5	LUCKY NUMBER (sh)	KENTON	PATHE EXCHANGE	1921
HR D-5	TELL IT TO THE JUDGE (sh)	MCCAREY, YATES	MGM	1928
HR D-6	FINGER PRINTS (sh)	CEDER	PATHE EXCHANGE	1923
HR D-6	PASS THE GRAVY (sh)	GUIOL, MCCAREY	MGM	1928
HR D-7	COLLARS AND CUFFS (sh)	JESKE	PATHE EXCHANGE	1923
HR D-7	DUMB DADDIES (sh)	YATES	MGM	1928
HR D-8	CAME THE DAWN (sh)	HEATH, MCCAREY	MGM	1928
HR D-8	LIVE WIRES (sh)	HOWE	PATHE EXCHANGE	1923
HR D-9	BLOW BY BLOW (sh)	MCCAREY	MGM	1928
HR D-9	GAS AND AIR (sh)	PEMBROKE	PATHE EXCHANGE	1923
HR D-10	POST NO BILLS (sh)	CEDER	PATHE EXCHANGE	1923
HR D-10	SHOULD WOMEN DRIVE? (sh)	MCCAREY	MGM	1928
HR D-11	FOR GUESTS ONLY (sh)	HOWE	PATHE EXCHANGE	1923
HR D-12	ORANGES AND LEMONS (sh)	JESKE	PATHE EXCHANGE	1923
HR D-13	TAKE THE AIR (sh)	CEDER	PATHE EXCHANGE	1923
HR D-14	SHORT ORDERS (sh)	PEMBROKE	PATHE EXCHANGE	1923

HR D-15	SAVE THE SHIP (sh)	JESKE, ROACH	PATHE EXCHANGE	1923
HR D-16	UNCOVERED WAGON (sh)	HOWE	PATHE EXCHANGE	1923
HR D-17	MAN ABOUT TOWN (sh)	JESKE	PATHE EXCHANGE	1923
HR D17	TOPPER (sh)	MCLEOD	MGM	1937
HR D-18	NO PETS (sh)	HOWE	PATHE EXCHANGE	1923
HR D-19	SCORCHING SANDS (sh)	WILLIAMSON, ROACH	PATHE EXCHANGE	1923
HR D-20	KNOCKOUT (sh)	POWERS	PATHE EXCHANGE	1923
HR D-21	JOIN THE CIRCUS (sh)	JESKE	PATHE EXCHANGE	1923
HR D-22	WHOLE TRUTH (sh)	CEDER	PATHE EXCHANGE	1923
HR D-23	GO WEST (sh)	POWERS	PATHE EXCHANGE	1923
HR D-24	DEAR OLD PAL (sh)		PATHE EXCHANGE	1923
HR D-25	LOVEY-DOVEY (sh)	POWERS	PATHE EXCHANGE	1923
HR D-26	GET BUSY (sh)	HAYES	PATHE EXCHANGE	1924
HR D-27	OLD WAR HORSE (sh)	JESKE	PATHE EXCHANGE	1926
HR D-28	AT FIRST SIGHT (sh)	ROACH	PATHE EXCHANGE	1924
HR D-29	IT'S A JOY (IT'S A BOY) (sh)	JESKE	PATHE EXCHANGE	1923
HR D-30	BAR-FLY (sh)	POWERS	PATHE EXCHANGE	1924
HR D-31	FULLY INSURED (sh)	JESKE	PATHE EXCHANGE	1923
HR D-32	FRIEND HUSBAND (WHY MARRY?) (sh)	HOWE	PATHE EXCHANGE	1924
HR D-33	BIG IDEA (sh)	JESKE	PATHE EXCHANGE	1924
HR D-34	MAN PAYS (sh)	POWERS	PATHE EXCHANGE	1924
HR D-35	PERFECT LADY (sh)	PARROTT	PATHE EXCHANGE	1924
HR D-36	POWDER AND SMOKE (sh)	PARROTT	PATHE EXCHANGE	1924
HR D-37	ONE OF THE FAMILY (sh)	PEMBROKE	PATHE EXCHANGE	1924
HR D-38	LOVE'S REWARD (sh)	POWERS	PATHE EXCHANGE	1924
HR D-39	JUST A MINUTE (sh)	PARROTT	PATHE EXCHANGE	1924
HR D-40	LOVE'S DETOUR (sh)	PARROTT	PATHE EXCHANGE	1924
HR D-41	OUR LITTLE NELL (sh)	POWERS	PATHE EXCHANGE	1924
HR D-42	HARD KNOCKS (sh)	PARROTT	PATHE EXCHANGE	1924
HR D-43	NORTH OF 50-50 (sh)	POWERS	PATHE EXCHANGE	1924
HR D-44	DON'T FORGET (sh)	PARROTT	PATHE EXCHANGE	1924
HR D-45	FRAIDY CAT (sh)	PARROTT	PATHE EXCHANGE	1924
HR D-46	UP AND AT 'EM (sh)	POWERS	PATHE EXCHANGE	1924
HR D-47	PUBLICITY PAYS (sh)	MCCAREY	PATHE EXCHANGE	1924
HR D-48	POSITION WANTED (sh)	CEDER	PATHE EXCHANGE	1924
HR D-49	BIG KICK (sh)	GUIOL, ROACH	PATHE EXCHANGE	1925
HR D-50	ONE AT A TIME (sh)	CEDER	PATHE EXCHANGE	1924
HR D-51	BOUNCER (sh)	CEDER, GUIOL	PATHE EXCHANGE	1925
HR D-52	APRIL FOOL (sh)	CEDER	PATHE EXCHANGE	1924
HR D-53	SOLID IVORY (sh)	CEDER	PATHE EXCHANGE	1925
HR D-54	STOLEN GOODS (sh)	MCCAREY	PATHE EXCHANGE	1924
HR D-55	BEFORE TAKING (sh)	CEDER	PATHE EXCHANGE	1924
HR D-56	YOUNG OLDFIELD (sh)	MCCAREY	PATHE EXCHANGE	1924
HR D-57	FAST BLACK (sh)	GARNETT	PATHE EXCHANGE	1924
HR D-58	JEFFRIES JR. (sh)	MCCAREY	PATHE EXCHANGE	1924
HR D-59	RIDER OF THE KITCHEN RANGE (sh)	GARNETT, JESKE	PATHE EXCHANGE	1925
HR D-60	WHY HUSBANDS GO MAD (sh)	MCCAREY	PATHE EXCHANGE	1924
HR D-61	ALL WOOL (sh)	GARNETT	PATHE EXCHANGE	1925
HR D-62	SEEING NELLIE HOME (sh)	MCCAREY	PATHE EXCHANGE	1924
HR D-63	GRIEF OF BAGDAD(SHEIKS IN BAGDAD) (sh)	LEDERMAN	PATHE EXCHANGE	1925
HR D-64	TEN MINUTE EGG (sh)	MCCAREY	PATHE EXCHANGE	1924
HR D-65	ACCIDENTAL ACCIDENTS (sh)	MCCAREY	PATHE EXCHANGE	1924
HR D-66	BIG RED RIDING HOOD (sh)	MCCAREY	PATHE EXCHANGE	1925
HR D-67	WHY MEN WORK (sh)	MCCAREY	PATHE EXCHANGE	1924
HR D-68	SWEET DADDY (sh)	MCCAREY	PATHE EXCHANGE	1924
HR D-69	OUTDOOR PAJAMAS (sh)	MCCAREY	PATHE EXCHANGE	1924
HR D-70	SITTIN' PRETTY (sh)	MCCAREY	PATHE EXCHANGE	1924
HR D-71	TOO MANY MAMMAS (sh)	MCCAREY	PATHE EXCHANGE	1924
HR D-72	BUNGALOW BOOBS (sh)	MCCAREY	PATHE EXCHANGE	1924
HR D-73	ALL WET (sh)	MCCAREY	PATHE EXCHANGE	1924
HR D-74	POOR FISH (sh)	MCCAREY	PATHE EXCHANGE	1924
HR D-75	ROYAL RAZZ (sh)	MCCAREY	PATHE EXCHANGE	1924
HR D-76	RAT'S KNUCKLES (sh)	MCCAREY	PATHE EXCHANGE	1925
HR D-77	HELLO BABY (sh)	MCCAREY	PATHE EXCHANGE	1925
HR D-78	FIGHTING FLUID (sh)	MCCAREY	PATHE EXCHANGE	1925
HR D-79	FAMILY ENTRANCE (sh)	MCCAREY	PATHE EXCHANGE	1925

HR D-80	SHOULD HUSBANDS BE WATCHED? (sh)	MCCAREY	PATHE EXCHANGE	1925
HR D-81	PLAIN AND FANCY GIRLS (sh)	MCCAREY	PATHE EXCHANGE	1925
HR D-82	IS MARRIAGE THE BUNK? (sh)	MCCAREY	PATHE EXCHANGE	1925
HR D-83	HOLD EVERYTHING (sh)	GUIOL, MCCAREY	PATHE EXCHANGE	1925
HR D-84	ARE HUSBANDS HUMAN? (sh)	BARROWS	PATHE EXCHANGE	1925
HR D-85	SURE MIKE (sh)	GUIOL	PATHE EXCHANGE	1925
HR D-86	TOL'ABLE ROMEO (sh)	ROBBINS	PATHE EXCHANGE	1925
HR D-87	IN THE GREASE (sh)	HOWE	PATHE EXCHANGE	1925
HR D-88	CHASING THE CHASER (sh)	LAUREL	PATHE EXCHANGE	1925
HR D-89	UNFRIENDLY ENEMIES (sh)	LAUREL	PATHE EXCHANGE	1925
HR D-90	YES, YES NANETTE (sh)	HENNECKE, LAUREL	PATHE EXCHANGE	1925
HR E-1	HOSS AND HOSS (sh)	(UNFINISHED)	PATHE EXCHANGE	1924
HR E-1	PICKANINNY (sh)	KERR, PARROTT	PATHE EXCHANGE	1921
HR E-1	YOU BRING THE DUCKS (sh)	YATES	MGM	1934
HR E-2	HOT HEELS (sh)	JESKE	PATHE EXCHANGE	1924
HR E-2	NOSED OUT (sh)	YATES	MGM	1934
HR E-3	BALLAD OF PADUCAH JAIL (sh)	GRINDE	MGM	1934
HR E-3	SKY PLUMBER (sh)	DAVISS	PATHE EXCHANGE	1924
HR E-4	LUCKY BEGINNERS (sh)	DOUGLAS, ROACH	MGM	1935
HR E-4	UNFINISHED ARTHUR STONE (sh)		PATHE EXCHANGE	1924
HR E-5	INFERNAL TRIANGLE (sh)	DOUGLAS	MGM	1935
HR E-5	SHOULD LANDLORDS LIVE? (sh)	BARROWS, DAVIS	PATHE EXCHANGE	1924
HR E-6	JUST A GOOD GUY (sh)	DEL RUTH	PATHE EXCHANGE	1924
HR E-6	UNFINISHED ROACH (sh)		PATHE EXCHANGE	1924
HR E-7	JUST A GOOD GUY (sh)	DEL RUTH	PATHE EXCHANGE	1924
HR E-8	TAME MEN AND WILD WOMEN (sh)	DE SANO	PATHE EXCHANGE	1925
HR E-9	HARD WORKING LOAFERS (sh)		PATHE EXCHANGE	1925
HR E-10	CHANGE THE NEEDLE (sh)	ROACH	PATHE EXCHANGE	1925
HR E-11	UNNAMED ARTHUR STONE (sh)		PATHE EXCHANGE	1925
HR E-12	SHERLOCK SLEUTH (sh)	CEDER	PATHE EXCHANGE	1925
HR E-13	HARD -BOILED (sh)	MCCAREY	PATHE EXCHANGE	1925
HR E-14	BAD BOY (sh)	MCCAREY	PATHE EXCHANGE	1925
HR E-15	LOOKING FOR SALLY (sh)	MCCAREY	PATHE EXCHANGE	1925
HR E-16	WHAT PRICE GOOFY? (sh)	MCCAREY	PATHE EXCHANGE	1925
HR E-17	ISN'T LIFE TERRIBLE? (sh)	MCCAREY	PATHE EXCHANGE	1925
HR E-18	INNOCENT HUSBANDS (sh)	MCCAREY	PATHE EXCHANGE	1925
HR E-19	NO FATHER TO GUIDE HIM (sh)	MCCAREY	PATHE EXCHANGE	1925
HR F-1	PARDON US	PARROTT	MGM	1931
HR F-1	ROUGHING IT (sh)	JACKMAN	PATHE EXCHANGE	1923
HR F-2	LET'S BUILD (sh)	PEMBROKE	PATHE EXCHANGE	1923
HR F-2	PACK UP YOUR TROUBLES (sh)	MARSHALL, MCCAREY	MGM	1932
HR F-3	DEVIL'S BROTHER	ROACH, ROGERS	MGM	1933
HR F-3	HEAVY SEAS (sh)	GUIOL, HOWE	PATHE EXCHANGE	1923
HR F-4	GREAT OUTDOORS (sh)	GUIOL	PATHE EXCHANGE	1923
HR F-5	BABES IN TOYLAND (MARCH OF THE WOODEN SOLDIERS)	MEINS, ROGERS	MGM	1934
HR F-5	DARKEST HOUR (sh)	HOWE	PATHE EXCHANGE	1923
HR F-6	POLITICAL PULL (sh)	CLEMENTS	PATHE EXCHANGE	1924
HR F-6	VAGABOND LADY	TAYLOR	MGM	1935
HR F-7	HELP ONE ANOTHER (sh)	GUIOL	PATHE EXCHANGE	1924
HR F-8	BOHEMIAN GIRL	HORNE, ROGERS	MGM	1936
HR F-8	HUNTERS BOLD (sh)	ROACH	PATHE EXCHANGE	1924
HR F-9	HIT THE HIGH SPOTS (sh)	GUIOL	PATHE EXCHANGE	1924
HR F-9	MR. CINDERELLA		MGM	1936
HR F-10	BOTTLE BABIES (sh)	HOWE, PEMBROKE	PATHE EXCHANGE	1924
HR F-10	KELLY THE SECOND	MEINS	MGM	1936
HR F-11	SUFFERING SHAKESPEARE (sh)	CEDER	PATHE EXCHANGE	1924
HR F-12	GENERAL SPANKY	DOUGLAS, NEWMEYER	MGM	1936
HR F-12	RADIO MAD (sh)	HOWE	PATHE EXCHANGE	1924
HR F-13	HARD-BOILED TENDERFOOT (sh)	HOWE	PATHE EXCHANGE	1924
HR F-13	UNRELEASED ROACH (sh)		MGM	1936
HR F-14	SOUTH O' THE NORTH POLE	HOWE	PATHE EXCHANGE	1924
HR F-15	LOST DOG (sh)	HOWE	PATHE EXCHANGE	1924
HR F-15	PICK A STAR	SEDGWICK	MGM	1937
HR F-16	HOT STUFF (sh)	HOWE	PATHE EXCHANGE	1924
HR F-16	NOBODY'S BABY	MEINS	MGM	1937
HR F-17	TOPPER (sh)	MCLEOD	MGM	1937

HR F-18	DEAF, DUMB AND DAFFY (sh)	HOWE	PATHE EXCHANGE	1924
HR F-18	UPSPECIFIEC TITLE	ROACH	MGM	1937
HR F-19	LAUGH THAT OFF (sh)	HOWE	PATHE EXCHANGE	1925
HR F-20	FOX HUNT (sh)	HOWE	PATHE EXCHANGE	1925
HR F-20	SWISS MISS	BLYSTONE	MGM	1938
HR F-21	EXCUSE MY GLOVE (sh)	HOWE	PATHE EXCHANGE	1925
HR F-21	THERE GOES MY HEART	MCLEOD	UNITED ARTISTS	1938
HR F-22	BLACK HAND BLUES (BLACK HANDS) (sh)	HOWE	PATHE EXCHANGE	1925
HR F-22	BLOCK-HEADS	BLYSTONE	MGM	1938
HR F-23	ROYAL FOUR-FLUSH (sh)	HOWE	PATHE EXCHANGE	1925
HR F-24	WILD PAPA (sh)	BARROWS, HOWE	PATHE EXCHANGE	1925
HR F-25	DON KEY (sh)	GUIOL, HORNE	PATHE EXCHANGE	1926
HR G-1	BIG EARS (sh)	MCGOWAN	MGM	1931
HR G-1	REGULAR PAL (sh)	ROACH	PATHE EXCHANGE	1920
HR G-1	YALE VS. HARVARD (sh)	MCGOWAN	MGM	1927
HR G-2	MERELY A MAID (sh)	ROACH	PATHE EXCHANGE	1920
HR G-2	OLD WALLOP (sh)	MCGOWAN	MGM	1927
HR G-2	SAILOR PAPA (sh)	GUIOL, WILDE	PATHE EXCHANGE	1925
HR G-2	SHIVER MY TIMBERS (sh)	MCGOWAN	MGM	1931
HR G-3	DOGS IS DOGS (sh)	MCGOWAN	MGM	1931
HR G-3	HEEBEE JEEBEES (sh)	MCGOWAN, MCGOWAN	MGM	1927
HR G-3	HELLO UNCLE (sh)	ROACH	PATHE EXCHANGE	1920
HR G-3	MEET THE MISSUS (sh)	CLEMENTS, GUIOL	PATHE EXCHANGE	1924
HR G-4	DOG HEAVEN	MCGOWAN	MGM	1927
HR G-4	READIN' AND WRITIN' (sh)	MCGOWAN	MGM	1932
HR G-4	START THE SHOW	ROACH	PATHE EXCHANGE	1920
HR G-4	WAGES OF TIN	CLEMENTS	PATHE EXCHANGE	1925
HR G-5	FREE EATS (sh)	MCCAREY	MGM	1932
HR G-5	SPOOK SPOOFING	MCGOWAN	MGM	1928
HR G-5	TELL IT TO A POLICEMAN	GUIOL	PATHE EXCHANGE	1925
HR G-6	HOLD MY BABY - WHOSE BABY ARE YOU?	HOWE	PATHE EXCHANGE	1925
HR G-6	RAINY DAYS (sh)	MCGOWAN, OELZE	MGM	1928
HR G-6	SPANKY	MCGOWAN	MGM	1932
HR G-7	EDISON, MARCONI & CO. (sh)	MCGOWAN	MGM	1928
HR G-7	HAUNTED HONEYMOON	GUIOL, WILDE	PATHE EXCHANGE	1925
HR G-8	BARNUM & RINGLING INC.	MCGOWAN	MGM	1928
HR G-8	POOCH (sh)	MCGOWAN	MGM	1932
HR G-8	THUNDERING LANDLORDS	HORNE	PATHE EXCHANGE	1925
HR G-9	DADDY GOES A' GRUNTING	HORNE	PATHE EXCHANGE	1925
HR G-9	FAIR AND MUDDY	OELZE	MGM	1928
HR G-9	HOOK AND LADDER (sh)	MCGOWAN	MGM	1932
HR G-10	CRAZY HOUSE (sh)	MCGOWAN	MGM	1928
HR G-10	FREE WHEELING (sh)	MCGOWAN	MGM	1932
HR G-10	MADAME SANS JANE	HORNE	PATHE EXCHANGE	1925
HR G-11	BIRTHDAY BLUES (sh)	MCGOWAN	MGM	1932
HR G-11	CUCKOO LOVE	GUIOL	PATHE EXCHANGE	1925
HR G-11	GROWING PAINS (sh)	MCGOWAN	MGM	1928
HR G-12	A LAD AN' A LAMP (sh)	MCGOWAN	MGM	1932
HR G-12	OL' GRAY HOSS (sh)	MCGOWAN	MGM	1928
HR G-12	PAPA, BE GOOD!	GUIOL	PATHE EXCHANGE	1925
HR G-13	FISH HOOKY (sh)	MCGOWAN	MGM	1933
HR G-13	SCHOOL BEGINS	MCGOWAN	MGM	1928
HR G-14	FORGOTTEN BABIES (sh)	MCGOWAN	MGM	1933
HR G-14	SPANKING AGE (sh)	MCGOWAN	MGM	1928
HR G-15	ELECTION DAY (sh)	MCGOWAN	MGM	1929
HR G-15	KID FROM BORNEO (sh)	MCGOWAN	MGM	1933
HR G-16	MUSH AND MILK (sh)	MCGOWAN	MGM	1933
HR G-16	NOISY NOISES	MCGOWAN	MGM	1929
HR G-17	BEDTIME WORRIES (sh)	MCGOWAN	MGM	1933
HR G-17	HOLY TERROR	MCGOWAN	MGM	1929
HR G-18	WIGGLE YOUR EARS (sh)	MCGOWAN	MGM	1929
HR G-18	WILD POSES (sh)	MCGOWAN	MGM	1933
HR G-19	FAST FREIGHT (sh)	MACK	MGM	1929
HR G-19	HI' NEIGHBOR! (sh)	MEINS	MGM	1934
HR G-20	FOR PETE'S SAKE!	MEINS	MGM	1934
HR G-20	LITTLE MOTHER	MCGOWAN	MGM	1929

HR G-21	CAT, DOG & CO. (sh)	MCGOWAN	MGM	1929
HR G-21	FIRST ROUNDUP (sh)	MEINS	MGM	1934
HR G-22	HONKY DONKEY (sh)	MEINS	MGM	1934
HR G-22	SATURDAY'S LESSON (sh)	MCGOWAN	MGM	1929
HR G-23	MIKE FRIGHT (sh)	MEINS	MGM	1934
HR G-23	SMALL TALK	MCGOWAN	MGM	1929
HR G-24	RAILROADIN' (sh)	MCGOWAN	MGM	1929
HR G-24	WASHEE IRONEE	PARROTT	MGM	1934
HR G-25	BOXING GLOVES (sh)	MCGOWAN	MGM	1929
HR G-25	MAMA'S LITTLE PIRATE	MEINS	MGM	1935
HR G-26	LAZY DAYS (sh)	MCGOWAN	MGM	1929
HR G-26	SHRIMPS FOR A DAY	MEINS	MGM	1935
HR G-27	ANNIVERSARY TROUBLE (sh)	MEINS	MGM	1935
HR G-27	BOUNCING BABIES	MCGOWAN	MGM	1929
HR G-28	BEGINNER'S LUCK (sh)	MEINS	MGM	1935
HR G-28	MOAN & GROAN INC. (sh)	MCGOWAN	MGM	1929
HR G-29	SHIVERING SHAKESPEARE (sh)	MCGOWAN	MGM	1930
HR G-29	TEACHER'S BEAU	MEINS	MGM	1935
HR G-30	FIRST SEVEN YEARS (sh)	MCGOWAN	MGM	1930
HR G-30	SPRUCIN' UP	MEINS	MGM	1935
HR G-31	LUCKY CORNER (sh)	MEINS	MGM	1936
HR G-31	WHEN THE WIND BLOWS (sh)	HORNE	MGM	1930
HR G-32	BEAR SHOOTERS (sh)	MCGOWAN	MGM	1930
HR G-32	LITTLE PAPA (sh)	MEINS	MGM	1935
HR G-33	LITTLE SINNER (sh)	MEINS	MGM	1935
HR G-33	TOUGH WINTER	MCGOWAN	MGM	1930
HR G-34	OUR GANG FOLLIES OF 1936 (sh)	MEINS	MGM	1935
HR G-34	PUPS IS PUPS (sh)	MCGOWAN	MGM	1930
HR G-35	PINCH SINGER (sh)	NEWMEYER	MGM	1936
HR G-35	TEACHER'S PET	MCGOWAN	MGM	1930
HR G-36	DIVOT DIGGERS	MCGOWAN	MGM	1936
HR G-36	SCHOOL'S OUT	MCGOWAN	MGM	1930
HR G-37	HELPING GRANDMA	MCGOWAN	MGM	1931
HR G-37	SECOND CHILDHOOD (sh)	MEINS	MGM	1936
HR G-38	ARBOR DAY (sh)	NEWMEYER	MGM	1936
HR G-38	LOVE BUSINESS	MCGOWAN	MGM	1931
HR G-39	LITTLE DADDY (sh)	MCGOWAN	MGM	1931
HR G-40	BARGAIN DAY	MCGOWAN	MGM	1931
HR G-41	FLY MY KITE	MCGOWAN	MGM	1931
HR H-1	ALL AT SEA	CHASE, GOULDING	PATHE EXCHANGE	1919
HR H-1	FLAMING FLAPPERS	GUIOL	PATHE EXCHANGE	1925
HR H-2	LONG PANTS	GUIOL	PATHE EXCHANGE	1926
HR H-2	START SOMETHING	GOULDING	PATHE EXCHANGE	1919
HR H-3	45 MINUTES FROM HOLLYWOOD	GUIOL	PATHE EXCHANGE	1926
HR H-3	CALL FOR MR. CAVEMAN	CHASE	PATHE EXCHANGE	1919
HR H-4	GIVING THE BRIDE AWAY	CHASE, ROACH	PATHE EXCHANGE	1919
HR H-4	HUG BUG	GUIOL	PATHE EXCHANGE	1926
HR H-5	ORDER IN THE COURT	CHASE	PATHE EXCHANGE	1919
HR H-5	UKULELE SHEIKS	GUIOL	PATHE EXCHANGE	1926
HR H-6	IT'S A HARD LIFE	ROACH	PATHE EXCHANGE	1919
HR H-6	SAY IT WITH BABIES	GUIOL	PATHE EXCHANGE	1926
HR H-7	COW'S KIMONO	GUIOL, PARROTT	PATHE EXCHANGE	1926
HR H-7	HOW DRY I AM	ROACH	PATHE EXCHANGE	1919
HR H-8	ALONG CAME AUNTIE	GUIOL, WALLACE	PATHE EXCHANGE	1926
HR H-8	UNFINISHED ROACH		PATHE EXCHANGE	1919
HR H-9	GETTING HIS GOAT	CHASE	PATHE EXCHANGE	1920
HR H-9	TWO TIME MAMA	GUIOL	PATHE EXCHANGE	1927
HR H-10	ONE HOUR MARRIED	STRONG, YATES	PATHE EXCHANGE	1927
HR H-10	TOUGH LUCK	CHASE	PATHE EXCHANGE	1919
HR H-11	LOOKING FOR TROUBLE	ROACH	PATHE EXCHANGE	1919
HR H-11	NICKEL HOPPER	JONES, YATES	PATHE EXCHANGE	1926
HR H-12	ANYTHING ONCE!	JONES, YATES	PATHE EXCHANGE	1927
HR H-12	FLOOR BELOW	CHASE, GOULDING	PATHE EXCHANGE	1919
HR H-13	RED HOT HOTTENTOTS	CHASE	PATHE EXCHANGE	1920
HR H-14	WHY GO HOME?	CHASE	PATHE EXCHANGE	1920
HR H-15	SHOULD MEN WALK HOME?	MCCAREY	PATHE EXCHANGE	1927

HR H-15	SLIPPERY SLICKERS	CHASE	PATHE EXCHANGE	1920
HR H-16	DIPPY DENTIST	GOULDING	PATHE EXCHANGE	1920
HR H-16	JEWISH PRUDENCE	MCCAREY	PATHE EXCHANGE	1927
HR H-17	ALL LIT UP	NEWMEYER	PATHE EXCHANGE	1920
HR H-17	EVE'S LOVE LETTERS	MCCAREY	PATHE EXCHANGE	1927
HR H-18	DON'T TELL EVERYTHING	MCCAREY	PATHE EXCHANGE	1927
HR H-18	WALTZ ME AROUND	CHASE	PATHE EXCHANGE	1920
HR H-19	RAISE THE RENT	NEWMEYER	PATHE EXCHANGE	1920
HR H-19	SHOULD SECOND HUSBANDS COME FIRST?	MCCAREY	PATHE EXCHANGE	1927
HR H-20	FIND THE GIRL	CHASE	PATHE EXCHANGE	1920
HR H-21	FLAT BROKE	CHASE	PATHE EXCHANGE	1920
HR H-22	FRESH PAINT	CHASE, GOULDING	PATHE EXCHANGE	1920
HR H-23	CUT THE CARDS	CHASE	PATHE EXCHANGE	1920
HR H-24	CRACKED WEDDING BELLS	LA ROSE	PATHE EXCHANGE	1920
HR H-25	DINNER HOUR	CHASE	PATHE EXCHANGE	1920
HR H-26	SPEED TO SPARE	CHASE	PATHE EXCHANGE	1920
HR H-27	SHOOT ON SIGHT	CHASE	PATHE EXCHANGE	1920
HR H-28	DON'T WEAKEN	GOULDING	PATHE EXCHANGE	1920
HR H-29	DRINK HEARTY	GOULDING	PATHE EXCHANGE	1920
HR H-30	TROTTING THROUGH TURKEY	CHASE	PATHE EXCHANGE	1920
HR H-31	ALL DRESSED UP	CHASE	PATHE EXCHANGE	1920
HR H-32	GRAB THE GHOST	GOULDING	PATHE EXCHANGE	1920
HR H-33	YOU'RE PINCHED	ROACH	PATHE EXCHANGE	1920
HR H-34	ALL IN A DAY	CHASE	PATHE EXCHANGE	1920
HR H-35	ANY OLD PORT	GOULDING	PATHE EXCHANGE	1920
HR H-36	DON'T ROCK THE BOAT	CHASE	PATHE EXCHANGE	1920
HR H-37	HOME STRETCH	CHASE	PATHE EXCHANGE	1920
HR H-38	CALL A TAXI	CHASE	PATHE EXCHANGE	1920
HR H-39	LIVE AND LEARN	CHASE	PATHE EXCHANGE	1920
HR H-40	RUN 'EM RAGGED	GOULDING	PATHE EXCHANGE	1920
HR H-41	LONDON BOBBY	CHASE	PATHE EXCHANGE	1920
HR H-42	MONEY TO BURN	NEWMEYER	PATHE EXCHANGE	1920
HR H-43	ROCK A BYE BABY	CHASE	PATHE EXCHANGE	1920
HR H-44	GO AS YOU PLEASE	GOULDING	PATHE EXCHANGE	1920
HR H-45	DOING TIME	GOULDING	PATHE EXCHANGE	1920
HR H-46	FELLOW CITIZENS	GOULDING	PATHE EXCHANGE	1920
HR H-47	WHEN THE WIND BLOWS	CHASE	PATHE EXCHANGE	1920
HR H-48	INSULTING THE SULTAN	GOULDING	PATHE EXCHANGE	1920
HR H-49	DEAR DEPARTED	CHASE	PATHE EXCHANGE	1920
HR H-50	CASH CUSTOMERS	GOULDING	PATHE EXCHANGE	1920
HR H-51	PARK YOUR CAR	GOULDING	PATHE EXCHANGE	1920
HR H-52	OPEN ANOTHER BOTTLE	GOULDING	PATHE EXCHANGE	1921
HR H-53	MORNING AFTER	GOULDING	PATHE EXCHANGE	1921
HR H-54	WHIRL OF THE WEST	BARROWS	PATHE EXCHANGE	1921
HR H-55	HIS BEST GIRL	CHASE	PATHE EXCHANGE	1921
HR H-56	MAKE IT SNAPPY		PATHE EXCHANGE	1921
HR H-57	FELLOW ROMANS	ROACH	PATHE EXCHANGE	1921
HR H-58	RUSH ORDERS	CHASE	PATHE EXCHANGE	1921
HR H-59	BUBBLING OVER	ROACH	PATHE EXCHANGE	1921
HR H-60	NO CHILDREN	GOULDING	PATHE EXCHANGE	1921
HR H-61	BIG GAME	GOULDING	PATHE EXCHANGE	1921
HR H-62	KILLJOYS (BLUE SUNDAY)	CHASE	PATHE EXCHANGE	1921
HR H-63	OWN YOUR OWN HOME	ROACH	PATHE EXCHANGE	1921
HR H-64	WHERE'S THE FIRE	ROACH	PATHE EXCHANGE	1921
HR H-65	HIGH ROLLERS	GOULDING	PATHE EXCHANGE	1921
HR H-66	YOU'RE NEXT	CHASE	PATHE EXCHANGE	1921
HR H-67	SAVE YOUR MONEY	ROACH	PATHE EXCHANGE	1921
HR H-68	BIKE BUG	ROACH	PATHE EXCHANGE	1921
HR H-69	NAME THE DAY	ROACH	PATHE EXCHANGE	1921
HR H-70	AT THE RING SIDE	CHASE	PATHE EXCHANGE	1921
HR H-71	NO STOP-OVER	ROACH	PATHE EXCHANGE	1921
HR H-72	LATE LODGERS	CHASE	PATHE EXCHANGE	1921
HR H-73	WHAT A WHOPPER	CHASE	PATHE EXCHANGE	1921
HR H-74	TEACHING THE TEACHER	ROACH	PATHE EXCHANGE	1921
HR H-75	SPOT CASH	CHASE	PATHE EXCHANGE	1921
HR H-77	GONE TO THE COUNTRY	CHASE	PATHE EXCHANGE	1921

HR H-78	LAW AND ORDER	CHASE	PATHE EXCHANGE	1921
HR H-79	FIFTEEN MINUTES	CHASE	PATHE EXCHANGE	1921
HR H-80	ON LOCATION	CHASE	PATHE EXCHANGE	1921
HR H-81	HOCUS POCUS	CHASE	PATHE EXCHANGE	1921
HR H-82	PENNY-IN-THE-SLOT	CHASE	PATHE EXCHANGE	1921
HR H-83	JOY RIDER	ROACH	PATHE EXCHANGE	1921
HR H-84	HUSTLER	CHASE	PATHE EXCHANGE	1921
HR H-85	SINK OR SWIM	CHASE	PATHE EXCHANGE	1921
HR H-86	SHAKE 'EM UP	CHASE	PATHE EXCHANGE	1921
HR H-87	STONE AGE	CHASE	PATHE EXCHANGE	1922
HR H-88	CORNER POCKET	CHASE	PATHE EXCHANGE	1921
HR H-89	LOSE NO TIME	CHASE	PATHE EXCHANGE	1922
HR H-90	CALL THE WITNESS	CHASE	PATHE EXCHANGE	1922
HR H-91	BLOW 'EM UP	CHASE	PATHE EXCHANGE	1922
HR H-92	YEARS TO COME	CHASE	PATHE EXCHANGE	1922
HR H-93	STAGE STRUCK	WATSON	PATHE EXCHANGE	1922
HR H-94	SOME BABY	CEDER	PATHE EXCHANGE	1922
HR H-95	DOWN AND OUT	CEDER	PATHE EXCHANGE	1922
HR H-96	PARDON ME	CEDER	PATHE EXCHANGE	1922
HR H-97	BOW WOWS	CEDER	PATHE EXCHANGE	1922
HR H-98	HOT OFF THE PRESS	CEDER, CHASE	PATHE EXCHANGE	1922
HR H-99	ANVIL CHORUS	CEDER	PATHE EXCHANGE	1922
HR H-100	JUMP YOUR JOB	CEDER	PATHE EXCHANGE	1922
HR H-101	KILL THE NERVE	CEDER	PATHE EXCHANGE	1922
HR H-102	FULL O' PEP	CHASE	PATHE EXCHANGE	1922
HR H-103	DO YOUR DUTY	CEDER	PATHE EXCHANGE	1926
HR H-104	DAYS OF OLD (DAYS OF GOLD)	CHASE	PATHE EXCHANGE	1922
HR H-105	LIGHT SHOWERS	CHASE	PATHE EXCHANGE	1922
HR H-106	DO ME A FAVOR	CHASE	PATHE EXCHANGE	1922
HR H-107	PUNCH THE CLOCK	BEAUDINE	PATHE EXCHANGE	1922
HR H-108	IN THE MOVIES	CHASE	PATHE EXCHANGE	1922
HR H-109	HALE AND HEARTY	SANTELL	PATHE EXCHANGE	1922
HR H-110	STRICTLY MODERN	BEAUDINE	PATHE EXCHANGE	1922
HR H-111	DUMB BELL	CHASE	PATHE EXCHANGE	1922
HR J-1	CALL OF THE WILD	JACKMAN	PATHE EXCHANGE	1923
HR J-2	KING OF WILD HORSES	JACKMAN	PATHE EXCHANGE	1924
HR J-3	BLACK CYCLONE	JACKMAN	PATHE EXCHANGE	1925
HR J-4	DEVIL HORSE	JACKMAN	PATHE EXCHANGE	1926
HR J-5	NO MAN'S LAW	JACKMAN	PATHE EXCHANGE	1927
HR K-1	BETTER MOVIES	MCGOWAN	PATHE EXCHANGE	1925
HR K-1	BORED OF EDUCATION	DOUGLAS	MGM	1936
HR K-1	HER DANGEROUS PATH (10 CH series)	CLEMENTS	PATHE EXCHANGE	1923
HR K-2	TWO TOO YOUNG	DOUGLAS	MGM	1936
HR K-2	YOUR OWN BACK YARD	MCGOWAN	PATHE EXCHANGE	1925
HR K-3	ONE WILD RIDE	MCGOWAN	PATHE EXCHANGE	1925
HR K-3	PAY AS YOU EXIT	DOUGLAS	MGM	1936
HR K-4	GOOD CHEER	MCGOWAN	PATHE EXCHANGE	1926
HR K-4	SPOOKY HOOKY	DOUGLAS	MGM	1936
HR K-5	BURIED TREASURE	MCGOWAN	PATHE EXCHANGE	1926
HR K-5	REUNION IN RHYTHM	DOUGLAS	MGM	1937
HR K-6	GLOVE TAPS	DOUGLAS	MGM	1937
HR K-6	MONKEY BUSINESS	MCGOWAN	PATHE EXCHANGE	1926
HR K-7	BABY CLOTHES	MCGOWAN	PATHE EXCHANGE	1926
HR K-7	HEARTS ARE THUMPS	DOUGLAS	MGM	1937
HR K-8	THREE SMART BOYS	DOUGLAS	MGM	1937
HR K-8	UNCLE TOM'S UNCLE	MCGOWAN	PATHE EXCHANGE	1926
HR K-9	RUSHIN' BALLET	DOUGLAS	MGM	1937
HR K-9	THUNDERING FLEAS	MCGOWAN	PATHE EXCHANGE	1926
HR K-10	ROAMIN' HOLIDAY	DOUGLAS	MGM	1937
HR K-10	SHIVERING SPOOKS	MCGOWAN	PATHE EXCHANGE	1926
HR K-11	FOURTH ALARM	MCGOWAN	PATHE EXCHANGE	1926
HR K-11	NIGHT 'N' GALES	DOUGLAS	MGM	1937
HR K-12	FISHY TALES	DOUGLAS	MGM	1937
HR K-12	WAR FEATHERS	MCGOWAN, MCGOWAN	PATHE EXCHANGE	1926
HR K-13	FRAMING YOUTH	DOUGLAS	MGM	1937
HR K-13	SEEING THE WORLD	MCGOWAN, MCGOWAN	PATHE EXCHANGE	1927

HR K-14	KWAIDAN (JAP)	KOBAYASHI	CONTINENTAL	1966
HR K-14	PIGSKIN PALOOKA	DOUGLAS	MGM	1937
HR K-14	TELLING WHOPPERS	MCGOWAN, MCGOWAN	PATHE EXCHANGE	1926
HR K-15	BRING HOME THE TURKEY	MCGOWAN, MCGOWAN	PATHE EXCHANGE	1927
HR K-15	MAIL AND FEMALE	NEWMEYER	MGM	1937
HR K-16	CANNED FISHING	DOUGLAS	MGM	1938
HR K-16	TEN YEARS OLD	MCGOWAN	PATHE EXCHANGE	1927
HR K-17	BEAR FACTS	DOUGLAS	MGM	1938
HR K-17	LOVE MY DOG	MCGOWAN	PATHE EXCHANGE	1927
HR K-18	THREE MEN IN A TUB	WATT	MGM	1938
HR K-18	TIRED BUSINESS MEN	MCGOWAN, OELZE	PATHE EXCHANGE	1927
HR K-19	BABY BROTHER	MCGOWAN, OELZE	PATHE EXCHANGE	1927
HR K-19	CAME THE BRAWN	DOUGLAS	MGM	1938
HR K-20	CHICKEN FEED	MCGOWAN, OELZE	PATHE EXCHANGE	1927
HR K-20	FEED 'EM AND WEEP	DOUGLAS	MGM	1938
HR K-21	AWFUL TOOTH	WATT	MGM	1938
HR K-21	OLYMPIC GAMES	MCGOWAN	PATHE EXCHANGE	1927
HR K-22	GLORIOUS FOURTH	MCGOWAN	PATHE EXCHANGE	1927
HR K-22	HIDE AND SHRIEK	DOUGLAS	MGM	1938
HR K-23	SMILE WINS	MCGOWAN	PATHE EXCHANGE	1928
HR K-24	PLAYIN' HOOKEY	MCGOWAN	PATHE EXCHANGE	1928
HR L-1	BUMPING INTO BROADWAY	ROACH	PATHE EXCHANGE	1919
HR L-1	COME CLEAN	HORNE	MGM	1931
HR L-1	OVER THE FENCE	LLOYD, MACDONALD	PATHE EXCHANGE	1917
HR L-1	ROUGHEST AFRICA	CEDER	PATHE EXCHANGE	1923
HR L-2	CAPTAIN KIDD'S KIDS	ROACH	PATHE EXCHANGE	1919
HR L-2	FROZEN HEARTS	HOWE	PATHE EXCHANGE	1923
HR L-2	ONE GOOD TURN	HORNE	MGM	1931
HR L-2	PINCHED	LLOYD, PRATT	PATHE EXCHANGE	1917
HR L-3	BEAU HUNKS	HORNE	MGM	1931
HR L-3	BY THE SAD SEA WAVES	GOULDING	PATHE EXCHANGE	1917
HR L-3	FROM HAND TO MOUTH	GOULDING	PATHE EXCHANGE	1919
HR L-3	SOILERS	CEDER	PATHE EXCHANGE	1923
HR L-4	ANY OLD PORT	HORNE	MGM	1932
HR L-4	HIS ROYAL SLYNESS	ROACH	PATHE EXCHANGE	1920
HR L-4	MOTHER'S JOY	CEDER	PATHE EXCHANGE	1923
HR L-4	RAINBOW ISLAND	GILBERT	PATHE EXCHANGE	1917
HR L-5	BLISS	GOULDING	PATHE EXCHANGE	1917
HR L-5	HAUNTED SPOOKS	ROACH	PATHE EXCHANGE	1920
HR L-5	HELPMATES	PARROTT	MGM	1932
HR L-5	NEAR DUBLIN	CEDER	PATHE EXCHANGE	1924
HR L-6	AN EASTERN WESTERNER	ROACH	PATHE EXCHANGE	1920
HR L-6	FLIRT	GILBERT	PATHE EXCHANGE	1917
HR L-6	MUSIC BOX	PARROTT	MGM	1932
HR L-6	SMITHY	JESKE, ROACH	PATHE EXCHANGE	1924
HR L-7	ALL ABOARD	GOULDING	PATHE EXCHANGE	1917
HR L-7	CHIMP	PARROTT	MGM	1932
HR L-7	HIGH AND DIZZY	ROACH	PATHE EXCHANGE	1920
HR L-7	ZEB VS. PAPRIKA	CEDER	PATHE EXCHANGE	1924
HR L-8	COUNTY HOSPITAL	PARROTT	MGM	1932
HR L-8	GET OUT AND GET UNDER	ROACH	PATHE EXCHANGE	1920
HR L-8	MOVE ON	PRATT, GILBERT	PATHE EXCHANGE	1917
HR L-8	POSTAGE DUE	JESKE	PATHE EXCHANGE	1924
HR L-9	BASHFUL	GOULDING	PATHE EXCHANGE	1917
HR L-9	BROTHER UNDER THE CHIN	CEDER	PATHE EXCHANGE	1924
HR L-9	NUMBER, PLEASE?	ROACH	PATHE EXCHANGE	1920
HR L-9	SCRAM!	MCCAREY	MGM	1932
HR L-10	NOW OR NEVER	ROACH	PATHE EXCHANGE	1921
HR L-10	TIP	PRATT, GILBERT	PATHE EXCHANGE	1918
HR L-10	WIDE OPEN SPACES	JESKE	PATHE EXCHANGE	1924
HR L-11	AMONG THOSE PRESENT	NEWMEYER	PATHE EXCHANGE	1921
HR L-11	RUPERT OF HEE HAW	PEMBROKE	PATHE EXCHANGE	1924
HR L-11	SHOULD MARRIED MEN GO HOME?	MCCAREY, PARROTT	MGM	1928
HR L-11	STEP LIVELY	GOULDING	PATHE EXCHANGE	1917
HR L-12	BIG IDEA	MOHR, PRATT	PATHE EXCHANGE	1918
HR L-12	EARLY TO BED	FLYNN	MGM	1928

HR L-12	I DO	NEWMEYER	PATHE EXCHANGE	1921
HR L-12	SHORT KILTS	JESKE	PATHE EXCHANGE	1924
HR L-12	TWICE TWO	PARROTT	MGM	1933
HR L-13	HELLO TEACHER	ROACH	PATHE EXCHANGE	1918
HR L-13	ME AND MY PAL	ROGERS	MGM	1933
HR L-13	NEVER WEAKEN	NEWMEYER	PATHE EXCHANGE	1921
HR L-13	TWO TARS	PARROTT	MGM	1928
HR L-14	HABEAS CORPUS	PARROTT, MCCAREY	MGM	1928
HR L-14	LAMB (GOAT)	LLOYD, PRATT	PATHE EXCHANGE	1918
HR L-14	MIDNIGHT PATROL	FRENCH	MGM	1933
HR L-14	SAILOR-MADE MAN	NEWMEYER	PATHE EXCHANGE	1921
HR L-15	BUSY BODIES	FRENCH	MGM	1933
HR L-15	GRANDMA'S BOY	NEWMEYER	ASSOC. EXHIBITORS	1922
HR L-15	LET'S GO	GOULDING	PATHE EXCHANGE	1918
HR L-15	WE FAW DOWN	MCCAREY	MGM	1928
HR L-16	BEAT IT	PRATT	PATHE EXCHANGE	1918
HR L-16	DIRTY WORK	FRENCH	MGM	1933
HR L-16	DR. JACK	NEWMEYER	PATHE EXCHANGE	1922
HR L-16	LIBERTY	MCCAREY	MGM	1929
HR L-17	GASOLINE WEDDING	GOULDING	PATHE EXCHANGE	1918
HR L-17	OLIVER THE EIGHTH	FRENCH	MGM	1934
HR L-17	SAFETY LAST!	TAYLOR, NEWMEYER	PATHE EXCHANGE	1923
HR L-17	WRONG AGAIN	MCCAREY	MGM	1929
HR L-18	GOING BYE-BYE!	ROGERS	MGM	1934
HR L-18	HIT HIM AGAIN	PRATT	PATHE EXCHANGE	1918
HR L-18	THAT'S MY WIFE	FRENCH	MGM	1929
HR L-19	BIG BUSINESS	HORNE, MCCAREY	MGM	1929
HR L-19	LOOK PLEASANT, PLEASE	GOULDING	PATHE EXCHANGE	1918
HR L-19	THEM THAR HILLS	ROGERS	MGM	1934
HR L-20	DOUBLE WHOOPEE	FOSTER	MGM	1929
HR L-20	HERE COME THE GIRLS	HIBBARD	PATHE EXCHANGE	1918
HR L-20	LIVE GHOST	ROGERS	MGM	1934
HR L-21	BACON GRABBERS	FOSTER	MGM	1929
HR L-21	ON THE JUMP	GOULDING	PATHE EXCHANGE	1918
HR L-21	TIT FOR TAT	ROGERS	MGM	1935
HR L-22	ANGORA LOVE	FOSTER	MGM	1929
HR L-22	HEY THERE!	GOULDING	PATHE EXCHANGE	1918
HR L-23	KICKED OUT	GOULDING	PATHE EXCHANGE	1918
HR L-23	THICKER THAN WATER	HORNE	MGM	1935
HR L-23	UNACCUSTOMED AS WE ARE	FOSTER, ROACH	MGM	1929
HR L-24	BERTH MARKS	FOSTER	MGM	1929
HR L-24	NON STOP KID	PRATT	PATHE EXCHANGE	1918
HR L-25	FOLLOW THE CROWD	GOULDING	PATHE EXCHANGE	1918
HR L-25	MEN O' WAR	FOSTER	MGM	1929
HR L-26	IT'S A WILD LIFE	PRATT	PATHE EXCHANGE	1918
HR L-27	PIPE THE WHISKERS	GOULDING	PATHE EXCHANGE	1918
HR L-27	THEY GO BOOM	PARROTT	MGM	1929
HR L-28	HOOSE-GOW	PARROTT	MGM	1929
HR L-28	SIC 'EM TOWSER	PRATT	PATHE EXCHANGE	1918
HR L-29	NIGHT OWLS	PARROTT	MGM	1930
HR L-29	TWO GUN GUSSIE	GOULDING	PATHE EXCHANGE	1918
HR L-30	BLOTTO	PARROTT	MGM	1930
HR L-30	LOVE'S YOUNG SCREAM	JEFFERSON	PATHE EXCHANGE	1919
HR L-31	FIREMAN SAVE MY CHILD	GOULDING	PATHE EXCHANGE	1918
HR L-32	CITY SLICKER	PRATT	PATHE EXCHANGE	1918
HR L-33	SOMEWHERE IN TURKEY	GOULDING	PATHE EXCHANGE	1918
HR L-34	ARE CROOKS DISHONEST	PRATT	PATHE EXCHANGE	1918
HR L-34	LAUREL-HARDY MURDER CASE	PARROTT	MGM	1930
HR L-35	OZARK ROMANCE	GOULDING	PATHE EXCHANGE	1918
HR L-36	THAT'S HIM	PRATT	PATHE EXCHANGE	1918
HR L-37	BE BIG!	HORNE, PARROTT	MGM	1931
HR L-37	BRIDE AND GLOOM	GOULDING	PATHE EXCHANGE	1918
HR L-38	CHICKENS COME HOME	HORNE	MGM	1931
HR L-38	TWO SCRAMBLED	PRATT	PATHE EXCHANGE	1918
HR L-39	KICKING THE GERM OUT OF GERMANY	GOULDING	PATHE EXCHANGE	1918
HR L-40	BEES IN HIS BONNET	PRATT	PATHE EXCHANGE	1918

HR L-40	OUR WIFE	HORNE	MGM	1931
HR L-41	SWING YOUR PARTNERS	GOULDING	PATHE EXCHANGE	1918
HR L-42	HEAR 'EM RAVE	PRATT	PATHE EXCHANGE	1918
HR L-43	NOTHING BUT TROUBLE	ROACH	PATHE EXCHANGE	1918
HR L-44	WHY PICK ON ME?	ROACH	PATHE EXCHANGE	1918
HR L-45	TAKE A CHANCE	GOULDING	PATHE EXCHANGE	1918
HR L-46	GOING! GOING! GONE!	PRATT	PATHE EXCHANGE	1919
HR L-47	SHE LOVES ME NOT		PATHE EXCHANGE	1918
HR L-48	WANTED $5000	PRATT	PATHE EXCHANGE	1919
HR L-49	I'M ON MY WAY	ROACH	PATHE EXCHANGE	1919
HR L-50	ASK FATHER	ROACH	PATHE EXCHANGE	1919
HR L-51	ON THE FIRE	ROACH	PATHE EXCHANGE	1919
HR L-52	LOOK OUT BELOW!	ROACH	PATHE EXCHANGE	1919
HR L-53	DUTIFUL DUB	GOULDING	PATHE EXCHANGE	1919
HR L-54	NEXT AISLE OVER	ROACH	PATHE EXCHANGE	1919
HR L-55	RING UP THE CURTAIN	GOULDING	PATHE EXCHANGE	1919
HR L-56	JUST DROPPED IN	ROACH	PATHE EXCHANGE	1919
HR L-57	CRACK YOUR HEELS	GOULDING	PATHE EXCHANGE	1919
HR L-58	YOUNG MR. JAZZ	ROACH	PATHE EXCHANGE	1919
HR L-59	SI, SENOR	GOULDING	PATHE EXCHANGE	1919
HR L-60	BEFORWE BREAKFAST	ROACH	PATHE EXCHANGE	1919
HR L-61	MARATHON	GOULDING	PATHE EXCHANGE	1919
HR L-62	BACK TO THE WOODS	ROACH	PATHE EXCHANGE	1919
HR L-63	PISTOLS FOR BREAKFAST	GOULDING	PATHE EXCHANGE	1919
HR L-64	SWAT THE CROOK	ROACH	PATHE EXCHANGE	1919
HR L-65	OFF THE TROLLEY	GOULDING	PATHE EXCHANGE	1919
HR L-66	AT THE OLD STAGE DOOR	ROACH	PATHE EXCHANGE	1919
HR L-67	JAZZED HONEYMOON	ROACH	PATHE EXCHANGE	1919
HR L-68	NEVER TOUCHED ME	GOULDING	PATHE EXCHANGE	1919
HR L-69	BILL BLAZES, ESQ.	ROACH	PATHE EXCHANGE	1919
HR L-70	COUNT YOUR CHANGE	GOULDING	PATHE EXCHANGE	1919
HR L-71	CHOP SUEY AND COMPANY	ROACH	PATHE EXCHANGE	1919
HR L-72	HEAP BIG CHIEF	GOULDING	PATHE EXCHANGE	1919
HR L-73	SAMMY IN SIBERIA	ROACH	PATHE EXCHANGE	1919
HR L-74	DON'T SHOVE	GOULDING	PATHE EXCHANGE	1919
HR L-75	BE MY WIFE	ROACH	PATHE EXCHANGE	1919
HR L-76	RAJAH	ROACH	PATHE EXCHANGE	1919
HR L-77	HE LEADS, OTHERS FOLLOW	ROACH	PATHE EXCHANGE	1919
HR L-78	SOFT MONEY	ROACH	PATHE EXCHANGE	1919
HR L-79	COUNT THE VOTES	ROACH	PATHE EXCHANGE	1919
HR L-80	PAY YOUR DUES	ROACH	PATHE EXCHANGE	1919
HR L-81	HIS ONLY FATHER	ROACH	PATHE EXCHANGE	1919
HR L-82	SPRING FEVER	ROACH	PATHE EXCHANGE	1919
HR L-83	JUST NEIGHBORS	LLOYD, TERRY	PATHE EXCHANGE	1919
HR LC-89	NOON WHISTLE	JESKE	PATHE EXCHANGE	1923
HR LC-91	WHITE WINGS	JESKE	PATHE EXCHANGE	1923
HR LC-92	PICK AND SHOVEL	JESKE	PATHE EXCHANGE	1923
HR LC-95	KILL OR CURE	PEMBROKE	PATHE EXCHANGE	1923
HR LC-97	COLLARS AND CUFFS	JESKE	PATHE EXCHANGE	1923
HR LC-99	GAS AND AIR	PEMBROKE	PATHE EXCHANGE	1923
HR LC-102	ORANGES AND LEMONS	JESKE	PATHE EXCHANGE	1923
HR LC-104	SHORT ORDERS	PEMBROKE	PATHE EXCHANGE	1923
HR LC-106	SAVE THE SHIP	JESKE, ROACH	PATHE EXCHANGE	1923
HR LC-112	SCORCHING SANDS	WILLIAMSON, ROACH	PATHE EXCHANGE	1923
HR LC-115	WHOLE TRUTH	CEDER	PATHE EXCHANGE	1923
HR LG-30	LOVE'S YOUNG SCREAM	JEFFERSON	PATHE EXCHANGE	1919
HR M-1	DESERT'S TOLL	SMITH	MGM	1926
HR M-1	ONE AT A TIME	CEDER	PATHE EXCHANGE	1924
HR M-1	RHAPSODY IN BREW	GILBERT	MGM	1934
HR M-2	KEG O' MY HEART	GILBERT	MGM	1933
HR M-2	VALLEY OF HELL	SMITH	MGM	1927
HR M-3	MUSIC IN YOUR HAIR	CHASE	MGM	1934
HR M-4	APPLES TO YOU!	JASON	MGM	1934
HR M-5	ROAMIN' VANDALS	JASON, YATES	MGM	1934
HR M-6	DUKE FOR A DAY	PARROTT	MGM	1934
HR M-7	BENNY, FROM PANAMA	PARROTT	MGM	1934

HR P-1	SPITBALL SADIE	ROACH	PATHE EXCHANGE	1915
HR P-2	TERRIBLY STUCK UP	ROACH	PATHE EXCHANGE	1915
HR P-3	DEVIL'S BROTHER	ROGERS	MGM	1933
HR P-3	RUSES, RHYMES AND ROUGHNECKS	ROACH	PATHE EXCHANGE	1915
HR P-4	MIXUP FOR MAZIE	ROACH	PATHE EXCHANGE	1915
HR P-5	SOME BABY	ROACH	PATHE EXCHANGE	1915
HR P-6	FRESH FROM THE FARM	ROACH	PATHE EXCHANGE	1915
HR P-7	FOOZLE AT THE TEE PARTY	ROACH	PATHE EXCHANGE	1915
HR P-8	GREAT WHILE IT LASTED	ROACH	PATHE EXCHANGE	1915
HR P-9	GIVING THEM FITS	ROACH	PATHE EXCHANGE	1915
HR P-10	TINKERING WITH TROUBLE	ROACH	PATHE EXCHANGE	1915
HR P-11	PECULIAR PATIENTS' PRANKS	ROACH	PATHE EXCHANGE	1915
HR P-12	LONESOME LUKE, SOCIAL GANGSTER	ROACH, MACDONALD	PATHE EXCHANGE	1915
HR P-13	BUGHOUSE BELLHOPS	ROACH	PATHE EXCHANGE	1915
HR P-14	RAGTIME SNAP SHOTS	ROACH	PATHE EXCHANGE	1915
HR P-15	LUKE LUGS LUGGAGE	ROACH	PATHE EXCHANGE	1916
HR P-16	LONESOME LUKE LEANS TO THE LITERARY	ROACH	PATHE EXCHANGE	1916
HR P-17	LONESOME LUKE LOLLS IN LUXURY	ROACH	PATHE EXCHANGE	1916
HR P-17	TOPPER (sh)	MCLEOD	MGM	1937
HR P-18	LUKE FOILS THE VILLAIN	ROACH	PATHE EXCHANGE	1916
HR P-19	LUKE, THE CANDY CUT-UP	ROACH	PATHE EXCHANGE	1916
HR P-20	LUKE AND THE RURAL ROUGHNECKS	ROACH	PATHE EXCHANGE	1916
HR P-21	LUKE PIPES THE PIPPINS	ROACH	PATHE EXCHANGE	1916
HR P-22	THEM WAS THE DAYS	ROACH	PATHE EXCHANGE	1916
HR P-23	LUKE'S DOUBLE	ROACH	PATHE EXCHANGE	1916
HR P-24	LONESOME LUKE, CIRCUS KING	ROACH	PATHE EXCHANGE	1916
HR P-25	LUKE'S LATE LUNCHERS	ROACH	PATHE EXCHANGE	1916
HR P-26	LUKE AND THE BOMB THROWERS	ROACH	PATHE EXCHANGE	1916
HR P-27	LUKE LAUGHS LAST	ROACH	PATHE EXCHANGE	1916
HR P-28	LUKE'S FATAL FLIVVER	ROACH	PATHE EXCHANGE	1916
HR P-29	LUKE'S SOCIETY MIX-UP	ROACH	PATHE EXCHANGE	1916
HR P-30	LUKE'S WASHFUL WAITING	ROACH	PATHE EXCHANGE	1916
HR PC-126	FRIEND HUSBAND (WHY MARRY?)	HOWE	PATHE EXCHANGE	1924
HR R-1	DO YOU LOVE YOUR WIFE?	ROACH	PATHE EXCHANGE	1919
HR R-1	JUS PASSIN' THROUGH	ROACH	PATHE EXCHANGE	1923
HR R-1	WHITE EAGLE (15 CH series)	JACKMAN, VAN DYKE	PATHE EXCHANGE	1922
HR R-2	JUST RAMBLING ALONG	ROACH	PATHE EXCHANGE	1918
HR R-2	TIMBER QUEEN (15 CH series)	JACKMAN	PATHE EXCHANGE	1922
HR R-3	HOOT MON!	ROACH	PATHE EXCHANGE	1919
HR R-3	UNCENSORED MOVIES	CLEMENTS	PATHE EXCHANGE	1923
HR R-4	GEE WHIZ, GENEVIEVE	HOWE	PATHE EXCHANGE	1924
HR R-4	NO PLACE LIKE JAIL	TERRY	PATHE EXCHANGE	1918
HR R-5	HUSTLING FOR HEALTH	TERRY	PATHE EXCHANGE	1919
HR R-5	TWO WAGONS, BOTH COVERED	WAGNER	PATHE EXCHANGE	1924
HR R-6	COWBOY SHEIK	HOWE	PATHE EXCHANGE	1924
HR R-7	CAKE EATER	HOWE	PATHE EXCHANGE	1924
HR R-8	UNNAMED WILL ROGERS		PATHE EXCHANGE	1924
HR R-9	BIG MOMENTS FROM LITTLE PICTURES	CLEMENTS	PATHE EXCHANGE	1924
HR R-11	GOING TO CONGRESS	WAGNER	PATHE EXCHANGE	1924
HR R-12	DON'T PARK THERE!	GUIOL	PATHE EXCHANGE	1924
HR R-13	OUR CONGRESSMAN	WAGNER	PATHE EXCHANGE	1924
HR R-14	TRUTHFUL LIAR	DEL RUTH	PATHE EXCHANGE	1924
HR S-1	CALL A COP	STEVENS	MGM	1931
HR S-1	DON KEY	GUIOL, HORNE	PATHE EXCHANGE	1926
HR S-1	SUGAR DADDIES	GUIOL, MCCAREY	MGM	1927
HR S-2	MAMA LOVES PAPA	STEVENS	MGM	1931
HR S-2	PUNCH IN THE NOSE	HOWE	PATHE EXCHANGE	1926
HR S-2	SECOND HUNDRED YEARS	GUIOL	MGM	1927
HR S-3	HATS OFF	YATES	MGM	1927
HR S-3	KICKOFF	STEVENS	MGM	1931
HR S-3	SOMEWHERE IN SOMEWHERE	HORNE	PATHE EXCHANGE	1925
HR S-4	LOVE PAINS	ROACH	MGM	1932
HR S-4	PUTTING PANTS ON PHILIP	BRUCKMAN	MGM	1927
HR S-4	THERE GOES THE BRIDE	HORNE	PATHE EXCHANGE	1925
HR S-5	BATTLE OF THE CENTURY	BRUCKMAN	MGM	1927
HR S-5	KNOCKOUT	FRENCH, MCGOWAN	MGM	1932

HR S-5	LAUGHING LADIES	HORNE	PATHE EXCHANGE	1925
HR S-6	LEAVE 'EM LAUGHING	BRUCKMAN	MGM	1928
HR S-6	YOUR HUSBAND'S PAST	GUIOL	PATHE EXCHANGE	1926
HR S-6	YOU'RE TELLING ME	FRENCH, MCGOWAN	MGM	1932
HR S-7	DIZZY DADDIES	WALLACE	PATHE EXCHANGE	1926
HR S-7	FINISHING TOUCH	BRUCKMAN, MCCAREY	MGM	1928
HR S-7	TOO MANY WOMEN	FRENCH, MCGOWAN	MGM	1932
HR S-8	FROM SOUP TO NUTS	KENNEDY	MGM	1928
HR S-8	LET GEORGE DO IT*	KENNEDY	MGM	1928
HR S-8	MADAME MYSTERY	WALLACE, LAUREL	PATHE EXCHANGE	1926
HR S-8	WILD BABIES	FRENCH, MCGOWAN	MGM	1932
HR S-9	NEVER TOO OLD	WALLACE	PATHE EXCHANGE	1926
HR S-9	YOU'RE DARN TOOTIN'	KENNEDY	MGM	1928
HR S-10	MERRY WIDOWER	WALLACE	PATHE EXCHANGE	1926
HR S-10	THEIR PURPLE MOMENT	PARROTT	MGM	1928
HR S-11	RAGGEDY ROSE	WALLACE	PATHE EXCHANGE	1926
HR S-11	THAT NIGHT	HEATH, MCCAREY	MGM	1928
HR S-12	DO GENTLEMEN SNORE?	MCCAREY	MGM	1928
HR S-12	WISE GUYS PREFER BRUNETTES	LAUREL	PATHE EXCHANGE	1926
HR S-13	BOY FRIEND	GUIOL	MGM	1928
HR S-13	GET 'EM YOUNG	GUIOL, LAUREL	PATHE EXCHANGE	1926
HR S-14	DUCK SOUP	GUIOL	PATHE EXCHANGE	1927
HR S-14	FEED 'EM AND WEEP	GUIOL, MCCAREY	MGM	1928
HR S-15	GOING GA GA	MCCAREY	MGM	1929
HR S-15	ON THE FRONT PAGE	PARROTT	PATHE EXCHANGE	1926
HR S-16	PAIR OF TIGHTS	YATES	MGM	1929
HR S-16	WHY GIRLS SAY NO	MCCAREY	PATHE EXCHANGE	1927
HR S-17	HONORABLE MR. BUGGS	JACKMAN	PATHE EXCHANGE	1927
HR S-17	WHEN MONEY COMES	MCCAREY	MGM	1929
HR S-18	SLIPPING WIVES	GUIOL	PATHE EXCHANGE	1927
HR S-18	UNKISSED MAN	ROACH, MCCAREY	MGM	1929
HR S-19	LOVE 'EM AND WEEP	GUIOL, JONES	PATHE EXCHANGE	1927
HR S-19	WHY IS A PLUMBER?	MCCAREY	MGM	1929
HR S-20	THUNDERING TOUPEES	MCGOWAN	MGM	1929
HR S-20	WHY GIRLS LOVE SAILORS	GUIOL	PATHE EXCHANGE	1927
HR S-21	WITH LOVE AND HISSES	GUIOL	PATHE EXCHANGE	1927
HR S-22	MADAME "Q"	MCCAREY	MGM	1929
HR S-22	SAILORS, BEWARE!	GUIOL	PATHE EXCHANGE	1927
HR S-23	COWBOYS CRY FOR IT*	GASNIER	PATHE EXCHANGE	1928
HR S-23	DAD'S DAY	MCCAREY	MGM	1929
HR S-23	SHOULD TALL MEN MARRY?	GASNIER	PATHE EXCHANGE	1928
HR S-24	DO DETECTIVES THINK?	GUIOL	PATHE EXCHANGE	1927
HR S-24	HOTTER THAN HOT	FOSTER	MGM	1929
HR S-25	FLAMING FATHERS	LAUREL, MCCAREY	PATHE EXCHANGE	1927
HR S-25	SKY BOY	ROGERS	MGM	1929
HR S-26	FLYING ELEPHANTS	ROACH, BUTLER	PATHE EXCHANGE	1928
HR S-26	SKIRT SHY	ROGERS	MGM	1929
HR S-27	HEAD GUY	ROACH	MGM	1930
HR S-28	FIGHTING PARSON	GUIOL, ROGERS	MGM	1930
HR S-29	BIG KICK	DOANE	MGM	1930
HR S-30	SHRIMP	ROGERS	MGM	1930
HR S-31	KING		MGM	1930
HR S-32	DOCTOR'S ORDERS	HEATH	MGM	1930
HR S-33	BIGGER AND BETTER	KENNEDY	MGM	1930
HR S-34	LADIES LAST	STEVENS	MGM	1930
HR S-35	BLOOD AND THUNDER	STEVENS	MGM	1931
HR S-36	LOVE FEVER	MCGOWAN	MGM	1931
HR S-37	HIGH GEAR	STEVENS	MGM	1931
HR S-38	AIR TIGHT	STEVENS	MGM	1931
HR T-1	BATTLING ORIOLES	GUIOL, WILDE	PATHE EXCHANGE	1924
HR T-1	MOVIE DUMMY (MOVIE MUMMY)	ROACH	PATHE EXCHANGE	1918
HR T-1	THUNDERING TAXIS	LORD, MEINS	MGM	1933
HR T-2	JUNKMAN	ROACH	PATHE EXCHANGE	1918
HR T-2	WHAT PRICE TAXI	LORD	MGM	1932
HR T-2	WHITE SHEEP	ROACH	PATHE EXCHANGE	1924
HR T-3	STRANGE INNERTUBE	LORD	MGM	1932

HR T-3	TOTO IN FARE PLEASE		PATHE EXCHANGE	1918
HR T-4	HOT SPOT	LORD	MGM	1932
HR T-4	TOTO IN ONE NIGHT ONLY	ROACH	PATHE EXCHANGE	1918
HR T-5	FIRE THE COOK (edited to create T-7)	ROACH	PATHE EXCHANGE	1918
HR T-5	TAXI FOR TWO	LORD	MGM	1932
HR T-6	BRING 'EM BACK A WIFE	LORD	MGM	1933
HR T-6	HIS BUSY DAY	ROACH	PATHE EXCHANGE	1918
HR T-7	DIPPY DAUGHTER	ROACH	PATHE EXCHANGE	1918
HR T-7	WRECKETY WRECKS	LORD	MGM	1933
HR T-8	CLEOPATSY - aka CLEO PROXY	ROACH	PATHE EXCHANGE	1918
HR T-8	TAXI BARONS	MEINS	MGM	1933
HR T-9	CALL HER SAUSAGE	MEINS	MGM	1933
HR T-9	FURNITURE MOVERS	ROACH	PATHE EXCHANGE	1918
HR T-10	CHECK YOUR BAGGAGE	ROACH	PATHE EXCHANGE	1918
HR T-10	RUMMY	LORD	MGM	1933
HR T-11	GREAT WATER PERIL (POOR CLARINE)	ROACH	PATHE EXCHANGE	1918
HR T-12	DO HUSBANDS DECEIVE?	ROACH	PATHE EXCHANGE	1918
HR T-13	BEACH NUTS	ROACH	PATHE EXCHANGE	1918
HR T-14	ENEMY OF SOAP	ROACH	PATHE EXCHANGE	1918
HRC	HERCULES	COZZI	CANNON	1983
HR-D17	TOPPER	MCLEOD	MGM	1937
HRZ	HARD ROCK ZOMBIES	SHAH	CANNON	1986
HS	HAUNTED SUMMER	PASSER	CANNON	1988
HS	HEART AND SOUL (MISCHIEF)	DAMSKI	20th CENTURY FOX	1984
HS	HEIDI'S SONG (t)	TAYLOR	PARAMOUNT	1982
HS	HELENE STANLEY	portrait	RKO	
HS	HIGH SPIRITS	JORDAN	TRI STAR	1988
HS	HOT SHOTS	ABRAHAMS	20th CENTURY FOX	1991
HS	HOTEL SPLENDIDE (UK)	POWELL	IDEAL	1932
HS2	HOT SHOTS! PART DEAUX	ABRAHAMS	20th CENTURY FOX	1993
HSH	HELL SQUAD	TOPPER	AIP	1958
HSH	HER AND SHE AND HIM	PECOS	GRIFFON FILMS	1970
HSH	HOME SWEET HOME (UK)	BLAKELEY	BUTCHER'S	1945
HSHC	HIGH SCHOOL HELLCATS	BERNDS	AIP	1958
HSKB	HONEY I SHRUNK THE KIDS	JOHNSTON	BUENA VISTA	1989
HS S7	BAR 20 (see HS 57) most stills look like an "S"			
HSU	HERCULES, SAMSON AND ULYSSES (IT: 1963)	FRANCISCI	MGM	1965
HSV	HORRIBLE SEXY VAMPIRE (GER: VAMPIRO AUTOPISTA 1971)	MADRID	PEPPERCORN-WORMSER	1976
HT	HAMMER THE TOFF (UK)	ROGERS	BUTCHER'S	1952
HT	HARD TIMES	HILL	COLUMBIA	1975
HT	HEAT	MANN	WARNER BROS	1995
HT	HELEN TALBOT	portrait		
HT	HIGH TREASON (UK)	BOULTING	MAYER-KINGLSEY	1951
HT	HOLLYWOOD THRILL-MAKERS	RAY	LIPPERT	1954
HT	HURRY UP OR I'LL BE 30	JACOBY	AVCO EMBASSY	1972
HTS	HOME TOWN STORY	PIERSON	MGM	1951
HV	HELEN VALKIS	portrait	WARNER BROS	
HV	HOLLYWOOD VARIETIES	LANDRES	LIPPERT	1950
HVR	VERA RALSTON	portrait	REP	
HW	HANNA'S WAR	GOLAN	CANNON	1988
HW	HARDLY WORKING	LEWIS	20th CENTURY FOX	1980
HW	HEADLINE WOMAN	NIGH	MASCOT	1935
HW	HEAT WAVE (UK: HOUSE ACROSS THE LAKE)	HUGHES	LIPPERT	1954
HW	HENRY WADSWORTH	portrait	MGM	
HW	HISTORY OF THE WORLD PART I	BROOKS	20th CENTURY FOX	1981
HW	HOLIDAY WEEK (UK: HINDLE WAKES)	CRABTREE	MONARCH	1952
HWD	HOUSE WHERE EVIL DWELLS	CONNOR	MGM	1982
HYLL	HOW'S YOUR LOVE LIFE?	VINCENT	CAL-TEX DIST.	1971
I	IDOL (UK)	PETRIE	EMBASSY	1966
I	IMPROMPTU	LAPINE	HEMSDALE	1991
I	IMPULSE	GREFE	CAMELOT	1974
I	IMPULSE	BAKER	20th CENTURY FOX	1984
I	IMPULSE	LOCKE	WARNER BROS	1990
I	INCORRIGIBLE, THE	DEBROCA	EDP FILMS	1975
I	INGA (SWE: JAG - EN OSKULD)	SARNO	CINEMATION	1968
I	INHERITOR (FR)	LABRO	HERA FILMS	1973

I	INNOCENTS (UK)	CLAYTON	20TH CENTURY FOX	1961
I	INTERVAL	MANN	AVCO EMBASSY	1973
I	IRONWEED	BABENCO	TRI STAR	1987
I1	WEDDING REHEARSAL (UK)	KORDA	IDEAL	1932
IA	INADMISSABLE EVIDENCE (UK)	PAGE	PARAMOUNT	1968
IA	INSIDE AMY	GARCUA	ADPIX	1974
IA	INTERNAL AFFAIRS	FIGGIS	PARAMOUNT	1990
IB	FIVE FINGERS OF DEATH (HK: TIAN XIA DI YI QUAN 1972)	CHANG	WARNER BROS	1973
IB	INNOCENT BLOOD (aka FRENCH VAMPIRE IN AMERICA)	LANDIS	WARNER BROS	1992
IB	INVISIBLE BOY	HOFFMAN	MGM	1957
IB	SEDUCTION OF THE SOUTH (BRIGANTI ITALIANI - IT)	CAMERINI	SCREEN GEMS	1961
IBD	ISLAND OF THE BURNING DOOMED (UK: NIGHT OF BIG HEAT)	FISHER	MARON	1967
IBS	BEAST (IT/FR: IL BESTIONE)	CORBUCCI	WARNER BROS	1974
IC	ICEMAN COMETH	FRANKENHEIMER	AMERICAN FILM THE.	1973
IC	ILLUSTRIOUS CORPSES (IT)	ROSI	UNITED ARTISTS	1976
IC	IMAGINARY CRIMES	DRAZAN	WARNER BROS	1994
IC	IN COUNTRY	JEWISON	WARNER BROS	1989
IC	IT'S A COP (UK)	ROGERS	UNITED ARTISTS	1934
IC-CX	ILLUSTRIOUS CORPSES (IT)	ROSI	UNITED ARTISTS	1976
ICFHW	FIRE MAIDENS OF OUTER SPACE	ROTH	SATURN	1956
ID	I'M DANCING AS FAST AS I CAN	HOFSISS	PARAMOUNT	1981
ID	INDEPENDENCE DAY	EMMERICH	20th CENTURY FOX	1996
IDH	IN THE DOGHOUSE (UK)	CONYERS	SCHOENFELD	1962
IE	IRON EAGLE	FURIE	TRI STAR	1985
IE2	IRON EAGLE 2	FURIE	TRI STAR	1988
IF	IF (UK)	ANDERSON	PARAMOUNT	1968
IF2	COLDITZ STORY (UK)	HAMILTON	DCA	1955
IFI	INTRUDER (UK)	HAMILTON	AAP	1953
IFM	INVADERS FROM MARS	MENZIES	20th CENTURY FOX	1953
IFM	INVADERS FROM MARS	HOOPER	CANNON	1986
IFT	INN FOR TROUBLE (UK)	PENNINGTON-RICHARDS	EROS	1960
IG	IRON GIANT	BIRD	WARNER BROS	1999
IG	STREET SINGER (UK)	DE MARGUENAT	ABFD	1937
IGY	LUCKY NICK CAIN (UK: I'LL GET YOU FOR THIS)	NEWMAN	20TH CENTURY FOX	1951
IH	CHINESE CONNECTION	HONG	NAT'L GENERAL	1973
IH	IVORY HUNTER (UK: WHERE NO VULTURES FLY)	WATT	UNIVERSAL	1951
II	SUMMER INTERLUDE/ILLICIT INTERLUDE (SWE: SOMMARLEK)	BERGMAN	GASTON HAKIM	1951
IJ	I, THE JURY	HEFFRON	20th CENTURY FOX	1982
IJL	IMAGINE	SOLT	WARNER BROS	1988
IJ-TD	INDIANA JONES AND THE TEMPLE OF DOOM	SPIELBERG	PARAMOUNT	1984
IK	INTENT TO KILL (UK)	CARDIFF	20TH CENTURY FOX	1958
IL	I'LL BE HOME FOR CHRISTMAS	SANFORD	BUENA VISTA	1998
IL	ILONA MASSEY	portrait	UNIV, UNITED ARTISTS	
IM	FIRST MAN INTO SPACE (UK)	DAY	MGM	1959
IM	ILONA MASSEY	portrait	MGM	
IM	IMAGES	ALTMAN	COLUMBIA	1971
IM	INSIDE MOVES	DONNER	ASSOCIATED FILM	1980
IMP-4	ELIZABETH OF LADYMEAD (UK)	WILCOX	BRITISH LION	1948
IMP-107	MAN IN THE DINGHY (UK: INTO THE BLUE)	WILCOX	SNADER	1950
IMP-108	LADY WITH THE LAMP (UK: LADY WITH A LAMP)	WILCOX	CONTINENTAL	1951
IMP-109	DERBY DAY (UK)	WILCOX	AAP	1952
IMS	I MARRIED A SHADOW	DAVIS	SPECTRAFILM	1983
IN	IN THE NICK (UK)	HUGHES	COLUMBIA	1960
IN	INCHON	YOUNG	MGM/UNITED ARTISTS	1982
IN	INDISCREET (UK)	DONEN	WARNER BROS	1958
INBB	INSIDER	MANN	BUENA VISTA	1999
INBB	INSTINCT	TURTELTAUB	BUENA VISTA	1999
INBB	SQUANTO	KOLLER	BUENA VISTA	1994
INS	NEVERENDING STORY II: NEXT CHAPTER	MILLER	WARNER BROS	1991
INT	INTERSECTION	RYDELL	PARAMOUNT	1994
INT-9500	BELLE OF THE YUKON	SEITER	RKO	1944
IP	IRENE PURCELL	portrait	MGM	
IP-103	SPRING IN PARK LANE (UK)	WILCOX	EAGLE-LION	1948
IP-107	MAYTIME IN MAYFAIR (UK)	WILCOX	REALART	1949
IPB	IS PARIS BURNING?	CLEMENT	PARAMOUNT	1966
IPL-15	NOTORIOUS GENTLEMAN (UK: RAKE'S PROGRESS)	GILLIAT	UNIVERSAL	1945

IPL-15A	NOTORIOUS GENTLEMAN (UK: RAKE'S PROGRESS)	GILLIAT	UNIVERSAL	1945
IPL-16	ADVENTURESS (UK: I SEE A DARK STRANGER)	LAUNDER	EAGLE-LION	1946
IPL-24	I KNOW WHERE I'M GOING! (UK)	POWELL, PRESSBURGER	UNIVERSAL	1945
IPL-26	BRIEF ENCOUNTER (UK)	LEAN	UNIVERSAL	1945
IPL-111	GREEN FOR DANGER (UK)	GILLIAT	EAGLE-LION	1946
IQ	I. Q.	SCHEPISI	PARAMOUNT	1994
IR-F-25	CAPTAIN FURY	ROACH	FAVORITE	R46
IS	ISLE OF SIN (GER: FLITTERWOCHEN IN DER HOLLE 1960)	KAI	MANSON FILM	1962
IS	INVINCIBLE SIX	NEGULESCO	PARAMOUNT	1969
ISBB	INDIAN SUMMER	BINDER	TOUCHSTONE	1993
ISF	SILENT DUST (UK)	COMFORT	STRATFORD	1949
ISF-4	HIDDEN ROOM (UK: OBSESSION)	DMYTRYK	EAGLE-LION	1949
ISR	INCREDIBLE SEX REVOLUTION	ZUGSMITH	FAMOUS PLAYERS	1965
IT	INFERNAL TRIO, THE (FR: LE TRIO INFERNAL)	GIROD	NEW LINE CINEMA	1974
IT	IT (GER)	SCHAMONI	WARNER BROS	1967
IT	IT (UK)	LEDER	WARNER BROS	1967
ITMA	IT'S THAT MAN AGAIN (UK)	FORDE	GFD	1943
ITS	PAWS, CLAWS AND JAWS (IT'S SHOWTIME)	MYERSON	UNITED ARTISTS	1976
IU	IRISH IN THE U.S.	BACON	WARNER BROS	1935
IV	FOR LOVE OF IVY	MANN	CINERAMA RELEASING	1968
IV	INTERVIEW WITH THE VAMPIRE	JORDAN	GEPPEN	1994
IV	YOUNG AND THE PASSIONATE (IT: I VITELLONI)	FELLINI	JANUS	1953
IWC	INTERVIEW WITH THE VAMPIRE	JORDAN	GEPPEN	1994
IY	I THANK YOU (UK)	VARNEL	GFD	1941
J	JAMILYA	POPLAVSKAYA	ARTKINO PICTURES	1972
J	JASON'S LYRIC	HOLLAND	GRAMERCY	1994
J	JERICHO (UK)	FREELAND	RECORD	1937
J	JINGLE ALL THE WAY	LEVANT	20th CENTURY FOX	1996
J	JOURNEY TOGETHER (UK)	BOULTING	ENGLISH	1945
J	JUGGERNAUT (UK)	EDWARDS	GRAND	1937
J	JUICE	DICKERSON	PARAMOUNT	1992
J	JULIETTA	ALLEGRET	KINGSLEY INT'L	1953
J	JUNGLE	BERKE	LIPPERT	1952
J	LAST MAN TO HANG (UK: AMAZING DAPHNE STROOD)	FISHER	COLUMBIA	1956
J-1	CALL OF THE WILD	JACKMAN	PATHE EXCHANGE	1923
J-2	KING OF WILD HORSES	JACKMAN	PATHE EXCHANGE	1924
J-3	BLACK CYCLONE	JACKMAN	PATHE EXCHANGE	1925
J-4	DEVIL HORSE	JACKMAN	PATHE EXCHANGE	1926
J-5	NO MAN'S LAW	JACKMAN	PATHE EXCHANGE	1927
J8	JENNIFER 8	ROBINSON	PARAMOUNT	1992
J81	TRENCHCOAT	TUCHNER	BUENA VISTA	1983
J-320	CANDLELIGHT IN ALGERIA (UK)	KING	20TH CENTURY FOX	1944
J-323	YOU CAN'T DO WITHOUT LOVE (UK: ONE EXCITING NIGHT)	FORDE	COLUMBIA	1944
JA	JOE'S APARTMENT	PAYSON	GEFFEN	1996
JB	JACK AND THE BEANSTALK	YARBROUGH	WARNER BROS	1952
JB	JACK THE BEAR (prerelease code copyright 1991 - see JTB)	HERSKOVITZ	20th CENTURY FOX	1993
JB	JAMES BELL	portrait	RKO	
JB	JAMES BURKE	portrait	RKO	
JB	JAMES BUSH	portrait	RKO	
JB	JEAN BROOKS	portrait	RKO	
JB	JOAN BROOKS aka JOAN LESLIE akaJOAN BRODEL	portrait		
JB	JOEY BOY (UK)	LAUNDER	BRITISH LION	1965
JB	JUNIOR BONNER	PECKINPAH	CINERAMA RELEASING	1972
JB	PRIME OF MISS JEAN BRODIE (UK)	NEAME	20TH CENTURY FOX	1969
JB	TERROR IN TINY TOWN	BUELL	COLUMBIA	1937
JB-1	LARCENY STREET (UK: SMASH AND GRAB)	WHELAN	FILM ALLIANCE	1937
JB-2	SKY'S THE LIMIT (UK)	BUCHANAN, GARMES	GFD	1938
JB-4	BREAK THE NEWS (UK)	CLAIR	MONOGRAM	1938
JBBB	JERKY BOYS THE MOVIE	MELKONIAN	BUENA VISTA	1995
JBBB	JUNGLE BOOK 2	TRENBIRTH	BUENA VISTA	2003
JBRNY	I'M ALL RIGHT. JACK	BOULTING	COLUMBIA	1959
JC	HALF BREED	GILMORE	RKO	1952
JC	JAMES CRAIG	portrait	RKO	
JC	JEROME COWAN	portrait	REP	
JC	JOHN CROMWELL	portrait	RKO	
JC	JOSEPH COTTON	portrait	UNIV, SELZNICK/UA	

JC	JUST CAUSE	GLIMCHER	WARNER BROS	1995
JD	JACK OF DIAMONDS	TAYLOR	MGM	1967
JD	JAMES DARREN		COL	
JD	JILL DONOHUE		COL	
JD	JUDGMENT DEFERRED (UK)	BAXTER	ASSO. BRITISH-PATHE	1952
JdW	JACQUELINE DeWIT	portrait	UNIV	
JE	JANE EYRE (R60S tv)	STEVENSON	NTA	1944
JEL	JOE E. LEWIS	portrait	UNIV	
JF	JACK FROST	MILLER	WARNER BROS	1998
JF	JAMES FOX	portrait	UNIV	
JF	JERUSALEM FILE	FLYNN	MGM	1972
JF	JOAN FONTAINE	portrait	UNITED ARTISTS	
JF	JOHNNY FRENCHMAN (UK 1945)	FREND	UNIVERSAL	1946
JFL-226	BROWNING VERSION (UK)	ASQUITH	UNIVERSAL	1951
JG	JETTA GOUDAL	portrait	PATHE-DE MILLE	
JG	JOHN GIELGUD	portrait	GAUMONT BRITISH	
JG	LOVES OF JOANNA GODDEN (UK)	FREND	GFD	1947
JG	NINE DAYS A QUEEN (UK: TUDOR ROSE)	STEVENSON	GAUMONT	1936
JH	JOHNNY HOLIDAY (BOY'S PRISON 1955)	GOLDBECK	UNITED ARTISTS	1950
JH	JUDY HOLLIDAY		COL	
JH-1	LIVING DEAD (GER 1932)	OSWALD	J H HOFFBERG	1940
JH-A	JOHNNY HOLIDAY (BOY'S PRISON 1955)	GOLDBECK	UNITED ARTISTS	1950
JHB	JIMI HENDRIX	BOYD	WARNER BROS	1973
JH-COL-1	NORTH OF OME	NIGH	COLUMBIA	1936
JHF-1	MAKE MINE A MILLION (UK)	COMFORT	SCHOENFELD	1959
JHP	BLUE MURDER AT ST. TRINIAN'S	LAUNDER	CONTINENTAL	1957
JHP-2	BLUE MURDER AT ST. TRINIAN'S (UK)	LAUNDER	CONTINENTAL	1957
JINX	JINX FALKENBURG		COL	
JJ	JESSE JAMES MEETS FRANKENSTEIN'S DAUGHTER	BEAUDINE	EMBASSY	1965
JJ	JOHN AND JULIE (UK)	FAIRCHILD	DCA	1955
JJ	JUMPIN' JACK FLASH	MARSHALL	20th CENTURY FOX	1986
JJ	RETURN OF JESSE JAMES	HILTON	LIPPERT	1950
JJR	GREAT JESSE JAMES RAID	LE BORG	LIPPERT	1953
JK	JACK KELLY	portrait	UNIV	
JK	JAMES KIRKWOOD	portrait		
JK	JEANNE KELLY aka JEAN BROOKS	portrait	UNIV	
JL	CONDEMNED TO DEATH (UK)	FORDE	FIRST DIVISION	1932
JL	DON'T RAISE THE BRIDGE, LOWER THE RIVER (UK)	PARIS	COLUMBIA	1968
JL	JACKIE LOUGHERY	portrait	UNIV	
JL	JANET LEIGH	portrait	UNIV	
JL	JOSEPH LOSEY	portrait	RKO	
JL-216	OPERATION DISASTER (UK: MORNING DEPARTURE 1950)	BAKER	UNIVERSAL	1951
JL-COL-1	ROLLING CARAVANS	LEVERING	COLUMBIA	1938
JL-COL-2	STAGECOACH DAYS	LEVERING	COLUMBIA	1938
JL-COL-3	PIONEER TRAIL	LEVERING	COLUMBIA	1938
JL-COL-4	PHANTOM GOLD	LEVERING	COLUMBIA	1938
JLNN	JUDY'S LITTLE NO-NO	PRICE	SCHOONER BAY	1969
JLP	FRONT PAGE STORY (UK)	PARRY	AAP	1954
JM	JAYNE MANSFIELD	portrait	WARNER BROS	
JM	JOANNA MOORE	portrait	UNIVERSAL	
JM	JOEL McCREA	portrait	UNIV	
JM	JUNE MARLOWE	portrait	WARNER BROS	
JMC	JOEL McCREA	portrait	UNIV	
JM-COL-11	STRANGE CASE OF DR. MEADE	COLLINS	COLUMBIA	1938
JMK	JOYCE MACKENZIE	portrait	RKO	
JML	JOAN MARIE LAWES	portrait		
JML	JUST MY LUCK (UK)	RAYMOND	WOOLF & FREEDMAN	1933
JN	INNOCENT AFFAIR (DON'T TRUST YOUR HUSBAND)	BACON	UNITED ARTISTS	1948
JN	JEWEL OF THE NILE	TEAGUE	20th CENTURY FOX	1985
JN	JOHNNY NOBODY (UK)	PATRICK	MEDALLION	1961
JO	JOANNA (UK)	SARNE	20TH CENTURY FOX	1968
JO	JONAS (GER: 1957)	DOMNICK	PRESIDENT FILMS	1959
JOA	JET OVER THE ATLANTIC	HASKIN	INTER-CONTINENT FILM	1959
JOAN.C.	JOAN CRAWFORD	portrait	WARNER BROS	
JP	HELL IS EMPTY	AINSWORTH	RANK	1967
JP	JEAN PARKER	portrait	MONOGRAM	

JP	JEAN PETERS	portrait		
JPBB	JEFFERSON IN PARIS	IVORY	BUENA VISTA	1995
JR	GOING PLACES (FR: LES VALSEUSES)	BERTRAND BLIER	CINEMA 5	1974
JR	JANICE RULE	portrait		
JR	JEAN RENOIR	portrait	RKO	
JR-11	RHYTHM RACKETEER (UK)	SEYMOUR	BRITISH INDEPENDENT	1937
JRB-1	JOSEPHINE AND MEN (UK)	BOULTING	CONTINENTAL	1955
JRB-2	PRIVATE'S PROGRESS (UK)	BOULTING	DCA	1956
JRB-3	BROTHERS IN LAW (UK)	BOULTING	CONTINENTAL	1957
JRB-3	MAN IN A COCKED HAT (UK: CARLTON-BROWNE OF THE F.O.)	DELL, BOULTING	SHOWCORPORATION	1959
JRB-4	I'M ALL RIGHT JACK (UK)	BOULTING	COLUMBIA	1959
JRB-4	LUCKY JIM (UK)	BOULTING	KINGSLEY INT'L	1957
JRB-5	THE RISK (UK: SUSPECT)	BOULTING, BOULTING	KINGSLEY INT'L	1960
JRB-6	FRENCH MISTRESS (UK)	BOULTING	FILMS AROUND THE WORL	1960
JRP-1	MYSTERIOUS MR. REEDER (UK: MIND OF MR. REEDER)	RAYMOND	GRAND NATIONAL	1939
JS	BUFFALO BILL RIDES AGAIN	RAY	SCREEN GUILD	1947
JS	JACQUES ("JACK") SERNAS	portrait	WARNER BROS	
JS	JAMES STEWART	portrait	UNIVERSAL	
JS	JEAN SEBERG	portrait	COL, UNIV	
JS	JEAN SHRIMPTON	portrait	UNIVERSAL	
JS	JEAN SULLIVAN	portrait	WARNER BROS	
JS	JET STORM (UK)	ENDFIELD	UNITED PRODUCERS	1959
JS	JOHNNY SOKKO AND HIS FLYING ROBOT (tv)		AIP	1967
JS	JULIET OF THE SPIRITS (IT)	FELLINI	CINERIZ	1965
JS	JUNGLE STREET GIRLS (UK: JUNGLE STREET)	SAUNDERS	AJAY	1960
JS-2	HOLLYWOOD BARN DANCE	RAY	SCREEN GUILD	1947
JSF	MY SEVEN LITTLE SINS (FR: J'AVAIS SEPT FILLES 1954)	BOYER	KINGSLEY INT'L	1956
JT	JACKTOWN	MARTIN	PICTORIAL INT'L	1962
JT	JUNGLE TREASURE (UK: MOTHER RILEY'S JUNGLE TREASURE)	ROGERS	RENOWN	1951
JT	TWO OF US (UK: JACK OF ALL TRADES)	HULBERT, STEVENSON	GAUMONT	1936
JTB	JACK THE BEAR	HERSKOVITZ	20th CENTURY FOX	1993
JTR	JOURNEY THROUGH ROSEBUD	GRIES	GSF PRODUCTIONS	1971
JU	JUDITH	MANN	PARAMOUNT	1966
JV	JOE VERSUS THE VOLCANO	SHANLEY	WARNER BROS	1990
JV	JOSEPH VITALI	portrait	RKO	
JVBB	JUST VISITING	GAUBERT	BUENA VISTA	2001
JW	JOHN WAYNE	portrait	PAR, UNIV	
JW	JUST LIKE A WOMAN (UK)	FUEST	MONARCH	1967
JW1	BIRTHDAY PRESENT (UK)	JACKSON	BRITISH LION	1957
JXK	JUNE KNIGHT	portrait	MGM	
JXM	JOHN MILJAN	portrait		
K	CACTUS IN THE SNOW	ZWEIBACH	GENERAL FILM	1971
K	HAPPY ROAD	KELLY	MGM	1956
K	KAGEMUSHA (JAP)	KUROSAWA	20th CENTURY FOX	1980
K	KANSAS	STEVENS	TRANS WORLD	1988
K	KEOMA (IT: 1976)	CASTELLARI	VADIB INT'L	1978
K	KERIMA	portrait	UNITED ARTISTS	
K	KIDNAPPED (UK)	STEVENSON	DISNEY	1960
K	KILLER IN THE FAMILY, A (tv movie)	HEFFRON	WARNER BROS	1983
K	KINDRED	CARPENTER, OBROW	FM ENTERTAINMENT	1987
K	KING OF THE DAMNED (UK)	FORDE	GAUMONT BRITISH	1935
K	KITCHEN (UK)	HILL	KINGSLEY INT'L	1961
K	KLANSMAN	YOUNG	PARAMOUNT	1974
K	MISSION TO GLORY (FATHER KINO STORY)	KENNEDY	ARIZONA FILM CORP	1977
K	OUTCAST OF THE ISLANDS	REED	LOPERT	1952
K	REMARKABLE MR. KIPPS (UK: KIPPS)	REED	20TH CENTURY FOX	1941
K	STAMBOUL (UK)	BUCHOWETZKI	TOBIS FORENFILMS	1931
K-1	BETTER MOVIES	MCGOWAN	PATHE EXCHANGE	1925
K-1	BORED OF EDUCATION	DOUGLAS	MGM	1936
K-1	HER DANGEROUS PATH (10 ch. series)	CLEMENTS	PATHE EXCHANGE	1923
K2	PECOS KID	FRASER	COMMODORE	1935
K-2	TWO TOO YOUNG	DOUGLAS	MGM	1936
K-2	YOUR OWN BACK YARD	MCGOWAN	PATHE EXCHANGE	1925
K-3	ONE WILD RIDE	MCGOWAN	PATHE EXCHANGE	1925
K-3	PAY AS YOU EXIT	DOUGLAS	MGM	1936
K-4	GOOD CHEER	MCGOWAN	PATHE EXCHANGE	1926

K-4	SPOOKY HOOKY	DOUGLAS	MGM	1936
K-5	BURIED TREASURE	MCGOWAN	PATHE EXCHANGE	1926
K-5	REUNION IN RHYTHM	DOUGLAS	MGM	1937
K-6	GLOVE TAPS	DOUGLAS	MGM	1937
K-6	MONKEY BUSINESS	MCGOWAN	PATHE EXCHANGE	1926
K-7	BABY CLOTHES	MCGOWAN	PATHE EXCHANGE	1926
K-7	HEARTS ARE THUMPS	DOUGLAS	MGM	1937
K-8	THREE SMART BOYS	DOUGLAS	MGM	1937
K-8	UNCLE TOM'S UNCLE	MCGOWAN	PATHE EXCHANGE	1926
K-9	RUSHIN' BALLET	DOUGLAS	MGM	1937
K-9	THUNDERING FLEAS	MCGOWAN	PATHE EXCHANGE	1926
K-10	ROAMIN' HOLIDAY	DOUGLAS	MGM	1937
K-10	SHIVERING SPOOKS	MCGOWAN	PATHE EXCHANGE	1926
K-11	FOURTH ALARM	MCGOWAN	PATHE EXCHANGE	1926
K-11	NIGHT 'N' GALES	DOUGLAS	MGM	1937
K-12	FISHY TALES	DOUGLAS	MGM	1937
K-12	WAR FEATHERS	MCGOWAN, MCGOWAN	PATHE EXCHANGE	1926
K-13	FRAMING YOUTH	DOUGLAS	MGM	1937
K-13	SEEING THE WORLD	MCGOWAN, MCGOWAN	PATHE EXCHANGE	1927
K-14	KWAIDAN (JAP)	KOBAYASHI	CONTINENTAL	1966
K-14	PIGSKIN PALOOKA	DOUGLAS	MGM	1937
K-14	TELLING WHOPPERS	MCGOWAN, MCGOWAN	PATHE EXCHANGE	1926
K-15	BRING HOME THE TURKEY	MCGOWAN, MCGOWAN	PATHE EXCHANGE	1927
K-15	MAIL AND FEMALE	NEWMEYER	MGM	1937
K-16	CANNED FISHING	DOUGLAS	MGM	1938
K-16	TEN YEARS OLD	MCGOWAN	PATHE EXCHANGE	1927
K-17	BEAR FACTS	DOUGLAS	MGM	1938
K-17	LOVE MY DOG	MCGOWAN	PATHE EXCHANGE	1927
K-18	THREE MEN IN A TUB	WATT	MGM	1938
K-18	TIRED BUSINESS MEN	MCGOWAN, OELZE	PATHE EXCHANGE	1927
K-19	BABY BROTHER	MCGOWAN, OELZE	PATHE EXCHANGE	1927
K-19	CAME THE BRAWN	DOUGLAS	MGM	1938
K-20	CHICKEN FEED	MCGOWAN, OELZE	PATHE EXCHANGE	1927
K-20	FEED 'EM AND WEEP	DOUGLAS	MGM	1938
K-21	AWFUL TOOTH	WATT	MGM	1938
K-21	OLYMPIC GAMES	MCGOWAN	PATHE EXCHANGE	1927
K-22	GLORIOUS FOURTH	MCGOWAN	PATHE EXCHANGE	1927
K-22	HIDE AND SHRIEK	DOUGLAS	MGM	1938
K-23	SMILE WINS	MCGOWAN	PATHE EXCHANGE	1928
K-24	PLAYIN' HOOKEY	MCGOWAN	PATHE EXCHANGE	1928
K101	THIEF OF BAGDAD (UK)	BERGER, POWELL	UNITED ARTISTS	1940
K101P	THIEF OF BAGDAD (UK)	BERGER, POWELL, WHALEN	UNITED ARTISTS	1940
K-106	GUSSIE'S DAY OF REST		MUTUAL FILM	1915
K-124	AMBROSE'S FURY	HENDERSON	MUTUAL FILM	1915
K-125	CAUGHT IN THE ACT	JONES	MUTUAL FILM	1915
K-126	SETTLED AT THE SEASIDE	GRIFFIN	MUTUAL FILM	1915
K-129	AMBROSE'S LOFTY PERCH	WRIGHT	MUTUAL FILM	1915
K-130	RENT JUMPERS	GRIFFIN	MUTUAL FILM	1915
K-131	DO-RE-ME-FA	CHASE	MUTUAL FILM	1915
K-132	AMBROSE'S NASTY TEMPER	HENDERSON	MUTUAL FILM	1915
K-139	BEAR AFFAIR	HENDERSON	MUTUAL FILM	1915
K-140	GUSSIE'S BACKWARD WAY		MUTUAL FILM	1915
K-141	CANNON BALL	WRIGHT	MUTUAL FILM	1915
K-144	THEIR SOCIAL SPLASH	GILLSTROM, JONES	MUTUAL FILM	1915
K-145	HUMAN HOUND'S TRIUMPH	HENDERSON	MUTUAL FILM	1915
K-146	HE WOULDN'T STAY DOWN	STERLING	MUTUAL FILM	1915
K-147	THOSE COLLEGE GIRLS	JONES	MUTUAL FILM	1915
K-148	CROSSED LOVE AND SWORDS	GRIFFIN	MUTUAL FILM	1915
K-150	LOVER'S LOST CONTROL	AVERY, CHAPLIN	MUTUAL FILM	1915
K-152	FOR BETTER-BUT WORSE	HENDERSON	MUTUAL FILM	1915
K-153	VERSATILE VILLAIN	GRIFFIN	MUTUAL FILM	1915
K-154	SUBMARINE PIRATE	AVERY, CHAPLIN	TRIANGLE	1915
K-155	LITTLE TEACHER	SENNETT	MUTUAL FILM	1915
K-157	COURT HOUSE CROOKS	STERLING	MUTUAL FILM	1915
K-158	THOSE BITTER SWEETS	HENDERSON	MUTUAL FILM	1915
K-160	WHEN AMBROSE DATED WALRUS		MUTUAL FILM	1915

K-161	HASH HOUSE FRAUD	CHASE	MUTUAL FILM	1915
K-162	HOME BREAKING HOUND	CHASE	MUTUAL FILM	1915
K-163	MERELY A MARRIED MAN	HENDERSON	MUTUAL FILM	1915
K-164	STOLEN MAGIC	SENNETT	TRIANGLE	1915
K-166	DIRTY WORK IN A LAUNDRY	SANTELL	MUTUAL FILM	1915
K-168	FIDO'S TIN-TYPE-TANGLE	ARBUCKLE	MUTUAL FILM	1915
K-169	RASCAL'S WOLFISH WAY	HENDERSON, SENNETT	MUTUAL FILM	1915
K-170	BATTLE OF AMBROSE AND WALRUS	WRIGHT	MUTUAL FILM	1915
K-171	MY VALET	SENNETT	TRIANGLE	1915
K-172	ONLY A MESSENGER BOY	GRIFFIN, STERLING	MUTUAL FILM	1915
K-175	GAME OLD KNIGHT	JONES	TRIANGLE	1915
K-177	FAVORITE FOOL	FRAZEE	TRIANGLE	1915
K-184	FICKLE FATTY'S FALL	ARBUCKLE	TRIANGLE	1915
K-187	MODERN ENOCH ARDEN	BADGER, AVERY	TRIANGLE	1916
K-190	GREAT PEARL TANGLE	HENDERSON	TRIANGLE	1916
K-195	CINDERS OF LOVE	WRIGHT	TRIANGLE	1916
K-201	GYPSY JOE	BADGER	TRIANGLE	1916
K-208	JUDGE	JONES	TRIANGLE	1916
K-209	WIFE AND AUTO TROUBLE	HENDERSON, SENNETT	TRIANGLE	1916
K-210	HE DID AND HE DIDN'T	ARBUCKLE	TRIANGLE	1916
K-212	DASH OF COURAGE	PARROTT	TRIANGLE	1916
K-214	HIS LAST LAUGH	WRIGHT	TRIANGLE	1916
K-230	BATH TUB PERILS	FRAZEE	TRIANGLE	1916
K-232	LOVE COMET	WRIGHT	TRIANGLE	1916
K-233	AMBROSE'S CUP OF WOE	FISHBACK	TRIANGLE	1916
K-234	SURF GIRL	EDWARDS	TRIANGLE	1916
K-235	PILLS OF PERIL	JONES	TRIANGLE	1916
K-236	HIS LAST SCENT	AVERY, CHAPLIN	TRIANGLE	1916
K-241	HIS LYING HEART	STERLING, AVERY	TRIANGLE	1916
K-243	TUGBOAT ROMEO	CAMPBELL, WILLIAMS	TRIANGLE	1916
K-245	SCOUNDREL'S TOLL	CAVENDER	TRIANGLE	1916
K-250	MAIDEN'S TRUST	HEERMAN	TRIANGLE	1916
K-251	HIS BUSTED TRUST	CLINE	TRIANGLE	1916
K-253	HAYSTACKS AND STEEPLES	BADGER	TRIANGLE	1916
K-255	STARS AND BARS	HEERMAN	TRIANGLE	1917
K-256	BOMBS!	GRIFFIN	TRIANGLE	1916
K-257	AMBROSE'S RAPID RISE	FISHBACK	TRIANGLE	1916
K-258	VILLA OF THE MOVIES	CLINE	TRIANGLE	1917
K-260	HER CIRCUS KNIGHT	WRIGHT	TRIANGLE	1917
K-261	HIS NAUGHTY THOUGHT	FISHBACK	TRIANGLE	1917
K-262	NICK OF TIME BABY	BADGER	TRIANGLE	1917
K-263	MAGGIE'S FIRST FALSE STEP	GRIFFIN	TRIANGLE	1917
K-264	DODGING HIS DOOM	WILLIAMS	TRIANGLE	1917
K-265	SAFETY FIRST AMBROSE	FISHBACK	TRIANGLE	1916
K-266	CACTUS NELL	FISHBACK	TRIANGLE	1917
K-267	HER NATURE DANCE	CAMPBELL	TRIANGLE	1917
K-268	SKIDDING HEARTS	WRIGHT	TRIANGLE	1917
K-269	HER FAME AND SHAME	GRIFFIN	TRIANGLE	1917
K-270	TEDDY AT THE THROTTLE	BADGER	TRIANGLE	1917
K-271	ROYAL ROGUE	KERR, HARTMAN	TRIANGLE	1917
K-272	DOG CATCHER'S LOVE	CLINE	TRIANGLE	1917
K-273	SECRETS OF A BEAUTY PARLOR	WILLIAMS	TRIANGLE	1917
K-274	HER TORPEDOED LOVE	GRIFFIN	TRIANGLE	1917
K-275	PINCHED IN THE FINISH	WRIGHT, WILLIAMS	TRIANGLE	1917
K-276	ORIENTAL LOVE	WRIGHT	TRIANGLE	1917
K-277	THIRST	FISHBACK	TRIANGLE	1917
K-278	WHOSE BABY	BADGER	TRIANGLE	1917
K-279	HULA-HULA LAND	CAMPBELL	TRIANGLE	1917
K-279	SHANGHAIED JONAH	CAMPBELL	TRIANGLE	1917
K-280	BETRAYAL OF MAGGIE	GRIFFIN	TRIANGLE	1917
K-281	DANGERS OF A BRIDE	KERR, HARTMAN	TRIANGLE	1917
K-282	TWO CROOKS	HEERMAN	TRIANGLE	1917
K-283	HIS UNCLE DUDLEY	JONES	TRIANGLE	1917
K-284	SHE NEEDED A DOCTOR	JONES	TRIANGLE	1917
K-285	SULTAN'S WIFE	BADGER	TRIANGLE	1917
K-286	HIS PRECIOUS LIFE	RAYMAKER	TRIANGLE	1917

K-287	PAWNBROKER'S HEART	CLINE	TRIANGLE	1917
K-288	CLEVER DUMMY	RAYMAKER	TRIANGLE	1917
K-289	LATE LAMENTED	WILLIAMS	TRIANGLE	1917
K-292	LOST, A COOK	JONES	TRIANGLE	1917
KA	KING ARTHUR WAS A GENTLEMAN (UK)	VARNEL	GFD	1942
KA	KNIVES OF THE AVENGER (IT)	BAVA	WORLD ENT	1966
KABB	KING ARTHUR	FUQUA	BUENA VISTA	2004
KB	KICKBOXER	DISALLE	CANNON	1989
KB	WHEN KNIGHTS WERE BOLD (UK)	RAYMOND	UNITY	1936
K B-14	KWAIDAN (JAP)	KOBAYASHI	CONTINENTAL	1966
KBK	KILL OR BE KILLED	NOSSECK	EAGLE LION	1950
KBS-111	FALSE FACES	SHERMAN	SONO ART-WORLDWIDE	1932
KBS-113	DEATH KISS	MARIN	SONO ART-WORLDWIDE	1932
KBS-116	CONSTANT WOMAN	SCHERTZINGER	SONO ART-WORLDWIDE	1933
KBS-117	STUDY IN SCARLET	MARIN	SONO ART-WORLDWIDE	1933
KC	KATHERINE CORNELL	portrait	UNITED ARTISTS	
KC	KEEP IT CLEAN (UK)	PALTENGHI	EROS	1956
KC	KING OF COMEDY	SCORSESE	PARAMOUNT	1983
KC	TO KILL A CLOWN	BLOOMFIELD	20th CENTURY FOX	1972
KC	WHO IS GUILTY? (UK: I KILLED THE COUNT)	ZELNIK	GRAND NATIONAL	1939
KCB	KANSAS CITY BOMBER	FREEDMAN	MGM	1972
KD	KING DINOSAUR	GORDON	LIPPERT	1955
KE	KEY EXCHANGE	KELLMAN	20th CENTURY FOX	1985
KE-L	KILLER ELITE	PECKINPAH	UNITED ARTISTS	1975
KF	PSYCHIC KILLER	DANTON	AVCO EMBASSY	1975
KFL	KNIFE FOR THE LADIES	SPANGLER	WARNER BROS	1974
KG	KATHRYN GRANT		COL	
KH	INVINCIBLE SIX	NEGULESCO	PARAMOUNT	1969
KH	KATHARINE HOUGHTON		COL	
KH	KELLY'S HEROES	HUTTON	MGM	1970
KJ	KAY JOHNSON	portrait	TIFFANY	early 30s
KJ	KIMBERLEY JIM	NOFAL	EMBASSY	1963
KJ	KINJITE: FORBIDDEN SUBJECTS	THOMPSON	CANNON	1989
KK	KAY KYSER	portrait	RKO	
KK	KITTY KELLY	portrait	RKO	
KK	KURT KREUGER	portrait	RKO	
KL	KIND OF LOVING (UK)	SCHLESINGER	GOVERNOR	1962
KL	KREMLIN LETTER	HUSTON	20th CENTURY FOX	1970
KM	KARL MALDEN	portrait	WARNER BROS	
KM2	FIDDLIN' BUCKAROO	MAYNARD	REALART	1933
KM7	HONOR OF THE RANGE (1934)	JAMES	FILM CLASSICS	R48
KM-COL-2	HEIR TO TROUBLE	BENNETT	COLUMBIA	1935
KN	KIM NOVAK		COL	
KNBB	KUNDUN	SCORSESE	BUENA VISTA	1997
KNY	KING IN NEW YORK (UK)	CHAPLIN	ARCHWAY	1957
KOD	KISS OF DEATH	SCHROEDER	20th CENTURY FOX	1995
KOG	KING OF THE GYPSIES	PIERSON	PARAMOUNT	1978
KP	KANSAS CITY PRINCESS	KEIGHLEY	WARNER BROS	1934
KR	KANE RICHMOND	portrait	MGM	
KR	KATHARINE ROSS	portrait	UNIV	
KRBB	KEEPING THE FAITH	NORTON	BUENA VISTA	2000
KS	KILLER SHREWS (ATTACK OF THE KILLER SHREWS)	KELLOGG	AIP	1959
KS	KING SISTERS	portrait	UNIV	
KT	KITCHEN TOTO	HOOK	CANNON	1987
KT29	BUG'S LIFE, A	LASSETER	BUENA VISTA	1998
KZ	KAZABLAN	GOLAN	MGM	1974
L	DEATH VALLEY	LANDERS	SCREEN GUILD	1946
L	LADY IN DISTRESS (UK: WINDOW IN LONDON)	MASON	TIMES	1940
L	LAIR OF THE WHITE WORM	RUSSELL	VESTRON	1988
L	LAND OF FURY (UK: SEEKERS)	ANNAKIN	UNIVERSAL	1954
L	LASH (UK)	EDWARDS	RKO	1934
L	LAWYER	FURIE	PARAMOUNT	1970
L	LIBERTINE	CAMPANILE	AUDUBON	1969
L	LINK	FRANKLIN	CANNON	1986
L	LOCUSTS, THE	KELLEY	ORION	1997
L	LODGER (UK)	HITCHCOCK	AMERANGLO	1927

L	LOOT (UK)	NARIZZANO	CINEVISION	1970
L	LUCAS	SELTZER	20th CENTURY FOX	1986
L	YOU LUCKY PEOPLE (UK)	ELVEY	ADELPHI	1955
L1	AUNT CLARA (UK)	KIMMINS	BRITISH LION	1954
L-1	BUMPING INTO BROADWAY	ROACH	PATHE EXCHANGE	1919
L-1	COME CLEAN	HORNE	MGM	1931
L1	OLD BILL AND SON (UK)	DALRYMPLE	GFD	1941
L-1	OVER THE FENCE	LLOYD, MACDONALD	PATHE EXCHANGE	1917
L-1	ROUGHEST AFRICA	CEDER	PATHE EXCHANGE	1923
L1-18	CAVALCADE	LLOYD	FOX FILM	1933
L-2	CAPTAIN KIDD'S KIDS	ROACH	PATHE EXCHANGE	1919
L2	CHARLEY MOON (UK)	HAMILTON	BRITISH LION	1956
L-2	FROZEN HEARTS	HOWE	PATHE EXCHANGE	1923
L-2	ONE GOOD TURN	HORNE	MGM	1931
L-2	PINCHED	LLOYD, PRATT	PATHE EXCHANGE	1917
L-2	TRAIL OF THE MOUNTIES	BRETHERTON	LIPPERT	1947
L-3	BEAU HUNKS	HORNE	MGM	1931
L-3	BY THE SAD SEA WAVES	GOULDING	PATHE EXCHANGE	1917
L-3	FROM HAND TO MOUTH	GOULDING	PATHE EXCHANGE	1919
L-3	SOILERS	CEDER	PATHE EXCHANGE	1923
L-4	ANY OLD PORT	HORNE	MGM	1932
L-4	HIS ROYAL SLYNESS	ROACH	PATHE EXCHANGE	1920
L-4	MOTHER'S JOY	CEDER	PATHE EXCHANGE	1923
L-4	RAINBOW ISLAND	GILBERT	PATHE EXCHANGE	1917
L-5	BLISS	GOULDING	PATHE EXCHANGE	1917
L-5	HAUNTED SPOOKS	ROACH	PATHE EXCHANGE	1920
L-5	HELPMATES	PARROTT	MGM	1932
L-5	NEAR DUBLIN	CEDER	PATHE EXCHANGE	1924
L-6	AN EASTERN WESTERNER	ROACH	PATHE EXCHANGE	1920
L-6	FLIRT	GILBERT	PATHE EXCHANGE	1917
L-6	MUSIC BOX	PARROTT	MGM	1932
L-6	SMITHY	JESKE, ROACH	PATHE EXCHANGE	1924
L-7	ALL ABOARD	GOULDING	PATHE EXCHANGE	1917
L-7	CHIMP	PARROTT	MGM	1932
L-7	HIGH AND DIZZY	ROACH	PATHE EXCHANGE	1920
L-7	ZEB VS. PAPRIKA	CEDER	PATHE EXCHANGE	1924
L-8	COUNTY HOSPITAL	PARROTT	MGM	1932
L-8	GET OUT AND GET UNDER	ROACH	PATHE EXCHANGE	1920
L-8	MOVE ON	PRATT, GILBERT	PATHE EXCHANGE	1917
L-8	POSTAGE DUE	JESKE	PATHE EXCHANGE	1924
L-9	BASHFUL	GOULDING	PATHE EXCHANGE	1917
L-9	BROTHER UNDER THE CHIN	CEDER	PATHE EXCHANGE	1924
L-9	BURN!	PONTECORVO	UNITED ARTISTS	1970
L-9	NUMBER, PLEASE?	ROACH	PATHE EXCHANGE	1920
L-9	SCRAM!	MCCAREY	MGM	1932
L-10	NOW OR NEVER	ROACH	PATHE EXCHANGE	1921
L-10	THEIR FIRST MISTAKE	MARSHALL	MGM	1932
L-10	TIP	PRATT, GILBERT	PATHE EXCHANGE	1918
L-10	WIDE OPEN SPACES	JESKE	PATHE EXCHANGE	1924
L-11	AMONG THOSE PRESENT	NEWMEYER	PATHE EXCHANGE	1921
L-11	RUPERT OF HEE HAW	PEMBROKE	PATHE EXCHANGE	1924
L-11	SHOULD MARRIED MEN GO HOME?	MCCAREY, PARROTT	MGM	1928
L-11	STEP LIVELY	GOULDING	PATHE EXCHANGE	1917
L-11	TOWED IN A HOLE	MARSHALL	MGM	1932
L-12	BIG IDEA	MOHR, PRATT	PATHE EXCHANGE	1918
L-12	EARLY TO BED	FLYNN	MGM	1928
L-12	I DO	NEWMEYER	PATHE EXCHANGE	1921
L-12	SHORT KILTS	JESKE	PATHE EXCHANGE	1924
L-12	TWICE TWO	PARROTT	MGM	1933
L-13	HELLO TEACHER	ROACH	PATHE EXCHANGE	1918
L-13	ME AND MY PAL	ROGERS	MGM	1933
L-13	NEVER WEAKEN	NEWMEYER	PATHE EXCHANGE	1921
L-13	TWO TARS	PARROTT	MGM	1928
L-14	HABEAS CORPUS	PARROTT, MCCAREY	MGM	1928
L-14	LAMB (GOAT)	LLOYD, PRATT	PATHE EXCHANGE	1918
L-14	MIDNIGHT PATROL	FRENCH	MGM	1933

L-14	SAILOR-MADE MAN	NEWMEYER	PATHE EXCHANGE	1921
L-15	BUSY BODIES	FRENCH	MGM	1933
L-15	GRANDMA'S BOY	NEWMEYER	ASSOC. EXHIBITORS	1922
L-15	LET'S GO	GOULDING	PATHE EXCHANGE	1918
L-15	WE FAW DOWN	MCCAREY	MGM	1928
L-16	BEAT IT	PRATT	PATHE EXCHANGE	1918
L-16	DIRTY WORK	FRENCH	MGM	1933
L-16	DR. JACK	NEWMEYER	PATHE EXCHANGE	1922.
L-17	GASOLINE WEDDING	GOULDING	PATHE EXCHANGE	1918
L-17	OLIVER THE EIGHTH	FRENCH	MGM	1934
L-17	SAFETY LAST!	TAYLOR, NEWMEYER	PATHE EXCHANGE	1923
L-17	WHITE LIES	LESAINT	FOX FILM	1920
L-18	GOING BYE-BYE!	ROGERS	MGM	1934
L-18	HIT HIM AGAIN	PRATT	PATHE EXCHANGE	1918
L18	MOTHER OF HIS CHILDREN	LESAINT	FOX FILM	1920
L-19	BIG BUSINESS	HORNE, MCCAREY	MGM	1929
L-19	LOOK PLEASANT, PLEASE	GOULDING	PATHE EXCHANGE	1918
L-19	THEM THAR HILLS	ROGERS	MGM	1934
L-20	HERE COME THE GIRLS	HIBBARD	PATHE EXCHANGE	1918
L-20	LIVE GHOST	ROGERS	MGM	1934
L-21	BACON GRABBERS	FOSTER	MGM	1929
L-21	ON THE JUMP	GOULDING	PATHE EXCHANGE	1918
L-21	TIT FOR TAT	ROGERS	MGM	1935
L-22	ANGORA LOVE	FOSTER	MGM	1929
L-22	FIXER-UPPERS	ROGERS	MGM	1935
L-22	HEY THERE!	GOULDING	PATHE EXCHANGE	1918
L-23	KICKED OUT	GOULDING	PATHE EXCHANGE	1918
L-23	THICKER THAN WATER	HORNE	MGM	1935
L-23	UNACCUSTOMED AS WE ARE	FOSTER, ROACH	MGM	1929
L-24	BERTH MARKS	FOSTER	MGM	1929
L-24	NON STOP KID	PRATT	PATHE EXCHANGE	1918
L-25	FOLLOW THE CROWD	GOULDING	PATHE EXCHANGE	1918
L-25	MEN O' WAR	FOSTER	MGM	1929
L-26	IT'S A WILD LIFE	PRATT	PATHE EXCHANGE	1918
L-26	PERFECT DAY	PARROTT	MGM	1929
L-27	PIPE THE WHISKERS	GOULDING	PATHE EXCHANGE	1918
L-27	THEY GO BOOM	PARROTT	MGM	1929
L-28	HOOSE-GOW	PARROTT	MGM	1929
L-28	SIC 'EM TOWSER	PRATT	PATHE EXCHANGE	1918
L-29	NIGHT OWLS	PARROTT	MGM	1930
L-29	TWO GUN GUSSIE	GOULDING	PATHE EXCHANGE	1918
L-30	BLOTTO	PARROTT	MGM	1930
L-30	LOVE'S YOUNG SCREAM	JEFFERSON	PATHE EXCHANGE	1919
L-31	BRATS	PARROTT	MGM	1930
L-31	FIREMAN SAVE MY CHILD	GOULDING	PATHE EXCHANGE	1918
L-32	BELOW ZERO	PARROTT	MGM	1930
L-32	CITY SLICKER	PRATT	PATHE EXCHANGE	1918
L-33	HOG WILD	PARROTT	MGM	1930
L-33	SOMEWHERE IN TURKEY	GOULDING	PATHE EXCHANGE	1918
L-34	ARE CROOKS DISHONEST	PRATT	PATHE EXCHANGE	1918
L-34	LAUREL-HARDY MURDER CASE	PARROTT	MGM	1930
L-35	OZARK ROMANCE	GOULDING	PATHE EXCHANGE	1918
L-35	PARDON US	PARROTT	MGM	1931
L-36	ANOTHER FINE MESS	PARROTT	MGM	1930
L-36	THAT'S HIM	PRATT	PATHE EXCHANGE	1918
L-37	BE BIG!	HORNE, PARROTT	MGM	1931
L-37	BRIDE AND GLOOM	GOULDING	PATHE EXCHANGE	1918
L-38	CHICKENS COME HOME	HORNE	MGM	1931
L-38	TWO SCRAMBLED	PRATT	PATHE EXCHANGE	1918
L-39	KICKING THE GERM OUT OF GERMANY	GOULDING	PATHE EXCHANGE	1918
L-39	LAUGHING GRAVY	HORNE	MGM	1931
L-40	BEES IN HIS BONNET	PRATT	PATHE EXCHANGE	1918
L-40	OUR WIFE	HORNE	MGM	1931
L-41	SWING YOUR PARTNERS	GOULDING	PATHE EXCHANGE	1918
L-42	HEAR 'EM RAVE	PRATT	PATHE EXCHANGE	1918
L-43	NOTHING BUT TROUBLE	ROACH	PATHE EXCHANGE	1918

L-44	WHY PICK ON ME?	ROACH	PATHE EXCHANGE	1918
L-45	TAKE A CHANCE	GOULDING	PATHE EXCHANGE	1918
L-46	GOING! GOING! GONE!	PRATT	PATHE EXCHANGE	1919
L-47	SHE LOVES ME NOT	ROACH	PATHE EXCHANGE	1918
L-48	WANTED $5000	PRATT	PATHE EXCHANGE	1919
L-49	I'M ON MY WAY	ROACH	PATHE EXCHANGE	1919
L-50	ASK FATHER	ROACH	PATHE EXCHANGE	1919
L-51	ON THE FIRE	ROACH	PATHE EXCHANGE	1919
L-52	LOOK OUT BELOW!	ROACH	PATHE EXCHANGE	1919
L-53	DUTIFUL DUB	GOULDING	PATHE EXCHANGE	1919
L-54	NEXT AISLE OVER	ROACH	PATHE EXCHANGE	1919
L-55	RING UP THE CURTAIN	GOULDING	PATHE EXCHANGE	1919
L-56	JUST DROPPED IN	ROACH	PATHE EXCHANGE	1919
L-57	CRACK YOUR HEELS	GOULDING	PATHE EXCHANGE	1919
L-58	YOUNG MR. JAZZ	ROACH	PATHE EXCHANGE	1919
L-59	SI, SENOR	GOULDING	PATHE EXCHANGE	1919
L-60	BEFORWE BREAKFAST	ROACH	PATHE EXCHANGE	1919
L-61	MARATHON	GOULDING	PATHE EXCHANGE	1919
L-62	BACK TO THE WOODS	ROACH	PATHE EXCHANGE	1919
L-63	PISTOLS FOR BREAKFAST	GOULDING	PATHE EXCHANGE	1919
L-64	SWAT THE CROOK	ROACH	PATHE EXCHANGE	1919
L-65	OFF THE TROLLEY	GOULDING	PATHE EXCHANGE	1919
L-66	AT THE OLD STAGE DOOR	ROACH	PATHE EXCHANGE	1919
L-67	JAZZED HONEYMOON	ROACH	PATHE EXCHANGE	1919
L-68	NEVER TOUCHED ME	GOULDING	PATHE EXCHANGE	1919
L-69	BILL BLAZES, ESQ.	ROACH	PATHE EXCHANGE	1919
L-70	COUNT YOUR CHANGE	GOULDING	PATHE EXCHANGE	1919
L-71	CHOP SUEY AND COMPANY	ROACH	PATHE EXCHANGE	1919
L-72	HEAP BIG CHIEF	GOULDING	PATHE EXCHANGE	1919
L-73	SAMMY IN SIBERIA	ROACH	PATHE EXCHANGE	1919
L-74	DON'T SHOVE	GOULDING	PATHE EXCHANGE	1919
L-75	BE MY WIFE	ROACH	PATHE EXCHANGE	1919
L-76	RAJAH	ROACH	PATHE EXCHANGE	1919
L-77	HE LEADS, OTHERS FOLLOW	ROACH	PATHE EXCHANGE	1919
L-78	SOFT MONEY	ROACH	PATHE EXCHANGE	1919
L-79	COUNT THE VOTES	ROACH	PATHE EXCHANGE	1919
L-80	PAY YOUR DUES	ROACH	PATHE EXCHANGE	1919
L-81	HIS ONLY FATHER	ROACH	PATHE EXCHANGE	1919
L-82	SPRING FEVER	ROACH	PATHE EXCHANGE	1919
L-83	JUST NEIGHBORS	LLOYD, TERRY	PATHE EXCHANGE	1919
L242	OLD WIVES FOR NEW	DEMILLE	PARAMOUNT	1918
L243	MISSING	YOUNG	PARAMOUNT	1918
L244	BRAVEST WAY	MELFORD	PARAMOUNT	1918
L245	HOW COULD YOU, JEAN?	TAYLOR	PARAMOUNT	1918
L246	CITY OF DIM FACES	MELFORD	PARAMOUNT	1918
L247	FIREFLY OF FRANCE	CRISP	PARAMOUNT	1918
L248	UNDER THE TOP	CRISP	PARAMOUNT	1919
L249	LESS THAN KIN	CRISP	PARAMOUNT	1918
L250	SOURCE	MELFORD	PARAMOUNT	1918
L251	CAPTAIN KIDD, JR.	TAYLOR	PARAMOUNT	1919
L252	WE CAN'T HAVE EVERYTHING	DEMILLE	PARAMOUNT	1918
L253	WOMAN'S WEAPONS	VIGNOLA	PARAMOUNT	1918
L254	GIRL WHO CAME BACK	VIGNOLA	PARAMOUNT	1918
L255	JOHANNA ENLISTS	TAYLOR	PARAMOUNT	1918
L256	SUCH A-LITTLE PIRATE	MELFORD	PARAMOUNT	1918
L258	TILL I COME BACK TO YOU	DEMILLE	PARAMOUNT	1918
L259	MYSTERY GIRL	DE MILLE	PARAMOUNT	1918
L260	JOHNNY GET YOUR GUN	CRISP	PARAMOUNT	1919
L261	CRUISE OF THE MAKE BELIEVES	MELFORD	PARAMOUNT	1918
L262	TOO MANY MILLIONS	CRUZE	PARAMOUNT	1918
L263	GOAT	CRISP	PARAMOUNT	1918
L264	SQUAW MAN	DEMILLE	PARAMOUNT	1918
L265	JANE GOES A-WOOING	MELFORD	PARAMOUNT	1919
L267	WAY OF A-MAN WITH A-MAID	CRISP	PARAMOUNT	1919
L268	IT PAYS TO ADVERTISE	CRISP	PARAMOUNT	1919
L269	MAGGIE PEPPER	WITHEY	PARAMOUNT	1919

L270	DUB	CRUZE	PARAMOUNT	1919
L271	PUPPY LOVE	NEILL	PARAMOUNT	1919
L272	ALIAS MIKE MORAN	CRUZE	PARAMOUNT	1919
L273	DON'T CHANGE YOUR HUSBAND	DEMILLE	PARAMOUNT	1919
L274	WOMAN NEXT DOOR (VICKEY VAN*)	VIGNOLA	PARAMOUNT	1919
L276	PRIVATE PETTIGREW'S GIRL		PARAMOUNT	1919
L277	POOR BOOB	CRISP	PARAMOUNT	1919
L278	WINNING GIRL	VIGNOLA	PARAMOUNT	1919
L279	FIRES OF FAITH	JOSE	PARAMOUNT	1919
L280	ROARING ROAD	CRUZE	PARAMOUNT	1919
L281	SOMETHING TO DO	CRISP	PARAMOUNT	1919
L286	FOR BETTER, FOR WORSE	DEMILLE	PARAMOUNT	1919
L287	PUTTING IT OVER	CRISP	PARAMOUNT	1919
L288	RUSTLING A-BRIDE	WILLAT	PARAMOUNT	1919
L289	VALLEY OF THE GIANTS	CRUZE	PARAMOUNT	1919
L290	SPORTING CHANCE	MELFORD	PARAMOUNT	1919
L291	MALE AND FEMALE	DEMILLE	PARAMOUNT	1919
L292	SECRET SERVICE	FORD	PARAMOUNT	1919
L293	DAUGHTER OF THE WOLF	WILLAT	PARAMOUNT	1919
L294	VERY GOOD YOUNG MAN	CRISP	PARAMOUNT	1919
L295	YOU'RE FIRED	CRUZE	PARAMOUNT	1919
L296	PEG O' MY HEART	DE MILLE	PARAMOUNT	1919
L297	TOLD IN THE HILLS	MELFORD	PARAMOUNT	1919
L298	GRIM GAME	WILLAT	PARAMOUNT	1919
L299	LOVE INSURANCE	CRISP	PARAMOUNT	1919
L300	LOVE BURGLAR	CRUZE	PARAMOUNT	1919
L301	ROSE OF THE RIVER	THORNBY	PARAMOUNT	1919
L302	LOTTERY MAN	CRUZE	PARAMOUNT	1919
L303	WHY SMITH LEFT HOME	CRISP	PARAMOUNT	1919
L304	IN MIZZOURA	FORD	PARAMOUNT	1919
L305	TREE OF KNOWLEDGE	DE MILLE	PARAMOUNT	1920
L306	EVERYWOMAN	MELFORD	PARAMOUNT	1919
L307	ADVENTURE IN HEARTS	CRUZE	PARAMOUNT	1919
L308	HEART OF YOUTH	VIGNOLA	PARAMOUNT	1919
L309	IT PAYS TO ADVERTISE	CRISP	PARAMOUNT	1919
L310	HAWTHORNE OF USA	CRUZE	PARAMOUNT	1919
L311	WHY CHANGE YOUR WIFE?	DEMILLE	PARAMOUNT	1920
L313	PHIL BROOKS ALASKAN EXPEDITION		PARAMOUNT	1920
L314	SEA WOLF	MELFORD	PARAMOUNT	1920
L315	DOUBLE SPEED	WOOD	PARAMOUNT	1920
L316	TOO MUCH JOHNSON	CRISP	PARAMOUNT	1920
L317	JACK STRAW	DE MILLE	PARAMOUNT	1920
L318	TERROR ISLAND	CRUZE	PARAMOUNT	1920
L319	EXCUSE MY DUST	WOOD	PARAMOUNT	1920
L320	SIX BEST CELLARS	CRISP	PARAMOUNT	1920
L321	YOUNG MRS. WINTHROP	EDWARDS	PARAMOUNT	1920
L322	THOU ART THE MAN	HEFFRON	PARAMOUNT	1920
L323	ROUND UP	MELFORD	PARAMOUNT	1920
L324	DANCIN' FOOL	WOOD	PARAMOUNT	1920
L326	FIGHTING CHANCE	MAIGNE	PARAMOUNT	1920
L327	PRINCE CHAP	DE MILLE	PARAMOUNT	1920
L328	SOMETHING TO THINK ABOUT	DEMILLE	PARAMOUNT	1920
L329	MRS. TEMPLE'S TELEGRAM	CRUZE	PARAMOUNT	1920
L330	LADY IN LOVE	EDWARDS	PARAMOUNT	1920
L331	HELD BY THE ENEMY	CRISP	PARAMOUNT	1920
L332	SICK ABED	WOOD	PARAMOUNT	1920
L333	CITY OF MASKS	HEFFRON	PARAMOUNT	1920
L334	LADDER OF LIES	FORMAN	PARAMOUNT	1920
L335	WHAT'S YOUR HURRY?	WOOD	PARAMOUNT	1920
L336	FOURTEENTH MAN	HENABERY	PARAMOUNT	1920
L337	CUMBERLAND ROMANCE	MAIGNE	PARAMOUNT	1920
L339	CROOKED STREETS	POWELL	PARAMOUNT	1920
L340	SOUL OF YOUTH	TAYLOR	PARAMOUNT	1920
L341	CONRAD IN QUEST OF HIS YOUTH	DE MILLE	PARAMOUNT	1920
L342	LIFE OF THE PARTY	HENABERY	PARAMOUNT	1920
L343	CITY SPARROW	WOOD	PARAMOUNT	1920

L344	CONSPIRACY OF HEARTS (UK)	THOMAS	PARAMOUNT	1960
L345	SINS OF ROSANNE	FORMAN	PARAMOUNT	1920
L346	FURNACE	TAYLOR	PARAMOUNT	1920
L347	JUCKLINS	MELFORD	PARAMOUNT	1920
L349	CHARM SCHOOL	CRUZE	PARAMOUNT	1921
L350	TRAVELING SALESMAN	HENABERY	PARAMOUNT	1921
L351	MIDSUMMER MADNESS	DE MILLE	PARAMOUNT	1920
L352	FORBIDDEN FRUIT	DEMILLE	PARAMOUNT	1921
L353	EYES OF THE HEART (REALART)	POWELL	PARAMOUNT	1920
L354	ALWAYS AUDACIOUS	CRUZE	PARAMOUNT	1920
L355	BREWSTER'S MILLIONS	HENABERY	PARAMOUNT	1921
L356	WITCHING HOUR	TAYLOR	PARAMOUNT	1921
L357	EASY ROAD	FORMAN	PARAMOUNT	1921
L357	TESTING BLOCK	HILLYER	PARAMOUNT	1920
L358	FAITH HEALER	MELFORD	PARAMOUNT	1921
L359	ALL SOULS EVE	FRANKLIN	PARAMOUNT	1921
L360	BAIT	TOURNEUR	PARAMOUNT	1921
L361	WHAT EVERY WOMAN KNOWS	DE MILLE	PARAMOUNT	1921
L362	WHAT DO MEN WANT?	WEBER	PARAMOUNT	1921
L363	DOLLAR A-YEAR MAN	CRUZE	PARAMOUNT	1921
L364	LITTLE CLOWN	HEFFRON	PARAMOUNT	1921
L365	LOVE SPECIAL	URSON	PARAMOUNT	1921
L366	WEALTH	TAYLOR	PARAMOUNT	1921
L368	SACRED AND PROFANE LOVE	TAYLOR, NEWMEYER	PARAMOUNT	1921
L370	LOST ROMANCE	DE MILLE	PARAMOUNT	1921
L372	CRAZY TO MARRY	CRUZE	PARAMOUNT	1921
L375	TOO MUCH SPEED	URSON	PARAMOUNT	1921
L376	GREAT MOMENT	WOOD	PARAMOUNT	1921
L377	GOLEM	BOESE, WEGENER	PARAMOUNT	1921
L378	GASOLINE GUS	CRUZE	PARAMOUNT	1921
L379	MOONLIGHT AND HONEYSUCKLE	HENABERY	PARAMOUNT	1921
L380	AT THE END OF THE WORLD	STANLAWS	PARAMOUNT	1921
L381	BEYOND	TAYLOR	PARAMOUNT	1921
L382	GREAT IMPERSONATION	MELFORD	PARAMOUNT	1921
L384	FOOLS PARADISE	DEMILLE	PARAMOUNT	1921
L385	GREAT IMPERSONATION	MELFORD	PARAMOUNT	1921
L386	EVERYTHING FOR SALE	O'CONNOR	PARAMOUNT	1921
LA	DEAF SMITH & JOHNNY EARS (IT: LOS AMIGOS)	CAVARA	MGM	1973
LA	IT LIVES AGAIN (IT'S ALIVE 2)	COHEN	WARNER BROS	1978
LA	KAY LINAKER	portrait	WARNER BROS	
LA	L. A. CONFIDENTIAL	HANSON	WARNER BROS	1997
LA	LA NOTTE (IT/FR: 1961)	ANTONIONI	LOPERT	1962
LA	LAWRENCE OF ARABIA (UK)	LEAN	COLUMBIA	1962
LA	LITTLE ANGEL		K. GORDON MURRAY	1961
LA	LONG AGO TOMORROW	FORBES	CINEMA 5	1971
LA	LOST ANGELS	HUDSON	ORION	1989
LA	LOVE AFFAIR	CARON	WARNER BROS	1994
LA	LOVE IN THE AFTERNOON	WILDER	ALLIED ARTISTS	1957
LA	LYONS ABROAD (UK: LYONS IN PARIS)	GUEST	EXCLUSIVE	1955
LA	TO LIVE AND DIE IN L.A.	FRIEDKIN	20TH CENTURY FOX	1985
LAD	LAWRENCE OF ARABIA (UK)	LEAN	COLUMBIA	1962
LADY	LADY & THE TRAMP (t)	GERONIMI	DISNEY	1955
LADY-NY	LADY & THE TRAMP (t)	GERONIMI	DISNEY	R62
LAL	LAWRENCE OF ARABIA (UK)	LEAN	COLUMBIA	1962
LAW	MILDRED LAW	portrait	WARNER BROS.	
LB	LA BALANCE	SWAIM	INT'L SPECTRAFILM	1983
LB	LEADBELLY	PARKS	PARAMOUNT	1975
LB	LOST BOUNDARIES	WERKER	FILM CLASSICS	1949
L-BAL	LITTLE BALLERINA (UK)	GILBERT	UNIVERSAL	1948
LBC	LEGEND OF BOGGY CREEK	PIERCE	HOWCO	1972
LBG	LINDA BE GOOD	MCDONALD	EAGLE LION	1948
LBH	LITTLE BIG HORN	WARREN	LIPPERT	1951
LBJ	LEGEND OF BILLIE JEAN	ROBBINS	TRI STAR	1985
LBS	LAST BOY SCOUT	SCOTT	GEFFEN	1991
LC	JOY HOUSE (FR: LES FELINS)	CLEMENS	MGM	1964
LC	LAST CONTINENT (UK)	CARRERAS	20TH CENTURY FOX	1968

LC	LINDA CRISTAL	portrait		
LC	LOST CONTINENT	NEWFIELD	LIPPERT	1951
LC	LOUISE CAMPBELL	portrait	RKO	
LC	LOVE IN THE CITY (IT: L'AMORE IN CITTA)	ANTONIONI, FELLINI	IFE	1953
LC	LA CAGE AUX FOLLES 3 (FR)	LAUTNER	TRI STAR	1985
LC-89	NOON WHISTLE	JESKE	PATHE EXCHANGE	1923
LC-91	WHITE WINGS	JESKE	PATHE EXCHANGE	1923
LC-92	PICK AND SHOVEL	JESKE	PATHE EXCHANGE	1923
LC-95	KILL OR CURE	PEMBROKE	PATHE EXCHANGE	1923
LC-97	COLLARS AND CUFFS	JESKE	PATHE EXCHANGE	1923
LC-99	GAS AND AIR	PEMBROKE	PATHE EXCHANGE	1923
LC-102	ORANGES AND LEMONS	JESKE	PATHE EXCHANGE	1923
LC-104	SHORT ORDERS	PEMBROKE	PATHE EXCHANGE	1923
LC-106	SAVE THE SHIP	JESKE, ROACH	PATHE EXCHANGE	1923
LC-112	SCORCHING SANDS	WILLIAMSON, ROACH	PATHE EXCHANGE	1923
LC-115	WHOLE TRUTH	CEDER	PATHE EXCHANGE	1923
LCD	LLOYD OF THE C.I.D. (UK) (serial)	MACRAE, TAYLOR	UNIVERSAL	1932
LCE	LADIES CRAVE EXCITEMENT	GRINDE	MASCOT	1935
LC-K	LOVING COUPLE	SMIGHT	20TH CENTURY FOX	1980
LCL	LADY CHATTERLEYS LOVER (FR: L'AMANT DI LADY CHATTERLEY)	ALLEGRET	KINGSLEY-INT'L	1955
LCT	LAW COMES TO TEXAS (1939)	LEVERING	ASTOR	R48
LD	DAVID AND LISA	PERRY	CONTINENTAL DIST.	1962
LD	LAST DRAGON	SCHULTZ	TRI STAR	1985
LD	LIFE IN DANGER (UK)	BISHOP	ALLIED ARTISTS	1964
LD	LIGHT OF DAY	SCHRADER	TRI STAR	1987
LD	LINDA DARNELL	portrait	RKO	
LD	LITTLE DARLINGS	MAXWELL	PARAMOUNT	1980
LD	LITTLE DORRIT	EDZARD	CANNON	1988
LD	LIVING DESERT	ALGAR	BUENA VISTA	1953
LD	LONG DAY'S DYING (UK)	COLLINSON	PARAMOUNT	1968
LD	LONG DUEL (UK)	ANNAKIN	PARAMOUNT	1967
LD	TRUTH ABOUT MURDER	LANDERS	RKO	1946
LDBB	LAST DANCE	BERESFORD	TOUCHSTONE	1996
L.D-COL-S-1	SHADOW (serial)	HORNE	COLUMBIA	1940
L.D-COL-S-2	TERRY AND THE PIRATES (serial)	HORNE	COLUMBIA	1940
L.D-COL-S-3	DEADWOOD DICK (serial)	HORNE	COLUMBIA	1940
L.D-COL-S-4	GREEN ARCHER (serial)	HORNE	COLUMBIA	1940
L.D-COL-S-5	WHITE EAGLE (serial)	HORNE	COLUMBIA	1941
L.D-COL-S-6	SPIDER RETURNS (serial)	HORNE	COLUMBIA	1941
L.D-COL-S-8	HOLT OF THE SECRET SERVICE (serial)	HORNE	COLUMBIA	1941
L.D-COL-S-10	PERILS OF THE ROYAL MOUNTED (serial)	HORNE	COLUMBIA	1942
L.D-COL-S-11	SECRET CODE (serial)	BENNET	COLUMBIA	1942
L.D-COL-S-13	BATMAN (serial)	HILLYER	COLUMBIA	1943
LDIA	LET'S DO IT AGAIN	POITIER	WARNER BROS	1975
LDV	LA DOLCE VITA (IT)	FELLINI	ASTOR	1960
LDW	LAST DAY OF THE WAR	BARDEM	MGM	1970
LE	LOVE IN EXILE (UK)	WERKER	CAPITOL-GFD	1936
LED	LEGEND OF EARL DURAND	PATTERSON	HOWCO	1974
LED	LORD EDGWARE DIES (UK)	EDWARDS	RKO	1934
LEHR-6	HOMESICK	LEHRMAN	FOX FILM	1928
LEOP	LEOPARD (IT: IL GATTOPARDO)	VISCONTI	TITANUS	1963
LEPKE	LEPKE	GOLAN	WARNER BROS	1974
LEW	LIGHT AT THE EDGE OF THE WORLD	BILLINGTON	MGM	1971
LF	EARTH DIES SCREAMING (UK)	FISHER	20TH CENTURY FOX	1964
LF	LADY FRANKENSTEIN	WELLES	NEW WORLD PICTURES	1972
LF	LESLIE FENTON	portrait		
LF	LIFEFORCE (SPACE VAMPIRES)	HOOPER	TRI STAR	1985
LF	LITTLE FUGITIVE	ASHLEY/ENGEL	BURNSTYN	1953
LF	LORD OF THE FLIES (UK)	BROOK	CONTINENTAL	1963
LF	LOST AND FOUND	FRANK	COLUMBIA	1979
LF	LOVING FEELING (UK)	WARREN	U-M	1968
LF	PLAYMATES	DAGUE	VIP DISTRIBUTORS	1968
LF	SCOTLAND YARD INSPECTOR (UK: LADY IN THE FOG)	NEWFIELD	LIPPERT	1952
LFBB	LADDER 49	RUSSELL	BUENA VISTA	2004
LFD	OVER THE MOON (UK)	FREELAND	UNITED ARTISTS	1939
LFLS	LIKE FATHER LIKE SON	DANIEL	TRI STAR	1987

LFP-8	ELEPHANT BOY (UK)	FLAHERTY, KORDA	UNITED ARTISTS	1937
LFP-20	I, CLAUDIUS (UK) (unfinished)	VON STERNBERG		1937
LFP-21	MEN ARE NOT GODS	REISCH	UNITED ARTISTS (UK)	1936
LFP-33	REBEL SON aka TARAS BULBA (FR/UK)	BRUNEL, DE COURVILLE		1938
LFP-102	ANNA KARENINA (UK)	DUVIVIER	20TH CENTURY FOX	1948
LFP-105	ANGEL WITH THE TRUMPET (UK)	BUSHELL	SNADER	1950
LFP-106	DEEP BLUE SEA (UK)	LITVAK	20TH CENTURY FOX	1955
LFP-106	IF THIS BE SIN (UK: THAT DANGEROUS AGE)	RATOFF	UNITED ARTISTS	1949
LFP-107	SMILEY (UK 1956)	KIMMINS	20th CENTURY FOX	1957
LG	LOVE GODDESSES: HISTORY OF SEX IN CINEMA	TURELL	PARAMOUNT	1965
LG	LITTLE GIANTS	DUNHAM	WARNER BROS	1994
LG-30	LOVE'S YOUNG SCREAM	JEFFERSON	PATHE EXCHANGE	1919
LGF	LONG GOOD FRIDAY	MCKENZIE	EMBASSY	1982
LGH	LET'S GET HARRY	ROSENBERG (SMITHEE)	TRI STAR	1986
LG/T/15	LEAGUE OF GENTLEMEN (UK)	DEARDEN	KINGSLEY-INT'L	1960
LGW	LOOKING GLASS WAR (UK)	PIERSON	COLUMBIA	1969
LH	BIG FRAME (UK: LOST HOURS)	MACDONALD	RKO	1952
LH	LAURENCE HARVEY	portrait	HAL WALLIS PRODS	
LH	LIBERTY HEIGHTS	LEVINSON	WARNER BROS	1999
LH	LLOYD HUGHES	portrait	FN	
LH	LOUISA HORTON	portrait		
LH	LOUISIANA HUSSY	SHOLEM	HOWCO	1959
LH	LOYAL HEART (UK)	MITCHELL	ANGLO-AMERICAN	1946
LHL	LOVERS, HAPPY LOVERS! (UK: LOVER BOY) (KNAVE OF HEARTS)	CLEMENT	AFE	1954
LI	LIVING IDOL	CARDONA	MGM	1957
LIB	LET IT BE (UK)	LINDSAY-HOGG	UNITED ARTISTS	1970
LIB-A	EX-FLAME	HALPERIN	LIBERTY	1930
LIM	LAND OF MINOTAUR	KARAGIANNUS	CROWN INTL	1977
LIM	SOCIAL HIGHWAYMAN	BEAUDINE	WARNER BROS	1926
LIO	RUSSIAN STORY, THE	FREEDLAND	ARKINO PICTURES	1943
LIP3	BOTH SIDES OF THE LAW (UK: STREET CORNER)	BOX	UNIVERSAL	1953
LIQ	LIQUIDATOR (UK)	CARDIFF	MGM	1965
LIR	LET IT RIDE	PYTKA	PARAMOUNT	1989
LIW	LADY IN WHITE	LALOGGIA	NEW CENTURY VISTA	1988
LJ	LORD JIM (UK)	BROOKS	COLUMBIA	1965
LJ	LUCKY JIM (UK)	BOULTING	KINGSLEY INTL	1957
LK	LORRAINE KRUEGER	portrait		
LK	LOUISE KING (KING SISTERS)	portrait	UNIV	
LK	LUCKY LADY	DONEN	20th CENTURY FOX	1975
LL	BASTARD (TV)	KATZIN	UNIVERSAL-TV	1978
LL	FAMILY AFFAIR (UK: LIFE WITH THE LYONS)	GUEST	LIPPERT	1954
LL	LADY L	USTINOV	MGM	1965
LL	LADY OF THE LAKE (UK 1928)	FITZPATRICK	FITZPATRICK PICTURES	1930
LL	LANCASHITE LUCK (UK)	CASS	PARAMOUNT BRITISH	1937
LL	LATE LIZ	ROSS	DICK ROSS & ASSOC.	1971
LL	LAUGHING LADY (UK)	STEIN	FOUR CONTINENTS	1946
LL	LAURA LA PLANTE	portrait		
LL	LESSON IN LOVE (SWE: EN LEKTION IN KARLEK)	BERGMAN	JANUS	1954
LL	LIFE WITH THE LYONS (UK) (FAMILY AFFAIR 1955)	GUEST	LIPPERT	1954
LL	LILA LEEDS	portrait		
LL	LITTLE MISS THOROUGHBRED	FARROW	WARNER BROS	1938
LL	LOLA LANE	portrait	TIFFANY, WARNER BROS	
LL	LONELINESS OF THE LONG DISTANCE RUNNER (UK)	RICHARDSON	CONTINENTAL	1962
LL	LOVE LINES	AMATEAU	TRI STAR	1984
LL	LUCKY LUCIANO	ROSI	AVCO EMBASSY	1973
LL	LUCKY LUKE (t) (FR: LA BALLADE LES DALTON)	GOSCINNY, GRUEL	DISNEY	1978
LL	PRIVATE AFFAIRS OF BEL AMI (WOMEN OF PARIS R1953)	LEWIN	UNITED ARTISTS	1947
LL	VOICE OF SCANDAL (HERE COMES CARTER)	CLEMENS	FIRST NATIONAL	1936
LLD	DANGEROUS LIAISONS	FREARS	WARNER BROS	1988
LLE	LADIES CRAVE EXCITEMENT	GRINDE	MASCOT	1935
LLL	LOVE, LIFE & LAUGHTER (UK)	ELVEY	ABFD	1934
LLOYD-1015	LITTLE GIRL OF THE ATTIC	LLOYD	UNIVERSAL	1915
LM	CAPTIVE HEART (UK)	DEARDEN	UNIVERSAL	1946
LM	DON'T GO NEAR THE WATER	WALTERS	MGM	1957
LM	GIRL IN THE STREET (UK: LONDON MELODY)	WILCOX	GAUMONT BRIT. AMER.	1937
LM	GOING TO BLAZES (doc-sh)	FRITSCH	MGM	1948

LM	KING SOLOMON'S MINES	BENNETT, MARTON	MGM	1950
LM	LADY OF MONZA, THE (IT: LA MONACA DI MONZA 1969)	VISCONTI	TOWER PROD.	1970
LM	LAST OF THE MOHICANS	MANN	20th CENTURY FOX	1992
LM	LEAN ON ME	ALVIDSEN	WARNER BROS	1989
LM	LIMPING MAN (UK)	SUMMERS	PATHE	1936
LM	LIMPING MAN (UK)	ENDFIELD	LIPPERT	1953
LM	LINDA MARSH	portrait	WARNER BROS	
LM	LISA MONTELL	portrait	BOGEAS-RKO	
LM	LITTLE MEN	ROSEN	MASCOT	1934
LM	LITTLE MURDERS	ARKIN	20th CENTURY FOX	1971
LM	UP GOES MAISIE	BEAUMONT	MGM	1946
LM	WEDDING OF LILLI MARLENE (UK)	CRABTREE	MONARCH	1953
LM228	JOHN HODIAK	portrait	MGM	
LM1046	ANN SOTHERN	portrait	MGM	
LM-1699	RICHARD CARLSON	portrait	MGM	
LM2573	JUNE ALLYSON	portrait	MGM	
LM2797	MAY WHITTY	portrait	MGM	
LM3057	FRANK MORGAN	portrait	MGM	
LM4831	WALTER PIDGEON	portrait	MGM	
LM8471	VAN JOHNSON	portrait	MGM	
LM8587	ELIZABETH TAYLOR	portrait	MGM	
LM8879	RICARDO MONTALBAN	portrait	MGM	
LM9407	JUNE ALLYSON	portrait	MGM	
LM10314	MICKEY ROONEY	portrait	MGM	
LM14363	JOHN HODIAK	portrait	MGM	
LM16391	NANCY DAVIS/REAGAN	portrait	MGM	
LM16511	ARLENE DAHL	portrait	MGM	
LM16512	ARLENE DAHL	portrait	MGM	
LM16695	KATHRYN GRAYSON	portrait	MGM	
LM16965	HOWARD KEEL	portrait	MGM	
LM16966	HOWARD KEEL	portrait	MGM	
LM16967	HOWARD KEEL	portrait	MGM	
LM17140	ELIZABETH TAYLOR	portrait	MGM	
LM17141	ELIZABETH TAYLOR	portrait	MGM	
LM17159	ELIZABETH TAYLOR	portrait	MGM	
LM17671	JUNE ALLYSON	portrait	MGM	
LM17672	JUNE ALLYSON	portrait	MGM	
LM18045	STEWART GRANGER	portrait	MGM	
LM18582	ANN HARDING	portrait	MGM	
LM18658	PIER ANGELI	portrait	MGM	
LM18693	PIER ANGELI	portrait	MGM	
LM18694	PIER ANGELI	portrait	MGM	
LM18696	PIER ANGELI	portrait	MGM	
LM18698	PIER ANGELI	portrait	MGM	
LM18815	MONICA LEWIS	portrait	MGM	
LM19341	DEBBIE REYNOLDS	portrait	MGM	
LM19471	ELIZABETH TAYLOR	portrait	MGM	
LM19622	LANA TURNER	portrait	MGM	
LM19627	ESTHER WILLIAMS	portrait	MGM	
LM19635	KEENAN WYNN	portrait	MGM	
LM19671	LANA TURNER	portrait	MGM	
LM19783	VAN JOHNSON	portrait	MGM	
LM19933	AVA GARDNER	portrait	MGM	
LM20060	LANA TURNER	portrait	MGM	
LM20168	AVA GARDNER	portrait	MGM	
LM20193	DIANA LYNN	portrait	MGM	
LM20363	GENE KELLY	portrait	MGM	
LM20385	FERNANDO LAMAS	portrait	MGM	
LM20567	JANET LEIGH	portrait	MGM	
LM20589	LESLIE CARON	portrait	MGM	
LM22051	DEBBIE REYNOLDS	portrait	MGM	
LM22674	JANET LEIGH	portrait	MGM	
LM22954	FERNANDO LAMAS	portrait	MGM	
LM25102	ESTHER WILLIAMS	portrait	MGM	
LM25300	JEAN HAGEN	portrait	MGM	
LM25302	JEAN HAGEN	portrait	MGM	

LM25312	ESTHER WILLIAMS	portrait	MGM	
LM25770	DAWN ADDAMS	portrait	MGM	
LM25771	DAWN ADDAMS	portrait	MGM	
LM25912	LESLIE CARON	portrait	MGM	
LM26230	ESTHER WILLIAMS	portrait	MGM	
LM26519	LESLIE CARON - LILI	portrait	MGM	
LM26691	JEAN SIMMONS	portrait	MGM	
LM26731	ESTHER WILLIAMS	portrait	MGM	
LM27226	GRACE KELLY	portrait	MGM	
LM27387	ROBERT TAYLOR	portrait	MGM	
LM27392	ROBERT TAYLOR	portrait	MGM	
LM27394	ROBERT TAYLOR	portrait	MGM	
LM27644	GENE TIERNEY	portrait	MGM	
LM27645	ELAINE STEWART	portrait	MGM	
LM28052	DEBBIE REYNOLDS	portrait	MGM	
LM28247	LESLIE CARON - LILI	portrait	MGM	
LM28882	ELAINE STEWART	portrait	MGM	
LM28888	ELAINE STEWART	portrait	MGM	
LM28893	ELAINE STEWART	portrait	MGM	
LM28955	LESLIE CARON	portrait	MGM	
LM29246	LESLIE CARON	portrait	MGM	
LM29421	ANN BLYTH	portrait	MGM	
LM30162	ESTHER WILLIAMS	portrait	MGM	
LM30198	JEAN SIMMONS	portrait	MGM	
LM30382	ELAINE STEWART	portrait	MGM	
LM30410	ELAINE STEWART	portrait	MGM	
LM31865	GENE KELLY	portrait	MGM	
LM32080	TRAILER FOR LONG, LONG TRAILER	portrait	MGM	1954
LM32680	JANE POWELL	portrait	MGM	
LM32816	ELEANOR PARKER	portrait	MGM	
LM33056	GENE KELLY	portrait	MGM	
LM33068	GREER GARSON, DONNA CORCORAN, CLAIRE SOMBERT	portrait	MGM	
LM33689	ELAINE STEWART	portrait	MGM	
LM33743	DONNA REED	portrait	MGM	
LM34442	ROBERT TAYLOR	portrait	MGM	
LM34526	ELAINE STEWART	portrait	MGM	
LM35636	JANE POWELL	portrait	MGM	
LM35952	ANNE FRANCIS	portrait	MGM	
LM35956	ANNE FRANCIS	portrait	MGM	
LM36084	WALTER PIDGEON	portrait	MGM	
LM36087	WALTER PIDGEON	portrait	MGM	
LM36097	WALTER PIDGEON	portrait	MGM	
LM36098	WALTER PIDGEON	portrait	MGM	
LM36818	JANE POWELL	portrait	MGM	
LM37456	CYD CHARISSE	portrait	MGM	
LM37467	LAUREN BACALL	portrait	MGM	
LM37601	LANA TURNER	portrait	MGM	
LM38043	LANA TURNER	portrait	MGM	
LM38061	DARLEEN ENGLE	portrait	MGM	
LM41177	CYD CHARISSE	portrait	MGM	
LM41323	RUBY DEE	portrait	MGM	
LM41543	GRACE KELLY	portrait	MGM	
LM42367	MITZI GAYNOR	portrait	MGM	
LM43154	JEAN SIMMONS	portrait	MGM	
LM43155	JEAN SIMMONS	portrait	MGM	
LM43938	ELIZABETH TAYLOR	portrait	MGM	
LM43979	JEAN SIMMONS	portrait	MGM	
LM44028	SANDRA DEE	portrait	MGM	
LM44035	SANDRA DEE	portrait	MGM	
LM44145	JULIE LONDON	portrait	MGM	
LM44530	LESLIE CARON - GIGI	portrait	MGM	
LM46226	WRECK OF THE MARY DEARE	portrait	MGM	
LM47361	ELIZABETH TAYLOR	portrait	MGM	
LMBB	LITTLE MERMAID	CLEMENTS	BUENA VISTA	1989
LMBB	LIZZIE MCGUIRE MOVIE	FALL	BUENA VISTA	2003
LMC	PARIS PICK-UP (FR: LE MONTE CHARGE 1962)	BLUWAL	PARAMOUNT	1963

LMT	LITTLE MAN TATE	FOSTER	ORION	1991
LN	LOVER'S NET* (FR) (LOVERS OF LISBON) (PORT OF SHAME)	VERNEUIL	TIMES FILM	1955
LNB	LIFE AND NOTHING BUT (FR)	TAVERNIER	ORION	1990
LNPL	LIVE NOW, PAY LATER (UK)	LEWIS	REGAL	1962
LOC	GREAT LOCOMOTIVE CHASE, THE	LYON	BUENA VISTA	1956
LOD	LAST OF THE DESPERADOS	NEWFIELD	ASSOCIATED FILM	1956
LOD	LAUGH IT OFF (UK)	BAXTER, ORTON	ANGLO-AMERICAN	1940
LOD	LOVE ON THE DOLE (UK)	BAXTER	UNITED ARTISTS	1941
LOD	SAVE A LITTLE SUNSHINE (UK)	LEE	PATHE	1938
LOF	LEAP OF FAITH	PEARCE	PARAMOUNT	1992
LOG	LOVE ON THE GROUND	RIVETTE	INT'L SPECTRAFILM	1984
LOR	SIGN OF THE GLADIATOR (IT)	BRIGNONE	AIP	1959
LP	AMAZING PANDA ADVENTURE, THE	CAIN	WARNER BROS	1995
LP	I DREAM TOO MUCH	CROMWELL	RKO	1935
LP	LA POUPEE (FR: 1962)	BARATIER	GASTON HAKIM INT'L	1964
LP	LARRY PARKS		COL	
LP	LAST PAGE/US: MAN BAIT (UK)	FISHER	LIPPERT	1952
LP	LAURA LA PLANTE	portrait	UNIV	
LP	LEE PATRICK	portrait	RKO	
LP	LILO PULVER	portrait	UNIV	
LP	LINDA PERRY	portrait	WARNER BROS	
LP	LOVE POTION #9	LAUNER	20th CENTURY FOX	1992
LP	LUANA PATTEN	portrait	UNIV	
LQ	LICKERISH QUARTET	METZGER	AUDUBON FILMS	1971
LR	LA RONDE	OPHUL	JANUS	1950
LR	LAST RITES	BELLISARIO	MGM	1988
LR	LAST RUN	FLEISCHER	MGM	1972
LR	LITTLE ROMANCE	HILL	WARNER BROS	1979
LR	LONG RIDE (BRADY'S ESCAPE)	GABOR	SONAR ENTERTAINMENT	1983
LR	ROOKIE, THE	O'HANLON	20th CENTURY FOX	1959
LRRH	LITTLE RED RIDING HOOD	RODRIGUEZ	J. GORDON MURRAY	1963
LS	LA STRADA	FELLINI	TRANS-LUX	1956
LS	LADY SURRENDERS (UK: LOVE STORY)	ARLISS	UNIVERSAL	1944
LS	LANE WATSON	portrait		
LS	LIFE STINKS	BROOKS	MGM	1991
LS	LISBON STORY (UK)	STEIN	FOUR CONTINENTS	1946
LS	LITTLE SAVAGE	HASKIN	20th CENTURY FOX	1959
LS	LITTLE SHEPHERD OF KINGDOM COME	MCLAGLEN	20th CENTURY FOX	1961
LS	LOAN SHARK	FRIEDMAN	LIPPERT	1952
LS	LONG SHOT, THE (TARGET OF AN ASSASSINATION)	COLLINSON	PRO INT'L	1978
LS	LOST IN THE STARS	WEILL	AMERICAN FILM	1973
LS	LOVE STREAMS	CASSAVETTES	CANNON	1983
LS	LOVES OF SALAMMBO	GRIECO	20th CENTURY FOX	1962
LS	LURE OF THE SWAMP	CORNFIELD	20th CENTURY FOX	1957
LS	TEMPTRESS (UK)	MITCHELL	AMBASSADOR	1949
LS20	SISTER TO SALOME	LESAINT	FOX FILM	1920
LSH	LITTLE SHOP OF HORRORS	OZ	GEFFEN	1986
LSP	LONE STAR PIONEERS	LEVERING	ASTOR	R48
LSYH	LAST SHOT YOU HEAR (UK)	HESSLER	20TH CENTURY FOX	1969
LT	LIFE AT THE TOP (UK)	KOTCHEFF	ROYAL	1965
LT	LITTLE TREASURE	SHARP	TRI STAR	1985
LT	LOST ONE (LA SIGNORA DALLE CAMELIE - 1947)	GALLONE	COLUMBIA	1948
LT	LOVE TEST (UK)	POWELL	FOX	1935
LT	LOVERS OF TERUEL	POWELL	CONTINENTAL DIST.	1962
LTA	LOSER TAKES ALL (UK)	ANNAKIN	DCA	1956
LTT	LULU THE TOOL (IT: LA CLASSE OPERAIA VA IN PARADISO 1971)	PETRI	NEW LINE CINEMA	1975
LU	LAUGHTER IN THE DARK (UK)	RICHARDSON	LOPERT	1969
LU	LUTHER	GREEN	AMERICAN FILM	1975
LUP	LUPO (ISRAEL 1970)	GOLAN	CANNON	1971
LUPO	LUPO (ISRAEL 1970)	GOLAN	CANNON	1971
LV	LEVIATHAN	COSMATOS	MGM	1989
LV	LIVING VENUS	LEWIS	MID-CONTINENT	1961
LV	LUTHER	GREEN	AMERICAN EXPRESS	1975
LV-36	LUTHER	GREEN	AMERICAN EXPRESS	1975
LVBY	LOVERBOY	SILVER	TRI STAR	1989
LVH	LAS VEGAS HILLBILLYS	PIERCE	WOOLNER BROTHERS	1966

LW	LAUGHING WOMAN (IT)	SCHIVAZAPPA	AUDUBON	1969
LW	LETHAL WEAPON	DONNOR	WARNER BROS	1987
LW	LONE WOLF MCQUADE	CARVER	ORION	1983
LW2	LETHAL WEAPON 2	DONNOR	WARNER BROS	1989
LW3	LETHAL WEAPON 3	DONNOR	WARNER BROS	1992
LW4	LETHAL WEAPON 4	DONNOR	WARNER BROS	1998
LWBB	LIFE WITH MIKEY	LAPINE	BUENA VISTA	1993
LWD	LADIES WHO DO (UK)	PENNINGTON-RICHARDS	CONTINENTAL	1963
LWFC	LIKE WATER FOR CHOCOLATE (MEX: COMO AGUA CHOCOLATE)	ARAU	MIRAMAX	1992
LWG	LUDWIG (IT)	VISCONTI	MGM	1972
LWH	LAST OF THE WILD HORSES	LIPPERT	SCREEN GUILD	1948
LXB	LORRAINE BRIDGES	portrait	MGM	
LY	LONGEST YARD	ALDRICH	PARAMOUNT	1974
LY	LORETTA YOUNG	portrait	COL, UNIVERSAL, WB	
LY	LOYALTIES (UK)	DEAN, DICKINSON	HAROLD AUTEN	1933
LYS	LYA LYS	portrait	WARNER BROS	
M	CANDLES AT NINE (UK)	HARLOW	ANGLO-AMERICAN	1944
M	GAMBLER AND THE LADY (UK)	JENKINS	LIPPERT	1952
M	MAFIA (TERROR OF SICILY)		PIC FILMS	
M	MAGIC	ATTENBOROUGH	20th CENTURY FOX	1978
M	MANIA (UK: FLESH AND THE FIENDS)	GILLING	VALIANT	1960
M	MARIE	DONALDSON	MGM/UA	1985
M	MASSACRE	KING	20th CENTURY FOX	1956
M	MATEWAN	SAYLES	CINECOM	1987
M	MATRIMONIAL BED	CURTIZ	WARNER BROS.	1930
M	MAURICE	IVORY	CINECOM	1987
M	MAVERICK	DONNER	WARNER BROS	1994
M	MAYERLING (UK)	YOUNG	MGM	1968
M	MCGUIRE, GO HOME! (UK: HIGH BRIGHT SUN)	THOMAS	CONTINENTAL	1964
M	MEMOIRS OF AN INVISIBLE MAN	CARPENTER	WARNER BROS	1992
M	METEOR MAN	TOWNSEND	MGM	1993
M	MIKADO (UK)	SCHERTZINGER	UNIVERSAL	1939
M	MILLENNIUM	ANDERSON	20th CENTURY FOX	1989
M	MIRACLE ON 34TH STREET	MAYFIELD	UNITED ARTISTS	1994
M	MISSION, THE	JOFFE	WARNER BROS	1986
M	MOONSTRUCK	JEWISON	MGM	1987
M	MORALS OF MARCUS (UK)	MANDER	GAUMONT BRITISH	1935
M	MOZAMBIQUE (UK)	LYNN	SEVEN ARTS	1965
M	MURIEL OR TIME OF RETURN (FR: MURIEL TEMPS D'UN RETOUR)	RESNAIS	LOPERT	1963
M	OF MICE AND MEN	SINISE	MGM	1992
M	ROADHOUSE GIRL (UK: MARILYN)	RILLA	ASTOR	1955
M-1	DESERT'S TOLL	SMITH	MGM	1926
M-1	ONE AT A TIME	CEDER	PATHE EXCHANGE	1924
M-1	RHAPSODY IN BREW	GILBERT	MGM	1934
M-2	KEG O' MY HEART	GILBERT	MGM	1933
M2	MANNEQUIN TWO: ON THE MOVE	RAFFILL	20th CENTURY FOX	1991
M-2	VALLEY OF HELL	SMITH	MGM	1927
M-3	MUSIC IN YOUR HAIR	CHASE	MGM	1934
M-4	APPLES TO YOU!	JASON	MGM	1934
M-5	ROAMIN' VANDALS	JASON, YATES	MGM	1934
M-6	DUKE FOR A DAY	PARROTT	MGM	1934
M-7	BENNY, FROM PANAMA	PARROTT	MGM	1934
M13	WHEN FATE DECIDES	MILLARDE	FOX FILM	1919
M-102	ANATOMY OF A MURDER	PREMINGER	COLUMBIA	1959
MA	MAIN ATTRACTION (UK)	PETRIE	MGM	1962
MA	MAKE MINE MINK (UK)	ASHER	CONTINENTAL	1960
MA	MALONE	COKLISS	ORION	1987
MA	MANNEQUIN	GOTTLEIB	20th CENTURY FOX	1987
MA	MARS ATTACKS!	BURTON	WARNER BROS	1996
MA	MAURIE	DANIEL MANN	NATIONAL GENERAL	1973
MA	MINI-MOB (UK: MINI AFFAIR)	AMRAM	UNITED SCREEN ARTS	1967
MA	MORNING AFTER, THE	LUMET	20th CENTURY FOX	1986
MA	MORO AFFAIR (IT: IL CASO MORO 1986)	FERRARA	ORION	1987
MA	WINDJAMMER; VOYAGE OF THE CHRISTIAN RADICH (doc)	DE ROCHEMONT III	NATIONAL THEATERS	1958
MA	MAMBO	ROSSEN	PARAMOUNT	1954
MAC6	TOP OF NEW YORK	TAYLOR	PARAMOUNT	1922

MAG	MAGUS (UK)	GREEN	20TH CENTURY FOX	1968
MAK	MIDDLE AGE CRAZY	TRENT	20th CENTURY FOX	1980
MAM	GHOST OF ST. MICHAEL'S (UK)	VARNEL	ABFD	1941
MAN	MANIFESTO	MAKAVEJEY	CANNON	1988
MAR	WILLIAM MARSHALL	portrait	WARNER BROS	
MAS-4	SHADOW OF THE EAGLE (serial)	BEEBE	MASCOT	1932
MAS-5	LAST OF THE MOHICANS (serial)	BEEBE, EASON	MASCOT	1932
MAS-6	HURRICANE EXPRESS (serial)	MCGOWAN, SCHAEFER	MASCOT	1932
MAS-8	DEVIL HORSE (serial)	BROWER	MASCOT	1932
MAS-9	WHISPERING SHADOW (serial)	CLARK, HERMAN	MASCOT	1933
MAS-10	3 MUSKETEERS (serial) (DESERT COMMAND 1949)	CLARK/SCHAEFER	MASCOT	1933
MAS-11	FIGHTING WITH KIT CARSON (RETURN OF KIT CARSON 1947)	CLARK/SCHAEFER	MASCOT	1933
MAS-13	LOST JUNGLE (serial)	HOWARD, SCHAEFER	MASCOT	1934
MAS-18	PHANTOM EMPIRE/G. AUTRY AND PHANTOM EMPIRE (serial)	BROWER, EASON	MASCOT	1935
MAW	MEN AT WORK	ESTEVEZ	TRIUMPH	1990
MAY	MAYERLING (UK)	YOUNG	MGM	1968
MB	M. BUTTERFLY	CRONENBERG	GEFFEN	1993
MB	MADAME BUTTERFLY	GALLONE	I.F.E.	1956
MB	MAGIC BOW (UK)	KNOWLES	UNIVERSAL	1947
MB	MAJOR BARBARA (UK)	PASCAL	UNITED ARTISTS	1941
MB	MALIBU BEACH	ROSENTHAL	CROWN INT'L	1978
MB	MAN AND BOY aka RIDE A DARK HORSE	SWACKHAMER	LEVITT-PICKMAN	1971
MB	MAN WITH BOGART'S FACE	DAY	20th CENTURY FOX	1980
MB	MEATBALLS	REITMAN	PARAMOUNT	1979
MB	MEMPHIS BELLE	CATON-JONES	WARNER BROS	1990
MB	MOTHER'S BOY	BARKER	PATHE	1929
MB	MRS. BROWN, YOU'VE GOT A LOVELY DAUGHTER (UK)	SWIMMER	MGM	1968
MB	MY BODYGUARD	BILL	20TH CENTURY FOX	1980
MB-2	MEATBALLS 2	WIEDERHORN	TRI STAR	1984
MB-81	MAD MONSTER	NEWFIELD	PRODUCERS RELEASING	1942
MBB	MY BABY IS BLACK (FR: LES LACHES VIVENT D'ESPOIR 1961)	BERNARD-AUBERT	AMERICAN FILM	1965
MBH	MAGIC BOY (JP)	DAIKUHARA	MGM	1961
MBH	MY BLUE HEAVEN	ROSS	WARNER BROS	1990
MBS	MONSTER FROM THE OCEAN FLOOR	ORDUNG	LIPPERT	1954
MBV	MY BLOODY VALENTINE	MIHALKA	PARAMOUNT	1981
MBW	MILLER'S BEAUTIFUL WIFE (LA BELLA MUGNAIA - IT)	CAMERINI	DISTRIBUTORS CORP	1955
MC	MAD CITY	GAVRAS	WARNER BROS	1997
MC	MADY CHRISTIANS	portrait	MGM	
MC	MAGIC CHRISTIAN (UK)	MCGRATH	COMMONWEALTH UNI.	1969
MC	MAIN CHANCE (UK)	KNIGHT	ANGLO-AMALGAMATED	1964
MC	MAN WHO LIVED AGAIN (UK: MAN WHO CHANGED HIS MIND)	STEVENSON	GAUMONT	1936
MC	MARINES ARE COMING	HOWARD	MASCOT	1934
MC	MATING CALL	CRUZE	PARAMOUNT	1928
MC	MIDNIGHT CROSSING	HOLZBERG	VESTRON	1988
MC	MILLER'S CROSSING	COEN BROS	20th CENTURY FOX	1990
MC	MIRROR CRACK'D	HAMILTON	ASSOCIATED FILM DIST.	1980
MC	MURDER IN THE CATHEDRAL (UK)	HOELLERING	CLASSIC	1951
MC	PRISONER OF CORBAL (UK: MARRIAGE OF CORBAL)	GRUNE	GFD	1936
MC	SECRET OF MONTE CRISTO (UK: TREASURE OF MONTE CRISTO)	BAKER, BERMAN	MGM	1961
MC	SLASHER (UK: COSH BOY)	GILBERT	LIPPERT	1953
MC2	MANIA (UK: FLESH AND THE FIENDS)	GILLING	VALIANT	1960
MC-108	SIEGE OF SIDNEY STREET (UK)	BAKER, BERMAN	UNITED PRODUCERS REL.	1960
MC 3400	GREEN PROMISE	RUSSELL	RKO	1949
MCA	MAN CALLED ADAM	PENN	EMBASSY	1966
MCE	MANIAC (UK)	CARRERAS	COLUMBIA	1963
M.CH.	MARGUERITE CHAPMAN	portrait	WARNER BROS	
MCP	ROARING SIX GUNS	MCGOWEN	CONN PICT (states rights)	1937
MCR	THOSE DARING YOUNG MEN IN THEIR JAUNTING JALOPIES (UK)	ANNAKIN	PARAMOUNT	1969
MCS	MAN CALLED SARGE	GILLARD	CANNON	1990
MCT	MARSEILLES CONTRACT (FR/UK: DESTRUCTORS)	PARRISH	WARNER BROS	1974
MCV	MY COUSIN VINNY	LYNN	20TH CENTURY FOX	1992
MCW	MAN WHO COULDN'T WALK (UK)	CASS	FALCON	1961
MCW	MONTE CARLO BABY (FR: NOUS IRONS A MONTE CARLO 1951)	BOYER	FILMMAKERS RELEASING	1953
MD	HEAVEN, HELL OR HOBOKEN (UK: I WAS MONTY'S DOUBLE)	GUILLERMIN	NTA	1958
MD	MAN CALLED DAGGER	RUSH	MGM	1968
MD	MARKED FOR DEATH	LITTLE	20TH CENTURY FOX	1990

MD	MARTIN'S DAY	GIBSON	MGM/UNITED ARTISTS	1985
MD	MAX DUGAN RETURNS	ROSS	20th CENTURY FOX	1983
MD	MOMMIE DEAREST	PERRY	PARAMOUNT	1981
MD	MRS. DOUBTFIRE	COLUMBUS	20th CENTURY FOX	1993
MD	MURDER BY DEATH	MOORE	COLUMBIA	1976
MD	MURDER BY DECREE	CLARK	AVCO EMBASSY	1979
MD	MURDER CAN BE DEADLY (UK: PAINTED SMILE)	COMFORT	COLORAMA	1962
MD	MYSTERY DATE	WACKS	ORION	1991
MD	PATIENT VANISHES (UK)	HUNTINGTON	FILM CLASSICS	1941
MD	RACE FOR LIFE (UK: MASK OF DUST)	FISHER	LIPPERT	1954
MD	MRS. DOUBTFIRE	COLUMBUS	20th CENTURY FOX	1993
MD-47	MYSTERY DATE	WACKS	ORION	1991
MDBB	MR. DESTINY	ORR	BUENA VISTA	1990
MDG	MAMA'S DIRTY GIRLS	HAYES	PREMIERE RELEASING	1974
MDL	MEN DON'T LEAVE	BRICKMAN	GEFFEN	1989
MDM	MOST DANGEROUS MAN ALIVE	DWAN	COLUMBIA	1961
MDR	MILLION DOLLAR RACKET	HILL	VICTORY (states rights)	1937
MDV	MEN IN THE WHITE VESTS (AUSTRIA)	STAUDTE	MGM	1970
MDXX	MARY DORAN	portrait	MGM	
ME	MAIN EVENT	ZIEFF	WARNER BROS	1979
ME	MAN ESCAPED, A	BRESSON	CONTINENTAL	1956
ME	METEOR	NEAME	AIP	1979
ME-146	METEOR	NEAME	AIP	1979
MF	AMOROUS ADVENTURES OF MOLL FLANDERS (UK)	YOUNG	PARAMOUNT	1965
MF	BEYOND THE CURTAIN (UK)	BENNETT	RANK	1960
MF	MAN FRIDAY	GOLD	AVCO EMBASSY	1975
MF	MAN OF FLOWERS	COX	INT'L SPECTRAFILM	1984
MF	MAN ON FIRE	CHOURAQUI	TRI STAR	1987
MF	MASCULINE-FEMININE	GODARD	ROYAL FILMS INT'L	1966
MF	MIKE FRANKOVICH/FRANKOVITCH		COL	
MF	MULHOLLAND FALLS	TAMAHORI	MGM	1996
MF	MURDER IN THE FIRST	ROCCO	WARNER BROS	1994
MF	MY FELLOW AMERICANS	SEGAL	WARNER BROS	1996
MF1	TWIST OF FATE (FR/UK: BEAUTIFUL STRANGER)	MILLER	UNITED ARTISTS	1954
MF-3	JAMAICA INN (UK)	HITCHCOCK	PARAMOUNT	1939
MFE	MAN WHO FELL TO EARTH	ROEG	CINEMA 5	1976
MFM	MAID FOR MURDER (UK: SHE'LL HAVE TO GO)	ASHER	JANUS	1962
MFM	MAN FROM MOROCCO (UK)	GREENBAUM	ENGLISH	1945
MG	BEAU HUNKS	HORNE	MGM	1931
MG	MAGIC HOUR (TWILIGHT)		PARAMOUNT	1997
MG	MIDNIGHT IN THE GARDEN OF GOOD AND EVIL	EASTWOOD	WARNER BROS	1997
MG	MINNA GOMBELL	portrait	RKO	
MG	MURDER GAME	SALKOW	20TH CENTURY FOX	1965
MG14	GRETA GARBO	portrait	MGM	
MG15	GRETA GARBO	portrait	MGM	
MG23	GRETA GARBO	portrait	MGM	
MG25	GRETA GARBO	portrait	MGM	
MG34	GRETA GARBO	portrait	MGM	
MG972	JOAN CRAWFORD	portrait	MGM	
MG976	JOAN CRAWFORD	portrait	MGM	
MG1040	GRETA GARBO	portrait	MGM	
MG1226	GRETA GARBO	portrait	MGM	
MG1306	ANITA PAGE	portrait	MGM	
MG1323	GRETA GARBO	portrait	MGM	
MG1328	GRETA GARBO	portrait	MGM	
MG1331	GRETA GARBO	portrait	MGM	
MG1336	GRETA GARBO	portrait	MGM	
MG1337	GRETA GARBO	portrait	MGM	
MG1758	GRETA GARBO	portrait	MGM	
MG1895	JACK CONWAY	portrait	MGM	
MG2073	JOAN CRAWFORD	portrait	MGM	
MG2240	BUSTER KEATON	portrait	MGM	
MG2259	RENEE ADOREE	portrait	MGM	
MG2404	BASIL RATHBONE	portrait	MGM	
MG2436	BASIL RATHBONE	portrait	MGM	
MG2444	BASIL RATHBONE	portrait	MGM	

MG2716	MARIE DRESSLER, POLLY MORAN	portrait	MGM	
MG3257	JOAN CRAWFORD	portrait	MGM	
MG3316	JOAN CRAWFORD	portrait	MGM	
MG3332	JOAN CRAWFORD	portrait	MGM	
MG3333	RAMON NOVARRO	portrait	MGM	
MG3500	NORMA SHEARER	portrait	MGM	
MG3722	LILIAN ROTH	portrait	MGM	
MG4146	SALLY EILERS	portrait	MGM	
MG4251	JOAN CRAWFORD	portrait	MGM	
MG4299	LIONEL BARRYMORE	portrait	MGM	
MG4471	SALLY EILERS	portrait	MGM	
MG4559	REGINALD DENNY	portrait	MGM	
MG4793	NORMA SHEARER	portrait	MGM	
MG5046	GRETA GARBO	portrait	MGM	
MG5102	GRETA GARBO	portrait	MGM	
MG5107	GRETA GARBO	portrait	MGM	
MG5202	GRETA GARBO	portrait	MGM	
MG5211	GRETA GARBO	portrait	MGM	
MG5238	GRETA GARBO	portrait	MGM	
MG5249	GRETA GARBO	portrait	MGM	
MG5337	GRETA GARBO	portrait	MGM	
MG5351	ANITA PAGE & MOTHER	portrait	MGM	
MG5361	GRETA GARBO	portrait	MGM	
MG5380	GAVIN GORDON	portrait	MGM	
MG5578	MARY PICKFORD	portrait	MGM	
MG5609	LILA LEE	portrait	MGM	
MG5617	JOAN CRAWFORD	portrait	MGM	
MG6224	ROBERT MONTGOMERY	portrait	MGM	
MG6354	ANITA PAGE + HER FATHER	portrait	MGM	
MG6374	RAMON NOVARRO	portrait	MGM	
MG6454	GRETA GARBO	portrait	MGM	
MG6476	ROBERT MONTGOMERY	portrait	MGM	
MG6847	JOAN CRAWFORD/XAVIER CUGAT	portrait	MGM	
MG7564	FIFI DORSAY	portrait	MGM	
MG7825	LUPE VELEZ	portrait	MGM	
MG7835X	GRETA GARBO	portrait	MGM	
MG7838X	GRETA GARBO	portrait	MGM	
MG7841X	GRETA GARBO	portrait	MGM	
MG7943	MARIE DRESSLER	portrait	MGM	
MG8153	JOAN CRAWFORD	portrait	MGM	
MG8555	WILLIAM BAKEWELL	portrait	MGM	
MG9124	JOAN CRAWFORD	portrait	MGM	
MG9143	JOAN CRAWFORD	portrait	MGM	
MG9436	KAY FRANCIS	portrait	MGM	
MG9492	WALLACE BEERY	portrait	MGM	
MG9592	POLLY MORAN	portrait	MGM	
MG9685	JOAN CRAWFORD	portrait	MGM	
MG9771	WALLACE BEERY	portrait	MGM	
MG9795	MARIE PREVOST	portrait	MGM	
MG9795	MARIE PREVOST	portrait	MGM	
MG9848	MARIE PREVOST	portrait	MGM	
MG10137	HEDDA HOPPER	portrait	MGM	
MG10257	MARJORIE RAMBEAU	portrait	MGM	
MG10632	CONSTANCE BENNETT	portrait	MGM	
MG10634	JOAN CRAWFORD, LESTER VAIL - DANCE FOOLS DANCE	portrait	MGM	
MG10657	BUSTER KEATON, WIFE NATALIE TALMADGE, SONS	portrait	MGM	
MG10848	BUSTER KEATON - SPITE MARRIAGE	portrait	MGM	
MG10938	JOAN CRAWFORD	portrait	MGM	
MG10946	JOAN CRAWFORD	portrait	MGM	
MG10952	JOAN CRAWFORD	portrait	MGM	
MG10957	BUSTER KEATON	portrait	MGM	
MG11201	JOAN CRAWFORD	portrait	MGM	
MG11269	JOAN CRAWFORD	portrait	MGM	
MG11271	JOAN CRAWFORD	portrait	MGM	
MG11283	NORMA SHEARER	portrait	MGM	
MG11418	GRETA GARBO	portrait	MGM	

MG11442	GRETA GARBO	portrait	MGM	
MG11443	GRETA GARBO	portrait	MGM	
MG11448	GRETA GARBO	portrait	MGM	
MG11449	GRETA GARBO	portrait	MGM	
MG11452	GRETA GARBO	portrait	MGM	
MG11453	GRETA GARBO	portrait	MGM	
MG11462	BUSTER KEATON	portrait	MGM	
MG11488	GRETA GARBO	portrait	MGM	
MG11578	JEAN HARLOWE	portrait	MGM	
MG11592	JOAN CRAWFORD	portrait	MGM	
MG11844	GRETA GARBO	portrait	MGM	
MG11890	MARY DUNCAN	portrait	MGM	
MG12384	ANITA PAGE	portrait	MGM	
MG12592	LEILA HYAMS	portrait	MGM	
MG12603	LILIAN BOND	portrait	MGM	
MG12785	HELEN CHANDLER	portrait	MGM	
MG12865	CLARK GABLE, JEAN HARLOW, W. BEERY, M. CARLISLE	portrait	MGM	
MG12964	JOAN CRAWFORD	portrait	MGM	
MG13025	JOAN CRAWFORD	portrait	MGM	
MG13145	NORMA SHEARER	portrait	MGM	
MG13152	NORMA SHEARER	portrait	MGM	
MG13169	NORMA SHEARER	portrait	MGM	
MG13173	NORMA SHEARER	portrait	MGM	
MG13174	NORMA SHEARER	portrait	MGM	
MG13311	ANITA PAGE	portrait	MGM	
MG13541	GRETA GARBO	portrait	MGM	
MG13547	GRETA GARBO	portrait	MGM	
MG13802	JOAN CRAWFORD	portrait	MGM	
MG13895	JOAN CRAWFORD	portrait	MGM	
MG13900	JOAN CRAWFORD	portrait	MGM	
MG13924	JOAN CRAWFORD	portrait	MGM	
MG14100	WARNER BAXTER	portrait	MGM	
MG14264	NORMA SHEARER	portrait	MGM	
MG14477	GRETA GARBO	portrait	MGM	
MG14571	WALLACE BEERY	portrait	MGM	
MG14643	LUPE VELEZ	portrait	MGM	
MG14694	LUPE VELEZ	portrait	MGM	
MG14784	CLARK GABLE	portrait	MGM	
MG15237	ROBERT MONTGOMERY	portrait	MGM	
MG15242	EDWINA BOOTH	portrait	MGM	
MG15437	IRENE DUNN	portrait	MGM	
MG15623	JANET CURRIE	portrait	MGM	
MG16529	JACKIE COOPER	portrait	MGM	
MG16538	JACKIE COOPER	portrait	MGM	
MG16555	JOAN CRAWFORD	portrait	MGM	
MG16585	GRETA GARBO	portrait	MGM	
MG16586	GRETA GARBO	portrait	MGM	
MG16610	GRETA GARBO	portrait	MGM	
MG16612	GRETA GARBO	portrait	MGM	
MG16613	GRETA GARBO	portrait	MGM	
MG16614	GRETA GARBO	portrait	MGM	
MG16617	GRETA GARBO	portrait	MGM	
MG16619	GRETA GARBO	portrait	MGM	
MG16621	GRETA GARBO	portrait	MGM	
MG16625	GRETA GARBO	portrait	MGM	
MG16628	GRETA GARBO	portrait	MGM	
MG16629	GRETA GARBO	portrait	MGM	
MG16939	WALLACE BEERY VISITING SET OF FLYING HIGH	portrait	MGM	
MG17057	KAREN MORLEY	portrait	MGM	
MG17342	ANITA PAGE	portrait	MGM	
MG17367	CLARK GABLE	portrait	MGM	
MG17479	ANITA PAGE	portrait	MGM	
MG17804	JOAN CRAWFORD	portrait	MGM	
MG17906	BUSTER KEATON	portrait	MGM	
MG18049	BUSTER KEATON	portrait	MGM	
MG18139	JOAN CRAWFORD	portrait	MGM	

MG18474	JOAN CRAWFORD	portrait	MGM	
MG18700	JOHN BARRYMORE, LIONEL BARRYMORE	portrait	MGM	
MG19015	JOAN MARSH	portrait	MGM	
MG19069	NORMA SHEARER	portrait	MGM	
MG19138	CLARK GABLE	portrait	MGM	
MG19156	ANITA PAGE	portrait	MGM	
MG19182	JOAN CRAWFORD	portrait	MGM	
MG19355	JOAN CRAWFORD	portrait	MGM	
MG19386	GRETA GARBO	portrait	MGM	
MG19387	GRETA GARBO	portrait	MGM	
MG19388	GRETA GARBO	portrait	MGM	
MG19389	GRETA GARBO	portrait	MGM	
MG19390	GRETA GARBO	portrait	MGM	
MG19391	GRETA GARBO	portrait	MGM	
MG19392	GRETA GARBO	portrait	MGM	
MG19393	GRETA GARBO	portrait	MGM	
MG19394	GRETA GARBO	portrait	MGM	
MG19395	GRETA GARBO	portrait	MGM	
MG19396	GRETA GARBO	portrait	MGM	
MG19397	GRETA GARBO	portrait	MGM	
MG19399	GRETA GARBO	portrait	MGM	
MG19404	GRETA GARBO	portrait	MGM	
MG19422	GRETA GARBO	portrait	MGM	
MG19576	GRETA GARBO	portrait	MGM	
MG19579	GRETA GARBO	portrait	MGM	
MG19583	GRETA GARBO	portrait	MGM	
MG19635	JOHNNY WEISSMULLER	portrait	MGM	
MG19673	ANITA PAGE	portrait	MGM	
MG19716	NORMA SHEARER	portrait	MGM	
MG20016	JOAN CRAWFORD	portrait	MGM	
MG20059	WALLACE BEERY	portrait	MGM	
MG20060	JACKIE COOPER	portrait	MGM	
MG20177	JOAN CRAWFORD	portrait	MGM	
MG20286	JOAN CRAWFORD	portrait	MGM	
MG20329	JOAN CRAWFORD	portrait	MGM	
MG20378	JOAN CRAWFORD	portrait	MGM	
MG20381	JOAN CRAWFORD	portrait	MGM	
MG20645	JOAN CRAWFORD	portrait	MGM	
MG20653	WALLACE BEERY	portrait	MGM	
MG20740	JOAN CRAWFORD	portrait	MGM	
MG20810	JOHN BARRYMORE	portrait	MGM	
MG20812	JOAN CRAWFORD	portrait	MGM	
MG20814	JOAN CRAWFORD	portrait	MGM	
MG20972	MARY CARLISLE	portrait	MGM	
MG21026	JOAN CRAWFORD	portrait	MGM	
MG21038	MYRNA LOY	portrait	MGM	
MG21073	LIONEL BARRYMORE	portrait	MGM	
MG21083	DOROTHY JORDAN	portrait	MGM	
MG21085	MAUREEN O'SULLIVAN	portrait	MGM	
MG21118	ANITA PAGE	portrait	MGM	
MG21359	NORMA SHEARER	portrait	MGM	
MG21371	JACKIE COOPER	portrait	MGM	
MG21640	WALTER HUSTON - NIGHT COURT	portrait	MGM	
MG21672	LAUREL & HARDY, BUSTER KEATON, JIMMY DURANTE	portrait	MGM	
MG21805	ANITA PAGE	portrait	MGM	
MG22021	MAUREEN O'SULLIVAN	portrait	MGM	
MG22038	ANITA PAGE	portrait	MGM	
MG22143	NORMA SHEARER	portrait	MGM	
MG22160	NORMA SHEARER	portrait	MGM	
MG22161	NORMA SHEARER	portrait	MGM	
MG22240	JOAN CRAWFORD	portrait	MGM	
MG22242	JOAN CRAWFORD	portrait	MGM	
MG22247	JOAN CRAWFORD	portrait	MGM	
MG22249	JOAN CRAWFORD	portrait	MGM	
MG22350	DICKIE MOORE	portrait	MGM	
MG22369	MAUREEN O'SULLIVAN	portrait	MGM	

MG22371	MAUREEN O'SULLIVAN	portrait	MGM	
MG22372	MAUREEN O'SULLIVAN	portrait	MGM	
MG22375	MAUREEN O'SULLIVAN	portrait	MGM	
MG22376	MAUREEN O'SULLIVAN	portrait	MGM	
MG22383	JACKIE COOPER	portrait	MGM	
MG22387	JACKIE COOPER	portrait	MGM	
MG22434	JOAN CRAWFORD	portrait	MGM	
MG22481	JACKIE COOPER	portrait	MGM	
MG22518	MAUREEN O'SULLIVAN	portrait	MGM	
MG22519	MAUREEN O'SULLIVAN	portrait	MGM	
MG22520	MAUREEN O'SULLIVAN	portrait	MGM	
MG22524	JACKIE COOPER	portrait	MGM	
MG22724	GRETA GARBO	portrait	MGM	
MG22725	GRETA GARBO	portrait	MGM	
MG22748	UNA MERKEL	portrait	MGM	
MG22759	JOAN CRAWFORD	portrait	MGM	
MG22760	JOAN CRAWFORD	portrait	MGM	
MG22822	GRETA GARBO	portrait	MGM	
MG22839	GRETA GARBO	portrait	MGM	
MG22843	GRETA GARBO	portrait	MGM	
MG22850	GRETA GARBO	portrait	MGM	
MG22851	GRETA GARBO	portrait	MGM	
MG22861	GRETA GARBO	portrait	MGM	
MG22935	ROBERT YOUNG, KAREN MORLEY	portrait	MGM	
MG22938	CLARK GABLE	portrait	MGM	
MG22958	JOAN CRAWFORD	portrait	MGM	
MG22966	ROBERT YOUNG, KAREN MORLEY	portrait	MGM	
MG22968	ROBERT YOUNG, KAREN MORLEY	portrait	MGM	
MG23089	CLARK GABLE	portrait	MGM	
MG23137	ANITA PAGE	portrait	MGM	
MG23416	THELMA TODD	portrait	MGM	
MG23545	JOHN GILBERT	portrait	MGM	
MG23737	JOHN BARRYMORE, ETHEL BARRYMORE	portrait	MGM	
MG23794	CHESTER MORRIS	portrait	MGM	
MG23833	COLLEEN MOORE	portrait	MGM	
MG23836	COLLEEN MOORE	portrait	MGM	
MG23949	GRETA GARBO	portrait	MGM	
MG24254	JOHN BARRYMORE, DOLORES COSTELLO, JOHN JR	portrait	MGM	
MG24320	JOAN CRAWFORD	portrait	MGM	
MG24336	MAUREEN O'SULLIVAN	portrait	MGM	
MG24349	KAREN MORLEY	portrait	MGM	
MG24352	FREDRIC MARCH, RALPH FORBES	portrait	MGM	
MG24373	MAUREEN O'SULLIVAN	portrait	MGM	
MG24522	KAREN MORLEY	portrait	MGM	
MG24557	GERTRUDE MICHAEL	portrait	MGM	
MG24748	JOHN GILBERT	portrait	MGM	
MG24799	KAREN MORLEY	portrait	MGM	
MG24981	MAUREEN O'SULLIVAN	portrait	MGM	
MG24986	MAUREEN O'SULLIVAN	portrait	MGM	
MG25308	JOAN CRAWFORD	portrait	MGM	
MG25350	CLARK GABLE	portrait	MGM	
MG25397	MYRNA LOY	portrait	MGM	
MG25484	LAUREL & HARDY, FRED QUIMBY, FELIX FEIST	portrait	MGM	
MG25621	UNA MERKEL	portrait	MGM	
MG25624	UNA MERKEL	portrait	MGM	
MG25625	UNA MERKEL	portrait	MGM	
MG25626	UNA MERKEL	portrait	MGM	
MG25701	LUPE VELEZ	portrait	MGM	
MG25826	WALLACE BEERY	portrait	MGM	
MG25843	MARY ASTOR	portrait	MGM	
MG26149	WALLACE BEERY	portrait	MGM	
MG26174	UNA MERKEL	portrait	MGM	
MG26238	JOHN BARRYMORE	portrait	MGM	
MG26252	BUSTER KEATON	portrait	MGM	
MG26302	WALLACE BEERY	portrait	MGM	
MG26303	WALLACE BEERY	portrait	MGM	

MG26425	JOAN CRAWFORD	portrait	MGM	
MG26429	JOAN CRAWFORD	portrait	MGM	
MG26458	JOAN CRAWFORD	portrait	MGM	
MG26559	RUTH SELWYN	portrait	MGM	
MG26754	ROBERT MONTGOMERY	portrait	MGM	
MG26787	JOAN CRAWFORD	portrait	MGM	
MG26797	MADGE EVANS	portrait	MGM	
MG27008	JOAN CRAWFORD	portrait	MGM	
MG27193	MAUREEN O'SULLIVAN	portrait	MGM	
MG27317	MYRNA LOY	portrait	MGM	
MG27349	MYRNA LOY	portrait	MGM	
MG27362	MAUREEN O'SULLIVAN	portrait	MGM	
MG27416	JOAN CRAWFORD	portrait	MGM	
MG27455	JOAN CRAWFORD	portrait	MGM	
MG27557	JOAN CRAWFORD	portrait	MGM	
MG27562	JOAN CRAWFORD	portrait	MGM	
MG27599	JOAN CRAWFORD	portrait	MGM	
MG27638	JOAN CRAWFORD	portrait	MGM	
MG27740	MARY CARLISLE	portrait	MGM	
MG27779	NORMA SHEARER	portrait	MGM	
MG28154	JOAN CRAWFORD	portrait	MGM	
MG28294	UNA MERKEL	portrait	MGM	
MG28295	UNA MERKEL	portrait	MGM	
MG28313	MAUREEN O'SULLIVAN	portrait	MGM	
MG28367	JOAN CRAWFORD	portrait	MGM	
MG28731	JOAN CRAWFORD	portrait	MGM	
MG28786	JOAN CRAWFORD	portrait	MGM	
MG28799	UNA MERKEL	portrait	MGM	
MG28947	JOAN CRAWFORD	portrait	MGM	
MG29007	JOHNNY WEISSMULLER	portrait	MGM	
MG29014	JOHNNY WEISSMULLER	portrait	MGM	
MG29053	LEE TRACY	portrait	MGM	
MG29082	JOHNNY WEISSMULLER	portrait	MGM	
MG29161	RAMON NOVARRO	portrait	MGM	
MG29193	MYRNA LOY	portrait	MGM	
MG29277	CLARK GABLE	portrait	MGM	
MG29333	MAUREEN O'SULLIVAN	portrait	MGM	
MG29667	UNA MERKEL	portrait	MGM	
MG29695	UNA MERKEL	portrait	MGM	
MG29780	UNA MERKEL	portrait	MGM	
MG29979	BILLIE BURKE	portrait	MGM	
MG29990	UNA MERKEL	portrait	MGM	
MG29991	UNA MERKEL	portrait	MGM	
MG30319	MARIE DRESSLER, RICHARD BOLESLAVSKY	portrait	MGM	
MG30586	MAUREEN O'SULLIVAN	portrait	MGM	
MG30594	JOAN CRAWFORD	portrait	MGM	
MG30607	MYRNA LOY	portrait	MGM	
MG30667	MYRNA LOY	portrait	MGM	
MG30687	MYRNA LOY	portrait	MGM	
MG30847	MARIE DRESSLER'S HOME	portrait	MGM	
MG31167	JOHN BARRYMORE	portrait	MGM	
MG31281	MADGE EVANS	portrait	MGM	
MG31402	MAUREEN O'SULLIVAN	portrait	MGM	
MG31501	IRVING THALBERG, WIFE NORMA SHEARER	portrait	MGM	
MG31502	IRVING THALBERG, WIFE NORMA SHEARER	portrait	MGM	
MG31834	GRETA GARBO	portrait	MGM	
MG32014	UNA MERKEL	portrait	MGM	
MG32016	UNA MERKEL	portrait	MGM	
MG32020	UNA MERKEL	portrait	MGM	
MG32129	GRETA GARBO	portrait	MGM	
MG32190	IRVING THALBERG, WIFE NORMA SHEARER, LOUIS B MAYER	portrait	MGM	
MG32432	MYRNA LOY	portrait	MGM	
MG32439	JOAN CRAWFORD	portrait	MGM	
MG32702	JEANETTE MACDONALD	portrait	MGM	
MG32742	JOAN CRAWFORD	portrait	MGM	
MG32754	JOAN CRAWFORD	portrait	MGM	

MG32822	UNA MERKEL	portrait	MGM	
MG32989	DOROTHY MACKAILL	portrait	MGM	
MG33003	LILLYAN ANDRUS	portrait	MGM	
MG33067	JOAN CRAWFORD	portrait	MGM	
MG33184	LUPE VELEZ	portrait	MGM	
MG33235	WALLACE BEERY	portrait	MGM	
MG33276	JEAN PARKER	portrait	MGM	
MG33329	ROBERT MONTGOMERY	portrait	MGM	
MG33485	MADGE EVANS	portrait	MGM	
MG33493	LUPE VELEZ	portrait	MGM	
MG33536	JOAN CRAWFORD	portrait	MGM	
MG33588	CLARK GABLE	portrait	MGM	
MG33592	CLARK GABLE	portrait	MGM	
MG33650	JEAN PARKER	portrait	MGM	
MG33722	JEAN HARLOW	portrait	MGM	
MG33723	NORMA SHEARER	portrait	MGM	
MG33875	JEANETTE MACDONALD	portrait	MGM	
MG33977	MYRNA LOY	portrait	MGM	
MG33979	MYRNA LOY	portrait	MGM	
MG34335	JOAN CRAWFORD	portrait	MGM	
MG34355	UNA MERKEL	portrait	MGM	
MG34510	JEAN HOWARD	portrait	MGM	
MG34566	JEANETTE MACDONALD	portrait	MGM	
MG34797	UNA MERKEL	portrait	MGM	
MG34864	MYRNA LOY	portrait	MGM	
MG34865	MYRNA LOY	portrait	MGM	
MG34915	MYRNA LOY	portrait	MGM	
MG35645	MAUREEN O'SULLIVAN	portrait	MGM	
MG35679	JOHNNY WEISSMULLER	portrait	MGM	
MG35694	JEAN HOWARD	portrait	MGM	
MG35748	MURIEL EVANS	portrait	MGM	
MG36061	JOAN CRAWFORD	portrait	MGM	
MG36075	JOAN CRAWFORD	portrait	MGM	
MG36201	FRANCHOT TONE	portrait	MGM	
MG36807	NORMA SHEARER	portrait	MGM	
MG36840	NORMA SHEARER	portrait	MGM	
MG36841	NORMA SHEARER	portrait	MGM	
MG37109	JOHNNY WEISMULLER	portrait	MGM	
MG37120	LUPE VELEZ	portrait	MGM	
MG37306	FRANCHOT TONE	portrait	MGM	
MG37310	NORMA SHEARER	portrait	MGM	
MG37488	JOHNNY WEISSMULLER	portrait	MGM	
MG37598	MYRNA LOY	portrait	MGM	
MG37749	MYRNA LOY	portrait	MGM	
MG38350	MYRNA LOY	portrait	MGM	
MG38402	MYRNA LOY	portrait	MGM	
MG38406	JOHNNY WEISSMULLER	portrait	MGM	
MG38642	ELIZABETH ALLAN	portrait	MGM	
MG38648	MAE CLARKE	portrait	MGM	
MG38894	JEANETTE MACDONALD	portrait	MGM	
MG38994	NORMA SHEARER	portrait	MGM	
MG39038	JEANETTE MACDONALD	portrait	MGM	
MG39619	CHARLES LAUGHTON	portrait	MGM	
MG39620	CHARLES LAUGHTON	portrait	MGM	
MG39849	KAREN MORLEY	portrait	MGM	
MG39911	MAUREEN O'SULLIVAN	portrait	MGM	
MG39913	MAUREEN O'SULLIVAN	portrait	MGM	
MG39922	MAUREEN O'SULLIVAN	portrait	MGM	
MG40147	BRIAN AHERNE	portrait	MGM	
MG40153	WILLIAM POWELL	portrait	MGM	
MG40271	NORMA SHEARER	portrait	MGM	
MG40480	JOAN CRAWFORD	portrait	MGM	
MG40518	JOAN CRAWFORD	portrait	MGM	
MG40528	JOAN CRAWFORD	portrait	MGM	
MG40532	NORMA SHEARER	portrait	MGM	
MG40584	MAURICE CHEVALIER	portrait	MGM	

MG40810	BASIL RATHBONE	portrait	MGM	
MG41026	EVELYN LAYE	portrait	MGM	
MG41053	MICKEY ROONEY	portrait	MGM	
MG41092	GRETA GARBO	portrait	MGM	
MG41093	GRETA GARBO	portrait	MGM	
MG41094	GRETA GARBO	portrait	MGM	
MG41100	GRETA GARBO	portrait	MGM	
MG41101	GRETA GARBO	portrait	MGM	
MG41102	GRETA GARBO	portrait	MGM	
MG41177	GRETA GARBO	portrait	MGM	
MG41187	GRETA GARBO	portrait	MGM	
MG41188	GRETA GARBO	portrait	MGM	
MG41189	GRETA GARBO	portrait	MGM	
MG41195	GRETA GARBO	portrait	MGM	
MG41201	GRETA GARBO	portrait	MGM	
MG41203	GRETA GARBO	portrait	MGM	
MG41204	GRETA GARBO	portrait	MGM	
MG41205	GRETA GARBO	portrait	MGM	
MG41206	GRETA GARBO	portrait	MGM	
MG41207	GRETA GARBO	portrait	MGM	
MG41208	GRETA GARBO	portrait	MGM	
MG41209	GRETA GARBO	portrait	MGM	
MG41211	GRETA GARBO	portrait	MGM	
MG41213	GRETA GARBO	portrait	MGM	
MG41215	GRETA GARBO	portrait	MGM	
MG41216	GRETA GARBO	portrait	MGM	
MG41217	GRETA GARBO	portrait	MGM	
MG41218	GRETA GARBO	portrait	MGM	
MG41219	GRETA GARBO	portrait	MGM	
MG41221	GRETA GARBO	portrait	MGM	
MG41223	GRETA GARBO	portrait	MGM	
MG41226	GRETA GARBO	portrait	MGM	
MG41227	GRETA GARBO	portrait	MGM	
MG41230	GRETA GARBO	portrait	MGM	
MG41233	GRETA GARBO	portrait	MGM	
MG41505	JEANETTE MACDONALD	portrait	MGM	
MG41582	MAUREEN O'SULLIVAN	portrait	MGM	
MG41611	BILLIE BURKE	portrait	MGM	
MG41785	CECILIA PARKER	portrait	MGM	
MG41796	JEAN PARKER	portrait	MGM	
MG41850	CHESTER MORRIS	portrait	MGM	
MG42039	NORMA SHEARER	portrait	MGM	
MG42237	JOAN CRAWFORD	portrait	MGM	
MG42248	JEANETTE MACDONALD	portrait	MGM	
MG42295	JOAN CRAWFORD	portrait	MGM	
MG42379	WILLIAM POWELL	portrait	MGM	
MG42477	WILLIAM POWELL	portrait	MGM	
MG42538	CLARK GABLE	portrait	MGM	
MG42560	KAREN MORLEY	portrait	MGM	
MG42613	JUNE KNIGHT	portrait	MGM	
MG42700	CONSTANCE BENNETT	portrait	MGM	
MG42748	MAUREEN O'SULLIVAN	portrait	MGM	
MG42976	BETTY FURNESS	portrait	MGM	
MG43171	MAUREEN O'SULLIVAN	portrait	MGM	
MG43334	WS VAN DYKE, CECILIA PARKER, I. HERVEY, L. ROSINE	portrait	MGM	
MG43451	ROBERT TAYLOR	portrait	MGM	
MG43455	HELEN HAYES	portrait	MGM	
MG43922	JUNE KNIGHT	portrait	MGM	
MG43928	CORA SUE COLLINS	portrait	MGM	
MG43968	FRANK MORGAN	portrait	MGM	
MG44011	NINA MAE MCKINNEY	portrait	MGM	
MG44076	WALLACE BEERY	portrait	MGM	
MG44313	FRANCHOT TONE	portrait	MGM	
MG44333	MAUREEN O'SULLIVAN	portrait	MGM	
MG44360	MAUREEN O'SULLIVAN	portrait	MGM	
MG44446	MAUREEN O'SULLIVAN	portrait	MGM	

MG44507	FREDDIE BARTHOLOMEW	portrait	MGM	
MG44911	FREDDIE BARTHOLOMEW	portrait	MGM	
MG44913	MAUREEN O'SULLIVAN	portrait	MGM	
MG44915	MAUREEN O'SULLIVAN	portrait	MGM	
MG44971	GREER GARSON, HUSBAND RICHARD NEY	portrait	MGM	
MG45068	MYRNA LOY	portrait	MGM	
MG45071	FREDDIE BARTHOLOMEW	portrait	MGM	
MG45082	MYRNA LOY	portrait	MGM	
MG45356	MYRNA LOY AT 3 MONTHS	portrait	MGM	
MG45383	ELEANOR POWELL	portrait	MGM	
MG45539	FREDDIE BARTHOLOMEW	portrait	MGM	
MG45548	NORMA SHEARER	portrait	MGM	
MG45582	JOAN CRAWFORD	portrait	MGM	
MG45972	VIRGINIA BRUCE	portrait	MGM	
MG46033	FREDDIE BARTHOLOMEW	portrait	MGM	
MG46078	WALLACE BEERY	portrait	MGM	
MG46167	NORMA SHEARER	portrait	MGM	
MG46217	JUNE KNIGHT	portrait	MGM	
MG46387	MAUREEN O'SULLIVAN	portrait	MGM	
MG46389	MAUREEN O'SULLIVAN	portrait	MGM	
MG46390	MAUREEN O'SULLIVAN	portrait	MGM	
MG46612	JUNE KNIGHT	portrait	MGM	
MG47020	ELIZABETH ALLAN	portrait	MGM	
MG47321	BRIAN AHERNE	portrait	MGM	
MG47475	LUCILE WATSON	portrait	MGM	
MG47842	THE MARX BROTHERS	portrait	MGM	
MG48052	JOSEPH L MANKIEWICZ	portrait	MGM	
MG48099	JUANITA QUIGLEY	portrait	MGM	
MG48534	UNA MERKEL	portrait	MGM	
MG48539	CECILIA PARKER	portrait	MGM	
MG48893	NORMA SHEARER	portrait	MGM	
MG48894	NORMA SHEARER	portrait	MGM	
MG48950	ROBERT YOUNG	portrait	MGM	
MG48951	JUDY GARLAND	portrait	MGM	
MG49109	JEANETTE MACDONALD	portrait	MGM	
MG49215	CECILIA PARKER	portrait	MGM	
MG49229	NORMA SHEARER	portrait	MGM	
MG49234	NORMA SHEARER	portrait	MGM	
MG49247	NORMA SHEARER	portrait	MGM	
MG49252	NORMA SHEARER	portrait	MGM	
MG49253	NORMA SHEARER	portrait	MGM	
MG49256	NORMA SHEARER	portrait	MGM	
MG49257	NORMA SHEARER	portrait	MGM	
MG49270	NORMA SHEARER	portrait	MGM	
MG49290	MADGE EVANS	portrait	MGM	
MG49351	NORMA SHEARER	portrait	MGM	
MG49469	MAUREEN O'SULLIVAN	portrait	MGM	
MG49601	JEANETTE MACDONALD	portrait	MGM	
MG49664	MAUREEN O'SULLIVAN	portrait	MGM	
MG49671	MAUREEN O'SULLIVAN	portrait	MGM	
MG49762	JEAN PARKER	portrait	MGM	
MG49849	MADGE EVANS	portrait	MGM	
MG50229	LUISE RAINER	portrait	MGM	
MG50232	LUISE RAINER	portrait	MGM	
MG50233	JOAN CRAWFORD	portrait	MGM	
MG50683	MAUREEN O'SULLIVAN	portrait	MGM	
MG50736	ROBERT TAYLOR	portrait	MGM	
MG50739	JEANETTE MACDONALD	portrait	MGM	
MG50742	JEANETTE MACDONALD	portrait	MGM	
MG50839	BETTY FURNESS	portrait	MGM	
MG51109	DARLA HOOD	portrait	MGM	
MG51523	MAUREEN O'SULLIVAN	portrait	MGM	
MG51574	ROBERT TAYLOR	portrait	MGM	
MG51589	ROBERT TAYLOR	portrait	MGM	
MG51717	LUISE RAINER	portrait	MGM	
MG51777	MAUREEN O'SULLIVAN	portrait	MGM	

MG52483	FRANCHOT TONE	portrait	MGM	
MG52525	JOAN CRAWFORD	portrait	MGM	
MG53205	FRANK MORGAN	portrait	MGM	
MG53297	JEANETTE MACDONALD	portrait	MGM	
MG53611	NELSON EDDY	portrait	MGM	
MG53820	ELEANOR POWELL	portrait	MGM	
MG54034	ELEANOR POWELL	portrait	MGM	
MG54396	FRANCHOT TONE	portrait	MGM	
MG54538	MYRNA LOY	portrait	MGM	
MG54765	JUNE KNIGHT	portrait	MGM	
MG54874	VIRGINIA GREY	portrait	MGM	
MG55067	MICKEY ROONEY	portrait	MGM	
MG55492	ROBERT YOUNG	portrait	MGM	
MG55516	UNA MERKEL	portrait	MGM	
MG55826	MYRNA LOY	portrait	MGM	
MG55945	MAUREEN O'SULLIVAN	portrait	MGM	
MG56003	UNA MERKEL	portrait	MGM	
MG56006	MAUREEN O'SULLIVAN	portrait	MGM	
MG56143	VIRGINIA GREY	portrait	MGM	
MG56231	MAUREEN O'SULLIVAN	portrait	MGM	
MG56310	JOAN CRAWFORD	portrait	MGM	
MG56436	DELLA LIND	portrait	MGM	
MG56707	MAUREEN O'SULLIVAN	portrait	MGM	
MG56743	JAMES STEWART	portrait	MGM	
MG56746	JAMES STEWART	portrait	MGM	
MG56761	CLARK GABLE, WILLAM POWELL, S. TRACY, R. TAYLOR	portrait	MGM	
MG56953	ROBERT YOUNG, DAUGHTER CAROL ANN	portrait	MGM	
MG57004	DOROTHY GISH	portrait	MGM	
MG57075	LUISE RAINER	portrait	MGM	
MG57210	MAUREEN O'SULLIVAN	portrait	MGM	
MG57353	GRETA GARBO	portrait	MGM	
MG57356	GRETA GARBO	portrait	MGM	
MG57357	GRETA GARBO	portrait	MGM	
MG57359	GRETA GARBO	portrait	MGM	
MG57360	GRETA GARBO	portrait	MGM	
MG57362	GRETA GARBO	portrait	MGM	
MG57363	GRETA GARBO	portrait	MGM	
MG57364	GRETA GARBO	portrait	MGM	
MG57365	GRETA GARBO	portrait	MGM	
MG57366	GRETA GARBO	portrait	MGM	
MG57367	GRETA GARBO	portrait	MGM	
MG57368	GRETA GARBO	portrait	MGM	
MG57369	GRETA GARBO	portrait	MGM	
MG57413	ROBERT TAYLOR	portrait	MGM	
MG57449	GRETA GARBO	portrait	MGM	
MG57450	GRETA GARBO	portrait	MGM	
MG57451	GRETA GARBO	portrait	MGM	
MG57452	GRETA GARBO	portrait	MGM	
MG57455	GRETA GARBO	portrait	MGM	
MG57456	GRETA GARBO	portrait	MGM	
MG57457	GRETA GARBO	portrait	MGM	
MG57458	GRETA GARBO	portrait	MGM	
MG57465	GRETA GARBO	portrait	MGM	
MG57468	GRETA GARBO	portrait	MGM	
MG57469	GRETA GARBO	portrait	MGM	
MG57470	GRETA GARBO	portrait	MGM	
MG57471	GRETA GARBO	portrait	MGM	
MG57473	GRETA GARBO	portrait	MGM	
MG57474	GRETA GARBO	portrait	MGM	
MG57475	GRETA GARBO	portrait	MGM	
MG57476	GRETA GARBO	portrait	MGM	
MG57478	GRETA GARBO	portrait	MGM	
MG57479	GRETA GARBO	portrait	MGM	
MG57481	GRETA GARBO	portrait	MGM	
MG57482	GRETA GARBO	portrait	MGM	
MG57483	GRETA GARBO	portrait	MGM	

MG57484	GRETA GARBO	portrait	MGM	
MG57485	GRETA GARBO	portrait	MGM	
MG57486	GRETA GARBO	portrait	MGM	
MG57487	GRETA GARBO	portrait	MGM	
MG57488	GRETA GARBO	portrait	MGM	
MG57489	GRETA GARBO	portrait	MGM	
MG57490	GRETA GARBO	portrait	MGM	
MG57492	GRETA GARBO	portrait	MGM	
MG57493	GRETA GARBO	portrait	MGM	
MG57494	GRETA GARBO	portrait	MGM	
MG57495	GRETA GARBO	portrait	MGM	
MG57496	GRETA GARBO	portrait	MGM	
MG57497	GRETA GARBO	portrait	MGM	
MG57499	GRETA GARBO	portrait	MGM	
MG57500	GRETA GARBO	portrait	MGM	
MG57502	GRETA GARBO	portrait	MGM	
MG57503	GRETA GARBO	portrait	MGM	
MG57504	GRETA GARBO	portrait	MGM	
MG57505	GRETA GARBO	portrait	MGM	
MG57506	GRETA GARBO	portrait	MGM	
MG57507	GRETA GARBO	portrait	MGM	
MG57508	GRETA GARBO	portrait	MGM	
MG57509	GRETA GARBO	portrait	MGM	
MG57510	GRETA GARBO	portrait	MGM	
MG57511	GRETA GARBO	portrait	MGM	
MG57512	GRETA GARBO	portrait	MGM	
MG57513	GRETA GARBO	portrait	MGM	
MG57514	GRETA GARBO	portrait	MGM	
MG57516	GRETA GARBO	portrait	MGM	
MG57517	GRETA GARBO	portrait	MGM	
MG57812	LUISE RAINER	portrait	MGM	
MG57888	JOHN BARRYMORE, MARY GARDEN	portrait	MGM	
MG57922	LUISE RAINER	portrait	MGM	
MG58038	BUDDY EBSEN	portrait	MGM	
MG58071	MYRNA LOY	portrait	MGM	
MG58414	WS VAN DYKE, PATIENCE ABBE, JOHN ABBE, RICHARD ABBE	portrait	MGM	
MG58641	LUISE RAINER	portrait	MGM	
MG58646	MAUREEN O'SULLIVAN	portrait	MGM	
MG59620	WS VAN DYKE	portrait	MGM	
MG60537	CECILIA PARKER, LILLIAN ROSINE	portrait	MGM	
MG60654	CECILIA PARKER, LILLIAN ROSINE	portrait	MGM	
MG60659	CECILIA PARKER, LILLIAN ROSINE	portrait	MGM	
MG60778	MYRNA LOY	portrait	MGM	
MG60871	MAUREEN O'SULLIVAN	portrait	MGM	
MG61696	MAUREEN O'SULLIVAN	portrait	MGM	
MG61798	MADGE EVANS	portrait	MGM	
MG61804	MYRNA LOY, DIRECTOR RICHARD THORPE	portrait	MGM	
MG62653	IRENE MANNING	portrait	MGM	
MG63203	ROBERT TAYLOR	portrait	MGM	
MG63232	LUISE RAINER	portrait	MGM	
MG63396	MAUREEN O'SULLIVAN	portrait	MGM	
MG63573	WALLACE BEERY - BAD MAN OF BRIMSTONE	portrait	MGM	
MG63685	ALLAN JONES	portrait	MGM	
MG63867	WALTER PIDGEON	portrait	MGM	
MG63958	GRETA GARBO	portrait	MGM	
MG63961	GRETA GARBO	portrait	MGM	
MG63963	GRETA GARBO	portrait	MGM	
MG63965	GRETA GARBO	portrait	MGM	
MG63966	GRETA GARBO	portrait	MGM	
MG63970	GRETA GARBO	portrait	MGM	
MG63973	GRETA GARBO	portrait	MGM	
MG63974	GRETA GARBO	portrait	MGM	
MG63975	GRETA GARBO	portrait	MGM	
MG63976	GRETA GARBO	portrait	MGM	
MG63977	GRETA GARBO	portrait	MGM	
MG63979	GRETA GARBO	portrait	MGM	

MG63980	GRETA GARBO	portrait	MGM	
MG63981	GRETA GARBO	portrait	MGM	
MG63983	GRETA GARBO	portrait	MGM	
MG63984	GRETA GARBO	portrait	MGM	
MG63986	GRETA GARBO	portrait	MGM	
MG63988	GRETA GARBO	portrait	MGM	
MG63989	GRETA GARBO	portrait	MGM	
MG63990	GRETA GARBO	portrait	MGM	
MG63994	GRETA GARBO	portrait	MGM	
MG63996	GRETA GARBO	portrait	MGM	
MG63997	GRETA GARBO	portrait	MGM	
MG63999	GRETA GARBO	portrait	MGM	
MG64001	GRETA GARBO	portrait	MGM	
MG64007	GRETA GARBO	portrait	MGM	
MG64017	GRETA GARBO	portrait	MGM	
MG64365	MICKEY ROONEY	portrait	MGM	
MG64480	LASZLO WILLINGER	portrait	MGM	
MG64812	FANNY BRICE	portrait	MGM	
MG65054	JOAN CRAWFORD	portrait	MGM	
MG65056	JOAN CRAWFORD	portrait	MGM	
MG65091	JOAN CRAWFORD	portrait	MGM	
MG65093	JOAN CRAWFORD	portrait	MGM	
MG65295	MAUREEN O'SULLIVAN	portrait	MGM	
MG65296	MAUREEN O'SULLIVAN	portrait	MGM	
MG65344	MYRNA LOY	portrait	MGM	
MG65356	FRANK MORGAN	portrait	MGM	
MG65394	CLARK GABLE, MYRNA LOY	portrait	MGM	
MG65586	MICKEY ROONEY	portrait	MGM	
MG65619	MICKEY ROONEY	portrait	MGM	
MG65639	ROSALIND RUSSELL	portrait	MGM	
MG65732	WS VAN DYKE, FRANK MORGAN	portrait	MGM	
MG65823	VIRGINIA GREY	portrait	MGM	
MG66098	GALE SONDERGAARD	portrait	MGM	
MG66116	ROBERT MORLEY	portrait	MGM	
MG66404	GRETA GARBO	portrait	MGM	
MG66580	ELEANOR POWELL	portrait	MGM	
MG66819	WALLACE BEERY	portrait	MGM	
MG66967	JEANETTE MACDONALD	portrait	MGM	
MG67026	LUISE RAINER	portrait	MGM	
MG67152	LUISE RAINER	portrait	MGM	
MG67484	HEDY LAMARR	portrait	MGM	
MG67550	MARGARET SULLAVAN	portrait	MGM	
MG67643	NORMA SHEARER	portrait	MGM	
MG67644	NORMA SHEARER	portrait	MGM	
MG67823	MAUREEN O'SULLIVAN	portrait	MGM	
MG67851	ROSALIND RUSSELL	portrait	MGM	
MG67907	FAY HOLDEN	portrait	MGM	
MG68327	NORMA SHEARER	portrait	MGM	
MG68545	ROBERT MONTGOMERY	portrait	MGM	
MG68547	ROBERT MONTGOMERY	portrait	MGM	
MG68609	UNA MERKEL	portrait	MGM	
MG68922	JANET GAYNOR	portrait	MGM	
MG68957	ELEANOR POWELL	portrait	MGM	
MG69279	TERRY KILBURN	portrait	MGM	
MG69284	UNA MERKEL	portrait	MGM	
MG69287	RUTH HUSSEY	portrait	MGM	
MG69294	ANN MORRISS	portrait	MGM	
MG69418	HEDY LAMARR	portrait	MGM	
MG69489	UNA MERKEL	portrait	MGM	
MG69608	RUTH HUSSEY	portrait	MGM	
MG69656	JOAN CRAWFORD	portrait	MGM	
MG69758	WALTER PIDGEON	portrait	MGM	
MG69936	SARA HADEN	portrait	MGM	
MG69974	MAUREEN O'SULLIVAN	portrait	MGM	
MG70124	HEDY LAMARR	portrait	MGM	
MG70181	GRETA GARBO	portrait	MGM	

MG70331	JEANETTE MACDONALD	portrait	MGM	
MG70450	JEANETTE MACDONALD	portrait	MGM	
MG70477	LENI LYNN	portrait	MGM	
MG70805	ROBERT BENCHLEY	portrait	MGM	
MG70957	GREER GARSON	portrait	MGM	
MG70962	MICKEY ROONEY	portrait	MGM	
MG71055	GREER GARSON	portrait	MGM	
MG71145	MAUREEN O'SULLIVAN	portrait	MGM	
MG71152	MAUREEN O'SULLIVAN	portrait	MGM	
MG71313	HEDY LAMARR	portrait	MGM	
MG71371	WALTER PIDGEON	portrait	MGM	
MG71379	WALTER PIDGEON	portrait	MGM	
MG71380	ROBERT YOUNG	portrait	MGM	
MG71383	FAY HOLDEN	portrait	MGM	
MG71491	RUTH HUSSEY	portrait	MGM	
MG71512	NORMA SHEARER	portrait	MGM	
MG71517	NORMA SHEARER	portrait	MGM	
MG71553	RUTH HUSSEY	portrait	MGM	
MG71554	JUNE PREISSER	portrait	MGM	
MG71555	ROBERT YOUNG	portrait	MGM	
MG71686	RUTH HUSSEY	portrait	MGM	
MG71687	ROBERT YOUNG	portrait	MGM	
MG71699	MARY HOWARD	portrait	MGM	
MG71786	NORMA SHEARER	portrait	MGM	
MG71856	ELEANOR POWELL	portrait	MGM	
MG71911	JOAN CRAWFORD	portrait	MGM	
MG72008	HEDY LAMARR	portrait	MGM	
MG72080	VIRGINIA GREY	portrait	MGM	
MG72159	VIRGINIA GREY	portrait	MGM	
MG72183	MYRNA LOY	portrait	MGM	
MG72197	MYRNA LOY	portrait	MGM	
MG72200	VIRGINIA GREY	portrait	MGM	
MG72320	ANN RUTHERFORD	portrait	MGM	
MG72357	HEDY LAMARR	portrait	MGM	
MG72518	LANA TURNER	portrait	MGM	
MG72542	LANA TURNER	portrait	MGM	
MG72898	GREER GARSON	portrait	MGM	
MG72947	VIRGINIA WEIDLER	portrait	MGM	
MG73260	ROBERT TAYLOR	portrait	MGM	
MG73296	MAUREEN O'SULLIVAN	portrait	MGM	
MG73371	ELEANOR POWELL	portrait	MGM	
MG73503	GREER GARSON	portrait	MGM	
MG73518	ANN SOTHERN	portrait	MGM	
MG73587	VIRGINIA WEIDLER	portrait	MGM	
MG74342	NORMA SHEARER	portrait	MGM	
MG74497	JOAN CRAWFORD	portrait	MGM	
MG74509	GRETA GARBO	portrait	MGM	
MG74512	GRETA GARBO	portrait	MGM	
MG74514	GRETA GARBO	portrait	MGM	
MG74516	GRETA GARBO	portrait	MGM	
MG74517	GRETA GARBO	portrait	MGM	
MG74523	GRETA GARBO	portrait	MGM	
MG74524	GRETA GARBO	portrait	MGM	
MG74525	GRETA GARBO	portrait	MGM	
MG74562	ILONA MASSEY	portrait	MGM	
MG74580	LANA TURNER	portrait	MGM	
MG74885	GREER GARSON	portrait	MGM	
MG74950	MARSHA HUNT	portrait	MGM	
MG75142	LARAINE DAY	portrait	MGM	
MG75280	LARAINE DAY	portrait	MGM	
MG75341	RUTH HUSSEY	portrait	MGM	
MG75342	RUTH HUSSEY	portrait	MGM	
MG75343	RUTH HUSSEY	portrait	MGM	
MG75352	LANA TURNER	portrait	MGM	
MG75429	GREER GARSON	portrait	MGM	
MG75448	JOAN CRAWFORD	portrait	MGM	

MG75515	GREER GARSON	portrait	MGM	
MG75731	MAUREEN O'SULLIVAN	portrait	MGM	
MG75741	ELEANOR POWELL	portrait	MGM	
MG75796	GRETA GARBO	portrait	MGM	
MG75800	GRETA GARBO	portrait	MGM	
MG75801	GRETA GARBO	portrait	MGM	
MG75802	GRETA GARBO	portrait	MGM	
MG75803	GRETA GARBO	portrait	MGM	
MG75804	GRETA GARBO	portrait	MGM	
MG75805	GRETA GARBO	portrait	MGM	
MG75806	GRETA GARBO	portrait	MGM	
MG75807	GRETA GARBO	portrait	MGM	
MG75809	GRETA GARBO	portrait	MGM	
MG75811	GRETA GARBO	portrait	MGM	
MG75812	GRETA GARBO	portrait	MGM	
MG75814	GRETA GARBO	portrait	MGM	
MG75815	GRETA GARBO	portrait	MGM	
MG75817	GRETA GARBO	portrait	MGM	
MG75821	GRETA GARBO	portrait	MGM	
MG75822	GRETA GARBO	portrait	MGM	
MG75823	GRETA GARBO	portrait	MGM	
MG75825	GRETA GARBO	portrait	MGM	
MG75826	GRETA GARBO	portrait	MGM	
MG75827	GRETA GARBO	portrait	MGM	
MG75828	GRETA GARBO	portrait	MGM	
MG75829	GRETA GARBO	portrait	MGM	
MG75830	GRETA GARBO	portrait	MGM	
MG75834	GRETA GARBO	portrait	MGM	
MG75836	GRETA GARBO	portrait	MGM	
MG75898	GRETA GARBO	portrait	MGM	
MG75928	INA CLAIRE	portrait	MGM	
MG75968	JUDY GARLAND	portrait	MGM	
MG76193	ANN RUTHERFORD	portrait	MGM	
MG76243	MICKEY ROONEY	portrait	MGM	
MG76251	WALTER PIDGEON	portrait	MGM	
MG76368	LARAINE DAY	portrait	MGM	
MG76591	FRED ASTAIRE	portrait	MGM	
MG76621	LANA TURNER	portrait	MGM	
MG76867	VIRGINIA WEIDLER	portrait	MGM	
MG76984	MARGARET SULLAVAN	portrait	MGM	
MG76987	MARGARET SULLAVAN	portrait	MGM	
MG77055	FRED ASTAIRE	portrait	MGM	
MG77056	FRED ASTAIRE	portrait	MGM	
MG77057	FRED ASTAIRE	portrait	MGM	
MG77058	FRED ASTAIRE	portrait	MGM	
MG77059	FRED ASTAIRE	portrait	MGM	
MG77502	DIANA LEWIS	portrait	MGM	
MG77761	DIANA LEWIS	portrait	MGM	
MG77805	DIANA LEWIS	portrait	MGM	
MG77880	LANA TURNER	portrait	MGM	
MG77996	MAUREEN O'SULLIVAN	portrait	MGM	
MG77997	MAUREEN O'SULLIVAN	portrait	MGM	
MG78000	ANN RUTHERFORD	portrait	MGM	
MG78004	FAY BAINTER	portrait	MGM	
MG78010	RUTH HUSSEY	portrait	MGM	
MG78014	DIANA LEWIS	portrait	MGM	
MG78031	ROBERT YOUNG	portrait	MGM	
MG78081	MAUREEN O'SULLIVAN	portrait	MGM	
MG78096	HEDY LAMARR	portrait	MGM	
MG78262	DIANA LEWIS, WILLIAM POWELL	portrait	MGM	
MG78264	VIRGINIA WEIDLER	portrait	MGM	
MG78598	RUTH HUSSEY	portrait	MGM	
MG78637	DIANA LEWIS	portrait	MGM	
MG78722	ANN RUTHERFORD	portrait	MGM	
MG78890	LAURENCE OLIVIER	portrait	MGM	
MG78917	SPENCER TRACY + HIS MOTHER	portrait	MGM	

MG78918	SPENCER TRACY	portrait	MGM	
MG79043	VIRGINIA WEIDLER	portrait	MGM	
MG79065	ELEANOR POWELL	portrait	MGM	
MG79069	DIANA LEWIS	portrait	MGM	
MG79075	RUTH HUSSEY	portrait	MGM	
MG79076	DIANA LEWIS	portrait	MGM	
MG79226	LANA TURNER AT 8	portrait	MGM	
MG80224	CLAUDETTE COLBERT	portrait	MGM	
MG80299	VIRGINIA WEIDLER	portrait	MGM	
MG80570	MYRNA LOY	portrait	MGM	
MG80686	KATHARINE HEPBURN	portrait	MGM	
MG80736	LARAINE DAY	portrait	MGM	
MG80969	KATHRYN GRAYSON	portrait	MGM	
MG80971	KATHRYN GRAYSON	portrait	MGM	
MG80974	HEDY LAMARR	portrait	MGM	
MG81006	KATHARINE HEPBURN	portrait	MGM	
MG81007	KATHARINE HEPBURN	portrait	MGM	
MG81012	VIRGINIA O'BRIEN	portrait	MGM	
MG81013	VIRGINIA O'BRIEN	portrait	MGM	
MG81032	KATHARINE HEPBURN	portrait	MGM	
MG81063	RUTH HUSSEY	portrait	MGM	
MG81102	RUTH HUSSEY	portrait	MGM	
MG81162	NORMA SHEARER	portrait	MGM	
MG81163	RUTH HUSSEY	portrait	MGM	
MG81173	LANA TURNER	portrait	MGM	
MG81178	ANN RUTHERFORD	portrait	MGM	
MG81180	DIANA LEWIS	portrait	MGM	
MG81239	MARY HOWARD	portrait	MGM	
MG81249	VIRGINIA O'BRIEN	portrait	MGM	
MG81377	ANN SOTHERN	portrait	MGM	
MG81385	RUTH HUSSEY	portrait	MGM	
MG81427	JEANETTE MACDONALD	portrait	MGM	
MG81479	MYRNA LOY	portrait	MGM	
MG81484	MYRNA LOY	portrait	MGM	
MG81514	LARAINE DAY	portrait	MGM	
MG81555	RUTH HUSSEY	portrait	MGM	
MG81560	SARA HADEN	portrait	MGM	
MG81685	NORMA SHEARER	portrait	MGM	
MG81695	SUSAN PETERS	portrait	MGM	
MG81881	MARJORIE MAIN	portrait	MGM	
MG81884	MARJORIE MAIN	portrait	MGM	
MG82098	RED SKELTON	portrait	MGM	
MG82100	RED SKELTON	portrait	MGM	
MG82120	RUTH HUSSEY	portrait	MGM	
MG82122	RUTH HUSSEY, EDWARD G. ROBINSON - BLACKMAIL	portrait	MGM	
MG82255	RUTH HUSSEY	portrait	MGM	
MG82259	HEDY LAMARR	portrait	MGM	
MG82397	RUTH HUSSEY + MOTHER, SISTER BETTY	portrait	MGM	
MG82398	RUTH HUSSEY, ROBERT YOUNG - RICH MAN, POOR GIRL	portrait	MGM	
MG82401	RUTH HUSSEY, CLIFF EDWARDS, ROBERT YOUNG - MAISIE	portrait	MGM	
MG82402	RUTH HUSSEY, MARY BETH HUGHES, NORMA SHEARER	portrait	MGM	
MG82405	RUTH HUSSEY, J. CRAWFORD, R. HOBART - SUSAN & GOD	portrait	MGM	
MG82410	RUTH HUSSEY	portrait	MGM	
MG82509	LANA TURNER	portrait	MGM	
MG82553	NORMA SHEARER	portrait	MGM	
MG82584	NORMA SHEARER	portrait	MGM	
MG82585	NORMA SHEARER	portrait	MGM	
MG82587	RUTH HUSSEY	portrait	MGM	
MG82713	GRETA GARBO	portrait	MGM	
MG82714	KATHARINE HEPBURN	portrait	MGM	
MG82957	MICKEY ROONEY	portrait	MGM	
MG82963	MYRNA LOY	portrait	MGM	
MG83104	ANN SOTHERN	portrait	MGM	
MG83108	ANN SOTHERN	portrait	MGM	
MG83278	LARAINE DAY	portrait	MGM	
MG83281	LARAINE DAY	portrait	MGM	

MG83448	LARAINE DAY	portrait	MGM	
MG83659	ROBERT YOUNG	portrait	MGM	
MG83690	JOAN CRAWFORD	portrait	MGM	
MG83700	JOAN CRAWFORD	portrait	MGM	
MG83949	MYRNA LOY	portrait	MGM	
MG83965	MYRNA LOY	portrait	MGM	
MG83989	JOAN CRAWFORD	portrait	MGM	
MG84057	ANN MORRISS, MARY HOWARD	portrait	MGM	
MG84135	ROBERT YOUNG, WIFE BETTY HENDERSON	portrait	MGM	
MG84138	ANN SOTHERN, HUSBAND ROGER PRYOR	portrait	MGM	
MG84152	ROBERT YOUNG	portrait	MGM	
MG84183	FAY HOLDEN	portrait	MGM	
MG84184	FAY HOLDEN	portrait	MGM	
MG84247	JOAN CRAWFORD	portrait	MGM	
MG84249	JOAN CRAWFORD	portrait	MGM	
MG84276	LANA TURNER	portrait	MGM	
MG84311	RED SKELTON	portrait	MGM	
MG84312	RED SKELTON	portrait	MGM	
MG84316	RED SKELTON	portrait	MGM	
MG84338	VIRGINIA GREY	portrait	MGM	
MG84367	JEANETTE MACDONALD	portrait	MGM	
MG84371	JEANETTE MACDONALD	portrait	MGM	
MG84539	ELEANOR POWELL	portrait	MGM	
MG84540	ELEANOR POWELL	portrait	MGM	
MG84594	LANA TURNER	portrait	MGM	
MG84663	DONALD MEEK	portrait	MGM	
MG84669	JOAN CRAWFORD	portrait	MGM	
MG84696	JOHNNY WEISSMULLER, WIFE BERYL, SON JOHN SCOTT	portrait	MGM	
MG84745	HEDY LAMARR	portrait	MGM	
MG84749	LARAINE DAY	portrait	MGM	
MG84921	GREER GARSON	portrait	MGM	
MG85212	VIRGINIA GREY	portrait	MGM	
MG85219	VIRGINIA GREY	portrait	MGM	
MG85244	GREER GARSON	portrait	MGM	
MG85370	RUTH HUSSEY	portrait	MGM	
MG85381	GREER GARSON	portrait	MGM	
MG85455	DONNA REED	portrait	MGM	
MG85536	ROBERT TAYLOR	portrait	MGM	
MG85679	BARRY NELSON	portrait	MGM	
MG85778	MARSHA HUNT	portrait	MGM	
MG85779	MARSHA HUNT	portrait	MGM	
MG85828	FAY HOLDEN	portrait	MGM	
MG85833	KATHRYN GRAYSON + HUSBAND JOHN SHELTON	portrait	MGM	
MG85852	MAUREEN O'SULLIVAN	portrait	MGM	
MG86066	BARRY NELSON	portrait	MGM	
MG86153	NORMA SHEARER	portrait	MGM	
MG86173	NORMA SHEARER	portrait	MGM	
MG86324	HEDY LAMARR	portrait	MGM	
MG86360	RUTH HUSSEY	portrait	MGM	
MG86366	RUTH HUSSEY	portrait	MGM	
MG86382	GRETA GARBO	portrait	MGM	
MG86383	GRETA GARBO	portrait	MGM	
MG86384	GRETA GARBO	portrait	MGM	
MG86393	GRETA GARBO	portrait	MGM	
MG86402	ANN SOTHERN	portrait	MGM	
MG86423	MAUREEN O'SULLIVAN	portrait	MGM	
MG86494	HEDY LAMARR	portrait	MGM	
MG86528	DONNA REED	portrait	MGM	
MG86579	BARRY NELSON	portrait	MGM	
MG86664	RUTH GORDON	portrait	MGM	
MG86677	ANN SOTHERN	portrait	MGM	
MG86679	ANN SOTHERN	portrait	MGM	
MG86803	RUTH HUSSEY	portrait	MGM	
MG86887	HEDY LAMARR	portrait	MGM	
MG86959	WALTER PIDGEON	portrait	MGM	
MG87048	MARSHA HUNT	portrait	MGM	

MG87063	KATHARINE HEPBURN	portrait	MGM	
MG87064	KATHARINE HEPBURN	portrait	MGM	
MG87079	KATHARINE HEPBURN	portrait	MGM	
MG87080	KATHARINE HEPBURN	portrait	MGM	
MG87202	WILLIAM LUNDIGAN	portrait	MGM	
MG87224	RUTH HUSSEY	portrait	MGM	
MG87318	LARAINE DAY	portrait	MGM	
MG87363	LARAINE DAY	portrait	MGM	
MG87377	KATHARINE HEPBURN	portrait	MGM	
MG87431	MARSHA HUNT	portrait	MGM	
MG87818	ANN SOTHERN	portrait	MGM	
MG87833	VIRGINIA O'BRIEN	portrait	MGM	
MG87836	VIRGINIA O'BRIEN	portrait	MGM	
MG87872	MAUREEN O'SULLIVAN	portrait	MGM	
MG87902	ANN SOTHERN	portrait	MGM	
MG87939	JEANETTE MACDONALD	portrait	MGM	
MG87950	JEANETTE MACDONALD	portrait	MGM	
MG87951	JEANETTE MACDONALD	portrait	MGM	
MG87953	JEANETTE MACDONALD	portrait	MGM	
MG87983	RUTH HUSSEY	portrait	MGM	
MG88078	RAGS RAGLAND	portrait	MGM	
MG88087	RED SKELTON	portrait	MGM	
MG88091	RED SKELTON	portrait	MGM	
MG88120	LARAINE DAY	portrait	MGM	
MG88160	DONNA REED AT 7, BROTHER KEITH, SISTER LAVONNE	portrait	MGM	
MG88183	MARJORIE MAIN	portrait	MGM	
MG88184	MARJORIE MAIN	portrait	MGM	
MG88186	JOHN GARFIELD	portrait	MGM	
MG88256	BASIL RATHBONE	portrait	MGM	
MG88496	VIRGINIA WEIDLER	portrait	MGM	
MG88657	MYRNA LOY	portrait	MGM	
MG88816	MYRNA LOY	portrait	MGM	
MG88853	VAN HEFLIN	portrait	MGM	
MG88995	DOROTHY MORRIS	portrait	MGM	
MG89131	FRANK MORGAN	portrait	MGM	
MG89177	VIRGINIA O'BRIEN	portrait	MGM	
MG89210	DICK SIMMONS	portrait	MGM	
MG89277	ANN SOTHERN	portrait	MGM	
MG89277	RED SKELTON, WIFE EDNA	portrait	MGM	
MG89362	DONNA REED	portrait	MGM	
MG89393	DONNA REED	portrait	MGM	
MG89395	DONNA REED	portrait	MGM	
MG89589	FAY HOLDEN	portrait	MGM	
MG89612	WILLIAM LUNDIGAN	portrait	MGM	
MG89616	DONNA REED	portrait	MGM	
MG89655	MYRNA LOY, HUSBAND JOHN D. HERTZ, JR	portrait	MGM	
MG89718	WILLIAM POWELL	portrait	MGM	
MG89753	RICHARD NEY	portrait	MGM	
MG89760	LANA TURNER	portrait	MGM	
MG89795	DOROTHY MORRIS	portrait	MGM	
MG89905	LARAINE DAY	portrait	MGM	
MG89956	DONNA REED	portrait	MGM	
MG90111	JEAN-PIERRE AUMONT	portrait	MGM	
MG90323	FAY BAINTER	portrait	MGM	
MG90338	GREER GARSON	portrait	MGM	
MG90369	FRANCES RAFFERTY	portrait	MGM	
MG90411	RUTH HUSSEY + HUSBAND C. ROBERT LONGENECKER	portrait	MGM	
MG90421	SIGNE HASSO	portrait	MGM	
MG90797	HEDY LAMARR	portrait	MGM	
MG90867	SUSAN PETERS	portrait	MGM	
MG90881	GREER GARSON, E. LAWRENCE - STARS OVER AMERICA	portrait	MGM	
MG90962	GREER GARSON, R. COLMAN, H. LAMARR, V. GILMORE	portrait	MGM	
MG91006	SUSAN PETERS	portrait	MGM	
MG91008	SUSAN PETERS	portrait	MGM	
MG91045	MARSHA HUNT	portrait	MGM	
MG91089	LANA TURNER	portrait	MGM	

MG91267	LARAINE DAY	portrait	MGM	
MG91324	NANCY WALKER	portrait	MGM	
MG91332	KATHARINE HEPBURN	portrait	MGM	
MG91553	MARILYN MAXWELL	portrait	MGM	
MG91583	JOAN CRAWFORD	portrait	MGM	
MG91584	SPRING BYINGTON	portrait	MGM	
MG91596	JOAN CRAWFORD	portrait	MGM	
MG91604	MARILYN MAXWELL	portrait	MGM	
MG91612	MARILYN MAXWELL	portrait	MGM	
MG91789	VIRGINIA O'BRIEN	portrait	MGM	
MG91996	RED SKELTON	portrait	MGM	
MG92114	ANN SOTHERN	portrait	MGM	
MG92153	LANA TURNER	portrait	MGM	
MG92169	LANA TURNER	portrait	MGM	
MG92273	GLORIA DE HAVEN	portrait	MGM	
MG92551	SPRING BYINGTON	portrait	MGM	
MG92752	DONNA REED	portrait	MGM	
MG92799	IRENE DUNNE	portrait	MGM	
MG92889	JOAN CRAWFORD	portrait	MGM	
MG93149	DAME MAY WHITTY	portrait	MGM	
MG93179	DONNA REED	portrait	MGM	
MG93538	PAMELA BLAKE	portrait	MGM	
MG93796	MARY ASTOR	portrait	MGM	
MG93797	MARY ASTOR	portrait	MGM	
MG93798	MARY ASTOR	portrait	MGM	
MG93799	MARY ASTOR	portrait	MGM	
MG93832	DONNA REED, HUSBAND BILL TUTTLE	portrait	MGM	
MG93863	JOAN CRAWFORD	portrait	MGM	
MG93877	ELEANOR POWELL	portrait	MGM	
MG93879	ELEANOR POWELL	portrait	MGM	
MG93881	ELEANOR POWELL	portrait	MGM	
MG93886	ELEANOR POWELL	portrait	MGM	
MG93924	ANN RICHARDS	portrait	MGM	
MG93940	LAURA LA PLANTE		MGM	
MG93995	MARY ASTOR	portrait	MGM	
MG94326	MARY ASTOR	portrait	MGM	
MG94377	FRANCES RAFFERTY	portrait	MGM	
MG94594	VIRGINIA WEIDLER	portrait	MGM	
MG94655	SARA HADEN	portrait	MGM	
MG94661	MICKEY ROONEY	portrait	MGM	
MG94737	MARILYN MAXWELL	portrait	MGM	
MG94910	FRANCES GIFFORD	portrait	MGM	
MG94969	GREER GARSON, HUSBAND RICHARD NEY	portrait	MGM	
MG94984	CONNIE GILCHRIST	portrait	MGM	
MG95005	LARAINE DAY	portrait	MGM	
MG95083	DONNA REED	portrait	MGM	
MG95155	DONNA REED	portrait	MGM	
MG95177	FAY BAINTER	portrait	MGM	
MG95215	TOMMY DIX	portrait	MGM	
MG95312	MARGARET SULLAVAN	portrait	MGM	
MG95386	MARILYN MAXWELL	portrait	MGM	
MG95388	MARILYN MAXWELL	portrait	MGM	
MG95389	MARILYN MAXWELL	portrait	MGM	
MG95390	MARILYN MAXWELL	portrait	MGM	
MG95481	ANN SOTHERN	portrait	MGM	
MG95511	BERT LAHR	portrait	MGM	
MG95629	HEDY LAMARR	portrait	MGM	
MG95719	GREER GARSON	portrait	MGM	
MG95776	GINNY SIMMS	portrait	MGM	
MG95793	ESTHER WILLIAMS	portrait	MGM	
MG95906	FRANCES GIFFORD	portrait	MGM	
MG96092	FRANCES GIFFORD	portrait	MGM	
MG96093	FRANCES GIFFORD	portrait	MGM	
MG96097	FRANCES GIFFORD	portrait	MGM	
MG96108	KATHRYN GRAYSON	portrait	MGM	
MG96304	GREER GARSON	portrait	MGM	

MG96499	LANA TURNER	portrait	MGM	
MG96591	FRANCES GIFFORD	portrait	MGM	
MG96592	FRANCES GIFFORD	portrait	MGM	
MG96622	HEDY LAMARR	portrait	MGM	
MG96626	HEDY LAMARR	portrait	MGM	
MG96684	JUNE LOCKHART	portrait	MGM	
MG96685	LANA TURNER	portrait	MGM	
MG96854	GLORIA DE HAVEN	portrait	MGM	
MG96861	JUNE ALLYSON	portrait	MGM	
MG96872	JOHN HODIAK	portrait	MGM	
MG96873	JOHN HODIAK	portrait	MGM	
MG96874	JOHN HODIAK	portrait	MGM	
MG97091	TOM DRAKE	portrait	MGM	
MG97126	KEENAN WYNN	portrait	MGM	
MG97149	HURD HATFIELD	portrait	MGM	
MG97151	ANN SOTHERN, HUSBAND ROBERT STERLING	portrait	MGM	
MG97191	IRENE DUNNE	portrait	MGM	
MG97192	LARAINE DAY	portrait	MGM	
MG97194	FRANCES GIFFORD	portrait	MGM	
MG97381	GLORIA DE HAVEN	portrait	MGM	
MG97393	FRANCES GIFFORD	portrait	MGM	
MG97487	GINNY SIMMS	portrait	MGM	
MG97522	ANN SOTHERN	portrait	MGM	
MG98088	GLORIA DE HAVEN	portrait	MGM	
MG98192	JOHN HODIAK	portrait	MGM	
MG98328	MARY ASTOR	portrait	MGM	
MG98377	LANA TURNER	portrait	MGM	
MG98525	JOHN HODIAK	portrait	MGM	
MG98972	ROBERT WALKER	portrait	MGM	
MGH	TAMING OF DOROTHY	SOLDATI	LUX	1950
MGM	TEMPTRESS, THE (see 265)	NIBLO	MGM	1926
MGM	TILLY THE TOILER (see 297)	HENLEY	MGM	1927
MGM-4	HAUNTED HONEYMOON (UK: BUSMAN'S HOLIDAY)	WOODS	MGM	1940
MGM-6	VACATION FROM MARRIAGE (UK: PERFECT STRANGERS)	KORDA	MGM	1945
MGM-8	EDWARD, MY SON (UK)	CUKOR	MGM	1949
MGM-28	SCAPEGOAT (UK)	HAMER	MGM	1959
MGM-32	INVASION QUARTET (UK)	LEWIS	MGM	1961
MGM-37	MURDER SHE SAID (UK)	POLLOCK	MGM	1961
MGM39	POSTMAN'S KNOCK (UK)	LYNN	MGM-UK	1962
MGM40	VILLAGE OF DAUGHTERS (UK)	POLLOCK	MGM-UK	1962
MGM-44	KILL OR CURE (UK)	POLLOCK	MGM	1962
MGM-46	COME FLY WITH ME (UK)	LEVIN	MGM	1963
MGM48	MURDER AT THE GALLOP (UK)	POLLOCK	MGM-UK	1963
MGM50	CHILDREN OF THE DAMNED (UK)	LEADER	MGM-UK	1964
MGM-52	NIGHT MUST FALL (UK)	REISZ	MGM	1964
MGM54	MURDER MOST FOUL (UK)	POLLOCK	MGM-UK	1964
MGM-57	MURDER AHOY (UK)	POLLOCK	MGM	1964
MGM-59	OPERATION CROSSBOW (UK)	ANDERSON	MGM	1965
MGM-60	ALPHABET MURDERS (UK)	TASHLIN	MGM	1965
MGM-80	SECRET OF MY SUCCESS (UK)	STONE	MGM	1965
MGM85	WHERE THE SPYS ARE (UK)	GUEST	MGM	1961
MGM-287	GRETA GARBO	portrait	MGM	
MGM529	LILLIAN GISH	portrait	MGM	
MGM682	NORMA SHEARER	portrait	MGM	
MGM-895	JOAN CRAWFORD	portrait	MGM	
MGM-965	GRETA GARBO	portrait	MGM	
MGM1076	CLAIRE WINDSOR	portrait	MGM	
MGM1086	CLAIRE WINDSOR	portrait	MGM	
MGM1100	CLAIRE WINDSOR	portrait	MGM	
MGM1123	KING VIDOR, E. BOARDMAN, J. GILBERT - BARDELYS...	portrait	MGM	
MGM-1254	GEORGE K. ARTHUR	portrait	MGM	
MGM-1330	JOAN CRAWFORD	portrait	MGM	
MGM-1657	SALLY O'NEIL	portrait	MGM	
MGM-1704	GRETA GARBO	portrait	MGM	
MGM2336	GWEN LEE	portrait	MGM	
MGM2603	GWEN LEE	portrait	MGM	

MGM-2781	JOAN CRAWFORD	portrait	MGM	
MGM2785	GWEN LEE	portrait	MGM	
MGM-2819	JOAN CRAWFORD	portrait	MGM	
MGM-2967	JOAN CRAWFORD	portrait	MGM	
MGM-3106	JOAN CRAWFORD	portrait	MGM	
MGM3158	CLAIRE WINDSOR, WILLIAM HAINES	portrait	MGM	
MGM4020	NORMA SHEARER	portrait	MGM	
MGM4022	NORMA SHEARER	portrait	MGM	
MGM4115	JOHN GILBERT	portrait	MGM	
MGM-4220	JOAN CRAWFORD	portrait	MGM	
MGM-4254	JOAN CRAWFORD	portrait	MGM	
MGM4385	NORMA SHEARER	portrait	MGM	
MGM4391	CLAIRE WINDSOR	portrait	MGM	
MGM-4398	JOAN CRAWFORD	portrait	MGM	
MGM5511	GWEN LEE	portrait	MGM	
MGM-5795	JOAN CRAWFORD	portrait	MGM	
MGM5826	GWEN LEE	portrait	MGM	
MGM-6071	WILLIAM HAINES	portrait	MGM	
MGM6769	GWEN LEE	portrait	MGM	
MGM-6862	JOAN CRAWFORD	portrait	MGM	
MGM-6970	JOAN CRAWFORD	portrait	MGM	
MGM-7125	JOAN CRAWFORD	portrait	MGM	
MGM-7457	JOAN CRAWFORD	portrait	MGM	
MGM8354	GWEN LEE	portrait	MGM	
MGM-8375	MARION DAVIES	portrait	MGM	
MGM8377	JOHN GILBERT	portrait	MGM	
MGM-8566	JOAN CRAWFORD	portrait	MGM	
MGM8575	GWEN LEE	portrait	MGM	
MGM8752	NORMA SHEARER	portrait	MGM	
MGM9223	NORMA SHEARER	portrait	MGM	
MGM9358	LON CHANEY	portrait	MGM	1927
MGM9801	GWEN LEE	portrait	MGM	
MGM9805	AILEEN PRINGLE	portrait	MGM	
MGM-9986	JOAN CRAWFORD	portrait	MGM	
MGM-10070	GRETA GARBO	portrait	MGM	
MGM-10544	FLASH, THE WONDER DOG	portrait	MGM	
MGM10573	GWEN LEE	portrait	MGM	
MGM-10837	JOAN CRAWFORD	portrait	MGM	
MGM11656	LILLIAN GISH	portrait	MGM	
MGM11827	NORMA SHEARER	portrait	MGM	
MGM-11851X	JOAN CRAWFORD	portrait	MGM	
MGM11891	MARCELINE DAY	portrait	MGM	
MGM-12213	JOAN CRAWFORD	portrait	MGM	
MGM-12214	JOAN CRAWFORD	portrait	MGM	
MGM12235	GWEN LEE	portrait	MGM	
MGM-12384	JOAN CRAWFORD	portrait	MGM	
MGM-13322	JOAN CRAWFORD	portrait	MGM	
MGM13804	STAN LAUREL, DOROTHY COBURN - FLYING ELEPHANTS	portrait	MGM	
MGM13903	LON CHANEY	portrait	MGM	
MGM13991	GWEN LEE	portrait	MGM	
MGM14109	GWEN LEE	portrait	MGM	
MGM14110	GWEN LEE	portrait	MGM	
MGM-14197	ANNA MAY WONG	portrait	MGM	
MGM N	MCMASTERS	KJELLEN	CHEVRON	1970
MGMP-746	EVELYN BRENT	portrait	MGM	
MGMP-959	KARL DANE	portrait	MGM	
MGMP-1122	GRETA GARBO	portrait	MGM	
MGMP-1134	ANNA MAY WONG	portrait	MGM	
MGMP-1405	JOAN CRAWFORD	portrait	MGM	
MGMP1464	GWEN LEE	portrait	MGM	
MGMP1566	GWEN LEE	portrait	MGM	
MGMP2096	CHARLEY CHASE	portrait	MGM	
MGMP-3375	LILLIAN GISH	portrait	MGM	
MGMP-3404	LILLIAN GISH	portrait	MGM	
MGMP-3612	JOAN CRAWFORD	portrait	MGM	
MGMP4179	ANITA PAGE, USC PRES. R. VON KLEIN, DEAN RAY K. IMMEL	portrait	MGM	

MGMP4593	BUSTER KEATON	portrait	MGM	
MGMP4688	DOROTHY REIVER	portrait	MGM	late 20's
MGMP4923	LAUREL & HARDY, MARION BYRON	portrait	MGM	
MGMP-5167	RAQUEL TORRES, MARIO CALVO - ESTRELLADOS	portrait	MGM	
MGMP-5889	JOAN CRAWFORD	portrait	MGM	
MGMP-5891	JOAN CRAWFORD	portrait	MGM	
MGMP-6092	JOAN CRAWFORD	portrait	MGM	
MGMP-6093	JOAN CRAWFORD	portrait	MGM	
MGMP-6094	JOAN CRAWFORD	portrait	MGM	
MGMP-6095	JOAN CRAWFORD	portrait	MGM	
MGMP-6371	JOAN CRAWFORD	portrait	MGM	
MGMP6877	EVA VON BERNE	portrait	MGM	
MGMP-7359	LILLIAN GISH	portrait	MGM	
MGMP8781	IRVING THALBERG, WIFE NORMA SHEARER	portrait	MGM	
MGMP 8783	CHANNING OF THE NORTHWEST	INCE	MGM (SELECT)	R
MGMP8883	BUSTER KEATON	portrait	MGM	
MGMP-9027	JOAN CRAWFORD	portrait	MGM	
MGMP-9028	JOAN CRAWFORD	portrait	MGM	
MGMP-9029	JOAN CRAWFORD	portrait	MGM	
MGMP-9037	JOAN CRAWFORD	portrait	MGM	
MGMP-9038	JOAN CRAWFORD	portrait	MGM	
MGMP-9048	JOAN CRAWFORD	portrait	MGM	
MGMP-9188	JOAN CRAWFORD	portrait	MGM	
MGMP9202	GWEN LEE	portrait	MGM	
MGMP-9418	ARTHUR FREED/NACIO HERB BROWN	portrait	MGM	
MGMP-9486	JOAN CRAWFORD	portrait	MGM	
MGMP9619	BUSTER KEATON	portrait	MGM	
MGMP-9839	GRETA GARBO	portrait	MGM	
MGMP-10382	JOAN CRAWFORD	portrait	MGM	
MGMP-10583	JOAN CRAWFORD	portrait	MGM	
MGMP10590	ANITA PAGE	portrait	MGM	
MGMP-11244	LON CHANEY	portrait	MGM	
MGMP11303	ANITA PAGE	portrait	MGM	
MGMP-11882	JOAN CRAWFORD	portrait	MGM	
MGMP12150	ANITA PAGE	portrait	MGM	
MGMP12778	BASIL RATHBONE	portrait	MGM	
MGMP12925	ANITA PAGE	portrait	MGM	
MGMP13199	BUSTER KEATON	portrait	MGM	
MGMP-14351	GRETA GARBO	portrait	MGM	
MGMP14390	LON CHANEY	portrait	MGM	
MGMP-14538	JOAN CRAWFORD	portrait	MGM	
MGMP-14759	JOAN CRAWFORD	portrait	MGM	
MGMP-14843	GRETA GARBO	portrait	MGM	
MGMP14866	CHARLEY CHASE	portrait	MGM	
MGMP15147	LAUREL & HARDY	portrait	MGM	
MGMP15773	NORMA SHEARER	portrait	MGM	
MGMP15786	JOHN GILBERT	portrait	MGM	
MGMP15817	ANITA PAGE	portrait	MGM	
MGMP-16417	JOAN CRAWFORD	portrait	MGM	
MGMP-16488	JOAN CRAWFORD	portrait	MGM	
MGMP16623X	NORMA SHEARER	portrait	MGM	
MGMP-17041	GRETA GARBO	portrait	MGM	
MGMP-17064	GRETA GARBO	portrait	MGM	
MGMP17455	LAUREL & HARDY	portrait	MGM	
MGMP-17656	GRETA GARBO	portrait	MGM	
MGMP-17961	GRETA GARBO	portrait	MGM	
MGMP17990	ROBERT MONTGOMERY	portrait	MGM	
MGMP-18015	GRETA GARBO	portrait	MGM	
MGMP18224	ROBERT MONTGOMERY	portrait	MGM	
MGMP-18649	GRETA GARBO	portrait	MGM	
MGMP18793	AILEEN PRINGLE	portrait	MGM	
MGMP19599	JOAN CRAWFORD	portrait	MGM	
MGMP19794	ANITA PAGE	portrait	MGM	
MGMP20126	LAUREL & HARDY	portrait	MGM	
MGMP20764	JACKIE COOPER	portrait	MGM	
MGMP21578	ANITA PAGE	portrait	MGM	

MGMP-22006	ANN DVORAK	portrait	MGM	
MGMP-22007	ANN DVORAK	portrait	MGM	
MGMP-22022	ANN DVORAK	portrait	MGM	
MGMP-22027	ANN DVORAK	portrait	MGM	
MGMP-22329	JOAN CRAWFORD	portrait	MGM	
MGMP-22360	RAQUEL TORRES	portrait	MGM	
MGMP-22416	JOAN CRAWFORD	portrait	MGM	
MGMP-22438	JOAN CRAWFORD	portrait	MGM	
MGMP22814	JACKIE COOPER	portrait	MGM	
MGMP-22847	JOAN CRAWFORD	portrait	MGM	
MH	MARIAN HALL	portrait	WARNER BROS	
MH	MEDITERRANEAN HOLIDAY (W. GER: FLYING CLIPPER 1962)	LEITNER	CONTINENTAL DIST	1964
MH	MONTE HALE	portrait	REP	
MH-INT	MOTEL HELL	CONNOR	UNITED ARTISTS	1980
MHP	MAN WHO HAD POWER OVER WOMEN (UK)	KRISH	AVCO EMBASSY	1970
MI	MATINEE IDOL (UK)	KING	UNITED ARTISTS	1933
MI	MURDER, INC.	BALABAN	20TH CENTURY FOX	1960
MI	MYSTERIOUS ISLAND	ENDFIELD	COLUMBIA	1961
MIA	MADE IN AMERICA	BENJAMIN	WARNER BROS	1993
MIA	MIAMI BLUES	ARMITAGE	ORION	1988
MIA	MISSING IN ACTION	ZITO	CANNON	1984
MIA2	MISSING IN ACTION 2	HOOL	CANNON	1985
MIG	MAN IN GREY (UK)	ARLISS	UNIVERSAL	1943
MIH	MADE IN HEAVEN	RUDOLPH	LORIMAR	1987
MIM	WINSTON AFFAIR (UK: MAN IN THE MIDDLE)	HAMILTON	20TH CENTURY FOX	1964
MIS	MARRIAGE ITALIAN STYLE	DE SICA	EMBASSY	1964
MITR	MIRACLE IN THE RAIN	MATE	WARNER BROS	1956
MJ	MOTHER, JUGS & SPEED	YATES	20TH CENTURY FOX	1976
MK	MAGIC OF THE KITE (FR:CERF-VOLANT DU BOUT DU MONDE 1958)	PIGAUT	PARAMOUNT	1971
MK	MAMBO KINGS	GLIMCHER	WARNER BROS	1992
MK	MAN WHO WOULD BE KING	HUSTON	ALLIED ARTISTS	1975
MK-1	KILLER DILL	COLLINS	SCREEN GUILD	1947
ML	JAZZMANIA	LEONARD	METRO PICTURES	1923
ML	MADAME GAMBLES (UK: MADAME LOUISE)	ROGERS	BUTCHER'S	1951
ML	MAGICIAN OF LUBLIN	STALIN	CANNON	1979
ML	MARGARET LANDRY	portrait	RKO	
ML	MARIA'S LOVERS	KONCHALOVSKY	CANNON	1984
ML	MARJORIE LORD	portrait	UNIV	
ML	MISS LONDON LTD. (UK)	GUEST	GFD	1943
ML	MOLLY LAMONT	portrait	RKO	
ML	MONA LISA	JORDAN	ISLAND PICTURES	1986
ML	MONTAGU LOVE	portrait	RKO	
ML	MURIEL LAWRENCE	portrait	REP	
ML	MUSIC LAND		RKO	1955
ML	MYRNA LOY	portrait	RKO	
ML	MAJOR LEAGUE	WARD	PARAMOUNT	1989
ML	MAJOR LEAGUE II	WARD	PARAMOUNT	1994
MLC	MONSTER OF LONDON CITY	DBONEK	PRODUCERS REL	1967
MLF	MY LEARNED FRIEND (UK)	DEARDEN, HAY	EALING	1943
MLM	KISS THE OTHER SHEIK (IT: OGGI, DOMANI, DOPODOMANI)	DE FILIPPO	MGM	1968
MLSN	MR. LORD SAYS NO (UK: HAPPY FAMILY)	BOX	SOUVAINE SELECTIVE	1952
MM	BOILING POINT	HARRIS	WARNER BROS	1993
MM	EFFECT OF GAMMA RAYS ON MAN-IN-THE-MOON MARIGOLDS	NEWMAN	20TH CENTURY FOX	1972
MM	INSIDER	MANN	BUENA VISTA	1999
MM	MAN FROM MOROCCO (UK)	GREENBAUM	ENGLISH	1945
MM	MAN IN THE MOON (UK)	DEARDEN	TRANS LUX	1960
MM	MARCY MCGUIRE	portrait	RKO	
MM	MARIE MCDONALD	portrait	UNITED ARTISTS	
MM	MARILYN MAXWELL	portrait	RKO	
MM	MARION MARTIN	portrait	RKO, UNIVERSAL	
MM	MARY MAGUIRE	portrait	RKO, WARNER BROS	
MM	MARY MASON	portrait	RKO	
MM	MATTER OF MURDER (UK)	GILLING	GRAND NATIONAL	1949
MM	MEMORIES OF ME	WINKLER	MGM	1988
MM	MICHELE MORGAN	portrait	UNIV, WARNER BROS	
MM	MILES MANDER	portrait	RKO	

MM	MILK MONEY	BENJAMIN	PARAMOUNT	1994
MM	MODEL FOR MURDER (UK)	BISHOP	CINEMA ASSOCIATES	1959
MM	MONA MARIS	portrait	RKO	1940s
MM	MY SIDE OF THE MOUNTAIN	RADNITZ	PARAMOUNT	R74
MM-112	MR. CELEBRITY	BEAUDINE	PRODUCERS RELEASING	1941
MMA	MY MAN ADAM	SIMON	TRI STAR	1985
MMC	MEET MR. CALLAGHAN (UK)	SAUNDERS	EROS	1954
MMD	MAKE MINE A DOUBLE (UK: NIGHT WE DROPPED A CLANGER)	CONYERS	ELLIS	1961
MMM	MARY MILES MINTER	portrait	REALART	
MMP	MAD MONSTER PARTY	BASS	EMBASSY	1967
MMPR	MIGHTY MORPHIN POWER RANGERS	SPICER	20th CENTURY FOX	1995
MMR	MAKING MR. RIGHT	SEIDELMAN	ORION	1987
MN	MURDER IN THE NIGHT (UK: MURDER IN SOHO)	LEE	FILM ALLIANCE	1939
MO	IN NAME ONLY (MEMORY OF LOVE*)	CROMWELL	RKO	1939
MO	MAUREEN O'HARA	portrait	UNIV	
MO	MONROE OWSLEY	portrait	MGM	
MO	SPOILERS	ENRIGHT	UNIVERSAL	1942
MOD	MESSENGER OF DEATH	THOMPSON	CANNON	1988
MOD	MY OLD DUTCH (UK)	HILL	GAUMONT BRITISH	1934
MOD	OPERATION MALAYA (UK: 1953)	MACDONALD	AMERICAN RELEASING	1955
MOF	MILL ON THE FLOSS (UK)	WHELAN	STANDARD	1937
MP	DOCTOR RHYTHM	TUTTLE	PARAMOUNT	1938
MP	MANHATTAN PROJECT	BRICKMAN	20th CENTURY FOX	1986
MP	MANITOU, THE	GIRDLER	AVCO EMBASSY	1978
MP	MARCO THE MAGNIFICENT	LEVY	MGM	1966
MP	MARGARET PERRY	portrait	MGM	
MP	MARIA PALMER	portrait	RKO	
MP	MARIE PREVOST	portrait	WARNER BROS	
MP	MASTER PLAN (UK)	ENDFIELD	ASTOR	1955
MP	MODERN PROBLEMS	SHAPIRO	20th CENTURY FOX	1981
MP	MONDO CANE	JACOPETTI	CINEMATION IND	1970
MP	MOON PILOT	NEILSON	BUENA VISTA	1961
MP	MORGAN THE PIRATE	DE TOTH, ZEGLIO	EMBASSY PICTURES	1961
MP	MURDER BY PROXY (UK) (US: BLACKOUT)	FISHER	EXCLUSIVE FILMS	1954
MP1	NEARLY A NASTY ACCIDENT (UK)	CHAFFEY	UNIVERSAL	1961
MP-9	DOCTOR RHYTHM	TUTTLE	PARAMOUNT	1938
MP-309	MAN OF COURAGE	THURN-TAXIS	PRODUCERS RELEASING	1943
MPBB	DANGEROUS MINDS	SMITH	BUENA VISTA	1995
MPGP	LA BOHEME	VIDOR	MGM	1926
MPGP-744	EVELYN BRENT	portrait	MGM	
MPGP2195	JOHN GILBERT	portrait	MGM	
MPGP2198	JOHN GILBERT	portrait	MGM	
MPGP2200	JOHN GILBERT	portrait	MGM	
MPGP2226	JOHN GILBERT	portrait	MGM	
MPGP2227	JOHN GILBERT	portrait	MGM	
MPGP2274	RAMON NOVARRO	portrait	MGM	
MPGP-2619	LON CHANEY	portrait	MGM	1924
MPGP-2620	LON CHANEY	portrait	MGM	1924
MPGP2770	NORMA SHEARER	portrait	MGM	
MPGP-2782	LON CHANEY	portrait	MGM	1924
MPGP2784	NORMA SHEARER	portrait	MGM	
MPGP3230	NORMA SHEARER	portrait	MGM	
MPGP3241	NORMA SHEARER	portrait	MGM	
MPGP3370	LILLIAN GISH	portrait	MGM	
MPGP3375	LILLIAN GISH	portrait	MGM	
MPGP3425	KING VIDOR, MARION DAVIES - ZANDER THE GREAT	portrait	MGM	
MPGP3916	CLAIRE WINDSOR, BERT LYTELL	portrait	MGM	
MPGP5135	NORMA SHEARER	portrait	MGM	
MPGP5260	NORMA SHEARER	portrait	MGM	
MPGP5262	NORMA SHEARER	portrait	MGM	
MPGP6142	RAMON NOVARRO	portrait	MGM	
MPGP6267	NORMA SHEARER	portrait	MGM	
MPGP6268	NORMA SHEARER	portrait	MGM	
MPGP6270	NORMA SHEARER	portrait	MGM	
MPGP6273	NORMA SHEARER	portrait	MGM	
MPGP6662	NORMA SHEARER	portrait	MGM	

MPGP6767	NORMA SHEARER	portrait	MGM	
MPGP7189	LILLIAN GISH	portrait	MGM	
MPGP7467	CLAIRE WINDSOR	portrait	MGM	
MPGP7517	GWEN LEE	portrait	MGM	
MPGP7687	NORMA SHEARER	portrait	MGM	
MPGP7723	GWEN LEE	portrait	MGM	
MPGP7838	GWEN LEE	portrait	MGM	
MPGP8163	CLAIRE WINDSOR	portrait	MGM	
MPGP8356	GERTRUDE OLMSTEAD	portrait	MGM	
MPGP-8588	KARL DANE	portrait	MGM	
MPGP8697	NORMA SHEARER	portrait	MGM	
MPGP8734	GWEN LEE	portrait	MGM	
MPGP8855	NORMA SHEARER	portrait	MGM	
MPGP8975	NORMA SHEARER	portrait	MGM	
MPGP-8989	LILYAN TASHMAN	portrait	MGM	
MPGP9303	NORMA SHEARER	portrait	MGM	
MPGP9452	GWEN LEE	portrait	MGM	
MPGP9736	GWEN LEE	portrait	MGM	
MPGP9790	GWEN LEE	portrait	MGM	
MPGP9799	GWEN LEE	portrait	MGM	
MPGP9806	GWEN LEE	portrait	MGM	
MPGP9952	CLAIRE WINDSOR	portrait	MGM	
MPI	HARRY BLACK AND THE TIGER	FREGONESE	20th CENTURY FOX	1958
MPJ/PS	MY BROTHER JONATHAN (UK)	FRENCH	ALLIED ARTISTS	1948
MPM3	LIFE AND DEATH OF COLONEL BLIMP (UK)	POWELL/ PRESSBURGER	GENERAL FILM	1943
MPM-6	SILVER FLEET (UK)	SEWELL, WELLESLEY	PRODUCERS RELEASING	1943
MPP	MISS PILGRIM'S PROGRESS (UK)	GUEST	GRAND NATIONAL	1949
MPX16	BERT LYTELL	portrait	METRO	
MPX19	ALICE LAKE	portrait	METRO	
MPX73	RUDOLPH VALENTINO	portrait	METRO	
MQ	MIGHTY QUINN	SCHENKEL	MGM	1989
MR	MARGARET RUTHERFORD	portrait		
MR	MARJORIE RAMBEAU	portrait	PATHE	
MR	MARJORIE REYNOLDS	portrait	MON, RKO, UNIV	
MR	MARTHA RAYE	portrait	UNIV	
MR	MARTIN RACKIN	portrait	FOX	
MR	MAY ROBSON	portrait	RKO	
MR	MIDAS RUN	KJELLIN	CINERAMA RELEASING	1969
MR	MIDNIGHT RIDE	BRALVER	CANNON	1990
MR	MIRACLE RIDER (serial)	EASON, SCHAEFER	MASCOT	1935
MR	OLD MOTHER RILEY (UK)	MITCHELL	BUTCHER'S	1937
MR	ROOM UPSTAIRS	LACOMBE	LOPERT	1948
MR	SHERLOCK HOLMES & MISSING REMBRANDT	HISCOTT	FIRST DIVISION	1932
MRB	OLD MOTHER RILEY IN BUSINESS (UK)	BAXTER	ANGLO-AMERICAN	1941
MRBB	MIAMI RHAPSODY	FRANKEL	BUENA VISTA	1995
MRBB	RUNAWAY BRAIN	BAILEY	BUENA VISTA	1995
MRD	OLD MOTHER RILEY DETECTIVE (UK)	COMFORT	ANGLO-AMERICAN	1943
MRH	OLD MOTHER RILEY AT HOME (UK)	MITCHELL	ANGLO-AMERICAN	1945
MRPM	MURDER AT 45 R.P.M. (FR: MEURTRE EN 45 TOURS 1960)	PERIER	MGM	1965
MRT	MAKE ROOM FOR TOMORROW (FR:AU BOUT BOUT BANC 1979)	KASSOVITZ	ROBERT MCNEIL	1980
MS	BEAST FROM 20,000 FATHOMS, THE	LOURIE	WARNER BROS	1953
MS	LITTLE MISS SOMEBODY (UK)	TENNYSON	BUTCHER'S	1937
MS	MADAME (IT/FR: MADAME SANS-GENE 1961)	JAQUE	EMBASSY	1963
MS	MAID IN SWEDEN	WOLMAN	CANNON	1971
MS	MARGOT STEVENSON	portrait	WARNER BROS	
MS	MARK STEVENS	portrait	RKO	
MS	MARTHA SCOTT	portrait	RKO	
MS	MAXIMILIAN SCHELL	portrait	UNIV	
MS	MEAN SEASON	BORSOS	ORION	1984
MS	MISSION STARDUST	ZEGLIO	TIMES FILM	1968
MS	MONSTER SQUAD	DEKKER	TRI STAR	1987
MS	MORALS SQUAD	MAHON	JOSEPH BRENNER	1960
MS	MRS. SOFFEL	ARMSTRONG	MGM	1984
MS	MUMMY'S SHROUD (UK)	GILLING	20TH CENTURY FOX	1967
MS	SEBASTIAN (UK)	GREENE	PARAMOUNT	1968
MS-18	SINGING BOXER (sh)	PEARCE	PARAMOUNT	1933

MS-20	LADIES FIRST	GRAINGER	PARAMOUNT (SENNETT)	1918
MS-27	BEWARE OF BORDERS	HIBBERT	PARAMOUNT (SENNETT)	1918
MS-33	KNOCKOUT KISSES	MARSHALL	PARAMOUNT (SENNETT)	1933
MS-33	NEVER TOO OLD (?)	JONES	PARAMOUNT	1933
MS-45	MS. 45	FERRERA	NAVARON FILM	1981
MSL	MY SECRET LIFE	THOMAS	HOWARD MAHLER FILMS	1971
MSM	MADONNA OF THE SEVEN MOONS (UK)	CRABTREE	GUNIVERSAL	1945
MSR	HELL'S CARGO (UK: MCGLUSKY THE SEA ROVER)	SUMMERS	FILM ALLIANCE	1935
MST	MADEMOISELLE STRIPTEASE (FR)	ALLEGRET	DCA	1957
MST	NUDE SET, THE (FR: MADEMOISELLE STRIPTEASE 1957)	ALLEGRET	AUDUBON	1960
MSUW	MAIN STREET UNDER SEA		ETERNAL FILM	1955
MSV	OLD MOTHER RILEY MEETS THE VAMPIRE/VAMPIRE LONDON	GILLING	BLUE CHIP	1952
MT	INSPECTOR MAIGRET (FR: MAIGRET TEND UN PIEGE)	DELANNOY	LOPERT	1958
MT	MAN TROUBLE	RAFELSON	20th CENTURY FOX	1992
MT	MELODY TIME (t)	GERONIMI	RKO	1948
MT	MERMAIDS OF TIBURON	LAMB	FILMGROUP	1962
MT	NEVER LET GO (UK)	GUILLERMIN	CONTINENTAL	1960
MTD	TEENAGE BAD GIRL (UK: MY TEENAGE DAUGHTER)	WILCOX	DCA	1956
MTG	MAKING THE GRADE	WALKER	CANNON	1984
MTK	MACK THE KNIFE	GOLAN	21ST CENTURY FILM	1990
MTM	MISSLE TO THE MOON	CUNHA	ASTOR	1959
MTM	MUPPETS TAKE MANHATTAN	OZ	TRI STAR	1984
MTO	MAID TO ORDER	JONES	NEW CENTURY	1987
MTS	MUCH TOO SHY (UK)	VARNEL	COLUMBIA BRITISH	1942
MU	MAN UPSTAIRS (UK)	CHAFFEY	KINGSLEY-UNION	1958
MU	MASTERS OF THE UNIVERSE	GODDARD	CANNON	1987
MU	MILLIONS LIKE US (UK)	GILLIAT, LAUNDER	GFD	1943
MU	MY UNCLE	TATI	CONTINENTAL DIST.	1958
MULAN	MULAN	COOK	BUENA VISTA	1998
MUS	FORBIDDEN MUSIC (IT: MUSICA PROIBITA 1942)	CAMPOGALLIANI	CONTINENTAL	1946
MV	MEETING VENUS	SZABO	WARNER BROS	1991
MV	MOVING VIOLATION	DUBIN	20th CENTURY FOX	1976
MV	MOVING VIOLATIONS	ISRAEL	20th CENTURY FOX	1985
MV	MY UNCLE	TATI	CONTINENTAL DIST.	1958
MV	TALK OF THE DEVIL (UK)	REED	GAUMONT	1936
MW	IT'S A MAD, MAD, MAD, MAD WORLD	KRAMER	UNITED ARTISTS	1964
MW	MAD AT THE WORLD	ESSEX	FILMAKERS RELEASING	1955
MW	MAN AND A WOMAN, A (FR: UN HOMME ET UNE FEMME)	LELOUCH	ALLIED ARTISTS	1966
MW	MAY WHITTY	portrait	UNIVERSAL	
MW	MIDDLE WATCH (UK)	BENTLEY	PATHE	1940
MW	MR. WONDERFUL	MINGHELLA	WARNER BROS	1993
MW	MURPHY'S WAR (UK)	YATES	PARAMOUNT	1971
MW	SMUGGLERS (UK)	KNOWLES	EAGLE LION	1948
MWC	MAN, WOMAN AND CHILD	RICHARDS	PARAMOUNT	1982
MWD	MORO, WITCH DOCTOR	ROMERO	20th CENTURY FOX	1954
MWF	MAN WITHOUT A FACE	GIBSON	WARNER BROS	1993
MWFD	MAN WHO FINALLY DIED (UK)	LAWRENCE	GOLDSTONE	1963
MWGE	MAN WITH THE GLASS EYE	VOHRER	SUNSET INT'L	1973
MWH	MAN WHO HAUNTED HIMSELF (UK)	DEARDEN	LEVITT-PICKMAN	1970
MWL	MY WIFE'S LODGER (UK)	ELVEY	ADELPHI	1952
MWM	DARK HIGHWAY*	RAY	RKO	1952
MWT	MAN WHO WOULDN'T TALK (UK)	WILCOX	SHOWCORPORATION	1958
MWU	BAD SISTER (UK: WHITE UNICORN)	KNOWLES	UNIVERSAL	1947
MWU	SMUGGLERS (UK: MAN WITHIN)	KNOWLES	EAGLE LION	1947
MX	MALCOLM X	LEE	WARNER BROS	1992
MXB	MARX BROTHERS	portrait	MGM	
MXC	MAE CLARKE	portrait	MGM	
MXKX	MILIZA KORJUS	portrait	MGM	
MY	MARYLA JONAS	portrait		
MZ	YOUR PAST IS SHOWING (UK: NAKED TRUTH)	ZAMPI	RANK	1957
MZ195	FIVE GOLDEN HOURS (UK)	ZAMPI	COLUMBIA	1961
N	BOYS WILL BE BOYS (UK)	BEAUDINE	GAUMONT	1935
N	NADINE	BENTON	TRI STAR	1987
N	NAPOLEON	GANCE	MGM	1929
N	NEGATIVES (UK)	MEDAK	CONTINENTAL	1968
N	NEGOTIATOR, THE	GRAY	WARNER BROS	1998

N	NELL	APTED	20th CENTURY FOX	1994
N	NETWORK	LUMET	MGM/UNITED ARTISTS	1976
N	NICKELODEON	BOGDANOVICH	COLUMBIA	19766
N	NIGHTBREED	BARKER	20th CENTURY FOX	1990
N	NIGHTWING	HILLER	COLUMBIA	1979
N	NIJINSKY	ROSS	PARAMOUNT	1980
N	NIKKI, WILD DOG OF THE NORTH	COUFFER, HALDANE	BUENA VISTA	1961
N	NOSFERATU THE VAMPYRE	HERZOG	20th CENTURY FOX	1979
N	TANK FORCE (UK: NO TIME TO DIE)	YOUNG	COLUMBIA	1958
N-1	HOT ROD RUMBLE (AA)	MARTINSON	MONOGRAM	1957
N-22	THY NAME IS WOMAN	NIBLO	METRO	1924
N-3100	SIREN OF ATLANTIS (ATLANTIS, THE LOST CONTINENT)	RIPLEY	UNITED ARTISTS	1947
NA	NARCO MEN, THE (SP: PERSECUCION HASTA VALENCIA 1968)	COLL	RAF IND	1971
NB	HOUSE ON THE WATERFRONT (FR: PORT DU DESIR)	GREVILLE	UNION FILM	1955
NB	NAKED AND BRAVE (SHIP OF DEAD) (GER: TOTENSCHIFF 1959)	TRESSLER	EAGLE AMERICAN FILM	R65
NB	NEWTON BOYS	LINKLATER	20th CENTURY FOX	1998
NB	NIGHT BOAT TO DUBLIN (UK)	HUNTINGTON	PATHE	1946
NB	NIGHT OF BLOODY HORROR	HOUCK JR	HOWCO	1969
NB	NONE BUT THE LONELY HEART	ODETS	RKO	1944
NB	NOW BARABBAS (UK)	PARRY	WARNER BROS.	1949
NBB	NIGHT OF THE BLOOD BEAST	KOWALSKI	AIP	1958
NBK	NEVER BEEN KISSED	GOSNELL	20th CENTURY FOX	1999
NC	CONVICTS AT LARGE	BEAL	PRINCIPAL DIST.	1938
NC	NARROWING CIRCLE (UK)	SAUNDERS	EROS	1956
NC	NEW CENTURIONS	FLEISCHER	COLUMBIA	1972
NC	NIGHT AND THE CITY	WINKLER	20th CENTURY FOX	1992
NC	NIGHTCOMERS	WINNER	AVCO EMBASSY	1972
NC	ROCKETSHIP X-M	NEUMANN	LIPPERT	1950
NCM	NORTHVILLE CEMETERY MASSACRE	DEAR	CANNON	1976
ND	NOT SO DUSTY (UK)	ROGERS	EROS	1956
NDD	NO MY DARLING DAUGHTER (UK)	THOMAS	ZENITH	1961
NDF	NORTH DALLAS FORTY	KOTCHEFF	PARAMOUNT	1979
NE	BURN, WITCH, BURN	HAYERS	AIP	1962
NE	NO ESCAPE	CAMPBELL	SAVOY	1994
NE	THERE IS NO ESCAPE (UK: DARK ROAD)	GOULDING	LIPPERT	1948
NF	FUGITIVE (UK: ON THE NIGHT OF THE FIRE)	HURST	UNIVERSAL	1939
NF	NIGHT WAS OUR FRIEND (UK)	ANDERSON	MONARCH	1951
NF	NIGHTFLYERS	BLAKE	NEW CENTURY	1987
NFH	IRON PETTICOAT (UK)	THOMAS	MGM	1956
NF-K	NINE TO FIVE	HIGGINS	20th CENTURY FOX	1980
NFM	IRON PETTICOAT (UK)	THOMAS	MGM	1956
NFR	NIGHT FULL OF RAIN (CAN/IT)	WERTMULLER	WARNER BROS	1978
NG	NAKED GUN	DEW	ASSOC. FILM RELEASING	1956
NG	NAME OF THE GAME (TV)	WYLIE	NBC-TV	1968
NG	NIGHT GAMES	ZETTERLING	MONDIAL FILMS	1966
NG	NIGHT OF THE GRIZZLY	PEVNEY	PARAMOUNT	1966
NG	NINTH GATE, THE	POLANSKI	WARNER BROS	1999
NG2 1/2	NAKED GUN 2 1/2: SMELL OF FEAR	ZUCKER	PARAMOUNT	1991
NGL	NICE GIRL LIKE ME (UK)	DAVIS	AVCO EMBASSY	1969
NHF	NIGHT HEAVEN FELL (FR: LES BIJOUTIERS DU CLAIRE DE LUNE)	VADIM	KINGSLEY INT'L	1958
NIC	NOTHING IN COMMON	MARSHALL	TRI STAR	1986
NIN	NINJA III - THE DOMINATION	FIRSTENBERG	CANNON	1984
NIN	REVENGE OF THE NINJA	FIRSTENBERG	CANNON	1983
NJ	NEW JACK CITY	VAN PEEBLES	WARNER BROS	1991
NJ	NIGHT OF THE JUGGLER	BUTLER	COLUMBIA	1980
NK	NANCY KWAN	portrait	PARAMOUNT`	
NK	NEXT OF KIN (UK)	DICKINSON	UNIVERSAL	1942
NK	NORMAN KERRY	portrait	MGM	
NKBB	3 NINJAS	TURTELTAUB	BUENA VISTA	1992
NL	NAKED LUNCH	CRONENBERG	20TH CENTURY FOX	1991
NL	NAVY LARK (UK)	PARRY	20TH CENTURY FOX	1959
NL	NEVER LET GO (UK)	GUILLERMIN	CONTINENTAL	1960
NL	NEW LEAF, A	MAY	PARAMOUNT	1971
NL	NO WAY TO TREAT A LADY	SMIGHT	PARAMOUNT	1967
NLB	NIGHTS OF THE LUCRETIA BORGIA (IT)	GRIECO	COLUMBIA	1959
NLBB	NOTHING TO LOSE	OEDEKERK	BUENA VISTA	1997

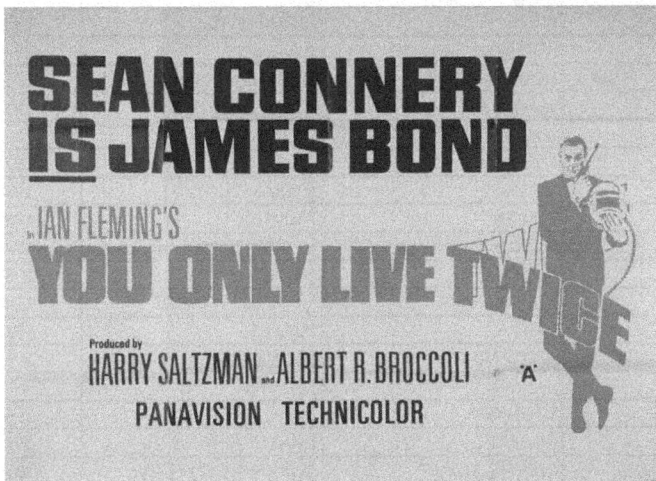

NLG	NIGHT THE LIGHTS WENT OUT IN GEORGIA	MAXWELL	AVCO EMBASSY	1981
NL-R	NEW LEAF	MAYFIELD	PARAMOUNT	1971
NM	NINE MONTHS	COLUMBUS	20th CENTURY FOX	1995
NM	NO MAN'S LAND	WERNER	ORION	1987
NM	NO MERCY	PEARCE	TRI STAR	1986
NM	NOREEN MICHAELS	portrait		
NM	PLATOON LEADER	NORRIS	CANNON	1988
NMF	NIGHT IS MY FUTURE/MUSIC IN DARKNESS (SWE)	BERGMAN	EMBASSY	1948
NN	99 AND 44/100% DEAD	FRANKENHEIMER	20TH CENTURY FOX	1974
NN	GHOSTS OF BERKELEY SQUARE (UK)	SEWELL	PATHE	1947
NN	LIFE AND ADVENTURES OF NICHOLAS NICKLEBY (UK)	CAVALCANTI	UNIVERSAL	1947
NN	NOTHING BUT THE NIGHT	SASDY	RANK	1973
NN	SAWDUST AND TINSEL/NAKED NIGHT (SWE: GYCKLARNAS AFTON)	BERGMAN	TIMES	1953
NNT	NEXT TO NO TIME (UK 1958)	CORNELIUS	SHOW CORPORATION	1960
NO	NINA ORLA	portrait	UNIV	
NO	NOAH'S ARK	CURTIZ	WARNER BROS	1928
NO	SEPTEMBER STORM	HASKIN	20th CENTURY FOX	1960
NOI	NIGHT OF THE IGUANA	HUSTON	MGM	1964
NOS	NEVER ON SUNDAY (GK: POTE TIN KYRIAKI)	DASSIN	LOPERT	1960
NOW	NUMBER ONE WITH A BULLET	SMIGHT	CANNON	1986
NOW	NURSE ON WHEELS (UK)	THOMAS	JANUS	1963
NP	ESCAPE BY NIGHT (UK)	GILLING	EROS	1953
NP	I, MOBSTER	CORMAN	20th CENTURY FOX	1958
NP	NAKED PARADISE (r: THUNDER OVER HAWAII)	CORMAN	AIP	1957
NP	NATURE'S PARADISE (UK: NUDIST PARADISE)	SAUNDERS	FANFARE	1959
NP	NEUTRAL PORT (UK)	VARNEL	GFD	1940
NP-49	I, Mobster	CORMAN	20th CENTURY-FOX	1958
NPT	PAUL TEMPLE'S TRIUMPH (UK)	ROGERS	BUTCHER'S	1950
NPW	NEVER PUT IT IN WRITING (UK)	STONE	ALLIED ARTISTS	1964
NQ	BEWARE OF BACHELORS	DEL RUTH	WARNER BROS	1928
NR	NAME OF THE ROSE, THE (FR: DER NAME DER ROSE)	ANNAUD	20th CENTURY FOX	1986
NR	NICKEL RIDE	MULLIGAN	20th CENTURY FOX	1974
NR	NO ROAD BACK (UK)	TULLY	RKO	1957
NR	NORMA RAE	RITT	20th CENTURY FOX	1979
NR	NUNS ON THE RUN	LYNN	20th CENTURY FOX	1990
NR	NURSES REPORT (GER)	BOOS		1977
NRI/PS	NO ROOM AT THE INN (UK)	BIRT	STRATFORD	1948
NRP	NO RESTING PLACE (UK)	ROTHA	LASSIC	1951
NS	FOR MEMBERS ONLY: NUDIST STORY	HERRINGTON	ART IN MOTION PICT	1959
NS	LIFE IN HER HANDS (UK)	LEACOCK	UNITED ARTISTS	1951
NS	NATALIE SCHAEFER	portrait	UNITED ARTISTS	
NS	NEXT STOP, GREENWICH VILLAGE	MAZURSKY	20th CENTURY FOX	1976
NS	NIGHT SCHOOL	HUGHES	PARAMOUNT	1981
NS	NIGHT STALKER	KLEVEN	ALMI	1985
NSP1	AVENGERS (UK: DAY WILL DAWN)	FRENCH	PARAMOUNT	1942
NT	NO TIME FOR TEARS (UK)	FRANKEL	PATHE	1957
NT	RUSSIAN STORY, THE	FREEDLAND	ARKINO PICTURES	1943
NT-16	ISLE OF CONQUEST	JOSE	SELECT	1919
NTH	NOWHERE TO HIDE	AZZOPARDI	NEW CENTURY	1987
NTK	NATALIE TALMADGE (KEATON)	portrait	METRO	
NTK	NO TIME TO KILL (UK)	YOUNGER	ADP	1959
NTL	TIME, GENTLEMEN, PLEASE! (UK)	GILBERT	MAYER-KINGLSEY	1952
NTN	NEVER TAKE NO FOR AN ANSWER (UK: SMALL MIRACLE)	CLOCHE, SMART	SOUVAINE SELECTIVE	1951
NTP	NIGHT TRAIN TO PARIS (UK)	DOUGLAS	20TH CENTURY FOX	1964
NW	NO PLACE LIKE HOMICIDE! (UK: WHAT A CARVE UP!)	JACKSON	EMBASSY	1961
NW	WINGS OF THE MORNING (UK)	SCHUSTER	20TH CENTURY FOX	1937
NW2	UNDER THE RED ROBE (UK)	SJOSTROM	20TH CENTURY FOX	1937
NW3	GREEN COCKATOO (UK)	MENZIES	20TH CENTURY FOX	1937
NWC	NUDE IN A WHITE CAR	HOSSEIN	TRANS-LUX	1958
NWO	NO WAY OUT	DONALDSON	ORION	1987
NY	NEW INTERNS	RICH	COLUMBIA	1964
NY-680	DOUBLE HARNESS	CROMWELL	RKO	1933
NY-695	LITTLE WOMEN	CUKOR	RKO	1933
NY-705	CHANCE AT HEAVEN	SEITER	RKO	1933
NY-803	ROBERTA	SEITER	RKO	1935
NY-827	LAST DAYS OF POMPEII	SCHOEDSACK	RKO	1935

NY-M	HORSE'S MOUTH (UK)	NEAME	UNITED ARTISTS	1958
NY-Q	MORNING GLORY	SHERMAN	RKO	1933
O	HANNAH LEE (OUTLAW TERRITORY)	GARMES	REALART	1953
O	OBSESSION	DE PALMA	COLUMBIA	1976
O	ODETTE (UK)	WILCOX	LOPERT	1950
O	OMOO - OMOO THE SHARK GOD	LEONARD	SCREEN GUILD	1949
O	OTHELLO (IT)	ZEFFIRELLI	CANNON	1986
O	OUTLAWED	FORDE	FBO	1929
O/BS	BLUE SCAR	CRAIGIE	BRITISH LION	1949
O03	IT'S ALIVE	COHEN	WARNER BROS	1974
O04	A STAR IS BORN	PIERSON	WARNER BROS	1976
O08	LISZTOMANIA	RUSSELL	WARNER BROS	1975
O12	STRAIGHT TIME	GROSBARD	WARNER BROS	1978
O16	SHARKY'S MACHINE	REYNOLDS	ORION (WARNER BROS)	1981
O18	THIEF WHO CAME TO DINNER	YORKIN	WARNER BROS	1973
O19	COME BACK CHARLESTON BLUE	WARREN	WARNER BROS	1972
O20	TRAIN ROBBERS	KENNEDY	WARNER BROS	1973
O21	EXCALIBUR	BOORMAN	ORION (WARNER BROS)	1981
O25	EXORCIST	FRIEDKIN	WARNER BROS	1973
O26	CLASS OF '44	BOGART	WARNER BROS	1973
O28	ROLLOVER	PAKULA	ORION (WARNER BROS)	1981
O28	SCARECROW	SHATZBERG	WARNER BROS	1973
O30	MAME	SAKS	WARNER BROS	1974
O31	CLEOPATRA JONES	STARRETT	WARNER BROS	1973
O32	FREEBIE AND THE BEAN	RUSH	WARNER BROS	1974
O33	BLAZING SADDLES	BROOKS	WARNER BROS	1974
O34	ZANDY'S BRIDE	TROELL	WARNER BROS	1974
O35	MAGNUM FORCE	POST	WARNER BROS	1973
O37	TERMINAL MAN	HODGES	WARNER BROS	1974
O38	NIGHT MOVES	PENN	WARNER BROS	1975
O39	OUR TIME	HYAMS	WARNER BROS	1974
O41	PRISONER OF SECOND AVENUE	FRANK	WARNER BROS	1975
O43	DOC SAVAGE: MAN OF BRONZE	ANDERSON	WARNER BROS	1975
O46	TOWERING INFERNO	GUILLERMIN	WARNER BROS	1974
O47	CLEOPATRA JONES & CASINO GOLD	BAIL	WARNER BROS	1975
O48	ULTIMATE WARRIOR	CLOUSE	WARNER BROS	1975
O50	SPARKLE	O'STEEN	WARNER BROS	1976
O56	ST. IVES	THOMPSON	WARNER BROS	1976
O57	EXORCIST II: HERETIC	BOORMAN	WARNER BROS	1977
O59	VIVA KNIEVEL	DOUGLAS	WARNER BROS	1977
O64	OH GOD	REINER	WARNER BROS	1977
O67	BIG WEDNESDAY	MILIUS	WARNER BROS	1978
O67	COME BACK CHARLESTON BLUE	WARREN	WARNER BROS	1972
O68	SWARM	ALLEN	WARNER BROS	1978
O72	EVERY WHICH WAY BUT LOOSE	FARGO	WARNER BROS	1978
O75	IN-LAWS	HILLER	WARNER BROS	1979
O76	BEYOND THE POSEIDON ADVENTURE	ALLEN	WARNER BROS	1979
O80	ALTERED STATES	RUSSELL	WARNER BROS	1980
O98	FANDANGO	REYNOLDS	WARNER BROS	1983
O360	BUT NOT FOR ME	LANG	PARAMOUNT	1959
OB	OLD BOYFRIENDS	TEWKESBURY	AVCO EMBASSY	1979
OB	ONCE BEFORE I DIE	DEREK	SEVEN ARTS	1966
OB	OPERATION BULLSHINE (UK)	GUNN	PATHE	1959
OB	OUTBREAK	PETERSEN	WARNER BROS	1995
OB	OUTLAW BLUES	HEFFRON	WARNER BROS	1977
OB	OVERBOARD	MARSHALL	MGM	1987
OB	OXFORD BLUES	BORIS	MGM	1984
OB	THREE STOPS TO MURDER (UK: BLOOD ORANGE)	FISHER	EXCLUSIVE	1953
OB	TO THE VICTOR (UK: OWD BOB)	STEVENSON	GAUMONT BRIT. AMER.	1938
OBB	OVER THE BROOKLYN BRIDGE	GOLAN	CANNON	1983
OBBB	OFF BEAT	DINNER	BUENA VISTA	1986
OC	OKLAHOMA CRUDE	KRAMER	COLUMBIA	1974
OC	ONCE A CROOK (UK)	MASON	20TH CENTURY FOX	1941
OC	OUTBREAK (on cast shot - should be OB)	PETERSEN	WARNER BROS	1995
OC2	ODD COUPLE II	DEUTCH	PARAMOUNT	1998
OD	OPERATION DAMES	STOUMEN	AIP	1959

OD	OPERATION DIPLOMAT (UK)	GUILLERMIN	BUTCHER'S	1953
OD	OWEN DAVIS JR	portrait	RKO	
OD 964	RECKLESS MOMENT	OPULS	COLUMBIA	1949
ODG	ON DEADLY GROUND	SEAGAL	WARNER BROS	1993
OE	MURDER ON THE ORIENT EXPRESS	LUMET	PARAMOUNT	1974
OE	OVER THE EDGE	KAPLAN	ORION (WARNER BROS)	1979
OF1	INVADERS (UK: 49TH PARALLEL)	POWELL, PRESSBURGER	COLUMBIA	1941
OFD	ONE FINE DAY	HOFFMAN	20th CENTURY FOX	1996
OFL	PLEASE NOT NOW (FR)	AUREL, TROP	INT'L CLASSICS	1961
OFN	ONE FRIGHTENED NIGHT	CABANNE	MASCOT	1935
OG	OFFICE GIRLS (GER: EROTIK IM BERUF) (SEX IN THE OFFICE)	HOFBAUER	ATLANTIC FILM	1972
OG	OLD GUN	ENRICO	SURROGATE	1975
OG	OUTLAW GIRL (IT)	CAMERINI	IFE RELEASING	1955
OH	OPERATION HAYLIFT	BERKE	LIPPERT	1950
OHBP	ON HER MAJESTY'S SECRET SERVICE (UK)	HUNTINGTON	UNITED ARTISTS	1969
OHGW	ON HER MAJESTY'S SECRET SERVICE (UK)	HUNTINGTON	UNITED ARTISTS	1969
OK	O-KAY FOR SOUND (UK)	VARNEL	GFD	1937
OK	ORDERS TO KILL (UK)	ASQUITH	UMPO	1958
OL	OPERATION LOVEBIRDS	BALLING	EMERSON FILM	1967
OLBB	OLIVER & COMPANY (t)	SCRIBNER	BUENA VISTA	1988
OM	ONCE MORE, WITH FEELING! (UK)	DONEN	COLUMBIA	1960
OM	OPERATION MERMAID (PATTERN FOR PLUNDER)	AINSWORTH	HERTS-LION INT'L	1964
OM/A	OUR MAN IN HAVANA	REED	COLUMBIA	1959
OMH	OUR MOTHER'S HOUSE (UK)	CLAYTON	MGM	1967
OMR	OLD MOTHER RILEY JOINS UP (UK)	ROGERS	ANGLO-AMERICAN	1940
OMR	SAID O'REILLY TO MCNAB (UK)	BEAUDINE	GAUMONT BRIT. AMER.	1937
ON	OVER NIGHT (UK: THAT NIGHT IN LONDON)	LEE	PARAMOUNT	1932
ONY	ONLY ONE NEW YORK	LEVINE	EMBASSY	1964
OO2	DIE LAUGHING	WERNER	ORION	1980
OOMA	OBJECT OF MY AFFECTION	HYTNER	20th CENTURY FOX	1998
OP	OH, MR. PORTER!	VARNEL	GFD	1937
OP	ONE POTATO, TWO POTATO	PEERCE	CINEMA V	1964
OP	ORDINARY PEOPLE	REDFORD	PARAMOUNT	1980
OP1	STOLEN LIFE (UK)	CZINNER	PARAMOUNT	1939
OP2	MOUSE THAT ROARED (UK)	ARNOLD	COLUMBIA	1959
OQ	PENNY POINT TO PARADISE (UK)	YOUNG	ADELPHI	1951
ORBB	OPEN RANGE	COSTNER	BUENA VISTA	2003
OS	OLIVER'S STORY	KORTY	PARAMOUNT	1978
OS	ONCE A SINNER (UK)	GILBERT	J.H. HOFFBERG	1950
OS	OPERATION SNATCH (UK)	DAY	CONTINENTAL	1962
OS	SPIES IN THE AIR (UK: SPIES OF THE AIR)	MACDONALD	FILM ALLIANCE	1940
OSBB	OSCAR	LANDIS	BUENA VISTA	1991
OSBB	OTHER SISTER, THE	MARSHALL	BUENA VISTA	1999
OSD	DOUBLE CONFESSION (UK)	ANNAKIN	STRATFORD	1950
OSF	IN OLD SANTA FE	HOWARD	MASCOT	1934
OSPC	YOU CAN'T CHEAT AN HONEST MAN	MARSHALL	UNIVERSAL	1939
OSS	GUMBALL RALLY - SEE #055	BAIL	WARNER BROS	1976
OSS	OSS 117: MISSION FOR KILLER (FR: FURIA DAHIA POUR OSS 117)	HUNEBELLE	EMBASSY	1966
OSTM	ONE SPY TOO MANY	SARGENT	MGM	1966
OT	DAMIEN-OMEN II	TAYLOR	20TH CENTURY FOX	1978
OT	OUTLAW TREASURE	DRAKE	AMERICAN RELEASING	1955
OT	OUT-OF-TOWNERS	WEISMAN	PARAMOUNT	1999
OTE	ON THE EDGE	NILSSON	SKOURAS	1986
OTL	ONLY THE LONELY	COLUMBUS	20th CENTURY FOX	1991
OTS	ONLY THE STRONG	LETTICH	20th CENTURY FOX	1993
OTTO4 ELVEY3	FOLLY OF VANITY	OTTO, ELVEY	FOX FILM	1924
OUF	ONCE UPON A FOREST (t)	GROSVENOR	20th CENTURY FOX	1993
OUI	ONCE UPON AN ISLAND	AXEL	ALLIED ARTISTS	1966
OW	OKLAHOMA WOMAN, THE	CORMAN	AMERICAN RELEASING	1956
OW	ONCE UPON WHEEL (tv doc)	WINTERS	SAGGITARIUS	1968
OW	OSCAR WILDE (UK)	RATOFF	FOUR CITY	1960
OW	OSKAR WERNER	portrait	UNIV	
OW	OSTERMAN WEEKEND	PECKINPAH	20TH CENTURY FOX	1983
OW	OUTLAW WOMEN	NEWFIELD	LIPPERT	1952
OWO	ONE WAY OUT (UK)	SEARLE	RANK	1955
OWO	ONE WILD OAT (UK)	SAUNDERS	EROS	1951

P	ADVENTURES OF PRISCILLA, QUEEN OF THE DESERT	ELLIOTT	GRAMERCY	1994
P	CAPTIVE WOMEN	GILMORE	RKO	1952
P	PAGEMASTER	HUNT, JOHNSTON	20th CENTURY FOX	1994
P	PAISAN (IT: PAISA)	ROSSELLINI	MAYER & BURSTYN	1946
P	PANTHER	VAN PEEBLES	GRAMERCY	1995
P	PARADISE	GILLARD	EMBASSY	1982
P	PARANOIA	LENZI	COMMONWEALTH	1969
P	PASSENGER 57	HOOKS	WARNER BROS	1992
P	PASSING OF THE THIRD FLOOR BACK (UK)	VIERTEL	GAUMONT BRITISH	1935
P	PASSION OF ANNA (SWE: EN PASSION 1969)	BERGMAN	UNITED ARTISTS	1970
P	PERSONA	BERGMAN	LOPERT	1967
P	PHYSICIAN (UK)	JACOBY	TIFFANY	1928
P	PIRATES	POLANSKI	CANNON	1986
P	PLENTY	SCHEPISI	20th CENTURY FOX	1985
P	POCO ...LITTLE DOG LOST	BROOKS	CINEMA SHARES	1977
P	POLYESTER	WATERS	NEW LINE CINEMA	1981
P	PORKY'S II: THE NEXT DAY	CLARK	20th CENTURY FOX	1982
P	POWER	LUMET	20th CENTURY FOX	1986
P	PRANCER	HANCOCK	ORION	1989
P	STRANGLER (UK: EAST OF PICCADILLY)	HUTH	PRODUCERS RELEASING	1941
P	TRAPPED IN PARADISE	GALLO	20th CENTURY FOX	1994
P	WITHOUT LIMITS	TOWNE	WARNER BROS	1998
P	YOUNG MR. PITT (UK)	REED	20TH CENTURY FOX	1942
P1	DAUGHTER OF DR. JEKYLL	ULMER	ALLIED ARTISTS	1957
P1	ESCAPE IN THE SUN (UK)	BREAKSTON	PARAMOUNT BRITISH	1956
P1	MEN OF TOMORROW (UK)	SAGAN	MUNDUA	1932
P1	PACIFIC DESTINY (UK)	RILLA	BRITISH LION	1956
P-1	PROJECT MOONBASE	TALMADGE	LIPPERT	1953
P-1	SPITBALL SADIE	ROACH	PATHE EXCHANGE	1915
P2	OVER NIGHT (UK: THAT NIGHT IN LONDON)	LEE	PARAMOUNT	1932
P-2	TERRIBLY STUCK UP	ROACH	PATHE EXCHANGE	1915
P-3	RUSES, RHYMES AND ROUGHNECKS	ROACH	PATHE EXCHANGE	1915
P-3	SIEGE AT RED RIVER	MATE	20th CENTURY FOX	1954
P4	COUNSEL'S OPINION (UK)	DWAN	PARAMOUNT BRITISH	1933
P4	GORILLA AT LARGE	JONES	20th CENTURY FOX	1954
P-4	MIXUP FOR MAZIE	ROACH	PATHE EXCHANGE	1915
P5	FOR LOVE OR MONEY (UK: CASH)	KORDA	HOFFBERG, MUNDUS	1933
P-5	SOME BABY	ROACH	PATHE EXCHANGE	1915
P-6	FRESH FROM THE FARM	ROACH	PATHE EXCHANGE	1915
P6	I MARRIED A SPY (UK: SECRET LIVES)	GREVILLE	GRAND NATIONAL	1937
P6	SCHOOL FOR HUSBANDS (UK)	MARTON	JH HOFFBERG	1937
P7	DANGEROUS SECRETS (UK: BRIEF ECSTASY)	GREVILLE	GRAND NATIONAL	1937
P-7	FOOZLE AT THE TEE PARTY	ROACH	PATHE EXCHANGE	1915
P-7	GAMBLER FROM NATCHEZ	LEVIN	20th CENTURY FOX	1954
P-8	GREAT WHILE IT LASTED	ROACH	PATHE EXCHANGE	1915
P8	PRISON BREAKER (UK)	BRUNEL	COLUMBIA	1936
P-9	GIVING THEM FITS	ROACH	PATHE EXCHANGE	1915
P-10	TINKERING WITH TROUBLE	ROACH	PATHE EXCHANGE	1915
P-11	PECULIAR PATIENTS' PRANKS	ROACH	PATHE EXCHANGE	1915
P-12	LONESOME LUKE, SOCIAL GANGSTER	ROACH, MACDONALD	PATHE EXCHANGE	1915
P-13	BUGHOUSE BELLHOPS	ROACH	PATHE EXCHANGE	1915
P-14	RAGTIME SNAP SHOTS	ROACH	PATHE EXCHANGE	1915
P-15	LUKE LUGS LUGGAGE	ROACH	PATHE EXCHANGE	1916
P-16	LONESOME LUKE LEANS TO THE LITERARY	ROACH	PATHE EXCHANGE	1916
P-17	LONESOME LUKE LOLLS IN LUXURY	ROACH	PATHE EXCHANGE	1916
P-17	LOST WORLD	HOYT	WARNER BROS	1925
P-18	LUKE FOILS THE VILLAIN	ROACH	PATHE EXCHANGE	1916
P-19	LUKE, THE CANDY CUT-UP	ROACH	PATHE EXCHANGE	1916
P-20	LUKE AND THE RURAL ROUGHNECKS	ROACH	PATHE EXCHANGE	1916
P-21	LUKE PIPES THE PIPPINS	ROACH	PATHE EXCHANGE	1916
P-22	THEM WAS THE DAYS	ROACH	PATHE EXCHANGE	1916
P-23	LUKE'S DOUBLE	ROACH	PATHE EXCHANGE	1916
P-24	LONESOME LUKE, CIRCUS KING	ROACH	PATHE EXCHANGE	1916
P-25	LUKE'S LATE LUNCHERS	ROACH	PATHE EXCHANGE	1916
P-26	LUKE AND THE BOMB THROWERS	ROACH	PATHE EXCHANGE	1916
P-27	LUKE LAUGHS LAST	ROACH	PATHE EXCHANGE	1916

P-28	LUKE'S FATAL FLIVVER	ROACH	PATHE EXCHANGE	1916
P-29	LUKE'S SOCIETY MIX-UP	ROACH	PATHE EXCHANGE	1916
P-30	LUKE'S WASHFUL WAITING	ROACH	PATHE EXCHANGE	1916
P68	SILENT LOVER	ARCHAINBAUD	FIRST NATIONAL	1926
P106	VIVIAN MARTIN	portrait	PARAMOUNT`	
P-165	GREAT DICTATOR	CHAPLIN	UNITED ARTISTS	1940
P242	ELLIOT DEXTER	portrait	PARAMOUNT`	
P264	DOUGLAS MACLEAN	portrait	PARAMOUNT`	
P510	RAYMOND HATTON	portrait	PARAMOUNT`	
P513	CHANGING HUSBANDS	IRIBE, URSON	PARAMOUNT	1924
P564	JOSEPH HENABERY	portrait	PARAMOUNT	
P598	SAZU PITTS	portrait	PARAMOUNT`	
P601	KING KONG	COOPER	RKO	1933
P678	DOROTHY SEBASTIAN	portrait	PARAMOUNT`	
P680	FLORENCE VIDOR	portrait	PARAMOUNT`	
P-691	ACE OF ACES	RUBEN	RKO	1933
P-696	ANN VICKERS	CROMWELL	RKO	1933
P-706	AFTER TONIGHT	ARCHAINBAUD	RKO	1933
P-710	LOST PATROL	FORD	RKO	1934
P712	MAN OF TWO WORLDS	RUBEN	RKO	1934
P-714	OLD MOTHER RILEY, HEADMISTRESS (UK)	HARLOW	RENOWN	1950
P720	LONG LOST FATHER	SCHOEDSACK	RKO	1934
P723	HIPS HIPS HOORAY	SANDRICH	RKO	1934
P-744	COCKEYED CAVALIERS	SANDRICH	RKO	1934
P746	LET'S TRY AGAIN	MINER	RKO	1934
P-780	KENTUCKY KERNELS	STEVENS	RKO	1934
P809	DOG OF FLANDERS	SLOMAN	RKO	1935
P-816	JEAN HERSHOLT	portrait	RKO	
P-827	LAST DAYS OF POMPEII	SCHOEDSACK	RKO	1935
P965	VAN NEST POLGLASE	portrait	PARAMOUNT`	
P1025	JEANNE EAGLES	portrait	PARAMOUNT`	
P1099	WESLEY RUGGLES AND WILLIAM LABARON	portrait	PARAMOUNT`	
P1134	RICHARD 'SKEETS' GALLAGHER	portrait	PARAMOUNT`	
P1143	GINGER ROGERS		PARAMOUNT	
P1167	MARLENE DIETRICH		PARAMOUNT	
P1186	PRISCILLA DEAN	portrait	PARAMOUNT	
P1277	ROBERT COOGAN	portrait	PARAMOUNT`	
P1298	HARPO MARX		PARAMOUNT	
P1383	MARY CARLISLE		PARAMOUNT	
P1400	GEORGE RAFT		PARAMOUNT	
P1446	MAE WEST		PARAMOUNT	
P1455	GRACIE ALLEN (also P1456) (MOSTLY W/O BURNS)		PARAMOUNT	
P1456	GRACIE ALLEN (also P1455), GEORGE BURNS		PARAMOUNT	
P1498	BUSTER CRABBE		PARAMOUNT	
P1581	LIVES OF A BENGAL LANCER	HATHAWAY	PARAMOUNT	1935
P1714	ANN SOTHERN	portrait	PARAMOUNT`	
P1837	ALAN CAMPBELL	portrait	PARAMOUNT`	
P1861	PLUMA NOISOM	portrait	PARAMOUNT	
P1909	ROAD TO DENVER	KANE	REPUBLIC	1955
P1921	RICHARD BARTHELMESS	portrait	PARAMOUNT`	
P1929	I DREAM OF JEANNIE	DWAN	REPUBLIC	1952
P1999	PSYCHO A GO-GO	ADAMSON	HEMISPHERE	1966
P2058	LESTER MATTHEWS	portrait	PARAMOUNT`	
P2075	CHARLES QUIGLEY	portrait	PARAMOUNT`	
P2204	LYLE TALBOT	portrait	PARAMOUNT`	
P2280	LAURIE LANE	portrait	PARAMOUNT`	
P2307	JANE DEWEY	portrait	PARAMOUNT	
P2365	ISA MIRANDA		PARAMOUNT	
P2442	FRITZ LANG	portrait	PARAMOUNT	
P2447	MARIAN WELDON	portrait	PARAMOUNT`	
P2601	DOROTHEA KENT	portrait	PARAMOUNT`	
P2670	KAY STEWART	portrait	PARAMOUNT	
P2717	ELLA NEAL	portrait	PARAMOUNT`	
P2719	STANLEY CLEMENTS	portrait	PARAMOUNT`	
P2817	LOUISE LA PLANCHE	portrait	PARAMOUNT`	
P2918	SIDNEY LANFIELD	portrait	PARAMOUNT`	

P2933	CHARLES QUIGLEY	portrait	PARAMOUNT`	
P2970	KAY SCOTT	portrait	PARAMOUNT`	
P3075	FRANK MCHUGH	portrait	PARAMOUNT	
P-4023	DOCTOR AT SEA	THOMAS	REPUBLIC	1956
P4074	DONNA PERCY	portrait	PARAMOUNT`	
P4102	JACQUELINE BEER	portrait	PARAMOUNT`	
P4104	ELAINE STRITCH	portrait	PARAMOUNT`	
P4112	DANEIL GELIN		PARAMOUNT	
P4160	PERRY WILSON	portrait	PARAMOUNT`	
P4209	COLOSSUS OF NEW YORK	LOURIE	PARAMOUNT	1958
P4248	PAUL FORD	portrait	PARAMOUNT`	
P-10008	I WALK ALONE	HASKIN	PARAMOUNT	1947
P-10009	SORRY, WRONG NUMBER	LITVAK	PARAMOUNT	1948
P-10010	ROPE OF SAND	DIETERLE	PARAMOUNT	1948
P-10011	THELMA JORDAN	SIODMAK	PARAMOUNT	1949
P-10012	MY FRIEND IRMA	MARSHALL	PARAMOUNT	1949
P-10013	FURIES	MANN	PARAMOUNT	1950
P-10015	THAT'S MY BOY	WALKER	PARAMOUNT	1951
P-10016	STOOGE	TAUROG	PARAMOUNT	1953
P-10017	SAILOR BEWARE	WALKER	PARAMOUNT	1952
P-10018	JUMPING JACKS	TAUROG	PARAMOUNT	1952
P-10019	SACRED STIFF	MARSHALL	PARAMOUNT	1953
P-10020	MONEY FROM HOME	MARSHALL	PARAMOUNT	1954
P-10054	A PLACE IN THE SUN	STEVENS	PARAMOUNT	1951
P-10056	CARRIE	WYLER	PARAMOUNT	1952
P&P	PRINCE AND THE PAUPER	GEISINGER	CHILDHOOD PROD.	1969
PA	MADE FOR EACH OTHER (UK)	CROMWELL	UNITED ARTISTS	1939
PA	PACIFIC ADVENTURE (aka SMITHY)	HALL	COLUMBIA	1946
PA	PINK ANGELS	BROWN	CROWN INT'L	1971
PA	POLICE ACADEMY	PARIS	WARNER BROS	1985
PA	POSEIDON ADVENTURE	NEAME	20th CENTURY FOX	1972
PA	POSTMARK FOR DANGER (UK: PORTRAIT OF ALISON)	GREEN	RKO	1955
PA	PRIVATE ANGELO (UK)	ANDERSON, USTINOV	PATHE	1949
PA2	RUTHLESS (R53: RUTHLESS MEN)	ULMER	EAGLE LION	1948
PAD	PROMISE AT DAWN	DASSIN	AVCO EMBASSY	1970
PAF	POPPY IS ALSO A FLOWER	YOUNG	COMET FILM DIST.	1966
PAG	CLOWN MUST LAUGH (UK: PAGLIACCI)	GRUNE	GAUMONT BRITISH	1936
PAR-BR1	HATTER'S CASTLE (UK)	COMFORT	PARAMOUNT	1942
PAS	PLAY IT AGAIN SAM	ROSS	PARAMOUNT	1972
PAT	PATTON	SCHAFFNER	20th CENTURY FOX	1970
PB	PELICAN BRIEF, THE	PAKULA	WARNER BROS	1993
PB	PHYLLIS BROOKS	portrait	UNIV	
PB	POINT BREAK	BIGELOW	20th CENTURY FOX	1991
PB	POSSE	DOUGLAS	PARAMOUNT	1975
PB	PRINCESS BRIDE, THE	REINER	20th CENTURY FOX	1987
PB	PRIVATE BENJAMIN	ZIEFF	WARNER BROS	1980
PB	PUSS N' BOOTS	1963	K. GORDON MURRAY	1963
PB-2	SPY FOR A DAY (UK)	ZAMPI	PARAMOUNT BRITISH	1940
PB-3	FRENCH WITHOUT TEARS (UK)	ASQUITH	PARAMOUNT	1941
PBBB	PIGLETS BIG MOVIE	GLEBAS	BUENA VISTA	2003
PC	ALEXANDRA (UK: PRINCESS CHARMING)	ELVEY	GAUMONT	1934
PC	PARATROOP COMMAND	WITNEY	AIP	1959
PC	PAT CROWLEY	portrait	UNIV	
PC	POOR COW (UK)	LOACH	NATIONAL GENERAL	1967
PC-126	FRIEND HUSBAND (WHY MARRY?)	HOWE	PATHE EXCHANGE	1924
PCU	PCU	BOCHNER	20th CENTURY FOX	1994
PCY	PERCY (UK)	THOMAS	MGM	1970
PD	PEG OF OLD DRURY (UK)	WILCOX	PARAMOUNT	1935
PD	PHILIP DORN	portrait	RKO, REPUBLIC, WB	
PD	PIPE DREAMS	VERONA	AVCO EMBASSY	1976
PD	PIT OF DARKNESS (UK)	COMFORT	BUTCHER'S	1961
PD	POACHER'S DAUGHTER (UK: SALLY'S IRISH ROGUE)	POLLOCK	SHOWCORPORATION	1958
PD	PROMISES IN THE DARK	HELLMAN	ORION	1979
PD2B	PRINCESS DIARIES 2	MARSHALL	BUENA VISTA	2004
PDBB	PARADISE	DONOGHUE	BUENA VISTA	1991
PDL	GATES OF PARIS (FR: PORTE DES LILAS)	CLAIR	LOPERT	1957

PE	LITTLE BOY BLUE AND PANCHO (HIDDEN PARADISE) (MEX 1962)	SELVILLA	J. GORDON MURRAY	1963
PE	PEOPLE'S ENEMY (RACKETEERS R1947)	WILBUR	RKO	1935
PE6	FACES IN THE DARK (UK)	EADY	SCHOENFELD	1960
PF	FEMALE FIENDS (UK: STRANGE AWAKENING)	TULLY	CINEMA ASSOCIATES	1958
PF	MRS. FITZHERBERT (UK)	TULLY	STRATFORD	1947
PF	PERFECT FRIDAY (UK)	HALL	CHEVRON	1970
PF	PETER FONDA		COL	
PF	THEY RAID BY NIGHT	BENNET	PRODUCERS RELEASING	1942
PF1	PYGMALION (UK)	ASQUITH, HOWARD	MGM	1938
PF4	COHEN AND KELLY'S IN TROUBLE	STEVENS	UNIVERSAL	1933
PF4	DO YOU KNOW THIS VOICE? (UK)	NESBITT	COLUMBIA	1964
PF8	HAIR OF THE DOG (UK)	BISHOP	RANK	1962
PFL	PLACE FOR LOVERS	DESICA	MGM	1969
PFR	PISTOL FOR RINGO	TESSARI	EMBASSY	1966
PFX	PHOEBE FOSTER	portrait	RKO	
PG	PAPER GALLOWS (UK: TORMENT)	GUILLERMIN	EAGLE-LION	1950
PG	PICNIC ON THE GRASS (FR: LE DEJEUNER SUR L'HERBE 1959)	RENOIR	KINGSLEY-UNION	1960
PG	PLEASURE GIRLS (UK)	O'HARA	TIMES	1965
PGP-20465	MIRIAM HOPKINS	portrait	PARAMOUNT	1930s
PH	BABY FACE KILLERS (R58) SEE PRIVATE HELL 36)	SIEGEL	FILMAKERS	1954
PH	PACIFIC HEIGHTS	SCHLESINGER	20th CENTURY FOX	1990
PH	PEGGY HYLAND	portrait		
PH	PENTHOUSE (UK)	COLLINSON	PARAMOUNT	1967
PH	PHAEDRA	DASSIN	LOPERT	1962
PH	PHANTASM	COSCARELLI	AVCO EMBASSY	1979
PH	PHYLLIS HAVER	portrait	PDC, PATHE	
PH	PLACES IN THE HEART	BENTON	TRI STAR	1984
PH	PRIVATE HELL 36 (r58 - BABY FACE KILLERS)	SIEGEL	FILMAKERS	1954
PH	PRIZZI'S HONOR	HUSTON	ABC MOTION PICTURE	1985
PHA	PROMISE HER ANYTHING (UK)	HILLER	PARAMOUNT	1965
PHBB	PHENOMENON	TURTELTAUB	BUENA VISTA	1996
PHST	PURE HELL OF ST. TRINIAN'S (UK)	LAUNDER	CONTINENTAL	1961
PI	DAUGHTER OF DR. JEKYLL	ULMER	ALLIED ARTISTS	1957
PI	DEADLY HERO	NAGY	AVCO EMBASSY	1976
PI	PASCALI'S ISLAND	DEARDEN	AVENUE ENT	1988
PI	PRESUMED INNOCENT	PAKULA	WARNER BROS	1990
PI	PRIVATE INFORMATION (UK)	MCDONELL	MONARCH	1952
PJ	POPE JOAN	ANDERSON	COLUMBIA	1972
PJ	PROJECTIONIST, THE	HURWITZ	MARON FILMS	1971
PJB	PRIME OF MISS JEAN BRODIE (UK)	NEAME	20TH CENTURY FOX	1969
PK	FIVE DAYS/US: PAID TO KILL (UK)	TULLY	LIPPERT	1954
PK	PAID TO KILL (UK: FIVE DAYS)	TULLY	LIPPERT	1954
PK	PATRIC KNOWLES	portrait	RKO, UNIV	
PK	PERCY KILBRIDE	portrait	UNIV	
PK	PERMISSION TO KILL (EXECUTIONER)	FRANKEL	AVCO EMBASSY	1975
PK	PRELUDE TO A KISS	RENE	20th CENTURY FOX	1992
PK	THUNDERHEART	APTED	TRI-STAR PICTURES	1992
PL	PALMER LEE	portrait	UNIV	
PL	PHANTOM LIGHT (UK)	POWELL	GAUMONT BRITISH	1935
PL	PLAYERS	HARVEY	PARAMOUNT	1979
PL	PLEASURE LOVERS (UK: NAKED FURY)	SAUNDERS	JOSEPH BRENNER	1959
PL	PRIEST OF LOVE	MILESTONE	FILMWAYS	1981
PL-3	SIDEWALKS OF LONDON (UK: ST. MARTIN'S LANE)	WHELAN	PARAMOUNT	1939
PLM	PEPE LE MOKO (FR)	DUVIVIER	JANUS	1937
PLX	COSMIC MONSTER (UK: STRANGE WORLD OF PLANET X)	GUNN	DCA	1958
PM	10:30 P.M. SUMMER	DASSIN	LOPERT	1966
PM	DANGEROUS CARGO (UK)	HARLOW	MONARCH	1954
PM	PATRICIA MEDINA	portrait	UNIV (40S-50S)	
PM	PATRICIA MORISON	portrait	UNIV	
PM	PETER MANN	portrait	UNIV	
PM	POCKET MONEY	TRUFFAUT	NEW WORLD PICTURES	1976
PM	POSTMAN, THE	COSTNER	WARNER BROS	1997
PM	PREACHERMAN	VIOLA	PREACHERMAN CORP	1971
PM	PREMIER MAY (FR: PREMIER MAI)	SASLAVSKY	CONTINENTAL DIST.	1958
PM	PICTURE MOMMY DEAD	GORDON	EMBASSY	1966
PM	SMALL CHANGE (FR)	TRUFFANT	NEW WORLD PICTURES	1976

PMC	PANDA AND THE MAGIC SERPENT (t) (JAP)	OKABE	GLOBE	1958
PMC	PATTI MCCARTY	portrait		
PMM	PLEASE MURDER ME	GODFREY	WARNER BROS	1956
PN	GIVE ME THE STARS (UK)	ROGERS	ANGLO-AMERICAN	1945
PN	PAUL NEWMAN	portrait	UNIV	
PN	POLICE NURSE	DEXTER	20th CENTURY FOX	1963
PN	PROM NIGHT	LYNCH	AVCO EMBASSY	1980
PN2-12	THAT MEN MAY LIVE - (This is America, 2nd series #12)		RKO	1944
PND	PEOPLE NEXT DOOR	GREENE	AVCO EMBASSY	1970
PO	PIRATES OF THE PRAIRIE	BRETHERTON	RKO	1942
PO	PLACE OF ONE'S OWN (UK)	KNOWLES	EAGLE-LION	1945
PO	POWER OF ONE	AVILDSEN	REGENCY	1992
POA	POSTMARK FOR DANGER (UK: PORTRAIT OF ALISON)	GREEN	RKO	1956
POB	PAT O'BRIEN	portrait	RKO	1940s
POC	PATSY O'CONNOR	portrait	UNIV	
POC	PIRATES OF THE COAST	PAOLELLA	SEVEN ARTS	1960
POC	PORT OF CALL (SWE: HAMNSTAD)	BERGMAN	JANUS	1948
POJ	PHANTOM OF THE JUNGLE	BENNET	LIPPERT	1955
POS	PLAN NINE FROM OUTER SPACE	WOOD	DCA	1959
PP	BEHOLD THE MAN! (UK)	RILLA	PHILOMENA	1951
PP	COURAGEOUS MR.PENN (UK: PENN OF PENNSYLVANIA)	COMFORT	JH HOFFBERG	1942
PP	CROSSED SWORDS	FLEISCHER	WARNER BROS	1977
PP	GIRL ON THE PIER (UK)	COMFORT	APEX	1953
PP	PATHER PANCHALI (IND)	RAY	EDWARD HARRISON	1955
PP	PENNY POOL (UK)	BLACK	MACUNIAN	1937
PP	PEYTON PLACE (tv series)	VARIOUS	20th CENTURY FOX	1964
PP	PHANTOM OF THE PARADISE	DE PALMA	20th CENTURY FOX	1974
PP	PICKWICK PAPERS (UK)	LANGLEY	MAYER-KINGSLEY	1952
PP	PIED PIPER, THE	DEMY	PARAMOUNT	1972
PP	PRIVATE PROPERTY	STEVENS	CITATION	1960
PP	PRIVATE'S PROGRESS (UK)	BOULTING	DCA	1956
PP	PUBLIC PIGEON NO. 1	MCLEOD	RKO	1956
PP	SANDOKAN THE GREAT (IT: SANDOKAN, TIGRE MOMPRACEM-63)	LANZI	MGM	1965
PP102	IDOL OF PARIS (UK)	ARLISS	WARNER BROS	1948
PP-B	POUND PUPPIES LEGEND OF BIG PAW (t)	DECELLES	CAROLCO, TRI STAR	1988
PPI	WHAT FOOLS MEN ARE	TERWILLIGER	AMERICAN RELEASING	1922
PPP	PETE, PEARL AND THE POLE (IT: PIAZZA PULITA 1972)	VANZI	NATIONAL GENERAL	1973
PPX1	MARTHA MANSFIELD	portrait	PYRAMID PICTURES	
PR	AFTER THE BALL (UK)	BENNETT	IFD	1957
PR	PATRICIA ROC	portrait	RKO	
PR	PETER RABBIT & TALES OF BEATRIX POTTER	MILLS	MGM	1971
PR	PLUNDER ROAD	CORNFIELD	20th CENTURY FOX	1957
PR	POPEYE	ALTMAN	PARAMOUNT	1980
PR	PORKY'S REVENGE	KOMACK	20th CENTURY FOX	1985
PR	PROPHECY	FRANKENHEIMER	PARAMOUNT	1979
PR	PROUD REBEL	CURTIZ	BUENA VISTA	1958
PR	PURPLE RAIN	MAGNOLI	WARNER BROS	1984
PR1	NOVEL AFFAIR (UK: PASSIONATE STRANGER)	BOX	CONTINENTAL	1957
PRBB	PRINCE AND THE PAUPER	SCRIBNER	BUENA VISTA	1990
PRC-101	PRISONER OF JAPAN	RIPLEY	PRODUCERS RELEASING	1942
PRC-114	VALLEY OF VENGEANCE	NEWFIELD	PRODUCERS RELEASING	1944
PRC-115	FUZZY SETTLES DOWN	NEWFIELD	PRODUCERS RELEASING	1944
PRC-119	OATH OF VENGEANCE	NEWFIELD	PRODUCERS RELEASING	1944
PRC-120	HIS BROTHER'S GHOST	NEWFIELD	PRODUCERS RELEASING	1945
PRC-122	SHADOWS OF DEATH	NEWFIELD	PRODUCERS RELEASING	1945
PRC-123	GANGSTER'S DEN	NEWFIELD	PRODUCERS RELEASING	1945
PRC-126	STAGECOACH OUTLAWS	NEWFIELD	PRODUCERS RELEASING	1945
PRC-127	BORDER BADMEN	NEWFIELD	PRODUCERS RELEASING	1945
PRC-128	FIGHTING BILL CARSON	NEWFIELD	PRODUCERS RELEASING	1945
PRC-130	PRAIRIE RUSTLERS	NEWFIELD	PRODUCERS RELEASING	1945
PRC-131	LIGHTNING RAIDERS	NEWFIELD	PRODUCERS RELEASING	1946
PRC-133	TERRORS ON HORSEBACK	NEWFIELD	PRODUCERS RELEASING	1946
PRC-134	GENTLEMEN WITH GUNS	NEWFIELD	PRODUCERS RELEASING	1946
PRC-135	LARCENY IN HER HEART	NEWFIELD	PRODUCERS RELEASING	1946
PRC-136	GHOST OF HIDDEN VALLEY	NEWFIELD	PRODUCERS RELEASING	1946
PRC-138	PRAIRIE BADMEN	NEWFIELD	PRODUCERS RELEASING	1946

PRC-139	OVERLAND RIDERS	NEWFIELD	PRODUCERS RELEASING	1946
PRC-140	OUTLAWS OF THE PLAINS	NEWFIELD	PRODUCERS RELEASING	1946
PRC-163	LONE RIDER RIDES ON	NEWFIELD	PRODUCERS RELEASING	1941
PRC-177	SWING HOSTESS	NEWFIELD	PRODUCERS RELEASING	1944
PRC-218	BOMBS OVER BURMA	LEWIS	PRODUCERS RELEASING	1942
PRC-221	YANK IN LIBYA	HERMAN	PRODUCERS RELEASING	1942
PRC-354	BORDER BUCKAROOS	DRAKE	PRODUCERS RELEASING	1943
PRC-407	DANGER! WOMEN AT WORK	NEWFIELD	PRODUCERS RELEASING	1943
PRC-411	HARVEST MELODY	NEWFIELD	PRODUCERS RELEASING	1943
PRC-412	GIRL FROM MONTERREY	FOX	PRODUCERS RELEASING	1943
PRC-417	DIXIE JAMBOREE	CABANNE	PRODUCERS RELEASING	1944
PRC-418	LADY IN THE DEATH HOUSE	SEKELY	PRODUCERS RELEASING	1944
PRC-423	SEVEN DOORS TO DEATH	CLIFTON	PRODUCERS RELEASING	1944
PRC-443	APOLOGY FOR MURDER	NEWFIELD	PRODUCERS RELEASING	1945
PRC-444	QUEEN OF BURLESQUE	NEWFIELD	PRODUCERS RELEASING	1946
PRC-445	DANNY BOY	MORSE	PRODUCERS RELEASING	1946
PRC-446	MASK OF DIIJON	LANDERS	PRODUCERS RELEASING	1946
PRC-451	DEVIL BAT'S DAUGHTER	WISBAR	PRODUCERS RELEASING	1946
PRC-452	WIFE OF MONTE CRISTO	ULMER	PRODUCERS RELEASING	1946
PRC-456	SPOOK TOWN	CLIFTON	PRODUCERS RELEASING	1944
PRC-477	BLUEBEARD	ULMER	PRODUCERS RELEASING	1944
PRC-479	WHEN THE LIGHTS GO ON AGAIN	HOWARD	PRODUCERS RELEASING	1944
PRC-480	TOWN WENT WILD	MURPHY	PRODUCERS RELEASING	1944
PRC-481	GREAT MIKE	FOX	PRODUCERS RELEASING	1944
PRC-484	MAN WHO WALKED ALONE	CABANNE	PRODUCERS RELEASING	1945
PRC-485	CRIME INC aka GANGSTER KELLY	LANDERS	PRODUCERS RELEASING	1945
PRC-489	PHANTOM OF 42ND STREET	HERMAN	PRODUCERS RELEASING	1945
PRC-493	DETOUR	ULMER	PRODUCERS RELEASING	1945
PRC-501	GANGSTERS OF THE FRONTIER	CLIFTON	PRODUCERS RELEASING	1944
PRC-502	DEAD OR ALIVE	CLIFTON	PRODUCERS RELEASING	1945
PRC-503	WHISPERING SKULL	CLIFTON	PRODUCERS RELEASING	1944
PRC-518	TOO MANY WINNERS	BEAUDINE	PRODUCERS RELEASING	1947
PRC-519	LAW OF THE LASH	TAYLOR	PRODUCERS RELEASING	1947
PRC-520	BORDER FEUD	TAYLOR	PRODUCERS RELEASING	1947
PRC-524	RETURN OF THE LASH	TAYLOR	PRODUCERS RELEASING	1947
PRC-525	WEST TO GLORY	TAYLOR	PRODUCERS RELEASING	1947
PRC-526	BIG FIX	FLOOD	PRODUCERS RELEASING	1947
PRC-528	GHOST TOWN RENEGADES	TAYLOR	PRODUCERS RELEASING	1947
PRC-529	PIONEER JUSTICE	TAYLOR	PRODUCERS RELEASING	1947
PRC-530	CHEYENNE TAKES OVER	TAYLOR	PRODUCERS RELEASING	1947
PRC-534	HEARTACHES	WRANGELL	PRODUCERS RELEASING	1947
PRC-535	CHECK YOUR GUNS	TAYLOR	PRODUCERS RELEASING	1947
PRC-536	BLACK HILLS	TAYLOR	PRODUCERS RELEASING	1947
PRC-537	WESTWARD TRAIL	TAYLOR	PRODUCERS RELEASING	1947
PRC-538	SHADOW VALLEY	TAYLOR	PRODUCERS RELEASING	1947
PRC-540	TIOGA KID	TAYLOR	PRODUCERS RELEASING	1947
PRC-553	WHY GIRLS LEAVE HOME	BERKE	PRODUCERS RELEASING	1945
PRC-555	STRANGLER OF THE SWAMP	WISBAR	PRODUCERS RELEASING	1946
PRC-557	HER SISTER'S SECRET	ULMER	PRODUCERS RELEASING	1946
PRC-562	ROMANCE OF THE WEST	TANSEY as EMMETT	PRODUCERS RELEASING	1946
PRC-563	NAVAJO KID	FRASER	PRODUCERS RELEASING	1945
PRC-564	SIX GUN MAN	FRASER	PRODUCERS RELEASING	1946
PRC-566	CARAVAN TRAILS (CARAVAN TRAIL)	TANSEY as EMMETT	PRODUCERS RELEASING	1946
PRC-569	AMBUSH TRAIL	FRASER	PRODUCERS RELEASING	1946
PRC-570	THUNDER TOWN	FRASER	PRODUCERS RELEASING	1946
PRC-574	COLORADO SERENADE	TANSEY	PRODUCERS RELEASING	1946
PRC-575	DOWN MISSOURI WAY	BERNE	PRODUCERS RELEASING	1946
PRC-578	PHILO VANCE RETURNS	BEAUDINE	PRODUCERS RELEASING	1947
PRC-587	GAS HOUSE KIDS	NEWFIELD	PRODUCERS RELEASING	1946
PRC-589	LADY CHASER	NEWFIELD	PRODUCERS RELEASING	1946
PRC-593	DRIFTIN' RIVER	TANSEY	PRODUCERS RELEASING	1946
PRC-595	STARS OVER TEXAS	TANSEY	PRODUCERS RELEASING	1946
PRC-599	DON RICARDO RETURNS	MORSE	PRODUCERS RELEASING	1946
PRC-603	DEVIL ON WHEELS	WILBUR	PRODUCERS RELEASING	1947
PRC-605	ACCOMPLICE	COLMES	PRODUCERS RELEASING	1946
PRC-663	CHEYENNE TAKES OVER	TAYLOR	PRODUCERS RELEASING	1947

PRO	PRODUCERS	BROOKS	EMBASSY	1967
PRO	SHADOW OF THE EAGLE (UK)	SALKOW	UNITED ARTISTS	1950
PRTS	POSTMAN ALWAYS RINGS TWICE, THE	RAFELSON	PARAMOUNT	1981
PRTS	PRIVATE PARTS	BARTEL	MGM	1972
PS	PASSPORT TO SHAME (UK) (ROOM 43)	RAKOFF	BRITISH LION	1959
PS	PHANTOM SHIP (UK: MYSTERY OF THE MARIE CELESTE)	CLIFT	GUARANTEED	1935
PS	PORT SINISTER (BEAST OF PARADISE R1957)	DANIELS	RKO	1953
PS	PRICE OF SILENCE (UK)	TULLY	EXCLUSIVE INTL	1959
PS	PRISON SHADOWS	HILL	MERCURY (states rights)	1936
PS	PRIVATE SECRETARY (UK)	EDWARDS	TWICKENHAM	1935
PS	ROOM 43 (UK: PASSPORT TO SHAME)	RAKOFF	CORY	1958
PS	WOMEN WITHOUT MEN (UK)	WILLIAMS, GLAZER	ASSOCIATED	1956
PS99	PARENTS WANTED (sh)	GUIOL	RKO PATHE	1931
PS101	PARADING PAJAMAS (sh)	FOX	RKO PATHE	1931
PS107	STAGE STRUCK (sh)	RAY	RKO PATHE	1931
PS111	WHAT A TIME (sh)	GREEN	RKO PATHE	1931
PS113	HOT WIRES (sh)	SWEET	RKO PATHE	1931
PS115	ROUGH HOUSE RHYTHM (sh)	SWEET	RKO PATHE	1931
PS116	TWISTED TALES (sh)	FOX	RKO PATHE	1931
PS117	OPENING HOUSE (sh)	FRASER	RKO PATHE	1931
PS120	THREE WISE CLUCKS (sh)	FOX	RKO PATHE	1931
PS121	NOT SO LOUD (sh)	SWEET	RKO PATHE	1931
PS123	NIGHT CLASS (sh)	FRASER	RKO PATHE	1931
PS191	STOUT HEARTS AND WILLING HANDS (sh)	FOY	RKO PATHE	1931
PS192	THAT'S NEWS TO ME (sh)	GILLSTROM	RKO PATHE	1931
PS193	SHE SNOOPS TO CONQUER (sh)	GUIOL	RKO PATHE	1931
PS194	THAT'S MY LINE (sh)	ARBUCKLE as GOODRICH	RKO PATHE	1931
PS195	LEMON MERINGUE (sh)	SWEET	RKO PATHE	1931
PS196	OH! OH! CLEOPATRA (sh)	SANTLEY	RKO PATHE	1931
PS197	MESSENGER BOY (sh)	LUDWIG	RKO PATHE	1931
PS198	OH! MARRY ME (sh)	WATSON	RKO PATHE	1931
PS201	THANKS AGAIN (sh)	SWEET	RKO PATHE	1931
PS204	TAKE 'EM AND SHAKE 'EM (sh)	ARBUCKLE as GOODRICH	RKO PATHE	1931
PS205	WHERE CANARIES SING BASS (sh)	GREEN	RKO PATHE	1931
PS206	HOT SPOT (sh)	GALLAHER	RKO PATHE	1931
PS211	SLOW POISON (sh)	SWEET	RKO PATHE	1931
PS214	SELLING SHORTS (sh)	EDWARDS	RKO PATHE	1931
PS215	ONLY MEN WANTED (sh)	CEDER	RKO PATHE	1931
PS218	STOP THAT RUN (sh)	BRETHERTON	RKO PATHE	1931
PS220	PROMOTER (sh)	CEDER	RKO PATHE	1931
PS222	WIDE OPEN SPACES (sh)	ROSSON	RKO PATHE	1931
PS223	NEWS HOUNDS (sh)		RKO PATHE	1931
PS225	PERFECT 36	CEDER	RKO PATHE	1931
PS227	NIAGARA FALLS (sh)	ARBUCKLE as GOODRICH	RKO PATHE	1931
PS228	MOTHER-IN-LAW'S DAY (sh)	SWEET	RKO PATHE	1932
PS229	WINNER TAKES ALL (sh)		RKO PATHE	1932
PS230	STEALIN' HOME (sh)	SWEET	RKO PATHE	1932
PS231	PETE BURKE, REPORTER (sh)		RKO PATHE	1932
PS232	RULE 'EM AND WEEP (sh)	SWEET	RKO PATHE	1932
PSG	PIRATE AND THE SLAVE GIRL	PIEROTTA	CREST FILM	1961
PSGM	PEGGY SUE GOT MARRIED	COPPOLA	TRI STAR	1986
PSW	PINK STRING AND SEALING WAX (UK)	HAMER	PENTAGON	1945
PT	BOMBAY WATERFRONT (UK: PAUL TEMPLE RETURNS)	ROGERS	BUTCHER'S	1952
PT	PEEPING TOM (UK)	POWELL	ASTOR	1960
PT	PHYLLIS THAXTER	portrait	WARNER BROS	
PT	POINT OF TERROR	NICOL	CROWN INT'L	1971
PT	PUSHING TIN	NEWELL	20TH CENTURY FOX	1999
PT2	CALLING PAUL TEMPLE (UK)	ROGERS	BUTCHER'S	1948
PTA	PASS THE AMMO	BEAIRD	NEW CENTURY VISTA	1987
PTBB	PARENT TRAP	MEYERS	BUENA VISTA	1998
PTBB	PLAY IT TO THE BONE	SHELTON	TOUCHSTONE	1999
PTS	PICCADILLY THIRD STOP (UK)	RILLA	GOLDSTONE	1960
PU	52 PICKUP	FRANKENHEIMER	CANNON	1986
PW	PERFECT WEAPON	DISALLE	PARAMOUNT	1991
PW	PREHISTORIC WOMEN	TALLAS	EAGLE LION	1950
PW	PREHISTORIC WOMEN (UK: SLAVE GIRLS)	CARRERAS	20TH CENTURY FOX	1967

PW	PREHISTORIC WORLD (TEENAGE CAVEMAN)	CORMAN	AIP	1958
PWBB	POWDER	SALVA	BUENA VISTA	1995
PWBB	PREACHERS WIFE, THE	MARSHALL	BUENA VISTA	1996
PWBB	PRETTY WOMAN	MARSHALL	TOUCHSTONE	1990
PWQ	POWAQQATSI	REGGIO	CANNON	1988
PX	PROJECT X	KAPLAN	20th CENTURY FOX	1987
PZ	PLAGUE OF THE ZOMBIES (UK)	GILLING	20th CENTURY FOX	1966
Q	QUADROON	JANNEKE, JR.	CONSOLIDATED	1971
Q	QUERY (UK: MURDER IN REVERSE)	TULLY	FOUR CONTINENTS	1945
Q	QUEST FOR CAMELOT (t)	DU CHAU	WARNER BROS	1998
Q	QUIGLEY DOWN UNDER	WINCER	PATHE	1990
Q	QUINTET	ALTMAN	20TH CENTURY FOX	1979
Q OF S	QUEEN OF SPADES (UK)	DICKINSON	MONOGRAM	1949
QA	QUESTION OF ADULTERY (UK)	CHAFFEY	EROS	1958
QB7	QB VII (tv miniseries '74-'76)	various	COLUMBIA	1974
QC	QUICK CHANGE	FRANKLIN	WARNER BROS	1990
QD	QUIGLEY DOWN UNDER	WINCER	WARNER BROS	1990
QDU	QUIGLEY DOWN UNDER	WINCER	MGM	1990
QF	QUILLAN FAMILY i.e. EDDIE QUILLAN & FAMILY	portrait	PATHE	
QK	JOEL KUPPERMAN (7-year-old 'Quiz Kid')	portrait	UNIV	
Q-K	QUEST FOR FIRE	ANNAUD	20TH CENTURY FOX	1982
QM	QUIET WOMAN (UK)	GILLING	EROS	1951
QOS	QUEEN OF SHEBA (IT: LA REGINA DI SABA)	FRANCISCI	LIPPERT	1952
QP	QUIET PLACE TO KILL	LENZI	AVCO EMBASSY	1973
QS	QUEEN OF SPADES (UK)	DICKINSON	MONOGRAM	1949
QW	QUIET WEEKEND (UK)	FRENCH	DISTINGUISHED	1946
QWE	QUIET WEEKEND (UK)	FRENCH	DISTINGUISHED	1946
R	BLACK DOLL	GARRETT	UNIVERSAL	1937
R	MURPHY'S LAW	THOMPSON	CANNON	1986
R	RAISE THE TITANIC	JAMESON	ASSOCIATED FILM DIST.	1980
R	RAMBO FIRST BLOOD PART II	COSMATOS	TRI-STAR	1985
R	RAT (UK)	RAYMOND	RKO	1937
R	REDS	BEATTY	PARAMOUNT	1981
R	RELIC, THE	HYAMS	PARAMOUNT	1996
R	RENDEZ-VOUS	TECHINE	INT'L SPECTRAFILM	1986
R	RENEGADES	SHOLDER	WARNER BROS	1989
R	RHINESTONE	CLARK	20TH CENTURY FOX	1984
R	RHINOCEROS	O'HORGAN	AMERICAN FILM THE.	1974
R	RIFIFI	DASSIN	UMPO	1955
R	RIMFIRE	EASON	LIPPERT	1949
R	RITUAL/RITE (SWE: RITEN)	BERGMAN	JANUS	1969
R	ROCKY	AVILDSEN	UNITED ARTISTS	1977
R	ROGER & ME	MOORE	WARNER BROS	1989
R	ROME, OPEN CITY (IT: ROMA CITTA APERTA)	ROSSELLINI	MAYER & BURSTYN	1945
R	ROOKIE	EASTWOOD	WARNER BROS	1990
R	ROOM TO LET (UK)	GRAYSON	EXCLUSIVE	1950
R	ROSE, THE	RYDELL	20th CENTURY FOX	1979
R	ROSSITER CASE (UK)	SEARLE	EXCLUSIVE	1951
R	RUMPLESTILTSKIN	IRVING	CANNON	1987
R	RUNAWAY	CRICHTON	TRI STAR	1984
R	RUSH	ZANUCK	MGM	1991
R	SUSPECT/US: RISK (UK)	BOULTING, BOULTING	KINGSLEY INT'L	1960
R	TOKOLOSHE: THE EVIL SPIRIT	PROWSE	ARTISTS INT'L	1971
R	UP THE CREEK	BUTLER	ORION	1984
R-1	DO YOU LOVE YOUR WIFE?	ROACH	PATHE EXCHANGE	1919
R-1	JUS PASSIN' THROUGH	ROACH	PATHE EXCHANGE	1923
R-1	WHITE EAGLE (15 ch. series)	JACKMAN, VAN DYKE	PATHE EXCHANGE	1922
R-2	JUST RAMBLING ALONG	ROACH	PATHE EXCHANGE	1918
R-2	TIMBER QUEEN (15 ch. series)	JACKMAN	PATHE EXCHANGE	1922
R-3	HOOT MON!	ROACH	PATHE EXCHANGE	1919
R3	RAMBO 3	MACDONALD	TRI STAR	1988
R-3	UNCENSORED MOVIES	CLEMENTS	PATHE EXCHANGE	1923
R-4	GEE WHIZ, GENEVIEVE	HOWE	PATHE EXCHANGE	1924
R-4	NO PLACE LIKE JAIL	TERRY	PATHE EXCHANGE	1918
R-4	SOLDIERS OF FORTUNE	DWAN	REALART	1919
R5	EVERYTHING IS RHYTHM (UK)	GOULDING	ASTOR	1936

R-5	HUSTLING FOR HEALTH	TERRY	PATHE EXCHANGE	1919
R-5	TWO WAGONS, BOTH COVERED	WAGNER	PATHE EXCHANGE	1924
R-6	COWBOY SHEIK	HOWE	PATHE EXCHANGE	1924
R6	MAN BEHIND THE MASK (UK)	POWELL	MGM	1936
R-7	CAKE EATER	HOWE	PATHE EXCHANGE	1924
R-8	UNNAMED WILL ROGERS		PATHE EXCHANGE	1924
R-9	BIG MOMENTS FROM LITTLE PICTURES	CLEMENTS	PATHE EXCHANGE	1924
R-11	GOING TO CONGRESS	WAGNER	PATHE EXCHANGE	1924
R11	PERMANENT RECORD	SILVER	PARAMOUNT	1988
R-12	DON'T PARK THERE!	GUIOL	PATHE EXCHANGE	1924
R-13	OUR CONGRESSMAN	WAGNER	PATHE EXCHANGE	1924
R-14	TRUTHFUL LIAR	DEL RUTH	PATHE EXCHANGE	1924
R-15	MY FAMILY	NAVA	NEW LINE CINEMA	1995
R74	WAITING FOR GUFFMAN	GUEST	CASTLE ROCK	1996
R101	SAFE PASSAGE	ACKERMAN	NEW LINE CINEMA	1994
R102	PERSUADER, THE	ROSS	ALLIED ARTISTS	1957
R122	INNOCENTS IN PARIS (UK)	PARRY	TUDOR	1953
R128	COURT MARTIAL (UK: CARRINGTON V.C.)	ASQUITH	KINGSLEY INT'L	1954
R133	I AM A CAMERA (UK)	CORNELIUS	DCA	1955
R141	PANIC IN THE PARLOR (UK: SAILOR BEWARE)	PARRY	DCA	1956
R142	DRY ROT (UK)	ELVEY	IFD	1956
R146	THREE MEN IN A BOAT (UK)	ANNAKIN	HAL ROACH	1956
R149	TEACHERS	HILLER	UNITED ARTISTS	1984
R156	ROOM AT THE TOP (UK)	CLAYTON	CONTINENTAL	1959
RA	RA EXPEDITIONS	EHRENBORG	INTERWEST FILM CORP	1971
RA	RADAR SECRET SERVICE	NEW FIELD	LIPPERT	1950
RA	RAMSBOTTOM RIDES AGAIN (UK)	BAXTER	BRITISH LION	1956
RA	RUNAWAY (UK)	YOUNG	COLUMBIA	1963
RA	SWORD OF THE CONQUEROR (IT: ROSMUNDA E ALBOINO)	CAMPOGALLIANI	UNITED ARTISTS	1961
RA1	ANGRY SILENCE (UK)	GREEN	VALIANT	1961
RA151	UP THE CREEK	BUTLER	ORION	1984
RA-COL-1	UNKNOWN RANGER	BENNET	COLUMBIA	1936
RA-COL-3	RIO GRANDE RANGER (BOB ALLEN series)	BENNET	COLUMBIA	1936
RA-COL-4	LAW OF THE RANGER (BOB ALLEN series)	BENNET	COLUMBIA	1937
RA-COL-5	RECKLESS RANGER	BENNET	COLUMBIA	1937
RA-COL-6	RANGERS STEP IN	BENNET	COLUMBIA	1937
RB	ABDULLAH'S HAREM (UK: ABDULLA THE GREAT)	RATOFF	20TH CENTURY FOX	1955
RB	RELUCTANT BRIDE (TWO GROOMS FOR A BRIDE 1957)	CASS	EROS FILMS	1955
RB	RIVER BEAT (UK)	GREEN	LIPPERT	1954
RB	ROBERT BARRAT	portrait	UNITED ARTISTS	
RB	ROCCO AND HIS BROTHERS	VISCONTI	ASTOR	1961
RB	RACING BLOOD	BARRY	20th CENTURY FOX	1954
RB-8	FUGITIVE VALLEY	LUBY	MONOGRAM	1941
RB-8	GIRL FROM OUTSIDE	BARKER	GOLDWYN	1919
RB-9	SILVER HORDE	LLOYD	GOLDWYN	1920
RB-131	ROSEMARY'S BABY	POLANSKI	PARAMOUNT	1968
RBA	TWO GROOMS FOR A BRIDE (UK: RELUCTANT BRIDE 1955)	CASS	20th CENTURY FOX	1957
RBD	RETURN OF BULLDOG DRUMMOND (UK)	SUMMERS	MUNDUS	1934
RBF	ROYAL BALLET	CZINNER	LOPERT PICTURES	1960
RBW	RING OF BRIGHT WATER (UK)	COUFFER	CINERAMA	1969
RC	HEAVEN IS ROUND THE CORNER (UK)	ROGERS	ANGLO-AMERICAN	1944
RC	RECORD CITY	STEINMETZ	AIP	1978
RC	RICARDO CORTEZ	portrait		
RC	RICHARD CARLSON	portrait		
RC	RICHARD CLAYTON	portrait	WARNER BROS	
RC	ROARING CITY	BERKE	LIPPERT	1951
RC	ROBINSON CRUSOE AND THE TIGER (MEX)	CARDONA JR	AVCO EMBASSY	1972
RC	ROTTEN TO THE CORE (UK)	BOULTING	CINEMA V	1965
RC	ROUGH CUT	SIEGEL	PARAMOUNT	1980
RC	WELCOME HOME, ROXY CARMICHAEL	ABRAHAMS	PARAMOUNT	1990
RC1	NIGHT WE GOT THE BIRD (UK)	CONYERS	BRITISH LION	1961
RCK	RECKLESS	FOLEY	MGM	1984
RCU	OLD MOTHER RILEY'S GHOSTS (UK)	BAXTER	ANGLO-AMERICAN	1941
RD	RED DAWN	MILLIUS	MGM	1984
RD	RED DESERT	BEEBE	LIPPERT	1949
RD	RED DESERT (IT: IL DESERTO ROSSO)	ANTONIONI	RIZZOLI	1964

RD	RED DRAGON	HOFBAUER	WOOLNER BROS	1961
RD	RUNAWAY DAUGHTERS (PROWL GIRLS)	MAHON	CHANCELLOR FILMS	1968
RD	RYAN'S DAUGHTER (UK)	LEAN	MGM	1970
RD	YOUNG, WILLING AND EAGER (UK: RAG DOLL)	COMFORT	MANSON	1961
RD1	CURE FOR LOVE (UK)	DONAT	BRITISH LION	1949
RDB	RETURN OF DANIEL BOONE	HILLYER	COLUMBIA	1941
RD-K	RACE WITH THE DEVIL	STARRETT	20th CENTURY FOX	1975
RE	REPULSION (UK)	POLANSKI	COLUMBIA	1965
RE	RICHARD EGAN	portrait	UNIV	
REBB	RECESS SCHOOL'S OUT	KEYES	BUENA VISTA	2001
REM	REMO WILLIAMS: THE ADVENTURE BEGINS	HAMILTON	ORION	1985
REV-22	GUNFIGHTER, THE	REYNOLDS	FOX FILM	1923
RF	NOBODY HOME (UK: RETURN OF THE FROG)	ELVEY	SELECT ATTRACTIONS	1938
RF	RAPID FIRE	LITTLE	20th CENTURY FOX	1992
RF1	FALLEN IDOL (UK)	REED	SELZNICK RELEASING	1948
RF2	THIRD MAN (UK)	REED	SELZNICK RELEASING	1949
RF-368	SKABENGA (KILLER LUST) (doc)	MICHAEL	ALLIED ARTISTS	1955
RFI	FALLEN IDOL (UK)	REED	BRITISH LION (UK)	1948
RF-P	THREE RUSSIAN GIRLS	OTSEP	UNITED ARTISTS	1943
RFTR	RISE AND FALL OF THE THIRD REICH	KAUFMAN	ABC-TV	1968
RG	BLUE LAGOON, THE	FRANKLIN	AVCO EMBASSY	1980
RG	REAL GENIUS	COOLIDGE	TRI STAR	1985
RG	RIAN GARRICK		COL	
RG	RICE GIRL	MATARAZZO	ULTRA PICTURES	1963
RG	RICHEST GIRL	SEITER	RKO	1934
RG	ROAD GAMES	FRANKLIN	AVCO EMBASSY	1980
RG	ROSE GARDEN	RADEMAKERS	CANNON	1989
RG	RUBY GENTRY	VIDOR	20th CENTURY FOX	1953
RG	RUNAWAY GIRL	PETROFF	LAUREL FILMS	1965
RH	CHALLENGE FOR ROBIN HOOD (UK)	PENNINGTON-RICHARDS	20TH CENTURY FOX	1967
RH	RED HEAT	HILL	TRI STAR	1988
RH	REGARDING HENRY	NICHOLS	PARAMOUNT	1991
RH	RELUCTANT HEROES (UK)	RAYMOND	ASSO. BRITISH-PATHE	1951
RH	RITA HAYWORTH		COL	1950s
RH	ROBIN HOOD: MEN IN TIGHTS	BROOKS	20th CENTURY FOX	1993
RH	ROBIN HOOD: PRINCE OF THIEVES	REYNOLDS	WARNER BROS	1991
RH	ROCKY HORROR PICTURE SHOW	SHARMAN	20th CENTURY FOX	1975
RH	ROSS HUNTER	portrait	UNIV	
RH	TALES OF ROBIN HOOD	TINLING	LIPPERT	1951
RHM	HE SNOOPS TO CONQUER (UK)	VARNEL	COLUMBIA BRITISH	1944
RIII	ROCKY III	STALLONE	MGM/UNITED ARTISTS	1982
RIO	BLAME IT ON RIO	DONEN	20th CENTURY FOX	1984
RIPC	RIDE IN A PINK CAR	EMERY	CLARION PICTURES	1974
RIT	RIFIFI IN TOKYO	DERAY	MGM	1963
RJ	ROMEO AND JULIET	ZEFFIRELLI	PARAMOUNT	1968
RJ	ROMEO AND JULIET (UK)	CASTELLANI	UNITED ARTISTS	1954
RJ	ROMEO AND JULIET (UK)	CZINNER	RANK	1966
RJ	WHITE GODDESS	FOX	LIPPERT	1953
RK	ROBERT KENT	portrait	UNIV	
RKO-9	GREAT DAY (UK)	COMFORT	RKO	1945
RL	REAL LIFE	BROOKS	PARAMOUNT	1979
RL	RICHARD LONG	portrait	UNIV	
RLA	RAIDERS OF THE LOST ARK	SPIELBERG	PARAMOUNT	1981
RLS	RALPH LEWIS	portrait	FBO	
RM	RACING WITH THE MOON	BENJAMIN	PARAMOUNT	1984
RM	RAY MONTGOMERY	portrait	WARNER BROS.	
RM	ROBERT MITCHUM	portrait	COL, RKO	
RM	ROOM 43 (UK: PASSPORT TO SHAME)	RAKOFF	CORY FILM	1959
RM	RUDOLPH MATE	portrait	UNIV	
RM	RUNNING MAN	GLASER	TRI STAR	1987
RM	RIVER AND DEATH (MEX)	BUNUEL	CLASA	1955
RM-55	ART OF SKIING (t)	KINNEY	RKO	1941
RMM	RETURN OF MR. MOTO (UK)	MORRIS	20TH CENTURY FOX	1965
RMP	OLD MOTHER RILEY, MP (UK)	MITCHELL	BUTCHER'S	1939
RN	RAPA NUI	REYNOLDS	WARNER BROS	1994
RN	RESTLESS NATIVES	HOFFMAN	ORION	1986

RNBB	RENAISSANCE MAN	MARSHALL	BUENA VISTA	1994
RO	OLD MOTHER RILEY OVERSEAS (UK)	MITCHELL	ANGLO-AMERICAN	1943
RO	RITA OEHMEN	portrait	RKO	
RO	ROBOCOP	VERHOEVEN	ORION	1987
RO	ROMA	FELLINI	UNITED ARTISTS	1972
ROB	ROBBERY (UK)	YATES	EMBASSY	1967
ROC	ROCKULA	BERCOVICI	CANNON	1989
ROD	RIVER OF DEATH	CARVER	CANNON	1989
ROP	RETURN OF THE PLAINSMAN	ROBINSON	ASTOR PICTURES	1953
ROR	RIDER ON THE RAIN	CLEMENT	AVCO EMBASSY	1970
RP	10 RILLINGTON PLACE (UK)	FLEISCHER	COLUMBIA	1971
RP	ALOHA	ROGELL	TIFFANY	1931
RP	PIRATES OF BLOOD RIVER (UK)	GILLING	COLUMBIA	1962
RP	RAMROD	DETOTH	UNITED ARTISTS	1947
RP	RETURN OF RIN-TIN-TIN	NOSSECK	PRODUCERS RELEASING	1947
RP	UNCENSORED (UK)	ASQUITH	20TH CENTURY FOX	1942
RP-2	13 LEAD SOLDIERS	MACDONALD	20th CENTURY FOX	1948
RPB	RUTHLESS PEOPLE	ABRAHAMS	TOUCHSTONE	1986
RR	HOUSE OF BLACKMAIL (UK)	ELVEY	MONARCH	1956
RR	RADAR SECRET SERVICE	NEWFIELD	LIPPERT	1950
RR	RAMBLING ROSE	COOLIDGE	WORLDVISION	1991
RR	RICHIE RICH	PETRIE	WARNER BROS	1994
RR	ROAD RACERS	SWERDLOFF	AIP	1959
RR	ROB ROY: HIGHLAND ROGUE (UK)	FRENCH	RKO	1954
RR	ROGUE RIVER	RAWLINS	EAGLE LION	1950
RR	RUSSIAN ROULETTE	LOMBARDO	AVCO EMBASSY	1975
RRH	RED RIDING HOOD	BROOKS	CANNON	1987
RS	FACE BEHIND THE SCAR (UK: RETURN OF A STRANGER)	HANBURY	FILM ALLIANCE	1937
RS	MAN WITH ONE RED SHOE	DRAGOTI	20TH CENTURY FOX	1985
RS	PORTRAIT OF A SINNER (UK: ROUGH AND THE SMOOTH)	SIODMAK	AIP	1959
RS	RED SONJA	FLEISCHER	MGM/UNITED ARTISTS	1985
RS	RED SUN	YOUNG	NATIONAL GENERAL PIC	1972
RS	RING OF TREASON (UK: RING OF SPIES)	TRONSON	PARAMOUNT	1964
RS	RINGSIDE	MCDONALD	LIPPERT	1949
RS	RISING SUN	KAUFMAN	20th CENTURY FOX	1993
RS	ROAD TO SALINA	LAUTNER	AVCO EMBASSY	1970
RS	ROCK STAR	HEREK	WARNER BROS	2001
RS	ROMANCING THE STONE	ZEMECKIS	20th CENTURY FOX	1984
RS	RUNNER STUMBLES	KRAMER	20TH CENTURY FOX	1979
RS	RUNNING SCARED	HYAMS	MGM	1986
RS-10	MERBABIES (t)	STALLINGS	RKO	1938
RS-101	HELL IS SOLD OUT (UK)	ANDERSON	REALART	1951
RSBT	RITA SUE & BOB TOO	CLARKE	ORION	1987
RSH	RUSSIA HOUSE	SCHEPISI	MGM	1990
RSM	RATTLE OF A SIMPLE MAN (UK)	BOX	CONTINENTAL	1964
RT	HE WHO RIDES THE TIGER (UK)	CRICHTON	SIGMA III	1965
RT	ON THE RIGHT TRACK	PHILIPS	20TH CENTURY FOX	1981
RT	RAGTIME	FORMAN	PARAMOUNT	1981
RT	RED TENT	KALATOZOV	PARAMOUNT	1969
RT	RED TERROR (GER: - GPU 1942)	RITTER	HOFFBERG PROD (UFA)	1960
RT	RICHARD TAYLOR aka JEFF RICHARDS	portrait		
RT	RICHARD THOMAS	portrait	UNIV	
RT	RUTH TERRY	portrait	UNIV	
RTM	RETURN TO ME	HUNT	MGM	2000
RU	GEORGE IN CIVVY STREET (UK)	VARNEL	COLUMBIA	1946
RU1	GLORY AT SEA (UK: GIFT HORSE)	BENNETT	SOUVAINE SELECTIVE	1952
RV	RETURN OF THE VIKINGS (UK)	FREND	ABFD	1945
RV	ROCKS OF VALPRE (UK)	EDWARDS	OLYMPIC	1935
RVM	RIDE A VIOLENT MILE	WARREN	20th CENTURY FOX	1957
RW	RAOUL WALSH		FOX	
RW	RED WAGON (UK)	STEIN	WARDOUR	1934
RW	RETURN OF WILDFIRE	TAYLOR	SCREEN GUILD	1948
RW	RICHARD WEBB		WB	
RW	ROBERT WAGNER	portrait	UNIV	
RW	RUNAWAY	CRICHTON	TRI STAR	1984
RW-5700	CORSAIR	WEST	UNITED ARTISTS	1931

RXL	ROSINA LAWRENCE	portrait	MGM	
RY	ROGUE'S YARN (UK)	SEWELL	EROS	1957
RY	ROOKIE OF THE YEAR	STERN	20th CENTURY FOX	1993
S	AMATEUR GENTLEMAN (UK)	FREELAND	UNITED ARTISTS	1936
S	FABULOUS SUZANNE	SEKELY	REPUBLIC	1946
S	GOLD RUSH	CHAPLIN	UNITED ARTISTS	R41
S	LAND OF FURY (UK: SEEKERS)	ANNAKIN	UNIVERSAL	1955
S	SABENA (GER 1971) HAY COUNTRY SWINGERS	BRUMMER	HEMISPHERE	1974
S	SAILOR WHO FELL FROM GRACE WITH THE SEA	CARLINO	AVCO EMBASSY	1976
S	SALOME	D'ANNA	CANNON	1986
S	SCAVENGERS, THE	CROMWELL	VALIANT FILMS	1959
S	SCROOGED	DONNER	PARAMOUNT	1988
S	SEBASTIAN (UK)	GREENE	PARAMOUNT	1968
S	SECRET OF STAMBOUL (UK)	MARTON	WORLD	1936
S	SERIAL	PERSKY	PARAMOUNT	1980
S	SERVANT (UK)	LOSEY	LANDAU RELEASING	1963
S	SHADOWLANDS	ATTENBOROUGH	SAVOY	1993
S	SHAFT	SINGLETON	PARAMOUNT	2000
S	SHALAKO (UK)	DMYTRYK	CINERAMA	1968
S	SHAME (SWE: SKAMMEN)	BERGMAN	LOPERT	1968
S	SHAMED	PAOLUCCI	CANTON-WEINER	1947
S	SHIPBUILDERS (UK)	BAXTER	ANGLO-AMERICAN	1943
S	SHOOT	HART	AVCO EMBASSY	1976
S	SICILIAN	CIMINO	20th CENTURY FOX	1987
S	SIDEWALK STORIES	LANE	ISLAND PICTURES	1989
S	SIEGE, THE	ZWICK	20th CENTURY FOX	1998
S	SINGLES	CROWE	WARNER BROS	1992
S	SKULL (UK)	FRANCIS	PARAMOUNT	1965
S	SLIVER	NOYCE	PARAMOUNT	1993
S	SMALL WORLD OF SAMMY LEE (UK)	HUGHES	BRYANSTON	1963
S	SOLDIER	ANDERSON	WARNER BROS	1998
S	SOME GIRLS	HOFFMAN	MGM	1988
S	SPACEWAYS (UK)	FISHER	LIPPERT	1953
S	SPEECHLESS	UNDERWOOD	MGM	1994
S	SPEED	DE BONT	20th CENTURY FOX	1994
S	SPEED 2: CRUISE CONTROL	DE BONT	20th CENTURY FOX	1997
S	SPLASH	HOWARD	BUENA VISTA	1984
S	SPRINGTIME (UK: SPRING SONG)	TULLY	ANGLO-AMERICAN	1946
S	SQUEEZE	YOUNG	TRI STAR	1987
S	STEAMING (UK)	LOSEY	COLUMBIA	1985
S	STEFANIA (I STEPANIA)	DALIANIDIS	CHANCELLOR FILMS	1966
S	STRANGER, THE	VISCONTI	PARAMOUNT	1967
S	SUBTERFUGE (UK)	SCOTT	COMMONWEALTH	1968
S	SUMMER	ROHMER	ORION	1986
S	SUNSET	EDWARDS	TRI STAR	1988
S	SUPER, THE	DANIEL	20th CENTURY FOX	1991
S	SUPERMAN	DONNER	WARNER BROS	1978
S	SUSPECT	YATES	TRI STAR	1987
S	SYLVIA	FIRTH	MGM	1985
S	TWO LOST WORLDS	DAWN	EAGLE LION	1951
S	UP JUMPED A SWAGMAN (UK)	MILES	WARNER-PATHE	1965
S-1	CALL A COP	STEVENS	MGM	1931
S-1	DON KEY	GUIOL, HORNE	PATHE EXCHANGE	1926
S-1	QUEEN OF THE AMAZON	FINNEY	SCREEN GUILD	1947
S-1	SHADOWS*		COLUMBIA	
S-2	MAMA LOVES PAPA	STEVENS	MGM	1931
S-2	PUNCH IN THE NOSE	HOWE	PATHE EXCHANGE	1926
S-2	SECOND HUNDRED YEARS	GUIOL	MGM	1927
S2	SMOKEY TRAILS	RAY	METROPOLITAN	1939
S-3	HATS OFF	YATES	MGM	1927
S-3	KICKOFF	STEVENS	MGM	1931
S-3	SOMEWHERE IN SOMEWHERE	HORNE	PATHE EXCHANGE	1925
S-4	LOVE PAINS	ROACH	MGM	1932
S-4	THERE GOES THE BRIDE	HORNE	PATHE EXCHANGE	1925
S-5	BATTLE OF THE CENTURY	BRUCKMAN	MGM	1927
S-5	KNOCKOUT	FRENCH, MCGOWAN	MGM	1932

S-5	LAUGHING LADIES	HORNE	PATHE EXCHANGE	1925
S-6	YOUR HUSBAND'S PAST	GUIOL	PATHE EXCHANGE	1926
S-6	YOU'RE TELLING ME	FRENCH, MCGOWAN	MGM	1932
S7	DEAD MAN'S TRAIL	COLLINS	MONOGRAM	1952
S-7	DIZZY DADDIES	WALLACE	PATHE EXCHANGE	1926
S-7	TOO MANY WOMEN	FRENCH, MCGOWAN	MGM	1932
S-8	LET GEORGE DO IT*	KENNEDY	MGM	1928
S-8	MADAME MYSTERY	WALLACE, LAUREL	PATHE EXCHANGE	1926
S-8	WILD BABIES	FRENCH, MCGOWAN	MGM	1932
S-9	NEVER TOO OLD	WALLACE	PATHE EXCHANGE	1926
S-9	YOU'RE DARN TOOTIN'	KENNEDY	MGM	1928
S-10	MERRY WIDOWER	WALLACE	PATHE EXCHANGE	1926
S-11	RAGGEDY ROSE	WALLACE	PATHE EXCHANGE	1926
S-11	THAT NIGHT	HEATH, MCCAREY	MGM	1928
S-12	DO GENTLEMEN SNORE?	MCCAREY	MGM	1928
S-12	WISE GUYS PREFER BRUNETTES	LAUREL	PATHE EXCHANGE	1926
S-13	BOY FRIEND	GUIOL	MGM	1928
S-13	GET 'EM YOUNG	GUIOL, LAUREL	PATHE EXCHANGE	1926
S-14	DUCK SOUP	GUIOL	PATHE EXCHANGE	1927
S-14	FEED 'EM AND WEEP	GUIOL, MCCAREY	MGM	1928
S-15	GOING GA GA	MCCAREY	MGM	1929
S-15	ON THE FRONT PAGE	PARROTT	PATHE EXCHANGE	1926
S-16	PAIR OF TIGHTS	YATES	MGM	1929
S-16	WHY GIRLS SAY NO	MCCAREY	PATHE EXCHANGE	1927
S-17	HONORABLE MR. BUGGS	JACKMAN	PATHE EXCHANGE	1927
S-17	WHEN MONEY COMES	MCCAREY	MGM	1929
S-18	SLIPPING WIVES	GUIOL	PATHE EXCHANGE	1927
S-18	STRANGER, THE	VISCONTI	PARAMOUNT	1967
S-18	UNKISSED MAN	ROACH, MCCAREY	MGM	1929
S-19	LOVE 'EM AND WEEP	GUIOL, JONES	PATHE EXCHANGE	1927
S-19	WHY IS A PLUMBER?	MCCAREY	MGM	1929
S-20	THUNDERING TOUPEES	MCGOWAN	MGM	1929
S-20	WHY GIRLS LOVE SAILORS	GUIOL	PATHE EXCHANGE	1927
S-21	HURDY GURDY	ROACH	MGM	1929
S-21	WITH LOVE AND HISSES	GUIOL	PATHE EXCHANGE	1927
S-22	MADAME "Q"	MCCAREY	MGM	1929
S-22	SAILORS, BEWARE!	GUIOL	PATHE EXCHANGE	1927
S-23	COWBOYS CRY FOR IT*	GASNIER	PATHE EXCHANGE	1928
S-23	DAD'S DAY	MCCAREY	MGM	1929
S-23	SHOULD TALL MEN MARRY?	GASNIER	PATHE EXCHANGE	1928
S-24	DO DETECTIVES THINK?	GUIOL	PATHE EXCHANGE	1927
S-24	HOTTER THAN HOT	FOSTER	MGM	1929
S-25	FLAMING FATHERS	LAUREL, MCCAREY	PATHE EXCHANGE	1927
S-25	SKY BOY	ROGERS	MGM	1929
S-26	FLYING ELEPHANTS	ROACH, BUTLER	PATHE EXCHANGE	1928
S-26	SKIRT SHY	ROGERS	MGM	1929
S-27	HEAD GUY	ROACH	MGM	1930
S-28	FIGHTING PARSON	GUIOL, ROGERS	MGM	1930
S-29	BIG KICK	DOANE	MGM	1930
S-30	SHRIMP	ROGERS	MGM	1930
S-31	KING		MGM	1930
S-32	DOCTOR'S ORDERS	HEATH	MGM	1930
S-33	BIGGER AND BETTER	KENNEDY	MGM	1930
S-34	LADIES LAST	STEVENS	MGM	1930
S-35	BLOOD AND THUNDER	STEVENS	MGM	1931
S-36	LOVE FEVER	MCGOWAN	MGM	1931
S-37	HIGH GEAR	STEVENS	MGM	1931
S-38	AIR TIGHT	STEVENS	MGM	1931
S-39	LET'S DO THINGS	ROACH	MGM	1931
S-320	SUBMARINE BASE	KELLEY	PRODUCERS RELEASING	1943
S1000	PIGSKIN CHAMPIONS (sh)	CLARKE	MGM	1937
S1002	MARRIED BEFORE BREAKFAST	MARIN	MGM	1937
S1003	THIRTEENTH CHAIR	SEITZ	MGM	1937
S1005	LONDON BY NIGHT	THIELE	MGM	1937
S1006	BETWEEN TWO WOMEN	SEITZ	MGM	1937
S1007	LIVE, LOVE AND LEARN	FITZMAURICE	MGM	1937

S1008	SPORTING BLOOD	SIMON	MGM	1940
S1010	BIG CITY	BORZAGE	MGM	1937
S1011	ROSALIE	VAN DYKE	MGM	1937
S1012	BAD GUY	CAHN	MGM	1937
S1013	MADAME X	WOOD	MGM	1937
S1014	WOMEN MEN MARRY	TAGGART	MGM	1937
S1015	MY DEAR MISS ALDRICH	SEITZ	MGM	1937
S1016	LAST GANGSTER	LUDWIG	MGM	1937
S1017	BAD MAN OF BRIMSTONE	RUBEN	MGM	1937
S1018	NAVY BLUE AND GOLD	WOOD	MGM	1937
S1020	EVERYBODY SING	MARIN	MGM	1938
S1021	MANNEQUIN	BORZAGE	MGM	1938
S1022	THOROUGHBREDS DON'T CRY	GREEN	MGM	1937
S1023	MAN-PROOF	THORPE	MGM	1937
S1024	YOU'RE ONLY YOUNG ONCE	SEITZ	MGM	1937
S1025	GIRL OF THE GOLDEN WEST	LEONARD	MGM	1938
S1026	OF HUMAN HEARTS	BROWN	MGM	1938
S1027	TEST PILOT	FLEMING	MGM	1938
S1028	BEG, BORROW OR STEAL	THIELE	MGM	1937
S1029	PORT OF THE SEVEN SEAS	WHALE	MGM	1938
S1030	MARIE ANTOINETTE	VAN DYKE	MGM	1938
S1032	ARSENE LUPIN RETURNS	FITZMAURICE	MGM	1938
S1033	PARADISE FOR THREE	BUZZELL	MGM	1938
S1034	LOVE IS A HEADACHE	THORPE	MGM	1938
S1035	FIRST HUNDRED YEARS	THORPE	MGM	1938
S1036	THREE COMRADES	BORZAGE	MGM	1938
S1037	JUDGE HARDY'S CHILDREN	SEITZ	MGM	1938
S1039	LORD JEFF	WOOD	MGM	1938
S1040	TOY WIFE	THORPE	MGM	1938
S1041	YELLOW JACK	SEITZ	MGM	1938
S1042	SHOPWORN ANGEL	POTTER	MGM	1938
S1043	HOLD THAT KISS	MARIN	MGM	1938
S1044	NORTHWEST PASSAGE	VIDOR	MGM	1940
S1045	SEA OF GRASS	KAZAN	MGM	1947
S1046	TOO HOT TO HANDLE	CONWAY	MGM	1938
S1047	WOMAN AGAINST WOMAN	SINCLAIR	MGM	1938
S1048	HONOLULU	BUZZELL	MGM	1939
S1049	CROWD ROARS	THORPE	MGM	1938
S1049	VIC DAMONE	portrait	MGM	
S1050	LOVE FINDS ANDY HARDY	SEITZ	MGM	1938
S1051	FAST COMPANY	BUZZELL	MGM	1938
S1052	THREE LOVES HAS NANCY	THORPE	MGM	1938
S1053	LISTEN, DARLING	MARIN	MGM	1938
S1054	BOYS TOWN	TAUROG	MGM	1938
S1055	SWEETHEARTS	VAN DYKE	MGM	1938
S1056	IDIOT'S DELIGHT	BROWN	MGM	1939
S1057	CHASER	MARIN	MGM	1938
S1058	RICH MAN, POOR GIRL	SCHUNZEL	MGM	1938
S1059	STABLEMATES	WOOD	MGM	1938
S1060	WIZARD OF OZ	FLEMING	MGM	1939
S1061	OUT WEST WITH THE HARDYS	SEITZ	MGM	1938
S1062	VACATION FROM LOVE	FITZMAURICE	MGM	1938
S1063	SHINING HOUR	BORZAGE	MGM	1938
S1064	DRAMATIC SCHOOL	SINCLAIR	MGM	1938
S1065	STAND UP AND FIGHT	VAN DYKE	MGM	1939
S1066	ICE FOLLIES OF 1939	SCHUNZEL	MGM	1939
S1067	YOUNG DR. KILDARE	BUCQUET	MGM	1938
S1068	CHRISTMAS CAROL	MARIN	MGM	1938
S1069	SPRING MADNESS	SIMON	MGM	1938
S1070	I TAKE THIS WOMAN	VAN DYKE	MGM	1940
S1071	GIRL DOWNSTAIRS	TAUROG	MGM	1938
S1072	BURN 'EM UP O'CONNOR	SEDGWICK	MGM	1939
S1073	ADVENTURES OF HUCKLEBERRY FINN	THORPE	MGM	1939
S1074	BROADWAY SERENADE	LEONARD	MGM	1939
S1075	LET FREEDOM RING	CONWAY	MGM	1939
S1076	FOUR GIRLS IN WHITE	SIMON	MGM	1939

S1077	TARZAN FINDS A SON	THORPE	MGM	1939
S1078	FAST AND LOOSE	MARIN	MGM	1939
S1079	KID FROM TEXAS	SIMON	MGM	1939
S1080	WITHIN THE LAW	MACHATY	MGM	1939
S1081	SERGEANT MADDEN	VON STERNBERG	MGM	1939
S1082	HARDYS RIDE HIGH	SEITZ	MGM	1939
S1083	IT'S A WONDERFUL WORLD	VAN DYKE	MGM	1939
S1085	CALLING DR. KILDARE	BUCQUET	MGM	1939
S1086	SOCIETY LAWYER	MARIN	MGM	1939
S1087	TELL NO TALES	FENTON	MGM	1939
S1088	BABES IN ARMS	BERKELEY	MGM	1939
S1089	FLORIAN	MARIN	MGM	1940
S1090	ON BORROWED TIME	BUCQUET	MGM	1939
S1091	WOMEN	CUKOR	MGM	1939
S1092	6,000 ENEMIES	SEITZ	MGM	1939
S1093	BALALAIKA	SCHUNZEL	MGM	1939
S1094	MAISIE	MARIN	MGM	1939
S1095	ANDY HARDY GETS SPRING FEVER	VAN DYKE	MGM	1939
S1096	STRONGER THAN DESIRE	FENTON	MGM	1939
S1097	LADY OF THE TROPICS	CONWAY	MGM	1939
S1098	BLACKMAIL	POTTER	MGM	1939
S1099	AT THE CIRCUS	BUZZELL	MGM	1939
S1100	NINOTCHKA	LUBITSCH	MGM	1939
S1101	MIRACLES FOR SALE	BROWNING	MGM	1939
S1102	THUNDER AFLOAT	SEITZ	MGM	1939
S1103	THESE GLAMOUR GIRLS	SIMON	MGM	1939
S1104	HENRY GOES ARIZONA	MARIN	MGM	1940
S1105	THEY ALL COME OUT	TOURNEUR	MGM	1939
S1106	DANCING CO-ED	SIMON	MGM	1939
S1107	ANOTHER THIN MAN	VAN DYKE	MGM	1939
S1108	REMEMBER?	MCLEOD	MGM	1940
S1112	BAD LITTLE ANGEL	THIELE	MGM	1939
S1113	JOE & ETHEL TURP CALL ON PRESIDENT	SINCLAIR	MGM	1939
S1114	JUDGE HARDY AND SON	SEITZ	MGM	1939
S1115	NICK CARTER, MASTER DETECTIVE	TOURNEUR	MGM	1939
S1116	SECRET OF DR. KILDARE	BUCQUET	MGM	1939
S1118	EARL OF CHICAGO	THORPE	MGM	1940
S1119	CONGO MAISIE	POTTER	MGM	1940
S1121	SHOP AROUND THE CORNER	LUBITSCH	MGM	1940
S1122	NEW MOON	LEONARD	MGM	1940
S1123	YOUNG TOM EDISON	TAUROG	MGM	1940
S1124	MAN FROM DAKOTA	FENTON	MGM	1940
S1125	EDISON THE MAN	BROWN	MGM	1940
S1126	FORTY LITTLE MOTHERS	BERKELEY	MGM	1940
S1127	20 MULE TEAM	THORPE	MGM	1940
S1128	GHOST COMES HOME	THIELE	MGM	1940
S1130	WATERLOO BRIDGE	LEROY	MGM	1940
S1131	SUSAN AND GOD	CUKOR	MGM	1940
S1135	MORTAL STORM	BORZAGE	MGM	1940
S1136	PRIDE AND PREJUDICE	LEONARD	MGM	1940
S1137	AND ONE WAS BEAUTIFUL	SINCLAIR	MGM	1940
S1139	ANDY HARDY MEETS DEBUTANTE	SEITZ	MGM	1940
S1140	WE WHO ARE YOUNG	BUCQUET	MGM	1940
S1141	STRIKE UP THE BAND	BERKELEY	MGM	1940
S1142	I LOVE YOU AGAIN	VAN DYKE	MGM	1940
S1143	PHANTOM RAIDERS	TOURNEUR	MGM	1940
S1144	CAPTAIN IS A LADY	SINCLAIR	MGM	1940
S1145	GOLD RUSH MAISIE	MARIN	MGM	1940
S1146	ESCAPE	LEROY	MGM	1940
S1147	WYOMING	THORPE	MGM	1940
S1148	GOLDEN FLEECING	FENTON	MGM	1940
S1150	FLIGHT COMMAND	BORZAGE	MGM	1940
S1151	BITTER SWEET	VAN DYKE	MGM	1940
S1152	PHILADELPHIA STORY	CUKOR	MGM	1940
S1153	LITTLE NELLIE KELLY	TAUROG	MGM	1940
S1156	SKY MURDER	SEITZ	MGM	1940

S1158	HULLABALOO	MARIN	MGM	1940
S1159	COMRADE X	VIDOR	MGM	1940
S1161	GALLANT SONS	SEITZ	MGM	1941
S1162	COME LIVE WITH ME	BROWN	MGM	1941
S1163	WILD MAN OF BORNEO	SINCLAIR	MGM	1941
S1166	KEEPING COMPANY	SIMON	MGM	1941
S1167	MAISIE WAS A LADY	MARIN	MGM	1941
S1168	BOYS TOWN	TAUROG	MGM	1938
S1169	BAD MAN	THORPE	MGM	1941
S1170	BLONDE INSPIRATION	BERKELEY	MGM	1941
S1174	ANDY HARDY'S PRIVATE SECRETARY	SEITZ	MGM	1941
S1175	TRIAL OF MARY DUGAN	MCLEOD	MGM	1941
S1176	PENALTY	BUCQUET	MGM	1941
S1177	WOMAN'S FACE	CUKOR	MGM	1941
S1178	DR. JEKYLL AND MR HYDE	FLEMING	MGM	1941
S1179	BLOSSOMS IN THE DUST	LEROY	MGM	1941
S1180	LOVE CRAZY	CONWAY	MGM	1941
S1181	THEY MET IN BOMBAY	BROWN	MGM	1941
S1182	LADY BE GOOD	MCLEOD	MGM	1941
S1183	WASHINGTON MELODRAMA	SIMON	MGM	1941
S1184	PEOPLE VS. DR. KILDARE	BUCQUET	MGM	1941
S1185	I'LL WAIT FOR YOU	SINCLAIR	MGM	1941
S1186	YEARLING	BROWN	MGM	1946
S1187	BIG STORE, THE	REISNER	MGM	1941
S1187	PETER LAWFORD	portrait	MGM	
S1188	SMILIN' THROUGH	BORZAGE	MGM	1941
S1189	GET-AWAY	BUZZELL	MGM	1941
S1190	TWO-FACED WOMAN	CUKOR	MGM	1941
S1191	BARNACLE BILL	THORPE	MGM	1941
S1192	TARZAN'S SECRET TREASURE	THORPE	MGM	1941
S1193	LIFE BEGINS FOR ANDY HARDY	SEITZ	MGM	1941
S1194	UNHOLY PARTNERS	LEROY	MGM	1941
S1196	WHEN LADIES MEET	LEONARD	MGM	1941
S1197	HONKY TONK	CONWAY	MGM	1941
S1199	CHOCOLATE SOLDIER	DEL RUTH	MGM	1941
S1201	WHISTLING IN THE DARK	SIMON	MGM	1941
S1202	MARRIED BACHELOR	BUZZELL	MGM	1941
S1203	FEMININE TOUCH	VAN DYKE	MGM	1941
S1204	BABES ON BROADWAY	BERKELEY	MGM	1941
S1205	PANAMA HATTIE	MCLEOD	MGM	1941
S1206	H. M. PULHAM, ESQ.	VIDOR	MGM	1941
S1207	KATHLEEN	BUCQUET	MGM	1941
S1209	WOMAN OF THE YEAR	STEVENS	MGM	1942
S1210	DESIGN FOR SCANDAL	TAUROG	MGM	1941
S1211	BUGLE SOUNDS	SIMON	MGM	1942
S1212	JOHNNY EAGER	LEROY	MGM	1942
S1213	VANISHING VIRGINIAN	BORZAGE	MGM	1942
S1214	WE WERE DANCING	LEONARD	MGM	1942
S1215	I MARRIED AN ANGEL	VAN DYKE	MGM	1942
S1217	MR. AND MRS. NORTH	SINCLAIR	MGM	1941
S1218	BORN TO SING	LUDWIG	MGM	1942
S1219	JOE SMITH AMERICAN	THORPE	MGM	1942
S1220	YANK ON THE BURMA ROAD	SEITZ	MGM	1942
S1221	MRS. MINIVER	WYLER	MGM	1942
S1222	RIO RITA	SIMON	MGM	1942
S1223	SHIPS AHOY	BUZZELL	MGM	1942
S1224	NAZI AGENT	DASSIN	MGM	1942
S1225	TORTILLA FLAT	FLEMING	MGM	1942
S1226	THIS TIME FOR KEEPS	REISNER	MGM	1942
S1227	KID GLOVE KILLER	ZINNEMANN	MGM	1942
S1228	TARZAN'S NEW YORK ADVENTURE	THORPE	MGM	1942
S1229	SOMEWHERE I'LL FIND YOU	RUGGLES	MGM	1942
S1230	COURTSHIP OF ANDY HARDY	SEITZ	MGM	1942
S1232	FINGERS AT THE WINDOW	LEDERER	MGM	1942
S1233	JACKASS MAIL	MCLEOD	MGM	1942
S1234	SUNDAY PUNCH	MILLER	MGM	1942

S1236	CALLING DR. GILLESPIE	BUCQUET	MGM	1942
S1237	STAND BY FOR ACTION	LEONARD	MGM	1943
S1238	APACHE TRAIL	THORPE	MGM	1942
S1239	CROSSROADS	CONWAY	MGM	1942
S1240	GRAND CENTRAL MURDER	SIMON	MGM	1942
S1241	PACIFIC RENDEZVOUS	SIDNEY	MGM	1942
S1242	AFFAIRS OF MARTHA	DASSIN	MGM	1942
S1243	MAISIE GETS HER MAN	RUTH	MGM	1942
S1244	FOR ME AND MY GAL	BERKELEY	MGM	1942
S1245	PIERRE OF THE PLAINS	SEITZ	MGM	1942
S1246	SEVEN SWEETHEARTS	BORZAGE	MGM	1943
S1247	YANK AT ETON	TAUROG	MGM	1942
S1248	CAIRO	VAN DYKE	MGM	1942
S1249	RANDOM HARVEST	LEROY	MGM	1942
S1250	TISH	SIMON	MGM	1942
S1251	OMAHA TRAIL	BUZZELL	MGM	1942
S1252	WAR AGAINST MRS. HADLEY	BUCQUET	MGM	1942
S1253	EYES IN THE NIGHT	ZINNEMANN	MGM	1942
S1254	WHITE CARGO	THORPE	MGM	1942
S1255	NORTHWEST RANGERS	NEWMAN	MGM	1942
S1256	KEEPER OF THE FLAME	CUKOR	MGM	1943
S1257	TENNESSEE JOHNSON	DIETERLE	MGM	1943
S1258	ANDY HARDY'S DOUBLE LIFE	SEITZ	MGM	1943
S1259	WHISTLING IN DIXIE	SIMON	MGM	1943
S1260	JOURNEY FOR MARGARET	VAN DYKE	MGM	1943
S1261	LASSIE COME HOME	WILCOX	MGM	1943
S1262	REUNION IN FRANCE	DASSIN	MGM	1943
S1263	PILOT NO. 5	SIDNEY	MGM	1943
S1264	PRESENTING LILY MARS	TAUROG	MGM	1943
S1266	DU BARRY WAS A LADY	DEL RUTH	MGM	1943
S1267	CABIN IN THE SKY	MINNELLI	MGM	1943
S1268	ASSIGNMENT IN BRITTANY	CONWAY	MGM	1943
S1269	HUMAN COMEDY	BROWN	MGM	1943
S1270	THREE HEARTS FOR JULIA	THORPE	MGM	1943
S1271	SLIGHTLY DANGEROUS	RUGGLES	MGM	1943
S1272	SALUTE TO THE MARINES	SIMON	MGM	1943
S1273	GENTLE ANNIE	MARTON	MGM	1945
S1274	THOUSANDS CHEER	SIDNEY	MGM	1943
S1275	AMERICAN ROMANCE	VIDOR	MGM	1944
S1276	YOUNGEST PROFESSION	BUZZELL	MGM	1943
S1277	HARRIGAN'S KID	REISNER	MGM	1943
S1278	ABOVE SUSPICION	THORPE	MGM	1943
S1279	STRANGER IN TOWN	ROWLAND	MGM	1943
S1280	BATAAN	GARNETT	MGM	1943
S1280	SERVANT	LOSEY	LANDAU RELEASING	1964
S1282	AIR RAID WARDENS	SEDGWICK	MGM	1943
S1283	CHRIS NOEL	portrait	MGM	
S1283	I DOOD IT	MINNELLI	MGM	1943
S1284	BEST FOOT FORWARD	BUZZELL	MGM	1943
S1285	GIRL CRAZY	TAUROG, BERKELEY	MGM	1943
S1286	SWING FEVER	WHELAN	MGM	1944
S1287	SWING SHIFT MAISIE	MCLEOD	MGM	1943
S1288	YOUNG IDEAS	DASSIN	MGM	1943
S1289	MARRIAGE IS A PRIVATE AFFAIR	LEONARD	MGM	1944
S1290	MADAME CURIE	LEROY	MGM	1943
S1291	GUY NAMED JOE	FLEMING	MGM	1944
S1292	MAN FROM DOWN UNDER	LEONARD	MGM	1943
S1293	SONG OF RUSSIA	RATOFF	MGM	1944
S1294	HITLER'S MADMAN	SIRK	MGM	1943
S1295	WHISTLING IN BROOKLYN	SIMON	MGM	1943
S1296	LOST ANGEL	ROWLAND	MGM	1943
S1298	CROSS OF LORRAINE	GARNETT	MGM	1944
S1299	CRY HAVOC	THORPE	MGM	1944
S1301	WHITE CLIFFS OF DOVER	BROWN	MGM	1944
S1302	MEET THE PEOPLE	REISNER	MGM	1944
S1303	BROADWAY RHYTHM	DEL RUTH	MGM	1944

S1304	SEE HERE, PRIVATE HARGROVE	RUGGLES	MGM	1944
S1305	DRAGON SEED	BUCQUET, CONWAY	MGM	1944
S1306	ANDY HARDY'S BLONDE TROUBLE	SEITZ	MGM	1944
S1307	RATIONING	GOLDBECK	MGM	1944
S1308	BATHING BEAUTY	SIDNEY	MGM	1944
S1309	KISMET	DIETERLE	MGM	1944
S1310	CANTERVILLE GHOST	DASSIN	MGM	1944
S1311	GASLIGHT	CUKOR	MGM	1944
S1312	QUO VADIS	LEROY	MGM	1951
S1313	TWO GIRLS AND A SAILOR	THORPE	MGM	1944
S1314	SEVENTH CROSS	ZINNEMANN	MGM	1944
S1315	NATIONAL VELVET	BROWN	MGM	1945
S1316	THIRTY SECONDS OVER TOKYO	LEROY	MGM	1944
S1317	MEET ME IN ST. LOUIS	MINNELLI	MGM	1944
S1318	THREE MEN IN WHITE	GOLDBECK	MGM	1944
S1319	PICTURE OF DORIAN GRAY	LEWIN	MGM	1945
S1320	THIS MAN'S NAVY	WELLMAN	MGM	1945
S1321	MRS. PARKINGTON	GARNETT	MGM	1944
S1323	MAISIE GOES TO RENO	BEAUMONT	MGM	1944
S1324	BARBARY COAST GENT	DEL RUTH	MGM	1944
S1325	ZIEGFELD FOLLIES	MINNELLI	MGM	1946
S1326	LOST IN A HAREM	REISNER	MGM	1945
S1327	SON OF LASSIE	SIMON	MGM	1945
S1328	THIN MAN GOES HOME	THORPE	MGM	1945
S1329	MUSIC FOR MILLIONS	KOSTER	MGM	1945
S1330	LOVE LAUGHS AT ANDY HARDY	GOLDBECK	MGM	1946
S1331	CLOCK	MINNELLI	MGM	1945
S1332	NOTHING BUT TROUBLE	TAYLOR	MGM	1945
S1333	ANCHORS AWEIGH	SIDNEY	MGM	1945
S1334	BLONDE FEVER	WHORF	MGM	1945
S1335	BETWEEN TWO WOMEN	GOLDBECK	MGM	1945
S1337	THRILL OF A ROMANCE	THORPE	MGM	1945
S1338	KEEP YOUR POWER DRY	BUZZELL	MGM	1945
S1339	COURAGE OF LASSIE	WILCOX	MGM	1946
S1341	VALLEY OF DECISION	GARNETT	MGM	1945
S1342	OUR VINES HAVE TENDER GRAPES	ROWLAND	MGM	1945
S1343	WEEK-END AT THE WALDORF	LEONARD	MGM	1945
S1344	TWICE BLESSED	BEAUMONT	MGM	1945
S1345	HIDDEN EYE	WHORF	MGM	1946
S1346	HER HIGHNESS AND THE BELLBOY	THORPE	MGM	1945
S1347	YOLANDA AND THE THIEF	MINNELLI	MGM	1945
S1348	HARVEY GIRLS	SIDNEY	MGM	1946
S1349	THEY WERE EXPENDABLE	FORD	MGM	1945
S1350	DANGEROUS PARTNERS	CAHN	MGM	1945
S1351	EASY TO WED	BUZZELL	MGM	1946
S1352	ADVENTURE	FLEMING	MGM	1946
S1353	SAILOR TAKES A WIFE	WHORF	MGM	1946
S1354	ABBOTT & COSTELLO IN HOLLYWOOD	SYLVAN	MGM	1945
S1355	POSTMAN ALWAYS RINGS TWICE	BARNETT	MGM	1946
S1356	SHE WENT TO THE RACES	GOLDBECK	MGM	1946
S1357	TWO SISTERS FROM BOSTON	KOSTER	MGM	1946
S1358	LETTER FOR EVIE	DASSIN	MGM	1946
S1359	BAD BASCOMB	SIMON	MGM	1946
S1360	HOLIDAY IN MEXICO	SIDNEY	MGM	1946
S1361	HOODLUM SAINT	TAUROG	MGM	1946
S1363	BOYS' RANCH	ROWLAND	MGM	1946
S1364	UP GOES MAISIE	BEAUMONT	MGM	1946
S1365	GREEN YEARS	SAVILLE	MGM	1946
S1366	NO LEAVE, NO LOVE	MARTIN	MGM	1946
S1368	GALLANT BESS	MARTON	MGM	1946
S1369	TILL THE CLOUDS ROLL BY	WHORF	MGM	1947
S1370	LITTLE MR. JIM	ZINNEMANN	MGM	1947
S1371	FIESTA	THORPE	MGM	1947
S1371	PEARLS AND DEVIL-FISH	AUSTIN	MGM	1931
S1371	SHARKS AND SWORDFISH	SMITH	MGM	1931
S1372	THREE WISE FOOLS	BUZZELL	MGM	1946

S1373	FAITHFUL IN MY FASHION	SALKOW	MGM	1946
S1374	COCKEYED MIRACLE	SIMON	MGM	1946
S1375	INSIDE STRAIGHT	MAYER	MGM	1951
S1376	UNDERCURRENT	MINNELLI	MGM	1946
S1377	BEGINNING OR THE END	TAUROG	MGM	1947
S1378	SHOW-OFF	BEAUMONT	MGM	1946
S1379	TENTH AVENUE ANGEL	ROWLAND	MGM	1948
S1380	MY BROTHER TALKS TO HORSES	ZINNEMANN	MGM	1947
S1380	WHIPPET RACING (sh)	WING	MGM	1931
S1381	DESIRE ME	CONWAY, CUKOR	MGM	1947
S1382	MIGHTY MCGURK	WATERS	MGM	1947
S1383	LADY IN THE LAKE	MONTGOMERY	MGM	1947
S1384	SECRET HEART	LEONARD	MGM	1946
S1385	HIGH BARBAREE	CONWAY	MGM	1947
S1386	SUMMER HOLIDAY	MAMOULIAN	MGM	1948
S1387	UNFINISHED DANCE	KOSTER	MGM	1947
S1388	IT HAPPENED IN BROOKLYN	WHORF	MGM	1947
S1389	THIS TIME FOR KEEPS	THORPE	MGM	1947
S1390	ROMANCE OF ROSY RIDGE	ROWLAND	MGM	1947
S1391	ARNELO AFFAIR	OBOLER	MGM	1947
S1392	LIVING IN A BIG WAY	LA CAVA	MGM	1947
S1393	MERTON OF THE MOVIES	ALTON	MGM	1947
S1395	CYNTHIA	LEONARD	MGM	1947
S1396	THREE DARING DAUGHTERS	WILCOX	MGM	1948
S1397	DARK DELUSION	GOLDBECK	MGM	1947
S1398	SONG OF LOVE	BROWN	MGM	1947
S1399	UNDERCOVER MAISIE	BEAUMONT	MGM	1947
S1401	HUCKSTERS	CONWAY	MGM	1947
S1402	SONG OF THE THIN MAN	BUZZELL	MGM	1947
S1403	CASS TIMBERLANE	SIDNEY	MGM	1948
S1404	GOOD NEWS	WALTERS	MGM	1947
S1405	ALIAS A GENTLEMAN	BEAUMONT	MGM	1948
S1406	KISSING BANDIT	BENEDEK	MGM	1949
S1407	IF WINTER COMES	SAVILLE	MGM	1948
S1409	HIGH WALL	BERNHARDT	MGM	1948
S1410	BRIDGE GOES WILD	TAUROG	MGM	1948
S1411	ON AN ISLAND WITH YOU	THORPE	MGM	1948
S1412	LUXURY LINER	WHORF	MGM	1948
S1413	HOMECOMING	LEROY	MGM	1948
S1414	STATE OF THE UNION	CAPRA	MGM	1948
S1415	HILLS OF HOME	WILCOX	MGM	1948
S1416	B.F.'S DAUGHTER	LEONARD	MGM	1948
S1417	BIG CITY	TAUROG	MGM	1948
S1418	EASTER PARADE	WALTERS	MGM	1948
S1419	DATE WITH JUDY	THORPE	MGM	1948
S1420	THREE MUSKETEERS	SIDNEY	MGM	1948
S1421	SECRET LAND (doc)		MGM	1948
S1422	JULIA MISBEHAVES	CONWAY	MGM	1948
S1423	SOUTHERN YANKEE	SEDGWICK	MGM	1948
S1424	STRATTON STORY	WOOD	MGM	1949
S1425	COMMAND DECISION	WOOD	MGM	1948
S1426	SUN COMES UP	THORPE	MGM	1949
S1427	WORDS AND MUSIC	TAUROG	MGM	1949
S1428	ACT OF VIOLENCE	ZINNEMANN	MGM	1949
S1429	NEPTUNE'S DAUGHTER	BUZZELL	MGM	1949
S1430	LITTLE WOMEN	LEROY	MGM	1949
S1431	BRIBE	LEONARD	MGM	1949
S1433	BARKLEYS OF BROADWAY	WALTERS	MGM	1949
S1435	SECRET GARDEN	WILCOX	MGM	1949
S1436	BIG JACK	THORPE	MGM	1949
S1438	THAT FORSYTE WOMAN	BENNETT	MGM	1950
S1439	RED DANUBE	SIDNEY	MGM	1950
S1440	IN THE GOOD OLD SUMMERTIME	LEONARD	MGM	1949
S1441	MADAME BOVARY	MINNELLI	MGM	1949
S1442	CHALLENGE TO LASSIE	THORPE	MGM	1950
S1443	THAT MIDNIGHT KISS	TAUROG	MGM	1949

S1444	ANY NUMBER CAN PLAY	LEROY	MGM	1949
S1445	EDWARD, MY SON (UK)	CUKOR	MGM	1949
S1447	SCENE OF THE CRIME	ROWLAND	MGM	1949
S1448	BORDER INCIDENT	MANN	MGM	1949
S1449	MALAYA	THORPE	MGM	1950
S1450	ANNIE GET YOUR GUN	SIDNEY	MGM	1950
S1451	INTRUDER IN THE DUST	BROWN	MGM	1949
S1452	BATTLEGROUND	WELLMAN	MGM	1949
S1453	ON THE TOWN	DONEN, KELLY	MGM	1949
S1455	SHADOW ON THE WALL	JACKSON	MGM	1950
S1456	DOCTOR AND THE GIRL	BERNHARDT	MGM	1949
S1457	ADAM'S RIB	CUKOR	MGM	1950
S1458	TENSION	BERRY	MGM	1950
S1459	STARS IN MY CROWN	TOURNEUR	MGM	1950
S1460	AMBUSH	WOOD	MGM	1950
S1461	NANCY GOES TO RIO	LEONARD	MGM	1950
S1462	PLEASE BELIEVE ME	TAUROG	MGM	1950
S1463	KEY TO THE CITY	SIDNEY	MGM	1950
S1464	EAST SIDE, WEST SIDE	LEROY	MGM	1949
S1466	BLACK HAND	THORPE	MGM	1950
S1467	KING SOLOMON'S MINES	BENNETT	MGM	1950
S1468	DEVIL'S DOORWAY	MANN	MGM	1950
S1469	OUTRIDERS	ROWLAND	MGM	1950
S1470	BIG HANGOVER	KRASNA	MGM	1950
S1471	YELLOW CAB MAN	DONOHUE	MGM	1950
S1472	MINIVER STORY	POTTER	MGM	1950
S1473	HAPPY YEARS	WELLMAN	MGM	1950
S1474	REFORMER AND THE REDHEAD	FRANK, PANAMA	MGM	1950
S1476	KIM	SAVILLE	MGM	1951
S1477	SUMMER STOCK	WALTERS	MGM	1950
S1478	LADY WITHOUT A PASSPORT	LEWIS	MGM	1950
S1479	ASPHALT JUNGLE	HUSTON	MGM	1950
S1480	SKIPPER SURPRISED HIS WIFE	NUGENT	MGM	1950
S1481	MYSTERY STREET	STURGES	MGM	1950
S1482	THREE LITTLE WORDS	THORPE	MGM	1950
S1483	TOAST OF NEW ORLEANS	TAUROG	MGM	1950
S1485	LIFE OF HER OWN	CUKOR	MGM	1950
S1486	CRISIS	BROOKS	MGM	1950
S1487	RIGHT CROSS	STURGES	MGM	1950
S1488	NEXT VOICE YOU HEAR	WELLMAN	MGM	1950
S1489	PAGAN LOVE SONG	ALTON	MGM	1950
S1490	DIAL 1119	MAYER	MGM	1950
S1491	TWO WEEKS WITH LOVE	ROWLAND	MGM	1950
S1492	RED HOT WHEELS (TO PLEASE A LADY 1950)	BROWN	MGM	R62
S1492	TO PLEASE A LADY	BROWN	MGM	1950
S1494	CAUSE FOR ALARM	GARNETT	MGM	1951
S1495	GROUNDS FOR MARRIAGE	LEONARD	MGM	1951
S1496	VENGEANCE VALLEY	THORPE	MGM	1951
S1497	WATCH THE BIRDIE	DONOHUE	MGM	1951
S1498	IT'S A BIG COUNTRY (INTERRUPTIONS episode)		MGM	1952
S1499	IT'S A BIG COUNTRY (CENSUS TAKER episode)		MGM	1952
S1500	IT'S A BIG COUNTRY (FOUR EYES episode)		MGM	1952
S1501	IT'S A BIG COUNTRY (ROSIKA episode)		MGM	1952
S1502	ROYAL WEDDING	DONEN	MGM	1951
S1503	MRS. O'MALLEY AND MR. MALONE	TAUROG	MGM	1951
S1504	PAINTED HILLS	KRESS	MGM	1951
S1505	IT'S A BIG COUNTRY (LOAD episode)		MGM	1952
S1506	MAGNIFICENT YANKEE	STURGES	MGM	1950
S1507	AMERICAN IN PARIS	MINNELLI	MGM	1951
S1508	ACROSS THE WIDE MISSOURI	WELLMAN	MGM	1951
S1509	THREE GUYS NAMED MIKE	WALTERS	MGM	1951
S1510	IT'S A BIG COUNTRY (MINISTER IN WASH episode)		MGM	1952
S1510	SHOWBOAT	SIDNEY	MGM	1951
S1511	MR. IMPERIUM	HARTMAN	MGM	1951
S1512	RED BADGE OF COURAGE	HUSTON	MGM	1951
S1513	CALLING BULLDOG DRUMMOND	SAVILLE	MGM	1951

S1514	GREAT CARUSO	THORPE	MGM	1951
S1515	IT'S A BIG COUNTRY (TEXAS episode)		MGM	1951
S1516	GO FOR BROKE	PIROSH	MGM	1951
S1517	SOLDIERS THREE	GARNETT	MGM	1951
S1518	EXCUSE MY DUST	ROWLAND	MGM	1951
S1519	FATHER'S LITTLE DIVIDEND	MINNELLI	MGM	1951
S1520	SHOW BOAT	SIDNEY	MGM	1951
S1521	KIND LADY	STURGES	MGM	1951
S1522	RICH, YOUNG AND PRETTY	TAUROG	MGM	1951
S1523	NIGHT INTO MORNING	MARKEL	MGM	1951
S1524	LOVE IS BETTER THAN EVER	DONEN	MGM	1952
S1525	IT'S A BIG COUNTRY (LETTER FROM KOREA episode)		MGM	1952
S1526	NO QUESTIONS ASKED	KRESS	MGM	1951
S1527	TALL TARGET	MANN	MGM	1951
S1528	STRIP	KARDOS	MGM	1951
S1529	UNKNOWN MAN	THORPE	MGM	1951
S1530	STRICTLY DISHONORABLE	FRANK, PANAMA	MGM	1951
S1531	LAW AND THE LADY	KNOPF	MGM	1951
S1532	TEXAS CARNIVAL	WALTERS	MGM	1951
S1533	SCARAMOUCHE	SIDNEY	MGM	1952
S1534	PEOPLE AGAINST O'HARA	STURGES	MGM	1951
S1535	WILD NORTH	MARTON	MGM	1952
S1536	WESTWARD THE WOMEN	WELLMAN	MGM	1951
S1537	ANGELS IN THE OUTFIELD	BROWN	MGM	1951
S1538	SHADOW IN THE SKY	WILCOX	MGM	1952
S1539	BANNERLINE	WEIS	MGM	1951
S1540	LIGHT TOUCH	BROOKS	MGM	1952
S1541	TOO YOUNG TO KISS	LEONARD	MGM	1951
S1542	CALLAWAY WENT THATAWAY	FRANK, PANAMA	MGM	1952
S1544	MAN WITH A CLOAK	MARKLE	MGM	1951
S1545	BELLE OF NEW YORK	WALTERS	MGM	1952
S1546	SINGIN' IN THE RAIN	DONEN, KELLY	MGM	1952
S1548	WHEN IN ROME	BROWN	MGM	1952
S1549	IVANHOE (UK)	THORPE	MGM	1952
S1550	JUST THIS ONCE	WEIS	MGM	1952
S1551	SELLOUT	MAYER	MGM	1952
S1552	PLYMOUTH ADVENTURE	BROWN	MGM	1952
S1553	BECAUSE YOU'RE MINE	HALL	MGM	1952
S1554	TALK ABOUT A STRANGER	BRADLEY	MGM	1952
S1555	LOVELY TO LOOK AT	LEROY	MGM	1952
S1556	SKIRTS AHOY	LANFIELD	MGM	1952
S1557	MERRY WIDOW	BERNHARDT	MGM	1952
S1559	YOUNG MAN WITH IDEAS	LEISEN	MGM	1952
S1560	HOUR OF 13	FRENCH	MGM	1952
S1561	GIRL IN WHITE	STURGES	MGM	1952
S1564	GLORY ALLEY	WALSH	MGM	1952
S1565	CARBINE WILLIAMS	THORPE	MGM	1952
S1566	PAT AND MIKE	CUKOR	MGM	1952
S1567	MILLION DOLLAR MERMAID	LEROY	MGM	1952
S1568	WASHINGTON STORY	PIROSH	MGM	1952
S1569	DEVIL MAKES THREE	MARTON	MGM	1952
S1570	HOLIDAY FOR SINNERS	MAYER	MGM	1952
S1571	STORY OF THREE LOVES (EQUILIBRIUM episode)	MINNELLI, REINHARDT	MGM	1953
S1572	STORY OF THREE LOVES (MADEMOISELLE episode)	MINNELLI, REINHARDT	MGM	1953
S1573	FEARLESS FAGAN	DONEN	MGM	1952
S1574	ABOVE AND BEYOND	FRANK, PANAMA	MGM	1953
S1575	LILI	WALTERS	MGM	1953
S1576	EVERYTHING I HAVE IS YOURS	LEONARD	MGM	1952
S1577	STORY OF THREE LOVES (BALLERINA episode)	MINNELLI, REINHARDT	MGM	1953
S1578	MY MAN AND I	WELLMAN	MGM	1952
S1579	PRISONER OF ZENDA	THORPE	MGM	1952
S1580	YOU FOR ME	WEIS	MGM	1952
S1581	BAD AND THE BEAUTIFUL	MINNELLI	MGM	1952
S1582	TERROR ON A TRAIN (TIME BOMB)	TETZLAFF	MGM	1953
S1583	SKY FULL OF MOON	FOSTER	MGM	1952
S1584	I LOVE MELVIN	WEIS	MGM	1953

S1585	ROGUE'S MARCH	DAVIS	MGM	1953
S1586	NAKED SPUR	MANN	MGM	1953
S1587	APACHE WAR SMOKE	KRESS	MGM	1952
S1588	SOMBRERO	FOSTER	MGM	1953
S1589	SMALL TOWN GIRL	WELLMAN	MGM	1953
S1590	DESPERATE SEARCH	LEWIS	MGM	1953
S1591	SCANDAL AT SCOURIE	NEGULESCO	MGM	1953
S1592	CONFIDENTIALLY CONNIE	BUZZELL	MGM	1953
S1593	NEVER LET ME GO	DAVES	MGM	1953
S1594	JEOPARDY	STURGES	MGM	1953
S1595	BATTLE CIRCUS	BROOKS	MGM	1953
S1596	STUDENT PRINCE	THORPE	MGM	1954
S1597	RIDE, VAQUERO	FARROW	MGM	1953
S1598	GIRL WHO HAD EVERYTHING	THORPE	MGM	1953
S1599	JULIUS CAESAR	MANKIEWICZ	MGM	1953
S1600	BRIGHT ROAD	MAYER	MGM	1953
S1601	STORY OF THREE LOVES	MINNELLI, REINHARDT	MGM	1953
S1602	DANGEROUS WHEN WET	WALTERS	MGM	1953
S1603	CRY OF THE HUNTED	LEWIS	MGM	1953
S1604	YOUNG BESS	SIDNEY	MGM	1953
S1605	INVITATION TO THE DANCE	KELLY	MGM	1957
S1606	HOAXTERS (doc)	HOFFMAN	MGM	1953
S1607	DREAM WIFE	SHELDON	MGM	1953
S1608	GIVE A GIRL A BREAK	DONEN	MGM	1954
S1609	CODE TWO	WILCOX	MGM	1953
S1610	BAND WAGON	MINNELLI	MGM	1953
S1611	CLOWN	LEONARD	MGM	1953
S1612	REMAINS TO BE SEEN	WEIS	MGM	1953
S1613	FAST COMPANY	STURGES	MGM	1953
S1614	ALL THE BROTHERS WERE VALIANT	THORPE	MGM	1953
S1617	ACTRESS	CUKOR	MGM	1953
S1619	SLIGHT CASE OF LARCENY	WEIS	MGM	1953
S1620	GREAT DIAMOND ROBBERY	LEONARD	MGM	1954
S1621	EASY TO LOVE	WALTERS	MGM	1954
S1622	SAADIA	LEWIN	MGM	1954
S1623	TAKE THE HIGH GROUND	BROOKS	MGM	1953
S1624	AFFAIRS OF DOBIE GILLIS	WEIS	MGM	1953
S1625	BIG LEAGUER	ALDRICH	MGM	1953
S1626	ARENA	FLEISCHER	MGM	1953
S1627	ESCAPE FROM FORT BRAVO	STURGES	MGM	1953
S1628	RHAPSODY	VIDOR	MGM	1954
S1630	HALF A HERO	WEIS	MGM	1953
S1631	TORCH SONG	WALTERS	MGM	1953
S1632	LONG, LONG TRAILER	MINNELLI	MGM	1954
S1634	KNIGHTS OF THE ROUND TABLE	THORPE	MGM	1953
S1635	FLAME AND THE FLESH	BROOKS	MGM	1954
S1636	TENNESSEE CHAMP	WILCOX	MGM	1954
S1637	ROSE MARIE	LEROY	MGM	1954
S1638	GYPSY COLT	MARTON	MGM	1954
S1639	HER TWELVE MEN	LEONARD	MGM	1954
S1640	EXECUTIVE SUITE	WISE	MGM	1954
S1641	MEN OF THE FIGHTING LADY	MARTON	MGM	1954
S1642	VALLEY OF THE KINGS	PIROSH	MGM	1954
S1644	BAD DAY AT BLACK ROCK	STURGES	MGM	1955
S1645	BRIGADOON	MINNELLI	MGM	1954
S1646	BETRAYED	REINHARDT	MGM	1954
S1647	BEAU BRUMMEL (UK)	BERNHARDT	MGM	1954
S1648	PRISONER OF WAR	MARTON	MGM	1954
S1649	LAST TIME I SAW PARIS	BROOKS	MGM	1954
S1650	ATHENA	THORPE	MGM	1954
S1651	GREEN FIRE	MARTON	MGM	1955
S1652	JUPITER'S DARLING	SIDNEY	MGM	1955
S1653	ROGUE COP	ROWLAND	MGM	1954
S1654	DEEP IN MY HEART	DONEN	MGM	1954
S1655	GLASS SLIPPER	WALTERS	MGM	1955
S1656	MANY RIVERS TO CROSS	ROWLAND	MGM	1955

S1657	INVITATION TO THE DANCE	KELLY	MGM	1957
S1658	PRODIGAL	THORPE	MGM	1955
S1659	HIT THE DECK	ROWLAND	MGM	1955
S1660	MOONFLEET	LANG	MGM	1955
S1661	INTERRUPTED MELODY	BERNHARDT	MGM	1955
S1662	BEDEVILLED	LEISEN	MGM	1955
S1663	IT'S ALWAYS FAIR WEATHER	DONEN, KELLY	MGM	1955
S1664	MARAUDERS	MAYER	MGM	1955
S1665	SCARLET COAT	STURGES	MGM	1955
S1666	BLACKBOARD JUNGLE	BROOKS	MGM	1955
S1667	COBWEB	MINNELLI	MGM	1955
S1669	KING'S THIEF	LEONARD	MGM	1955
S1670	IT'S A DOG'S LIFE	HOFFMAN	MGM	1955
S1671	FORBIDDEN PLANET	WILCOX	MGM	1956
S1672	BHOWANI JUNCTION	CUKOR	MGM	1956
S1673	TRIBUTE TO A BADMAN	WISE	MGM	1956
S1674	QUENTIN DURWARD (UK)	THORPE	MGM	1955
S1675	DIANE	MILLER	MGM	1956
S1676	KISMET	MINNELLI	MGM	1955
S1677	TRIAL	ROBSON	MGM	1955
S1678	LAST HUNT	BROOKS	MGM	1956
S1679	I'LL CRY TOMORROW	MANN	MGM	1955
S1680	MEET ME IN LAS VEGAS	ROWLAND	MGM	1956
S1681	TENDER TRAP	WALTERS	MGM	1955
S1682	LUST FOR LIFE	MINNELLI	MGM	1956
S1683	GABY	BERNHARDT	MGM	1956
S1684	SWAN	VIDOR	MGM	1956
S1685	RANSOM	SEGAL	MGM	1956
S1686	RACK	LAVEN	MGM	1956
S1687	CATERED AFFAIR	BROOKS	MGM	1956
S1688	OPPOSITE SEX	MILLER	MGM	1956
S1689	FASTEST GUN ALIVE	ROUSE	MGM	1956
S1690	HIGH SOCIETY	WALTERS	MGM	1956
S1691	SOMEBODY UP THERE LIKES ME	WISE	MGM	1956
S1692	RAINTREE COUNTY	DMYTRYK	MGM	1957
S1693	TEAHOUSE OF THE AUGUST MOON	MANN	MGM	1956
S1694	TEA AND SYMPATHY	MINNELLI	MGM	1956
S1695	52 MILES TO TERROR (HOT RODS TO HELL)	BRAHM	MGM	1967
S1696	THESE WILDER YEARS	ROWLAND	MGM	1956
S1697	POWER AND THE PRIZE	KOSTER	MGM	1956
S1698	BARRETTS OF WIMPOLE STREET	FRANKLIN	MGM	1957
S1699	GREAT AMERICAN PASTIME	HOFFMAN	MGM	1956
S1700	SOMETHING OF VALUE	BROOKS	MGM	1957
S1701	WINGS OF EAGLES	FORD	MGM	1957
S1702	VINTAGE	HAYDEN	MGM	1957
S1703	HOT SUMMER NIGHT	FRIEDKIN	MGM	1957
S1704	SLANDER	ROWLAND	MGM	1957
S1705	TEN THOUSAND BEDROOMS	THORPE	MGM	1957
S1706	DESIGNING WOMAN	MINNELLI	MGM	1957
S1707	LES GIRLS	CUKOR	MGM	1957
S1708	THIS COULD BE THE NIGHT	WISE	MGM	1957
S1709	SILK STOCKINGS	MAMOULIAN	MGM	1957
S1710	SEVENTH SIN	NEAME	MGM	1957
S1711	GUN GLORY	ROWLAND	MGM	1957
S1712	UNTIL THEY SAIL	WISE	MGM	1957
S1713	MAN ON FIRE	MACDOUGALL	MGM	1957
S1714	HOUSE OF NUMBERS	ROUSE	MGM	1957
S1715	DON'T GO NEAR THE WATER	WALTERS	MGM	1957
S1716	TIP ON A DEAD JOCKEY	THORPE	MGM	1957
S1718	MERRY ANDREW	KIDD	MGM	1958
S1719	JAILHOUSE ROCK	THORPE	MGM	1957
S1720	BROTHERS KARAMAZOV	BROOKS	MGM	1958
S1721	SADDLE THE WIND	PARRISH	MGM	1958
S1722	HIRED GUN	NAZARRO	MGM	1957
S1723	GIGI	MINNELLI	MGM	1958
S1724	BEN-HUR	WYLER	MGM	1959

S1725	HIGH COST OF LOVING	FERRER	MGM	1958
S1726	SHEEPMAN	MARSHALL	MGM	1958
S1727	HANDLE WITH CARE	FRIEDKIN	MGM	1958
S1728	LAW AND JAKE WADE	STURGES	MGM	1958
S1729	TUNNEL OF LOVE	KELLY	MGM	1958
S1730	RELUCTANT DEBUTANTE	MINNELLI	MGM	1958
S1731	IMITATION GENERAL	MARSHALL	MGM	1958
S1732	BADLANDERS	DAVES	MGM	1958
S1733	HIGH SCHOOL CONFIDENTIAL	ARNOLD	MGM	1958
S1734	GREEN MANSIONS	FERRER	MGM	1959
S1735	CAT ON A HOT TIN ROOF	BROOKS	MGM	1958
S1737	WORLD, FLESH AND THE DEVIL	MACDOUGALL	MGM	1958
S1738	TORPEDO RUN	PEVNEY	MGM	1958
S1739	ANDY HARDY COMES HOME	KOCH	MGM	1958
S1740	WATUSI	NEUMANN	MGM	1959
S1742	COUNT YOUR BLESSINGS	NEGULESCO	MGM	1959
S1743	NORTH BY NORTHWEST	HITCHCOCK	MGM	1959
S1744	NIGHT OF THE QUARTER MOON	HAAS	MGM	1959
S1746	BEAT GENERATION	HAAS	MGM	1959
S1747	ASK ANY GIRL	WALTERS	MGM	1959
S1748	NEVER SO FEW	STURGES	MGM	1959
S1749	BIG OPERATOR	HAAS	MGM	1959
S1750	WRECK OF THE MARY DEARE	ANDERSON	MGM	1959
S1751	IT STARTED WITH A KISS	MARSHALL	MGM	1959
S1752	TARZAN THE APE MAN	NEWMAN	MGM	1959
S1753	GIRLS TOWN	HAAS	MGM	1960
S1754	HOME FROM THE HILL	MINNELLI	MGM	1960
S1755	TIME MACHINE	PAL	MGM	1960
S1756	PLEASE DON'T EAT THE DAISIES	WALTERS	MGM	1960
S1757	SUBTERRANEANS	MACDOUGALL	MGM	1960
S1758	GAZEBO	MARSHALL	MGM	1959
S1759	KEY WITNESS	KARLSON	MGM	1960
S1760	BELLS ARE RINGING	MINNELLI	MGM	1960
S1761	ADVENTURES OF HUCKLEBERRY FINN	CURTIZ	MGM	1960
S1762	PLATINUM HIGH SCHOOL	HAAS	MGM	1960
S1763	CIMARRON	MANN	MGM	1960
S1764	ALL THE FINE YOUNG CANNIBALS	ANDERSON	MGM	1960
S1765	BUTTERFIELD 8	MANN	MGM	1960
S1766	GO NAKED IN THE WORLD	MACDOUGALL	MGM	1961
S1767	ATLANTIS, THE LOST CONTINENT	PAL	MGM	1961
S1768	WHERE THE BOYS ARE	LEVIN	MGM	1960
S1769	MUTINY ON THE BOUNTY	MILESTONE	MGM	1962
S1770	TWO LOVES	WALTERS	MGM	1961
S1771	FOUR HORSEMEN OF THE APOCALYPSE	MINNELLI	MGM	1962
S1773	ADA	MANN	MGM	1961
S1774	HONEYMOON MACHINE	THORPE	MGM	1961
S1775	THUNDER OF DRUMS	NEWMAN	MGM	1961
S1776	HOW THE WEST WAS WON	FORD, HATHAWAY	MGM	1963
S1777	HOW THE WEST WAS WON	FORD, HATHAWAY	MGM	1963
S1778	HOW THE WEST WAS WON	FORD, HATHAWAY	MGM	1963
S1779	HOW THE WEST WAS WON	FORD, HATHAWAY	MGM	1963
S1780	HOW THE WEST WAS WON	FORD, HATHAWAY	MGM	1963
S1781	HOW THE WEST WAS WON	FORD, HATHAWAY	MGM	1963
S1782	HOW THE WEST WAS WON	FORD, HATHAWAY	MGM	1963
S1783	BACHELOR IN PARADISE	ARNOLD	MGM	1961
S1784	SWEET BIRD OF YOUTH	BROOKS	MGM	1962
S1785	WONDERFUL WORLD OF BROTHERS GRIMM (t)	LEVIN, PAL	MGM	1962
S1789	WONDERFUL WORLD OF BROTHERS GRIMM (t)	LEVIN, PAL	MGM	1962
S1790	WONDERFUL WORLD OF BROTHERS GRIMM (t)	LEVIN, PAL	MGM	1962
S1791	ALL FALL DOWN	FRANKENHEIMER	MGM	1962
S1792	HORIZONTAL LIEUTENANT	THORPE	MGM	1962
S1793	RIDE THE HIGH COUNTRY	PECKINPAH	MGM	1962
S1794	TWO WEEKS IN ANOTHER TOWN	MINNELLI	MGM	1962
S1795	BOYS' NIGHT OUT	GORDON	MGM	1962
S1796	BILLY ROSES' JUMBO	WALTERS	MGM	1962
S1797	PERIOD OF ADJUSTMENT	HILL	MGM	1962

S1798	HOOK	SEATON	MGM	1963
S1801	COURTSHIP OF EDDIE'S FATHER	MINNELLI	MGM	1963
S1802	IT HAPPENED AT THE WORLD'S FAIR	TAUROG	MGM	1963
S1803	DRUMS OF AFRICA	CLARK	MGM	1963
S1804	TICKLISH AFFAIR	SIDNEY	MGM	1963
S1805	WHEELER DEALERS	HILLER	MGM	1963
S1806	TWILIGHT OF HONOR	SAGAL	MGM	1963
S1807	SUNDAY IN NEW YORK	TEWKSBURY	MGM	1964
S1808	PRIZE	ROBSON	MGM	1963
S1809	GLOBAL AFFAIR	ARNOLD	MGM	1964
S1810	ADVANCE TO THE REAR	MARSHALL	MGM	1964
S1811	7 FACES OF DR. LAO	PAL	MGM	1964
S1813	MAIL ORDER BRIDE	KENNEDY	MGM	1964
S1814	HOOTENANNY HOOT	NELSON	MGM	1963
S1815	UNSINKABLE MOLLY BROWN	WALTERS	MGM	1963
S1816	HONEYMOON HOTEL	LEVIN	MGM	1964
S1817	LOOKING FOR LOVE	WEIS	MGM	1964
S1818	SIGNPOST TO MURDER	ENGLUND	MGM	1965
S1819	KISSIN' COUSINS	NELSON	MGM	1964
S1820	AMERICANIZATION OF EMILY	HILLER	MGM	1964
S1823	OUTRAGE	RITT	MGM	1964
S1824	QUICK, BEFORE IT MELTS	MANN	MGM	1965
S1825	ROUNDERS	KENNEDY	MGM	1965
S1826	36 HOURS	SEATON	MGM	1965
S1827	YOUR CHEATIN' HEART	NELSON	MGM	1965
S1828	JOY IN THE MORNING	SEGAL	MGM	1965
S1829	GIRL HAPPY	SAGAL	MGM	1965
S1830	GET YOURSELF A COLLEGE GIRL	MILLER	MGM	1964
S1831	SANDPIPER	MINNELLI	MGM	1965
S1832	ONCE A THIEF	NELSON	MGM	1965
S1833	CINCINNATI KID	JEWISON	MGM	1965
S1834	MONEY TRAP	KENNEDY	MGM	1966
S1835	7 WOMEN	FORD	MGM	1966
S1836	MISTER BUDDWING	MANN	MGM	1966
S1837	PATCH OF BLUE	GREEN	MGM	1965
S1838	HARUM SCARUM	NELSON	MGM	1965
S1839	MADE IN PARIS	SAGAL	MGM	1966
S1840	ICE STATION ZEBRA	STURGES	MGM	1968
S1841	WHEN THE BOYS MEET THE GIRLS	GANZER	MGM	1965
S1842	GLASS BOTTOM BOAT	TASHLIN	MGM	1966
S1843	SINGING NUN	KOSTER	MGM	1966
S1844	HOLD ON!	LUBIN	MGM	1966
S1845	SPINOUT	TAUROG	MGM	1966
S1846	DOCTOR, YOU'VE GOT TO BE KIDDING	TEWKSBURY	MGM	1967
S1847	VENETIAN AFFAIR	THORPE	MGM	1967
S1848	PENELOPE	HILLER	MGM	1967
S1851	FASTEST GUITAR ALIVE	MOORE	MGM	1967
S1852	LAST CHALLENGE	THORPE	MGM	1967
S1853	POINT BLANK	BOORMAN	MGM	1967
S1854	GUNS FOR SAN SEBASTIAN	VERNEUIL	MGM	1968
S1855	EXTRAORDINARY SEAMAN	FRANKENHEIMER	MGM	1969
S1857	SOL MADRID	HUTTON	MGM	1968
S1858	PHANTOM TOLLBOOTH (t)	JONES, LEVITOW	MGM	1970
S1859	LEGEND OF LYLAH CLARE	ALDRICH	MGM	1968
S1860	SPEEDWAY	TAUROG	MGM	1968
S1861	WHERE WERE YOU WHEN LIGHTS WENT OUT	AVERBACK	MGM	1968
S1862	DAY OF THE EVIL GUN	THORPE	MGM	1968
S1863	IMPOSSIBLE YEARS	GORDON	MGM	1969
S1864	STAY AWAY, JOE	TEWKSBURY	MGM	1968
S1866	TIME TO SING	DREIFUSS	MGM	1968
S1867	SPLIT	FLEMYNG	MGM	1968
S1868	LIVE A LITTLE, LOVE A LITTLE	TAUROG	MGM	1968
S1869	HEAVEN WITH A GUN	KATZIN	MGM	1969
S1870	YOUNG RUNAWAYS	DREIFUSS	MGM	1968
S1871	GYPSY MOTHS	FRANKENHEIMER	MGM	1969
S1872	MARLOWE	BOGART	MGM	1969

S1873	ZABRISKIE POINT	ANTONIONI	MGM	1970
S1875	TROUBLE WITH GIRLS	TEWKSBURY	MGM	1969
S1876	MALTESE BIPPY	PANAMA	MGM	1969
S1877	TICK … TICK … TICK	NELSON	MGM	1970
S1878	MAGIC GARDEN STANLEY SWEETHEART	HORN	MGM	1970
S1879	MOONSHINE WAR	QUINE	MGM	1970
S1880	ZIGZAG	COLLA	MGM	1970
S1881	STRAWBERRY STATEMENT	HAGMANN	MGM	1970
S1884	DIRTY DINGUS MAGEE	KENNEDY	MGM	1970
S1885	TRAVELING EXECUTIONER	SMIGHT	MGM	1970
S1886	HOUSE OF DARK SHADOWS	CURTIS	MGM	1970
S1887	ALEX IN WONDERLAND	MAZURSKY	MGM	1970
S1888	BREWSTER MCCLOUD	ALTMAN	MGM	1971
S1889	ELVIS- THAT'S THE WAY IT IS (doc)	SANDERS	MGM	1970
S1890	PRETTY MAIDS ALL IN A ROW	VADIM	MGM	1971
S1891	CORKY	HORN	MGM	1973
S1892	BELIEVE IN ME	HAGMANN	MGM	1971
S1893	FORTUNE AND MEN'S EYES	HART	MGM	1971
S1894	WILD ROVERS	EDWARDS	MGM	1971
S1895	SHAFT	PARKS	MGM	1971
S1896	NIGHT OF DARK SHADOWS	CURTIS	MGM	1971
S1897	GANG THAT COULDN'T SHOOT STRAIGHT	GOLDSTONE	MGM	1971
S1898	GOING HOME	LEONARD	MGM	1971
S1899	EVERY LITTLE CROOK AND NANNY	HOWARD	MGM	1972
S1901	WRATH OF GOD	NELSON	MGM	1972
S1902	CAREY TREATMENT	EDWARDS	MGM	1971
S1903	ONE IS A LONELY NUMBER (TWO IS A HAPPY NUMBER)	STUART	MGM	1972
S1904	NIGHTMARE HONEYMOON	SILVERSTEEN	MGM	1973
S1906	SKYJACKED	GUILLERMIN	MGM	1972
S1907	NIGHT OF THE LEPUS	CLAXTON	MGM	1972
S1908	SHAFT'S BIG SCORE	PARKS	MGM	1972
S1909	MELINDA	ROBERTSON	MGM	1972
S1910	THEY ONLY KILL THEIR MASTERS	GOLDSTONE	MGM	1972
S1911	ELVIS ON TOUR (doc)	ABEL, ADIDGE	MGM	1972
S1912	LOLLY-MADONNA XXX	SARAFIAN	MGM	1973
S1914	WICKED, WICKED	BARE	MGM	1973
S1915	SOYLENT GREEN	FLEISCHER	MGM	1973
S1916	PAT GARRETT AND BILLY THE KID	PECKINPAH	MGM	1973
S1917	SHAFT IN AFRICA	GUILLERMIN	MGM	1973
S1918	MAN WHO LOVED CAT DANCING	SARAFIAN	MGM	1973
S1919	TRADER HORN	BADIYI	MGM	1973
S1921	WESTWORLD	CRICHTON	MGM	1973
S1924	THAT'S ENTERTAINMENT	HALEY JR.	MGM	1974
S1926	HEARTS OF THE WEST	ZIEFF	MGM	1975
S1927	SUNSHINE BOYS	ROSS	MGM	1975
S1928	THAT'S ENTERTAINMENT, PART 2	KELLY	MGM	1976
S1933	DEMON SEED	CAMMELL	MGM	1977
S1938	COMA	CRICHTON	MGM	1978
S1939	CORVETTE SUMMER	ROBBINS	MGM	1978
S1941	CHAMP	ZEFFIRELLI	MGM	1979
S1942	HIDE IN PLAIN SIGHT	CAAN	MGM	1980
S1947	WHY WOULD I LIE?	PEERCE	MGM	1980
S1948	FORMULA	AVILDSEN	MGM	1980
S1950	RICH AND FAMOUS	CUKOR	MGM	1981
S1952	BUDDY EBSEN	portrait	MGM	
S1953	PENNIES FROM HEAVEN	ROSS	MGM	1981
S1954	WHOSE LIFE IS IT ANYWAY?	BADHAM	MGM	1982
S1956	BUDDY, BUDDY	WILDER	MGM	1981
S2056	NOSTRADAMUS SAYS SO	LANDAU	MGM	1953
S2078	DENISE DARCEL	portrait	MGM	
S2504	CARNIVAL IN PARIS	THIELE	MGM	1937
S2505	SONG OF REVOLT	ROWLAND	MGM	1937
S2506	IT MAY HAPPEN TO YOU	BUCQUET	MGM	1937
S2507	HAVE COURAGE	SHERMAN	MGM	1937
S2509	HOW TO START THE DAY	ROWLAND	MGM	1937
S2510	SOAK THE POOR	BUCQUET	MGM	1937

S2511	BOSS DIDN'T SAY GOOD MORNING	TOURNEUR	MGM	1937
S2512	GIVE TILL IT HURTS	FEIST	MGM	1937
S2513	KING WITHOUT A CROWN	TOURNEUR	MGM	1937
S2517	BEHIND THE CRIMINAL	BUCQUET	MGM	1937
S2518	MAN IN THE BARN	TOURNEUR	MGM	1937
S2518	NIGHT AT THE MOVIES	ROWLAND	MGM	1937
S2521	CANARY COMES ACROSS	JASON	MGM	1938
S2526	CAPTAIN KIDD'S TREASURE	FENTON	MGM	1938
S2532	WHAT PRICE SAFETY		MGM	1918
S2533	LIFE IN SOMETOWN U.S.A.	KEATON	MGM	1938
S2534	SHIP THAT DIED	TOURNEUR	MGM	1938
S2537	OPTICAL POEM (t)	FISCHINGER	MGM	1938
S2538	FACE BEHIND THE MASK	TOURNEUR	MGM	1938
S2540	SNOW GETS IN YOUR EYES	JASON	MGM	1938
S2541	MIRACLE MONEY	FENTON	MGM	1938
S2542	MUSIC MADE SIMPLE	ROWLAND	MGM	1938
S2543	EVENING ALONE	ROWLAND	MGM	1938
S2545	BILLY ROSE'S CASE MANANA REVUE	SIDNEY	MGM	1938
S2547	THAT MOTHERS MIGHT LIVE	ZINNEMANN	MGM	1938
S2549	COME ACROSS	BUCQUET	MGM	1938
S2550	TUPAPAOO	TOURNEUR	MGM	1938
S2551	MAGICIAN'S DAUGHTER	FEIST	MGM	1938
S2552	TRACKING THE SLEEPING DEATH	ZINNEMANN	MGM	1938
S2553	JOAQUIN MURIETTA	WILCOX	MGM	1938
S2554	ANESTHESIA	JASON	MGM	1938
S2555	IT'S IN THE STARS	MILLER	MGM	1938
S2556	CRIMINAL IS BORN	FENTON	MGM	1938
S2557	STRANGE GLORY	TOURNEUR	MGM	1938
S2558	HOLLYWOOD HANDICAP	KEATON	MGM	1938
S2559	HOW TO RAISE A BABY	ROWLAND	MGM	1938
S2561	BRAVEST OF THE BRAVE	CAHN	MGM	1938
S2562	COURTSHIP OF THE NEWT	ROWLAND	MGM	1938
S2564	MIRACLE OF SALT LAKE	WRANGELL	MGM	1938
S2566	LITTLE RANGER	DOUGLAS	MGM	1938
S2567	HOW TO READ	ROWLAND	MGM	1938
S2568	PARTY FEVER	SIDNEY	MGM	1938
S2570	MAN ON THE ROCK	CAHN	MGM	1938
S2572	THEY'RE ALWAYS CAUGHT	BUCQUET	MGM	1938
S2573	ALADDIN'S LANTERN	DOUGLAS	MGM	1938
S2575	THINK IT OVER	TOURNEUR	MGM	1938
S2576	NOSTRADAMUS	MILLER	MGM	1938
S2577	STREAMLINED SWING	KEATON	MGM	1938
S2578	UNSEEN GUARDIANS	WRANGELL	MGM	1939
S2579	HOW TO WATCH FOOTBALL	ROWLAND	MGM	1938
S2580	MEN IN FRIGHT	SIDNEY	MGM	1938
S2581	CITY OF LITTLE MEN	LOUD	MGM	1938
S2583	THEY LIVE AGAIN	ZINNEMANN	MGM	1938
S2584	OPENING DAY	ROWLAND	MGM	1938
S2585	ALICE WEAVER	portrait	MGM	
S2586	MEN OF STEEL	LEE	MGM	1938
S2588	ONCE OVER LIGHTLY	JASON	MGM	1938
S2589	FOOTBALL ROMEO	SIDNEY	MGM	1938
S2590	GREAT HEART	MILLER	MGM	1938
S2593	MENTAL POISE	ROWLAND	MGM	1938
S2594	STORY OF ALFRED NOBEL	NEWMAN	MGM	1939
S2595	PRACTICAL JOKERS	SIDNEY	MGM	1938
S2596	WRONG WAY OUT	MACHATY	MGM	1938
S2597	HOUR FOR LUNCH	ROWLAND	MGM	1939
S2598	HOW TO SUBLET	ROWLAND	MGM	1939
S2600	ALFALFA'S AUNT	SIDNEY	MGM	1939
S2602	HAPPILY BURIED	FEIST	MGM	1939
S2605	ANGEL OF MERCY	CAHN	MGM	1939
S2606	TINY TROUBLES	SIDNEY	MGM	1939
S2607	DREAM OF LOVE	FITZPATRICK	MGM	1939
S2609	SOMEWHAT SECRET	LEE	MGM	1939
S2610	DUEL PERSONALITIES	SIDNEY	MGM	1939

S2611	MONEY TO LOAN	NEWMAN	MGM	1939
S2613	CLOWN PRINCES	SIDNEY	MGM	1939
S2614	WHILE AMERICA SLEEPS	ZINNEMANN	MGM	1939
S2615	ICE ANTICS	MILLER	MGM	1939
S2616	GIANT OF NORWAY	CAHN	MGM	1939
S2617	PROPHET WITHOUT HONOR	FEIST	MGM	1939
S2618	COUSSIN WILBUR	SIDNEY	MGM	1939
S2619	STORY THAT COULDN'T BE PRINTED	NEWMAN	MGM	1939
S2623	YANKEE DOODLE GOES TO WAR		MGM	1939
S2624	HOLLYWOOD HOBBIES	SIDNEY	MGM	1939
S2625	HELP WANTED	ZINNEMANN	MGM	1939
S2626	HOW TO EAT	ROWLAND	MGM	1939
S2627	HOME EARLY	ROWLAND	MGM	1939
S2628	DARK MAGIC	ROWLAND	MGM	1939
S2629	IT CAN'T BE DONE		MGM	1948
S2630	JOY SCOUTS	CAHN	MGM	1939
S2631	DOG DAZE	SIDNEY	MGM	1939
S2632	AUTO ANTICS	CAHN	MGM	1939
S2633	ONE AGAINST THE WORLD	ZINNEMANN	MGM	1939
S2637	SEE YOUR DOCTOR	WRANGELL	MGM	1939
S2638	DAY OF REST	WRANGELL	MGM	1939
S2639	THINK FIRST	ROWLAND	MGM	1939
S2640	CAPTAIN SPANKY'S SHOW BOAT	CAHN	MGM	1939
S2642	FAILURE AT FIFTY	JASON	MGM	1939
S2644	MIRACLE AT LOURDES	DUNN	MGM	1939
S2645	CHARLTON HESTON	portrait	MGM	
S2645	DAD FOR A DAY	CAHN	MGM	1939
S2647	RHUMBA RHYTHM HOLLYWOOD LA CONGO	LEE	MGM	1939
S2648	DRUNK DRIVING	MILLER	MGM	1939
S2649	GOODBYE, MISS TURLOCK	CAHN	MGM	1948
S2652	FORGOTTEN VICTORY	ZINNEMANN	MGM	1939
S2654	THAT INFERIOR FEELING	WRANGELL	MGM	1940
S2655	TIME OUT FOR LESSONS	CAHN, MURRAY	MGM	1939
S2656	ALFALFA'S DOUBLE	CAHN	MGM	1940
S2657	MENDELSSOHN'S WEDDING MARCH	FITZPATRICK	MGM	1939
S2658	FLAG SPEAKS	MILLER	MGM	1940
S2659	POUND FOOLISH	FEIST	MGM	1939
S2661	WHERE TURF MEETS SURF	LEE	MGM	1940
S2662	THIRD DIMENSIONAL MURDER	SIDNEY	MGM	1941
S2663	KNOW YOUR MONEY	NEWMAN	MGM	1940
S2664	OLD SOUTH (trailer for GONE WITH THE WIND)	ZINNEMANN	MGM	1940
S2665	TRIFLES OF IMPORTANCE	WRANGELL	MGM	1940
S2667	NORTHWARD HO	LOUD	MGM	1940
S2668	BUBBLING TROUBLES	CAHN	MGM	1940
S2669	BIG PREMIERE	CAHN	MGM	1940
S2672	JACK POT	ROWLAND	MGM	1940
S2673	WHAT'S YOUR I.Q.		MGM	1940
S2674	ALL ABOUT HASH	CAHN	MGM	1940
S2675	HIDDEN MASTER	LEE	MGM	1940
S2676	XXX MEDICO	WRANGELL	MGM	1940
S2677	NEW PUPIL	CAHN	MGM	1940
S2678	SERVANT OF MANKIND (trailer for EDISON THE MAN)		MGM	1940
S2680	GOIN' FISHIN'	CAHN	MGM	1940
S2681	WAY IN THE WILDERNESS	ZINNEMANN	MGM	1940
S2684	GOOD BAD BOYS (1940)	CAHN	MGM	R54
S2685	WOMEN IN HIDING	NEWMAN	MGM	1940
S2686	WALDO'S LAST STAND	CAHN	MGM	1940
S2687	KIDDIE KURE	CAHN	MGM	1940
S2689	RODEO DOUGH	LEE	MGM	1940
S2690	EYES OF THE NAVY		MGM	1940
S2691	BUYER BEWARE	NEWMAN	MGM	1940
S2693	SOAK THE OLD	LEE	MGM	1940
S2695	UTOPIA OF DEATH		MGM	1940
S2696	FIGHTIN' FOOLS	CAHN	MGM	1941
S2697	GREAT MEDDLER	ZINNEMANN	MGM	1940
S2698	DREAMS	FEIST	MGM	1940

S2698	FAMILY TROUBLES	GLAZER	MGM	1943
S2699	BARON AND THE ROSE	WRANGELL	MGM	1940
S2700	MORE ABOUT NOSTRADAMUS	MILLER	MGM	1941
S2702	AMERICAN SPOKEN HERE	WRANGELL	MGM	1940
S2703	HAPPIEST MAN ON EARTH	MILLER	MGM	1940
S2704	YOU, THE PEOPLE	ROWLAND	MGM	1940
S2706	BABY BLUES	CAHN	MGM	1941
S2707	AMERICAN SPOKEN HERE	WRANGELL	MGM	1940
S2708	RESPECT THE LAW	NEWMAN	MGM	1941
S2709	WHISPERS	WRANGELL	MGM	1941
S2710	1-2-3- GO	CAHN	MGM	1941
S2711	FORBIDDEN PASSAGE	ZINNEMANN	MGM	1941
S2714	OUT OF DARKNESS	LEE	MGM	1941
S2716	YE OLDE MINSTRELS	CAHN	MGM	1941
S2719	THIS IS THE BOWERY	VON FRITSCH	MGM	1941
S2720	COME BACK MISS PIPPS	CAHN	MGM	1941
S2721	GREENER HILLS	LEE	MGM	1939
S2721	MAN WHO CHANGED THE WORLD	LEE	MGM	1941
S2724	TRIUMPH WITHOUT DRUMS	NEWMAN	MGM	1941
S2725	LISTEN, BOYS	FRITSCH	MGM	1942
S2726	COFFINS ON WHEELS	NEWMAN	MGM	1941
S2728	WILLIE AND THE MOUSE	SIDNEY	MGM	1941
S2729	BATTLE (sh)		MGM	1941
S2730	YOUR LAST ACT	ZINNEMANN	MGM	1941
S2731	GHOST TREASURE	JASON	MGM	1941
S2732	ROBOT WRECKS	CAHN	MGM	1941
S2735	STROKE OF GENIUS	ROSS	MGM	1938
S2735	SUCKER LIST	ROWLAND	MGM	1941
S2736	TELL TALE HEART	DASSIN	MGM	1941
S2739	MAIN STREET ON THE MARCH	CAHN	MGM	1942
S2741	MEMORIES OF EUROPE	FITZPATRICK	MGM	1941
S2742	HOBBIES	LABROUSSE	MGM	1941
S2743	CHANGED IDENTITY	ROWLAND	MGM	1941
S2746	SOARING STARS	WRANGELL	MGM	1942
S2747	STRANGE TESTAMENT	LEE	MGM	1941
S2748	WE DO IT BECAUSE	WRANGELL	MGM	1942
S2750	GREENIE	ZINNEMANN	MGM	1942
S2751	WEDDING WORRIES	CAHN	MGM	1941
S2753	VIVA MEXICO	LEWYN	MGM	1941
S2755	MELODIES OLD AND NEW	CAHN	MGM	1942
S2757	LADY OR THE TIGER?	ZINNEMANN	MGM	1942
S2758	GOING TO PRESS	CAHN	MGM	1942
S2760	FILM THAT WAS LOST	LEE	MGM	1942
S2762	FLAG OF MERCY	CAHN	MGM	1942
S2765	FURTHER PROPHECIES OF NOSTRADAMS	MILLER	MGM	1942
S2768	WOMAN IN THE HOUSE	LEE	MGM	1942
S2769	INCREDIBLE STRANGER	TOURNEUR	MGM	1942
S2770	SURPRISED PARTIES	CAHN	MGM	1942
S2771	DOIN' THEIR BIT	GLAZER	MGM	1942
S2773	MR. BLABBERMOUTH	WRANGELL	MGM	1942
S2774	GOOD JOB		MGM	1942
S2776	VENDETTA	NEWMAN	MGM	1942
S2777	FOR THE COMMON DEFENSE	KENWARD	MGM	1942
S2780	ROVER'S BIG CHANCE	GLAZER	MGM	1942
S2783	MIGHTY LAK A GOAT	GLAZER	MGM	1942
S2784	MAGIC ALPHABET	TOURNEUR	MGM	1942
S2785	A.T.C.A.		MGM	1942
S2787	PORTRAIT OF A GENIUS	LEE	MGM	1943
S2789	GREATEST GIFT	DANIELS	MGM	1942
S2790	BRIEF INTERVAL	LEE	MGM	1943
S2791	FAMOUS BONERS	FOSTER	MGM	1942
S2792	MADERO OF MEXICO	CAHN	MGM	1942
S2794	UNEXPECTED RICHES	GLAZER	MGM	1942
S2795	BENJAMIN FRANKLIN, JR.	GLAZER	MGM	1943
S2796	KEEP 'EM SAILING	WRANGELL	MGM	1942
S2797	INCA GOLD	JASON	MGM	1943

S2799	THAT'S WHY I LEFT YOU	CAHN	MGM	1943
S2800	LAST LESSON	KENWARD	MGM	1942
S2801	JOURNEY TO YESTERDAY	DANIELS	MGM	1943
S2804	TRIFLES THAT WIN WARS	DANIELS	MGM	1943
S2805	ELECTION DAZE	GLAZER	MGM	1943
S2806	FIRST AID	JASON	MGM	1943
S2807	PLAN FOR DESTRUCTION	CAHN	MGM	1943
S2809	HERE AT HOME	HART	MGM	1943
S2810	CALLING ALL KIDS	BAERWITZ	MGM	1943
S2815	WHO'S SUPERSTITIOUS	LEE	MGM	1943
S2816	DOG HOUSE (t)	HANNA, BARBERA	MGM	1943
S2818	INFLATION	ENDFIELD	MGM	1943
S2819	FARM HANDS	GLAZER	MGM	1943
S2821	FORGOTTEN TREASURE	LEE	MGM	1943
S2827	NURSERY RHYME MYSTERIES	CAHN	MGM	1943
S2828	PEOPLE OF RUSSIA		MGM	1942
S2829	HEAVENLY MUSIC	BERNE	MGM	1943
S2830	LITTLE MISS PINKERTON	GLAZER	MGM	1943
S2832	WOOD GOES TO WAR		MGM	1943
S2833	STORM	BURNFORD	MGM	1943
S2834	ODE TO VICTORY	CAHN	MGM	1943
S2835	SHOE SHINE BOY	HART	MGM	1943
S2838	TO MY UNBORN SON	KARDOS	MGM	1943
S2840	NOSTRADAMUS IV	BURNFORD, ENDFIELD	MGM	1944
S2844	THREE SMART GUYS	CAHN	MGM	1943
S2846	THIS IS TOMORROW	NESBITT	MGM	1943
S2849	MEMORIES OF AUSTRALIA		MGM	1943
S2854	KID IN UPPER FOUR		MGM	1943
S2857	NO NEWS IS GOOD NEWS	JASON	MGM	1943
S2858	SOMEWHERE U.S.A.	KNOX, VON FRITSCH	MGM	1944
S2859	MY TOMATO	JASON	MGM	1943
S2860	RADIO BUGS	ENDFIELD	MGM	1944
S2861	DANCING ROMEO	ENDFIELD	MGM	1944
S2863	IMPORTANT BUSINESS	JASON	MGM	1944
S2864	WHY DADDY?	JASON	MGM	1944
S2866	TALE OF A DOG (OUR GANG series)	ENDFIELD	MGM	1944
S2868	RETURN FROM NOWHERE	BURNFORD	MGM	1944
S2869	EASY LIFE	HART	MGM	1944
S2871	MAIN STREET TODAY	CAHN	MGM	1944
S2874	PATROLLING THE ETHER	BURNFORD	MGM	1944
S2876	GREAT DAY'S COMING	ELWYN	MGM	1944
S2877	IMMORTAL BLACKSMITH	LEE	MGM	1944
S2878	GRANDPA CALLED IT ART	HART	MGM	1944
S2879	LADY FIGHTS BACK		MGM	1944
S2886	DARK SHADOWS	BURNFORD, HART	MGM	1944
S2888	STRANGE DESTINY	BURNFORD	MGM	1945
S2892	SPREADIN' THE JAM	WALTERS	MGM	1945
S2893	LAST INSTALLMENT	HART	MGM	1945
S2894	SEESAW AND THE SHOES	FOSTER	MGM	1945
S2895	GETTIN' GLAMOUR	ANDERSON	MGM	1946
S2900	PHANTOMS	YOUNG	MGM	1945
S2901	LITTLE WHITE LIE	BURNFORD	MGM	1945
S2902	MUSICAL MASTERPIECES	PYE	MGM	1946
S2903	MIRACLE IN A CORNFIELD	NESBITT	MGM	1947
S2909	FALL GUY	BURNFORD	MGM	1945
S2910	GREAT AMERICAN MUG	ENDFIELD	MGM	1945
S2915	GOLDEN HUNCH		MGM	1945
S2918	MAGIC ON A STICK	ENDFIELD	MGM	1946
S2920	PEOPLE ON PAPER	MORGAN	MGM	1945
S2921	OUR OLD CAR	ENDFIELD	MGM	1946
S2922	GUN IN HIS HAND	LOSEY	MGM	1945
S2924	STAIRWAY TO LIGHT	LEE	MGM	1945
S2926	PURITY SQUAD	KRESS	MGM	1945
S2938	BIKINI, THE ATOM ISLAND	WILSON	MGM	1946
S2945	I LOVE MY HUSBAND, BUT	O'BRIEN	MGM	1946
S2946	REALLY IMPORTANT PERSON	WRANGELL	MGM	1947

S2947	LUCKIEST GUY IN THE WORLD	NEWMAN	MGM	1947
S2949	GOODBYE, MISS TURLOCK	CAHN	MGM	1948
S2952	AMAZING MR. NORDILL	NEWMAN	MGM	1947
S2962	MY OLD TOWN	NESBITT	MGM	1948
S2966	TENNIS IN RHYTHM	MURRAY	MGM	1949
S2967	GIVE US THE EARTH	VON FRITSCH	MGM	1947
S2969	IT CAN'T BE DONE		MGM	1948
S2977	TEX BENEKE		MGM	1948
S2978	CITY OF CHILDREN	NESBITT	MGM	1949
S2984	FABULOUS FRAUD	CAHN	MGM	1948
S2985	SOUVENIRS OF DEATH	CAHN	MGM	1948
S2998	SCREEN ACTORS		MGM	1950
S3001	GOING TO BLAZES	VON FRITSCH	MGM	1948
S3002	CLUES TO ADVENTURE	NESBITT	MGM	1949
S3005	ANNIE WAS A WONDER	CAHN	MGM	1949
S3006	STUFF FOR STUFF		MGM	1949
S3009	MR. WHITNEY HAD A NOTION	MAYER	MGM	1949
S3016	MOMENTS IN MUSIC		MGM	1950
S3017	HEART TO HEART	VON FRITSCH	MGM	1949
S3019	IN CASE YOU'RE CURIOUS	O'BRIEN	MGM	1951
S3020	I LOVE CHILDREN, BUT	O'BRIEN	MGM	1952
S3033	AIN'T IT AGGRAVATIN'	O'BRIEN	MGM	1954
S3038	MEALTIME MAGIC	O'BRIEN	MGM	1952
S3041	THIS IS A LIVING?	SMITH	MGM	1953
S3042	DO SOMEONE A FAVOR	O'BRIEN	MGM	1954
S3047	LANDLORDING IT	O'BRIEN	MGM	1953
S3049	FILM ANTICS	O'BRIEN	MGM	1954
S3054	IT WOULD SERVE 'EM RIGHT	O'BRIEN	MGM	1953
S3055	OUT FOR FUN	O'BRIEN	MGM	1954
S3056	NOSTRADAMUS SAYS SO	LANDAU	MGM	1953
S3066	FISH TALES	DUDLEY	MGM	1954
S3068	NOSTRADAMUS AND THE QUEEN (1942)		MGM	R53
S3069	THINGS WE CAN DO WITHOUT	O'BRIEN	MGM	1953
S3070	SAFE AT HOME	O'BRIEN	MGM	1954
S3072	MERRY WIVES OF WINDSOR		MGM	1954
S3073	POET AND PEASANT OVERTURE		MGM	1954
S3075	MGM JUBILEE		MGM	1954
S3602	LITTLE JOURNEY	LEONARD	MGM	1927
S3699	MITCHELL BROTHER	portrait	MGM	
S3700	MITCHELL BROTHER	portrait	MGM	
S3701	MITCHELL BROTHER	portrait	MGM	
S3702	MITCHELL BROTHER	portrait	MGM	
S4001	CAPITAL CITY, WASHINGTON D.C.	FITZPATRICK	MGM	1940
S4002	CATERED AFFAIR	BROOKS	MGM	1956
S4002	CAVALCADE OF SAN FRANCISCO	FITZPATRICK	MGM	1940
S4003	OLD NEW MEXICO	FITZPATRICK	MGM	1940
S4004	BEAUTIFUL BALI	FITZPATRICK	MGM	1940
S4005	OLD NEW ORLEANS	FITZPATRICK	MGM	1940
S4006	MEDITERRANEAN PORTS OF CALL	FITZPATRICK	MGM	1941
S4007	RED MEN ON PARADE	FITZPATRICK	MGM	1941
S4008	ALLURING ALASKA	FITZPATRICK	MGM	1941
S4009	GLIMPSES OF KENTUCKY	FITZPATRICK	MGM	1941
S4010	YOSEMITE THE MAGNIFICENT	FITZPATRICK	MGM	1941
S4011	GLIMPSES OF WASHINGTON STATE	FITZPATRICK	MGM	1941
S4012	HAITI, LAND OF DARK MAJESTY	FITZPATRICK	MGM	1941
S4013	GLIMPSES OF FLORIDA	FITZPATRICK	MGM	1941
S4014	INSIDE PASSAGE	FITZPATRICK	MGM	1941
S4015	GEORGETOWN, PRIDE OF PENANG	FITZPATRICK	MGM	1941
S4016	SCENIC GRANDEUR	FITZPATRICK	MGM	1941
S4017	MINNESOTA, LAND OF PLENTY	FITZPATRICK	MGM	1942
S4018	HISTORIC MARYLAND	FITZPATRICK	MGM	1941
S4019	WEST POINT ON THE HUDSON	FITZPATRICK	MGM	1942
S4020	COLORFUL NORTH CAROLINA	FITZPATRICK	MGM	1942
S4021	LAND OF THE QUINTUPLETS	FITZPATRICK	MGM	1942
S4022	GLACIER PARK AND WATERTON LAKES	FITZPATRICK	MGM	1942
S4023	PICTURESQUE PATZCUARO	FITZPATRICK	MGM	1942

S4024	EXOTIC MEXICO	FITZPATRICK	MGM	1942
S4025	PICTURESQUE MASSACHUSETTS	FITZPATRICK	MGM	1942
S4026	MODERN MEXICO CITY	FITZPATRICK	MGM	1942
S4027	GLIMPSES OF ONTARIO	FITZPATRICK	MGM	1942
S4028	LAND OF ORIZABA	FITZPATRICK	MGM	1943
S4029	MIGHTY NIAGARA	FITZPATRICK	MGM	1943
S4030	MEXICAN POLICE ON PARADE	FITZPATRICK	MGM	1943
S4031	MOTORING IN MEXICO	FITZPATRICK	MGM	1943
S4032	ON THE ROAD TO MONTEREY	FITZPATRICK	MGM	1943
S4033	ROMANTIC NEVADA	FITZPATRICK	MGM	1943
S4034	SCENIC OREGON	FITZPATRICK	MGM	1943
S4035	GLIMPSES OF MEXICO	FITZPATRICK	MGM	1943
S4036	OVER THE ANDES	FITZPATRICK	MGM	1943
S4037	THROUGH THE COLORADO ROCKIES	FITZPATRICK	MGM	1943
S4038	GRAND CANYON, PRIDE OF CREATION	FITZPATRICK	MGM	1943
S4039	DAY IN DEATH VALLEY	FITZPATRICK	MGM	1944
S4040	SALT LAKE DIVERSIONS	FITZPATRICK	MGM	1943
S4041	MACKINAC ISLAND	FITZPATRICK	MGM	1944
S4042	VISITING ST. LOUIS	FITZPATRICK	MGM	1944
S4043	ALONG THE CACTUS TRAIL	FITZPATRICK	MGM	1944
S4044	ROAMING THROUGH ARIZONA	FITZPATRICK	MGM	1944
S4045	COLORFUL COLORADO	FITZPATRICK	MGM	1944
S4046	CITY OF BRIGHAM YOUNG	FITZPATRICK	MGM	1944
S4047	MONUMENTAL UTAH	FITZPATRICK	MGM	1944
S4048	WANDERING HERE AND THERE	FITZPATRICK	MGM	1944
S4049	SEEING EL SALVADOR	FITZPATRICK	MGM	1945
S4051	LAND OF THE MAYAS	FITZPATRICK	MGM	1946
S4052	MERIDA AND CAMPECHE	FITZPATRICK	MGM	1945
S4053	MODERN GUATEMALA CITY	FITZPATRICK	MGM	1945
S4054	WHERE TIME STANDS STILL	FITZPATRICK	MGM	1945
S4055	GLIMPSES OF GUATEMALA	FITZPATRICK	MGM	1946
S4056	VISITING VERA CRUZ	FITZPATRICK	MGM	1946
S4057	MISSION TRAIL	FITZPATRICK	MGM	1946
S4058	CALLING ON COSTA RICA	FITZPATRICK	MGM	1947
S4059	GLIMPSES OF CALIFORNIA	FITZPATRICK	MGM	1946
S4060	AROUND THE WORLD IN CALIFORNIA	FITZPATRICK	MGM	1947
S4061	ON THE SHORES OF NOVA SCOTIA	FITZPATRICK	MGM	1947
S4062	LOOKING AT LONDON	FITZPATRICK	MGM	1946
S4063	VISITING VIRGINIA	SMITH	MGM	1947
S4064	CRADLE OF A NATION	SMITH	MGM	1947
S4065	CAPE BRETON ISLAND	FITZPATRICK	MGM	1948
S4066	GLIMPSES OF NEW SCOTLAND	FITZPATRICK	MGM	1947
S4067	OVER THE SEAS TO BELFAST	FITZPATRICK	MGM	1946
S4068	WANDERING THROUGH WALES	FITZPATRICK	MGM	1948
S4069	FROM LIVERPOOL TO STRATFORD	DONALDSON	MGM	1949
S4070	SCHOLASTIC ENGLAND	FITZPATRICK	MGM	1948
S4071	GLIMPSES OF OLD ENGLAND	FITZPATRICK	MGM	1949
S4072	ROAMING THROUGH NORTHERN IRELAND	FITZPATRICK	MGM	1949
S4073	TO THE COAST OF DEVON	FITZPATRICK	MGM	1950
S4074	LAND OF TRADITION	FITZPATRICK	MGM	1950
S4075	WEE BIT OF SCOTLAND	FITZPATRICK	MGM	1949
S4076	TOURING NORTHERN ENGLAND	FITZPATRICK	MGM	1950
S4077	LAND OF AULD LANG SYNE	FITZPATRICK	MGM	1950
S4078	LIFE ON THE THAMES	FITZPATRICK	MGM	1950
S4079	PASTORAL PANORAMAS	FITZPATRICK	MGM	1950
S4080	CHICAGO THE BEAUTIFUL	FITZPATRICK	MGM	1948
S4081	NIGHT LIFE IN CHICAGO	FITZPATRICK	MGM	1948
S4082	CALLING ON MICHIGAN	FITZPATRICK	MGM	1949
S4083	MIGHTY MANHATTAN, NEW YORK'S WONDER CITY	SMITH	MGM	1949
S4084	QUEBEC IN SUMMERTIME	FITZPATRICK	MGM	1949
S4085	ONTARIO, LAND OF LAKES	FITZPATRICK	MGM	1949
S4086	PLAYLANDS OF MICHIGAN	FITZPATRICK	MGM	1949
S4087	ROAMING THROUGH MICHIGAN	FITZPATRICK	MGM	1950
S4088	IN OLD AMSTERDAM	DONALDSON	MGM	1949
S4089	COLORFUL HOLLAND	DONALDSON	MGM	1950
S4090	LAND OF THE ZUIDER ZEE	FITZPATRICK	MGM	1951

S4091	SPRINGTIME IN THE NETHERLANDS	FITZPATRICK	MGM	1951
S4092	VOICES OF VENICE	FITZPATRICK	MGM	1951
S4093	EGYPT SPEAKS	FITZPATRICK	MGM	1951
S4094	WORD FOR THE GREEKS	FITZPATRICK	MGM	1951
S4095	ROMANTIC RIVIERA	FITZPATRICK	MGM	1951
S4096	GLIMPSES OF MOROCCO & ALGIERS	FITZPATRICK	MGM	1951
S4097	VISITING ITALY	FITZPATRICK	MGM	1951
S4098	GLIMPSES OF ARGENTINA	FITZPATRICK	MGM	1951
S4099	BEAUTIFUL BRAZIL	FITZPATRICK	MGM	1951
S4100	PICTURESQUE NEW ZEALAND	FITZPATRICK	MGM	1952
S4101	LIFE IN THE ANDES	FITZPATRICK	MGM	1952
S4102	LAND OF THE TAJ MAHAL	FITZPATRICK	MGM	1952
S4103	SEEING CEYLON	FITZPATRICK	MGM	1952
S4104	JASPER NATIONAL PARK	FITZPATRICK	MGM	1952
S4105	ANCIENT INDIA	FITZPATRICK	MGM	1952
S4106	PRETORIA TO DURBAN	FITZPATRICK	MGM	1952
S4107	IN THE LAND OF DIAMONDS	FITZPATRICK	MGM	1952
S4108	CALLING ON CAPETOWN	FITZPATRICK	MGM	1952
S4110	LAND OF THE UGLY DUCKING	FITZPATRICK	MGM	1953
S4111	JOHANNESBURG – CITY OF GOLD	FITZPATRICK	MGM	1953
S4112	DELIGHTFUL DENMARK	FITZPATRICK	MGM	1953
S4113	COPENHAGEN, CITY OF TOWERS	FITZPATRICK	MGM	1953
S4114	SEEING SPAIN	FITZPATRICK	MGM	1953
S4115	IN THE VALLEY OF THE RHINE	FITZPATRICK	MGM	1953
S4116	LOOKING AT LISBON	FITZPATRICK	MGM	1953
S4117	GLIMPSES OF WESTERN GERMANY	FITZPATRICK	MGM	1954
S4660	RAGS RAGLAND	portrait	MGM	
S4662	RAGS RAGLAND	portrait	MGM	
S4744	PETER LAWFORD	portrait	MGM	
S4804	HOLLYWOOD PARTY (1934) SHOWGIRLS	portrait	MGM	
S4813	HOLLYWOOD PARTY (1934) SHOWGIRLS	portrait	MGM	
S4925	HURD HATFIELD	portrait	MGM	
S5025	LAST VOYAGE	STONE	MGM	1960
S5033	VILLAGE OF THE DAMNED	RILLA	MGM	1960
S5047	SECRET PARTNER	DEARDEN	MGM	1961
S5061	VERY PRIVATE AFFAIR	MALLE	MGM	1962
S5074	CAPTAIN SINBAD	HASKIN	MGM	1963
S5075	TARZAN GOES TO INDIA	GUILLERMIN	MGM	1962
S5170	GONE WITH THE WIND (1939)	FLEMING	MGM	R68
S5174	GONE WITH THE WIND (1939)	FLEMING	MGM	R68
S5233	SHOOT THE MOON	PARKER	MGM	1982
S5302	IN THE COOL OF THE DAY	STEVENS	MGM	1963
S5303	HAUNTING	WISE	MGM	1963
S5304	COME FLY WITH ME	LEVIN	MGM	1963
S5308	RHINO!	TORS	MGM	1964
S5309	V.I.P.'S	ASQUITH	MGM	1963
S5316	LOVED ONE	RICHARDSON	MGM	1965
S5587	ELISABETH MUELLER	portrait	MGM	
S5593	WHERE THE BOYS ARE	LEVIN	MGM	1960
S5710	PETER LAWFORD	portrait	MGM	
S6025	KARATE KILLERS	SHEAR	MGM	1967
S6050	HOT RODS TO HELL	BRAHM	MGM	1967
S6400	RAGS RAGLAND	portrait	MGM	
S7004	SING AND BE HAPPY	KEMP	UNIVERSAL	1946
S7005	SING AND BE HAPPY	KEMP	UNIVERSAL	1946
S7006	SIX GUN MUSIC	WATT	UNIVERSAL	1948
S7007	CHEYENNE COWBOY	WATT	UNIVERSAL	1948
S7009	TED WEEMS	portrait	MGM	
S7011	WEST OF LARAMIE	COWAN	UNIVERSAL	1948
S7012	PRAIRIE PIRATES	COWAN	UNIVERSAL	1948
S7015	DUKE ELLINGTON	portrait	MGM	
S7018	SILVER BUTTE	COWAN	UNIVERSAL	1948
S7019	NEVADA TRAIL	MARTELL	UNIVERSAL	1948
S7020	PECOS PISTOL (GIRL FROM GUNSIGHT)	COWAN	UNIVERSAL	1948
S7022	TED FRENTA	portrait	MGM	
S7023	DEL COURTNEY	portrait	MGM	

S7025	SPADE COOLEY	portrait	MGM	
S7027	WESTERN COURAGE	COWAN	UNIVERSAL	1949
S7034	COYOTE CANYON	COWAN	UNIVERSAL	1949
S7035	FARGO PHANTOM	COWAN	UNIVERSAL	1949
S7036	GOLD STRIKE	COWAN	UNIVERSAL	1949
S7037	RUSTLER'S RANSOM	COWAN	UNIVERSAL	1949
S7045	CACTUS CARAVAN/READY TO RIDE	COWAN	UNIVERSAL	1949
S7755	HOW GRINCH STOLE CHRISTMAS (t)	JONES	MGM	1966
S9433	IT'S A WISE CHILD	LEONARD	MGM	1931
S9676	HURD HATFIELD	portrait	MGM	
S II	SOUNDER PART 2	GRAHAM	ABC	1976
SA	SAINTS AND SINNERS (UK)	ARLISS	LOPERT	1949
SA	SAY ANYTHING	CROWE	20th CENTURY FOX	1989
SA	SEVERED ARM, THE	ALDERMAN	MEDIA CINEMA	1974
SA	SEX AND THE ANIMALS (doc)	DWAIN	FALCON INT'L	1969
SA	SHOGUN ASSASSIN	HOUSTON	UNITED ARTISTS	1981`
SA	SHOOT TO KILL	BERKE	SCREEN GUILD	1947
SA	SILKEN AFFAIR (UK)	KELLINO	DCA	1956
SA	SPY 77 (UK: ON SECRET SERVICE)	WOODS	FIRST DIVISION	1933
SA	STAYING ALIVE	STALLONE	PARAMOUNT	1983
SABB	SISTER ACT	ARDOLINO	BUENA VISTA	1992
SAC	SPARE A COPPER (UK)	CARSTAIRS	ABFD	1940
SAE	SIN OF ADAM AND EVE (MEX: PECADO D ADAN Y EVA 1969)	ZACHARY	DEMENSION	1972
SAG	SON OF A GUNFIGHTER	LANDRES	MGM	1966
SAH	SAHARA	MCLAGLEN	CANNON	1983
SAL	SONS AND LOVERS (UK)	CARDIFF	20TH CENTURY FOX	1960
SAN	SANDWICH MAN (UK)	HARTFORD-DAVIS	RANK	1966
S-ARWIN	JULIE	STONE	MGM	1956
SAWM	SING ALONG WITH ME (UK)	SCOTT	BRITISH LION	1952
SB	FIGHTING BACK	LUPONE	PARAMOUNT	1987
SB	MEET SEXTON BLAKE (UK)	HARLOW	ANGLO-AMERICAN	1945
SB	PANIC IN THE PARLOR (UK: SAILOR BEWARE)	PARRY	DCA	1956
SB	SALOON BAR (UK)	FORDE	ABFD	1940
SB	SECOND BUREAU (UK)	HANBURY	RKO	1936
SB	SHARK BOY (BEYOND THE REEF)	CLARKE	20th CENTURY FOX	1980
SB	SHE BEAST (UK)	REEVES		1966
SB	SIERRA BARON	CLARK	20th CENTURY FOX	1958
SB	SILVER BEARS	PASSER	COLUMBIA	1977
SB	SILVER BULLET	ATTAIS	PARAMOUNT	1985
SB	SLEEPING BEAUTY (RUS: SPYASHCHAYA KRASAVITSA)	DUDKO	ROYAL FILMS	1966
SB	SLEEPING BEAUTY (t)	GERONIMI	BUENA VISTA	R70S
SB	SMOKE BELLEW	DUNLAP	FIRST DIVISION	1929
SB	SOLARBABIES	JOHNSON	MGM	1986
SB	SOLDIER BLUE	NELSON	AVCO EMBASSY	1970
SB	SPIDER AND THE FLY (UK)	HAMER	UNIVERSAL	1949
SB	SPRING BYINGTON	portrait	RKO	
SB	STEPHEN BROOKS	portrait	WARNER BROS-TV	
SB	STUDENT BODIES	ROSE	PARAMOUNT	1981
SB	SUNBURN	SARAFIAN	PARAMOUNT	1979
SB	VILLAGE SQUIRE (UK)	DENHAM	PARAMOUNT BRITISH	1935
SB8900	LUCKY LUKE		UNITED ARTISTS	1943
SBBB	SIMON BIRCH	JOHNSON	BUENA VISTA	1998
SBBB	SORORITY BOYS	WOLODARSKY	BUENA VISTA	2002
SBS	2ND BEST SECRET AGENT ...WIDE WORLD (UK:LICENSED TO KILL)	SHONTEFF	EMBASSY	1965
SBV	BELOVED VAGABOND (UK)	BERNHARDT	COLUMBIA	1936
SC	7TH COMMANDMENT	BERWICK	CROWN INT'L	1961
SC	MORGAN! (UK: MORGAN: A SUITABLE CASE FOR TREATMENT)	REISZ	CINEMA V	1966
SC	SALZBURG CONNECTION, THE	KATZIN	20th CENTURY FOX	1972
SC	SANTA CLAUS (MEX: 1959)	CARDONA	K. GORDON MURRAY	1960
SC	SANTA CLAUS THE MOVIE	SZWARC	TRI STAR	1985
SC	SEA CREATURE	CAHN	AIP	1956
SC	SERIOUS CHARGE (UK)	YOUNG	GOVERNOR	1959
SC	SHORT CIRCUIT	BADHAM	TRI STAR	1986
SC	SILENT CALL, THE	BUSHELMAN	20th CENTURY FOX	1961
SC	SOMETHING IN THE CITY (UK)	ROGERS	BUTCHER'S	1950
SC	SOMEWHERE IN CAMP (UK)	BLAKELEY	BUTCHER'S	1942

SC	SOMEWHERE IN CIVVIES (UK)	ROGERS	BUTCHER'S	1943
SC	SOUTHERN COMFORT	HILL	20th CENTURY FOX	1981
SC	SQUAD CAR	LEFTWICH	20th CENTURY FOX	1960
SC	STAR CHAMBER	HYAMS	20th CENTURY FOX	1983
SC	STOCK CAR (UK)	RILLA	BUTCHER'S	1955
SC	STRANGERS CAME (UK: YOU CAN'T FOOL AN IRISHMAN)	TRAVERS	BELL	1949
SC	STREETCAR NAMED DESIRE	KAZAN	WARNER BROS	R93
SC	SUGAR COOKIES	GERSHUNY	GENERAL	1972
SC	SUNDAY IN THE COUNTRY	TAVERNIER	MGM	1984
SC	SWEETEST CONFESSIONS (SWEET TORTURE)	MOLINARO	TRIANON	1971
SC	SWORD OF THE CONQUEROR (IT: ROSMUNDA E ALBOINO)	CAMPOGALLIANI	UNITED ARTISTS	1961
S-C	SCROOGED	DONNER	PARAMOUNT	1989
SC2	SHORT CIRCUIT 2	JOHNSON	TRI STAR	1988
SCA	SCANNERS	CRONENBERG	AVCO EMBASSY	1981
SCBB	SANTA CLAUSE, THE	PASQUIN	BUENA VISTA	1994
SCDM	STRANGE CASE OF DR. MANNING (UK: MORNING CALL)	CRABTREE	REPUBLIC	1957
SCH-GG	GREAT GADSBY	CLAYTON	PARAMOUNT	1974
SCM	SLEEPING CAR MURDER (FR: COMPARTIMENT TUEURS)	GAVRAS	SEVEN ARTS	1966
SCN	SPY WITH A COLD NOSE (UK)	PETRIE	EMBASSY	1966
SCT	CRY TERROR	STONE	MGM	1958
SD	MALA HEMBRA	DELGADO	MAYA	1950
SD	SAN DEMETRIO LONDON (UK)	FREND	20TH CENTURY FOX	1943
SD	SAVAGE DRUMS	BERKE	LIPPERT	1951
SD	SCARS OF DRACULA (UK)	BAKER	CONTINENTAL	1971
SD	SILVER DARLINGS (UK)	ELDER	PATHE	1947
SD	SIN & DESIRE	ROZIER	ATLANTIS	1960
SD	SNOW DAY	KOCH	PARAMOUNT	2000
SD	SOAP DISH	HOFFMAN	PARAMOUNT	1991
SD	SON OF DRACULA	FRANCIS	CINEMATION	1974
SD	SPLIT DECISIONS	DRURY	NEW CINEMA	1988
SD	STRANGE DECEPTION (IT: IL CRISTO PROIBITO)	MALAPARTE	CASINO	1951
SD	STRIKE ME DEADLY	MIKELS	HANSEN ENTERPRISE	1964
SD	SWEET DREAMS	REISZ	TRI STAR	1985
SD	SYMPATHY FOR THE DEVIL	GODARD	NEW LINE CINEMA	1970
SDBB	SIX DAYS, SEVEN NIGHTS	REITMAN	BUENA VISTA	1998
SDER	SAFECRACKER (UK)	MILLAND	MGM	1958
SDL	SERVICE DELUXE	LEE	UNIVERSAL	1938
SDSN	SHE DIDN'T SAY NO! (UK)	FRANKEL	SEVEN ARTS	1958
SDW	SHE-DEVILS ON WHEELS	LEWIS	MAYFLOWER	1968
SE	SAMANTHA EGGAR		COL	
SE	SAVAGE EYE, THE	MADDOW	TRANS-LUX	1960
SE	SCUM OF THE EARTH	BROWNRIGG	DIMENSIONS PICTURES	1974
SE	SHORT EYES	YOUNG	FILM LEAGUE	1977
SE	SO EVIL, SO YOUNG (UK)	GRAYSON	UNITED ARTISTS	1961
SE	SOMEWHERE IN ENGLAND (UK)	BLAKELEY	BUTCHER'S	1940
SE	STARS IN YOUR EYES (UK)	ELVEY	BRITISH LION	1956
SE	STREAMLINE EXPRESS	FIELDS	MASCOT	1935
SE	STUART ERWIN	portrait	GRAND NATIONAL	
SE5	DANCING WITH CRIME (UK)	CARSTAIRS	PARAMOUNT BRITISH	1947
SEA	DECKS RAN RED	STONE	MGM	1958
SEA	SEA GYPSIES	RAFFILL	WARNER BROS	1978
SEI-25	OUTLAWS OF RED RIVER	SEILER	FOX	1927
SEL	SELENA	NAVA	WARNER BROS	1997
SEL-2	GAY INTRUDERS, THE	MCCAREY	20th CENTURY FOX	1948
SEN	BAREFOOT SAVAGE (IT: SENSUALITA)	FRACASSI	PARAMOUNT	1952
SER	SERPICO	LUMET	PARAMOUNT	1973
SF	DAY THEY ROBBED THE BANK OF ENGLAND (UK)	GUILLERMIN	MGM	1960
SF	MEN OF SHERWOOD FOREST (UK: 1954)	GUEST	ASTOR	1956
SF	ROCK 'N ROLL REVUE	KOHN	STUDIO FILMS	1955
SF	SAINT OF FORT WASHINGTON	HUNTER	WARNER BROS	1993
SF	SECOND FIDDLE (UK)	ELVEY	BRITISH LION	1957
SF	SKY SPIDER	THORPE	ACTION PICTURES	1931
SF	SOUL FOOD	TILLMAN	20th CENTURY FOX	1997
SF	SPACEFLIGHT IC-1 (UK)	KNOWLES	LIPPERT	1965
SF	STARS FELL ON HENRIETTA	KEACH	WARNER BROS	1995
SF	STOLEN FACE (UK)	FISHER	LIPPERT	1952

SF	SWISS FAMILY ROBINSON, THE	ANNAKIN	BUENA VISTA	1960
SF8223	BOOLOO	ELLIOTT	PARAMOUNT	1938
SFB1	OPERATION SNAFU (UK: ON THE FIDDLE)	FRANKEL	AIP	1961
SFH	SECRET FILE HOLLYWOOD	CUSUMANO	CROWN INT'L	1961
SFS	SCHOOL FOR SEX (UK)	WALKER	PAUL MART	1969
SG	KILLING OF SISTER GEORGE	ALDRICH	PALOMAR	1968
SG	LET'S TRY AGAIN	MINER	RKO	1934
SG	SECRET GARDEN	HOLLAND	WARNER BROS	1993
SG	SMARTEST GIRL IN TOWN	SANTLEY	RKO	1936
SG	STREETS OF GOLD	ROTH	20th CENTURY FOX	1986
SG	SUPERGIRL	SZWARC	TRI STAR	1984
SG	WHITE FIRE (UK: THREE STEPS TO THE GALLOWS)	GILLING	LIPPERT	1953
SG-1200	BARBARY COAST (R54 - PORT OF WICKEDNESS)	HAWKS	UNITED ARTISTS	1935
SG-9100	BELOVED ENEMY	POTTER	GOLDWYN	1936
SG-9400	PRINCESS AND THE PIRATE	BUTLER	RKO	1944
SGB	SINDERELLA AND THE GOLDEN BRA	MINARDI	MANSON DISTRIBUTING	1964
SGH	STAGE MADNESS	SCHERTZINGER	FOX FILM	1927
SH	CALL HIM MR. SHATTER (UK: SHATTER)	CARRERAS	AVCO EMBASSY	1975
SH	HOME, SWEET HOME (UK)	COOPER	RKO	1933
SH	SAD HORSE	CLARK	20th CENTURY FOX	1959
SH	SAVAGE HARVEST	COLLINS	UNITED ARTISTS	1981
SH	SCAVENGER HUNT	SCHULTZ	20th CENTURY FOX	1979
SH	SCRATCH HARRY	MATTER	CANNON	1969
SH	SHAKESPEARE WALLAH (IND)	IVORY	CONTINENTAL	1965
SH	SHALAKO (UK)	DMYTRYK	CINERAMA	1968
SH	STEPHANIE HILL		COL	
SH	STRANGER'S HAND (UK)	SOLDATI	DCA	1954
SH	STRIKE AND HYDE		UNITED ARTISTS	1978
SH	SUGAR HILL	ICHASO	20th CENTURY FOX	1994
SHD	SWEET HEARTS DANCE	GREENWALD	TRI STAR	1988
SHE	SHE (UK)	DAY	MGM	1965
SHH	SWEDEN HEAVEN AND HELL (IT: SVEZIA, INFERNO E PARADISO)	SCATTINI	AVCO EMBASSY	1969
SHM	SHE SHALL HAVE MURDER (UK)	BIRT	IFD	1950
SHR	SEVEN HILLS OF ROME (IT: ARRIVEDERCI ROMA)	ROWLAND	MGM	1958
SHTJ	SEVEN HOURS TO JUDGMENT	BRIDGES	TRANS WORLD	1988
SHY	SAY HELLO TO YESTERDAY (UK)	RAKOFF	CINERAMA	1970
SI	SAVAGE ISLANDS		PARAMOUNT	1983
SIB	INVISIBLE BOY	HOFFMAN	MGM	1957
SIBB	SPACED INVADERS	JOHNSON	BUENA VISTA	1990
SIH	COP-OUT (UK: STRANGER IN THE HOUSE)	ROUVE	CINERAMA	1967
SIN	RUNAWAY BUS (UK)	GUEST	KRAMER-HYAMS	1954
SING	SING	BASKIN	TRI STAR	1989
SIT	STRANGER IN TOWN (UK)	POLLOCK	ASTOR	1957
SITN	SKIMPY IN THE NAVY (UK)	DICKENS	ADELPHI	1949
SJ	PASSING STRANGER (UK)	ARNOLD	CONTINENTAL	1954
SJ	SHIRLEY JONES		COL	early 1960s
SJ	SINS OF JEZEBEL	LE BORG	LIPPERT	1953
SJ	SISTER TO JUDAS	HOPPER	MAYFAIR	1932
SJ	SPACE JAM	PYTKA	WARNER BROS	1996
SK	BROTHERLY LOVE (COUNTRY DANCE)	THOMPSON	MGM	1970
SK	SANDS OF THE KALAHARI (UK)	ENDFIELD	PARAMOUNT	1965
SK	SHAKEDOWN (UK)	LEMONT	UNIVERSAL	1960
SK	SKULL (UK)	FRANCIS	PARAMOUNT	1965
SK	SUMMERTIME KILLER	ISASI	AVCO EMBASSY	1973
SK	SKULL	FRANCIS	PARAMOUNT	1965
SK-5	CHAMPION	ROBSON	UNITED ARTISTS	1949
SK9	STEEL KEY (UK)	BAKER	EROS	1953
SK-101	LOVEABLE CHEAT, THE	OSWALD	FILM CLASSICS	1949
SKBB	SHANGHAI KNIGHTS	DOBKIN	BUENA VISTA	2003
SKBB	SHOOT TO KILL	SPOTTISWOODE	TOUCHSTONE	1988
SKC	WHO IS KILLING THE GREAT CHIEFS OF EUROPE?	KOTCHEFF	WARNER BROS	1978
SKH	SOME KIND OF HERO	PRESSMAN	PARAMOUNT	1981
SKH-5124	SOME KIND OF HERO	PRESSMAN	PARAMOUNT	1981
SK-R	CHAMPION	KRAMER	UNITED ARTISTS	1955
SK-R-130	NOT AS A STRANGER	LARDNER	UNITED ARTISTS	1949
SK-S	NOT AS A STRANGER	LARDNER	UNITED ARTISTS	1949

S LZ	LIZZIE	HAAS	MGM	1957
SL	SANDLOT	EVANS	20th CENTURY FOX	1993
SL	SHAMELESS OLD LADY	ALLIO	RANK	1966
SL	SILENCE OF THE LAMBS	DEMME	ORION	1991
SL	SUMMER LOVERS	KLEISER	FILMWAYS	1982
SL	SUNDAY LOVERS	FORBES	UNITED ARTISTS	1980
SL	THIS SPORTING LIFE (UK)	ANDERSON	CONTINENTAL	1963
SL	TOO BAD SHE'S BAD	BLASETTI	GETZ-KINGSLEY	1955
SL-16	SILENCE OF THE LAMBS	DEMME	ORION	1991
SLBB	SCARLET LETTER	JOFFE	BUENA VISTA	1995
SLD	STARS LOOK DOWN (UK)	REED	MGM	1940
SLU	SPIES LIKE US	LANDIS	WARNER BROS	1985
SLW	DR. STRANGELOVE (UK)	KUBRICK	COLUMBIA	1964
SM	DENNIS MORGAN / STANLEY MORNER	portrait	MGM	
SM	SAVAGE MESSIAH	RUSSELL	MGM	1972
SM	SCENES FROM A MARRIAGE (SWE: SCENER UR ETT AKTENSKAP)	BERGMAN	CINEMA 5	1973
SM	SECOND MATE (UK)	BAXTER	ASSO. BRITISH-PATHE	1950
SM	SHADOW MAN (UK: STREET OF SHADOWS)	VERNON	LIPPERT	1953
SM	SHIRLEY MACLAINE	portrait	UNIV	
SM	SILVANA MANGANO	portrait	PARAMOUNT`	
SM	SOUTHERN MAID (UK)	HUGHES	WARDOUR	1933
SM	STEPHEN MCNALLY	portrait		
SM	STRANGLER'S MORGUE (UK: CURSE OF THE WRAYDONS)	GOVER	JH HOFFBERG	1946
SM	SUMMER MAGIC	NEILSON	BUENA VISTA	1963
SM223	MR. MUGGS RIDES AGAIN	FOX	MONOGRAM	1945
SMBB	SIXTH MAN, THE	MILLER	BUENA VISTA	1997
SMS	STOP MAKING SENSE	DEMME	CINECOM PICTURES	1984
SMW	DANGEROUS MILLIONS	TINLING	20th CENTURY FOX	1946
SMW2	DEADLINE FOR MURDER	TINLING	20th CENTURY FOX	1946
SN	SATURDAY NIGHT & SATURDAY MORNING (UK)	REISZ	CONTINENTAL	1961
SN	SECRET OF NIMH (t)	BLUTH	MGM/UNITED ARTISTS	1982
SN	SONG OF NORWAY	STONE	CINERAMA RELEASING	1970
SNDN	SILENT NIGHT DEADLY NIGHT	SELLIER JR	TRI STAR	1984
SNE	SEE NO EVIL, HEAR NO EVIL	HILLER	TRI STAR	1989
SNO	SATURDAY NIGHT OUT (UK)	HARTFORD-DAVIS	CAMEO	1964
SO	SMILES OF A SUMMER NIGHT (SWE: SOMMARNATTENS LEENDE)	BERGMAN	RANK FILMS AMERICA	1955
SO	SOUNDER	RITT	20th CENTURY FOX	1972
SO	STARTING OVER	PAKULA	PARAMOUNT	1979
SOA	BAREFOOT EXECUTIVE	BUTLER	BUENA VISTA	1971
SOA	SIGN OF AQUARIUS (GHETTO FREAKS, LOVE COMMUNE)	EMERY	CINAR PROD	1970
SOB	S. O. B.	EDWARDS	PARAMOUNT	1981
SOB	SON OF BLOB (BEWARE! THE BLOB)	HAGMAN	HARRIS ENT.	1972
SOBB	STAKEOUT	BADHAM	BUENA VISTA	1987
SOE	SHADOW OF THE EAGLE (UK)	SALKOW	UNITED ARTISTS	1950
SOF	SHOES OF THE FISHERMAN	ANDERSON	MGM	1968
SON	SLAVE, THE (IT: IL FIGLIO DI SPARTACUS 1962)	CORBUCCI	MGM	1963
SON	SPY OF NAPOLEON (UK)	ELVEY	GRAND NATIONAL	1936
SONY	SLAVES OF NEW YORK	IVORY	TRI STAR	1989
SOR	SCOTCH ON THE ROCKS (UK: LAXDALE HALL)	ELDRIDGE	KINGSLEY INT'L	1953
SOS	SOS PACIFIC (UK)	GREEN	UNIVERSAL	1959
SOS	SOS SUBMARINE (IT: UOMINI SUL FONDO 1941)	DE ROBERTIS	SCREEN GUILD	1948
SOV	SQUARE OF VIOLENCE	BERCOVICI	MGM	1962
SP	ABOUT LAST NIGHT (SEXUAL PERVERSITY IN CHICAGO*)	ZWICK	TRI STAR	1986
SP	CHRISTMAS CAROL	HURST	UNITED ARTISTS	1951
SP	CURSE OF THE DEMON (UK: NIGHT OF THE DEMON)	TOURNEUR	COLUMBIA	1957
SP	DEBT OF HONOUR (UK)	WALKER	GFD	1936
SP	GO TELL THE SPARTANS	POST	AVCO EMBASSY	1978
SP	SCANDALS OF PARIS (UK: THERE GOES SUSIE)	HANBURY, STAFFORD	REGAL	1934
SP	SECRET PLACES	BARRON	20th CENTURY FOX	1985
SP	SHOOT THE PIANO PLAYER	TRUFFAUT	ASTOR PICTURES	1960
SP	SHY PEOPLE	KONCHALOVSKY	CANNON	1987
SP	SIX PACK	PETRIE	20th CENTURY FOX	1982
SP	SKI PATROL	CORRELL	TRIUMPH RELEASING	1990
SP	SOME PEOPLE (UK)	DONNER	AAIP	1962
SP	SPACE BALLS	BROOKS	MGM	1987
SP	SPACE: 1999 (tv)	various	ITC	1975

SP	SPARROWS CAN'T SING (UK)	LITTLEWOOD	JANUS	1963
SP	SPECIES II	MEDAK	MGM	1998
SP	SPETTERS (NETH)	VERHOEVEN	SAMUEL GOLDWYN	1981
SP	SPHERE	LEVINSON	WARNER BROS	1998
SP	S*P*Y*S	KERSHNER	20th CENTURY FOX	1974
SP	SURVIVING PICASSO	IVORY	WARNER BROS	1996
SP	SUSPECTED PERSON (UK)	HUNTINGTON	PRODUCERS RELEASING	1942
SP	SUZANNE PLESHETTE	portrait	UNIV	
SP	TWO LIVING, ONE DEAD (UK)	ASQUITH	BRITISH LION	1961
SP1	TWO WAY STRETCH (UK)	DAY	SHOWCORPORATION	1960
SP2	ROAD TO THE BIG HOUSE	COLMES	SCREEN GUILD	1947
SPBB	SACRED PLANET	LONG	BUENA VISTA	2003
SPC-5064	SERPICO	LUMET	PARAMOUNT	1973
SPRA-MCF-3	THEIR MAD MOMENT	SPRAGUE, MCFADDEN	FOX FILM	1931
SR	SECRET RITES	FORDE	AVCO EMBASSY	1971
SR	SECRETS OF THE REEF	LERNER	MARINE STUDIOS	1956
SR	SHUTTERED ROOM (UK)	GREENE	WARNER BROS.	1967
SR	SKY RIDERS	HICKOX	20th CENTURY FOX	1976
SR	SOLDIER OF ORANGE (NETH: SOLDAAT VAN ORANJE 1977)	VERHOEVEN	INT'L PICTURE SHOW	1979
SR	SONG OF THE ROAD (UK)	BAXTER	SELECT ATTRACTIONS	1937
SR	STORM RIDER	BERNDS	20th CENTURY FOX	1957
SR	STRYKER OF THE YARD (UK)	CRABTREE	REPUBLIC	1953
SR	SUBJECT WAS ROSES	GROSBARD	MGM	1968
SR	SUMMER RENTAL	REINER	PARAMOUNT	1985
SR	SUMMER TO REMEMBER (IT)	MARTINO	TITANUS	1974
SRBB	RETURN TO SNOWY RIVER	BURROWES	BUENA VISTA	1987
SRK	SIDNEY R. KENT	portrait	FOX	
SR-P8	SAINT'S GIRL FRIDAY (SAINT'S RETURN)	FRIEDMAN	RKO	1954
SS	BACKSTAGE (UK: LIMELIGHT) STREET SINGER'S SERENADE*	WILCOX	GAUMONT BRIT. AMER.	1937
SS	GREAT MANHUNT (UK: STATE SECRET)	GILLIAT	BRITISH LION	1950
SS	MAGIC GARDEN OF STANLEY SWEETHEART	HORN	MGM	1970
SS	S. Z. SAKALL	portrait	WARNER BROS	
SS	SALLY STARR	portrait	MGM	
SS	SATAN'S SADIST	ADAMSON	INDEPENDENT INT'L	1959
SS	SAVANNAH SMILES	DE MORO	GOLD COAST	1982
SS	SCREAMING SKULL	NICOL	AIP	1958
SS	SEASIDE SWINGERS (UK: EVERY DAY'S A HOLIDAY)	HILL	EMBASSY	1964
SS	SECOND SIGHT	ZWICK	WARNER BROS	1989
SS	SEVENTH SIGN	SCHULTZ	TRI STAR	1988
SS	SHADOW MAN (UK: STREET OF SHADOWS)	VERNON	LIPPERT	1953
SS	SHIPYARD SALLY (UK)	BANKS	20TH CENTURY FOX	1939
SS	SHOESHINE (IT: SCIUSCIA 1946)	DE SICA	LOPERT	1947
SS	SHOW OF SHOWS	ADOLFI	WARNER BROS	1929
SS	SILVER STAR	BARLETT	LIPPERT	1955
SS	SILVER STREAK	HILLER	20th CENTURY FOX	1976
SS	SIMONE SIGNORET	portrait	UNIV	
SS	SING AND SWING (UK: LIVE IT UP!)	COMFORT	UNIVERSAL	1963
SS	SIXTH SENSE, THE	SHYAMALAN	BUENA VISTA	1999
SS	SON OF SAMSON	CAMPOGALLIANI	MEDALLION	1962
SS	SOUL SOLDIER (RED, WHITE AND BLACK 1970)	CARDOS	FANFARE	1972
SS	SPLIT SECOND	POWELL	RKO	1953
SS	STOWAWAY IN THE SKY (FR: LE VOYAGE EN BALLOON 1960)	LAMORISSE	LOPERT	1962
SS	STREET SMART	SCHATZBERG	CANNON	1986
SS	STREET SONG (UK)	VORHAUS	RKO	1935
SS	STREETS OF SHANGHAI	GASNIER	TIFFANY	1927
SS3	LADY FROM LISBON (UK)	HISCOTT	ANGLO-AMERICAN	1942
SSBB	SUMMER OF SAM	LEE	BUENA VISTA	1999
SSCT	SEVEN SEAS TO CALAIS (IT: IL DOMINATORE DEI 7 MARI 1962	MATE	MGM	1963
SSF	STREETS OF SAN FRANCISCO (tv series)	VARIOUS	WARNER BROS TV	1972
SSF	SWORD OF SHERWOOD FOREST (UK)	FISHER	COLUMBIA	1960
SSG	STAR SPANGLED GIRL	KOCH	PARAMOUNT	1971
SSI	CINDERELLA SWINGS IT	CABANNE	RKO	1943
SSI	STARSHIP INVASIONS	HUNT	WARNER BROS	1977
SSM	SHE SHALL HAVE MUSIC (UK)	HISCOTT	IMPERIAL	1935
SSOE	BIG TIME OPERATORS (UK: SMALLEST SHOW ON EARTH)	DEARDEN	TIMES	1957
SSS	SIEGE OF SIDNEY STREET (UK)	BAKER, BERMAN	UNITED PRODUCERS REL.	1960

SSW	SHAME OF THE SABINE WOMEN	GOUT	UNITED PRODUCERS REL.	1962
ST	BLONDE BLACKMAILER (UK: STOLEN TIME)	DEANE	ALLIED ARTISTS	1955
ST	BRIGHTHAVEN EXPRESS (UK: SALUTE THE TOFF)	ROGERS	BUTCHER'S	1952
ST	CLIMAX (IT: L'IMMORALE)	GERMI	LOPERT	1967
ST	PARIS EXPRESS (UK: MAN WHO WATCHED TRAINS GO BY)	FRENCH	MACDONALD	1952
ST	SCARLET THREAD (UK)	GILBERT	REALART	1951
ST	SECRET TUNNEL (UK)	HAMMOND	GFD	1948
ST	SHARKYS' TREASURE	WILDE	UNITED ARTISTS	1975
ST	SHINING THROUGH	SELTZER	20th CENTURY FOX	1992
ST	SHIRLEY TEMPLE	portrait	WARNER BROS	1930s-40s
ST	SHORT TIME	CHAMPION	20th CENTURY FOX	1990
ST	SLEEPING TIGER	ALLEN	RKO	1951
ST	SLEEPING TIGER (UK)	LOSEY	ASTOR	1954
ST	SMASHING TIME (UK)	DAVIS	PARAMOUNT	1967
ST	SMOOTH TALK	CHOPRA	INT'L SPECTRAFILM	1985
ST	SOMETHING TO TALK ABOUT	HALSTROM	WARNER BROS	1995
ST	SPEED TRAP	BELLAMY	FIRST ARTISTS	1977
ST	STAR TREK	WISE	PARAMOUNT	1979
ST	STAY TUNED	HYAMS	WARNER BROS	1992
ST	STORK TALK (UK)	FORLONG	PARADE RELEASING	1962
ST	STORYVILLE	FROST	20th CENTURY FOX	1992
ST	STUD, THE (UK: 1978)	MASTERS	AIP	1979
ST	SUNRISE TRAIL	MCCARTHY	TIFFANY	1931
ST	SURE THING	REINER	EMBASSY	1985
ST	SWAMP THING	CRAVEN	EMBASSY	1982
ST2	STAR TREK: WRATH OF KHAN	MEYER	PARAMOUNT	1982
ST3	STAR TREK III	NIMOY	PARAMOUNT	1984
ST4	HEADIN' NORTH	MCCARTHY	TIFFANY	1930
ST4	STAR TREK IV	NIMOY	PARAMOUNT	1986
ST5	STAR TREK V	SHATNER	PARAMOUNT	1989
ST-7	NEAR THE TRAIL'S END	FOX	ALBERT DEZEL	R48
STAR	BATTLE BEYOND THE STARS	MURAKAMI	ORION	1980
STB	STAB (WT FOR STILL OF THE NIGHT)	BENTON	UNITED ARTISTS	1982
STB	STILL OF THE NIGHT	BENTON	MGM/UNITED ARTISTS	1982
STC	STOP THAT CAB	DE LIGUORO	LIPPERT	1951
STF	STAGECOACH TO FURY	CLAXTON	LIPPERT	1956
ST-K	STUNT MAN	RUSH	20th CENTURY FOX	1980
STN-101	QUEEN OF BROADWAY	NEWFIELD	PRODUCERS RELEASING	1942
STO	SHE'S THE ONE	BURNS	20th CENTURY FOX	1996
STO-22	CIRCUS ACE	STOLOFF	FOX	1927
STO-32	JUST LIKE HEAVEN	NEILL	TIFFANY	1930
STO-32	NEW FOX MOVIETONE FOLLIES OF 1930	STOLOFF	FOX FILM	1930
STS	SANDY THE SEAL (UK)	LYNN	TIGON	1968
STS	SMALL TOWN STORY (UK)	TULLY	GFD	1953
STVI	STAR TREK VI	MEYER	PARAMOUNT	1991
SU	SEVEN-UPS	D'ANTONI	20th CENTURY FOX	1974
SV	SACCO & VANZETTI	MONTALDO	UMC PICTURES	1971
SV	SEVENTH VEIL (UK)	BENNETT	UNIVERSAL	1945
SV	SHIRLEY VALENTINE	GILBERT	PARAMOUNT	1989
SV	SORCERER'S VILLAGE, THE (doc)	DAVIS	CONTINENTAL	1958
SV	SUPER VIXEN	MEYER	R.M. FILMS	1975
SV	UNTOUCHED (MEX: SOMBRA VERDE 1954)	GAVALDON	EXCELSIOR PICTURES	1956
SW	JANE WYMAN	ARCHAINBAUD	RKO	1950
SW	SEA WIFE (UK)	MCNAUGHT	20th CENTURY FOX	1957
SW	SHOCK WAVES	WIEDERHORN	JOSEPH BRENNER ASSO.	1977
SW	SIDEWINDER ONE	BELLAMY	AVCO EMBASSY	1977
SW	SOMETHING WILD	DEMME	ORION	1986
SW	SWITCHING CHANNELS	KOTCHEFF	TRI STAR	1987
SW1	STAR WARS PHANTOM MENACE	LUCAS	20th CENTURY FOX	1999
SWBB	SWING KIDS	CARTER	BUENA VISTA	1993
SW-C	SWORD AND THE STONE (t)	REITHERMAN	BUENA VISTA	1964
SWE	SLEEPING WITH THE ENEMY	RUBEN	20th CENTURY FOX	1991
SWF	SAY IT WITH FLOWERS (UK)	BAXTER	RKO	1934
SWG	SWIMMING POOL	DERAY	AVCO EMBASSY	1970
SWL	SPY WHO LOVED ME	GILBERT	UNITED ARTISTS	1977
SY	SINS OF YOUTH	DUCHESNE	JANUS FILMS	1958

SYM				
SYM	LIVING DEAD (UK: SCOTLAND YARD MYSTERY)	BENTLEY	FIRST DIVISION	1934
T	ADVENTURES OF ICHOBOD AND MR. TOAD	GERONIMI	RKO	1949
T	ESCAPE (TUNNEL 28)	SIODMAK	MGM	1962
T	LADY CRAVED EXCITEMENT (UK)	GRAYSON, SEARLE	EXCLUSIVE	1950
T	PARIS EXPRESS (UK: MAN WHO WATCHED TRAINS GO BY)	FRENCH	MACDONALD	1952
T	PLAYGIRL AFTER DARK	YOUNG	TOPAZ	1962
T	PROUD VALLEY (UK)	TENNYSON	SUPREME	1940
T	RING-A-DING RHYTHM (UK: IT'S TRAD, DAD!)	LESTER	COLUMBIA	1962
T	SUMMER LOVERS	KLEISER	FILMWAYS PICTURES	1982
T	TAKE MY TIP (UK)	MASON	GFD	1937
T	TAMAHINE	LEACOCK	ASSOC. BRITISH	1964
T	TAMANGO	BERRY	HAL ROACH DIST.	1959
T	TAP	CASTLE	TRI STAR	1989
T	TEACHERS	HILLER	MGM	1984
T	TEMP, THE	HOLLAND	PARAMOUNT	1993
T	TERMINATOR	CAMERON	ORION	1984
T	TESTAMENT	LITTMAN	PARAMOUNT	1983
T	THE TOY	DONNOR	COLUMBIA	1982
T	THUMBELINA (t)	BLEUTH	WARNER BROS	1994
T	THUNDERBALL	YOUNG	UNITED ARTISTS	R68
T	TOM THUMB (UK)	PAL	MGM	1958
T	TORMENT (SWE: HETS 1944)	SJOBERG	LOPERT	1947
T	TORSO (IT)	MARTINO	JOSEPH BRENNER	1973
T	TOYS	LEVINSON	20th CENTURY FOX	1992
T	TRANS-ATLANTIC TUNNEL (UK: TUNNEL)	ELVEY	GAUMONT BRIT. AMER.	1935
T	TROJAN BROTHERS (UK)	ROGERS	ANGLO-AMERICAN	1946
T	TROUBLE (UK)	ROGERS	UNITED ARTISTS	1933
T	TROUBLEMAKER, THE	FLICKER	JANUS	1964
T	TRUNK (UK)	WINTER	COLUMBIA	1961
T	TURK 182!	CLARK	20th CENTURY FOX	1985
T	TWILIGHT'S LAST GLEAMING	ALDRICH	LORIMAR	1977
T	TWISTER	DE BONT	UNIVERSAL	1996
T-1	BATTLING ORIOLES	GUIOL, WILDE	PATHE EXCHANGE	1924
T-1	MOVIE DUMMY (MOVIE MUMMY)	ROACH	PATHE EXCHANGE	1918
T-1	MY VALET	SENNETT	TRIANGLE	1915
T-1	THUNDERING TAXIS	LORD, MEINS	MGM	1933
T-2	GAME OLD KNIGHT	JONES	TRIANGLE	1915
T-2	JUNKMAN		PATHE EXCHANGE	1918
T-2	WHAT PRICE TAXI	LORD	MGM	1932
T-2	WHITE SHEEP	ROACH	PATHE EXCHANGE	1924
T-3	FARE PLEASE		PATHE EXCHANGE	1918
T-3	HER PAINTED HERO	JONES	TRIANGLE	1915
T-3	STRANGE INNERTUBE	LORD	MGM	1932
T-4	FAVORITE FOOL	FRAZEE	TRIANGLE	1915
T-4	HOT SPOT	LORD	MGM	1932
T-4	TOTO IN ONE NIGHT ONLY	ROACH	PATHE EXCHANGE	1918
T-5	FIRE THE COOK (edited to create T-7)	ROACH	PATHE EXCHANGE	1918
T-5	STOLEN MAGIC	SENNETT	TRIANGLE	1915
T-5	TAXI FOR TWO	LORD	MGM	1932
T-6	BRING 'EM BACK A WIFE	LORD	MGM	1933
T-6	HIS BUSY DAY	ROACH	PATHE EXCHANGE	1918
T-7	DIPPY DAUGHTER	ROACH	PATHE EXCHANGE	1918
T-7	FICKLE FATTY'S FALL	ARBUCKLE	TRIANGLE	1915
T-7	WRECKETY WRECKS	LORD	MGM	1933
T-8	CLEOPATSY (CLEO PROXY)	ROACH	PATHE EXCHANGE	1918
T-8	NAMELESS MEN	CABANNE	TIFFANY	1928
T-8	TAXI BARONS	MEINS	MGM	1933
T-9	CALL HER SAUSAGE	MEINS	MGM	1933
T-9	FURNITURE MOVERS	ROACH	PATHE EXCHANGE	1918
T-10	CHECK YOUR BAGGAGE	ROACH	PATHE EXCHANGE	1918
T-10	JANITOR'S WIFE'S TEMPTATION	HENDERSON	TRIANGLE	1915
T-10	RUMMY	LORD	MGM	1933
T-11	GREAT WATER PERIL (POOR CLARINE)	ROACH	PATHE EXCHANGE	1918
T-11	SUBMARINE PIRATE	AVERY, CHAPLIN	TRIANGLE	1915
T-12	DO HUSBANDS DECEIVE?	ROACH	PATHE EXCHANGE	1918
T-13	BEACH NUTS	ROACH	PATHE EXCHANGE	1918

T-14	CROOKED TO THE END	FRAZEE, REED	TRIANGLE	1915
T-14	ENEMY OF SOAP	ROACH	PATHE EXCHANGE	1918
T-15	FATTY AND THE BROADWAY STARS	ARBUCKLE	TRIANGLE	1915
T-16	HUNT	STERLING, PARROTT	TRIANGLE	1915
T-17	DIZZY HEIGHTS AND DARING HEARTS	WRIGHT	TRIANGLE	1916
T-19	GREAT PEARL TANGLE	HENDERSON	TRIANGLE	1916
T19	MAN IN THE MOON (UK)	DEARDEN	TRANS LUX	1960
T-20	FATTY AND MABEL ADRIFT	ARBUCKLE	TRIANGLE	1916
T-21	BECAUSE HE LOVED HER	HENDERSON	TRIANGLE	1916
T-22	MODERN ENOCH ARDEN	BADGER, AVERY	TRIANGLE	1916
T24	BEWARE OF CHILDREN (UK: NO KIDDING)	THOMAS	AIP	1961
T-24	MOVIE STAR	CLINE	TRIANGLE	1916
T-26	HE DID AND HE DIDN'T	ARBUCKLE	TRIANGLE	1916
T27	CARRY ON REGARDLESS (UK)	THOMAS	GOVERNOR	1961
T-27	HIS HEREAFTER	JONES	TRIANGLE	1916
T-28	FIDO'S FATE	GRIFFIN	TRIANGLE	1916
T28	VICTIM (UK)	DEARDEN	ASTOR	1961
T-29	BETTER LATE THAN NEVER	GRIFFIN	TRIANGLE	1916
T29	WHISTLE DOWN THE WIND (UK)	FORBES	ASTOR	1961
T-30	HIS AUTO RUINATION	FISHBACK	TRIANGLE	1916
T30	ROOMMATES (UK: RAISING THE WIND)	THOMAS	HERTS-LION	1961
T-32	CINDERS OF LOVE	WRIGHT	TRIANGLE	1916
T32	WHAT A WHOPPER (UK)	GUNN	REGAL	1961
T-33	JUDGE	JONES	TRIANGLE	1916
T34	WALTZ OF THE TOREADORS (UK)	GUILLERMIN	CONTINENTAL	1962
T-35	WIFE AND AUTO TROUBLE	HENDERSON, SENNETT	TRIANGLE	1916
T36	TWICE ROUND THE DAFFODILS (UK)	THOMAS	ANGLO-AMALGAMATED	1962
T-38	GYPSY JOE	BADGER	TRIANGLE	1916
T-39	BY STORK DELIVERY	FISHBACK	TRIANGLE	1916
T39	CARRY ON CRUISING (UK)	THOMAS	ANGLO-AMALGAMATED	1962
T-40	LOVE RIOT	JONES	TRIANGLE	1916
T40	PLAY IT COOL (UK)	WINNER	ALLIED ARTISTS	1962
T-41	OILY SCOUNDREL	FRAZEE	TRIANGLE	1916
T-42	HIS LAST LAUGH	WRIGHT	TRIANGLE	1916
T-43	HIS WIFE'S MISTAKE	ARBUCKLE	TRIANGLE	1916
T-46	BUCKING SOCIETY	CAMPBELL	TRIANGLE	1916
T46	MIND BENDERS (UK)	DEARDEN	AIP	1963
T49	CALL ME BWANA (UK)	DOUGLAS	UNITED ARTISTS	1963
T-49	HIS BITTER PILL	FISHBACK	TRIANGLE	1916
T-50	DASH OF COURAGE	PARROTT	TRIANGLE	1916
T50	NURSE ON WHEELS (UK)	THOMAS	JANUS	1963
T-53	BATH TUB PERILS	FRAZEE	TRIANGLE	1916
T-54	LOVE COMET	WRIGHT	TRIANGLE	1916
T55	SÉANCE ON A WET AFTERNOON (UK)	FORBES	ARTIXO	1964
T-57	AMBROSE'S CUP OF WOE	FISHBACK	TRIANGLE	1916
T57	THIS IS MY STREET (UK)	HAYERS	PATHE	1964
T59	CARRY ON JACK (UK)	THOMAS	ANGLO-AMALGAMATED	1963
T68	CARRY ON CLEO (UK)	THOMAS	GOVERNOR	1964
T-71	HIS LYING HEART	STERLING, AVERY	TRIANGLE	1916
T72	THREE HATS FOR LISA (UK)	HAYERS	ANGLO-AMALGAMATED	1966
T-73	RECKLESS ROMEO	ARBUCKLE	TRIANGLE	1916
T79	CARRY ON COWBOY (UK)	THOMAS	ANGLO-AMALGAMATED	1965
T-79	SCOUNDREL'S TOLL	CAVENDER	TRIANGLE	1916
T-81	AMBROSE'S RAPID RISE	FISHBACK	TRIANGLE	1916
T-82	HIS BUSTED TRUST	CLINE	TRIANGLE	1916
T-83	HAYSTACKS AND STEEPLES	BADGER	TRIANGLE	1916
T-84	TUGBOAT ROMEO	CAMPBELL, WILLIAMS	TRIANGLE	1916
T-85	BOMBS!	GRIFFIN	TRIANGLE	1916
T85	CARRY ON SCREAMING! (UK)	THOMAS	SIGMA III	1966
T-86	HONEST THIEVES	MATTHEWS	TRIANGLE	1917
T-88	HIS LAST SCENT	AVERY, CHAPLIN	TRIANGLE	1916
T-93	BLACK EYES AND BLUE	KERR	TRIANGLE	1916
T-96	SAFETY FIRST AMBROSE	FISHBACK	TRIANGLE	1916
T99	CARRY ON PIMPERNEL (UK: DON'T LOSE YOUR HEAD)	THOMAS	RANK	1966
T-100	HER CIRCUS KNIGHT	WRIGHT	TRIANGLE	1917
T-101	TELEPHONE BELLE	RAYMAKER	TRIANGLE	1917

T-103	BACHELOR'S FINISH	DILLION	TRIANGLE	1917
T-105	DONE IN OIL	AVERY	TRIANGLE	1917
T-106	STONE AGE	HARTMAN	TRIANGLE	1917
T-107	FILM EXPOSURE	MCCOY	TRIANGLE	1917
T108	CARRY ON IN THE LEGION (UK: FOLLOW THAT CAMEL)	THOMAS	SCHOENFELD	1967
T-108	DODGING HIS DOOM	WILLIAMS	TRIANGLE	1917
T-109	VILLA OF THE MOVIES	CLINE	TRIANGLE	1917
T-110	HOBBLED HARTS	DILLION	TRIANGLE	1917
T-111	HER FAME AND SHAME	GRIFFIN	TRIANGLE	1917
T112	CARRY ON DOCTOR (UK)	THOMAS	RANK	1967
T-114	HER CANDY KID	AVERY	TRIANGLE	1917
T-115	FINISHED PRODUCT	MORRIS	TRIANGLE	1917
T117	CARRY ON... UP THE KHYBER (UK)	THOMAS	RANK	1968
T-117	TUNER OF NOTE	MCCOY	TRIANGLE	1917
T-123	DOG'S OWN TALE	RAYMAKER	TRIANGLE	1917
T-131	HER NATURE DANCE	CAMPBELL	TRIANGLE	1917
T-134	HIS ONE NIGHT STAND	MCCOY	TRIANGLE	1917
T-137	HIS SOCIAL RISE	MORRIS	TRIANGLE	1917
T-139	CARRY ON CRUISING	THOMAS	ANGLO-AMALGAMATED	1962
T-141	MAIDEN'S TRUST	HEERMAN	TRIANGLE	1916
T-146	HIS MARRIAGE FAILURE	RAYMAKER	TRIANGLE	1917
T-147	HIS BITTER FATE	WILLIAMS	TRIANGLE	1917
T-151	AIRED IN COURT	DILLION	TRIANGLE	1917
T-152	HIS PERFECT DAY	MCCOY	TRIANGLE	1917
T-154	HIS THANKLESS JOB	MORRIS	TRIANGLE	1917
T-155	DAD'S DOWNFALL	RAYMAKER	TRIANGLE	1917
T-156	CACTUS NELL	FISHBACK	TRIANGLE	1917
T-158	HIS SUDDEN RIFVAL	DILLION	TRIANGLE	1917
T-159	TOY OF FATE	MCCOY	TRIANGLE	1917
T-160	INNOCENT VILLAIN	WILLIAMS	TRIANGLE	1917
T-162	HIS WIDOW'S MIGHT	KERNAN	TRIANGLE	1917
T-164	HIS FATAL MOVE	MORRIS	TRIANGLE	1917
T-166	HIS COOL NERVE	MCCOY	TRIANGLE	1917
T-167	MATRIMONIAL ACCIDENT	AVERY	TRIANGLE	1917
T-168	HIS HIDDEN TALENT (UK)	MORRIS	TRIANGLE	1917
T-169	LOVE CASE	KERNAN	TRIANGLE	1917
T-170	DOG CATCHER'S LOVE	CLINE	TRIANGLE	1917
T-172	HOTEL DISGRACE	DILLION	TRIANGLE	1917
T-173	HER DONKEY LOVE	AVERY	TRIANGLE	1917
T-175	HIS FOOT-HILL FOLLY	MORRIS	TRIANGLE	1917
T-176	FALLEN STAR	MCCOY	TRIANGLE	1917
T-177	DANGERS OF A BRIDE	KERR, HARTMAN	TRIANGLE	1917
T-178	DARK ROOM SECRET	KERNAN	TRIANGLE	1917
T-179	WARM RECEPTION	DILLION	TRIANGLE	1917
T-180	HIS BABY DOLL	WILLIAMS	TRIANGLE	1917
T-181	HIS UNCONSCIOUS CONSCIENCE	AVERY	TRIANGLE	1917
T-182	CLEVER DUMMY	RAYMAKER	TRIANGLE	1917
T&C	TANGO AND CASH	KONCHALOVSKY	WARNER BROS	1989
T&L	THELMA AND LOUISE (intl-1990 copyright)	SCOTT	PATHE	1990
T&theGL	TARZAN AND THE GOLDEN LION	MCGOWAN	RKO	1927
TA	ABYSS	CAMERON	20th CENTURY FOX	1989
TA	ADVENTURER, THE	CHAPLIN	RKO	R32
TA	ANNIVERSARY (UK)	BAKER	20TH CENTURY FOX	1968
TA	ASPHYX	NEWBROOK	PARAGON PICTURES	1972
TA	SHIRLEY O'HARA	portrait		
TA	TANGIER ASSIGNMENT (UK)	ARDAVIN, LEVERSUCH	AAP	1955
TA	THEY ALL DIED LAUGHING (UK: JOLLY BAD FELLOW)	CHAFFEY	CONTINENTAL	1964
TA	THREE AMIGOS, THE	LANDIS	ORION	1988
TA	TOUGH ASSIGNMENT	BEAUDINE	SCREEN GUILD	1949
TA L	THE APARTMENT (pre-prod -see APT)	WILDER	UNITED ARTISTS	1960
TAWM	THEY'RE A WEIRD MOB (UK)	POWELL	RANK	1966
TB	BAXTER	JEFFRIES	NATIONAL GENERAL	1973
TB	BELIEVERS, THE	SCHLESINGER	ORION	1987
TB	BIBLE: IN THE BEGINNING, THE	HUSTON	20TH CENTURY FOX	1966
TB	BLOB	RUSSELL	TRI STAR	1988
TB	BORROWER	MCNAUGHTON	CANNON	1991

TB	TANK BATTALION	ROSE	AIP	1958
TB	TERMINAL BLISS	ALAN	CANNON	1992
TB	THIS BOY'S LIFE	CATON-JONES	WARNER BROS	1993
TB	TIGER BAY (UK) (MYSTERY OF TIGER BAY 1961)	THOMPSON	CONTINENTAL DIST.	1959
TB	TIME BANDITS (UK)	GILLIAM	EMBASSY	1981
TB	TO BE OR NOT TO BE	JOHNSON	20TH CENTURY FOX	1983
TB	TOD BROWNING	portrait	MGM	
TB	TOGETHER BROTHERS	GRAHAM	20TH CENTURY FOX	1974
TB	TROUBLE BREWING (UK)	KIMMINS	ABFD	1939
TBA	THREE BITES OF THE APPLE	GANZER	MGM	1967
TBB	BANK RAIDERS (UK)	MUNDEN	RANK	1958
TBC	BIG CITY (INDIA: MAHANAGAR)	RAY	EDWARD HARRISON	1963
TBC	BIG DIAMOND ROBBERY	CONNOR	WARNER BROS	1976
T-BDR	BIG DIAMOND ROBBERY	FORDE	FILM BOOKING (RKO)	1929
T-BDR	TRIAL BY COMBAT (UK)(DIRTY KNIGHT'S WORK)	FORDE	FILM BOOKING (RKO)	1929
TBFL4	CARRY ON TEACHER (UK)	THOMAS	GOVERNOR	1959
TBJ	BELL JAR, THE	PEERCE	AVCO EMBASSY	1979
TBJ	TRIAL BY JURY	GOULD	WARNER BROS	1994
TBL	THREE BLONDS IN HIS LIFE	CHOOLUCK	CINEMA ASSOCIATES	1960
TBS	BLACK STALLION, THE	BALLARD	UNITED ARTISTS	1979
TBS	TWO IF BY SEA (STOLEN HEARTS*)	BENNETT	WARNER BROS	1996
TC	BIG CHASE	HILTON	LIPPERT	1954
TC	CAT, THE (FACE OF THE CAT) (FR: LA CHATTE 1958)	DECOIN	ELLIS FILMS	1959
TC	CAVERN, THE	ULMER	20TH CENTURY FOX	1965
TC	CHAIRMAN (UK)	THOMPSON	20TH CENTURY FOX	1969
TC	CHALLENGE	FRANKENHEIMER	EMBASSY	1982
TC	CHAMP, THE	ZEFFIRELLI	UNITED ARTISTS	1979
TC	CLIENT, THE	SCHUMACHER	WARNER BROS	1994
TC	CLOWNS, THE (IT)	FELLINI	LEVITT-PICKMAN	1971
TC	COMEDIAN, THE	GLENVILLE	MGM	1967
TC	CONFORMIST, THE	BERTOLUCCI	PARAMOUNT	1971
TC	CRUCIBLE, THE	HYTNER	20TH CENTURY FOX	1996
TC	MURDER GO ROUND (FR/IT:UN CONDE)(NIGHT EXECUTIONERS)	BOISSET	AUDUBON	1973
TC	NIGHT OF THE EXECUTIONER (SP)	NASCHY	AUDUBON	1992
TC	THREE'S COMPANY (tv)	VARIOUS	ABC-TV	1976
TC	THURSDAY'S CHILD (UK)	ACKLAND	ABPC-PATHE	1943
TC	TOUCH OF CLASS, A	FRANK	AVCO EMBASSY	1973
TC	TROPIC OF CANCER	STRICK	PARAMOUNT	1970
TC	TRUE COLORS	ROSS	PARAMOUNT	1991
TC	TRUE CRIME	EASTWOOD	WARNER BROS	1999
TC-6	UNPUBLISHED STORY (UK)	FRENCH	COLUMBIA	1942
TC-8	ADVENTURE FOR TWO (UK: DEMI-PARADISE)	ASQUITH	UNIVERSAL	1943
TC-9	GENTLE SEX (UK)	HOWARD	GFD	1943
TC-10	FLEMISH FARM (UK)	DELL	GFD	1943
TC-16	LAMP STILL BURNS (UK)	ELVEY	GFD	1943
TC-17	MEN OF TWO WORLDS (UK: WITCH DOCTOR)	DICKINSON	INT'L RELEASING	1946
TC-19	TAWNY PIPIT (UK)	MILES, SAUNDERS	UNIVERSAL	1944
TC-20	HER MAN GILBEY (UK: ENGLISH WITHOUT TEARS)	FRENCH	UNIVERSAL	1944
TC-21	WAY AHEAD (UK)	REED	20TH CENTURY FOX	1944
TC-27	DON'T TAKE IT TO HEART (UK)	DELL	EAGLE-LION	1944
TC-30A	JOHNNY IN THE CLOUDS (UK: WAY TO THE STARS)	ASQUITH	UNITED ARTISTS	1945
TC-33	CARNIVAL (UK)	HAYNES	GFD	1946
TC-34	BEWARE OF PITY (UK)	ELVEY	EAGLE-LION	1946
TC-107	WAY WE LIVE (UK)	CRAIGIE	GFD	1946
TC-110	HUNGRY HILL (UK)	HURST	UNIVERSAL	1947
TC-120	FAME IS THE SPUR (UK)	BOULTING	TOXFORD	1947
TC-124	INHERITANCE (UK: UNCLE SILAS)	FRANK	FINE ARTS	1947
TC-126	OCTOBER MAN (UK)	BAKER	EAGLE LION	1947
TC-131	VICE VERSA (UK)	USTINOV	GFD	1948
TC-132	MARK OF CAIN (UK)	HURST	GFD	1947
TC-133	HAMLET (UK)	OLIVIER	UNIVERSAL	1949
TC-142	ONE NIGHT WITH YOU (UK)	YOUNG	UNIVERSAL	1948
TC-142	THIS HAPPY BREED (UK)	LEAN	UNIVERSAL	1944
TC-159	MR. PERRIN AND MR. TRAILL (UK)	HUNTINGTON	EAGLE-LION	1948
TC-160	SLEEPING CAR TO TRIESTE (UK)	CARSTAIRS	EAGLE-LION	1948
TC-164	WOMAN HATER (UK)	YOUNG	UNIVERSAL	1948

TC-168	WEAKER SEX (UK)	BAKER	EAGLE-LION	1948
TC-172	HISTORY OF MR. POLLY (UK)	PELISSIER	INT'L RELEASING	1949
TC-183	CARDBOARD CAVALIER (UK)	FORDE	GFD	1949
TC-185	THE GAY LADY (UK: TROTTIE TRUE)	HURST	EAGLE-LION	1949
TC-188	ADAM AND EVALYN (UK: ADAM AND EVELYNE)	FRENCH	UNIVERSAL	1949
TC-193	MADNESS OF THE HEART (UK)	BENNETT	UNIVERSAL	1949
TC-196	PERFECT WOMAN (UK)	KNOWLES	EAGLE-LION	1949
TC-199	AMAZING MR. BEECHAM (UK: CHILTERN HUNDREDS)	CARSTAIRS	EAGLE-LION	1949
TC-205	ROCKING HORSE WINNER (UK)	PELISSIER	UNIVERSAL	1949
TC-209	PRELUDE TO FAME (UK)	MCDONNELL	UNIVERSAL	1950
TC-233	ENCORE (UK)	FRENCH, JACKSON	PARAMOUNT	1951
TC-223	HIGHLY DANGEROUS (UK)	BAKER	LIPPERT	1950
TCA	THOMAS CROWN AFFAIR	MCTIERNAN	MGM	1999
TCBB	TAKING CARE OF BUSINESS	HILLER	BUENA VISTA	1990
TCC	THEY CAME TO A CITY (UK)	DEARDEN	AFE	1944
TCF1	WE'RE GOING TO BE RICH (UK)	BANKS	20TH CENTURY FOX	1938
TCG	TERROR CREATURES FROM GRAVE	ZUCKER	PACEMAKER	1967
TCM	TEXAS CHAINSAW MASSACRE	HOOPER	BRYANSTON	1974
TCM2	TEXAS CHAINSAW MASSACRE 2	HOOPER	CANNON	1986
TCP-4	INSPECTOR HORNLEIGH (UK)	FORDE	20TH CENTURY FOX	1939
TD	BLOOD FIEND (UK: THEATRE OF DEATH)	GALLU	HEMISPHERE	1967
TD	DAMNED, THE	VISCONTI	WARNER BROS	1970
TD	DEERSLAYER	NEUMANN	20TH CENTURY FOX	1957
TD	DISH, THE	SITCH	WARNER BROS	2000
TD	DOCTORS, THE (FR: LES HOMMES EN BLANC 1955)	HABIB	KINGSLEY INTL	1956
TD	POLYESTER	WATERS	NEW LINE CINEMA	1981
TD	THAT'S DANCING	HALEY	MGM	1985
TD	THREE DESPERATE MEN	NEWFIELD	LIPPERT	1951
TD	TIDALWAVE (JAP: NIPPON CHINBOTSU 1973)	MORITANI	NEW WORLD	1975
TD	TILL DEATH US DO PART (UK)	COHEN	SHERPIX	1969
TD	TIME OF DESIRE, THE	HOLMSEN	JANUS	1954
TD	TONY DEVLIN	portrait	EDWARD SMALL	
TD	TURKISH DELIGHT (NETH: TURKS FRUIT 1973) (SENSUALIST)	VERHOEVEN	CINEMATION	1974
TDT	DEVIL'S TRADEMARK	MEEHAN	FBO	1928
TE	3 EVIL MASTERS (THE MASTER) (HK: BEI PAN SHE MEN)	CHIN-KU LU	WORLD NORTHAL	1980
TE	20,000 EYES	LEEWOOD	20TH CENTURY FOX	1961
TE	BEST OF ENEMIES (IT)	HAMILTON	COLUMBIA	1961
TE	ENTERTAINER (UK)	RICHARDSON	CONTINENTAL	1960
TE	IN TROUBLE WITH EVE	SEARLE	SEYMOUR BORDE ASSO	1964
TE	TANGLED EVIDENCE (UK)	COOPER	RKO	1934
TE	THIS ENGLAND (UK)	MACDONALD	WORLD	1941
TE	THUNDER IN THE EAST (UK: THE BATTLE)	FARKAS	UNITED ARTISTS	1935
TE	TOUGH ENOUGH	FLEISCHER	20TH CENTURY FOX	1982
TEX	LONE TEXAN	LANDRES	20TH CENTURY FOX	1959
TF	BACHELOR OF HEARTS (UK)	RILLA	CONTINENTAL	1958
TF	FAN, THE	BIANCHI	PARAMOUNT	1981
TF	FIXER	FRANKENHEIMER	MGM	1968
TF	FROG (UK)	RAYMOND	20TH CENTURY FOX	1937
TF	RACKET, THE	CROMWELL	RKO	1951
TF	TIME FLIES (UK)	FORDE	GFD	1944
TF	TONGFATHER	TIEN	SINO-AMERICAN	1974
TFL	TALENT FOR LOVING (UK)	QUINE	PARAMOUNT	1969
TFL	TARZAN'S FIGHT FOR LIVE	HUMBERSTONE	MGM	1958
TFT	EDGE OF THE CITY	RITT	MGM	1957
TFW	TALE OF FIVE WOMEN (UK: TALE OF FIVE CITIES)	TULLY	UNITED ARTISTS	1951
TG	GETAWAY, THE	PECKINPAH	NATIONAL GENERAL	1972
TG	GUEST (UK: CARETAKER)	DONNER	JANUS	1963
TG	LAST GRENADE (UK)	FLEMYNG	CINERAMA	1970
TG	MAGIC WORLD OF TOPO GIGIO (IT: AVVENTURE DI TOPO GIGIO 1961)	CALDURA, DE RICO	COLUMBIA	1965
TG	THANK GOD IT'S FRIDAY	KLANE	COLUMBIA	1978
TG	TIME GOES BY	BLASETTI	I. F. E. RELEASING	1953
TG	TOUCH AND GO	MANDEL	TRI STAR	1986
TG	TRAITOR'S GATE (UK)	FRANCIS	COLUMBIA	1964
TG	TWO ARE GUILTY (FR: LE GLAIVE ET LA BALANCE 1963)	CAYATTE	MGM	1964
TGD	THROUGH A GLASS DARKLY (SWE: SASOM I EN SPEGEL)	BERGMAN	JANUS	1961
TGDD	TOUGH GUYS DON'T DANCE	MAILER	CANNON	1987

TGG	BATTLE HELL (UK: YANGTSE INCIDENT)	ANDERSON	DCA	1957
TGH	GRASSHOPPER, THE	PARIS	NATIONAL GENERAL	1970
TGIK	NAME OF THE GAME IS KILL	HELLSTROM	FANFARE	1968
TGM	GREEN MILE, THE	DARABONT	WARNER BROS	1999
TGR	TARZAN AND THE GREAT RIVER	DAY	PARAMOUNT	1967
TGT	GLASS TOMB (UK: GLASS CAGE)	TULLY	LIPPERT	1955
TH	HERO (UK: BLOOMFIELD 1971)	HARRIS	AVCO EMBASSY	1972
TH	HILL (UK)	LUMET	MGM	1965
TH	HOSTAGE (UK)	HUTH	EROS	1956
TH	HOTTENTOT, THE	RUTH	WARNER BROS	1929
TH	HUNTER, THE	KULIK	PARAMOUNT	1980
TH	I'LL GET YOU (UK: ESCAPE ROUTE)	FRIEDMAN, SCOTT	LIPPERT	1952
TH	TASTE OF HONEY (UK)	RICHARDSON	CONTINENTAL	1961
TH	TEMPTATION HARBOR (UK: TEMPTATION HARBOUR)	COMFORT	MONOGRAM	1947
TH	THELMA AND LOUISE *(1990 copyright)*	SCOTT	MGM	1990
TH	THIEF OF HEARTS	STEWART	PARAMOUNT	1984
TH	THIEVES	BERRY	PARAMOUNT	1976
TH	TREASURE HUNT (UK)	CARSTAIRS	CARDINAL	1952
TH	TWILIGHT HOUR (UK)	STEIN	ANGLO-AMERICAN	1945
THE MEDIUM	MEDIUM	MENOTTI	LOPPERT	1951
THH	HANOI HILTON	CHETWYND	CANNON	1987
THN	THINGS HAPPEN AT NIGHT (UK)	SEARLE	RENOWN	1948
THUNDERBOLT	THUNDERBOLT	STURGES	MONOGRAM	1947
TI	TEN LITTLE INDIANS (UK)	COLLINSON	AVCO EMBASSY	1974
TI	TOWERING INFERNO, THE	GUILLERMIN	20TH CENTURY FOX	1974
TI	VISCOUNT (FR: LE VICOMTE REGLE SES COMPTES)	CLOCHE	WARNER BROS	
TI21	INDIAN IN THE CUPBOARD, THE	OZ	PARAMOUNT	1995
TI55	SÉANCE ON A WET AFTERNOON (UK)	FORBES	ARTIXO PRODUCTIONS	1964
TIBB	REMEMBER THE TITANS - *mistake?*	YAKIN	BUENA VISTA	2000
TIBB	TRUE IDENTITY	LANE	BUENA VISTA	1991
TIC	INDIAN IN THE CUPBOARD, THE	OZ	PARAMOUNT	1995
TICO	TIKO AND THE SHARK	QUILICI	MGM	1962
TIGG	TIGGER MOVIE (t)	FALKENSTEIN	BUENA VISTA	2000
TIML	THIS IS MY LIFE	EPHRON	20th CENTURY FOX	1992
TISS	SÉANCE ON A WET AFTERNOON (UK)	FORBES	ARTIXO PRODUCTIONS	1964
TJ	TERROR IN THE JUNGLE	DESIMONE	CROWN INT'L	1968
TJ	TWO JAKES	NICHOLSON	PARAMOUNT	1990
TJ-R	THUNDERING JETS	DANTINE	20TH CENTURY FOX	1958
TJS	JAZZ SINGER, THE	FLEISCHER	ASSOCIATED FILM	1980
TK	KEEP	MANN	PARAMOUNT	1983
TK	KISS	DENSHAM	TRI STAR	1988
TK	SACRED KNIVES OF VENGEANCE (HK: DA SHA SHOU)	CHOR	WARNER BROS	1972
TK	TIME TO KILL, A	SCHUMACHER	WARNER BROS	1996
TK	TRIBUTE	CLARK	20TH CENTURY FOX	1980
TK	TWO OF A KIND	HERZFELD	20TH	1983
TKCFA	TEN KILLERS COME FROM AFAR	BOSCH	PEPPERCORN WORMSER	1974
TKCFA	THREE KINGS	RUSSELL	WARNER BROS	1999
TKG	THAT KIND OF GIRL (UK)	O'HARA	TOPAZ	1963
TKH	THREE KINDS OF HEAT	STEVENS	CANNON	1987
TL	LAW IS THE LAW, THE (FR: LA LEGGE E LEGGE)	JAQUE	CONTINENTAL DIST	1958
TL	LAW, THE (FR: WHERE THE HOT WIND BLOWS 1959)	DASSIN	MGM	1960
TL	LAWYER, THE	FURIE	PARAMOUNT	1970
TL	TEN LITTLE INDIANS (UK)	POLLOCK	SEVEN ARTS	1965
TL	THANK YOU ALL VERY MUCH (UK: TOUCH OF LOVE)	HUSSEIN	COLUMBIA	1969
TL	THELMA AND LOUISE *(1991 copyright)*	SCOTT	MGM	1991
TL	THELMA LEEDS	portrait	RKO	
TL	THUNDER AND LIGHTNING	ALLEN	20TH CENTURY FOX	1977
TL	TILT	DURAND	WARNER BROS	1979
TL	TIME LOCK (UK)	THOMAS	DCA	1957
TL	TIME LOST AND TIME REMEMBERED (UK: I WAS HAPPY HERE)	DAVIS	CONTINENTAL	1966
TL	TINA LOUISE	portrait		
TL	TO BE A LADY (UK)	KING	PARAMOUNT BRITISH	1934
TL	TRUE LIES	CAMERON	20th CENTURY FOX	1994
TL	WHERE THE HOT WIND BLOWS (FR/IT: LA LEGGE)	DASSIN	MGM	1960
TL-12	TARZAN AND THE LOST SAFARI (UK)	HUMBERSTONE	MGM	1957
TLB	TO LOVE AND TO BE LOVED		SONNEY AMUSEMENT	1960

TLB	TWO LITTLE BEARS	HOOD	20th CENTURY FOX	1961
TLBB	THREE MEN AND A LITTLE LADY	ARDOLINO	BUENA VISTA	1990
TLG	TWILIGHT'S LAST GLEAMING	ALDRICH	LORIMAR	1977
TLH	TOO LATE THE HERO	ALDRICH	ABC PICTURES	1970
TLM	THE LADIES MAN	HUDLIN	PARAMOUNT	2000
TLOD	TWO LIVING, ONE DEAD (UK)	ASQUITH	BRITISH LION	1961
TLOP	LORD OF THE RINGS	BAKSHI	UNITED ARTISTS	1978
TLP	TO LIVE IN PEACE (IT: VIVERE IN PACE)	ZAMPA	TIMES	1947
TLW	LAST WINTER	NISSIMOFF	TRI STAR	1984
TM	MAGICIAN (SWE: ANSIKTET)	BERGMAN	JANIS	1958
TM	MAN, THE	SARGENT	PARAMOUNT	1972
TM	MARK (UK)	GREEN	CONTINENTAL	1961
TM	MAYOR OF 44TH STREET	GREEN	RKO	1942
TM	MIRROR HAS TWO FACES (FR: LE MIRIOR A DEUX FACES 1958)	CAYATTE	CONTINENTAL DIST	1959
TM	PROFFESSIONAL GUN (IT: THE MERCENARY 1968)	CORBUCCI	UNITED ARTISTS	1970
TM	SHOW GOES ON (UK: THREE MAXIMS)	WILCOX	GAUMONT BRIT. AMER.	1936
TM	TARGET FOR MURDER		ELLIS FILMS	
TM	TARZAN THE MAGNIFICENT (UK)	DAY	PARAMOUNT	1960
TM	TERROR IS A MAN	DE LEON	VALIANT FILMS	1959
TM	TERRY MOORE	portrait	RKO	
TM	THIS TIME I'LL MAKE YOU RICH (IT)	PAROLINI	AVCO EMBASSY	1974
TM	THREE MUSKETEERS	LESTER	20TH CENTURY FOX	1974
TM	THROW MAMA FROM THE TRAIN	DEVITO	ORION	1987
TM	TIM MCCOY	portrait		
TM2	TEENAGE MUTANT NINJA TURTLES 2	PRESSMAN	20th CENTURY FOX	1991
TM-K	THIS TIME I'LL MAKE YOU RICH (IT/GER: QUESTA VOLTA RICCO)	KRAMER (PAROLINI)	AVCO EMBASSY	1975
TMP	THREE MUSKETEERS	LESTER	20TH CENTURY FOX	1974
TMS	MOD SQUAD, THE	SILVER	MGM	1999
TMT	TOMORROW IS MY TURN (FR: LE PASSAGE DU RHIN 1960)	CAYATTE	SHOWCORPORATION	1962
TMT	TOO MANY THIEVES	BIBERMAN	MGM	1968
TN	BUTLER'S DILEMMA (UK)	HISCOTT	ANGLO-AMERICAN	1943
TN	NANNY (UK)	HOLT	20TH CENTURY FOX	1965
TN	TWISTED NERVE (UK 1968)	BOULTING	NATIONAL GENERAL	1969
TO	3 DESPERATE MEN	NEWFIELD	LIPPERT	1950
TO	DEADFALL (UK)	WATT	UNIVERSAL	1946
TO	TOO OUTRAGEOUS!	BENNER	SPECTRAFILM	1987
TO	TOUCHABLES (UK)	FREEMAN	20TH CENTURY FOX	1968
TOB	THIEF OF BAGDAD (IT)	LUBIN	MGM	1961
TOE	TERMS OF ENDEARMENT	BROOKS	PARAMOUNT	1983
TOF	ONION FIELD, THE	BECKER	AVCO EMBASSY	1979
TOS	THUNDER OVER SANGOLAND	NEWFIELD	LIPPERT	1955
TP	PACKAGE, THE	DAVIS	ORION	1989
TP	PASSENGER	ANTONIONI	MGM	1975
TP	PHOTOGRAPHER, THE	HILLMAN	AVCO EMBASSY	1974
TP	PRESS FOR TIME (UK)	ASHER	RANK	1966
TP	PRINCIPAL, THE	CAIN	TRI STAR	1987
TP	PSYCHOPATH (UK)	FRANCIS	PARAMOUNT	1966
TP	TEENAGE PLAYMATES (GER)	HOFBAUER	HEMISPHERE	1974
TP	THOSE PEOPLE NEXT DOOR (UK)	HARLOW	EROS	1953
TP	THUNDER IN THE PINES	GORDON	LIPPERT	1948
TP	THUNDER PASS	MCDONALD	LIPPERT	1954
TP	TIDES OF PASSION (FR: LA FOIRE AUX FEMMES 1956)	STELLI	JANUS	1959
TP	TURNING POINT	ROSS	20th CENTURY FOX	1977
TP-7	OUTLAW ROUNDUP	FRASER	PRODUCERS RELEASING	1944
TPR	BIG DEADLY GAME (UK: THIRD PARTY RISK)	BIRT	LIPPERT	1954
TPR	FORCE OF EVIL	POLONSKY	MGM	1948
TPR	TILLIE'S PUNCTURED ROMANCE	SUTHERLAND	PARAMOUNT	1928
TPROC	THE PURPLE ROSE OF CAIRO	ALLEN	ORION	1985
TQM	20 QUESTIONS MURDER MYSTERY (UK)	STEIN	GRAND NATIONAL	1950
TR	RACKET, THE	CROMWELL	RKO	1951
TR	REPTILE (UK)	GILLING	20TH CENTURY FOX	1966
TR	THEATRE ROYAL (UK)	BAXTER	ANGLO-AMERICAN	1943
TR	THELMA RITTER	portrait	FOX	
TR	THUNDER ROCK (UK)	BOULTING	ENGLISH	1942
TR	THUNDER RUN	HUDSON	CANNON	1986
TR	TONY RANDALL	portrait	UNIV	

TR	TRAITORS (UK)	TRONSON	UNIVERSAL	1962
TR-2	WHERE THE BUFFALO ROAM	HERMAN	MONOGRAM	1938
TR-108	GAMBLING DAUGHTERS	NOSSECK	PRODUCERS RELEASING	1941
TR-113	BLONDE COMET	BEAUDINE	PRODUCERS RELEASING	1941
TRA	TRAMPLERS (IT/FR: GLI UOMINI DAL PASSO PESANTE 1965)	BAND	EMBASSY	1966
TRB	T. R. BASKIN	ROSS	PARAMOUNT	1971
TRBB	RECRUIT	DONALDSON	BUENA VISTA	2003
TRH	TOM THUMB AND LITTLE RED RIDING HOOD (MEX)	RODRIGUEZ	K. GORDON MURRAY	1962
TRI-122	GOOD-TIME GIRL (UK)	MACDONALD	EAGLE-LION	1948
TRI-154	ONCE UPON A DREAM (UK)	THOMAS	EAGLE-LION	1949
TRI-198	DON'T EVER LEAVE ME (UK)	CRABTREE	TRITON-GFD	1949
TRL	TRAIL OF THE PINK PANTHER	EDWARDS	UNITED ARTISTS	1982
TS	ASSASSIN, THE (POINT OF NO RETURN)	BADHAM	WARNER BROS	1993
TS	BABYSITTER, THE	HENDERSON	CROWN INT'L	19969
TS	POCATELLO KID	ROSEN	ALBERT DEZEL	1931
TS	SEDUCTION	SCHMOELLER	AVCO EMBASSY	1982
TS	SHADOW (UK)	COOPER	GLOBE	1933
TS	SIEGE, THE	ZWICK	20TH CENTURY FOX	1998
TS	SILENCE (SWE: TYSTNADEN)	BERGMAN	JANUS	1963
TS	SOLDIER, THE	GLICKENHAUS	EMBASSY	1982
TS	SORCERER, THE	FREIDKIN	FILM PROPERTIES	1977
TS	SPECIALIST	LLOSA	WARNER BROS	1994
TS	STEPDAUGHTER, THE (WINTER LOVE)	WALL	FALCON FILM	1973
TS	STRANGERS IN THE CITY	CARRIER	EMBASSY	1962
TS	SVENGALI (UK)	LANGLEY	MGM	1954
TS	TAMARIND SEED	EDWARDS	AVCO EMBASSY	1974
TS	TENDER SCOUNDREL (FR: TENDRE VOYOU 1966)	BECKER	EMBASSY	1967
TS	TEQUILA SUNRISE	TOWNE	WARNER BROS	1988
TS	TERROR SHIP (UK: DANGEROUS VOYAGE)	SEWELL	LIPPERT	1954
TS	THIRD SEX, THE (GER: ANDERS ICH) (BEWILDERED YOUTH)	HARLAN	FFF FILMS	1957
TS	THREE SISTERS	OLIVIER	AMERICAN FILM THE.	1974
TS	THRILL SEEKERS (YELLOW TEDDY BEARS)	HARTFORD-DAVIS	TOPAZ FILMS	1964
TS	TOMMY SANDS	portrait	FOX	
TS	TOP SECRET	ABRAHAMS, ZUCKER	PARAMOUNT	1984
TS	TORSO MURDER MYSTERY (UK: TRAITOR SPY)	SUMMERS	ARTHUR ZIEHM	1939
TS	TRAIN TO TOMBSTONE	BERKE	LIPPERT	1950
TS	TRIO (UK)	ANNAKIN, FRENCH	PARAMOUNT	1950
TS	TRUE STORIES	BYRNE	WARNER BROS	1986
TS2	DUKE WORE JEANS (UK)	THOMAS	ALLIED ARTISTS	1958
TS-15	PEACOCK ALLEY	DE SANO	TIFFANY	1930
TS-17	TOILERS	BARKER	TIFFANY	1928
TS-19	MARRIAGE BY CONTRACT	FLOOD	TIFFANY	1928
TS-26	PROWLERS OF THE SEA	ADOLFI	TIFFANY	1928
TS-28	GRAIN OF DUST	ARCHAINBAUD	TIFFANY	1928
TS-32	LUCKY BOY	TAUROG, WILSON	TIFFANY	1928
TS-34	MEDICINE MAN	PEMBROKE	TIFFANY	1930
TS-44	MIDSTREAM	FLOOD	TIFFANY	1929
TS-47	PAINTED FACES	ROGELL	TIFFANY	1929
TS-49	MOLLY AND ME	RAY	TIFFANY	1929
TS-54	LOST ZEPPELIN	SLOMAN	TIFFANY	1929
TS-64	SUNDOWN RIDERS	HILLYER	ASTOR	1948
TS-75	HIGH TREASON	ELVEY	TIFFANY	1929
TS-82	UTAH KID	THORPE	TIFFANY	1930
TS-89	BORDER ROMANCE	THORPE	TIFFANY	1929
TS-93	HOT CURVES	TAUROG	TIFFANY	1930
TSBB	UNDER THE TUSCAN SUN	WELLS	BUENA VISTA	2003
TSC	SWORD AND THE CROSS (IT: LE SCHIAVE DI CARTAGINE 1956)	BRIGNONE	VALIANT FILMS	1960
TSD	SHE GOT WHAT SHE WANTED	CRUZE	TIFFANY	1930
TSD	THREE STEPS IN THE DARK (UK)	BIRT	PATHE	1953
TSE	THEODORA, SLAVE EMRESS	FREDA	I. F. E. RELEASING	1954
TSH	THEY SHOOT HORSES, DON'T THEY?	POLLACK	CINERAMA RELEASING	1969
TSN	DEAD BY MORNING (UK: MISS TULIP STAYS THE NIGHT)	ARLISS	ADELPHI	1955
TSS	TREAD SOFTLY STRANGER (UK)	PARRY	ATLANTIC	1958
TST	TOO SHY TO TRY (FR: I'M SHY BUT I'LL HEAL)	RICHARD	QUARTET FILMS	1978
TSV	HIDEOUT (UK: SMALL VOICE)	MCDONELL	SNADER	1948
TSX-1	WOMAN TO WOMAN	SAVILLE	TIFFANY-STAHL	1929

TT	AFRICA IN FLAMES (UK: STAMPEDE)	HINDS	BRITISH INT'L	1930
TT	ALIAS JOHN PRESTON (UK)	MACDONALD	AAP	1955
TT	CRAZY FOR LOVE	NORMAND	ELLIS FILM	1960
TT	DEADLY HERO	NAGY	AVCO EMBASSY	1976
TT	GASBAGS (UK)	FORDE, VARNEL	GFD	1941
TT	GREAT ST. TRINIAN'S TRAIN ROBBERY (UK)	GILLIAT, LAUNDER	GARY DARTNELL	1966
TT	SONS OF THUNDER (IT)	TESSARI	UNITED ARTISTS	1963
TT	TALL TEXAN	WILLIAMS	LIPPERT	1953
TT	TERROR TRAIN	SPOTTISWOODE	20TH CENTURY FOX	1980
TT	THAT THING YOU DO	HANKS	20th CENTURY FOX	1996
TT	THUMB TRIPPING	LEVINE	AVCO EMBASSY	1970
TT	TOMBSTONE TERROR	BRADBURY	STEINER (states rights)	1935
TT	TOWER OF TERROR (UK)	HUNTINGTON	MONOGRAM	1941
TT	TRAP (UK)	HAYERS	CONTINENTAL	1966
TT	TROJAN BROTHERS (UK)	ROGERS	ANGLO-AMERICAN	1946
TTG	THREE TOUGH GUYS	TESSARI	PARAMOUNT	1973
TTH	TELL-TALE HEART (UK)	MORRIS	DANBRIGADIER	1960
TTJ	TAKE THIS JOB AND SHOVE IT	TRIKONIS	AVCO EMBASSY	1981
TTL	THIRD TIME LUCKY (UK)	FORDE	WOOLF & FREEDMAN	1931
TTRL	THIN RED LINE	MALICK	20TH CENTURY FOX	1998
TTT	FOR THEM THAT TRESPASS (UK)	CAVALCANTI	ASSSTRATFORD	1949
TU	TUCKER: THE MAN AND HIS DREAM	COPPOLA	PARAMOUNT	1988
TU	TWO OF US, THE (FR: LE VIEIL HOMME ET L'ENFANT 1967)	BERRI	CINEMA 5	1968
TUL	TULIPS	BROMFIELD	AVCO EMBASSY	1981
TUN	GHOST GOES WEST (UK)	CLAIR	UNITED ARTISTS	1935
TUV	AND NOW MY LOVE	LELOUCH	AVCO EMBASSY	1974
TV	10TH VICTIM, THE	LEVINE	EMBASSY	1965
TV	MAN AND THE MOON	KIMBALL	DISNEY - TV	1955
TV	MAN IN SPACE	KIM	BUENA VISTA	1956
TV	SWAMP FOX (series)	VARIOUS	DISNEY - TV	1959-61
TV	VIOLATORS, THE	FLEISCHER	UNITED ARTISTS	1958
TVBB	TERMINAL VELOCITY	SARAFIAN	BUENA VISTA	1994
TVM	THANK YOU VERY MUCH	HUSSEIN	COLUMBIA	1969
TW	29TH STREET	GALLO	20th CENTURY FOX	1991
TW	TEEN WITCH	WALKER	TRANS WORLD ENT.	1989
TW	THREE WOMEN	ALTMAN	20TH CENTURY FOX	1977
TW	TWO THOUSAND WOMEN (UK)	LAUNDER	ELLIS	1944
TW	TWO WOMEN (IT: LA CIOCIARA 1960)	DE SICA	MGM	1961
TW	WALK A TIGHTROPE (UK)	NESBITT	PARAMOUNT	1965
TW	WORLD IS NOT ENOUGH	APTED	MGM	1999
TWBB	13TH WARRIOR	MCTIERNAN	BUENA VISTA	1999
TWGM	ADVENTURES OF WILL BILL HICKOK (tv series)	VARIOUS		1951-58
TWM	TALES THAT WITNESS MADNESS	FRANCIS	PARAMOUNT	1973
TWM	WISHING MACHINE, THE (CZ: AUTOMAT NA PRANI 1968)	PINKAVA	PARAMOUNT	1974
TWO	CITY AFTER MIDNIGHT (UK: THAT WOMAN OPPOSITE)	BENNETT	RKO	1957
TWP	TOWN WITHOUT PITY	TULLY	RKO	1956
TWS	THEY WERE SISTERS (UK)	CRABTREE	UNIVERSAL	1945
TWS	THREE WEIRD SISTERS (UK)	BIRT	PATHE	1948
TWT	THAT WAS THEN ... THIS IS NOW	CAIN	PARAMOUNT	1985
TX-2	JOURNEY'S END (UK)	WHALE	TIFFANY	1930
TY	THEY WERE SO YOUNG	NEUMANN	LIPPERT	1953
TY T	TYPHOON TREASURE (AUS)	MONKMAN	UNITED ARTISTS	1938
TYOF	THIRTY YEARS OF FUN	YOUNGSON	20th CENTURY FOX	1963
U	UNDERNEATH	SODERBERGH	GRAMERCY	1995
U	UNFORGETTABLE	DAHL	MGM	1996
U	UNTIL THE END OF THE WORLD (GER/FR: BIS...DER WELT)	WINDERS	WARNER BROS	1991
UA-12	I STAND CONDEMNED (UK: MOSCOW NIGHTS)	ASQUITH	UNITED ARTISTS	1935
UA-18	FOREVER YOURS (UK: FORGET ME NOT)	KORDA	GRAND NATIONAL	1936
UBW	A MAN, A WOMAN AND A BANK	BLACK	EMBASSY	1979
UC	UNDER COVER	STOCKWELL	CANNON	1987
UC	UNDERGROUND GUERRILLAS (UK: UNDERCOVER)	NOLBANDOV	COLUMBIA	1943
UC	URBAN COWBOY	BRIDGES	PARAMOUNT	1980
UCA	ANDALUSIAN DOG (FR: UN CHIEN ANDALOU) (sh)	BUNUEL		1929
UCBB	UP CLOSE AND PERSONAL	AVNET	BUENA VISTA	1996
UE	UNLAWFUL ENTRY	KAPLAN	20th CENTURY FOX	1992
UF	UNDER FIRE	SPOTTISWOODE	ORION	1983

UF	UNFORGIVEN	EASTWOOD	WARNER BROS	1992
UF	UNHOLY FOUR (UK: STRANGER CAME HOME)	FISHER	LIPPERT	1954
UFC	UP FOR THE CUP (UK)	RAYMOND	ASSO. BRITISH-PATHE	1950
UG	UNCERTAIN GLORY	WALSH	WARNER BROS	1944
UHF	UHF	LEVEY	ORION	
UHF	UPPER HAND, THE (FR)	LA PATELLIERE	PARAMOUNT	1967
UI	INFORMERS (UK) (US: UNDERWORLD INFORMERS)	ANNAKIN	CONTINENTAL	1963
UIS	UP IN SMOKE	ADLER	PARAMOUNT	1978
UK	UP THE JUNCTION (UK)	COLLINSON	PARAMOUNT	1968
UN	UNA MERKEL	portrait		
UN	UNEARTHLY	PETROFF	AB-PT	1957
UNBB	UNBREAKABLE	SHYAMALAN	BUENA VISTA	2000
UP	NINE MEN (UK)	WATT	UNITED ARTISTS	1943
UP	USED PEOPLE	KIDRON	20TH CENTURY FOX	1992
UPS	UNDER PARIS SKIES (SOUS LE CIL DE PARIS)	DUVIVIER	DISCINA INT'L	1952
UPT	UPTOWN SATURDAY NIGHT	POITIER	WARNER BROS	1974
US	I, MONSTER (UK 1971)	WEEKS	CANNON	1973
US	U. S. MARSHALS	BAIRD	WARNER BROS	1998
US	UNDER SEIGE	DAVIS	WARNER BROS	1992
US	UNFINISHED SYMPHONY (UK)	ASQUITH, FORST	GAUMONT BRITISH	1934
US	UNTIL SEPTEMBER	MARQUAND	UNITED ARTISTS	1984
US	USUAL SUSPECTS	SINGER	GRAMERCY	1995
US2	UNDER SEIGE 2: DARK TERRITORY	MURPHY	WARNER BROS	1995
UTC	UP THE CREEK (UK)	GUEST	DOMINANT	1958
UT/PS	UNEASY TERMS (UK)	SEWELL	PATHE	1948
UV	UNCLE VANYA (UK)	BURGE	ARTHUR CANTOR	1963
UW	UNDERWATER WARRIOR	MARTON	MGM	1958
UW	UNMARRIED WOMAN	MAZURSKY	20TH CENTURY FOX	1978
UY	UNFAITHFULLY YOURS	ZIEFF	20TH CENTURY FOX	1984
UYA	UP YOUR ALLEY	LIEBERMAN	GROUP I FILMS	1972
V	DANGEROUS BEAUTY	HERSKOVITZ		
V	NOTHING BUT TROUBLE	AKYROYD	WARNER BROS	1991
V	OUR VIRGIN ISLAND (UK: VIRGIN ISLAND)	JACKSON	FILMS AROUND WORLD	1959
V	SINCE YOU WENT AWAY	CROMWELL	UNITED ARTISTS	1944
V	SON OF THE SHEIK	FITZMAURICE	UNITED ARTISTS	1926
V	VANISHING, THE	SLUIZER	20TH CENTURY FOX	1993
V	VENOM	HAGGARD	PARAMOUNT	1981
V	VERDICT, THE	LUMET	20TH CENTURY FOX	1982
V	VICTORY (ESCAPE TO VICTORY)	HUSTON	PARAMOUNT	1981
V	VIRILITY (IT: VIRILITA)	CAVARA	COLISEUM	1974
V	VOLUNTEERS	MEYER	TRI STAR	1985
V1	MISSILES FROM HELL (UK: BATTLE OF THE V1)	SEWELL	EROS	1958
V2	LEFT RIGHT AND CENTRE (UK)	GILLIAT	BCG	1959
V-3	SON OF THE SHEIK	FITZMAURICE	UNITED ARTISTS	1926
V32	SON OF THE SHEIK	FITZMAURICE	UNITED ARTISTS	1926
V-1253	ALLISON HAYES	portrait	UNIVERSAL	Spanish
VAM	VAMPIRE'S COFFIN (MEX: ATAUD DEL VAMPIRO 1957)	MENDEZ	YOUNG AMERICA PROD.	1964
VB	FAST LADY (UK)	ANNAKIN	CONTINENTAL	1962
VB	VIRGINIA BRUCE	portrait	REP	
VBW	MAN A WOMAN AND A BANK, A (A VERY BIG WITHDRAWAL)	BLACK	AVCO EMBASSY	1979
VCH	MATTER OF RESISTANCE (FR: LA VIE DE CHATEAU)	RAPPENEAU	ROYAL	1966
V-CH	VIVA CHIHUAHUA	SOLARES	PEL MEX	1961
VD	GUNS DON'T ARGUE	KAHN	VISUAL DRAMA	1957
VE	VERY EDGE (UK)	FRANKEL	BRITISH LION	1963
VE	VICTORY AT ENTEBBE (tv movie)	CHOMSKY	WARNER BROS	1976
VER	VERDICT (FR/IT) (JURY OF ONE)	CAYATTE	WARNER BROS	1975
VF	VALERIE FRENCH		COL	
VF	VENUS IN FURS (UK: PAROXISMUS)	FRANCO	AIP	1970
VF	VICTOR FRANCEN	portrait		
VF-3	PURE HELL OF ST. TRINIAN'S (UK)	LAUNDER	CONTINENTAL	1960
VFM	VENGEANCE OF FU MANCHU (UK)	SUMMERS	WARNER BROS.	1967
VG	VILLAGE OF THE GIANTS	GORDON	EMBASSY	1965
VG	VIRGIN AND THE GYPSY (UK)	MILES	CHEVRON	1970
VGBB	VERONICA GUERIN	SCHUMACHER	BUENA VISTA	2003
VH	VAN HEFLIN	portrait	RKO, UNIV	
VH	VINCENT & THEO	ALTMAN	HEMDALE	1990

VHR	VERA RALSTON	portrait	REP	
VIK	STORY OF VICKIE	MARISCHKA	BUENA VISTA	1958
VK	FEARLESS VAMPIRE KILLERS	POLANSKI	MGM	1967
VK	VIEW TO A KILL, A	GLEN	MGM/UA	1985
VKC	VIOLET KEMBLE COOPER	portrait	RKO	
VL	VARIETY LIGHTS (IT: LUCI DEL VARIETA)	FELLINI, LATTUADA	PATHE CONTEMPORARY	1950
VL	VIRGINIA LEITH	portrait	US	
VM	VICTOR MATURE	portrait	RKO	
VM-10	MURDER WILL OUT (UK: VOICE OF MERRILL)	GILLING	KRAMER-HYAMS	1952
VMN	VIRGEN DE MEDIA NOCHE	GALINDO	MUNDIAL	1942
VN	HORROR CASTLE (IT: VERGINE DE NORIMBERGA 1963)	DAWSON (MARGHERITI)	ZODIAC	1964
VN	MAN FROM U.N.C.L.E.	ROLFE	NATIONAL BROADCAST.	1964
VNB	VAN NUYS BLVD.	SACHS	CROWN INT'L	1979
VOB	VICAR OF BRAY (UK)	EDWARDS	ABFD	1937
VOF	TRIUMPH OF SHERLOCK HOLMES (UK)	HISCOTT	OLYMPIC	1935
VOL	VOLCANO	JACKSON	20TH CENTURY FOX	1997
VOP	VARIETIES ON PARADE	ORMOND	LIPPERT	1951
VP	LI'L ABNER	ROGELL	RKO	1940
VP	MAIDEN FOR THE PRINCE (IT)	CAMPANILE	COLUMBIA	1966
VP	VANISHING PRAIRIE	ALGAR	BUENA VISTA	1954
VP	VICTIMAS DEL PICADO	EERNANDEZ	PELICULAS MEX.	1951
VP	VINCENT PRICE	portrait	UNIVERSAL	
VP	VIOLENT PROFESSIONALS	MARTINO	SCOTIA AMERICAN	1974
VP1	LET'S GET MARRIED (UK)	SCOTT	EROS	1960
VQ	VIKING QUEEN (UK)	CHAFFEY	20TH CENTURY FOX	1967
VS	SUICIDE LEGION (UK: SUNSET IN VIENNA)	WALKER	FILM ALLIANCE	1940
VS	VENGEANCE OF SHE (UK)	OWEN	20TH CENTURY FOX	1968
VS	VICE SQUAD	SHERMAN	AVCO EMBASSY	1982
VS	VIRGIN SPRING	BERGMAN	JANUS	1960
VS	VITAL SIGNS	SILVER	20th CENTURY FOX	1990
VT	MAYA	BERRY	MGM	1966
VUK	INTERVIEW WITH THE VAMPIRE	JORDAN	GEPPEN	1994
VUL	VULTURE (UK)	HUNTINGTON	PARAMOUNT	1966
VV	ANITA LOUISE	portrait	WARNER BROS	1930s
VV	VANINA VANINI	ROSSELLINI	COLUMBIA	1961
VV	VEGAS VACATION	KESSLER	WARNER BROS	1997
VV	VICE AND VIRTUE (FR: LE VICE ET LA VERTU 1963)	VADIM	MGM	1965
VVK	FEARLESS VAMPIRE KILLERS (UK: DANCE OF THE VAMPIRES)	POLANSKI	MGM	1967
VW	VIOLENT WOMEN	MAHON	EXPLOIT FILMS	1959
VWSS	VIKING WOMAN AND THE SEA SERPENT	CORMAN	AIP	1957
VX5	BESSIE LOVE	portrait	VITAGRAPH	
W	FIGHTING MUSTANG	DRAKE	ASTOR	1948
W	MYSTERY AT THE BURLESQUE (UK: MURDER AT THE WINDMILL)	GUEST	MONOGRAM	1949
W	SEX IS A WOMAN(UK: DEATH IS WOMAN 1966)(LOVE IS WOMAN)	GOODE	AIP	1967
W	WEAPON (UK)	GUEST	REPUBLIC	1956
W	WEDDING, A	ALTMAN	20TH CENTURY FOX	1978
W	WETHERBY	HARE	MGM	1985
W	WHAT THE BUTLER SAW (UK)	GRAYSON	EXCLUSIVE	1950
W	WILLOW	HOWARD	MGM	1988
W	WINDSPLITTER	FEIGELSON	FUTURAMA	1971
W	WIRED	PEERCE	TAURUS ENTERTAINMET	1989
W	WITNESS	WEIR	PARAMOUNT	1985
W	WOMAN	ROSSELLINI	CANTON-WEINER	1950
W-1	MARKSMAN	COLLINS	ALLIED ARTISTS	1953
W1	SEE HOW THEY RUN (UK)	ARLISS	BRITISH LION	1955
W1	SINGING OUTLAW	LEWIS	FILM CLASSICS	R48
W2	FREE WILLY 2: ADVENTURE HOME	LITTLE	WARNER BROS	1995
W6	OUTLAW EXPRESS	WAGGNER	FILM CLASSICS	R48
W11	WEST 11 (UK)	WINNER	SEVEN ARTS	1963
W15	DAWN RIDER	BRADBURY	WESTERN ADVENTURES	R47
W16	DAWN RIDER	BRADBURY	MONOGRAM	1935
W49-1	NO PLACE FOR JENNIFER (UK)	CASS	STRATFORD	1950
W49-2	LAST HOLIDAY (UK)	CASS	STRATFORD	1950
W49-3	CAIRO ROAD (UK)	MACDONALD	REALART	1950
W50-1	MURDER WITHOUT CRIME (UK)	THOMPSON	STRATFORD	1950
W50-2	FRANCHISE AFFAIR (UK)	HUNTINGTON	STRATFORD	1951

W50-3	TALK OF A MILLION (UK)	CARSTAIRS	STRATFORD	1951
W515	BLUEBEARD'S 10 HONEYMOONS (UK)	WILDER	ALLIED ARTISTS	1960
WA	AWAKENING, THE (IT: SUOR LETIZIA)	CAMERINI	KINGSLEY INT'L	1956
WA	BANANAS	ALLEN	UNITED ARTISTS	1971
WA	WILD AMERICA	DEAR	WARNER BROS	1997
WA	WOMEN AREN'T ANGELS (UK)	HUNTINGTON	PATHE	1943
WA	WONDERS OF ALADDIN (FR: LE MERAVIGLIE DI ALADINO)	BAVA	MGM	1961
WA	WRONG ARM OF THE LAW (UK)	OWEN	CONTINENTAL	1963
WABB	V. I. WARSHAWSKI	KANEW	BUENA VISTA	1991
WAL	WE ALL LOVED EACH OTHER SO MUCH (IT)	SCOLA	CINEMA 5	1974
WAL-24	COCK-EYED WORLD	WALSH	FOX FILM	1929
WAP-4	OUTLAW COUNTRY	TAYLOR	SCREEN GUILD	1948
WAP-6	SON OF A BADMAN	TAYLOR	SCREEN GUILD	1949
WAP-8	DALTONS' WOMEN	CARR	WESTERN ADVENTURES	1950
WAP-9	DALTONS' WOMEN	CARR	WESTERN ADVENTURES	1950
WB	WALTER BRENNAN	portrait	UNIV	
WB	WEEKEND AT BERNIE'S	KOTCHEFF	20th CENTURY FOX	1989
WB	WHERE THE RIVER RUNS BLACK	CAIN	MGM	1986
WB	WIDE BOY (UK)	HUGHES	REALART	1952
WB	WILD BILL	HILL	UNITED ARTISTS	1995
WB	WILD BOY (UK)	DE COURVILLE	GAUMONT BRITISH	1934
WB	WOMEN ON THE VERGE OF A BREAKDOWN	ALMOVODAR	ORION PICTURES	1988
WB-2	WORLD BY NIGHT NO. 2 (IT: IL MONDO DI NOTTE NUMERO 2)	PROIA	WARNER BROS	1961
WBA	WHERE THE BOYS ARE	AVERBACK	TRI STAR	1984
WBF-IV	MAN OF THE MOMENT (UK)	BANKS	WARNER BROS.	1935
WBH	ADVENTURES OF WILL BILL HICKOK (tv series)	VARIOUS		1951-58
WBP	WAR BETWEEN THE PLANETS	MARGHERITI	FANFARE FILM	1971
WC	CAUGHT	OPHULS	MGM	1949
WC	WAITING FOR CAROLINE	KELLY	LOPERT	1969
WC	WARE CASE (UK)	STEVENSON	20TH CENTURY FOX	1938
WC	WE WANT A CHILD (DEN: VI VIL HA' ET BARN)	LAURITZEN	LIPPERT	1949
WC	WHEATON CHAMBERS	portrait	RKO	
WC	WING COMMANDER	ROBERTS	20th CENTURY FOX	1998
WCB7	WOMEN IN CELL BLOCK 7	DISILVESTRO	AQUARIUS FILM	1973
WCK	WHEN COMEDY WAS KING	YOUNGSON	20th CENTURY FOX	1960
WD	DR. WHO AND THE DALEKS (UK)	FLEMYNG	CONTINENTAL	1966
WD	WALL OF DEATH (UK: THERE IS ANOTHER SUN)	GILBERT	REALART	1951
WD	WARM DECEMBER (UK)	POITIER	NATIONAL GENERAL	1973
WD	WATERSHIP DOWN	ROSEN	AVCO EMBASSY	1978
WD	WEB OF EVIDENCE (UK: BEYOND THIS PLACE)	CARDIFF	ALLIED ARTISTS	1959
WD	WHITE DOG	FULLER	PARAMOUNT	1981
WD	WICKED DIE SLOW	HENNIGAR	CANNON	1968
WD	WOLF DOG	NEWFIELD	LIPPERT	1958
WDIH	WHERE DOES IT HURT?	AMATEAU	CINERAMA RELEASING	1972
WE	GERT AND DAISY'S WEEKEND (UK)	ROGERS	BUTCHERS'	1942
WE	WAITING TO EXHALE	WHITAKER	20th CENTURY FOX	1995
WE	WEEK END	GODARD	GROVE PRESS	1968
WE	WEST 11 (UK)	WINNER	PATHE	1963
WE	WRESTLING ERNEST HEMINGWAY	HAINES	WARNER BROS	1993
WEH	WEEK END HUSBANDS	GRIFFITH	EQUITY PICTURES	1924
WEL	WEEKEND WITH LULU (UK)	CARSTAIRS	COLUMBIA	1961
WEL-1	GAME OF DANGER (UK: BANG! YOU'RE DEAD)	COMFORT	AAP	1954
WES-19	RAISING A RIOT (UK)	TOYE	CONTINENTAL	1955
WEV	WORM'S EYE VIEW (UK)	RAYMOND	ASSO. BRITISH-PATHE	1951
W-F	LADY IN THE IRON MASK	MURPHY	20th CENTURY FOX	1952
WF	MY WIFE'S FAMILY (UK)	MYCROFT	ABPC-PATHE	1941
WF	WHERE'S THAT FIRE? (UK)	VARNEL	20TH CENTURY FOX	1940
WFP7	KILLERS OF KILIMANJARO (UK)	THORPE	COLUMBIA	1959
WFTL	WAITING FOR THE LIGHT	MONGER	VISION INT'L	1990
WG	SAFECRACKER (UK)	MILLAND	MGM	1958
WG	SECRETS OF A WINDMILL GIRL (UK)	MILLER	COMPTON-CAMEO	1966
WG	WAR GAME (UK)	WATKINS	PATHE CONTEMPORARY	1965
WG	WILD GEESE	MCLAGLEN	ALLIED ARTISTS	1978
WGG	WHAT'S GOOD FOR THE GOOSE (UK)	GOLAN	NATIONAL SHOWMAN.	1969
WGI	INSPECTOR CALLS (UK)	HAMILTON	AAP	1954
WGI	SAFECRACKER (UK)	MILLAND	MGM	1958

WGL	WIFE OF GENERAL LING (UK)	VAJDA	GAUMONT BRIT. AMER.	1937
WH	WANDA HENDRIX	portrait	UNIVERSAL	
WH	WESTWARD HO THE WAGONS	BEAUDINE	BUENA VISTA	1957
WH	WHITE HELL OF PITZ PALU (GER: WEIBE HOLLE PIZ PALU 1929)	PABST	IFE RELEASING	1954
WH	WHITE HUNTER BLACK HEART	EASTWOOD	WARNER BROS	1990
WH	WOMAN HUNT	DEXTER	20TH CENTURY FOX	1962
WHC	WHO'S HARRY CRUMB?	FLAHERTY	TRI STAR	1989
WHO	MATTER OF WHO	CHAFFEY	MGM	1961
WI	AFFAIRS OF SUSAN	SEITER	PARAMOUNT	1945
WI	MARKSMAN	COLLINS	ALLIED ARTISTS	1953
WI	SINGING OUTLAW	LEWIS	FILM CLASSICS	R48
WI	WOMEN IN LOVE (UK)	RUSSELL	UNITED ARTISTS	1969
WIC	SIN OF NORA MORAN	GOLDSTONE	MAJESTIC	1934
WIGD	WEREWOLF IN A GIRL'S DOMITORY (IT: LYCANTHROPUS 1961)	HEUSCH (BENSON)	MGM	1963
WIH	WALK INTO HELL (AUS: WALK INTO PARADISE)	ROBINSON	PATRIC	1957
WII	WILLIAM COMES TO TOWN	GUEST	UNITED ARTISTS	1948
WIP	WORLD IN MY POCKET (GER: EINEM FREITAG UM HALB ZWOLF)	RAKOFF	MGM	1962
WITD	WHISPERS IN THE DARK	CROWE	PARAMOUNT	1992
WIW	WEDDING IN WHITE	FRUET	AVCO EMBASSY	1973
WJ	WANDERING JEW (UK)	ELVEY	OLYMPIC	1933
WJ	WHERE'S JACK? (UK)	CLAVELL	PARAMOUNT	1969
WK	SAVAGE WEEKEND	PAULSEN	CANNON	1979
WK	WAKE UP AND KILL (IT)	LIZZANI	CINEMATION	1966
WK	WILD FOR KICKS (UK: BEAT GIRL)	GREVILLE	TIMES	1960
WK	WINTER KILLS	RICHERT	AVCO EMBASSY	1979
WKP	WILLIE & PHIL	MAZURSKY	20TH CENTURY FOX	1980
WL	WALTER LANTZ	portrait	UNIV	
WL	WHITE LIGHTNING	SARGENT	UNITED ARTISTS	1973
WL	WICKED LADY	WINNER	COLUMBIA	1983
WL	WICKED LADY (UK)	ARLISS	UNIVERSAL	1945
WL	WILLARD LEWIS	portrait	WARNER BROS	
WL	WILLIAM LUNDIGAN	portrait	UNIV	
WL	WIND AND THE LION	MILIUS	MGM	1975
WL	WINNIE LIGHTNER	portrait		
WL	WINTER LIGHT (SWE: NATTVARDSGASTERNA)	BERGMAN	JANUS	1963
WLA	WICKED LADY (UK)	ARLISS	UNIVERSAL	1945
WM	AND WOMEN SHALL WEEP (UK)	LEMONT	RANK	1960
WM	MOST WONDERFUL MOMENT (IT: IL MOMENTO PIU BELLO 1957)	EMMER	ELLIS FILMS	1959
WM	WARN THAT MAN (UK)	HUNTINGTON	ABPC-PATHE	1943
WM	WATERMELON MAN	VAN PEBBLES	COLUMBIA	1970
WM	WHEN WE ARE MARRIED (UK)	COMFORT	ANGLO-AMERICAN	1943
WM	WHOLLY MOSES	WEIS	COLUMBIA	1980
WM	WICKER MAN (UK-1973)	HARDY	WARNER BROS	1975
WMCJ	WHITE MEN CAN'T JUMP	SHELTON	20th CENTURY FOX	1992
WMP	WICKER MAN (UK-1973)	HARDY	WARNER BROS	1975
WMT	MISSOURI TRAVELER	HOPPER	BUENA VISTA	1958
WN	WHITE NIGHTS	HACKFORD	COLUMBIA	1985
WN	WHITE NIGHTS (IT: LE NOTTI DI BIANCHI)	VISCONTI	UMPO	1957
WN	WORLD BY NIGHT	VANZI	WARNER BROS	1960
WNA	WE'RE NO ANGELS	JORDAN	PARAMOUNT	1989
WNY	WHOLE NINE YARDS	LYNN	WARNER BROS	2000
WO	WHITE ORCHID (MEX) (CREATURES OF THE JUNGLE 1957)	LE BORG	UNITED ARTISTS	1954
WO	WORTH WINNING	MACKENZIE	20th CENTURY FOX	1989
WOA	WORLD OF APU (IND: APUR SANSAR)	RAY	EDWARD HARRISON	1959
WOB	WILD ON THE BEACH	DEXTER	20th CENTURY FOX	1965
WOF	HOUR OF THE WOLF (SWE: VARGTIMMEN)	BERGMAN	LOPERT	1968
WOL	WOLFEN	WADLEIGH	ORION	1981
WOR	WAR OF THE ROSES	DEVITO	20th CENTURY FOX	1989
WOS	LURE OF THE SILA (IT 1949)	COLETTI	IFE RELEASING	1954
WOZ	WEST OF ZANZIBAR (UK)	WATT	UNIVERSAL	1954
WP	WESTERN PACIFIC AGENT	NEWFIELD	LIPPERT	1950
WP	WILD PUSSYCAT (GR)	DADIRAS	CROWN INT'L	1969
WP	WILLIAM PERLBERG	portrait	PARAMOUNT`	
WP	WILLIAM POWELL	portrait	UNIV	
WP	WITHOUT PITY (IT: SENZA PIETA)	LATTUADA	LUX	1948
WPM	WHAT PRICE MURDER (FR: 1957) (KISS FOR A KILLER)	VERNEUIL	20th CENTURY FOX	1960

WPS	WAR AND PEACE	VIDOR	PARAMOUNT	1956
WR	WEDDING REHEARSAL (UK)	KORDA	IDEAL	1932
WR	WHEN YOU COMIN' BACK, RED RYDER	KATSELAS	COLUMBIA	1978
WR	WILLIAM REYNOLDS	portrait	UNIV	
WR	WOMAN IN RED	WILDER	ORION	1984
WR	WORLD FOR RANSOM	ALDRICH	ALLIED ARTISTS	1954
WRFG	WHERE THE RED FERN GROWS	TOKAR	DOTY-DAYTON REL.	1974
WS	FEMALE (FR: LA FEMME ET LE PANTIN 1959)	DUVIVIER	LOPERT	1960
WS	MIRACLE OF THE WHITE STALLIONS	HILLER	BUENA VISTA	1962
WS	WALK IN THE SHADOW (UK: LIFE FOR RUTH)	DEARDEN	CONTINENTAL	1962
WS	WALKING STICK (UK)	TILL	MGM	1970
WS	WALTER SODERLING	portrait	RKO	
WS	WARNING SIGN	BARWOOD	20th CENTURY FOX	1985
WS	WHITE SANDS	DONALDSON	WARNER BROS	1992
WS	WHITE SHEIK (IT: LO SCEICCO BIANCO)	FELLINI	JANUS	1952
WS	WILD STRAWBERRIES (SWE: SMULTRONSTALLET 1957)	BERGMAN	JANIS	1959
WS	WINDBAG THE SAILOR (UK)	BEAUDINE	GAUMONT BRITISH	1936
WS	WOMAN LIKE SATAN	DUVIVIER	LOPERT	1959
WS	WONDERFUL STORY (UK)	FOGWELL	STERLING	1932
WSBB	WHITE SQUALL	SCOTT	BUENA VISTA	1996
WSG	WARRIOR AND SLAVE GIRL (IT: RIVOLTA DEI GLADIATORI 1958)	COTTAFAVI	COLUMBIA	1959
WSR	WE SHALL RETURN	GOODMAN	UNITED INT'L	1963
WSR	WORLD SEX REPORT (GER)	RIMMEL	WHITE	1971
WSS	SWEDISH WEDDING NIGHT (SWED: BROLLOPSBESVAR 1964)	FALCK	ROYAL FILMS INT'L	1965
WSS	WHILE THE SUN SHINES (UK)	ASQUITH	STRATFORD	1947
WT	TWILIGHT WOMEN (UK: WOMEN OF TWILIGHT)	PARRY	LIPPERT	1952
WT	WALTZ OF THE TOREADORS (UK)	GUILLERMIN	CONTINENTAL	1962
WT	WALTZ TIME (UK)	THIELE	GAUMONT	1933
WT	WALTZ TIME (UK)	STEIN	FOUR CONTINENTS	1945
WT	WESTERN TERROR (orig: BUZZY RIDES THE RANGE 1940)	KAHN	ASTOR	R48
WT	WHITE TOWER	TETZLAFF	RKO	1950
WT	WHOLE TRUTH	GUILLERMIN	COLUMBIA	1958
WT	WHOLE TRUTH (UK)	GUILLERMIN	COLUMBIA	1958
WT	WITHOUT A TRACE	JAFFE	20th CENTURY FOX	1982
WT	WON TON TON, THE DOG WHO SAVED HOLLYWOOD	WINNER	PARAMOUNT	1975
WTC	UP THE CREEK (UK)	GUEST	DOMINANT	1958
WTM	MAN WHO KNEW TOO LITTLE, THE	AMIEL	WARNER BROS	1997
WTO	WORLD TEN TIMES OVER (UK)	RILLA	GOLDSTONE	1963
WTS	WOMAN TIMES SEVEN	DE SICA	EMBASSY	1967
WTT	WAVELL'S 30,000 (UK)	MONCK	MGM	1942
WUF	WHAT'S UP FRONT	WEHLING	FAIRWAY	1964
WV	STRAUSS' GREAT WALTZ (UK: WALTZES FROM VIENNA)	HITCHCOCK	GAUMONT BRITISH	1934
WW	3 MURDERESS (FR)	BOISROND	20th CENTURY FOX	1960
WW	CRIMES AT THE DARK HOUSE (UK)	KING	EXPLOITATION	1940
WW	HAL TALIAFERRO aka WALLY WALES	portrait		
WW	WAITING WOMEN (SWE: KVINNORS VANTAN)	BERGMAN	JANUS	1952
WW	WASP WOMAN	CORMAN	FILM GROUP	1959
WW	WATERFRONT WOMEN (UK: WATERFRONT)	ANDERSON	BELL	1950
WW	WAYNE'S WORLD	SPHEERIS	PARAMOUNT	1992
WW	WAYWARD WIFE (FR: LA PROVINIALE 1953)	SOLDATI	IFE	1955
WW	WELCOME TO WOOP WOOP	ELLIOTT	MGM	1997
WW	WHEN THE WHALES CAME	REES	20th CENTURY FOX	1989
WW	WICKED WIFE (UK: GRAND NATIONAL NIGHT)	MCNAUGHT	ALLIED ARTISTS	1953
WW	YOUNG AND WILLING (UK: WEAK AND THE WICKED)	THOMPSON	ALLIED ARTISTS	1954
WW.14	PICCADILLY (UK)	DUPONT	SONO ART-WORLDWIDE	1929
WW93	CAIRO ROAD (UK - 1950)	MACDONALD	REALART	1952
WWN	WOMEN WITHOUT NAMES (IT: DONNE SENZA NOME 1950)	RADVANYI	LOPERT	1951
WWP	WILD, WILD PLANET (IT: I CRIMINALI DELLA GALASSIA 1966)	MARGHERETTI	MGM	1967
WWS	WORLD WITHOUT SHAME (UK)	WINTER	GALAXY	1962
WWS12	WINE, WOMEN AND SONG	BRENON	CHADWICK	1933
WWW	WILD WILD WORLD	SOKOLER	SOKOLER FILM	1965
WY	I'LL WALK BESIDE YOU (UK)	ROGERS	BUTCHER'S	1943
WY	WILD YOUTH	SCHREYER	CINEMA ASSOC	1960
WYCH	WHEN YOU COME HOME (UK)	BAXTER	BUTCHER'S	1948
X	KANGAROO KID (UK)	SELANDER	EAGLE-LION	1950
X-1	LOVE UNDER COVER	MACDONALD	TRIANGLE	1917

X-2	PIPE OF DISCONTENT	MATTHEWS	TRIANGLE	1917
X-3	HEART STRATEGY	MACDONALD	TRIANGLE	1917
X-4	HONEST THIEVES	MATTHEWS	TRIANGLE	1917
X-5	NOBLE FRAUD	WILLIAMS	TRIANGLE	1917
X-6	MALE GOVERNESS	DILLION	TRIANGLE	1917
X-7	WON BY A FOOT	FAY	TRIANGLE	1917
X-8	BLACK EYES AND BLUE	KERR	TRIANGLE	1916
X-9	ROAD AGENT		TRIANGLE	1917
X-10	GRAB BAG BRIDE	HARTMAN	TRIANGLE	1917
X-11	DONE IN OIL	AVERY	TRIANGLE	1917
X-12	TELEPHONE BELLE	RAYMAKER	TRIANGLE	1917
X-13	HIS DEADLY UNDERTAKING	MCCOY	TRIANGLE	1917
X-14	WHEN HEARTS COLLIDE	KERR	TRIANGLE	1917
X-15	STONE AGE	HARTMAN	TRIANGLE	1917
X-16	BACHELOR'S FINISH	DILLION	TRIANGLE	1917
X-17	FILM EXPOSURE	MCCOY	TRIANGLE	1917
X-18	CAUGHT WITH THE GOODS	KAUFMAN	TRIANGLE	1917
X-19	INNOCENT SINNERS	RAYMAKER	TRIANGLE	1917
X-20	HOBBLED HARTS	DILLION	TRIANGLE	1917
X-21	HER CANDY KID	AVERY	TRIANGLE	1917
X-22	FINISHED PRODUCT	MORRIS	TRIANGLE	1917
X-23	SELF-MADE HERO	HARTMAN	TRIANGLE	1917
X-24	HIS RISE AND TUMBLE	MCCOY	TRIANGLE	1917
X-25	BERTH SCANDAL	DILLION	TRIANGLE	1917
X-26	BOOKWORM TURNS	AVERY	TRIANGLE	1917
X-27	TUNER OF NOTE	MCCOY	TRIANGLE	1917
X-28	DOG'S OWN TALE	RAYMAKER	TRIANGLE	1917
X-29	WINNING LOSER	HARTMAN	TRIANGLE	1917
X-30	PETTICOAT PERILS	MORRIS	TRIANGLE	1917
X-31	HIS PARLOR ZOO	MCCOY	TRIANGLE	1917
X-32	HER BIRTHDAY KNIGHT	AVERY	TRIANGLE	1917
X-33	HER FINISHING TOUCH	DILLION	TRIANGLE	1917
X-34	LOVE AND FISH	MORRIS	TRIANGLE	1917
X-35	LAUNDRY CLEAN-UP	HARTMAN	TRIANGLE	1917
X-36	CAMERA CURE	RAYMAKER	TRIANGLE	1917
X-37	HIS ONE NIGHT STAND	MCCOY	TRIANGLE	1917
X-38	DISHONEST BURGLAR	DILLION	TRIANGLE	1917
X-39	SKIRT STRATEGY	AVERY	TRIANGLE	1917
X-40	HIS SOCIAL RISE	MORRIS	TRIANGLE	1917
X-41	TWIN TROUBLES	DILLION	TRIANGLE	1917
X-42	GIRL AND THE RING	AVERY	TRIANGLE	1917
X-43	HIS CRIMINAL CAREER	HARTMAN	TRIANGLE	1917
X-44	HIS MARRIAGE FAILURE	RAYMAKER	TRIANGLE	1917
X-45	PERILS OF THE BAKERY	MCCOY	TRIANGLE	1917
X-46	WHEELS AND WOE	DILLION	TRIANGLE	1917
X-47	HIS SPEEDY FINISH	MORRIS	TRIANGLE	1917
X-48	JANITOR'S VENGEANCE	AVERY	TRIANGLE	1917
X-49	THEIR WEAK MOMENTS	MCCOY	TRIANGLE	1917
X-50	HIS BITTER FATE	WILLIAMS	TRIANGLE	1917
X-51	AIRED IN COURT	DILLION	TRIANGLE	1917
X-52	DAD'S DOWNFALL	RAYMAKER	TRIANGLE	1917
X-53	HIS PERFECT DAY	MCCOY	TRIANGLE	1917
X-55	HOUSE OF SCANDAL	AVERY	TRIANGLE	1917
X-56	HIS SUDDEN RIFVAL	DILLION	TRIANGLE	1917
X-57	INNOCENT VILLAIN	WILLIAMS	TRIANGLE	1917
X-58	HIS WIDOW'S MIGHT	KERNAN	TRIANGLE	1917
X-59	SOLE MATES	RAYMAKER	TRIANGLE	1917
X-60	TOY OF FATE	MCCOY	TRIANGLE	1917
X-61	HIS FATAL MOVE	MORRIS	TRIANGLE	1917
X-62	MATRIMONIAL ACCIDENT	AVERY	TRIANGLE	1917
X-63	LOVE CASE	KERNAN	TRIANGLE	1917
X-64	HIS COOL NERVE	MCCOY	TRIANGLE	1917
X-65	HOTEL DISGRACE	DILLION	TRIANGLE	1917
X-66	HIS HIDDEN TALENT	MORRIS	TRIANGLE	1917
X-67	THEIR DOMESTIC DECEPTION	WILLIAMS	TRIANGLE	1917
X-68	CLEVER DUMMY	RAYMAKER	TRIANGLE	1917

X-69	HER DONKEY LOVE	AVERY	TRIANGLE	1917
X-70	FALLEN STAR	MCCOY	TRIANGLE	1917
X-71	HIS FOOT-HILL FOLLY	MORRIS	TRIANGLE	1917
X-72	HIS BABY DOLL	WILLIAMS	TRIANGLE	1917
X-73	DARK ROOM SECRET	KERNAN	TRIANGLE	1917
X-74	WARM RECEPTION	DILLION	TRIANGLE	1917
X-75	HIS UNCONSCIOUS CONSCIENCE	AVERY	TRIANGLE	1917
X-76	HIS SAVING GRACE	MCCOY	TRIANGLE	1917
X-77	HIS TAKING WAYS	DILLION	TRIANGLE	1917
X-78	HALF AND HALF	MORRIS	TRIANGLE	1917
X-79	HER FICKLE FORTUNE	KERNAN	TRIANGLE	1917
X-80	CAUGHT IN THE END	AVERY	TRIANGLE	1917
X-81	ALL AT SEA		TRIANGLE	1917
X-82	THEIR LOVE LESSON		TRIANGLE	1917
X-83	PRAIRIE HEIRESS		TRIANGLE	1917
X-84	HIS BUSY DAY		TRIANGLE	1917
X-85	MODERN SHERLOCK		TRIANGLE	1917
X-86	THEIR HUSBAND		TRIANGLE	1917
X-118	COUNTERFEIT SCENT	MORRIS	TRIANGLE	1917
X537	GEOGRAPHY LESSON (sh) (# 538 crossed out and X537 written)		MGM	1931
XBL	BEN LYON	portrait	MGM	
XFOX	BRIMSTONE (tv series)	REIFF	20TH CENTURY FOX	1998
XLXB	LUCILLE BREMER	portrait	MGM	
XM	X-MEN	SINGER	20TH CENTURY FOX	2000
XW	THIS MAN IS MINE (UK)	VARNEL	COLUMBIA BRITISH	1946
XWP	WAR AND PEACE (RUS: VOYNA I MIR 1966)	BONDARCHUK	CONTINENTAL	1968
XX	HAL ROACH PORTRAIT SERIES	portrait		
XXC-8800	BORN TO BE BAD	SHERMAN	UNITED ARTISTS	1934
Y	BIG RED	TOKAR	BUENA VISTA	1962
Y	OLD YELLER	STEVENSON	BUENA VISTA	1957
Y166	NEVER MENTION MURDER (UK)	NELSON-BURTON	ANGLO-AMALGAMATED	1964
YA	FOR YOU ALONE (UK)	FAITHFULL	BUTCHER'S	1945
YAD	YOUNG AND DANGEROUS	CLAXTON	20TH CENTURY FOX	1957
YB	YEARS BETWEEN (UK)	BENNETT	UNIVERSAL	1946
YB	YELLOW BIRD		CENTURY CINEMA	1970
YB	YOUNG AND BEAUTIFUL	SANTLEY	MASCOT	1934
YC	YOUNG CASSIDY (UK)	CARDIFF	MGM	1965
YD	YEAR OF THE DRAGON	CIMINO	MGM	1985
YD	YOUNG DOCTORS IN LOVE	MARSHALL	20TH CENTURY FOX	1982
YE	YANK IN ERMINE (UK)	PARRY	M&A ALEXANDER	1955
YE	YOUNG EINSTEIN	SERIOUS	WARNER BROS	1989
YF	YOUNG FRANKENSTEIN	BROOKS	20TH CENTURY FOX	1974
YG	YOUNG GIRLS OF GOOD FAMILIES	MONTAZEL	EMBASSY	1963
YG2	YOUNG GUNS 2	MURPHY	20th CENTURY FOX	1990
YJJ	YOUNG JESSE JAMES	CLAXTON	20TH CENTURY FOX	1960
YL	YOU LIGHT UP MY LIFE	BROOKS	SPECTRAFILM	1977
YLM	YOU MADE ME LOVE YOU (UK)	BANKS	MAJESTIC	1933
YL-M	YOUNG LOVERS	GOLDWIN JR.	MGM	1964
YM	YOUR MONEY OR YOUR WIFE (UK)	SIMMONS	ELLIS	1960
YMB	YES, MR. BROWN (UK)	BUCHANAN, WILCOX	WOOLF & FREEDMAN	1933
YMF	YOUNG MAN'S FANCY (UK)	STEVENSON	ABFD	1939
YMM	YOU MUST GET MARRIED (UK)	PEARCE	GFD	1936
YN	YIELD TO THE NIGHT	THOMPSON	ALLIED ARTISTS	1957
YO	WONDERFUL TO BE YOUNG! (UK: YOUNG ONES)	FURIE	PARAMOUNT	1961
YP	AT WAR WITH THE ARMY	WALKER	PARAMOUNT	1950
YP-1	AT WAR WITH THE ARMY	WALKER	PARAMOUNT	1950
YR	YELLOW ROLLS ROYCE (UK)	ASQUITH	MGM	1965
YRC	YELLOW ROLLS ROYCE (UK)	ASQUITH	MGM	1965
YS	YOUNG STRANGER, THE	FRANKENHEIMER	UNIVERSAL	1957
YS	YOUNG SWINGERS	DEXTER	20TH CENTURY FOX	1963
YSH	YOUNG SHERLOCK HOLMES	LEVINSON	PARAMOUNT	1985
YTT	YESTERDAY, TODAY AND TOMORROW	DE SICA	EMBASSY	1964
YW	YOUNG WORLD (IT: UN MONDE NOUVEAU)	DE SICA	LOPERT	1966
YWE	YOUNG, WILLING AND EAGER (UK: RAG DOLL)	COMFORT	MANSON	1961
Z	WEST OF ZANZIBAR (UK)	WATT	UNIVERSAL	1954
Z	ZACHARIAH	ENGLUND	CINERAMA REL.	1971

Z	ZARAK (UK)	YOUNG	COLUMBIA	1956
Z	ZOOLANDER	STILLER	PARAMOUNT	2001
Z	ZULU (UK)	ENDFIELD	EMBASSY	1964
ZEX	ELECTRONIC MONSTER (UK: ESCAPEMENT)	TULLY, PALTENGHI	COLUMBIA	1958
ZH	ZERO HOUR	BARTLETT	PARAMOUNT	1957
ZO	ZERO HOUR (CAN) (doc - sh)	LEGG	UNITED ARTISTS	1944
ZP	ZABRISKIE POINT	ANTONIONI	MGM	1970
ZP1	FRIGHTENED CITY (UK)	LEMONT	RANK	1961
ZPG	Z.P.G.	CAMPUS	PARAMOUNT	1971
ZRA	ZORRO RIDES AGAIN	ENGLISH, WHITNEY	REPUBLIC	1959
ZZ	DESERT PATROL (UK: SEA OF SAND)	GREEN	UNIVERSAL	1958

8x10" Still Clear Poly Sleeves

8x10" Matted Print Show Boxes

8x10" Art Presentation Books

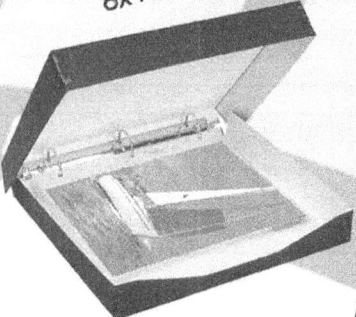

3-Ring Binders & Pages

8x10" Backings

8X10"StillS

Collection Protection Supplies

8x10" Museum-Grade Storage Boxes

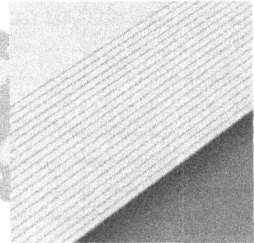

Decorative Matboards with Window

8x10" Sectional Aluminum Frame Kits

8x10" Ultra-PRO Toploaders

8x10" Rigid Mailer

8x10" Photo Storage Boxes

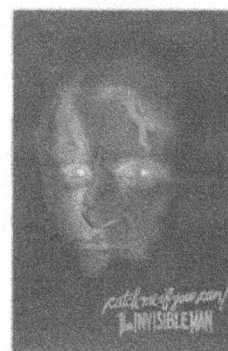

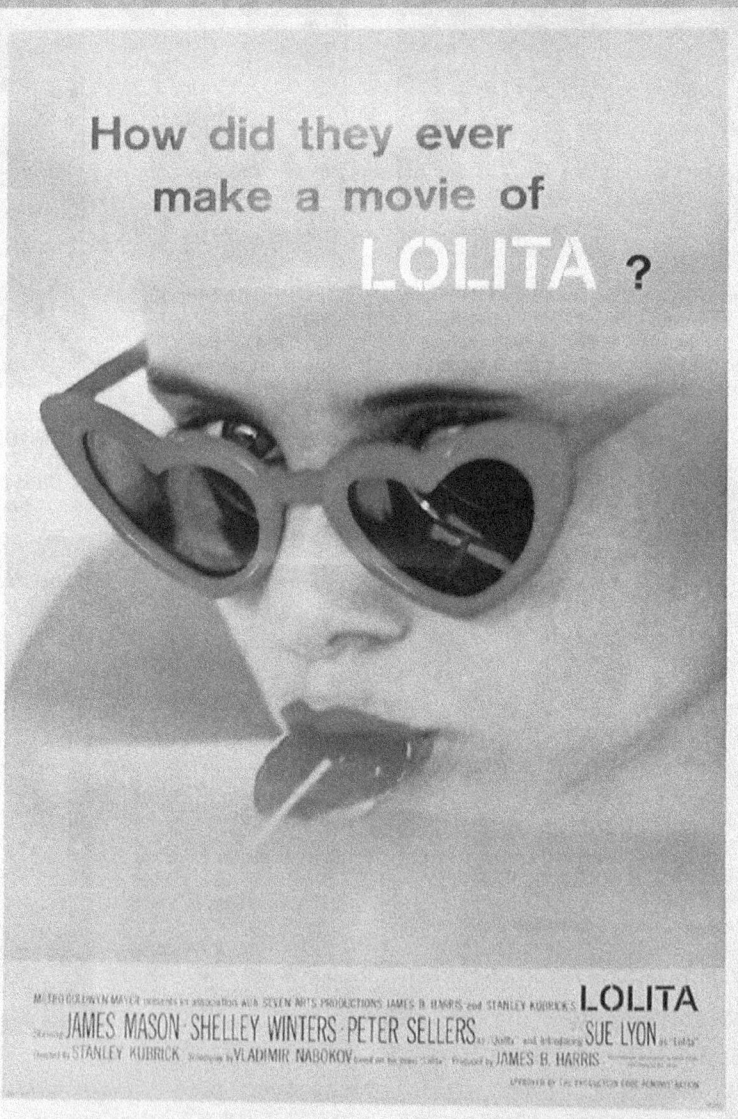

CODE	TITLE/NAME	DIRECTOR/TYPE	STUDIO/DISTRIBUTOR	YEAR
001	HIS NEW JOB	CHAPLIN	ESSANAY	1915
002	UNNAMED HAL ROACH PROJECT (sh)	CHAPLIN	ESSANAY	1915
002	DIE LAUGHING	WERNER	ORION	1980
003	CHAMPION, THE	CHAPLIN	ESSANAY	1915
003	IT'S ALIVE	COHEN	WARNER BROS	1974
004	IN THE PARK	CHAPLIN	ESSANAY	1915
004	STAR IS BORN	PIERSON	WARNER BROS	1976
005	JITNEY ELOPEMENT, A	CHAPLIN	ESSANAY	1915
006	TRAMP, THE	CHAPLIN	ESSANAY	1915
008	LISZTOMANIA	RUSSELL	WARNER BROS	1975
05-B3	ANCIENT MARINER	OTTO, BENNETT	FOX FILM	1925
06F	ADVENTURES OF SADIE	LANGLEY	20TH CENTURY FOX	1955
010	SELLOUT (IS)	COLLINSON	WARNER BROS	1976
012	STRAIGHT TIME	GROSBARD	WARNER BROS	1978
016	SHARKY'S MACHINE	REYNOLDS	ORION (WARNER BROS)	1981
018	THIEF WHO CAME TO DINNER	YORKIN	WARNER BROS	1973
019	COME BACK CHARLESTON BLUE	WARREN	WARNER BROS	1972
020	TRAIN ROBBERS	KENNEDY	WARNER BROS	1973
021	EXCALIBUR (see O21)	BOORMAN	WARNER BROS	1981
025	EXORCIST	FRIEDKIN	WARNER BROS	1973
026	CLASS OF '44	BOGART	WARNER BROS	1973
027	BLUME IN LOVE	MAZURSKI	WARNER BROS	1973
028	ROLLOVER	PAKULA	ORION (WARNER BROS)	1981
028	SCARECROW	SHATZBERG	WARNER BROS	1973
030	MAME	SAKS	WARNER BROS	1974
031	CLEOPATRA JONES	STARRETT	WARNER BROS	1973
032	FREEBIE AND THE BEAN	RUSH	WARNER BROS	1974
033	BLAZING SADDLES	BROOKS	WARNER BROS	1974
034	ZANDY'S BRIDE	TROELL	WARNER BROS	1974
035	MAGNUM FORCE	POST	WARNER BROS	1973
036	MCQ	STURGES	WARNER BROS	1974
037	TERMINAL MAN	HODGES	WARNER BROS	1974
038	NIGHT MOVES	PENN	WARNER BROS	1975
039	OUR TIME	HYAMS	WARNER BROS	1974
041	PRISONER OF SECOND AVENUE	FRANK	WARNER BROS	1975
042	RAFFERTY AND THE GOLD DUST TWINS	RICHARDS	WARNER BROS	1975
043	DOC SAVAGE: MAN OF BRONZE	ANDERSON	WARNER BROS	1975
044	ALICE DOESN'T LIVE HERE ANYMORE	SCORSESE	WARNER BROS	1974
046	TOWERING INFERNO	GUILLERMIN	WARNER BROS	1974
048	ULTIMATE WARRIOR	CLOUSE	WARNER BROS	1975
049	DOG DAY AFTERNOON	LUMET	WARNER BROS	1975
050	PIECE OF THE ACTION	POITIER	WARNER BROS	1977
050	SPARKLE	O'STEEN	WARNER BROS	1976
051	LONG DARK NIGHT (THE PACK)	CLOUSE	WARNER BROS	1977
055	GUMBALL RALLY	BAIL	WARNER BROS	1976
056	ST. IVES	THOMPSON	WARNER BROS	1976
057	EXORCIST II: HERETIC	BOORMAN	WARNER BROS	1977
059	VIVA KNIEVEL	DOUGLAS	WARNER BROS	1977
060	ENFORCER	FARGO	WARNER BROS	1976
063	ONE ON ONE	JOHNSON	WARNER BROS	1977
064	OH GOD	REINER	WARNER BROS	1977
065	GAUNTLET	EASTWOOD	WARNER BROS	1977
066	BLOOD BROTHERS		WARNER BROS	
067	BIG WEDNESDAY	MILIUS	WARNER BROS	1978
068	SWARM	ALLEN	WARNER BROS	1978
070	AGATHA	APTED	WARNER BROS	1979
071	HOOPER	NEEDHAM	WARNER BROS	1978
072	EVERY WHICH WAY BUT LOOSE	FARGO	WARNER BROS	1978
073	TIME AFTER TIME	MEYER	WARNER BROS	1979
074	FRISCO KID	ALDRICH	WARNER BROS	1979
075	IN-LAWS	HILLER	WARNER BROS	1979
076	BEYOND THE POSEIDON ADVENTURE	ALLEN	WARNER BROS	1979
077	JUST TELL ME WHAT YOU WANT	LUMET	WARNER BROS	1980
078	WHEN TIME RAN OUT	GOLDSTONE	WARNER BROS	1980
079	GOING IN STYLE	BREST	WARNER BROS	1979

080	ALTERED STATES	RUSSELL	WARNER BROS	1980
082	HONEYSUCKLE ROSE	SCHATZBERG	WARNER BROS	1980
089	PERSONAL BEST	TOWNE	WARNER BROS	1982
098	FANDANGO	REYNOLDS	WARNER BROS	1983
0101	MILLION DOLLAR MELODY (sh)	WHITE	EDUCATIONAL FILM	1933
0102	MR. ADAM (sh)	CHRISTIE	EDUCATIONAL FILM	1933
0103	POPPIN' THE CORK (sh)	WHITE	EDUCATIONAL FILM	1933
0104	EXPECTANT FATHER (sh)		EDUCATIONAL FILM	1934
0105	GOLD GHOST (sh)	LAMONT	EDUCATIONAL FILM	1934
0106	GOING SPANISH (sh)	CHRISTIE	EDUCATIONAL FILM	1934
0107	LOVE AND BABIES (sh)		EDUCATIONAL FILM	1934
0108	ELOPEMENT (sh)		EDUCATIONAL FILM	1934
0110	ALLEZ OOP (sh)	LAMONT	EDUCATIONAL FILM	1934
0201	BLUE BLACKBIRDS (sh)	LAMONT	EDUCATIONAL FILM	1933
0202	DORA'S DUNKING DOUGHNUTS	EDWARDS	FOX FILM	1933
0203	STATIC (sh)	CHRISTIE	EDUCATIONAL FILM	1933
0204	FARMER'S FATAL FOLLY (sh)		EDUCATIONAL FILM	1933
0205	HIS WEAK MOMENT (sh)	EDWARDS	EDUCATIONAL FILM	1933
0206	FROZEN ASSETS (sh)	EDWARDS	EDUCATIONAL FILM	1933
0207	DIVORCE SWEETS (sh)		EDUCATIONAL FILM	1933
0208	FREEZE OUT (sh)		EDUCATIONAL FILM	1933
0210	SUPER SNOOPER (sh)	EDWARDS	EDUCATIONAL FILM	1934
0211	BIG MEOW (sh)		EDUCATIONAL FILM	1934
0212	HELLO PROSPERITY (sh)	LAMONT	EDUCATIONAL FILM	1934
0214	HALF BAKED RELATIONS (sh)	LAMONT	EDUCATIONAL FILM	1934
0215	WRONG BOTTLE (sh)		EDUCATIONAL FILM	1934
0301	HOOKS AND JABS (sh)	GILLSTROM	EDUCATIONAL FILM	1933
0302	STAGE HAND (sh)	EDWARDS	EDUCATIONAL FILM	1933
0303	MERRILY YOURS (sh)	LAMONT	EDUCATIONAL FILM	1933
0304	LEAVE IT TO DAD (sh)	EDWARDS	EDUCATIONAL FILM	1933
0305	WHAT A WIFE (sh)		EDUCATIONAL FILM	1933
0306	WHAT'S TO DO? (sh)	LAMONT	EDUCATIONAL FILM	1933
0307	GOOD BAD MAN (sh)	BLACK	EDUCATIONAL FILM	1933
0308	POP'S PAL (sh)	EDWARDS	EDUCATIONAL FILM	1933
0309	INVENTORS (sh)	CHRISTIE	EDUCATIONAL FILM	1934
0310	PARDON MY PUPS (sh)	LAMONT	EDUCATIONAL FILM	1934
0311	TRIMMED IN FURS (sh)	LAMONT	EDUCATIONAL FILM	1934
0312	NORTH OF ZERO (sh)	WHITE	EDUCATIONAL FILM	1934
0313	MANAGED MONEY (sh)	LAMONT	EDUCATIONAL FILM	1934
0314	NO SLEEP ON THE DEEP (sh)	LAMONT	EDUCATIONAL FILM	1934
0315	HOTEL ANCHOVY (sh)	CHRISTIE	EDUCATIONAL FILM	1934
0316	EDUCATING PAPA (sh)	LAMONT	EDUCATIONAL FILM	1934
0360	BUT NOT FOR ME	LANG	PARAMOUNT	1959
0501	GRAND UPROAR (t) (sh)	MOSER	EDUCATIONAL FILM	1933
0502	PICK NECKING (t) (sh)	MOSER	EDUCATIONAL FILM	1933
0503	FANNY'S WEDDING DAY (t) (sh)	MOSER	EDUCATIONAL FILM	1933
0504	GYPSY FIDDLER (t) (sh)	MOSER	EDUCATIONAL FILM	1933
0505	BEAN STALK JACK (t) (sh)	MOSER	EDUCATIONAL FILM	1933
0506	VILLAGE BLACKSMITH (t) (sh)	MOSER	EDUCATIONAL FILM	1933
0507	ROBINSON CRUSOE (t) (sh)	MOSER	EDUCATIONAL FILM	1933
0508	LITTLE BOY BLUE (t) (sh)	MOSER	EDUCATIONAL FILM	1933
0509	IN VENICE (t) (sh)	MOSER	EDUCATIONAL FILM	1933
0510	SUNNY SOUTH (t) (sh)	MOSER	EDUCATIONAL FILM	1933
0511	HOLLAND DAYS (t) (sh)	MOSER	EDUCATIONAL FILM	1934
0512	THREE BEARS (t) (sh)	MOSER	EDUCATIONAL FILM	1934
0513	RIP VAN WINDLE (t) (sh)	MOSER	EDUCATIONAL FILM	1934
0514	LAST STRAW (t) (sh)	MOSER	EDUCATIONAL FILM	1934
0515	OWL AND THE PUSSYCAT (t) (sh)	MOSER	EDUCATIONAL FILM	1934
0516	MAD HOUSE (t) (sh)	MOSER	EDUCATIONAL FILM	1934
0517	JOE'S LUNCH WAGON (t) (sh)	MOSER	EDUCATIONAL FILM	1934
0518	JUST A CLOWN (t) (sh)	MOSER	EDUCATIONAL FILM	1934
0519	KING'S DAUGHTER (t) (sh)	MOSER	EDUCATIONAL FILM	1934
0520	LION'S FRIEND (t) (sh)	MOSER	EDUCATIONAL FILM	1934
0521	PANDORA (t) (sh)	MOSER	EDUCATIONAL FILM	1934
0522	SLOW BUT SURE (t) (sh)	MOSER	EDUCATIONAL FILM	1934
0523	SEE THE WORLD (t) (sh)	MOSER	EDUCATIONAL FILM	1934

0524	MY LADY'S GARDEN (t) (sh)	MOSER	EDUCATIONAL FILM	1934
0525	IRISH SWEEPSTAKES (t) (sh)	MOSER	EDUCATIONAL FILM	1934
0526	BUSTED BLOSSOMS (t) (sh)	MOSER	EDUCATIONAL FILM	1934
0601	YOUR LIFE IS IN YOUR HANDS (sh)		EDUCATIONAL FILM	1933
0602	SONG OF VIENNA (sh)		EDUCATIONAL FILM	1933
0603	SHORTS (sh)	JUDELS	EDUCATIONAL FILM	1933
0604	DAY DREAMS (sh)	MILTON	EDUCATIONAL FILM	1933
0605	WHAT DOES 1934 HOLD? (sh)	WATSON	EDUCATIONAL FILM	1933
0606	AIR MANIACS (sh)		EDUCATIONAL FILM	1933
0607	HULA HONEYMOON (sh)		EDUCATIONAL FILM	1934
0608	BOSOM FRIENDS (sh)		EDUCATIONAL FILM	1934
0609	PAGLIACCI (sh)		EDUCATIONAL FILM	1934
0701	KID IN AFRICA (sh)	LAMONT	EDUCATIONAL FILM	1933
0702	GIMME MY QUARTERBACK (sh)	HAYS	EDUCATIONAL FILM	1933
0801	ENCHANTED TRAIL (sh)		EDUCATIONAL FILM	1933
0802	ACROSS THE SEA (sh)		EDUCATIONAL FILM	1933
0803	CANYON OF ROMANCE (sh)		EDUCATIONAL FILM	1933
0804	MEDITERANEAN BLUES (sh)		EDUCATIONAL FILM	1934
0805	LOST RACE (sh)		EDUCATIONAL FILM	1934
0806	PARADISE OF THE PACIFIC (sh)		EDUCATIONAL FILM	1934
0901	SLOW POKE (sh)	HERZIG	EDUCATIONAL FILM	1932
0902	GIT ALONG LITTLE DOGGIES (sh)		EDUCATIONAL FILM	1933
0903	MANHATTAN LULLABY (sh)		EDUCATIONAL FILM	1933
0904	TRAV'LLING THE ROAD (sh)	WATSON	EDUCATIONAL FILM	1934
0905	DOCTOR (sh)		EDUCATIONAL FILM	1934
1	CLOTHES MAKE THE PIRATE	TOURNEUR	FIRST NATIONAL	1925
1	COUNSEL FOR CRIME	BRAHM	COLUMBIA	1937
1	GOOD COMPANIONS (UK)	SAVILLE	FOX FILM	1933
1	ONE PLUS ONE	OBOLER	SELECTED FILMS	1961
1	PAPER ORCHID (UK)	BAKER	COLUMBIA	1949
1	RIO CONCHOS	DOUGLAS	20TH CENTURY FOX	1964
1	ROME EXPRESS (UK)	FORDE	UNIVERSAL	1932
1	ROPING HER ROMEO (sh)	FISHBACK	PARAMOUNT	1917
1	UNNAMED HAL ROACH PROJECT (sh)	ROACH	ROLIN	1914
2	ACE HIGH	REYNOLDS	FOX FILM	1918
2	COWBOY AND THE PRIZE FIGHTER	COLLINS	EAGLE LION	1950
2	LIGHTNING CONDUCTOR (UK)	ELVEY	GFD	1938
2	MURDER IN GREENWICH VILLAGE	ROGELL	COLUMBIA	1937
2	NIGHT WORK	MACK	PATHE	1930
2	PULLMAN BRIDE (sh)	BADGER	PARAMOUNT	1917
2	UNNAMED HAL ROACH PROJECT (sh)	ROACH	ROLIN	1914
2A	THREE LIVES OF THOMASINA (UK)	CHAFFEY	BUENA VISTA	1963
2HCBB	25TH HOUR	LEE	BUENA VISTA	2002
2-S-2	DESPERADO	CARR	ALLIED ARTISTS	1954
2WH	HAPPENING	SILVERSTEIN	COLUMBIA	1967
2WT	PART 2 WALKING TALL	BELLAMY	AIP	1975
3	BEDROOM BLUNDER (sh)	CLINE	PARAMOUNT	1917
3	DUKE FOR A DAY (sh)	ROACH	ROLIN	1914
3	DUKE FOR A DAY (sh)	CURTIS	UNIVERSAL	1915
3	GOD'S COUNTRY	TANSEY	SCREEN GUILD	1947
3	INTO HER KINGDOM	GADE	FIRST NAT'L	1926
3	MIDSHIPMAID GOB (UK: MIDSHIPMAID)	DE COURVILLE	WOOLF & FREEDMAN	1932
3V	LOS TRES VIVALES (MEX 1958)	BALEDON	COLUMBIA	1959
4	AMERICAN METHODS	LLOYD	FOX FILM	1918
4	ARE WAITRESSES SAFE? (sh)	HEERMAN	PARAMOUNT	1917
4	LIFE BEGINS WITH LOVE	MCCAREY	COLUMBIA	1937
4	MR. LOGAN U.S.A.	REYNOLDS	FOX FILM	1918
4	SCARLET ROAD	LESAINT	FOX FILM	1918
4	UNNAMED HAL ROACH PROJECT (sh)	ROACH	ROLIN	1914
4F	FATHER CAME TOO! (UK)	SCOTT	RANK	1964
5	DURAND OF THE BADLANDS	STANTON	FOX FILM	1917
5	GULLIVER'S TRAVELS (t)	FLEISCHER	PARAMOUNT	1939
5	INTERNATIONAL SNEAK (sh)	FISHBACK	PARAMOUNT	1917
5	SELF MADE NUT (sh)	ROACH	ROLIN	1914
5A	DR. SYN, ALIAS THE SCARECROW (UK)	NEILSON	WALT DISNEY	1963
5B	MISADVENTURES OF MERLINE JONES	STEVENSON	BUENA VISTA	1963

5F	STRICTLY FOR THE BIRDS (UK)	SEWELL	RANK	1963
5P	MODERN TIMES	CHAPLIN	UNITED ARTISTS	1936
6	BIRDY	PARKER	TRI STAR	1984
6	FALL OF LADY SAMPSON (sh)	ROACH	ROLIN	1914
6	MISS IN THE DARK, A	ANDREWS	FBO	1924
6	SHE MARRIED AN ARTIST	GERING	COLUMBIA	1937
6	THAT NIGHT (sh)	CLINE	PARAMOUNT	1917
6	YESTERDAY'S WIFE	LESAINT	COLUMBIA	1923
6-14	LITTLE HUT, THE	ROBSON	MGM	1957
6A	DR. SYN, ALIAS THE SCARECROW (UK)	NEILSON	WALT DISNEY	1963
7	END OF THE LINE (UK)	SAUNDERS	FORTRESS-EROS	1957
7	HIS HIDDEN PURPOSE (sh)	CLINE, BADGER	PARAMOUNT	1917
7	PRIVATE'S AFFAIR, A	WALSH	20TH CENTURY FOX	1959
7	SHRINE FOR A DIME (sh)	ROACH	ROLIN	1914
7A	MARY POPPINS	STEVENSON	BUENA VISTA	1964
7B	GRETA, THE MISFIT GREYHOUND (tv) (doc)		BUENA VISTA	1963
7S	SEVEN SLAVES AGAINST ROME (IT: 1964)	LUPO	PARAMOUNT	1965
8	BARBER FOR A DAY (sh)	ROACH	ROLIN	1914
8	MARRIAGE MARKET	LESAINT	COLUMBIA	1923
8	SIX SHOOTER ANDY	FRANKLIN	FOX FILM	1918
8	TAMING TARGET CENTER (sh)	CAMPBELL	PARAMOUNT	1917
8	TIMBER WAR	NEWFIELD	AMBASSADOR	1936
8-S	CAN CAN	LANG	20TH CENTURY FOX	1960
9	CALL OF THE SOUL	LESAINT	FOX FILM	1919
9	DUSTY ROMANCE (sh)	ROACH	ROLIN	1914
9	HANNAH AND HER SISTERS	ALLEN	ORION	1985
9	LITTLE MISS ROUGHNECK	SCOTTO	COLUMBIA	1938
9	WATCH YOUR NEIGHBOR (sh)	HEERMAN	PARAMOUNT	1917
9A	MOON-SPINNERS (UK)	NEILSON	WALT DISNEY	1964
10	HELL ROARIN' REFORM	LESAINT	FOX FILM	1919
10	KITCHEN LADY (sh)	CLINE	PARAMOUNT	1917
10	SLEEPING CAR (UK)	LITVAK	IDEAL	1933
10	TEN	EDWARDS	WB	1979
10	TROUBLES OF THE WORK FAMILY (sh)	ROACH	ROLIN	1914
10W	TENTH WOMAN, THE	FLOOD	WARNER BROS.	1924
11	OPIUM FIRE (sh)	ROACH	ROLIN	1914
11	RIDERS OF THE PURPLE SAGE	LLOYD	FOX FILM	1918
11	SHERIFF NELL'S TUSSLE (sh)	CAMPBELL	PARAMOUNT	1918
11A	EMIL AND THE DETECTIVES	TEWKSBURY	BUENA VISTA	1964
12	DEADLY NIGHTSHADE (UK)	GILLING	GFD	1953
12	FRIEND HUSBAND (sh)	WRIGHT	PARAMOUNT	1918
12	PENITENTIARY	BRAHM	COLUMBIA	1938
12	TWO BUM HEROES (TWO BORN HEROES) (sh)	ROACH	ROLIN	1914
12-S	IS LOVE EVERYTHING?	CABANNE	ASSOC. EXHIBITORS	1924
13	MAN HUNTER	LLOYD	FOX FILM	1919
13	OH MARY BE CAREFUL	ASHLEY	GOLDWYN	1921
13	THOSE ATHLETIC GIRLS (sh)	CLINE	PARAMOUNT	1918
13	WILLIE RUNS THE PARK (WILLIE RUNS THE PACK)	ROACH	WARNER BROS	1915
14	IT PAYS TO EXERCISE (sh)	JONES	PARAMOUNT	1918
14	MARRIED LIFE	KENTON	ASSOC. FIRST NAT'L	1920
14	PAINTED DESERT	HIGGIN	RKO-PATHE	1931
14	SMELL THERE WAS (sh)	ROACH	ROLIN	1914
15	LOVE LOOPS THE LOOP (sh)	WRIGHT	PARAMOUNT	1918
15	PEACOCK ALLEY	DE SANO	TIFFANY	1930
15	THERE'S ALWAYS A WOMAN	HALL	COLUMBIA	1938
15	WILLIE WORKS THE HAREM (sh)	ROACH	ROLIN	1914
16	SAUCY MADELINE (sh)	JONES	PARAMOUNT	1918
16	WOMAN ON THE JURY, THE	HOYT	FIRST NATIONAL	1924
16	YOU CAN'T TAKE IT WITH YOU	CAPRA	COLUMBIA	1938
16A	BLACKBEARD'S GHOST	STEVENSON	BUENA VISTA	1968
17	HIS SMOTHERED LOVE (sh)	CLINE	PARAMOUNT	1918
17	HOLIDAY	CUKOR	COLUMBIA	1938
17	PICCADILLY (UK)	DUPONT	SONO ART-WORLD WIDE	1929
17	TOILERS	BARKER	TIFFANY	1928
17A	WINNIE THE POOH (t) (sh)		BUENA VISTA	1966
18	COUNTRY GIRL - (not released) (sh)	SENNETT	MACK SENNETT	1918

18	EMBEZZLER (UK)	GILLING	GFD	1954
18	MANXMAN (UK)	HITCHCOCK	SONO ART-WORLD WIDE	1929
19	AS YOU LIKE IT (UK)	CZINNER	20TH CENTURY FOX	1936
19	BATTLE ROYAL (sh)	JONES	PARAMOUNT	1918
19	CITY STREETS (CITY SHADOWS*)	ROGELL	COLUMBIA	1938
19	MARRIAGE BY CONTRACT	FLOOD	TIFFANY	1928
19C	CHARLEY'S AUNT	CHRISTIE	COLUMBIA	1930
20	GHOUL (UK)	HUNTER	GAUMONT	1933
20	GIRL'S SCHOOL	BRAHM	COLUMBIA	1938
20	LADIES FIRST! (sh)	GRAINGER	PARAMOUNT	1918
20	RICH PEOPLE	GRIFFITH	PATHE	1929
20A	FOLLOW ME, BOYS	TOKAR	BUENA VISTA	1966
21	GILDED CAGE (UK)	GILLING	MEDALLION	1955
21	I AM THE LAW	HALL	COLUMBIA	1938
21	ORDERS IS ORDERS (UK)	FORDE	GAUMONT BRIT. AMER.	1934
21	TWO TOUGH TENDERFEET (sh)	JONES	PARAMOUNT	1918
21A	CONFESSIONS OF A QUEEN	SJOSTROM	MGM	1925
21A	JUNGLE BOOK (t)	REITHERMAN	BUENA VISTA	1967
22	HER BLIGHTED LOVE (sh)	WRIGHT	PARAMOUNT	1918
22	MOST WANTED	HOGAN	NEW LINE CINEMA	1997
22	NO SMOKING (UK)	CASS	EROS	1955
22A	FIGHTING PRINCE OF DONEGAL	O'HERLIHY	BUENA VISTA	1966
23	COUCH TRIP	RITCHIE	ORION	1988
23	HER SCREEN IDOL (sh)	CLINE	PARAMOUNT	1918
23	I WAS A SPY (UK)	SAVILLE	FOX FILM	1933
23	LADY OBJECTS	KENTON	COLUMBIA	1938
23	PATH OF GLORY (UK)	BOWER	ABFD	1934
23	WHEN KNIGHTHOOD WAS IN FLOWER	VIGNOLA	COSMOPOLITAN	1922
23-321	SECRET VALLEY	BRETHERTON	20th CENTURY-FOX	1937
24	21 DAYS TOGETHER (UK: 21 DAYS)	DEAN	COLUMBIA	1940
24	FLIGHT TO FAME	COLEMAN	COLUMBIA	1938
24	MURDER PARTY (UK: NIGHT OF THE PARTY)	POWELL	GAUMONT BRITISH	1935
24	SHE LOVED HIM PLENTY (sh)	JONES	PARAMOUNT	1918
24HK	24 HOURS TO KILL (UK)	BEZENCENET	SEVEN ARTS	1965
24-NW2	UNDER THE RED ROBE (UK)	SJOSTROM	20TH CENTURY FOX	1937
24S	SWORDSMAN OF SIENA	BANDINI	MGM	1962
25	25TH HOUR (FR: LA VINGT CINQUIEME HEURE)	VERNEUIL	MGM	1967
25	BEAR (FR: L'OURS 1988)	ANNAUD	TRI STAR	1989
25	CHANNEL CROSSING (UK)	ROSMER	GAUMONT BRIT. AMER.	1933
25	COMPULSORY HUSBAND (UK)	BANKS, LACHMAN	WARDOUR	1930
25	I'LL TAKE ROMANCE	GRIFFITH	COLUMBIA	1937
25	SUMMER GIRLS (sh)	CLINE	PARAMOUNT	1918
26	BEWARE OF BOARDERS! (sh)	FISHBACK	PARAMOUNT	1918
26	CUCKOO IN THE NEST (UK)	WALLS	WOOLF & FREEDMAN	1933
26	GODDESS OF LOST LAKE	WORSLEY	HODKINSON	1918
26	PROWLERS OF THE SEA	ADOLFI	TIFFANY	1928
27	FIRE RAISERS (UK)	POWELL	WOOLF & FREEDMAN	1934
27C	HIS WIFE'S FRIEND (sh)	WRIGHT	PARAMOUNT	1918
27	LONELY WIVES	MACK	RKO	1931
27A	HAPPIEST MILLIONAIRE	TOKAR	BUENA VISTA	1967
28	ADELE	WORSLEY	UNITED PICTURE	1919
28	BLACKMAIL (UK)	HITCHCOCK	SONO ART-WORLD WIDE	1928
28	BOND OF FEAR (UK)	CASS	EROS	1956
28	CONSTANT NYMPH (UK)	DEAN	FOX	1933
28	GRAIN OF DUST	ARCHAINBAUD	TIFFANY	1928
28	SLEUTHS! (sh)	JONES	PARAMOUNT	1918
28	THERE'S THAT WOMAN AGAIN	HALL	COLUMBIA	1939
29	AMAZING GRACE AND CHUCK (SILENT VOICE*)	NEWELL	TRI STAR	1987
29	PASSPORT TO TREASON (UK)	BAKER	ASTOR	1956
29	STRIKE! (UK: RED ENSIGN)	POWELL	GAUMONT BRITISH	1934
29	WHOSE LITTLE WIFE ARE YOU? (sh)	CLINE	PARAMOUNT	1918
29A	WINNIE THE POOH AND THE BLUSTERY DAY (t) (sh)	REITHERMAN	BUENA VISTA	1969
30	BLONDIE	STRAYER	COLUMBIA	1938
30	DOUBLE TROUBLE		20TH CENTURY FOX	
30	HER FIRST MISTAKE (sh)	JONES	PARAMOUNT	1918
30	JACK AHOY (UK)	FORDE	GAUMONT BRIT. AMER.	1934

30	MAN WHO COULD CHEAT DEATH (UK)	FISHER	PARAMOUNT	1959
30A	BLACKBEARD'S GHOST	STEVENSON	BUENA VISTA	1968
31	COMMON LAW	STEIN	PATHE	1931
31	SMASHING THE SPY RING	CABANNE	COLUMBIA	1939
31	YANKEE DOODLE IN BERLIN	JONES	SOL LESSER	1919
31A	WHY BEACHES ARE POPULAR (sh)	JONES	SOL LESSER	1919
32	BILL & TED'S BOGUS JOURNEY	HEWITT	ORION	1991
32	HIDE AND SEEK, DETECTIVES (sh)	CLINE	PARAMOUNT	1918
32	LADY AND THE MOB	STOLOFF	COLUMBIA	1939
32	LUCKY BOY	TAUROG, WILSON	TIFFANY	1928
32	POWER (UK: JEW SUSS)	MENDES	GAUMONT BRIT. AMER.	1934
32B	LEGEND OF EL BLANCO	VITERELLA	NATIONAL BROADCASTING	1966
33	FROM SOUP TO NUTS (sh)	KENNEDY	MGM	1928
33	LONE WOLF SPY HUNT	GODFREY	COLUMBIA	1939
33	NEVER TOO OLD (sh)	JONES	PARAMOUNT	1919
33-NW4	DINNER AT THE RITZ (UK)	SCHUSTER	20TH CENTURY FOX	1937
34	EVERGREEN (UK)	V SAVILLE	GAUMONT BRIT. AMER.	1934
34	MEDICINE MAN	PEMBROKE	TIFFANY	1930
34	VILLAGE CHESTNUT (sh)	WRIGHT, GRIFFITH	PARAMOUNT	1918
34A	NEVER A DULL MOMENT	PARIS	BUENA VISTA	1968
34-TCF1	WE'RE GOING TO BE RICH (UK)	BANKS	20TH CENTURY FOX	1938
35	CUP OF KINDNESS (UK)	WALLS	GAUMONT BRITISH	1934
35	CUPID'S DAY OFF (sh)	CLINE	PARAMOUNT	1919
35	DONNA REED	portrait	MGM	
35-328	HAWAIIAN BUCKAROO	TAYLOR	GUARANTEE PICTURES	1938
36	DONNA REED	portrait	MGM	
36	LITTLE FRIEND (UK)	VIERTEL	GAUMONT BRIT. AMER.	1934
36	ONLY ANGELS HAVE WINGS	HAWKS	COLUMBIA	1939
36	RIP & STITCH, TAILORS (sh)	WATSON, ST. CLAIR	PARAMOUNT	1919
36	TROLLENBERG TERROR (UK) (CRAWLING EYE)	LAWRENCE	EROS	1958
36H	TERROR STREET (UK: 36 HOURS)	TULLY	LIPPERT	1953
37	COAST GUARD	LUDWIG	COLUMBIA	1939
37	EAST LYNNE WITH VARIATIONS (sh)	CLINE	PARAMOUNT	1919
37	ONE NIGHT STAND	FIGGIS	NEW LINE CINEMA	1997
37	SONG FOR YOU (UK: MY SONG FOR YOU)	ELVEY	GAUMONT BRIT. AMER.	1934
37A	LOVE BUG	STEVENSON	BUENA VISTA	1969
37-TCP2	SMILING ALONG (UK: KEEP SMILING)	BANKS	20TH CENTURY FOX	1938
38	EVENSONG (UK)	V SAVILLE	GAUMONT BRIT. AMER.	1934
38	LOVE, HONOR AND BEHAVE	JONES, KENTON	ASSOC. FIRST NAT'L	1920
38	ROMANCE OF THE REDWOODS	VIDOR	COLUMBIA	1939
38	VILLAGE SMITHY (sh)	JONES	PARAMOUNT	1919
38-ATCP3	SO THIS IS LONDON (UK)	FREELAND	20TH CENTURY FOX	1939
39	BLONDIE MEETS THE BOSS	STRAYER	COLUMBIA	1939
39	MAN WHO KNEW TOO MUCH	HITCHCOCK	GAUMONT BRITISH	1934
39	PARADISE ISLAND	GLENNON	TIFFANY	1930
39	REILLY'S WASH DAY (sh)	JONES	PARAMOUNT	1919
40	GOLDEN BOY	MAMOULIAN	COLUMBIA	1939
40	MARINES LET'S GO	WALSH	20TH CENTURY FOX	1961
40	MICKEY ROONEY	portrait	MGM	
40	WHEN LOVE IS BLIND (sh)	CLINE	PARAMOUNT	1919
40A	SMITH	OHERLIHY	BUENA VISTA	1969
41	BLIND ALLEY	VIDOR	COLUMBIA	1939
41	LITTLE WIDOW (sh)	ST. CLAIR, ROACH	PARAMOUNT	1919
41	ROAD HOUSE (UK)	ELVEY	GAUMONT BRITISH	1934
41A	RASCAL	TOKAR	BUENA VISTA	1969
41-SS	SHIPYARD SALLY (UK)	BANKS	20TH CENTURY FOX	1939
42	ALL HANDS ON DECK	TAUROG	20th CENTURY-FOX	1961
42	FLAME OF LOVE (UK: ROAD TO DISHONOUR)	EICHBERG, SUMMERS	BRITISH INTERNATIONAL	1930
42	FOOLISH AGE (sh)	JONES	PARAMOUNT`	1919
42	GOOD GIRLS GO TO PARIS	HALL	COLUMBIA	1939
42A	KING OF THE GRIZZLIES	KELLY	BUENA VISTA	1970
43	LOVE'S FALSE FACES (sh)	JONES	PARAMOUNT	1919
43	MR. SMITH GOES TO WASHINGTON	CAPRA	COLUMBIA	1939
43	MY HEART IS CALLING (UK)	GALLONE	GAUMONT BRITISH	1935
43A	APPLE DUMPLING GANG RIDES AGAIN, THE	MCEVEETY	BUENA VISTA	1979
43-TC	THEY CAME BY NIGHT (UK)	LACHMAN	20TH CENTURY FOX	1940

44	ELSTREE CALLING (UK)	CHARLOT, HITCHCOCK	WARDOUR	44
44	MIDSTREAM	FLOOD	TIFFANY	1929
44	NABONGA	NEWFIELD	PRC	1944
44	NO MOTHER TO GUIDE HIM (sh)	ST. CLAIR, KENTON	PARAMOUNT	1919
45	I LOVE MONEY		20th CENTURY-FOX	1962
45	BLONDIE TAKES A VACATION	STRAYER	COLUMBIA	1939
45	HEARTS AND FLOWERS (sh)	CLINE	PARAMOUNT	1919
45	IRON DUKE (UK)	SAVILLE	GAUMONT BRITISH	1934
45	LOCK UP	FLYNN	TRI STAR	1989
45	MR. TOPAZE/US: I LIKE MONEY		20th CENTURY-FOX	1962
45	RAINY DAY WITH THE BEAR FAMILY (t) (sh)		MGM	1940
45A	ARISTOCATS	REITHERMAN	BUENA VISTA	1971
45B	OWL THAT DIDN'T GIVE A HOOT	ZUNIGA	NATIONAL BROADCASTING	1968
45G	NIGHT TRAIN TO MUNICH (UK)	REED	20TH CENTURY FOX	1940
46	FIVE LITTLE PEPPERS AND HOW THEY GREW	BARTON	COLUMBIA	1939
46	FRIGHT NIGHT PART 2	WALLACE	TRI STAR	1988
46	IRENE	GREEN	FIRST NATIONAL	1926
46	ROMANCE IN FLANDERS (UK)	ELVEY	STANDARD	1937
46	TRYING TO GET ALONG (sh)	JONES	PARAMOUNT	1919
46A	BEDKNOBS AND BROOMSTICKS	STEVENSON	BUENA VISTA	1971
47	ALIAS BULLDOG DRUMMOND (UK: BULLDOG JACK)	FORDE	GAUMONT BRIT. AMER.	1935
47	AMONG THOSE PRESENT (sh)	KENTON, GREY	PARAMOUNT	1919
47	DONNA REED	portrait	MGM	
47	MYSTERY DATE	WACKS	ORION	1991
47	PAINTED FACES	ROGELL	TIFFANY	1929
47	THOSE HIGH GRAY WALLS	VIDOR	COLUMBIA	1939
48	DONNA REED	portrait	MGM	
48	HEAVEN KNOWS MR. ALLISON (should be 948)	HUSTON	20th CENTURY-FOX	1957
48	ME AND MARLBOROUGH (UK)	SAVILLE	GAUMONT BRITISH	1935
48	UNCLE TOM WITHOUT THE CABIN (sh)	HUNT	PARAMOUNT	1919
48	WAITING FOR GUFFMAN	GUEST	CASTLE ROCK	1996
48A	BOATNIKS, THE	TOKAR	BUENA VISTA	1970
49	39 STEPS (UK)	HITCHCOCK	GAUMONT BRIT. AMER.	1935
49	BEWARE SPOOKS	SEDGWICK	COLUMBIA	1939
49	GREAT WHITE WAY	HOPPER	COSMOPOLITAN	1924
49	MICKEY ROONEY	portrait	MGM	
49	MOLLY AND ME	RAY	TIFFANY	1929
49	TREATING 'EM ROUGH (sh)	JACKMAN	PARAMOUNT	1919
49	WHO'S HARRY CRUMB?	FLAHERTY	TRI STAR	1989
49A	BEDKNOBS AND BROOMSTICKS	STEVENSON	BUENA VISTA	1971
50	DENTIST (sh)	JONES	PARAMOUNT	1919
50	GREER GARSON	portrait	MGM	
50	INNOCENTS, THE	CLAYTON	20TH CENTURY FOX	1961
50A	BAREFOOT EXECUTIVE	BUTLER	BUENA VISTA	1971
50-TC21	WAY AHEAD (UK)	REED	20TH CENTURY FOX	1944
51	BLONDIE BRINGS UP BABY	STRAYER	COLUMBIA	1939
51	FRIGHT NIGHT PART 2	WALLACE	TRI STAR	1988
51	FUED OF THE RANGE	WEBB	METROPOLITAN	1939
51	JANICE MEREDITH	HOPPER	MGM	1924
51	LADY'S TAILOR (sh)	KENTON, GREY	PARAMOUNT	1919
51A	$1,000,000 DUCK	MCEVEETY	BUENA VISTA	1971
52	ARIZONA	RUGGLES	COLUMBIA	1940
52	BACK TO THE KITCHEN (sh)	MORRIS, BELMONT	PARAMOUNT	1919
52	KING OF THE DAMNED (UK)	FORDE	GAUMONT BRIT. AMER.	1935
52	MICKEY ROONEY	portrait	MGM	
52	NO GREATER LOVE	SEILER	COLUMBIA	1932
52	OUT COLD	MOWBRAY	HEMSDALE	1989
52	YANK IN LONDON (UK: I LIVE IN GROSVENOR SQUARE)	WILCOX	20TH CENTURY FOX	1945
52A	SCANDALOUS JOHN	BUTLER	BUENA VISTA	1971
53	GREER GARSON	portrait	MGM	
53	SALOME VS. SHENANDOAH (sh)	GREY, HUNT	PARAMOUNT	1919
53	SCANDAL SHEET	GRINDE	COLUMBIA	1939
53-3	HOLD THAT WOMAN!	NEWFIELD (SCOTT)	PRC	1940
54	AMAZING MR. WILLIAMS	HALL	COLUMBIA	1939
54	LOST ZEPPELIN	SLOMAN	TIFFANY	1929
54	UP IN ALF'S PLACE (sh)	JONES	PARAMOUNT	1919

54	VERSAILLES AFFAIR, THE (FR: MONSIEUR SUZUKI)	VERNAY	ELYSEE FILMS	1960
54A	SNOWBALL EXPRESS	TOKAR	BUENA VISTA	1972
55	CAFE HOSTESS	SALKOW	COLUMBIA	1940
55	HIS LAST FALSE STEP (sh)	JONES	PARAMOUNT	1919
55	I ONLY ARSKED! (UK)	TULLY	COLUMBIA	1958
55	UNCHAINED	BARTLETT	WARNER BROS	1955
55A	WORLD'S GREATEST ATHLETE	SCHEERER	BUENA VISTA	1973
56	DOWN ON THE FARM	GREY, JONES	UNITED ARTISTS	1920
56	GREER GARSON	portrait	MGM	
56	MY SON IS GUILTY	BARTON	COLUMBIA	1939
56	SECRETS OF LIFE (documentary)	ALGAR	BUENA VISTA	1956
56B	VARDA THE PEREGRINE FALCON		NATIONAL BROADCASTING	1969
56 EH	PLEASURE SEEKERS, THE	ARCHAINBAUD	SELZNICK	1920
57	ELLA CINDERS	GREEN	FIRST NAT'L	1926
57	INSPECTOR (UK) (US: LISA)	DUNNE	20TH CENTURY FOX	1962
57	LISA	DUNNE	20th CENTURY-FOX	1962
57	MARRIED LIFE	KENTON	ASSOC. FIRST NAT'L	1920
57	MILITARY ACADEMY	LEDERMAN	COLUMBIA	1940
57	PANAMA PATROL	LAMONT	FINE ARTS GRAND	1939
57	RHODES (UK: RHODES OF AFRICA)	VIERTEL	GAUMONT BRIT. AMER.	1936
57	SKIN GAME (UK)	HITCHCOCK	BRITISH INTERNATIONAL	1931
57A	CHARLEY AND THE ANGEL	MCEVEETY	BUENA VISTA	1973
58	FIRST OFFENCE	MASON	GAUMONT BRITISH	1936
58	FIVE LITTLE PEPPERS AT HOME	BARTON	COLUMBIA	1940
58	SPEAK-EASY (sh)	JONES	PARAMOUNT	1919
58 (LD)	LONGEST DAY	MARTON	20th CENTURY-FOX	1962
59	ANN-MARGRET	portrait	20th CENTURY-FOX	1960s
59	OPERATION CROSSBOW	ANDERSON	MGM	1965
59	SECRET AGENT (UK)	HITCHCOCK	GAUMONT BRIT. AMER.	1936
59	STAR BOARDER (sh)	DAVIS	PARAMOUNT	1920
59A	SUPERDAD	MCEVEETY	BUENA VISTA	1974
60	IT'S LOVE AGAIN (UK)	V SAVILLE	GAUMONT BRIT. AMER.	1936
60	LOVE, HONOR AND BEHAVE	JONES, KENTON	ASSOC. FIRST NAT'L	1920
60	SWISS FAMILY ROBINSON, THE	ANNAKIN	BUENA VISTA	1960
60	UGLY DUCKLING (UK)	COMFORT	COLUMBIA	1959
61	DOOMED CARGO (UK: SEVEN SINNERS)	DE COURVILLE	GAUMONT BRIT. AMER.	1936
61	GINGHAM GIRL (sh)	DAVIS	PARAMOUNT	1920
61	GREER GARSON	portrait	MGM	
61	STRANGLERS OF BOMBAY (UK)	FISHER	COLUMBIA	1959
62	EVERYTHING IS THUNDER (UK)	ROSMER	GAUMONT BRIT. AMER.	1936
62	FRESH FROM THE CITY (sh)	WRIGHT	PARAMOUNT	1920
62	NEVER TAKE SWEETS FROM A STANGER	FRANKEL	COLUMBIA - UK	1960
63	EAST MEETS WEST (UK)	MASON	GAUMONT BRITISH	1936
63	GEE WHIZ! (sh)	JONES	PARAMOUNT	1920
63	SON OF FLUBBER	STEVENSON	BUENA VISTA	1962
63A	ISLAND AT TOP OF THE WORLD	STEVENSON	BUENA VISTA	1974
64	ALIAS THE BAD MAN	ROSEN	TIFFANY	1931
64	BY GOLLY! (sh)	MURRAY	PARAMOUNT	1920
64	ONE WEEK OF LOVE	ARCHAINBAUD	SELZNICK	1922
64	SILENT BARRIERS (UK: GREAT BARRIER)	ROSMER	GAUMONT BRIT. AMER.	1937
64	THREE LIVES OF THOMASINA (UK)	CHAFFEY	WALT DISNEY	1963
64A	RESCUERS	REITHERMAN	BUENA VISTA	1977
65	LET 'ER GO! (sh)	DAVIS	PARAMOUNT	1920
65	MAGNOLIA	ANDERSON	NEW LINE CINEMA	1999
65	VERY BRADY SEQUEL, A	SANFORD	PARAMOUNT	1996
65A	WINNIE THE POOH AND TIGGER TOO (t) (sh)	LOUNSBERY	BUENA VISTA	1974
66	BLOOD BROTHERS (KUNG FU INVADERS)	CHANG	WARNER BROS	1974
66	SABOTAGE	HITCHCOCK	GAUMONT BRITISH	1936
66	WOMAN ALONE (UK: SABOTAGE)	HITCHCOCK	GAUMONT BRIT. AMER.	1936
66	YOU WOULDN'T BELIEVE IT! (sh)	KENTON	PARAMOUNT	1920
66A	CASTAWAY COWBOY	MCEVEETY	BUENA VISTA	1974
67	QUACK DOCTOR (sh)	GRAY, BEVAN	PARAMOUNT	1920
68	GREAT SCOTT! (sh)	MURRAY	PARAMOUNT	1920
68	WHAT'S YOUR HUSBAND DOING?	INGRAHAM	PARAMOUNT - ARTCRAFT	1920
69	CURSE OF THE WEREWOLF (UK)	FISHER	UNIVERSAL	1961
69	SHE SIGHED BY THE SEASIDE (sh)	KENTON	ASSOC. FIRST NAT'L	1921

69	YOU'RE IN THE ARMY NOW (UK: O.H.M.S.)	WALSH	GAUMONT BRIT. AMER.	1937
69A	APPLE DUMPLING GANG	TOKAR	BUENA VISTA	1975
70	CARRY ON AGAIN DOCTOR (UK)	THOMAS	RANK	1969
70	KING SOLOMON'S MINES (UK)	STEVENSON	GAUMONT BRIT. AMER.	1937
70	ROMAN SLAVE STORY	UNFINISHED	USED IN 'HOME TALENT'	1920
71	BEDKNOBS AND BROOMSTICKS	STEVENSON	BUENA VISTA	1971
71	BREAKIN' 2 ELECTRIC BOOGALOO	FIRSTENBERG	TRI-STAR	1984
71	IT'S A BOY! (sh)	SMITH	PARAMOUNT	1920
71	TAKE MY TIP (UK)	MASON	GFD	1937
72	BILLY THE KID WANTED	NEWFIELD	PRC	1941
72	DON'T WEAKEN! (sh)	ST. CLAIR	PARAMOUNT	1920
72	NON-STOP NEW YORK (UK: LISBON CLIPPER MYSTERY)	STEVENSON	GAUMONT BRIT. AMER.	1937
73	MY GOODNESS (sh)	SMITH	PARAMOUNT	1920
73A	BEST OF WALT DISNEY'S TRUE-LIFE ADVENTURES		BUENA VISTA	1975
74	BILLY THE KID ROUNDUP	NEWFIELD	PRC	1941
74	EAST OF SHANGHAI (UK: RICH AND STRANGE)	HITCHCOCK	POWERS	1931
74	GIRL WAS YOUNG	HITCHCOCK	GAUMONT BRITISH	1937
74	HIS YOUTHFUL FANCY (sh)	ST. CLAIR	PARAMOUNT	1920
74A	GUS	MCEVEETY	BUENA VISTA	1976
75	HIGH TREASON	ELVEY	TIFFANY	1929
75	SMALL TOWN IDOL	KENTON	ASSOC. PRODUCERS	1921
76	NORTHVILLE CEMETERY MASSACRE	DEAR	CANNON	1976
76	STRANGE BOARDERS (UK)	MASON	GAUMONT BRIT. AMER.	1938
76A	MADE IN THE KITCHEN (sh)	SMITH	ASSOC. PRODUCERS	1921
76B	FIRESIDE BREWER (sh)	SMITH	PARAMOUNT	1920
77	MAN WITH 100 FACES (UK: CRACKERJACK)	DE COURVILLE	GAUMONT BRIT. AMER.	1938
77	MOVIE FANS (sh)	KENTON	PARAMOUNT	1920
78	BILLY THE KID TRAPPED	NEWFIELD	PRC	1942
78	CLIMBING HIGH (UK)	REED	20TH CENTURY FOX	1938
78	DIANE CILENTO	portrait	20TH CENTURY FOX	1960s
78	NIGHT CREATURES (UK: CAPTAIN CLEGG)	SCOTT	UNIVERSAL	1962
78	RAMSHACKLE HOUSE	WEIGHT	PDC	1924
78	SHOCK WAVES	WIEDERHORN	JOSEPH BRENNER	1977
78A	FICKLE FANCY (sh)	KENTON	PARAMOUNT	1920
78B	DABBLING IN ART (sh)	KENTON	PARAMOUNT	1921
78b	STRANGE MONSTER OF STRAWBERRY COVE	SHEA	NATIONAL BROADCASTING	1971
79	SEVEN	FINCHER	NEW LINE CINEMA	1995
79	UNHAPPY FINISH (sh)	DAVIS	PARAMOUNT	1921
79A	SHAGGY D.A.	STEVENSON	BUENA VISTA	1976
80	ALARM CLOCK ANDY	STORM	ARTCRAFT	1920
80	BUNGALOW TROUBLES (sh)	AUSTIN	PARAMOUNT	1921
80	DON IS DEAD	FLEISCHER	UNIVERSAL	1973
80-638	REAL BRUCE LEE	MARKOVIC	CINEMATIC RELEASING CORP	1973
81	CROSSED SWORDS	FLEISCHER	WB	1977
82	BILLY THE KID SMOKING GUNS	NEWFIELD	PRC	1943
82	CALL A COP (sh)	ST. CLAIR	ASSOC. PRODUCERS	1921
82	DOMINICK AND EUGENE	YOUNG	ORION	1988
82	MOTHER OF HIS CHILDREN	LESAINT	FOX FILM	1920
82	UTAH KID	THORPE	TIFFANY	1930
82A	PETE'S DRAGON	CHAFFY	BUENA VISTA	1977
83	BONITA GRANVILLE	portrait	MGM	
83	CROSSROADS OF NEW YORK (sh)	JONES	ASSOC. FIRST NAT'L	1922
83	KISS OF THE VAMPIRE (UK)	SHARP	UNIVERSAL	1963
83	SHERIFF OF SAGE VALLEY	NEWFIELD	PRC	1943
84	CLASS OF 1984	LESTER	UNITED FILM DIST.	1982
84	ON A SUMMER'S DAY (sh)	AUSTIN	PARAMOUNT	1921
85	AMADEUS	FORMAN	ORION	1984
85	ASTRAY FROM THE STEERAGE (sh)	POWELL	PARAMOUNT	1921
85	NAKED HILLS, THE	SHAFTEL	ALLIED ARTISTS	1956
85	RADIO DAYS	ALLEN	ORION	1987
85A	RETURN FROM WITCH MOUNTAIN	HOUGH	BUENA VISTA	1978
86	KITCHEN CINDERELLA (unreleased)	ST. CLAIR	MACK SENNETT	1920
86	LAW AND ORDER	NEWFIELD	PRC	1942
86	NO WAY OUT	DONALDSON	ORION	1987
87	LEFTOVER LADIES	KENTON	TIFFANY	1931
87	WEDDING BELLS OUT OF TUNE (sh)	ST. CLAIR	PARAMOUNT	1921

88	BORDERLINE	FREEDMAN	ASSOCIATED FILM DIST	1980
88	FIRST OFFENCE	MASON	GAUMONT BRITISH	1936
88	LOVE'S OUTCAST (sh)	WALDRON	ASSOC. PRODUCERS	1921
89	BORDER ROMANCE	THORPE	TIFFANY	1929
89	SORROWS OF LOVE	GIBLYN	TRIANGLE	1916
89	SWEETHEART DAYS (sh)	ST. CLAIR	PARAMOUNT	1921
89A	NORTH AVENUE IRREGULARS	BILSON	BUENA VISTA	1979
90	HOUSE ON CARROLL STREET	YATES	ORION	1988
90	OFFICER CUPID (sh)	POWELL	PARAMOUNT	1921
90	TIME OUT FOR RHYTHM (sh)	SALKOW	COLUMBIA	1941
90	TIN PAN ALLEY	LANG	20TH CENTURY FOX	1940
90A	BLACK CAULDRON	BERMAN	BUENA VISTA	1985
91	HOME TALENT	SENNETT, ABBE	ASSOC. PRODUCERS	1921
92	BRIGHT EYES (sh)	ST. CLAIR	ASSOC. FIRST NAT'L	1921
92	MEN LIKE THESE (UK)	SUMMERS	BRITISH INTERNATIONAL	1932
93	BILLY THE KID - THE MYSTERIOUS RIDER	NEWFIELD	PRC	1943
93	GIOVANNI MARTINELLI	portrait	VITAPHONE	
93	HARD KNOCKS AND LOVE TAPS (sh)	DEL RUTH	ASSOC. PRODUCERS	1921
94	HOME FOR THE HOLIDAYS	FOSTER	PARAMOUNT	1995
94	LETTY LANDS A LIVE ONE (unreleased)	SENNETT	MACK SENNETT	1921
94	MAN WHO WON (UK: MR. BILL THE CONQUEROR)	WALKER	POWERS	1932
95	BILLY THE KID - THE KID RIDES AGAIN	NEWFIELD	PRC	1943
95	BLIND FURY	NOYCE	TRI STAR	1989
95	UP FROM THE BEACH (UK)	PARRISH	20TH CENTURY FOX	1965
95A	LOVE AND DOUGHNUTS (sh)	DEL RUTH	ASSOC. FIRST NAT'L	1921
95B	BE REASONABLE (sh)	DEL RUTH	ASSOC. FIRST NAT'L	1921
96	BILLY THE KID - FUGITIVE OF THE PLAINS	NEWFIELD	PRC	1943
96	HER HUSBAND'S FRIEND	NIBLO	INCE	1920
96	SUZANNA	JONES	ALLIED PRODUCERS	1923
96A	LONDON CONNECTION	CLOUSE	BUENA VISTA	1979
97	BORDER LINE (unfinished)		MACK SENNETT	1921
97	WILD HORSE RUSTLERS	NEWFIELD	TIFFANY	1943
98	BILLY THE KID - WESTERN CYCLONE	NEWFIELD	PRC	1943
98	BY HECK (sh)	DEL RUTH	ASSOC. FIRST NAT'L	1921
98	GREATER CLAIM	RUGGLES	METRO	1921
98	RAD	NEEDHAM	TRI STAR	1986
98	RUPERT OF HENTZAU	LYTELL	SELZNICK	1923
98	SUNSET	EDWARDS	TRI STAR	1988
99	COMMON LAW	ARCHAINBEAU	SELZNICK	1923
99	DUCK HUNTER (sh)	DEL RUTH	ASSOC. FIRST NAT'L	1922
99W	99 WOMEN (UK)	FRANCO	COMMONWEALTH	1969
100	GREAT BALLS OF FIRE	MCBRIDE	ORION	1989
100	STEP FORWARD (sh)	MEINS	ASSOC. FIRST NAT'L	1922
101	BILLY THE KID - RENEGADES	NEWFIELD	PRC	1943
101	NO ORCHIDS FOR MISS BLANDISH (UK)	CLOWES	RKO	1948
101	ON PATROL (sh)	DEL RUTH	ASSOC. FIRST NAT'L	1922
101	UNCHARTED SEAS	RUGGLES	METRO	1921
102	BILLY THE KID - BLAZING FRONTIER	NEWFIELD	PRC	1943
102	HOMEMADE MOVIES	GREY, MEINS	ASSOC. FIRST NAT'L	1922
102	PROTOCOL	ROSS	WARNER BROS.	1984
103	AMERICAN FLYERS	BADHAM	WARNER BROS	1985
103	CAMILLE	SMALLWOOD	METRO	1921
103	HELL FIRE AUSTIN	SHELTON	TIFFANY	1932
103	HORNET'S NEST (UK)	SAUNDERS	GFD	1955
103	MARY ANNE (unfinished)		MACK SENNETT	1923
103	SHE'S GOT EVERYTHING (mistake - 1003)	SANTLEY	RKO	1937
103 (IP)	STAIRWAY TO HEAVEN (UK: MATTER OF LIFE AND DEATH)	POWELL, PRESSBURGER	UNIVERSAL	1946
104	BILLY THE KID - CATTLE STAMPEDE	NEWFIELD	PRC	1943
104	BROTHER ALFRED (UK)	EDWARDS	WARDOUR	1932
104	GYMNASIUM JIM (sh)	DEL RUTH	ASSOC. FIRST NAT'L	1922
104	PEE WEE'S BIG ADVENTURE	BURTON	WARNER BROS	1985
104-1	MISBEHAVING HUSBANDS	BEAUDINE	PRC	1940
105	LIFE'S DARN FUNNY	FITZGERALD	METRO	1921
105	MA AND PA (sh)	DEL RUTH	ASSOC. FIRST NAT'L	1922
105	WILDCATS	RITCHIE	WARNER BROS	1985
105-DB	DEVIL BAT	YARBROUGH	PRC	1940

106	WHEN SUMMER COMES (sh)	DEL RUTH	ASSOC. FIRST NAT'L	1922
106 (IP)	GREAT EXPECTATIONS (UK)	LEAN	CINEGUILD	1946
106Q	STRANGERS OF THE EVENING	HUMBERSTONE	TIFFANY	1932
107	BOW WOW (sh)	JACKMAN	ASSOC. FIRST NAT'L	1922
107	DEVIL RIDERS	NEWFIELD	PRC	1943
107	FIG LEAF FOR EVE	BRODIE	MONOGRAM	1944
107	FIRES OF FATE (UK)	WALKER	POWERS	1932
107	LENA RIVERS	ROSEN	TIFFANY	1932
107	MOTHER O' MINE	NIBLO	INCE	1921
108	BOILING POINT	MELFORD	ALLIED	1932
108	CONQUERING POWER	INGRAM	METRO	1921
108	LUCKY GIRL (UK)	GERRARD, MILLER	WARDOUR	1932
108	SHRIEK OF ARABY (sh)	JONES	ALLIED PRODUCERS	1923
108	SMALL TOWN IDOL	KENTON	ASSOC. FIRST NAT'L	1921
108Q	MAN CALLED BACK	FLOREY	TIFFANY	1932
109	MILLION DOLLAR CAT (t) (sh)	HANNA, BARBERA	MGM	1944
109	NIP AND TUCK (sh)	DEL RUTH	PATHE EXCHANGE	1923
110	EXTRA GIRL	JONES	ASSOC. EXHIBITORS	1923
110	FACE VALUE	FLOREY	STERLING	1927
110	HAIL THE WOMAN	WRAY	INCE	1921
110	LAST COUPON (UK)	LAUNDER	WARDOUR	1932
110	NABONGA	NEWFIELD	PRC	1944
111	ARMS AND THE MAN (UK)	LEWIS	WARDOUR	1932
111	COME DANCE WITH ME (UK)	ZAMPI	COLUMBIA	1950
111	FRONTIER OUTLAWS	NEWFIELD	PRC	1944
111	HOME TALENT (sh)	SENNETT, ABBE	ASSOC. FIRST NAT'L	1921
111	ONE CYLINDER LOVE	LORD	PATHE EXCHANGE	1923
112	JEAN-PIERRE AUMONT	portrait	MGM	
112	MAN IN THE MIRROR (UK)	ELVEY	GRAND NATIONAL	1936
112	OVER THE EDGE	KAPLAN	WB	1979
112	SKYLARKING (sh)	DEL RUTH	PATHE EXCHANGE	1923
112	THERE ARE NO VILLAINS	VEILLER	METRO	1921
112	THUNDERING GUN STINGERS	NEWFIELD	PRC	1944
112	WOMAN HATERS (sh)	GOTTLER	COLUMBIA	1934
113	FLASH GORDON CONQUERS UNIVERSE (serial)	BEEBE, TAYLOR	UNIVERSAL	1940
113	WHERE'S MY WANDERING BOY THIS EVENING? (sh)	WALDRON	PATHE EXCHANGE	1923
114	LET ME EXPLAIN, DEAR (UK)	GERRARD, MILLER	WARDOUR	1932
114	PITFALLS OF A BIG CITY (sh)	WALDRON	PATHE EXCHANGE	1923
114	VALLEY OF VENGEANCE	NEWFIELD	PRC	1944
114	WOMAN IN RED, THE	WILDER	ORION	1984
114 (IP)	BLACK NARCISSUS (UK)	POWELL, PRESSBURGER	UNIVERSAL	1947
115	DOWN TO THE SEA IN SHOES (sh)	LORD	PATHE EXCHANGE	1923
115	FUZZY SETTLES DOWN	NEWFIELD	PRC	1944
115	HOW WOMEN LOVE	WEBB	BETTY BLYTHE	1922
115	TIGHTROPE	TUGGLE	WARNER BROS	1984
115	TWO IN A TAXI	FLOREY	COLUMBIA	1941
116	ASLEEP AT THE SWITCH (sh)	DEL RUTH	PATHE EXCHANGE	1923
116	LOVE NEVER DIES	VIDOR	ASSOCIATED PRODUCERS	1921
116	OUR WIFE	STAHL	COLUMBIA	1941
116	PUNCH DRUNKS (sh)	BRESLOW	COLUMBIA	1934
116	RUSTLERS HIDEOUT	NEWFIELD	PRC	1944
116	SLEEPLESS NIGHTS (UK)	BENTLEY	REMINGTON	1932
116 (IP)	TAKE MY LIFE (UK)	NEAME	EAGLE-LION	1947
117	END OF THE RIVER (UK 1947)	TWIST	UNIVERSAL	1948
117	HERE COMES MR. JORDAN	HALL	COLUMBIA	1941
117	RENEGADE TRAIL	SELANDER	PARAMOUNT	1939
117	ROUGH AND READY (sh)	CAMPBELL	PATHE EXCHANGE	1923
117 (IP)	END OF THE RIVER (UK)	TWIST	UNIVERSAL	1947
118	DARE-DEVIL (sh)	LORD	PATHE EXCHANGE	1923
118	WILD HORSE PHANTOM	NEWFIELD	PRC	1944
118	YOU'LL NEVER GET RICH	LANFIELD	COLUMBIA	1941
118 (IP)	CAPTAIN BOYCOTT (UK)	LAUNDER	UNIVERSAL	1947
119	FLIP FLOPS (sh)	DEL RUTH	PATHE EXCHANGE	1923
119	MYSTERY SHIP	LANDERS	COLUMBIA	1941
119	OATH OF VENGEANCE	NEWFIELD	PRC	1944
120	CHALLENGE, THE (UK) IT TAKES A THIEF	GILLING	ALLIANCE FILM	1960

120	IT TAKES A THIEF (UK: CHALLENGE)	GILLING	VALIANT	1960
120	TEN DOLLARS OR TEN DAYS (sh)	LORD	PATHE EXCHANGE	1924
120	TWO LATINS FROM MANHATTAN	BARTON	COLUMBIA	1941
121	MOLLY O'	JONES	ASSOC. FIRST NAT'L	1921
121G	JASSY (UK)	KNOWLES	UNIVERSAL	1947
122	COUNTER-ESPIONAGE	DMYTRYK	COLUMBIA	1942
122	HOLE IN THE WALL		METRO	1922
122	SMILE PLEASE (sh)	WALDRON	PATHE EXCHANGE	1924
123	DEAR MURDERER (UK)	CRABTREE	UNIVERSAL	1947
123	ONE SPOOKY NIGHT (sh)	LORD	PATHE EXCHANGE	1924
124	ALONG CAME RUTH	CLINE	METRO GOLDWYN	1924
124	PICKING PEACHES (sh)	KENTON	PATHE EXCHANGE	1924
124	THREE GIRLS ABOUT TOWN	JASON	COLUMBIA	1941
125	BINNIE BARNES	portrait		
125	GO WEST YOUNG LADY	STRAYER	COLUMBIA	1941
125	HALF-BACK OF NOTRE DAME (sh)	LORD	PATHE EXCHANGE	1924
125G	HOLIDAY CAMP (UK)	ANNAKIN	UNIVERSAL	1947
126	HARMON OF MICHIGAN	BARTON	COLUMBIA	1941
126	PRISONER OF ZENDA	INGRAM	METRO	1922
126	SHANGHAIED LOVERS (sh)	DEL RUTH	PATHE EXCHANGE	1924
127	KISSES		METRO	1922
127	MAUREEN O'SULLIVAN	portrait	MGM	
127	SCAREM MUCH (sh)	LORD	PATHE EXCHANGE	1924
127	STORK PAYS OFF	LANDERS	COLUMBIA	1941
127 (IP)	BLANCHE FURY (UK)	ALLEGRET	EAGLE LION	1948
128	SECRETS OF THE LONE WOLF	DMYTRYK	COLUMBIA	1941
128	YUKON JAKE (sh)	LORD	PATHE EXCHANGE	1924
128 (IP)	WOMAN IN THE HALL (UK)	LEE	EAGLE-LION	1947
129	BLOOD RED	MASTERSON	HEMDALE	1989
129	FLICKERING YOUTH (sh)	KENTON	PATHE EXCHANGE	1924
129	LADY IS WILLING	LEISEN	COLUMBIA	1942
129	WHEN THE BOUGH BREAKS (UK)	HUNTINGTON	GFD	1947
130	BLACK OXFORDS (sh)	LORD	PATHE EXCHANGE	1924
130	SING FOR YOUR SUPPER	BARTON	COLUMBIA	1941
131	CAT'S MEOW (sh)	DEL RUTH	PATHE EXCHANGE	1924
132	HARVARD, HERE I COME	LANDERS	COLUMBIA	1941
132	HIS NEW MAMMA (sh)	DEL RUTH	PATHE EXCHANGE	1924
133	SONG YOU GAVE ME (UK)	STEIN	COLUMBIA	1933
133	TRIFLING WOMEN	INGRAM	METRO	1922
134	BLONDIE GOES TO COLLEGE	STRAYER	COLUMBIA	1942
134	LION AND THE SOUSE (sh)	EDWARDS	PATHE EXCHANGE	1924
134	LOVE IN THE DARK	BEAUMONT	METRO PICTURES	1922
135	BLONDE SAVAGE	SEELEY	EAGLE LION	1947
135	CITY HEAT	BENJAMIN	WARNER BROS	1984
135	FIRST 100 YEARS (sh)	SWEET	PATHE EXCHANGE	1924
135	HONOLULU LU	BARTON	COLUMBIA	1941
135	LARCENY IN HER HEART	NEWFIELD	PRC	1946
135	THEY MADE ME A FUGITIVE (US: I BECAME A CRIMINAL)	CAVALCANTI	WARNER BROS	1947
135G	BROKEN JOURNEY (UK)	ANNAKIN, CHORLTON	EAGLE LION	1948
136	CADETS ON PARADE	LANDERS	COLUMBIA	1942
136	COUCH TRIP	RITCHIE	ORION	1988
136	DAUGHTER OF DARKNESS (UK)	COMFORT	PARAMOUNT BRITISH	1948
136	DESERT FLOWER	CUMMINGS	FIRST NAT'L	1925
136	RED SHOES	POWELL-PRESSBURGER	EAGLE LION	1949
136	WALL STREET BLUES (sh)	LORD	PATHE EXCHANGE	1924
136 (IP)	RED SHOES (UK)	POWELL, PRESSBURGER	EAGLE-LION	1948
137	EAST OF THE WATER PLUG (sh)	MARTIN	PATHE EXCHANGE	1924
137	MAYFAIR GIRL (UK)	KING	WARNER BROS.	1933
137	NEW FACES	SILLMAN	20TH CENTURY FOX	1954
137	SHUT MY BIG MOUTH	BARTON	COLUMBIA	1942
137 (PA)	SO EVIL MY LOVE (UK)	ALLEN	PARAMOUNT	1948
138	LUCK O' THE FOOLISH (sh)	EDWARDS	PATHE EXCHANGE	1924
138	OLIVIER TWIST	LEAN	EAGLE LION	1951
138	TWO YANKS IN TRINIDAD	RATOFF	COLUMBIA	1942
138	WHERE THE PAVEMENT ENDS	INGRAM	METRO	1923
138 (IP)	OLIVER TWIST (UK)	LEAN	EAGLE-LION	1948

139	HUMAN WRECKAGE	WRAY	FBO	1923
139	LIZZIES OF THE FIELD (sh)	LORD	PATHE EXCHANGE	1924
139	MAN WHO RETURNED TO LIFE	LANDERS	COLUMBIA	1942
139	RED WAGON (UK - BIP 1934)	STEIN	ALLIANCE	1935
140	ALL THE BROTHERS WERE VALIANT	WILLAT	METRO	1923
140	AMERICAN BEAUTY	MENDES	DREAMWORKS	1999
140	BREAK (UK)	COMFORT	PLANET	1963
140	CANAL ZONE	LANDERS	COLUMBIA	1942
140	ROMEO AND JULIET (sh)	MORRIS, SWEET	PATHE EXCHANGE	1924
140G	HELTER SKELTER (UK)	THOMAS	GFD	1949
141	CRIME ON THE HILL (UK)	VORHAUS	WARDOUR	1933
141	DUNKIRK (UK)	NORMAN	MGM	1958
141	HANSOM CABMAN (sh)	EDWARDS	PATHE EXCHANGE	1924
141	MIRANDA	ANNAKIN	EAGLE LION	1948
141	TRAMP TRAMP TRAMP	BARTON	COLUMBIA	1942
141	YOUNG MASTER	CHAN	GOLDEN HARVEST	1980
142	DAVY (UK)	RELPH	MGM	1958
142	LITTLE ROBINSON CORKSCREW (sh)	CEDER	PATHE EXCHANGE	1924
143	ALL AT SEA (UK: BARNACLE BILL)	FREND	MGM	1957
143	HIS CAPTIVE WOMAN	FITZMAURICE	FIRST NATIONAL	1929
143	JACKIE COLLINS	portrait		
143	LIVING DEAD (UK: SCOTLAND YARD MYSTERY)	BENTLEY	FIRST DIVISION	1934
143	PAINTED DESERT	HIGGINS	RKO PATHE	1930
143	WANDERING WAISTLINES (sh)	CEDER	PATHE EXCHANGE	1924
144	ALIAS BOSTON BLACKIE	LANDERS	COLUMBIA	1942
144	MIRACLE MILE	DE JARNETT	HEMDALE RELEASING	1989
144	SPY 77 (UK: ON SECRET SERVICE)	WOODS	FIRST DIVISION	1933
144	SUPREME SECRET (UK)	WALKER	CHURCH AND CHAPEL	1958
144	THREE FOOLISH WEEKS (sh)	KENNEDY, MORRIS	PATHE EXCHANGE	1924
145	PALE RIDER	EASTWOOD	WARNER BROS	1985
145	SEA SQUAWK (sh)	EDWARDS	PATHE EXCHANGE	1925
145 (IP)	SIN OF ESTHER WATERS (UK: ESTHER WATERS)	DALRYMPLE, PROUD	INTERNATIONAL RELEASING	1948
146	GALLOPING BUNGALOWS (sh)	LORD	PATHE EXCHANGE	1924
146	TALK OF THE TOWN	STEVENS	COLUMBIA	1942
146 (IP)	BLUE LAGOON (UK)	LAUNDER	UNIVERSAL	1949
147	ANNA CHRISTIE	WRAY	ASSOC. FIRST NAT'L	1923
147	ART OF LOVE	JEWISON	UNIVERSAL	1965
147	GREYSTOKE	HUDSON	WARNER BROS	1984
147	NOT A LADIES MAN	LANDERS	COLUMBIA	1942
147	RIDERS OF THE PURPLE COWS (sh)	CEDER	PATHE EXCHANGE	1924
147	ROBOCOP 2	KERSHNER	ORION	1990
147	SCARAMOUCHE	INGRAM	METRO	1923
148	BARBARA FRIETCHIE	HILLYER	PDC	1924
148	HELLO ANAPOLIS	BARTON	COLUMBIA	1942
148	REEL VIRGINIAN (sh)	MORRIS, KENNEDY	PATHE EXCHANGE	1924
149	EAGLE'S FEATHER, THE	SLOMAN	METRO	1923
149	FISH PICTURE	SENNETT	UNF. MACK SENNETT	1924
149	MEET THE STEWARTS	GREEN	COLUMBIA	1942
149G	EASY MONEY (UK)	KNOWLES	EAGLE LION	1948
150	CANNON BALL EXPRESS (sh)	LORD	PATHE EXCHANGE	1924
150	MADE IN THE KITCHEN	SMITH	ASSOC. FIRST NAT'L	1921
150	THEY ALL KISSED THE BRIDE	HALL	COLUMBIA	1942
150G	BAD LORD BYRON (UK)	MACDONALD	INTERNATIONAL RELEASING	1949
151	ALL I WANT FOR CHRISTMAS	LIEBERMAN	PARAMOUNT	1991
151	ALL NIGHT LONG (sh)	EDWARDS	PATHE EXCHANGE	1924
151	FRIGHT NIGHT PART 2	WALLACE	TRI STAR	1988
151	PARACHUTE NURSE	BARTON	COLUMBIA	1942
151	SOCIAL CODE	APFEL	METRO PICTURES	1923
152	CUPID'S BOOTS (sh)	KENNEDY, MORRIS	PATHE EXCHANGE	1925
152	DULCIMER STREET (UK: LONDON BELONGS TO M 1948)	GILLIAT	UNIVERSAL	1949
152	MEN IN BLACK (sh)	R MCCAREY	COLUMBIA	1934
152	SWEETHEART OF THE FLEET	BARTON	COLUMBIA	1942
153	BULL AND SAND (sh)	LORD	PATHE EXCHANGE	1924
153	SUBMARINE RAIDER	LANDERS	COLUMBIA	1942
153	WHO'S HARRY CRUMB?	FLAHERTY	TRI STAR	1989
153/H	PENNY AND THE POWNALL CASE (UK)	HAND	GFD	1948

154	FEET OF MUD (sh)	EDWARDS	PATHE EXCHANGE	1924
154	RETURN OF BULLDOG DRUMMOND (UK)	SUMMERS	MUNDUS	1934
154	SOMETHING ALWAYS HAPPENS (UK)	POWELL	WARNER BROS.	1934
154	YOU WERE NEVER LOVELIER	SEITER	COLUMBIA	1942
155	ATLANTIC CONVOY	LANDERS	COLUMBIA	1942
155	GIVE HER A RING	WOODS	BRITISH INTERNATIONAL	1934
155	MARRIAGE CIRCUS (sh)	MORRIS, KENNEDY	PATHE EXCHANGE	1925
155G	CHRISTOPHER COLUMBUS (UK)	MACDONALD	UNIVERSAL	1949
156	FLIGHT LIEUTENANT	SALKOW	COLUMBIA	1942
156	GIRL IN THE CROWD (UK)	POWELL	WARNER BROS.	1935
156	HONEYMOON HARDSHIPS (sh)	CEDER	PATHE EXCHANGE	1925
156	THREE LITTLE PIGSKINS (sh)	MCCAREY	COLUMBIA	1934
156H	TROUBLE IN THE AIR (UK)	SAUNDERS	GFD	1948
157	BLIND GODDESS (UK)	FRENCH	UNIVERSAL	1948
157	LOVES OF MADAME DUBARRY (UK: I GIVE MY HEART)	VARNEL	JH HOFFBERG	1935
157	LOVE'S SWEET PIFFLE (sh)	KENNEDY	PATHE EXCHANGE	1924
157	MARRIAGE CHEAT	WRAY	ASSOC. FIRST NAT'L	1924
157	ONE DANGEROUS NIGHT	GORDON	COLUMBIA	1943
157G	BLIND GODDESS (UK)	FRENCH	UNIVERSAL	1948
158	APRIL BLOSSOMS (UK: BLOSSOM TIME)	STEIN	FILM ALLIANCE	1934
158	BLONDIE FOR VICTORY	STRAYER	COLUMBIA	1942
158	OFF HIS TROLLEY (sh)	CLINE	PATHE EXCHANGE	1924
158G	MY BROTHER'S KEEPER (UK)	ROOME	EAGLE LION	1948
159	BOOBS IN THE WOODS (sh)	EDWARDS	PATHE EXCHANGE	1925
159	FISHERMAN'S PARADISE		MGM	1931
159	GIRL LIKE THAT, A	HENDERSON	PARAMOUNT	1917
159	HAPPINESS	VIDOR	METRO	1924
159	HORSES' COLLARS (sh)	BRUCKMAN	COLUMBIA	1935
159	MAN'S WORLD	BARTON	COLUMBIA	1942
160	GIRLS WILL BE BOYS (UK)	VARNEL	WARDOUR	1934
160	RESTLESS KNIGHTS (sh)	LAMONT	COLUMBIA	1935
160	REVELATION	BAKER	METRO GOLDWYN	1924
160	SABOTAGE SQUAD	LANDERS	COLUMBIA	1942
160	THIS WAY PLEASE	FLOREY	PARAMOUNT	1937
160	WATER WAGONS (sh)	LORD	PATHE EXCHANGE	1925
161	CROSSROADS OF NEW YORK	JONES	ASSOC. FIRST NAT'L	1922
161	DYNAMITE SMITH	INCE	PATHE EXCHANGE	1924
161	FRANCES GIFFORD	portrait	MGM	
161	MY SISTER EILEEN	HALL	COLUMBIA	1942
161	RASPBERRY ROMANCE (sh)	BACON	PATHE EXCHANGE	1925
161 (IP)	PASSIONATE FRIENDS (UK)	LEAN	UNIVERSAL	1949
162	GIDDAP! (sh)	LORD	PATHE EXCHANGE	1925
162	ISLE OF SUNKEN GOLD	WEBB	MASCOT PICTURES	1927
162	LUCKY LEGS	BARTON	COLUMBIA	1942
163	DESPERADOES	VIDOR	COLUMBIA	1943
163	LONE RIDER RIDES ON	NEWFIELD	PRC	1941
163	MISTER CINDERS (UK)	ZELNIK	WARDOUR	1934
163	PLUMBER (sh)	CLINE	PATHE EXCHANGE	1925
163	POP GOES THE EASEL (sh)	LORD	COLUMBIA	1935
163	QUARTET (UK)	ANNAKIN,CRABTREE, FRENCH	EAGLE LION	1948
164	ALONG CAME RUTH	CLINE	METRO GOLDWYN	1924
164	HIS MARRIAGE WOW (sh)	EDWARDS	PATHE EXCHANGE	1925
164	STAND BY ALL NETWORKS	LANDERS	COLUMBIA	1942
165	BREAD	SCHERTZINGER	METRO GOLDWYN	1924
165	CHRISTINE OF THE HUNGRY HEART	ARCHAINBAUD	FIRST NAT'L	1924
165	LION'S WHISKERS (sh)	LORD	PATHE EXCHANGE	1925
165	SPIRIT OF STANFORD	BARTON	COLUMBIA	1942
165	UNCIVIL WARRIORS (sh)	LORD	COLUMBIA	1935
166	DESTROYER	SEITER	COLUMBIA	1943
166	OLD CURIOSITY SHOP (UK)	BENTLEY	FIRST DIVISION	1934
166	WILD GOOSE CHASER (sh)	BACON	PATHE EXCHANGE	1925
166 (IP)	MANIACS ON WHEELS (UK: ONCE A JOLLY SWAGMAN)	LEE	INTERNATIONAL RELEASING	1949
167	DON'T MARRY (SPANISH)		FOX FILM	1928
167	LET'S HAVE FUN	BARTON	COLUMBIA	1943
167	MURDER AT MONTE CARLO (UK)	INCE	WARNER BROS.	1935
167	SKINNERS IN SILK (sh)	LORD	PATHE EXCHANGE	1925

167G	LOST DAUGHTER (UK: PORTRAIT FROM LIFE)	FISHER	UNIVERSAL	1948
168	BELOVED BOZO (sh)	CLINE	PATHE EXCHANGE	1925
168	DARING YOUNG MAN	STRAYER	COLUMBIA	1942
168	HELL'S CARGO (UK: MCGLUSKY THE SEA ROVER)	SUMMERS	FILM ALLIANCE	1935
168	PARDON MY SCOTCH (sh)	LORD	COLUMBIA	1935
169	BOSTON BLACKIE GOES HOLLYWOOD	GORDON	COLUMBIA	1942
169	DANDY DICK (UK)	BEAUDINE	WARDOUR	1935
169	HERE COME THE HUGGETTS (UK)	ANNAKIN	PENTAGON	1948
169	PLAIN CLOTHES (sh)	EDWARDS	PATHE EXCHANGE	1925
169G	HERE COME THE HUGGETTS (UK)	ANNAKIN	PENTAGON	1948
170	ABDUL THE DAMNED (UK)	GRUNE	COLUMBIA	1935
170	DON'T FAIL (sh)	BACON	EDUCATIONAL	1924
170	SMITH OF MINNESOTA	LANDERS	COLUMBIA	1942
170	SNEEZING BEEZERS! (sh)	LORD	PATHE EXCHANGE	1925
171	BASHFUL JIM (sh)	CLINE	PATHE EXCHANGE	1925
171	BOOGIE MAN WILL GET YOU	LANDERS	COLUMBIA	1942
171	MIMI (UK)	STEIN	UNITED ARTISTS	1935
171	NIGHT SHIFT	HOWARD	WARNER BROS	1982
171AQ	WARNING TO WANTONS (UK)	WILSON	GFD	1949
172	DANCE BAND (UK)	VARNEL	FIRST DIVISION	1935
172	FRANCES GIFFORD	portrait	MGM	
172	SUPER-HOOPER-CYNE LIZZIES (sh)	LORD	PATHE EXCHANGE	1925
172	UNDERGROUND AGENT	GORDON	COLUMBIA	1942
172	WHEEL OF FATE (UK)	SEARLE	GFD	1953
172A	BEN-HUR	WYLER	MGM	1959
173	DRAKE THE PIRATE (UK: DRAKE OF ENGLAND)	WOODS	GRAND NATIONAL	1935
173	MAN OF THE MOMENT (UK)	BANKS	WARNER BROS.	1935
173	NIGHT TO REMEMBER	WALLACE	COLUMBIA	1943
173	SQUAWK MAN	SENNETT	UNR. MACK SENNETT	1925
173AQ	FLOODTIDE (UK)	WILSON	AQUILA-GFD	1949
174	CRIME UNLIMITED (UK)	R INCE	WARNER BROS.	1935
174	LAUGH YOUR BLUES AWAY	BARTON	COLUMBIA	1942
174	MARILYN MAXWELL	portrait	MGM	
174	REGAL CAVALCADE (UK: ROYAL CAVALCADE)	BRENON, KELLINO, LEE	FILM ALLIANCE	1935
174	REMEMBER WHEN? (sh)	EDWARDS	PATHE EXCHANGE	1925
175	BREAKING THE ICE (sh)	SANTELL	PATHE EXCHANGE	1925
175	CHEAP KISSES	INCE	FBO	1924
175	JUNIOR ARMY	LANDERS	COLUMBIA	1942
175	STUDENT'S ROMANCE (UK)	KANTUREK	BIP	1935
175	WHO'S HARRY CRUMB?	FLAHERTY	TRI STAR	1989
175G	IT'S NOT CRICKET (UK)	INCE	WARNER BROS.	1937
176	FRANCES GIFFORD	portrait	MGM	
176	LOVE AND KISSES (sh)	CLINE	PATHE EXCHANGE	1925
176	MORE THE MERRIER	STEVENS	COLUMBIA	1943
177	BROWN WALLET (UK)	POWELL	WARNER BROS.	1936
177	HEART'S DESIRE (UK)	STEIN	GAUMONT BRIT. AMER.	1936
177	HIS FIRST FLAME (sh)	EDWARDS	PATHE EXCHANGE	1927
177	POWER OF THE PRESS	LANDERS	COLUMBIA	1943
177	SWING HOSTESS	NEWFIELD	PRC	1944
178	CLAUDINE AT SCHOOL (FR)	POLIGNY	PHOENIX FILM	1940
178	COLD TURKEY (sh)	CLINE	PATHE EXCHANGE	1925
178	HONOURS EASY (UK)	BRENON	WARDOUR	1935
178	WHAT'S BUZZIN COUSIN?	BARTON	COLUMBIA	1943
178/H	LOVE IN WAITING (UK)	PEIRCE	GFD	1948
179	IRON NAG (sh)	LORD	PATHE EXCHANGE	1925
179	MUSIC HATH CHARMS (UK)	BENTLEY	WARDOUR	1935
179	REVELIE WITH BEVERLY	BARTON	COLUMBIA	1943
179G	BOY, A GIRL AND A BIKE, A (UK)	SMART	GFD	1949
180	HE WHO GETS SMACKED (sh)	BACON	PATHE EXCHANGE	1925
180	HUGGETTS ABROAD (UK)	ANNAKIN	GFD	1949
180	ONCE IN A MILLION (UK)	WOODS	GAUMONT BRIT. AMER.	1936
180G	HUGGETTS ABROAD (UK)	ANNAKIN	GFD	1949
181	CROWN V. STEVENS (UK)	POWELL	WARNER BROS.	1936
181	LIVING DANGEROUSLY (UK)	BRENON	GAUMONT BRITISH	1936
181	SAHARA	KORDA	COLUMBIA	1943
181	TEE FOR TWO (sh)	CLINE	PATHE EXCHANGE	1925

181G	VOTE FOR HUGGETT (UK)	ANNAKIN	GFD	1949
182	APPOINTMENT IN BERLIN	GREEN	COLUMBIA	1943
182	BRAVADOS, THE	KING	20th CENTURY-FOX	1958
182	GOOD MORNING, NURSE! (sh)	BACON	PATHE EXCHANGE	1925
183	AFTER MIDNIGHT WITH BOSTON BLACKIE	LANDERS	COLUMBIA	1943
183	BUTTER FINGERS (sh)	LORD	PATHE EXCHANGE	1925
183	EDUCATED EVANS (UK)	BEAUDINE	WARNER BROS.	1936
183	RIVER OF UNREST (UK: OURSELVES ALONE)	HURST, SUMMERS	GAUMONT BRITISH	1936
184	ANN SOTHERN	portrait	MGM	
184	FIRST COMES COURAGE	ARZNER	COLUMBIA	1943
184	MONTE CRISTO	FLYNN	FOX FILM	1922
184	RAINY KNIGHT (sh)	BACON	PATHE EXCHANGE	1925
184	VIRGIN	JAMES	TRUART	1924
184G	LOST PEOPLE (UK)	BOX, KNOWLES	FRACKMAN GOLDBERG	1949
185	GOSH-DARN MORTGAGE (sh)	CLINE	PATHE EXCHANGE	1926
185	SHE HAS WHAT IT TAKES	BARTON	COLUMBIA	1943
185	TENTH MAN (UK)	HURST	GAUMONT BRITISH	1936
186	IT'S A GREAT LIFE	STRAYER	COLUMBIA	1943
186	OVER THERE-ABOUTS (sh)	ROSSON	PATHE EXCHANGE	1925
186	WELCOME STRANGER	YOUNG	PDC	1924
186 (IP)	ALL OVER THE TOWN (UK)	TWIST	UNIVERSAL	1949
187	BOY FROM STALINGRAD	SALKOW	COLUMBIA	1943
187	DANGEROUS CURVES BEHIND (sh)	CLINE	PATHE EXCHANGE	1925
187	DOMINANT SEX (UK)	BRENON	ABFD	1937
187AQ	STOP PRESS GIRL (UK)	BARRY	GFD	1949
188	ISN'T LOVE CUCKOO? (sh)	BACON	PATHE EXCHANGE	1925
188	LOVE RACKET	SEITER	WARNER BROS	1929
188	REDHEAD FROM MANHATTAN	LANDERS	COLUMBIA	1943
188	SUBMARINE D-1	BACON	WARNER BROS	1937
189	FROM RAGS TO BRITCHES (sh)	LORD	PATHE EXCHANGE	1925
189	ONCE UPON A TIME	HALL	COLUMBIA	1944
189	WALLACE BEERY + DAUGHTER CAROL ANN	portrait	MGM	
189 (IP)	FOOLS RUSH IN (UK)	CARSTAIRS	GFD	1949
190	SWEET PICKLE (sh)	ROSSON	PATHE EXCHANGE	1925
190	TWO SENORITAS FROM CHICAGO	WOODRUFF	COLUMBIA	1943
190 (IP)	BULLDOG DRUMMOND AT BAY (UK)	LEE	REPUBLIC	1937
190 (IP)	DEAR MR. PROHACK (UK)	FREELAND	PENTAGON	1949
191	SMITH'S BABY (sh)	CLINE	PATHE EXCHANGE	1926
191	WHO'S HARRY CRUMB?	FLAHERTY	TRI STAR	1989
191G	MARRY ME (UK)	FISHER	ELLIS	1949
192	GOOD LUCK MR. YATES	ENRIGHT	COLUMBIA	1943
192	LUCKY STARS (sh)	EDWARDS	PATHE EXCHANGE	1925
192	PERMIT ME (sh)	RAY	EDUCATIONAL	1925
192	SPRING HANDICAP (UK)	BRENON	ABPC	1937
192	THREE WISE FOOLS	VIDOR	GOLDWYN	1923
192	WALLACE BEERY	portrait	MGM	
192G	DIAMOND CITY (UK)	MACDONALD	FAVORITE	1949
193	CHAMBER, THE	FOLEY	UNIVERSAL	1996
193	DON'T TELL DAD (sh)	PRATT	PATHE EXCHANGE	1925
193	DOUGHBOYS IN IRELAND	LANDERS	COLUMBIA	1943
193	LOCK OUT (sh)		EDUCATIONAL	1925
194	COVER GIRL	VIDOR	COLUMBIA	1944
194	NEVER AGAIN (sh)	ST. JOHN	EDUCATIONAL	1924
194	POET'S PUB (UK)	WILSON	GFD	1949
194	SOAPSUDS LADY (sh)	ROSSON	PATHE EXCHANGE	1925
194	THIEF IN PARADISE	FITZMAURICE	FIRST NAT'L	1925
195	MY KINGDOM FOR A COOK	WALLACE	COLUMBIA	1943
195	WHISPERING WHISKERS (sh)	LORD	PATHE EXCHANGE	1926
196	LOVE MANIA (sh)	ST. JOHN	EDUCATIONAL	1925
196	MYSTERY OF ROOM 13 (UK: MR. REEDER IN ROOM 13)	LEE	FILM ALLIANCE	1938
196	TERROR (UK)	BIRD	FILM ALLIANCE	1938
196	TRIMMED IN GOLD (sh)	LORD	PATHE EXCHANGE	1926
196	VULTURE (UK)	INCE	WARNER BROS.	1937
197	DYNAMITE DOGGIE (sh)	ST. JOHN	EDUCATIONAL	1925
197	PASSPORT TO SUEZ	DE TOTH	COLUMBIA	1943
197	SMITH'S VACATION (sh)	CLINE	PATHE EXCHANGE	1926

197G	TRAVELLER'S JOY (UK)	THOMAS	GFD	1950
198	BRIGHT LIGHTS	CURTIZ	WARNER BROS	1930
198	DANGEROUS BLONDES	JASON	COLUMBIA	1943
198	HOUSEMASTER (UK)	BRENON	ALLIANCE	1938
198	THERE HE GOES	EDWARDS	PATHE EXCHANGE	1925
199	HOTSY TOTSY (sh)	GOULDING	PATHE EXCHANGE	1925
199	THERE'S SOMETHING ABOUT A SOLDIER	GREEN	COLUMBIA	1943
200	EXTORTION	HILLYER	COLUMBIA	1938
200	HURRY, DOCTOR! (sh)	BACON	PATHE EXCHANGE	1925
200	JANE STEPS OUT (UK)	STEIN	ABFD	1938
200	KING OF KINGS	DEMILLE	PATHE EXCHANGE	1927
200 (IP)	MADELEINE (UK)	LEAN	UNIVERSAL	1950
201	I WAS A TEENAGE WEREWOLF	FOWLER	AIP	1957
201	SMITH'S LANDLORD (sh)	CLINE	PATHE EXCHANGE	1926
201G	BOYS IN BROWN (UK)	TULLY	GFD	1949
202	DORA'S DUNKING DOUGHNUTS	EDWARDS	FOX FILM	1933
202	EVERY DAY'S A HOLIDAY	SUTHERLAND	PARAMOUNT	1937
202	IRVING THALBERG, WIFE NORMA SHEARER	portrait	MGM	
202	SOLDIER MAN	EDWARDS	PATHE EXCHANGE	1928
202	VIRGINIA GREY	portrait	MGM	
203	CIRCUS TODAY (sh)	LORD	PATHE EXCHANGE	1926
203	FOOTSTEPS IN THE SAND (UK: BLACK LIMELIGHT)	STEIN	FILM ALLIANCE	1939
203	MAIN EVENT	DARE	COLUMBIA	1938
204	HOLD MY HAND (UK)	FREELAND	ABFD	1938
204	HOT CAKES FOR TWO (sh)	GOULDING	PATHE EXCHANGE	1926
204	PAID TO DANCE (HARD TO HOLD)	COLEMAN	COLUMBIA	1937
204G	ASTONISHED HEART (UK)	DARNBOROUGH, FISHER	UNIVERSAL	1950
205	ALL AMERICAN SWEETHEART	HILLYER	COLUMBIA	1937
205	GOOD MORNING, MADAM! (sh)	BACON	PATHE EXCHANGE	1925
206	WANDERING WILLIES (sh)	LORD	PATHE EXCHANGE	1926
206 (IP)	GOLDEN SALAMANDER (UK)	NEAME	EAGLE-LION	1950
207	DEVIL'S ISLAND	O'CONNOR	CHADWICK PICTURES	1926
207	GOOSE-LAND (sh)	GOULDING	PATHE EXCHANGE	1926
207	HOI POLLOI (sh)	LORD	COLUMBIA	1935
207	SQUADRON OF HONOR	COLEMAN	COLUMBIA	1938
207 (IP)	SPIDER AND THE FLY (UK)	HAMER	UNIVERSAL	1949
208	WOMEN IN PRISON	HILLYER	COLUMBIA	1938
209	OLD GYPSY CUSTOM (sh)	EDWARDS	EDUCATIONAL FILM	1934
209	ROOT OF ALL EVIL (UK)	WILLIAMS	GFD	1947
209	TAKE YOUR TIME! (sh)	BACON	PATHE EXCHANGE	1925
209	WHO KILLED GAIL PRESTON?	BARSHA	COLUMBIA	1938
210	HAYFOOT, STRAWFOOT! (sh)	PRATT, MOFFITT	PATHE EXCHANGE	1926
210	MURDER IN THE NIGHT (UK: MURDER IN SOHO)	LEE	FILM ALLIANCE	1939
210	THREE LITTLE BEERS (sh)	LORD	COLUMBIA	1935
210	WHEN G-MEN STEP IN	COLEMAN	COLUMBIA	1938
210-M	DOUGHNUTS AND SOCIETY	COLLINS	REPUBLIC	1936
211	FALSE RAPTURE (UK: BLACK EYES)	BRENON	FILM ALLIANCE	1939
211	HIGHWAY PATROL	COLEMAN	COLUMBIA	1938
211	SPANKING BREEZES (sh)	CLINE	PATHE EXCHANGE	1926
211PIN	NAUGHTY ARLETTE (UK: ROMANTIC AGE)	GREVILLE	EAGLE LION	1949
212	FIDDLESTICKS (sh)	EDWARDS	PATHE EXCHANGE	1927
212	HOMICIDE BUREAU	COLEMAN	COLUMBIA	1939
212 MPC	FORTUNE IN DIAMONDS (UK: ADVENTURERS)	MACDONALD	LIPPERT	1951
213	GOOD SCOUT (sh)		EDUCATIONAL FILM	1934
213	JUVENILE COURT	LEDERMAN	COLUMBIA	1938
213	MOVIE MANIACS (sh)	LORD	COLUMBIA	1936
213	SLAVES OF PRIDE	TERWILLIGER	VITAGRAPH	1920
213	WINDOW DUMMY (sh)	BACON	PATHE EXCHANGE	1925
214	ADVENTURE IN SAHARA	LEDERMAN	COLUMBIA	1938
214	FIGHT NIGHT (sh)	PRATT, MOFFITT	PATHE EXCHANGE	1926
214	JUST WILLIAM'S LUCK (UK)	CUTTS	PATHE	1940
215	DEAD MAN'S SHOES (UK)	BENTLEY	MONOGRAM	1940
215	INSIDE THE LAW	MCFADDEN	PRODUCERS RELEASING	1942
215	LOVE SUNDAE (sh)	CLINE	PATHE EXCHANGE	1926
215	NORTH OF SHANGHAI	LEDERMAN	COLUMBIA	1939
216	MY SON IS A CRIMINAL	COLEMAN	COLUMBIA	1939

216	WIDE OPEN FACES (sh)	BACON	PATHE EXCHANGE	1926
216	YUKON GOLD (see 215)	MCDONALD	MONOGRAM	1952
217	DISORDER IN THE COURT (sh)	WHITE	COLUMBIA	1936
217	FIRST OFFENDERS	MCDONALD	COLUMBIA	1939
217	MUSCLE-BOUND MUSIC (sh)	GOULDING	PATHE EXCHANGE	1926
217 CON	WATERFRONT WOMEN (UK: WATERFRONT)	ANDERSON	BELL	1950
218	ALICE BE GOOD (sh)	CLINE	PATHE EXCHANGE	1926
218	ANTS IN THE PANTRY (sh)	WHITE	COLUMBIA	1936
218	BOMBS OVER BURMA	LEWIS	PRC	1942
218	CRAWLING EYE (UK: TROLLENBERG TERROR)	LAWRENCE	DCA	1958
218	MILLION DOLLAR HANDICAP	SIDNEY	METROPOLITAN	1925
218	OUTSIDE THESE WALLS	MCCAREY	COLUMBIA	1939
218	TERROR FROM THE YEAR 5000	GURNEY	AIP	1958
218 PIN	TONY DRAWS A HORSE (UK)	CARSTAIRS	FINE ARTS	1950
219	GHOST OF FOLLY	CLINE	PATHE EXCHANGE	1926
219	MISSING DAUGHTERS	COLEMAN	COLUMBIA	1939
219G	TRIO (UK)	ANNAKIN, FRENCH	ARAMOUNT	1950
220	PARENTS ON TRIAL	NELSON	COLUMBIA	1939
220	VALKYRIE	NOWLAND	THANHOUSER	1915
220	WHEN A MAN'S A PRINCE (sh)	CLINE	PATHE EXCHANGE	1926
221	JANET GAYNOR	portrait	MGM	
221	PUPPY LOVETIME (sh)	CLINE	PATHE EXCHANGE	1926
221	SLIPPERY SILKS (sh)	WHITE	COLUMBIA	1936
221	WOMAN IS THE JUDGE	GRINDE	COLUMBIA	1939
221	YANK IN LIBYA	HERMAN	PRC	1942
222	BEHIND PRISON GATES	BARTON	COLUMBIA	1939
222	FUNNYMOONERS (sh)	LORD	PATHE EXCHANGE	1926
220CB	GRETA GARBO	portrait	MGM	
222 MPC	GREAT ADVENTURE, THE (FORTUNE IN DIAMONDS)	MACDONALD	LIPPERT	1951
223	JEZEBEL	WYLER	WARNER BROS	1938
223	LOVE'S LAST LAUGH (sh)	LORD	PATHE EXCHANGE	1926
223	MAN THEY COULD NOT HANG	GRINDE	COLUMBIA	1939
223	PAIN IN THE PULLMAN (sh)	WHITE	COLUMBIA	1936
223	THANK EVANS (UK)	NEILL	WB-FIRST NATIONAL	1938
224	BIG PARADE	VIDOR	MGM	1925
224	FALSE ALARMS (sh)	LORD	COLUMBIA	1936
224	KONGA, THE WILD STALLION	NELSON	COLUMBIA	1940
224	MEET MY GIRL (sh)	BACON	PATHE EXCHANGE	1926
224	RAILROAD RAIDERS - CH. 4	HURST	MUTUAL	1917
224	SEVENTH SIGN	SCHULTZ	TRI STAR	1988
224 HH	BLACKMAILED (UK)	ALLEGRET	BELL	1951
225	HALF SHOT SHOOTERS (sh)	WHITE	COLUMBIA	1936
225	HER ACTOR FRIEND (sh)	CLINE	PATHE EXCHANGE	1926
225 EF	NIGHT WITHOUT STARS (UK)	PELISSIER	RKO	1951
2251E	LESLIE CARON	portrait	MGM	
226	ICE COLD COCOS (sh)	LORD	PATHE EXCHANGE	1926
226	WHOOPS, I'M AN INDIAN! (sh)	LORD	COLUMBIA	1936
227	SMITH'S VISITOR (sh)	PRATT	PATHE EXCHANGE	1926
227 TF	HOTEL SAHARA (UK)	ANNAKIN	UNITED ARTISTS	1951
228	HESITATING HORSES (sh)	CLINE	PATHE EXCHANGE	1926
228	SPIDER, THE (EARTH VS. THE SPIDER)	GORDON	AIP	1958
228 VIC	WHITE CORRIDORS (UK)	JACKSON	GENERAL FILM	1951
229	ESTHER WILLIAMS	portrait	MGM	
229	SEA DOG'S TALE (sh)	LORD	PATHE EXCHANGE	1926
229 CON	HIGH TREASON (UK)	R BOULTING	MAYER-KINGLSEY	1951
230	EVERYTHING HAPPENS TO ME (UK)	NEILL	WARNER BROS.	1938
230	SMITH'S SURPRISE (sh)	PRATT	PATHE EXCHANGE	1927
230 ISF	VALLEY OF THE EAGLES (UK: VALLEY OF EAGLES 1951)	YOUNG	LIPPERT	1952
231	HOOKED AT THE ALTAR (sh)	RUGGLES, RIPLEY	PATHE EXCHANGE	1926
231 BFM	ISLAND RESCUE (UK: APPOINTMENT WITH VENUS)	THOMAS	UNIVERSAL	1951
232	SMITH'S UNCLE (sh)	PRATT	PATHE EXCHANGE	1926
233	GILDED LILY	LEONARD	PARAMOUNT	1921
233	MANY TANKS MR. ATKINS (UK)	NEILL	WARNER BROS.	1938
233	PERILS OF PETERSBORO (sh)	RODNEY	PATHE EXCHANGE	1926
234	HOBOKEN TO HOLLYWOOD (sh)	LORD	PATHE EXCHANGE	1926
234	STRANGER IN BETWEEN (UK: HUNTED)	CRICHTON	UNIVERSAL	1952

234CB	GRETA GARBO	portrait	MGM	
235	CARD/US: PROMOTER (UK)	NEAME	UNIVERSAL	1952
235	YANKEE DOODLE DUKE (sh)	LAMONT	PATHE EXCHANGE	1926
236	ANITA PAGE	portrait	MGM	
236	IMPORTANCE OF BEING EARNEST (UK)	ASQUITH	UNIVERSAL	1952
236	PRODIGAL BRIDEGROOM (sh)	BACON	PATHE EXCHANGE	1926
237	GOOD OLD DAYS (UK)	NEILL	WARNER BROS.	1940
237	PREY, THE	SARGENT	VITAGRAPH	1920
237	SHOULD SLEEP WALKERS MARRY? (sh)	LORD	PATHE EXCHANGE	1927
237 CPL	PENNY PRINCESS (UK)	GUEST	UNIVERSAL	1952
238	SHOULD HUSBANDS MARRY? (sh)	CLINE	PATHE EXCHANGE	1926
239	HUBBY'S QUIET LITTLE GAME (sh)	LORD	PATHE EXCHANGE	1926
239	SOMETHING MONEY CAN'T BUY (UK)	JACKSON	UNIVERSAL	1952
240	ANITA PAGE	portrait	MGM	
240	FIFTH AVENUE	VIGNOLA	PDC	1926
240	SMITH'S CUSTOMER (sh)	BACON	PATHE EXCHANGE	1927
240	VICE OF FOOLS, THE	GRIFFITH	VITAGRAPH	1920
241	BROKE IN CHINA (sh)	CLINE	PATHE EXCHANGE	1927
241	DEAD MEN TELL NO TALES (UK)	MACDONALD	FILM ALLIANCE	1939
241	FOREVER	FITZMAURICE	PARAMOUNT	1921
241	IT STARTED IN PARADISE (UK)	BENNETT	ASTOR	1952
242	KITTY FROM KILLARNEY (sh)	CLINE	PATHE EXCHANGE	1926
242	TONIGHT AT 8:30 (UK: MEET ME TONIGHT)	PELISSIER	CONTINENTAL	1952
243	HAREM KNIGHT (sh)	PRATT	PATHE EXCHANGE	1926
243	MADE IN HEAVEN (UK)	CARSTAIRS	GFD	1952
244	LONG MEMORY (UK)	HAMER	ASTOR	1953
244	MASKED MAMAS (sh)	LORD	PATHE EXCHANGE	1926
245	PROJECT M-7 (UK - THE NET)	ASQUITH	UNIVERSAL	1953
245	SMITH'S PETS (sh)	GOULDING	PATHE EXCHANGE	1927
246	RAILROAD RAIDERS - CH. 8	HURST	MUTUAL	1917
246	SMITH'S NEW HOME (sh)	GOULDING	PATHE EXCHANGE	1927
247	OVER HERE	CLINE	UNR. MACK SENNETT	1926
247	TOP OF THE FORM (UK)	CARSTAIRS	GFD	1953
248	DESPERATE MOMENT (UK)	BENNETT	UNIVERSAL	1953
248	DIVORCE DODGER (sh)	LORD	PATHE EXCHANGE	1926
248	HERE COMES TROUBLE (BLACK GANG*)	SEILER	20TH CENTURY FOX	1936
249	GENEVIEVE	CORNELIUS	RANK (UK)	1953
249	PLUMBER'S DAUGHTER (sh)	SEMON	PATHE EXCHANGE	1927
250	BURKE STORY (sh)		UNR. MACK SENNETT	1926
250	ROBERT TAYLOR	portrait	MGM	
251	FINAL TEST (UK)	ASQUITH	CONTINENTAL	1954
251	PRIDE OF PIKEVILLE (sh)	GOULDING	PATHE EXCHANGE	1927
251	RAILROAD RAIDERS - CH. 10	HURST	MUTUAL	1917
252	SMITH'S PICNIC (sh)	GOULDING	PATHE EXCHANGE	1926
252	TURN THE KEY SOFTLY (UK)	LEE	ASTOR	1953
253	ALWAYS A BRIDE (UK)	SMART	UNIVERSAL	1953
253	SMALL TOWN PRINCESS (sh)	CLINE	PATHE EXCHANGE	1927
254	BATHING GIRLS SCENARIO		UNR. MACK SENNETT	1927
255	DR. O'DOWD (UK)	MASON	WARNER BROS.	1940
255	PASS THE DUMPLINGS (sh)	SEMON	PATHE EXCHANGE	1927
256	BLONDE'S REVENGE (sh)	LORD	PATHE EXCHANGE	1926
256	DAY TO REMEMBER (UK)	THOMAS	REPUBLIC	1953
257	MATRIMONIAL WEB	JOSE	VITAGRAPH	1921
257	PEACHES AND PLUMBERS (sh)	CLINE	PATHE EXCHANGE	1927
258	SMITH'S KINDERGARTEN (sh)	GOULDING	PATHE EXCHANGE	1927
259	DOZEN SOCKS (sh)	RODNEY	PATHE EXCHANGE	1927
259	GRIPS, GRUNTS AND GROANS (sh)	WHITE	COLUMBIA	1937
260	CURED IN THE EXCITEMENT (sh)	LORD	PATHE EXCHANGE	1927
260	GEORGE AND MARGARET (UK)	KING	WARNER BROS.	1940
260	TROUBLE IN STORE (UK)	CARSTAIRS	REPUBLIC	1953
261	FAST AND LOOSE (UK)	PARRY	GFD	1954
261	JOLLY JILTER (sh)	CLINE	PATHE EXCHANGE	1927
262	SMITH'S FISHING TRIP (sh)	GOULDING	PATHE EXCHANGE	1927
263	CRAZY TO ACT (sh)	RODNEY	PATHE EXCHANGE	1927
263	DIZZY DOCTORS (sh)	LORD	COLUMBIA	1937
263	FINGERS (UK)	MASON	WARNER BROS.	1941

264	FORBIDDEN CARGO (UK)	FRENCH	FINE ARTS	1954
264	HOLLYWOOD HERO (sh)	EDWARDS	PATHE EXCHANGE	1926
264	PRIME MINISTER (UK)	DICKINSON	WARNER BROS.	1941
265	FLIRTY FOUR-FLUSHERS (sh)	CLINE	PATHE EXCHANGE	1926
266	3 DUMB CLUCKS (sh)	LORD	COLUMBIA	1937
266	BETTY FURNESS	portrait	MGM	
266	COLLEGE KIDDO (sh)	RODNEY	PATHE EXCHANGE	1927
267	SMITH'S CANDY SHOP (sh)	GOULDING	PATHE EXCHANGE	1927
267	THIS WAS PARIS (UK)	HARLOW	WARNER BROS.	1942
268	BACK TO THE WOODS (sh)	WHITE	COLUMBIA	1937
268	BROWN OF HARVARD	CONWAY	MGM	1926
268	CHANCE MEETING (UK: YOUNG LOVERS)	ASQUITH	GENERAL FILM	1954
268	IT PAYS TO ADVERTISE	CRISP	PARAMOUNT	1919
268	LOVE'S LANGUID LURE (sh)	CONLEY	PATHE EXCHANGE	1927
269	GOOD-BYE KISS	SENNETT	FIRST NAT'L	1928
269	UP TO HIS NECK (UK)	CARSTAIRS	GFD	1955
270	SIMBA (UK)	HURST	LIPPERT	1955
270	SMITH'S PONY (sh)	GOULDING	PATHE EXCHANGE	1927
271	LOVE IN A POLICE STATION (sh)	RODNEY	PATHE EXCHANGE	1927
271	MAD ABOUT MEN (UK)	THOMAS	GFD	1954
272	ONE GOOD TURN (UK)	CARSTAIRS	GFD	1955
272	SMITH'S COOK (sh)	GOULDING	PATHE EXCHANGE	1927
273	CATALINA, HERE I COME (sh)	RODNEY	PATHE EXCHANGE	1927
273	NIGHT INVADER (UK)	MASON	WARNER BROS.	1943
273	TO PARIS WITH LOVE (UK)	HAMER	CONTINENTAL	1955
274	AS LONG AS THEY'RE HAPPY (UK)	THOMPSON	RANK	1955
274	CHARIOTS OF FIRE	HUDSON	WARNER BROS	1981
274	GOOFS AND SADDLES (sh)	LORD	COLUMBIA	1937
274	SMITH'S COUSIN (sh)	GOULDING	PATHE EXCHANGE	1927
275	FOR SALE A BUNGALOW (sh)	RODNEY	PATHE EXCHANGE	1927
275	PASSAGE HOME (UK)	BAKER	GFD	1955
276	ABOVE US THE WAVES (UK)	THOMAS	REPUBLIC	1955
276	DADDYBOY (sh)	EDWARDS	PATHE EXCHANGE	1927
276	DARK TOWER (UK)	HARLOW	WARNER BROS.	1943
277	HUNDRED POUND WINDOW (UK)	HURST	WARNER BROS.	1944
277	SMITH'S MODISTE SHOP (sh)	GOULDING	PATHE EXCHANGE	1927
278	BULL FIGHTER (sh)	RODNEY	PATHE EXCHANGE	1927
278	FLIGHT FROM FOLLY (UK)	MASON	WARNER BROS.	1945
278	INGRID BERGMAN	portrait	MGM	
278	LOVERS?	STAHL	MGM	1927
278	VALUE FOR MONEY (UK)	ANNAKIN	RANK	1955
279	DOCTOR AT SEA (UK)	THOMAS	REPUBLIC	1955
279	SMITH'S HOLIDAY (sh)	GOULDING	PATHE EXCHANGE	1928
280	GOLF NUT (sh)	EDWARDS	PATHE EXCHANGE	1927
280	TERRY KILBURN	portrait	MGM	
280	WOMAN FOR JOE (UK)	O'FERRALL	RANK	1955
281	MAN OF THE MOMENT (UK)	CARSTAIRS	RANK	1955
281	SMITH'S ARMY LIFE (sh)	GOULDING	PATHE EXCHANGE	1928
281	TERRY KILBURN	portrait	MGM	
282	ALLIGATOR NAMED DAISY (UK)	THOMPSON	RANK	1955
282	GOLD DIGGER OF WEEPAH	EDWARDS	PATHE EXCHANGE	1927
282	OUTLAW JOSEY WALES	EASTWOOD	WARNER BROS	1976
283	ROSE MARIE	HUBBARD	MGM	1928
283	SIMON AND LAURA (UK)	BOX	UNIVERSAL	1955
283	SMITH'S FARM DAYS (sh)	WHITMAN	PATHE EXCHANGE	1928
284	ALL FOR MARY (UK)	TOYE	RANK	1955
284	BEACH CLUB (sh)	EDWARDS	PATHE EXCHANGE	1928
285	BACHELORS' BABIES (sh)	LAMONT	EDUCATIONAL	1925
285	SMITH'S RESTAURANT (sh)	WHITMAN	PATHE EXCHANGE	1928
285	SQUEEZE	YOUNG	TRI STAR	1987
285	TOWN LIKE ALICE (UK)	LEE	RANK	1956
286	BEST MAN (sh)	EDWARDS	PATHE EXCHANGE	1928
286	DAVID KNIGHT	portrait	RANK	
286	GETTING GERTIE'S GARTER	HOPPER	PRODUCERS	1927
286	JOHN BARCLAY	portrait	VITAPHONE	
287	REACH FOR THE SKY (UK)	GILBERT	RANK	1956

288	BLACK TENT (UK)	HURST	RANK	1956
288	CATALINA ROWBOAT RACES (sh)	WHITMAN	PATHE EXCHANGE	1928
289	EXCESS BAGGAGE (sh)	LAMONT	EDUCATIONAL	1926
289	JUMPING FOR JOY (UK)	CARSTAIRS	RANK	1956
289	MOTORBOAT MAMAS (sh)	EDWARDS	PATHE EXCHANGE	1928
290	BICYCLE FLIRT (sh)	EDWARDS	PATHE EXCHANGE	1928
291	IRON PETTICOAT	THOMAS	MGM	1956
291	LOVE AT FIRST FLIGHT (sh)	CLINE	PATHE EXCHANGE	1928
291	MAUREEN O'SULLIVAN	portrait	MGM	
292	BABY'S BIRTHDAY (sh)	WHITMAN	PATHE EXCHANGE	1929
292	JACQUELINE (UK)	BAKER	RANK	1956
293	EYE WITNESS (UK: YOUR WITNESS)	MONTGOMERY	EAGLE LION	1950
293	EYEWITNESS (UK)	BOX	RANK	1956
293	HIS UNLUCKY NIGHT (sh)	EDWARDS	PATHE EXCHANGE	1928
294	BIG MONEY (UK)	CARSTAIRS	LOPERT	1958
294	RUN, GIRL, RUN (sh)	GOULDING	PATHE EXCHANGE	1928
295	CHICKEN (sh)	WHITMAN	PATHE EXCHANGE	1928
295	ROMANCE OF THE HOLLOW TREE, THE		THANHOUSER	1916
295	SPANISH GARDENER (UK)	LEACOCK	RANK	1956
296	ART JARRETT	portrait	MGM	
296	HUBBY'S WEEK-END TRIP (sh)	EDWARDS	PATHE EXCHANGE	1928
296	TRIPLE DECEPTION (UK: HOUSE OF SECRETS - 1956)	GREEN	RANK	1957
297	BARGAIN HUNT (sh)	WHITMAN	PATHE EXCHANGE	1928
297	CHECKPOINT (UK)	THOMAS	RANK	1956
298	CALLING HUBBY'S BLUFF (sh)	EDWARDS	PATHE EXCHANGE	1929
298	NO WAY OUT	DONALDSON	ORION	1987
298	ROBOCOP 2	KERSHNER	ORION	1990
298	TIGER IN THE SMOKE (UK)	BAKER	RANK	1956
299	SECRET PLACE (UK)	DONNER	RANK	1957
299	SWIM PRINCESS (sh)	GOULDING	PATHE EXCHANGE	1928
300	BURGLAR (sh)	WHITMAN	PATHE EXCHANGE	1928
300	OUTLAWS OF THE PRAIRIE	NELSON	COLUMBIA	1937
300	TRUE AS A TURTLE (UK)	TOYE	RANK	1957
301	CAMPUS CARMEN (sh)	GOULDING	PATHE EXCHANGE	1928
301	CATTLE RAIDERS	NELSON	COLUMBIA	1938
301	STOKER (UK)	C FRANKLIN	ALLIED PICTURES	1932
302	OLD WYOMING TRAIL	BLANGSTED	COLUMBIA	1937
302	UNCLE TOM (sh)	WHITMAN	PATHE EXCHANGE	1929
302	UP IN THE WORLD (UK)	CARSTAIRS	RANK	1956
303	CALL OF THE ROCKIES	JAMES	COLUMBIA	1938
303	FOOLISH HUSBANDS (sh)	WHITMAN	PATHE EXCHANGE	1929
303	NIGHT AMBUSH (UK: ILL MET BY MOONLIGHT)	POWELL, PRESSBURGER	RANK	1957
304	CAMPUS VAMP (sh)	EDWARDS	PATHE EXCHANGE	1928
304	HIGH TIDE AT NOON (UK)	LEACOCK	RANK	1957
304	LAW OF THE PLAINS	NELSON	COLUMBIA	1938
305	DOCTOR AT LARGE (UK)	THOMAS	RANK	1957
305	DONNA REED	portrait	MGM	
305	GIRL FROM NOWHERE	EDWARDS	PATHE EXCHANGE	1928
305	WEST OF CHEYENNE	NELSON	COLUMBIA	1938
306	HELL DRIVERS (UK)	ENDFIELD	RANK	1957
306	RODEO (sh)	GOULDING	PATHE EXCHANGE	1929
306	SOUTH OF ARIZONA	NELSON	COLUMBIA	1938
307	DON'T GET JEALOUS (sh)	WHITMAN	PATHE EXCHANGE	1929
307	MIRACLE IN SOHO (UK)	AMYES	RANK	1957
307	WEST OF SANTA FE	NELSON	COLUMBIA	1938
308	ACROSS THE BRIDGE (UK)	ANNAKIN	RANK DIST. OF AMERICA	1957
308	COLORADO TRAIL	NELSON	COLUMBIA	1938
308	MATCHMAKING MAMMA (sh)	EDWARDS	PATHE EXCHANGE	1929
309	NEW AUNT (sh)	RODNEY	PATHE EXCHANGE	1929
309	RIO GRANDE	NELSON	COLUMBIA	1938
309	ROBBERY UNDER ARMS (UK)	LEE	RANK	1957
310	CAMPBELL'S KINGDOM (UK)	THOMAS	RANK	1957
310	SENNETT ALL-STAR TROUPE STORY		UNR. MACK SENNETT	1928
310	THUNDERING WEST	NELSON	COLUMBIA	1939
311	DANGEROUS EXILE (UK)	HURST	RANK	1957
311	SMITH FAMILY HOLLYWOOD STORY		UNR. MACK SENNETT	1928

311	TEXAS STAMPEDE	NELSON	COLUMBIA	1939
312	JACKIE COOPER	portrait	MGM	
312	NORTH OF THE YUKON	NELSON	COLUMBIA	1939
312	ONE THAT GOT AWAY (UK)	BAKER	RANK	1957
312	PAY OFF	DRIEFUSS	PRC	1942
312	SMITH FAMILY PICNIC STORY		UNR. MACK SENNETT	1928
313	BEASTS OF MARSEILLES (UK: SEVEN THUNDERS)	FREGONESE	LOPERT	1957
313	HUBBY'S LATEST ALIBI (sh)	WHITMAN	PATHE EXCHANGE	1928
313	SPOILERS OF THE RANGE	COLEMAN	COLUMBIA	1939
314	NIGHT WATCHMAN'S MISTAKE (sh)	EDWARDS	PATHE EXCHANGE	1929
314	WESTERN CARAVANS	NELSON	COLUMBIA	1939
314	WINDOM'S WAY (UK)	NEAME	RANK	1957
315	CLOSE SHAVE (sh)	EDWARDS	PATHE EXCHANGE	1929
315	JUST MY LUCK (UK)	CARSTAIRS	RANK	1957
315	MAN FROM SUNDOWN	NELSON	COLUMBIA	1939
315	TWO AND TWO MAKE SIX (UK: GIRL SWAPPERS)	FRANCIS	UNION	1962
316	GYPSY AND THE GENTLEMAN (UK)	LOSEY	RANK	1958
316	MAN FROM TORONTO (UK)	S HILL	IDEAL	1933
316	OUTPOST OF THE MOUNTIES	COLEMAN	COLUMBIA	1939
316	SUBMARINE SEAHAWK	BENNETT	AIP	1958
316	TAXI SCANDAL (sh)	LORD	PATHE EXCHANGE	1928
317	BUTTON MY BACK (sh)	WHITMAN	PATHE EXCHANGE	1929
317	JOHN BREWSTER'S WIFE		THANHOUSER	1916
317	STRANGER FROM TEXAS	NELSON	COLUMBIA	1939
317	TALE OF TWO CITIES (UK)	THOMAS	RANK	1958
318	CARVE HER NAME WITH PRIDE (UK)	GILBERT	LOPERT	1958
318	KING LEAR	WARDE	THANHOUSER	1916
318	RIDERS OF BLACK RIVER	DEMING	COLUMBIA	1939
318	TAXI FOR TWO (sh)	LORD	PATHE EXCHANGE	1928
319	TAMING OF THE WEST	DEMING	COLUMBIA	1939
319	TAXI DOLLS (sh)	LORD	PATHE EXCHANGE	1929
319	VIOLENT PLAYGROUND (UK)	DEARDEN	RANK	1958
320	HIS NEW STENOGRAPHER (sh)	WHITMAN	PATHE EXCHANGE	1928
320	INNOCENT SINNERS (UK)	LEACOCK	RANK	1958
320	MAN FROM TUMBLEWEEDS	LEWIS	COLUMBIA	1940
320	O LUCKY MAN	ANDERSON	WB	1973
321	CLUNKED ON THE CORNER (sh)	EDWARDS	PATHE EXCHANGE	1929
321	ROONEY (UK)	POLLOCK	RANK	1958
321	TWO FISTED RANGERS	LEWIS	COLUMBIA	1939
322	BULLETS FOR RUSTLERS	NELSON	COLUMBIA	1940
322	CAUGHT IN THE KITCHEN	WHITMAN	PATHE EXCHANGE	1928
322	NIGHT TO REMEMBER (UK)	BAKER	RANK	1958
322	SHINE GIRL, THE	PARKE	THANHOUSER	1916
323	ELEANOR POWELL	portrait	MGM	
323	ELEPHANT GUN (UK: NOR THE MOON BY NIGHT)	ANNAKIN	LOPERT	1958
323	LADIES MUST EAT (sh)	EDWARDS	PATHE EXCHANGE	1929
323	LEGEND OF EL BLANCO	VITERELLA	NATIONAL BROADCASTING	1966
323	NIGHT FLYER	LANG	PATHE	1927
323	PIONEERS OF THE FRONTIER	NELSON	COLUMBIA	1940
324	BLAZING SIX SHOOTERS	LEWIS	COLUMBIA	1940
324	MYRNA LOY	portrait	MGM	
324	SING	BASKIN	TRI STAR	1989
324	TAXI SPOOKS (sh)	LORD	PATHE EXCHANGE	1929
324	WIND CANNOT READ (UK)	THOMAS	20th CENTURY-FOX	1958
325	PINK PAJAMAS (sh)	WHITMAN	PATHE EXCHANGE	1929
325	SEA FURY (UK)	ENDFIELD	LOPERT	1958
325	THUNDERING FRONTIER	LEDERMAN	COLUMBIA	1940
326	DUMB WAITER (sh)	EDWARDS	PATHE EXCHANGE	1928
326	TEXAS STAGECOACH	LEWIS	COLUMBIA	1940
327	MAD LITTLE ISLAND (UK: ROCKETS GALORE)	RELPH	RANK (UK)	1958
327	MOTORING MAMMAS (sh)	WHITMAN	PATHE EXCHANGE	1929
327	PINTO KID	HILLYER	COLUMBIA	1941
328	CAUGHT IN A TAXI (sh)	LORD	PATHE EXCHANGE	1929
328	WEST OF ABILENE	CEDER	COLUMBIA	1940
329	ELEANOR POWELL	portrait	MGM	
329	RETURN OF WILD BILL	LEWIS	COLUMBIA	1940

329	STORM OVER JAMAICA (UK: PASSIONATE SUMMER)	CARTIER	RANK	1958
329	TAXI BEAUTIES (sh)	LORD	PATHE EXCHANGE	1928
330	DURANGO KID	HILLYER	COLUMBIA	1940
330	FLOODS OF FEAR (UK)	CRICHTON	UNIVERSAL	1958
330	JIM JAM JANITOR (sh)	EDWARDS	PATHE EXCHANGE	1928
331	DAY FOR NIGHT (FRANCE)	TRUFFAUT	WARNER BROS	1973
331	LION'S ROAR (sh)	SENNETT	EDUCATIONAL FILM	1928
331	PRAIRIE SCHOONERS	NELSON	COLUMBIA	1940
331	SQUARE PEG (UK)	CARSTAIRS	RANK	1958
332	CAPTAIN'S TABLE (UK)	LEE	20TH CENTURY FOX	1959
332	OUTLAWS OF THE PANHANDLE	NELSON	COLUMBIA	1941
332	TEMPTRESS	NIBLO	MGM	1926
332	WHAT AM I DOING IN THE MIDDLE OF A REVOLUTION? (IT)	CORBUCCI	WARNER BROS	1973
333	ELEANOR POWELL	portrait	MGM	
333	OPERATION AMSTERDAM (UK)	MCCARTHY	20TH CENTURY FOX	1959
334	BEYOND THE SACRAMENTO	HILLYER	COLUMBIA	1940
334	BROADWAY BLUES (sh)	SENNETT	EDUCATIONAL FILM	1929
334	MACINTOSH MAN	HILL	WB	1973
334	PRUDENCE THE PIRATE	PARKE	THANHOUSER	1916
334	TOO MANY CROOKS (UK)	ZAMPI	LOPERT	1959
335	ACROSS THE SIERRAS	LEDERMAN	COLUMBIA	1941
335	BRIDE'S RELATIONS (sh)	SENNETT	EDUCATIONAL FILM	1929
335	DONNA REED	portrait	MGM	
335	WHIRLPOOL (UK)	ALLEN	CONTINENTAL	1959
336	39 STEPS (UK)	THOMAS	20TH CENTURY FOX	1959
336	DONNA REED	portrait	MGM	
337	DONNA REED	portrait	MGM	
337	FERRY TO HONG KONG (UK)	GILBERT	20TH CENTURY FOX	1959
337	I DD IT! (IT: SONO STATO IO!)	LATTUADA	WARNER BROS	1973
337	THEIR NEIGHBOR'S BABY	EDWARDS	TRIANGLE	1918
337	WHIRLS AND GIRLS (sh)	SENNETT	EDUCATIONAL FILM	1929
337	WILDCAT OF TUCSON	HILLYER	COLUMBIA	1940
338	ELEANOR POWELL	portrait	MGM	
338	JAZZ MAMMAS (sh)	SENNETT	EDUCATIONAL FILM	1929
338	NORTH FROM THE LONE STAR	HILLYER	COLUMBIA	1941
338	SAPPHIRE (UK)	DEARDEN	UNIVERSAL	1959
339	BEES' BUZZ (sh)	SENNETT	EDUCATIONAL FILM	1929
339	ENTER THE DRAGON	CLOUSE	WB	1973
339	ROYAL BALLET	CZINNER	RANK	1960
340	HANDS ACROSS THE ROCKIES	HILLYER	COLUMBIA	1941
340	HEART OF A MAN (UK)	WILCOX	RANK	1959
340	MIDNIGHT DADDIES	SENNETT	SONO ART-WORLD WIDE	1930
341	FAINTING LOVER (sh)	SENNETT	EDUCATIONAL FILM	1931
341	SON OF DAVY CROCKETT	HILLYER	COLUMBIA	1941
341	UPSTAIRS AND DOWNSTAIRS (UK)	THOMAS	20TH CENTURY FOX	1959
342	BIG PALOOKA	GOULDING	EDUCATIONAL FILM	1929
342	DONNA REED	portrait	MGM	
342	MEDICO OF PAINTED SPRINGS	HILLYER	COLUMBIA	1941
342	NORTH WEST FRONTIER (UK: FLAME OVER INDIA)	THOMPSON	20TH CENTURY FOX	1959
343	COLLEGE CAPERS (sh)		UNR. MACK SENNETT	1929
343	DONNA REED	portrait	MGM	
343	FOLLOW A STAR (UK)	ASHER	ZENITH	1959
343	KING OF DODGE CITY	HILLYER	COLUMBIA	1941
344	CONSPIRACY OF HEARTS (UK)	THOMAS	PARAMOUNT	1960
344	THUNDER OVER THE PRAIRIE	HILLYER	COLUMBIA	1941
345	ABDICATION	HARVEY	WB	1974
345	CONSTABULE (sh)	SENNETT	EDUCATIONAL FILM	1929
345	MAKE MINE MINK (UK)	ASHER	CONTINENTAL	1960
345	ROARING FRONTIERS	HILLYER	COLUMBIA	1941
346	DOCTOR IN LOVE (UK)	THOMAS	GOVERNOR	1960
346	GIRL CRAZY	GOULDING	EDUCATIONAL FILM	1929
346	LOVE AT LARGE	RUDOLPH	ORION	1990
346	PRAIRIE STRANGER	HILLYER	COLUMBIA	1941
347	BARBER'S DAUGHTER (sh)	SENNETT	EDUCATIONAL FILM	1929
347	LONE STAR VIGILANTES	FOX	COLUMBIA	1942
348	LUNKHEAD (sh)	SENNETT, RODNEY	EDUCATIONAL FILM	1929

348	MALICIOUS (MALIZIA - IT)	SAMPERI	WARNER BROS	1973
348	NO LOVE FOR JOHNNIE (UK)	THOMAS	EMBASSY	1961
348	ROYAL MOUNTED PATROL	HILLYER	COLUMBIA	1941
348	WHEN TOMORROW COMES (mistake 948- unassigned)	STAHL	UNIVERSAL	1939
349	BULLDOG BREED (UK)	ASHER	RANK	1960
349	BULLETS FOR BANDITS	FOX	COLUMBIA	1942
349	GOLFERS (sh)	SENNETT	EDUCATIONAL FILM	1929
349	MEAN STREETS	SCORSESE	WARNER BROS	1973
350	HOLLYWOOD STAR (sh)	SENNETT	EDUCATIONAL FILM	1929
350	HOUSE OF MYSTERY (UK: AT THE VILLA ROSE)	SUMMERS	MONOGRAM	1940
350	RIDERS OF THE BADLANDS	BRETHERTON	COLUMBIA	1941
351	BARRIER	HILL	MGM	1926
351	CLANCY AT THE BAT (sh)	RODNEY	EDUCATIONAL FILM	1929
351	FLAME IN THE STREETS (UK)	BAKER	ATLANTIC	1961
351	NORTH OF THE ROCKIES	HILLYER	COLUMBIA	1942
351	YAKUZA, THE	POLLACK	WB	1974
352	DEVIL'S TRAIL	HILLYER	COLUMBIA	1942
352	NEW HALFBACK (sh)	SENNETT	EDUCATIONAL FILM	1929
352	NO, MY DARLING DAUGHTER (UK)	THOMAS	EMBASSY	1961
352	THUNDERGAP OUTLAWS	HERMAN	PRODUCERS RELEASING	1943
353	IN THE DOGHOUSE (UK)	CONYERS	SCHOENFELD	1962
353	UPPERCUT' O'BRIEN (sh)	RODNEY	EDUCATIONAL FILM	1929
353	WEST OF TOMBSTONE	BRETHERTON	COLUMBIA	1942
354	ALL NIGHT LONG (UK)	DEARDEN	COLORAMA	1962
354	BORDER BUCKAROOS	DRAKE	PRC	1943
354	LAWLESS PLAINSMEN	BERKE	COLUMBIA	1942
354	SCOTCH (sh)	SENNETT	EDUCATIONAL FILM	1930
355	DOWN RIO GRANDE WAY	BERKE	COLUMBIA	1942
355	SUCCESSFUL FAILURE	LUBIN	MONOGRAM	1934
355	SUGAR PLUM PAPA (sh)	SENNETT	EDUCATIONAL FILM	1930
356	BULLS AND BEARS (sh)	SENNETT	EDUCATIONAL FILM	1930
356	PAIR OF BRIEFS (UK)	THOMAS	DAVIS	1962
356	PRAIRIE GUNSMOKE	HILLYER	COLUMBIA	1942
357	MATCH PLAY (sh)	SENNETT	EDUCATIONAL FILM	1930
357	OVERLAND TO DEADWOOD	BERKE	COLUMBIA	1942
357	YOUNG AND WILLING (UK: WILD AND WILLING)	THOMAS	UNIVERSAL	1962
358	BADMEN OF THE HILLS	BERKE	COLUMBIA	1942
358	BLACK SAMSON	BAIL	WB	1974
358	HONEYMOON ZEPPELIN (sh)	SENNETT	EDUCATIONAL FILM	1930
359	HE TRUMPED HER ACE (sh)	PEARCE	EDUCATIONAL FILM	1930
359	MYSTERIES OF THE DEEP (sh) (doc)		BUENA VISTA	1959
359	RIDERS OF THE NORTHLAND	BERKE	COLUMBIA	1942
360	80,000 SUSPECTS (UK)	GUEST	CONTINENTAL	1963
360	RADIO KISSSES (sh)	PEARCE	EDUCATIONAL FILM	1930
360	VENGEANCE OF THE WEST	HILLYER	COLUMBIA	1942
361	DOCTOR IN DISTRESS (UK)	THOMAS	GOVERNOR	1963
361	FAT WIVES FOR THIN (sh)	SENNETT	EDUCATIONAL FILM	1930
362	CAMPUS CRUSHES (sh)	SENNETT	EDUCATIONAL FILM	1930
362	RIDING THROUGH NEVADA	BERKE	COLUMBIA	1942
363	CHUMPS (sh)	SENNETT	EDUCATIONAL FILM	1930
363	PARDON MY GUN	BERKE	COLUMBIA	1942
363	TEACHER, TEACHER (sh)	TAUROG	EDUCATIONAL FILM	1926
364	CONTEST GIRL (UK: BEAUTY JUNGLE)	GUEST	CONTINENTAL	1964
364	GOOD-BYE LEGS (sh)	SENNETT	EDUCATIONAL FILM	1930
364	ONE SUNDAY MORNING (sh)	ARBUCKLE	EDUCATIONAL FILM	1926
364	TORNADO IN THE SADDLE	BERKE	COLUMBIA	1942
365	HELLO TELEVISION (sh)	PEARCE	EDUCATIONAL FILM	1930
365	LONE PRAIRIE	BERKE	COLUMBIA	1942
365	MCGUIRE, GO HOME! (UK: HIGH BRIGHT SUN)	THOMAS	CONTINENTAL	1964
366	CHINESE THEATRE OPENING		UNR. MACK SENNETT	1930
366	FIGHTING BUCKAROO	BERKE	COLUMBIA	1943
367	AVERAGE HUSBAND (sh)	SENNETT	EDUCATIONAL FILM	1930
367	BREEZING ALONG (sh)	TAUROG	EDUCATIONAL FILM	1927
367	LAW OF THE NORTHWEST	BERKE	COLUMBIA	1943
368	ANITA PAGE	portrait	MGM	
368	EARLY BIRD (UK)	ASHER	RANK	1965

368	GOOSE FLESH (sh)	TAUROG	EDUCATIONAL FILM	1927
368	SILVER CITY RAIDERS	BERKE	COLUMBIA	1943
368	VACATION LOVES (sh)	SENNETT	EDUCATIONAL FILM	1930
369	CARNABY, M.D. (UK: DOCTOR IN CLOVER)	THOMAS	CONTINENTAL	1966
369	GRANDMA'S GIRL (sh)	SENNETT	EDUCATIONAL FILM	1930
369	HIS BETTER HALF (sh)	TAUROG	EDUCATIONAL FILM	1927
369	RIDERS OF THE NORTHWEST MOUNTED	BERKE	COLUMBIA	1943
370	DIVORCED SWEETHEARTS (sh)	SENNETT	EDUCATIONAL FILM	1930
370	HAIL TO THE RANGERS	BERKE	COLUMBIA	1943
370	THAT RIVIERA TOUCH (UK)	OWEN	CONTINENTAL	1966
371	MAGNIFICENT TWO (UK)	OWEN	RANK	1967
371	RACKET CHEERS (sh)	SENNETT	EDUCATIONAL FILM	1930
371	ROBIN HOOD OF THE RANGE	BERKE	COLUMBIA	1943
372	DON'T BITE YOUR DENTIST (sh)	CLINE	EDUCATIONAL FILM	1930
372	SADDLES AND THE SAGEBRUSH	BERKE	COLUMBIA	1943
373	ROUGH IDEA OF LOVE (sh)	SENNETT	EDUCATIONAL FILM	1930
373	VIGILANTES RIDE	BERKE	COLUMBIA	1943
374	BLUFFER (sh)	CLINE	EDUCATIONAL FILM	1930
374	WYOMING HURRICANE	BERKE	COLUMBIA	1944
375	LAST HORSEMAN	BERKE	COLUMBIA	1944
375	NO, NO, LADY (sh)	CLINE	EDUCATIONAL FILM	1931
376	DANCE HALL MARGE (sh)	SENNETT, LORD	EDUCATIONAL FILM	1931
376	RIDING WEST	BERKE	COLUMBIA	1944
377	FRONTIER FURY	BERKE	COLUMBIA	1943
377	TAKE YOUR MEDICINE (sh)	CLINE	EDUCATIONAL FILM	1930
378	ONE YARD TO GO (sh)	BEAUDINE	EDUCATIONAL FILM	1931
378	TONIGHT'S THE NIGHT (UK: HAPPILY EVER AFTER)	ZAMPI	ALLIED ARTISTS	1954
379	GOODBYE GIRL	ROSS	WB	1977
379	HIS MAJESTY O'KEEFE	HASKIN	WARNER BROS	1954
379	HOLLYWOOD THEME SONG (sh)	BEAUDINE	EDUCATIONAL FILM	1930
381	COLLEGE VAMP (sh)	BEAUDINE	EDUCATIONAL FILM	1931
382	BRIDE'S MISTAKE (sh)	RODNEY	EDUCATIONAL FILM	1931
383	STRANGE BIRDS (sh)		EDUCATIONAL FILM	1930
383	WHAT'S UP? (sh)	ROBBINS	EDUCATIONAL FILM	1925
383A	MOVIE-TOWN (sh)	SENNETT	EDUCATIONAL FILM	1931
384	DOG DOCTOR (sh)	WHITMAN	EDUCATIONAL FILM	1931
385	GREAT IMPERSONATION	MELFORD	PARAMOUNT	1921
385	MAVERICK		AMERICAN BROADCASTING	1957
385	SPEED (sh)	SENNETT	EDUCATIONAL FILM	1931
386	JUST A BEAR (sh)	STAFFORD	EDUCATIONAL FILM	1931
387	EX-SWEETIES (sh)	NEILAN	EDUCATIONAL FILM	1931
388	BARRICADE (WHITE LADY OF THE ORIENT)	RATOFF	20th CENTURY-FOX	1939
388	DON'T TELL EVERYTHING	WOOD	PARAMOUNT	1921
388	FOUR FEATHERS (UK)	Z KORDA	UNITED ARTISTS	1939
388	POOR FISH (sh)	SENNETT	EDUCATIONAL FILM	1931
389	IN CONFERENCE (sh)	CLINE	EDUCATIONAL FILM	1931
389	LOST IN AMERICA	BROOKS	GEFFEN	1985
390	COWCATCHER'S DAUGHTER (sh)	STAFFORD	EDUCATIONAL FILM	1931
391	LITTLE DRUMMER GIRL	HILL	WARNER BROS	1984
392	NATIONAL LAMPOON'S EUROPEAN VACATION	HECKERLING	WARNER BROS	1985
392	SOMEBODY'S WRONG (sh)	WHITE	EDUCATIONAL FILM	1926
393	GHOST PARADE (sh)	SENNETT	EDUCATIONAL FILM	1931
393	WHO'S BOSS? (sh)	WHITE	EDUCATIONAL FILM	1926
394	HOLD 'ER SHERIFF (sh)	SENNETT	EDUCATIONAL FILM	1931
394	WHAT A LIFE!	WHITE	EDUCATIONAL FILM	1926
395	MEET MY DOG (sh)	WHITE	EDUCATIONAL FILM	1926
395	MONKEY BUSINESS IN AFRICA (sh)	SENNETT	EDUCATIONAL FILM	1931
396	SLIDE, SPEEDY, SLIDE (sh)	STAFFORD	EDUCATIONAL FILM	1931
397	ALBANY BRANCH	SENNETT	EDUCATIONAL FILM	1931
399	ANIMAL WORLD	ALLEN	WARNER BROS	1956
399	DONNA REED	portrait	MGM	
399	I SURRENDER, DEAR (sh)	SENNETT	EDUCATIONAL FILM	1931
400	CANNONBALL (sh)	LORD	EDUCATIONAL FILM	1931
400	CASH AND CARRY (sh)	LORD	COLUMBIA	1937
401	PLAYGROUND OF THE MAMMALS (sh)	SENNETT	EDUCATIONAL FILM	1932
401	PLAYING THE PONIES (sh)	LAMONT	COLUMBIA	1937

402	ONE MORE CHANCE (sh)	SENNETT	EDUCATIONAL FILM	1931
402	SITTER DOWNERS (sh)	LORD	COLUMBIA	1937
403	HYPNOTIZED	SENNETT	SONO ART-WORLD WIDE	1932
404	TOO MANY HUSBANDS (sh)	PEARCE	EDUCATIONAL FILM	1931
404	WEE WEE MONSIEUR (sh)	LORD	COLUMBIA	1938
405	TAXI TROUBLES (sh)	LORD	EDUCATIONAL FILM	1931
406	POKER WIDOWS (sh)	PEARCE	EDUCATIONAL FILM	1931
407	ALASKA LOVE (sh)	STAFFORD	EDUCATIONAL FILM	1932
407	DANGER! WOMEN AT WORK	NEWFIELD	PRC	1943
407	GRACIE AT THE BAT (sh)	LORD	COLUMBIA	1937
409	BILLBOARD GIRL (sh)	PEARCE	EDUCATIONAL FILM	1932
410	CRAIG'S WIFE	DEMILLE	PATHE	1928
410	WORLD FLIER (sh)	LORD	EDUCATIONAL FILM	1931
411	BOY AND THE LAUGHING DOG, THE (GOOD-BYE MY LADY)	WELLMAN	WARNER BROS	1956
411	DREAM HOUSE (sh)	LORD	EDUCATIONAL FILM	1932
411	HARVEST MELODY	NEWFIELD	PRC	1943
411	RIO BRAVO	HAWKS	WARNER BROS	1959
411	UNA MERKEL	portrait	MGM	
412	GIRL FROM MONTERREY	FOX	PRC	1943
412	HALF HOLIDAY (sh)	STAFFORD	EDUCATIONAL FILM	1931
413	SEA-GOING BIRDS	SENNETT	EDUCATIONAL FILM	1932
413	UNA MERKEL	portrait	MGM	
414	ANN SOTHERN	portrait	MGM	
414	GREAT PIE MYSTERY (sh)	LORD	EDUCATIONAL FILM	1931
414	TRAVELIN' ON	HILLYER	PARAMOUNT	1922
415	ANN SOTHERN	portrait	MGM	
415	BRONCO BILLY	EASTWOOD	WARNER BROS	1980
415	FAT MAN AND LITTLE BOY	JOFFE	PARAMOUNT	1989
416	MAN-EATING SHARKS (sh)		EDUCATIONAL FILM	1932
416	TERMITES OF 1938 (sh)	LORD	COLUMBIA	1938
417	DIXIE JAMBOREE	CABANNE	PRC	1944
417	WHO'S WHO IN THE ZOO (sh)	STAFFORD	EDUCATIONAL FILM	1931
418	ALIBI	WEST	MGM	1929
418	LADY IN THE DEATH HOUSE	SEKELY	PRC	1944
418	SHOPPING WITH WIFIE (sh)	STAFFORD	EDUCATIONAL FILM	1932
419	ALL-AMERICAN KICKBACK (sh)	LORD	EDUCATIONAL FILM	1931
419	THREE LITTLE SEW AND SEWS (sh)	LORD	COLUMBIA	1939
420	TASSELS IN THE AIR (sh)	CHASE	COLUMBIA	1938
422	HEALTHY, WEALTHY AND DUMB (sh)	LORD	COLUMBIA	1938
422	OLD HOMESTEAD	CRUZE	PARAMOUNT	1922
422	SPEED IN THE GAY NINETIES (sh)	LORD	EDUCATIONAL FILM	1932
423	POTTSVILLE PALOOKA (sh)	PEARCE	EDUCATIONAL FILM	1931
423	VIOLENT IS THE WORD FOR CURLY (sh)	CHASE	COLUMBIA	1938
424	MACHINE GUN MAMA	YOUNG	PRC PICTURES	1944
424	SMALL TOWN IDOL (revamp version from 1921)	KENTON	EDUCATIONAL FILM	1933
425	GIRL IN THE TONNEAU	STAFFORD	EDUCATIONAL FILM	1932
426	HEAVENS! MY HUSBAND! (sh)	STAFFORD	EDUCATIONAL FILM	1932
426	THREE MISSING LINKS (sh)	WHITE	COLUMBIA	1938
427	LADY! PLEASE! (sh)	STAFFORD	EDUCATIONAL FILM	1932
427	MUTTS TO YOU (sh)	CHASE	COLUMBIA	1938
427	TIGHT LITTLE ISLAND (UK: WHISKY GALORE)	MACKENDRICK	UNIVERSAL	1949
428	ENCHANTED FOREST	LANDERS	PRC	1945
428	LISTENING IN (sh)	PEARCE	EDUCATIONAL FILM	1932
429	FLIRTY SLEEPWALKER (sh)	LORD	EDUCATIONAL FILM	1932
430	BITTER SPRINGS (AUSTRALIA/UK)	SPRINGS	BELL	1950
430	BOUDOIR BUTLER (sh)	PEARCE	EDUCATIONAL FILM	1932
430	SAVED BY THE BELLE (sh)	CHASE	COLUMBIA	1939
431	MEET THE SENATOR (sh)	LORD	PARAMOUNT PUBLIX	1932
432	FREAKS OF THE DEEP (sh)		EDUCATIONAL FILM	1932
432	WIND ACROSS THE EVERGLADES	RAY	WARNER BROS	1958
434	SPOT ON THE RUG (sh)	LORD	EDUCATIONAL FILM	1932
435	DIVORCE A LA MODE (sh)	PEARCE	EDUCATIONAL FILM	1932
436	HIS ROYAL SHYNESS (sh)	PEARCE	EDUCATIONAL FILM	1932
436	OLYMPIC DAMES (sh)		UNR. MACK SENNETT	1932
436	SOUP TO NUTS (sh)	WATSON	EDUCATIONAL FILM	1925
437	LIGHTHOUSE LOVE (sh)	DELMER	PARAMOUNT PUBLIX	1932

438	HATTA MARRI (sh)	STAFFORD	EDUCATIONAL FILM	1932
438	YES, WE HAVE NO BANANAS (sh)	LORD	COLUMBIA	1939
439	FLAT FOOT STOOGES (sh)	CHASE	COLUMBIA	1938
439	MY SWEDIE (sh)	BEAUDINE	EDUCATIONAL FILM	1925
440	JIMMY'S NEW YACHT (sh)	LORD	PARAMOUNT PUBLIX	1932
441	LOUD MOUTH (sh)	LORD	PARAMOUNT PUBLIX	1932
441	RUN TIN CAN (sh)	THORNBY	EDUCATIONAL FILM	1926
442	GIDDY AGE (sh)	STAFFORD	EDUCATIONAL FILM	1932
442	MAUREEN O'SULLIVAN	portrait	MGM	
443	APOLOGY FOR MURDER	NEWFIELD	PRC	1945
443	FOR THE LOVE OF LUDWIG (sh) (mistake)	HARBERGER	EDUCATIONAL FILM	1932
443	SHORE SHY (sh)	WATSON	EDUCATIONAL FILM	1926
443	SINGING PLUMBER (sh)	PEARCE	PARAMOUNT PUBLIX	1932
443	WE WANT OUR MUMMY (sh)	LORD	COLUMBIA	1939
444	CANDID CAMERA (sh)	PEARCE	EDUCATIONAL FILM	1932
444	DUCKING THEY DID GO (sh)	LORD	COLUMBIA	1939
444	MAUREEN O'SULLIVAN	portrait	MGM	
444	PAPA'S PEST (sh)	WATSON	EDUCATIONAL FILM	1926
444	QUEEN OF BURLESQUE	NEWFIELD	PRC	1946
445	CALLING ALL CURS (sh)	WHITE	COLUMBIA	1939
445	DANNY BOY	MORSE	PRC	1946
445	MISTER WIFE (sh)	BEAUDINE	EDUCATIONAL FILM	1926
445	NEIGHBOR TROUBLE (sh)	PEARCE	EDUCATIONAL FILM	1932
446	ELEANOR POWELL	portrait	MGM	
446	MASK OF DIIJON	LANDERS	PRC	1946
446	RATTLING ROMEO (sh)	LORD	COLUMBIA	1939
446	UP POPPED THE GHOST (sh)	STAFFORD	PARAMOUNT PUBLIX	1932
447	ASK DAD (sh)	FAULCON	EDUCATIONAL FILM	1929
447	SINGING BOXER (sh)	PEARCE	PARAMOUNT PUBLIX	1933
448	ELEANOR POWELL	portrait	MGM	
448	MA'S PRIDE AND JOY (sh)	PEARCE	PARAMOUNT PUBLIX	1932
448	NOW IT CAN BE SOLD (sh)	LORD	COLUMBIA	1939
448	RIGHT BED (sh)	FAULCON	EDUCATIONAL FILM	1929
449	ELEANOR POWELL	portrait	MGM	
449	HAWKINS AND WATKINS, INC. (sh)	SENNETT	PARAMOUNT PUBLIX	1932
449	OILY TO BED, OILY TO RISE (sh)	WHITE	COLUMBIA	1939
449	TRUSTING WIVES	PEARCE	EDUCATIONAL FILM	1929
450	PRINCE GABBY (sh)	PEARCE	EDUCATIONAL FILM	1929
450	RISE AND FALL OF LEGS DIAMOND	BOETTICHER	WARNER BROS	1960
450	WHEREEVER SHE GOES (UK/AUS)	GORDON	ASTRAL	1951
450	YOUNG ONIONS (sh)	EMESS	EDUCATIONAL FILM	1932
451	DEVIL BAT'S DAUGHTER	WISBAR	PRC	1946
451	SING, BING, SING (sh)	STAFFORD	PARAMOUNT	1933
451	THREE SAPPY PEOPLE (sh)	WHITE	COLUMBIA	1939
452	BLUE OF THE NIGHT (sh)	PEARCE	PARAMOUNT PUBLIX	1932
452	MARSHA HUNT	portrait	MGM	
452	OUR LEADING CITIZEN	GREEN	PARAMOUNT	1922
452	SUNRISE AT CAMPOBELLO	DONEHUE	WARNER BROS	1960
452	TEACHER'S PEST (sh)	KRAMER, ULLMAN	COLUMBIA	1939
452	WIFE OF MONTE CRISTO	ULMER	PRC	1946
453	ELEANOR POWELL	portrait	MGM	
453	FALSE IMPRESSIONS (sh)	PEARCE	PARAMOUNT PUBLIX	1932
453	STATIC IN THE ATTIC (sh)	CHASE	COLUMBIA	1939
454	COURTING TROUBLE (sh)	PEARCE	PARAMOUNT PUBLIX	1932
454	DRAMA DELUXE	TAUROG	EDUCATIONAL FILM	1927
454	MARSHA HUNT	portrait	MGM	
454	PEST FROM THE WEST (sh)	LORD	COLUMBIA	1939
455	BLOOD AND SAND	NIBLO	PARAMOUNT	1922
455	COOKOO CAVALIERS (sh)	WHITE	COLUMBIA	1940
455	DOUBLING IN THE QUICKIES (sh)	STAFFORD	PARAMOUNT PUBLIX	1932
455	ELEANOR POWELL	portrait	MGM	
456	BRING 'EM BACK SOBER (sh)	STAFFORD	PARAMOUNT PUBLIX	1932
456	HEDY LAMARR	portrait	MGM	
456	SPOOK TOWN	CLIFTON	PRC	1944
456	WHO'S AFRAID? (sh)	LAMONT	EDUCATIONAL FILM	1927
457	ELEANOR POWELL	portrait	MGM	

457	HUMAN FISH (sh)	BRUCKMAN	PARAMOUNT PUBLIX	1932
457	MONTY OF THE MOUNTED (sh)	SANDRICH	EDUCATIONAL FILM	1927
458	DENTIST (sh)	JONES	PARAMOUNT PUBLIX	1932
458	HOW HIGH IS UP? (sh)	LORD	COLUMBIA	1940
459	LION AND THE HOUSE (sh)	STAFFORD	PARAMOUNT PUBLIX	1932
460	ALL AMERICAN BLONDES (sh)	LORD	COLUMBIA	1939
460	WRESTLER'S BRIDE (sh)	STAFFORD	PARAMOUNT PUBLIX	1933
461	ELEANOR POWELL	portrait	MGM	
461	FATAL GLASS OF BEER (sh)	BRUCKMAN	PARAMOUNT	1933
461	ROCKIN' THRU THE ROCKIES (sh)	WHITE	COLUMBIA	1940
462	DON'T PLAY BRIDGE WITH YOUR WIFE (sh)	PEARCE	PARAMOUNT PUBLIX	1933
462	PLUMBING WE WILL GO (sh)	LORD	COLUMBIA	1940
463	ANDY CLYDE GETS SPRING CHICKEN (sh)	WHITE	COLUMBIA	1939
463	ELEANOR POWELL	portrait	MGM	
463	PLUMBER AND THE LADY (sh)	STAFFORD	PARAMOUNT	1933
463	YOUNG RAJAH	ROSEN	PARAMOUNT	1922
464	TOO MANY HIGHBALLS	BRUCKMAN	PARAMOUNT	1933
465	EASY ON THE EYES (sh)	MARSHALL	PARAMOUNT	1933
465	NUTTY BUT NICE (sh)	WHITE	COLUMBIA	1940
466	CALIENTE LOVE (sh)	MARSHALL	PARAMOUNT	1933
466	ELEANOR POWELL	portrait	MGM	
467	HECKLER (sh)	LORD	COLUMBIA	1940
467	HEDY LAMARR	portrait	MGM	
467	SWEET COOKIE (sh)	MARSHALL	PARAMOUNT	1933
468	FROM NURSE TO WORSE (sh)	WHITE	COLUMBIA	1940
468	UNCLE JAKE (sh)	CLINE	PARAMOUNT	1933
469	DREAM STUFF (sh)	CROWLEY	PARAMOUNT	1933
470	DADDY KNOWS BEST (sh)	PEARCE	PARAMOUNT	1933
471	PHARMACIST (sh)	RIPLEY	PARAMOUNT	1933
471	YOU NAZTY SPY! (sh)	WHITE	COLUMBIA	1940
472	SEE YOU TONIGHT (sh)	CROWLEY	PARAMOUNT	1933
473	ROADHOUSE QUEEN (sh)	PEARCE	PARAMOUNT	1933
473	SOUTH OF THE BOUDOIR (sh)	LORD	COLUMBIA	1940
474	KNOCKOUT KISSES (sh)	MARSHALL	PARAMOUNT	1933
474	NO CENSUS, NO FEELING (sh)	LORD	COLUMBIA	1940
475	BIG FIBBER (sh)	MARSHALL	PARAMOUNT	1933
475	DEAR HEART	MANN	WARNER BROS	1964
476	HUSBAND'S REUNION (sh)	MARSHALL	PARAMOUNT	1933
477	BARBER SHOP (sh)	RIPLEY	PARAMOUNT	1933
477	BLUEBEARD	ULMER	PRC	1944
479	WHEN THE LIGHTS GO ON AGAIN	HOWARD	PRC	1944
480	TOWN WENT WILD	MURPHY	PRC	1944
481	GREAT MIKE	FOX	PRC	1944
481	LARAINE DAY	portrait	MGM	
482	IN THE SWEET PIE AND PIE (sh)	WHITE	COLUMBIA	1941
483	BLONDES AND BLUNDERS (sh)	LORD	COLUMBIA	1940
484	MAN WHO WALKED ALONE	CABANNE	PRC	1945
484	SO LONG MR. CHUMPS (sh)	WHITE	COLUMBIA	1941
485	CRIME INC aka GANGSTER KELLY	LANDERS	PRC	1945
485	DUTIFUL BUT DUMB (sh)	LORD	COLUMBIA	1941
486	BOOBS IN ARMS (sh)	WHITE	COLUMBIA	1940
486	ROBERT MONTGOMERY	portrait	MGM	
487	ALL THE WORLD'S A STOOGE (sh)	LORD	COLUMBIA	1941
488	ACHE IN EVERY STAKE (sh)	LORD	COLUMBIA	1941
489	PHANTOM OF 42ND STREET	HERMAN	PRC	1945
492	I RING DOORBELLS	STRAYER	PRC	1946
493	DETOUR	ULMER	PRC	1945
496	WEAK, BUT WILLING (sh)	MAYO	EDUCATIONAL FILM	1926
498	YANKEE DOODLE ANDY (sh)	WHITE	COLUMBIA	1941
500	ALICE	ALLEN	ORION	1990
500	I'LL NEVER HEIL AGAIN (sh)	WHITE	COLUMBIA	1941
500	LIGHTHOUSE	WISBAR	PRC	1947
501	GANGSTERS OF THE FRONTIER	CLIFTON	PRC	1944
501	LOVE AT FIRST FRIGHT (sh)	LORD	COLUMBIA	1941
502	DEAD OR ALIVE	CLIFTON	PRC	1944
503	FRENCH FRIED PATOOTIE (sh)	WHITE	COLUMBIA	1941

503	WHISPERING SKULL	CLIFTON	PRC	1944
506	HALF SHOT AT SUNRISE (sh)	LORD	COLUMBIA	1941
507	EVEN AS IOU (sh)	LORD	COLUMBIA	1942
508	BUNKER BEAN	HAMILTON, KILLY	RKO	1936
508	GENERAL NUISANCEE (sh)	WHITE	COLUMBIA	1941
508	MARE NOSTRUM	INGRAM	MGM	1926
509	BATTLE CRY	WALSH	WARNER BROS	1955
509	SOCIETY GOES SPAGHETTI (sh)	SANDRICH	RKO	1930
510	GARDEN OF ALLAH	INGRAM	MGM	1927
510	LOCO BOY MAKES GOOD (sh)	WHITE	COLUMBIA	1942
511	BABES IN TOYLAND (unfinished)		RKO	1930
511	ODE TO BILLY JOE	BAER, JR	WB	1976
511	SOME MORE OF SAMOA (sh)	LORD	COLUMBIA	1941
512	MITT ME TONIGHT (sh)	WHITE	COLUMBIA	1941
513	ADAM'S RIB	DEMILLE	PARAMOUNT	1923
513	CACTUS MAKES PERFECT (sh)	LORD	COLUMBIA	1942
513	HEY DIDDLE DIDDLE (sh)	MARSHALL	RKO	1930
514	JOAN CRAWFORD	portrait	MGM	
514	MOONLIGHT & MONKEY BUSINESS (sh)	SANDRICH	RKO	1930
515	PHONY CRONIES (sh)	EDWARDS	COLUMBIA	1942
515	RAZORED IN OLD KENTUCKY (sh)	SANDRICH	RKO	1930
517	AUNT'S IN THE PANTS (sh)	SANDRICH	RKO	1930
517	DANCE PRETTY LADY (UK)	ASQUITH	WARDOUR	1932
518	BLUEBEARD'S 8TH WIFE	WOOD	PARAMOUNT	1923
518	DIANA LEWIS	portrait	MGM	
518	TOO MANY WINNERS	BEAUDINE	PRC	1947
519	LESLIE BROOKS		COLUMBIA	
519	WHAT'S THE MATADOR? (sh)	WHITE	COLUMBIA	1942
520	ROBERT ARMSTRONG		MGM	
520	TRADER GINSBERG (sh)	SANDRICH	RKO	1930
521	CREATION	O'BRIEN	RKO	1931
521	SWEET SPIRITS OF NIGHTER (sh)	LORD	COLUMBIA	1941
522	BACK FROM THE FRONT (sh)	WHITE	COLUMBIA	1943
523	GROOM AND BORED (sh)	LORD	COLUMBIA	1942
523	HE LOVED HER NOT (sh)	MARSHALL	RKO	1931
523	RANGE BEYOND THE BLUE	TAYLOR	PRODUCERS RELEASING	1947
524	TALKING TURKEY (sh)	SANDRICH	RKO	1930
525	GLOVE AFFAIR (sh)	WHITE	COLUMBIA	1941
525	WEST TO GLORY	TAYLOR	PRC	1947
526	BIG FIX	FLOOD	PRC	1947
526	WIFE O'RILEY (sh)	SANDRICH	RKO	1931
527	MATRI-PHONY (sh)	H EDWARDS	COLUMBIA	1942
528	OLAF LAUGHS LAST (sh)	WHITE	COLUMBIA	1942
528	SHE WENT FOR A TRAMP (sh)	BROCK	RKO	1931
529	DIZZY DETECTIVES (sh)	WHITE	COLUMBIA	1943
531	FORBIDDEN PARADISE	LUBITSCH	PARAMOUNT	1924
531	QUACK SERVICE (sh)	EDWARDS	COLUMBIA	1943
532	RITZ	LESTER	WB	1976
532	THREE SMART SAPS (sh)	WHITE	COLUMBIA	1942
533	THEY STOOGE TO CONGA (sh)	LORD	COLUMBIA	1943
534	FEMALE	WOOD	PARAMOUNT	1924
534	HEARTACHES	WRANGELL	PRC	1947
535	CHECK YOUR GUNS	TAYLOR	PRC	1947
536	BLACK HILLS	TAYLOR	PRC	1947
536	CARRY HARRY (sh)	EDWARDS	COLUMBIA	1942
536	PISCATORIAL PLEASURES (sh)	AUSTIN	MGM	1931
537	BLITZ ON THE FRITZ (sh)	WHITE	COLUMBIA	1943
537	WESTWARD TRAIL	TAYLOR	PRC	1947
538	SHADOW VALLEY	TAYLOR	PRC	1947
538	SLIP AT THE SWITCH (sh) (mistake - 583)		RKO	1932
538	WAY OF ALL FISH (sh)	SANDRICH	RKO	1931
538	WOLF IN THIEF'S CLOTHING (sh)	WHITE	COLUMBIA	1943
539	SOCK-A-BYE BABY (sh)	WHITE	COLUMBIA	1942
540	TIOGA KID	TAYLOR	PRC	1947
541	DEALING: OR THE BOSTON TO BERKELEY...	WILLIAMS	WARNER BROS	1972
541	HIS WEDDING SCARE (sh)	LORD	COLUMBIA	1943

543	CLEANUP ON THE CURB	FRENCH	RKO	1931
543	FRED BECKNER	portrait	MGM	
543	GOLDEN RULE KATE	BARKER	TRIANGLE	1917
544	LONE STARVED RANGER (sh)	SCHWARTZ	RKO	1931
544	SIX STUTTER SHERIFF*		RKO	1931
545	COUNTY SEAT (sh)	SANDRICH	RKO	1931
545	HIS GIRL'S WORST FRIEND (sh)	WHITE	COLUMBIA	1943
546	FARMER FOR A DAY (sh)	WHITE	COLUMBIA	1943
546	NED SPARKS #2		RKO	1931
546	ROBERT YOUNG, DAUGHTERS CAROLE ANN, BARBARA QUEEN	portrait	MGM	
546	STRIFE OF THE PARTY (sh)	SANDRICH	RKO	1931
547	MAID MADE MAD (sh)	LORD	COLUMBIA	1943
547	ROBERT YOUNG	portrait	MGM	
547	STEELYARD BLUES	MYERSON	WARNER BROS	1972
548	LAS VEGAS SHAKEDOWN	SALKOW	ALLIED ARTISTS	1955
548	SOCKS APPEAL (sh)	EDWARDS	COLUMBIA	1943
549	SPOOK LOUDER (sh)	LORD	COLUMBIA	1943
550	I SPIED FOR YOU (sh)	WHITE	COLUMBIA	1943
551	ROBERT YOUNG, WIFE, DAUGHTERS CAROLE, BARBARA	portrait	MGM	
551	THREE LITTLE TWIRPS (sh)	H EDWARDS	COLUMBIA	1943
552	BLONDE AND GROOM (sh)	EDWARDS	COLUMBIA	1943
552	HEADLINER #2 (sh)		RKO	1931
553	COWSLIPS (sh)	SANDRICH	RKO	1931
553	WHY GIRLS LEAVE HOME	BERKE	PRC	1945
554	HERE COMES MR. ZERK (sh)	EDWARDS	COLUMBIA	1943
555	DIZZY PILOTS (sh)	WHITE	COLUMBIA	1943
555	STRANGLER OF THE SWAMP	WISBAR	PRC	1946
555	TOURIST (sh)	ARBUCKLE	EDUCATIONAL FILM	1925
556	ONE SHOT ROSS	SMITH	TRIANGLE	1917
556	TWO SAPLINGS (sh)	EDWARDS	COLUMBIA	1943
557	HER SISTER'S SECRET	ULMER	PRC	1946
558	FALSE ROOMERS (sh)	SANDRICH	RKO	1931
558	FRANCES RAFFERTY	portrait	MGM	
558	WHAT A SOLDIER (sh) NOT RELEASED		COLUMBIA	1943
559	MR. CINDERELLA (sh)	TAUROG	EDUCATIONAL FILM	1926
559	ROBERT YOUNG, DAUGHTERS CAROLE ANN, BARBARA QUEEN	portrait	MGM	
559	SHOT IN THE ESCAPE (sh)	WHITE	COLUMBIA	1943
559	WHEN SUMMONS COME (sh)		RKO	1931
560	FRANCES RAFFERTY	portrait	MGM	
560	HONEST INJUN (sh)	TAUROG	EDUCATIONAL FILM	1926
561	GLAND PARADE (sh)	SCHWARTZ	RKO	1931
561	HE WAS ONLY FEUDIN' (sh)	EDWARDS	COLUMBIA	1943
562	ROMANCE OF THE WEST	TANSEY as EMMETT	PRC	1946
562	ROOKIE'S COOKIE (sh)	WHITE	COLUMBIA	1943
563	BOOBS IN THE NIGHT (sh)	LORD	COLUMBIA	1943
563	FRANCES RAFFERTY	portrait	MGM	
563	USE YOUR NOODLE (sh)	FRENCH	RKO	1931
564	EX-ROOSTER (sh)	SANDRICH	RKO	1932
564	NO DOUGH BOYS (sh)	WHITE	COLUMBIA	1944
565	HUGH HERBERT (sh)		COLUMBIA	
565	SCRATCH AS CATCH CAN (sh)	SANDRICH	RKO	1931
566	CARAVAN TRAILS (CARAVAN TRAIL)	TANSEY as EMMETT	PRC	1946
566	PITCHIN' IN THE KITCHEN (sh)	WHITE	COLUMBIA	1943
567	HULLABALOO		RKO	1931
567-X	ATHLETIC DAZE (SHORT)	MCCAREY	MGM	1932
567-X	OLYMPIC EVENTS (SHORT)	MCCAREY	MGM	1932
567-X	TIMBER TOPPERS (SHORT)		MGM	1932
568	HIGHER THAN A KITE (sh)	LORD	COLUMBIA	1943
568	MARILYN MAXWELL	portrait	MGM	
568	MELON DRAMA (sh)	SANDRICH	RKO	1931
569	PHONY EXPRESS (sh)	LORD	COLUMBIA	1943
570	I CAN HARDLY WAIT (sh)	WHITE	COLUMBIA	1943
571	MAUREEN O'SULLIVAN	portrait	MGM	
571	YOKE'S ON ME (sh)	WHITE	COLUMBIA	1944
572	TO HEIR IS HUMAN (sh)	GODSOE	COLUMBIA	1944
573	GARDEN OF EATIN' (sh)	EDWARDS	COLUMBIA	1943

574	COLORADO SERENADE	TANSEY	PRC	1946
574	NEVER THE TWINS SHALL MEET (sh)	SCHWARTZ	RKO	1932
574	WHO'S HUGH (sh)	EDWARDS	COLUMBIA	1943
575	DOWN MISSOURI WAY	BERNE	PRC	1946
575	GEM OF A JAM (sh)	LORD	COLUMBIA	1943
575	MANY A SIP (sh)	SANDRICH	RKO	1932
576	BIG DAME HUNTING (sh)	MARSHALL	RKO	1932
576	CLAN OF THE CAVE BEAR	CHAPMAN	WARNER BROS	1986
576	NED SPARKS @4		RKO	1932
578	HURRY CALL (sh)		RKO	1931
578	PHILO VANCE RETURNS	BEAUDINE	PRC	1947
579	CHICHI AND HER PAPAS (unfinished)		RKO	1932
581	FRONTIER*		RKO	1932
583	SLIP AT THE SWITCH (sh)		RKO	1932
585	HASSAN		PARAMOUNT	1926
587	GAS HOUSE KIDS	NEWFIELD	PRC	1946
589	LADY CHASER	NEWFIELD	PRC	1946
591	BEYOND THE ROCKIES	ALLEN	RKO	1932
595	STOOGES (sh)		COLUMBIA	
597	ENGINEER'S DAUGHTER; OR, IRON MINNIE'S REVENGE (sh)	HILL	RKO	1932
598	DONNA REED	portrait	MGM	
598	JUST A PAIN IN THE PARLOR (sh)	MARSHALL	RKO	1932
600	FREDDIE BARTHOLOMEW	portrait	MGM	
601	CAST A DARK SHADOW (UK 1955)	GILBERT	DCA	1957
601	DONNA REED	portrait	MGM	
602	BORN TO SPEED	CAHN	GIBRALTAR	R61
602	TOM DRAKE	portrait	MGM	
603	DEVIL ON WHEELS	WILBUR	PRC	1947
603	GOLF CHUMP (sh)	SWEET	RKO	1932
603	TOM DRAKE	portrait	MGM	
604	MILLIONAIRE CAT (sh)	SANDRICH	RKO	1932
604	TOM DRAKE	portrait	MGM	
605	ACCOMPLICE	COLMES	PRC	1946
605	BOSS OF THE LAZY Y	SMITH	TRIANGLE	1918
605	TOM DRAKE	portrait	MGM	
606	REPEAT PERFORMANCE	WERKER	EAGLE LION	1947
606	TOM DRAKE	portrait	MGM	
607	IT'S A JOKE, SON	STOLOFF	EAGLE LION	1947
607	TOM DRAKE	portrait	MGM	
608	FIREHOUSE HONEYMOON (sh)	MARSHALL	RKO	1932
608	HUMMING BIRD	OLCOTT	PARAMOUNT	1924
608	LOST HONEYMOON	JASON	EAGLE-LION	1947
608	PRICE OF A SONG (UK)	POWELL	FOX	1935
608	TOM DRAKE	portrait	MGM	
609	TOM DRAKE	portrait	MGM	
609	TWO LIPS AND JULEPS (sh)	SLOMAN	RKO	1932
610	FORLORN RIVER	WATERS	PARAMOUNT	1926
610	JITTERS THE BUTLER (sh)	SANDRICH	RKO	1932
610	TOM DRAKE	portrait	MGM	
612	CALLAHANS AND THE MURPHYS	HILL	MGM	1927
614	LIGHT THAT FAILED	MELFORD	PARAMOUNT	1923
615	HOCUS FOCUS (sh)		RKO	1932
616	CARMEN MARANDA	portrait	20TH CENTURY FOX	
616	LATE EXTRA (UK)	PARKER	FOX	1935
617	MICKEY	MURPHY	EAGLE LION	1948
617	SHAM POO, THE MAGICIAN (sh)	SWEET	RKO	1932
618	BLUE SMOKE (UK)	R INCE	FOX	1935
618	BRIDE'S BEREAVEMENTS (sh)	HILL	RKO	1932
619	BY THE SUN'S RAYS	GIBLYN	NESTOR	1914
620	WRATH OF JEALOUSY (UK: WEDDING GROUP)	BRYCE, GULLAN	20TH CENTURY FOX	1936
621	DRUGGIST'S DILEMMA (sh)	SANDRICH	RKO	1932
623	PARLOR, BEDROOM AND WRATH (sh)	SWEET	RKO	1932
625	CANON CITY	WILBUR	EAGLE LION	1948
626	HE WALKED BY NIGHT	WERKER	EAGLE-LION	1948
628	BIG IDEA (sh)	BEAUDINE	MGM	1934
628	GAY NINETIES*		RKO	1932

629	DONNA REED	portrait	MGM	
629	FISH FEATHERS (sh)	SWEET	RKO	1932
631	FLY GOD	SMITH	TRIANGLE	1918
631	MAKING LOOPIE (sh)		RKO	1932
631	REIGN OF TERROR	MANN	EAGLE LION	1949
631	WALLACE BEERY	portrait	MGM	
632	DONNA REED	portrait	MGM	
632	PORT OF NEW YORK	BENEDEK	EAGLE LION	1949
633	THRU THIN AND THICKET (sh)	SANDRICH	RKO	1933
634	DOWN MEMORY LANE	KARLSON	EAGLE LION	1949
635	FORCED RESPONSE	CULBERTSON	RKO	1933
635	RUTH HUSSEY	portrait	MGM	
636	FELIX THE CAT USES HIS HEAD (t) (sh)	MESSMER	EDUCATIONAL FILM	1926
637	MARRIAGE WHIRL	SANTELL	FIRST NATIONAL	1925
641	FELIX THE CAT RINGS THE RINGER (t) (sh)	MESSMER	EDUCATIONAL FILM	1926
641	PRIVATE WIVES (sh)	SANDRICH	RKO	1933
641	TODAY WE LIVE (mistake - 651)	HAWKS, ROSSON	MGM	1933
641 #1	PIGSKIN	MCCAREY	MGM	1932
641 #2	BLOCK AND TACKLE	HANLEY	MGM	1932
642	ART IN THE RAW (sh)	SWEET	RKO	1933
642	MYRNA LOY	portrait	MGM	
646	FOOLS WHO MADE HISTORY-ELIAS HOWE	LEMAN	COLUMBIA	1939
647	FOOLS WHO MADE HISTORY-CHARLES GOODYEAR		COLUMBIA	1939
647	MERCHANT OF MENACE (sh)	SWEET	RKO	1933
648	HIP ZIP HOORAY (sh) HEADLINER #4		RKO	1933
650	SWORD OF THE AVENGER	SALKOW	EAGLE LION	1948
650	THROWN OUT OF JOINT (sh)	SWEET	RKO	1933
651	MANHANDLED	DWAN	PARAMOUNT	1924
653	WHAT NO TO DO IN BRIDGE	CULBERTSON	RKO	1933
654	ANITA PAGE	portrait	MGM	
654	DECLASSE AND OTHER PLAYS (unfinished - # reassigned)		RKO	1933
654	TUNED OUT	GOULDING	RKO	1933
656	MURDER AT THE BRIDGE TABLE	CULBERTSON	RKO	1933
656	TRIANGLE MARRIAGE (ME, HIM AND I)		UNIVERSAL	1914
657	SHAKESPEARE WITH TIN EARS (sh)	SWEET	RKO	1933
658	SOCIETY CHEATERS (sh)	CULBERTSON	RKO	1933
661	ELEANOR POWELL	portrait	MGM	
662	DIVORCE COURTSHIP (sh)	STEVENS	RKO	1933
662-C	SILVER FOX AND SAM DAVENPORT (tv)		NATIONAL BROADCASTING	1962
663	CHEYENNE TAKES OVER	TAYLOR	PRC	1947
663	FEMALE, THE	WOOD	PARAMOUNT	1924
663	MOONSHINER'S DAUGHTER (sh)	RAY	RKO	1933
664	LOVE'S PAY DAY	HOPPER	TRIANGLE	1918
664	THREE KNAVES AND A QUEEN	CULBERTSON	RKO	1933
665	KAREN MORLEY	portrait	MGM	
665	TRANSATLANTIC BRIDGE TRICKS	CULBERTSON	RKO	1933
666	GOOD HOUSEWRECKING (sh)	SWEET	RKO	1933
668	BE CAREFUL (sh)	BEAUDINE	EDUCATIONAL FILM	1925
668	FAST SET, THE	DEMILLE	PARAMOUNT	1924
668	LUCILLE LOVE: GIRL OF MYSTERY - EP. 15	FORD	UNIVERSAL	1914
669	FAIR BUT FOOLISH (sh)	WATSON	EDUCATIONAL FILM	1925
670	FOR SADIE'S SAKE (sh)	BEAUDINE	EDUCATIONAL FILM	1926
670	RESTLESS SOULS	DOWLAN	TRIANGLE	1919
671	ANN RUTHERFORD	portrait	MGM	
671	WHOA, EMMA! (sh)	THORNBY	EDUCATIONAL FILM	1926
672	DINNER AT EIGHT	CUKOR	MGM	1933
672	ANN RUTHERFORD	portrait	MGM	
672	GIMME STRENGTH (sh)	ST. JOHN	EDUCATIONAL FILM	1926
673	CHASE YOURSELF (sh)	WATSON	EDUCATIONAL FILM	1926
673	SHE OUTDONE HIM (sh)	SWEET	RKO	1933
674	BEAUTY A LA MUD (sh)	BEAUDINE	EDUCATIONAL FILM	1926
675	DENNIS MORGAN	portrait		
675	SHELL SOCKED (sh)	GRAHAM	EDUCATIONAL FILM	1926
675	WORLDLY GOODS	BERN	PARAMOUNT	1924
676	STOLEN BY GYPSIES	RAY	RKO	1933
676	WILD AND WOOZY (sh)	BEAUDINE	EDUCATIONAL FILM	1927

677	HERE COMES PRECIOUS (sh)	RODNEY	EDUCATIONAL FILM	1927
677	KICKIN' THE CROWN AROUND (sh)	WHITE	RKO	1933
677	LOOKING THE CROWN AROUND*		RKO	1933
678	VOICE OF THE TURTLE	RAPPER	WARNER BROS	1948
679	MEET THE FOLKS (sh)	CHRISTIE, KERR	EDUCATIONAL FILM	1927
679	QUIET PLEASE (sh)	STEVENS	RKO	1933
682	YES, YES BABETTE (sh)	RODNEY	EDUCATIONAL FILM	1925
683	MAN MUST LIVE	SLOANE	PARAMOUNT	1925
684	LUCILLE BREMER	portrait	MGM	
685	SUITS TO NUTS (sh)	SWEET	RKO	1933
686	DIPPY TAR (sh)	RODNEY	EDUCATIONAL FILM	1926
686	HOW COMEDIES ARE BORN (sh)	SWEET	RKO	1933
687	FITS IN A FIDDLE (sh)	WHITE	RKO	1933
690	DUMB BELLES (sh)	WATSON	EDUCATIONAL FILM	1927
690	LOVE AND HISSES (sh)	WHITE	RKO	1933
692	FLIRTING IN THE PARK (sh)	STEVENS	RKO	1933
692	KAREN MORLEY	portrait	MGM	
692	MOVIES (sh)	ARBUCKLE	EDUCATIONAL FILM	1925
692	THROWN TO THE LIONS	HENDERSON	UNIVERSAL	1916
693	FRAMED (sh)	ROBERTS	EDUCATIONAL FILM	1925
693	KNEE DEEP IN MUSIC (sh)	GOULDING	RKO	1933
694	PREFFERED LIST (sh)	JASON	RKO	1933
695	NOBODY'S BUSINESS (sh)	TAUROG	EDUCATIONAL FILM	1926
697	MOVE ALONG (sh)	TAUROG	EDUCATIONAL FILM	1926
697	MR. SMUG (sh)		COLUMBIA	1943
697	SNUG IN THE JUG (sh)	HOLMES	RKO	1933
698	BARRETTS OF WIMPOLE STREET (UK)	FRANKLIN	MGM	1957
698	CALIFORNIA WEATHER (sh)	GOULDING	RKO	1933
698	DOROTHY MAGUIRE	portrait		
698	EMBRACEABLE YOU	JACOVES	WARNER BROS	1948
699	GRIN AND BEAR IT (sh)	STEVENS	RKO	1933
699	KISS IN THE DARK	DAVES	WARNER BROS	1949
700	HALF A BRIDE	LA CAVA	PARAMOUNT	1928
700	MOONLIGHT AND PRETZELS	FREUND	UNIVERSAL	1933
701	HEY, NANNY NANNY (sh)	HOLMES	RKO	1933
702	AIR TONIC	WHITE	RKO	1933
704	VIRGINIA WEIDLER	portrait	MGM	
706	SCOTT OF THE ANTARCTIC (UK)	FREND	EAGLE LION	1948
708	IN THE DEVILDOG HOUSE (sh)	HOLMES	RKO	1934
711	TORCH TANGO (sh)	GOULDING	RKO	1934
712	LOOK BACK IN ANGER (UK)	RICHARDSON	WARNER BROS.	1959
712	OLD MOTHER RILEY'S NEW VENTURE (UK)	HARLOW	BELL	1949
713	COLORADO TERRITORY	WALSH	WARNER BROS	1949
713	WHAT FUR? (sh)	STEVENS	RKO	1934
714	AGAINST THE WIND (UK)	CRICHTON	EAGLE LION	1948
714	AUTOBUYOGRAPHY (sh)	BOASBERG	RKO	1934
714	UNIVERSAL IKE JUNIOR IN DANGERS OF A GREAT CITY		UNIVERSAL	1914
715	SCUDDA HOO; SCUDDA HAY (SUMMER LIGHTNING)	HERBERT	20th CENTURY-FOX	1948
715	THREE SMART GIRLS - error on some R49 - should be 795	KOSTER	UNIVERSAL	1936
715	WALKING BACK HOME (sh)		RKO	1934
716	DIZZY DAISY (sh)	WHITE	EDUCATIONAL FILM	1924
716	IT ALWAYS RAINS ON SUNDAY (UK)	HAMER	EAGLE LION	1947
716	ODOR IN THE COURT (sh)	HOLMES	RKO	1934
717	BEDLAM OF BEARDS (sh)	HOLMES	RKO	1934
717	HERE COMES CHARLIE (sh)	TAUROG	EDUCATIONAL FILM	1926
717	SARABAND (UK: SARABAND FOR DEAD LOVERS)	DEARDEN	EAGLE LION	1948
718	HER BOY FRIEND	SEMON	EDUCATIONAL FILM	1924
718	SPLENDID LIE	HORAN	ARROW	1922
719	DONNA REED	portrait	MGM	
720	DOME DOCTOR (sh)	SEMON	EDUCATIONAL FILM	1925
720	DONNA REED	portrait	MGM	
720	MASSACRE HILL (UK: EUREKA STOCKADE)	WATT	PENTAGON	1949
721	KIND HEARTS AND CORONETS (UK)	HAMER	EAGLE LION	1949
722	ANOTHER SHORE (UK)	CRICHTON	PENTAGON	1948
722	WELCOME HOME	CRUZE	PARAMOUNT	1925
723	PASSPORT TO PIMLICO (UK)	CORNELIUS	EAGLE LION	1949

724	DERBY DECADE (sh)	GOULDING	RKO	1934
724	GHOST TOWN GOLD	KANE	REPUBLIC	1936
725	BRIDAL BAIL (sh)	STEVENS	RKO	1934
725	ELEANOR POWELL	portrait	MGM	
725	LOST: A WIFE	DE MILLE	PARAMOUNT	1925
726	ALIAS MARY DOW	NEUMANN	UNIVERSAL	1935
726	LOVE ON A LADDER (sh)	WHITE	RKO	1934
727	TIGHT LITTLE ISLAND (UK: WHISKY GALORE)	MACKENDRICK	UNIVERSAL	1949
729	CITY WITHOUT MEN	SALKOW	COLUMBIA	1943
729	TRAIN OF EVENTS (UK)	CRICHTON, DEARDEN, COLE	FINE ARTS	1949
730	BITTER SPRINGS (UK)	SMART	BELL	1950
730	BROKEN FETTERS	INGRAM	UNIVERSAL	1916
730	UNDIE-WORLD (sh)	STEVENS	RKO	1934
731	RUN FOR YOUR MONEY (UK)	FREND	UNIVERSAL	1949
731	WRONG DIRECTION (sh)	GOULDING	RKO	1934
732	BLUE LAMP (UK)	DEARDEN	EAGLE LION	1950
732	HALF AN HOUR		PARAMOUNT	1928
732	IN-LAWS ARE OUT (sh)	WHITE	RKO	1934
732	PRINCE OF BAVARIA	LLOYD	REX	1914
733	DANCE HALL (UK)	CRICHTON	EALING-GFD	1950
733	ROUGH NECKING (sh)	STEVENS	RKO	1934
733	UNIVERSAL IKE JUNIOR AT THE DANCE OF LITTLE L.O.		UNIVERSAL	1914
734	CAGE OF GOLD (UK)	DEARDEN	ELLIS	1950
734	COLORADO RANGER	CARR	LIPPERT	1950
734	CONTENTED CALVES (sh)	WHITE	RKO	1934
734	CRY OF THE CITY (MARTIN ROME)	SIODONAK	20th CENTURY-FOX	1948
734	IN THE CLUTCHES OF A VILLIAN		UNIVERSAL	1914
734	MAN OF CONQUEST	NICHOLS JR.	REPUBLIC	1939
735	HEAT'S ON	RATOFF	COLUMBIA	1943
735	MAGNET (UK)	FREND	UNIVERSAL	1950
736	IVORY HUNTER (UK: WHERE NO VULTURES FLY)	WATT	UNIVERSAL	1951
736	TIME FLIES (sh)	ROBBINS	EDUCATIONAL FILM	1926
738	LAVENDER HILL MOB (UK)	CRICHTON	UNIVERSAL	1951
738	OLD MAID'S MISTAKE (sh)	BOASBERG	RKO	1934
739	POOL OF LONDON (UK)	DEARDEN	UNIVERSAL	1951
740	DAFFY DILL	WATSON	EDUCATIONAL FILM	1926
740	MAN IN THE WHITE SUIT (UK)	MACKENDRICK	UNIVERSAL	1951
741	BETTY FURNESS	portrait	MGM	
741	SECRET PEOPLE (UK)	DICKINSON	LIPPERT	1952
741	UNIVERSAL IKE JUNIOR NEARLY GETS MARRIED		UNIVERSAL	1914
741	UPPER CUTS (sh)	GRAHAM	EDUCATIONAL FILM	1926
742	HIS EXCELLENCY (UK)	HAMER	JOSEPH BRENNER	1952
742	HOLD STILL (sh)	WATSON	EDUCATIONAL FILM	1926
742	WELL CURED HAM (sh - HEADLINER #5)		RKO	1934
743	BREAKTHROUGH	SEILER	WARNER BROS	1950
743	DODGING TROUBLE (sh)	BEAUDINE	EDUCATIONAL FILM	1926
743	GENTLE GUNMAN (UK)	DEARDEN	UNIVERSAL	1952
743	STRICTLY FRESH YEGGS (sh)	STEVENS	RKO	1934
744	I BELIEVE IN YOU (UK)	DEARDEN, RELPH	UNIVERSAL	1952
745	BREAK AWAY! (sh)	BEAUDINE	EDUCATIONAL FILM	1927
745	CRACKED SHOTS (sh)	STEVENS	RKO	1934
746	CRASH OF SILENCE aka STORY OF MANDY (UK: MANDY)	MACKENDRICK	UNIVERSAL	1952
747	CASH AND CARRY (sh)	GILLSTROM	EDUCATIONAL FILM	1927
747	CRUEL SEA (UK)	FREND	UNIVERSAL	1953
748	QUEER DUCKS (sh)	BEAUDINE	EDUCATIONAL FILM	1927
748	WIFE VS. SECRETARY	BROWN	MGM	1936
749	GIDDY GOBBLERS (sh)	GILLSTROM	EDUCATIONAL FILM	1927
749	MYSTERIOUS DR. FU MANCHU (INSIDIOUS DR. FU MANCHU*)	LEE	PARAMOUNT	1929
749	TITFIELD THUNDERBOLT (UK)	CRICHTON	UNIVERSAL	1953
750	FORBIDDEN STREET	NEGULESCO	20th CENTURY-FOX	1949
750	IMPULSE (FORBIDDEN STREET - BRITTANIA MEWS*)	NEGULESCO	20th CENTURY-FOX	1949
750	WHEREEVER SHE GOES (UK/AUSTRALIA)	GORDON	ASTRAL	1951
751	CRY BABY KILLER	ADDISS	ALLIED ARTISTS	1958
751	FULLER GUSH MAN (sh)	BOASBERG	RKO	1934
751	LOVE LOTTERY (UK)	CRICHTON	CONTINENTAL	1954
751	MAMBA	ROGELL	TIFFANY	1930

751	UNIVERSAL IKE JUNIOR IN SCARECROW AND THE CHAPERONE		UNIVERSAL	1914
752	FERRY GO ROUND (sh)	WHITE	RKO	1934
754	MEET MR. LUCIFER (UK)	PELISSIER	GFD	1953
758	POISONED IVORY (sh)	GOULDING	RKO	1934
759	UNLUCKY STRIKE (sh)	HOLMES	RKO	1934
760	HIGH AND DRY (UK: MAGGIE)	MACKENDRICK	UNIVERSAL	1954
760	TRAILING ALONG (sh)	GUIOL	RKO	1934
761	EVERYTHING'S DUCKY (sh)	SANDRICH	RKO	1934
761	UNIVERSAL IKE JUNIOR IN THE DEAR HUNTER		UNIVERSAL	1914
762	CRIME DR.'S STRANGEST CASE	FORDE	COLUMBIA	1943
762	LEASE OF LIFE (UK)	FREND	IFE RELEASING	1954
762	WHAT, NO GROCERIES (sh)		RKO	1934
763	BLASTED EVENT (sh)	GOULDING	RKO	1934
764	FLYING DOWN TO ZERO (sh)	HOLMES	RKO	1935
764	NIGHT MY NUMBER CAME UP (UK)	NORMAN	CONTINENTAL	1955
765	PT RAIDERS (UK: SHIP THAT DIED OF SHAME)	DEARDEN	CONTINENTAL	1955
765	SHIP WAS LOADED (UK: CARRY ON ADMIRAL)	GUEST	GO	1957
765	THIS BAND AGE (sh)	WHITE	RKO	1935
766	OUT OF THE CLOUDS (UK 1955)	DEARDEN	RANK FILM	1957
767	IF THIS ISN'T LOVE (sh)		RKO	1934
768	TOUCH AND GO (US: THE LIGHT TOUCH)	TRUMAN	UNIVERSAL	1955
769	BRICK A BRAC (sh)	WHITE	RKO	1935
769	WHO DONE IT? (UK)	DEARDEN	RANK	1956
770	GENTLE TOUCH (UK: FEMININE TOUCH)	JACKSON	RANK	1956
770	IN A PIG'S EYE (sh)	HOLMES	RKO	1934
770	SECRET COMMAND	SUTHERLAND	COLUMBIA	1944
771	OCEAN SWELLS (sh)	STEVENS	RKO	1934
772	SOUTHERN STYLE (sh)	GOULDING	RKO	1934
772	THIRD KEY (UK: LONG ARM)	FREND	RANK	1956
773	ADDRESS UNKNOWN	MENZIES	COLUMBIA	1944
773	FIXING A STEW (sh)	BOASBERG	RKO	1934
773	MARY HOWARD	portrait	MGM	
773	SHIRALEE (UK)	NORMAN	MGM	1957
775	SONGS OF THE SOUTH (sh - HEADLINER #3)		RKO	1934
776	ALIBI BYE BYE (sh)	HOLMES	RKO	1935
778	DANCING MILLIONAIRE	WHITE	RKO	1934
779	MELVYN DOUGLAS	portrait	MGM	
780	AT EASE (sh)	TAUROG	EDUCATIONAL FILM	1927
781	NEW WRINKLES (sh)	TAUROG	EDUCATIONAL FILM	1927
782	BIG MOUTHPIECE (sh)	GUIOL	RKO	1934
782	PAPA'S BOY (sh)	TAUROG	EDUCATIONAL FILM	1927
783	ALWAYS A GENTLEMAN (sh)	TAUROG	EDUCATIONAL FILM	1928
783	BANDITS AND BALLADS (sh)	HOLLAENDER	RKO	1934
783	FLEET'S IN, THE	ST. CLAIR	PARAMOUNT	1928
784	BETWEEN JOBS (sh)	TAUROG	EDUCATIONAL FILM	1928
785	BLAZING AWAY (sh)	TAUROG	EDUCATIONAL FILM	1928
785	WILLIAM POWELL	portrait	MGM	
786	HOME MADE MAN (sh)	TAUROG	EDUCATIONAL FILM	1928
786	OLD SPANISH ONION (sh)	GOULDING	RKO	1934
786 F	SLIGHTLY SCARLET (French version)	GASNIER, KNOPF	PARAMOUNT	1930
786 S	SLIGHTLY SCARLET (Spanish version)	GASNIER, KNOPF	PARAMOUNT	1930
787	LISTEN CHILDREN (sh)	TAUROG	EDUCATIONAL FILM	1928
787	WHISTLER	CASTLE	COLUMBIA	1944
788	JAZZ MAMMAS	SENNETT	EDUCATIONAL FILM	1929
788	LIONEL BARRYMORE	portrait	MGM	
788	TEXAS	MARSHALL	COLUMBIA	1941
788S	BENSON MURDER CASE	TUTTLE	PARAMOUNT	1930
789	MATCH PLAY	SENNETT	EDUCATIONAL FILM	1930
789	SHADOWS IN THE NIGHT	FORDE	COLUMBIA	1944
790	TICKET OR LEAVE IT (sh)	GOULDING	RKO	1934
791	EVER SINCE VENUE	DREIFUSS	COLUMBIA	1944
791	JAMES STEWART	portrait	MGM	
794	HOW TO BREAK 90 AT CROQUET (sh)	JASON	RKO	1934
797	HUNGER PAINS (sh)	STEVENS	RKO	1935
798	HORSE HEIR (sh)	GUIOL	RKO	1934
799	NILS ASTHER	portrait	MGM	

799	WIG-WAG (sh)	WHITE	RKO	1934
801	SIMP-PHONEY CONCERT (sh)		RKO	1935
802	SPIRIT OF 1976 (sh)	JASON	RKO	1934
803	MARK OF THE WHISTLER	CASTLE	COLUMBIA	1944
804	PICKLED PEPPERS (sh)	HOLMES	RKO	1934
805	ANN RUTHERFORD	portrait	MGM	
805	RAISED AND CALLED (sh)	GUIOL	RKO	1935
806 S	GRUMPY (Spanish versin)	CUKOR, GARDNER	PARAMOUNT	1930
808	BRENDA STARR – REPORTER serial	FOX	COLUMBIA	1945
808	COAST OF FOLLY	DWAN	PARAMOUNT	1925
808	SOUTH SEASICKNESS (sh)	RIPLEY	RKO	1935
809	YOU'RE IN THE NAVY NOW (U.S.S. TEAKETTLE)	HATHAWAY	20th CENTURY-FOX	1951
809 S	SEA GOD (Spanish version)	ABBOTT	PARAMOUNT	1930
810	COBRA	HENABERY	PARAMOUNT	1925
810	LADDIE	STEVENS	RKO	1935
810	PLAYBOY OF PARIS (LITTLE CAFE, THE*) English version	BERGER	PARAMOUNT	1930
810 F	LITTLE CAFE, THE (French version) (see PLAYBOY OF PARIS)	BERGER	PARAMOUNT	1930
811	FRANCES GIFFORD	portrait	MGM	
811	KANGAROO (AUSTRALIA: THE AUSTRALIAN STORY)	MILESTONE	20th CENTURY-FOX	1952
811	RIDERS OF THE WHISTLING PINES	ENGLISH	COLUMBIA	1949
812	CRIME DR.'S COURAGE	SHERMAN	COLUMBIA	1945
812	FRANCES GIFFORD	portrait	MGM	
813	POWER OF THE WHISTLER	LANDERS	COLUMBIA	1945
814	FRANCES GIFFORD	portrait	MGM	
814	GOONIES	DONNER	WARNER BROS	1985
814	KISS AND TELL	WALLACE	COLUMBIA	1945
815	I'LL NEVER FORGET YOU (UK: HOUSE IN THE SQUARE)	BAKER	20th CENTURY-FOX	1951
815	MAN OF TWO WORLDS (see - I'LL NEVER FORGET YOU)	BAKER	20th CENTURY-FOX	1951
815	SOCK ME TO SLEEP (sh)	HOLMES	RKO	1935
816	FRANCES GIFFORD	portrait	MGM	
816	UNA MERKEL	portrait	MGM	
816	VANISHING AMERICAN, THE	SEITZ	PARAMOUNT	1925
818	HIT AND RUM (sh)	HOLMES	RKO	1935
818	MONSTER AND THE APE	BRETHERTON	COLUMBIA	1945
820	REGINALD OWEN	portrait	MGM	
821	RED SKELTON	portrait	MGM	
821	SHE SIGHED BY THE SEASIDE	HOLDEN, PICHEL	RKO	1935
822	DRAWING RUMORS (sh)	HOLMES	RKO	1934
822	OVER 21	VIDOR	COLUMBIA	1945
824	CAPTAIN THUNDER	CROSLAND	PARAMOUNT	1930
825	NIGHT AT THE BILTMORE BOWL (sh)	GOULDING	RKO	1935
826	EDGAR HAMLET (sh)	RIPLEY	RKO	1935
828	QUIET FOURTH (sh)	GUIOL	RKO	1935
830	ADVENTURES OF RUSTY	BURNFORD	COLUMBIA	1945
830	FINN AND HATTIE (FINN AND HATTIE ABROAD*)	MCLEOD, TAUROG	PARAMOUNT	1931
830	NIGHT LIFE (sh)	GOULDING	RKO	1935
833	NEWLY REWEDS (sh)		RKO	1935
834	SALESMANSHIP AHOY (sh)	BOASBERG	RKO	1935
834	SNAFU	MOSS	COLUMBIA	1945
835	JUNGLE RAIDERS (serial)	SELANDER	COLUMBIA	1945
835	MIS MANAGED (sh)		RKO	1935
837	METROPOLITAN NOCTURNE (sh)	JASON	RKO	1935
838	CRIME DR.'S WARNING	CASTLE	COLUMBIA	1945
839	HOME WORK (sh)	GOULDING	RKO	1935
840	DAMN YANKEE	ABBOTT	WARNER BROS	1958
840 S	HONEYMOON HATE (Spanish version)	REED	PARAMOUNT	1927
841	PERILOUS HOLIDAY	GRIFFITH	COLUMBIA	1946
843	HAPPY THO MARRIED (sh)	RIPLEY	RKO	1935
844	JEAN MADEIRA	portrait		
844	WHO'S GUILTY?	BRETHERTON, GRISSELL	COLUMBIA	1945
845	WHERE THERE'S A WILL (sh)		RKO	1935
846	RETURNED ENGAGEMENT (sh)		RKO	1935
850	JOHNNY O'CLOCK	ROSSEN	COLUMBIA	1947
850	MY MAN GODFREY	KOSTER	UNIVERSAL	1957
851	MR. DISTRICT ATTORNEY	SINCLAIR	COLUMBIA	1947
851	WESTWARD HO	BRADBURY	REPUBLIC	1935

853	NEW FRONTIER	PIERSON	REPUBLIC	1935
854	TUNED OUT (sh)	GOULDING	RKO	1935
855	COUNSELITIS (sh)	BOASBERG	RKO	1935
855	HOP HARRIGAN	ABRAHAMS	COLUMBIA	1946
856	ALLADIN FROM MANHATTAN (sh)	HOLMES	RKO	1936
856	JOHNNY TREMAIN	STEVENSON	BUENA VISTA	1957
856	TO THE ENDS OF THE EARTH	STEVENSON	COLUMBIA	1948
857	DARK AT THE TOP OF THE STAIRS	MANN	WARNER BROS	1960
857	JAMES STEWART	portrait	MGM	
858	QUIET FOURTH (WORM BURNS*) (sh)	GUIOL	RKO	1936
859	DOWN THE RIBBER (sh)	BOASBERG	RKO	1936
860	GASALOONS (sh)		RKO	1936
861	TOO MANY SURPRISES (sh)	GUIOL	RKO	1936
862	CHICK CARTER DETECTIVE	ABRAHAMS	COLUMBIA	1946
862	FOOLISH HEARTS (sh)	HOLMES	RKO	1936
863	RETURN OF MONTE CRISTO	LEVIN	COLUMBIA	1946
863	WE'RE ONLY HUMAN	FLOOD	RKO	1936
865	UPPER CUTLETS (sh)	BOASBERG	RKO	1936
866	BROKEN LULLABY (UK: MAN I KILLED)	LUBITSCH	PARAMOUNT	1932
866	FRANCES GIFFORD, WALTER PIDGEON	portrait	MGM	
866	MELODY IN MAY (sh)	HOLMES	RKO	1936
867	IT HAPPENED IN HOLLYWOOD*		RKO	1936
868	CAMERA CRANKS (sh)	TOWNLEY	RKO	1936
868	SON OF THE GUARDSMAN	ABRAHAMS	COLUMBIA	1946
869	LAST OF THE REDMEN	SHERMAN	COLUMBIA	1947
869	SLEEPY TIME (sh)	HOLMES	RKO	1936
870	CHATTERBOX	NICHOLS JR.	RKO	1936
871	TWO O'CLOCK COURAGE		RKO	1936
872	YELLOW DUST	FOX	RKO	1936
873	BETTY CO-ED	DREIFUSS	COLUMBIA	1946
873	FRANCES GIFFORD, LAURITZ MELCHIOR	portrait	MGM	
873	MUSS 'EM UP	VIDOR	RKO	1936
874	FOLLOW THE FLEET	SANDRICH	RKO	1936
875	WILL POWER (sh)	RIPLEY	RKO	1936
876	ALL BUSINESS (sh)	YARBROUGH	RKO	1936
876	CORPSE CAME C.O.D.	LEVIN	COLUMBIA	1947
877	FRAMING FATHER (sh)	GOODWINS	RKO	1936
878	JACK ARMSTRONG	FOX	COLUMBIA	1947
878	LOVE ON A BET	JASON	RKO	1936
879	GUNFIGHTERS	WAGGNER	COLUMBIA	1947
879	LADY CONSENTS	ROBERTS	RKO	1936
880	CHESTER MORRIS, FATHER WILLIAM MORRIS	portrait	MGM	
880	SILLY BILLIES (sh)	GUIOL	RKO	1936
881	HE MET A FRENCH GIRL*		PARAMOUNT	1932
881	RADIO BARRED	GOODWINS	RKO	1936
882	VIGILANTE - serial	FOX	COLUMBIA	1947
882	WEDTIME STORY (HEADLINER #4)		RKO	1936
883	ARMORED CAR	FOSTER	UNIVERSAL	1937
883	RELENTLESS	SHERMAN	COLUMBIA	1948
883	SAILOR OF THE KING (UK: SINGLE-HANDED)	BOWLING	20th CENTURY-FOX	1953
883	TWO IN REVOLT	TRYON	RKO	1936
884	FARMER IN THE DELL	HOLMES	RKO	1936
884	LITTLE MISS BROADWAY	DREIFUSS	COLUMBIA	1947
885	GREEN SLIME, THE	FUKASAKU	MGM	1969
885	HER HUSBANDS AFFAIRS	SIMON	COLUMBIA	1947
885	LISTEN TO FREEZIN' (sh)	BOASBERG	RKO	1936
885	WHAT A NIGHT! (sh)	TAUROG	EDUCATIONAL FILM	1924
886	MOTOR MAD (sh)	TAUROG	EDUCATIONAL FILM	1924
886	SEA HOUND	EASON, WRIGHT	COLUMBIA	1947
886	SWING IT (sh)	GOODWINS	RKO	1936
887	LOW TIDE (ASLEEP IN THE DEEP)	GILLSTROM	EDUCATIONAL FILM	1925
887	MURDER ON A BRIDAL PATH	HAMILTON, KILLY	RKO	1936
887	PRINCE OF THIEVES	BRETHERTON	COLUMBIA	1948
888	I LOVE TROUBLE	SIMON	COLUMBIA	1948
888	WILD GAME (sh)	TAUROG	EDUCATIONAL FILM	1924
888	WITNESS CHAIR	NICHOLS JR.	RKO	1936

889	AMERICAN DREAM (SEE YOU IN HELL, DARLING)	GIST	WARNER BROS	1966
889	MUSIC IN MY HEART	SANTLEY	COLUMBIA	1940
889	SPECIAL INVESTIGATOR	KING	RKO	1936
889	STEP LIGHTLY (sh)	TAUROG	EDUCATIONAL FILM	1925
889	STRAWBERRY ROAN	ENGLISH	COLUMBIA	1948
890	FIGHT IS RIGHT (sh)	GOODWINS	RKO	1936
890	HIS HIGH HORSE (sh)	GILLSTROM	EDUCATIONAL FILM	1925
890	JOHNNY WEISSMULLER, WIFE BERYL, SON JOHN SCOTT	portrait	MGM	
890	SWEET GENEVIEVE	DREIFUSS	COLUMBIA	1947
891	EX MRS. BRADFORD	ROBERTS	RKO	1936
891	HELLO HOLLYWOOD (sh)		EDUCATIONAL FILM	1925
891	TWO BLONDES AND A REDHEAD	DREIFUSS	COLUMBIA	1947
892	BAD MEDICINE (sh)	YARBROUGH	RKO	1936
892	LAST ROUNDUP	ENGLISH	COLUMBIA	1947
893	BIG SOMBRERO	MCDONALD	COLUMBIA	1949
893	MARY OF SCOTLAND	FORD	RKO	1936
894	FARES, PLEASE ! (sh)	ROBERTS	EDUCATIONAL FILM	1925
894	WHOLESALING ALONG (sh)	BOASBERG	RKO	1936
895	AND SO TO WED (sh)		RKO	1936
895	TEX GRANGER - serial	ABRAHAMS	COLUMBIA	1948
896	HIGH BEER PRESSURE (sh)	GOODWINS	RKO	1936
896	SIGN OF THE RAM	STURGES	COLUMBIA	1948
897	BLACK ARROW	DOUGLAS	COLUMBIA	1948
897	DUMMY ACHE (sh)	GOODWINS	RKO	1936
898	LAST OUTLAW	CABANNE	RKO	1936
899	BEWARE! (sh)		EDUCATIONAL FILM	1925
899	BRICK BRADFORD (serial)	BENNET, CARR	COLUMBIA	1947
899	BUNKER BEAN (some marked 508)	HAMILTON, KILLY	RKO	1936
899	MAN ON THE MOON	FORMAN	WARNER BROS	1999
900	GREAT ADV OF WILD BILL HICKOK (serial)	NELSON, WRIGHT	COLUMBIA	1938
900	MARY LOU	DREIFUSS	COLUMBIA	1948
900	VOCALIZING (sh)	GOODWINS	RKO	1936
901	DOG BLIGHT (sh)	YARBROUGH	RKO	1936
901	SPIDER'S WEB (serial)	HORNE, TAYLOR	COLUMBIA	1938
902	ALL THE KING'S MEN	ROSSEN	COLUMBIA	1950
902	BRIDE WALKS OUT	JASON	RKO	1936
902	CRIME OF DOCTOR HALLET	SIMON	UNIVERSAL	1938
902	FLYING G-MEN (serial)	HORNE, TAYLOR	COLUMBIA	1939
902	WAIT UNTIL DARK	YOUNG	WARNER BROS -7 ARTS	1967
903	MANDRAKE THE MAGICIAN (serial)	DEMING, NELSON	COLUMBIA	1939
903	M'LISS	NICHOLS JR.	RKO	1936
904	ONE LIVE GHOST	GOODWINS	RKO	1936
904	OVERLAND WITH KIT CARSON	DEMING, NELSON	COLUMBIA	1939
904	WILL HUTCHINS	portrait		
905	LOADED PISTOLS	ENGLISH	COLUMBIA	1948
905	SWING TIME	STEVENS	RKO	1936
906	SO AND SEW	ROBERTS	RKO	1936
907	MUMMY'S BOYS	GUIOL	RKO	1936
908	GLAMOUR GIRL	DREIFUSS	COLUMBIA	1948
908	WHO'S LOONEY NOW? (sh)	GOODWINS	RKO	1936
909	MANHATTAN ANGEL	DREIFUSS	COLUMBIA	1949
909	THAT MAN SAMSON		RKO	1936
910	GRAND JURY	ROGELL	RKO	1936
910	SUPERMAN - serial	BENNET, CARR	COLUMBIA	1948
911	ADVENTURE IN WASHINGTON	GREEN	COLUMBIA	1941
911	MARIE DRESSLER	portrait	MGM	
911	RIDERS OF THE WHISTLING PINES	ENGLISH	COLUMBIA	1949
911	WALKING ON AIR	SANTLEY	RKO	1936
912	I SURRENDER DEAR	DREIFUSS	COLUMBIA	1948
912	LALAPALOOSA		RKO	1936
912	MARIE DRESSLER	portrait	MGM	
913	FULLER BRUSH MAN	SIMON	COLUMBIA	1948
914	RACING LUCK	BERKE	COLUMBIA	1948
914	WOMAN REBELS	SANDRICH	RKO	1936
915	DON'T TURN 'EM LOOSE	STOLOFF	RKO	1936
915	LOVES OF CARMEN	VIDOR	COLUMBIA	1948

916	PLOW AND THE STARS (sh)		RKO	1936
916	SHE KNEW ALL THE ANSWERS	WALLACE	COLUMBIA	1941
917	DON'T BE LIKE THAT (sh)	YARBROUGH	RKO	1936
918	BIG GAME	NICHOLS JR., KILLY	RKO	1936
918	MUTINEERS	YARBROUGH	COLUMBIA	1949
919	LULU BELLE	FENTON	COLUMBIA	1948
919	WINTERSET	SANTELL	RKO	1936
920	UNDERCOVER MAN	LEWIS	COLUMBIA	1949
920	WE WHO ARE ABOUT TO DIE	CABANNE	RKO	1937
921	HILLBILLY GOAT (sh)	GOODWINS	RKO	1937
921	SONS OF NEW MEXICO	ENGLISH	COLUMBIA	1949
922	WITHOUT ORDERS	LANDERS	RKO	1936
923	ANNA LUCASTA	RAPPER	COLUMBIA	1949
923	MAKE WAY FOR A LADY	JASON	RKO	1936
924	CAMP MEETIN' (sh)	GOODWINS	RKO	1936
924	COMMAND DECISION	WOOD	MGM	1948
924	COWBOY AND THE INDIANS	ENGLISH	COLUMBIA	1949
924	WALLACE BEERY	portrait	MGM	
925	SMARTEST GIRL IN TOWN	SANTLEY	RKO	1936
926	CONGO BILL	BENNET, CARR	COLUMBIA	1948
926	GRANDMA'S BOUYS (sh)	GOODWINS	RKO	1936
927	UNTAMED BREED	LAMONT	COLUMBIA	1948
927	WANTED! JANE TURNER	KILLY	RKO	1936
928	LADIES OF THE CHORUS	KARLSON	COLUMBIA	1948
928	SINGING IN THE AIR (sh) HEADLINER #2		RKO	1936
929	RACING LADY	FOX	RKO	1936
930	BORN TO THE WEST	WATERS	PARAMOUNT	1926
930	PLOT THICKENS (sh)	HOLMES	RKO	1936
931	ADAM HAD FOUR SONS	RATOFF	COLUMBIA	1941
931	AFFAIR TO REMEMBER	MCCAREY	20TH CENTURY FOX	1957
931	KNOCK ON ANY DOOR	RAY	COLUMBIA	1949
931	NIGHT WAITRESS (sh)	LANDERS	RKO	1936
932	THAT GIRL FROM PARIS	JASON	RKO	1937
932	TOKYO JOE	HEISLER	COLUMBIA	1949
933	BAD HOUSEKEEPING (sh)	GOODWINS	RKO	1937
933	JOSEPH CALLEIA	portrait	MGM	
933	TRIPLE THREAT	YARBROUGH	COLUMBIA	1948
934	QUALITY STREET	STEVENS	RKO	1937
934	SONG OF INDIA	ROGELL	COLUMBIA	1949
934	TRIPLE THREAT (mistake? 933)	YARBROUGH	COLUMBIA	1948
934	YOU NEVER KNOW WOMEN	WELLMAN	PARAMOUNT	1926
935	CRIMINAL LAWYER	CABANNE, KILLY	RKO	1937
935	JUNGLE JIM	BERKE	COLUMBIA	1948
935	MANTRAP	FLEMING	PARAMOUNT	1926
935	PEGGY CUMMINS	portrait	20TH CENTURY FOX	1950S
936	DEEP SOUTH (sh)	GOODWINS	RKO	1937
937	BRUCE GENTRY	BENNET, CARR	COLUMBIA	1949
937	IDENTITY UNKNOWN		PARAMOUNT	1937
937	SEA DEVILS	STOLOFF	RKO	1937
938	THEY WANTED TO MARRY	LANDERS	RKO	1937
939	HORSEPLAY (sh)		RKO	1937
939	WE WERE STRANGERS	HUSTON	COLUMBIA	1949
940	WE'RE ON THE JURY	HOLMES	RKO	1937
941	DON'T TELL THE WIFE (sh)	CABANNE	RKO	1937
941	PALM BEACH STORY	STURGES	PARAMOUNT	1942
942	LOST TRIBE	BERKE	COLUMBIA	1949
942	SOLDIER AND THE LADY	NICHOLS JR.	RKO	1937
943	TOAST OF NEW YORK	LEE	RKO	1937
944	ADVENTURES OF BATMAN AND ROBIN	BENNET	COLUMBIA	1949
944	CHINA PASSAGE	KILLY	RKO	1937
945	DOOLINS OF OKLAHOMA	DOUGLAS	COLUMBIA	1949
945	WOMAN I LOVE	LITVAK	RKO	1937
946	BRIDAL GRIEFS (sh) (SUPERBA #2*)		RKO	1937
946	JOLSON SINGS AGAIN	LEVIN	COLUMBIA	1949
947	LOCKS AND BONDS (sh)	GOODWINS	RKO	1937
947	RIM OF THE CANYON	ENGLISH	COLUMBIA	1949

948	SHALL WE DANCE (sh)	SANDRICH	RKO	1937
949	LADIES IN RETIREMENT	VIDOR	COLUMBIA	1941
949	RHYTHM ON THE RAMPAGE (sh)		RKO	1937
950	KAREN MORLEY	portrait	MGM	
950	MAN WHO FOUND HIMSELF	LANDERS	RKO	1937
950	STATE PENITENTIARY	LANDERS	COLUMBIA	1950
951	BARBARY PIRATE	LANDERS	COLUMBIA	1949
951	OUTCASTS OF POKER FLATS	CABANNE	RKO	1937
951	WAY TO LOVE - (English Version) see 952	TAUROG	PARAMOUNT	1933
952	COW TOWN	ENGLISH	COLUMBIA	1950
952	ELEANOR POWELL	portrait	MGM	
952	TOO MANY WIVES	HOLMES	RKO	1937
952	TRUE-LIFE ADVENTURE FESTIVAL		BUENA VISTA	1964
952	WAY TO LOVE - (French Version) see 951	TAUROG	PARAMOUNT	1933
953	ADVENTURES OF SIR GALAHAD (serial)	BENNET	COLUMBIA	1949
953	DUMB'S THE WORD (sh)	GOODWINS	RKO	1937
953	LET NOT MAN PUT ASUNDER	BLACKTON	VITAGRAPH	1924
953	MEN IN HER LIFE	RATOFF	COLUMBIA	1941
954	CAPTIVE GIRL	BERKE	COLUMBIA	1950
954	INLAWFUL (sh)	YARBROUGH	RKO	1937
954	MARIE DRESSLER	portrait	MGM	
955	MARK OF THE GORILLA	BERKE	COLUMBIA	1950
955	ROBERT MONTGOMERY	portrait	MGM	
955	YOU CAN'T BUY LUCK	LANDERS	RKO	1937
956	ATOM MAN VS. SUPERMAN	BENNET	COLUMBIA	1950
956	WRONG ROMANCE (sh)	GOODWINS	RKO	1937
957	CODY OF THE PONY EXPRESS	BENNET	COLUMBIA	1950
957	MINADO, THE WOLVERINE		NATIONAL BROADCASTING	1965
957	WHITE WILDERNESS	ALGAR	BUENA VISTA	1958
957	WIFE INSURANCE (sh)	YARBROUGH	RKO	1937
958	CHINATOWN AT MIDNIGHT	FRIEDMAN	COLUMBIA	1949
958	MISSISSIPPI MOODS	GOODWINS	SACK (RKO)	1937
959	THERE GOES MY GIRL	HOLMES	RKO	1937
960	MEET THE MISSUS (sh)	SANTLEY	RKO	1937
961	BEHIND THE HEADLINES (sh)	ROSSON	RKO	1937
962	NEW FACES OF 1937	JASON	RKO	1937
962	TYRANT OF THE SEA	LANDERS	COLUMBIA	1950
963	BORDER CAFÉ	LANDERS	RKO	1937
964	ADVENTURES OF MARTIN EDEN	SALKOW	COLUMBIA	1942
964	RECKLESS MOMENT	OPHULS	COLUMBIA	1949
964	TRAMP TROUBLE (sh)	GOODWINS	RKO	1937
965	TRAVELING SALESWOMAN	REISNER	COLUMBIA	1950
965	YOU CAN'T BEAT LOVE	CABANNE	1937	
966	AND BABY MAKES THREE	LEVIN	COLUMBIA	1949
966	SWING FEVER (sh)	YARBROUGH	RKO	1937
967	BLAZING SUN	ENGLISH	COLUMBIA	1950
967	ON AGAIN OFF AGAIN (sh)	CLINE	RKO	1937
968	NEVADAN	DOUGLAS	COLUMBIA	1950
969	MORNING JUDGE (sh)	GOODWINS	RKO	1937
970	IN A LONELY PLACE	RAY	COLUMBIA	1950
970	SUNSHINE BY SUNNY MOAT* (mistake)		RKO	1935
970	SUPER SLEUTH	STOLOFF	RKO	1937
971	RIDERS IN THE SKY	ENGLISH	COLUMBIA	1949
971	TRAILING ALONG (sh)	YARBROUGH	RKO	1937
973	BIG SHOT (TAKE THE HEIR*)	KILLY	RKO	1937
973	BUSTER KEATON, JIMMY DURANTE, TED FIORITA - SPEAK EASILY	portrait	MGM	
973	CATHERINE THE GREAT*	VON STERNBURG	PARAMOUNT	1934
974	HIDEAWAY (sh)	ROSSON	RKO	1937
974	JONAH JONES (sh)	HIBBARD	EDUCATIONAL FILM	1924
975	ANNAPOLIS*		RKO	1937
975	BRAVE BULLS	ROSSON	COLUMBIA	1951
976	MULE TRAIN	ENGLISH	COLUMBIA	1950
976	RHYTHM WRANGLERS (sh)	ROBERTS	RKO	1937
977	BEYOND THE PURPLE HILLS	ENGLISH	COLUMBIA	1950
977	HALF A HERO (sh)	HIBBARD	EDUCATIONAL FILM	1925
977	LIFE OF THE PARTY	SEITER	RKO	1937

977	NO MORE WOMEN	ROGELL	PARAMOUNT	1934
978	MADONNA OF THE STREETS	CAREWE	FIRST NAT'L	1924
978	MANY UNHAPPY RETURNS (sh)	ROBERTS	RKO	1937
979	HARRIS IN THE SPRING (sh)	GOODWINS	RKO	1937
979	WAITING (sh)	ROBERTS	EDUCATIONAL FILM	1925
980	HELL BENT KID	HATHAWAY	20th CENTURY-FOX	1958
980	STAGE DOOR	LACAVA	RKO	1937
981	INDIAN TERRITORY	ENGLISH	COLUMBIA	1950
981	MUSIC FOR MADAME	BLYSTONE	RKO	1937
982	FIGHT FOR GLORY*		RKO	1937
982	SOMETHING TO SHOUT ABOUT	RATOFF	COLUMBIA	1943
983	SHOULD WIVES WORK? (sh)	GOODWINS	RKO	1937
984	BREAKFAST FOR TWO	SANTELL	RKO	1937
984	JAMES STEWART	portrait	MGM	
985	HIGH FLYERS	CLINE	RKO	1937
986	LAST OF THE BUCCANEERS	LANDERS	COLUMBIA	1950
986	RENTED RIOT (sh)	YARBROUGH	RKO	1937
987	SATURDAY'S HEROES (sh)	KILLY	RKO	1937
988	DON'T FORGET TO REMEMBER (sh)		RKO	1937
988	GENE AUTRY AND THE MOUNTIES	ENGLISH	COLUMBIA	1951
989	FORTY NAUGHTY GIRLS	CLINE	RKO	1937
989	REVENUE AGENT	LANDERS	COLUMBIA	1950
990	FIGHT FOR YOUR LADY	STOLOFF	RKO	1937
990	PIRATES OF THE HIGH SEAS	BENNET, CARR	COLUMBIA	1950
991	DAMSEL IN DISTRESS	STEVENS	RKO	1937
991	SIROCCO	BERNHARDT	COLUMBIA	1951
992	HURRICANE ISLAND	LANDERS	COLUMBIA	1951
992	LIVING ON LOVE	LANDERS	RKO	1937
993	CHAIN GANG	LANDERS	COLUMBIA	1950
993	EDGAR AND GOLIATH (sh)	GOODWINS	RKO	1937
994	EARS OF EXPERIENCE (sh)	GOODWINS	RKO	1938
994	PYGMY ISLAND	BERKE	COLUMBIA	1950
995	DUMMY OWNER (sh)	YARBROUGH	RKO	1937
995	FURY OF THE CONGO	BERKE	COLUMBIA	1951
996	COMMANDOES STRIKE AT DAWN	FARROW	COLUMBIA	1942
996	MUSIC WILL TELL (sh) (HEADLINER #2)		RKO	1938
997	HITTING A NEW HIGH	WALSH	RKO	1938
998	SATURDAY'S HERO	MILLER	COLUMBIA	1951
998	WISE GIRL	JASON	RKO	1938
999	APPOINTMENT WITH CRIME (UK)	HARLOW	FOUR CONTINENTS	1946
999	BRINGING UP BABY	HAWKS	RKO	1938
999	FAMILY SECRET	LEVIN	COLUMBIA	1951
1000	ANGELA LANSBURY	portrait	MGM	
1001	ANGELA LANSBURY	portrait	MGM	
1001	CITY OF WAX (sh)		EDUCATIONAL FILM	1934
1001	FOOTLIGHT GLAMOUR	STRAYER	COLUMBIA	1943
1002	ANGELA LANSBURY	portrait	MGM	
1002	BECAUSE YOU'RE MINE	HALL	MGM	1952
1002	BORN TO DIE (sh)		EDUCATIONAL FILM	1934
1002	IS EVERYBODY HAPPY?	BARTON	COLUMBIA	1943
1002	MUTINY ON THE BLACKHAWK	CABANNE	UNIVERSAL	1939
1003	ANGELA LANSBURY	portrait	MGM	
1003	JANET LEIGH	portrait	MGM	
1003	MUTINY ON THE BLACKHAWK (mistake - 1002)	CABANNE	UNIVERSAL	1939
1003	SPOTTED WINGS (sh)		EDUCATIONAL FILM	1934
1003	UNDER-PUP	WALLACE	UNIVERSAL	1939
1004	ANGELA LANSBURY	portrait	MGM	
1004	NATURE'S GANGSTER (sh)		EDUCATIONAL FILM	1934
1004	WHAT A WOMAN	CUMMINGS	COLUMBIA	1943
1005	ANGELA LANSBURY	portrait	MGM	
1005	CHAD EVERETT	portrait	MGM	
1005	HIS BIG MINUTE (sh)	WATSON	EDUCATIONAL FILM	1929
1005	NINE GIRLS	JASON	COLUMBIA	1944
1006	ANGELA LANSBURY	portrait	MGM	
1006	NONE SHALL ESCAPE	DE TOTH	COLUMBIA	1944
1007	ANGELA LANSBURY	portrait	MGM	

1007	ESTHER WILLIAMS	portrait	MGM	
1008	ANGELA LANSBURY	portrait	MGM	
1008	JANET LEIGH	portrait	MGM	
1008	PEACEFUL ALLEY (sh)	GOULDING	EDUCATIONAL FILM	1929
1009	ANGELA LANSBURY	portrait	MGM	
1009	RACKET MAN	LEDERMAN	COLUMBIA	1944
1009S	DOUBLE WEDDING	THORPE	MGM	1937
1010	CLARK GABLE/SYLVIA ASHLEY	portrait	MGM	
1010	CYD CHARISSE	portrait	MGM	
1010	RETURN OF THE VAMPIRE	LANDERS	COLUMBIA	1944
1011	CLARK GABLE/SYLVIA ASHLEY	portrait	MGM	
1011	CYD CHARISSE	portrait	MGM	
1011	SONG TO REMEMBER	VIDOR	COLUMBIA	1945
1011E	YVONNE CRAIG	portrait	MGM	
1012	CHANCE OF A LIFETIME	CASTLE	COLUMBIA	1943
1012	CLARK GABLE/SYLVIA ASHLEY	portrait	MGM	
1012	CYD CHARISSE	portrait	MGM	
1012	MOTHER	BROOKS	PARAMOUNT	1996
1013	CLARK GABLE/SYLVIA ASHLEY	portrait	MGM	
1013	CYD CHARISSE	portrait	MGM	
1014	CLARK GABLE/SYLVIA ASHLEY	portrait	MGM	
1014	CYD CHARISSE	portrait	MGM	
1014	FIRE AWAY	ROBERTS	EDUCATIONAL FILM	1925
1014	MR. WINKLE GOES TO WAR	GREEN	COLUMBIA	1944
1014E	YVONNE CRAIG	portrait	MGM	
1015	CLARK GABLE/SYLVIA ASHLEY	portrait	MGM	
1015	CYD CHARISSE	portrait	MGM	
1015	HOTEL IMPERIAL	STILLER	PARAMOUNT	1927
1015	KLONDIKE KATE	CASTLE	COLUMBIA	1943
1015	ON EDGE (sh)	TAUROG	EDUCATIONAL FILM	1926
1016	CLARK GABLE/SYLVIA ASHLEY	portrait	MGM	
1016	SWING OUT OF THE BLUES	ST. CLAIR	COLUMBIA	1943
1017	BEAUTIFUL BUT BROKE	BARTON	COLUMBIA	1944
1017	CLARK GABLE/SYLVIA ASHLEY	portrait	MGM	
1017	CYD CHARISSE	portrait	MGM	
1017	LIVE COWARDS (sh)	ROBERTS	EDUCATIONAL FILM	1926
1017E	YVONNE CRAIG	portrait	MGM	
1018	CLARK GABLE/SYLVIA ASHLEY	portrait	MGM	
1018	CYD CHARISSE	portrait	MGM	
1019	CLARK GABLE/SYLVIA ASHLEY	portrait	MGM	
1019	GHOST THAT WALKS ALONE	LANDERS	COLUMBIA	1944
1020	CLARK GABLE/SYLVIA ASHLEY	portrait	MGM	
1021	CLARK GABLE/SYLVIA ASHLEY	portrait	MGM	
1021	GIRL IN THE CASE	BERKE	COLUMBIA	1944
1022	CLARK GABLE/SYLVIA ASHLEY	portrait	MGM	
1022	TONIGHT AND EVERY NIGHT	SAVILLE	COLUMBIA	1945
1023	CLARK GABLE/SYLVIA ASHLEY	portrait	MGM	
1023	SAILOR'S HOLIDAY	BERKE	COLUMBIA	1944
1023E	YVONNE CRAIG	portrait	MGM	
1024	CLARK GABLE/SYLVIA ASHLEY	portrait	MGM	
1024	CREEPS (sh)	TAUROG	EDUCATIONAL FILM	1926
1024	TOGETHER AGAIN	VIDOR	COLUMBIA	1944
1025	CLARK GABLE/SYLVIA ASHLEY	portrait	MGM	
1025	TWO MAN SUBMARINE	LANDERS	COLUMBIA	1944
1026	CAROLINA BLUES	JASON	COLUMBIA	1944
1026	CLARK GABLE/SYLVIA ASHLEY	portrait	MGM	
1026	ESTHER WILLIAMS, CHILDREN KIMBALL, BENJAMIN, SUSAN	portrait	MGM	
1026	WHO HIT ME? (sh)	ROBERTS	EDUCATIONAL FILM	1926
1027	CLARK GABLE/SYLVIA ASHLEY	portrait	MGM	
1027	ESTHER WILLIAMS, CHILDREN KIMBALL, BENJAMIN, SUSAN	portrait	MGM	
1027	SOLID GOLD (sh)	ROBERTS	EDUCATIONAL FILM	1926
1027	STARS ON PARADE	LANDERS	COLUMBIA	1944
1027E	MARY ANN MOBLEY	portrait	MGM	
1028	BLACK PARACHUTE	LANDERS	COLUMBIA	1944
1028	CLARK GABLE/SYLVIA ASHLEY	portrait	MGM	
1028	KISS PAPA (sh)	ROBERTS	EDUCATIONAL FILM	1926

1029	CLARK GABLE/SYLVIA ASHLEY	portrait	MGM	
1029	MY KID (sh)	LAMONT	EDUCATIONAL FILM	1926
1029	SHE'S A SOLDIER TOO	CASTLE	COLUMBIA	1944
1030	JOLSON STORY (some marked 1130)	GREEN	COLUMBIA	1946
1030	OPEN SPACES (sh)	LAMONT	EDUCATIONAL FILM	1926
1030	VAN JOHNSON	portrait	MGM	
1031	COUNTER-ATTACK	KORDA	COLUMBIA	1945
1031	FUNNY FACE (sh)	LAMONT	EDUCATIONAL FILM	1927
1032	GRANDPA'S BOY (sh)	LAMONT	EDUCATIONAL FILM	1927
1032	THEY LIVE IN FEAR	BERNE	COLUMBIA	1944
1033	ATTA BOY (sh)		EDUCATIONAL FILM	1927
1033	U-BOAT PRISONER	LANDERS	COLUMBIA	1944
1034	CYD CHARISSE	portrait	MGM	
1034	KID TRICKS (sh)	LAMONT	EDUCATIONAL FILM	1927
1035	LOUISIANA HAYRIDE	BARTON	COLUMBIA	1944
1036	HOW AM I DOING?		PARAMOUNT	1933
1036	IMPATIENT YEARS	CUMMINGS	COLUMBIA	1944
1036	YOU CAN'T CHEAT AN HONEST MAN	MARSHALL	UNIVERSAL	1939
1037	CRY OF THE WEREWOLF	LEVIN	COLUMBIA	1944
1038	UNWRITTEN CODE	ROTSTEN	COLUMBIA	1944
1039	EVE KNEW HER APPLES	JASON	COLUMBIA	1945
1040	KANSAS CITY KITTY	LORD	COLUMBIA	1944
1041	BRINGING OUT THE DEAD	SCORSESE	PARAMOUNT	1999
1041E	ANJANETTE COMER	portrait	MGM	
1042	MEET MISS BOBBY SOCKS	TRYON	COLUMBIA	1944
1043	STRANGE AFFAIR	GREEN	COLUMBIA	1944
1043	UNA MERKEL	portrait	MGM	
1043	VAN JOHNSON	portrait	MGM	
1043E	ANJANETTE COMER	portrait	MGM	
1044	SOUL OF A MONSTER	JASON	COLUMBIA	1944
1045	ONE MYSTERIOUS NIGHT	BOETTICHER	COLUMBIA	1944
1046	SERGEANT MIKE	LEVIN	COLUMBIA	1944
1047	ELAINE STEWART	portrait	MGM	
1047	MISSING JUROR	BOETTICHER	COLUMBIA	1944
1048	ESCAPE IN THE FOG	BOETTICHER	COLUMBIA	1945
1049	SHE'S A SWEETHEART	LORD	COLUMBIA	1944
1049	VIC DAMONE	portrait	MGM	
1050	TARS AND SPARS	GREEN	COLUMBIA	1946
1051	EADIE WAS A LADY	DREIFUSS	COLUMBIA	1945
1051	SNOW WHITE AND THE SEVEN DWARFS (t)	HAND	DISNEY	1937
1052	DANCING IN MANHATTAN	LELVIN	COLUMBIA	1944
1053	WEDDING BILL$	KENTON	PARAMOUNT	1927
1054	BLIND ALLEYS	TUTTLE	PARAMOUNT	1927
1054	THOUSAND AND ONE NIGHTS	GREEN	COLUMBIA	1945
1054	UNDERWORLD	VON STERNBERG	PARAMOUNT	1927
1055	CLARK GABLE	portrait	MGM	
1055	TAHITI NIGHTS	JASON	COLUMBIA	1944
1056	CYD CHARISSE	portrait	MGM	
1056	LEAVE IT TO BLONDIE	BERLIN	COLUMBIA	1945
1056E	ANJANETTE COMER	portrait	MGM	
1057	JAMES STEWART	portrait	MGM	
1057	LET'S GO STEADY	LORD	COLUMBIA	1945
1058	CYD CHARISSE	portrait	MGM	
1058	I LOVE A MYSTERY	LEVIN	COLUMBIA	1945
1059	JAMES STEWART	portrait	MGM	
1059	YOUTH ON TRIAL	BOETTICHER	COLUMBIA	1945
1060	JAMES STEWART	portrait	MGM	
1060	SHE WOULDN'T SAY YES	HALL	COLUMBIA	1945
1061	JAMES STEWART	portrait	MGM	
1061	MEET ME ON BROADWAY	JASON	COLUMBIA	1946
1062	CLARK GABLE	portrait	MGM	
1062	CYD CHARISSE	portrait	MGM	
1062	GENE TIERNEY	portrait	MGM	
1062	GUY, A GAL AND A PAL	BOETTICHER	COLUMBIA	1945
1062	JAMES STEWART	portrait	MGM	
1063	JAMES STEWART	portrait	MGM	

1063	KLONDIKE ANNIE (KLONDIKE LOU*)	WALSH	PARAMOUNT	1936
1063	ROUGH TOUGH AND READY	LORD	COLUMBIA	1945
1064	FIGHTING GUARDSMAN	LEVIN	COLUMBIA	1946
1065	ANN BLYTH	portrait	MGM	
1066	JAMES STEWART	portrait	MGM	
1066	TEN CENTS A DANCE	JASON	COLUMBIA	1945
1067	JAMES STEWART	portrait	MGM	
1068	JAMES STEWART	portrait	MGM	
1068	WINNIE THE POOH AND THE BLUSTERY DAY (t) (sh)	REITHERMAN	BUENA VISTA	1969
1069	BOSTON BLACKIE HOOKED ON SUSPICION	DREIFUSS	COLUMBIA	1945
1070	BLONDE FROM BROOKLYN	LORD	COLUMBIA	1945
1071	GAY SENORITA	DREIFUSS	COLUMBIA	1945
1071	JAMES STEWART	portrait	MGM	
1072	BOSTON BLACKIE'S RENDEZVOUS	DREIFUSS	COLUMBIA	1945
1072	JAMES STEWART	portrait	MGM	
1072	VAN JOHNSON	portrait	MGM	
1073	ANGELA LANSBURY	portrait	MGM	
1073	NAKED GUN	ZUCKER	PARAMOUNT	1988
1074	ANGELA LANSBURY	portrait	MGM	
1074	BANDIT OF SHERWOOD FOREST	LEVIN, SHERMAN	COLUMBIA	1946
1074	MAUREEN O'SULLIVAN	portrait	MGM	
1075	ANGELA LANSBURY	portrait	MGM	
1075	I LOVE A BANDLEADER	LORD	COLUMBIA	1945
1076	ANGELA LANSBURY	portrait	MGM	
1076	VOICE OF THE WHISTLER	CASTLE	COLUMBIA	1945
1077	ANGELA LANSBURY	portrait	MGM	
1078	ANGELA LANSBURY	portrait	MGM	
1078	GIRL OF THE LIMBERLOST	FERRER	COLUMBIA	1945
1079	ANGELA LANSBURY	portrait	MGM	
1079	RENEGADES	SHERMAN	COLUMBIA	1946
1080	ANGELA LANSBURY	portrait	MGM	
1080	HULA	FLEMING	PARAMOUNT	1927
1080	ONE WAY TO LOVE	ENRIGHT	COLUMBIA	1946
1081	ANGELA LANSBURY	portrait	MGM	
1081	HIT THE HAY	LORD	COLUMBIA	1945
1081	SPEEDY	WILDE	PARAMOUNT	1928
1081E	DEBORAH KERR	portrait	MGM	
1082	ANGELA LANSBURY	portrait	MGM	
1082	MY NAME IS JULIA ROSS	LEWIS	COLUMBIA	1945
1082E	GENE TIERNEY	portrait	MGM	
1083	ANGELA LANSBURY	portrait	MGM	
1083	OUT OF THE DEPTHS	LEDERMAN	COLUMBIA	1945
1084	ANGELA LANSBURY	portrait	MGM	
1084	LIFE WITH BLONDIE	BERLIN	COLUMBIA	1945
1084	VAN JOHNSON + WIFE EVIE	portrait	MGM	
1085	ANGELA LANSBURY	portrait	MGM	
1086	ANGELA LANSBURY	portrait	MGM	
1086	BIG TOP PEE WEE	KLEISER	PARAMOUNT	1988
1086	PRISON SHIP	DREIFUSS	COLUMBIA	1945
1086	VAN JOHNSON	portrait	MGM	
1087	ANGELA LANSBURY	portrait	MGM	
1087	GILDA	VIDOR	COLUMBIA	1946
1088	ANGELA LANSBURY	portrait	MGM	
1088	BLONDIE'S LUCKY DAY	BERLIN	COLUMBIA	1946
1088	SECRET HOUR	LEE	PARAMOUNT	1928
1089	CLOSE CALL FOR BOSTON BLACKIE	LANDERS	COLUMBIA	1946
1089E	ANNE FRANCIS	portrait	MGM	
1090	CARIBBEAN HOLIDAY*	SUTHERLAND	UNIVERSAL	1940
1090	SO DARK THE NIGHT	LEWIS	COLUMBIA	1946
1091	NOTORIOUS LONE WOLF	LEDERMAN	COLUMBIA	1946
1092	GENTLEMEN MISBEHAVES	SHERMAN	COLUMBIA	1946
1092	NEW LIFE, A	ALDA	PARAMOUNT	1988
1093	ESTHER WILLIAMS	portrait	MGM	
1093	JUST BEFORE DAWN	CASTLE	COLUMBIA	1946
1094	ESTHER WILLIAMS	portrait	MGM	
1094	WALLS CAME TUMBLING DOWN	MENDES	COLUMBIA	1946

1095	DEVIL'S MASK	LEVIN	COLUMBIA	1946
1096	DANGEROUS BUSINESS	LEDERMAN	COLUMBIA	1946
1097	TALK ABOUT A LADY	SHERMAN	COLUMBIA	1946
1098	MYSTERIOUS INTRUDER	CASTLE	COLUMBIA	1946
1099	NIGHT EDITOR	LEVIN	COLUMBIA	1946
1100	DOWN TO EARTH	HALL	COLUMBIA	1947
1101	PHANTOM THIEF	LEDERMAN	COLUMBIA	1946
1102	MAN WHO DARED	STURGES	COLUMBIA	1946
1103	GALLANT JOURNEY	WELLMAN	COLUMBIA	1946
1104	THRILL OF BRAZIL	SIMON	COLUMBIA	1946
1105	HOWARD KEEL	portrait	MGM	
1105	RETURN OF RUSTY	CASTLE	COLUMBIA	1946
1106	PLAIN CLOTHES	COOLIDGE	PARAMOUNT	1987
1106	SIGNE HASSO	portrait	MGM	
1106	UNKNOWN	LEVIN	COLUMBIA	1946
1106E	JANE POWELL	portrait	MGM	
1107	BLONDIE KNOWS BEST	BERLIN	COLUMBIA	1946
1108	SING WHILE YOU DANCE	LEDERMAN	COLUMBIA	1946
1109	CYD CHARISSE	portrait	MGM	
1109	PERSONALITY KID	SHERMAN	COLUMBIA	1946
1110	CRIME DR.'S MANHUNT	CASTLE	COLUMBIA	1946
1111	CYD CHARISSE	portrait	MGM	
1111	DEAD RECKONING	CROMWELL	COLUMBIA	1947
1112	CYD CHARISSE	portrait	MGM	
1112	IT'S GREAT TO BE YOUNG	LORD	COLUMBIA	1946
1113	CALL ON THE PRESIDENT, A	SINCLAIR	MGM	1939
1113	CYD CHARISSE	portrait	MGM	
1113	FRAMED	WALLACE	COLUMBIA	1947
1114	CYD CHARISSE	portrait	MGM	
1114	EASY TO TAKE (RIGHT IN YOUR LAP*)	TRYON	PARAMOUNT	1936
1114	SECRET OF THE WHISTLER	SHERMAN	COLUMBIA	1946
1115	GUILT OF JANET AMES	LEVIN	COLUMBIA	1947
1115E	CYD CHARISSE	portrait	MGM	
1116	SHADOWED	STURGES	COLUMBIA	1946
1116E	CYD CHARISSE	portrait	MGM	
1117	LANA TURNER	portrait	MGM	
1117	SHOWDOWN	SCHERTZINGER	PARAMOUNT	1928
1117	SWORDSMAN	LEWIS	COLUMBIA	1948
1118	LANA TURNER	portrait	MGM	
1118	SINGING IN THE CORN	LORD	COLUMBIA	1946
1119	BLONDIE'S BIG MOMENT	BERLIN	COLUMBIA	1947
1120	BOSTON BLACKIE AND THE LAW	LEDERMAN	COLUMBIA	1946
1121	LANA TURNER	portrait	MGM	
1121	RETURN OF OCTOBER	LEWIS	COLUMBIA	1948
1122	LANA TURNER	portrait	MGM	
1122	LONE WOLF IN MEXICO	LEDERMAN	COLUMBIA	1947
1123	ALIAS MR. TWILIGHT	STURGES	COLUMBIA	1946
1124	BLIND SPOT	GORDON	COLUMBIA	1947
1125	MILLIE'S DAUGHTER	SALKOW	COLUMBIA	1947
1126	BARBARA LANG	portrait	MGM	
1126	LADY FROM SHANGHAI		COLUMBIA	1947
1126	LANA TURNER	portrait	MGM	
1127	CIGARETTE GIRL	VON FRITSCH	COLUMBIA	1947
1127	LANA TURNER	portrait	MGM	
1128	THIRTEENTH HOUR	CLEMENS	COLUMBIA	1947
1129	GOOD SPIRITS (sh)	MAYO	EDUCATIONAL FILM	1925
1129	KING OF THE WILD HORSES	ARCHAINBAUD	COLUMBIA	1947
1129	LANA TURNER	portrait	MGM	
1130	BLONDIE'S HOLIDAY	BERLIN	COLUMBIA	1947
1130	JOLSON STORY (some marked 1030)	GREEN	COLUMBIA	1946
1131	MILLERSON CASE	ARCHAINBAUD	COLUMBIA	1947
1132	BULLDOG DRUMMOND AT BAY	SALKOW	COLUMBIA	1947
1132S	DR. KILDARE'S STRANGE CASE	BUCQUET	MGM	1940
1133	FOR THE LOVE OF RUSTY	STURGES	COLUMBIA	1947
1134	BRIGHT LIGHTS (sh)	GRAHAM	EDUCATIONAL FILM	1924
1134	FRED ASTAIRE	portrait	MGM	

1135	BOOMTOWN			
1135	MAN FROM COLORADO	LEVIN	COLUMBIA	1948
1136	BLONDIE IN THE DOUGH	BERLIN	COLUMBIA	1947
1136	FRENCH PASTRY (sh)	BEAUDINE	EDUCATIONAL FILM	1925
1136	GREER GARSON	portrait	MGM	
1137	GREAT GUNS (sh)	BEAUDINE	EDUCATIONAL FILM	1925
1137	SPORT OF KINGS	GORDON	COLUMBIA	1947
1138	ANJANETTE COMER	portrait	MGM	
1138	IT HAD TO BE YOU	HARTMAN, MATE	COLUMBIA	1947
1139	AIR TIGHT (sh)	BEAUDINE	EDUCATIONAL FILM	1925
1139	KEEPER OF THE BEES	STURGES	COLUMBIA	1947
1140	SON OF RUSTY	LANDERS	COLUMBIA	1947
1141	KEY WITNESS	LEDERMAN	COLUMBIA	1947
1141	NAKED GUN	ZUCKER	PARAMOUNT	1988
1142	BULLDOG DRUMMOND STRIKES AGAIN	MCDONALD	COLUMBIA	1947
1142	FRED ASTAIRE	portrait	MGM	
1143	MATING OF MILLIE	LEVIN	COLUMBIA	1948
1144	WHEN A GIRL'S BEAUTIFUL	MCDONALD	COLUMBIA	1947
1145	BEGGAR'S OF LIFE	WELLMAN	PARAMOUNT	1928
1145	SLIGHTLY FRENCH	SIRK	COLUMBIA	1949
1146	LONE WOLF IN LONDON	GOODWINS	COLUMBIA	1947
1148	CRIME DR.'S GAMBLE	CASTLE	COLUMBIA	1947
1148	DOCKS OF NEW YORK	FOX	PARAMOUNT	1945
1149	DEVIL SHIP	LANDERS	COLUMBIA	1947
1151	LAMBERT, THE SHEEPISH LION (t) (sh)	HANNAH	RKO	1952
1152	ADVENTURES IN SILVERADO	KARLSON	COLUMBIA	1948
1153	WRECK OF THE HESPERUS	HOFFMAN	COLUMBIA	1948
1154	PORT SAID	LE BORG	COLUMBIA	1948
1154	PRESIDIO, THE	HYAMS	PARAMOUNT	1988
1154S	DR. KILDARE GOES HOME	BUCQUET	MGM	1940
1155	BLONDIE'S REWARD	BERLIN	COLUMBIA	1948
1155	INTERFERENCE	MENDES, POMEROY	PARAMOUNT	1928
1156	BLONDIE'S ANNIVERSARY	BERLIN	COLUMBIA	1947
1156	OUR FRIEND THE ATOM	LUSKE	DISNEY-TV	1957
1156	WILD PARTY, THE	ARZNER	PARAMOUNT	1929
1157	WOMAN FROM TANGIER	DANIELS	COLUMBIA	1948
1159	RETURN OF THE WHISTLER	LEDERMAN	COLUMBIA	1948
1159	RIVER OF ROMANCE	WALLACE	PARAMOUNT	1929
1159	VINCENTE MINNELLI	portrait	MGM	
1160	GALLANT BLADE	LEVIN	COLUMBIA	1948
1160	SAVAGE LOVE (sh)	SIDNEY	EDUCATIONAL FILM	1924
1160S	DR. KILDARE'S CRISIS	BUCQUET	MGM	1941
1161	COURT PLASTER (sh)	PRATT	EDUCATIONAL FILM	1924
1161	MY DOG RUSTY	LANDERS	COLUMBIA	1948
1161	SCANDAL STREET (THEY KNEW WHAT HAPPENED*)	HOGAN	PARAMOUNT	1938
1162	BEST MAN WINS	STURGES	COLUMBIA	1948
1162	LESLIE CARON	portrait	MGM	
1162	SHOPWORN ANGEL	WALLACE	PARAMOUNT	1928
1162	WHY HURRY? (sh)	BEAUDINE	EDUCATIONAL FILM	1924
1163	JEAN HAGEN	portrait	MGM	
1163	TRAPPED BY BOSTON BLACKIE	FRIEDMAN	COLUMBIA	1948
1164	LESLIE CARON	portrait	MGM	
1164	STEP FAST (sh)	BEAUDINE	EDUCATIONAL FILM	1925
1164	THUNDERHOOF	KARLSON	COLUMBIA	1948
1165	LEATHER GLOVES	ASHER, QUINIE	COLUMBIA	1948
1165	SEA LEGS (sh)	PRATT	EDUCATIONAL FILM	1925
1166	JEAN HAGEN	portrait	MGM	
1166	LESLIE CARON	portrait	MGM	
1166	LOVE GOOFY (sh)	PRATT	EDUCATIONAL FILM	1925
1166	RUSTY LEADS THE WAY	JASON	COLUMBIA	1948
1167	WALKING HILLS	STURGES	COLUMBIA	1949
1168	DARK PAST	MATE	COLUMBIA	1948
1169	BLACK EAGLE	GORDON	COLUMBIA	1948
1169	LESLIE CARON	portrait	MGM	
1170	GENTLEMEN FROM NOWHERE	CASTLE	COLUMBIA	1948
1171	RUSTY SAVES A LIFE	FRIEDMAN	COLUMBIA	1949

1172	BLONDIE'S SECRET	BERNDS	COLUMBIA	1948
1172	DEBORAH KERR	portrait	MGM	
1173	BOSTON BLACKIE'S CHINESE VENTURE	FRIEDMAN	COLUMBIA	1949
1174	SHOCKPROOF	SIRK	COLUMBIA	1949
1175	MR. SOFT TOUCH	DOUGLAS, LEVIN	COLUMBIA	1949
1175	VIRGINIA O'BRIEN, HUSBAND KIRK ALYN, DAUGHTER TERESA	portrait	MGM	
1175E	LESLIE CARON	portrait	MGM	
1176	HOLIDAY IN HAVANA	YARBROUGH	COLUMBIA	1949
1177	LAW OF THE BARBARY COAST	LANDERS	COLUMBIA	1949
1177a	BOOLOO	ELLIOTT	PARAMOUNT	1938
1178	LONE WOLF AND HIS LADY	HOFFMAN	COLUMBIA	1949
1178S	DR. JEKYLL AND MR. HYDE	FLEMING	MGM	1941
1179	CRIME DR.'S DIARY	FRIEDMAN	COLUMBIA	1949
1180	ANN SOTHERN	portrait	MGM	
1180	BLONDIE'S BIG DEAL	BERNDS	COLUMBIA	1949
1181	AIR HOSTESS	LANDERS	COLUMBIA	1949
1182	ANN SOTHERN	portrait	MGM	
1182	MAKE BELIEVE BALLROOM	SANTLEY	COLUMBIA	1949
1183	ANN SOTHERN	portrait	MGM	
1183	LUST FOR GOLD	SIMON	COLUMBIA	1949
1185	BLONDIE HITS THE JACKPOT	BERNDS	COLUMBIA	1949
1186	DEVIL'S HENCHMEN	FRIEDMAN	COLUMBIA	1949
1187	JOHNNY ALLEGRO	TETZLAFF	COLUMBIA	1949
1187	PETER LAWFORD	portrait	MGM	
1187E	LESLIE CARON	portrait	MGM	
1188	RIDE A CROOKED MILE (LAST MILE, THE*)	GREEN	PARAMOUNT	1938
1188	SECRET OF ST. IVES	ROSEN	COLUMBIA	1949
1189	DANGEROUS WOMAN	GROVE, LEE	PARAMOUNT	1929
1189	KAZAN	JASON	COLUMBIA	1949
1190	RUSTY'S BIRTHDAY	FRIEDMAN	COLUMBIA	1949
1191	MISS GRANT TAKES RICHMOND	BACON	COLUMBIA	1949
1192	DUMMY LOVE (sh)	BEAUDINE	EDUCATIONAL FILM	1926
1192	TELL IT TO THE JUDGE	FOSTER	COLUMBIA	1949
1193	PALOMINO	NAZARRO	COLUMBIA	1950
1194	HOOT MON! (sh)	BEAUDINE	EDUCATIONAL FILM	1926
1194	PRISON WARDEN	FRIEDMAN	COLUMBIA	1949
1194	THANKS FOR THE MEMORY	ARCHAINBAUD	PARAMOUNT	1938
1195	BLONDIE'S HERO	BERNDS	COLUMBIA	1950
1196	GOOD HUMOR MAN	BACON	COLUMBIA	1950
1197	ADVENTURE	FLEMING	MGM	1945
1197	BORN YESTERDAY	CUKOR	COLUMBIA	1950
1197	JAIL BIRDIES (sh)		EDUCATIONAL FILM	1927
1198	CARGO TO CAPETOWN	MCEVOY	COLUMBIA	1950
1198S	DOWN IN SAN DIEGO	SINCLAIR	MGM	1941
1199	MARY RYAN, DETECTIVE	BERLIN	COLUMBIA	1949
1200	GIRL'S SCHOOL	BRAHM	COLUMBIA	1938
1200S	DR. KILDARE'S WEDDING DAY	BUCQUET	MGM	1941
1201	ROGUES OF SHERWOOD FOREST	DOUGLAS	COLUMBIA	1950
1202	WOMAN OF DISTINCTION	BUZZELL	COLUMBIA	1950
1203	MICKEY ROONEY	portrait	MGM	
1204	FATHER IS A BACHELOR	BERLIN, FOSTER	COLUMBIA	1950
1204	MICKEY ROONEY	portrait	MGM	
1205	BODYHOLD	FRIEDMAN	COLUMBIA	1949
1206	FORTUNES OF CAPTAIN BLOOD	DOUGLAS	COLUMBIA	1950
1207	PETTY GIRL, THE	LEVIN	COLUMBIA	1950
1208	BEWARE OF BLONDIE	BERNDS	COLUMBIA	1950
1208	UNMARRIED (NIGHT SPOT HOSTESS*)	NEUMANN	PARAMOUNT	1939
1209	KILL THE UMPIRE	BACON	COLUMBIA	1950
1210	MILITARY ACADEMY WITH THAT 10TH AVENUE GANG	LEDERMAN	COLUMBIA	1950
1211	FULLER BRUSH GIRL	BACON	COLUMBIA	1950
1211	RICHARD CONTE	portrait	MGM	
1212	FRIGHTENED CITY (KILLER THAT STALKED NEW YORK)	MCEVOY	COLUMBIA	1950
1213	BEAUTY ON PARADE	LANDERS	COLUMBIA	1950
1214	NO SAD SONGS FOR ME	MATE	COLUMBIA	1950
1215	CUSTOMS AGENT	FRIEDMAN	COLUMBIA	1950
1216S	DR. KILDARE'S VICTORY	VAN DYKE	MGM	1942

1217	MIGHTY	CROMWELL	PARAMOUNT	1929
1218	WHEN YOU'RE SMILING	SANTLEY	COLUMBIA	1950
1219	CONVICTED	LEVIN	COLUMBIA	1950
1220	ROOKIE FIREMAN	FRIEDMAN	COLUMBIA	1950
1221	DAVID HARDING, COUNTERSPY	NAZARRO	COLUMBIA	1950
1222	BETWEEN MIDNIGHT AND DAWN	DOUGLAS	COLUMBIA	1950
1222	WELCOME DANGER	BRUCKMAN	PARAMOUNT	1929
1223	HE'S A COCKEYED WONDER	GODFREY	COLUMBIA	1950
1224	HARRIET CRAIG	SHERMAN	COLUMBIA	1950
1225	DOLORES GRAY - KISMET	portrait	MGM	
1225	LENA HORNE	portrait	MGM	
1225	ON THE ISLE OF SAMOA	BERKE	COLUMBIA	1950
1226	RICARDO MONTALBAN	portrait	MGM	
1226	TWO OF A KIND	LEVIN	COLUMBIA	1951
1227	GUNSMOKE MESA	FRASER	PRC	1944
1227	NIGHT OF NIGHTS (HAPPY ENDING*)	MILESTONE	PARAMOUNT	1939
1227	SEVEN DAYS LEAVE	WALLACE	PARAMOUNT	1930
1228	STAGE TO TUCSON	MURPHY	COLUMBIA	1950
1230	EMERGENCY WEDDING	BUZZELL	COLUMBIA	1950
1230	HONEYMOON IN BALI (MY LOVE FOR YOURS*)	GRIFFITH	PARAMOUNT	1939
1231	AL JENNINGS OF OKLAHOMA	NAZARRO	COLUMBIA	1951
1232	FLYING MISSING	LEVIN	COLUMBIA	1950
1232	RICARDO MONTALBAN	portrait	MGM	
1233	MASK OF THE AVENGER	KARLSON	COLUMBIA	1951
1234	COUNTERSPY MEETS SCOTLAND YARD	FRIEDMAN	COLUMBIA	1950
1234	GLORIA GRAHAME	portrait	MGM	
1235	GLORIA GRAHAME	portrait	MGM	
1235	HER FIRST ROMANCE	FRIEDMAN	COLUMBIA	1951
1237	TOUGHER THEY COME	NAZARRO	COLUMBIA	1950
1238	FLAME OF STAMBOUL	NAZARRO	COLUMBIA	1951
1239	ADVENTURE IN DIAMONDS (DIAMONDS ARE DANGEROUS)	FITZMAURICE	PARAMOUNT	1940
1239	LADY AND THE BANDIT	MURPHY	COLUMBIA	1951
1239	MOVIE MAD (sh)	BEAUDINE	EDUCATIONAL FILM	1921
1240	GASOLINE ALLEY	BERNDS	COLUMBIA	1951
1240	PAROLE FIXER (FEDERAL OFFENSE*)	FLOREY	PARAMOUNT	1940
1241	BAREFOOT MAILMAN	MCEVOY	COLUMBIA	1951
1242	SUNNY SIDE OF THE STREET	QUINE	COLUMBIA	1951
1243	NEVER TRUST A GAMBLER	MURPHY	COLUMBIA	1951
1244	FRANCES GIFFORD	portrait	MGM	
1244	SMUGGLERS GOLD	BERKE	COLUMBIA	1951
1244E	DEBBIE REYNOLDS	portrait	MGM	
1245	MOB	PARRISH	COLUMBIA	1951
1246	CRIMINAL LAWYER	FRIEDMAN	COLUMBIA	1951
1246	STUDY IN TERROR (UK)	HILL	COLUMBIA	1965
1248	LET ME EXPLAIN (sh)	SIDNEY	EDUCATIONAL FILM	1921
1248	PAULA	MATE	COLUMBIA	1952
1249	MY TRUE STORY	ROONEY	COLUMBIA	1951
1250	CHINA CORSAIR	NAZARRO	COLUMBIA	1951
1250	GIRL OF THE JUNGLE		REPUBLIC	
1251	BIG GUSHER	LANDERS	COLUMBIA	1951
1251	JOAN BLONDELL	portrait	MGM	
1252	JOAN BLONDELL	portrait	MGM	
1252	SON OF DR. JEKYL	FRIEDMAN	COLUMBIA	1951
1253	ASSIGNMENT-PARIS	PARRISH	COLUMBIA	1952
1253	JOAN BLONDELL	portrait	MGM	
1253	THOSE WERE THE DAYS (AT GOOD OLD SIWASH*)	REED	PARAMOUNT	1940
1254	CHAIN OF CIRCUMSTANCES	JASON	COLUMBIA	1951
1254	JOAN BLONDELL	portrait	MGM	
1254	LEWIS STONE	portrait	MGM	
1255	CORKY OF GASOLINE ALLEY	BERNDS	COLUMBIA	1951
1255	JOAN BLONDELL	portrait	MGM	
1256	GREAT MCGINTY (DOWN WENT MCGINTY*)	STURGES	PARAMOUNT	1940
1256	JOAN BLONDELL	portrait	MGM	
1256	SOUND OFF	QUINE	COLUMBIA	1952
1257	CAPTAIN PIRATE (CAPTAIN BLOOD, FUGITIVE)	MURPHY	COLUMBIA	1952
1257	JOAN BLONDELL	portrait	MGM	

1257	MOONSHINE (sh)	CHASE	EDUCATIONAL FILM	1920
1258	MAD DOCTOR (A DATE WITH DYNASTY*)	WHELAN	PARAMOUNT	1941
1258	MARRYING KIND, THE	CUKOR	COLUMBIA	1952
1259	OKINAWA	JASON	COLUMBIA	1952
1260	FLESH & FANTASY ep #1	DUVIVIER	UNIVERSAL	1943
1260	FLESH & FANTASY ep #2	DUVIVIER	UNIVERSAL	1943
1260	GREYFRIARS BOBBY	CHAFFEY	RANK INTL	1961
1260	MONTANA TERRITORY	NAZARRO	COLUMBIA	1952
1261	HAREM GIRL	BERNDS	COLUMBIA	1952
1261	LESLIE CARON	portrait	MGM	
1262	WITH BYRD AT THE SOUTH POLE (DOC.)		PARAMOUNT	1930
1263	LAST OF THE COMMANCHES	DE TOTH	COLUMBIA	1953
1264	LESLIE CARON	portrait	MGM	
1264	RAINBOW 'ROUND MY SHOULDER	QUINE	COLUMBIA	1952
1265	TARGET HONG KONG	SEARS	COLUMBIA	1953
1265S	DR. GILLESPIE'S NEW ASSISTANT	GOLDBECK	MGM	1943
1266	ALL ASHORE	QUINE	COLUMBIA	1953
1266	ESTHER WILLIAMS, LA COLLEGE FOOTBALL TEAM	portrait	MGM	
1267	AMBUSH AT TOMAHAWK GAP	SEARS	COLUMBIA	1953
1267	ESTHER WILLIAMS, JIMMY MCHUGH	portrait	MGM	
1268	LET'S DO IT AGAIN	HALL	COLUMBIA	1953
1269	MISSION OVER KOREA	SEARS	COLUMBIA	1953
1270	LAST POSSE	WERKER	COLUMBIA	1953
1270	PITTSBURG (SEE 1271)	SEILER	UNIVERSAL	1942
1270	RITA MORENO	portrait	MGM	
1271	FLESH & FANTASY ep #3	DUVIVIER	UNIVERSAL	1943
1271	FROM HERE TO ETERNITY	ZINNEMANN	COLUMBIA	1953
1271	RITA MORENO	portrait	MGM	
1272	CRUISIN' DOWN THE RIVER	QUINE	COLUMBIA	1953
1272	HARD BOILED CANARY (THERE'S MAGIC IN MUSIC*)	STONE	PARAMOUNG	1941
1272A	BLOOD AND SAND	NIBLO	PARAMOUNT	1922
1273	EL ALAMEIN (GER: THAT WAS OUR ROMMEL)	WIGANKO	COLUMBIA	1953
1273	RITA MORENO	portrait	MGM	
1274	CHINA VENTURE	SIEGEL	COLUMBIA	1953
1274	RITA MORENO	portrait	MGM	
1275	RITA MORENO	portrait	MGM	
1276	BIG HEAT	LANG	COLUMBIA	1953
1276	RITA MORENO	portrait	MGM	
1277	CLARK GABLE, ROBERT MONTGOMERY	portrait	MGM	
1277	RITA MORENO	portrait	MGM	
1278	DESTINY (FLESH & FANTASY ep #4)	DUVIVIER	UNIVERSAL	1944
1278	GUN FURY	WALSH	COLUMBIA	1953
1280	MAN IN THE DARK	LANDERS	COLUMBIA	1953
1281	HUMAN DESIRE	LANG	COLUMBIA	1954
1281S	DR. GILLESPIE'S CRIMINAL CASE	GOLDBECK	MGM	1943
1283	CHRIS NOEL	portrait	MGM	
1283	NEBRASKAN	SEARS	COLUMBIA	1953
1284	BAD FOR EACH OTHER	RAPPER	COLUMBIA	1953
1285	IT SHOULD HAPPEN TO YOU	CUKOR	COLUMBIA	1954
1286	MAUREEN O'SULLIVAN	portrait	MGM	
1287	THREE FOR THE SHOW	POTTER	COLUMBIA	1955
1288	JEAN SIMMONS	portrait	MGM	
1288	MASSACRE CANYON	SEARS	COLUMBIA	1954
1289	DRIVE A CROOKED MILE	QUINE	COLUMBIA	1954
1290	JEAN SIMMONS	portrait	MGM	
1290	MAUREEN O'SULLIVAN	portrait	MGM	
1290	THEY RODE WEST	KARLSON	COLUMBIA	1954
1291	PUSHOVER	QUINE	COLUMBIA	1954
1292	OUTLAW STALLION	SEARS	COLUMBIA	1954
1293	THREE HOUSE TO FILL	WERKER	COLUMBIA	1954
1294	GANG BUSTER	SUTHERLAND	PARAMOUNT	1931
1295	BLACK DAKOTAS	NAZARRO	COLUMBIA	1954
1298	JEAN SIMMONS	portrait	MGM	
1298	PHFFFT	ROBSON	COLUMBIA	1954
1298	TIGER WOMAN (serial) (R51: PERILS OF THE DARKEST JUNGLE)	BENNET, GRISSELL	REPUBLIC	1944
1299	JEAN SIMMONS	portrait	MGM	

1299	WYOMING RENEGADES	SEARS	COLUMBIA	1954
1300	BATTER UP (sh)	ROBERTS	EDUCATIONAL FILM	1927
1300	JEAN SIMMONS	portrait	MGM	
1300	TIGHT SPOT	KARLSON	COLUMBIA	1955
1301	FOX TALES (sh)	ROBERTS	EDUCATIONAL FILM	1927
1301	MY SISTER EILEEN	QUINE	COLUMBIA	1955
1302	CELL 2455-DEATH ROW	SEARS	COLUMBIA	1955
1302	JEAN SIMMONS	portrait	MGM	
1303	BRUNETTES PREFER GENTLEMEN (sh)	LAMONT	EDUCATIONAL FILM	1927
1303	JEAN SIMMONS	portrait	MGM	
1303	THREE STRIPES IN THE SUN	MURPHY	COLUMBIA	1955
1304	LUISE RAINER	portrait	MGM	
1304	RED HOT BULLETS (sh)	ROBERTS	EDUCATIONAL FILM	1927
1305	BRING YOUR SMILE ALONG	EDWARDS	COLUMBIA	1955
1305	NOTHING FLAT (sh)	ROBERTS	EDUCATIONAL FILM	1927
1306	LAST FRONTIER	MANN	COLUMBIA	1955
1306	RACING MAD (sh)	ROBERTS	EDUCATIONAL FILM	1928
1307	APACHE AMBUSH	SEARS	COLUMBIA	1955
1307	HIGH STRUNG (sh)	ROBERTS	EDUCATIONAL FILM	1928
1308	HIS MAIDEN VOYAGE (sh)	ROBERTS	EDUCATIONAL FILM	1928
1308	QUEEN BEE	MACDOUGALL	COLUMBIA	1955
1309	BEYOND THE BLUE HORIZON (MALAYA*)	SANTELL	PARAMOUNT	1942
1309	INDISCREET PETE (sh)	SWEET	EDUCATIONAL FILM	1928
1309	PICNIC	LOGAN	COLUMBIA	1955
1310	JUBAL	DAVES	COLUMBIA	1956
1310	KITCHEN TALENT (sh)	ROBERTS	EDUCATIONAL FILM	1928
1311	AT IT AGAIN	TAUROG	EDUCATIONAL FILM	1928
1311	EDDIE DUCHIN STORY	SIDNEY	COLUMBIA	1956
1311	PACIFIC BLACKOUT (MIDNIGHT ANGEL*)	MURPHY	PARAMOUNT	1942
1312	MYRNA LOY	portrait	MGM	
1312	WHO'S LYIN'? (sh)	ROBERTS	EDUCATIONAL FILM	1928
1313	FURY AT GUNSIGHT PASS	SEARS	COLUMBIA	1956
1313	LADIES PREFERRED (sh)	ROBERTS	EDUCATIONAL FILM	1928
1313	RITA MORENO	portrait	MGM	
1314	DUKE COMES BACK (1937)	PICHEL	REPUBLIC	R-ONLY
1314	LEAPING LUCK (sh)	ROBERTS	EDUCATIONAL FILM	1928
1314	YOU CAN'T RUN AWAY FROM IT	POWELL	COLUMBIA	1956
1315	HARDER THEY FALL	ROBSON	COLUMBIA	1956
1315	JUST DANDY (sh)	ROBERTS	EDUCATIONAL FILM	1928
1316	DELUXE #18		REPUBLIC	
1316	MYRNA LOY	portrait	MGM	
1316	SECRET OF TREASURE MOUNTAIN	FRIEDMAN	COLUMBIA	1956
1318	SOLID GOLD CADILLAC	QUINE	COLUMBIA	1956
1319	INNOCENTS (UK)	CLAYTON	20TH CENTURY FOX	1961
1319	OVER-EXPOSED	SEILER	COLUMBIA	1956
1320	BILL CRACKS DOWN (1937	NIGH	REPUBLIC	R52
1320	HE LAUGHED LAST	EDWARDS	COLUMBIA	1956
1320	YOUNG AND WILLING (OUT OF THE FRYING PAN*)	GRIFFITH	PARAMOUNT	1942
1321	CAROLYN JONES	portrait	MGM	
1322	FULL OF LIFE	QUINE	COLUMBIA	1957
1322	MICKEY ROONEY	portrait	MGM	
1323	CLARK GABLE + WIFE SYLVIA	portrait	MGM	
1323	MICKEY ROONEY	portrait	MGM	
1323	SHADOW ON THE WINDOW	ASHER	COLUMBIA	1957
1324	MICKEY ROONEY	portrait	MGM	
1326	MICKEY ROONEY	portrait	MGM	
1329	CLARK GABLE + WIFE SYLVIA	portrait	MGM	
1329	GUNMAN'S WALK	KARLSON	COLUMBIA	1958
1332	CLARK GABLE + WIFE SYLVIA	portrait	MGM	
1332	GUNMEN FROM LAREDO	MACDONALD	COLUMBIA	1959
1334	GIDGET	WENDKOS	COLUMBIA	1959
1336	LANA TURNER	portrait	MGM	
1337	FELIX THE CAT IN SURE-LOCKED HOMES (t) (sh)	MESSMER	EDUCATIONAL FILM	1928
1337	GREAT MOMENT (TRIUMPH OVER PAIN* GREAT WITHOUT GLORY*)	STURGES	PARAMOUNT	1942
1340	DIANA LEWIS	portrait	MGM	
1342	CRYSTAL BALL	NUGENT	PARAMOUNT	1943

1344	RAY DANTON	portrait	MGM	
1351	BARBARA STANWYCK	portrait	MGM	
1352	GOOD MORNING SHERIFF (sh)	GOULDING	EDUCATIONAL FILM	1930
1353	HONK YOUR HORN (sh)	GOULDING	EDUCATIONAL FILM	1930
1354	PRIZE PUPPIES (sh)	GOULDING	EDUCATIONAL FILM	1930
1354	TAINA ELG	portrait	MGM	
1356	BARBARA STANWYCK	portrait	MGM	
1356	SHANGHAI EXPRESS	VON STERNBERG	PARAMOUNT	1932
1357	BARBARA STANWYCK	portrait	MGM	
1360	LION'S ROAR	SENNETT	EDUCATIONAL FILM	1928
1361	OLD BARN (sh)	SENNETT	EDUCATIONAL FILM	1929
1362	BROADWAY BLUES (sh)	SENNETT	EDUCATIONAL FILM	1929
1362	GLORIA DE HAVEN	portrait	MGM	
1363	BRIDE'S RELATIONS (sh)	SENNETT	EDUCATIONAL FILM	1929
1364	HOWARD KEEL	portrait	MGM	
1364	MIRACLE MAN	MCLEOD	PARAMOUNT	1932
1364	WHIRLS AND GIRLS	SENNETT	EDUCATIONAL FILM	1929
1365	BEES' BUZZ (sh)	SENNETT	EDUCATIONAL FILM	1929
1365	HOWARD KEEL	portrait	MGM	
1366	BIG PALOOKA	GOULDING	EDUCATIONAL FILM	1929
1366	HOWARD KEEL	portrait	MGM	
1367	BIG PALOOKA (MISTAKE)	GOULDING	EDUCATIONAL FILM	1929
1367	GIRL CRAZY	GOULDING	EDUCATIONAL FILM	1929
1367	HOWARD KEEL	portrait	MGM	
1368	BARBER'S DAUGHTER (sh)	SENNETT	EDUCATIONAL FILM	1929
1368	FRENCHMAN'S CREEK	LEISEN	PARAMOUNT	1944
1368	HOWARD KEEL	portrait	MGM	
1369	CONSTABULE	SENNETT	EDUCATIONAL FILM	1929
1369	HOWARD KEEL	portrait	MGM	
1369	LUCILLE BALL	portrait	MGM	
1370	HOWARD KEEL	portrait	MGM	
1370	LUNKHEAD	SENNETT, RODNEY	EDUCATIONAL FILM	1929
1371	CYD CHARISSE	portrait	MGM	
1371	GOLFERS	SENNETT	EDUCATIONAL FILM	1929
1371	HOWARD KEEL	portrait	MGM	
1371	PEARLS AND DEVIL-FISH	AUSTIN	MGM	1931
1371	SHARKS AND SWORDFISH	SMITH	MGM	1931
1371-X	FISHERMAN'S PARADISE		MGM	1931
1371-X	PEARLS AND DEVIL-FISH	AUSTIN	MGM	1931
1371-X	SHARKS AND SWORDFISH	SMITH	MGM	1931
1372	HOLLYWOOD STAR (sh)	SENNETT	EDUCATIONAL FILM	1929
1372	HOWARD KEEL	portrait	MGM	
1373	CLANCY AT THE BAT (sh)	RODNEY	EDUCATIONAL FILM	1929
1373	CYD CHARISSE	portrait	MGM	
1374	NEW HALFBACK (sh)	SENNETT	EDUCATIONAL FILM	1929
1375	RESERVED FOR LADIES (UK: SERVICE FOR LADIES)	KORDA	PARAMOUNT	1932
1375	UPPERCUT' O'BRIEN (sh)	RODNEY	EDUCATIONAL FILM	1929
1376	CYD CHARISSE	portrait	MGM	
1376	SCOTCH (sh)	SENNETT	EDUCATIONAL FILM	1930
1376	WHEN I COME BACK*	SANDRICH	PARAMOUNT	1944
1377	SUGAR PLUM PAPA	SENNETT	EDUCATIONAL FILM	1930
1377	TOMORROW'S HARVEST*	BORZAGE	PARAMOUNT	1944
1378	BULLS AND BEARS (sh)	SENNETT	EDUCATIONAL FILM	1930
1379	HE TRUMPED HER ACE	PEARCE	EDUCATIONAL FILM	1930
1380	HONEYMOON ZEPPELIN (sh)	SENNETT	EDUCATIONAL FILM	1930
1380	WHIPPET RACING (sh)	WING	MGM	1931
1380-X	WHIPPET RACING (SHORT)	WING	MGM	1931
1381	RADIO KISSSES (sh)	PEARCE	EDUCATIONAL FILM	1930
1382	ANITA PAGE	portrait	MGM	
1382	FAT WIVES FOR THIN (sh)	SENNETT	EDUCATIONAL FILM	1930
1383	CAMPUS CRUSHES (sh)	SENNETT	EDUCATIONAL FILM	1930
1384	CHUMPS (sh)	SENNETT	EDUCATIONAL FILM	1930
1385	GOOD-BYE LEGS (sh)	SENNETT	EDUCATIONAL FILM	1930
1386	HELLO TELEVISION (sh)	PEARCE	EDUCATIONAL FILM	1930
1386	LILY CHJRISTINE (UK)	STEIN	PARAMOUNT	1932
1387	AVERAGE HUSBAND (sh)	SENNETT	EDUCATIONAL FILM	1930

1388	CAROLYN JONES	portrait	MGM	
1388	INNOCENTS (UK)	CLAYTON	20TH CENTURY FOX	1961
1388	VACATION LOVES (sh)	SENNETT	EDUCATIONAL FILM	1930
1388	VERA-ELLEN	portrait	MGM	
1389	FEAR* (HER HEART IN HER THROAT*)	ALLEN	PARAMOUNT	1945
1389	VERA-ELLEN	portrait	MGM	
1390	VERA-ELLEN	portrait	MGM	
1392	CAROLYN JONES	portrait	MGM	
1392	MAUREEN O'SULLIVAN	portrait	MGM	
1392	VERA-ELLEN	portrait	MGM	
1394	CAROLYN JONES	portrait	MGM	
1394	MISS SUSIE SLAGLE	BERRY	PARAMOUNT	1945
1394	THERE IT IS (sh)	MULLER	EDUCATIONAL FILM	1928
1394	VERA-ELLEN	portrait	MGM	
1395	CAROLYN JONES	portrait	MGM	
1395	DUFFY'S TAVERN	WALKER	PARAMOUNT	1945
1395	SAY AH-H! (sh)	BOWERS	EDUCATIONAL FILM	1928
1395	VERA-ELLEN	portrait	MGM	
1396	NIGHT OF JUNE 13TH	ROBERTS	PARAMOUNT	1932
1396	VERA-ELLEN	portrait	MGM	
1396	VIRGINIAN	GILMORE	PARAMOUNT	1946
1396	WHOOZIT (sh)	BOWERS, MULLER	EDUCATIONAL FILM	1928
1397	PIER ANGELI	portrait	MGM	
1397	VERA-ELLEN	portrait	MGM	
1397	YOU'LL BE SORRY (sh)	MULLER	EDUCATIONAL FILM	1928
1398	HOLD THAT BLONDE	MARSHALL	PARAMOUNT	1945
1398	HOP OFF (sh)	BOWERS, MULLER	EDUCATIONAL FILM	1928
1398	VERA-ELLEN	portrait	MGM	
1399	GOOFY BIRDS (sh)	BOWERS, MULLER	EDUCATIONAL FILM	1928
1399	VERA-ELLEN	portrait	MGM	
1400	VERA-ELLEN	portrait	MGM	
1401	VERA-ELLEN	portrait	MGM	
1402	LOLA ALBRIGHT	portrait	MGM	
1402	VERA-ELLEN	portrait	MGM	
1403	TWO IS A HAPPY NUMBER	STUART	MGM	1972
1403	VERA-ELLEN	portrait	MGM	
1404	VERA-ELLEN	portrait	MGM	
1405	VERA-ELLEN	portrait	MGM	
1406	VERA-ELLEN	portrait	MGM	
1407	GREER GARSON, HUSBAND RICHARD NEY	portrait	MGM	
1407	VERA-ELLEN	portrait	MGM	
1408	VERA-ELLEN	portrait	MGM	
1409	JOAN BLONDELL	portrait	MGM	
1409	MICKEY ROONEY	portrait	MGM	
1409	VERA-ELLEN	portrait	MGM	
1410	VERA-ELLEN	portrait	MGM	
1411	EARL CARROLL VANITIES	SANTLEY	REPUBLIC	1945
1411	VERA-ELLEN	portrait	MGM	
1412	HALF PINT HERO (sh)	LAMONT	EDUCATIONAL FILM	1927
1412	VERA-ELLEN	portrait	MGM	
1413	SOME SCOUT (sh)	SANDRICH	EDUCATIONAL FILM	1927
1413	VERA-ELLEN	portrait	MGM	
1414	HELLO SAILOR (sh)	SANDRICH	EDUCATIONAL FILM	1927
1414	VERA-ELLEN	portrait	MGM	
1415	PIER ANGELI	portrait	MGM	
1415	SWORD POINTS (sh)	SANDRICH	EDUCATIONAL FILM	1928
1415	VERA-ELLEN	portrait	MGM	
1416	ESTHER WILLIAMS, KEENAN WYNN, LARRY PARKS, BETTY GARRETT	portrait	MGM	
1416	JOAN BLONDELL	portrait	MGM	
1416	LISTEN SISTER (sh)	BEAUCHAMP	EDUCATIONAL FILM	1928
1416	VERA-ELLEN	portrait	MGM	
1417	FANDANGO (sh)	LANE	EDUCATIONAL FILM	1928
1417	LIGHTNING RAIDERS	NEWFIELD	PRC	1945
1417	VERA-ELLEN	portrait	MGM	
1418	HECTIC DAYS (sh)	LANE	EDUCATIONAL FILM	1928
1418	VERA-ELLEN	portrait	MGM	

1419	ROAMING ROMEO (sh)	LANE	EDUCATIONAL FILM	1928
1419	VERA-ELLEN	portrait	MGM	
1420	VERA-ELLEN	portrait	MGM	
1421	VERA-ELLEN	portrait	MGM	
1422	VERA-ELLEN	portrait	MGM	
1423	VERA-ELLEN	portrait	MGM	
1424	VERA-ELLEN	portrait	MGM	
1425	VERA-ELLEN	portrait	MGM	
1427	ANGELA LANSBURY	portrait	MGM	
1427E	ANN-MARGRET	portrait	MGM	
1428	MARSHA HUNT	portrait	MGM	
1428	MAUREEN O'SULLIVAN	portrait	MGM	
1429	MARSHA HUNT	portrait	MGM	
1435	MARSHA HUNT	portrait	MGM	
1436	CRAZY NUT (sh)	LAMONT	EDUCATIONAL FILM	1929
1436	MARGO	portrait	MGM	
1437	MARGO	portrait	MGM	
1437	TICKLISH BUSINESS (sh)	WHITE	EDUCATIONAL FILM	1929
1440	BIG JEWEL CASE (sh)	ROBERTS	EDUCATIONAL FILM	1930
1440	WALLACE BEERY	portrait	MGM	
1441	WESTERN KNIGHTS (sh)	ROBERTS	EDUCATIONAL FILM	1930
1442	MARGO	portrait	MGM	
1442	PEACE AND HARMONY (sh)	ROBERTS	EDUCATIONAL FILM	1930
1443	HOW'S MY BABY? (sh)	ROBERTS	EDUCATIONAL FILM	1930
1444	ESTHER WILLIAMS	portrait	MGM	
1445	INNOCENTS (UK)	CLAYTON	20TH CENTURY FOX	1961
1446	INNOCENTS (UK)	CLAYTON	20TH CENTURY FOX	1961
1448	VERA-ELLEN	portrait	MGM	
1451	ALICE IN WONDERLAND	MCLEOD	PARAMOUNT	1933
1460	VERA-ELLEN	portrait	MGM	
1461	POLLY BERGEN	portrait	MGM	
1466	AMBUSH - (mistake 1460)	WOOD	MGM	1950
1472	GRACE KELLY - THE SWAN	portrait	MGM	
1472	WILDCAT WILLIE (sh)	GILLSTROM	EDUCATIONAL FILM	1925
1474	OH, TEACHER! (sh)	GILLSTROM	EDUCATIONAL FILM	1924
1475S	DUCHESS OF IDAHO	LEONARD	MGM	1950
1476	ELIZABETH TAYLOR, NICKY HILTON	portrait	MGM	
1476	MAUREEN O'SULLIVAN	portrait	MGM	
1478	GRACE KELLY - THE SWAN	portrait	MGM	
1478	SIX OF A KIND	MCCAREY	PARAMOUNT	1934
1478E	ELKE SOMMER	portrait	MGM	
1478X	GRACE KELLY - THE SWAN	portrait	MGM	
1479	ASSIGNMENT TO KILL	REYNOLDS	WARNER BROS	1968
1480	THAT SON OF A SHEIK (sh)	CHRISTIE, SIDNEY	EDUCATIONAL FILM	1922
1483	ANNE FRANCIS	portrait	MGM	
1484	HEDY LAMARR	portrait	MGM	
1486	HEDY LAMARR	portrait	MGM	
1488	HEDY LAMARR	portrait	MGM	
1488	PASSKEY TO DANGER	SELANDER	REPUBLIC	1946
1489	HEDY LAMARR	portrait	MGM	
1490	HEDY LAMARR	portrait	MGM	
1490	KAREN MORLEY	portrait	MGM	
1491	HEDY LAMARR	portrait	MGM	
1492	BRUTE MAN	YARBROUGH	PRC	1946
1492	HEDY LAMARR	portrait	MGM	
1493	HEDY LAMARR	portrait	MGM	
1494	BELLE OF THE NINETIES	MCCAREY	PARAMOUNT	1934
1494	MARISA PAVAN	portrait	MGM	
1495	MAUREEN O'SULLIVAN	portrait	MGM	
1496	KAREN MORLEY	portrait	MGM	
1497	ELIZABETH TAYLOR	portrait	MGM	
1500	DR. WASSEL*	ROSSON-DEMILLE	PARAMOUNT	1944
1502	AVA GARDNER	portrait	MGM	
1502	SHE SIGHED BY THE SEASIDE	KENTON	ASSOC. FIRST NAT'L	1921
1503	CALL A COP	ST. CLAIR	ASSOC. FIRST NAT'L	1921
1503	HERE COME THE WAVES	SANDRICH-TEMPLETON	PARAMOUNT	1944

1504	HARD KNOCKS AND LOVE TAPS	DEL RUTH	ASSOC. PRODUCERS	1921
1505	BE REASONABLE	DEL RUTH	ASSOC. FIRST NAT'L	1921
1506	BY HECK	DEL RUTH	ASSOC. FIRST NAT'L	1921
1507	DUCK HUNTER	DEL RUTH	ASSOC. FIRST NAT'L	1922
1508	ON PATROL (sh)	DEL RUTH	ASSOC. FIRST NAT'L	1922
1510	SHOWBOAT	SIDNEY	MGM	1951
1512	MAUREEN O'SULLIVAN	portrait	MGM	
1513	MARISA PAVAN	portrait	MGM	
1513	MAUREEN O'SULLIVAN	portrait	MGM	
1515	MAUREEN O'SULLIVAN	portrait	MGM	
1517	MAUREEN O'SULLIVAN	portrait	MGM	
1518	FIGHTING VIGILANTES	TAYLOR	PRC	1947
1518	TUESDAY WELD	portrait	MGM	
1519	JUNE ALLYSON	portrait	MGM	
1519	TUESDAY WELD	portrait	MGM	
1520	TUESDAY WELD	portrait	MGM	
1521E	TUESDAY WELD	portrait	MGM	
1522	NAVY BLUES (1937)	STAUB	REPUBLIC	R-ONLY
1523E	TUESDAY WELD	portrait	MGM	
1524	BEHOLD MY WIFE	LEISEN	PRAMOUNT	1934
1525	MAUREEN O'SULLIVAN	portrait	MGM	
1527	NAVY BORN (1936)	WATT	REPUBLIC	R-ONLY
1530	DEVIL IS A WOMAN	VON STERNBERG	PARAMOUNT	1935
1530	ELIZABETH TAYLOR	portrait	MGM	
1534	HIT PARADE (1937)	MEINS	REPUBLIC	R-ONLY
1538	BETTA ST. JOHN	portrait	MGM	
1541	MARY CARLISLE	portrait	MGM	
1544	CRUSADES	DEMILLE	PARAMOUNT	1935
1545	MARY CARLISLE	portrait	MGM	
1555	CAMPUS HONEYMOON	SALE	REPUBLIC	1948
1557	LAST OUTPOST	BARTON, GASNIER	PARAMOUNT	1935
1559	GEORGE CUKOR	portrait	MGM	
1560	GEORGE CUKOR	portrait	MGM	
1561	PAULA RAYMOND	portrait	MGM	
1561	WALLACE BEERY'S HOME	portrait	MGM	
1563	WHEEL OF FORTUNE (MAN BETRAYED 1936)	AUER	REPUBLIC	R55
1564	PAULA RAYMOND	portrait	MGM	
1565	PAULA RAYMOND	portrait	MGM	
1566	GUSSIE MORRAN	portrait		
1586	PRETZELS (t) (sh)	MOSER	EDUCATIONAL FILM	1930
1588	JAMES STEWART	portrait	MGM	
1589	INDIAN PUDDING (t) (sh)	MOSER	EDUCATIONAL FILM	1930
1590	HOT TURKEY (t) (sh)	MOSER	EDUCATIONAL FILM	1930
1591	DEBBIE REYNOLDS	portrait	MGM	
1591	HAWAIIAN PINEAPPLES (t) (sh)	MOSER	EDUCATIONAL FILM	1930
1591	SCANDAL AT SCOURIE	NEGULESCO	MGM	1953
1592	SWISS CHEESE (t) (sh)	MOSER	EDUCATIONAL FILM	1930
1593	CODFISH BALLS (t) (sh)	MOSER	EDUCATIONAL FILM	1930
1594	HUNGARIAN GOULASH (t) (sh)	MOSER	EDUCATIONAL FILM	1930
1595	BULLY BEEF (t) (sh)	MOSER	EDUCATIONAL FILM	1930
1596	KANGAROO STEAK (t) (sh)	MOSER	EDUCATIONAL FILM	1930
1596	WRONG, WRONG TRAIL (sh)	HENABERY	WARNER BROS.	1934
1597	MONKEY MEAT (t) (sh)	MOSER	EDUCATIONAL FILM	1930
1601	LOVE'S OUTCAST (sh)	WALDRON	ASSOC. FIRST NAT'L	1921
1602	LOVE AND DOUGHNUTS	DEL RUTH	ASSOC. FIRST NAT'L	1921
1603	BRIGHT EYES (sh)	ST. CLAIR	ASSOC. FIRST NAT'L	1921
1604	STEP FORWARD (sh)	MEINS	ASSOC. FIRST NAT'L	1922
1610	CYD CHARISSE	portrait	MGM	
1610	FRANCIS (FRANCIS THE TALKING MULE)	LUBIN	UNIVERSAL	1949
1610	LUCILLE BREMER	portrait	MGM	
1613	CALIFORNIA FIREBRAND	FORD	REPUBLIC	1948
1619	CYD CHARISSE	portrait	MGM	
1620	ELEANOR POWELL	portrait	MGM	
1626	JAMES STEWART	portrait	MGM	
1631	RUTH SELWYN	portrait	MGM	
1633	CREST OF THE WAVE (UK: SEAGULLS OVER SORRENTO)	BOULTING, BOULTING	MGM	1954

1634	ELEANOR POWELL	portrait	MGM	
1638	CLAIRE BLOOM	portrait	MGM	
1641E	JEAN SIMMONS	portrait	MGM	
1642E	JEAN SIMMONS	portrait	MGM	
1643E	JEAN SIMMONS	portrait	MGM	
1644E	JEAN SIMMONS	portrait	MGM	
1645E	JEAN SIMMONS	portrait	MGM	
1646	GRACE KELLY	portrait	MGM	
1646	JEAN SIMMONS	portrait	MGM	
1648	GRACE KELLY	portrait	MGM	
1648	MAID OF SALEM	LLOYD	PARAMOUNT	1936
1649	GRACE KELLY	portrait	MGM	
1650	GRACE KELLY	portrait	MGM	
1651	VAGRANT (sh)	WHITE	EDUCATIONAL FILM	1921
1652	GRACE KELLY	portrait	MGM	
1653	ARLENE DAHL	portrait	MGM	
1653	MILK MAN*		UNIVERSAL	1950
1655	ELEANOR POWELL	portrait	MGM	
1656	INSIDE STORY, THE (BIG GAMBLE R1954)	DWAN	REPUBLIC	1948
1661	JANIS PAIGE	portrait	MGM	
1662	FREDDIE BARTHOLOMEW	portrait	MGM	
1663	NANCY DAVIS/REAGAN	portrait	MGM	
1663	ZIP! BOOM! BANG! (sh)	WHITE	EDUCATIONAL FILM	1929
1664	ELAINE STEWART	portrait	MGM	
1666	LOOK OUT BELOW (sh)	ROBERTS	EDUCATIONAL FILM	1929
1667	HUNTING THE HUNTER (sh)	ROBERTS	EDUCATIONAL FILM	1929
1668	MADHOUSE (sh)	ROBERTS	EDUCATIONAL FILM	1929
1669	NANCY DAVIS/REAGAN	portrait	MGM	
1670	JOHN CASSAVETES	portrait	MGM	
1674	HOWARD KEEL	portrait	MGM	
1674	KAREN MORLEY	portrait	MGM	
1675	ANGEL ON THE AMAZON	AUER	REPUBLIC	1948
1675	HOWARD KEEL	portrait	MGM	
1675	JUNGLE WILDERNESS (ANGEL ON THE AMAZON)	AUER	REPUBLIC	1948
1676	PEST OF THE STORM COUNTRY (sh)	WHITE	EDUCATIONAL FILM	1923
1677	HOWARD KEEL	portrait	MGM	
1678	HOWARD KEEL	portrait	MGM	
1678	JUNE ALLYSON	portrait	MGM	
1679	ELEANOR POWELL	portrait	MGM	
1679	HOWARD KEEL	portrait	MGM	
1680	HOWARD KEEL	portrait	MGM	
1681	HOWARD KEEL	portrait	MGM	
1682	HOWARD KEEL	portrait	MGM	
1683	HOWARD KEEL	portrait	MGM	
1684	HOWARD KEEL	portrait	MGM	
1685	HOWARD KEEL	portrait	MGM	
1686	AIR DERBY (sh)	BROWN	EDUCATIONAL FILM	1929
1686	DONNA REED	portrait	MGM	
1686	GREER GARSON, HUSBAND RICHARD NEY	portrait	MGM	
1686	HOWARD KEEL	portrait	MGM	
1687	HOWARD KEEL	portrait	MGM	
1688	HOWARD KEEL	portrait	MGM	
1689	SOUTH OF RIO	FORD	REPUBLIC	1949
1692	ESTHER WILLIAMS, HUSBAND BEN GAGE	portrait	MGM	
1698	WILLIAM LUNDIGAN, WIFE RONA MORGAN	portrait	MGM	
1700	AVA GARDNER	portrait	MGM	
1700	SOMETHING OF VALUE (r62 - AFRICA ABLAZE!)	BROOKS	MGM	1957
1701	AMAZING DOBERMANS, THE (r78 - LUCKY)	CHUDNOW	GOLDEN FILMS	1976
1702	OUT OF CONTROL (BAD GEORGIA ROAD)	BRODERICK	GOLDEN FILMS	1976
1706	LESLIE HOWARD, OP HEGGIE	portrait	MGM	
1708	AVA GARDNER	portrait	MGM	
1709	LANA TURNER	portrait	MGM	
1709	MEET ME AT THE FAIR (mistake 1705)	SIRK	UNIVERSAL	1952
1710	LANA TURNER	portrait	MGM	
1711	LANA TURNER	portrait	MGM	
1712	LANA TURNER	portrait	MGM	

1713	BIG BROADCAST OF 1938	LEISEN	PARAMOUNT	1938
1713	LANA TURNER	portrait	MGM	
1714	LANA TURNER	portrait	MGM	
1715	LANA TURNER	portrait	MGM	
1715S	DON'T GO NEAR THE WATER	WALTERS	MGM	1957
1716	LANA TURNER	portrait	MGM	
1716E	SHIRLEY EATON	portrait	MGM	
1717	LANA TURNER	portrait	MGM	
1717E	SHIRLEY EATON	portrait	MGM	
1718	LANA TURNER	portrait	MGM	
1719	LANA TURNER	portrait	MGM	
1719E	SHIRLEY EATON	portrait	MGM	
1720	LANA TURNER	portrait	MGM	
1721	LANA TURNER	portrait	MGM	
1722	LANA TURNER	portrait	MGM	
1723	LANA TURNER	portrait	MGM	
1724	LANA TURNER	portrait	MGM	
1725	LANA TURNER	portrait	MGM	
1726	LANA TURNER	portrait	MGM	
1727	LANA TURNER	portrait	MGM	
1728	LANA TURNER	portrait	MGM	
1733E	SHIRLEY EATON	portrait	MGM	
1738	ESTHER WILLIAMS	portrait	MGM	
1738	JANE POWELL	portrait	MGM	
1738	MARY ASTOR	portrait	MGM	
1749	MAUREEN O'SULLIVAN	portrait	MGM	
1753	LANA TURNER	portrait	MGM	
1753	PLUNDERERS, THE	KANE	REPUBLIC	1948
1757	RED MENACE (UNDERGROUND SPY)	SPRINGSTEEN	REPUBLIC	1949
1758	KATHRYN CRAWFORD	portrait	MGM	
1758	POLTERGEIST	HOOPER	MGM	1982
1765	AUDREY TOTTER	portrait	MGM	
1771	JUNE ALLYSON	portrait	MGM	
1772	ADVENTURES OF TARTU (UK)	BUCQUET	MGM	1943
1775	GREER GARSON	portrait	MGM	
1776	1776	HUNT	COLUMBIA	1972
1777	JUNE ALLYSON	portrait	MGM	
1780	BUSTER KEATON	portrait	MGM	
1782	JANE POWELL	portrait	MGM	
1783	JANE POWELL	portrait	MGM	
1784	JUNE ALLYSON	portrait	MGM	
1785	JANE POWELL	portrait	MGM	
1785	JUNE ALLYSON	portrait	MGM	
1786	MYRNA LOY	portrait	MGM	
1786	WONDERFUL WORLD BROTHERS GRIMM-Dancing Princess (t)	LEVIN, PAL	MGM	1962
1787	WONDERFUL WORLD BROTHERS GRIMM-Cobbler & Elves (t)	LEVIN, PAL	MGM	1962
1788	JANE POWELL	portrait	MGM	
1788	JUNE ALLYSON	portrait	MGM	
1788	WONDERFUL WORLD BROTHERS GRIMM-Singing Bone (t)	LEVIN, PAL	MGM	1962
1789	JANE POWELL	portrait	MGM	
1790	JANE POWELL	portrait	MGM	
1791	MARGARET SULLAVAN	portrait	MGM	
1793	THIS MAN IS NEWS (UK)	MACDONALD	PARAMOUNT	1938
1796	ILONA MASSEY	portrait	MGM	
1797	ILONA MASSEY	portrait	MGM	
1797	MYRNA LOY	portrait	MGM	
1798	ILONA MASSEY	portrait	MGM	
1799	ESTHER WILLIAMS	portrait	MGM	
1799	ILONA MASSEY	portrait	MGM	
1800	ILONA MASSEY	portrait	MGM	
1801	ILONA MASSEY	portrait	MGM	
1801	PAULA RAYMOND	portrait	MGM	
1802	PAULA RAYMOND	portrait	MGM	
1803	PAULA RAYMOND	portrait	MGM	
1803	WALTER PIDGEON	portrait	MGM	
1804	PAULA RAYMOND	portrait	MGM	

1804	WALTER PIDGEON	portrait	MGM	
1805	PAULA RAYMOND	portrait	MGM	
1805	PIER ANGELI	portrait	MGM	
1806	ILONA MASSEY	portrait	MGM	
1806	OUR LEADING CITIZEN	SANTELL	PARAMOUNT	1939
1806	PAULA RAYMOND	portrait	MGM	
1807	ILONA MASSEY	portrait	MGM	
1807	PAULA RAYMOND	portrait	MGM	
1808	ILONA MASSEY	portrait	MGM	
1808	PAULA RAYMOND	portrait	MGM	
1809	ILONA MASSEY	portrait	MGM	
1809	PAULA RAYMOND	portrait	MGM	
1810	PAULA RAYMOND	portrait	MGM	
1810	SIDEWALKS OF LONDON (UK: ST. MARTIN'S LANE)	WHELAN	PARAMOUNT	1938
1811	PAULA RAYMOND	portrait	MGM	
1812	PAULA RAYMOND	portrait	MGM	
1812	RODDY MCDOWALL	portrait	MGM	
1813	PAULA RAYMOND	portrait	MGM	
1813	RODDY MCDOWALL	portrait	MGM	
1814	OPEN HOUSE (sh)	LAMONT	EDUCATIONAL FILM	1926
1814	VERA-ELLEN	portrait	MGM	
1815	HUMDINGER (sh)	TAUROG	EDUCATIONAL FILM	1926
1815	PIER ANGELI	portrait	MGM	
1815	VERA-ELLEN	portrait	MGM	
1816	CLOSE SHAVES (sh)	LAMONT	EDUCATIONAL FILM	1926
1816	VERA-ELLEN	portrait	MGM	
1817	BELLE OF OLD MEXICO	SPRINGSTEEN	REPUBLIC	1950
1817	VERA-ELLEN	portrait	MGM	
1817	WEDDING YELLS (sh)	LAMONT	EDUCATIONAL FILM	1927
1818	DRAW-BACK (sh)	TAUROG	EDUCATIONAL FILM	1927
1818	RODDY MCDOWALL	portrait	MGM	
1818	VERA-ELLEN	portrait	MGM	
1819	DONNA REED	portrait	MGM	
1819	ROBERT MONTGOMERY	portrait	MGM	
1819	RODDY MCDOWALL	portrait	MGM	
1819	VERA-ELLEN	portrait	MGM	
1820	BELLE LE GRAND	DWAN	REPUBLIC	1951
1820	ELIZABETH TAYLOR	portrait	MGM	
1820	VERA-ELLEN	portrait	MGM	
1821	ELIZABETH TAYLOR AT 2 1/2, MOTHER & BROTHER	portrait	MGM	
1821	KISS ME KATE (sh)	BEAUCHAMP	EDUCATIONAL FILM	1926
1822	PLUMB GOOFY (sh)	BEAUCHAMP	EDUCATIONAL FILM	1926
1823	BARBARA KENT	portrait	MGM	
1826	SWEET BABY (sh)	FAY	EDUCATIONAL FILM	1926
1826	VERA-ELLEN	portrait	MGM	
1827	BARBARA KENT	portrait	MGM	
1827	VERA-ELLEN	portrait	MGM	
1828	GREAT VICTOR HERBERT	STONE	PARAMOUNT	1939
1829	TYPHOON	KING	PARAMOUNT	1939
1830	BLONDE BANDIT	KELLER	REPUBLIC	1950
1830	RICARDO MONTALBAN	portrait	MGM	
1831	RICARDO MONTALBAN	portrait	MGM	
1834	TRIGGER JR.	WITNEY	REPUBLIC	1950
1836	VERA-ELLEN	portrait	MGM	
1838	APPOINTMENT WITH A SHADOW	PEVNEY	UNIVERSAL	1958
1839	ROBERT TAYLOR	portrait	MGM	
1840	LOST PLANET AIRMEN	BRANNON	REPUBLIC	1951
1840	NIGHT OWLS (sh)	SANDRICH	EDUCATIONAL FILM	1927
1842E	CHAD EVERETT	portrait	MGM	
1845	JANE POWELL	portrait	MGM	
1848	ROBERT TAYLOR	portrait	MGM	
1849S	DON'T MAKE WAVES	MACKENDRICK	MGM	1967
1850	GHOST BREAKERS	MARSHALL	PARAMOUNT	1940
1850S	DOUBLE TROUBLE	TAUROG	MGM	1967
1852	NANCY DAVIS/REAGAN	portrait	MGM	
1852	TOM DRAKE	portrait	MGM	

1853	ELAINE STEWART	portrait	MGM	
1854	ELAINE STEWART	portrait	MGM	
1856	MALAGA (UK: MOMENT OF DANGER)	SALE	WARNER BROS	1954
1859	HOPALONG RIDES AGAIN	SELANDER	PARAMOUNT	1937
1862	MICKEY ROONEY	portrait	MGM	
1866E	PIER ANGELI	portrait	MGM	
1867	BETTA ST. JOHN	portrait	MGM	
1871	JEFF RICHARDS	portrait	MGM	
1873	SEA DEVILS (UK)	WALSH	RKO	1953
1879	JEFF RICHARDS	portrait	MGM	
1882	DRUMMING IT IN (sh)	LAMONT	EDUCATIONAL FILM	1930
1882	ELEANOR POWELL	portrait	MGM	
1883	ELEANOR POWELL	portrait	MGM	
1883	TROUBLE FOR TWO (sh)	ROBERTS	EDUCATIONAL FILM	1930
1885	ELEANOR POWELL	portrait	MGM	
1885	FRENCH KISSES (sh)	ROBERTS	EDUCATIONAL FILM	1930
1886	ELEANOR POWELL	portrait	MGM	
1886	JUNE ALLYSON	portrait	MGM	
1888	JUNE ALLYSON	portrait	MGM	
1889	PIER ANGELI	portrait	MGM	
1890	ELEANOR POWELL	portrait	MGM	
1890	RED SKELTON	portrait	MGM	
1891	PIER ANGELI	portrait	MGM	
1892	ELEANOR POWELL	portrait	MGM	
1892	JUNE ALLYSON	portrait	MGM	
1892	SHE'S A BOY (sh)	LAMONT	EDUCATIONAL FILM	1927
1893	ELEANOR POWELL	portrait	MGM	
1894	GREER GARSON	portrait	MGM	
1894	PIER ANGELI	portrait	MGM	
1895	ELEANOR POWELL	portrait	MGM	
1896	NO FARE (sh)	LAMONT	EDUCATIONAL FILM	1928
1897	ELIZABETH TAYLOR	portrait	MGM	
1897	GREER GARSON	portrait	MGM	
1898	GLOOM CHASER (sh)	LAMONT	EDUCATIONAL FILM	1928
1898	NAVY BEANS (sh)	LAMONT	EDUCATIONAL FILM	1928
1899	MR BUG GOES TO TOWN (t) (HOPPITY GOES TO TOWN 1959)	FLEISCHER	PARAMOUNT	1941
1900	1900	BERTOLUCCI	PARAMOUNT	1976
1902	GUNS A POPPIN' (sh)	WHITE	COLUMBIA	1957
1903	FIFI BLOWS HER TOP (sh)	WHITE	COLUMBIA	1958
1904	RUSTY ROMEOS (sh)	WHITE	COLUMBIA	1957
1905	MICKEY ROONEY	portrait	MGM	
1905	TRICKY CHICKS (sh)	WHITE	COLUMBIA	1957
1906	FLYING SAUCER DAFFY (sh)	WHITE	COLUMBIA	1958
1907	QUIZ WHIZZ (sh)	WHITE	COLUMBIA	1958
1908	PIES AND GUYS (sh)	WHITE	COLUMBIA	1958
1908	RULES OF ENGAGEMENT	FRIEDKIN	VIACOM	2000
1909	OUTER SPACE JITTERS (sh)	WHITE	COLUMBIA	1957
1909	UNA MERKEL	portrait	MGM	
1910	SWEET AND HOT (sh)	WHITE	COLUMBIA	1958
1911	OIL'S WELL THAT ENDS WELL (sh)	WHITE	COLUMBIA	1958
1912	SAPPY BULLFIGHTERS (sh)	WHITE	COLUMBIA	1959
1913	TRIPLE CROSSED (sh)	WHITE	COLUMBIA	1959
1915	JUNE ALLYSON	portrait	MGM	
1916	MAN OF CONQUEST (1939)	NICHOLS JR.	REPUBLIC	R-ONLY
1920	NAVY BLUES (sh)	BEAUDINE	EDUCATIONAL FILM	1923
1921	BEYOND THE BLUE HORIZON	SANTELL	PARAMOUNT	1942
1921	PIER ANGELI	portrait	MGM	
1925	GENE KELLY	portrait	MGM	
1926	GREER GARSON	portrait	MGM	
1928	GENE KELLY	portrait	MGM	
1931	ESTHER WILLIAMS	portrait	MGM	
1935	NANCY DAVIS/REAGAN	portrait	MGM	
1936	ELIZABETH TAYLOR	portrait	MGM	
1937	NERVE TONIC (sh)	BEAUDINE	EDUCATIONAL FILM	1924
1938	DUKE OF WEST POINT	GREEN	UNITED ARTISTS	1938
1939	CORVETTE SUMMER	ROBBINS	MGM	1978

1939	ELIZABETH TAYLOR	portrait	MGM	
1942	ANDY	SARAFIAN	UNIVERSAL	1965
1943	HERO AT LARGE	DAVIDSON	MGM	1980
1944	VERA-ELLEN	portrait	MGM	
1946	JULES MUNSHIN	portrait	MGM	
1952	BUDDY EBSEN	portrait	MGM	
1955	UNA MERKEL	portrait	MGM	
1956	I MARRIED A WITCH	CLAIR	UNITED ARTISTS	1942
1959	ANGIE DICKINSON	portrait	MGM	
1961	DEBORAH KERR	portrait	MGM	
1961	END OF THE AFFAIR	RUDOLPH	MGM/UA	1982
1962	LOST CANYON	SELANDER	UNITED ARTISTS	1942
1963	FOR WHOM THE BELL TOLLS	WOOD	PARAMOUNT	1943
1967	DEBORAH KERR	portrait	MGM	
1971	LUCKY JORDAN	TUTTLE	PARAMOUNT	1943
1973	VERA-ELLEN	portrait	MGM	
1974	AVENGERS (UK: DAY WILL DAWN)	FRENCH	PARAMOUNT	1942
1976	JELLY FISH (sh)	ADOLFI	EDUCATIONAL FILM	1926
1977	PINK ELEPHANTS (sh)	ROBERTS	EDUCATIONAL FILM	1926
1978	MIDNIGHT FOLLIES (sh)	JONES	EDUCATIONAL FILM	1926
1980	SO PROUDLY WE HAIL	SANDRICH	PARAMOUNT	1943
1981	HIGH SEA BLUES (sh)	JONES	EDUCATIONAL FILM	1927
1981	MIRACLE OF MORGAN'S CREEK	STURGES	PARAMOUNT	1944
1982	BUSY LIZZIE (sh)	JONES	EDUCATIONAL FILM	1927
1983	HEADLINE HUNTERS	WHITNEY	REPUBLIC	1955
1983	LISTEN LENA (sh)	BEAUCHAMP	EDUCATIONAL FILM	1927
1984	HOT LIGHTNING (sh)	ROBERTS	EDUCATIONAL FILM	1927
1985	ALASKA HIGHWAY	MCDONALD	PARAMOUNT	1943
1985	ROPED IN (sh)	LAMONT	EDUCATIONAL FILM	1927
1985	TERROR AT MIDNIGHT	ADREON	REPUBIC	1956
1986	JUNE ALLYSON	portrait	MGM	
1988	CIRCUS CAPERS (sh)	JONES	EDUCATIONAL FILM	1927
1988	JUNE ALLYSON	portrait	MGM	
1988	MAN IS ARMED	ADREON	REPUBLIC	1956
1989	JUNE ALLYSON	portrait	MGM	
1989	QUEENS WILD (sh)	ROBERTS	EDUCATIONAL FILM	1927
1990	I COVER THE UNDERWORLD	SPRINGSTEEN	REPUBLIC	1955
1990	NO CHEATING (sh)	ROBERTS	EDUCATIONAL FILM	1927
1991	DOUBLE JEOPARDY	SPRINGSTEEN	REPUBLIC	1955
1991E	PIER ANGELI	portrait	MGM	
1992	FRANCES RAFFERTY	portrait	MGM	
1992	HIGH SPOTS (sh)	ROBERTS	EDUCATIONAL FILM	1927
1992	JUNE ALLYSON	portrait	MGM	
1992E	PIER ANGELI	portrait	MGM	
1993	KING'S PIRATE	WEIS	UNIVERSAL	1967
1993	PLUMB DUMB (sh)	TAUROG	EDUCATIONAL FILM	1927
1993E	PIER ANGELI	portrait	MGM	
1994	BRONCHO EXPRESS (sh)	AUSTIN	EDUCATIONAL FILM	1924
1994	ROBERT TAYLOR	portrait	MGM	
1995E	PIER ANGELI	portrait	MGM	
1997	LESLIE CARON	portrait	MGM	
1999	GALE STORM SHOW: SUSANNA, THE BABYSITTER	SEITER	CBS-TV	1959
1999E	PIER ANGELI	portrait	MGM	
2000	MARIO LANZA	portrait	MGM	
2001	MARIO LANZA	portrait	MGM	
2002	HAIL, THE CONQUERING HERO	STURGES	PARAMOUNT	1944
2002	LESLIE CARON	portrait	MGM	
2002	MARIO LANZA	portrait	MGM	
2002E	PIER ANGELI	portrait	MGM	
2003	MARIO LANZA	portrait	MGM	
2004	MARIO LANZA	portrait	MGM	
2004	ROBERT TAYLOR	portrait	MGM	
2004	STORY OF DR. WASSELL	DEMILLE	PARAMOUNT	1944
2005	FRENCHMAN'S CREEK	LEISEN	PARAMOUNT	1944
2005	LESLIE CARON	portrait	MGM	
2005	MARIO LANZA	portrait	MGM	

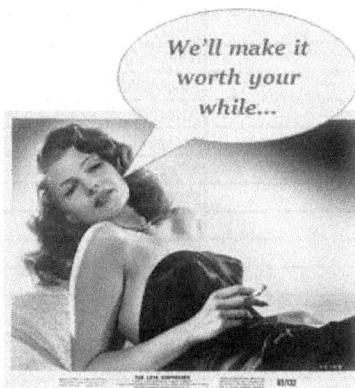

2005	ROBERT TAYLOR	portrait	MGM	
2006	MARIO LANZA	portrait	MGM	
2007	MARIO LANZA	portrait	MGM	
2008	JOAN CRAWFORD	portrait	MGM	
2013	MAURICE CHEVALIER	portrait	MGM	
2014	ROBERT TAYLOR	portrait	MGM	
2020	TILL WE MEET AGAIN	BORZAGE	PARAMOUNT	1944
2024	KAREN MORLEY	portrait	MGM	
2024	ONE BODY TOO MANY	MCDONALD	PARAMOUNT	1944
2026	BARBARA STANWYCK	portrait	MGM	
2026	JEAN HAGEN	portrait	MGM	
2027	JEAN HAGEN	portrait	MGM	
2028	JEAN HAGEN	portrait	MGM	
2028	WALLACE BEERY	portrait	MGM	
2029	JEAN HAGEN	portrait	MGM	
2030	JEAN HAGEN	portrait	MGM	
2031	JEAN HAGEN	portrait	MGM	
2032	JEAN HAGEN	portrait	MGM	
2033	HOWARD KEEL	portrait	MGM	
2033	JEAN HAGEN	portrait	MGM	
2034	JEAN HAGEN	portrait	MGM	
2035	JEAN HAGEN	portrait	MGM	
2036	FRANK MORGAN	portrait	MGM	
2037	FRANK MORGAN	portrait	MGM	
2043	FRANK MORGAN	portrait	MGM	
2043E	DEBBIE REYNOLDS	portrait	MGM	
2044	FRANK MORGAN	portrait	MGM	
2045	FRANK MORGAN	portrait	MGM	
2045	I LOVE MY HUSBAND BUT ...	O'BRIEN	MGM	1946
2048	FRANK MORGAN	portrait	MGM	
2048	MARJORIE MAIN	portrait	MGM	
2053	FERNANDO LAMAS	portrait	MGM	
2054	FERNANDO LAMAS	portrait	MGM	
2055	FERNANDO LAMAS	portrait	MGM	
2056	ELIZABETH TAYLOR	portrait	MGM	
2059	VIRGINIA GREY	portrait	MGM	
2067	HEDY LAMARR	portrait	MGM	
2070	GRETA GARBO	portrait	MGM	
2078	DENISE DARCEL	portrait	MGM	
2081	RED SKELTON, WIFE, CHILDREN	portrait	MGM	
2084	DEBORAH KERR	portrait	MGM	
2084	WALLACE BEERY	portrait	MGM	
2093	RAMON NOVARRO	portrait	MGM	
2102	MICKEY ROONEY	portrait	MGM	
2110	RAMON NOVARRO	portrait	MGM	
2111	RAMON NOVARRO	portrait	MGM	
2114	KATHRYN GRAYSON	portrait	MGM	
2115	KATHRYN GRAYSON	portrait	MGM	
2116	KATHRYN GRAYSON	portrait	MGM	
2117	KATHRYN GRAYSON	portrait	MGM	
2121	GREER GARSON. MOTHER, HUSBAND RICHARD NEY	portrait	MGM	
2127	GREER GARSON. MOTHER, HUSBAND RICHARD NEY	portrait	MGM	
2131	GREER GARSON. MOTHER, HUSBAND RICHARD NEY	portrait	MGM	
2132	SMOKEY AND THE BANDIT II	NEEDHAM	UNIVERSAL	1980
2134	ALL NIGHT LONG	TRAMONT	UNIVERSAL	1981
2135	DEBORAH KERR	portrait	MGM	
2135	FOUR SEASONS	ALDA	UNIVERSAL	1981
2136	HEARTBEEPS	ARKUSH	UNIVERSAL	1981
2137	BORDER	RICHARDSON	UNIVERSAL-RKO	1982
2138	RAGGEDY MAN	FISK	UNIVERSAL	1981
2140	CONTINENTAL DIVIDE	APTED	UNIVERSAL	1981
2140	EVA GABOR	portrait	MGM	
2141	GHOST STORY	IRVIN	UNIVERSAL	1981
2142	ZOOT SUIT	VALDEZ	UNIVERSAL	1981
2144	ELAINE STEWART	portrait	MGM	
2144	MISSING	GAVRAS	UNIVERSAL	1982

2145	ELAINE STEWART	portrait	MGM	
2145	STING II	KAGAN	UNIVERSAL	1983
2146	THING	CARPENTER	UNIVERSAL	1982
2147	FAST TIMES AT RIDGEMONT HIGH	HECKERLING	UNIVERSAL	1982
2148	EDDIE MACON'S RUN	KANEW	UNIVERSAL	1983
2149	MYRNA LOY	portrait	MGM	
2149	PSYCHO II	FRANKLIN	UNIVERSAL	1983
2150	DOCTOR DETROIT	PRESSMAN	UNIVERSAL	1983
2151	GOING BERSERK	STEINBERG	UNIVERSAL	1983
2154	SCARFACE	DE PALMA	UNIVERSAL	1983
2156	D. C. CAB	SCHUMACHER	UNIVERSAL	1983
2158	NIGHTMARES	SARGENT	UNIVERSAL	1983
2159	SIXTEEN CANDLES	HUGHES	UNIVERSAL	1984
2160	CLOCK & DAGGER	FRANKLIN	UNIVERSAL	1984
2161	RIVER	RYDELL	UNIVERSAL	1984
2162	STICK	REYNOLDS	UNIVERSAL	1985
2163	WILD LIFE, THE	LINSON	UNIVERSAL	1984
2165	MASK	BOGDANOVICH	UNIVERSAL	1984
2166	BREWSTER'S MILLIONS	HILL	UNIVERSAL	1985
2167	FLETCH	RITCHIE	UNIVERSAL	1985
2170	ESTHER WILLIAMS	portrait	MGM	
2170	GOTCHA!	KANEW	UNIVERSAL	1984
2171	BACK TO THE FUTURE	SPIELBERG	UNIVERSAL	1985
2172	OUT OF AFRICA	POLLACK	UNIVERSAL	1985
2174	SWEET LIBERTY	ALDA	UNIVERSAL	1986
2175	PSYCHO III	PERKINS	UNIVERSAL	1986
2177	LEGAL EAGLES	REITMAN	UNIVERSAL	1986
2178	HARRY AND THE HENDERSONS	DEAR	UNIVERSAL	1987
2179	SECRET OF MY SUCCESS	ROSS	RASTAR	1987
2180	DEBBIE REYNOLDS	portrait	MGM	
2183	CROSS MY HEART	BERNSTEIN	UNIVERSAL	1987
2184	DEBBIE REYNOLDS	portrait	MGM	
2184	JAWS THE REVENGE	SARGENT	UNIVERSAL	1987
2185	BILOXI BLUES	NICHOLS	RASTAR	1988
2186	MOON OVER PARADOR	MAZURSKY	UNIVERSAL	1988
2188	DEBBIE REYNOLDS	portrait	MGM	
2188	MIDNIGHT RUN	BREST	UNIVERSAL	1988
2189	SEA OF LOVE	BECKER	UNIVERSAL	1989
2190	DEBBIE REYNOLDS	portrait	MGM	
2193	DAD	GOLDBERG	UNIVERSAL	1989
2193	DEBBIE REYNOLDS	portrait	MGM	
2194	BIRD ON A WIRE	BADHAM	UNIVERSAL	1990
2194	DEBBIE REYNOLDS	portrait	MGM	
2197	DEBBIE REYNOLDS	portrait	MGM	
2199	HARD WAY, THE	BADHAM	UNIVERSAL	1990
2199	ROBERT YOUNG	portrait	MGM	
2200	ANN SOTHERN	portrait	MGM	
2201	SHOUT	HORNADAY	UNIVERSAL	1991
2207	WE'RE BACK! A DINOSAUR'S STORY (t)	NIBBELINK, WELLS	UNIVERSAL	1993
2208	ELAINE STEWART	portrait	MGM	
2209	STOP! OR MY MOM WILL SHOOT	SPOTTISWOODE	UNIVERSAL	1992
2210	SNEAKERS	ROBINSON	UNIVERSAL	1992
2212	ELAINE STEWART	portrait	MGM	
2212	ROBERT TAYLOR	portrait	MGM	
2214	ELAINE STEWART	portrait	MGM	
2215	HEART AND SOULS	UNDERWOOD	UNIVERSAL	1993
2216	SCHINDLER'S LIST	SPIELBERG	UNIVERSAL	1993
2217	BALTO (t)	WELLS	UNIVERSAL	1995
2219	ELAINE STEWART	portrait	MGM	
2219	ROBERT TAYLOR	portrait	MGM	
2220	BEETHOVEN'S 2ND	DANIEL	UNIVERSAL	1993
2221	ELAINE STEWART	portrait	MGM	
2221	GREEDY	LYNN	UNIVERSAL	1994
2222	THE PAPER	HOWARD	UNIVERSAL	1994
2223	RIVER WILD	HANSON	UNIVERSAL	1994
2224	COWBOY WAY, THE	CHAMPION	UNIVERSAL	1994

2225	LITTLE RASCALS	SPHEERIS	UNIVERSAL	1994
2226	CASPER	SILBERLING	UNIVERSAL	1995
2227	JUNIOR	REITMAN	UNIVERSAL	1994
2228	TOO WONG FOO, THANKS FOR EVERYTHING JULIE NEWMAR	KIDRON	UNIVERSAL	1995
2228	UNA MERKEL	portrait	MGM	
2229	APOLLO 13	HOWARD	UNIVERSAL	1995
2230	ELAINE STEWART	portrait	MGM	
2230	HOW TO MAKE AN AMERICAN QUILT	MOORHOUSE	UNIVERSAL	1995
2232	BEVERLY TYLER	portrait	MGM	
2234	CASINO	SCORSESE	UNIVERAL	1995
2235	NUTTY PROFESSOR	SHADYAC	UNIVERSAL	1996
2235	UNA MERKEL	portrait	MGM	
2237	BETTA ST. JOHN, HUSBAND PETER GRANT	portrait	MGM	
2240	LOST WORLD: JURASSIC PARK	SPIELBERG	UNIVERSAL	1997
2241	CHAMBER, THE	FOLEY	UNIVERSAL	1996
2242	BULLETPROOF	DICKERSON	UNIVERSAL	1996
2243	LIAR LIAR	SHADYAC	UNIVERSAL	1997
2244	DANTE'S PEAK	DONALDSON	UNIVERSAL	1997
2252	RICARDO MONTALBAN	portrait	MGM	
2254	KEENAN WYNN, FATHER ED WYNN	portrait	MGM	
2258	FLINTSTONES IN VIVA ROCK VEGAS	LEVANT	UNIVERSAL	2000
2260	MAN ON THE MOON	FORMAN	UNIVERSAL	1999
2262	NUTTY PROFESSOR II: THE KLUMPS	SEGAL	UNIVERSAL	2000
2263	LESLIE CARON	portrait	MGM	
2264	GINNY SIMMS	portrait	MGM	
2273	GINNY SIMMS	portrait	MGM	
2273	LANA TURNER, DAUGHTER CHERYL	portrait	MGM	
2273	MARSHA HUNT, HUSBAND ROBERT PRESNELL JR	portrait	MGM	
2274	GINNY SIMMS	portrait	MGM	
2275	LESLIE CARON	portrait	MGM	
2275	MARSHA HUNT, HUSBAND ROBERT PRESNELL JR	portrait	MGM	
2276	LESLIE CARON	portrait	MGM	
2277	LESLIE CARON	portrait	MGM	
2278	LESLIE CARON	portrait	MGM	
2279	AMERICAN PIE 2	ROGERS	UNIVERSAL	2001
2279	LESLIE CARON	portrait	MGM	
2281	BIG FAT LIAR	LEVY	UNIVERSAL	2002
2281	DONNA REED	portrait	MGM	
2282	DONNA REED	portrait	MGM	
2283	GINNY SIMMS	portrait	MGM	
2292	DONNA REED	portrait	MGM	
2305	ANN BLYTH	portrait	MGM	
2310	PIER ANGELI	portrait	MGM	
2316	PIER ANGELI	portrait	MGM	
2325	ANITA PAGE	portrait	MGM	
2327	ANN BLYTH	portrait	MGM	
2328	JOAN CRAWFORD	portrait	MGM	
2339	COLLEEN MOORE	portrait	MGM	
2340	CHESTER MORRIS	portrait	MGM	
2347	CHESTER MORRIS, DAUGHTER CYNTHIA	portrait	MGM	
2355	ROBERT TAYLOR	portrait	MGM	
2358	ROBERT TAYLOR	portrait	MGM	
2360	ROBERT TAYLOR	portrait	MGM	
2361	JANE POWELL	portrait	MGM	
2362	JANE POWELL	portrait	MGM	
2362	JANE POWELL	portrait	MGM	
2363	JANE POWELL	portrait	MGM	
2366	JANE POWELL	portrait	MGM	
2370	JANE POWELL	portrait	MGM	
2371	ANITA PAGE	portrait	MGM	
2373	JANE POWELL	portrait	MGM	
2374	ANITA PAGE	portrait	MGM	
2377	CALL YOUR SHOTS (sh)	ROBERTS	EDUCATIONAL FILM	1928
2378	POLAR PERILS (sh)	ROBERTS	EDUCATIONAL FILM	1928
2379	STAGE FRIGHTS (sh)	ROBERTS	EDUCATIONAL FILM	1928
2380	HOLD THAT MONKEY (sh)	WHITE	EDUCATIONAL FILM	1928

2381	HOT OR COLD (sh)	ROBERTS	EDUCATIONAL FILM	1928
2382	SOCIAL PRESTIGE (sh)	ROBERTS	EDUCATIONAL FILM	1928
2383	GOING PLACES (sh)		EDUCATIONAL FILM	1928
2384	WHOOPEE BOYS (sh)	ROBERTS	EDUCATIONAL FILM	1929
2385	SMART STEPPERS (sh)	ROBERTS	EDUCATIONAL FILM	1929
2386	PARLOR PESTS (sh)	ROBERTS	EDUCATIONAL FILM	1929
2387	HOWLING HOLLYWOOD (sh)	ROBERTS	EDUCATIONAL FILM	1929
2388	ROBERT TAYLOR	portrait	MGM	
2390	WHAT A DAY! (sh)	ROBERTS	EDUCATIONAL FILM	1929
2394	MISPLACED HUSBANDS (sh)	LAMONT	EDUCATIONAL FILM	1928
2394	UNA MERKEL	portrait	MGM	
2395	AUNTIE'S MISTAKE (sh)	LAMONT	EDUCATIONAL FILM	1929
2396	LONGEST DAY	MARTON	20th CENTURY FOX	1962
2400	HIGH LIFE (sh)	FAY	EDUCATIONAL FILM	1923
2410	HOT AIR (sh)	TAUROG	EDUCATIONAL FILM	1924
2411	PATRICIA OWENS	portrait	MGM	
2420	BARRY NELSON	portrait	MGM	
2420	PIER ANGELI (?)	portrait	MGM	
2421	GREER GARSON	portrait	MGM	
2421	PIER ANGELI	portrait	MGM	
2423	PIER ANGELI	portrait	MGM	
2428	ANGELA LANSBURY, RICHARD CROMWELL	portrait	MGM	
2436	GREER GARSON + MOTHER	portrait	MGM	
2437	MARTHA SLEEPER	portrait	MGM	
2438	GEORGE CUKOR	portrait	MGM	
2442	EATS FOR TWO (sh)	WHITE	EDUCATIONAL FILM	1927
2443	SHOOTING WILD (sh)	SANDRICH	EDUCATIONAL FILM	1927
2444	HE TRIED TO PLEASE (sh)	SWEET	EDUCATIONAL FILM	1927
2445	REST DAY (sh)	WHITE	EDUCATIONAL FILM	1927
2447	CLARK GABLE	portrait	MGM	
2449	VERA-ELLEN	portrait	MGM	
2453	BATTLING BELL BOY	BEAUDINE	UNIVERSAL	1917
2454	VERA-ELLEN	portrait	MGM	
2455	ELIZABETH ALLAN	portrait	MGM	
2459	THREE TOUGH ONIONS (sh)	WHITE	EDUCATIONAL FILM	1928
2460	CROWN ME (sh)	LANE	EDUCATIONAL FILM	1928
2462	OH, MAMA! (sh)	WHITE	EDUCATIONAL FILM	1928
2463	LOST LAUGH (sh)	ROBERTS	EDUCATIONAL FILM	1928
2463	MAUREEN O'SULLIVAN	portrait	MGM	
2463	ROBERT TAYLOR	portrait	MGM	
2464	HARD WORK (sh)	WHITE	EDUCATIONAL FILM	1928
2464	LANA TURNER	portrait	MGM	
2465	WEDDED BLISTERS (sh)	WHITE	EDUCATIONAL FILM	1928
2467	HUSBANDS MUST PLAY (sh)	WHITE	EDUCATIONAL FILM	1929
2472	PATRICIA OWENS	portrait	MGM	
2474	DUMMIES (sh)	SEMON	EDUCATIONAL FILM	1928
2474	MAUREEN O'SULLIVAN	portrait	MGM	
2475	LANA TURNER	portrait	MGM	
2478	CLARK GABLE	portrait	MGM	
2494	BE MY KING (sh)	LANE	EDUCATIONAL FILM	1928
2495	ONLY ME (sh)	LANE	EDUCATIONAL FILM	1929
2497	GOOD NIGHT NURSE (sh)	LANE	EDUCATIONAL FILM	1929
2498	BATTLING SISTERS (sh)	LANE	EDUCATIONAL FILM	1929
2499	JOY LAND (sh)	LANE	EDUCATIONAL FILM	1929
2500	HOT LUCK (sh)	LAMONT	EDUCATIONAL FILM	1928
2501	COME TO PAPA (sh)	LAMONT	EDUCATIONAL FILM	1928
2502	FOLLOW TEACHER (sh)	LAMONT	EDUCATIONAL FILM	1928
2503	FIXER (sh)	LAMONT	EDUCATIONAL FILM	1929
2504	GINGER SNAPS (sh)	LAMONT	EDUCATIONAL FILM	1929
2505	JOY TONIC (sh)	LAMONT	EDUCATIONAL FILM	1929
2506	HELTER SKELTER (sh)	LAMONT	EDUCATIONAL FILM	1929
2507	SOLE SUPPORT (sh)	LAMONT	EDUCATIONAL FILM	1929
2510	BARBARA LANG	portrait	MGM	
2510	TROUBLES GALORE (sh)	MARTIN	EDUCATIONAL FILM	1928
2512	SPENCER TRACY	portrait	MGM	
2516	PIER ANGELI	portrait	MGM	

2518	MURDER WILL OUT (sh)	WHITE	EDUCATIONAL FILM	1928
2519	IN THE MORNING (sh)	MARTIN	EDUCATIONAL FILM	1928
2523	PEP UP (sh)	MARTIN	EDUCATIONAL FILM	1929
2523S	WHAT DO YOU THINK #2	FEIST	MGM	1937
2524	HER BIG BEN (sh)	WHITE	EDUCATIONAL FILM	1929
2525	TIME TO EXPIRE (sh)	MARTIN	EDUCATIONAL FILM	1929
2527	DELICIOUS AND REFRESHING (sh)	MARTIN	EDUCATIONAL FILM	1929
2527S	WHAT DO YOU THINK #3	TOURNEUR	MGM	1938
2530	HOUSEHOLD BLUES (sh)	WHITE	EDUCATIONAL FILM	1929
2531E	CYD CHARISSE	portrait	MGM	
2532	RUBBING IT IN (sh)	MARTIN	EDUCATIONAL FILM	1929
2533	JACKIE COOPER	portrait	MGM	
2535	HOT SPORTS (sh)	WHITE	EDUCATIONAL FILM	1929
2535E	CYD CHARISSE	portrait	MGM	
2545	CYD CHARISSE	portrait	MGM	
2546	MARSHALL THOMPSON	portrait	MGM	
2547	CYD CHARISSE	portrait	MGM	
2551	MARSHALL THOMPSON	portrait	MGM	
2552	GIRLIES BEHAVE (sh)	LAMONT	EDUCATIONAL FILM	1928
2553	QUIET WORKER (sh)	LAMONT	EDUCATIONAL FILM	1928
2554	WIVES WON'T WEAKEN (sh)	ROBERTS	EDUCATIONAL FILM	1928
2556	WISE WIMMIN (sh)	ROBERTS	EDUCATIONAL FILM	1929
2557	ONLY HER HUSBAND (sh)	LAMONT	EDUCATIONAL FILM	1929
2558	STUDIO PESTS (sh)	ROBERTS	EDUCATIONAL FILM	1929
2559	FAKE FLAPPERS (sh)	LAMONT	EDUCATIONAL FILM	1929
2572	LITTLE RUBE (sh)	TAUROG	EDUCATIONAL FILM	1927
2574	CIRCUS BLUES (sh)	LAMONT	EDUCATIONAL FILM	1928
2578	JEAN HAGEN + HER CHILDREN	portrait	MGM	
2578 (3)	UNSEEN GUARDIANS	WRANGELL	MGM	1939
2580	CLARK GABLE	portrait	MGM	
2580	LIVE NEWS (sh)	LAMONT	EDUCATIONAL FILM	1927
2581	SCARED SILLY (sh)	LAMONT	EDUCATIONAL FILM	1927
2582	WILDCAT VALLEY (sh)	LAMONT	EDUCATIONAL FILM	1927
2583	VISITORS WELCOME (sh)	SWEET	EDUCATIONAL FILM	1928
2584	SLIPPERY HEAD (sh)	TAUROG	EDUCATIONAL FILM	1928
2584E	BETTA ST. JOHN	portrait	MGM	
2585	ALICE WEAVER	portrait	MGM	
2585	BLONDES BEWARE (sh)	TAUROG	EDUCATIONAL FILM	1928
2593	AVA GARDNER	portrait	MGM	
2594E	ELAINE STEWART	portrait	MGM	
2608	GREER GARSON	portrait	MGM	
2608	JEAN SIMMONS	portrait	MGM	
2608	PIER ANGELI	portrait	MGM	
2609	JEAN SIMMONS	portrait	MGM	
2609	PIER ANGELI	portrait	MGM	
2610	JEAN SIMMONS	portrait	MGM	
2611	GREER GARSON	portrait	MGM	
2612	BUYING A GUN (sh)	LANE	EDUCATIONAL FILM	1929
2612	JEAN SIMMONS	portrait	MGM	
2613	PIER ANGELI	portrait	MGM	
2614	FIRE PROOF (sh)	LAMONT	EDUCATIONAL FILM	1929
2614	JAMES STEWART	portrait	MGM	
2614	JEAN SIMMONS	portrait	MGM	
2615	PURELY CIRCUMSTANTIAL (sh)	LANE	EDUCATIONAL FILM	1929
2616	JEAN SIMMONS	portrait	MGM	
2616	PIER ANGELI	portrait	MGM	
2617	JEAN SIMMONS	portrait	MGM	
2618	JEAN SIMMONS	portrait	MGM	
2619	HAIL THE PRINCESS (sh)	ROBERTS	EDUCATIONAL FILM	1930
2619	JEAN SIMMONS	portrait	MGM	
2620	RICHARD NEY	portrait	MGM	
2621	GREER GARSON + HUSBAND RICHARD NEY	portrait	MGM	
2622	JEAN SIMMONS	portrait	MGM	
2622	OVER THE FENCE (sh)	MONTGOMERY	EDUCATIONAL FILM	1923
2623	ABOUT FACE (sh)	GILLSTROM	EDUCATIONAL FILM	1924
2624	BARNUM JUNIOR (sh)	GILLSTROM	EDUCATIONAL FILM	1924

2624	JEAN SIMMONS	portrait	MGM	
2625	JEAN SIMMONS	portrait	MGM	
2625	MICKEY ROONEY	portrait	MGM	
2626	GREER GARSON + HUSBAND RICHARD NEY	portrait	MGM	
2626	JEAN SIMMONS	portrait	MGM	
2627	JEAN SIMMONS	portrait	MGM	
2629	JEAN SIMMONS	portrait	MGM	
2631	FRONT! (sh)		EDUCATIONAL FILM	1923
2632	WALLACE BEERY	portrait	MGM	
2633	WALLACE BEERY	portrait	MGM	
2634	NEW SHERIFF (sh)		EDUCATIONAL FILM	1924
2634	WALLACE BEERY	portrait	MGM	
2635	BONEHEAD (sh)		EDUCATIONAL FILM	1924
2636	HIS FIRST CAR (sh)	ST. JOHN	EDUCATIONAL FILM	1924
2640	GRANDMA'S GIRL (sh)	SENNETT	EDUCATIONAL FILM	1930
2640	JEAN SIMMONS	portrait	MGM	
2641	DIVORCED SWEETHEARTS	SENNETT	EDUCATIONAL FILM	1930
2642	RACKET CHEERS (sh)	SENNETT	EDUCATIONAL FILM	1930
2643	DON'T BITE YOUR DENTIST (sh)	CLINE	EDUCATIONAL FILM	1930
2644	NO, NO, LADY	CLINE	EDUCATIONAL FILM	1931
2645	CHUNG TUY TREASURE (unfinished)		UNIVERSAL	
2645	ROUGH IDEA OF LOVE (sh)	SENNETT	EDUCATIONAL FILM	1930
2646	HOLLYWOOD THEME SONG (sh)	BEAUDINE	EDUCATIONAL FILM	1930
2647	DANCE HALL MARGE (sh)	SENNETT, LORD	EDUCATIONAL FILM	1931
2648	ONE YARD TO GO (sh)	BEAUDINE	EDUCATIONAL FILM	1931
2648E	PIER ANGELI	portrait	MGM	
2649	COLLEGE VAMP	BEAUDINE	EDUCATIONAL FILM	1931
2649	ROBERT MONTGOMERY	portrait	MGM	
2649E	PIER ANGELI	portrait	MGM	
2650	BRIDE'S MISTAKE (sh)	RODNEY	EDUCATIONAL FILM	1931
2650	ROBERT MONTGOMERY	portrait	MGM	
2650E	PIER ANGELI	portrait	MGM	
2650S	DOOR WILL OPEN	SIDNEY	MGM	1940
2651	DOG DOCTOR (sh)	WHITMAN	EDUCATIONAL FILM	1931
2652	GRETA GARBO	portrait	MGM	
2652	JUST A BEAR (sh)	STAFFORD	EDUCATIONAL FILM	1931
2652	ROBERT MONTGOMERY	portrait	MGM	
2653	EX-SWEETIES (sh)	NEILAN	EDUCATIONAL FILM	1931
2653E	PIER ANGELI	portrait	MGM	
2654	IN CONFERENCE (sh)	CLINE	EDUCATIONAL FILM	1931
2654E	PIER ANGELI	portrait	MGM	
2655	SPEED (sh)		EDUCATIONAL FILM	1931
2656	COWCATCHER'S DAUGHTER (sh)	STAFFORD	EDUCATIONAL FILM	1931
2657	GHOST PARADE (sh)	SENNETT	EDUCATIONAL FILM	1931
2658	HOLD 'ER SHERIFF (sh)	SENNETT	EDUCATIONAL FILM	1931
2659	MOVIE TOWN	SENNETT	EDUCATIONAL FILM	1931
2660	MONKEY BUSINESS IN AFRICA (sh)	SENNETT	EDUCATIONAL FILM	1931
2661	SLIDE, SPEEDY, SLIDE (sh)	STAFFORD	EDUCATIONAL FILM	1931
2662	ALBANY BRANCH (sh)	SENNETT	EDUCATIONAL FILM	1931
2663	FAINTING LOVER	SENNETT	EDUCATIONAL FILM	1931
2664	I SURRENDER, DEAR (sh)	SENNETT	EDUCATIONAL FILM	1931
2664	TOO MANY HUSBANDS (sh)	PEARCE	EDUCATIONAL FILM	1931
2665	POKER WIDOWS (sh)	PEARCE	EDUCATIONAL FILM	1931
2667	UP A TREE (sh)	ARBUCKLE	EDUCATIONAL FILM	1930
2668	MARRIAGE ROWS (sh)	ARBUCKLE	EDUCATIONAL FILM	1931
2669	EX-PLUMBER (sh)	ARBUCKLE	EDUCATIONAL FILM	1931
2679	EXPENSIVE KISSES (sh)	WATSON	EDUCATIONAL FILM	1930
2680	GIRLS WILL BE BOYS (sh)	WATSON	EDUCATIONAL FILM	1931
2681	BRIDE AND GLOOMY (sh)	PEARCE	EDUCATIONAL FILM	1931
2682	DON'T DIVORCE HIM (sh)	WATSON	EDUCATIONAL FILM	1931
2683	ELIZABETH TAYLOR, HUSBAND MICHAEL & SON	portrait	MGM	
2683	GRETA GARBO	portrait	MGM	
2683	WHAT A HEAD! (sh)	HALL	EDUCATIONAL FILM	1931
2684	ILONA MASSEY	portrait	MGM	
2684	JOHNNY'S WEEK END (sh)	WATSON	EDUCATIONAL FILM	1930
2685	OUR NAGGING WIVES (sh)	GILLSTROM	EDUCATIONAL FILM	1930

2686	DON'T LEAVE HOME (sh)	WATSON	EDUCATIONAL FILM	1930
2687	COME TO PAPA (sh)	WATSON	EDUCATIONAL FILM	1931
2687	KATY JURADO	portrait	MGM	
2688	FOWL AFFAIR (sh)		EDUCATIONAL FILM	1931
2688	KATY JURADO	portrait	MGM	
2690	KATY JURADO	portrait	MGM	
2691	DON'T GIVE UP (sh)	WATSON	EDUCATIONAL FILM	1930
2692	COLLEGE CUTIES (sh)	ROSS	EDUCATIONAL FILM	1930
2693	ESTHER WILLIAMS AT 3	portrait	MGM	
2693	HAPPY LITTLE HONEYMOON (sh)	BEAUDINE	EDUCATIONAL FILM	1931
2694	SHOTGUN WEDDING (sh)	WATSON	EDUCATIONAL FILM	1931
2695	COLLEGE RACKET (sh)	BEAUDINE	EDUCATIONAL FILM	1931
2695	VIRGINIA GREY	portrait	MGM	
2695	WALLACE BEERY + FATHER NOAH BEERY	portrait	MGM	
2697	LOVE A LA MODE (sh)	ROBERTS	EDUCATIONAL FILM	1930
2698	THEIR WIVES VACATION (sh)	WATSON	EDUCATIONAL FILM	1930
2699	LOVE BARGAIN (sh)	GILLSTROM	EDUCATIONAL FILM	1931
2700	SHOOTING OF DAN, THE DUCK (sh)	GILLSTROM	EDUCATIONAL FILM	1931
2701	WINDY RILEY GOES HOLLYWOOD (sh)	ARBUCKLE	EDUCATIONAL FILM	1931
2702	BACK PAGE (sh)	ARBUCKLE	EDUCATIONAL FILM	1931
2705	MY HAREM (sh)	ROBERTS	EDUCATIONAL FILM	1930
2706	THREE HOLLYWOOD GIRLS (sh)	ARBUCKLE	EDUCATIONAL FILM	1931
2707	PETE AND REPEAT (sh)	ARBUCKLE	EDUCATIONAL FILM	1931
2708	CRASHING HOLLYWOOD (sh)	ARBUCKLE	EDUCATIONAL FILM	1931
2709	LURE OF HOLLYWOOD (sh)	ARBUCKLE	EDUCATIONAL FILM	1931
2710	CHOP SUEY (t) (sh)	MOSER	EDUCATIONAL FILM	1930
2711	FRENCH FRIED (t) (sh)	MOSER	EDUCATIONAL FILM	1930
2712	DUTCH TREAT (t) (sh)	MOSER	EDUCATIONAL FILM	1930
2713	IRISH STEW (t) (sh)	MOSER	EDUCATIONAL FILM	1930
2714	FRIED CHICKEN (t) (sh)	MOSER	EDUCATIONAL FILM	1930
2715	JUMPING BEAN (t) (sh)	MOSER	EDUCATIONAL FILM	1930
2715E	KATY JURADO	portrait	MGM	
2716	SCOTCH HIGHBALL (sh)			
2716E	KATY JURADO	portrait	MGM	
2717	SALT WATER TUFFY (t) (sh)	MOSER	EDUCATIONAL FILM	1930
2717E	KATY JURADO	portrait	MGM	
2718	KATY JURADO	portrait	MGM	
2719	LANA TURNER	portrait	MGM	
2719	PIGSKIN CAPERS (t) (sh)	MOSER	EDUCATIONAL FILM	1930
2720	POPCORN (t) (sh)	MOSER	EDUCATIONAL FILM	1931
2721	CLUB SANDWICH (t) (sh)	MOSER	EDUCATIONAL FILM	1931
2722	MARSHA HUNT, HUSBAND ROBERT PRESNELL JR	portrait	MGM	
2722	RAZZBERRIES (t) (sh)	MOSER	EDUCATIONAL FILM	1931
2723	GO WEST, BIG BOY (t) (sh)	MOSER	EDUCATIONAL FILM	1931
2724	QUACK, QUACK (t) (sh)	MOSER	EDUCATIONAL FILM	1931
2725	EXPLORER (t) (sh)	MOSER	EDUCATIONAL FILM	1931
2726	CLOWNING (t) (sh)	MOSER	EDUCATIONAL FILM	1931
2727	SING SING SONG (t) (sh)	MOSER	EDUCATIONAL FILM	1931
2728	FIREMAN'S BRIDE (t) (sh)	MOSER	EDUCATIONAL FILM	1931
2729	SULTAN'S CAT (t) (sh)	MOSER	EDUCATIONAL FILM	1931
2730	DAY TO LIVE (t) (sh)	MOSER	EDUCATIONAL FILM	1931
2730	DEBBIE REYNOLDS	portrait	MGM	
2731	2000 B.C. (t) (sh)	MOSER	EDUCATIONAL FILM	1930
2732	BLUES (t) (sh)	MOSER	EDUCATIONAL FILM	1931
2733	BY THE SEA (t) (sh)	MOSER	EDUCATIONAL FILM	1931
2734	HER FIRST EGG (t) (sh)	MOSER	EDUCATIONAL FILM	1931
2735	JAZZ MAD (t) (sh)	MOSER	EDUCATIONAL FILM	1931
2735	WALLACE BEERY	portrait	MGM	
2736	FLYING TRIP (sh) (Hodge Podge #83)	HOWE	EDUCATIONAL FILM	1930
2737	OVER THE AIR (sh) (Hodge Podge #84)	HOWE	EDUCATIONAL FILM	1930
2737	WALLACE BEERY	portrait	MGM	
2738	MEDLEY OF RIVERS (sh) (Hodge Podge #85)	HOWE	EDUCATIONAL FILM	1930
2740	TIDBITS (sh) (Hodge Podge #87)	HOWE	EDUCATIONAL FILM	1931
2741	MONEYMAKERS OF MANHATTAN (sh) (Hodge Podge #89)	HOWE	EDUCATIONAL FILM	1931
2742	DEBBIE REYNOLDS	portrait	MGM	
2742	JUNGLE GIANTS (sh) (Hodge Podge #88)	HOWE	EDUCATIONAL FILM	1931

2743	VAGABOND MELODIES (sh) (Hodge Podge #90)	HOWE	EDUCATIONAL FILM	1931
2744	HIGHLIGHTS OF TRAVEL (sh) (Hodge Podge #91)	HOWE	EDUCATIONAL FILM	1931
2748	BLUFFER (sh)	SENNETT	EDUCATIONAL FILM	1930
2748	DEBBIE REYNOLDS	portrait	MGM	
2749	TAKE YOUR MEDICINE (sh)	CLINE	EDUCATIONAL FILM	1930
2751	POOR FISH (sh)	SENNETT	EDUCATIONAL FILM	1931
2752S	DON'T LIE	CAHN	MGM	1942
2754	DEBBIE REYNOLDS	portrait	MGM	
2760	JOHNNY WEISSMULLER, JACKIE COOPER	portrait	MGM	
2760	WILKINS MURDER MYSTERS (sh)	REID	EDUCATIONAL FILM	1931
2761	COSTA RICAN CASE (sh)	REID	EDUCATIONAL FILM	1931
2761	DEBBIE REYNOLDS	portrait	MGM	
2761S	DON'T TALK	NEWMAN	MGM	1942
2762	ULRICH CASE	REID	EDUCATIONAL FILM	1931
2763	SUPPRESSED CRIME (sh)	REID	EDUCATIONAL FILM	1930
2765	ASBURY PARK MURDER MYSTERS (sh)	REID	EDUCATIONAL FILM	1930
2766	ANONYMOUS LETTER (sh)	REID	EDUCATIONAL FILM	1931
2767	BANK SWINDLE (sh)	REID	EDUCATIONAL FILM	1931
2768	BLACK WIDOW (sh)	REID	EDUCATIONAL FILM	1931
2768	WOMAN IN THE HOUSE	LEE	MGM	1942
2769	CYD CHARISSE + SON	portrait	MGM	
2769	TRIANGLE MURDER (sh)	REID	EDUCATIONAL FILM	1931
2770	RING LEADER (sh)	REID	EDUCATIONAL FILM	1931
2772	DEATH HOUSE (sh)	REID	EDUCATIONAL FILM	1931
2773	FRAMED (sh)	REID	EDUCATIONAL FILM	1931
2774	THAYER TRIAL (sh)		EDUCATIONAL FILM	1931
2775	STARBRITE DIAMOND (sh)	REID	EDUCATIONAL FILM	1931
2776	MEADE TRIAL (sh)	REID	EDUCATIONAL FILM	1931
2777	DOUBLE CROSS (sh)	REID	EDUCATIONAL FILM	1931
2777	JACKIE COOPER	portrait	MGM	
2778	FOILED (sh)	REID	EDUCATIONAL FILM	1931
2779	ANTHONY CASE (sh)	REID	EDUCATIONAL FILM	1931
2784	CYD CHARISSE	portrait	MGM	
2786	HONEYMOON LAND (sh)		EDUCATIONAL FILM	1931
2787	CROSSROADS (sh)		EDUCATIONAL FILM	1931
2788	CYD CHARISSE	portrait	MGM	
2788	DREAM WORLD (sh)		EDUCATIONAL FILM	1931
2789	HAREM SECRETS (sh)		EDUCATIONAL FILM	1931
2791	PEASANTS PARADISE (sh)		EDUCATIONAL FILM	1931
2792	ACROSS THE SEA (sh)		EDUCATIONAL FILM	1931
2792	FRANCES GIFFORD	portrait	MGM	
2793	ROAD TO ROMANCE (sh)		EDUCATIONAL FILM	1931
2794	ELIZABETH TAYLOR AT 9, BROTHER HOWARD	portrait	MGM	
2794	TREASURE ISLE (sh)		EDUCATIONAL FILM	1932
2795	CYD CHARISSE	portrait	MGM	
2795	JOHN BARRYMORE	portrait	MGM	
2795	LAST RACE (sh)		EDUCATIONAL FILM	1932
2796	CYD CHARISSE	portrait	MGM	
2796	MEDITERRANEAN BLUES (sh)		EDUCATIONAL FILM	1932
2797A	CYD CHARISSE	portrait	MGM	
2798	CYD CHARISSE	portrait	MGM	
2799	CYD CHARISSE	portrait	MGM	
2800	CANNONBALL (sh)	LORD, SENNETT	EDUCATIONAL FILM	1931
2801	CYD CHARISSE	portrait	MGM	
2801	TAXI TROUBLES (sh)	LORD	EDUCATIONAL FILM	1931
2802	CYD CHARISSE	portrait	MGM	
2802	HALF HOLIDAY (sh)	STAFFORD	EDUCATIONAL FILM	1931
2803	CYD CHARISSE	portrait	MGM	
2803	SHOPPING WITH WIFIE (sh)	STAFFORD	EDUCATIONAL FILM	1932
2804	CYD CHARISSE	portrait	MGM	
2804	SPEED IN THE GAY NINETIES (sh)	LORD	EDUCATIONAL FILM	1932
2805	FOR THE LOVE OF LUDWIG (sh)	HARBERGER	EDUCATIONAL FILM	1932
2805	HEAVENS! MY HUSBAND! (sh)	STAFFORD	EDUCATIONAL FILM	1932
2806	BOUDOIR BUTLER (sh)	PEARCE	EDUCATIONAL FILM	1932
2807	ALASKA LOVE	STAFFORD	EDUCATIONAL FILM	1932
2807	CYD CHARISSE	portrait	MGM	

2807	HIS ROYAL SHYNESS (sh)	PEARCE	EDUCATIONAL FILM	1932
2808	CYD CHARISSE	portrait	MGM	
2808	I SURRENDER, DEAR (sh)	SENNETT	EDUCATIONAL FILM	1931
2808	NORMA SHEARER	portrait	MGM	
2809	CYD CHARISSE	portrait	MGM	
2809	NORMA SHEARER	portrait	MGM	
2809	ONE MORE CHANCE (sh)	SENNETT	EDUCATIONAL FILM	1931
2810	BILLBOARD GIRL (sh)	PEARCE	EDUCATIONAL FILM	1932
2810	CYD CHARISSE	portrait	MGM	
2810	NORMA SHEARER	portrait	MGM	
2811	CYD CHARISSE	portrait	MGM	
2811	DREAM HOUSE (sh)	LORD	EDUCATIONAL FILM	1932
2811	NORMA SHEARER	portrait	MGM	
2812	NORMA SHEARER	portrait	MGM	
2812	SPOT ON THE RUG (sh)	LORD	EDUCATIONAL FILM	1932
2813	HATTA MARRI (sh)	STAFFORD	EDUCATIONAL FILM	1932
2813	NORMA SHEARER	portrait	MGM	
2814	GREAT PIE MYSTERY (sh)	LORD	EDUCATIONAL FILM	1931
2814	NORMA SHEARER	portrait	MGM	
2815	ALL AMERICAN KICKBACK (sh)	LORD	EDUCATIONAL FILM	1931
2815	CYD CHARISSE	portrait	MGM	
2815	NORMA SHEARER	portrait	MGM	
2816	CYD CHARISSE	portrait	MGM	
2816	POTTSVILLE PALOOKA (sh)	PEARCE	EDUCATIONAL FILM	1931
2817	CYD CHARISSE	portrait	MGM	
2817	GIRL IN THE TONNEAU (sh)	STAFFORD	EDUCATIONAL FILM	1932
2817S	DON'T YOU BELIEVE IT	CAHN	MGM	1943
2818	CYD CHARISSE	portrait	MGM	
2818	LADY! PLEASE! (sh)	STAFFORD	EDUCATIONAL FILM	1932
2819	FLIRTY SLEEPWALKER (sh)	LORD	EDUCATIONAL FILM	1932
2820	LISTENING IN (sh)	PEARCE	EDUCATIONAL FILM	1932
2821	DIVORCE A LA MODE (sh)	PEARCE	EDUCATIONAL FILM	1932
2821	MEET THE SENATOR (changed)	LORD	EDUCATIONAL FILM	1932
2822	CANDID CAMERA (sh)	PEARCE	EDUCATIONAL FILM	1932
2823	ALASKA LOVE (sh)	STAFFORD	EDUCATIONAL FILM	1932
2823	HATTA MARRI (sh) (mistake)	STAFFORD	EDUCATIONAL FILM	1932
2824	NEIGHBOR TROUBLE (sh)	PEARCE	EDUCATIONAL FILM	1932
2825	YOUNG ONIONS (sh)	EMMES	EDUCATIONAL FILM	1932
2826	FRESHMAN'S FINISH (sh)	WATSON	EDUCATIONAL FILM	1931
2827	GIRL RUSH (sh)	WATSON	EDUCATIONAL FILM	1931
2828	FOR THE LOVE OF FANNY (sh)	CHRISTIE	EDUCATIONAL FILM	1931
2829	GRACE KELLY - MOGAMBO	portrait	MGM	
2829	THAT RASCAL (sh)	CHRISTIE	EDUCATIONAL FILM	1932
2830	HE'S A HONEY (sh)	CHRISTIE	EDUCATIONAL FILM	1932
2831	NOW'S THE TIME (sh)		EDUCATIONAL FILM	1932
2832	DONNA REED	portrait	MGM	
2832	SHIP A HOOEY! (sh)	EDWARDS	EDUCATIONAL FILM	1932
2834	GRACE KELLY - MOGAMBO	portrait	MGM	
2834	UP POPS THE DUKE (sh)	ARBUCKLE	EDUCATIONAL FILM	1931
2835	ONCE A HERO (sh)	ARBUCKLE	EDUCATIONAL FILM	1931
2836	KEEP LAUGHING (sh)	ARBUCKLE	EDUCATIONAL FILM	1932
2837	DONNA REED	portrait	MGM	
2837	IT'S A CINCH (sh)	ARBUCKLE	EDUCATIONAL FILM	1932
2840	TAMALE VENDOR (sh)	ARBUCKLE	EDUCATIONAL FILM	1931
2841	FIRST AID	JASON	MGM	1943
2841	QUEENIE OF HOLLYWOOD (sh)	ARBUCKLE	EDUCATIONAL FILM	1931
2842	MOONLIGHT AND CACTUS (sh)	ARBUCKLE	EDUCATIONAL FILM	1932
2843	CLAIRE KELLY	portrait	MGM	
2843	HOLLYWOOD LUCK (sh)	ARBUCKLE	EDUCATIONAL FILM	1932
2844	HOLLYWOOD LIGHTS (sh)	ARBUCKLE	EDUCATIONAL FILM	1932
2846	TORCHY (sh)	BURR	EDUCATIONAL FILM	1931
2847	TORCHY PASSES THE BUCK (sh)	BURR	EDUCATIONAL FILM	1931
2848	TORCHY TURNS THE TRICK (sh)	BURR	EDUCATIONAL FILM	1932
2849	TORCHY'S NIGHT CAP (sh)	BURR	EDUCATIONAL FILM	1932
2850	TORCHY RAISES THE AUNTIE (sh)	BURR	EDUCATIONAL FILM	1932
2851	TORCHY'S TWO TOOTS (sh)	BURR	EDUCATIONAL FILM	1932

2852	CANADIAN CAPERS (t) (sh)	MOSER	EDUCATIONAL FILM	1931
2853	JESSE AND JAMES (t) (sh)	MOSER	EDUCATIONAL FILM	1931
2854	ANN BLYTH	portrait	MGM	
2854	CHAMP (t) (sh)	MOSER	EDUCATIONAL FILM	1931
2854	GLORIA GRAHAME	portrait	MGM	
2854	NORMA SHEARER	portrait	MGM	
2856	GLORIA GRAHAME	portrait	MGM	
2857	BLACK SPIDER (t) (sh)	MOSER	EDUCATIONAL FILM	1931
2858	CHINA (t) (sh)	MOSER	EDUCATIONAL FILM	1931
2859	JOAN CRAWFORD	portrait	MGM	
2859	LORELEI (t) (sh)	MOSER	EDUCATIONAL FILM	1931
2860	GLORIA GRAHAME	portrait	MGM	
2860	SUMMERTIME (t) (sh)	MOSER	EDUCATIONAL FILM	1931
2861	ALADDIN'S LAMP (t) (sh)	MOSER	EDUCATIONAL FILM	1931
2862	GLORIA GRAHAME	portrait	MGM	
2862	VILLAIN'S CURSE (t) (sh)	MOSER	EDUCATIONAL FILM	1931
2863	NOAH'S OUTING (t) (sh)	MOSER	EDUCATIONAL FILM	1931
2864	SPIDER TALKS (t) (sh)	MOSER	EDUCATIONAL FILM	1932
2865	GLORIA GRAHAME	portrait	MGM	
2865	PEG LEG PETE (t) (sh)	MOSER	EDUCATIONAL FILM	1932
2866	PLAY BALL (t) (sh)	MOSER	EDUCATIONAL FILM	1932
2867	YE OLDE SONGS (t) (sh)	MOSER	EDUCATIONAL FILM	1932
2868	BULL-ERO (t) (sh)	MOSER	EDUCATIONAL FILM	1932
2869	RADIO GIRL (t) (sh)	MOSER	EDUCATIONAL FILM	1932
2870	WOODLAND (t) (sh)	MOSER	EDUCATIONAL FILM	1932
2871	ROMANCE (t) (sh)	MOSER	EDUCATIONAL FILM	1932
2872	BLUEBEARD'S BROTHER (t) (sh)	MOSER	EDUCATIONAL FILM	1932
2872	FRANCES GIFFORD	portrait	MGM	
2873	FARMER ALFALFA'S BEDTIME STORY (t) (sh)	MOSER	EDUCATIONAL FILM	1932
2874	MAD KIND (t) (sh)	MOSER	EDUCATIONAL FILM	1932
2875	COCKY COCKROACH (t) (sh)	MOSER	EDUCATIONAL FILM	1932
2876	SPRING IS HERE (t) (sh)	MOSER	EDUCATIONAL FILM	1932
2877	FARMER ALFALFA'S APE GIRL (t) (sh)	MOSER	EDUCATIONAL FILM	1932
2878	HONEYMOON TRIO (sh)	ARBUCKLE	EDUCATIONAL FILM	1931
2878	UNA MERKEL	portrait	MGM	
2879	THAT'S MY MEAT (sh)	ARBUCKLE	EDUCATIONAL FILM	1931
2880	ONE QUIET NIGHT (sh)	ARBUCKLE	EDUCATIONAL FILM	1931
2881	IDLE ROOMERS (sh)	ARBUCKLE	EDUCATIONAL FILM	1931
2882	ROBERT MONTGOMERY	portrait	MGM	
2882	SMART WORK (sh)	ARBUCKLE	EDUCATIONAL FILM	1931
2883	ANYBODY'S GOAT (sh)	ARBUCKLE	EDUCATIONAL FILM	1932
2884	BRIDGE WIVES (sh)	ARBUCKLE	EDUCATIONAL FILM	1932
2885	MOTHER'S HOLIDAY (sh)	ARBUCKLE	EDUCATIONAL FILM	1932
2891	WORLD FLIER (sh)	LORD	EDUCATIONAL FILM	1931
2892	WHO'S WHO IN THE ZOO (sh)	STAFFORD	EDUCATIONAL FILM	1931
2893	FRED ZINNEMANN	portrait	MGM	
2894	CYD CHARISSE	portrait	MGM	
2895	CYD CHARISSE	portrait	MGM	
2895	ROBERT MONTGOMERY	portrait	MGM	
2896	CYD CHARISSE	portrait	MGM	
2898	CYD CHARISSE	portrait	MGM	
2898	ROBERT MONTGOMERY	portrait	MGM	
2901	FRANCES GIFFORD	portrait	MGM	
2903	TRAIL OF THE SWORDFISH (sh)	SENNETT	EDUCATIONAL FILM	1931
2904	WRESTLING SWORDFISH (sh)		EDUCATIONAL FILM	1931
2905	PLAYGROUND OF THE MAMMALS (sh)	SENNETT	EDUCATIONAL FILM	1932
2906	FRANCES GIFFORD	portrait	MGM	
2906	MAN-EATING SHARKS (sh)		EDUCATIONAL FILM	1932
2909	VELDT (sh) (Hodge Podge #93)	HOWE	EDUCATIONAL FILM	1931
2910	DONNA REED	portrait	MGM	
2910	PIER ANGELI	portrait	MGM	
2910	WONDER TRAIL (sh) (Hodge Podge #92)	HOWE	EDUCATIONAL FILM	1931
2911	ALL AROUND THE TOWN (sh) (Hodge Podge #94)	HOWE	EDUCATIONAL FILM	1932
2911	HEDY LAMARR	portrait	MGM	
2911	PIER ANGELI	portrait	MGM	
2912	PROWLERS (sh) (Hodge Podge #95)	HOWE	EDUCATIONAL FILM	1932

2913	FURY OF THE STORM (sh) (Hodge Podge #97)	HOWE	EDUCATIONAL FILM	1932
2914	BUBBLE BLOWERS (sh) (Hodge Podge #97)	HOWE	EDUCATIONAL FILM	1932
2914	NORMA SHEARER	portrait	MGM	
2915	NO HOLDS BARRED (sh)		EDUCATIONAL FILM	1931
2916	INSIDE BASEBALL (sh)	BROWN	EDUCATIONAL FILM	1931
2917	CANINE CAPERS (sh)	BROWN	EDUCATIONAL FILM	1931
2918	HE MAN HOCKEY (sh)	BROWN	EDUCATIONAL FILM	1931
2919	JEAN HAGEN	portrait	MGM	
2919	SPEEDWAY (sh)	BROWN	EDUCATIONAL FILM	1932
2920	HEDY LAMARR	portrait	MGM	
2920	JEAN HAGEN	portrait	MGM	
2920	THRILLS AND SPILLS (SLIDES AND GLIDES) (sh)	BROWN	EDUCATIONAL FILM	1932
2922	JEAN HAGEN	portrait	MGM	
2925	JEAN HAGEN	portrait	MGM	
2926	JEAN HAGEN	portrait	MGM	
2927	JEAN HAGEN	portrait	MGM	
2929	GINNY SIMMS	portrait	MGM	
2932	CYD CHARISSE	portrait	MGM	
2933	CYD CHARISSE	portrait	MGM	
2934	HEAVENS! MY HUSBAND! (sh)	STAFFORD	EDUCATIONAL FILM	1932
2935	GIDDY AGE (sh) (changed to 320101)	STAFFORD	EDUCATIONAL FILM	1932
2936	MILADY'S ESCAPADE (sh)		EDUCATIONAL FILM	1932
2937	VENDETTA (sh)		EDUCATIONAL FILM	1932
2938	IDOL OF SEVILLE (sh)		EDUCATIONAL FILM	1932
2942	WAR IN CHINA (sh)		EDUCATIONAL FILM	1932
2950	CYD CHARISSE	portrait	MGM	
2952	CYD CHARISSE	portrait	MGM	
2962	MICKEY ROONEY	portrait	MGM	
2965	MAUREEN O'SULLIVAN	portrait	MGM	
2977	FRANCES GIFFORD	portrait	MGM	
2982	ROBERT MONTGOMERY	portrait	MGM	
2987X	ELEANOR PARKER	portrait	MGM	
2995	ROBERT MONTGOMERY	portrait	MGM	
2999	WRONG SON	VON FRITSCH	MGM	1950
3000	3000 MILES TO GRACELAND	LICHTENSTEIN	WARNER BROS	2001
3000	AUDREY TOTTER	portrait	MGM	
3000	RED SKELTON + WIFE	portrait	MGM	
3000E	DEBBIE REYNOLDS	portrait	MGM	
3001	COWBOY FROM LONESOME RIVER	KLINE	COLUMBIA	1944
3002	CYCLONE PRAIRIE RANGERS	KLINE	COLUMBIA	1944
3003	COWBOY IN THE CLOUDS	KLINE	COLUMBIA	1943
3004	SUNDOWN VALLEY	KLINE	COLUMBIA	1944
3005	COWBOY CANTEEN	LANDERS	COLUMBIA	1944
3006	SADDLE LEATHER LAW	KLINE	COLUMBIA	1944
3007	SAGEBRUSH HEROES	KLINE	COLUMBIA	1945
3008	ROUGH RIDING JUSTICE	ABRAHAMS	COLUMBIA	1945
3009	SWING IN THE SADDLE	LANDERS	COLUMBIA	1944
3010	ANTHONY QUINN	portrait	MGM	
3010	AUDREY TOTTER	portrait	MGM	
3010	RETURN OF THE DURANGO KID	ABRAHAMS	COLUMBIA	1945
3011	BOTH BARRELS BLAZING	ABRAHAMS	COLUMBIA	1945
3012	AUDREY TOTTER	portrait	MGM	
3012	RUSTLERS OF THE BADLANDS	ABRAHAMS	COLUMBIA	1945
3013	AUDREY TOTTER	portrait	MGM	
3013	FRONTIER GUNLAW	ABRAHAMS	COLUMBIA	1946
3014	SING ME A SONG OF TEXAS	KEAYS	COLUMBIA	1945
3015	AUDREY TOTTER	portrait	MGM	
3015	BLAZING THE WESTERN TRAIL	KEAYS	COLUMBIA	1945
3016	LAWLESS EMPIRE	KEAYS	COLUMBIA	1945
3017	ROCKIN' IN THE ROCKIES	KEAYS	COLUMBIA	1945
3018	DO YOU REMEMBER? (series) (changed to 321201)		EDUCATIONAL FILM	1932
3018	LEON AMES	portrait	MGM	
3018	RHYTHM ROUNDUP	KEAYS	COLUMBIA	1945
3019	OUTLAWS OF THE ROCKIES	NAZARRO	COLUMBIA	1945
3020	TEXAS PANHANDLE	NAZARRO	COLUMBIA	1945
3021	SONG OF THE PRAIRIE	NAZARRO	COLUMBIA	1945

3022	DESERT HORSEMAN	NAZARRO	COLUMBIA	1946
3022	LEON AMES	portrait	MGM	
3023	ALFRED HITCHCOCK	portrait	MGM	
3023	GUNNING FOR VENGEANCE	NAZARRO	COLUMBIA	1946
3024	AUDREY TOTTER	portrait	MGM	
3024	ROARING RANGERS	NAZARRO	COLUMBIA	1946
3025	AUDREY TOTTER	portrait	MGM	
3025	LYNN ARLEN	portrait	MGM	
3025	THROW A SADDLE ON A STAR	NAZARRO	COLUMBIA	1946
3026	AUDREY TOTTER	portrait	MGM	
3026	HEADING WEST	NAZARRO	COLUMBIA	1946
3027	AUDREY TOTTER	portrait	MGM	
3027	GALLOPING THUNDER	NAZARRO	COLUMBIA	1946
3028	AUDREY TOTTER	portrait	MGM	
3028	TWO-FISTED STRANGER	NAZARRO	COLUMBIA	1946
3029	AUDREY TOTTER	portrait	MGM	
3029	THAT TEXAS JAMBOREE	NAZARRO	COLUMBIA	1946
3030	AUDREY TOTTER	portrait	MGM	
3030	TERROR TRAIL	NAZARRO	COLUMBIA	1946
3031	AUDREY TOTTER	portrait	MGM	
3031	LANDRUSH	KEAYS	COLUMBIA	1946
3032	AUDREY TOTTER	portrait	MGM	
3032	COWBOY BLUES	NAZARRO	COLUMBIA	1946
3033	AUDREY TOTTER	portrait	MGM	
3033	SINGING ON THE TRAIL	NAZARRO	COLUMBIA	1946
3034	AUDREY TOTTER	portrait	MGM	
3034	FIGHTING FRONTIERSMAN	ABRAHAMS	COLUMBIA	1946
3035	AUDREY TOTTER	portrait	MGM	
3035	SOUTH OF THE CHISHOLM TRAIL	ABRAHAMS	COLUMBIA	1947
3036	AUDREY TOTTER	portrait	MGM	
3036	LONE STAR MOONLIGHT	NAZARRO	COLUMBIA	1946
3037	AUDREY TOTTER	portrait	MGM	
3037	OVER THE SANTA FE TRAIL	NAZARRO	COLUMBIA	1947
3038	AUDREY TOTTER	portrait	MGM	
3038	SALLY FORREST	portrait	MGM	
3038	WEST OF DODGE CITY	NAZARRO	COLUMBIA	1947
3039	AUDREY TOTTER	portrait	MGM	
3039	LONE HAND TEXAS	NAZARRO	COLUMBIA	1947
3040	AUDREY TOTTER	portrait	MGM	
3040	ELAINE STEWART	portrait	MGM	
3040	LAW OF THE CANYON	NAZARRO	COLUMBIA	1947
3041	AUDREY TOTTER	portrait	MGM	
3041	PRAIRIE RAIDERS	ABRAHAMS	COLUMBIA	1947
3042	AUDREY TOTTER	portrait	MGM	
3042	STRANGER FROM PONCA CITY	ABRAHAMS	COLUMBIA	1947
3043	AUDREY TOTTER	portrait	MGM	
3043	ELAINE STEWART	portrait	MGM	
3043	RIDERS OF THE LONE STAR	ABRAHAMS	COLUMBIA	1947
3044	AUDREY TOTTER	portrait	MGM	
3044	SWING THE WESTERN WAY	ABRAHAMS	COLUMBIA	1947
3045	AUDREY TOTTER	portrait	MGM	
3045	SMOKEY RIVER SERENADE	ABRAHAMS	COLUMBIA	1947
3046	AUDREY TOTTER	portrait	MGM	
3046	ELAINE STEWART	portrait	MGM	
3046	SIX GUN LAW	NAZARRO	COLUMBIA	1948
3047	AUDREY TOTTER	portrait	MGM	
3047	BUCKAROO FROM POWDER RIVER	NAZARRO	COLUMBIA	1947
3048	AUDREY TOTTER	portrait	MGM	
3048	PHANTOM VALLEY	NAZARRO	COLUMBIA	1948
3048E	CYD CHARISSE	portrait	MGM	
3049	AUDREY TOTTER	portrait	MGM	
3049	ELAINE STEWART	portrait	MGM	
3049	LAST DAYS OF BOOTHILL	NAZARRO	COLUMBIA	1947
3050	ELAINE STEWART	portrait	MGM	
3050	ROSE OF SANTA ROSA	NAZARRO	COLUMBIA	1947
3051	ELAINE STEWART	portrait	MGM	

3051	WHIRLWIND RAIDERS	KEAYS	COLUMBIA	1948
3052	WEST OF SONORA	NAZARRO	COLUMBIA	1948
3053	SONG OF IDAHO	NAZARRO	COLUMBIA	1948
3054	BLAZING ACROSS THE PECOS	NAZARRO	COLUMBIA	1948
3055	TRAIL TO LAREDO	NAZARRO	COLUMBIA	1948
3056	ARKANSAS SWING	NAZARRO	COLUMBIA	1948
3057	BASIL RATHBONE	portrait	MGM	
3057	SINGIN' SPURS	NAZARRO	COLUMBIA	1948
3058	EL DORADO PASS	NAZARRO	COLUMBIA	1948
3059	ELIZABETH TAYLOR	portrait	MGM	
3059	QUICK ON THE TRIGGER	NAZARRO	COLUMBIA	1948
3060	CHALLENGE OF THE RANGE	NAZARRO	COLUMBIA	1949
3061	SMOKY MOUNTAIN MELODY	NAZARRO	COLUMBIA	1948
3062	ELIZABETH TAYLOR	portrait	MGM	
3062	SOUTH OF DEATH VALLEY	NAZARRO	COLUMBIA	1949
3063	DESERT VIGILANTE	SEARS	COLUMBIA	1949
3063	ELAINE STEWART	portrait		
3063	JACKIE COOPER	portrait		
3064	LARAMIE	NAZARRO	COLUMBIA	1949
3065	HOME IN SAN ANTONE	NAZARRO	COLUMBIA	1949
3066	BLAZING TRAIL	NAZARRO	COLUMBIA	1949
3067	HORSEMEN OF THE SIERRAS	SEARS	COLUMBIA	1949
3068	AVA GARDNER	portrait	MGM	
3068	BANDITS OF EL DORADO	NAZARRO	COLUMBIA	1949
3069	RENEGADES OF THE SAGE	NAZARRO	COLUMBIA	1949
3070	HOEDOWN	NAZARRO	COLUMBIA	1950
3071	FEUDIN' RHYTHM	BERNDS	COLUMBIA	1949
3072	OUTCAST OF BLACK MESA	NAZARRO	COLUMBIA	1950
3073	FRONTIER OUTPOST	NAZARRO	COLUMBIA	1950
3074	TRAIL OF THE RUSTLERS	NAZARRO	COLUMBIA	1950
3075	TEXAS DYNAMO	NAZARRO	COLUMBIA	1950
3076	STREETS OF GHOST TOWN	NAZARRO	COLUMBIA	1950
3077	ACROSS THE BADLANDS	SEARS	COLUMBIA	1950
3078	RAIDERS OF TOMAHAWK CREEK	SEARS	COLUMBIA	1950
3079	LIGHTNING GUNS	SEARS	COLUMBIA	1950
3080	PRAIRIE ROUNDUP	SEARS	COLUMBIA	1951
3081	RIDIN' THE OUTLAW TRAIL	SEARS	COLUMBIA	1951
3082	CLARK GABLE	portrait		
3082	ELIZABETH TAYLOR	portrait		
3082	FORT SAVAGE RAIDERS	NAZARRO	COLUMBIA	1951
3083	SNAKE RIVER DESPERADOES	SEARS	COLUMBIA	1951
3084	BONANZA TOWN	SEARS	COLUMBIA	1951
3085	CYCLONE FURY	NAZARRO	COLUMBIA	1951
3086	KID FROM AMARILLO	NAZARRO	COLUMBIA	1951
3087	KID FROM AMARILLO (error on some - should be 3086)	NAZARRO	COLUMBIA	1951
3087	PECOS RIVER	SEARS	COLUMBIA	1951
3088	AVA GARDNER	portrait	MGM	
3088	SMOKY CANYON	SEARS	COLUMBIA	1952
3089	HAWK OF WILD RIVER	SEARS	COLUMBIA	1952
3090	LARAMIE MOUNTAINS	NAZARRO	COLUMBIA	1952
3091	ELIZABETH TAYLOR	portrait		
3091	ROUGH TOUGH WEST	NAZARRO	COLUMBIA	1952
3092	JUNCTION CITY	NAZARRO	COLUMBIA	1952
3092	LESLIE CARON	portrait		
3093	KID FROM BROKEN GUN	SEARS	COLUMBIA	1952
3095	CLARK GABLE	portrait		
3120	ROBERT MONTGOMERY	portrait		
3125	LESLIE CARON	portrait		
3126	LESLIE CARON	portrait		
3127	LESLIE CARON	portrait		
3128	LESLIE CARON	portrait		
3129	LESLIE CARON	portrait		
3130	LESLIE CARON	portrait		
3130	RICARDO MONTALBAN	portrait		
3131	LESLIE CARON	portrait		
3131	RICARDO MONTALBAN	portrait		

3132	LESLIE CARON	portrait		
3138	LESLIE CARON	portrait		
3139	LESLIE CARON	portrait		
3143	HOWARD KEEL	portrait		
3145	HOWARD KEEL	portrait		
3147	CLARK GABLE	portrait		
3147	HOWARD KEEL	portrait		
3152	JAMES STEWART	portrait		
3154	NORMA SHEARER, WILL HAYS	portrait		
3155	JAMES STEWART	portrait		
3158E	GREER GARSON	portrait		
3162	WALLACE BEERY	portrait		
3168	WALLACE BEERY	portrait		
3171	BARRY SULLIVAN	portrait	MGM	
3193	AUDREY TOTTER	portrait		
3193	LARAINE DAY	portrait		
3215	UNA MERKEL	portrait		
3216	UNA MERKEL	portrait		
3221	UNA MERKEL	portrait		
3221	WALLACE BEERY + DAUGHTER CAROL ANN	portrait		
3232	SUSAN PETERS, HUSBAND RICHARD QUINE	portrait		
3239	PAMELA BROWN	portrait	MGM	
3240	PAMELA BROWN	portrait	MGM	
3241	PAMELA BROWN	portrait	MGM	
3244E	ANN BLYTH	portrait	MGM	
3246	PAMELA BROWN	portrait	MGM	
3263	PATRICIA DANE	portrait		
3279	WALTER PIDGEON	portrait		
3283	MICKEY ROONEY	portrait		
3286	MICKEY ROONEY	portrait		
3290	LESLIE CARON	portrait		
3294	PIER ANGELI	portrait	MGM	
3296	GLORIA DE HAVEN	portrait		
3298	ANGELA LANSBURY	portrait		
3298	LESLIE CARON	portrait		
3299	LESLIE CARON	portrait		
3300	LESLIE CARON	portrait		
3300	PIER ANGELI	portrait	MGM	
3301	BEDROOM BLUNDER (sh)	CLINE	PARAMOUNT	1917
3301	LESLIE CARON	portrait		
3302	ROPING HER ROMEO (sh)	FISHBACK	PARAMOUNT	1917
3303	PULLMAN BRIDE (sh)	BADGER	PARAMOUNT	1917
3304	ARE WAITRESSES SAFE? (sh)	HEERMAN	PARAMOUNT	1917
3305	INTERNATIONAL SNEAK (sh)	FISHBACK	PARAMOUNT	1917
3306	THAT NIGHT (sh)	CLINE	PARAMOUNT	1917
3307	TAMING TARGET CENTER (sh)	CAMPBELL	PARAMOUNT	1917
3308	KITCHEN LADY (sh)	CLINE	PARAMOUNT	1917
3309	HIS HIDDEN PURPOSE (sh)	CLINE, BADGER	PARAMOUNT	1917
3310	WATCH YOUR NEIGHBOR (sh)	HEERMAN	PARAMOUNT	1917
3311	IT PAYS TO EXERCISE (sh)	JONES	PARAMOUNT	1918
3312	SHERIFF NELL'S TUSSLE (sh)	CAMPBELL	PARAMOUNT	1918
3313	THOSE ATHLETIC GIRLS (sh)	CLINE	PARAMOUNT	1918
3314	FRIEND HUSBAND (sh)	WRIGHT	PARAMOUNT	1918
3315	SAUCY MADELINE (sh)	JONES	PARAMOUNT	1918
3316	HIS SMOTHERED LOVE (sh)	CLINE	PARAMOUNT	1918
3317	BATTLE ROYAL (sh)	JONES	PARAMOUNT	1918
3318	CYD CHARISSE	portrait		
3318	LOVE LOOPS THE LOOP (sh)	WRIGHT	PARAMOUNT	1918
3319	TWO TOUGH TENDERFEET (sh)	JONES	PARAMOUNT	1918
3320	HER SCREEN IDOL (sh)	CLINE	PARAMOUNT	1918
3321	LADIES FIRST! (sh)	GRAINGER	PARAMOUNT	1918
3322	HER BLIGHTED LOVE (sh)	WRIGHT	PARAMOUNT	1918
3322	NANCY DAVIS/REAGAN	portrait		
3323	HEDY LAMARR	portrait		
3323	SHE LOVED HIM PLENTY (sh)	JONES	PARAMOUNT	1918
3324	SUMMER GIRLS (sh)	CLINE	PARAMOUNT	1918

3325	HIS WIFE'S FRIEND (sh)	WRIGHT	PARAMOUNT	1918
3326	SLEUTHS! (sh)	JONES	PARAMOUNT	1918
3327	BEWARE OF BOARDERS! (sh)	FISHBACK	PARAMOUNT	1918
3327	MAUREEN O'SULLIVAN	portrait		
3328	WHOSE LITTLE WIFE ARE YOU? (sh)	CLINE	PARAMOUNT	1918
3329	HER FIRST MISTAKE (sh)	JONES	PARAMOUNT	1918
3330	CYD CHARISSE	portrait		
3330	HIDE AND SEEK, DETECTIVES (sh)	CLINE	PARAMOUNT	1918
3330	MAUREEN O'SULLIVAN	portrait		
3331	FRANCES GIFFORD	portrait		
3331	VILLAGE CHESTNUT (sh)	WRIGHT, GRIFFITH	PARAMOUNT	1918
3332	CUPID'S DAY OFF (sh)	CLINE	PARAMOUNT	1919
3333	NEVER TOO OLD (sh)	JONES	PARAMOUNT	1919
3334	BETTY GARRETT	portrait		
3334	RIP & STITCH, TAILORS (sh)	WATSON, ST. CLAIR	PARAMOUNT	1919
3335	BETTY GARRETT	portrait		
3335	EAST LYNNE WITH VARIATIONS (sh)	CLINE	PARAMOUNT	1919
3336	BETTY GARRETT	portrait		
3336	CYD CHARISSE	portrait		
3336	VILLAGE SMITHY (sh)	JONES	PARAMOUNT	1919
3337	BETTY GARRETT	portrait		
3337	REILLY'S WASH DAY (sh)	JONES	PARAMOUNT	1919
3338	BETTY GARRETT	portrait		
3338	FOOLISH AGE (sh)	JONES	PARAMOUNT`	1919
3339	BETTY GARRETT	portrait		
3339	LITTLE WIDOW (sh)	ST. CLAIR, ROACH	PARAMOUNT	1919
3340	BETTY GARRETT	portrait		
3340	VIRGINIA GREY	portrait		
3340	WHEN LOVE IS BLIND (sh)	CLINE	PARAMOUNT	1919
3341	BETTY GARRETT	portrait		
3341	LOVE'S FALSE FACES (sh)	JONES	PARAMOUNT	1919
3342	BETTY GARRETT	portrait		
3342	NO MOTHER TO GUIDE HIM (sh)	ST. CLAIR, KENTON	PARAMOUNT	1919
3343	BETTY GARRETT	portrait		
3343	HEARTS AND FLOWERS (sh)	CLINE	PARAMOUNT	1919
3343	LESLIE CARON	portrait		
3344	BETTY GARRETT	portrait		
3344	TRYING TO GET ALONG (sh)	JONES	PARAMOUNT	1919
3345	AMONG THOSE PRESENT (sh)	KENTON, GREY	PARAMOUNT	1919
3345	BETTY GARRETT	portrait		
3345	POLLY BERGEN	portrait	MGM	
3346	BETTY GARRETT	portrait		
3346	TREATING 'EM ROUGH (sh)	JACKMAN	PARAMOUNT	1919
3347	BETTY GARRETT	portrait		
3347	DENTIST (sh)	JONES	PARAMOUNT	1919
3348	BETTY GARRETT	portrait		
3348	HEDY LAMARR	portrait		
3349	BETTY GARRETT	portrait		
3350	BETTY GARRETT	portrait		
3350E	CYD CHARISSE	portrait		
3351	BETTY GARRETT	portrait		
3351	UNCLE TOM WITHOUT THE CABIN (sh)	HUNT	PARAMOUNT	1919
3352	BACK TO THE KITCHEN (sh)	MORRIS, BELMONT	PARAMOUNT	1919
3352	BETTY GARRETT	portrait		
3352E	CYD CHARISSE	portrait		
3353	BETTY GARRETT	portrait		
3353	JEAN SIMMONS	portrait	MGM	
3353	UP IN ALF'S PLACE (sh)	JONES	PARAMOUNT	1919
3354	BETTY GARRETT	portrait		
3354	SALOME VS. SHENANDOAH (sh)	GREY, HUNT	PARAMOUNT	1919
3354E	CYD CHARISSE	portrait		
3355	BETTY GARRETT	portrait		
3355	HIS LAST FALSE STEP (sh)	JONES	PARAMOUNT	1919
3356	BETTY GARRETT	portrait		
3356	LADY'S TAILOR (sh)	KENTON, GREY	PARAMOUNT	1919
3357	BETTY GARRETT	portrait		

3357	SPEAK-EASY (sh)	JONES	PARAMOUNT	1919
3358	BETTY GARRETT	portrait		
3358	STAR BOARDER (sh)	DAVIS	PARAMOUNT	1920
3358E	CYD CHARISSE	portrait		
3359	GEE WHIZ! (sh)	JONES	PARAMOUNT	1920
3359	MAUREEN O'SULLIVAN	portrait		
3360	GINGHAM GIRL (sh)	DAVIS	PARAMOUNT	1920
3360	NITA TALBOT	portrait	MGM	
3361	FRESH FROM THE CITY (sh)	WRIGHT	PARAMOUNT	1920
3361	NITA TALBOT	portrait	MGM	
3361	SUSAN PETERS, HUSBAND RICHARD QUINE, 2-MONTH-OLD SON	portrait		
3362	LET 'ER GO! (sh)	DAVIS	PARAMOUNT	1920
3362	NITA TALBOT	portrait	MGM	
3363	BY GOLLY! (sh)	MURRAY	PARAMOUNT	1920
3363	NITA TALBOT	portrait	MGM	
3364	NITA TALBOT	portrait	MGM	
3364	YOU WOULDN'T BELIEVE IT! (sh)	KENTON	PARAMOUNT	1920
3364E	CYD CHARISSE	portrait		
3365	NITA TALBOT	portrait	MGM	
3365	QUACK DOCTOR (sh)	GRAY, BEVAN	PARAMOUNT	1920
3365E	CYD CHARISSE	portrait		
3366	GREAT SCOTT! (sh)	MURRAY	PARAMOUNT	1920
3367	DON'T WEAKEN! (sh)	ST. CLAIR	PARAMOUNT	1920
3368	IT'S A BOY! (sh)	SMITH	PARAMOUNT	1920
3369	HIS YOUTHFUL FANCY (sh)	ST. CLAIR	PARAMOUNT	1920
3370	MY GOODNESS	SMITH	PARAMOUNT	1920
3371	MOVIE FANS (sh)	KENTON	PARAMOUNT	1920
3372	FICKLE FANCY (sh)	KENTON	PARAMOUNT	1920
3373	FIRESIDE BREWER (sh)	SMITH	PARAMOUNT	1920
3374	DABBLING IN ART (sh)	KENTON	PARAMOUNT	1921
3375	BUNGALOW TROUBLES (sh)	AUSTIN	PARAMOUNT	1921
3375	MAUREEN O'SULLIVAN	portrait		
3376	MAUREEN O'SULLIVAN	portrait		
3379	MAUREEN O'SULLIVAN	portrait		
3380	MAUREEN O'SULLIVAN	portrait		
3380	OFFICER CUPID	POWELL	PARAMOUNT	1921
3381	ASTRAY FROM THE STEERAGE (sh)	POWELL	PARAMOUNT	1921
3384	MAUREEN O'SULLIVAN	portrait		
3392	MAUREEN O'SULLIVAN	portrait		
3393	MAUREEN O'SULLIVAN	portrait		
3398	KATHARINE HEPBURN	portrait		
3399E	DEBORAH KERR	portrait		
3400	CORONER CREEK	ENRIGHT	COLUMBIA	1948
3403E	DEBORAH KERR	portrait	MGM	
3405	KATHARINE HEPBURN	portrait	MGM	
3405E	SHIRLEY MACLAINE	portrait		
3406	ANN SOTHERN	portrait		
3406E	DEBORAH KERR	portrait	MGM	
3407	ANN SOTHERN	portrait		
3413	ANN SOTHERN	portrait		
3415	KATHARINE HEPBURN	portrait		
3416	KATHARINE HEPBURN	portrait		
3418	KATHARINE HEPBURN	portrait		
3419	ANN SOTHERN	portrait		
3419	GLORIA DE HAVEN	portrait		
3420	GLORIA DE HAVEN	portrait		
3421	GLORIA DE HAVEN	portrait		
3422	ANN SOTHERN	portrait		
3422	GLORIA DE HAVEN	portrait		
3422	KATHARINE HEPBURN	portrait		
3422	MAMIE VAN DOREN	portrait	MGM	
3422	UNA MERKEL	portrait		
3423	GLORIA DE HAVEN	portrait		
3424	ANN SOTHERN	portrait		
3426	GLORIA DE HAVEN	portrait		
3433	GLORIA DE HAVEN	portrait		

3442	WALTER PIDGEON	portrait	MGM	
3449	VERA-ELLEN	portrait	MGM	
3450	CLARK GABLE	portrait		
3452	JEAN SIMMONS	portrait	MGM	
3455	ELKE SOMMER	portrait	MGM	
3459	JEAN SIMMONS	portrait	MGM	
3463	ELKE SOMMER	portrait	MGM	
3463	VERA-ELLEN	portrait	MGM	
3464	VERA-ELLEN	portrait	MGM	
3465	VERA-ELLEN	portrait	MGM	
3466	VERA-ELLEN	portrait	MGM	
3467	VERA-ELLEN	portrait	MGM	
3468	VERA-ELLEN	portrait	MGM	
3471	VERA-ELLEN	portrait	MGM	
3481E	DEBBIE REYNOLDS	portrait		
3495	DEBBIE REYNOLDS	portrait		
3496	DEBBIE REYNOLDS	portrait		
3501	COAST OF CATALONIA (sh)		FOX FILM	1934
3502	IN FAIR MANDALAY (sh)		FOX FILM	1934
3503	PICTURESQUE PORTUGAL (sh)		FOX FILM	1934
3503	RED SKELTON	portrait		
3504	CROSSROADS OF THE WORLD (sh)		FOX FILM	1934
3505	ISLE OF BERMUDA (sh)		FOX FILM	1934
3506	GENEVA BY THE LAKE (sh)		FOX FILM	1934
3511	MAUREEN O'SULLIVAN	portrait		
3526	ANN SOTHERN	portrait		
3527	VERA-ELLEN	portrait	MGM	
3542E	MICKEY ROONEY	portrait		
3545	SOUND OF MUSIC	WISE	20TH CENTURY FOX	1965
3548	MAUREEN O'SULLIVAN	portrait		
3551	AVA GARDNER	portrait	MGM	
3556	ANN SOTHERN	portrait		
3556	VERA-ELLEN	portrait	MGM	
3557	ANN SOTHERN	portrait		
3558	ANN SOTHERN	portrait		
3559E	CYD CHARISSE	portrait	MGM	
3562	DORE SCHARY	portrait		
3563	ANN SOTHERN	portrait		
3565	LARAINE DAY	portrait		
3565	WALLACE BEERY	portrait		
3578	MAUREEN O'SULLIVAN	portrait		
3581	MAUREEN O'SULLIVAN	portrait		
3597	ROBERT WALKER	portrait		
3598	ROBERT WALKER	portrait		
3599	ROBERT WALKER	portrait		
3600	ROBERT WALKER	portrait		
3601	MOROCCO MIRAGE (sh)		FOX FILM	1935
3601	ROBERT WALKER	portrait		
3602	LITTLE JOURNEY	LEONARD	MGM	1927
3602	ROBERT WALKER	portrait		
3603	ROBERT WALKER	portrait	MGM	
3604	ARGENTINE ARGOSY (sh)		20TH CENTURY FOX	1935
3604	ROBERT WALKER	portrait		
3605	ROBERT WALKER	portrait		
3605	WINTER MAGIC (sh)		20TH CENTURY FOX	1935
3606	HONG KONG HIGHLIGHTS (sh)		20TH CENTURY FOX	1936
3606	ROBERT WALKER	portrait		
3607	ROBERT WALKER	portrait		
3608	ROBERT WALKER	portrait		
3609	ROBERT MITCHUM	portrait		
3609	ROBERT WALKER	portrait		
3610	ROBERT MITCHUM	portrait		
3610	ROBERT WALKER	portrait		
3611	ROBERT MITCHUM	portrait		
3611	ROBERT WALKER	portrait		
3612	ROBERT MITCHUM	portrait		

3612	ROBERT WALKER	portrait		
3613	ROBERT MITCHUM	portrait		
3613	ROBERT WALKER	portrait		
3615	VAN JOHNSON	portrait		
3617	ELEANOR POWELL	portrait		
3625	KING VIDOR, GARY COOPER	portrait		
3630	ESTHER WILLIAMS	portrait		
3638	KATHRYN GRAYSON	portrait		
3646	MAUREEN O'SULLIVAN	portrait		
3650	GLORIA DE HAVEN	portrait		
3670	KATHARINE HEPBURN	portrait		
3685	SPENCER TRACY	portrait	MGM	
3686	SPENCER TRACY	portrait	MGM	
3687	SPENCER TRACY	portrait	MGM	
3688	SPENCER TRACY	portrait	MGM	
3689	LUISE RAINER	portrait	MGM	
3689	SPENCER TRACY	portrait	MGM	
3694	HEDY LAMARR	portrait		
3699	MITCHELL BROTHER	portrait	MGM	
3700	MITCHELL BROTHER	portrait	MGM	
3702	MITCHELL BROTHER	portrait	MGM	
3704	TOURING BRAZIL (sh)		20TH CENTURY FOX	1936
3705	LAND OF GENGHIS KHAN (sh)		20TH CENTURY FOX	1936
3706	WESTERN GRANDEUR (sh)		20TH CENTURY FOX	1937
3707	IRENE DUNNE	portrait		
3728	ANITA PAGE	portrait		
3728	ANN SOTHERN	portrait		
3729	ANN SOTHERN	portrait		
3731	ANN SOTHERN	portrait		
3732	ANN SOTHERN	portrait		
3732	MAUREEN O'SULLIVAN	portrait		
3735	CLINTON SUNDBERG	portrait	MGM	
3737	SPENCER TRACY	portrait	MGM	
3738	SPENCER TRACY	portrait	MGM	
3739	SPENCER TRACY	portrait	MGM	
3740	ANN SOTHERN, HUSBAND ROBERT STERLING	portrait		
3741	GREER GARSON + HUSBAND RICHARD NEY	portrait		
3745	GREER GARSON + HUSBAND RICHARD NEY	portrait		
3748	AVA GARDNER	portrait	MGM	
3748	GREER GARSON + HUSBAND RICHARD NEY	portrait		
3748	MYRNA LOY	portrait		
3749	AVA GARDNER	portrait	MGM	
3750	AVA GARDNER	portrait	MGM	
3751	AVA GARDNER	portrait	MGM	
3751	GREER GARSON + HUSBAND RICHARD NEY	portrait		
3752	AVA GARDNER	portrait	MGM	
3753	AVA GARDNER	portrait	MGM	
3753	MYRNA LOY	portrait		
3754	AVA GARDNER	portrait	MGM	
3754	SPENCER TRACY	portrait		
3755	AVA GARDNER	portrait	MGM	
3755	MYRNA LOY	portrait		
3755	SPENCER TRACY	portrait		
3756	AVA GARDNER	portrait	MGM	
3756	MAUREEN O'SULLIVAN	portrait		
3757	AVA GARDNER	portrait	MGM	
3758	AVA GARDNER	portrait	MGM	
3758	MAUREEN O'SULLIVAN	portrait		
3759	AVA GARDNER	portrait	MGM	
3759	SPENCER TRACY	portrait		
3760	AVA GARDNER	portrait	MGM	
3761	AVA GARDNER	portrait	MGM	
3761	SPENCER TRACY	portrait		
3762	AVA GARDNER	portrait	MGM	
3762	SPENCER TRACY	portrait		
3763	AVA GARDNER	portrait	MGM	

3763	SPENCER TRACY	portrait		
3764	AVA GARDNER	portrait	MGM	
3765	AVA GARDNER	portrait	MGM	
3766	AVA GARDNER	portrait	MGM	
3767	AVA GARDNER	portrait	MGM	
3768	AVA GARDNER	portrait	MGM	
3770	DEBBIE REYNOLDS	portrait	MGM	
3779	NORMA SHEARER'S LIVING ROOM	portrait		
3785	VERA-ELLEN	portrait	MGM	
3786	VERA-ELLEN	portrait	MGM	
3787	VERA-ELLEN	portrait	MGM	
3788	VERA-ELLEN	portrait	MGM	
3789	VERA-ELLEN	portrait	MGM	
3790	VERA-ELLEN	portrait	MGM	
3791	VERA-ELLEN	portrait	MGM	
3792	VERA-ELLEN	portrait	MGM	
3793	VERA-ELLEN	portrait	MGM	
3794	VERA-ELLEN	portrait	MGM	
3795	VERA-ELLEN	portrait	MGM	
3796	VERA-ELLEN	portrait	MGM	
3797	VERA-ELLEN	portrait	MGM	
3798	VERA-ELLEN	portrait	MGM	
3799	VERA-ELLEN	portrait	MGM	
3800	MARSHA HUNT	portrait		
3800	VERA-ELLEN	portrait	MGM	
3801	VERA-ELLEN	portrait	MGM	
3802	VERA-ELLEN	portrait	MGM	
3803	VERA-ELLEN	portrait	MGM	
3804	VERA-ELLEN	portrait	MGM	
3809	JULIA (tv series)	VARIOUS	20TH CENTURY FOX	1968
3810	PAULA RAYMOND	portrait		
3823	FRANCES GIFFORD	portrait		
3829	WANTED BY SCOTLAND YARD (UK)	LEE	MONOGRAM	1939
3841	ESTHER WILLIAMS	portrait	MGM	
3842	ESTHER WILLIAMS	portrait	MGM	
3843	ESTHER WILLIAMS	portrait	MGM	
3844	ESTHER WILLIAMS	portrait	MGM	
3845	ESTHER WILLIAMS	portrait	MGM	
3846	ESTHER WILLIAMS	portrait	MGM	
3847	ESTHER WILLIAMS	portrait	MGM	
3848	ESTHER WILLIAMS	portrait	MGM	
3849	ESTHER WILLIAMS	portrait	MGM	
3850	ESTHER WILLIAMS	portrait	MGM	
3851	ESTHER WILLIAMS	portrait	MGM	
3852	ESTHER WILLIAMS	portrait	MGM	
3853	ESTHER WILLIAMS	portrait	MGM	
3854	ESTHER WILLIAMS	portrait	MGM	
3855	ESTHER WILLIAMS	portrait	MGM	
3856	CATHERINE MOYLAN	portrait		
3856	ESTHER WILLIAMS	portrait	MGM	
3857	ESTHER WILLIAMS	portrait	MGM	
3857	JEAN HAGEN	portrait	MGM	
3858	ESTHER WILLIAMS	portrait	MGM	
3859	ESTHER WILLIAMS	portrait	MGM	
3860	ESTHER WILLIAMS	portrait	MGM	
3861	ESTHER WILLIAMS	portrait	MGM	
3861	JEAN HAGEN	portrait	MGM	
3862	ESTHER WILLIAMS	portrait	MGM	
3863	SANTA FE STAMPEDE	SHERMAN	REPUBLIC	1938
3863	ESTHER WILLIAMS	portrait	MGM	
3864	ESTHER WILLIAMS	portrait	MGM	
3865	ESTHER WILLIAMS	portrait	MGM	
3866	ESTHER WILLIAMS	portrait	MGM	
3867	JANET LEIGH	portrait		
3868	JANET LEIGH	portrait		
3868	JEAN HAGEN	portrait	MGM	

3869	JANET LEIGH	portrait		
3870	JANET LEIGH	portrait		
3871	JANET LEIGH	portrait		
3872	JANET LEIGH	portrait		
3873	JANET LEIGH	portrait		
3874	JANET LEIGH	portrait		
3875	JANET LEIGH	portrait		
3876	JANET LEIGH	portrait		
3878	JANET LEIGH	portrait		
3879	JANET LEIGH	portrait		
3880	JANE POWELL	portrait		
3881	JANE POWELL	portrait		
3882	DIVIDEND, THE	EDWARDS	TRIANGLE	1916
3882	JANE POWELL	portrait		
3883	JANE POWELL	portrait		
3884	JANE POWELL	portrait		
3885	JANE POWELL	portrait		
3886	JANE POWELL	portrait		
3887	JAMES STEWART, BRIDE GLORIA HATRICK MCLEAN	portrait		
3887	JANE POWELL	portrait		
3888	JANE POWELL	portrait		
3889	JANE POWELL	portrait		
3890	JANE POWELL	portrait		
3891	JAMES STEWART, BRIDE GLORIA HATRICK MCLEAN	portrait		
3891	JANE POWELL	portrait		
3892	JANE POWELL	portrait		
3893	JANE POWELL	portrait		
3896	ESTHER WILLIAMS	portrait		
3896	MAUREEN O'SULLIVAN	portrait		
3897	ESTHER WILLIAMS	portrait		
3897	JAMES STEWART, BRIDE GLORIA MCLEAN, BILLY GRADY	portrait		
3899	DOROTHY JORDAN AT 3	portrait		
3902	MAUREEN O'SULLIVAN	portrait		
3910	ROBERT TAYLOR	portrait		
3911	MARSHA HUNT	portrait		
3919	FAY HOLDEN	portrait	MGM	
3923	PHANTOM STRIKES (UK: GAUNT STRANGER 1938)	FORDE	MONOGRAM	1939
3926	CIRCUS BOY (UK)	MUSK	GFD	1947
3940	UNA MERKEL	portrait		
3940	WHO IS GUILTY? (UK: I KILLED THE COUNT)	ZELNIK	GRAND NATIONAL	1939
3949	ELIZABETH TAYLOR	portrait		
3951	ROBERT MONTGOMERY	portrait		
3953	ELIZABETH TAYLOR	portrait		
3956	ELIZABETH TAYLOR	portrait		
3985	JEAN HAGEN	portrait		
3988	IRENE HERVEY	portrait		
3993	BETTY GARRETT	portrait		
4000	DEBBIE REYNOLDS	portrait		
4001	BUSY BUDDIES (sh)	LORD	COLUMBIA	1944
4002	CATERED AFFAIR	BROOKS	MGM	1956
4002	WEDDED BLISS (sh)	EDWARDS	COLUMBIA	1944
4003	BACHELOR DAZE (sh)	WHITE	COLUMBIA	1943
4003	GRACE KELLY	portrait	MGM	
4004	YOU DEAR BOY (sh)	WHITE	COLUMBIA	1943
4005	DOCTOR, FEEL MY PULSE (sh)	WHITE	COLUMBIA	1944
4005	ILONA MASSEY	portrait	MGM	
4006	BOOBY DUPES (sh)	LORD	COLUMBIA	1945
4007	CYD CHARISSE	portrait		
4007	HIS TALE IS TOLD (sh)	EDWARDS	COLUMBIA	1944
4008	YOU WERE NEVER UGLIER (sh)	WHITE	COLUMBIA	1944
4009	GOLD IS WHERE YOU LOSE IT (sh)	WHITE	COLUMBIA	1944
4010	CRASH GOES THE HASH (sh)	WHITE	COLUMBIA	1944
4010	DOCTOR IN THE HOUSE	THOMAS	REPUBLIC	1955
4011	CRAZY LIKE A FOX (sh)	WHITE	COLUMBIA	1944
4012	HIS HOTEL SWEET (sh)	EDWARDS	COLUMBIA	1944
4013	IDLE ROOMERS (sh)	LORD	COLUMBIA	1943

4014	OH, BABY (sh)	WHITE	COLUMBIA	1944
4015	MICKEY ROONEY	portrait		
4015	OFF AGAIN, ON AGAIN (sh)	WHITE	COLUMBIA	1945
4016	FERNANDO LAMAS	portrait		
4016	GREEN BUDDHA (US: GREEN CARNATION)	LEMONT	REPUBLIC	1955
4016	OPEN SEASON FOR SAPS (sh)	WHITE	COLUMBIA	1944
4017	DEFECTIVE DETECTIVES (sh)	EDWARDS	COLUMBIA	1944
4018	PICK A PECK OF PLUMBERS (sh)	WHITE	COLUMBIA	1944
4019	DYNAMITERS (UK: GELIGNITE GANG)	SEARLE	ASTOR	1956
4019	MOPEY DOPE (sh)	LORD	COLUMBIA	1944
4019X	CYD CHARISSE	portrait		
4020	GENTS WITHOUT CENTS (sh)	WHITE	COLUMBIA	1944
4021	CYD CHARISSE	portrait		
4021	HEATHER AND YON (sh)	EDWARDS	COLUMBIA	1944
4022	THREE PESTS IN A MESS (sh)	LORD	COLUMBIA	1945
4023	DOCTOR AT SEA	THOMAS	REPUBLIC	1956
4023	WOO WOO (I SHOULD WORRY*)	WHITE	COLUMBIA	1945
4024	TWO LOCAL YOKELS (sh)	WHITE	COLUMBIA	1945
4025	KNIGHT AND A BLONDE (sh)	EDWARDS	COLUMBIA	1944
4025	WOO WOO (I SHOULD WORRY*)	WHITE	COLUMBIA	1945
4026	SHE SNOOPS TO CONQUER (sh)	WHITE	COLUMBIA	1944
4027	STRIFE OF THE PARTY (sh)	EDWARDS	COLUMBIA	1944
4028	DANCE DUNCE, DANCE (sh)	WHITE	COLUMBIA	1945
4028	MAUREEN O'SULLIVAN	portrait		
4029	SNOOPER SERVICE (sh)	EDWARDS	COLUMBIA	1945
4030	IDIOTS DELUXE (sh)	WHITE	COLUMBIA	1945
4030	MAUREEN O'SULLIVAN	portrait		
4031	JURY GOES ROUND AND ROUND (sh)	WHITE	COLUMBIA	1945
4031	NORMA SHEARER	portrait		
4032	HISS AND YELL (sh)	WHITE	COLUMBIA	1946
4033	IF A BODY MEETS A BODY (sh)	WHITE	COLUMBIA	1945
4034	GREER GARSON	portrait		
4035	PISTOL PACKIN' NITWITS (sh)	EDWARDS	COLUMBIA	1945
4035	SOUND OF MUSIC (SEE 79)	WISE	20TH CENTURY FOX	1965
4036	WIFE DECOY (sh)	EDWARDS	COLUMBIA	1945
4037	FERNANDO LAMAS	portrait		
4037	JEAN HAGEN	portrait	MGM	
4037	SPOOK TO ME (sh)	EDWARDS	COLUMBIA	1945
4038	HIT WITH A MISS (sh)	EDWARDS, WHITE	COLUMBIA	1945
4039	MAYOR'S HUSBAND (sh)	EDWARDS	COLUMBIA	1945
4040	MINER AFFAIR (sh)	WHITE	COLUMBIA	1945
4041	BLONDE STAYED ON (sh)	EDWARDS	COLUMBIA	1946
4042	CALLING ALL FIBBERS (sh)	WHITE	COLUMBIA	1945
4042	FERNANDO LAMAS	portrait		
4043	BIRD IN THE HEAD (sh)	BERNDS	COLUMBIA	1946
4044	MICRO-PHONIES (sh)	BERNDS	COLUMBIA	1945
4045	BEER BARREL POLECATS (sh)	WHITE	COLUMBIA	1946
4046	THREE TROUBLEDOERS (sh)	BERNDS	COLUMBIA	1946
4047	WHEN THE WIFE'S AWAY (sh)	BERNDS	COLUMBIA	1946
4048	JIGGERS, MY WIFE (sh)	WHITE	COLUMBIA	1946
4048	WHERE THE PEST BEGINS	EDWARDS	COLUMBIA	1945
4049	YOU CAN'T FOOL A FOOL (sh)	WHITE	COLUMBIA	1946
4050	UNCIVIL WAR BIRDS (sh)	WHITE	COLUMBIA	1946
4051	HIGH BLOOD PLEASURE (sh)	WHITE	COLUMBIA	1945
4052	JOAN CRAWFORD	portrait	MGM	
4052	SOCIETY MUGS (sh)	BERNDS	COLUMBIA	1946
4053	THREE LOAN WOLVES (sh)	WHITE	COLUMBIA	1946
4054	MR. NOISY (sh)	BERNDS	COLUMBIA	1946
4055	GET ALONG LITTLE ZOMBIE (sh)	BERNDS	COLUMBIA	1946
4056	HALF-WITS HOLIDAY (sh)	WHITE	COLUMBIA	1947
4057	RHYTHM AND WEEP (sh)	WHITE	COLUMBIA	1946
4058	MONKEY BUSINESSMEN (sh)	BERNDS	COLUMBIA	1946
4059	ANDY PLAYS HOOKEY (sh)	BERNDS	COLUMBIA	1946
4059	HUSBANDS FOR RENT	LEHRMAN	WARNER BROS	1927
4060	HEADIN' FOR A WEDDIN' (sh)	WHITE	COLUMBIA	1946
4061	SCOOPER DOOPER (sh)	BERNDS	COLUMBIA	1947

4062	AIN'T LOVE CUCKOO (sh)	WHITE	COLUMBIA	1946
4063	G.I. WANNA HOME (sh)	WHITE	COLUMBIA	1946
4064	BRIDE AND GLOOM (sh)	BERNDS	COLUMBIA	1947
4065	MR. WRIGHT GOES WRONG (sh)	WHITE	COLUMBIA	1946
4066	HOT WATER (sh)	BERNDS	COLUMBIA	1946
4066	JOAN CRAWFORD	portrait	MGM	
4067	THREE LITTLE PIRATES (sh)	BERNDS	COLUMBIA	1946
4068	PARDON MY TERROR (sh)	BERNDS	COLUMBIA	1946
4069	JOAN CRAWFORD	portrait	MGM	
4069	SUNK IN THE SINK (sh)	WHITE	COLUMBIA	1949
4070	BARBARA STANWYCK	portrait	MGM	
4070	FIDDLERS THREE (sh)	WHITE	COLUMBIA	1948
4071	BARBARA STANWYCK	portrait	MGM	
4071	FRIGHT NIGHT (sh)	BERNDS	COLUMBIA	1947
4072	SHOULD HUSBANDS MARRY? (sh)	LORD	COLUMBIA	1947
4073	CRABBIN' IN THE CABIN (sh)	WHITE	COLUMBIA	1948
4074	HONEYMOON BLUES (sh)	BERNDS	COLUMBIA	1946
4075	BARBARA STANWYCK	portrait	MGM	
4075	HOT HEIR (sh)	BERNDS	COLUMBIA	1947
4076	HECTIC HONEYMOON (sh)	BERNDS	COLUMBIA	1947
4077	OUT WEST (sh)	BERNDS	COLUMBIA	1947
4078	SO'S YOUR ANTENNA (sh)	WHITE	COLUMBIA	1946
4079	TWO JILLS AND A JACK (sh)	WHITE	COLUMBIA	1947
4080	SLAPPILY MARRIED (sh)	BERNDS	COLUMBIA	1946
4081	MEET MR. MISCHIEF (sh)	BERNDS	COLUMBIA	1947
4082	SQUAREHEADS OF THE ROUND TABLE (sh)	BERNDS	COLUMBIA	1948
4083	RENO-VATED (sh)	WHITE	COLUMBIA	1946
4084	NERVOUS SHAKEDOWN (sh)	LORD	COLUMBIA	1947
4085	MORON THAN OFF (sh)	WHITE	COLUMBIA	1946
4086	GOOD BAD EGG (sh)	WHITE	COLUMBIA	1947
4087	HOLD THAT LION (sh)	WHITE	COLUMBIA	1947
4088	BROKEN HEARTS OF BROADWAY	CUMMINGS	IRVING CUMMINGS PROD	1923
4088	SING A SONG OF SIX PANTS (sh)	WHITE	COLUMBIA	1947
4089	ROLLING DOWN TO RENO (sh)	WHITE	COLUMBIA	1947
4091	I'M A MONKEY'S UNCLE (sh)	WHITE	COLUMBIA	1948
4093	PARDON MY CLUTCH (sh)	BERNDS	COLUMBIA	1948
4094	HOT SCOTS (sh)	BERNDS	COLUMBIA	1948
4095	BRIDELESS GROOM (sh)	BERNDS	COLUMBIA	1947
4096	WIFE TO SPARE (sh)	BERNDS	COLUMBIA	1947
4097	CUPID GOES NUTS (sh)	WHITE	COLUMBIA	1947
4097	MAUREEN O'SULLIVAN	portrait		
4098	TRAINING FOR TROUBLE (sh)	WHITE	COLUMBIA	1947
4099	WEDDING BELLE (sh)	BERNDS	COLUMBIA	1947
4100	TALL, DARK AND GRUESOME (sh)	LORD	COLUMBIA	1948
4101	WAITING IN THE LURCH (sh)	BERNDS	COLUMBIA	1949
4102	STOOGES (sh)		COLUMBIA	
4103	MARK STEVENS	portrait	MGM	
4103	SHIVERING SHERLOCKS (sh)	LORD	COLUMBIA	1948
4104	ALL GUMMED UP (sh)	WHITE	COLUMBIA	1947
4105	MUMMY'S DUMMIES (sh)	BERNDS	COLUMBIA	1948
4106	WEDLOCK DEADLOCK (sh)	BERNDS	COLUMBIA	1947
4107	THREE HAMS ON RYE (sh)	WHITE	COLUMBIA	1950
4108	GHOST TALKS (sh)	WHITE	COLUMBIA	1949
4109	RADIO ROMEO (sh)	BERNDS	COLUMBIA	1947
4110	MAN OR MOUSE (sh)	WHITE	COLUMBIA	1948
4111	CRIME ON THEIR HANDS (sh)	BERNDS	COLUMBIA	1948
4112	WHO DONE IT? (sh)	BERNDS	COLUMBIA	1949
4113	EIGHT BALL ANDY (sh)	BERNDS	COLUMBIA	1948
4114	UNNAMED WOMAN	HOYT	UNIVERSAL	1925
4115	HUGS AND MUGS (sh)	WHITE	COLUMBIA	1950
4116	FERNANDO LAMAS	portrait		
4116	HOKUS POKUS (sh)	WHITE	COLUMBIA	1949
4117	FERNANDO LAMAS	portrait		
4117	FLAT FEAT (sh)	BERNDS	COLUMBIA	1948
4118	FERNANDO LAMAS	portrait		
4118	GO CHASE YOURSELF (sh)	WHITE	COLUMBIA	1948

4119	FERNANDO LAMAS	portrait		
4119	MALICE IN THE PALACE (sh)	WHITE	COLUMBIA	1949
4120	FERNANDO LAMAS	portrait		
4120	JITTER BUGHOUSE (sh)	WHITE	COLUMBIA	1948
4121	FERNANDO LAMAS	portrait		
4121	GENE KELLY	portrait		
4121	PARDON MY LAMBCHOP (sh)	WHITE	COLUMBIA	1948
4122	FERNANDO LAMAS	portrait		
4122	SILLY BILLY (sh)	WHITE	COLUMBIA	1948
4123	FERNANDO LAMAS	portrait		
4123	HE'S IN AGAIN (sh)	BERNDS	COLUMBIA	1949
4124	FERNANDO LAMAS	portrait		
4124	GRACE KELLY	portrait		
4124	TWO NUTS IN A RUT (sh)	BERNDS	COLUMBIA	1948
4125	BILLIE GETS HER MAN (sh)	BERNDS	COLUMBIA	1948
4125	FERNANDO LAMAS	portrait		
4125	MAGGIE PIERCE	portrait		
4126	FERNANDO LAMAS	portrait		
4126	SHEEPISH WOLF (sh)	BERNDS	COLUMBIA	1948
4127	FERNANDO LAMAS	portrait		
4127	PARLOR, BEDROOM AND WRATH (sh)	WHITE	COLUMBIA	1948
4128	FERNANDO LAMAS	portrait		
4128	GENE KELLY	portrait		
4128	PINCH IN TIME (sh)	LORD	COLUMBIA	1948
4129	FERNANDO LAMAS	portrait		
4129	LOVE AT FIRST BITE (sh)	WHITE	COLUMBIA	1950
4130	FERNANDO LAMAS	portrait		
4130	MICROSPOOK (sh)	BERNDS	COLUMBIA	1949
4131	DOPEY DICKS (sh)	BERNDS	COLUMBIA	1950
4132	RADIO RIOT (sh)	BERNDS	COLUMBIA	1949
4133	ELAINE STEWART	portrait	MGM	
4133	GENE KELLY	portrait		
4133	TRAPPED BY A BLOND (sh)	LORD	COLUMBIA	1949
4134	FLUNG BY A FLING (sh)	BERNDS	COLUMBIA	1949
4135	CLUNKED IN THE CLINK (sh)	WHITE	COLUMBIA	1949
4136	MISS IN A MESS (sh)	WHITE	COLUMBIA	1949
4137	DUNKED IN THE DEEP (sh)	WHITE	COLUMBIA	1949
4137	ELAINE STEWART	portrait		
4138	DIZZY YARDBIRD (sh)	WHITE	COLUMBIA	1950
4139	SLAPHAPPY SLEUTHS (sh)	WHITE	COLUMBIA	1950
4140	VAGABOND LOAFERS (sh)	BERNDS	COLUMBIA	1949
4141	SELF MADE MAIDS (sh)	WHITE	COLUMBIA	1950
4142	PUNCHY COWPUNCHERS (sh)	BERNDS	COLUMBIA	1950
4143	LARAINE DAY	portrait		
4143	STUDIO STOOPS (sh)	BERNDS	COLUMBIA	1950
4144	HOLD THAT MONKEY (sh)	WHITE	COLUMBIA	1950
4145	HIS BAITING BEAUTY (sh)	BERNDS	COLUMBIA	1950
4146	SUPER WOLF (sh)	LORD	COLUMBIA	1949
4147	LET DOWN YOUR AERIAL (sh)	BERNDS	COLUMBIA	1949
4148	LUCILLE BALL	portrait		
4148	ONE SHIVERY NIGHT (sh)	LORD	COLUMBIA	1950
4149	WHA' HAPPEN? (sh)	WHITE	COLUMBIA	1949
4150	NURSIE BEHAVE (sh)	WHITE	COLUMBIA	1950
4151	FRENCH FRIED FROLIC (sh)	WHITE	COLUMBIA	1949
4152	HOUSE ABOUT IT (sh)	WHITE	COLUMBIA	1950
4153	MARINATED MARINER (sh)	WHITE	COLUMBIA	1950
4154	SNITCH IN TIME (sh)	BERNDS	COLUMBIA	1950
4155	BABY SITTERS JITTERS (sh)	WHITE	COLUMBIA	1951
4155	JANE POWELL	portrait		
4156	THREE ARABIAN NUTS (sh)	BERNDS	COLUMBIA	1951
4157	SCRAMBLED BRAINS (sh)	WHITE	COLUMBIA	1951
4157	UNA MERKEL	portrait		
4158	DON'T THROW THAT KNIFE (sh)	WHITE	COLUMBIA	1951
4158	GRACE KELLY	portrait	MGM	
4159	MALICE IN THE PALACE (sh) (see 4119)	WHITE	COLUMBIA	1949
4159	MISSED FORTUNE (sh)	WHITE	COLUMBIA	1952

4160	BLUNDERFUL TIME (sh)	WHITE	COLUMBIA	1949
4160	GRACE KELLY	portrait	MGM	
4161	MERRY MAVERICKS (sh)	BERNDS	COLUMBIA	1951
4161	ROBERT STACK	portrait		
4162	GRACE KELLY	portrait	MGM	
4162	TOOTH WILL OUT (sh)	BERNDS	COLUMBIA	1951
4163	GRACE KELLY	portrait	MGM	
4163	PEST MAN WINS (sh)	WHITE	COLUMBIA	1951
4164	GRACE KELLY	portrait	MGM	
4164	WINE, WOMEN AND BONG (sh)	WHITE	COLUMBIA	1951
4165	GRACE KELLY	portrait	MGM	
4165	TWO ROAMING CHAMPS (sh)	BERNDS	COLUMBIA	1950
4166	GRACE KELLY	portrait	MGM	
4166	HE FLEW THE SHREW (sh)	WHITE	COLUMBIA	1951
4167	FUN ON THE RUN (sh)	WHITE	COLUMBIA	1951
4167	GRACE KELLY	portrait	MGM	
4167	JOHN HODIAK, ANNE BAXTER, HODIAK'S PARENTS	portrait		
4168	GRACE KELLY	portrait		
4168	SLIP AND A MISS (sh)	MCCOLLUM	COLUMBIA	1950
4169	WOO WOO BLUES (sh)	QUINE	COLUMBIA	1951
4170	BLONDE ATOM BOMB (sh)	WHITE	COLUMBIA	1951
4170	MARY CARLISLE	portrait	MGM	
4171	MARY CARLISLE	portrait	MGM	
4171	PLEASURE TREASURE (sh)	WHITE	COLUMBIA	1951
4172	INNOCENTLY GUILTY (sh)	WHITE	COLUMBIA	1950
4173	AWFUL SLEUTH (sh)	QUINE	COLUMBIA	1951
4173	RITA GAM	portrait		
4174	DAREDEVIL JACK	VAN DYKE	PATHE	1920
4174	FOY MEETS GIRL (sh)	ULLMAN	COLUMBIA	1950
4174	RITA GAM	portrait		
4175	MARY CARLISLE	portrait	MGM	
4175	RITA GAM	portrait		
4175	WEDDING YELLS (sh)	WHITE	COLUMBIA	1951
4176	HAPPY GO WACKY (sh)	WHITE	COLUMBIA	1952
4176	RITA GAM	portrait		
4177	SHE TOOK A POWDER (sh)	WHITE	COLUMBIA	1951
4178	CORNY CASANOVAS (sh)	WHITE	COLUMBIA	1952
4178	RITA GAM	portrait		
4179	HULA-LA-LA (sh)	MCCOLLUM	COLUMBIA	1951
4179E	CYD CHARISSE	portrait		
4180	LISTEN, JUDGE (sh)	BERNDS	COLUMBIA	1952
4181	HE COOKED HIS GOOSE (sh)	WHITE	COLUMBIA	1952
4182	UP IN DAISY'S PENTHOUSE (sh)	WHITE	COLUMBIA	1953
4183	GENTS IN A JAM (sh)	BERNDS	COLUMBIA	1952
4184	TROUBLE IN-LAWS (sh)	MCCOLLUM	COLUMBIA	1951
4185	CHAMPS STEP OUT (sh)	BERNDS	COLUMBIA	1951
4185	FRANCES LANGFORD	portrait		
4186	ROOTIN' TOOTIN' TENDERFEET (sh)	WHITE	COLUMBIA	1952
4187	GINK AT THE SINK (sh)	WHITE	COLUMBIA	1952
4188	HEEBIE GEE-GEES (sh)	BERNDS	COLUMBIA	1952
4189	FOOL AND HIS HONEY (sh)	WHITE	COLUMBIA	1952
4189E	HAYA HARAREET	portrait	MGM	
4190	BLISSFUL BLUNDER (sh)	WHITE	COLUMBIA	1952
4191	HOOKED AND ROOKED (sh)	WHITE	COLUMBIA	1952
4192	FRAIDY CAT (sh)	WHITE	COLUMBIA	1951
4192	MARY CARLISLE	portrait	MGM	
4193	AIM, FIRE, SCOOT (sh)	WHITE	COLUMBIA	1952
4194	CUCKOO ON A CHOO CHOO (sh)	WHITE	COLUMBIA	1952
4195	CAUGHT ON THE BOUNCE (sh)	WHITE	COLUMBIA	1952
4195	LARAINE DAY	portrait		
4197	AVA GARDNER	portrait	MGM	
4197	LOOSE LOOT (sh)	WHITE	COLUMBIA	1953
4198	AVA GARDNER	portrait	MGM	
4198	STROP, LOOK AND LISTEN (sh)	WHITE	COLUMBIA	1952
4199	MAXWELL ARCHER, DETECTIVE (UK: MEET MAXWELL ARCHER)	CARSTAIRS	MONOGRAM	1940
4199	TRICKY DICKS (sh)	WHITE	COLUMBIA	1953

4200	THREE DARK HORSES (sh)	WHITE	COLUMBIA	1952
4201	BUBBLE TROUBLE (sh) (2- 4201's - error?)	WHITE	COLUMBIA	1953
4201	RIP, SEW AND STITCH (sh) (2- 4201's - error?)	WHITE	COLUMBIA	1953
4203	GOOF ON THE ROOF (sh)	WHITE	COLUMBIA	1953
4204	HE POPPED HIS PISTOL (sh)	WHITE	COLUMBIA	1953
4205	SPIES AND GUYS (sh)	WHITE	COLUMBIA	1953
4206	LOVE'S A POPPIN' (sh)	WHITE	COLUMBIA	1953
4207	KATHRYN GRAYSON	portrait		
4207	OH, SAY CAN YOU SUE (sh)	WHITE	COLUMBIA	1953
4207	TWO JILLS AND A JACK (sh) (see 4079)	WHITE	COLUMBIA	1947
4208	INCOME TAX SAPPY (sh)	WHITE	COLUMBIA	1954
4209	LINDA CHRISTIAN	portrait		
4209	MUSTY MUSKATEERS (sh)	WHITE	COLUMBIA	1954
4210	SPOOKS (sh)	WHITE	COLUMBIA	1953
4211	FRANK MORGAN	portrait	MGM	
4211	PALS AND GALS (sh)	WHITE	COLUMBIA	1954
4212	PARDON MY BACKFIRE (sh)	WHITE	COLUMBIA	1953
4213	A-HUNTING THEY DID GO	WHITE	COLUMBIA	1948
4213	LINDA CHRISTIAN	portrait		
4214	DOGGIE IN THE BEDROOM (sh)	WHITE	COLUMBIA	1954
4215	DOWN THE HATCH (sh)	WHITE	COLUMBIA	1953
4216	SHOT IN THE FRONTIER (sh)	WHITE	COLUMBIA	1954
4217	KNUTZY KNIGHTS (sh)	WHITE	COLUMBIA	1954
4218	SCOTCHED IN SCOTLAND (sh)	WHITE	COLUMBIA	1954
4219	TOOTING TOOTERS (sh)	WHITE	COLUMBIA	1954
4220	MINER AFFAIR	WHITE	COLUMBIA	1945
4220	TWO APRIL FOOLS (sh)	WHITE	COLUMBIA	1954
4221	KIDS WILL BE KIDS (sh)	WHITE	COLUMBIA	1954
4222	BLUNDER BOYS (sh)	WHITE	COLUMBIA	1955
4223	FLING IN THE RING	WHITE	COLUMBIA	1955
4224	GYPPED IN THE PENTHOUSE (sh)	WHITE	COLUMBIA	1955
4224	KATHRYN GRAYSON	portrait		
4225	OF CASH AND HASH (sh)	WHITE	COLUMBIA	1955
4226	FIRE CHASER (sh)	WHITE	COLUMBIA	1954
4227	CREEPS (sh)	WHITE	COLUMBIA	1956
4227	G. I. DOOD IT (sh)	WHITE	COLUMBIA	1955
4228	BEDLAM IN PARADISE (sh)	WHITE	COLUMBIA	1955
4228	HEAVENLY DAZE (sh)	WHITE	COLUMBIA	1948
4229	KATHRYN GRAYSON	portrait		
4229	STONE AGE ROMEOS (sh)	WHITE	COLUMBIA	1955
4230	HIS PEST FRIEND (sh)	WHITE	COLUMBIA	1955
4231	NOBODY'S HOME (sh)	WHITE	COLUMBIA	1955
4232	WHAM-BAM-SLAM! (sh)	WHITE	COLUMBIA	1955
4233	HOT ICE (sh)	WHITE	COLUMBIA	1955
4234	ONE SPOOKY NIGHT (sh)	WHITE	COLUMBIA	1955
4235	JUNE ALLYSON	portrait		
4235	SCRATCH SCRATCH SCRATCH	WHITE	COLUMBIA	1955
4236	HUSBANDS BEWARE (sh)	WHITE	COLUMBIA	1956
4238	FLAGPOLE JITTERS (sh)	WHITE	COLUMBIA	1956
4239	FOR CRIMIN' OUT LOUD (sh)	WHITE	COLUMBIA	1956
4240	HOOK A CROOK (sh)	WHITE	COLUMBIA	1955
4241	HE TOOK A POWDER (sh)	WHITE	COLUMBIA	1955
4242	ARMY DAZE (sh)	WHITE	COLUMBIA	1956
4242	JACKIE COOPER	portrait		
4243	COME ON SEVEN (sh)	WHITE	COLUMBIA	1956
4244	RUMPUS IN THE HAREM (sh)	WHITE	COLUMBIA	1956
4245	HOT STUFF (sh)	WHITE	COLUMBIA	1956
4246	SCHEMING SCHEMERS (sh)	WHITE	COLUMBIA	1956
4247	COMMOTION ON THE OCEAN (sh)	WHITE	COLUMBIA	1956
4248	ANDY GOES WILD (sh)	WHITE	COLUMBIA	1956
4248	DEBBIE REYNOLDS	portrait		
4249	PARDON MY NIGHTSHIRT (sh)	WHITE	COLUMBIA	1956
4250	MUSCLE UP A LITTLE CLOSER (sh)	WHITE	COLUMBIA	1957
4251	HOOFS AND GOOFS (sh)	WHITE	COLUMBIA	1957
4252	MERRY MIXUP (sh)	WHITE	COLUMBIA	1957
4253	SPACE SHIP SAPPY (sh)	WHITE	COLUMBIA	1957

4256	DEBBIE REYNOLDS	portrait		
4269	CLARK GABLE	portrait		
4270	CLARK GABLE	portrait		
4271	CLARK GABLE	portrait		
4272	CLARK GABLE	portrait		
4273	CLARK GABLE	portrait		
4273	JANE POWELL	portrait		
4274	CLARK GABLE	portrait		
4276	HIS NEW SUIT	MYERS	UNIVERSAL	1925
4282	TWO-FISTED JONES	SEDGWICK	UNIVERSAL	1925
4283	ILONA MASSEY	portrait	MGM	
4285	SMOULDERING FIRES	BROWN	UNIVERSAL	1925
4286	AUDREY TOTTER	portrait	MGM	
4287	AUDREY TOTTER	portrait	MGM	
4290	WESTERN PLUCK	VALE	UNIVERSAL	1926
4291	AUDREY TOTTER	portrait	MGM	
4293	AUDREY TOTTER	portrait	MGM	
4296	STEWART GRANGER	portrait	MGM	
4298	MAUREEN O'SULLIVAN	portrait		
4306	JEAN SIMMONS/STEWART GRANGER	portrait	MGM	
4314	ELEANOR POWELL	portrait		
4314	GINNY SIMMS	portrait		
4314	ROBERT YOUNG	portrait		
4316	ROBERT TAYLOR	portrait	MGM	
4323	ROBERT TAYLOR	portrait	MGM	
4330	MAUREEN O'SULLIVAN	portrait		
4333	JANE POWELL	portrait		
4346	EDMUND PURDOM	portrait	MGM	
4348	ELAINE STEWART	portrait		
4360	NORMA SHEARER	portrait		
4363	RUTH HUSSEY	portrait		
4365	ROBERT TAYLOR	portrait		
4367	EILEEN HECKART	portrait		
4372	RUTH HUSSEY	portrait		
4379	CLARK GABLE	portrait		
4387	LESLIE CARON	portrait		
4388	LESLIE CARON	portrait	MGM	
4403E	DEBBIE REYNOLDS	portrait		
4405E	DEBBIE REYNOLDS	portrait		
4406	MAUREEN O'SULLIVAN	portrait		
4414	DOROTHY MORRIS	portrait		
4414	VAN JOHNSON	portrait		
4418	DOROTHY MORRIS	portrait		
4420	DOROTHY MORRIS	portrait		
4422	ELIZABETH TAYLOR	portrait	MGM	
4423	ELIZABETH TAYLOR	portrait		
4426	ELIZABETH TAYLOR	portrait	MGM	
4429	ELIZABETH TAYLOR	portrait	MGM	
4430	ELIZABETH TAYLOR	portrait		
4432	JEAN HAGEN	portrait	MGM	
4435	JEAN HAGEN	portrait	MGM	
4436	JEAN HAGEN	portrait	MGM	
4437	JEAN HAGEN	portrait	MGM	
4438	JEAN HAGEN	portrait	MGM	
4439	JEAN HAGEN	portrait	MGM	
4440	JEAN HAGEN	portrait	MGM	
4441	JEAN HAGEN	portrait	MGM	
4441	JOHN HODIAK	portrait		
4442	JEAN HAGEN	portrait	MGM	
4443	JEAN HAGEN	portrait	MGM	
4444	JEAN HAGEN	portrait	MGM	
4445	JEAN HAGEN	portrait	MGM	
4445	JOHN HODIAK	portrait		
4446	JEAN HAGEN	portrait	MGM	
4447	JEAN HAGEN	portrait	MGM	
4448	JEAN HAGEN	portrait	MGM	

4449	JEAN HAGEN	portrait	MGM	
4449E	DORIS DAY	portrait		
4450	JEAN HAGEN	portrait	MGM	
4451	JEAN HAGEN	portrait	MGM	
4452	JEAN HAGEN	portrait	MGM	
4452	JOHN HODIAK	portrait		
4453	JEAN HAGEN	portrait	MGM	
4454	JEAN HAGEN	portrait	MGM	
4455	JEAN HAGEN	portrait	MGM	
4456	JEAN HAGEN	portrait	MGM	
4457	JEAN HAGEN	portrait	MGM	
4458	JEAN HAGEN	portrait	MGM	
4459	JEAN HAGEN	portrait	MGM	
4460	FRANCES GIFFORD	portrait		
4460	JEAN HAGEN	portrait	MGM	
4461	VAN JOHNSON	portrait		
4462	VAN JOHNSON	portrait		
4463	VAN JOHNSON	portrait		
4464	VAN JOHNSON	portrait		
4465	VAN JOHNSON	portrait		
4466	VAN JOHNSON	portrait		
4467	VAN JOHNSON	portrait		
4468	VAN JOHNSON	portrait		
4469	VAN JOHNSON	portrait		
4470	VAN JOHNSON	portrait		
4471	VAN JOHNSON	portrait		
4472	CELESTE HOLM	portrait		
4472	VAN JOHNSON	portrait		
4473	JEFF RICHARDS	portrait		
4473	VAN JOHNSON	portrait		
4474	JEFF RICHARDS	portrait		
4474	JOAN BLONDELL	portrait	MGM	
4474	VAN JOHNSON	portrait		
4475	VAN JOHNSON	portrait		
4476	JEFF RICHARDS	portrait		
4476	JOAN BLONDELL	portrait	MGM	
4476	VAN JOHNSON	portrait		
4477	JOAN BLONDELL	portrait	MGM	
4477	VAN JOHNSON	portrait		
4478	JANIS PAIGE	portrait	MGM	
4478	JOAN BLONDELL	portrait	MGM	
4478	MANHUNT IN THE JUNGLE	MCGOWAN	WARNER BROS	1958
4479	JEFF RICHARDS	portrait		
4481	JEFF RICHARDS	portrait		
4482	JEFF RICHARDS	portrait		
4483	ROBERT MONTGOMERY	portrait		
4484	UNA MERKEL	portrait		
4485	CLARK GABLE	portrait		
4486	WHO KILLED SANTA CLAUS? (FR: L'ASSASSINAT DU PERE NOEL 1941)	CHAPATTE	LOPERT	1948
4486E	DEBBIE REYNOLDS	portrait		
4493	ROBERT YOUNG	portrait		
4497	ESTHER WILLIAMS	portrait		
4498	ESTHER WILLIAMS	portrait		
4499	ESTHER WILLIAMS	portrait		
4500	ESTHER WILLIAMS	portrait		
4501	ESTHER WILLIAMS	portrait		
4502	ESTHER WILLIAMS	portrait		
4503	ESTHER WILLIAMS	portrait		
4504	ESTHER WILLIAMS	portrait		
4505	ESTHER WILLIAMS	portrait		
4506	ESTHER WILLIAMS	portrait		
4507	ESTHER WILLIAMS	portrait		
4508	ESTHER WILLIAMS	portrait		
4509	ESTHER WILLIAMS	portrait		
4510	ESTHER WILLIAMS	portrait		
4511	ESTHER WILLIAMS	portrait		

4512	ESTHER WILLIAMS	portrait		
4513	ESTHER WILLIAMS	portrait		
4513	SHANGHAI COBRA	KARLSON	MONOGRAM	1945
4514	ESTHER WILLIAMS	portrait		
4515	ESTHER WILLIAMS	portrait		
4515	MAUREEN O'SULLIVAN	portrait		
4516	ESTHER WILLIAMS	portrait		
4517	ESTHER WILLIAMS	portrait		
4518	ESTHER WILLIAMS	portrait		
4519	ESTHER WILLIAMS	portrait		
4520	ESTHER WILLIAMS	portrait		
4521	ESTHER WILLIAMS	portrait		
4522	ESTHER WILLIAMS	portrait		
4522	UNA MERKEL	portrait		
4523	ESTHER WILLIAMS	portrait		
4523	JANET LEIGH	portrait		
4524	ESTHER WILLIAMS	portrait		
4524	JANET LEIGH	portrait		
4525	ESTHER WILLIAMS	portrait		
4525	JANET LEIGH	portrait		
4526	ESTHER WILLIAMS	portrait		
4526	JANET LEIGH	portrait		
4527	ESTHER WILLIAMS	portrait		
4527	JANET LEIGH	portrait		
4528	ESTHER WILLIAMS	portrait		
4528	JANET LEIGH	portrait		
4529	ESTHER WILLIAMS	portrait		
4529	JANET LEIGH	portrait		
4530	ESTHER WILLIAMS	portrait		
4530	JANET LEIGH	portrait		
4531	JANET LEIGH	portrait		
4532	JANET LEIGH	portrait		
4532	WALLACE BEERY	portrait		
4533	JANET LEIGH	portrait		
4534	JANET LEIGH	portrait		
4535	JANET LEIGH	portrait		
4536	JANET LEIGH	portrait		
4537	JANET LEIGH	portrait		
4538	JANET LEIGH	portrait		
4539	JANET LEIGH	portrait		
4540	JANET LEIGH	portrait		
4546	VERA-ELLEN	portrait	MGM	
4560	JOAN CRAWFORD	portrait		
4563	MARIE DRESSLER	portrait		
4566	MARIE DRESSLER	portrait		
4570	MICKEY ROONEY	portrait		
4575	MARIE DRESSLER	portrait		
4581	MARIE DRESSLER	portrait		
4582	MARIE DRESSLER	portrait		
4583	MARIE DRESSLER	portrait		
4583	MYRNA LOY	portrait		
4590	JUNE ALLYSON	portrait		
4598	NINA MAE MCKINNEY	portrait		
4605	DARK ALIBI	KARLSON	MONOGRAM	1946
4607	GINNY SIMMS	portrait		
4607	MAUREEN O'SULLIVAN	portrait		
4610	KAREN MORLEY	portrait		
4630	WALLACE BEERY + DAUGHTER CAROL ANN	portrait		
4645	MAUREEN O'SULLIVAN	portrait		
4660	RAGS RAGLAND	portrait	MGM	
4662	RAGS RAGLAND	portrait	MGM	
4674	FRANCES GIFFORD	portrait		
4676	MARSHA HUNT	portrait		
4684	VAN JOHNSON	portrait		
4685	DONNA REED	portrait		
4685	SUSAN KOHNER	portrait	MGM	

4688	SUSAN KOHNER	portrait	MGM	
4689	JACKIE 'BUTCH' JENKINS	portrait	MGM	
4690	JACKIE 'BUTCH' JENKINS	portrait	MGM	
4690	VIRGINIA O'BRIEN	portrait		
4691	JACKIE 'BUTCH' JENKINS	portrait	MGM	
4692	JACKIE 'BUTCH' JENKINS	portrait	MGM	
4693	JACKIE 'BUTCH' JENKINS	portrait	MGM	
4693	LARAINE DAY	portrait		
4694	JACKIE 'BUTCH' JENKINS	portrait	MGM	
4694	SUSAN KOHNER	portrait	MGM	
4695	JACKIE 'BUTCH' JENKINS	portrait	MGM	
4696	JACKIE 'BUTCH' JENKINS	portrait	MGM	
4696	KAREN MORLEY	portrait		
4697	JACKIE 'BUTCH' JENKINS	portrait	MGM	
4698	JACKIE 'BUTCH' JENKINS	portrait	MGM	
4698	SUSAN KOHNER	portrait	MGM	
4699	JACKIE 'BUTCH' JENKINS	portrait	MGM	
4701	PORTRAITS OF PORTUGAL (sh)		20TH CENTURY FOX	1937
4702	MEXICAN MURAL (sh)		20TH CENTURY FOX	1937
4703	DUDE RANCH (sh)		20TH CENTURY FOX	1937
4704	ITALIAN LIBYA (sh)		20TH CENTURY FOX	1937
4705	LAND OF THE MAPLE LEAF (sh)		20TH CENTURY FOX	1937
4706	MAUREEN O'SULLIVAN	portrait		
4706	MODERN DIXIE (sh)		20TH CENTURY FOX	1938
4709	GINNY SIMMS	portrait		
4710	GINNY SIMMS	portrait		
4711	GINNY SIMMS	portrait		
4712	GINNY SIMMS	portrait		
4713	GINNY SIMMS	portrait		
4714	GINNY SIMMS	portrait		
4715	GINNY SIMMS	portrait		
4716	GINNY SIMMS	portrait		
4717	GINNY SIMMS	portrait		
4718	GINNY SIMMS	portrait		
4719	GINNY SIMMS	portrait		
4720	GINNY SIMMS	portrait		
4720	GREER GARSON	portrait		
4721	GINNY SIMMS	portrait		
4722	GOOD MORNING JUDGE	SEITER	UNIVERSAL	1928
4722E	RUSS TAMBLYN	portrait		
4723	ROBERT YOUNG	portrait		
4725	NELSON EDDY	portrait		
4727X	FRANCES GIFFORD	portrait		
4730	MARGARET O'BRIEN	portrait		
4731	ROBERT TAYLOR	portrait		
4732	JACKIE 'BUTCH' JENKINS	portrait	MGM	
4733	JACKIE 'BUTCH' JENKINS	portrait	MGM	
4734	JACKIE 'BUTCH' JENKINS	portrait	MGM	
4735	JACKIE 'BUTCH' JENKINS	portrait	MGM	
4738	PETER LAWFORD	portrait		
4739	PETER LAWFORD	portrait		
4739	UNA MERKEL	portrait		
4740	PETER LAWFORD	portrait		
4741	PETER LAWFORD	portrait		
4742	PETER LAWFORD	portrait		
4743	PETER LAWFORD	portrait		
4744	PETER LAWFORD	portrait		
4744	PETER LAWFORD	portrait	MGM	
4745	PETER LAWFORD	portrait		
4745	VIRGINIA GREY	portrait		
4746	PETER LAWFORD	portrait		
4746	UNA MERKEL	portrait		
4747	PETER LAWFORD	portrait		
4748	PETER LAWFORD	portrait		
4748	UNA MERKEL	portrait		
4750	UNA MERKEL	portrait		

4755	MAUREEN O'SULLIVAN	portrait		
4766	GEORGE PEPPARD	portrait		
4773	VIRGINIA GREY	portrait		
4791	PIER ANGELI	portrait	MGM	
4792	PIER ANGELI	portrait	MGM	
4793	PIER ANGELI	portrait	MGM	
4800	SECOND TIME AROUND (mistake? - 53)	SHERMAN	20th CENTURY-FOX	1961
4802	AVA GARDNER	portrait	MGM	
4803	BUDDY EBSEN	portrait		
4804	BUDDY EBSEN	portrait		
4804	HOLLYWOOD PARTY (1934) (SHOWGIRLS)	portrait	MGM	
4805	BUDDY EBSEN	portrait		
4813	HOLLYWOOD PARTY (1934) (SHOWGIRLS)	portrait	MGM	
4821	VIRGINIA GREY	portrait		
4828	VIRGINIA GREY	portrait		
4831	MEL TORME	portrait		
4833	ELAINE STEWART	portrait		
4842	TARZAN THE MIGHTY (serial)	NELSON	UNIVERSAL	1928
4844	MYRNA LOY	portrait		
4859	SPENCER TRACY	portrait		
4862	GREER GARSON	portrait		
4868	JUNE ALLYSON	portrait		
4869	GREER GARSON	portrait		
4871	GREER GARSON	portrait		
4872	FRANCES GIFFORD	portrait		
4874	FRANCES GIFFORD	portrait		
4875	WALLACE BEERY	portrait		
4877	WALLACE BEERY	portrait		
4878	FRANCES GIFFORD	portrait		
4879	WALLACE BEERY	portrait		
4880	JOAN BLONDELL	portrait	MGM	
4881	FRANCES GIFFORD	portrait		
4881	JOAN BLONDELL	portrait	MGM	
4882	FRANCES GIFFORD	portrait		
4888	ELAINE STEWART	portrait		
4889	MAUREEN O'SULLIVAN	portrait		
4890	MY BROTHER JONATHAN (UK)	FRENCH	ALLIED ARTISTS	1948
4890	UNA MERKEL	portrait		
4891	TEMPTATION HARBOR (UK: TEMPTATION HARBOUR)	COMFORT	MONOGRAM	1947
4895	GRACE KELLY	portrait		
4896	GRACE KELLY	portrait	MGM	
4899	FRANCES GIFFORD, RICHARD SIMMONS	portrait		
4900	HOWARD KEEL	portrait		
4901	MICHAEL KIRBY	portrait		
4902	HOWARD KEEL	portrait		
4910	PHYLLIS POVAH	portrait		
4917	DEBBIE REYNOLDS	portrait		
4918	ELIZABETH TAYLOR	portrait		
4919	DEBBIE REYNOLDS	portrait		
4923	HURD HATFIELD	portrait		
4923	MARJORIE MAIN	portrait		
4924	HURD HATFIELD	portrait		
4925	HURD HATFIELD	portrait	MGM	
4926	HURD HATFIELD	portrait		
4926	MYSTERY AT THE BURLESQUE (UK: MURDER AT THE WINDMILL)	GUEST	MONOGRAM	1949
4927	HURD HATFIELD	portrait		
4927	JEAN PARKER	portrait		
4928	HURD HATFIELD	portrait		
4929	HURD HATFIELD	portrait		
4930	HURD HATFIELD	portrait		
4930	KATHRYN GRAYSON	portrait		
4931	HURD HATFIELD	portrait		
4933	BETTY LOU KEIM	portrait		
4933	GREER GARSON	portrait		
4937	MAUREEN O'SULLIVAN	portrait		
4938	BETTY LOU KEIM	portrait		

4938	MAUREEN O'SULLIVAN	portrait		
4939	GLORIA GRAHAME	portrait		
4939	MAUREEN O'SULLIVAN	portrait		
4944	MAUREEN O'SULLIVAN	portrait		
4947	GLORIA GRAHAME	portrait		
4948	ESTHER WILLIAMS	portrait		
4949	ESTHER WILLIAMS	portrait		
4950	ESTHER WILLIAMS	portrait		
4951	ESTHER WILLIAMS	portrait		
4952	ESTHER WILLIAMS	portrait		
4953	ESTHER WILLIAMS	portrait		
4954	ESTHER WILLIAMS	portrait		
4955	ESTHER WILLIAMS	portrait		
4956	ESTHER WILLIAMS	portrait		
4957	ESTHER WILLIAMS	portrait		
4958	ESTHER WILLIAMS	portrait		
4959	ESTHER WILLIAMS	portrait		
4960	ESTHER WILLIAMS	portrait		
4969	JUNE ALLYSON	portrait		
4969	MYRNA LOY	portrait		
4973	MYRNA LOY	portrait		
4977	SPENCER TRACY	portrait		
4981	SPENCER TRACY	portrait		
4982	SPENCER TRACY	portrait		
4983	ESTHER WILLIAMS	portrait		
4985	SPENCER TRACY	portrait		
4988	NELSON EDDY	portrait		
4989	DEBORAH KERR	portrait	MGM	
4992	FRANCES RAFFERTY	portrait		
4992	KAREN MORLEY	portrait		
4997	KAREN MORLEY	portrait		
5000	GODFATHER PART 3	COPPOLA	PARAMOUNT	1990
5003	FAHRENHEIT 451 (UK)	TRUFFAUT	UNIVERSAL	1966
5004	COUNTESS FROM HONG KONG	CHAPLIN	UNIVERSAL	1967
5004	TRUE COLORS	ROSS	PARAMOUNT	1991
5005	CHAMPAGNE MURDERS, THE	CHABROL	UNIVERSAL	1967
5006	JOKERS (UK)	WINNER	UNIVERSAL	1967
5007	DEADLIER THAN THE MALE (UK)	THOMAS	UNIVERSAL	1967
5008	PROJECTED MAN (UK)	CURTEIS	UNIVERSAL	1966
5008	REVENGERS	MANN	NATIONAL GENERAL	1972
5009	ISLAND OF TERROR (UK)	FISHER	UNIVERSAL	1966
5009	MILK MONEY	BENJAMIN	PARAMOUNT	1994
5010	PRIVILEGE (UK)	WATKINS	UNIVERSAL	1967
5011	JOURNEY, THE	LITVAK	MGM	1959
5011	MATTER OF INNOCENCE (UK: PRETTY POLLY)	GREEN	UNIVERSAL	1967
5011	SOUTHSIDE 1-1000	INGSTER	MONOGRAM	1950
5012	CHARLIE BUBBLES (UK)	FINNEY	REGIONAL	1967
5015	RIO LOBO	HAWKS	NATIONAL GENERAL	1970
5016	ANGRY HILLS (UK)	ALDRICH	MGM	1959
5016	WORK IS A 4-LETTER WORD (UK)	HALL	UNIVERSAL	1968
5019	HOUSE OF THE SEVEN HAWKS (UK)	THORPE	MGM	1959
5020	APRIL FOOLS	ROSENBERG	NAT'L GENERAL	1969
5021	DOCTOR'S DILEMMA (UK)	ASQUITH	MGM	1958
5021	OEDIPUS THE KING	SAVILLE	UNIVERSAL	1968
5021	SWITCHBACK	STUART	PARAMOUNT	1997
5022	ANDRE	MILLER	PARAMOUNT	1994
5025	LAST VOYAGE, THE	STONE	MGM	1960
5025	LOVES OF ISADORA (UK: ISADORA)	REISZ	UNIVERSAL	1968
5026	LIBEL (UK)	ASQUITH	MGM	1959
5028	BUTCHER'S WIFE, THE	HUGHES	PARAMOUNT	1991
5030	BOOM! (UK)	LOSEY	UNIVERSAL	1968
5031	DAY THEY ROBBED THE BANK OF ENGLAND (UK)	GUILLERMIN	MGM	1960
5032	ANGEL WORE RED	JOHNSON	MGM	1960
5033	VILLAGE OF THE DAMNED	RILLA	MGM	1960
5034	BIRDS IN PERU (FR)	GARY	UNIVERSAL	1968
5034	SOAPDISH	HOFFMAN	PARAMOUNT	1991

5035	KING OF KINGS	RAY	MGM	1961
5035	SERGEANT RYKER	KULIK	UNIVERSAL	1968
5036	GREEN HELMET (UK)	FORLONG	MGM	1961
5036	NIGHT OF THE FOLLOWING DAY	CORNFIELD	UNIVERSAL	1968
5036	RED HELMET (UK)	FORLONG	MGM	1961
5036	REIVERS, THE	RYDELL	NAT'L GENERAL	1970
5037	RING OF FIRE	STONE	MGM	1961
5038	FATAL ATTRACTION	LYNE	PARAMOUNT	1987
5038	INVASION QUARTET (UK)	LEWIS	MGM	1961
5039	DORE SCHARY	portrait		
5039	I, TARTARI (IT)	THORPE	LUX (MGM)	1961
5039	KING KONG ESCAPES (JAP)	HONDA	UNIVERSAL	1968
5041	LITTLE BIG MAN	PENN	NAT'L GENERAL	1971
5042	FOLLOW THE BOYS	THORPE	MGM	1963
5043	BADGE 373	KOCH	PARAMOUNT	1973
5045	BLUE WATER WHITE DEATH	GIMBEL, LIPSCOMB	NAT'L GENERAL	1971
5045	BOFORS GUN (UK)	GOLD	REGIONAL	1968
5046	COLOSSUS OF RHODES (IT: IL COLOSSO DI RODI)	LEONI	MGM	1961
5046	THREE INTO TWO WON'T GO	HALL	UNIVERSAL	1969
5047	BODY PARTS	DICKERSON	PARAMOUNT	1991
5048	SECRET CEREMONY (UK)	LOSEY	UNIVERSAL	1968
5049	TWO LANE BLACKTOP	HELLMAN	UNIVERSAL	1971
5050	ADDING MACHINE (UK)	EPSTEIN	REGIONAL	1969
5050	HAIL HERO!	MILLER	CINEMA CENTER	1969
5051	HEDY LAMARR	portrait	MGM	
5053	CAN HEIRONYMUS MERKIN EVER FORGET MERCY HUMPPE (UK)	NEWLEY	REGIONAL	1969
5054	MAN CALLED HORSE	SILVERSTEIN	NAT'L GENERAL	1970
5055	JOURNEY TO THE FAR SIDE OF THE SUN (UK: DOPPELGANGER)	PARRISH	UNIVERSAL	1969
5057	AUDREY TOTTER	portrait	MGM	
5057	LE MANS	KATZIN	NAT'L GENERAL	1971
5060	FIGURES IN A LANDSCAPE (UK)	LOSEY	NATIONAL GENERAL	1970
5060	PASSWORD IS COURAGE (UK)	STONE	MGM	1963
5061	PSYCHO	HITCHCOCK	UNIVERSAL	R69
5062	ISTANBUL EXPRESS (tv movie) MARY ANN MOBLEY	IRVING	UNIVERSAL	1968
5062	LIGHT IN THE PIAZZA	GREEN	MGM	1962
5063	JOAN CRAWFORD	portrait	MGM	
5064	ONCE IS NOT ENOUGH	GREEN	PARAMOUNT	1974
5070	ANNE OF THE THOUSAND DAYS (UK)	JARROTT	UNIVERSAL	1969
5071	NUN AT THE CROSSROADS	BUCHS	UNIVERSAL	1967
5074	CAPTAIN SINDBAD	HASKIN	MGM	1963
5075	ACTIVIST, THE	NAPOLEON	UNIVERSAL	1969
5075	TARZAN GOES TO INDIA	GUILLERMIN	MGM	1962
5076	BIG JAKE	SHERMAN	NATIONAL GENERAL	1971
5076	DAY AND THE HOUR, THE (FR: LE JOUR ET L'HEURE 1963)	CLEMENT	MGM	1964
5077	SCROOGE (UK)	NEAME	NATIONAL GENERAL	1970
5079	JUNE ALLYSON	portrait		
5079	ROYAL HUNT OF THE SUN (UK)	LERNER	NATIONAL GENERAL	1969
5080	LAST MOVIE	HOPPER	UNIVERSAL	1971
5082	VAMPIRE IN BROOKLYN	CRAVEN	PARAMOUNT	1995
5083	AFRICAN ELEPHANT	TREVOR	NATIONAL GENERAL	1971
5083	JANE POWELL	portrait		
5084	PET SEMATARY TWO	LAMBERT	PARAMOUNT	1992
5084	STARTING OVER	PAKULA	PARAMOUNT	1979
5087	COMPANY OF KILLERS	THORPE	UNIVERSAL-TV	1971
5087	MUSIC BOX	GAVRAS	CAROLCO	1989
5088	LAST TYCOON, THE	KAZAN	PARAMOUNT	1976
5090	TAKING OFF	FORMAN	UNIVERSAL	1971
5096	YOUNG AND THE BRAVE, THE	LYON	MGM	1963
5097	CATTLE KING	GARNETT	MGM	1963
5097	JUNE ALLYSON	portrait		
5097	MILK MONEY	BENJAMIN	PARAMOUNT	1994
5101	GOOD LUCK - BEST WISHES (sh) (BLESS YOU*)	CHRISTIE	FOX FILM	1934
5102	CONGO	MARSHALL	PARAMOUNT	1995
5102	HIS LUCKY DAY (sh)	CHRISTIE	EDUCATIONAL FILM	1934
5102	RAILWAY CHILDREN (UK)	JEFFRIES	UNIVERSAL	1970
5102	TARZAN'S THREE CHALLENGES (UK)	DAY	MGM	1963

5103	NOBODY'S FOOL	BENTON	PARAMOUNT	1995
5103	SHE'S MY LILY, I'M HER WILLIE (sh)	GRANET, WATSON	EDUCATIONAL FILM	1934
5104	BIG BUSINESS (sh)	BOASBERG	EDUCATIONAL FILM	1934
5105	I.Q.	SCHEPISI	PARAMOUNT	1994
5105	NIFTY NURSES (sh)	JASON	EDUCATIONAL FILM	1934
5106	GIRL FROM PARADISE (sh)		EDUCATIONAL FILM	1934
5107	FRANCES GIFFORD	portrait		
5107	PALOOKA FROM PADUCAH (sh)	LAMONT	EDUCATIONAL FILM	1935
5108	ANN SOTHERN	portrait		
5108	GENTLEMEN OF THE BAR (sh)	CHRISTIE	EDUCATIONAL FILM	1934
5109	MR. WIDGET (sh)	CHRISTIE	EDUCATIONAL FILM	1934
5110	FRANCES GIFFORD	portrait		
5110	FRANKIE & JOHNNY	MARSHALL	PARAMOUNT	1991
5110	ONE RUN ELMER (sh)	LAMONT	EDUCATIONAL FILM	1935
5111	FRANCES GIFFORD	portrait		
5111	OBJECT NOT MATRIMONY (sh)	CHRISTIE	EDUCATIONAL FILM	1935
5112	HAYSEED ROMANCE (sh)	LAMONT	EDUCATIONAL FILM	1935
5113	HAIL BROTHER (sh)	JASON	EDUCATIONAL FILM	1935
5114	NOSE FOR NEWS (sh)	LAMONT	EDUCATIONAL FILM	1935
5114	PRIMAL FEAR	HOBLIT	PARAMOUNT	1996
5114	WAYNE'S WORLD 2	SURJIK	PARAMOUNT	1993
5115	ONLY THE BRAVE (sh)	LAMONT	EDUCATIONAL FILM	1935
5116	GROUNDSTAR CONSPIRACY	JOHNSON	UNIVERSAL	1972
5116	TARS AND STRIPES (sh)	LAMONT	EDUCATIONAL FILM	1935
5117	LIGHT FANTASTIC (sh)	CHRISTIE	EDUCATIONAL FILM	1935
5118	FLIPPERS NEW ADVENTURE	BENSON	MGM	1964
5118	FRIENDLY SPIRITS (sh)	CHRISTIE	EDUCATIONAL FILM	1935
5121	DAYS OF THUNDER	SCOTT	PARAMOUNT	1990
5121	PUBLIC EYE, THE	REED	UNIVERSAL	1972
5121E	TERRY MOORE	portrait	MGM	
5122	KATHRYN GRAYSON	portrait		
5123	SNOOPY COME HOME	MELENDEZ	NAT'L GENERAL	1972
5126	SOMETHING BIG	MCLAGLEN	NAT'L GENERAL	1971
5128	PRIME CUT	RITCHIE	NAT'L GENERAL	1972
5129	PLAY IT AS IT LAYS	PERRY	UNIVERSAL	1972
5130	BOPHA!	FREEMAN	PARAMOUNT	1993
5131	AVA GARDNER	portrait	MGM	
5131	CLUELESS	HECKERLING	PARAMOUNT	1995
5138	LOSING ISAIAH	GYLLENHAAL	PARAMOUNT	1995
5139	JOAN BLONDELL	portrait	MGM	
5141	LESLIE CARON, HOWARD KEEL	portrait		
5144	SLIVER	NOYCE	PARAMOUNT	1993
5145	DAY OF THE JACKAL (UK)	ZINNEMANN	UNIVERSAL	1973
5145	LADY IN ERMINE	FLOOD	FIRST NAT'L	1927
5146	ADDAMS FAMILY VALUES	SONNENFELD	PARAMOUNT	1993
5146	AVA GARDNER	portrait	MGM	
5147	FACE/OFF	WOO	PARAMOUNT	1997
5149	EXPLORERS	DANTE	PARAMOUNT	1985
5151	LESLIE CARON	portrait		
5151	MAN OF THE YEAR (ITALY/FRANCE: HOMO EROTICUS 1971)	VICARIO	UNIVERSAL	1973
5152	GUNS OF A STRANGER	HINKLE	UNIVERSAL	1973
5153	NELSON AFFAIR (UK: BEQUEST TO THE NATION)	JONES	UNIVERSAL	1973
5155	BARBARA STANWYCK	portrait	MGM	
5156	BOY WHO CRIED WEREWOLF	JURAN	UNIVERSAL	1973
5157	DEBORAH KERR, HUSBAND ANTHONY BARTLEY	portrait		
5161	BLACK WINDMILL	SIEGEL	UNIVERSAL	1974
5166	JIM... THE WORLD'S GREATEST (STORY OF A TEENAGER)	COSCARELLI	UNIVERSAL	1975
5166E	AVA GARDNER	portrait	MGM	
5167	RA EXPEDITIONS, THE	BROWNE	UNIVERSAL	1971
5169	DOROTHY PATRICK	portrait	MGM	
5169	LESLIE CARON	portrait		
5170	LESLIE CARON	portrait		
5175	BAWDY ADVENTURES OF TOM JONES, THE	OWEN	UNIVERSAL	1976
5175	CRAZY PEOPLE	BILL	PARAMOUNT	1990
5175	JOAN BLONDELL	portrait	MGM	
5176	JOAN BLONDELL	portrait	MGM	

5177	LESLIE CARON	portrait		
5178	HUNT FOR RED OCTOBER	MCTIERNAN	PARAMOUNT	1990
5182X	AVA GARDNER	portrait	MGM	
5191	DEER HUNTER	CIMINO	UNIVERSAL	1978
5191	JOAN CRAWFORD	portrait	MGM	
5192	FAST CHARLIE... THE MOONBEAM RIDER	CARVER	UNIVERSAL	1979
5192	GYPSY FURY (FR: SINGOALLA 1949)(WIND IS MY LOVER)	JAQUE	MONOGRAM	1951
5192	STEVE FORREST	portrait	MGM	
5194	CHOIRBOYS	ALDRICH	UNIVERSAL	1977
5195	MARILYN MAXWELL	portrait		
5197	PROMISE, THE	CATES	UNIVERSAL	1978
5199	ANN SOTHERN	portrait		
5199	FIVE DAYS FROM HOME	PEPPARD	UNIVERSAL	1978
5200	BLUE COLLAR	SCHRADER	UNIVERSAL	1978
5200	ESTHER WILLIAMS, DAUGHTER SUSAN	portrait		
5201	BRINK'S JOB	FRIEDKIN	UNIVERSAL	1978
5201	HELLO SAILORS (sh)	CHRISTIE	EDUCATIONAL FILM	1934
5201	MARILYN MAXWELL	portrait		
5202	SUPER STUPID (sh)	JASON	EDUCATIONAL FILM	1934
5203	AFRICAN TREASURE	BEEBE	MONOGRAM	1952
5203	SECOND HAND HUSBAND (sh)	CHRISTIE	EDUCATIONAL FILM	1934
5203	SGT. PEPPER'S LONELY HEARTS CLUB BAND	SCHULT	UNIVERSAL	1978
5204	RURAL ROMEOS (sh)	PEARCE	EDUCATIONAL FILM	1934
5205	TWO LAME DUCKS (sh)	GOULDING	EDUCATIONAL FILM	1934
5206	EASY MONEY (sh)	WATSON	EDUCATIONAL FILM	1935
5206	MOMENT BY MOMENT	WAGNER	UNIVERSAL	1978
5207	EAR FOR MUSIC (sh)	WATSON	EDUCATIONAL FILM	1935
5207	MARILYN MAXWELL	portrait		
5208	GROOMS IN GLOOM (sh)	CHRISTIE	EDUCATIONAL FILM	1935
5210	CYD CHARISSE	portrait		
5210	MORE AMERICAN GRAFFITI	NORTON	UNIVERSAL	1979
5214	CATLOW	WANAMAKER	MGM	1971
5215	1941	SPIELBURG	UNIVERSAL	1979
5215	ANN MILLER	portrait		
5216	RETURN OF THE FLY	BERNDS	ALLIED ARTISTS	1959
5216	SITTING TARGET	HICKOX	MGM	1972
5220	RUNNING	STERN	UNIVERSAL	1979
5221	FFOLKES	MCLAGLEN	UNIVERSAL	1979
5222	INTERNATIONAL VELVET	FORBES	UNITED ARTISTS	1978
5223	JERK, THE	REINER	UNIVERSAL	1979
5225	BRASS TARGET	HOUGH	UNITED ARTISTS	1978
5227	CLASH OF THE TITANS	DAVIS	UNITED ARTISTS	1981
5230	DEBBIE REYNOLDS	portrait	MGM	
5233	SHOOT THE MOON	PARKER	MGM	1982
5234	VICTOR/VICTORIA	EDWARDS	MGM	1982
5235	GUYANA CULT OF THE DAMNED	CARDONA	UNIVERSAL	1980
5235	WAYNE'S WORLD 2	SURJIK	PARAMOUNT	1993
5239	PINK FLOYD THE WALL	PARKER	MGM/UA	1982
5240	YEAR OF LIVING DANGEROUSLY	WEIR	MGM	1982
5242	GLORIA DE HAVEN	portrait		
5243	GLORIA DE HAVEN	portrait		
5243	PURSUIT OF D. B. COOPER	SPOTTISWOODE	UNIVERSAL	1981
5243	STRANGE BREW	THOMAS/MORANIS	MGM	1983
5244	GLORIA DE HAVEN	portrait		
5245	GLORIA DE HAVEN	portrait		
5246	GLORIA DE HAVEN	portrait		
5247	GLORIA DE HAVEN	portrait		
5248	AMERICAN WEREWOLF IN LONDON	LANDIS	UNIVERSAL	1981
5250	VAN JOHNSON, DAUGHTER, CHERYL CRANE, ET AL	portrait		
5251	KING OF THE MOUNTAIN	NOSSECK	UNIVERSAL	1981
5255	E.T. THE EXTRA-TERRESTRIAL	SPIELBURG	UNIVERSAL	1982
5256	LITTLE SEX, A	PALTROW	UNIVERSAL	1982
5260	GREAT MUPPET CAPER, THE	HENSON	UNIVERSAL	1981
5260	VIRGINIA BRUCE	portrait		
5261	HONKY TONK FREEWAY	SCHLESINGER	UNIVERSAL	1981
5264	ON GOLDEN POND	RYDELL	UNIVERSAL	1981

5264	VIRGINIA BRUCE	portrait		
5266	BARBAROSA	SCHEPISI	UNIVERSAL	1982
5267	ANN SHERIDAN	portrait		
5269	STEVE FORREST	portrait	MGM	
5273	EVIL UNDER THE SUN	HAMILTON	UNIVERSAL	1982
5273	KATHRYN GRAYSON	portrait		
5274	KATHRYN GRAYSON	portrait		
5275	DEAN MEN DON'T WEAR PLAID	REINER	UNIVERSAL	1982
5275	KATHRYN GRAYSON	portrait		
5276	KATHRYN GRAYSON	portrait		
5277	KATHRYN GRAYSON	portrait		
5278	KATHRYN GRAYSON	portrait		
5279	KATHRYN GRAYSON	portrait		
5279	TENDER MERCIES	BERESFORD	UNIVERSAL	1983
5280	KATHRYN GRAYSON	portrait		
5280	SIX WEEKS	BILL	UNIVERSAL	1982
5281	KATHRYN GRAYSON	portrait		
5282	KATHRYN GRAYSON	portrait		
5283	KATHRYN GRAYSON	portrait		
5284	KATHRYN GRAYSON	portrait		
5285	ICEMAN	SCHEPISI	UNIVERSAL	1984
5285	KATHRYN GRAYSON	portrait		
5285	MAUREEN O'SULLIVAN	portrait		
5286	KATHRYN GRAYSON	portrait		
5287	KATHRYN GRAYSON	portrait		
5288	KATHRYN GRAYSON	portrait		
5289	KATHRYN GRAYSON	portrait		
5290	KATHRYN GRAYSON	portrait		
5291	CROSS CREEK	RITT	UNIVERSAL	1983
5291	KATHRYN GRAYSON	portrait		
5292	KATHRYN GRAYSON	portrait		
5293	BAD BOYS	ROSENTHAL	UNIVERSAL	1983
5293	KATHRYN GRAYSON	portrait		
5294	KATHRYN GRAYSON	portrait		
5295	RUMBLE FISH	COPPOLA	UNIVERSAL	1983
5296	LONELY LADY, THE	SASDY	UNIVERSAL	1983
5300	JAWS 3-D	ALVES	LANDSBURG	1983
5301	EDUCATING PAPA (sh)	LAMONT	EDUCATIONAL FILM	1934
5301	I THANK A FOOL (UK)	STEVENS	MGM-UK	1962
5302	DOMESTIC BLISS-TERS (sh)	PEARCE	EDUCATIONAL FILM	1934
5302	IN THE COOL OF THE DAY	STEVENS	MGM	1963
5302	MAUREEN O'SULLIVAN	portrait		
5303	DEBBIE REYNOLDS	portrait		
5303	HAUNTING	WISE	MGM	1963
5303	THREE CHEERS FOR LOVE (sh)	CHRISTIE	EDUCATIONAL FILM	1934
5304	CAMPUS HOOFER (sh)	GOULDING	EDUCATIONAL FILM	1934
5304	CLEAR AND PRESENT DANGER	NOYCE	PARAMOUNT	1994
5304	COME FLY WITH ME (UK)	LEVIN	MGM	1963
5305	FLIPPER	CLARK	MGM	1963
5305	HANNA K.	GAVRAS	UNIVERSAL	1983
5305	HOW AM I DOING? (sh)	PEARCE	EDUCATIONAL FILM	1934
5306	BOOSTING DAD (sh)	FREDERIC	EDUCATIONAL FILM	1934
5306	DUNE	LYNCH	UNIVERSAL	1984
5307	DIME WITH A HALO	SAGAL	MGM	1963
5307	DUMB LUCK (sh)	HENABERY	EDUCATIONAL FILM	1935
5308	LITTLE BIG TOP (sh)	GOULDING	EDUCATIONAL FILM	1935
5308	RHINO!	TORS	MGM	1964
5309	MOON OVER MANHATTAN (sh)	CHRISTIE	EDUCATIONAL FILM	1935
5309	V.I.P.'S	ASQUITH	MGM	1963
5310	LOVE IN A HURRY (sh)	CHRISTIE	EDUCATIONAL FILM	1935
5311	IT NEVER RAINS (sh)	GOULDING	EDUCATIONAL FILM	1935
5311	JACK CUMMINGS, DEBBIE REYNOLDS	portrait		
5312	ALL FOR ONE (sh)	CHRISTIE	EDUCATIONAL FILM	1935
5312	ELAINE STEWART	portrait		
5312	ZEBRA IN THE KITCHEN	TORS	MGM	1965
5313	ELAINE STEWART	portrait		

5313	REAR WINDOW	HITCHCOCK	UNIVERSAL	R83
5313	TIME OUT (sh)	CHRISTIE	EDUCATIONAL FILM	1935
5314	AROUND THE WORLD UNDER THE SEA	MARTON	MGM	1966
5314	MAGIC WORD (sh)	CHRISTIE	EDUCATIONAL FILM	1935
5315	CLARENCE, THE CROSS EYED LION	MARTON	MGM	1965
5316	LAST STARFIGHTER, THE	CASTLE	UNIVERSAL	1984
5316	LOVED ONES	RICHARDSON	MGM	1965
5317	TANK	CHOMSKY	UNIVERSAL	1984
5319	ELAINE STEWART	portrait		
5320	REPO MAN	COX	UNIVERSAL	1984
5322	MERRY CHRISTMAS, MR. LAWRENCE	OSHIMA	UNIVERSAL	1983
5323	PUBERTY BLUES (AUST 1981)	BERESFORD	UNIVERSAL	1983
5325	CONAN THE DESTROYER	FLEISCHER	UNIVERSAL	1984
5325	ELAINE STEWART	portrait		
5326	FIRESTARTER	LESTER	UNIVERSAL	1984
5326	KENNER	SEKELY	MGM	1969
5327	UNDER THE VOLCANO	HUSTON	UNIVERSAL	1984
5329	ELAINE STEWART	portrait		
5333	COMFORT AND JOY	FORSYTH	UNIVERSAL	1984
5333	ELAINE STEWART	portrait		
5336	ALL OF ME	REINER	UNIVERSAL	1984
5337	CREATOR	PASSER	UNIVERSAL	1985
5340	BRAZIL	GILLIAM	UNIVERSAL	1985
5342	HOWARD KEEL	portrait		
5342	TEST OF LOVE, A	BREALEY	UNIVERSAL	1985
5343	BEST OF TIMES	SPOTTISWOODE	UNIVERSAL	1986
5345	AMERICAN TAIL, AN (t)	BLUTH	UNIVERSAL	1986
5351	NIGHT, MOTHER	MOORE	UNIVERSAL	1986
5352	AMAZON WOMEN ON THE MOON	DANTE	UNIVERSAL	1987
5352	ELAINE STEWART	portrait		
5358	MILAGRO BEANFIELD WAR	REDFORD	UNIVERSAL	1987
5359	LAND BEFORE TIME (t)	BLUTH	UNIVERSAL	1988
5360	NORTH SHORE	PHELPS	UNIVERSAL	1987
5361	KEENAN WYNN	portrait		
5362	BORN IN EAST L. A.	MARIN	UNIVERSAL	1987
5363	GORILLAS IN THE MIST	APTED	UNIVERSAL	1988
5364	WALKER	COX	UNIVERSAL	1987
5365	SERPENT AND THE RAINBOW	CRAVEN	UNIVERSAL	1987
5369	CASUAL SEX?	ROBERT	UNIVERSAL	1987
5370	PRINCE OF DARKNESS	CARPENTER	UNIVERSAL	1987
5371	FORCED VENGEANCE	FARGO	MGM	1982
5372E	BROOKE BUNDY	portrait		
5373	EXPOSED	TOBACK	MGM	1983
5373	THEY LIVE	ARMITAGE	UNIVERSAL	1988
5375	SHAKEDOWN	GLICKENHAUS	UNIVERSAL	1988
5376	DREAM TEAM	ZIEFF	UNIVERSAL	1989
5377	GUARDIAN, THE	FRIEDKIN	UNIVERSAL	1990
5378	FIELD OF DREAMS	ROBINSON	UNIVERSAL	1989
5378	HUNGER, THE	SCOTT	UNIVERSAL	1983
5379	BURBS, THE	DANTE	UNIVERSAL	1989
5381	ROBERT TAYLOR	portrait	MGM	
5382	MAUREEN O'SULLIVAN	portrait		
5382	WATCHERS	HESS	UNIVERSAL	1988
5385	RETURN OF THE MUSKETEERS	LESTER	UNIVERSAL	1989
5386	RENEGADES	SHOLDER	UNIVERSAL	1989
5389	CHRISTMAS STORY	CLARK	MGM	1983
5390	PARENTHOOD	HOWARD	UNIVERSAL	1989
5391	SHOCKER	CRAVEN	TRI STAR	1989
5393	LUISE RAINER	portrait		
5394	DARKMAN	RAIMI	UNIVERSAL	1990
5395	MAUREEN O'SULLIVAN	portrait		
5396	MAUREEN O'SULLIVAN	portrait		
5396	WIZARD, THE	HOLLAND	UNIVERSAL	1989
5397	COUPE DE VILLE	ROTH	UNIVERSAL	1990
5398	MAUREEN O'SULLIVAN	portrait		
5399	OPPORTUNITY KNOCKS	PETRIE	UNIVERSAL	1990

5401	HAVANA	POLLACK	UNIVERSAL	1990
5401	I SURRENDER, DEAR (sh)	SENNETT	EDUCATIONAL FILM	R34 ONLY
5402	ONE MORE CHANCE (sh)	SENNETT	EDUCATIONAL FILM	R34 ONLY
5403	DREAM HOUSE (sh)	LORD	EDUCATIONAL FILM	R34 ONLY
5403	PROBLEM CHILD	DUGAN	UNIVERSAL	1990
5404	BILLBOARD GIRL (sh)	PEARCE	EDUCATIONAL FILM	R34 ONLY
5405	DEBBIE REYNOLDS AT 6 MONTHS	portrait		
5406	MO' BETTER BLUES	LEE	UNIVERSAL	1990
5407	WHITE PALACE	MANDOKI	UNIVERSAL	1990
5408	SPENCER TRACY	portrait		
5409	DEBBIE REYNOLDS AT 18 MONTHS	portrait		
5409	KISS BEFORE DYING, A	DEARDEN	UNIVERSAL	1990
5410	DEBBIE REYNOLDS IN HIGH SCHOOL	portrait		
5410	MAUREEN O'SULLIVAN	portrait		
5410	MICKEY ROONEY	portrait		
5410	ONCE AROUND	HALLSTROM	UNIVERSAL	1990
5411	KING RALPH	WARD	UNIVERSAL	1990
5413	BACKDRAFT	HOWARD	UNIVERSAL	1990
5413	DEBBIE REYNOLDS	portrait		
5414	CAPE FEAR	SCORSESE	UNIVERSAL	1991
5414	MICKEY ROONEY	portrait	MGM	
5415	JUNGLE FEVER	LEE	UNIVERSAL	1991
5417	ARMY OF DARKNESS	RAIMI	UNIVERSAL	1992
5417	DEBBIE REYNOLDS AT 10	portrait		
5418	FRIED GREEN TOMATOES	AVNET	UNIVERSAL	1991
5419	PURE LUCK	TASS	UNIVERSAL	1991
5420	MR. BASEBALL	SCHEPISI	UNIVERSAL	1992
5421	MAD DOG AND GLORY	MCNAUGHTON	UNIVERSAL	1992
5426	FAR AND AWAY	HOWARD	UNIVERSAL	1992
5427	PEOPLE UNDER THE STAIRS	CRAVEN	UNIVERSAL	1991
5428	LORENZO'S OIL	MILLER	UNIVERSAL	1992
5429	PUBLIC EYE, THE	FRANKLIN	UNIVERSAL	1992
5431	HOUSESITTER	OZ	UNIVERSAL	1992
5433	AT PLAY IN FIELDS OF THE LORD	BABENCO	UNIVERSAL	1991
5434	MATINEE	DANTE	UNIVERSAL	1993
5434	MICKEY ROONEY	portrait		
5435	SPLITTING HEIRS	YOUNG	UNIVERSAL	1993
5436	FOR LOVE OR MONEY	SONNENFELD	UNIVERSAL	1993
5437	DRAGON: THE BRUCE LEE STORY	COHEN	UNIVERSAL	1993
5438	COP AND A HALF	WINKLER	UNIVERSAL	1993
5439	DOROTHY MORRIS	portrait		
5439	DR. GIGGLES	COTO	UNIVERSAL	1992
5442	CB4	DAVIS	UNIVERSAL	1992
5442	DOROTHY MORRIS	portrait		
5443	HARD TARGET	WOO	UNIVERSAL	1993
5444	PIER ANGELI	portrait	MGM	
5446	DOROTHY MORRIS	portrait		
5446	JUDGMENT NIGHT	HOPKINS	UNIVERSAL	1993
5447	MICKEY ROONEY	portrait		
5448	DOROTHY MORRIS	portrait		
5448	PIER ANGELI	portrait	MGM	
5449	IN THE NAME OF THE FATHER	SHERIDAN	UNIVERSAL	1993
5451	DEBORAH KERR	portrait	MGM	
5451	DOROTHY MORRIS	portrait		
5452	GETAWAY	DONALDSON	UNIVERSAL	1994
5453	REALITY BITES	STILLER	UNIVERSAL	1994
5454	CROOKLYN	LEE	UNIVERSAL	1994
5455	SHADOW	MULCAHY	UNIVERSAL	1994
5456	WAR, THE	AVNET	UNIVERSAL	1994
5459	RADIOLAND MURDERS	SMITH	UNIVERSAL	1994
5460	WATERWORLD	REYNOLDS	UNIVERSAL	1995
5461	HOWARD KEEL	portrait		
5467	MAJOR PAYNE	CASTLE	UNIVERSAL	1995
5468	CLOCKERS	LEE	UNIVERSAL	1995
5474	SUDDEN DEATH	HYAMS	UNIVERSAL	1995
5478	12 MONKEYS	GILLIAM	UNIVERSAL	1995

5479	JEAN SIMMONS/STEWART GRANGER	portrait		MGM	
5480E	DEBORAH KERR	portrait		MGM	
5483	ELIZABETH TAYLOR	portrait			
5483	QUEST, THE	VAN DAMME		UNIVERSAL	1996
5484E	DEBORAH KERR	portrait		MGM	
5485	DONNA REED	portrait			
5485	HOWARD KEEL	portrait			
5486	DRAGONHEART	COHEN		UNIVERSAL	1996
5487	FLIPPER	SHAPIRO		UNIVERSAL	1996
5488E	DEBORAH KERR	portrait			
5490	EILEEN SEDGWICK	portrait			
5491	DOROTHY PORTER	portrait			
5491	HOWARD KEEL	portrait			
5493	DAYLIGHT	COHEN		UNIVERSAL	1996
5497	MCHALE'S NAVY	SPICER		UNIVERSAL	1997
5501	JACKAL	CATON-JONES		UNIVERSAL	1997
5501	MICE IN COUNCIL (t) (sh)	MOSER		EDUCATIONAL FILM	1934
5501	ROMANTIC COMEDY	HILLER		UNITED ARTISTS	1983
5502	POPE OF GREENWICH VILLAGE (VILLAGE DREAMS)	ROSENBERG		MGM	1984
5502	WHY MULES LEAVE HOME (t) (sh)	MOSER		EDUCATIONAL FILM	1934
5502E	ELIZABETH TAYLOR	portrait		MGM	
5503	JAIL BIRDS (t) (sh)	MOSER		EDUCATIONAL FILM	1934
5503E	ELIZABETH TAYLOR	portrait			
5504	BLACK SHEEP (t) (sh)	MOSER		EDUCATIONAL FILM	1934
5505	MAGIC FISH (t) (sh)	MOSER		EDUCATIONAL FILM	1934
5506	HOT SANDS (t) (sh)	MOSER		EDUCATIONAL FILM	1934
5507	TOM TOM THE PIPER'S SON (t) (sh)	MOSER		EDUCATIONAL FILM	1934
5508	JACK'S SHACK (t) (sh)	MOSER		EDUCATIONAL FILM	1934
5509	SOUTH POLE OR BUST (t) (sh)	MOSER		EDUCATIONAL FILM	1934
5510	DOG SHOW (t) (sh)	MOSER		EDUCATIONAL FILM	1934
5511	FIRST SNOW (t) (sh)	MOSER		EDUCATIONAL FILM	1935
5512	WHAT A NIGHT (t) (sh)	MOSER		EDUCATIONAL FILM	1935
5512E	ELIZABETH TAYLOR	portrait		MGM	
5513	BULL FIGHT (t) (sh)	MOSER		EDUCATIONAL FILM	1935
5514	FIREMAN SAVE MY CHILD (t) (sh)	MOSER		EDUCATIONAL FILM	1935
5515	DEBBIE REYNOLDS	portrait			
5515	MOTH AND THE SPIDER (t) (sh)	MOSER		EDUCATIONAL FILM	1935
5516	OLD DOG TRAY (t) (sh)	MOSER		EDUCATIONAL FILM	1935
5517	FLYING OIL (t) (sh)	MOSER		EDUCATIONAL FILM	1935
5518	FIVE PUPLETS (t) (sh)	MOSER		EDUCATIONAL FILM	1935
5519	PEG LEG PETE THE PIRATE (t) (sh)	MOSER		EDUCATIONAL FILM	1935
5520	MODERN RED RIDING HOOD (t) (sh)	MOSER		EDUCATIONAL FILM	1935
5521	OPERA NIGHT (t) (sh)	MOSER		EDUCATIONAL FILM	1935
5522	KING LOONEY XIV (t) (sh)	MOSER		EDUCATIONAL FILM	1935
5523	MOANS AND GROANS (t) (sh)	MOSER		EDUCATIONAL FILM	1935
5524	AMATEUR NIGHT (t) (sh)	MOSER		EDUCATIONAL FILM	1935
5524	CYD CHARISSE	portrait		MGM	
5525	FOXY FOX (t) (sh)	MOSER		EDUCATIONAL FILM	1935
5526	CHAIN LETTERS (t) (sh)	MOSER		EDUCATIONAL FILM	1935
5528	JANET LEIGH	portrait			
5529	END OF DAYS	HYAMS		UNIVERSAL	1999
5529	JANET LEIGH	portrait			
5530	JANET LEIGH	portrait			
5532	JANET LEIGH	portrait			
5533	MARY BISHOP	portrait			
5534	SKULLS, THE	COHEN		UNIVERSAL	2000
5538E	CYD CHARISSE	portrait		MGM	
5540	CAPTAIN CORELLI'S MANDOLIN	MADDEN		UNIVERSAL	2001
5540E	PIER ANGELI	portrait		MGM	
5541	FAMILY MAN	RATNER		UNIVERSAL	2000
5541E	PIER ANGELI	portrait		MGM	
5545E	PIER ANGELI	portrait			
5547E	JANE POWELL	portrait			
5548E	CYD CHARISSE	portrait		MGM	
5551E	JANE POWELL	portrait			
5554	ESTHER WILLIAMS, HUSBAND BEN GAGE, SON	portrait			

5557	JANET LEIGH	portrait		
5558	JANET LEIGH	portrait		
5558E	DEBBIE REYNOLDS	portrait		
5559	JANET LEIGH	portrait		
5560	JANET LEIGH	portrait		
5560E	DEBBIE REYNOLDS	portrait		
5561	JANET LEIGH	portrait		
5562	JANET LEIGH	portrait		
5562E	DEBBIE REYNOLDS	portrait	MGM	
5563	JANET LEIGH	portrait		
5563E	DEBBIE REYNOLDS	portrait		
5564	JANET LEIGH	portrait		
5564E	DEBBIE REYNOLDS	portrait	MGM	
5565	JANET LEIGH	portrait		
5566	DEBBIE REYNOLDS	portrait		
5566	JANET LEIGH	portrait		
5566E	DEBBIE REYNOLDS	portrait		
5567	JANET LEIGH	portrait		
5568	JANET LEIGH	portrait		
5569	JANET LEIGH	portrait		
5570	JANET LEIGH	portrait		
5571	JANET LEIGH	portrait		
5572	JANET LEIGH	portrait		
5573	DEBBIE REYNOLDS	portrait		
5573	JANET LEIGH	portrait		
5574	DEBBIE REYNOLDS	portrait		
5574	JANET LEIGH	portrait		
5575	JANET LEIGH	portrait		
5577	BARBARA STANWYCK	portrait	MGM	
5586	ANN MILLER	portrait		
5587	ELISABETH MUELLER	portrait	MGM	
5591	DONNA REED	portrait		
5593	WHERE THE BOYS ARE	LEVIN	MGM	1960
5594	DONNA REED	portrait		
5597	JANET LEIGH	portrait		
5601	THEN CAME THE YAWN (sh)	BLAKE, HAYES	EDUCATIONAL FILM	1934
5602	HOLLYWOOD GAD-ABOUT (sh)	LEWYN	EDUCATIONAL FILM	1934
5603	YOUR STARS FOR 1935 (sh)	WATSON	EDUCATIONAL FILM	1934
5604	HOLLYWOOD MOVIE PARADE (sh)		EDUCATIONAL FILM	1934
5604E	DEBBIE REYNOLDS	portrait		
5605	DEBBIE REYNOLDS	portrait		
5605	HARLEM HARMONY (sh)	GOULDING	EDUCATIONAL FILM	1934
5606	CHUMS (sh)		EDUCATIONAL FILM	1935
5607	TAMING THE WILD (sh)		EDUCATIONAL FILM	1935
5608	PERSONALITY AND THE PEN (sh)	WATSON	EDUCATIONAL FILM	1935
5609	SKI SCRAPERS (sh)		EDUCATIONAL FILM	1935
5610	DOG DAYS (sh)		EDUCATIONAL FILM	1935
5612	DONNA REED	portrait		
5622	GRACE KELLY, ESTHER WILLIAMS	portrait		
5628	LYNNE CARVER	portrait		
5642	CYD CHARISSE	portrait		
5646	ANN RUTHERFORD	portrait		
5655	ELEANOR PARKER	portrait	MGM	
5662	ELEANOR PARKER	portrait	MGM	
5679E	BARBARA NICHOLS	portrait	MGM	
5689	BARBARA NICHOLS	portrait	MGM	
5689	ESTHER WILLIAMS	portrait		
5690	BARBARA NICHOLS	portrait	MGM	
5690	ESTHER WILLIAMS	portrait	MGM	
5691	BARBARA LANG	portrait	MGM	
5692	BARBARA NICHOLS	portrait	MGM	
5693	BARBARA LANG	portrait		
5693	ESTHER WILLIAMS	portrait		
5694	ESTHER WILLIAMS	portrait		
5696	BARBARA NICHOLS	portrait	MGM	
5696	ESTHER WILLIAMS	portrait		

5697	BARBARA NICHOLS	portrait	MGM	
5698	ESTHER WILLIAMS	portrait	MGM	
5702	ESTHER WILLIAMS	portrait	MGM	
5703	ESTHER WILLIAMS	portrait		
5704	CALYPSO JOE	DEIN	ALLIED ARTISTS	1957
5704	ESTHER WILLIAMS	portrait	MGM	
5705	DEATH IN SMALL DOSES	NEWMAN	MONOGRAM	1957
5705	ESTHER WILLIAMS	portrait	MGM	
5706	ESTHER WILLIAMS	portrait		
5710	PETER LAWFORD	portrait	MGM	
5711	BEAST OF BUDAPEST	JONAS	ALLIED ARTISTS	1958
5717	LANA TURNER	portrait		
5719E	ELIZABETH TAYLOR	portrait		
5738	ANN SOTHERN	portrait		
5778	ESTHER WILLIAMS + FAMILY AT SUSAN'S CHRISTENING	portrait		
5784	HEDY LAMARR	portrait		
5789	HEDY LAMARR	portrait		
5803	QUEEN OF OUTER SPACE (mistake 5801)	BERNDS	ALLIED ARTISTS	1958
5804	King of the Wild Stallions	SPRINGSTEEN	MONOGRAM	1959
5812	DEAN MARTIN	portrait		
5813	STEVE FORREST	portrait		
5817	DONNA REED	portrait		
5817	ELIZABETH TAYLOR AT 2	portrait		
5821	ELIZABETH TAYLOR	portrait		
5834	VAN JOHNSON	portrait	MGM	
5835	VAN JOHNSON	portrait	MGM	
5836	VAN JOHNSON	portrait	MGM	
5837	RUTH HUSSEY	portrait		
5837	UNA MERKEL	portrait		
5837	VAN JOHNSON	portrait	MGM	
5838	VAN JOHNSON	portrait	MGM	
5839	VAN JOHNSON	portrait	MGM	
5840	RUTH HUSSEY	portrait		
5840	VAN JOHNSON	portrait	MGM	
5841	VAN JOHNSON	portrait	MGM	
5842	VAN JOHNSON	portrait	MGM	
5843	VAN JOHNSON	portrait	MGM	
5845	PIER ANGELI	portrait	MGM	
5846	PIER ANGELI	portrait	MGM	
5846	VIRGINIA GREY	portrait		
5847	PIER ANGELI	portrait	MGM	
5862	BARBARA LANG	portrait		
5869	BARBARA LANG	portrait		
5869E	JANE POWELL	portrait		
5884	VERA-ELLEN	portrait	MGM	
5888	UNA MERKEL	portrait		
5901	BUCKET OF BLOOD, A	CORMAN	AIP	1959
5901	THEM THAR HILLS (sh)	ROGERS	EDUCATIONAL FILM	1934
5902	TIME ON THEIR HANDS (sh)	WATSON	EDUCATIONAL FILM	1934
5903	HOUSE WHERE I WAS BORN (sh)	WATSON	EDUCATIONAL FILM	1934
5904	BOUNDING MAIN (sh)	WATSON	EDUCATIONAL FILM	1934
5905	WAY DOWN YONDER (sh)	WATSON	EDUCATIONAL FILM	1934
5906	GAY OLD DAYS (sh)	WATSON	EDUCATIONAL FILM	1935
5907	SONG PLUGGER (sh)	WATSON	EDUCATIONAL FILM	1935
5908	OLD CAMP GROUND (sh)	WATSON	EDUCATIONAL FILM	1935
5909	FIREMAN'S DAY OFF (sh)	WATSON	EDUCATIONAL FILM	1935
5910	LIFE OF THE PARTY (sh)	WATSON	EDUCATIONAL FILM	1935
5913	JANE POWELL	portrait		
5930	PIER ANGELI	portrait	MGM	
5931	PIER ANGELI	portrait	MGM	
5935	DEBORAH KERR	portrait		
5937	DEBORAH KERR	portrait		
5938	DEBORAH KERR	portrait		
5950	ROGER MOORE	portrait		
5955	ANN SOTHERN	portrait		
5958	BETTY GARRETT	portrait		

5960	MAUREEN O'SULLIVAN	portrait		
5960	MYRNA LOY	portrait		
5962	FREDDIE BARTHOLOMEW	portrait		
5976	NAKED DAWN	ULMER	UNIVERSAL	1955
5979	WARREN WILLIAM	portrait		
5994	JANE POWELL	portrait		
6007	GUNS OF DIABLO	SAGAL	MGM	1965
6008	BEYOND THE TIME BARRIER	ULMER	AIP	1960
6009	AMAZING TRANSPARENT MAN, THE	ULMER	AIP	1960
6009	CYD CHARISSE	portrait		
6010	CYD CHARISSE	portrait		
6011	CYD CHARISSE	portrait		
6011	SPY IN THE GREEN HAT (on some stills)	SARGENT	MGM	1967
6011	SPY WITH MY FACE	NEWLAND	MGM	1965
6012	CYD CHARISSE	portrait		
6013	CYD CHARISSE	portrait		
6014	CYD CHARISSE	portrait		
6015	CYD CHARISSE	portrait		
6018	HAND (UK)	CASS	AIP	1960
6021	MYRNA LOY	portrait		
6022	AGNES MOOREHEAD	portrait	MGM	
6022	MYRNA LOY	portrait		
6023	AGNES MOOREHEAD	portrait	MGM	
6024	AGNES MOOREHEAD	portrait	MGM	
6025	AGNES MOOREHEAD	portrait	MGM	
6025	KARATE KILLERS	SHEAR	MGM	1967
6026	AGNES MOOREHEAD	portrait	MGM	
6026	HELICOPTER SPIES	SAGAL	MGM-TV	1968
6027	AGNES MOOREHEAD	portrait	MGM	
6027	HOW TO STEAL THE WORLD	ROLEY	MGM	1968
6028	AGNES MOOREHEAD	portrait	MGM	
6029	AGNES MOOREHEAD	portrait	MGM	
6030	AGNES MOOREHEAD	portrait	MGM	
6038E	ANN BLYTH	portrait	MGM	
6044	ANN BLYTH	portrait	MGM	
6051	DANGEROUS DAYS OF KIOWA JONES	MARCH	MGM	1967
6052	SCORPIO LETTERS	THORPE	MGM	1967
6053	RETURN OF THE GUNFIGHTER	NEILSON	MGM	1968
6055	WELCOME TO HARD TIMES	KENNEDY	MGM	1967
6056	HONDO AND THE APACHES	KATZIN	MGM	1967
6059	TESS OF THE STORM COUNTRY	GUILFOYLE	LIPPERT	1960
6066	GENE KELLY + BROTHER FRED - DEEP IN MY HEART	portrait		
6067	GENE KELLY + BROTHER FRED - DEEP IN MY HEART	portrait		
6068	GENE KELLY + BROTHER FRED - DEEP IN MY HEART	portrait		
6069	GENE KELLY + BROTHER FRED - DEEP IN MY HEART	portrait		
6070	GENE KELLY + BROTHER FRED - DEEP IN MY HEART	portrait		
6072	FRANCES GIFFORD	portrait		
6072	GENE KELLY + BROTHER FRED - DEEP IN MY HEART	portrait		
6073	GENE KELLY + BROTHER FRED - DEEP IN MY HEART	portrait		
6077	ANN BLYTH	portrait	MGM	
6082	ANN BLYTH	portrait	MGM	
6089	FIVE GATES TO HELL	CLAVELL	20TH CENTURY FOX	1959
6095	CYD CHARISSE	portrait		
6097	MYRNA LOY	portrait		
6098	MYRNA LOY	portrait		
6099	MYRNA LOY	portrait		
6100	MYRNA LOY	portrait		
6101	DOMESTIC EARTHQUAKE (sh)		EDUCATIONAL FILM	1935
6101	MYRNA LOY	portrait		
6102	CYD CHARISSE	portrait		
6102	E FLAT MAN (sh)	LAMONT	EDUCATIONAL FILM	1935
6102	MYRNA LOY	portrait		
6102	TWENTY PLUS TWO	GRUBER	ALLIED ARTISTS	1961
6103	DAUGHTER OF THE SUN GOD	HARTFORD	HERTS-LION INT'L	1963
6103	MOONLIGHT AND ME LADY (sh)		EDUCATIONAL FILM	1935
6103	MYRNA LOY	portrait		

6104	KARL BOEHM	portrait	MGM	
6104	MYRNA LOY	portrait		
6104	PENNY WISE (sh)	CHRISTIE	EDUCATIONAL FILM	1935
6105	LADIES LOVE HATS (sh)	MCCARDELL	EDUCATIONAL FILM	1935
6106	RHYTHM OF PAREE (sh)	CHRISTIE	EDUCATIONAL FILM	1935
6107	TIMID YOUNG MAN (sh)	SENNETT	EDUCATIONAL FILM	1935
6107	WILLIAM POWELL	portrait		
6108	PERFECT THIRTY-SIXES (sh)		EDUCATIONAL FILM	1935
6109	THREE ON A LIMB (sh)	LAMONT	EDUCATIONAL FILM	1936
6110	THANKS MR. CUPID (sh)	LAMONT	EDUCATIONAL FILM	1936
6111	GRAND SLAM OPERA (sh)	LAMONT	EDUCATIONAL FILM	1936
6112	GIVE 'IM AIR (sh)	CHRISTIE	EDUCATIONAL FILM	1936
6113	GOLD BRICKS (sh)	WATSON	EDUCATIONAL FILM	1936
6114	CYD CHARISSE	portrait		
6114	WHITE HOPE (sh)	GRAHAM	EDUCATIONAL FILM	1936
6115	TRIPLE TROUBLE (sh)	CHRISTIE	EDUCATIONAL FILM	1936
6116	HOME ON THE RANGE (sh)	CHRISTIE	EDUCATIONAL FILM	1936
6117	JEANETTE MACDONALD/GENE RAYMOND	portrait	MGM	
6122	ILONA MASSEY	portrait		
6125	DEBORAH KERR	portrait	MGM	
6126	RUSS TAMBLYN	portrait		
6127	RUSS TAMBLYN	portrait		
6130	MUMMY (UK)	FISHER	UNIVERSAL	1959
6137	CYD CHARISSE	portrait		
6143	CYD CHARISSE	portrait		
6145	CYD CHARISSE	portrait		
6152	CYD CHARISSE	portrait		
6155	CYD CHARISSE	portrait		
6157	CYD CHARISSE	portrait		
6161	RED SKELTON	portrait		
6162	CYD CHARISSE	portrait		
6166	CYD CHARISSE	portrait		
6171	CYD CHARISSE	portrait		
6175	VAN JOHNSON	portrait		
6176	CYD CHARISSE	portrait		
6178	CLARK GABLE	portrait		
6179	CYD CHARISSE	portrait		
6179	GENE KELLY + DAUGHTER KERRY	portrait		
6181	GRACE KELLY AT 2, BROTHER JACK, SISTER PEGGY	portrait		
6182	DEBORAH KERR	portrait	MGM	
6182	GRACE KELLY AT 18 MONTHS	portrait		
6183	DEBORAH KERR	portrait	MGM	
6183	GRACE KELLY AT 3, SISTER LIZANN	portrait		
6184	DEBORAH KERR	portrait	MGM	
6185	DEBORAH KERR	portrait	MGM	
6186	DEBORAH KERR	portrait	MGM	
6186	GRACE KELLY	portrait	MGM	
6187	DEBORAH KERR	portrait	MGM	
6188	DEBORAH KERR	portrait	MGM	
6189	DEBORAH KERR	portrait	MGM	
6189	GENE KELLY + DAUGHTER KERRY	portrait		
6189	GRACE KELLY	portrait	MGM	
6190	DEBORAH KERR	portrait	MGM	
6190	GRACE KELLY	portrait		
6191	DEBORAH KERR	portrait	MGM	
6191	GRACE KELLY	portrait		
6193	GRACE KELLY	portrait		
6194	GRACE KELLY	portrait		
6195	GRACE KELLY	portrait		
6199	KARL BOEHM	portrait	MGM	
6200	BURN, WITCH, BURN (UK: NIGHT OF THE EAGLE)	HAYERS	AIP	1962
6201	DAME SHY (sh)		EDUCATIONAL FILM	1936
6201	VINCENTE MINNELLI	portrait		
6203	STYLISH STOUTS (sh)	CHRISTIE	EDUCATIONAL FILM	1935
6204	ROBERT YOUNG	portrait		
6204	YE OLD SAW MILL (sh)	SENNETT	EDUCATIONAL FILM	1935

6205	PANIC IN YEAR ZERO (END OF THE WORLD)	MILLAND	AIP	1962
6206	HE'S A PRINCE (sh)	CHRISTIE	EDUCATIONAL FILM	1935
6207	ONE BIG HAPPY FAMILY (sh)	CHRISTIE	EDUCATIONAL FILM	1935
6208	BRAIN BUSTERS (sh)	EDWARDS	EDUCATIONAL FILM	1936
6209	MIXED POLICIES (sh)	CHRISTIE	EDUCATIONAL FILM	1936
6210	JUST PLAIN FOLKS (sh)	WATSON	EDUCATIONAL FILM	1936
6210	ROBERT YOUNG	portrait		
6211	WHERE IS WALL STREET? (sh)	KANE	EDUCATIONAL FILM	1936
6212	HAPPY HEELS (sh) (changed to 7101)	WATSON	EDUCATIONAL FILM	1936
6212	RAIL BIRDS (sh)	WATSON	EDUCATIONAL FILM	1936
6213	SLEEPLESS HOLLOW (sh)	WATSON	EDUCATIONAL FILM	1936
6213	TOO SOON TO LOVE	RUSH	UNIVERSAL	1960
6214	FRESH FROM THE FLEET (sh)	CHRISTIE	EDUCATIONAL FILM	1936
6218	JEAN SIMMONS/STEWART GRANGER	portrait	MGM	
6219	GRACE KELLY	portrait		
6220	JEAN SIMMONS/STEWART GRANGER	portrait	MGM	
6222	GRACE KELLY	portrait		
6223	GRACE KELLY	portrait		
6225	GRACE KELLY	portrait		
6226	CITY BENEATH THE SEA (tv)	ALLEN	WBTV	1971
6227	JEAN SIMMONS/STEWART GRANGER	portrait	MGM	
6230	GRACE KELLY	portrait		
6231	JEAN SIMMONS/STEWART GRANGER	portrait	MGM	
6232	GRACE KELLY	portrait		
6234	GRACE KELLY	portrait		
6234	HEAD OF A TYRANT (IT: GUIDITTA E OLOFERNE 1959)	CERCHIO	UNIVERSAL	1960
6236	GRACE KELLY	portrait		
6237	GRACE KELLY	portrait		
6239	GRACE KELLY	portrait		
6240	GRACE KELLY	portrait		
6241	GRACE KELLY	portrait		
6242	ESTHER WILLIAMS	portrait		
6242	GRACE KELLY	portrait		
6243	GRACE KELLY	portrait		
6244	GRACE KELLY	portrait		
6246	DONNA REED	portrait		
6247	SPENCER TRACY	portrait	MGM	
6250	DONNA REED	portrait		
6256	NATALIE SCHAFER	portrait		
6260	JANET LEIGH	portrait		
6263	ELIZABETH TAYLOR	portrait		
6263	JANET LEIGH	portrait		
6265	ELIZABETH TAYLOR	portrait		
6266	ANN RUTHERFORD	portrait		
6269	CHARTROOSE CABOOSE	REYNOLDS	UNIVERSAL	1960
6279	SHAKEDOWN (UK)	LEMONT	UNIVERSAL	1960
6280	DOROTHY MORRIS	portrait		
6285	DIANA LEWIS	portrait		
6296	MARIO VAN PEEBLES	portrait	WARNER BROS	
6298	MARIO VAN PEEBLES, (dad) MELVIN, & (brother) MAX	portrait	WARNER BROS	
6301	ESTHER WILLIAMS	portrait	MGM	
6301	MICHELE MORGAN	portrait	MGM	
6301	WAY UP THAR (sh)	SENNETT	EDUCATIONAL FILM	1935
6303	KNOCKOUT DROPS (sh)	LAMONT	EDUCATIONAL FILM	1935
6304	ANNE FRANCIS	portrait	MGM	
6304	CHOOSE YOUR PARTNERS (sh)	LAMONT	EDUCATIONAL FILM	1935
6305	BEWARE OF BLONDES (sh)	CHRISTIE	EDUCATIONAL FILM	1936
6306	LOVE IN SEPTEMBER (sh)	CLINE	EDUCATIONAL FILM	1936
6307	IT HAPPENED ALL RIGHT (sh)	WATSON	EDUCATIONAL FILM	1936
6308	JANET LEIGH	portrait		
6308	PEACEFUL RELATIONS (sh)	WATSON	EDUCATIONAL FILM	1936
6309	JANET LEIGH	portrait		
6313	KATHRYN GRAYSON	portrait		
6314	ANNE FRANCIS	portrait	MGM	
6315	ANNE FRANCIS	portrait	MGM	
6316	ANNE FRANCIS	portrait	MGM	

6317	CLAUDE JARMAN JR	portrait	MGM	
6317	DONNA REED	portrait		
6318	DONNA REED	portrait		
6319	ANNA MARIA ALBERGHETTI	portrait	MGM	
6319	DONNA REED	portrait		
6320	DONNA REED	portrait		
6321	DONNA REED	portrait		
6322	DONNA REED	portrait		
6323	DONNA REED	portrait		
6324	DONNA REED	portrait		
6325	DONNA REED	portrait		
6325	LISA MONTELL	portrait		
6326	DONNA REED	portrait		
6326	TOMBOY AND THE CHAMP	LYON	UNIVERSAL	1961
6327	DONNA REED	portrait		
6327	TROUBLE IN THE SKY (UK: CONE OF SILENCE)	FREND	UNIVERSAL	1960
6328	DEMENTIA 13	COPPOLA	AIP	1963
6328	DONNA REED	portrait		
6329	DONNA REED	portrait		
6330	DONNA REED	portrait		
6331	DONNA REED	portrait		
6331	MESSALINA (IT: MESSALINA VENERE IMPERATRICE 1960)	COTTAFAVI	AIP-TV	1964
6332	DONNA REED	portrait		
6332	LISA MONTELL	portrait		
6332	THOR AND THE AMAZON WOMEN (IT: LE GLADIATRICI)	LEONVIOLA	AIP-TV	1963
6333	DONNA REED	portrait		
6333	QUEEN OF THE SEAS(FR: ADVVENTURE DE MARY READ 1961)	LENZI	AIP-TV	1964
6334	COLOSSUS OF THE ARENA (IT: 1962)	LUPO	AIP-TV	1964
6334	DONNA REED	portrait		
6335	DONNA REED	portrait		
6335	ROME 1585 (IT: L MASNADIERI 1961)	BONNARD	AIP-TV	1964
6336	DONNA REED	portrait		
6337	AVA GARDNER	portrait	MGM	
6337	COLOSSUS AND THE HEADHUNTERS (IT: 1963)	MALATESTA	AIP-TV	1964
6337	DONNA REED	portrait		
6338	AVA GARDNER	portrait	MGM	
6339	AVA GARDNER	portrait	MGM	
6339	REVENGE OF THE BARBARIANS (IT: 1960)	VARI	AIP-TV	1964
6340	AVA GARDNER	portrait	MGM	
6340	TAUR THE MIGHTY (IT: TAUR, RE DELLA FORZA BRUTA 1963)	LEONVIOLA	AIP-TV	1964
6341	AVA GARDNER	portrait	MGM	
6342	AVA GARDNER	portrait	MGM	
6343	AVA GARDNER	portrait	MGM	
6344	AVA GARDNER	portrait	MGM	
6345	AVA GARDNER	portrait	MGM	
6346	AVA GARDNER	portrait	MGM	
6348	LANA TURNER	portrait		
6356	JANE POWELL, DEBBIE REYNOLDS	portrait		
6356	JUNE ALLYSON	portrait	MGM	
6366	MYRNA LOY	portrait		
6367	MYRNA LOY	portrait		
6368	MYRNA LOY	portrait		
6369	MYRNA LOY	portrait		
6370	MYRNA LOY	portrait		
6371	MYRNA LOY	portrait		
6372	MYRNA LOY	portrait		
6373	MYRNA LOY	portrait		
6374	MYRNA LOY	portrait		
6374	SHADOW OF THE CAT (UK)	GILLING	UNIVERSAL	1961
6375	MYRNA LOY	portrait		
6376	ELIZABETH TAYLOR	portrait		
6376	MYRNA LOY	portrait		
6376	ROBERT TAYLOR	portrait		
6377	MYRNA LOY	portrait		
6378	MYRNA LOY	portrait		
6379	MYRNA LOY	portrait		

6380	MYRNA LOY	portrait		
6381	MYRNA LOY	portrait		
6382	MYRNA LOY	portrait		
6383	MYRNA LOY	portrait		
6384	MYRNA LOY	portrait		
6385	MYRNA LOY	portrait		
6386	MYRNA LOY	portrait		
6387	MYRNA LOY	portrait		
6389E	CARROLL BAKER	portrait	MGM	
6391E	CARROLL BAKER	portrait		
6400	RAGS RAGLAND	portrait	MGM	
6402	SECRET INVASION	CORMAN	UNITED ARTISTS	1964
6403	HERCULES AND THE MASKED RIDER (IT: 1963)	PIEROTTI	AIP-TV	1964
6405	ATTACK OF THE NORMANS (IT: I NORMANNI 1962)	VARI	AIP-TV	1964
6406	ATTACK OF THE MOORS (IT: I REALI DI FRANCIA 1959)	COSTA	AIP-TV	1964
6407	TAUR THE MIGHTY (IT: TAUR, RE DELLA FORZA BRUTA 1963)	LEONVIOLA	AIP-TV	1964
6408	WOMEN OF DEVIL'S ISLAND (FR: 1962)	PAOLELLA	AIP-TV	1964
6410	COLOSSUS AND THE AMAZON QUEEN (IT: 1960)	SALA	AIP-TV	1964
6411	MASKED CONQUEROR, THE (IT: 1962)	CAPUANO	AIP-TV	1964
6412	FAY BAINTER	portrait		
6413	REVENGE OF THE MUSKETEERS (IT: 1963)	TULUI	AIP-TV	1964
6414	FAY BAINTER	portrait		
6415	MASK OF THE MUSKETEERS (IT: 1963)	CAPUANO	AIP-TV	1964
6416	SARACENS, THE (IT: IL PIRATA DEL DIAVOLO 1963)	MAURI	AIP-TV	1964
6419	TEN GLADIATORS (IT: I DIECI GLADIATORI 1963)	PAROLINI	AIP-TV	1964
6420	79 A. D. (IT: ANNO 79: DISTRUZIONE DI ERCOLANO 1962)	PAROLINI	AIP-TV	1964
6421	AUDREY TOTTER	portrait	MGM	
6422	AUDREY TOTTER	portrait	MGM	
6423	AUDREY TOTTER	portrait	MGM	
6424	AUDREY TOTTER	portrait	MGM	
6425	AUDREY TOTTER	portrait	MGM	
6426	UNDER AGE	BUCHANAN	FALCON INTERNATIONAL	1964
6427	HERCULES AND THE BLACK PIRATES (IT)	CAPUANO	AIP-TV	1964
6428	HERCULES AGAINST THE MONGOLS (IT: 1963)	PAOLELLA	AIP-TV	1964
6429	BLACK INVADERS (IT: ODIO MORTALE 1962)	MONTEMURRO	AIP-TV	1964
6429	FRANCES GIFFORD	portrait		
6430	MUSKETEERS OF THE SEA (IT: 1962)	PATRIZI	AIP-TV	1964
6431	KING OF THE VIKINGS (IT: PRINCIPE ENCADENADO 1960)	LUCIA	AIP-TV	1964
6432	HERCULES AGAINST ROME (IT: ERCOLE CONTRO ROMA)	PIEROTTI	AIP-TV	1964
6433	BRENNUS, ENEMY OF ROME (IT: 1963)	GENTILOMO	AIP-TV	1964
6435	HERCULES AGAINST THE BARBARIANS (IT)	PAOLELLA	AIP-TV	1964
6437	GENE KELLY	portrait	MGM	
6438	GENE KELLY	portrait	MGM	
6439	GENE KELLY	portrait	MGM	
6440	GENE KELLY	portrait	MGM	
6441	GENE KELLY	portrait	MGM	
6442	GENE KELLY	portrait	MGM	
6443	GENE KELLY	portrait	MGM	
6444	GENE KELLY	portrait	MGM	
6445	GENE KELLY	portrait	MGM	
6445	INVISIBLE CREATURE (HOUSE IN MARSH ROAD)	TULLY	AIP	1964
6446	GENE KELLY	portrait	MGM	
6447	GENE KELLY	portrait	MGM	
6448	GENE KELLY	portrait	MGM	
6448	OPERATION SNAFU (UK: ON THE FIDDLE)	FRANKEL	AIP	1965
6449	GENE KELLY	portrait	MGM	
6449	PHANTOM PLANET, THE	MARSHALL	AIP	1961
6450	DESERT PATROL (UK: SEA OF SAND)	GREEN	UNIVERSAL	1958
6450	GENE KELLY	portrait	MGM	
6451	DAY THE EARTH FROZE, THE (FIN: SAMPO 1959)	PTUSHKO	AIP-TV	1964
6451	GENE KELLY	portrait	MGM	
6452	ASSIGNMENT OUTER SPACE (IT: SPACE MEN 1960)	MARGHERITI (DAISIES)	AIP	1961
6452	GENE KELLY	portrait	MGM	
6453	BLANCHEVILLE MONSTER, THE (IT: HORROR 1963)	DE MARTINO (HERBERT)	AIP-TV	1964
6453	GENE KELLY	portrait	MGM	
6454	JOAN McCRACKEN	portrait	MGM	

6454	NEARLY A NASTY ACCIDENT (UK)	CHAFFEY	UNIVERSAL	1961
6455	APEMAN OF THE JUNGLE (IT: 1964)	VEO (FOSTER)	AIP-TV	1965
6455	JOAN McCRACKEN	portrait	MGM	
6456	HAWK OF BAGDAD (ALI BABA & THE 7 SARACENS) (IT)	SALVI	AIP	1964
6456	JOAN McCRACKEN	portrait	MGM	
6471	ILONA MASSEY	portrait	MGM	
6474	TOM DRAKE	portrait	MGM	
6475	TOM DRAKE	portrait	MGM	
6476	TOM DRAKE	portrait	MGM	
6477	TOM DRAKE	portrait	MGM	
6478	TOM DRAKE	portrait	MGM	
6483	DOLORES GRAY	portrait		
6497	NIGHT CREATURES (UK: CAPTAIN CLEGG)	SCOTT	UNIVERSAL-INT'L	1962
6500	GREER GARSON	portrait		
6501	BIRD LAND (t) (sh)	MOSER	EDUCATIONAL FILM	1935
6501	GREER GARSON	portrait		
6501	LOST WORLD OF SINBAD, THE (JAP: DAI TOZOKU 1963	TANIGUCHI	AIP	1965
6502	GREER GARSON	portrait		
6502	SLAVE QUEEN OF BABYLON (IT: IO SEMIRAMIDE 1963)	ZEGLIO	AIP-TV	1964
6503	HEY DIDDLE DIDDLE (t) (sh)	MOSER	EDUCATIONAL FILM	1935
6504	DOE AVEDON	portrait	MGM	
6505	CYD CHARISSE	portrait		
6507	ALADDIN'S LAMP (t) (sh)	MOSER	EDUCATIONAL FILM	1935
6507	MAN IN OUTER SPACE (CZ: MUZ Z PRVNIHO STOLETI 1962)	LIPSKY	AIP-TV	1965
6508	FIRE OVER ROME (IT: L'INCENDIO DI ROMA)	MALATESTA	AIP-TV	1965
6508	SOUTHERN HORSE-PITALITY (t) (sh)	MOSER	EDUCATIONAL FILM	1935
6509	SWORD OF THE EMPIRE (IT: UNA SPADA PER L'IMPERO)	GRIECO	AIP-TV	1964
6509	YE OLDE TOY SHOP (t) (sh)	MOSER	EDUCATIONAL FILM	1935
6509E	PIER ANGELI	portrait	MGM	
6510	HERCULES, PRISONER OF EVIL (IT)	MARGHERITI (DAWSON)	AIP-TV	1964
6510	MAYFLOWER (t) (sh)	MOSER	EDUCATIONAL FILM	1935
6511	FEUD (t) (sh)	MOSER	EDUCATIONAL FILM	1936
6511	WAR OF THE ZOMBIES (IT) (mistake - see 6512)	VARI	AIP	1965
6512	19TH HOLE CLUB (t) (sh)	MOSER	EDUCATIONAL FILM	1936
6512	LARAINE DAY	portrait		
6513	ATTACK OF THE MUSHROOM PEOPLE (JAP: MATANGO 1963)	HONDA	AIP-TV	1965
6513	HOMETOWN OLYMPICS (t) (sh)	MOSER	EDUCATIONAL FILM	1936
6513	LARAINE DAY	portrait		
6514	ALPINE YODELER (t) (sh)	MOSER	EDUCATIONAL FILM	1936
6514	LARAINE DAY	portrait		
6514	NO MAN IS AN ISLAND	GOLDSTONE	UNIVERSAL	1962
6514	VAMPIRE, THE (MEX: EL VAMPIRO 1957)	MENDEZ	AIP-TV	1964
6515	BARNYARD AMATEURS (t) (sh)	MOSER	EDUCATIONAL FILM	1936
6515	LARAINE DAY	portrait		
6515	LIVING HEAD, THE (MEX: LA CABEZA VIVIENTI 1963)	URUETA	AIP-TV	1965
6516	BRAINIAC, THE (MEX: EL BARON DEL TERROR 1962)	URUETA	AIP-TV	1965
6516	GREER GARSON	portrait		
6516	LARAINE DAY	portrait		
6516	OFF TO CHINA (t) (sh)	MOSER	EDUCATIONAL FILM	1936
6517	INVASION OF THE VAMPIRES (MEX: 1963)	MORAYTA	AIP-TV	1965
6517	LARAINE DAY	portrait		
6517	LAUREN BACALL	portrait	MGM	
6517	WESTERN TRAIL (t) (sh)	DAVIS	EDUCATIONAL FILM	1936
6518	DEBBIE REYNOLDS	portrait		
6518	LARAINE DAY	portrait		
6518	WITCH'S MIRROR, THE (MEX: ESPEJO DE LA BRUJA 1962)	URUETA	AIP-TV	1965
6518	WOLF IN CHEAP CLOTHING (t) (sh)	DAVIS	EDUCATIONAL FILM	1936
6519	CURSE OF THE CRYING WOMAN (MEX: 1963)	BALEDON	AIP-TV	1965
6519	LARAINE DAY	portrait		
6519	ROLLING STONES (t) (sh)	DAVIS	EDUCATIONAL FILM	1936
6520	FARMER ALFALFA AND THE RUNT (t) (sh)		EDUCATIONAL FILM	1936
6520	SAMSOM VS THE VAMPIRE WOMEN (MEX: 1962)	BLAKE	AIP-TV	1965
6521	BUSY BEE (t) (sh)	DAVIS	EDUCATIONAL FILM	1936
6521	DESERT RAIDERS (IT: DOMINATORE DEL DESERTO 1964)	BOCCIA (ANTON)	AIP-TV	1965
6522	CURSE OF THE DOLL PEOPLE (MEX: 1961)	ALARAKI	AIP-TV	1965
6522	SAILOR'S HOME (t) (sh)		EDUCATIONAL FILM	1936

6523	TOUGH EGG (t) (sh)	DAVIS	EDUCATIONAL FILM	1936
6524	DOCTOR OF DOOM (MEX: 1963)	CARDONA	AIP-TV	1965
6524	HOT SPELL (t) (sh)	DAVIS	EDUCATIONAL FILM	1936
6525	PUDDY THE PUP AND THE GYPSIES (t) (sh)	DAVIS	EDUCATIONAL FILM	1936
6525	VAMPIRE'S COFFIN (MEX: ATAUD DEL VAMPIRO 1958)	MENDEZ	AIP-TV	1965
6526	CURSE OF NOSTRADAMUS (MEX: 1961)	CURIEL	AIP-TV	1965
6526	ESTHER WILLIAMS	portrait		
6526	PRIZE PACKAGE (t) (sh)	GORDON	EDUCATIONAL FILM	1936
6527	DEBBIE REYNOLDS	portrait		
6527	SAMSON IN THE WAX MUSEUM (MEX: 1963)	BLAKE	AIP-TV	1965
6527	WOMAN'S WORLD	NEGULESCO	20TH CENTURY FOX	1954
6529	GENII OF DARKNESS (MEX: 1962)	CURIEL	AIP-TV	1965
6531	MAN AND THE MONSTER (MEX: 1959)	BALEDON	AIP-TV	1965
6532	CURSE OF THE ATEC MUMMY (MEX: 1957)	PORTILLO	AIP-TV	1965
6533	BLOODY VAMPIRE (MEX: VAMPIRO SANGRIENTO 1962)	MORAYTA	AIP-TV	1965
6535	CHALLENGE OF THE GLADIATOR (IT)	PAOLELLA	AIP-TV	1965
6536	GREER GARSON	portrait		
6536	SWINGER'S PARADISE (UK: WONDERFUL LIFE)	FURIE	AIP	1965
6537	GREER GARSON	portrait		
6539	GREER GARSON	portrait		
6541	SOUTH OF TANA RIVER (DEN: SYD FOR TANA RIVER 1963)	CHRISTENSEN	AIP-TV	1965
6542	HERCULES OF THE DESERT (IT)	BOCCIA (ANTON)	AIP-TV	1964
6542	ROGER MOORE	portrait	MGM	
6543	REVENGE OF THE GLADIATORS(IT: VENDETTA DI SPARTACUS)	LUPO	AIP-TV	1964
6544	HERCULES AND THE TREASURE OF THE INCAS (IT)	PIEROTTI	AIP-TV	1964
6545	BEACH GIRLS AND THE MONSTER (r: SURF TERROR)	HALL	AIP-TV	1966
6546	INCIDENT IN SAIGON (FR: TRANSIT A SAIGON 1963)	LEDUC	AIP-TV	1965
6547	OUTPOST IN INDO-CHINA (FR: FORT-DU-FOU 1963)	JOANNON	AIP-TV	1965
6548	MARILYN MAXWELL	portrait		
6550	CRY OF THE BEWITCHED (CUBA: YAMBAO 1957)	CREVENNA	AIP-TV	1965
6551	GREER GARSON	portrait		
6553	GREER GARSON	portrait		
6554	ESCAPE FROM SIAGON (FR: LE CAPTIF 1963)	LABRO	AIP-TV	1965
6555	ADVENTURES IN INDOCHINA (FR: 1958)	BASTIA	AIP-TV	1965
6556	ESCAPADE (FR: 1957)	HABIB	AIP-TV	1965
6558	BLACK MONOCLE, THE (FR: LE MONOCLE NOIR 1961)	LAUTNER	AIP-TV	1965
6561	WALLS OF FEAR (THE HIDEOUT) (FR: LA PLANQUE 1962)	ANDRE	AIP-TV	1965
6563	DANGER IN THE MIDDLE EAST (FR: 1960)	CLEMENT	AIP-TV	1965
6564	JEAN-PIERRE AUMONT	portrait		
6565	JEAN-PIERRE AUMONT	portrait		
6566	JANE POWELL	portrait		
6566	JEAN-PIERRE AUMONT	portrait		
6567	EYE FOR AN EYE, AN (FR: OEIL POUR OEIL 1957)	CAYATTE	AIP-TV	1965
6568	DIANA LEWIS	portrait		
6569	ATOMIC AGENT (FR: NATHALIE, AGENT SECRET 1959)	DECOIN	AIP-TV	1965
6569	JANE POWELL	portrait		
6570	JANE POWELL	portrait		
6571	DAGORA, THE SPACE MONSTER (DOGORA) (JAP: 1964)	HONDA	AIP-TV	1965
6571	JANE POWELL	portrait		
6572	JANE POWELL	portrait		
6573	JANE POWELL	portrait		
6574	JANE POWELL	portrait		
6575	JANE POWELL	portrait		
6575	SWORD OF LANCELOT (UK: LANCELOT AND GUINEVERE)	WILDE	UNIVERSAL	1963
6576	GIANT OF THE EVIL ISLAND (IT)	PIEROTTI	AIP-TV	1965
6576	JANE POWELL	portrait		
6576	MYSTERY SUBMARINE (UK)	PENNINGTON-RICHARDS	UNIVERSAL	1963
6577	FRANCES RAFFERTY	portrait		
6577	JANE POWELL	portrait		
6578	JANE POWELL	portrait	MGM	
6579	ARLENE DAHL	portrait		
6579	JANE POWELL	portrait		
6580	ARLENE DAHL	portrait		
6580	JANE POWELL	portrait		
6581	ARLENE DAHL	portrait		
6582	ARLENE DAHL	portrait		

6583	ARLENE DAHL	portrait		
6583	TRAPPED BY FEAR (FR: LES DISTRACTIONS 1960)	DUPONT	AIP-TV	1965
6584	ARLENE DAHL	portrait		
6585	ARLENE DAHL	portrait		
6585	JANE POWELL	portrait		
6586	ARLENE DAHL	portrait		
6587	DESTINATION FURY (MANI IN ALTO 1961)	BIANCHI	AIP-TV	1965
6587	LANA TURNER	portrait		
6588	WHEREABOUTS UNKNOWN (FR)	STELLI	AIP-TV	1965
6589	NEST OF SPIES (FR: ALERTE AU DEUXIEME BUREAU 1956)	STELLI	AIP-TV	1965
6591	PARANOIAC (UK)	FRANCIS	UNIVERSAL	1963
6598E	PAULA PRENTISS	portrait		
6601	CLEVER CRITTERS (sh)		EDUCATIONAL FILM	1935
6602	FAY HOLDEN	portrait	MGM	
6602	INVASION (UK)	BRIDGES	AIP-TV	1966
6603	DESERT FIGHTERS (SP: TRES HOMBRES VAN A MORIR 1954)	CATALAN	AIP-TV	1965
6603	MANHATTAN TAPESTRY (sh)		EDUCATIONAL FILM	1936
6605	SPACE PROBE TAURUS	KATZMAN	AIP-TV	1965
6606	FAY HOLDEN	portrait	MGM	
6606	SEEING EYE (sh)		EDUCATIONAL FILM	1936
6607	BLOOD BATH (TRACK OF THE VAMPIRE)	HILL, ROTHMAN	AIP	1966
6607	FAY HOLDEN	portrait	MGM	
6607	GAME OF JAI ALAI (sh)		EDUCATIONAL FILM	1935
6608	FAY HOLDEN	portrait	MGM	
6608	QUEEN OF BLOOD (PLANET OF BLOOD)	HARRINGTON	AIP	1966
6608	SWORDFISH (FISHERMAN'S LUCK) (sh)		EDUCATIONAL FILM	1936
6609	FAST FRIENDS (sh)	FOSTER	EDUCATIONAL FILM	1936
6609	FAY HOLDEN	portrait	MGM	
6609	LEGEND OF THE LEI (sh) (changed to 7606)		EDUCATIONAL FILM	1936
6609	SCARLET BARONESS (GER: DIE FEUERROTE BARONESS 1959)	JUGERT	AIP-TV	1966
6610	ANIMAL CUNNING (sh)		EDUCATIONAL FILM	1936
6610	FAY HOLDEN	portrait	MGM	
6611	HEADHUNTERS OF THE AMAZON		AIP-TV	1966
6620	DESERT WAR (IT: QUATTRO NOTTI CON ALBA)	D'AMICO	AIP-TV	1962
6623	JANE POWELL	portrait		
6623	TOMMY DORSEY	portrait		
6624	M.M.M. 83 (IT: MISSIONE MORTE MOLO 83)	BERGONZELLI	AIP-TV	1966
6625	JEAN HAGEN	portrait		
6625	KILLERS ARE CHALLENGED (IT: A 077, SFIDA AI KILLERS)	MARGHERITI (DAWSON)	AIP-TV	1966
6628	IL BIDONE (IT)	FELLINI	ASTOR	1955
6628	SWINDLE, THE (IT: IL BIDONE 1955)	FELLINI	AIP-TV	1966
6629E	BRIGID BAZLEN	portrait		
6631	DEVIL'S BLAST, THE (FR) (doc)	TAZIEFF	AIP-TV	1965
6632	IVORY COAST ADVENTURE (FR: GENTLEMAN DE COCODY)	JAQUE	AIP	1965
6641	DEBBIE REYNOLDS	portrait		
6641	SECRET AGENTS (GER: DIRTY GAME)	JAQUE, KLINGLER	AIP	1966
6644	CASTLE OF THE LIVING DEAD (IT)	KIEFER, RICCI	AIP	1964
6645	DEBBIE REYNOLDS	portrait		
6646	DEBBIE REYNOLDS	portrait	MGM	
6646	GIRL GETTERS, THE (UK: THE SYSTEM 1964)	WINNER	AIP	1966
6646	JANIS PAIGE	portrait	MGM	
6650	VIOLENT JOURNEY, A (FOOL KILLER)	GONZALEZ	AIP	1966
6658	SERVANT	LOSEY	LANDAU RELEASING	1964
6659E	PIER ANGELI	portrait	MGM	
6660	JANE POWELL	portrait		
6661	BANG, BANG YOU'RE DEAD (UK: OUR MAN IN MARRAKESH)	SHARP	AIP	1966
6661	JANE POWELL	portrait		
6662	MACABRO	MARSHALL	AIP	1966
6670	MARY ASTOR	portrait	MGM	
6671	MARY ASTOR	portrait	MGM	
6672	MARY ASTOR	portrait	MGM	
6673	GLASS SPHINX, THE (IT: LA SFINGE D'ORO)	SCATTINI	AIP	1967
6673	HALLUCINATION GENERATION (mistake? See 6676)	MANN	AIP	1966
6673	MARY ASTOR	portrait	MGM	
6674	MARY ASTOR	portrait	MGM	
6674	PSYCHO CIRCUS (UK: CIRCUS OF FEAR)	MOXEY	AIP	1967

6675	FRANCES GIFFORD	portrait		
6675	MARY ASTOR	portrait	MGM	
6676	FRANCES GIFFORD	portrait		
6676	MARY ASTOR	portrait	MGM	
6677	MARY ASTOR	portrait	MGM	
6678	MARY ASTOR	portrait	MGM	
6685E	ELIZABETH TAYLOR	portrait		
6687	ELIZABETH TAYLOR	portrait		
6693	ELIZABETH TAYLOR	portrait		
6699	ELIZABETH TAYLOR	portrait		
6702	IT'S A BIKINI WORLD (THE GIRL IN DADDY'S BIKINI)	ROTHMAN	AIP	1967
6703	ELIZABETH TAYLOR	portrait	MGM	
6705	MONDO-TEENO (TEENAGE REBELLION)	HERMAN	AIP	AIP
6706E	JEAN SIMMONS	portrait	MGM	
6707	FORTUNA (ISR)	GOLAN	AIP	1966
6707	JANET LEIGH	portrait		
6708	CURSE OF THE SWAMP CREATURE	BUCHANONA	AIP	1966
6708E	JEAN SIMMONS	portrait	MGM	
6711E	JEAN SIMMONS	portrait	MGM	
6714	MAJIN MONSTER OF TERROR (JAP: DIAMAJIN 1966)	YASUDA	AIP-TV	1968
6715	BARBARA LANG	portrait		
6715	MONSTER FROM A PREHISTORIC PLANET (JAP: 1967)	NOGUCHI	AIP-TV	1968
6716	BARBARA LANG	portrait		
6716	BEAST OF MOROCCO (UK: HAND OF NIGHT)	GOODE	AIP-TV	1968
6716	NAKED RUNNER (UK)	FURIE	WARNER BROS.	1967
6717	ELIZABETH TAYLOR	portrait	MGM	
6718	EDWARD ARNOLD	portrait		
6719	EDWARD ARNOLD	portrait		
6720	EDWARD ARNOLD	portrait		
6720	ELIZABETH TAYLOR	portrait		
6720	MANEATER OF HYDRA (ISLAND OF THE DOOMED)	WELLES	AIP	1967
6721	BARBARA LANG	portrait		
6721	EDWARD ARNOLD	portrait		
6721	MARS NEEDS WOMEN	BUCHANAN	AIP	1967
6722	ELIZABETH TAYLOR	portrait		
6722	SADISMO (doc)		AIP	1967
6723	WAR OF THE MONSTERS (JAP: KAIJU DAISENSO 1965)	HONDA	AIP-TV	1967
6724	BARBARA LANG	portrait		
6724	DEATH IS A WOMAN (LOVE IS A WOMAN)	GOODE	AIP	1966
6725	BARBARA LANG	portrait		
6725	ISLAND AFFAIR (IT: PECCATI D'ESTATE 1962)	BIANCHI	AIP-TV	1968
6726	ELIZABETH TAYLOR	portrait	MGM	
6727	BARBARA LANG	portrait	MGM	
6727	RUN PSYCHO RUN (IT: PIU TARDI, CLAIRE, PIU TARDI)	RONDI	AIP-TV	1968
6728	SAPPHIRE (UK)	DEARDEN	UNIVERSAL	1959
6730	TRANS EUROPE EXPRESS	ROBBE-GRILLET	TRANSAMERICA	1968
6731	DANIELLE DARRIEUX	portrait	MGM	
6732	DANIELLE DARRIEUX	portrait	MGM	
6732	ELIZABETH TAYLOR	portrait	MGM	
6733	DANIELLE DARRIEUX	portrait	MGM	
6734	DANIELLE DARRIEUX	portrait	MGM	
6734	TRANS EUROPE EXPRESS	ROBBE-GRILLET	AIP	1967
6735	IN THE YEAR 2889	BUCHANAN	AIP-TV	1967
6741	ARLENE DAHL	portrait		
6745	JEAN SIMMONS	portrait	MGM	
6747	DEBORAH KERR	portrait		
6748	ARTHUR FREED	portrait		
6748	DEBORAH KERR	portrait		
6749	DEBORAH KERR	portrait		
6750	DEBORAH KERR	portrait		
6751	DEBORAH KERR	portrait		
6752	DEBORAH KERR	portrait	MGM	
6753	DEBORAH KERR	portrait		
6754	DEBORAH KERR	portrait		
6754	MYRNA LOY	portrait		
6755	CYD CHARISSE	portrait		

6755	DEBORAH KERR	portrait		
6755	INGER STEVENS	portrait		
6755	INGER STEVENS	portrait	MGM	
6756	DEBORAH KERR	portrait		
6757	DEBORAH KERR	portrait		
6757	LENA HORNE	portrait		
6758	DEBORAH KERR	portrait		
6759	DEBORAH KERR	portrait		
6759	LESLIE CARON	portrait		
6760	DEBORAH KERR	portrait		
6760	LESLIE CARON	portrait		
6761	DEBORAH KERR	portrait	MGM	
6761	LESLIE CARON	portrait		
6762	DEBORAH KERR	portrait		
6763	DEBORAH KERR	portrait		
6763E	RHONDA FLEMING	portrait	MGM	
6764	DEBORAH KERR	portrait		
6764	LESLIE CARON	portrait		
6764	LEWIS STONE	portrait		
6765	DEBORAH KERR	portrait		
6765	LESLIE CARON	portrait		
6765	PHYLLIS KIRK	portrait		
6765E	JEAN SIMMONS	portrait	MGM	
6766	LESLIE CARON	portrait		
6768	LESLIE CARON	portrait		
6769	LESLIE CARON	portrait		
6770	LESLIE CARON	portrait		
6771	LESLIE CARON	portrait		
6774	ELIZABETH TAYLOR, SON MICHAEL	portrait		
6774	RHONDA FLEMING	portrait	MGM	
6775	RHONDA FLEMING	portrait	MGM	
6777	BETTY GARRETT	portrait	MGM	
6788	NATALIE SCHAFER	portrait		
6800	NOBODY'S WIDOW	CRISP	PDC	1927
6804	DIANA LEWIS, WILLIAM POWELL	portrait		
6806	X FROM OUTER SPACE (JAP: UCHU DAIKAIJU GIRARA 1967)	NIHONMATSU	AIP-TV	1968
6807	DIANA LEWIS, WILLIAM POWELL	portrait		
6807	YOUNG REBEL (SP: CERVANTES 1967)	SHERMAN	AIP-TV	1969
6808	FIVE GOLDEN DRAGONS (UK)	SUMMERS	ALLIED ARTISTS	1967
6809	HIGH, WILD AND FREE	EASTMAN	AIP	1968
6812	CYD CHARISSE	portrait		
6813	HELL RAIDERS	BUCHANAN	AIP-TV	1968
6814	IT'S ALIVE	BUCHANAN	AIP-TV	1969
6815	CREATURE OF DESTRUCTION	BUCHANAN	AIP-TV	1968
6816	BETTY GARRETT	portrait		
6816	HONEYMOONS WILL KILL YOU (IT: 1966)	AMENDOLA	AIP-TV	1968
6819	SALLY FORREST	portrait		
6820	HORROR OF DRACULA (UK: DRACULA)	FISHER	UNIVERSAL	1958
6821	CYD CHARISSE	portrait		
6821	LUCILLE BREMER	portrait	MGM	
6821	SALLY FORREST	portrait	MGM	
6824	AGNES MOOREHEAD	portrait	MGM	
6825	AGNES MOOREHEAD	portrait	MGM	
6827	CAN'T STOP THE MUSIC	WALKER	ASSOCIATED FILM DIST	1980
6827	JEFF RICHARDS	portrait		
6828	AGNES MOOREHEAD	portrait	MGM	
6829	AGNES MOOREHEAD	portrait	MGM	
6832	VERA-ELLEN	portrait	MGM	
6834	JEAN SIMMONS/STEWART GRANGER	portrait	MGM	
6835	LEON AMES	portrait		
6836E	CYD CHARISSE	portrait		
6839	CARLETON CARPENTER	portrait		
6839	LEON AMES	portrait		
6842	VERA-ELLEN	portrait	MGM	
6843	CARLETON CARPENTER	portrait		
6847	RED SKELTON, DAUGHTER VALENTINE MARIE	portrait		

6848	CECILIA PARKER	portrait		
6860	VIRGINIA WEIDLER	portrait		
6863	ROBERT YOUNG	portrait		
6870	VERA-ELLEN	portrait	MGM	
6873	FRED ASTAIRE	portrait		
6877	FREDDIE BARTHOLOMEW	portrait		
6877	VERA-ELLEN	portrait	MGM	
6881	JANIS PAIGE	portrait	MGM	
6882	CYD CHARISSE	portrait		
6888E	DEBBIE REYNOLDS	portrait		
6892	LESLIE CARON	portrait		
6893	ESTHER WILLIAMS, HUSB. BEN GAGE, SONS BENJAMIN, KIMBALL	portrait		
6898	ESTHER WILLIAMS, SONS BENJAMIN, KIMBALL	portrait		
6900	BARBARA LANG	portrait		
6900	DOROTHY MORRIS	portrait		
6901	LESLIE CARON	portrait		
6901	RADIO RASCALS (sh)	WATSON	EDUCATIONAL FILM	1935
6902	HURRAY FOR RHYTHM (sh)	WATSON	EDUCATIONAL FILM	1935
6903	COLLEGE CAPERS (sh)	WATSON	EDUCATIONAL FILM	1935
6903	ESTHER WILLIAMS, SONS BENJAMIN, KIMBALL	portrait		
6903	GRETA GARBO	portrait	MGM	
6905	AUDREY TOTTER	portrait	MGM	
6905	WAY OUT WEST (sh)	WATSON	EDUCATIONAL FILM	1935
6906	AUDREY TOTTER	portrait	MGM	
6906	SUCCUBUS (GER: NECRONOMICON-GETRAUMTE SUNDEN)	FRANCO	AIP-TV	1968
6907	AUDREY TOTTER	portrait	MGM	
6907	PIER ANGELI	portrait	MGM	
6907	SEEING NELLIE HOME (sh)	WATSON	EDUCATIONAL FILM	1935
6908	AUDREY TOTTER	portrait	MGM	
6908	SORORITY BLUES (sh)	WATSON	EDUCATIONAL FILM	1935
6909	ANGEL, ANGEL, DOWN WE GO (CULT OF THE DAMNED)	THOM	AIP	1969
6909	AUDREY TOTTER	portrait	MGM	
6909	EASY PICKIN'S (sh)	WATSON	EDUCATIONAL FILM	1935
6910	AUDREY TOTTER	portrait	MGM	
6910	LESLIE CARON	portrait		
6910	SPOOKS (sh)	WATSON	EDUCATIONAL FILM	1936
6911	AUDREY TOTTER	portrait	MGM	
6911	LESLIE CARON	portrait		
6914	DANIELLE DARRIEUX	portrait	MGM	
6916	YONGARY MONSTER FROM THE DEEP (JAP: 1967)	KIM	AIP-TV	1970
6917	DANIELLE DARRIEUX	portrait	MGM	
6919	DANIELLE DARRIEUX	portrait	MGM	
6921	BLOOD OF THE VAMPIRE	CASS	UNIVERSAL	1958
6921	DANIELLE DARRIEUX	portrait	MGM	
6922	DANIELLE DARRIEUX	portrait	MGM	
6922	HONEYMOON KILLERS	KASTLE	AIP	1970
6923	DANIELLE DARRIEUX	portrait	MGM	
6924	GENE KELLY	portrait		
6927	HELEN O'HARA	portrait		
6927	SILENT ENEMY (UK)	FAIRCHILD	UNIVERSAL	1958
6929	HELEN O'HARA	portrait		
6931	HELEN O'HARA	portrait		
6932	HELEN O'HARA	portrait		
6942	LORRAINE MILLER	portrait	MGM	
6943	RUSS TAMBLYN, BARBARA LANG	portrait		
6945	ESTHER WILLIAMS	portrait	MGM	
6946	BLACK GOLD (mistake - 946)	MARTINSON	WARNER BROS	1962
6946	JEAN SIMMONS	portrait	MGM	
6949	JEAN SIMMONS	portrait	MGM	
6950	JEAN SIMMONS	portrait	MGM	
6951	FBI CODE 98	MARTINSON	WARNER BROS	1963
6952	JEAN SIMMONS	portrait	MGM	
6953	ANN RUTHERFORD	portrait		
6953	AVA GARDNER	portrait	MGM	
6954	JEAN SIMMONS	portrait	MGM	
6956	ANN RUTHERFORD	portrait		

6963	FRANCES DONELIN	portrait	MGM	
6968	SOPHIE TUCKER	portrait		
6979	DOROTHY MORRIS	portrait		
6982	GLORIA GRAHAME	portrait		
6983	GLORIA GRAHAME	portrait		
6984	GLORIA GRAHAME	portrait		
6985	GLORIA GRAHAME	portrait		
6986	GLORIA GRAHAME	portrait		
6987	GLORIA GRAHAME	portrait		
6988	GLORIA GRAHAME	portrait		
6989	GLORIA GRAHAME	portrait		
6990	GLORIA GRAHAME	portrait		
6991	GLORIA GRAHAME	portrait		
6995	FLOODS OF FEAR (UK)	CRICHTON	UNIVERSAL	1958
7004	HORROR HOUSE (UK: HAUNTED HOUSE OF HORROR)	ARMSTRONG	AIP	1970
7008	JEAN SIMMONS/STEWART GRANGER	portrait	MGM	
7008	WEDDING NIGHT (UK: I CAN'T... I CAN'T)	HAGGARD	AIP	1970
7011	FRANCES GIFFORD	portrait		
7012E	LANA TURNER	portrait	MGM	
7013	JOAN BLONDELL	portrait	MGM	
7016	LANA TURNER	portrait		
7021	COUNT DRACULA (GER: NACHT, WENN DRACULA ERWACHT)	FRANCO	AIP	1970
7024	LANA TURNER	portrait		
7025	LANA TURNER	portrait		
7033	LINA ROMAY	portrait		
7037	WESTERN COURAGE (sh) (mistake)	COWAN	UNIVERSAL	1949
7039	JEAN SIMMONS/STEWART GRANGER	portrait	MGM	
7042	MARIE DRESSLER'S HOME	portrait		
7045	ELEANOR POWELL	portrait		
7046	JOAN BLONDELL	portrait	MGM	
7048	SALLY FORREST	portrait		
7049	JOAN BLONDELL	portrait	MGM	
7052	GRETA GARBO	portrait	MGM	
7053	AVA GARDNER	portrait	MGM	
7061	SALLY FORREST	portrait	MGM	
7068	CLARK GABLE	portrait	MGM	
7076	CLARK GABLE	portrait	MGM	
7081	ELEANOR POWELL	portrait		
7087	CLARK GABLE	portrait	MGM	
7091E	DEBBIE REYNOLDS	portrait		
7092E	DEBBIE REYNOLDS	portrait		
7094E	DEBBIE REYNOLDS	portrait		
7101	HAPPY HEELS (sh)	WATSON	EDUCATIONAL FILM	1936
7103	BLUE BLAZES (sh)	KANE	EDUCATIONAL FILM	1936
7104	IT'S YOUR MOVE (IT: 1968)	FIZ	AIP-TV	1970
7105	GAGS AND GALS (sh)	KANE	EDUCATIONAL FILM	1936
7105	WARNING FROM SPACE (JAP 1956)	SHIMA	AIP-TV	1967
7106	DIAMONDS IN THE ROUGH (sh)	HALL	EDUCATIONAL FILM	1936
7107	MAJIN THE HIDEOUS IDOL (JAP: DAIMAJIN 1966)	YASUDA	AIP-TV	1968
7107	WHOSE BABY ARE YOU? (sh)	CHRISTIE	EDUCATIONAL FILM	1936
7108	CHEMIST (sh)	CHRISTIE	EDUCATIONAL FILM	1936
7108	FREDDIE BARTHOLOMEW	portrait		
7108	MISSION STARDUST (IT: ...4...3...2...1...MORTE 1967)	ZEGLIO	AIP-TV	1968
7109	MAGIC SERPENT (JAP: KAIRYU DAIKESSEN)	YAMAUCHI	AIP-TV	1966
7110	FREDDIE BARTHOLOMEW	portrait		
7110	MIXED MAGIC (sh)	KANE	EDUCATIONAL FILM	1936
7111	DESTROY ALL PLANETS (GAMERA VS VIRAS) (JAP)	YUASA	AIP-TV	1968
7112	AMUSE YOURSELF (sh)		EDUCATIONAL FILM	1936
7112	FREDDIE BARTHOLOMEW	portrait		
7113	SCREEN TEST (sh)	WATSON	EDUCATIONAL FILM	1936
7113	YEAR OF THE CANNIBALS (IT: I CANNIBALI 1970)	CAVANI	AIP	1971
7114	HIGH C HONEYMOON (sh)	CHRISTIE	EDUCATIONAL FILM	1937
7115	TRANSATLANTIC LOVE (sh)	WATSON	EDUCATIONAL FILM	1936
7116	FUN'S FUN (sh)	CHRISTIE	EDUCATIONAL FILM	1937
7117	DR. PHIBES	FUEST	AIP	1971
7117	JAIL BAIT (sh)	LAMONT	EDUCATIONAL FILM	1937

7118	PRACTICALLY PERFECT (sh)	WATSON	EDUCATIONAL FILM	1937
7119	DITTO (sh)	LAMONT	EDUCATIONAL FILM	1937
7120	OFF THE HORSES (sh)	WATSON	EDUCATIONAL FILM	1937
7122	PLEASURE PIT (FR: 1969) (r: DIRTY DOLLS OF KATMANDU)	CAYATTE	AIP-TV	1972
7125	STORY OF DAVID (UK: 1960)	MCNAUGHT	AIP-TV	1962
7128	SWEDISH FLY GIRLS (DEN: CHRISTA 1971)	O'CONNELL	AIP	1972
7129	CARRY ON CAMPING (UK)	THOMAS	AIP	1969
7131	JACK AND THE WITCH (JAP: 1967)	YABUSHITA	AIP-TV	1971
7134	WALTER PIDGEON	portrait		
7136	DEVIL'S WIDOW (UK: BALLAD OF TAM LIN)	MCDOWELL	AIP	1972
7136	ESTHER WILLIAMS, HUSBAND BEN & SONS	portrait		
7138	ESTHER WILLIAMS, HUSBAND BEN & SONS	portrait		
7139	ESTHER WILLIAMS, HUSBAND BEN & SONS	portrait		
7145	ANNE FRANCIS	portrait	MGM	
7146	ANNE FRANCIS	portrait	MGM	
7151	ANNE FRANCIS	portrait	MGM	
7152	ANNE FRANCIS	portrait	MGM	
7153	ANNE FRANCIS	portrait	MGM	
7156	ANNE FRANCIS	portrait	MGM	
7157	ANNE FRANCIS	portrait	MGM	
7160	ANNE FRANCIS	portrait	MGM	
7160	FRANCES GIFFORD	portrait		
7161	DEBORAH KERR	portrait	MGM	
7163	FRANCES GIFFORD	portrait		
7164	FRANCES GIFFORD	portrait		
7165	ESTHER WILLIAMS	portrait		
7165	WILDEST	COHAN	UNIVERSAL	1958
7167	LARAINE DAY	portrait	MGM	
7167	SALLY FORREST	portrait	MGM	
7168	LARAINE DAY	portrait	MGM	
7169	LARAINE DAY	portrait	MGM	
7169	SALLY FORREST	portrait		
7170	LARAINE DAY	portrait	MGM	
7171	LARAINE DAY	portrait	MGM	
7172	LARAINE DAY	portrait	MGM	
7173	LARAINE DAY	portrait	MGM	
7174	LARAINE DAY	portrait	MGM	
7175	LARAINE DAY	portrait	MGM	
7176	LARAINE DAY	portrait	MGM	
7177	LARAINE DAY	portrait	MGM	
7178	LARAINE DAY	portrait	MGM	
7179	LARAINE DAY	portrait	MGM	
7180	LARAINE DAY	portrait	MGM	
7181	LARAINE DAY	portrait	MGM	
7182	AVA GARDNER	portrait	MGM	
7182	LARAINE DAY	portrait	MGM	
7183	AVA GARDNER	portrait	MGM	
7183	LARAINE DAY	portrait	MGM	
7184	LARAINE DAY	portrait	MGM	
7185	AVA GARDNER	portrait	MGM	
7185	LARAINE DAY	portrait	MGM	
7186	LESLIE CARON	portrait		
7194	LESLIE CARON	portrait		
7200	MYRNA LOY	portrait		
7201	BLOOD FROM THE MUMMY'S TOMB	HOLT, CARRERAS	AIP	1972
7201	LOVE NEST ON WHEELS (sh)	LAMONT	EDUCATIONAL FILM	1937
7202	MAN TO MAN (BOY FRIEND*) (sh)	KANE	EDUCATIONAL FILM	1937
7203	READY TO SERVE (sh)	WATSON	EDUCATIONAL FILM	1937
7204	MELDOY GIRL (sh)	CHRISTIE	EDUCATIONAL FILM	1937
7205	COMIC ARTIST'S HOME LIFE (sh)	CHRISTIE	EDUCATIONAL FILM	1937
7207	LOVE IN ARMS (sh)	CHRISTIE	EDUCATIONAL FILM	1937
7208	GIRLS AHOY (sh)	CHRISTIE	EDUCATIONAL FILM	1937
7210	ESTHER WILLIAMS	portrait		
7212	ESTHER WILLIAMS	portrait		
7213	ESTHER WILLIAMS	portrait		
7214-SG	WILD PACK (SANDPIT GENERALS)	GARNETT	AIP	1972

7215	EVENING OF EDGAR ALLAN POE (1970)	JOHNSON	AIP-TV	1973
7221	MICKEY ROONEY	portrait		
7223	FEMALE RESPONSE, THE	KINCAID	TRANS-AMERICAN	1972
7224	GREER GARSON + MOTHER	portrait		
7233	KATHRYN GRAYSON + DAUGHTER PATTY	portrait		
7234	LANA TURNER, DAUGHTER CHERYL, & MOTHER	portrait		
7239	ANGELA LANSBURY	portrait		
7255	GREER GARSON, LAURITZ MELCHIOR	portrait		
7259	LANA TURNER	portrait		
7267	ROBERT MONTGOMERY	portrait		
7271	HEDY LAMARR, ROBERT MONTGOMERY	portrait		
7275	ESTHER WILLIAMS	portrait		
7276	ESTHER WILLIAMS	portrait		
7277	ESTHER WILLIAMS	portrait		
7281	ANNE FRANCIS	portrait	MGM	
7282	ANNE FRANCIS	portrait	MGM	
7286	ANNE FRANCIS	portrait	MGM	
7287	ANNE FRANCIS	portrait	MGM	
7295	ANNE FRANCIS	portrait	MGM	
7296	ANNE FRANCIS	portrait	MGM	
7299	ILONA MASSEY	portrait	MGM	
7300	RUSH HOUR	HOPPER	PATHE	1928
7301	BASHFUL BUDDIES (sh)	WATSON	EDUCATIONAL FILM	1936
7302	DONNA REED	portrait		
7303	DONNA REED	portrait		
7303	RAH! RAH! RHYTHM! (sh)	WATSON	EDUCATIONAL FILM	1936
7304	DONNA REED	portrait		
7304	MODERN HOME (sh)	WATSON	EDUCATIONAL FILM	1936
7305	DONNA REED	portrait		
7305	JUST THE TYPE (sh)	WATSON	EDUCATIONAL FILM	1936
7306	DONNA REED	portrait		
7306	HOLD IT (sh)	WATSON	EDUCATIONAL FILM	1937
7307	BIG COURTSHIP (sh)	WATSON	EDUCATIONAL FILM	1937
7307	DONNA REED	portrait		
7308	DONNA REED	portrait		
7308	PIXILATED (sh)	WATSON	EDUCATIONAL FILM	1937
7308	SPY IN THE SKY! (UK)	WL WILDER	ALLIED ARTISTS	1958
7309	DONNA REED	portrait		
7309	FRESHIES (sh)	WATSON	EDUCATIONAL FILM	1937
7309	MANSON (doc)	HENDRICKSON	AIP-TV	1973
7310	DONNA REED	portrait		
7310	HIS PEST GIRL (sh)	GRAHAM	EDUCATIONAL FILM	1937
7311	DONNA REED	portrait		
7311	HOLDING THE BAG (sh)	WATSON	EDUCATIONAL FILM	1937
7311	SCHOOL FOR UNCLAIMED GIRLS (UK: SMASHING BIRD..1969)	HARTFORD-DAVIS	AIP	1973
7312	DONNA REED	portrait		
7312	EQUINOX (1970)	WOODS	AIP-TV	1974
7312	HER ACCIDENTAL HERO (sh)	WATSON	EDUCATIONAL FILM	1937
7313	DONNA REED	portrait		
7313	HAMLET AND EGGS (sh)	WATSON	EDUCATIONAL FILM	1937
7314	THAT'S THE SPIRIT (sh)	KANE	EDUCATIONAL FILM	1937
7315	ANNE FRANCIS	portrait	MGM	
7315	DRACULA VS FRANKENSTEIN (1971)	ADAMSON	AIP-TV	1973
7316	FRANKENSTEIN'S BLOODY TERROR (SP: 1968)	EGUILUZ	AIP-TV	1971
7319	ASSIGNMENT TERROR (SP: 1970)	DEMICHELLI	AIP-TV	1976
7320	SALLY FORREST	portrait		
7347	JANE POWELL	portrait	MGM	
7355	VERA-ELLEN	portrait	MGM	
7359	GENE KELLY	portrait		
7363	GENE KELLY	portrait		
7379	GLORIA DE HAVEN	portrait		
7380	GLORIA DE HAVEN	portrait		
7381	GLORIA DE HAVEN	portrait		
7382	GLORIA DE HAVEN	portrait		
7383	GLORIA DE HAVEN	portrait		
7384	GLORIA DE HAVEN	portrait		

7384	GREER GARSON	portrait		
7385	GLORIA DE HAVEN	portrait		
7386	GLORIA DE HAVEN	portrait		
7387	GLORIA DE HAVEN	portrait		
7388	GLORIA DE HAVEN	portrait		
7389	GLORIA DE HAVEN	portrait		
7389	PIER ANGELI	portrait	MGM	
7390	GLORIA DE HAVEN	portrait		
7390	PIER ANGELI	portrait	MGM	
7392	GLORIA DE HAVEN	portrait		
7393	GLORIA DE HAVEN	portrait		
7393	PIER ANGELI	portrait	MGM	
7394	GLORIA DE HAVEN	portrait		
7394	PIER ANGELI	portrait	MGM	
7395	GLORIA DE HAVEN	portrait		
7396	GLORIA DE HAVEN	portrait		
7397	GLORIA DE HAVEN	portrait		
7398	GLORIA DE HAVEN	portrait		
7399	GLORIA DE HAVEN	portrait		
7400	AMAZONS, THE (WAR GODDESS) (IT: 1973)	YOUNG	AIP-TV	1975
7400	GLORIA DE HAVEN	portrait		
7401	GLORIA DE HAVEN	portrait		
7402	GLORIA DE HAVEN	portrait		
7403	GLORIA DE HAVEN	portrait		
7404	GLORIA DE HAVEN	portrait		
7404	IT LIVES BY NIGHT	JAMESON	AIP	1974
7405	GLORIA DE HAVEN	portrait		
7406	GLORIA DE HAVEN	portrait		
7407	GLORIA DE HAVEN	portrait		
7408	GLORIA DE HAVEN	portrait		
7409	GLORIA DE HAVEN	portrait		
7410	GLORIA DE HAVEN	portrait		
7411	GLORIA DE HAVEN	portrait		
7412	DOLORES GRAY	portrait		
7412	GLORIA DE HAVEN	portrait		
7412	SUPER STOOGES VS. THE WONDER WOMEN (IT: 1974)	BRESCIA	AIP-TV	1975
7413	GLORIA DE HAVEN	portrait		
7414	DOLORES GRAY	portrait		
7414	GLORIA DE HAVEN	portrait		
7415	GLORIA DE HAVEN	portrait		
7415	HOUSE THAT VANISHED (UK: SCREAM.. AND DIE 1973)	LARRAZ	AIP-TV	1974
7416	GLORIA DE HAVEN	portrait		
7417	GLORIA DE HAVEN	portrait		
7418	FRANCES GIFFORD	portrait		
7418	GLORIA DE HAVEN	portrait		
7419	GLORIA DE HAVEN	portrait		
7420	DOLORES GRAY	portrait		
7420	GLORIA DE HAVEN	portrait		
7421	GLORIA DE HAVEN	portrait		
7421	MARK OF THE DEVIL PART 2 (GER: 1973)	HOVEN	AIP-TV	1974
7422	DEADLY WEAPONS	WISHMAN	AIP	1974
7422	GLORIA DE HAVEN	portrait		
7423	FRANCES GIFFORD	portrait		
7423	GLORIA DE HAVEN	portrait		
7424	FRANCES GIFFORD	portrait		
7424	GLORIA DE HAVEN	portrait		
7425	GLORIA DE HAVEN	portrait		
7426	GLORIA DE HAVEN	portrait		
7427	GLORIA DE HAVEN	portrait		
7427	SHAG	BARRON	HEMDALE	1989
7428	GLORIA DE HAVEN	portrait		
7429	GLORIA DE HAVEN	portrait		
7430	GLORIA DE HAVEN	portrait		
7431	GLORIA DE HAVEN	portrait		
7432	GLORIA DE HAVEN	portrait		
7433	GLORIA DE HAVEN	portrait		

7434	GLORIA DE HAVEN	portrait		
7435	GLORIA DE HAVEN	portrait		
7436	GLORIA DE HAVEN	portrait		
7437	GLORIA DE HAVEN	portrait		
7438	GLORIA DE HAVEN	portrait		
7439	GLORIA DE HAVEN	portrait		
7439E	PIER ANGELI	portrait	MGM	
7440	GLORIA DE HAVEN	portrait		
7441	GLORIA DE HAVEN	portrait		
7454	ARLENE DAHL	portrait		
7464	ARLENE DAHL	portrait		
7466	VIVECA LINDFORS	portrait		
7476	ESTHER WILLIAMS	portrait		
7484	FRANCES RAFFERTY	portrait		
7485	FRANCES RAFFERTY	portrait		
7507	ROBIN HOOD IN AN ARROW ESCAPE (t) (sh)	DAVIS	EDUCATIONAL FILM	1936
7508	FARMER ALFALFA'S 20TH ANNIVERSARY (t) (sh)	DAVIS	EDUCATIONAL FILM	1936
7509	CATS IN A BAG (t) (sh)	DAVIS	EDUCATIONAL FILM	1936
7509	WILD McCULLOUCHS	BAER JR.	AIP	1975
7510	SKUNKED AGAIN (t) (sh)	DAVIS	EDUCATIONAL FILM	1936
7510	TAINE ELG	portrait		
7511	ROBERT MONTGOMERY	portrait		
7511	SALTY McGUIRE (t) (sh)	DAVIS	EDUCATIONAL FILM	1936
7512	TIN CAN TOURIST (t) (sh)	DAVIS	EDUCATIONAL FILM	1937
7513	BOOK SHOP (t) (sh)	DAVIS	EDUCATIONAL FILM	1937
7514	BIG GAME HUNT (t) (sh)	DAVIS	EDUCATIONAL FILM	1937
7515	RED HOT MUSIC (t) (sh)	DAVIS	EDUCATIONAL FILM	1937
7516	FLYING SOUTH (t) (sh)	DAVIS	EDUCATIONAL FILM	1937
7517	HAYRIDE (t) (sh)	DAVIS	EDUCATIONAL FILM	1937
7518	BUG CARNIVAL (t) (sh)	DAVIS	EDUCATIONAL FILM	1937
7519	SCHOOL BIRDS (t) (sh)	DAVIS	EDUCATIONAL FILM	1937
7520	PUDDY'S CORONATION (t) (sh)	DAVIS	EDUCATIONAL FILM	1937
7521	OZZIE OSTRICH COMES TO TOWN (t) (sh)	DAVIS	EDUCATIONAL FILM	1937
7522	PLAY BALL (t) (sh)	DAVIS	EDUCATIONAL FILM	1937
7523	MECHANICAL COW (t) (sh)	ZANDER	EDUCATIONAL FILM	1937
7524	PINK ELEPHANTS (t) (sh)	GORDON	EDUCATIONAL FILM	1937
7525	HOMELESS PUP (t) (sh)	GORDON	EDUCATIONAL FILM	1937
7526	PAPER HANGERS (t) (sh)	DAVIS	EDUCATIONAL FILM	1937
7533	DEBBIE REYNOLDS	portrait		
7539	DONNA REED	portrait		
7542	DONNA REED	portrait		
7551	GREER GARSON	portrait		
7563	ELEANOR POWELL	portrait		
7564	ELEANOR POWELL	portrait		
7571	LESLIE CARON	portrait	MGM	
7589	DIANA LYNN	portrait	MGM	
7593	ROBERT WALKER	portrait		
7594	ROBERT WALKER	portrait		
7595	ROBERT WALKER	portrait		
7596	ROBERT WALKER	portrait		
7597	ROBERT WALKER	portrait		
7598	ROBERT WALKER	portrait		
7599	ROBERT WALKER	portrait		
7600	ROBERT WALKER	portrait		
7601	ROBERT WALKER	portrait		
7602	ROBERT WALKER	portrait		
7603	ROBERT WALKER	portrait		
7604	ROBERT WALKER	portrait		
7606	LEGEND OF THE LEI (sh)		EDUCATIONAL FILM	1936
7606	SMALL TOWN IN TEXAS	STARRETT	AIP	1976
7607	CHESAPEAKE BAY RETRIEVER (sh)	FREYLINGHUYSEN	EDUCATIONAL FILM	1936
7608	SONGS OF THE DANUBE (sh)		EDUCATIONAL FILM	1937
7609	CRYSTAL BALLET (sh)	SPARLING	EDUCATIONAL FILM	1937
7610	HEDY LAMARR	portrait	MGM	
7610	ORNAMENTAL SWIMMING (sh)	SPARLING	EDUCATIONAL FILM	1937
7614	DAY THAT SHOOK THE WORLD (YUGO: 1974)	BULAJIC	AIP	1977

7617	MADAM KITTY (IT: SALON KITTY 1976)	BRASS	AIP	1977
7621	HOUSE BY THE LAKE (CAN: DEATH WEEKEND 1976)	FRUET	AIP	1977
7622	LITTLE GIRL WHO LIVES DOWN THE LANE (CAN: 1976)	GESSNER	AIP	1977
7623	TOWN THAT DREADED SUNDOWN, THE	PIERCE	AIP	1976
7624	JARMA LEWIS	portrait		
7640	ANNE FRANCIS	portrait	MGM	
7647	GLORIA DE HAVEN	portrait		
7648	ANNE FRANCIS	portrait	MGM	
7648	PETER LAWFORD	portrait		
7649	PETER LAWFORD	portrait		
7650	PETER LAWFORD	portrait		
7651	PETER LAWFORD	portrait		
7652	ANNE FRANCIS	portrait	MGM	
7652	PETER LAWFORD	portrait		
7653	DIANA LYNN	portrait	MGM	
7653	PETER LAWFORD	portrait		
7654	PETER LAWFORD	portrait		
7655	PETER LAWFORD	portrait		
7656	PETER LAWFORD	portrait		
7657	PETER LAWFORD	portrait		
7661	DIANA LYNN	portrait	MGM	
7662	DIANA LYNN	portrait	MGM	
7694	GREER GARSON, R. COLMAN, H. LAMARR, V. GILMORE	portrait		
7695	GREER GARSON, EDWARD LAWRENCE	portrait		
7698	JANE POWELL	portrait		
7708	JANE POWELL	portrait		
7715	INCREDIBLE MELTING MAN, THE	SACHS	AIP	1977
7716	GRAYEAGLE	PIERCE	AIP	1977
7717	ELIZABETH TAYLOR	portrait		
7723	ELIZABETH TAYLOR	portrait	MGM	
7728	JANE POWELL	portrait		
7731	ELIZABETH TAYLOR	portrait		
7731E	LANA TURNER	portrait		
7734	KEENAN WYNN	portrait		
7738	ELIZABETH TAYLOR	portrait		
7742	ELIZABETH TAYLOR	portrait		
7755	HOW GRINCH STOLE CHRISTMAS (t)	JONES	MGM	1966
7770	ELIZABETH TAYLOR	portrait	MGM	
7770	TOM DRAKE	portrait		
7775	GREER GARSON	portrait		
7777	GREER GARSON	portrait		
7779	RUTH HUSSEY	portrait	MGM	
7787	JAMES STEWART	portrait		
7791	MARSHA HUNT	portrait		
7793	MARSHA HUNT	portrait		
7793	RUTH HUSSEY	portrait		
7796	MARSHA HUNT	portrait		
7798	MARSHA HUNT	portrait		
7800	CYD CHARISSE	portrait		
7800	HEDY LAMARR	portrait	MGM	
7801	CYD CHARISSE	portrait		
7801	JANE POWELL, ANN BLYTH, PIER ANGELI	portrait		
7803	JANE POWELL, ANN BLYTH, PIER ANGELI, D. REYNOLDS	portrait		
7809	ELEANOR POWELL	portrait		
7811	CYD CHARISSE	portrait		
7816	CYD CHARISSE	portrait		
7817	GIRLS ON THE LOOSE	HENREID	UNIVERSAL	1958
7821	ESTHER WILLIAMS, SONS BENJAMIN, KIMBALL	portrait		
7823	JAMES STEWART	portrait		
7824	ANNE FRANCIS	portrait	MGM	
7826	CORA SUE COLLINS	portrait		
7827	CORA SUE COLLINS	portrait		
7828	CORA SUE COLLINS	portrait		
7828	JAMES STEWART	portrait		
7829	ANNE FRANCIS	portrait	MGM	
7829	CORA SUE COLLINS	portrait		

7829	JUNE ALLYSON	portrait		
7829	LANA TURNER	portrait		
7830	CORA SUE COLLINS	portrait		
7831	CORA SUE COLLINS	portrait		
7832	CORA SUE COLLINS	portrait		
7833	CORA SUE COLLINS	portrait		
7834	CORA SUE COLLINS	portrait		
7835	ANNE FRANCIS	portrait	MGM	
7836	ANNE FRANCIS	portrait	MGM	
7837	ANNE FRANCIS	portrait	MGM	
7837	AVA GARDNER	portrait	MGM	
7838	ANNE FRANCIS	portrait	MGM	
7838	AVA GARDNER	portrait	MGM	
7839	AVA GARDNER	portrait	MGM	
7840	AVA GARDNER	portrait	MGM	
7841	AVA GARDNER	portrait	MGM	
7842	AVA GARDNER	portrait	MGM	
7843	ANNE FRANCIS	portrait	MGM	
7843	AVA GARDNER	portrait	MGM	
7844	AVA GARDNER	portrait	MGM	
7845	AVA GARDNER	portrait	MGM	
7845	ESTHER WILLIAMS	portrait	MGM	
7846	AVA GARDNER	portrait	MGM	
7847	AVA GARDNER	portrait	MGM	
7848	AVA GARDNER	portrait	MGM	
7849	AVA GARDNER	portrait	MGM	
7850	AVA GARDNER	portrait	MGM	
7850	VIRGINIA GREY	portrait		
7852	ROBERT TAYLOR	portrait		
7857	ROBERT TAYLOR	portrait		
7870	AUDREY TOTTER	portrait		
7871	AUDREY TOTTER	portrait		
7872	AUDREY TOTTER	portrait		
7873	AUDREY TOTTER	portrait		
7874	AUDREY TOTTER	portrait		
7875	AUDREY TOTTER	portrait		
7876	AUDREY TOTTER	portrait		
7877	AUDREY TOTTER	portrait		
7878	AUDREY TOTTER	portrait		
7879	AUDREY TOTTER	portrait		
7879	ESTHER WILLIAMS	portrait		
7879	MAUREEN O'SULLIVAN	portrait		
7880	AUDREY TOTTER	portrait		
7881	AUDREY TOTTER	portrait		
7882	AUDREY TOTTER	portrait		
7882	BONITA GRANVILLE	portrait		
7883	AUDREY TOTTER	portrait		
7883	PIER ANGELI	portrait	MGM	
7884	AUDREY TOTTER	portrait		
7885	AUDREY TOTTER	portrait		
7886	AUDREY TOTTER	portrait		
7887	AUDREY TOTTER	portrait		
7888	AUDREY TOTTER	portrait		
7889	AUDREY TOTTER	portrait		
7890	AUDREY TOTTER	portrait		
7894	JANET LEIGH, MARGE CHAMPION, MIRIAM NELSON	portrait		
7895	JANET LEIGH, LILLIAN BURNS (MRS. GEORGE SIDNEY)	portrait		
7901	ALPINE RENDEZVOUS (sh)	WATSON	EDUCATIONAL FILM	1936
7902	EVICTORS, THE	PIERCE	AIP	1979
7904	QUEEN'S BIRTHDAY (sh)	WATSON	EDUCATIONAL FILM	1936
7905	ANN SOTHERN, DAUGHTER PATRICIA ANN STERLING	portrait		
7905	PINK LEMONADE (sh)	HAMMONS	EDUCATIONAL FILM	1936
7906	DEFIANCE	FLYNN	AIP	1980
7906	GIFTS IN RHYTHM (sh)		EDUCATIONAL FILM	1936
7907	PLAY! GIRLS (sh)	GRAHAM	EDUCATIONAL FILM	1936
7908	STRIKE! YOU'RE OUT (sh)	HALL	EDUCATIONAL FILM	1936

7908	SUNNYSIDE	GALFAS	AIP	1979
7909	BUCK ROGERS IN 25TH CENTURY - (tv)		UNIVERSAL	1979
7909	SEE UNCLE SOL (sh)	HALL	EDUCATIONAL FILM	1937
7910	NOTHING BUT THE TOOTH*		EDUCATIONAL FILM	1937
7911	GLORIA GRAHAME	portrait	MGM	
7911	SOMETHING SHORT OF PARADISE	HELPERN	AIP	1979
7912	GLORIA GRAHAME	portrait	MGM	
7913	GLORIA GRAHAME	portrait	MGM	
7914	GLORIA GRAHAME	portrait	MGM	
7915	GLORIA GRAHAME	portrait	MGM	
7916	GLORIA GRAHAME	portrait	MGM	
7917	GLORIA GRAHAME	portrait	MGM	
7918	GLORIA GRAHAME	portrait	MGM	
7919	GLORIA GRAHAME	portrait	MGM	
7919	LANA TURNER	portrait	MGM	
7919	SEVEN	SIDARIS	AIP	1979
7920	GLORIA GRAHAME	portrait	MGM	
7921	GLORIA GRAHAME	portrait	MGM	
7921	LANA TURNER	portrait	MGM	
7922	GLORIA GRAHAME	portrait	MGM	
7923	GLORIA GRAHAME	portrait	MGM	
7924	GLORIA GRAHAME	portrait	MGM	
7925	GLORIA GRAHAME	portrait	MGM	
7931	RUSS TAMBLYN	portrait		
7932	PIER ANGELI	portrait	MGM	
7932	RUSS TAMBLYN	portrait		
7936	MARGARET SULLAVAN	portrait		
7937	MARGARET SULLAVAN	portrait		
7938	MARGARET SULLAVAN	portrait		
7940	DONNA REED	portrait		
7942	MARGARET SULLAVAN	portrait	MGM	
7944	MARGARET SULLAVAN	portrait	MGM	
7945	DENISE DARCEL	portrait		
7946	DENISE DARCEL	portrait		
7948	MARGARET SULLAVAN	portrait		
7954	GRETA GARBO	portrait	MGM	
7955	JUNE ALLYSON	portrait		
7958	JUNE ALLYSON	portrait		
7960	JUNE ALLYSON	portrait		
7960	MARGARET SULLAVAN	portrait	MGM	
7963	MARGARET SULLAVAN	portrait		
7964	MARGARET SULLAVAN	portrait		
7970	ESTHER WILLIAMS	portrait		
7973	ESTHER WILLIAMS	portrait		
7975	MARILYN MAXWELL	portrait		
7988	SANDRA DEE	portrait		
7990	PIER ANGELI	portrait	MGM	
8006	DONNA REED	portrait		
8007	DONNA REED	portrait		
8007	LORNA DOONE	KARLSON	COLUMBIA	1951
8008	DONNA REED	portrait		
8008	ROAR OF THE IRON HORSE	BENNET, CARR	COLUMBIA	1951
8009	DONNA REED	portrait		
8009	TEXANS NEVER CRY	MCDONALD	COLUMBIA	1951
8010	DONNA REED	portrait		
8010	VALLEY OF FIRE	ENGLISH	COLUMBIA	1951
8011	DONNA REED	portrait		
8011	MAGIC CARPET	LANDERS	COLUMBIA	1951
8011	MYSTERIOUS ISLAND (serial)	BENNET	COLUMBIA	1951
8012	DONNA REED	portrait		
8013	DONNA REED	portrait		
8013	WHEN THE REDSKINS RODE	LANDERS	COLUMBIA	1951
8014	DONNA REED	portrait		
8014	TEXAS RANGERS	KARLSON	COLUMBIA	1951
8015	BRIGAND	KARLSON	COLUMBIA	1952
8015	DONNA REED	portrait		

Sir Arthur Conan Doyle's

THE HOUND OF THE BASKERVILLES

WITH Richard GREENE · Basil RATHBONE · Wendy BARRIE

Nigel Lionel John Barlowe
BRUCE · ATWILL · CARRADINE · BORLAND

Beryl MERCER · Morton LOWRY · Ralph FORBES

A 20th CENTURY-FOX PICTURE

DIRECTED BY Darryl F. Zanuck IN CHARGE OF PRODUCTION SIDNEY LANFIELD

ASSOCIATE PRODUCER Gene Markey SCREEN PLAY BY ERNEST PASCAL

8015	JUNE ALLYSON	portrait		
8016	DONNA REED	portrait		
8016	SILVER CANYON	ENGLISH	COLUMBIA	1951
8017	DONNA REED	portrait		
8017	SCANDAL SHEET	KARLSON	COLUMBIA	1952
8018	DONNA REED	portrait		
8019	DONNA REED	portrait		
8020	DONNA REED	portrait		
8021	DONNA REED	portrait		
8022	DONNA REED	portrait		
8022	ROGER MOORE	portrait	MGM	
8023	ROGER MOORE	portrait	MGM	
8025	FRANCES GIFFORD	portrait		
8026	WHIRLWIND	ENGLISH	COLUMBIA	1951
8029	INDIAN UPRISING	NAZARRO	COLUMBIA	1952
8030	CALIFORNIA CONQUEST	LANDERS	COLUMBIA	1952
8031	YANK IN KOREA	LANDERS	COLUMBIA	1951
8032	HILLS OF UTAH	ENGLISH	COLUMBIA	1951
8033	HARLEM GLOBETROTTERS	BROWN, JASON	COLUMBIA	1951
8035	MAN IN THE SADDLE	DE TOTH	COLUMBIA	1951
8036	PURPLE HEART DIARY	QUINE	COLUMBIA	1951
8037	JUNGLE JIM IN THE FORBIDDEN LAND	LANDERS	COLUMBIA	1952
8038	JUNGLE MAN-HUNT	LANDERS	COLUMBIA	1951
8039	KING OF THE CONGO (serial)	BENNET, GRISSELL	COLUMBIA	1952
8040	CAPTAIN VIDEO (serial)	BENNET, GRISSELL	COLUMBIA	1951
8041	BOOTS MALONE	DIETERLE	COLUMBIA	1952
8042	CYD CHARISSE, TONY MARTIN	portrait		
8042	TEN TALL MEN	GOLDBECK	COLUMBIA	1951
8043	FIRST TIME	TASHLIN	COLUMBIA	1952
8044	BRAVE WARRIOR	BENNET	COLUMBIA	1952
8045	OLD WEST	ARCHAINBAUD	COLUMBIA	1952
8047	MEMBER OF THE WEDDING	ZINNEMANN	COLUMBIA	1952
8048	CAROLYN JONES	portrait	MGM	
8049	CAROLYN JONES	portrait	MGM	
8049	GOLDEN HAWK	SALKOW	COLUMBIA	1952
8049	PIER ANGELI	portrait	MGM	
8053	PRINCE OF PIRATES	SALKOW	COLUMBIA	1953
8054	MY SIX CONVICTS	FREGONESE	COLUMBIA	1952
8055	BLACKHAWK	BENNET	COLUMBIA	1952
8055	ESTHER WILLIAMS	portrait	MGM	
8056	DEATH OF A SALESMAN	BENEDEK	COLUMBIA	1951
8057	FOUR POSTER	REIS	COLUMBIA	1952
8061	AUDREY TOTTER	portrait	MGM	
8061	CRIPPLE CREEK	NAZARRO	COLUMBIA	1952
8062	AUDREY TOTTER	portrait	MGM	
8062	SNIPER	DMYTRYK	COLUMBIA	1952
8063	AUDREY TOTTER	portrait	MGM	
8063	NIGHT STAGE TO GALVESTON	ARCHAINBAUD	COLUMBIA	1952
8064	5000 FINGERS OF DR. T	ROWLAND	COLUMBIA	1953
8064	AUDREY TOTTER	portrait	MGM	
8064	PIER ANGELI	portrait		
8065	AUDREY TOTTER	portrait	MGM	
8066	AFFAIR IN TRINIDAD	SHERMAN	COLUMBIA	1952
8066	AUDREY TOTTER	portrait	MGM	
8066	ESTHER WILLIAMS	portrait		
8067	AUDREY TOTTER	portrait	MGM	
8067	BLUE CANADIAN ROCKIES	ARCHAINBAUD	COLUMBIA	1952
8068	AUDREY TOTTER	portrait	MGM	
8068	PRISONERS OF THE CASBAH	BARE	COLUMBIA	1953
8069	AUDREY TOTTER	portrait	MGM	
8070	AUDREY TOTTER	portrait	MGM	
8071	AUDREY TOTTER	portrait	MGM	
8071	HAPPY TIME	FLEISCHER	COLUMBIA	1952
8072	APACHE COUNTRY	ARCHAINBAUD	COLUMBIA	1952
8072	AUDREY TOTTER	portrait	MGM	
8073	AUDREY TOTTER	portrait	MGM	

8074	AUDREY TOTTER	portrait	MGM	
8074	MEMBER OF THE WEDDING	ZINNEMANN	COLUMBIA	1952
8075	AUDREY TOTTER	portrait		
8076	ESTHER WILLIAMS	portrait		
8078	EIGHT IRON MEN	DMYTRYK	COLUMBIA	1952
8079	BARBED WIRE	ARCHAINBAUD	COLUMBIA	1952
8082	CAINE MUTINY	DMYTRYK	COLUMBIA	1954
8082	MAUREEN O'SULLIVAN	portrait		
8083E	CYD CHARISSE	portrait		
8085	YANK IN INDO-CHINA	GRISSELL	COLUMBIA	1952
8086	BETTY FURNESS	portrait		
8087	SERPENT OF THE NILE	CASTLE	COLUMBIA	1953
8088	LAST TRAIN FROM BOMBAY	SEARS	COLUMBIA	1952
8089	SAVAGE MUTINY	BENNET	COLUMBIA	1953
8090	VOODOO TIGER	BENNET	COLUMBIA	1952
8091	JUGGLER	DMYTRYK	COLUMBIA	1953
8092	JACK MCCALL – DESPERADO	SALKOW	COLUMBIA	1953
8093	PIRATES OF TRIPOLI	FEIST	COLUMBIA	1955
8094	WAGON TEAM	ARCHAINBAUD	COLUMBIA	1952
8095	LOST PLANET	BENNET	COLUMBIA	1953
8096	LANA TURNER	portrait		
8100	SON OF GERONIMO (serial)	BENNET	COLUMBIA	1952
8101	AFFAIRS OF PIERRE (sh)		EDUCATIONAL FILM	1937
8101	ESTHER WILLIAMS	portrait	MGM	
8102	MONTAGUE THE MAGNIFICENT (sh)	CHRISTIE	EDUCATIONAL FILM	1937
8103	PATHFINDER	SALKOW	COLUMBIA	1952
8103	SLACKS APPEAL (sh)	CHRISTIE	EDUCATIONAL FILM	1937
8104	BASHFUL BALLERINA (sh)	WATSON	EDUCATIONAL FILM	1937
8105	SMART WAY (sh)	WATSON	EDUCATIONAL FILM	1937
8106	SILLY NIGHT (sh)	CHRISTIE	EDUCATIONAL FILM	1937
8107	GOING, GOING, GONE (sh)	CHRISTIE	EDUCATIONAL FILM	1937
8108	BON VOYAGE* (sh)		EDUCATIONAL FILM	1937
8109	DAWN ADDAMS	portrait	MGM	
8109	SLAVES OF BABYLON	CASTLE	COLUMBIA	1953
8109	WHO'S WHO (sh)		EDUCATIONAL FILM	1937
8109E	DORIS DAY	portrait	MGM	
8110	KOO KOO KORRESPONDENCE SKOOL (sh)	CHRISTIE	EDUCATIONAL FILM	1937
8111	HURRAY FOR HOLLIGAN (sh)	WATSON	EDUCATIONAL FILM	1937
8112	DEBBIE REYNOLDS	portrait		1950
8112	DIME A DANCE (sh)	CHRISTIE	EDUCATIONAL FILM	1937
8112	PRIEST OF LOVE	MILES	FILMWAYS	1981
8113	AIR PARADE (sh)	CHRISTIE	EDUCATIONAL FILM	1938
8114	MISS THEY MISSED (sh)	CHRISTIE	EDUCATIONAL FILM	1938
8114	WALTER PIDGEON	portrait	MGM	
8115	CUPID TAKES A HOLIDAY (sh)	WATSON	EDUCATIONAL FILM	1938
8115	SKY COMMANDS	SEARS	COLUMBIA	1953
8115E	ELIZABETH TAYLOR	portrait		
8116	DAWN ADDAMS	portrait		
8116	HANGMAN'S KNOT	HUGGINS	COLUMBIA	1952
8116	WANNA BE A MODEL? (sh)	CHRISTIE	EDUCATIONAL FILM	1938
8117	BEAUTIFUL BUT DUMMIES (sh)	WATSON	EDUCATIONAL FILM	1938
8117	SALOME	DIETERLE	COLUMBIA	1953
8117E	ELIZABETH TAYLOR	portrait		
8118	CUTE CRIME (sh)		EDUCATIONAL FILM	1938
8118	ON TOP OF OLD SMOKY	ARCHAINBAUD	COLUMBIA	1953
8118-52	BLOW OUT	DE PALMA	FILMWAYS	1981
8119	JITTERBUGS (sh)	GRAHAM	EDUCATIONAL FILM	1938
8120	FLAME OF CALCUTTA	FRIEDMAN	COLUMBIA	1953
8120	PARDON MY ACCIDENT (sh)	CHRISTIE	EDUCATIONAL FILM	1938
8120E	ELIZABETH TAYLOR	portrait		
8121	STRANGE FASCINATION	HAAS	COLUMBIA	1952
8122	SIREN OF BAGDAD	QUINE	COLUMBIA	1953
8122	UNA MERKEL	portrait		
8125	WINNING OF THE WEST, THE	ARCHAINBAUD	COLUMBIA	1953
8127	IRON GLOVE, THE	CASTLE	COLUMBIA	1954
8128	GOLDTOWN GHOST RIDERS	ARCHAINBAUD	COLUMBIA	1953

8130	CONQUEST OF COCHISE	CASTLE	COLUMBIA	1953
8130E	DEBBIE REYNOLDS	portrait		
8132	CHARGE OF THE LANCERS	CASTLE	COLUMBIA	1954
8133	RUSS TAMBLYN	portrait		
8138	VERA-ELLEN	portrait	MGM	
8140	CYD CHARISSE	portrait		
8140	ONE GIRL'S CONFESSION	HAAS	COLUMBIA	1953
8146	PACK TRAIN	ARCHAINBAUD	COLUMBIA	1953
8146	VERA-ELLEN	portrait	MGM	
8148	VERA-ELLEN	portrait	MGM	
8149	GREAT ADV OF CAPTAIN KIDD (serial)	ABRAHAMS, GOULD	COLUMBIA	1953
8149	VERA-ELLEN	portrait	MGM	
8150	KILLER APE	BENNET	COLUMBIA	1953
8150	VERA-ELLEN	portrait	MGM	
8151	SAGINAW TRAIL	ARCHAINBAUD	COLUMBIA	1953
8151	VERA-ELLEN	portrait	MGM	
8152	VERA-ELLEN	portrait	MGM	
8157	49TH MAN	SEARS	COLUMBIA	1953
8157	CYD CHARISSE	portrait	MGM	
8158	CYD CHARISSE	portrait		
8165	ELAINE STEWART	portrait		
8166	ARLENE DAHL	portrait		
8166	ELAINE STEWART	portrait		
8166	LARAINE DAY	portrait		
8170	MISS SADIE THOMPSON	BERNHARDT	COLUMBIA	1953
8172	VALLEY OF HEADHUNTERS	BERKE	COLUMBIA	1953
8173	FORT TI	CASTLE	COLUMBIA	1953
8173	FRANCES RAFFERTY	portrait		
8178	STRANGER WORE A GUN	DE TOTH	COLUMBIA	1953
8180	ARLENE DAHL	portrait		
8180	AUDREY TOTTER	portrait	MGM	
8182	AUDREY TOTTER	portrait	MGM	
8183	DONNA REED, ESTHER WILLIAMS, J. ALLYSON + CHILDREN	portrait		
8188	LAST OF THE PONY RIDERS	ARCHAINBAUD	COLUMBIA	1953
8190	FRANCES RAFFERTY	portrait		
8191	JESSE JAMES VS DALTONS	CASTLE	COLUMBIA	1954
8193	DRUMS OF TAHITI	CASTLE	COLUMBIA	1954
8194	GUNFIGHTERS OF THE NORTHWEST	BENNET, GOULD	COLUMBIA	1954
8197	SARACEN BLADE	CASTLE	COLUMBIA	1954
8198E	JANE FONDA	portrait		
8199	ROBERT WALKER	portrait		
8200	MYRNA LOY AT 6, BROTHER DAVID	portrait		
8201	MYRNA LOY AT 3	portrait		
8201	TIMID GHOST (sh)	WATSON	EDUCATIONAL FILM	1937
8202	BASHFUL BUCKAROO (sh)	WATSON	EDUCATIONAL FILM	1937
8203	HI HO HOLLYWOOD (sh)	WATSON	EDUCATIONAL FILM	1938
8204	ARLENE DAHL	portrait		
8204	GETTING AN EYEFUL (sh)	WATSON	EDUCATIONAL FILM	1938
8204	JUNGLE MAN-EATERS	SHOLEM	COLUMBIA	1954
8205	DAVID WILLIAMS (MYRNA LOY'S FATHER) AT 16	portrait		
8205	MONEY ON YOUR LIFE (sh)	WATSON	EDUCATIONAL FILM	1938
8205	RIDING WITH BUFFALO BILL (serial)	BENNET	COLUMBIA	1954
8206	CACTUS CABALLEROS (sh)	WATSON	EDUCATIONAL FILM	1938
8206	LAW VS. BILLY THE KID	CASTLE	COLUMBIA	1954
8209	ARLENE DAHL	portrait		
8210	ROBERT WALKER	portrait		
8211	TEENAGE CRIME WAVE	SEARS	COLUMBIA	1955
8214	BATTLE OF ROGUE RIVER	CASTLE	COLUMBIA	1954
8217	CYD CHARISSE	portrait		
8230	ANN SOTHERN	portrait		
8232	ANN SOTHERN	portrait		
8232	FRANCES RAFFERTY	portrait		
8236	ANN SOTHERN	portrait		
8243	FRANCES GIFFORD	portrait		
8244	CLARK GABLE	portrait		
8244	FERNANDO LAMAS	portrait		

8247	MIAMI STORY	SEARS	COLUMBIA	1954
8249	CHICAGO SYNDICATE	SEARS	COLUMBIA	1955
8250	SEMINOLE UPRISING	BELLAMY	COLUMBIA	1955
8252	MASTERSON OF KANSAS	CASTLE	COLUMBIA	1954
8253	DORETTA MORROW	portrait		
8253	MAD MAGICIAN	BRAHM	COLUMBIA	1954
8254	KAY WILLIAMS	portrait	MGM	
8255	ANN SOTHERN	portrait		
8257	ADVENTURES OF CAPTAIN AFRICA (serial)	BENNET	COLUMBIA	1955
8260	IT CAME FROM BENEATH THE SEA	GORDON	COLUMBIA	1955
8262	CANNIBAL ATTACK	SHOLEM	COLUMBIA	1954
8263	DEVIL GODDESS	BENNET	COLUMBIA	1955
8264	BAMBOO PRISON	SEILER	COLUMBIA	1954
8265	JUNGLE MOON-MEN	GOULD	COLUMBIA	1955
8267	JOHN HODIAK	portrait		
8268	JOHN HODIAK	portrait		
8269	JOHN HODIAK	portrait		
8270	JOHN HODIAK	portrait		
8271	JOHN HODIAK	portrait		
8271	MAN FROM LARAMIE	MANN	COLUMBIA	1955
8272	JOHN HODIAK	portrait		
8273	JOHN HODIAK	portrait		
8273	TEN WANTED MEN	HUMBERSTONE	COLUMBIA	1955
8274	WOMEN'S PRISON	SEILER	COLUMBIA	1955
8281	NEW ORLEANS UNCENSORED	CASTLE	COLUMBIA	1955
8283	BUDDY EBSEN + WIFE RUTH CAMBRIDGE	portrait		
8283	GREER GARSON	portrait		
8284	BARBARA STANWYCK	portrait	MGM	
8284	GRETA GARBO	portrait	MGM	
8284	GUN THAT WON THE WEST	CASTLE	COLUMBIA	1955
8285	CREATURE WITH THE ATOM BRAIN	CAHN	COLUMBIA	1955
8285	VIRGINIA O'BRIEN	portrait		
8286	DUEL ON THE MISSISSIPPI	CASTLE	COLUMBIA	1955
8289	BARBARA STANWYCK	portrait	MGM	
8289	BATTLE STATIONS	SEILER	COLUMBIA	1956
8289	BROTHERS RICO	KARLSON	COLUMBIA	1957
8291	BARBARA STANWYCK	portrait	MGM	
8293	AUDREY TOTTER	portrait		
8294	BARBARA STANWYCK	portrait	MGM	
8294	LONG GREY LINE	FORD	COLUMBIA	1955
8295	GRETA GARBO	portrait	MGM	
8299	BATTLE STATIONS	SEILER	COLUMBIA	1956
8300	BARBARA STANWYCK	portrait	MGM	
8301	FIVE AGAINST THE HOUSE	KARLSON	COLUMBIA	1955
8301	WHO'S CRAZY? (sh)	WATSON	EDUCATIONAL FILM	1937
8302	SWEETIES (sh)	HALL	EDUCATIONAL FILM	1937
8303	UNCLE SOL SOLVES IT (sh)	KANE	EDUCATIONAL FILM	1938
8304	WILL YOU STOP! (sh)	WATSON	EDUCATIONAL FILM	1937
8305	HEIR TODAY (sh)	WATSON	EDUCATIONAL FILM	1937
8305	NIGHT HOLDS TERROR	STONE	COLUMBIA	1955
8306	LAWLESS STREET	LEWIS	COLUMBIA	1955
8306	MEED THE BRIDE (sh)	HALL	EDUCATIONAL FILM	1937
8307	DATES AND NUTS (sh)	HALL	EDUCATIONAL FILM	1937
8307	EARTH VS. THE FLYING SAUCERS	SEARS	COLUMBIA	1956
8308	COUNT THREE AND PRAY	SHERMAN	COLUMBIA	1955
8308	LOVE AND ONIONS (sh)	WATSON	EDUCATIONAL FILM	1938
8309	SING FOR SWEETIE (sh)	CHRISTIE	EDUCATIONAL FILM	1938
8310	HOUSTON STORY	CASTLE	COLUMBIA	1956
8310	WINNER LOSE ALL (sh)	WATSON	EDUCATIONAL FILM	1938
8311	BLACKJACK KETCHUM-DESPERADO	BELLAMY	COLUMBIA	1956
8311	SPENCER TRACY, CONTEST WINNER ROY HARRIS	portrait		
8312	JOHN HODIAK	portrait		
8313	EDDIE AND THE CRUISERS	DAVIDSON	EMBASSY	1983
8313	INSIDE DETROIT	SEARS	COLUMBIA	1956
8316	URANIUM BOOM	CASTLE	COLUMBIA	1956
8319	FLYING FONTAINES	SHERMAN	COLUMBIA	1959

8321	CROOKED WEB	JURAN	COLUMBIA	1955
8322	AUTUMN LEAVES	ALDRICH	COLUMBIA	1956
8322	ILONA MASSEY	portrait		
8323	BELL BOOK AND CANDLE	QUINE	COLUMBIA	1958
8324	DEBBIE REYNOLDS	portrait		
8325	DEBBIE REYNOLDS	portrait		
8327	DEBBIE REYNOLDS	portrait		
8328	FRANCES GIFFORD	portrait		
8330	NIGHTFALL	TOURNEUR	COLUMBIA	1957
8332	JUNE ALLYSON	portrait		
8333	DEBBIE REYNOLDS	portrait		
8333	STORM CENTER	TARADASH	COLUMBIA	1956
8334	DEBBIE REYNOLDS	portrait		
8335	HOT BLOOD	RAY	COLUMBIA	1956
8335	MERVYN LEROY	portrait		
8336	BLAZING THE OVERLAND TRAIL (serial)	BENNET	COLUMBIA	1956
8342	GUNS OF FORT PETTICOAT	MARSHALL	COLUMBIA	1957
8344	SEVENTH CALVARY	LEWIS	COLUMBIA	1956
8345	WEREWOLF	SEARS	COLUMBIA	1955
8346	REPRISAL	SHERMAN	COLUMBIA	1956
8349	DEBBIE REYNOLDS	portrait		
8352	ROCK AROUND THE CLOCK	SEARS	COLUMBIA	1956
8354	RUMBLE ON THE DOCKS	SEARS	COLUMBIA	1956
8355	MIAMI EXPOSE	SEARS	COLUMBIA	1956
8356	JANE POWELL	portrait		
8357	27TH DAY	ASHER	COLUMBIA	1957
8359	GIANT CLAW	SEARS	COLUMBIA	1957
8359	WHITE SQUAW	NAZARRO	COLUMBIA	1956
8361	JANE POWELL	portrait		
8364	ANN SOTHERN	portrait		
8364	PHANTOM STAGECOACH	NAZARRO	COLUMBIA	1957
8365	20 MILLION MILES TO EARTH	JURAN	COLUMBIA	1957
8366	NIGHT THE WORLD EXPLODED	SEARS	COLUMBIA	1957
8367	ILONA MASSEY	portrait		
8368	CHA CHA CHA BOOM	SEARS	COLUMBIA	1956
8369	JANE POWELL, SON GEARY STEFFIN III	portrait		
8371	ELIZABETH TAYLOR	portrait		
8372	LINEUP	SIEGEL	COLUMBIA	1958
8373	ELIZABETH TAYLOR	portrait		
8373	MAN WHO TURNED TO STONE	KARDOS	COLUMBIA	1957
8376	ELIZABETH TAYLOR	portrait		
8376	HELLCATS OF THE NAVY	JURAN	COLUMBIA	1957
8377	ANN SOTHERN	portrait		
8377	GREER GARSON	portrait		
8378	ANN SOTHERN	portrait		
8378	GREER GARSON	portrait		
8378	ZOMBIES OF MORA TAU	CAHN	CLOVER	1957
8379	GREER GARSON	portrait		
8379	TALL T	BOATTICHER	COLUMBIA	1957
8380	ANN SOTHERN	portrait		
8380	GREER GARSON	portrait		
8381	GREER GARSON	portrait		
8381	UTAH BLAINE	SEARS	COLUMBIA	1957
8382	GREER GARSON	portrait		
8383	DON'T KNOCK THE ROCK	SEARS	COLUMBIA	1956
8383	GREER GARSON	portrait		
8384	GREER GARSON	portrait		
8385	GREER GARSON	portrait		
8385	YOUNG DON'T CRY	WERKER	COLUMBIA	1957
8386	ANN SOTHERN	portrait		
8386	GREER GARSON	portrait		
8386	JANE POWELL, HUSBAND PATRICK NERNEY	portrait		
8387	ANN SOTHERN	portrait		
8387	GREER GARSON	portrait		
8388	ANN SOTHERN	portrait		
8388	GREER GARSON	portrait		

8389	GREER GARSON	portrait		
8389	TIJUANA STORY, THE	KARDOS	COLUMBIA	1957
8390	GREER GARSON	portrait		
8391	GREER GARSON	portrait		
8392	GREER GARSON	portrait		
8393	GREER GARSON	portrait		
8394	GREER GARSON	portrait		
8394	RETURN TO WARBOW	NAZARRO	COLUMBIA	1958
8395	GARMENT JUNGLE	SHERMAN	COLUMBIA	1957
8395	GREER GARSON	portrait		
8396	GREER GARSON	portrait		
8396	NO TIME TO BE YOUNG	RICH	COLUMBIA	1957
8397	3:10 TO YUMA	DAVES	COLUMBIA	1957
8397	GREER GARSON	portrait		
8398	ESCAPE FROM SAN QUENTIN	SEARS	COLUMBIA	1957
8398	GREER GARSON	portrait		
8399	DONNA REED	portrait		
8399	GREER GARSON	portrait		
8400	GENE KELLY	portrait		
8400	GREER GARSON	portrait		
8400	SEVENTH VOYAGE OF SINBAD	JURAN	COLUMBIA	1958
8401	GREER GARSON	portrait		
8402	GREER GARSON	portrait		
8403	JEANNE EAGELS	SIDNEY	COLUMBIA	1957
8404	GENE KELLY	portrait		
8406	CRASH LANDING	SEARS	COLUMBIA	1958
8407	PAL JOEY	SIDNEY	COLUMBIA	1957
8410	DONNA REED	portrait		
8411	PIER ANGELI	portrait		
8414	HARD MAN	SHERMAN	COLUMBIA	1957
8417	THIS ANGRY AGE	CLEMENT	COLUMBIA	1958
8418	DOMINO KID	NAZARRO	COLUMBIA	1957
8418	UNA MERKEL	portrait		
8420	DECISION AT SUNDOWN	BROWN	COLUMBIA	1957
8422	LIFE BEGINS AT 17	DREIFUSS	COLUMBIA	1958
8423	OPERATION MADBALL	QUINE	COLUMBIA	1957
8426	BATTLE OF THE CORAL SEA	WENDKOS	COLUMBIA	1959
8427	TARAWA BEACHHEAD	WENDKOS	COLUMBIA	1958
8428	CASE AGAINST BROOKLYN	WENDKOS	COLUMBIA	1958
8429	GOING STEADY	SEARS	COLUMBIA	1958
8430	CALYPSO HEAT WAVE	SEARS	COLUMBIA	1957
8431	SCREAMING MIMI	OSWALD	COLUMBIA	1958
8438	ANN SOTHERN	portrait		
8439	UNA MERKEL	portrait		
8442	NANCY DAVIS/REAGAN	portrait		
8449	TRUE STORY OF LYNN STUART	SEILER	COLUMBIA	1958
8450	BUCHANAN RIDES ALONE	BOETTICHER	COLUMBIA	1958
8453	COWBOY	DAVES	COLUMBIA	1958
8453	KATHRYN GRAYSON	portrait		
8461	LAST BLITZKRIEG	DREIFUSS	COLUMBIA	1959
8462	1001 ARABIAN NIGHTS (t)	KINNEY	COLUMBIA	1959
8464	13 WEST STREET	LEACOCK	COLUMBIA	1962
8465	GODDESS	CROMWELL	COLUMBIA	1958
8468	JUKE BOX RHYTHM	DREIFUSS	COLUMBIA	1959
8469	KATHRYN GRAYSON	portrait		
8470	FORBIDDEN ISLAND	GRIFFITH	COLUMBIA	1959
8472	APACHE TERRITORY	NAZARRO	COLUMBIA	1958
8472	KATHRYN GRAYSON	portrait		
8475	ME AND THE COLONEL	GLENVILLE	COLUMBIA	1958
8476	PEPE	SIDNEY	COLUMBIA	1960
8479	GIDEON OF SCOTLAND YARD (UK: GIDEON'S DAY)	FORD	COLUMBIA	1958
8484	13 WEST STREET	LEACOCK	COLUMBIA	1962
8485	ESTHER WILLIAMS	portrait		
8485	LAST HURRAH	FORD	COLUMBIA	1958
8490	LEON AMES	portrait	MGM	
8490	MAUREEN O'SULLIVAN	portrait		

8495	GOOD DAY FOR A HANGING	JURAN	COLUMBIA	1959
8496	IT HAPPENED TO JANE	QUINE	COLUMBIA	1959
8498	GENE KRUPA STORY	WEIS	COLUMBIA	1959
8500	CHASE		COLUMBIA	1958
8501	GUNS OF NAVARONE (UK)	THOMPSON	COLUMBIA	1961
8501	TRAILER LIFE (t) (sh)	DAVIS	EDUCATIONAL FILM	1937
8502	PIER ANGELI	portrait	MGM	
8502	SONG WITHOUT END	VIDOR	COLUMBIA	1960
8502	VILLAIN STILL PURSUED HER (t) (sh)	DAVIS	EDUCATIONAL FILM	1937
8503	ESTHER WILLIAMS	portrait	MGM	
8503	KIKO'S CLEANING DAY (t) (sh)	DAVIS	EDUCATIONAL FILM	1937
8503	PIER ANGELI	portrait	MGM	
8503	THEY CAME TO CORDURA	ROSSEN	COLUMBIA	1959
8504	CLOSE SHAVE (t) (sh)	DAVIS	EDUCATIONAL FILM	1937
8504	ESTHER WILLIAMS	portrait	MGM	
8504	MOUNTAIN ROAD	MANN	COLUMBIA	1960
8505	DANCING BEAR (t) (sh)	DAVIS	EDUCATIONAL FILM	1937
8505	ESTHER WILLIAMS	portrait	MGM	
8506	RIDE LONESOME	BOETTICHER	COLUMBIA	1959
8506	SAW MILL MYSTERY (t) (sh)	DAVIS	EDUCATIONAL FILM	1937
8507	DOG AND THE BONE (t) (sh)	DAVIS	EDUCATIONAL FILM	1937
8507	SENIOR PROM	RICH	COLUMBIA	1958
8508	LET NO MAN WRITE MY EPITAPH	LEACOCK	COLUMBIA	1960
8508	TIMID RABBIT (t) (sh)	DAVIS	EDUCATIONAL FILM	1937
8509	BILLY GOAT'S WHISKERS (t) (sh)	FOSTER	EDUCATIONAL FILM	1937
8510	BARNYARD BOSS (t) (sh)	RASINSKI	EDUCATIONAL FILM	1937
8510	JOAN CRAWFORD	portrait	MGM	
8511	I AIM AT THE STARS	THOMPSON	COLUMBIA	1960
8511	LION HUNT (t) (sh)	DAVIS	EDUCATIONAL FILM	1937
8512	BUGS BETTLE AND HIS ORCHESTRA (t) (sh)	FOSTER	EDUCATIONAL FILM	1938
8512	SURPRISE PACKAGE	DONEN	COLUMBIA	1960
8513	HEY BOY HEY GIRL	RICH	COLUMBIA	1959
8513	HIS OFF DAY (t) (sh)	RASINSKI	EDUCATIONAL FILM	1938
8514	JUST ASK JUPITER (t) (sh)	DAVIS	EDUCATIONAL FILM	1938
8514	MAN ON A STRING	DE TOTH	COLUMBIA	1960
8515	GANDY THE GOOSE (t) (sh)	FOSTER	EDUCATIONAL FILM	1938
8515	JANE POWELL	portrait		
8515	MYSTERIOUS ISLAND	ENDFIELD	COLUMBIA	1962
8516	FACE OF A FUGITIVE	WENDKOS	COLUMBIA	1959
8516	HAPPY AND LUCKY (t) (sh)	RASINSKI	EDUCATIONAL FILM	1938
8516	JANE POWELL	portrait		
8517	JANE POWELL	portrait		
8517	MOUNTAIN ROMANCE (t) (sh)	DAVIS	EDUCATIONAL FILM	1938
8518	ROBINSON CRUSOE'S BROADCAST (t) (sh)	FOSTER	EDUCATIONAL FILM	1938
8518	WHO WAS THAT LADY?	SIDNEY	COLUMBIA	1960
8519	CRIMSON KIMONO	FULLER	COLUMBIA	1959
8519	MAID IN CHINA (t) (sh)	RASINSKI	EDUCATIONAL FILM	1938
8520	BIG TOP (t) (sh)		EDUCATIONAL FILM	1938
8520	LAST ANGRY MAN	MANN	COLUMBIA	1959
8521	DEVIL OF THE DEEP (t) (sh)	FOSTER	EDUCATIONAL FILM	1938
8522	ARLENE DAHL	portrait		
8522	HERE'S TO THE GOOD OLD JAIL (t) (sh)	DONNELLY	EDUCATIONAL FILM	1938
8523	LAST INDIAN (t) (sh)	RASINSKI	EDUCATIONAL FILM	1938
8524	ARLENE DAHL	portrait	MGM	
8524	MILK FOR BABY (t) (sh)	DAVIS	EDUCATIONAL FILM	1938
8525	ARLENE DAHL	portrait	MGM	
8525	DEVIL AT 4 O'CLOCK	LEROY	COLUMBIA	1961
8525	MRS. O'LEARY'S COW (t) (sh)	DONNELLY	EDUCATIONAL FILM	1938
8526	ARLENE DAHL	portrait	MGM	
8526	ELIZA RUNS AGAIN (t) (sh)	RASINSKI	EDUCATIONAL FILM	1938
8527	ARLENE DAHL	portrait	MGM	
8527	VIRGINIA O'BRIEN	portrait		
8528	ARLENE DAHL	portrait	MGM	
8529	ARLENE DAHL	portrait	MGM	
8533	WACKIEST SHIP IN THE ARMY, THE	MURPHY	COLUMBIA	1960
8535	30 FOOT BRIDE OF CANDY ROCK	MILLER	COLUMBIA	1959

8536	ESTHER WILLIAMS	portrait	MGM	
8536	MIDDLE OF THE NIGHT	MANN	COLUMBIA	1959
8539	STRANGERS WHEN WE MEET	QUINE	COLUMBIA	1960
8540	ROBERT YOUNG, DAUGHTERS CAROLE, BARBARA, BETTY	portrait		
8543	NOTORIOUS LANDLADY	QUINE	COLUMBIA	1962
8546	EDGE OF ETERNITY	SIEGEL	COLUMBIA	1959
8548	JANE POWELL	portrait		
8548	ROBERT YOUNG, DAUGHTER BETTY LOU	portrait		
8550	LEGEND OF TOM DOOLEY	POST	COLUMBIA	1959
8554	ANN MILLER	portrait		
8556	HAVE ROCKET WILL TRAVEL	RICH	COLUMBIA	1959
8557	COMANCHE STATION	BOETTICHER	COLUMBIA	1960
8558	ESTHER WILLIAMS	portrait		
8559	TINGLER	CASTLE	COLUMBIA	1959
8564	JEAN SIMMONS/STEWART GRANGER	portrait	MGM	
8565	KATHARINE HEPBURN	portrait		
8566	CRY FOR HAPPY	MARSHALL	COLUMBIA	1961
8569	BECAUSE THEY'RE YOUNG	WENDKOS	COLUMBIA	1960
8569E	DINA MERRILL	portrait		
8570	KATHARINE HEPBURN	portrait		
8570	RAISIN IN THE SUN	PETRIE	COLUMBIA	1961
8571	KATHARINE HEPBURN	portrait		
8572	ENEMY GENERAL	SHERMAN	COLUMBIA	1960
8573	ALL THE YOUNG MEN	BARTLETT	COLUMBIA	1960
8574	MARY HOWARD	portrait		
8577	JEFF RICHARDS	portrait		
8578	JEFF RICHARDS	portrait		
8580E	STELLA STEVENS	portrait	MGM	
8581	GIDGET GOES HAWAIIAN	WENDKOS	COLUMBIA	1961
8582	JEAN SIMMONS/STEWART GRANGER	portrait	MGM	
8583	THIRTEEN GHOSTS	CASTLE	COLUMBIA	1960
8585E	STELLA STEVENS	portrait	MGM	
8588	DIAMOND HEAD	GREEN	COLUMBIA	1963
8589	MARSHA HUNT	portrait		
8590E	DINA MERRILL	portrait		
8591	STOP, LOOK AND LAUGH	APPELL, BRANDT	COLUMBIA	1960
8594	HOMICIDAL	CASTLE	COLUMBIA	1961
8596	INTERNS, THE	SWIFT	COLUMBIA	1962
8596	RED SKELTON	portrait		
8599	ANGELA LANSBURY	portrait		
8601	HOW TO SKI (sh)		EDUCATIONAL FILM	1937
8602	PRIVATE LIFE OF THE GANNETS (sh)	HUXLEY	EDUCATIONAL FILM	1937
8602	SAIL A CROOKED SHIP	BRECHER	COLUMBIA	1961
8603	ANGELA LANSBURY	portrait		
8603	FERNANDO LAMAS	portrait	MGM	
8603	FIVE FINGER EXERCISE	MANN	COLUMBIA	1962
8603	NOT SO DUMB(sh)	ALEXANDER	EDUCATIONAL FILM	1937
8604	KINGDOM FOR A HORSE (sh)	RENNIE	EDUCATIONAL FILM	1938
8605	GREY OWL'S LITTLE BROTHER (sh)		EDUCATIONAL FILM	1937
8606	SONG BIRDS OF THE NORTH WOODS (sh)		EDUCATIONAL FILM	1938
8606	VERA-ELLEN	portrait	MGM	
8607	SKY FISHING (sh) (CAN)	SPARLING	EDUCATIONAL FILM	1938
8608	RETURN OF THE BUFFALO (sh) (CAN)	SPARLING	EDUCATIONAL FILM	1938
8609	VERA-ELLEN	portrait	MGM	
8609	WE LIVE IN TWO WORLDS (sh) (UK)	CAVALCANTI	EDUCATIONAL FILM	1938
8610	MR. SARDONICUS	CASTLE	COLUMBIA	1961
8610	MUSIC FROM THE STARS (sh) (CAN)	SPARLING		
8617	THREE STOOGES MEET HERCULES	BERNDS	COLUMBIA	1962
8623	AVA GARDNER	portrait	MGM	
8624	AVA GARDNER	portrait	MGM	
8624	EVERYTHING'S DUCKY	TAYLOR	COLUMBIA	1962
8625	BYE BYE BIRDIE	SIDNEY	COLUMBIA	1963
8626	EXPERIMENT IN TERROR	EDWARDS	COLUMBIA	1962
8627	AVA GARDNER	portrait	MGM	
8629	WALK ON THE WILD SIDE	DYMTRYK	COLUMBIA	1962
8631	AVA GARDNER	portrait	MGM	

8632	AVA GARDNER	portrait	MGM	
8633	MAN FROM THE DINER'S CLUB	TASHLIN	COLUMBIA	1963
8634	LOVE HAS MANY FACES	SINGER	COLUMBIA	1965
8636	LARAINE DAY	portrait		
8637	AVA GARDNER	portrait	MGM	
8637	LARAINE DAY	portrait		
8638	LARAINE DAY	portrait		
8639	LARAINE DAY	portrait	MGM	
8640	LARAINE DAY	portrait		
8641	LARAINE DAY	portrait		
8642	LARAINE DAY	portrait		
8643	LARAINE DAY	portrait		
8644	LARAINE DAY	portrait		
8645	LARAINE DAY	portrait		
8646	LARAINE DAY	portrait		
8647	LARAINE DAY	portrait		
8648	LARAINE DAY	portrait		
8649	LARAINE DAY	portrait		
8650	13 FRIGHTENED GIRLS	CASTLE	COLUMBIA	1963
8650	JANET LEIGH	portrait		
8650	LARAINE DAY	portrait		
8651	LARAINE DAY	portrait		
8652	LARAINE DAY	portrait		
8652	WILD WESTERNERS	RUDOLPH	COLUMBIA	1962
8653	LARAINE DAY	portrait		
8654	LARAINE DAY	portrait		
8655	LARAINE DAY	portrait		
8656	LARAINE DAY	portrait		
8657	DON'T KNOCK THE TWIST	RUDOLPH	COLUMBIA	1962
8660	JANET LEIGH	portrait		
8661	JANET LEIGH	portrait		
8662	JANE POWELL	portrait		
8664	JANE POWELL	portrait		
8666	THREE STOOGES IN ORBIT	BERNDS	COLUMBIA	1962
8669	JANET LEIGH	portrait		
8677	JANET LEIGH	portrait		
8678	JANET LEIGH	portrait		
8679	JANET LEIGH	portrait		
8687	JANET LEIGH	portrait		
8689	JANET LEIGH	portrait		
8689	KING RAT	FORBES	COLUMBIA	1965
8691	STRAIGHT-JACKET	CASTLE	COLUMBIA	1964
8692	NEW INTERNS	RICH	COLUMBIA	1964
8696	JANET LEIGH	portrait		
8697	ANN SOTHERN	portrait	MGM	
8697	MAUREEN O'SULLIVAN	portrait		
8699	GOOD NEIGHBOR SAM	SWIFT	COLUMBIA	1964
8701	CAT BALLOU	SILVERSTEIN	COLUMBIA	1965
8704	PETER LAWFORD	portrait		
8705	3 STOOGES GO AROUND THE WORLD IN A DAZE	MAURER	COLUMBIA	1963
8706	FRED ASTAIRE	portrait		
8706	LIONEL BARRYMORE	portrait		
8708	FRED ASTAIRE	portrait		
8709	BABY THE RAIN MUST FALL	MULLIGAN	COLUMBIA	1965
8712	PROFESSIONALS	BROOKS	COLUMBIA	1966
8712	VIRGINIA O'BRIEN	portrait		
8715	MAJOR DUNDEE	PECKINPAH	COLUMBIA	1965
8716	DEBBIE REYNOLDS	portrait		
8717	DEBBIE REYNOLDS	portrait		
8719	COLLECTOR	WYLER	COLUMBIA	1965
8720	HEY THERE IT'S YOGI BEAR (t)	HANNA, BARBERA	COLUMBIA	1964
8722	LIFE BEGINS AT 17	DREIFUSS	COLUMBIA	1958
8724	QUICK GUN	SALKOW	COLUMBIA	1964
8728	DEBBIE REYNOLDS	portrait		
8731	OUTLAWS IS COMING	MAURER	COLUMBIA	1965
8732	RIDE THE WILD SURF	TAYLOR	COLUMBIA	1964

8734	MAUREEN O'SULLIVAN	portrait		
8741	SILENCERS	KARLSON	COLUMBIA	1966
8744	ALVAREZ KELLY	DMYTRYK	COLUMBIA	1966
8747	DEBBIE REYNOLDS	portrait	MGM	
8748	LANA TURNER	portrait		
8750	JANET LEIGH	portrait		
8755	WALK DON'T RUN	WALTERS	COLUMBIA	1966
8761	ARIZONA RAIDERS	WITNEY	COLUMBIA	1965
8765	ANN SOTHERN	portrait		
8768	ANN SOTHERN	portrait		
8769	ANN SOTHERN	portrait		
8772	VERA-ELLEN	portrait	MGM	
8775	ANN SOTHERN	portrait		
8778	VERA-ELLEN	portrait	MGM	
8786	VERA-ELLEN	portrait	MGM	
8798	ARLENE DAHL	portrait		
8802	RIDE BEYOND VENGEANCE	MCEVEETY	COLUMBIA	1966
8803	JANET LEIGH	portrait		
8804	JANET LEIGH	portrait		
8805	JANET LEIGH	portrait		
8806	JANET LEIGH	portrait		
8808	JANET LEIGH	portrait		
8809	JANET LEIGH	portrait		
8817	CYD CHARISSE	portrait		
8817	THREE ON A COUCH	LEWIS	COLUMBIA	1966
8818	BIRDS DO IT	MARTON	COLUMBIA	1966
8825	CYD CHARISSE	portrait		
8825E	SHIRLEY JONES	portrait		
8826	RAGE	GAZCON	COLUMBIA	1966
8833	JANET LEIGH	portrait		
8833	JOHNNY WEISSMULLER	portrait		
8834	JANET LEIGH	portrait		
8837	JANET LEIGH	portrait		
8839	JANET LEIGH	portrait		
8841	DEBBIE REYNOLDS	portrait		
8845	JANET LEIGH	portrait		
8845E	SHIRLEY JONES	portrait	MGM	
8852	JANET LEIGH	portrait		
8869	DEBBIE REYNOLDS	portrait		
8871	JAMES STEWART, WIFE GLORIA	portrait		
8872	VIRGINIA O'BRIEN	portrait		
8873	JAMES STEWART, STEPSONS RONALD, MICHAEL	portrait		
8874	JAMES STEWART, WIFE GLORIA, TWIN DAUGHTERS	portrait		
8875	JAMES STEWART, WIFE GLORIA, TWIN DAUGHTERS	portrait		
8876	JAMES STEWART, WIFE GLORIA, TWIN DAUGHTERS	portrait		
8878	JAMES STEWART, WIFE GLORIA, TWIN DAUGHTERS	portrait		
8879	GLORIA GRAHAME	portrait		
8880	GLORIA GRAHAME	portrait		
8881	GLORIA GRAHAME	portrait		
8882	JAMES STEWART, STEPSONS RONALD, MICHAEL	portrait		
8889	ANN MORRISS	portrait		
8890	CYD CHARISSE	portrait		
8890	JAMES STEWART, WIFE GLORIA, TWIN DAUGHTERS	portrait		
8891	JAMES STEWART, WIFE GLORIA, TWIN DAUGHTERS	portrait		
8892	JAMES STEWART, WIFE GLORIA, TWIN DAUGHTERS	portrait		
8893	JANET LEIGH	portrait		
8899	JAMES STEWART, STEPSONS RONALD, MICHAEL	portrait		
8900E	CAROLYN JONES	portrait	MGM	
8901	BIG APPLE (sh)	GRAHAM	EDUCATIONAL FILM	1937
8902	BETTY GARRETT	portrait		
8902	POT LUCK (sh)	HALL	EDUCATIONAL FILM	1937
8903	BETTY GARRETT	portrait		
8903	HEDY LAMARR, CPL. NICK SZABADOS	portrait		
8903	MISS LONELY HEARTS (sh)	HALL	EDUCATIONAL FILM	1937
8903E	CAROLYN JONES	portrait	MGM	
8904	ASK UNCLE SOL (sh)	KANE	EDUCATIONAL FILM	1937

8904	BETTY GARRETT	portrait		
8905	BETTY GARRETT	portrait		
8905	RHYTHM SAVES THE DAY (sh)	KANE	EDUCATIONAL FILM	1937
8905E	CAROLYN JONES	portrait	MGM	
8906	BETTY GARRETT	portrait		
8906	TRAILER PARADISE (sh)	HALL	EDUCATIONAL FILM	1937
8907	CALLING ALL CROONERS (sh)	GRAHAM	EDUCATIONAL FILM	1937
8908	LOVE GOES WEST (sh)	HALL	EDUCATIONAL FILM	1937
8909	HOW TO DANCE THE SHAG (sh)	CHRISTIE	EDUCATIONAL FILM	1937
8909	MYRNA LOY	portrait		
8909E	CAROLYN JONES	portrait	MGM	
8910	ALL'S FAIR (sh)	HALL	EDUCATIONAL FILM	1938
8910	HEDY LAMARR	portrait		
8913	ANN MILLER	portrait	MGM	
8914E	CAROLYN JONES	portrait	MGM	
8915E	CAROLYN JONES	portrait	MGM	
8924	AILEEN PRINGLE	portrait		
8928	VERA-ELLEN	portrait	MGM	
8929	VERA-ELLEN	portrait	MGM	
8931	MAUREEN O'SULLIVAN	portrait		
8967	LANA TURNER	portrait	MGM	
8970E	CAROLYN JONES	portrait	MGM	
8978	RUTH HUSSEY	portrait		
8979	CAROLYN JONES	portrait	MGM	
8981	ELIZABETH TAYLOR	portrait		
8999	JUNE ALLYSON	portrait		
9000	RED SKELTON	portrait		
9005	VAN JOHNSON	portrait		
9006	VAN JOHNSON	portrait		
9008	VAN JOHNSON, DAUGHTER SCHUYLER	portrait		
9010	VAN JOHNSON + WIFE EVIE	portrait		
9011	VAN JOHNSON	portrait		
9012	VAN JOHNSON, WIFE EVIE, DAUGHTER SCHUYLER	portrait		
9013	VAN JOHNSON + WIFE EVIE	portrait		
9015	VAN JOHNSON	portrait		
9016	SAFEGUARDING MILITARY INFORMATION (sh) training proj. #187		PARAMOUNT	1943
9017	CRYPTOGRAPHIC SECURITY (sh) training film		PARAMOUNT	1943
9018	SAFEGUARDING MILITARY INFORMATION (sh) training film		PARAMOUNT	1943
9023	PATROL FLIGHT OVER SEAS (sh) training film		PARAMOUNT	1943
9033	ESTHER WILLIAMS	portrait		
9034	DEBBIE REYNOLDS + MOTHER	portrait		
9039	MARDI GRAS (sh) (Musical Parade series #1 [of 6])	BENNETT	PARAMOUNT	1943
9042	JOEY HEATHERTON	portrait		
9043	LAST WILL & TESTAMENT OF TOM SMITH (sh)	BUCQUET	PARAMOUNT	1943
9044	CARIBBEAN ROMANCE (sh) MUSICAL PARADE SERIES #2	FULLER	PARAMOUNT	1943
9051	TELEPHONE TIME: SAM HOUSTON'S DECISION	TAYLOR	ABC-TV	1957
9053	ARMY TRAINING FILM PROJECT #7146		PARAMOUNT	1944
9054	HIDDEN ARMY, THE (sh) Army training film		PARAMOUNT	1944
9054	TELEPHONE TIME: MAN THE NAVY COULDN'T SINK	MINER	ABC-TV	1957
9055	TELEPHONE TIME: WAR AGAINST WAR	TAYLOR	ABC-TV	1958
9055	USE OF VOICE RADIO (sh) Army training film		PARAMOUNT	1944
9057	ELIZABETH TAYLOR, SON CHRISTOPHER WILDING	portrait		
9057	TIMBER TO TOKYO (sh) (Army training film)		PARAMOUNT	1945
9058	TELEPHONE TIME: DEATH OF A NOBODY		ABC-TV	1957
9059	ELIZABETH TAYLOR, HUSBAND MICHAEL & TWO SONS	portrait		
9059	INTRODUCTION TO THE ARMY PROJ. 7209		PARAMOUNT	1945
9059	TELEPHONE TIME: ALICE'S WEDDING GOWN		ABC-TV	1957
9060	STAR BRIGHT (ah)	BENNETT	PARAMOUNT	1944
9061	BONNIE LASSIE (sh) (MUSICAL PARADE SERIES #1)	SHEA	PARAMOUNT	2944
9061	ELIZABETH TAYLOR	portrait		
9062	ELIZABETH TAYLOR, MICHAEL & SONS	portrait		
9062	TELEPHONE TIME: RESCUE		ABC-TV	1957
9063	PIER ANGELI	portrait	MGM	
9063	RECONDITIONING CONVELESCENTS FOR RETURN TO DUTY (sh)		PARAMOUNT	1945
9063	TELEPHONE TIME: FLIGHT FOR LIFE	HILLER	ABC-TV	1958
9064	TELEPHONE TIME: MAN OF PRINCIPLE	TEWKSBURY	ABC-TV	1958

9065	INSIDE STORY OF SEAMAN JONES (training film)		PARAMOUNT	1945
9065	TELEPHONE TIME: CAVALRY SURGEON	WAGGNER	ABC-TV	1958
9066	ISLE OF TABU (sh)	SHEA	PARAMOUNT	1945
9066	TELEPHONE TIME: IMMORTAL EYE	SINCLAIR	ABC-TV	1958
9067	BOMBALERA (sh) MUSICAL PARADE SERIES #3	MADISON	PARAMOUNT	1945
9067	TELEPHONE TIME: VESTRIS	HILLER	ABC-TV	1958
9069	TELEPHONE TIME: CHECKERED FLAG	LANDON	ABC-TV	1958
9070	FREEDOM COMES HIGH (sh) (U. S. NAVY)	ALLEN	PARAMOUNT	1943
9071	JANE POWELL	portrait		
9071	PIER ANGELI	portrait	MGM	
9072	JANE POWELL	portrait		
9072	TELEPHONE TIME: RECIPE FOR SUCCESS	WAGGNER	ABC-TV	1958
9073	JANE POWELL	portrait		
9074	JANE POWELL	portrait		
9075	JANE POWELL	portrait		
9075	TELEPHONE TIME: TRAIL BLAZER	MINER	ABC-TV	1958
9076	JANE POWELL	portrait		
9077	JANE POWELL	portrait		
9078	JANE POWELL	portrait		
9078	TELEPHONE TIME: QUALITY OF MERCY	SINCLAIR	ABC-TV	1958
9079	JANE POWELL	portrait		
9079	RUTH HUSSEY	portrait		
9080	JUNE ALLYSON	portrait	MGM	
9081	JUNE ALLYSON	portrait	MGM	
9082	JUNE ALLYSON	portrait	MGM	
9083	JUNE ALLYSON	portrait	MGM	
9084	JUNE ALLYSON	portrait	MGM	
9085	JUNE ALLYSON	portrait	MGM	
9086	JUNE ALLYSON	portrait	MGM	
9087	JUNE ALLYSON	portrait	MGM	
9088	JUNE ALLYSON	portrait	MGM	
9089	JUNE ALLYSON	portrait	MGM	
9090	JUNE ALLYSON	portrait	MGM	
9091	JUNE ALLYSON	portrait	MGM	
9099	SALLY FORREST	portrait	MGM	
9103E	DEBBIE REYNOLDS	portrait		
9107	NORMA SHEARER	portrait		
9112	NORMA SHEARER	portrait	MGM	
9114	NORMA SHEARER	portrait		
9119	VIRGINIA GREY	portrait		
9125	VIRGINIA GREY	portrait		
9131E	CLAIRE BLOOM	portrait	MGM	
9136	GALE SONDERGAARD	portrait	MGM	
9141	RUSS TAMBLYN	portrait		
9143	ANN SOTHERN	portrait		
9146	RUSS TAMBLYN	portrait		
9148	RUTH HUSSEY + MOTHER, SISTER BETTY	portrait		
9151	RUTH HUSSEY AT 3 MONTHS	portrait		
9154	FERNANDO LAMAS	portrait		
9154	RUTH HUSSEY AT 5, BROTHER ROBERT, SISTER BETTY	portrait		
9155	FERNANDO LAMAS	portrait		
9155	RUTH HUSSEY	portrait		
9156	RUTH HUSSEY AT 3	portrait		
9158	RUTH HUSSEY, CLIFF EDWARDS, ROBERT YOUNG - MAISIE	portrait		
9159	FERNANDO LAMAS	portrait		
9159	RUTH HUSSEY, ROBERT YOUNG - RICH MAN, POOR GIRL	portrait		
9162	RUTH HUSSEY, MARY BETH HUGHES, NORMA SHEARER	portrait		
9163	RUTH HUSSEY, JOAN CRAWFORD, ROSE HOBART	portrait		
9165	RUTH HUSSEY, EDWARD G. ROBINSON - BLACKMAIL	portrait		
9172	GALE STORM SHOW: ON THE DOT		CBS-TV	1959
9177	GALE STORM SHOW: JAILMATES	SEITER	CBS-TV	1959
9189	ROBERT TAYLOR	portrait	MGM	
9189	VERA-ELLEN	portrait	MGM	
9193	MICKEY ROONEY	portrait		
9212	AVA GARDNER	portrait	MGM	
9218	DOROTHY MCGUIRE	portrait		

9239	LUISE RAINER	portrait		
9242	KATY JURADO	portrait	MGM	
9244	KATY JURADO	portrait	MGM	
9245	KATY JURADO	portrait	MGM	
9246	KATY JURADO	portrait	MGM	
9249	KATY JURADO	portrait	MGM	
9250	ARLENE DAHL	portrait		
9251	ARLENE DAHL	portrait		
9257	VERA-ELLEN	portrait	MGM	
9258	VERA-ELLEN	portrait	MGM	
9259	VAN JOHNSON, WIFE EVIE, DAUGHTER SCHUYLER	portrait		
9260	VAN JOHNSON, WIFE EVIE, DAUGHTER SCHUYLER	portrait		
9261	VAN JOHNSON, WIFE EVIE, DAUGHTER SCHUYLER	portrait		
9261	VERA-ELLEN	portrait	MGM	
9262	VERA-ELLEN	portrait	MGM	
9263	VAN JOHNSON, WIFE EVIE, DAUGHTER SCHUYLER	portrait		
9267	VAN JOHNSON, WIFE EVIE, DAUGHTER SCHUYLER	portrait		
9268	VAN JOHNSON, WIFE EVIE, DAUGHTER SCHUYLER	portrait		
9268	VERA-ELLEN	portrait	MGM	
9269	VAN JOHNSON, WIFE EVIE, DAUGHTER SCHUYLER	portrait		
9272	DONNA REED	portrait		
9273	VAN JOHNSON, DAUGHTER SCHUYLER	portrait		
9274	VAN JOHNSON, DAUGHTER SCHUYLER	portrait		
9275	VAN JOHNSON, WIFE EVIE, DAUGHTER SCHUYLER	portrait		
9276	VAN JOHNSON, WIFE EVIE, DAUGHTER SCHUYLER	portrait		
9282	ELIZABETH TAYLOR	portrait		
9283	ELIZABETH TAYLOR	portrait		
9284	ELIZABETH TAYLOR	portrait		
9285	ELIZABETH TAYLOR	portrait		
9286	ELIZABETH TAYLOR	portrait		
9287	ELIZABETH TAYLOR	portrait		
9288	ELIZABETH TAYLOR	portrait		
9289	ELIZABETH TAYLOR	portrait		
9291	VERA-ELLEN	portrait	MGM	
9292	VERA-ELLEN	portrait	MGM	
9293	ROBERT TAYLOR	portrait		
9293	VERA-ELLEN	portrait	MGM	
9294	VERA-ELLEN	portrait	MGM	
9295	VERA-ELLEN	portrait	MGM	
9296	VERA-ELLEN	portrait	MGM	
9297	VERA-ELLEN	portrait	MGM	
9298	VERA-ELLEN	portrait	MGM	
9338	ELKE SOMMER	portrait	MGM	
9343	AUDREY TOTTER	portrait	MGM	
9347	NORMA SHEARER	portrait		
9349	NORMA SHEARER	portrait		
9359	AUDREY TOTTER	portrait	MGM	
9362E	MICHELE MERCIER	portrait		
9364E	ELAINE STEWART	portrait		
9369	MYRNA LOY	portrait		
9375	DONNA REED	portrait		
9377	DONNA REED	portrait		
9382	MYRNA LOY	portrait		
9383	MYRNA LOY	portrait		
9384	MYRNA LOY	portrait		
9387	MYRNA LOY	portrait		
9389	MYRNA LOY	portrait		
9394	AUDREY TOTTER	portrait	MGM	
9395	AUDREY TOTTER	portrait	MGM	
9396	AUDREY TOTTER	portrait	MGM	
9397	AUDREY TOTTER	portrait	MGM	
9398	AUDREY TOTTER	portrait	MGM	
9399	AUDREY TOTTER	portrait	MGM	
9400	AUDREY TOTTER	portrait	MGM	
9401	AUDREY TOTTER	portrait	MGM	
9402	AUDREY TOTTER	portrait	MGM	

9403	AUDREY TOTTER	portrait	MGM	
9403	MARNIE	HITCHCOCK	UNIVERSAL	1964
9404	AUDREY TOTTER	portrait	MGM	
9405	AUDREY TOTTER	portrait	MGM	
9406	AUDREY TOTTER	portrait	MGM	
9407	AUDREY TOTTER	portrait	MGM	
9408	AUDREY TOTTER	portrait	MGM	
9409	AUDREY TOTTER	portrait	MGM	
9418	MYRNA LOY	portrait		
9429	MARSHALL THOMPSON	portrait	MGM	
9442	GREER GARSON	portrait		
9444	DONNA REED	portrait		
9449	DONNA REED	portrait		
9453	DONNA REED	portrait		
9453	GRACE KELLY	portrait		
9455	GRACE KELLY	portrait		
9456	GENE KELLY	portrait		
9457	AUDREY TOTTER	portrait		
9457	GRACE KELLY	portrait		
9458	AUDREY TOTTER	portrait		
9458	DEBBIE REYNOLDS	portrait		1950s
9458	ELAINE STEWART	portrait		
9459	JOHNNY MACK BROWN	portrait		
9461	GRACE KELLY	portrait		
9464	GRACE KELLY	portrait		
9480	VIRGINIA O'BRIEN	portrait		
9486	JANET LEIGH	portrait		
9491	ESTHER WILLIAMS	portrait	MGM	
9492	VAN JOHNSON	portrait		
9497	JOHN HODIAK	portrait		
9498	DEBBIE REYNOLDS	portrait	MGM	
9501	CHRIS COLUMBO (t) (sh)	DONNELLY	EDUCATIONAL FILM	1938
9502	GOOSE FLIES HIGH (t) (sh)	FOSTER	EDUCATIONAL FILM	1938
9502	LYNNE CARVER	portrait	MGM	
9503	WOLF'S SIDE OF THE STORY (t) (sh)	RASINSKI	EDUCATIONAL FILM	1938
9504	NEW COMER (t) (sh)	DAVIS	EDUCATIONAL FILM	1938
9505	JOHN HODIAK	portrait		
9505	STRANGER RIDES AGAIN (t) (sh)	DAVIS	EDUCATIONAL FILM	1938
9505	WALTER PIDGEON	portrait		
9506	WALTER PIDGEON	portrait		
9507	WALTER PIDGEON	portrait		
9508	WALTER PIDGEON	portrait		
9509	WALTER PIDGEON	portrait		
9510	WALTER PIDGEON	portrait		
9511	WALTER PIDGEON	portrait		
9512	DEBBIE REYNOLDS	portrait		
9512	WALTER PIDGEON	portrait		
9513	WALTER PIDGEON	portrait		
9514	WALTER PIDGEON	portrait		
9515	WALTER PIDGEON	portrait		
9516	WALTER PIDGEON	portrait		
9517	WALTER PIDGEON	portrait		
9518	VAN JOHNSON	portrait		
9518	WALTER PIDGEON	portrait		
9519	WALTER PIDGEON	portrait		
9520	VAN JOHNSON	portrait		
9520	WALTER PIDGEON	portrait		
9521	WALTER PIDGEON	portrait		
9522	VAN JOHNSON	portrait		
9522	WALTER PIDGEON	portrait		
9523	VAN JOHNSON	portrait		
9523	WALTER PIDGEON	portrait		
9524	WALTER PIDGEON	portrait		
9525	VAN JOHNSON	portrait		
9525	WALTER PIDGEON	portrait		
9526	WALTER PIDGEON	portrait		

9527	VAN JOHNSON	portrait		
9527	WALTER PIDGEON	portrait		
9528	WALTER PIDGEON	portrait		
9529	WALTER PIDGEON	portrait		
9530	WALTER PIDGEON	portrait		
9531	WALTER PIDGEON	portrait		
9532	WALTER PIDGEON	portrait		
9545	JANE POWELL	portrait		
9554	DEBORAH KERR	portrait	MGM	
9556	DEBORAH KERR	portrait		
9556	ESTHER WILLIAMS	portrait		
9559	ESTHER WILLIAMS, HUSBAND BEN GAGE, HER PARENTS	portrait		
9567	DEBORAH KERR	portrait	MGM	
9569	JANE POWELL, A. DAHL, B. GARRETT, K. GRAYSON	portrait		
9571	JOAN CRAWFORD	portrait	MGM	
9576	JANE POWELL, MOTHER-IN-LAW, AMANDA BLAKE	portrait		
9581	MARILYN MAXWELL	portrait		
9588	NANCY DAVIS	portrait	MGM	
9589	ESTHER WILLIAMS, HUSBAND BEN GAGE	portrait		
9589	MARILYN MAXWELL	portrait		
9590	MARILYN MAXWELL	portrait		
9593	ESTHER WILLIAMS, HUSBAND BEN GAGE	portrait		
9597	ELEANOR POWELL	portrait		
9601	GOOD MORNING, MISS DOVE	KOSTER	20th CENTURY-FOX	1955
9605	ROBERT YOUNG	portrait		
9610	GOOD MORNING, MISS DOVE	KOSTER	20th CENTURY-FOX	1955
9611	GOOD MORNING, MISS DOVE	KOSTER	20th CENTURY-FOX	1955
9612	GOOD MORNING, MISS DOVE	KOSTER	20th CENTURY-FOX	1955
9616	ROBERT YOUNG	portrait		
9623	GOOD MORNING, MISS DOVE	KOSTER	20th CENTURY FOX	1955
9625	GOOD MORNING, MISS DOVE	KOSTER	20th CENTURY FOX	1955
9632	GOOD MORNING, MISS DOVE	KOSTER	20th CENTURY FOX	1955
9633	DONNA REED	portrait		
9635	JEANETTE MACDONALD	portrait		
9636	JEANETTE MACDONALD	portrait		
9637	JEANETTE MACDONALD	portrait		
9638	JEANETTE MACDONALD	portrait		
9639	JEANETTE MACDONALD	portrait		
9640	FRANCES GIFFORD	portrait		
9640	JANE POWELL, HUSBAND GEARY STEFFIN	portrait		
9640	JEANETTE MACDONALD	portrait		
9641	JANE POWELL, HUSBAND GEARY STEFFIN	portrait		
9641	JEANETTE MACDONALD	portrait		
9642	JEANETTE MACDONALD	portrait		
9643	JANE POWELL, HUSBAND GEARY STEFFIN	portrait		
9643	JEANETTE MACDONALD	portrait		
9644	JEANETTE MACDONALD	portrait		
9645	JANE POWELL, HUSBAND GEARY STEFFIN	portrait		
9645	JEANETTE MACDONALD	portrait		
9646	JEANETTE MACDONALD	portrait		
9647	JEANETTE MACDONALD	portrait		
9648	JANE POWELL, HUSBAND GEARY STEFFIN	portrait		
9648	JEANETTE MACDONALD	portrait		
9649	JANE POWELL, HUSBAND GEARY STEFFIN	portrait		
9649	JEANETTE MACDONALD	portrait		
9650	JEANETTE MACDONALD	portrait		
9652	JAMES STEWART, TWIN DAUGHTERS JUDY, KELLY	portrait		
9676	HURD HATFIELD	portrait	MGM	
9683	JEANETTE MACDONALD	portrait		
9684	JEANETTE MACDONALD	portrait		
9687	ANGELA LANSBURY	portrait		
9688	JEAN SIMMONS/STEWART GRANGER	portrait	MGM	
9692	MARSHALL THOMPSON	portrait	MGM	
9711	GLORIA DE HAVEN	portrait		
9736	ELAINE STEWART	portrait		
9737	RICARDO MONTALBAN	portrait		

9747	ELAINE STEWART	portrait	MGM	
9773	ELAINE STEWART	portrait		
9773	MYRNA LOY AT 6, COUSIN LAURA BELLE WILDER	portrait		
9774	ELAINE STEWART	portrait		
9774	MYRNA LOY - MASK OF FU MANCHU	portrait		
9775	ELAINE STEWART	portrait		
9775	MYRNA LOY AT 5	portrait		
9779	ELAINE STEWART	portrait		
9779	SALLY FORREST	portrait	MGM	
9784	SALLY FORREST	portrait	MGM	
9787	ELIZABETH TAYLOR	portrait		
9787	VAN HEFLIN	portrait	MGM	
9788	MYRNA LOY AT 10, BROTHER DAVID	portrait		
9797	ESTHER WILLIAMS	portrait		
9797	LANA TURNER	portrait	MGM	
9798	ESTHER WILLIAMS	portrait		
9799	ESTHER WILLIAMS	portrait		
9800	ESTHER WILLIAMS	portrait		
9801	ESTHER WILLIAMS	portrait		
9801	MYRNA LOY AT 3	portrait		
9803	FRANCES GIFFORD	portrait	MGM	
9803	LANA TURNER	portrait	MGM	
9804	ARLENE DAHL	portrait		
9804	FRANCES GIFFORD	portrait	MGM	
9812	CYD CHARISSE	portrait		
9812	MYRNA LOY AT 10, BROTHER DAVID	portrait		
9817	MYRNA LOY	portrait	MGM	
9821	MARJORIE MAIN	portrait		
9823	MARJORIE MAIN	portrait		
9829	JANE POWELL	portrait		
9832	AVA GARDNER	portrait		
9836	STELLA STEVENS	portrait	MGM	
9866	AUDREY TOTTER	portrait		
9868	PIER ANGELI	portrait	MGM	
9871	STEVE FORREST	portrait	MGM	
9872	AUDREY TOTTER	portrait		
9874	RAMON NOVARRO	portrait		
9876	STEVE FORREST	portrait	MGM	
9877	GREER GARSON + MOTHER	portrait		
9879	GREER GARSON	portrait		
9884	FRANK MORGAN	portrait	MGM	
9887	AUDREY TOTTER	portrait	MGM	
9888	FRANK MORGAN	portrait	MGM	
9888	LUCILLE BALL	portrait		
9889	FRANK MORGAN	portrait		
9890	FRANK MORGAN	portrait	MGM	
9892	AUDREY TOTTER	portrait		
9893	LUCILLE BALL	portrait		
9894	AUDREY TOTTER	portrait	MGM	
9895	ESTHER WILLIAMS	portrait		
9896	ESTHER WILLIAMS	portrait		
9898	DEBBIE REYNOLDS	portrait		
9899	DEBBIE REYNOLDS	portrait		
9900	DEBBIE REYNOLDS	portrait		
9901	DEBBIE REYNOLDS	portrait		
9901	ELIZABETH TAYLOR	portrait		
9903	DEBBIE REYNOLDS	portrait		
9906	DEBBIE REYNOLDS	portrait		
9908	DEBBIE REYNOLDS	portrait		
9912	ESTHER WILLIAMS	portrait		
9913	ESTHER WILLIAMS	portrait		
9914	ESTHER WILLIAMS	portrait		
9918	ESTHER WILLIAMS	portrait	MGM	
9918	WILLIAM POWELL	portrait		
9919	ESTHER WILLIAMS	portrait	MGM	
9920	ESTHER WILLIAMS	portrait	MGM	

9921	ESTHER WILLIAMS	portrait	MGM	
9922	ESTHER WILLIAMS	portrait	MGM	
9923	ESTHER WILLIAMS	portrait	MGM	
9924	ESTHER WILLIAMS	portrait	MGM	
9925	ESTHER WILLIAMS	portrait	MGM	
9926	ESTHER WILLIAMS	portrait	MGM	
9927	ESTHER WILLIAMS	portrait	MGM	
9928	ESTHER WILLIAMS	portrait	MGM	
9929	ESTHER WILLIAMS	portrait	MGM	
9930	ESTHER WILLIAMS	portrait	MGM	
9931	ESTHER WILLIAMS	portrait	MGM	
9932	ESTHER WILLIAMS	portrait	MGM	
9933	ESTHER WILLIAMS	portrait	MGM	
9934	ESTHER WILLIAMS	portrait	MGM	
9935	ESTHER WILLIAMS	portrait	MGM	
9936	ESTHER WILLIAMS	portrait	MGM	
9939	ELEANOR POWELL	portrait		
9939	PIER ANGELI	portrait	MGM	
9942	PIER ANGELI	portrait	MGM	
9943	ESTHER WILLIAMS	portrait		
9944	JANE POWELL	portrait		
9944	JOHN HODIAK	portrait		
9945	TELEPHONE TIME: PICTURE OF THE MAGI	SINCLAIR	ABC-TV	1957
9949	CYD CHARISSE	portrait	MGM	
9951	JOHN HODIAK	portrait		
9955	TELEPHONE TIME: ARITHMETIC SAILOR		ABC-TV	1957
9956	TELEPHONE TIME: UNDER SEVENTEEN	SINCLAIR	ABC-TV	1957
9959	CYD CHARISSE	portrait	MGM	
9961	TELEPHONE TIME: NOVEL APPEAL	HILLER	ABC-TV	1957
9962	ANGELA LANSBURY	portrait		
9962	TELEPHONE TIME: STUBBORN FOOL	TAYLOR	ABC-TV	1958
9965	CLAIRE BLOOM	portrait	MGM	
9965	GLORIA DE HAVEN	portrait		
9966	TELEPHONE TIME: OTHER VAN GOGH	SINCLAIR	ABC-TV	1957
9968	GLORIA DE HAVEN	portrait	MGM	
9968	TELEPHONE TIME: FRYING PAN		ABC-TV	1957
9969	TELEPHONE TIME: I GET ALONG WITHOUT YOU VERY WELL	BERLIN	ABC-TV	1957
9970	GLORIA DE HAVEN	portrait		
9972	AVA GARDNER	portrait	MGM	
9976	MARY ASTOR	portrait		
9977	MARY ASTOR	portrait	MGM	
9977	ROBERT TAYLOR	portrait		
9978	MARY ASTOR	portrait		
9979	MARY ASTOR	portrait		
9981	MARY ASTOR	portrait	MGM	
9991	ANN RUTHERFORD	portrait		
9995	ANGELA LANSBURY	portrait		
9995E	DEBBIE REYNOLDS	portrait		
9996	ANGELA LANSBURY	portrait		
9997	ANGELA LANSBURY	portrait		
9998	ANGELA LANSBURY	portrait		
9999	ANGELA LANSBURY	portrait		
10007	DESERT FURY (see 11007)	ALLEN	PARAMOUNT	R58(47)
10007	DESERT TOWN*	ALLEN	PARAMOUNT	1947
10017	AT SEA WITH THE NAVY*	WALKER	PARAMOUNT	1952
10051	ROAD TO RIO	MCLEOD	PARAMOUNT	1947
10052	HEIRESS	WYLER	PARAMOUNT	1949
10053	RIDING HIGH	CAPRA	PARAMOUNT	1950
10055	SOMETHING TO LIVE FOR (MR. & MISS ANONYMOUS*)	STEVENS	PARAMOUNT	1950
10057	DETECTIVE STORY	WYLER	PARAMOUNT	1951
10064	STORM IN A TEACUP	SEVILLE	UNITED ARTISTS	1937
10102	EASY DOES IT*	HALL	PARAMOUNT	1950
10102	GREAT LOVER	HALL	PARAMOUNT	1950
10102	LEMON DROP KID	LANFIELD	PARAMOUNT	1951
10103	LEMON DROP KID	LANFIELD	PARAMOUNT	1951
10104	SON OF PALEFACE	TASHLIN	PARAMOUNT	1952

10105	HERE COME THE GIRLS	BINYON	PARAMOUNT	1953
10106	EDDIE FOY STORY	SHAVELSON	PARAMOUNT	1955
10151	TOP O' THE MORNING	MILLER	PARAMOUNT	1949
10152	ROAD TO BALI	WALKER	PARAMOUNT	1953
10157	MR. & MISS ANONYMOUS - (2nd unit* see 10055)	GUIOL	PARAMOUNT	1950
10202	QUANTRELL'S RAIDERS*	DIETERLE	PARAMOUNT	1951
10212	LOVING YOU (LONESOME COWBOY*)	KANTER	PARAMOUNT	1957
10215	A WOMAN OBSESSED*	CUKOR	PARAMOUNT	1957
10215	OBSESSION*	CUKOR	PARAMOUNT	1957
10217	ONE ANGRY DAY*	STURGES	PARAMOUNT	1959
10217	SHOWDOWN AT GUN HILL*	STURGES	PARAMOUNT	1959
10223	SUMMER AND SMOKE	GLENVILLE	PARAMOUNT	1961
10224	BLUE HAWAII	TAUROG	PARAMOUNT	1961
10229	BECKET	GLENVILLE	PARAMOUNT	1963
10301	MY SON JOHN	MCCAREY	PARAMOUNT	1951
10322	YOU'RE NEVER TOO YOUNG	TAUROG	PARAMOUNT	1955
10337	LADY EVE*	TAUROG	PARAMOUNT	1956
10339	FLAME OF GRANADA*	SIEGEL	PARAMOUNT	1956
10339	SPANISH AFFAIR (FLAMENCO*)	SIEGEL	PARAMOUNT	1956
10344	VERTIGO (FROM AMONGST THE DEAD*)	HITCHCOCK	PARAMOUNT	1958
10347	DESIRE UNDER THE ELMS	MANN	PARAMOUNT	1957
10354	AS YOUNG AS WE ARE (TOO YOUNG FOR LOVE*)	GIRARD	PARAMOUNT	1958
10358	GUNS UP* (ONE EYED JACKS)	KUBRICK*	PARAMOUNT	1958
10361	NO BAIL FOR THE JUDGE*	HITCHCOCK	PARAMOUNT	1960
10362	BAY OF NAPLES*	SHAVELSON	PARAMOUNT	1960
10371	HATARI (AFRICAN STORY*)	HAWKS	PARAMOUNT	1962
10373	ON THE DOUBLE	SHAVELSON	PARAMOUNT	1961
10374	LADY SITTER*	LEWIS*	PARAMOUNT	1961
10381	PARIS WHEN IT SIZZLES (TOGETHER IN PARIS*)	QUINE	PARAMOUNT	1964
10383	PAPA'S DELICATE CONDITION	MARSHALL	PARAMOUNT	1963
10393	ROBINSON CRUSOE ON MARS	HASKINS	PARAMOUNT	1964
10397	JUDITH	MANN	PARAMOUNT	1964
10399	AMOUROUS ADV. OF MOLL FLANDERS	YOUNG	PARAMOUNT	1964
10403	VANQUISHED (ROCK GRAYSON'S WOMEN*)	LUDWIG	PARAMOUNT	1953
10407	JIVARO (LOST TREASURE OF THE AMAZON*)	LUDWIG	PARAMOUNT	1954
10409	HELL'S ISLAND (LOVE IS A WEAPON*)	KARLSON	PARAMOUNT	1954
10410	FAR HORIZONS (TWO CAPTAINS WEST*)	MATE	PARAMOUNT	1954
10414	SPY WHO CAME IN FROM THE COLD	RITT	PARAMOUNT	1965
10417	ALFIE	GILBERT	PARAMOUNT	1965
10418	EASY COME EASY GO	SHEAR	PARAMOUNT	1965
10419	SCHIZOID	FRANCIS	PARAMOUNT	1965
10421	FUNERAL IN BERLIN	HAMILTON	PARAMOUNT	1966
10425	IDOL	PETRIE	PARAMOUNT	1966
10427	DEADLY BEES	FRANCIS	PARAMOUNT	1966
10429	SPY WITH THE COLD NOSE	PETRIE	PARAMOUNT	1966
10434	HUNTSVILLE	SPRINGSTEEN	PARAMOUNT	1966
10436	WATERHOLE #3	GRAHAM	PARAMOUNT	1966
10438	BUSHWACKERS	SELANDER	PARAMOUNT	1966
10441	ISABEL	ALMOND	PARAMOUNT	1966
10442	BLUE	NARIZZANO	PARAMOUNT	1966
10445	HIS, HERS AND THEIRS	SHAVELSON	PARAMOUNT	1966
10447	ROGUES GALLERY	HORN	PARAMOUNT	1966
10448	BROTHERHOOD	RITT	PARAMOUNT	1966
10517	MR. AND MISS ANONYMOUS (2nd unit*)	GUIOL	PARAMOUNT	1950
10517	SOMETHING TO LIVE FOR (2nd unit*)	GUIOL	PARAMOUNT	1950
11001	AFFAIRS OF SUSAN	SEITER	PARAMOUNT	1945
11004	STRANGE LOVE OF MARTHA IVERS (LOVE, LIES, BLEEDING*)	MILESTONE	PARAMOUNT	1946
11007	DESERT FURY (DESERT TOWN*)	ALLEN	PARAMOUNT	1947
11008	DEADLOCK* (see 10008)	HASKINS	PARAMOUNT	1947
11050	STORK CLUB	WALKER	PARAMOUNT	1946
11051	ROAD TO RIO	MCLEOD	PARAMOUNT	1947
11101	MY FAVORITE BRUNETTE	NUGENT	PARAMOUNT	1947
11387	TWO YEARS BEFORE THE MAST	FARROW	PARAMOUNT	1945
11391	KITTY	LEISEN	PARAMOUNT	1944
11393	SALTY O'ROURKE	WALSH	PARAMOUNT	1945
11409	IMPERFECT LADY (TAKE THIS WOMAN*)	ALLEN	PARAMOUNT	1947

11421	BIG HAIR CUT (WILD HARVEST*)	GARNETT	PARAMOUNT	1947
11428	SAINTED SISTERS*	LEISEN	PARAMOUNT	1947
11434	BEYOND GLORY (LONG GREY LINE*)	FARROW	PARAMOUNT	1948
11439	ABIGAIL, DEAR HEART* (See SONG OF SURRENDER)	LEISEN	PARAMOUNT	1949
11439	NOW AND FOREVER*	LEISEN	PARAMOUNT	1949
11439	SONG OF SURRENDER (SIN OF ABBY HUNT*)	LEISEN	PARAMOUNT	1949
11445	ALIAS NICK BEAL (DARK CIRCLE)	FARROW	PARAMOUNT	1949
11445	STRANGE TEMPTATION*	FARROW	PARAMOUNT	1949
11446	LADY FROM LARIAT LOOP (?)	MARSHALL	PARAMOUNT	1949
11446	PAID IN FULL (BITTER VICTORY *)	DIETERLE	PARAMOUNT	1950
11450	BRIDE OF VENGEANCE (A MASK FOR LUCRETIA*)	LEISEN	PARAMOUNT	1949
11451	BROADWAY STORY*	FARROW	PARAMOUNT	1949
11453	CAPTAIN CAREY USA (AFTER MIDNIGHT*)	LEISEN	PARAMOUNT	1950
11456	NO MAN OF HER OWN (I MARRIED A DEAD MAN*) (THE LIE*)	LEISEN	PARAMOUNT	1950
11457	BLUES SKIES	HEISLER	PARAMOUNT	1946
11458	APPOINTMENT WITH DANGER (POSTAL INSPECTOR*)	ALLEN	PARAMOUNT	1951
11459	WHERE MEN ARE MEN*	MARSHALL	PARAMOUNT	1950
11463	BRANDED (MONTANA RIDES*)	MATE	PARAMOUNT	1950
11464	REDHEAD AND THE COWBOY (BEYOND THE SUNSET*)	FENTON	PARAMOUNT	1950
11467	GOLDBERGS	HART	PARAMOUNT	1950
11470	RENDEZVOUS*	LEISEN	PARAMOUNT	1951
11475	RAGE OF THE VULTURE*	VIDOR	PARAMOUNT	1951
11479	SAVAGE (WARBONNET*)	MARSHALL	PARAMOUNT	1952
11484	LOS ALAMOS*	HOPPER	PARAMOUNT	1952
11485	JUST FOR YOU (FAMOUS*)	NUGENT	PARAMOUNT	1952
11486	ROSALIND	EPSTEIN	PARAMOUNT	1952
11488	OFF LIMITS (MILITARY POLICE MEN*)	MARSHALL	PARAMOUNT	1953
11496	FOREVER FEMALE (REACHING FOR THE STARS*)	RAPPER	PARAMOUNT	1953
11497	ARROWHEAD (ADOBE WALLS*)	WARREN	PARAMOUNT	1953
11498	ELEPHANT WALK	DIETERLE	PARAMOUNT	1954
11500	SECRET OF THE INCAS (LEGEND OF THE INCAS*)	HOPPER	PARAMOUNT	1954
11503	CASANOVA'S BIG NIGHT (MR. CASANOVA*)	MCLEOD	PARAMOUNT	1954
11504	UNCONQUERED (2nd unit*)	ROSSON	PARAMOUNT	1947
11505	UNCONQUERED (3rd unit*)	JENNINGS	PARAMOUNT	1947
11506	BIG HAIR CUT (2nd unit*)	HASKIN	PARAMOUNT	1947
11506	SABRINA (SABRINA FAIR*)	WILDER	PARAMOUNT	1954
11506	WILD HARVEST (2nd unit)	HASKIN	PARAMOUNT	1947
11507	BLAZE OF NOON (2nd unit*)	FARROW	PARAMOUNT	1947
11508	BLAZE OF NOON (3rd unit*)	JENNINGS	PARAMOUNT	1947
11509	WHISPERING SMITH (2nd unit*)	COLMAN JR.	PARAMOUNT	1948
11510	A FOREIGN AFFAIR (2nd unit*)	WILDER	PARAMOUNT	1948
11511	LONG GREY LINE (advance unit*)	FARROW	PARAMOUNT	1949
11512	SEALED VERDICT (2nd unit*)	ALLEN	PARAMOUNT	1949
11513	SAMSON AND DELILAH - (MOROCO) (2nd unit*)	JESTER	PARAMOUNT	1949
11514	SAMSON AND DELILAH - (STUDIO) (3rd unit*)	JENNINGS	PARAMOUNT	1949
11515	SAMSON AND DELILAH - (MINIATURE) (4th unit*)	JENNINGS	PARAMOUNT	1949
11516	SEPTEMBER AFFAIR (ITALIAN unit*)	DIETERLE	PARAMOUNT	1950
11516	TOO LATE MY LOVE*	CURTIZ	PARAMOUNT	1955
11517	PROUD AND THE PROFANE (MAGNIFICIENT DEVILS*)	SEATON	PARAMOUNT	1956
11521	MAVERICK*	MATE	PARAMOUNT	1957
11522	OMAR KHAYYAM (LOVES OF OMAR KHAYYAM*)	DIETERLE	PARAMOUNT	1957
11525	FEAR STRIKES OUT (JIM PIERSALL STORY*)	MULLIGAN	PARAMOUNT	1957
11534	HELLER IN PINK TIGHTS (HELLER WITH A GUN*)	CUKOR	PARAMOUNT	1959
11535	OLYMPIA*	CURTIZ	PARAMOUNT	1960
11537	BLUEPRINT FOR ROBBERY (BIG BOSTON ROBBERY*)	HOPPER	PARAMOUNT	1961
11538	MAN-TRAP (DEADLOCK*)	O'BRIEN	PARAMOUNT	1961
11541	ESCAPE FROM ZAHRAIN	NEAME	PARAMOUNT	1962
11542	IRON MEN	CASSAVETES	PARAMOUNT	1962
11546	HARLOW	DOUGLAS	PARAMOUNT	1965
11549	HALF A SIX PENCE	SIDNEY	PARAMOUNT	1967
11552	LAST SAFARI	HATHAWAY	PARAMOUNT	1967
11554	ODD COUPLE	SAKS	PARAMOUNT	1967
11555	MR. SEBASTIAN	GREENE	PARAMOUNT	1967
11556	FADE IN	TAYLOR	PARAMOUNT	1967
11557	VILLA RIDES	KULIK	PARAMOUNT	1967
11558	MY SIDE OF THE MOUNTAIN	CLARK	PARAMOUNT	1967

11559	BARBARELLA	VADIM	PARAMOUNT	1967
13061	JOAN CRAWFORD	portrait	MGM	
14430	ANN DVORAK	portrait	MGM	
14486	SWAMP FOX (series)	VARIOUS	DISNEY - TV	1959
14565	FORTY THIEVES	SELANDER	UNITED ARTIST	1944
14954	MARION SCHILLING	portrait		
14956	MARION SCHILLING	portrait		
15622	RAGE	SCOTT	WARNER BROS	1972
16058	CANADIANS, THE	KENNEDY	20th CENTURY FOX	1961
16173	SWAMP FOX (series)	VARIOUS	DISNEY - TV	1960
17022	TOUCH OF LARCENY (UK)	HAMILTON	PARMOUNT	1959
17023	MAN WHO COULD CHEAT DEATH (UK)	FISHER	PARAMOUNT	1959
17026	CHANCE MEETING (UK: BLIND DATE)	LOSEY	PARAMOUNT	1959
18529	SWAMP FOX (series)	VARIOUS	DISNEY - TV	1961
20002	LAW OF THE LAWLESS (INVITATION TO A HANGING*)	CLAXTON	PARAMOUNT	1964
20003	SOLDIER IN THE RAIN	NELSON	PARAMOUNT	1964
20004	GUNFIGHT AT COMANCHE CREEK	MCDONALD	PARAMOUNT	1964
20005	FOR THOSE WHO THINK YOUNG	MARTINSON	PARAMOUNT	1964
20006	STRANGLER	TOPPER	PARAMOUNT	1964
20007	SEX AND THE SINGLE GIRL	QUINE	PARAMOUNT	1964
20008	OUT OF TOWNERS	MANN	PARAMOUNT	1964
20009	STAGE TO THUNDER ROCK (STAGECOACH TO HELL*)	CLAXTON	PARAMOUNT	1964
20011	HOUSE IS NOT A HOME	ROUSE	EMBASSY	1964
20012	CHEYENNE AUTUMN	WB	PARAMOUNT	1964
20013	HOW TO MURDER YOUR WIFE	CHARLESTON	PARAMOUNT	1964
20014	REACHING FOR THE STARS	CAPRA	PARAMOUNT	1964
20015	YOUNG FURY	NYBY	PARAMOUNT	1964
20016	IN HARM'S WAY	PREMINGER	PARAMOUNT	1964
20017	OSCAR	ROUSE	EMBASSY	1964
20018	SHIP OF FOOLS	KRAMER	PARAMOUNT	1964
20020	TICKLE ME	TAUROG	PARAMOUNT	1964
20021	BLACK SPURS	SPRINGSTEEN	PARAMOUNT	1964
20022	GLORY GUYS	LAVEN	PARAMOUNT	1964
20023	BOUNTY KILLER	BENNET	PARAMOUNT	1964
20024	REQUIEM FOR A GUNFIGHTER	BENNET	PARAMOUNT	1964
20025	TOWN TAMER	SELANDER	PARAMOUNT	1965
20026	O DAD, POOR DAD, MAMMA'S HUNG YOU IN THE CLOSET...	QUINE	PARAMOUNT	1965
20027	BABY SITTER*	HILLER	PARAMOUNT	1965
20027	PROMISE HER ANYTHING	HILLER	PARAMOUNT	1965
20028	FIFTH COFFIN		PARAMOUNT	1965
20029	THIS PROPERTY IS CONDEMNED	HUSTON	PARAMOUNT	1965
20030	OWL AND THE PUSSYCAT		PARAMOUNT	1965
20031	DEEP FREEZE GIRLS		PARAMOUNT	1965
20033	YOU JUST KILLED ME	HUGHES	PARAMOUNT	1966
20034	ASSAULT ON A QUEEN	DONAHUE	PARAMOUNT	1966
20035	BILLIE (GINGER*)	WEIS	PARAMOUNT	1965
20036	VILLAGE OF THE GIANTS	GORDON	PARAMOUNT	1965
20037	IS PARIS BURNING?	CLEMENT	PARAMOUNT	1966
20038	NIGHT OF THE TIGER	MCEVEETY	PARAMOUNT	1965
20039	APACHE UPRISING	SPRINGSTEEN	PARAMOUNT	1965
20045	JOHNNY RENO	SPRINGSTEEN	PARAMOUNT	1966
20047	PICTURE MOMMY DEAD	GORDON	PARAMOUNT	1966
20048	WACO	SPRINGSTEEN	PARAMOUNT	1966
20050	EYE FOR AN EYE	MOORE	PARAMOUNT	1966
20051	GOOD TIMES (I GOT YOU BABE*)	FRIEDKIN	PARAMOUNT	1966
20052	SCILLETO	BERRY	PARAMOUNT	1967
20055	GRADUATE	NICHOLS	PARAMOUNT	1967
20057	DEVIL'S BRIGADE	MCLAGLAN	PARAMOUNT	1967
20192	DIANA LYNN	portrait	MGM	
21002	V. D. CONTROL IN THE NAVY		PARAMOUNT	1949
21003	CURRENCY OF OPPORTUNITY (U.S. Army training film)		PARAMOUNT	
21004	HERE'S YOUR LETTER SAILOR (sh) (training film)		PARAMOUNT	1944
21006	LATE COMPANY "B", THE (sh) (Army training film)		PARAMOUNT	1944
21008	ELECTION DAY (sh) (U.S. Army)		PARAMOUNT	
21172	ALIAS JESSE JAMES	MCLEOD	PARAMOUNT	1959
21190	BROTHERHOOD OF EVIL	PARRISH	PARAMOUNT	1961

21200	POCKET FULL OF MIRACLES	CAPRA	PARAMOUNT	1962
21717	I ACCUSE!	FERRER	MGM	1958
23912	HONEYMOONIACS (sh)	ROBERTS	EDUCATIONAL FILM	1929
26001	MAUREEN O'SULLIVAN	portrait	MGM	
26558	FEAR NO EVIL (tv)	WENDKOS	NATIONAL BROADCASTING	1969
26858	FEAR NO EVIL	WENDKOS	NATIONAL BROADCASTING	1969
29001	BOOGIE WOOGIE (sh) (MUSICAL PARADE SERIES 5)	MADISON	PARAMOUNT	1945
29003	YOU HIT THE SPOT (sh)	TEMPLETON	PARAMOUNT	1945
29004	LITTLE WITCH	TEMPLETON	PARAMOUNT	1946
29005	NAUGHTY NANETTE	TEMPLETON	PARAMOUNT	1946
29006	COLLEGE QUEEN	TEMPLETON	PARAMOUNT	1946
29007	TALE OF TWO CAFES, A	TEMPLETON	PARAMOUNT	1946
29008	DOUBLE RHYTHM	TEMPLETON	PARAMOUNT	1946
29010	GOLDEN SLIPPERS	TEMPLETON	PARAMOUNT	1946
29011	SWEET AND LOW (PARIS IN THE SPRING*) (sh)	HOPPER	PARAMOUNT	1947
29012	CHAMPAIGNE FOR TWO (sh)	EPSTEIN	PARAMOUNT	1947
29013	CURTAIN TIME	EPSTEIN	PARAMOUNT	1947
29014	SMOOTH SAILING (sh)	HOPPER	PARAMOUNT	1947
29015	MIDNIGHT SERENADE	GANZER	PARAMOUNT	1948
29016	JINGLE, JANGLE, JINGLE (sh)	HOPPER	PARAMOUNT	1948
29018	SAMBA-MANIA (sh)	DANIELS	PARAMOUNT	1948
29019	FOOTLIGHT RHYTHM (sh)	DANIELS	PARAMOUNT	1948
29020	GYPSY HOLIDAY	DAY	PARAMOUNT	1948
29021	TROPICAL MASQUERADE (sh)	GANZER	PARAMOUNT	1948
29022	BIG SISTER BLUES	GANZER	PARAMOUNT	1948
29023	CATALINA INTERLUDE (sh)	GANZER	PARAMOUNT	1949
29047	WILLIAMSBURG	SEATON	PARAMOUNT	1956
29200	QUEBEC	TEMPLETON	PARAMOUNT	1951
29409	COLOR-SONICS - OFFICIAL FILMS		PARAMOUNT	1966
30008	DRACULA HAS RISEN FROM GRAVE (UK)	FRANCIS	WARNER BROS -7 ARTS	1969
30009	START THE REVOLUTION WITHOUT ME (TWO TIMES TWO)	YORKIN	WARNER BROS	1970
30011	SEA GULL (UK)	LUMET	WARNER BROS.	1968
30014	SOPHIE'S PLACE (UK: CROOKS AND CORONETS)	O'CONNELLY	WARNER BROS.	1969
30016	WHEN DINOSAURS RULED THE EARTH (UK)	GUEST	WARNER BROS.	1970
30018	ADAM'S WOMAN (AUS)	LEACOCK	WARNER BROS	1970
30022	FRANKENSTEIN MUST BE DESTROYED (UK)	FISHER	WARNER BROS	1969
30026	BOX 13	HOPPER	PARAMOUNT	1959
30029	TROG (UK)	FRANCIS	WARNER BROS.	1970
30037	TASTE THE BLOOD OF DRACULA (UK)	SASDY	WARNER BROS.	1970
30042	ZEPPELIN (UK)	PERIER	WARNER BROS	1971
30045	PRIEST'S WIFE (IT)	RISI	WARNER BROS	1971
30050	MCCABE AND MRS. MILLER	ALTMAN	WARNER BROS.	1971
30055	LADY LIBERTY (IT/FR)	MONTICELLO	WARNER BROS	1972
30059	SNOW JOB	ENGLUND	WB	1972
30100	LINCOLN JONES (tv pilot)	SMIGHT	PARAMOUNT	1959
30150	GUNSMOKE (tv series)	series	PARAMOUNT	1960
30151	GUNSMOKE (tv series)	series	PARAMOUNT	1960
30152	GUNSMOKE (tv series)	series	PARAMOUNT	1960
30153	GUNSMOKE (tv series)	series	PARAMOUNT	1960
30154	GUNSMOKE (tv series)	series	PARAMOUNT	1960
30155	GUNSMOKE (tv series)	series	PARAMOUNT	1960
30156	GUNSMOKE (tv series)	series	PARAMOUNT	1960
30157	GUNSMOKE (tv series)	series	PARAMOUNT	1960
30158	GUNSMOKE (tv series)	series	PARAMOUNT	1960
30159	GUNSMOKE (tv series)	series	PARAMOUNT	1960
30160	GUNSMOKE (tv series)	series	PARAMOUNT	1960
30161	GUNSMOKE (tv series)	series	PARAMOUNT	1960
30162	GUNSMOKE (tv series)	series	PARAMOUNT	1960
30163	GUNSMOKE (tv series)	series	PARAMOUNT	1960
30164	GUNSMOKE (tv series)	series	PARAMOUNT	1960
30165	GUNSMOKE (tv series)	series	PARAMOUNT	1960
30166	GUNSMOKE (tv series)	series	PARAMOUNT	1960
30167	GUNSMOKE (tv series)	series	PARAMOUNT	1960
30168	GUNSMOKE (tv series)	series	PARAMOUNT	1960
30169	GUNSMOKE (tv series)	series	PARAMOUNT	1960
30170	GUNSMOKE (tv series)	series	PARAMOUNT	1960

30171	GUNSMOKE (tv series)	series	PARAMOUNT	1960
30172	GUNSMOKE (tv series)	series	PARAMOUNT	1960
30173	GUNSMOKE (tv series)	series	PARAMOUNT	1960
30174	GUNSMOKE (tv series)	series	PARAMOUNT	1960
30175	GUNSMOKE (tv series)	series	PARAMOUNT	1960
30176	GUNSMOKE (tv series)	series	PARAMOUNT	1960
30177	GUNSMOKE (tv series)	series	PARAMOUNT	1960
30178	GUNSMOKE (tv series)	series	PARAMOUNT	1960
30179	GUNSMOKE (tv series)	series	PARAMOUNT	1960
30180	GUNSMOKE (tv series)	series	PARAMOUNT	1960
30181	GUNSMOKE (tv series)	series	PARAMOUNT	1960
30182	GUNSMOKE (tv series)	series	PARAMOUNT	1960
30183	GUNSMOKE (tv series)	series	PARAMOUNT	1960
30184	GUNSMOKE (tv series)	series	PARAMOUNT	1960
30185	GUNSMOKE (tv series)	series	PARAMOUNT	1960
30186	GUNSMOKE (tv series)	series	PARAMOUNT	1960
30187	GUNSMOKE (tv series)	series	PARAMOUNT	1960
30188	GUNSMOKE (tv series)	series	PARAMOUNT	1960
30189	GUNSMOKE (tv series)	series	PARAMOUNT	1960
30190	GUNSMOKE (tv series)	series	PARAMOUNT	1960
30191	GUNSMOKE (tv series)	series	PARAMOUNT	1960
30192	GUNSMOKE (tv series)	series	PARAMOUNT	1960
30193	GUNSMOKE (tv series)	series	PARAMOUNT	1960
30194	GUNSMOKE (tv series)	series	PARAMOUNT	1960
30195	GUNSMOKE (tv series)	series	PARAMOUNT	1960
30196	GUNSMOKE (tv series)	series	PARAMOUNT	1960
30197	GUNSMOKE (tv series)	series	PARAMOUNT	1960
30198	GUNSMOKE (tv series)	series	PARAMOUNT	1960
30199	GUNSMOKE (tv series)	series	PARAMOUNT	1960
30200	THIRD PLATOON (tv pilot)	KOCH	PARAMOUNT	1959
30250	HAVE GUN WILL TRAVEL - (tv series)	series	PARAMOUNT	1960
30251	HAVE GUN WILL TRAVEL - (tv series)	series	PARAMOUNT	1960
30252	HAVE GUN WILL TRAVEL - (tv series)	series	PARAMOUNT	1960
30253	HAVE GUN WILL TRAVEL - (tv series)	series	PARAMOUNT	1960
30254	HAVE GUN WILL TRAVEL - (tv series)	series	PARAMOUNT	1960
30255	HAVE GUN WILL TRAVEL - (tv series)	series	PARAMOUNT	1960
30256	HAVE GUN WILL TRAVEL - (tv series)	series	PARAMOUNT	1960
30257	HAVE GUN WILL TRAVEL - (tv series)	series	PARAMOUNT	1960
30258	HAVE GUN WILL TRAVEL - (tv series)	series	PARAMOUNT	1960
30259	HAVE GUN WILL TRAVEL - (tv series)	series	PARAMOUNT	1960
30260	HAVE GUN WILL TRAVEL - (tv series)	series	PARAMOUNT	1960
30261	HAVE GUN WILL TRAVEL - (tv series)	series	PARAMOUNT	1960
30262	HAVE GUN WILL TRAVEL - (tv series)	series	PARAMOUNT	1960
30263	HAVE GUN WILL TRAVEL - (tv series)	series	PARAMOUNT	1960
30264	HAVE GUN WILL TRAVEL - (tv series)	series	PARAMOUNT	1960
30265	HAVE GUN WILL TRAVEL - (tv series)	series	PARAMOUNT	1960
30266	HAVE GUN WILL TRAVEL - (tv series)	series	PARAMOUNT	1960
30267	HAVE GUN WILL TRAVEL - (tv series)	series	PARAMOUNT	1960
30268	HAVE GUN WILL TRAVEL - (tv series)	series	PARAMOUNT	1960
30269	HAVE GUN WILL TRAVEL - (tv series)	series	PARAMOUNT	1960
30270	HAVE GUN WILL TRAVEL - (tv series)	series	PARAMOUNT	1960
30271	HAVE GUN WILL TRAVEL - (tv series)	series	PARAMOUNT	1960
30272	HAVE GUN WILL TRAVEL - (tv series)	series	PARAMOUNT	1960
30273	HAVE GUN WILL TRAVEL - (tv series)	series	PARAMOUNT	1960
30274	HAVE GUN WILL TRAVEL - (tv series)	series	PARAMOUNT	1960
30275	HAVE GUN WILL TRAVEL - (tv series)	series	PARAMOUNT	1960
30276	HAVE GUN WILL TRAVEL - (tv series)	series	PARAMOUNT	1960
30277	HAVE GUN WILL TRAVEL - (tv series)	series	PARAMOUNT	1960
30278	HAVE GUN WILL TRAVEL - (tv series)	series	PARAMOUNT	1960
30279	HAVE GUN WILL TRAVEL - (tv series)	series	PARAMOUNT	1960
30280	HAVE GUN WILL TRAVEL - (tv series)	series	PARAMOUNT	1960
30281	HAVE GUN WILL TRAVEL - (tv series)	series	PARAMOUNT	1960
30282	HAVE GUN WILL TRAVEL - (tv series)	series	PARAMOUNT	1960
30283	HAVE GUN WILL TRAVEL - (tv series)	series	PARAMOUNT	1960
30284	HAVE GUN WILL TRAVEL - (tv series)	series	PARAMOUNT	1960
30285	HAVE GUN WILL TRAVEL - (tv series)	series	PARAMOUNT	1960

30286	HAVE GUN WILL TRAVEL - (tv series)	series	PARAMOUNT	1960
30287	HAVE GUN WILL TRAVEL - (tv series)	series	PARAMOUNT	1960
30288	HAVE GUN WILL TRAVEL - (tv series)	series	PARAMOUNT	1960
30289	HAVE GUN WILL TRAVEL - (tv series)	series	PARAMOUNT	1960
30290	HAVE GUN WILL TRAVEL - (tv series)	series	PARAMOUNT	1960
30291	HAVE GUN WILL TRAVEL - (tv series)	series	PARAMOUNT	1960
30292	HAVE GUN WILL TRAVEL - (tv series)	series	PARAMOUNT	1960
30293	HAVE GUN WILL TRAVEL - (tv series)	series	PARAMOUNT	1960
30294	HAVE GUN WILL TRAVEL - (tv series)	series	PARAMOUNT	1960
30295	HAVE GUN WILL TRAVEL - (tv series)	series	PARAMOUNT	1960
30296	HAVE GUN WILL TRAVEL - (tv series)	series	PARAMOUNT	1960
30297	HAVE GUN WILL TRAVEL - (tv series)	series	PARAMOUNT	1960
30298	HAVE GUN WILL TRAVEL - (tv series)	series	PARAMOUNT	1960
30299	HAVE GUN WILL TRAVEL - (tv series)	series	PARAMOUNT	1960
30301	BONANZA - (tv series) pilot	LUDWIG	PARAMOUNT	1959
30302	BONANZA-(tv series)-MR. HENRY COMSTOCK	BRAHM	PARAMOUNT	1959
30303	BONANZA-NEWCOMERS	NYBY	PARAMOUNT	1959
30304	BONANZA-MARK BURDETTE STORY	LANDRES	PARAMOUNT	1959
30304	BONANZA-SUN MOUNTAIN HERD*	LANDRES	PARAMOUNT	1959
30305	BONANZA-SAGA OF ANNIE O'TOOLE	KANE	PARAMOUNT	1959
30306	BONANZA-PAIUTE WAR	LANDRES	PARAMOUNT	1959
30307	BONANZA-PHILIP DIEDESHIEMER STORY	KANE	PARAMOUNT	1959
30308	BONANZA-JULIA BULETTE STORY	NYBY	PARAMOUNT	1959
30309	BONANZA-ENTER MARK TWAIN	LANDRES	PARAMOUNT	1959
30310	BONANZA-NAKED LADY	NYBY	PARAMOUNT	1959
30311	BONANZA-TRUCKEE STRIP	NYBY	PARAMOUNT	1959
30312	BONANZA-HANGING POSSEE	NYBY	PARAMOUNT	1959
30313	BONANZA-VENDETTA	KANE	PARAMOUNT	1959
30314	BONANZA-SISTERS	KANE	PARAMOUNT	1959
30315	BONANZA-EL TORO GRANDE	NYBY	PARAMOUNT	1960
30316	BONANZA-OUTCASTS	ALLEN	PARAMOUNT	1960
30317	BONANZA-LAST HUNT	NYBY	PARAMOUNT	1960
30318	BONANZA-HOUSE DIVIDED	ALLEN	PARAMOUNT	1960
30319	BONANZA-GUNMAN	NYBY	PARAMOUNT	1960
30320	BONANZA-FEAR MERCHANTS	ALLEN	PARAMOUNT	1960
30321	BONANZA -(tv series)	series	PARAMOUNT	1959
30322	BONANZA -(tv series)	series	PARAMOUNT	1959
30323	BONANZA -(tv series)	series	PARAMOUNT	1959
30324	BONANZA -(tv series)	series	PARAMOUNT	1959
30325	BONANZA -(tv series)	series	PARAMOUNT	1959
30326	BONANZA -(tv series)	series	PARAMOUNT	1959
30327	BONANZA -(tv series)	series	PARAMOUNT	1959
30328	BONANZA -(tv series)	series	PARAMOUNT	1959
30329	BONANZA -(tv series)	series	PARAMOUNT	1959
30330	BONANZA -(tv series)	series	PARAMOUNT	1959
30331	BONANZA -(tv series)	series	PARAMOUNT	1959
30332	BONANZA -(tv series)	series	PARAMOUNT	1959
30333	BONANZA -(tv series)	series	PARAMOUNT	1959
30334	BONANZA -(tv series)	series	PARAMOUNT	1959
30335	BONANZA -(tv series)	series	PARAMOUNT	1959
30336	BONANZA -(tv series)	series	PARAMOUNT	1959
30337	BONANZA -(tv series)	series	PARAMOUNT	1959
30338	BONANZA -(tv series)	series	PARAMOUNT	1959
30339	BONANZA -(tv series)	series	PARAMOUNT	1959
30340	BONANZA -(tv series)	series	PARAMOUNT	1959
30341	BONANZA -(tv series)	series	PARAMOUNT	1959
30342	BONANZA -(tv series)	series	PARAMOUNT	1959
30343	BONANZA -(tv series)	series	PARAMOUNT	1959
30344	BONANZA -(tv series)	series	PARAMOUNT	1959
30345	BONANZA -(tv series)	series	PARAMOUNT	1959
30346	BONANZA -(tv series)	series	PARAMOUNT	1959
30347	BONANZA -(tv series)	series	PARAMOUNT	1959
30348	BONANZA -(tv series)	series	PARAMOUNT	1959
30349	BONANZA -(tv series)	series	PARAMOUNT	1959
30350	BONANZA -(tv series)	series	PARAMOUNT	1959
30351	REBEL-(tv series) PILOT	KERSHNER	PARAMOUNT	1959

30352	REBEL-(tv series)-JUDGEMENT	KERSHNER	PARAMOUNT	1959
30353	REBEL-(tv series)-PANIC	KERSHNER	PARAMOUNT	1959
30354	REBEL-(tv series)-YELLOWHAIR	KERSHNER	PARAMOUNT	1959
30355	REBEL-(tv series)-IN MEMORIUM	KERSHNER	PARAMOUNT	1959
30356	REBEL-(tv series)-MISFITS	KERSHNER	PARAMOUNT	1959
30357	REBEL-(tv series)-VICIOUS	KOWALSKI	PARAMOUNT	1959
30358	REBEL-(tv series)-DARK SECRET	KERSHNER	PARAMOUNT	1959
30359	REBEL-(tv series)-SCAVENGERS	MILLER	PARAMOUNT	1959
30360	REBEL-(tv series)-LAND	KERSHNER	PARAMOUNT	1959
30361	REBEL-(tv series)-CRIME	KERSHNER	PARAMOUNT	1959
30362	REBEL-(tv series)-SCHOOL DAYS	KERSHNER	PARAMOUNT	1959
30363	REBEL-(tv series)-VAGRANTS	KERSHNER	PARAMOUNT	1959
30364	REBEL-(tv series)-GUN CITY	KERSHNER	PARAMOUNT	1959
30365	REBEL-(tv series)-GOLD SEEKER	MCEVEETY	PARAMOUNT	1959
30366	REBEL-(tv series)-CAPTIVE OF TEMBLOR	KERSHNER	PARAMOUNT	1959
30367	REBEL-(tv series)-TAKE DEAD AIM	BAUR	PARAMOUNT	1959
30368	REBEL-(tv series)-GLORY	KERSHNER	PARAMOUNT	1959
30369	REBEL-(tv series)-DASH OF GRAY	KOWALSKI	PARAMOUNT	1960
30370	REBEL-(tv series)-NIGHT ON A RAINBOW	KERSHNER	PARAMOUNT	1960
30371	REBEL-(tv series)-ANGRY TOWN	KOWALSKI	PARAMOUNT	1960
30372	REBEL-(tv series)-UNWANTED	KERSHNER	PARAMOUNT	1960
30373	REBEL-(tv series)-NOBLESS OBLIGE	KOWALSKI	PARAMOUNT	1960
30374	REBEL-(tv series)-RATTLER	KERSHNER	PARAMOUNT	1960
30375	REBEL-(tv series)-HE'S ONLY A BOY	KOWALSKI	PARAMOUNT	1960
30376	REBEL-(tv series)-BLIND MARRIAGE	KERSHNER	PARAMOUNT	1960
30379	REBEL-(tv series)	series	PARAMOUNT	1960
30380	REBEL-(tv series)	series	PARAMOUNT	1960
30381	REBEL-(tv series)	series	PARAMOUNT	1960
30382	REBEL-(tv series)	series	PARAMOUNT	1960
30383	REBEL-(tv series)	series	PARAMOUNT	1960
30384	REBEL-(tv series)	series	PARAMOUNT	1960
30385	REBEL-(tv series)	series	PARAMOUNT	1960
30386	REBEL-(tv series)	series	PARAMOUNT	1960
30387	REBEL-(tv series)	series	PARAMOUNT	1960
30388	REBEL-(tv series)	series	PARAMOUNT	1960
30389	REBEL-(tv series)	series	PARAMOUNT	1960
30390	REBEL-(tv series)	series	PARAMOUNT	1960
30391	REBEL-(tv series)	series	PARAMOUNT	1960
30392	REBEL-(tv series)	series	PARAMOUNT	1960
30393	REBEL-(tv series)	series	PARAMOUNT	1960
30394	REBEL-(tv series)	series	PARAMOUNT	1960
30395	REBEL-(tv series)	series	PARAMOUNT	1960
30396	REBEL-(tv series)	series	PARAMOUNT	1960
30397	REBEL-(tv series)	series	PARAMOUNT	1960
30398	REBEL-(tv series)	series	PARAMOUNT	1960
30399	REBEL-(tv series)	series	PARAMOUNT	1960
30400	REBEL-(tv series)	series	PARAMOUNT	1960
30401	DESTINATION SPACE - TV	PEVNEY	PARAMOUNT	1959
30451	COUNT DOWN - TV	GIRARD	PARAMOUNT	1959
30461	BRANDED - (tv series)		PARAMOUNT	1965
30481	DEATH VALLEY DAYS - (tv series)		PARAMOUNT	1965
30501	GET SMART - (tv series)	series	PARAMOUNT	1966
30501	ON GUARD - TV	YARBOROUGH	PARAMOUNT	1959
30502	GET SMART - (tv series)	series	PARAMOUNT	1966
30503	GET SMART - (tv series)	series	PARAMOUNT	1966
30504	GET SMART - (tv series)	series	PARAMOUNT	1966
30505	GET SMART - (tv series)	series	PARAMOUNT	1966
30506	GET SMART - (tv series)	series	PARAMOUNT	1966
30507	GET SMART - (tv series)	series	PARAMOUNT	1966
30508	GET SMART - (tv series)	series	PARAMOUNT	1966
30509	GET SMART - (tv series)	series	PARAMOUNT	1966
30510	GET SMART - (tv series)	series	PARAMOUNT	1966
30511	GET SMART - (tv series)	series	PARAMOUNT	1966
30512	GET SMART - (tv series)	series	PARAMOUNT	1966
30513	GET SMART - (tv series)	series	PARAMOUNT	1966
30514	GET SMART - (tv series)	series	PARAMOUNT	1966

30515	GET SMART - (tv series)	series	PARAMOUNT	1966
30516	GET SMART - (tv series)	series	PARAMOUNT	1966
30517	GET SMART - (tv series)	series	PARAMOUNT	1966
30518	GET SMART - (tv series)	series	PARAMOUNT	1966
30519	GET SMART - (tv series)	series	PARAMOUNT	1966
30520	GET SMART - (tv series)	series	PARAMOUNT	1966
30521	GET SMART - (tv series)	series	PARAMOUNT	1966
30522	GET SMART - (tv series)	series	PARAMOUNT	1966
30523	GET SMART - (tv series)	series	PARAMOUNT	1966
30524	GET SMART - (tv series)	series	PARAMOUNT	1966
30525	GET SMART - (tv series)	series	PARAMOUNT	1966
30526	GET SMART - (tv series)	series	PARAMOUNT	1966
30527	GET SMART - (tv series)	series	PARAMOUNT	1966
30528	GET SMART - (tv series)	series	PARAMOUNT	1966
30529	GET SMART - (tv series)	series	PARAMOUNT	1966
30530	GET SMART - (tv series)	series	PARAMOUNT	1966
30531	GET SMART - (tv series)	series	PARAMOUNT	1966
30532	GET SMART - (tv series)	series	PARAMOUNT	1966
30533	GET SMART - (tv series)	series	PARAMOUNT	1966
30534	GET SMART - (tv series)	series	PARAMOUNT	1966
30535	GET SMART - (tv series)	series	PARAMOUNT	1966
30536	GET SMART - (tv series)	series	PARAMOUNT	1966
30537	GET SMART - (tv series)	series	PARAMOUNT	1966
30538	GET SMART - (tv series)	series	PARAMOUNT	1966
30539	GET SMART - (tv series)	series	PARAMOUNT	1966
30540	GET SMART - (tv series)	series	PARAMOUNT	1966
30541	GET SMART - (tv series)	series	PARAMOUNT	1966
30542	GET SMART - (tv series)	series	PARAMOUNT	1966
30543	GET SMART - (tv series)	series	PARAMOUNT	1966
30544	GET SMART - (tv series)	series	PARAMOUNT	1966
30545	GET SMART - (tv series)	series	PARAMOUNT	1966
30546	GET SMART - (tv series)	series	PARAMOUNT	1966
30547	GET SMART - (tv series)	series	PARAMOUNT	1966
30548	GET SMART - (tv series)	series	PARAMOUNT	1966
30549	GET SMART - (tv series)	series	PARAMOUNT	1966
30551	HEAVE HO HARRIGAN - tv	GRAUMAN	PARAMOUNT	1959
30700	BONANZA -(tv series)	series	PARAMOUNT	1960
30701	BONANZA -(tv series)	series	PARAMOUNT	1960
30702	BONANZA -(tv series)	series	PARAMOUNT	1960
30703	BONANZA -(tv series)	series	PARAMOUNT	1960
30704	BONANZA -(tv series)	series	PARAMOUNT	1960
30705	BONANZA -(tv series)	series	PARAMOUNT	1960
30706	BONANZA -(tv series)	series	PARAMOUNT	1960
30707	BONANZA -(tv series)	series	PARAMOUNT	1960
30708	BONANZA -(tv series)	series	PARAMOUNT	1960
30709	BONANZA -(tv series)	series	PARAMOUNT	1960
30710	BONANZA -(tv series)	series	PARAMOUNT	1960
30711	BONANZA -(tv series)	series	PARAMOUNT	1960
30712	BONANZA -(tv series)	series	PARAMOUNT	1960
30713	BONANZA -(tv series)	series	PARAMOUNT	1960
30714	BONANZA -(tv series)	series	PARAMOUNT	1960
30715	BONANZA -(tv series)	series	PARAMOUNT	1960
30716	BONANZA -(tv series)	series	PARAMOUNT	1960
30717	BONANZA -(tv series)	series	PARAMOUNT	1960
30718	BONANZA -(tv series)	series	PARAMOUNT	1960
30719	BONANZA -(tv series)	series	PARAMOUNT	1960
30720	BONANZA -(tv series)	series	PARAMOUNT	1960
30721	BONANZA -(tv series)	series	PARAMOUNT	1960
30722	BONANZA -(tv series)	series	PARAMOUNT	1960
30723	BONANZA -(tv series)	series	PARAMOUNT	1960
30724	BONANZA -(tv series)	series	PARAMOUNT	1960
30725	BONANZA -(tv series)	series	PARAMOUNT	1960
30726	BONANZA -(tv series)	series	PARAMOUNT	1960
30727	BONANZA -(tv series)	series	PARAMOUNT	1960
30728	BONANZA -(tv series)	series	PARAMOUNT	1960
30729	BONANZA -(tv series)	series	PARAMOUNT	1960

30730	BONANZA -(tv series)	series	PARAMOUNT	1960
30731	BONANZA -(tv series)	series	PARAMOUNT	1960
30732	BONANZA -(tv series)	series	PARAMOUNT	1960
30733	BONANZA -(tv series)	series	PARAMOUNT	1960
30734	BONANZA -(tv series)	series	PARAMOUNT	1960
30735	BONANZA -(tv series)	series	PARAMOUNT	1960
30736	BONANZA -(tv series)	series	PARAMOUNT	1960
30737	BONANZA -(tv series)	series	PARAMOUNT	1960
30738	BONANZA -(tv series)	series	PARAMOUNT	1960
30739	BONANZA -(tv series)	series	PARAMOUNT	1960
30740	BONANZA -(tv series)	series	PARAMOUNT	1960
30741	BONANZA -(tv series)	series	PARAMOUNT	1960
30742	BONANZA -(tv series)	series	PARAMOUNT	1960
30743	BONANZA -(tv series)	series	PARAMOUNT	1960
30744	BONANZA -(tv series)	series	PARAMOUNT	1960
30745	BONANZA -(tv series)	series	PARAMOUNT	1960
30746	BONANZA -(tv series)	series	PARAMOUNT	1960
30747	BONANZA -(tv series)	series	PARAMOUNT	1960
30748	BONANZA -(tv series)	series	PARAMOUNT	1960
30749	BONANZA -(tv series)	series	PARAMOUNT	1960
30750	PETE AND GLADYS - (tv series)	series	PARAMOUNT	1960
30751	PETE AND GLADYS - (tv series)	series	PARAMOUNT	1960
30752	PETE AND GLADYS - (tv series)	series	PARAMOUNT	1960
30753	PETE AND GLADYS - (tv series)	series	PARAMOUNT	1960
30754	PETE AND GLADYS - (tv series)	series	PARAMOUNT	1960
30755	PETE AND GLADYS - (tv series)	series	PARAMOUNT	1960
30756	PETE AND GLADYS - (tv series)	series	PARAMOUNT	1960
30757	PETE AND GLADYS - (tv series)	series	PARAMOUNT	1960
30758	PETE AND GLADYS - (tv series)	series	PARAMOUNT	1960
30759	PETE AND GLADYS - (tv series)	series	PARAMOUNT	1960
30760	PETE AND GLADYS - (tv series)	series	PARAMOUNT	1960
30761	PETE AND GLADYS - (tv series)	series	PARAMOUNT	1960
30762	PETE AND GLADYS - (tv series)	series	PARAMOUNT	1960
30763	PETE AND GLADYS - (tv series)	series	PARAMOUNT	1960
30764	PETE AND GLADYS - (tv series)	series	PARAMOUNT	1960
30765	PETE AND GLADYS - (tv series)	series	PARAMOUNT	1960
30766	PETE AND GLADYS - (tv series)	series	PARAMOUNT	1960
30767	PETE AND GLADYS - (tv series)	series	PARAMOUNT	1960
30768	PETE AND GLADYS - (tv series)	series	PARAMOUNT	1960
30769	PETE AND GLADYS - (tv series)	series	PARAMOUNT	1960
30770	PETE AND GLADYS - (tv series)	series	PARAMOUNT	1960
30771	PETE AND GLADYS - (tv series)	series	PARAMOUNT	1960
30772	PETE AND GLADYS - (tv series)	series	PARAMOUNT	1960
30773	PETE AND GLADYS - (tv series)	series	PARAMOUNT	1960
30774	PETE AND GLADYS - (tv series)	series	PARAMOUNT	1960
30775	PETE AND GLADYS - (tv series)	series	PARAMOUNT	1960
30776	PETE AND GLADYS - (tv series)	series	PARAMOUNT	1960
30777	PETE AND GLADYS - (tv series)	series	PARAMOUNT	1960
30778	PETE AND GLADYS - (tv series)	series	PARAMOUNT	1960
30779	PETE AND GLADYS - (tv series)	series	PARAMOUNT	1960
30780	PETE AND GLADYS - (tv series)	series	PARAMOUNT	1960
30781	PETE AND GLADYS - (tv series)	series	PARAMOUNT	1960
30782	PETE AND GLADYS - (tv series)	series	PARAMOUNT	1960
30783	PETE AND GLADYS - (tv series)	series	PARAMOUNT	1960
30784	PETE AND GLADYS - (tv series)	series	PARAMOUNT	1960
30785	PETE AND GLADYS - (tv series)	series	PARAMOUNT	1960
30786	PETE AND GLADYS - (tv series)	series	PARAMOUNT	1960
30787	PETE AND GLADYS - (tv series)	series	PARAMOUNT	1960
30788	PETE AND GLADYS - (tv series)	series	PARAMOUNT	1960
30789	PETE AND GLADYS - (tv series)	series	PARAMOUNT	1960
30790	PETE AND GLADYS - (tv series)	series	PARAMOUNT	1960
30791	PETE AND GLADYS - (tv series)	series	PARAMOUNT	1960
30792	PETE AND GLADYS - (tv series)	series	PARAMOUNT	1960
30793	PETE AND GLADYS - (tv series)	series	PARAMOUNT	1960
30794	PETE AND GLADYS - (tv series)	series	PARAMOUNT	1960
30795	PETE AND GLADYS - (tv series)	series	PARAMOUNT	1960

30796	PETE AND GLADYS - (tv series)	series	PARAMOUNT	1960
30797	PETE AND GLADYS - (tv series)	series	PARAMOUNT	1960
30798	PETE AND GLADYS - (tv series)	series	PARAMOUNT	1960
30799	PETE AND GLADYS - (tv series)	series	PARAMOUNT	1960
30800	REBEL-(tv series)	series	PARAMOUNT	1960
30801	REBEL-(tv series)	series	PARAMOUNT	1960
30802	REBEL-(tv series)	series	PARAMOUNT	1960
30803	REBEL-(tv series)	series	PARAMOUNT	1960
30804	REBEL-(tv series)	series	PARAMOUNT	1960
30805	REBEL-(tv series)	series	PARAMOUNT	1960
30806	REBEL-(tv series)	series	PARAMOUNT	1960
30807	REBEL-(tv series)	series	PARAMOUNT	1960
30808	REBEL-(tv series)	series	PARAMOUNT	1960
30809	REBEL-(tv series)	series	PARAMOUNT	1960
30810	REBEL-(tv series)	series	PARAMOUNT	1960
30811	REBEL-(tv series)	series	PARAMOUNT	1960
30812	REBEL-(tv series)	series	PARAMOUNT	1960
30813	REBEL-(tv series)	series	PARAMOUNT	1960
30814	REBEL-(tv series)	series	PARAMOUNT	1960
30815	REBEL-(tv series)	series	PARAMOUNT	1960
30816	REBEL-(tv series)	series	PARAMOUNT	1960
30817	REBEL-(tv series)	series	PARAMOUNT	1960
30818	REBEL-(tv series)	series	PARAMOUNT	1960
30819	REBEL-(tv series)	series	PARAMOUNT	1960
30820	REBEL-(tv series)	series	PARAMOUNT	1960
30821	REBEL-(tv series)	series	PARAMOUNT	1960
30822	REBEL-(tv series)	series	PARAMOUNT	1960
30823	REBEL-(tv series)	series	PARAMOUNT	1960
30824	REBEL-(tv series)	series	PARAMOUNT	1960
30825	REBEL-(tv series)	series	PARAMOUNT	1960
30826	REBEL-(tv series)	series	PARAMOUNT	1960
30827	REBEL-(tv series)	series	PARAMOUNT	1960
30828	REBEL-(tv series)	series	PARAMOUNT	1960
30829	REBEL-(tv series)	series	PARAMOUNT	1960
30830	REBEL-(tv series)	series	PARAMOUNT	1960
30831	REBEL-(tv series)	series	PARAMOUNT	1960
30832	REBEL-(tv series)	series	PARAMOUNT	1960
30833	REBEL-(tv series)	series	PARAMOUNT	1960
30834	REBEL-(tv series)	series	PARAMOUNT	1960
30835	REBEL-(tv series)	series	PARAMOUNT	1960
30836	REBEL-(tv series)	series	PARAMOUNT	1960
30837	REBEL-(tv series)	series	PARAMOUNT	1960
30838	REBEL-(tv series)	series	PARAMOUNT	1960
30839	REBEL-(tv series)	series	PARAMOUNT	1960
30840	REBEL-(tv series)	series	PARAMOUNT	1960
30841	REBEL-(tv series)	series	PARAMOUNT	1960
30842	REBEL-(tv series)	series	PARAMOUNT	1960
30843	REBEL-(tv series)	series	PARAMOUNT	1960
30844	REBEL-(tv series)	series	PARAMOUNT	1960
30845	REBEL-(tv series)	series	PARAMOUNT	1960
30846	REBEL-(tv series)	series	PARAMOUNT	1960
30847	REBEL-(tv series)	series	PARAMOUNT	1960
30848	REBEL-(tv series)	series	PARAMOUNT	1960
30849	REBEL-(tv series)	series	PARAMOUNT	1960
30850	OUTLAWS - (tv series)	series	PARAMOUNT	1962
30851	OUTLAWS - (tv series)	series	PARAMOUNT	1962
30852	OUTLAWS - (tv series)	series	PARAMOUNT	1962
30853	OUTLAWS - (tv series)	series	PARAMOUNT	1962
30854	OUTLAWS - (tv series)	series	PARAMOUNT	1962
30855	OUTLAWS - (tv series)	series	PARAMOUNT	1962
30856	OUTLAWS - (tv series)	series	PARAMOUNT	1962
30857	OUTLAWS - (tv series)	series	PARAMOUNT	1962
30858	OUTLAWS - (tv series)	series	PARAMOUNT	1962
30859	OUTLAWS - (tv series)	series	PARAMOUNT	1962
30860	OUTLAWS - (tv series)	series	PARAMOUNT	1962
30861	OUTLAWS - (tv series)	series	PARAMOUNT	1962

30862	OUTLAWS - (tv series)	series	PARAMOUNT	1962
30863	OUTLAWS - (tv series)	series	PARAMOUNT	1962
30864	OUTLAWS - (tv series)	series	PARAMOUNT	1962
30865	OUTLAWS - (tv series)	series	PARAMOUNT	1962
30866	OUTLAWS - (tv series)	series	PARAMOUNT	1962
30867	OUTLAWS - (tv series)	series	PARAMOUNT	1962
30868	OUTLAWS - (tv series)	series	PARAMOUNT	1962
30869	OUTLAWS - (tv series)	series	PARAMOUNT	1962
30870	OUTLAWS - (tv series)	series	PARAMOUNT	1962
30871	OUTLAWS - (tv series)	series	PARAMOUNT	1962
30872	OUTLAWS - (tv series)	series	PARAMOUNT	1962
30873	OUTLAWS - (tv series)	series	PARAMOUNT	1962
30874	OUTLAWS - (tv series)	series	PARAMOUNT	1962
30875	OUTLAWS - (tv series)	series	PARAMOUNT	1962
30876	OUTLAWS - (tv series)	series	PARAMOUNT	1962
30877	OUTLAWS - (tv series)	series	PARAMOUNT	1962
30878	OUTLAWS - (tv series)	series	PARAMOUNT	1962
30879	OUTLAWS - (tv series)	series	PARAMOUNT	1962
30880	OUTLAWS - (tv series)	series	PARAMOUNT	1962
30881	OUTLAWS - (tv series)	series	PARAMOUNT	1962
30882	OUTLAWS - (tv series)	series	PARAMOUNT	1962
30883	OUTLAWS - (tv series)	series	PARAMOUNT	1962
30884	OUTLAWS - (tv series)	series	PARAMOUNT	1962
30885	OUTLAWS - (tv series)	series	PARAMOUNT	1962
30886	OUTLAWS - (tv series)	series	PARAMOUNT	1962
30887	OUTLAWS - (tv series)	series	PARAMOUNT	1962
30888	OUTLAWS - (tv series)	series	PARAMOUNT	1962
30889	OUTLAWS - (tv series)	series	PARAMOUNT	1962
30890	OUTLAWS - (tv series)	series	PARAMOUNT	1962
30891	OUTLAWS - (tv series)	series	PARAMOUNT	1962
30892	OUTLAWS - (tv series)	series	PARAMOUNT	1962
30893	OUTLAWS - (tv series)	series	PARAMOUNT	1962
30894	OUTLAWS - (tv series)	series	PARAMOUNT	1962
30895	OUTLAWS - (tv series)	series	PARAMOUNT	1962
30896	OUTLAWS - (tv series)	series	PARAMOUNT	1962
30897	OUTLAWS - (tv series)	series	PARAMOUNT	1962
30898	OUTLAWS - (tv series)	series	PARAMOUNT	1962
30899	OUTLAWS - (tv series)	series	PARAMOUNT	1962
30943	ALEXANDER THE GREAT - tv pilot		PARAMOUNT	1964
30944	S. D. I. - THE PRELUDE - tv pilot		PARAMOUNT	1964
30950	HAVE GUN WILL TRAVEL - (tv series)	series	PARAMOUNT	1963
30951	HAVE GUN WILL TRAVEL - (tv series)	series	PARAMOUNT	1963
30952	HAVE GUN WILL TRAVEL - (tv series)	series	PARAMOUNT	1963
30953	HAVE GUN WILL TRAVEL - (tv series)	series	PARAMOUNT	1963
30954	HAVE GUN WILL TRAVEL - (tv series)	series	PARAMOUNT	1963
30955	HAVE GUN WILL TRAVEL - (tv series)	series	PARAMOUNT	1963
30956	HAVE GUN WILL TRAVEL - (tv series)	series	PARAMOUNT	1963
30957	HAVE GUN WILL TRAVEL - (tv series)	series	PARAMOUNT	1963
30958	HAVE GUN WILL TRAVEL - (tv series)	series	PARAMOUNT	1963
30959	HAVE GUN WILL TRAVEL - (tv series)	series	PARAMOUNT	1963
30960	HAVE GUN WILL TRAVEL - (tv series)	series	PARAMOUNT	1963
30961	HAVE GUN WILL TRAVEL - (tv series)	series	PARAMOUNT	1963
30962	HAVE GUN WILL TRAVEL - (tv series)	series	PARAMOUNT	1963
30963	HAVE GUN WILL TRAVEL - (tv series)	series	PARAMOUNT	1963
30964	HAVE GUN WILL TRAVEL - (tv series)	series	PARAMOUNT	1963
30965	HAVE GUN WILL TRAVEL - (tv series)	series	PARAMOUNT	1963
30966	HAVE GUN WILL TRAVEL - (tv series)	series	PARAMOUNT	1963
30967	HAVE GUN WILL TRAVEL - (tv series)	series	PARAMOUNT	1963
30968	HAVE GUN WILL TRAVEL - (tv series)	series	PARAMOUNT	1963
30969	HAVE GUN WILL TRAVEL - (tv series)	series	PARAMOUNT	1963
30970	HAVE GUN WILL TRAVEL - (tv series)	series	PARAMOUNT	1963
30971	HAVE GUN WILL TRAVEL - (tv series)	series	PARAMOUNT	1963
30972	HAVE GUN WILL TRAVEL - (tv series)	series	PARAMOUNT	1963
30973	HAVE GUN WILL TRAVEL - (tv series)	series	PARAMOUNT	1963
30974	HAVE GUN WILL TRAVEL - (tv series)	series	PARAMOUNT	1963
30975	HAVE GUN WILL TRAVEL - (tv series)	series	PARAMOUNT	1963

30976	HAVE GUN WILL TRAVEL - (tv series)	series	PARAMOUNT	1963
30977	HAVE GUN WILL TRAVEL - (tv series)	series	PARAMOUNT	1963
30978	HAVE GUN WILL TRAVEL - (tv series)	series	PARAMOUNT	1963
30979	HAVE GUN WILL TRAVEL - (tv series)	series	PARAMOUNT	1963
30980	HAVE GUN WILL TRAVEL - (tv series)	series	PARAMOUNT	1963
30981	HAVE GUN WILL TRAVEL - (tv series)	series	PARAMOUNT	1963
30982	HAVE GUN WILL TRAVEL - (tv series)	series	PARAMOUNT	1963
30983	HAVE GUN WILL TRAVEL - (tv series)	series	PARAMOUNT	1963
30984	HAVE GUN WILL TRAVEL - (tv series)	series	PARAMOUNT	1963
30985	HAVE GUN WILL TRAVEL - (tv series)	series	PARAMOUNT	1963
30986	HAVE GUN WILL TRAVEL - (tv series)	series	PARAMOUNT	1963
30987	HAVE GUN WILL TRAVEL - (tv series)	series	PARAMOUNT	1963
30988	HAVE GUN WILL TRAVEL - (tv series)	series	PARAMOUNT	1963
30989	HAVE GUN WILL TRAVEL - (tv series)	series	PARAMOUNT	1963
30990	HAVE GUN WILL TRAVEL - (tv series)	series	PARAMOUNT	1963
30991	HAVE GUN WILL TRAVEL - (tv series)	series	PARAMOUNT	1963
30992	HAVE GUN WILL TRAVEL - (tv series)	series	PARAMOUNT	1963
30993	HAVE GUN WILL TRAVEL - (tv series)	series	PARAMOUNT	1963
30994	HAVE GUN WILL TRAVEL - (tv series)	series	PARAMOUNT	1963
30995	HAVE GUN WILL TRAVEL - (tv series)	series	PARAMOUNT	1963
30996	HAVE GUN WILL TRAVEL - (tv series)	series	PARAMOUNT	1963
30997	HAVE GUN WILL TRAVEL - (tv series)	series	PARAMOUNT	1963
30998	HAVE GUN WILL TRAVEL - (tv series)	series	PARAMOUNT	1963
30999	HAVE GUN WILL TRAVEL - (tv series)	series	PARAMOUNT	1963
31000	GUNSMOKE (tv series)	series	PARAMOUNT	1963
31001	GUNSMOKE (tv series)	series	PARAMOUNT	1963
31002	GUNSMOKE (tv series)	series	PARAMOUNT	1963
31003	GUNSMOKE (tv series)	series	PARAMOUNT	1963
31004	GUNSMOKE (tv series)	series	PARAMOUNT	1963
31005	GUNSMOKE (tv series)	series	PARAMOUNT	1963
31006	GUNSMOKE (tv series)	series	PARAMOUNT	1963
31007	GUNSMOKE (tv series)	series	PARAMOUNT	1963
31008	GUNSMOKE (tv series)	series	PARAMOUNT	1963
31009	GUNSMOKE (tv series)	series	PARAMOUNT	1963
31010	GUNSMOKE (tv series)	series	PARAMOUNT	1963
31011	GUNSMOKE (tv series)	series	PARAMOUNT	1963
31012	GUNSMOKE (tv series)	series	PARAMOUNT	1963
31013	GUNSMOKE (tv series)	series	PARAMOUNT	1963
31014	GUNSMOKE (tv series)	series	PARAMOUNT	1963
31015	GUNSMOKE (tv series)	series	PARAMOUNT	1963
31016	GUNSMOKE (tv series)	series	PARAMOUNT	1963
31017	GUNSMOKE (tv series)	series	PARAMOUNT	1963
31018	GUNSMOKE (tv series)	series	PARAMOUNT	1963
31019	GUNSMOKE (tv series)	series	PARAMOUNT	1963
31020	GUNSMOKE (tv series)	series	PARAMOUNT	1963
31021	GUNSMOKE (tv series)	series	PARAMOUNT	1963
31022	GUNSMOKE (tv series)	series	PARAMOUNT	1963
31023	GUNSMOKE (tv series)	series	PARAMOUNT	1963
31024	GUNSMOKE (tv series)	series	PARAMOUNT	1963
31025	GUNSMOKE (tv series)	series	PARAMOUNT	1963
31026	GUNSMOKE (tv series)	series	PARAMOUNT	1963
31027	GUNSMOKE (tv series)	series	PARAMOUNT	1963
31028	GUNSMOKE (tv series)	series	PARAMOUNT	1963
31029	GUNSMOKE (tv series)	series	PARAMOUNT	1963
31030	GUNSMOKE (tv series)	series	PARAMOUNT	1963
31031	GUNSMOKE (tv series)	series	PARAMOUNT	1963
31032	GUNSMOKE (tv series)	series	PARAMOUNT	1963
31033	GUNSMOKE (tv series)	series	PARAMOUNT	1963
31034	GUNSMOKE (tv series)	series	PARAMOUNT	1963
31035	GUNSMOKE (tv series)	series	PARAMOUNT	1963
31036	GUNSMOKE (tv series)	series	PARAMOUNT	1963
31037	GUNSMOKE (tv series)	series	PARAMOUNT	1963
31038	GUNSMOKE (tv series)	series	PARAMOUNT	1963
31039	GUNSMOKE (tv series)	series	PARAMOUNT	1963
31040	GUNSMOKE (tv series)	series	PARAMOUNT	1963
31041	GUNSMOKE (tv series)	series	PARAMOUNT	1963

31042	GUNSMOKE (tv series)	series	PARAMOUNT	1963
31043	GUNSMOKE (tv series)	series	PARAMOUNT	1963
31044	GUNSMOKE (tv series)	series	PARAMOUNT	1963
31045	GUNSMOKE (tv series)	series	PARAMOUNT	1963
31046	GUNSMOKE (tv series)	series	PARAMOUNT	1963
31047	GUNSMOKE (tv series)	series	PARAMOUNT	1963
31048	GUNSMOKE (tv series)	series	PARAMOUNT	1963
31049	GUNSMOKE (tv series)	series	PARAMOUNT	1963
31050	OUTLAWS - (tv series)	series	PARAMOUNT	1963
31051	OUTLAWS - (tv series)	series	PARAMOUNT	1963
31052	OUTLAWS - (tv series)	series	PARAMOUNT	1963
31053	OUTLAWS - (tv series)	series	PARAMOUNT	1963
31054	OUTLAWS - (tv series)	series	PARAMOUNT	1963
31055	OUTLAWS - (tv series)	series	PARAMOUNT	1963
31056	OUTLAWS - (tv series)	series	PARAMOUNT	1963
31057	OUTLAWS - (tv series)	series	PARAMOUNT	1963
31058	OUTLAWS - (tv series)	series	PARAMOUNT	1963
31059	OUTLAWS - (tv series)	series	PARAMOUNT	1963
31060	OUTLAWS - (tv series)	series	PARAMOUNT	1963
31061	OUTLAWS - (tv series)	series	PARAMOUNT	1963
31062	OUTLAWS - (tv series)	series	PARAMOUNT	1963
31063	OUTLAWS - (tv series)	series	PARAMOUNT	1963
31064	OUTLAWS - (tv series)	series	PARAMOUNT	1963
31065	OUTLAWS - (tv series)	series	PARAMOUNT	1963
31066	OUTLAWS - (tv series)	series	PARAMOUNT	1963
31067	OUTLAWS - (tv series)	series	PARAMOUNT	1963
31068	OUTLAWS - (tv series)	series	PARAMOUNT	1963
31069	OUTLAWS - (tv series)	series	PARAMOUNT	1963
31070	OUTLAWS - (tv series)	series	PARAMOUNT	1963
31071	OUTLAWS - (tv series)	series	PARAMOUNT	1963
31072	OUTLAWS - (tv series)	series	PARAMOUNT	1963
31073	OUTLAWS - (tv series)	series	PARAMOUNT	1963
31074	OUTLAWS - (tv series)	series	PARAMOUNT	1963
31075	OUTLAWS - (tv series)	series	PARAMOUNT	1963
31076	OUTLAWS - (tv series)	series	PARAMOUNT	1963
31077	OUTLAWS - (tv series)	series	PARAMOUNT	1963
31078	OUTLAWS - (tv series)	series	PARAMOUNT	1963
31079	OUTLAWS - (tv series)	series	PARAMOUNT	1963
31080	OUTLAWS - (tv series)	series	PARAMOUNT	1963
31081	OUTLAWS - (tv series)	series	PARAMOUNT	1963
31082	OUTLAWS - (tv series)	series	PARAMOUNT	1963
31083	OUTLAWS - (tv series)	series	PARAMOUNT	1963
31084	OUTLAWS - (tv series)	series	PARAMOUNT	1963
31085	OUTLAWS - (tv series)	series	PARAMOUNT	1963
31086	OUTLAWS - (tv series)	series	PARAMOUNT	1963
31087	OUTLAWS - (tv series)	series	PARAMOUNT	1963
31088	OUTLAWS - (tv series)	series	PARAMOUNT	1963
31089	OUTLAWS - (tv series)	series	PARAMOUNT	1963
31090	OUTLAWS - (tv series)	series	PARAMOUNT	1963
31091	OUTLAWS - (tv series)	series	PARAMOUNT	1963
31092	OUTLAWS - (tv series)	series	PARAMOUNT	1963
31093	OUTLAWS - (tv series)	series	PARAMOUNT	1963
31094	OUTLAWS - (tv series)	series	PARAMOUNT	1963
31095	OUTLAWS - (tv series)	series	PARAMOUNT	1963
31096	OUTLAWS - (tv series)	series	PARAMOUNT	1963
31097	OUTLAWS - (tv series)	series	PARAMOUNT	1963
31098	OUTLAWS - (tv series)	series	PARAMOUNT	1963
31099	OUTLAWS - (tv series)	series	PARAMOUNT	1963
31150	HAVE GUN WILL TRAVEL - (tv series)	series	PARAMOUNT	1963
31151	HAVE GUN WILL TRAVEL - (tv series)	series	PARAMOUNT	1963
31152	HAVE GUN WILL TRAVEL - (tv series)	series	PARAMOUNT	1963
31153	HAVE GUN WILL TRAVEL - (tv series)	series	PARAMOUNT	1963
31154	HAVE GUN WILL TRAVEL - (tv series)	series	PARAMOUNT	1963
31155	HAVE GUN WILL TRAVEL - (tv series)	series	PARAMOUNT	1963
31156	HAVE GUN WILL TRAVEL - (tv series)	series	PARAMOUNT	1963
31157	HAVE GUN WILL TRAVEL - (tv series)	series	PARAMOUNT	1963

31158	HAVE GUN WILL TRAVEL - (tv series)	series	PARAMOUNT	1963
31159	HAVE GUN WILL TRAVEL - (tv series)	series	PARAMOUNT	1963
31160	HAVE GUN WILL TRAVEL - (tv series)	series	PARAMOUNT	1963
31161	HAVE GUN WILL TRAVEL - (tv series)	series	PARAMOUNT	1963
31162	HAVE GUN WILL TRAVEL - (tv series)	series	PARAMOUNT	1963
31163	HAVE GUN WILL TRAVEL - (tv series)	series	PARAMOUNT	1963
31164	HAVE GUN WILL TRAVEL - (tv series)	series	PARAMOUNT	1963
31165	HAVE GUN WILL TRAVEL - (tv series)	series	PARAMOUNT	1963
31166	HAVE GUN WILL TRAVEL - (tv series)	series	PARAMOUNT	1963
31167	HAVE GUN WILL TRAVEL - (tv series)	series	PARAMOUNT	1963
31168	HAVE GUN WILL TRAVEL - (tv series)	series	PARAMOUNT	1963
31169	HAVE GUN WILL TRAVEL - (tv series)	series	PARAMOUNT	1963
31170	HAVE GUN WILL TRAVEL - (tv series)	series	PARAMOUNT	1963
31171	HAVE GUN WILL TRAVEL - (tv series)	series	PARAMOUNT	1963
31172	HAVE GUN WILL TRAVEL - (tv series)	series	PARAMOUNT	1963
31173	HAVE GUN WILL TRAVEL - (tv series)	series	PARAMOUNT	1963
31174	HAVE GUN WILL TRAVEL - (tv series)	series	PARAMOUNT	1963
31175	HAVE GUN WILL TRAVEL - (tv series)	series	PARAMOUNT	1963
31176	HAVE GUN WILL TRAVEL - (tv series)	series	PARAMOUNT	1963
31177	HAVE GUN WILL TRAVEL - (tv series)	series	PARAMOUNT	1963
31178	HAVE GUN WILL TRAVEL - (tv series)	series	PARAMOUNT	1963
31179	HAVE GUN WILL TRAVEL - (tv series)	series	PARAMOUNT	1963
31180	HAVE GUN WILL TRAVEL - (tv series)	series	PARAMOUNT	1963
31181	HAVE GUN WILL TRAVEL - (tv series)	series	PARAMOUNT	1963
31182	HAVE GUN WILL TRAVEL - (tv series)	series	PARAMOUNT	1963
31183	HAVE GUN WILL TRAVEL - (tv series)	series	PARAMOUNT	1963
31184	HAVE GUN WILL TRAVEL - (tv series)	series	PARAMOUNT	1963
31185	HAVE GUN WILL TRAVEL - (tv series)	series	PARAMOUNT	1963
31186	HAVE GUN WILL TRAVEL - (tv series)	series	PARAMOUNT	1963
31187	HAVE GUN WILL TRAVEL - (tv series)	series	PARAMOUNT	1963
31188	HAVE GUN WILL TRAVEL - (tv series)	series	PARAMOUNT	1963
31189	HAVE GUN WILL TRAVEL - (tv series)	series	PARAMOUNT	1963
31190	HAVE GUN WILL TRAVEL - (tv series)	series	PARAMOUNT	1963
31191	HAVE GUN WILL TRAVEL - (tv series)	series	PARAMOUNT	1963
31192	HAVE GUN WILL TRAVEL - (tv series)	series	PARAMOUNT	1963
31193	HAVE GUN WILL TRAVEL - (tv series)	series	PARAMOUNT	1963
31194	HAVE GUN WILL TRAVEL - (tv series)	series	PARAMOUNT	1963
31195	HAVE GUN WILL TRAVEL - (tv series)	series	PARAMOUNT	1963
31196	HAVE GUN WILL TRAVEL - (tv series)	series	PARAMOUNT	1963
31197	HAVE GUN WILL TRAVEL - (tv series)	series	PARAMOUNT	1963
31198	HAVE GUN WILL TRAVEL - (tv series)	series	PARAMOUNT	1963
31199	HAVE GUN WILL TRAVEL - (tv series)	series	PARAMOUNT	1963
31200	GUNSMOKE - (tv series)	series	PARAMOUNT	1963
31201	GUNSMOKE - (tv series)	series	PARAMOUNT	1963
31202	GUNSMOKE - (tv series)	series	PARAMOUNT	1963
31203	GUNSMOKE - (tv series)	series	PARAMOUNT	1963
31204	GUNSMOKE - (tv series)	series	PARAMOUNT	1963
31205	GUNSMOKE - (tv series)	series	PARAMOUNT	1963
31206	GUNSMOKE - (tv series)	series	PARAMOUNT	1963
31207	GUNSMOKE - (tv series)	series	PARAMOUNT	1963
31208	GUNSMOKE - (tv series)	series	PARAMOUNT	1963
31209	GUNSMOKE - (tv series)	series	PARAMOUNT	1963
31210	GUNSMOKE - (tv series)	series	PARAMOUNT	1963
31211	GUNSMOKE - (tv series)	series	PARAMOUNT	1963
31212	GUNSMOKE - (tv series)	series	PARAMOUNT	1963
31213	GUNSMOKE - (tv series)	series	PARAMOUNT	1963
31214	GUNSMOKE - (tv series)	series	PARAMOUNT	1963
31215	GUNSMOKE - (tv series)	series	PARAMOUNT	1963
31216	GUNSMOKE - (tv series)	series	PARAMOUNT	1963
31217	GUNSMOKE - (tv series)	series	PARAMOUNT	1963
31218	GUNSMOKE - (tv series)	series	PARAMOUNT	1963
31219	GUNSMOKE - (tv series)	series	PARAMOUNT	1963
31220	GUNSMOKE - (tv series)	series	PARAMOUNT	1963
31221	GUNSMOKE - (tv series)	series	PARAMOUNT	1963
31222	GUNSMOKE - (tv series)	series	PARAMOUNT	1963
31223	GUNSMOKE - (tv series)	series	PARAMOUNT	1963

31224	GUNSMOKE - (tv series)	series	PARAMOUNT	1963
31225	GUNSMOKE - (tv series)	series	PARAMOUNT	1963
31226	GUNSMOKE - (tv series)	series	PARAMOUNT	1963
31227	GUNSMOKE - (tv series)	series	PARAMOUNT	1963
31228	GUNSMOKE - (tv series)	series	PARAMOUNT	1963
31229	GUNSMOKE - (tv series)	series	PARAMOUNT	1963
31230	GUNSMOKE - (tv series)	series	PARAMOUNT	1963
31231	GUNSMOKE - (tv series)	series	PARAMOUNT	1963
31232	GUNSMOKE - (tv series)	series	PARAMOUNT	1963
31233	GUNSMOKE - (tv series)	series	PARAMOUNT	1963
31234	GUNSMOKE - (tv series)	series	PARAMOUNT	1963
31235	GUNSMOKE - (tv series)	series	PARAMOUNT	1963
31236	GUNSMOKE - (tv series)	series	PARAMOUNT	1963
31237	GUNSMOKE - (tv series)	series	PARAMOUNT	1963
31238	GUNSMOKE - (tv series)	series	PARAMOUNT	1963
31239	GUNSMOKE - (tv series)	series	PARAMOUNT	1963
31240	GUNSMOKE - (tv series)	series	PARAMOUNT	1963
31241	GUNSMOKE - (tv series)	series	PARAMOUNT	1963
31242	GUNSMOKE - (tv series)	series	PARAMOUNT	1963
31243	GUNSMOKE - (tv series)	series	PARAMOUNT	1963
31244	GUNSMOKE - (tv series)	series	PARAMOUNT	1963
31245	GUNSMOKE - (tv series)	series	PARAMOUNT	1963
31246	GUNSMOKE - (tv series)	series	PARAMOUNT	1963
31247	GUNSMOKE - (tv series)	series	PARAMOUNT	1963
31248	GUNSMOKE - (tv series)	series	PARAMOUNT	1963
31249	GUNSMOKE - (tv series)	series	PARAMOUNT	1963
31250	BONANZA - (tv series)	series	PARAMOUNT	1963
31251	BONANZA - (tv series)	series	PARAMOUNT	1963
31252	BONANZA - (tv series)	series	PARAMOUNT	1963
31253	BONANZA - (tv series)	series	PARAMOUNT	1963
31254	BONANZA - (tv series)	series	PARAMOUNT	1963
31255	BONANZA - (tv series)	series	PARAMOUNT	1963
31256	BONANZA - (tv series)	series	PARAMOUNT	1963
31257	BONANZA - (tv series)	series	PARAMOUNT	1963
31258	BONANZA - (tv series)	series	PARAMOUNT	1963
31259	BONANZA - (tv series)	series	PARAMOUNT	1963
31260	BONANZA - (tv series)	series	PARAMOUNT	1963
31261	BONANZA - (tv series)	series	PARAMOUNT	1963
31262	BONANZA - (tv series)	series	PARAMOUNT	1963
31263	BONANZA - (tv series)	series	PARAMOUNT	1963
31264	BONANZA - (tv series)	series	PARAMOUNT	1963
31265	BONANZA - (tv series)	series	PARAMOUNT	1963
31266	BONANZA - (tv series)	series	PARAMOUNT	1963
31267	BONANZA - (tv series)	series	PARAMOUNT	1963
31268	BONANZA - (tv series)	series	PARAMOUNT	1963
31269	BONANZA - (tv series)	series	PARAMOUNT	1963
31270	BONANZA - (tv series)	series	PARAMOUNT	1963
31271	BONANZA - (tv series)	series	PARAMOUNT	1963
31272	BONANZA - (tv series)	series	PARAMOUNT	1963
31273	BONANZA - (tv series)	series	PARAMOUNT	1963
31274	BONANZA - (tv series)	series	PARAMOUNT	1963
31275	BONANZA - (tv series)	series	PARAMOUNT	1963
31276	BONANZA - (tv series)	series	PARAMOUNT	1963
31277	BONANZA - (tv series)	series	PARAMOUNT	1963
31278	BONANZA - (tv series)	series	PARAMOUNT	1963
31279	BONANZA - (tv series)	series	PARAMOUNT	1963
31280	BONANZA - (tv series)	series	PARAMOUNT	1963
31281	BONANZA - (tv series)	series	PARAMOUNT	1963
31282	BONANZA - (tv series)	series	PARAMOUNT	1963
31283	BONANZA - (tv series)	series	PARAMOUNT	1963
31284	BONANZA - (tv series)	series	PARAMOUNT	1963
31285	BONANZA - (tv series)	series	PARAMOUNT	1963
31286	BONANZA - (tv series)	series	PARAMOUNT	1963
31287	BONANZA - (tv series)	series	PARAMOUNT	1963
31288	BONANZA - (tv series)	series	PARAMOUNT	1963
31289	BONANZA - (tv series)	series	PARAMOUNT	1963

31290	BONANZA - (tv series)	series	PARAMOUNT	1963
31291	BONANZA - (tv series)	series	PARAMOUNT	1963
31292	BONANZA - (tv series)	series	PARAMOUNT	1963
31293	BONANZA - (tv series)	series	PARAMOUNT	1963
31294	BONANZA - (tv series)	series	PARAMOUNT	1963
31295	BONANZA - (tv series)	series	PARAMOUNT	1963
31296	BONANZA - (tv series)	series	PARAMOUNT	1963
31297	BONANZA - (tv series)	series	PARAMOUNT	1963
31298	BONANZA - (tv series)	series	PARAMOUNT	1963
31299	BONANZA - (tv series)	series	PARAMOUNT	1963
31300	PETE AND GLADYS - (tv series)	series	PARAMOUNT	1963
31301	PETE AND GLADYS - (tv series)	series	PARAMOUNT	1963
31302	PETE AND GLADYS - (tv series)	series	PARAMOUNT	1963
31303	PETE AND GLADYS - (tv series)	series	PARAMOUNT	1963
31304	PETE AND GLADYS - (tv series)	series	PARAMOUNT	1963
31305	PETE AND GLADYS - (tv series)	series	PARAMOUNT	1963
31306	PETE AND GLADYS - (tv series)	series	PARAMOUNT	1963
31307	PETE AND GLADYS - (tv series)	series	PARAMOUNT	1963
31308	PETE AND GLADYS - (tv series)	series	PARAMOUNT	1963
31309	PETE AND GLADYS - (tv series)	series	PARAMOUNT	1963
31310	PETE AND GLADYS - (tv series)	series	PARAMOUNT	1963
31311	PETE AND GLADYS - (tv series)	series	PARAMOUNT	1963
31312	PETE AND GLADYS - (tv series)	series	PARAMOUNT	1963
31313	PETE AND GLADYS - (tv series)	series	PARAMOUNT	1963
31314	PETE AND GLADYS - (tv series)	series	PARAMOUNT	1963
31315	PETE AND GLADYS - (tv series)	series	PARAMOUNT	1963
31316	PETE AND GLADYS - (tv series)	series	PARAMOUNT	1963
31317	PETE AND GLADYS - (tv series)	series	PARAMOUNT	1963
31318	PETE AND GLADYS - (tv series)	series	PARAMOUNT	1963
31319	PETE AND GLADYS - (tv series)	series	PARAMOUNT	1963
31320	PETE AND GLADYS - (tv series)	series	PARAMOUNT	1963
31321	PETE AND GLADYS - (tv series)	series	PARAMOUNT	1963
31322	PETE AND GLADYS - (tv series)	series	PARAMOUNT	1963
31323	PETE AND GLADYS - (tv series)	series	PARAMOUNT	1963
31324	PETE AND GLADYS - (tv series)	series	PARAMOUNT	1963
31325	PETE AND GLADYS - (tv series)	series	PARAMOUNT	1963
31326	PETE AND GLADYS - (tv series)	series	PARAMOUNT	1963
31327	PETE AND GLADYS - (tv series)	series	PARAMOUNT	1963
31328	PETE AND GLADYS - (tv series)	series	PARAMOUNT	1963
31329	PETE AND GLADYS - (tv series)	series	PARAMOUNT	1963
31330	PETE AND GLADYS - (tv series)	series	PARAMOUNT	1963
31331	PETE AND GLADYS - (tv series)	series	PARAMOUNT	1963
31332	PETE AND GLADYS - (tv series)	series	PARAMOUNT	1963
31333	PETE AND GLADYS - (tv series)	series	PARAMOUNT	1963
31334	PETE AND GLADYS - (tv series)	series	PARAMOUNT	1963
31335	PETE AND GLADYS - (tv series)	series	PARAMOUNT	1963
31336	PETE AND GLADYS - (tv series)	series	PARAMOUNT	1963
31337	PETE AND GLADYS - (tv series)	series	PARAMOUNT	1963
31338	PETE AND GLADYS - (tv series)	series	PARAMOUNT	1963
31339	PETE AND GLADYS - (tv series)	series	PARAMOUNT	1963
31340	PETE AND GLADYS - (tv series)	series	PARAMOUNT	1963
31341	PETE AND GLADYS - (tv series)	series	PARAMOUNT	1963
31342	PETE AND GLADYS - (tv series)	series	PARAMOUNT	1963
31343	PETE AND GLADYS - (tv series)	series	PARAMOUNT	1963
31344	PETE AND GLADYS - (tv series)	series	PARAMOUNT	1963
31345	PETE AND GLADYS - (tv series)	series	PARAMOUNT	1963
31346	PETE AND GLADYS - (tv series)	series	PARAMOUNT	1963
31347	PETE AND GLADYS - (tv series)	series	PARAMOUNT	1963
31348	PETE AND GLADYS - (tv series)	series	PARAMOUNT	1963
31349	PETE AND GLADYS - (tv series)	series	PARAMOUNT	1963
31350	HERO - (tv series)	series	PARAMOUNT	1966
31351	HERO - (tv series)	series	PARAMOUNT	1966
31352	HERO - (tv series)	series	PARAMOUNT	1966
31353	HERO - (tv series)	series	PARAMOUNT	1966
31354	HERO - (tv series)	series	PARAMOUNT	1966
31355	HERO - (tv series)	series	PARAMOUNT	1966

31356	HERO - (tv series)	series	PARAMOUNT	1966
31357	HERO - (tv series)	series	PARAMOUNT	1966
31358	HERO - (tv series)	series	PARAMOUNT	1966
31359	HERO - (tv series)	series	PARAMOUNT	1966
31360	HERO - (tv series)	series	PARAMOUNT	1966
31361	HERO - (tv series)	series	PARAMOUNT	1966
31362	HERO - (tv series)	series	PARAMOUNT	1966
31363	HERO - (tv series)	series	PARAMOUNT	1966
31364	HERO - (tv series)	series	PARAMOUNT	1966
31365	HERO - (tv series)	series	PARAMOUNT	1966
31366	HERO - (tv series)	series	PARAMOUNT	1966
31367	HERO - (tv series)	series	PARAMOUNT	1966
31368	HERO - (tv series)	series	PARAMOUNT	1966
31369	HERO - (tv series)	series	PARAMOUNT	1966
31370	HERO - (tv series)	series	PARAMOUNT	1966
31371	HERO - (tv series)	series	PARAMOUNT	1966
31372	HERO - (tv series)	series	PARAMOUNT	1966
31373	HERO - (tv series)	series	PARAMOUNT	1966
31374	HERO - (tv series)	series	PARAMOUNT	1966
31375	HERO - (tv series)	series	PARAMOUNT	1966
31376	HERO - (tv series)	series	PARAMOUNT	1966
31377	HERO - (tv series)	series	PARAMOUNT	1966
31378	HERO - (tv series)	series	PARAMOUNT	1966
31379	HERO - (tv series)	series	PARAMOUNT	1966
31380	HERO - (tv series)	series	PARAMOUNT	1966
31381	HERO - (tv series)	series	PARAMOUNT	1966
31382	HERO - (tv series)	series	PARAMOUNT	1966
31383	HERO - (tv series)	series	PARAMOUNT	1966
31384	HERO - (tv series)	series	PARAMOUNT	1966
31385	HERO - (tv series)	series	PARAMOUNT	1966
31386	HERO - (tv series)	series	PARAMOUNT	1966
31387	HERO - (tv series)	series	PARAMOUNT	1966
31388	HERO - (tv series)	series	PARAMOUNT	1966
31389	HERO - (tv series)	series	PARAMOUNT	1966
31390	HERO - (tv series)	series	PARAMOUNT	1966
31391	HERO - (tv series)	series	PARAMOUNT	1966
31392	HERO - (tv series)	series	PARAMOUNT	1966
31393	HERO - (tv series)	series	PARAMOUNT	1966
31394	HERO - (tv series)	series	PARAMOUNT	1966
31395	HERO - (tv series)	series	PARAMOUNT	1966
31396	HERO - (tv series)	series	PARAMOUNT	1966
31397	HERO - (tv series)	series	PARAMOUNT	1966
31398	HERO - (tv series)	series	PARAMOUNT	1966
31399	HERO - (tv series)	series	PARAMOUNT	1966
31400	BONANZA - (tv series)	series	PARAMOUNT	1963
31401	BONANZA - (tv series)	series	PARAMOUNT	1963
31402	BONANZA - (tv series)	series	PARAMOUNT	1963
31403	BONANZA - (tv series)	series	PARAMOUNT	1963
31404	BONANZA - (tv series)	series	PARAMOUNT	1963
31405	BONANZA - (tv series)	series	PARAMOUNT	1963
31406	BONANZA - (tv series)	series	PARAMOUNT	1963
31407	BONANZA - (tv series)	series	PARAMOUNT	1963
31408	BONANZA - (tv series)	series	PARAMOUNT	1963
31409	BONANZA - (tv series)	series	PARAMOUNT	1963
31410	BONANZA - (tv series)	series	PARAMOUNT	1963
31411	BONANZA - (tv series)	series	PARAMOUNT	1963
31412	BONANZA - (tv series)	series	PARAMOUNT	1963
31413	BONANZA - (tv series)	series	PARAMOUNT	1963
31414	BONANZA - (tv series)	series	PARAMOUNT	1963
31415	BONANZA - (tv series)	series	PARAMOUNT	1963
31416	BONANZA - (tv series)	series	PARAMOUNT	1963
31417	BONANZA - (tv series)	series	PARAMOUNT	1963
31418	BONANZA - (tv series)	series	PARAMOUNT	1963
31419	BONANZA - (tv series)	series	PARAMOUNT	1963
31420	BONANZA - (tv series)	series	PARAMOUNT	1963
31421	BONANZA - (tv series)	series	PARAMOUNT	1963

31422	BONANZA - (tv series)	series	PARAMOUNT	1963
31423	BONANZA - (tv series)	series	PARAMOUNT	1963
31424	BONANZA - (tv series)	series	PARAMOUNT	1963
31425	BONANZA - (tv series)	series	PARAMOUNT	1963
31426	BONANZA - (tv series)	series	PARAMOUNT	1963
31427	BONANZA - (tv series)	series	PARAMOUNT	1963
31428	BONANZA - (tv series)	series	PARAMOUNT	1963
31429	BONANZA - (tv series)	series	PARAMOUNT	1963
31430	BONANZA - (tv series)	series	PARAMOUNT	1963
31431	BONANZA - (tv series)	series	PARAMOUNT	1963
31432	BONANZA - (tv series)	series	PARAMOUNT	1963
31433	BONANZA - (tv series)	series	PARAMOUNT	1963
31434	BONANZA - (tv series)	series	PARAMOUNT	1963
31435	BONANZA - (tv series)	series	PARAMOUNT	1963
31436	BONANZA - (tv series)	series	PARAMOUNT	1963
31437	BONANZA - (tv series)	series	PARAMOUNT	1963
31438	BONANZA - (tv series)	series	PARAMOUNT	1963
31439	BONANZA - (tv series)	series	PARAMOUNT	1963
31440	BONANZA - (tv series)	series	PARAMOUNT	1963
31441	BONANZA - (tv series)	series	PARAMOUNT	1963
31442	BONANZA - (tv series)	series	PARAMOUNT	1963
31443	BONANZA - (tv series)	series	PARAMOUNT	1963
31444	BONANZA - (tv series)	series	PARAMOUNT	1963
31445	BONANZA - (tv series)	series	PARAMOUNT	1963
31446	BONANZA - (tv series)	series	PARAMOUNT	1963
31447	BONANZA - (tv series)	series	PARAMOUNT	1963
31448	BONANZA - (tv series)	series	PARAMOUNT	1963
31449	BONANZA - (tv series)	series	PARAMOUNT	1963
31450	GET SMART - (tv series)	series	PARAMOUNT	1966
31451	GET SMART - (tv series)	series	PARAMOUNT	1966
31452	GET SMART - (tv series)	series	PARAMOUNT	1966
31453	GET SMART - (tv series)	series	PARAMOUNT	1966
31454	GET SMART - (tv series)	series	PARAMOUNT	1966
31455	GET SMART - (tv series)	series	PARAMOUNT	1966
31456	GET SMART - (tv series)	series	PARAMOUNT	1966
31457	GET SMART - (tv series)	series	PARAMOUNT	1966
31458	GET SMART - (tv series)	series	PARAMOUNT	1966
31459	GET SMART - (tv series)	series	PARAMOUNT	1966
31460	GET SMART - (tv series)	series	PARAMOUNT	1966
31461	GET SMART - (tv series)	series	PARAMOUNT	1966
31462	GET SMART - (tv series)	series	PARAMOUNT	1966
31463	GET SMART - (tv series)	series	PARAMOUNT	1966
31464	GET SMART - (tv series)	series	PARAMOUNT	1966
31465	GET SMART - (tv series)	series	PARAMOUNT	1966
31466	GET SMART - (tv series)	series	PARAMOUNT	1966
31467	GET SMART - (tv series)	series	PARAMOUNT	1966
31468	GET SMART - (tv series)	series	PARAMOUNT	1966
31469	GET SMART - (tv series)	series	PARAMOUNT	1966
31470	GET SMART - (tv series)	series	PARAMOUNT	1966
31471	GET SMART - (tv series)	series	PARAMOUNT	1966
31472	GET SMART - (tv series)	series	PARAMOUNT	1966
31473	GET SMART - (tv series)	series	PARAMOUNT	1966
31474	GET SMART - (tv series)	series	PARAMOUNT	1966
31475	GET SMART - (tv series)	series	PARAMOUNT	1966
31476	GET SMART - (tv series)	series	PARAMOUNT	1966
31477	GET SMART - (tv series)	series	PARAMOUNT	1966
31478	GET SMART - (tv series)	series	PARAMOUNT	1966
31479	GET SMART - (tv series)	series	PARAMOUNT	1966
31480	GET SMART - (tv series)	series	PARAMOUNT	1966
31481	GET SMART - (tv series)	series	PARAMOUNT	1966
31482	GET SMART - (tv series)	series	PARAMOUNT	1966
31483	GET SMART - (tv series)	series	PARAMOUNT	1966
31484	GET SMART - (tv series)	series	PARAMOUNT	1966
31485	GET SMART - (tv series)	series	PARAMOUNT	1966
31486	GET SMART - (tv series)	series	PARAMOUNT	1966
31487	GET SMART - (tv series)	series	PARAMOUNT	1966

31488	GET SMART - (tv series)	series	PARAMOUNT	1966
31489	GET SMART - (tv series)	series	PARAMOUNT	1966
31490	GET SMART - (tv series)	series	PARAMOUNT	1966
31491	GET SMART - (tv series)	series	PARAMOUNT	1966
31492	GET SMART - (tv series)	series	PARAMOUNT	1966
31493	GET SMART - (tv series)	series	PARAMOUNT	1966
31494	GET SMART - (tv series)	series	PARAMOUNT	1966
31495	GET SMART - (tv series)	series	PARAMOUNT	1966
31496	GET SMART - (tv series)	series	PARAMOUNT	1966
31497	GET SMART - (tv series)	series	PARAMOUNT	1966
31498	GET SMART - (tv series)	series	PARAMOUNT	1966
31499	GET SMART - (tv series)	series	PARAMOUNT	1966
31500	BONANZA - (tv series)	series	PARAMOUNT	1963
31501	BONANZA - (tv series)	series	PARAMOUNT	1963
31502	BONANZA - (tv series)	series	PARAMOUNT	1963
31503	BONANZA - (tv series)	series	PARAMOUNT	1963
31504	BONANZA - (tv series)	series	PARAMOUNT	1963
31505	BONANZA - (tv series)	series	PARAMOUNT	1963
31506	BONANZA - (tv series)	series	PARAMOUNT	1963
31507	BONANZA - (tv series)	series	PARAMOUNT	1963
31508	BONANZA - (tv series)	series	PARAMOUNT	1963
31509	BONANZA - (tv series)	series	PARAMOUNT	1963
31510	BONANZA - (tv series)	series	PARAMOUNT	1963
31511	BONANZA - (tv series)	series	PARAMOUNT	1963
31512	BONANZA - (tv series)	series	PARAMOUNT	1963
31513	BONANZA - (tv series)	series	PARAMOUNT	1963
31514	BONANZA - (tv series)	series	PARAMOUNT	1963
31515	BONANZA - (tv series)	series	PARAMOUNT	1963
31516	BONANZA - (tv series)	series	PARAMOUNT	1963
31517	BONANZA - (tv series)	series	PARAMOUNT	1963
31518	BONANZA - (tv series)	series	PARAMOUNT	1963
31519	BONANZA - (tv series)	series	PARAMOUNT	1963
31520	BONANZA - (tv series)	series	PARAMOUNT	1963
31521	BONANZA - (tv series)	series	PARAMOUNT	1963
31522	BONANZA - (tv series)	series	PARAMOUNT	1963
31523	BONANZA - (tv series)	series	PARAMOUNT	1963
31524	BONANZA - (tv series)	series	PARAMOUNT	1963
31525	BONANZA - (tv series)	series	PARAMOUNT	1963
31526	BONANZA - (tv series)	series	PARAMOUNT	1963
31527	BONANZA - (tv series)	series	PARAMOUNT	1963
31528	BONANZA - (tv series)	series	PARAMOUNT	1963
31529	BONANZA - (tv series)	series	PARAMOUNT	1963
31530	BONANZA - (tv series)	series	PARAMOUNT	1963
31531	BONANZA - (tv series)	series	PARAMOUNT	1963
31532	BONANZA - (tv series)	series	PARAMOUNT	1963
31533	BONANZA - (tv series)	series	PARAMOUNT	1963
31534	BONANZA - (tv series)	series	PARAMOUNT	1963
31535	BONANZA - (tv series)	series	PARAMOUNT	1963
31536	BONANZA - (tv series)	series	PARAMOUNT	1963
31537	BONANZA - (tv series)	series	PARAMOUNT	1963
31538	BONANZA - (tv series)	series	PARAMOUNT	1963
31539	BONANZA - (tv series)	series	PARAMOUNT	1963
31540	BONANZA - (tv series)	series	PARAMOUNT	1963
31541	BONANZA - (tv series)	series	PARAMOUNT	1963
31542	BONANZA - (tv series)	series	PARAMOUNT	1963
31543	BONANZA - (tv series)	series	PARAMOUNT	1963
31544	BONANZA - (tv series)	series	PARAMOUNT	1963
31545	BONANZA - (tv series)	series	PARAMOUNT	1963
31546	BONANZA - (tv series)	series	PARAMOUNT	1963
31547	BONANZA - (tv series)	series	PARAMOUNT	1963
31548	BONANZA - (tv series)	series	PARAMOUNT	1963
31549	BONANZA - (tv series)	series	PARAMOUNT	1963
31551	SHANE - (tv series)	series	PARAMOUNT	1966
31552	SHANE - (tv series)	series	PARAMOUNT	1966
31553	SHANE - (tv series)	series	PARAMOUNT	1966
31554	SHANE - (tv series)	series	PARAMOUNT	1966

31555	SHANE - (tv series)	series	PARAMOUNT	1966
31556	SHANE - (tv series)	series	PARAMOUNT	1966
31557	SHANE - (tv series)	series	PARAMOUNT	1966
31558	SHANE - (tv series)	series	PARAMOUNT	1966
31559	SHANE - (tv series)	series	PARAMOUNT	1966
31560	SHANE - (tv series)	series	PARAMOUNT	1966
31561	SHANE - (tv series)	series	PARAMOUNT	1966
31562	SHANE - (tv series)	series	PARAMOUNT	1966
31563	SHANE - (tv series)	series	PARAMOUNT	1966
31564	SHANE - (tv series)	series	PARAMOUNT	1966
31565	SHANE - (tv series)	series	PARAMOUNT	1966
31566	SHANE - (tv series)	series	PARAMOUNT	1966
31567	SHANE - (tv series)	series	PARAMOUNT	1966
31600	BONANZA - (tv series)	series	PARAMOUNT	1964
31601	BONANZA - (tv series)	series	PARAMOUNT	1964
31602	BONANZA - (tv series)	series	PARAMOUNT	1964
31603	BONANZA - (tv series)	series	PARAMOUNT	1964
31604	BONANZA - (tv series)	series	PARAMOUNT	1964
31605	BONANZA - (tv series)	series	PARAMOUNT	1964
31606	BONANZA - (tv series)	series	PARAMOUNT	1964
31607	BONANZA - (tv series)	series	PARAMOUNT	1964
31608	BONANZA - (tv series)	series	PARAMOUNT	1964
31609	BONANZA - (tv series)	series	PARAMOUNT	1964
31610	BONANZA - (tv series)	series	PARAMOUNT	1964
31611	BONANZA - (tv series)	series	PARAMOUNT	1964
31612	BONANZA - (tv series)	series	PARAMOUNT	1964
31613	BONANZA - (tv series)	series	PARAMOUNT	1964
31614	BONANZA - (tv series)	series	PARAMOUNT	1964
31615	BONANZA - (tv series)	series	PARAMOUNT	1964
31616	BONANZA - (tv series)	series	PARAMOUNT	1964
31617	BONANZA - (tv series)	series	PARAMOUNT	1964
31618	BONANZA - (tv series)	series	PARAMOUNT	1964
31619	BONANZA - (tv series)	series	PARAMOUNT	1964
31620	BONANZA - (tv series)	series	PARAMOUNT	1964
31621	BONANZA - (tv series)	series	PARAMOUNT	1964
31622	BONANZA - (tv series)	series	PARAMOUNT	1964
31623	BONANZA - (tv series)	series	PARAMOUNT	1964
31624	BONANZA - (tv series)	series	PARAMOUNT	1964
31625	BONANZA - (tv series)	series	PARAMOUNT	1964
31626	BONANZA - (tv series)	series	PARAMOUNT	1964
31627	BONANZA - (tv series)	series	PARAMOUNT	1964
31628	BONANZA - (tv series)	series	PARAMOUNT	1964
31629	BONANZA - (tv series)	series	PARAMOUNT	1964
31630	BONANZA - (tv series)	series	PARAMOUNT	1964
31631	BONANZA - (tv series)	series	PARAMOUNT	1964
31632	BONANZA - (tv series)	series	PARAMOUNT	1964
31633	BONANZA - (tv series)	series	PARAMOUNT	1964
31634	BONANZA - (tv series)	series	PARAMOUNT	1964
31635	BONANZA - (tv series)	series	PARAMOUNT	1964
31636	BONANZA - (tv series)	series	PARAMOUNT	1964
31637	BONANZA - (tv series)	series	PARAMOUNT	1964
31638	BONANZA - (tv series)	series	PARAMOUNT	1964
31639	BONANZA - (tv series)	series	PARAMOUNT	1964
31640	BONANZA - (tv series)	series	PARAMOUNT	1964
31641	BONANZA - (tv series)	series	PARAMOUNT	1964
31642	BONANZA - (tv series)	series	PARAMOUNT	1964
31643	BONANZA - (tv series)	series	PARAMOUNT	1964
31644	BONANZA - (tv series)	series	PARAMOUNT	1964
31645	BONANZA - (tv series)	series	PARAMOUNT	1964
31646	BONANZA - (tv series)	series	PARAMOUNT	1964
31647	BONANZA - (tv series)	series	PARAMOUNT	1964
31648	BONANZA - (tv series)	series	PARAMOUNT	1964
31649	BONANZA - (tv series)	series	PARAMOUNT	1964
31652	CAPTAIN NICE - (tv series)	series	PARAMOUNT	1967
31653	CAPTAIN NICE - (tv series)	series	PARAMOUNT	1967
31654	CAPTAIN NICE - (tv series)	series	PARAMOUNT	1967

31655	CAPTAIN NICE - (tv series)	series	PARAMOUNT	1967
31656	CAPTAIN NICE - (tv series)	series	PARAMOUNT	1967
31657	CAPTAIN NICE - (tv series)	series	PARAMOUNT	1967
31658	CAPTAIN NICE - (tv series)	series	PARAMOUNT	1967
31659	CAPTAIN NICE - (tv series)	series	PARAMOUNT	1967
31660	CAPTAIN NICE - (tv series)	series	PARAMOUNT	1967
31661	CAPTAIN NICE - (tv series)	series	PARAMOUNT	1967
31662	CAPTAIN NICE - (tv series)	series	PARAMOUNT	1967
31663	CAPTAIN NICE - (tv series)	series	PARAMOUNT	1967
31664	CAPTAIN NICE - (tv series)	series	PARAMOUNT	1967
31665	CAPTAIN NICE - (tv series)	series	PARAMOUNT	1967
31666	CAPTAIN NICE - (tv series)	series	PARAMOUNT	1967
31700	BONANZA - (tv series)	series	PARAMOUNT	1965
31701	BONANZA - (tv series)	series	PARAMOUNT	1965
31702	BONANZA - (tv series)	series	PARAMOUNT	1965
31703	BONANZA - (tv series)	series	PARAMOUNT	1965
31704	BONANZA - (tv series)	series	PARAMOUNT	1965
31705	BONANZA - (tv series)	series	PARAMOUNT	1965
31706	BONANZA - (tv series)	series	PARAMOUNT	1965
31707	BONANZA - (tv series)	series	PARAMOUNT	1965
31708	BONANZA - (tv series)	series	PARAMOUNT	1965
31709	BONANZA - (tv series)	series	PARAMOUNT	1965
31710	BONANZA - (tv series)	series	PARAMOUNT	1965
31711	BONANZA - (tv series)	series	PARAMOUNT	1965
31712	BONANZA - (tv series)	series	PARAMOUNT	1965
31713	BONANZA - (tv series)	series	PARAMOUNT	1965
31714	BONANZA - (tv series)	series	PARAMOUNT	1965
31715	BONANZA - (tv series)	series	PARAMOUNT	1965
31716	BONANZA - (tv series)	series	PARAMOUNT	1965
31717	BONANZA - (tv series)	series	PARAMOUNT	1965
31718	BONANZA - (tv series)	series	PARAMOUNT	1965
31719	BONANZA - (tv series)	series	PARAMOUNT	1965
31720	BONANZA - (tv series)	series	PARAMOUNT	1965
31721	BONANZA - (tv series)	series	PARAMOUNT	1965
31722	BONANZA - (tv series)	series	PARAMOUNT	1965
31723	BONANZA - (tv series)	series	PARAMOUNT	1965
31724	BONANZA - (tv series)	series	PARAMOUNT	1965
31725	BONANZA - (tv series)	series	PARAMOUNT	1965
31726	BONANZA - (tv series)	series	PARAMOUNT	1965
31727	BONANZA - (tv series)	series	PARAMOUNT	1965
31728	BONANZA - (tv series)	series	PARAMOUNT	1965
31729	BONANZA - (tv series)	series	PARAMOUNT	1965
31730	BONANZA - (tv series)	series	PARAMOUNT	1965
31731	BONANZA - (tv series)	series	PARAMOUNT	1965
31732	BONANZA - (tv series)	series	PARAMOUNT	1965
31733	BONANZA - (tv series)	series	PARAMOUNT	1965
31734	BONANZA - (tv series)	series	PARAMOUNT	1965
31735	BONANZA - (tv series)	series	PARAMOUNT	1965
31736	BONANZA - (tv series)	series	PARAMOUNT	1965
31737	BONANZA - (tv series)	series	PARAMOUNT	1965
31738	BONANZA - (tv series)	series	PARAMOUNT	1965
31739	BONANZA - (tv series)	series	PARAMOUNT	1965
31740	BONANZA - (tv series)	series	PARAMOUNT	1965
31741	BONANZA - (tv series)	series	PARAMOUNT	1965
31742	BONANZA - (tv series)	series	PARAMOUNT	1965
31743	BONANZA - (tv series)	series	PARAMOUNT	1965
31744	BONANZA - (tv series)	series	PARAMOUNT	1965
31745	BONANZA - (tv series)	series	PARAMOUNT	1965
31746	BONANZA - (tv series)	series	PARAMOUNT	1965
31747	BONANZA - (tv series)	series	PARAMOUNT	1965
31748	BONANZA - (tv series)	series	PARAMOUNT	1965
31749	BONANZA - (tv series)	series	PARAMOUNT	1965
31750	BRANDED - (tv series)	series	PARAMOUNT	1965
31751	BRANDED - (tv series)	series	PARAMOUNT	1965
31752	BRANDED - (tv series)	series	PARAMOUNT	1965
31753	BRANDED - (tv series)	series	PARAMOUNT	1965

31754	BRANDED - (tv series)	series	PARAMOUNT	1965
31755	BRANDED - (tv series)	series	PARAMOUNT	1965
31756	BRANDED - (tv series)	series	PARAMOUNT	1965
31757	BRANDED - (tv series)	series	PARAMOUNT	1965
31758	BRANDED - (tv series)	series	PARAMOUNT	1965
31759	BRANDED - (tv series)	series	PARAMOUNT	1965
31760	BRANDED - (tv series)	series	PARAMOUNT	1965
31761	BRANDED - (tv series)	series	PARAMOUNT	1965
31762	BRANDED - (tv series)	series	PARAMOUNT	1965
31763	BRANDED - (tv series)	series	PARAMOUNT	1965
31764	BRANDED - (tv series)	series	PARAMOUNT	1965
31765	BRANDED - (tv series)	series	PARAMOUNT	1965
31766	BRANDED - (tv series)	series	PARAMOUNT	1965
31767	BRANDED - (tv series)	series	PARAMOUNT	1965
31768	BRANDED - (tv series)	series	PARAMOUNT	1965
31769	BRANDED - (tv series)	series	PARAMOUNT	1965
31770	BRANDED - (tv series)	series	PARAMOUNT	1965
31771	BRANDED - (tv series)	series	PARAMOUNT	1965
31772	BRANDED - (tv series)	series	PARAMOUNT	1965
31773	BRANDED - (tv series)	series	PARAMOUNT	1965
31774	BRANDED - (tv series)	series	PARAMOUNT	1965
31775	BRANDED - (tv series)	series	PARAMOUNT	1965
31776	BRANDED - (tv series)	series	PARAMOUNT	1965
31777	BRANDED - (tv series)	series	PARAMOUNT	1965
31778	BRANDED - (tv series)	series	PARAMOUNT	1965
31779	BRANDED - (tv series)	series	PARAMOUNT	1965
31780	BRANDED - (tv series)	series	PARAMOUNT	1965
31781	BRANDED - (tv series)	series	PARAMOUNT	1965
31782	BRANDED - (tv series)	series	PARAMOUNT	1965
31783	BRANDED - (tv series)	series	PARAMOUNT	1965
31784	BRANDED - (tv series)	series	PARAMOUNT	1965
31785	BRANDED - (tv series)	series	PARAMOUNT	1965
31786	BRANDED - (tv series)	series	PARAMOUNT	1965
31787	BRANDED - (tv series)	series	PARAMOUNT	1965
31788	BRANDED - (tv series)	series	PARAMOUNT	1965
31789	BRANDED - (tv series)	series	PARAMOUNT	1965
31790	BRANDED - (tv series)	series	PARAMOUNT	1965
31791	BRANDED - (tv series)	series	PARAMOUNT	1965
31792	BRANDED - (tv series)	series	PARAMOUNT	1965
31793	BRANDED - (tv series)	series	PARAMOUNT	1965
31794	BRANDED - (tv series)	series	PARAMOUNT	1965
31795	BRANDED - (tv series)	series	PARAMOUNT	1965
31796	BRANDED - (tv series)	series	PARAMOUNT	1965
31797	BRANDED - (tv series)	series	PARAMOUNT	1965
31798	BRANDED - (tv series)	series	PARAMOUNT	1965
31799	BRANDED - (tv series)	series	PARAMOUNT	1965
31800	BONANZA - (tv series)	series	PARAMOUNT	1966
31801	BONANZA - (tv series)	series	PARAMOUNT	1966
31802	BONANZA - (tv series)	series	PARAMOUNT	1966
31803	BONANZA - (tv series)	series	PARAMOUNT	1966
31803	DRUMS OF AFRICA	CLARK	MGM	1963
31804	BONANZA - (tv series)	series	PARAMOUNT	1966
31805	BONANZA - (tv series)	series	PARAMOUNT	1966
31806	BONANZA - (tv series)	series	PARAMOUNT	1966
31807	BONANZA - (tv series)	series	PARAMOUNT	1966
31808	BONANZA - (tv series)	series	PARAMOUNT	1966
31809	BONANZA - (tv series)	series	PARAMOUNT	1966
31810	BONANZA - (tv series)	series	PARAMOUNT	1966
31811	BONANZA - (tv series)	series	PARAMOUNT	1966
31812	BONANZA - (tv series)	series	PARAMOUNT	1966
31813	BONANZA - (tv series)	series	PARAMOUNT	1966
31814	BONANZA - (tv series)	series	PARAMOUNT	1966
31815	BONANZA - (tv series)	series	PARAMOUNT	1966
31816	BONANZA - (tv series)	series	PARAMOUNT	1966
31817	BONANZA - (tv series)	series	PARAMOUNT	1966
31818	BONANZA - (tv series)	series	PARAMOUNT	1966

31819	BONANZA - (tv series)	series	PARAMOUNT	1966
31820	BONANZA - (tv series)	series	PARAMOUNT	1966
31821	BONANZA - (tv series)	series	PARAMOUNT	1966
31822	BONANZA - (tv series)	series	PARAMOUNT	1966
31823	BONANZA - (tv series)	series	PARAMOUNT	1966
31824	BONANZA - (tv series)	series	PARAMOUNT	1966
31825	BONANZA - (tv series)	series	PARAMOUNT	1966
31826	BONANZA - (tv series)	series	PARAMOUNT	1966
31827	BONANZA - (tv series)	series	PARAMOUNT	1966
31828	BONANZA - (tv series)	series	PARAMOUNT	1966
31829	BONANZA - (tv series)	series	PARAMOUNT	1966
31830	BONANZA - (tv series)	series	PARAMOUNT	1966
31831	BONANZA - (tv series)	series	PARAMOUNT	1966
31832	BONANZA - (tv series)	series	PARAMOUNT	1966
31833	BONANZA - (tv series)	series	PARAMOUNT	1966
31834	BONANZA - (tv series)	series	PARAMOUNT	1966
31835	BONANZA - (tv series)	series	PARAMOUNT	1966
31836	BONANZA - (tv series)	series	PARAMOUNT	1966
31837	BONANZA - (tv series)	series	PARAMOUNT	1966
31838	BONANZA - (tv series)	series	PARAMOUNT	1966
31839	BONANZA - (tv series)	series	PARAMOUNT	1966
31840	BONANZA - (tv series)	series	PARAMOUNT	1966
31841	BONANZA - (tv series)	series	PARAMOUNT	1966
31842	BONANZA - (tv series)	series	PARAMOUNT	1966
31843	BONANZA - (tv series)	series	PARAMOUNT	1966
31844	BONANZA - (tv series)	series	PARAMOUNT	1966
31845	BONANZA - (tv series)	series	PARAMOUNT	1966
31846	BONANZA - (tv series)	series	PARAMOUNT	1966
31847	BONANZA - (tv series)	series	PARAMOUNT	1966
31848	BONANZA - (tv series)	series	PARAMOUNT	1966
31849	BONANZA - (tv series)	series	PARAMOUNT	1966
31900	BONANZA - (tv series)	series	PARAMOUNT	1967
31901	BONANZA - (tv series)	series	PARAMOUNT	1967
31902	BONANZA - (tv series)	series	PARAMOUNT	1967
31903	BONANZA - (tv series)	series	PARAMOUNT	1967
31904	BONANZA - (tv series)	series	PARAMOUNT	1967
31905	BONANZA - (tv series)	series	PARAMOUNT	1967
31906	BONANZA - (tv series)	series	PARAMOUNT	1967
31907	BONANZA - (tv series)	series	PARAMOUNT	1967
31908	BONANZA - (tv series)	series	PARAMOUNT	1967
31909	BONANZA - (tv series)	series	PARAMOUNT	1967
31910	BONANZA - (tv series)	series	PARAMOUNT	1967
31911	BONANZA - (tv series)	series	PARAMOUNT	1967
31912	BONANZA - (tv series)	series	PARAMOUNT	1967
31913	BONANZA - (tv series)	series	PARAMOUNT	1967
31914	BONANZA - (tv series)	series	PARAMOUNT	1967
31915	BONANZA - (tv series)	series	PARAMOUNT	1967
31916	BONANZA - (tv series)	series	PARAMOUNT	1967
31917	BONANZA - (tv series)	series	PARAMOUNT	1967
31918	BONANZA - (tv series)	series	PARAMOUNT	1967
31919	BONANZA - (tv series)	series	PARAMOUNT	1967
31920	BONANZA - (tv series)	series	PARAMOUNT	1967
31921	BONANZA - (tv series)	series	PARAMOUNT	1967
31922	BONANZA - (tv series)	series	PARAMOUNT	1967
31923	BONANZA - (tv series)	series	PARAMOUNT	1967
31924	BONANZA - (tv series)	series	PARAMOUNT	1967
31925	BONANZA - (tv series)	series	PARAMOUNT	1967
31926	BONANZA - (tv series)	series	PARAMOUNT	1967
31927	BONANZA - (tv series)	series	PARAMOUNT	1967
31928	BONANZA - (tv series)	series	PARAMOUNT	1967
31929	BONANZA - (tv series)	series	PARAMOUNT	1967
31930	BONANZA - (tv series)	series	PARAMOUNT	1967
31931	BONANZA - (tv series)	series	PARAMOUNT	1967
31932	BONANZA - (tv series)	series	PARAMOUNT	1967
31933	BONANZA - (tv series)	series	PARAMOUNT	1967
31934	BONANZA - (tv series)	series	PARAMOUNT	1967

31935	BONANZA - (tv series)	series	PARAMOUNT	1967
31936	BONANZA - (tv series)	series	PARAMOUNT	1967
31937	BONANZA - (tv series)	series	PARAMOUNT	1967
31938	BONANZA - (tv series)	series	PARAMOUNT	1967
31939	BONANZA - (tv series)	series	PARAMOUNT	1967
31940	BONANZA - (tv series)	series	PARAMOUNT	1967
31941	BONANZA - (tv series)	series	PARAMOUNT	1967
31942	BONANZA - (tv series)	series	PARAMOUNT	1967
31943	BONANZA - (tv series)	series	PARAMOUNT	1967
31944	BONANZA - (tv series)	series	PARAMOUNT	1967
31945	BONANZA - (tv series)	series	PARAMOUNT	1967
31946	BONANZA - (tv series)	series	PARAMOUNT	1967
31947	BONANZA - (tv series)	series	PARAMOUNT	1967
31948	BONANZA - (tv series)	series	PARAMOUNT	1967
31949	BONANZA - (tv series)	series	PARAMOUNT	1967
32001	PATTY DUKE SHOW - (tv series)	series	PARAMOUNT	1966
32002	PATTY DUKE SHOW - (tv series)	series	PARAMOUNT	1966
32003	PATTY DUKE SHOW - (tv series)	series	PARAMOUNT	1966
32004	PATTY DUKE SHOW - (tv series)	series	PARAMOUNT	1966
32005	PATTY DUKE SHOW - (tv series)	series	PARAMOUNT	1966
32006	PATTY DUKE SHOW - (tv series)	series	PARAMOUNT	1966
32007	PATTY DUKE SHOW - (tv series)	series	PARAMOUNT	1966
32008	PATTY DUKE SHOW - (tv series)	series	PARAMOUNT	1966
32009	PATTY DUKE SHOW - (tv series)	series	PARAMOUNT	1966
32010	PATTY DUKE SHOW - (tv series)	series	PARAMOUNT	1966
32011	PATTY DUKE SHOW - (tv series)	series	PARAMOUNT	1966
32012	PATTY DUKE SHOW - (tv series)	series	PARAMOUNT	1966
32013	PATTY DUKE SHOW - (tv series)	series	PARAMOUNT	1966
32014	PATTY DUKE SHOW - (tv series)	series	PARAMOUNT	1966
32015	PATTY DUKE SHOW - (tv series)	series	PARAMOUNT	1966
32016	PATTY DUKE SHOW - (tv series)	series	PARAMOUNT	1966
32017	PATTY DUKE SHOW - (tv series)	series	PARAMOUNT	1966
32018	PATTY DUKE SHOW - (tv series)	series	PARAMOUNT	1966
32019	PATTY DUKE SHOW - (tv series)	series	PARAMOUNT	1966
32020	PATTY DUKE SHOW - (tv series)	series	PARAMOUNT	1966
32021	PATTY DUKE SHOW - (tv series)	series	PARAMOUNT	1966
32022	PATTY DUKE SHOW - (tv series)	series	PARAMOUNT	1966
32023	PATTY DUKE SHOW - (tv series)	series	PARAMOUNT	1966
32024	PATTY DUKE SHOW - (tv series)	series	PARAMOUNT	1966
32025	PATTY DUKE SHOW - (tv series)	series	PARAMOUNT	1966
32026	PATTY DUKE SHOW - (tv series)	series	PARAMOUNT	1966
32027	PATTY DUKE SHOW - (tv series)	series	PARAMOUNT	1966
32028	PATTY DUKE SHOW - (tv series)	series	PARAMOUNT	1966
32029	PATTY DUKE SHOW - (tv series)	series	PARAMOUNT	1966
32030	PATTY DUKE SHOW - (tv series)	series	PARAMOUNT	1966
32031	PATTY DUKE SHOW - (tv series)	series	PARAMOUNT	1966
32032	PATTY DUKE SHOW - (tv series)	series	PARAMOUNT	1966
32033	PATTY DUKE SHOW - (tv series)	series	PARAMOUNT	1966
32034	PATTY DUKE SHOW - (tv series)	series	PARAMOUNT	1966
32035	PATTY DUKE SHOW - (tv series)	series	PARAMOUNT	1966
32036	PATTY DUKE SHOW - (tv series)	series	PARAMOUNT	1966
32037	PATTY DUKE SHOW - (tv series)	series	PARAMOUNT	1966
32038	PATTY DUKE SHOW - (tv series)	series	PARAMOUNT	1966
32039	PATTY DUKE SHOW - (tv series)	series	PARAMOUNT	1966
32040	PATTY DUKE SHOW - (tv series)	series	PARAMOUNT	1966
32041	PATTY DUKE SHOW - (tv series)	series	PARAMOUNT	1966
32042	PATTY DUKE SHOW - (tv series)	series	PARAMOUNT	1966
32043	PATTY DUKE SHOW - (tv series)	series	PARAMOUNT	1966
32044	PATTY DUKE SHOW - (tv series)	series	PARAMOUNT	1966
32045	PATTY DUKE SHOW - (tv series)	series	PARAMOUNT	1966
32046	PATTY DUKE SHOW - (tv series)	series	PARAMOUNT	1966
32047	PATTY DUKE SHOW - (tv series)	series	PARAMOUNT	1966
32048	PATTY DUKE SHOW - (tv series)	series	PARAMOUNT	1966
32049	PATTY DUKE SHOW - (tv series)	series	PARAMOUNT	1966
32100	T. H. E. CAT - (tv series)	series	PARAMOUNT	1966
32101	T. H. E. CAT - (tv series)	series	PARAMOUNT	1966

32102	T. H. E. CAT - (tv series)	series	PARAMOUNT	1966
32103	T. H. E. CAT - (tv series)	series	PARAMOUNT	1966
32104	T. H. E. CAT - (tv series)	series	PARAMOUNT	1966
32105	T. H. E. CAT - (tv series)	series	PARAMOUNT	1966
32106	T. H. E. CAT - (tv series)	series	PARAMOUNT	1966
32107	T. H. E. CAT - (tv series)	series	PARAMOUNT	1966
32108	T. H. E. CAT - (tv series)	series	PARAMOUNT	1966
32109	T. H. E. CAT - (tv series)	series	PARAMOUNT	1966
32110	T. H. E. CAT - (tv series)	series	PARAMOUNT	1966
32111	T. H. E. CAT - (tv series)	series	PARAMOUNT	1966
32112	T. H. E. CAT - (tv series)	series	PARAMOUNT	1966
32113	T. H. E. CAT - (tv series)	series	PARAMOUNT	1966
32114	T. H. E. CAT - (tv series)	series	PARAMOUNT	1966
32115	T. H. E. CAT - (tv series)	series	PARAMOUNT	1966
32116	T. H. E. CAT - (tv series)	series	PARAMOUNT	1966
32117	T. H. E. CAT - (tv series)	series	PARAMOUNT	1966
32118	T. H. E. CAT - (tv series)	series	PARAMOUNT	1966
32119	T. H. E. CAT - (tv series)	series	PARAMOUNT	1966
32120	T. H. E. CAT - (tv series)	series	PARAMOUNT	1966
32121	T. H. E. CAT - (tv series)	series	PARAMOUNT	1966
32122	T. H. E. CAT - (tv series)	series	PARAMOUNT	1966
32123	T. H. E. CAT - (tv series)	series	PARAMOUNT	1966
32124	T. H. E. CAT - (tv series)	series	PARAMOUNT	1966
32125	T. H. E. CAT - (tv series)	series	PARAMOUNT	1966
32126	T. H. E. CAT - (tv series)	series	PARAMOUNT	1966
32127	T. H. E. CAT - (tv series)	series	PARAMOUNT	1966
32128	T. H. E. CAT - (tv series)	series	PARAMOUNT	1966
32129	T. H. E. CAT - (tv series)	series	PARAMOUNT	1966
32130	T. H. E. CAT - (tv series)	series	PARAMOUNT	1966
32131	T. H. E. CAT - (tv series)	series	PARAMOUNT	1966
32132	T. H. E. CAT - (tv series)	series	PARAMOUNT	1966
32133	T. H. E. CAT - (tv series)	series	PARAMOUNT	1966
32134	T. H. E. CAT - (tv series)	series	PARAMOUNT	1966
32135	T. H. E. CAT - (tv series)	series	PARAMOUNT	1966
32136	T. H. E. CAT - (tv series)	series	PARAMOUNT	1966
32137	T. H. E. CAT - (tv series)	series	PARAMOUNT	1966
32138	T. H. E. CAT - (tv series)	series	PARAMOUNT	1966
32139	T. H. E. CAT - (tv series)	series	PARAMOUNT	1966
32140	T. H. E. CAT - (tv series)	series	PARAMOUNT	1966
32141	T. H. E. CAT - (tv series)	series	PARAMOUNT	1966
32142	T. H. E. CAT - (tv series)	series	PARAMOUNT	1966
32143	T. H. E. CAT - (tv series)	series	PARAMOUNT	1966
32144	T. H. E. CAT - (tv series)	series	PARAMOUNT	1966
32145	T. H. E. CAT - (tv series)	series	PARAMOUNT	1966
32146	T. H. E. CAT - (tv series)	series	PARAMOUNT	1966
32147	T. H. E. CAT - (tv series)	series	PARAMOUNT	1966
32148	T. H. E. CAT - (tv series)	series	PARAMOUNT	1966
32149	T. H. E. CAT - (tv series)	series	PARAMOUNT	1966
32200	HIGH CHAPARRAL - (tv series)	series	PARAMOUNT	1967
32201	HIGH CHAPARRAL - (tv series)	series	PARAMOUNT	1967
32202	HIGH CHAPARRAL - (tv series)	series	PARAMOUNT	1967
32203	HIGH CHAPARRAL - (tv series)	series	PARAMOUNT	1967
32204	HIGH CHAPARRAL - (tv series)	series	PARAMOUNT	1967
32205	HIGH CHAPARRAL - (tv series)	series	PARAMOUNT	1967
32206	HIGH CHAPARRAL - (tv series)	series	PARAMOUNT	1967
32207	HIGH CHAPARRAL - (tv series)	series	PARAMOUNT	1967
32208	HIGH CHAPARRAL - (tv series)	series	PARAMOUNT	1967
32209	HIGH CHAPARRAL - (tv series)	series	PARAMOUNT	1967
32210	HIGH CHAPARRAL - (tv series)	series	PARAMOUNT	1967
32211	HIGH CHAPARRAL - (tv series)	series	PARAMOUNT	1967
32212	HIGH CHAPARRAL - (tv series)	series	PARAMOUNT	1967
32213	HIGH CHAPARRAL - (tv series)	series	PARAMOUNT	1967
32214	HIGH CHAPARRAL - (tv series)	series	PARAMOUNT	1967
32215	HIGH CHAPARRAL - (tv series)	series	PARAMOUNT	1967
32216	HIGH CHAPARRAL - (tv series)	series	PARAMOUNT	1967
32217	HIGH CHAPARRAL - (tv series)	series	PARAMOUNT	1967

32218	HIGH CHAPARRAL - (tv series)	series	PARAMOUNT	1967
32219	HIGH CHAPARRAL - (tv series)	series	PARAMOUNT	1967
32220	HIGH CHAPARRAL - (tv series)	series	PARAMOUNT	1967
32221	HIGH CHAPARRAL - (tv series)	series	PARAMOUNT	1967
32222	HIGH CHAPARRAL - (tv series)	series	PARAMOUNT	1967
32223	HIGH CHAPARRAL - (tv series)	series	PARAMOUNT	1967
32224	HIGH CHAPARRAL - (tv series)	series	PARAMOUNT	1967
32225	HIGH CHAPARRAL - (tv series)	series	PARAMOUNT	1967
32226	HIGH CHAPARRAL - (tv series)	series	PARAMOUNT	1967
32227	HIGH CHAPARRAL - (tv series)	series	PARAMOUNT	1967
32228	HIGH CHAPARRAL - (tv series)	series	PARAMOUNT	1967
32229	HIGH CHAPARRAL - (tv series)	series	PARAMOUNT	1967
32230	HIGH CHAPARRAL - (tv series)	series	PARAMOUNT	1967
32231	HIGH CHAPARRAL - (tv series)	series	PARAMOUNT	1967
32232	HIGH CHAPARRAL - (tv series)	series	PARAMOUNT	1967
32233	HIGH CHAPARRAL - (tv series)	series	PARAMOUNT	1967
32234	HIGH CHAPARRAL - (tv series)	series	PARAMOUNT	1967
32235	HIGH CHAPARRAL - (tv series)	series	PARAMOUNT	1967
32236	HIGH CHAPARRAL - (tv series)	series	PARAMOUNT	1967
32237	HIGH CHAPARRAL - (tv series)	series	PARAMOUNT	1967
32238	HIGH CHAPARRAL - (tv series)	series	PARAMOUNT	1967
32239	HIGH CHAPARRAL - (tv series)	series	PARAMOUNT	1967
32240	HIGH CHAPARRAL - (tv series)	series	PARAMOUNT	1967
32241	HIGH CHAPARRAL - (tv series)	series	PARAMOUNT	1967
32242	HIGH CHAPARRAL - (tv series)	series	PARAMOUNT	1967
32243	HIGH CHAPARRAL - (tv series)	series	PARAMOUNT	1967
32244	HIGH CHAPARRAL - (tv series)	series	PARAMOUNT	1967
32245	HIGH CHAPARRAL - (tv series)	series	PARAMOUNT	1967
32246	HIGH CHAPARRAL - (tv series)	series	PARAMOUNT	1967
32247	HIGH CHAPARRAL - (tv series)	series	PARAMOUNT	1967
32248	HIGH CHAPARRAL - (tv series)	series	PARAMOUNT	1967
32249	HIGH CHAPARRAL - (tv series)	series	PARAMOUNT	1967
34100	MR. GARLUND - (tv series)	series	PARAMOUNT	1960
34101	MR. GARLUND - (tv series)	series	PARAMOUNT	1960
34102	MR. GARLUND - (tv series)	series	PARAMOUNT	1960
34103	MR. GARLUND - (tv series)	series	PARAMOUNT	1960
34104	MR. GARLUND - (tv series)	series	PARAMOUNT	1960
34105	MR. GARLUND - (tv series)	series	PARAMOUNT	1960
34106	MR. GARLUND - (tv series)	series	PARAMOUNT	1960
34107	MR. GARLUND - (tv series)	series	PARAMOUNT	1960
34108	MR. GARLUND - (tv series)	series	PARAMOUNT	1960
34109	MR. GARLUND - (tv series)	series	PARAMOUNT	1960
34110	MR. GARLUND - (tv series)	series	PARAMOUNT	1960
34111	MR. GARLUND - (tv series)	series	PARAMOUNT	1960
34112	MR. GARLUND - (tv series)	series	PARAMOUNT	1960
34113	MR. GARLUND - (tv series)	series	PARAMOUNT	1960
34114	MR. GARLUND - (tv series)	series	PARAMOUNT	1960
34115	MR. GARLUND - (tv series)	series	PARAMOUNT	1960
34116	MR. GARLUND - (tv series)	series	PARAMOUNT	1960
34117	MR. GARLUND - (tv series)	series	PARAMOUNT	1960
34118	MR. GARLUND - (tv series)	series	PARAMOUNT	1960
34119	MR. GARLUND - (tv series)	series	PARAMOUNT	1960
34120	MR. GARLUND - (tv series)	series	PARAMOUNT	1960
34121	MR. GARLUND - (tv series)	series	PARAMOUNT	1960
34122	MR. GARLUND - (tv series)	series	PARAMOUNT	1960
34123	MR. GARLUND - (tv series)	series	PARAMOUNT	1960
34124	MR. GARLUND - (tv series)	series	PARAMOUNT	1960
34125	MR. GARLUND - (tv series)	series	PARAMOUNT	1960
34126	MR. GARLUND - (tv series)	series	PARAMOUNT	1960
34127	MR. GARLUND - (tv series)	series	PARAMOUNT	1960
34128	MR. GARLUND - (tv series)	series	PARAMOUNT	1960
34129	MR. GARLUND - (tv series)	series	PARAMOUNT	1960
34130	MR. GARLUND - (tv series)	series	PARAMOUNT	1960
34131	MR. GARLUND - (tv series)	series	PARAMOUNT	1960
34132	MR. GARLUND - (tv series)	series	PARAMOUNT	1960
34133	MR. GARLUND - (tv series)	series	PARAMOUNT	1960

34134	MR. GARLUND - (tv series)	series		PARAMOUNT	1960
34135	MR. GARLUND - (tv series)	series		PARAMOUNT	1960
34136	MR. GARLUND - (tv series)	series		PARAMOUNT	1960
34137	MR. GARLUND - (tv series)	series		PARAMOUNT	1960
34138	MR. GARLUND - (tv series)	series		PARAMOUNT	1960
34139	MR. GARLUND - (tv series)	series		PARAMOUNT	1960
34140	MR. GARLUND - (tv series)	series		PARAMOUNT	1960
34141	MR. GARLUND - (tv series)	series		PARAMOUNT	1960
34142	MR. GARLUND - (tv series)	series		PARAMOUNT	1960
34143	MR. GARLUND - (tv series)	series		PARAMOUNT	1960
34144	MR. GARLUND - (tv series)	series		PARAMOUNT	1960
34145	MR. GARLUND - (tv series)	series		PARAMOUNT	1960
34146	MR. GARLUND - (tv series)	series		PARAMOUNT	1960
34147	MR. GARLUND - (tv series)	series		PARAMOUNT	1960
34148	MR. GARLUND - (tv series)	series		PARAMOUNT	1960
34149	MR. GARLUND - (tv series)	series		PARAMOUNT	1960
39053	OFF WE GO - tv pilot			PARAMOUNT	1966
39057	SAGUARO - tv pilot			PARAMOUNT	1966
39058	CAPTAIN NICE - tv pilot			PARAMOUNT	1966
39061	RHUBARB - tv pilot			PARAMOUNT	1967
39063	TWO MEN & A GIRL IN A MEATGRINDER (tv pilot)			PARAMOUNT	1967
42306	BARETTA - TV	CANNELL		UNIVERSAL-TV	1975
47008	WAR AND PEACE	VIDOR		PARAMOUNT	1956
47011	ANOTHER TIME, ANOTHER PLACE (UK)	ALLEN		PARAMOUNT	1958
47017	TEMPEST (IT: LA TEMPESTA)	LATTUADA		PARAMOUNT	1958
47018	HIGH HELL (UK)	BALABAN		PARAMOUNT	1958
47025	SAVAGE INNOCENTS (UK)	RAY		PARAMOUNT	1960
47029	UNDER TEN FLAGS (IT: SOTTO DIECI BANDIERE)	COLETTI		PARAMOUNT	1960
47031	TARZAN THE MAGNIFICENT (UK)	DAY		PARAMOUNT	1960
47034	CONSPIRACY OF HEARTS (UK)	THOMAS		PARAMOUNT	1960
47035	IN THE WAKE OF A STRANGER (UK 1958)	EADY		PARAMOUNT	1960
47036	BOY WHO STOLE A MILLION (UK)	CRICHTON		PARAMOUNT	1960
47037	FOXHOLE IN CAIRO (UK)	MOXEY		PARAMOUNT	1961
47039	FOREVER MY LOVE (AUSTRIA)	MARISCHKA		PARAMOUNT	1962
47041	BRUSHFIRE!	WARNER		PARAMOUNT	1962
47046	DUEL OF THE TITANS (IT: ROMOLO E REMO 1961)	CORBUCCI		PARAMOUNT	1963
47049	SON OF CAPTAIN BLOOD (SP)	DEMICHILI		PARAMOUNT	1964
47052	YOUNG FURY	NYBY		PARAMOUNT	1965
47054	CRACK IN THE WORLD	MARTON		PARAMOUNT	1965
47056	DR. TERROR'S HOUSE OF HORRORS (UK)	FRANCIS		PARAMOUNT	1965
47064	BEACH BALL	WEINRIB		PARAMOUNT	1965
51208	SHADOW OF THE THIN MAN	VAN DYKE		MGM	1941
51225	TORTILLA FLATS	FLEMING		MGM	1942
51243	MAISIE GETS HER MAN	RUTH		MGM	1942
51250	SUSAN PETERS	portrait			
51395	CYNTHIA	LEONARD		MGM	1947
51482	THREE LITTLE WORDS	THORPE		MGM	1950
51680	MEET ME IN LAS VEGAS	ROWLAND		MGM	1956
53308	MARIA SCHELL	portrait		MGM	
63019	UNCHAINED	BARTLETT		WARNER BROS	1955
63104	BLACK SCORPION, THE	LUDWIG		WARNER BROS	1957
63712	LOOK BACK IN ANGER (UK)	RICHARDSON		WARNER BROS.	1959
81458	BARBARA NICHOLS	portrait		WARNER BROS	
83358	ALIAS SMITH AND JONES (tv)	LARSON		UNIVERSAL	1971
86585	MAUREEN O'SULLIVAN	portrait		MGM	
89222	AMOUROUS ADV. OF MOLL FLANDERS	YOUNG		PARAMOUNT	1964
90032	TRAITORSTHE (UK 1962)	TRONSON		UNIVERSAL	1963
90168	NIGHTMARE (UK)	FRANCIS		UNIVERSAL	1964
90201	HIDE AND SEEK (UK)	ENDFIELD		UNIVERSAL	1964
90204	YOUNG AND WILLING	THOMAS		UNIVERSAL	1964
90204	YOUNG AND WILLING (UK: WILD AND WILLING)	THOMAS		UNIVERSAL	1962
90226	DREAM MAKER (UK: IT'S ALL HAPPENING)	SHARP		UNIVERSAL	1963
90265	EVIL OF FRANKENSTEIN (UK)	FRANCIS		UNIVERSAL	1964
92580	PINOCCHIO IN OUTER SPACE (t)	GOOSSENS		UNIVERSAL	1965
95008	KILLERS	SIEGEL		UNIVERSAL	1964
95179	SECRET OF BLOOD ISLAND (UK)	LAWRENCE		UNIVERSAL	1965

95186	IPCRESS FILE (UK)	FURIE	UNIVERSAL	1965
95263	BOY CRIED MURDER (UK)	BREAKSTON	UNIVERSAL	1966
95295	AGENT FOR H.A.R.M.	OSWALD	UNIVERSAL	1966
320101	GIDDY AGE (sh) (see 2935)	STAFFORD	EDUCATIONAL FILM	1932
320102	SUNKISSED SWEETIES (sh)	EDWARDS	EDUCATIONAL FILM	1932
320103	FOOL ABOUT WOMEN (sh)	EDWARDS	EDUCATIONAL FILM	1932
320104	BOY, OH BOY! (sh)	EDWARDS	EDUCATIONAL FILM	1932
320105	ARTIST'S MUDDLES (sh)	EDWARDS	EDUCATIONAL FILM	1933
320106	FEELING ROSY (sh)	EDWARDS	EDUCATIONAL FILM	1933
320107	LOOSE RELATIONS (sh)	EDWARDS	EDUCATIONAL FILM	1933
320108	DORA'S DUNKING DOUGHNUTS (sh)(changed to 0202)	EDWARDS	EDUCATIONAL FILM	1933
320201	AS THE CROWS FLY (sh)	EDWARDS	EDUCATIONAL FILM	1933
320202	TWO BLACK CROWS IN AFRICA (sh)	LAMONT	EDUCATIONAL FILM	1933
320203	HOT HOOFS (sh)	EDWARDS	EDUCATIONAL FILM	1933
320204	PAIR OF SOCKS (sh)	LAMONT	EDUCATIONAL FILM	1933
320205	BLUE BLACKBIRDS (sh)	LAMONT	EDUCATIONAL FILM	1933
320301	BIG FLASH (sh)	GILLSTROM	EDUCATIONAL FILM	1932
320302	VEST WITH A TALE (sh)	SCOTTO	EDUCATIONAL FILM	1932
320303	TIRED FEET (sh)	GILLSTROM	EDUCATIONAL FILM	1933
320304	HITCHHIKER (sh)	GILLSTROM	EDUCATIONAL FILM	1933
320305	KNIGHT DUTY (sh)	GILLSTROM	EDUCATIONAL FILM	1933
320306	TIED FOR LIFE (sh)	GILLSTROM	EDUCATIONAL FILM	1933
320307	HOOKS AND JABS (sh)	GILLSTROM	EDUCATIONAL FILM	1933
320401	HONEYMOON BEACH (sh)	EDWARDS	EDUCATIONAL FILM	1932
320402	HOLLYWOOD RUNAROUND (sh)	CHRISTIE	EDUCATIONAL FILM	1932
320403	KEYHOLE KATIE (sh)	LAMONT	EDUCATIONAL FILM	1933
320404	TECHNO CRAZY (sh)	LAMONT	EDUCATIONAL FILM	1933
320501	TORCHY'S BUSY DAY (sh)	BURR	EDUCATIONAL FILM	1932
320502	TORCHY ROLLS HIS OWN (sh)	BURR	EDUCATIONAL FILM	1932
320503	TORCHY'S KITTY COUP (sh)	BURR	EDUCATIONAL FILM	1933
320504	TORCHY TURNS TURTLE (sh)	BURR	EDUCATIONAL FILM	1933
320505	TORCHY'S LOUD SPOOKER (sh)	BURR	EDUCATIONAL FILM	1933
320506	TRYING OUT TORCHY (sh)	BURR	EDUCATIONAL FILM	1933
320601	OFF HIS BASE (sh)	GLEASON	EDUCATIONAL FILM	1932
320602	ALWAYS KICKIN' (sh)	GLEASON	EDUCATIONAL FILM	1932
320603	HOCKEY HICK (sh)	GLEASON	EDUCATIONAL FILM	1932
320701	HYPNOTIZING FOR LOVE (sh)		EDUCATIONAL FILM	1932
320702	BURNED AT THE STEAK (sh)		EDUCATIONAL FILM	1932
320703	IN THE CLUTCHWS OF DEATH (sh)		EDUCATIONAL FILM	1932
320704	EVIL EYE CONQUERS (sh)		EDUCATIONAL FILM	1933
320705	ON THE BRINK OF DISASTER (sh)		EDUCATIONAL FILM	1933
320804	WALPURGIS NIGHT (sh)	HIGGIN	EDUCATIONAL FILM	1932
320805	BRAHMIN'S DAUGHTER (sh)		EDUCATIONAL FILM	1933
320901	SHERMAN WAS RIGHT (t) (sh)	MOSER	EDUCATIONAL FILM	1932
320902	BURLESQUE (t) (sh)	MOSER	EDUCATIONAL FILM	1932
320903	SOUTHERN RHYTHM (t) (sh)	MOSER	EDUCATIONAL FILM	1932
320904	FARMER ALFALFA'S BIRTHDAY PARTY (t) (sh)	MOSER	EDUCATIONAL FILM	1932
320905	COLLEGE SPIRIT (t) (sh)	MOSER	EDUCATIONAL FILM	1932
320906	HOOK AND LADDER NO. 1 (t) (sh)	MOSER	EDUCATIONAL FILM	1932
320907	FORTY THIEVES (t) (sh)	MOSER	EDUCATIONAL FILM	1932
320908	TOYLAND (t) (sh)	MOSER	EDUCATIONAL FILM	1932
320909	HOLLYWOOD DIET (t) (sh)	MOSER	EDUCATIONAL FILM	1932
320910	IRELAND OR BUST (t) (sh)	MOSER	EDUCATIONAL FILM	1932
320911	JEALOUS LOVER (t) (sh)	MOSER	EDUCATIONAL FILM	1933
320912	ROBIN HOOD (t) (sh)	MOSER	EDUCATIONAL FILM	1933
320913	HANSEL UND GRETEL (t) (sh)	MOSER	EDUCATIONAL FILM	1933
320914	TALE OF A SHIRT (t) (sh)	MOSER	EDUCATIONAL FILM	1933
320915	DOWEN ON THE LEVEE (t) (sh)	MOSER	EDUCATIONAL FILM	1933
320916	WHO KILLED COCK ROBIN? (t) (sh)	MOSER	EDUCATIONAL FILM	1933
320917	OH! SUSANNA (t) (sh)	MOSER	EDUCATIONAL FILM	1933
320918	ROMEO AND JULIET (t) (sh)	MOSER	EDUCATIONAL FILM	1933
320919	PIRATE SHIP (t) (sh)	MOSER	EDUCATIONAL FILM	1933
320920	TROPICAL FISH (t) (sh)	MOSER	EDUCATIONAL FILM	1933
320921	CINDERELLA (t) (sh)	MOSER	EDUCATIONAL FILM	1933
320922	KING ZILCH (t) (sh)	MOSER	EDUCATIONAL FILM	1932
320923	BANKER'S DAUGHTER (t) (sh)	MOSER	EDUCATIONAL FILM	1933

320924	OIL CAN MYSTERY (t) (sh)	MOSER	EDUCATIONAL FILM	1933
320925	FANNIE IN THE LION'S DEN (t) (sh)	MOSER	EDUCATIONAL FILM	1933
320926	HYPNOTIC EYES (t) (sh)	MOSER	EDUCATIONAL FILM	1933
321001	WAR BABIES (sh)	LAMONT	EDUCATIONAL FILM	1932
321002	PIE COVERED WAGON (sh)	LAMONT	EDUCATIONAL FILM	1932
321003	GLAD RAGS TO RICHES (sh)	LAMONT	EDUCATIONAL FILM	1933
321004	KID'S LAST FIGHT (sh)	LAMONT	EDUCATIONAL FILM	1933
321005	KID 'N' HOLLYWOOD (sh)	LAMONT	EDUCATIONAL FILM	1933
321006	POLLY TIX IN WASHINGTON (sh)	LAMONT	EDUCATIONAL FILM	1933
321101	BATTLE OF THE CENTURIES (sh)		EDUCATIONAL FILM	1932
321102	KILLERS (sh)		EDUCATIONAL FILM	1932
321103	DESERT DEMONS (sh)		EDUCATIONAL FILM	1932
321104	SEA (sh)		EDUCATIONAL FILM	1933
321105	BENEATH OUR FEET (sh)		EDUCATIONAL FILM	1933
321201	DO YOU REMEMBER? - OLD NEW YORK (sh)		EDUCATIONAL FILM	1932
321202	DO YOU REMEMBER? - GASLIT NINETIES (sh)		EDUCATIONAL FILM	1932
321203	DO YOU REMEMBER? - WHEN DAD WAS A BOY (sh)		EDUCATIONAL FILM	1933
321204	DO YOU REMEMBER? - PUFFS AND BUSTLES (sh)		EDUCATIONAL FILM	1933
321205	DO YOU REMEMBER? - HIGHLIGHTS OF THE PAST (sh)		EDUCATIONAL FILM	1933
321206	DO YOU REMEMBER? - OLD FASHIONED NEWSREEL (sh)		EDUCATIONAL FILM	1933
321301	FORGOTTEN ISLAND (sh)	DOWLING	EDUCATIONAL FILM	1932
321302	ICELESS ARCTIC (sh)	DOWLING	EDUCATIONAL FILM	1932
321303	TAMING THE WILDCAT (sh)	DOWLING	EDUCATIONAL FILM	1933
321304	TWO HUNDRED FATHOMS DEEP (sh)	DOWLING	EDUCATIONAL FILM	1933
321305	COUGAR'S MISTAKE (sh)	DOWLING	EDUCATIONAL FILM	1933
321401	WOMEN'S WORK (sh) (Hodge Podge #98)	HOWE	EDUCATIONAL FILM	1932
321402	LITTLE THRILLS (sh) (Hodge Podge #99)	HOWE	EDUCATIONAL FILM	1932
321403	TRAFFIC (sh) (Hodge Podge #100)	HOWE	EDUCATIONAL FILM	1932
321404	WONDER CITY (sh) (Hodge Podge #101)	HOWE	EDUCATIONAL FILM	1932
321405	DOWN ON THE FARM (sh) (Hodge Podge #102)	HOWE	EDUCATIONAL FILM	1932
321406	ACROSS AMERICA IN 10 MINUTES (sh) (H. Podge #103)	HOWE	EDUCATIONAL FILM	1933
321407	ANIMAL FAIR (sh) (Hodge Podge #104)	HOWE	EDUCATIONAL FILM	1932
321408	SKIPPING ABOUT THE UNIVERSE (sh) (H. Podge #105)	HOWE	EDUCATIONAL FILM	1933
321409	OUT OF THE ORDINARY (sh) (Hodge Podge #107)	HOWE	EDUCATIONAL FILM	1933
321410	WOMEN OF MANY LANDS (sh) (Hodge Podge #106)	HOWE	EDUCATIONAL FILM	1933
321411	SAWDUST SIDELIGHTS (sh) (Hodge Podge #108)	HOWE	EDUCATIONAL FILM	1933
321501	OREGON CAMERA HUNT (sh)	BRAY	EDUCATIONAL FILM	1932
321502	OUR BIRD CITIZENS (sh)	BRAY	EDUCATIONAL FILM	1932
321503	STABLE MANNERS (sh)	BRAY	EDUCATIONAL FILM	1932
321504	OUR NOBLE ANCESTORS (sh)	BRAY	EDUCATIONAL FILM	1932
321505	WILD COMPANY (sh)	BRAY	EDUCATIONAL FILM	1933
321506	WOODLAND PALS (sh)	BRAY	EDUCATIONAL FILM	1933
321507	PIRATES OF THE DEEP (sh)	BRAY	EDUCATIONAL FILM	1933
321508	GIANTS OF THE NORTH (sh)	BRAY	EDUCATIONAL FILM	1933
321509	WILD LIFE AT HOME (sh)	BRAY	EDUCATIONAL FILM	1933
321601	SPIRIT OF THE CAMPUS - CORNELL (sh)	SCOTTO	EDUCATIONAL FILM	1932
321602	SPIRIT OF THE CAMPUS - YALE (sh)	SCOTTO	EDUCATIONAL FILM	1932
321603	SPIRIT OF THE CAMPUS - MICHIGAN (sh)	SCOTTO	EDUCATIONAL FILM	1932
321604	SPIRIT OF THE CAMPUS - CALIFORNIA (sh)	SCOTTO	EDUCATIONAL FILM	1933
321605	SPIRIT OF THE CAMPUS (sh)	SCOTTO	EDUCATIONAL FILM	1933
321606	SPIRIT OF THE CAMPUS (sh)	SCOTTO	EDUCATIONAL FILM	1933
321607	SPIRIT OF THE CAMPUS - MCGILL (sh)	SCOTTO	EDUCATIONAL FILM	1933
321701	ACES WILD (sh)	SCOTTO	EDUCATIONAL FILM	1933
321702	MOUSE TRAPPER (sh)	SCOTTO	EDUCATIONAL FILM	1932
321703	ACID TEST (sh)	SCOTTO	EDUCATIONAL FILM	1932
321704	DRUG ON THE MARKET (sh)	SCOTTO	EDUCATIONAL FILM	1933
321705	HONESTY PAYS - BUT NOT MUCH (sh)	SCOTTO	EDUCATIONAL FILM	1933
321801	BROADWAY GOSSIP (sh)	DONNELLY	EDUCATIONAL FILM	1932
321802	BROADWAY GOSSIP NO. 2 (sh)	DONNELLY	EDUCATIONAL FILM	1932
321803	BROADWAY GOSSIP NO. 3 (sh)	DONNELLY	EDUCATIONAL FILM	1932
321804	BROADWAY GOSSIP NO. 4 (sh)	DONNELLY	EDUCATIONAL FILM	1933
321805	BROADWAY GOSSIP NO. 5 (sh)	DONNELLY	EDUCATIONAL FILM	1933
321806	BROADWAY GOSSIP NO. 6 (sh)	DONNELLY	EDUCATIONAL FILM	1933
322001	KRAKATOA (sh)		EDUCATIONAL FILM	1933

MPA

Movie Poster Archives

Are You a Friend of the Archives?

Join a distinguished philanthropic effort. Friends of the Archives help
make possible the rescue and preservation of endangered movie posters,
create a world-class collection, advance groundbreaking research, and
support development of digital and educational resources.

Your membership fee is tax-deductible,
minus the value of your tangible benefits such as books.

FRIEND $25.00	ENTHUSIAST $50.00	BENEFACTOR $100,00	PATRON $250,00
• Gift Subscription to *Learn About Movie Posters Newsletter* • Your name on the MPA Gratitude Page	• A Movie Still from the Lagniappe Collection • Gift Subscription to Learn About Movie Posters Newsletter • Your name on the MPA Gratitude Page	• A Poster from the Lagniappe Collection • A Movie Still from the Lagniappe Collection • Gift Subscription to Learn About Movie Posters Newsletter • Your name on the MPA Gratitude Page	• Your own copy of Movie Poster Artists Volume 1: United States and Canada • A Poster from the Lagniappe Collection • A Movie Still from the Lagniappe Collection • Gift Subscription to Learn About Movie Posters Newsletter • Your name on the MPA Gratitude Page.

JOIN TODAY

Major credit cards, PayPal or checks accepted.
email: mpa@movieposterarchies.org

Movie Poster Archives, Inc.

2112 Belle Chasse Hwy, Ste 8-131, Gretna, LA 70053
225 283 4498 http://movieposterarchives.org

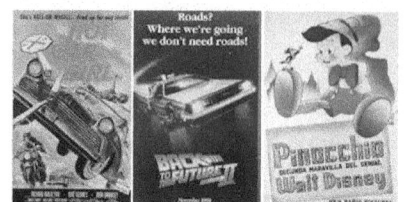

LAMP SPONSORS

Aston's Auctioneers

Bags Unlimited

Bonhams Auctions

Channing Posters

Cinema Retro

Conway's Vintage Treasures

Dominique Besson

eMoviePoster.com

Ewbank's Auction

FFF Movie Posters

Film Art Gallery

French Movie Poster

Heritage Auctions back cover

Hollywood Poster Frames

Illustration Gallery

KinoArt

L'Imagerie Gallery

Last Moving Picture Show

Limited Runs

Mauvais Genres

Movie Art GmbH

Movie Art of Austin

Movie Ink

Movie Poster Archives

Movie Poster Page

MovieMem Original Movie
Posters

Original Poster

Partners 65

Past Posters

Picture Palace Movie Posters

Posteropolis

Simon Dwyer

Spotlight Displays

Unshredded Nostalgia

Vintage Movie Posters Forum

Please take time to notice the ads throughout
this book and support these wonderful people as
they have invested financially in YOUR education
by sponsoring this book.

www.ingramcontent.com/pod-product-compliance
Lightning Source LLC
Chambersburg PA
CBHW082350270326
41935CB00013B/1566